writing about

the world

third edition

Susan McLeod

*University of California,
Santa Barbara*

John Jarvis

Bay Path College

Shelley Spear

*University of California,
Santa Barbara*

THOMSON

WADSWORTH

Australia • Canada • Mexico • Singapore • Spain
United Kingdom • United States

THOMSON

WADSWORTH

Writing about the World/Third Edition

McLeod • Jarvis • Spear

Publisher: *Michael Rosenberg*
Acquisitions Editor: *Dickson Musslewhite*
Development Editor: *Laurie Runion*
Production Editor: *Brett Palana-Shanahan*
Marketing Manager: *Katrina Byrd*
Manufacturing Coordinator: *Marcia Locke*
Compositor: *Shepherd Incorporated*

Photography Manager: *Sheri Blaney*
Permissions Manager: *Cheri Throop*
Photo Researcher: *Cheri Throop*
Cover Designer: *Diana Coe*
Text Designer: *Shepherd Incorporated*
Printer/Binder: *Maple Vail*
Cover Printer: *Phoenix Color Corp.*

Cover Image: © Nevada Weir/CORBIS

For more information contact Thomson Wadsworth, 25 Thomson Place, Boston, Massachusetts 02210 USA, or you can visit our Internet site at http://www.thomson.com

For permission to use material from this text or product, submit a request online at http://www.thomsonrights.com. Any additional questions about permissions can be submitted by email to thomsonrights@thomson.com.

ISBN: 1-4130-0238-2

PCN number: 2003116065

CONTENTS

CHAPTER 3   Art and Literature   270

CHAPTER 4   Science and Technology   402

PREFACE

A recent report from the American Council on Education (entitled "Mapping Internationalization on U.S. Campuses") stresses the need for college graduates to have international knowledge and skills, knowledge about the world. Although many colleges have moved to internationalize curricula, this report states that most fail to provide their students with a sufficiently internationalized education.

Writing About the World, Third Edition, addresses the gaps in students' knowledge about the world. Our work is also in line with a resolution passed by the Conference on College Composition and Communication in 1989: "Resolved, that CCCC adopt a curriculum policy that represents the inclusion of women and people of color in the curriculum on all levels." We are pleased to implement that curriculum policy in this book of readings.

Writing About the World includes readings that are both ancient and contemporary, focusing on themes of interest across the disciplines. We also provide a guide to reading and writing critically in college in Chapter 1, using Aristotle's *Rhetoric* as a framework and providing guiding questions and writing assignments. This book takes a writing-across-the-curriculum approach, suggesting writing assignments that provide students with the kinds of writing tasks they will encounter in their other classes (e.g., definition, summary, argument). The reading journal, perhaps the single most important writing assignment, is designed to improve students' reading as well as their writing skills. We also provide sample student essays from students who have studied abroad, so that undergraduates can read for themselves about the value of examining another culture while living in it.

In this new edition, we have kept many of the classic texts, updated most of the modern selections, and provided a set of thematic focuses for each of the four sections of readings. In the set of readings on the environment, we have included new readings on globalization and its discontents, as well as up-to-date readings on oppression in various parts of the world. We have also included a set of readings that pertain to the war on terrorism and to the ever-increasing connection between religion, politics, and war.

It is no secret that today's students are very sophisticated about and responsive to visual information. For that reason we have found it useful to approach cultural issues through videotape/DVD as well as through reading. There are a number of multi-program series readily available from PBS that we recommend: "Millennium" (especially the introduction, "Shock of the Other and Strange Relations"), the "American Indian Collection," "Legacy," and "Eyes on the Prize," to name a few. We have included a section in Chapter 1 on visual literacy to help both teachers and students think about how to analyze visual images rhetorically.

We hope it is clear that this is a book for our students and students like them; we have chosen the readings with students in mind and have used both the readings and the writing assignments with success in several different universities.

Given Americans' general lack of knowledge about the rest of the world, it is our hope that the readings and assignments will help students not only with their writing but also with their understanding of the complexity and richness of other cultures.

NEW TO THIS EDITION

- New introduction, "How Will *You* Learn about the World?" helps students begin to think about their view of the world.
- New Chapter 1, "Reading and Writing in College," provides students with a model for analysis using Aristotle's *Rhetoric,* provides a primary source introduction to the framework of the book, and introduces students to the topic of visual rhetoric.
- Forty-one of 129 readings are new.
- Each chapter includes a set of readings on race, gender, and oppression and includes such important readings as Nobel Peace Prize Winner Daw Aung San Suu Kyi's Keynote Address at the Beijing Forum on Women; Sultana Yusufali's "Why Do I Wear Hijab?"; and Kofi Annan's Nobel Peace Prize lecture.
- New pedagogy enhances students' understanding of readings and provides the information and exercises they need to approach the readings rhetorically. This new structure includes: thorough chapter introductions, headnotes, discussion and reading journal questions focused on rhetorical and thematic concerns, and end-of-chapter writing assignments that ask students to respond to chapter readings by analyzing, critiquing, synthesizing, comparing/contrasting, and writing persuasively.
- **Instructor's Manual** An updated Instructor's Manual is available to adopters of this text. The Instructor's Manual includes: sample syllabi for both a quarter and a semester course, based on themes or on sections of the book; pedagogical advice about the teaching of writing, such as leading discussions, using groups, using peer review, responding to writing and grading, integrating library research into the assignments; suggestions for further reading; and a sample student paper.

ACKNOWLEDGMENTS

We would like to acknowledge the people who helped develop earlier versions of this book, in particular, Richard Law, Director of General Education at Washington State University; without his help, we would not have written the first edition. We would also like to thank our co-editors for that first edition, Alan Hunt and Stacia Bates, and our present institutions, the University of California, Santa Barbara, and Bay Path College, for the support we have received while working on this edition of the book. We would also like to thank the reviewers whose comments helped us make decisions about the new edition:

Sue Beebe, Southwest Texas State University; Lara Gary, Sacramento City College; Annabel Servat, Southeastern Louisiana University; Gordon Thomas, University of Idaho; Laurie Vickroy, Bradley University.

Finally, we thank our families, who have been most patient with us during what must have seemed like endless revisions.

RHETORICAL TABLE OF CONTENTS

Based on James Kinneavy's Modes and Aims (Source: *A Theory of Discourse*)

BY MODE

Description

Classification and Definition

Narration

Evaluation

BY AIM

Expressive

Referential (or Expository: Convey Information, Prove a Point, Explore a Subject)

INTRODUCTION

How Will *You* Learn about the World?

John Jarvis

In the aftermath of the terrible events of September 11, 2001, it became clear that there are two very different ways in America to learn about other peoples who share this planet with us. As is often the case, different approaches lead to different results. Robb Svenson, a middle-aged businessman in Chicago, illustrates the most common way in which Americans have learned about other cultures in the past. As a young man, Svenson joined the U.S. Navy and fought in the Vietnam War. What he learned about other cultures through his war experiences surfaced in the news recently as Americans debated helping Afghanistan after American bombing had made a harsh winter even more devastating for people there. He told a reporter for *USA Today:* "The people of Afghanistan do not matter; Americans matter. I have a whole way of life that's being damaged by these (terrorists), and I am not concerned about Afghanistan."[1]

Ms. Mary Pat Larocca and her 26 kindergarten students in Countryside, Illinois, had a very different response to the suffering of human beings in Afghanistan. Speaking of the events of September 11, Ms. Larocca told her class of 5- and 6-year-olds, "[B]ecause of this tragedy, we have children in a faraway country called Afghanistan that might not be having any food this winter, and they need some help. And President Bush asked if we could all send in a dollar." As is often the case with young minds and hearts, the results were instantaneous.

The 26 children went to work. They pitched in to clean up their classroom and to keep it clean for a day. In return, Ms. Larocca paid them each one dollar. Then they joined together to make a large poster with the photo of each of them on it. The final step in the project was for each child to attach his or her crisp new one-dollar bill to the poster so that Ms. Larocca could mail it to the White House. Each child did so, and the poster went out promptly.

Ms. Larocca's students were learning about the world through very different means and in different circumstances than the way that Robb Svenson did so. They were learning under the guidance and support of a caring teacher. As young as they were, this teacher was asking them to give as much as they got as they reached out across cultural borders. At the heart of it all, she was teaching them to understand the suffering of others and the value of taking positive action to ease that suffering. They mastered the lesson quickly.

These are all skills that will serve Ms. Larocca's charges well as they continue learning about the world through high school and perhaps later in college. This first lesson taught them to care about other people in general. Future lessons will teach them to care about (and to understand) more specific things, such as other people's languages, cultures, histories, arts, religions, and day-to-day lives, as well as their social, political, and economic systems. Should they someday choose to study abroad, they will find themselves welcomed and appreciated among other peoples. Then they will make friends face-to-face, not just through the mail. It is a healthy way to learn about the world. Unfortunately, for most young Americans, it is also a rare way to learn about the world.

The truth is, like Robb Svenson, many Americans have had and continue to have their first face-to-face encounters with people in other cultures through war, not through peace. The statistics tell the story. A total of 3.1 million young Americans fought alongside Svenson in the Vietnam War. Some 1,137,000 more traveled abroad to fight the Gulf War in the early 1990s.[2] Currently 250,000 are deployed in other lands to fight the War on Terrorism.[3] These are sobering statistics. They mean, quite simply, that in the last generation some 4.5 million young Americans have gone abroad with the express mission of killing people in other lands. When they return, it is not surprising that they tend to feel as Robb Svenson feels, that people in other lands "do not matter" and that it is Americans who "matter."

The good news, of course, is that young Americans are increasingly going abroad for reasons other than war. Student interest in travel and study abroad has more than doubled in the last decade. The number of young Americans who studied overseas went from 70,727 in the 1989–90 school year to 143,590 in 1999–2000. Not only are more students going in peace to other cultures, but they are going to places few Americans have gone before. While the percentage of students going to Europe is declining, the percentage going to more unusual destinations is booming. A total of 2,949 young Americans studied in China in the 1999–2000 school year. Thousands more went to Brazil, Cuba, Egypt, Nepal, India, Kenya, and Vietnam.[4]

Each year adventuresome young Americans visit the Great Wall of China, they work on environmental projects in the Amazon Rain Forest, they learn to see life through the eyes of young people in Cuba, they study Islamic history and culture in the shadows of the pyramids, and they trek through the Himalayan Mountains of Nepal. In each place, they make friends. They experience other people's lives. They laugh together. They dance together. They learn new songs and new ways of being. In each place they share friendship, hope, and peace with people who might otherwise have been their enemies.

When these young Americans return from their time overseas, they return with very different attitudes than those of Robb Svenson. They know that a world in which only "Americans matter" is a frightening place that will always be filled with hatred and war. They not only understand that other peoples matter but also have the knowledge and the skills to build on that understanding in peaceful ways. They do it through business partnerships, sharing advancements in health care, effective global communication, responsible journalism, positive international relations, informed governmental policy-making, conscientious international banking, teaching better foreign language skills and deeper cultural understanding, and through hundreds of other meaningful life careers.

If Ms. Larocco's kindergarten students continue on the path they first began by helping children in Afghanistan through a deadly winter, they too will one day qualify for these kinds of careers. The decision to take this journey toward global understanding will enrich their lives, the life of our nation, and the world itself. In the end, we can all pitch in and find ways to make the world a better place. All we have to do is follow the examples of 26 kindergarten children in Countryside, Illinois. They attend classes, by the way, at a place called "Ideal Public School."

NOTES

1. Greg Zoroya, "Suffering Afghan Children Touch American Hearts," *USA Today* (6 December 2001): 1A, 2A.
2. Department of Veterans Affairs, "America's Wars" (May 2001), retrieved online February 19, 2002, from http://www.va.gov/pressrel/amwars01.htm
3. The White House Office of Management and Budget, "Budget Highlights," retrieved online February 19, 2002, from http://www.whitehouse.gov/omb/budget/fy2003
4. Institute of International Education, "Study Abroad Enrollment Since 1985," Opendoors on the Web, retrieved February 18, 2002, from http://www.opendoorsweb.org/2001%20files/STAB_since_1985.htm

If we could shrink the earth's population to a village of precisely 100 people, with all the existing human ratios remaining the same, it would look something like the following:

There would be

57 Asians
21 Europeans
14 from the Western Hemisphere, both north and south
8 Africans

52 would be female.
48 would be male.

70 would be nonwhite.
30 would be white.

70 would be non-Christian.
30 would be Christian.

89 would be heterosexual.
11 would be homosexual.

6 people would possess 59 percent of the entire world's wealth, and all 6 would be from the United States.

80 would live in substandard housing.
70 would be unable to read.
50 would suffer from malnutrition.
1 would be near death; 1 would be near birth.
1 (yes, only 1) would have a college education.
1 would own a computer.

CHAPTER 1

Reading and Writing in College

One thing that nearly all college writing tasks have in common is this: they require you to read and understand other texts and, sometimes, use the ideas in (perhaps quotations from) those texts. The readings included in this textbook are intended to give you practice with the kinds of reading and writing tasks you will experience in your other college classes, but they are also designed to help you think and write about important ideas associated with world cultures. The readings are not necessarily models for you to follow (although some are excellent models); they are intended to provide you with a mini-library of sources from which to write papers. Some are primary sources (e.g., the selections from the Bible), and some are secondary sources (e.g., they write about primary texts, for example, McNeil and Sedlar's introduction to Confucius). Many are challenging but no more so than readings in other courses in the university.

We have chosen to focus on world cultures because we feel that this focus is important, given Americans' general lack of knowledge about the rest of the world in a time of increasing global interdependence. It is our hope that the readings will help you not only with developing your critical reading and writing skills but also with your understanding of the complexity and richness of other cultures. We also hope that after having read and written about other cultures, you will want to spend some time living in another culture in order to understand it better, perhaps through a study-abroad program or through an organization that encourages international exchanges. To that end, we have included essays in each section of the book written by students who have participated in such programs. The focus for the readings should not obscure the fact that this is a writing textbook. The writing assignments we suggest to go with this book are reading-based.

The following premises have informed our choices of readings and our crafting of writing assignments:

- Reading and writing are interrelated: you learn to write by both reading and writing.
- One of the purposes of a college writing class is to help you develop the critical reading, writing, and thinking strategies you need for other classes in the college curriculum.
- The best way to learn these strategies is to work with readings similar to those you will encounter in other classes.
- Writing is a mode of learning and a tool you can use to help you learn, as well as a method of testing that learning.
- Reading texts from other cultures poses special challenges that an understanding of Aristotle's rhetorical theory helps to overcome.

READING RHETORICALLY

Before we introduce Aristotle's ideas about rhetoric, we would like you to think for a moment about how you read texts in college. For the most part, you read to get information, to learn the subject matter; that much is obvious. But reading critically involves more than that; it involves pulling back from the text asking yourself questions about the information, about *how* it is presented and *why* it might be presented that way. Let us say you are checking Web sites to try to find information about a topic for a research paper on the ethics of cloning. Since anyone can post anything on the Web, you need to ask yourself questions about other issues; about the information itself—Is this information really accurate, given what I already know? Is this argument for or against cloning really logical?; about the author—Who is this person? Is he or she an authority or just someone with an opinion?; and about how the author seems to want you to feel as you take in the information—Are the words loaded emotionally? Is the picture of an adorable cloned kitten there to explain the text or to make you react emotionally and agree with the argument in favor of cloning? The same questions should be asked as you are reading a printed text. As you read, you should be thinking not only about the information you need to get from that text but also about whether or not that information is reliable and logical, whether or not the author is someone who is a credible source of information, and how that author is working upon your emotions as well as your intellect to persuade you that he or she is presenting information fairly and reasonably. In other words, you should read a text rhetorically.

RHETORIC, ARISTOTLE'S *RHETORIC*, AND READING ACROSS CULTURES

Rhetoric may be defined as the art that deals with the effective use of language—either spoken or written—to inform, persuade, or motivate an audience (sometimes just one person). We can trace the beginnings of rhetoric to the Greeks; one of the first written treatises[1] on the subject was by Aristotle (384–322 BCE), a philosopher known also for being a pupil of Plato and a tutor to Alexander the Great. *Philosopher* means literally "lover of wisdom," and that Aristotle certainly was. No one before him had contributed so much to learning and knowledge; although many of his works are now lost, we know that he wrote at least 150 treatises on such subjects as logic, language, intellectual and constitutional history, zoology, botany, chemistry, astronomy, mathematics, psychology, ethics, and metaphysics. His work on rhetoric reflected just one of his many interests.

Aristotle's work is not easy reading, as you will see. Some of it was never actually published (that is, copied by scribes and sold) but was available in his own library for others to study. These works were most probably his own notes for his lectures; thus, they have a highly compressed style. In fact, modern translations add information in brackets [like this] in order to make the prose more understandable. Further, Greek culture was an oral culture. The arenas in which rhetoric was useful (at trials, for example, or during political deliberations) required speeches; thus, Aristotle refers to "the speech" when he discusses means of persuasion. Although Aristotle intended his discussion of rhetoric to apply to public speaking, most of what he has to say applies as well to writing; it can also be used as a tool for reading as you try to decipher an unfamiliar text.

We believe Aristotle's *Rhetoric* is particularly useful for reading works from other cultures, since his focus is not just on logical argument (something we value highly in Western culture) but also on the emotions of the audience (or reader) and the credibility of the speaker/writer. For example, if we look at the *Analects* of Confucius (pp. 680–683 in this book), we see short, pithy sayings that are clearly meant to be persuasive—words to live by—but they do not use point-by-point logical arguments to persuade. Here is an example:

> The Master said, "The gentleman understands what is moral. The small man understands what is profitable." (IV: 16)

The beginning of the analect announces who is telling us this—the Master, Confucius himself, an authority on wisdom and how to live one's life; we are alerted by this beginning that we should pay attention, since what follows will be from someone important. What follows are two short, parallel sentences about the difference between a gentleman (someone of virtue) and a "small" man (someone we would not want to be); these appeal to the emotions of the listener/reader—none of us wants to be a small person. Finally, there is an implied connection between the two sentences that the listener/reader can make: if I want to be a gentleman/woman myself, I need to understand that what is moral is more important than what is profitable. This is not a logical connection; it is an emotional one. The two persuasive elements used here are what Aristotle called *ethos* and *pathos.*

DEFINING *RHETORIC, LOGOS, PATHOS,* AND *ETHOS*

Aristotle defines the art of rhetoric as the ability or power of discovering (for each individual situation) the available means of persuasion. Note that this definition focuses on "discovering," that is, on figuring out which means of persuasion is best for each particular situation. Each communication situation we face (for example, reading an unfamiliar text in order to understand it or writing a paper for a class) involves not only thinking about what we want to say but also whom we are saying it to and why. Aristotle's definition reminds us that in each communication act, we need to discover or think through what the persuasive strategy is, given the audience and purpose, and how we need to read rhetorically, thinking about the writer's own credibility, his or her purpose in writing, the logical arguments used, and the way the author appeals to our emotions as well as to our reason.

In his *Rhetoric,* Aristotle gives us three ways that an author or speaker can persuade audience members: by appealing to their reason, or *logos;* by appealing to their emotions, or *pathos;* and by appealing to our own character or credibility, or *ethos.* Thus, if you are reading an essay arguing that no war is a just war, you would want to first know something about the writer; if the person is a retired general with combat experience, his *ethos* lends great credibility to his argument. If you are writing a research paper that has as its thesis that in fact some wars *can* be defined as just wars, you would present a reasoned argument *(logos)* but you would build your own *ethos* by making sure that you cite respected or credible sources and that you have a substantial "works cited" page showing that you had read and evaluated a range of material to arrive at your conclusions. You may also want to include a narrative from a war survivor to illustrate the justness of that particular war from his or her point of view and to appeal to the emotions *(pathos)* of your reader.

ARISTOTLE AND READING RHETORICALLY: KEEPING A READING JOURNAL

In a moment, you will read a selection from Aristotle's *Rhetoric* yourself. To understand this or any other text, you need to read rhetorically, as we stated earlier; one of the best ways to read is to read a passage first with a pencil (NOT a highlighting pen) in your hand, underlining key words and phrases and summarizing key points in the margins of your texts. You will note that for this text, since it is a difficult one, we have already summarized these points for you. You should also keep a reading journal—a small, spiral-bound notebook that you can keep with your textbook. The purpose of keeping such a journal is to help you understand the readings by writing about them, but the journal is also a place where you can jot down ideas for the texts that you will be creating—where you can try out sample thesis statements or ask yourself questions about how you might fit ideas together. In other words, the reading journal gives you some raw material for the papers you will write.

Some suggestions follow for keeping your reading journal.[2]

1. First, summarize the main ideas of the selection you are reading. This need not be a long summary, but it should be as complete as possible. A good way to do a summary is to look before you start reading at the first paragraph of a piece; then look at the last paragraph; and then ask yourself questions about how the author got from beginning to end—what came in between, what were the steps in reasoning that led from the first to the last point? Then skim the entire piece, underlining the ideas that seem most important. Finally, go back and read carefully, noting the main ideas in your reading journal.
2. Analyze the rhetoric of the piece according to Aristotle's categories of *logos*, *pathos*, and *ethos*. Which of these does the author use most predominantly? Why, do you think?
3. Focusing on *logos*, reason along with the writer. What do you agree with and why? Imagine the writer is there to talk with you, and jot down the points that you would like to talk about with the writer, points where there is a meeting of the minds.

4. Again, focusing on *logos* and imagining that the writer is there to talk with you, argue with the writer. What do you disagree with and why? What seems strange to you and why? Write down your points of disagreement.

5. Still focusing on *logos*, ask questions about the material (these can be questions you could ask in class). Why does the author structure his or her argument in a particular way? What perplexes you about the material? Try beginning your questions with such phrases as "I don't understand why . . ." or "I was surprised when . . . ."

6. Focusing on *pathos*, write about how the piece affects you, or make connections to your own experience. What does this reading make you think of? How does it connect with other readings in this class or in your other classes? Are there other issues that are related to the issues raised in this reading that are important to you?

7. Focusing on *ethos*, write about the author and the author's point of view. What is the context (historical or cultural) for the piece? For what audience is the author writing? What seems to be his or her attitude toward the subject matter and the audience? How can you tell?

Selection from Aristotle's *Rhetoric*

As you read the following selection, underline what you think are the main points and jot down notes about how you would answer the seven preceding questions for a reading journal. Then compare your notes to the sample reading journal that follows.

[Definition of Rhetoric. Modes and Means of Persuasion.] Let Rhetoric be defined as the faculty [power] of discovering in the particular case what are the available means of persuasion. This is the function of no other art. The others are each instructive or persuasive with regard to some special subject-matter. Thus medicine informs us about the conditions of health and disease; geometry about the properties of magnitudes; arithmetic about numbers; and so with the rest of the arts and sciences. But Rhetoric, it would seem, has the function of discovering the means of persuasion for every case, so to speak, that is offered; and hence we say that the art as such has no special application to any distinct class of subjects. *(margin: Rhetoric defined)*

Proofs [persuasions] are of two kinds, artistic and non-artistic. By 'non-artistic' proofs are meant all such as are not supplied by our own efforts, but existed beforehand, such as witnesses, admissions under torture, written contracts, and the like. By 'artistic' proofs [means of persuasion] are meant those that may be furnished by the method of Rhetoric through our own efforts. The first sort have only to be used; the second have to be found. *(margin: Rhetorical proofs (persuasions); Non-artistic proofs; Artistic proofs)*

Of the means of persuasion supplied by the speech itself there are three kinds. The first kind reside in the character [*ethos*] of the speaker; the second consist in producing a certain [the right] attitude [*pathos*] in *(margin: Means of persuasion in the speech)* the hearer; the third appertain to the argument proper [*logos*], in so far as it actually or seemingly demonstrates.

The *ethos* of the speaker

The character [*ethos*] of the speaker is a cause of persuasion when the speech is so uttered as to make him worthy of belief; for as a rule we trust men of probity [honesty] more, and more quickly, about things in general, while on points outside the realm of exact knowledge, where opinion is divided, we trust them absolutely. This trust, however, should be created by the speech itself, and not left to depend upon an antecedent impression that the speaker is this or that kind of man. It is not true, as some writers on the art maintain, that the probity of the speaker contributes nothing to his persuasiveness; on the contrary, we might almost affirm that his character [*ethos*] is the most potent of all the means to persuasion.

Emotion in the hearers (*pathos*)

Secondly, persuasion is effected through the audience, when they are brought by the speech into a state of emotion; for we give very different decisions under the sway of pain or joy, and liking or hatred. This, we contend, is the sole aspect of the art with which technical writers of the day have tried to deal. We shall elucidate it in detail when we come to discuss the emotions.

Argument proper (*logos*)

Thirdly, persuasion is effected by the arguments, when we demonstrate the truth, real or apparent, by such means as inhere in particular cases.

What a mastery of Rhetoric calls for

Such being the instruments of persuasion, to master all three obviously calls for a man who can reason logically, can analyze the types of human character, along with the virtues, and, thirdly, can analyze the emotions—the nature and quality of each several emotion, with the means by which, and the manner in which, it is excited.

SAMPLE READING JOURNAL ENTRY

Summary: Aristotle defines rhetoric as the power of discovering in a particular case the available means of persuasion. There are two kinds of proof, artistic (ones we create ourselves) and non-artistic (ones that existed before, like contracts). There are three means of persuasion you can use in a speech: *ethos* (appealing to the character of the speaker), *pathos* (appealing to the emotions of the audience), and *logos* (appealing to logical argument).

The rhetoric: Aristotle uses what looks like pretty logical reasoning, defining a term and then making lists of types. *Logos* all the way. He sounds like my biology teacher.

Logos: *Reasoning and arguing with Aristotle:* I'm not sure I can do this until I know a little more. I'm confused. I'm going to go on to my questions.

Questions: Why does he only talk about men? Didn't women need to persuade people as well? If he's talking about speeches in a trial, I understand why he talks about witnesses and written contracts as "non-artistic," but why does he include admissions under torture? That's weird. And I'm also not clear about *pathos* and *ethos* as ways of persuading people. Logical argument makes sense, but not the others.

Pathos: *Connection to my own experience:* I really can't find anything here that connects to my own experience (except that I argue all the time with my brother and I'd like to figure out how to persuade him that I'm right more often. I guess that is a connection.)

Ethos: *The author and the context:* OK, I just figured something out. The reason I'm having trouble connecting to this reading is that he was writing for Greek guys more than 2,000 years ago. There's a lot about that context I don't know, so I need to know more before I can understand this.

Let us make a few observations about this journal entry. First, the writer has learned something by the end; she knew she was having difficulty understanding the passage completely, but until she began to think on paper about it, she did not know why. By the end, she had figured it out; she needed to know more about the historical context and about Aristotle's own *ethos* in order to understand the text. The audience for this journal is you, so make it useful to you; keeping a reading journal can help you process the information you are reading but can also help to clarify and perhaps even answer your own questions. Second, she now has some very specific questions to ask in class when the teacher opens the discussion. She would find out, for example, that Greek education and public life were entirely male; she would also find out that torturing was common practice and that confessions under torture were considered true. Finally, it did not take her long to write the entry—only about 10 minutes. The reading journal is a thinking/writing/study tool. You need to invest a little time in it at the beginning; but, once you get into a routine, it becomes part of the way you read and prepare to write.

VISUAL RHETORIC

Aristotle's culture was primarily oral; it depended primarily on the spoken word for getting things done. Modern Western culture—our culture—is primarily dependent on the written word, but it is also a profoundly visual culture. Pictures as well as words can persuade. But we can use Aristotle's categories to understand visual rhetoric as well. For example, look at the two advertisements that follow, the first for CARE, an international nondenominational organization that works to fight global poverty, and the second from World Vision, an international Christian humanitarian organization.

Both of these ads are excellent examples of the integration of visual and verbal persuasion. Let us examine the first one, published in 2003. CARE's purpose in publishing this ad is to get its audience—readers of the magazine in which this ad appeared—to care about the effects of poverty on the world, and CARE wants to motivate readers to do something about it (by contributing to their humanitarian aid). The name of the organization is itself an example of *ethos*—this is an organization that cares about helping people. We see a smiling, healthy baby girl (at least, the jewelry suggests that this is a girl) with

Source: CARE, 151 Ellis St. NE, Atlanta, GA

large, liquid eyes—appealing to our emotions *(pathos)* and pulling us in to look more closely, to look back at her since she appears to be looking right at us. There is a heading to the left, the place where Western readers always start when they scan a page (unlike some other writing systems, where one reads from right to left or from top to bottom). We read the heading to the left, and we are told (shockingly) that she died because of poverty, malnutrition, and lack of medical care and is survived by her mother who was powerless to help and by us, who could have helped. The contrast between the apparently healthy baby and the news that she died creates a logical contradiction, until we see that the date of her death is in the future, 2006. We are then led to the conclusion *(logos)* that if we contribute now, we can prevent her death. Our eyes are led downward from the text on the left to the coupon we can cut out to send with a contribution, so that we can "rewrite the future." The combination of visual and verbal persuasion is powerful, emphasizing *pathos* but also using *ethos* and *logos*.

The second ad is more conventional in its layout; at the top is a picture of a young girl (here the dress is the clue to her gender), looking not at us but at some point far into the distance and looking very sad. There are two pieces of text embedded in the photograph, one announcing an initiative called "Hope," the other announcing the organization, World Vision, with a graphic representation of something that looks like a star with a cross-like shape, perhaps the symbol of the organization. The photo has a caption just below telling us why she is so pensive: she represents one of the 25 million children who will be orphaned by AIDS. The combination of the picture and the caption are an appeal to *pathos*. On the left side, under the caption (again where Western readers

the Hope Initiative

World Vision

in **seven years**
25 million children
will be **orphaned by AIDS.**

World Vision. 52 years of getting results, plus a commitment to showing God's love. That's the kind of combination you need to bring hope to children affected by the HIV/AIDS crisis around the world.

Our new Hope Initiative is bringing together caring Americans, churches, and private and public partners to reach out to millions of children and families affected by AIDS. Together we're providing hurting families with things like food, clean water, health care, education, and prevention that works in the fight against AIDS. In Rakai, Uganda, we're working with local partners to help make history: the rate of HIV infection has reversed and school graduation rates have doubled.

Join us and help turn the tide against AIDS.
www.worldvision.org • 1.888.56.CHILD

Founded in 1950, World Vision is an international Christian humanitarian organization serving the world's poorest children and families in nearly 100 countries.

Source: www.worldvision.org

start to scan a page), we again see the phrase "World Vision" as the sponsor of this Hope Initiative; the name of the organization suggests its *ethos*—an organization that has a vision about the world or, perhaps, what the world should be. The rest of the text on the left expands on this ethos: the organization has had 52 years of getting results and also has a religious commitment. The concluding sentence of this text states, "That's the kind of combination you need to bring hope to children affected by the HIV/AIDS Crisis around the world." There is no logical connection between those two ideas (getting results plus commitment to showing God's love equals bringing hope to affected children): the persuasive tactic here is *ethos* (52 years of getting results) plus *pathos* (we are committed to living our religion, implying that readers should be too). The text on the right, the last place we usually look when scanning a page, announces a new program (called the Hope Initiative) and gives two facts to support the claim of getting results *(logos)*—increased school graduation rates and a lower rate of HIV infection in Rakai, Uganda. Finally, there is an appeal to the reader to help, with contact information; this is an appeal to *pathos* (join us to help turn the tide against AIDS), with an implication—because of the picture—that this will help save such a child from becoming an orphan. As with the other ad, the appeal is primarily to *pathos* and *ethos,* persuasive modes that get people to reach for their checkbooks.

READING AND WRITING ABOUT LITERATURE AND ART

It is a short jump from visual rhetoric to a discussion of reading literature and "reading" works of art. Alfred North Whitehead (1861–1947), a philosopher and mathematician, said, "Art is the imposing of a pattern on experience, and our aesthetic enjoyment is recognition of the pattern."[3] Works of art and literature are not necessarily meant to persuade or to present an argument of some sort (although some do: see Hardy's "The Man He Killed," p. 346). There is a further discussion of how to read and write about literature and art in the introduction to that section of this book; what we would like you to think about now is reading aesthetically—that is, looking at the visual arts and literature in order to understand and appreciate their formal elements (line, shape and space, light and value, balance, proportion, rhythm and repetition, the sound as well as the sense of the words, the shape of the plot, character development, etc.), recognize the principles of their design, consider their historical context, and enjoy them as well as understand their value. Although you read these works aesthetically, when you write about works of art, you still write rhetorically; that is, you need to think about your audience and purpose and how to persuade them that your understanding of a work is complete or that your evaluation of it is credible.

READING, WRITING, AND THINKING RHETORICALLY

We hope that it is clear by now that the three modes of persuasion Aristotle suggested—*logos* (appeal to reasoned argument), *pathos* (appeal to emotions), and *ethos* (appeal to the character of the speaker or writer)—are useful concepts for reading college texts and for writing college papers. In the notes on the readings, we ask you to think about the rhetoric of what you are reading; in the writing assignments, we also refer to Aristotle's modes of persuasion as we ask you to think about your audience and purpose for writing.

But we hope that these concepts are useful to you in other ways as well, giving you ways to think about other communicative acts. When you listen to campaign speeches, what are the appeals that the candidates are making? On talk shows and in newspaper editorials, what sorts of persuasive tactics are being used? When your friends are trying to convince you to go to one party rather than another, how do they try to persuade you? We are not suggesting that these three modes of persuasion are all that you need to know about rhetoric; if you are interested in learning more about classical rhetoric, we give a suggestion in Question 4 for further reading. But we hope that by introducing you to Aristotle's concepts, we have given you a useful tool not only for your college reading and writing tasks but also for your life outside of and beyond school.

Notes

1. A *treatise* is a formal and systematic exposition on a particular subject; thus, many of Aristotle's titles resemble one another ("On Justice," "On the Poets," "On Plants," "On Motion," etc.).
2. Adapted from Sharon Flitterman-King, "The Role of the Response Journal in Active Reading," *The Quarterly* 10 (July 1988): 4–11.
3. Alfred North Whitehead, *Dialogues of Alfred North Whitehead, as Recorded by Lucien Price* (Boston: Little Brown, 1954): June 10, 1943.

Questions for Discussion and Your Reading Journal

1. Which of the two ads discussed in this chapter do you think is most persuasive? Why?
2. Both ads picture young girls, and there are suggestions in both ads that the girls are African (the name of one, and the fact that the text of the other mentions Uganda). Poverty is not exclusively African. Why do you suppose both of these organizations chose African girls to be part of their appeal for support?
3. Another definition of *rhetoric* is "pompous or pretentious speech." Speculate about how such a definition might have come about.
4. Choose another of the *Analects* of Confucius (pp. 680–683) and analyze it according to the modes of persuasion discussed in this chapter: *logos*, *pathos*, and *ethos*.

Suggestions for Further Reading

Corbett, Edward P. J. *Classical Rhetoric for the Modern Student*, 3rd. New York: Oxford University Press, 1990.

Crowley, Sharon. *Ancient Rhetorics for Contemporary Students*. New York: Macmillan, 1994.

CHAPTER 2

Government and Politics

© John Madere/CORBIS

A recent report issued by the American Council on Education (ACE) in Washington, D.C., and endorsed by 35 of the nation's top educational associations underscores in no uncertain terms the importance America's educational leaders place upon awareness of other peoples, their societies, their governments, and their political systems in the 21st century. At the very time that the terrorist attacks of September 11 and the worldwide "War on Terror" are putting new demands upon the United States for citizens "with expanded knowledge and skills" for working with other cultures, the ACE study found "a dangerous shortfall of individuals with global competence." Warning that it will take "a generation of education and reform" to meet this global challenge, the report called upon Americans at all levels of education, government, and the private sector to come up with a "comprehensive agenda on international education" to teach global understanding more effectively to our citizens. If we do not do so, the report warned, we face "serious costs in terms of potential foreign-policy failures, military blunders, terrorism, and a decline in U.S. competitiveness in the global marketplace . . . ."[1]

This chapter of *Writing About the World* represents an explicit response to ACE's call for better understanding in a global world. The chapter starts with the assumption that you, the student, must have essential background knowledge about the governments and politics of other nations in order to understand how and why they function in the ways that they do today (ways that are often radically different from, and sometimes in opposition to, your own). Therefore, the first collection of readings under "Definitions and Cultural Contexts" offers opportunities to explore, to think about, and to write about some of the most important ideas evolved by humans throughout history to guide their myriad forms of government and politics.

In the second half of the chapter, readings build upon the foundational knowledge of earlier readings. Here, you will find essays and articles on some of the most intensely debated political issues of our time, issues such as the globalization of wealth and poverty, war, terrorism, racism, and oppression. The second section, like the first, draws upon readings from some of the most important thinkers and participants in global politics to open wider the doors of ideas and knowledge to students.

However, entering these "doors of knowledge" is not easy. Governmental and political texts written in China over 2,000 years ago or similar texts written in far off parts of the world today can be equally daunting to students who live in very different times and in different places from the writers. Here, as throughout this book, the key we offer to unlocking knowledge and meaning across challenging historical and cultural barriers is Aristotle's rhetoric. You, as a student, will constantly be asked to draw upon the conceptual tools of *logos, ethos,* and *pathos* to gain a deeper understanding (1) of what authors are trying to say and how they are saying it *(logos);* (2) of how and why they present themselves as they do in their texts *(ethos);* (3) and of what they are doing in their writing to help intended audiences see and feel the importance of their various messages *(pathos).*

The problem you will constantly face, of course, is that you are quite often *not* the intended audience for these great writers and thinkers from the past and present. If you want them to "speak to you," you must do the work of becoming part of their audience. This means making an added effort to interpret the historical contexts and cultural mindsets of the writers and their original audiences. Headnotes provide much of this essential background. Read them. Take notes on headnotes the same as you do on the actual readings. In addition to key background information, headnotes regularly indicate other readings in the text that can help you to grasp the larger picture of the topics and issues being treated. Finally, the questions after each reading can be most useful in guiding your attention deeper into key ideas and can provide excellent starting points for writing in your Reading Journal, as well as for opening class discussions.

Government and politics are difficult and challenging areas of study. Many students in the United States and elsewhere may prefer to pursue a wide variety of other fields of knowledge. However, Arundhati Roy, a young woman novelist and social critic from India, gives a particularly compelling reason for why citizens, in general, and young Americans, in particular, need to be educated about global politics. (A selection of her writing is included near the end of the chapter.) While many observers speak of the American military as the greatest armed force the earth has ever known and of the U.S. government in similar terms, Roy makes a deeper assessment of American might from a perspective *outside* of the United States of America. As she puts it, "The fact is that the only institution in the world today that is more powerful than the American government is American civil society. American citizens have a huge responsibility riding on their shoulders. How can we not salute and support those who not only acknowledge but act upon that responsibility? They are our allies, our friends."[2] As the American Council on Education has underscored, as well, the global alliances and worldwide friendships of which Roy writes must be nourished and sustained by knowledge and understanding to endure. If they do not endure, war and conflict will continue to be the focus of the governments and the political bodies of the world, in the place of peace, education, better health care, trade, and a greater prosperity that is shared by all the citizens of the world instead of a beleaguered few.

Notes

1. American Council on Education, *Beyond September 11: A Comprehensive National Policy on International Education,* 2002: pp. 7, 15, 11.
2. Arundhati Roy, "Mesopotamia. Babylon. The Tigris and Euphrates." *The Guardian* (UK), Wednesday, April 2, 2003.

CYNTHIA REBELO Little Flag, Full of Hope

Cynthia Rebelo (1982–) is a major in International/Peace Studies at Bay Path College in Longmeadow, Massachusetts. During the summer after her first year of college, she spent 3 weeks living and working as a volunteer in a shantytown of 300,000 people on the outskirts of Lima, Peru. Her work involved caring for 2-year-olds in a community day-care center, allowing their mothers to go to work to help their families financially. In the following article, Rebelo attempts to communicate the ideas and emotions that she encountered as she journeyed into a new culture quite different from her own in North America.

Reading Rhetorically

The main point of Rebelo's message is that even the poorest of citizens in third-world countries have deep resources of dignity and pride that can lead to hope and amazing community achievements when their own governments and political systems fail them. As you read, note how Rebelo uses evidence to make her message persuasive, evidence grounded in her own personal experiences in Peru (her *ethos*). Note also how she presents herself in her text. Although she labels herself as a "*gringa,* a foreigner," there is more to her persona than a visiting tourist or casual outside observer. In the end, she bonds with the people she serves in a manner that makes her more than simply another "foreigner." It is through this human bond that she offers her readers the deepest insight into the community that opened to her. Finally, note how her use of language to describe such things as stray dogs, encounters with children, and interactions with the elderly helps to stimulate an emotional response in her readers (*pathos*). All of these rhetorical elements work together to make her writing especially powerful for a student writer.

I had only been in Peru for a few days when I led a group of 14 two-year-olds   1
through the courtyard of a daycare center in a small parade. It was June 7th, Flag Day, and we marched with red and white Peruvian flags made from thin tissue paper and a Popsicle stick held high. I had no idea it was Flag Day, nor that I would be marching among the two-year-olds, until I was hustled out along with them. Only minutes before, the teacher had taught us the song we would be singing over and over through the courtyard for the principal, teachers, older students and *abuelitos,* the affectionate name for the elderly which means "little grandparents," who cheered as we passed with our small wrinkled flags. The song went to the tune of *Frere Jacques* with the simple lyrics:

Villa El Salvador. Courtesy of Cynthia Rebelo.

Bandelito, bandelito	Little flag, little flag,
de Perú, de Perú,	of Peru, of Peru,
rojo y blanco,	red and white,
rojo y blanco,	red and white,
eres tu, eres tu!	are you, are you!

2   I can only imagine what the *abuelitos* thought of this *gringa,* a foreigner, as she sang in *castellano* (Spanish) along with the inaudible voices of the small children. They were laughing with me and they were happy. After only being in Peru for a couple of days, I was surprised that the people I was surrounded by were so willing to celebrate. They lived in poverty, but as I learned more about the remarkable shantytown that I was working in, it became clear to me that they had plenty to celebrate.

3   The daycare center was located in *Villa El Salvador,* or "Village of the Savior," a squatter settlement about 25 km south of Lima, the capital of Peru, and home to an estimated 300,000 people. *Villa El Salvador* is a model shantytown, which has given hope to its members by following the principle of equality through organization and local community services, such as daycare, health and community centers for the development of its people as individuals and also as a community.

4   Nothing could have prepared me for my first day in a shantytown. No news report or magazine article, not a textbook or class lecture, not even a "Save the Children" commercial could have made poverty as realistic to me as the three weeks I spent in Peru. I went through a non-profit organization called Cross-Cultural Solutions which organizes groups of volunteers in countries throughout the world in communities such as *Villa El Salvador.* Volunteers are given placements in schools, daycare centers, health facilities, and in other grass roots community services depending on experience and interest. I was placed in a daycare center with 14 two-year-olds, although I also spent time with equally energetic *abuelitos.*

5   The first day that other new volunteers and I were taken to *Villa,* we piled into two vans and were busy getting to know one another. Most of the volunteers were

students who wanted to experience something outside of our fortunate lifestyles in the U.S. Every one was talking until the moment we drove into *Villa*. Then complete and deafening silence fell over the van that had been noisy only seconds before. Our driver, Juan Carlos, wasn't surprised, as he has been taking American volunteers into *Villa* for over two years. Stunned silence was the effect that the poverty had on us. We simply were not used to such extreme conditions of life.

Villa is located on a desert strip along the coast of Peru. The homes in the 6 sandy neighborhood we were brought to were made of straw and wooden poles. Many of the homes were covered with a sheet of plastic, thrown over in a desperate attempt for a roof. It appeared as though a gust of wind would knock a house down, bringing the surrounding houses down along with it. It was one of the newly settled parts of *Villa* and so there was still no running water. As we entered more established neighborhoods the straw and wooden poles gave way to cement and brick and the plastic roofs to large flat pieces of wood. In some places, there was even electricity and running water.

One of the most striking moments of my experience in Peru was a few days 7 later while riding in the van with Juan Carlos. Stray dogs roam *Villa* in a constant attempt to find food, and by the looks of them they are rarely successful. I was watching as a dog was sniffing and digging into a large trash pile. As we drove past the pile I saw that on the other side there was also a person digging through the same pile. This struck me for two reasons. A man, *a human being*, was searching through garbage along side mangy dogs. Even more depressing was the fact that he was going through another poor man's trash. Everyone is struggling and it is difficult to imagine that the man would find anything in that pile, yet he was still there digging through it. This scene haunted me the entire time I was in Peru and continued to follow me after leaving the Andean country.

When I was taken to my placement for the first time I was met by the curious 8 stares of 14 two-year-olds. The daycare center in which I was placed was called *INABIF*, which stands for National Institute for the Welfare of Infants and the Family. Partially government funded, *INABIF* offers educational and recreational services for children from age 1 to age 16. Older children go to school in the morning and younger children go to school in the afternoon. *INABIF* is a place for children to go before and after school. Younger children, such as the two-year-olds that I worked with, stay all day until their parents are able to pick them up. This constant push for education in school and in daycare centers has proven successful with amazing results. The national illiteracy rate in Peru is 27%, while in *Villa* the illiteracy rate is only 2%. Over half of the residents are high school graduates, while the national average is less than 10% (Ruiz 1989).

A problem facing *INABIF* is proper funding, as parents are only expected to 9 pay a very small sum every month, which includes meals and supervision. Most teachers are also stressed and tired, with a large ratio of children to adults, and are paid very small wages. My classroom had 14 two-year-olds with one teacher and sometimes an aid. Coordinating activities and feeding the children could become a lengthy process with so many, causing the children to get cranky and rowdy. Every day the children played with the same building blocks and puzzles, which were worn and had lost their color. The teacher would also sing songs with them and sometimes would color. I noticed that we repeated the same activities every day, making the very most out of the few resources available.

10   One little girl grew especially attached to me and would cry whenever she wasn't sitting in my lap or holding my hand. The teacher and I laughed about this but at the same time it was sad because I knew that all she needed was attention. Unlike in the U.S. where most children are sheltered from life's harsh realities, in Peru they are subject to a very different lifesyle, especially when they are living in poverty. Responsibility seems to come at a much younger age because of the conditions that they are living in. Parents are busy trying to make ends meet and as a result many children don't get the personal attention that they crave.

11   I was surprised to find that there were *abuelitos*, "little grandparents," sitting around *INABIF*. They had their own garden where they grew vegetables and they would also make crafts with their skilled hands. The elderly are oftentimes forgotten in a struggling society like the one in *Villa*, and there are not very many options for them. They sometimes find their way into centers like *INABIF*, although it is not directed towards the elderly. *Los Martincitos* is a program in *Villa El Salvador*, partially sponsored by the Catholic Church, that provides two hot meals, recreational activities, health care, and counseling for about 120 *abuelitos* twice a week. Every Wednesday and Friday they come together to share their meals, talk, exercise, dance, and pray.

12   However, *Los Martincitos* has trouble finding financial support because funding groups often assume that the elderly are unable to give anything back to the community. Sponsors feel that by supporting younger generations they will someday give back to those who helped them along the way. The *abuelitos* who participate in *Los Martincitos* have been abandoned by their families, have often been abused, are in poor health, or are otherwise alone. For many, these meals twice a week are the only times that they eat and they look forward to the time that they can spend with one another. Out of all the centers that I visited, the one with *abuelitos* was the most fun and lively. They truly appreciated the center and all it had to offer them. And yet without stable financial support, *Los Martinicitos* is constantly at risk of being reduced to one or no days a week.

13   During my time in Peru, I was fortunate enough to visit the homes of three *abuelitos* with the director of *Los Martincitos*, Tony. All three *abuelitos* had been abandoned by their children and two were left to take care of their grandchildren. One woman was left to care for her mentally handicapped granddaughter, and an elderly gentleman was left to care for his two young granddaughters. When we entered his home he told us he had just found out that his water had been turned off. He didn't know what to do because both of his granddaughters were very sick and he didn't know how they were going to survive.

14   The third man had also been abandoned by his family. He rented out half of his home to a young man in order to earn some income. He told Tony that he wanted to leave what little he had to him when he died because he hadn't seen or heard from his son in years. He led us into his home, and muttered his apologies the entire time we were visiting. It bothered me that he was apologizing for his situation. No one should have to apologize for living in poverty. As we walked away from his home there was a small puppy whimpering in the middle of the sandy road, and I knew exactly how he felt.

15   Despite these scenes of struggle and suffering, *Villa El Salvador* has still managed to become one of the most successful shantytowns in the world. For many of

the members, the shantytown is considered a "desert dream" offering hope for a better future. Every family that arrives in *Villa* is given ownership of an equal piece of land. This is important to the people of *Villa* for two reasons. The first is that they *own* their own property. No one can take it away from them. The second reason is that it is an *equal* piece of land. Everyone is given an equal opportunity to build his or her future. *Villa* is also recognized as home to the first women's rights group in Peru, a further reflection of the goal for complete social equality.

Despite financial setbacks, community based services continue to strive in *Villa* El Salvador, setting *Villa* apart from other shantytowns. In the center of every city in Latin America there is a central plaza. Most are given a military name, but in *Villa El Salvador* it is called "Solidarity Square" in honor of its citizens' mission to work together as a community. *Villa's* efforts have not gone unnoticed. In 1987 the United Nations named *Villa El Salvador* an "Official Messenger of Peace" and a year earlier *Villa* was even nominated for the Nobel Peace Prize (Hart *et al.* 1989).

Peru taught me more in three weeks than I ever dreamed possible. It is an experience that I will carry with me for the rest of my life. I left Lima wanting to return with my friends and family so they could do what I did, see what I saw, and feel what I felt. *Villa El Salvador* is without a doubt a remarkable community. The achievements and successes of *Villa* have gone beyond the expectations of the first families to arrive on a sandy strip of land near the capital. Every community, whether poverty stricken or wealthy, has something to learn from this city which has brought so many people together to create their own hope. They have earned the right to wave their flags high with dignity and with pride.

References

Hart, R., Cote, L., Bertomeu, J. (Directors). (1989). *Villa El Salvador, A desert dream.* [Videotape]. Montreal: Adobe Foundations.

Ruiz, W. (1989). Listening and learning: An interview with the mayor of a peruvian shantytown. *IDRC Reports,* 6–7.

Questions for Discussion and Your Reading Journal

1. What seems to be the rhetorical purpose of Rebelo's article? Of what is she trying to persuade her audience?
2. What is Rebelo's first-world response to living conditions in a third-world shantytown?
3. Rebelo mentions "dogs" a couple of times in her piece. What effect do her comments about dogs have overall on the article?
4. Many people feel that if able-bodied adults live in poverty, it is their own fault for not working harder to raise their living standards. How does Rebelo's focus on children and old people in *Villa El Salvador* subtly counter this argument?
5. Does Rebelo succeed in changing your perspective on the shantytown *Villa El Salvador* by the end of her essay? Explain.

DEFINITIONS AND CULTURAL CONTEXT

CONFUCIUS

The Chinese philosopher, teacher, and political reformer, K'ung Fu-tzu ("Master K'ung," 551–479 BCE) is known in the West as Confucius and is considered one of the greatest thinkers of all time. He lived near the end of an extremely violent period of warring feudal states in Chinese history and sought to reform the government so as to alleviate the sufferings of the people. To begin to appreciate Confucius, you must understand just how troubled his times were. For 300 years, the common people of China had regularly faced death and the destruction of their homes, their families, and their villages as opposing armies waged brutal warfare back and forth across their lands. Even in the best of times, the people often starved as regional warlords violently took what they needed to maintain their armies for ongoing wars with rivals. Confucius taught that the way to end this painful and destructive social chaos was through a focus upon ethics and education as building blocks of good government. In the following reading, you will note the repetition of the Chinese words jen *(humanity),* li *(order), and* yi *(understanding or empathy). According to Confucius, an education stressing proper ethical behavior toward all other human beings was a means to strengthen a political ruler's character and personal conduct. The right to govern depended upon the ruler's virtue—his love for the people and his ability to understand the governed and to make them happy. Such teachings took deep roots in Chinese society, so much so that, for the following 2,000 years, the Chinese government required ambitious young men who wanted to enter government service to pass grueling civil service examinations based entirely upon Confucius's ideas. Women were excluded from these exams, as is pointed out by the poet Yü Hsüan-Chi in "On a Visit to Ch'ung Chên Taoist Temple" (in the Art and Literature chapter of this book). Confucius did not come up with entirely new ideas born from his own genius. Like other important thinkers, he built upon ideas that were passed on to him as part of his culture. It is not surprising, therefore, that Confucius's political thought has roots in the ideas of Taoism, one of the most significant Chinese religions/philosophies of his time. Perhaps his greatest genius is in the way that he applied the concept of the Tao, best understood as "the way of nature and the universe," to human relations, translating harmony with the Tao into a complex set of rules for governing people who would be in harmony with each other. The result was a political system based upon maintaining ethical and peaceful relations between the rulers and the ruled, and between all members of society. At the very core of Confucian ethics are eight Chinese written characters that translate into: "A ruler rules; a minister ministers; a father fathers; a son sons." The meaning of this deceptively simple ethical code is the imperative that each member of society learn his or her social role and then carry it out in harmony with the ethical rules that govern that role. For further background information on Confucius and the world in which he lived, see McNeill and Sedlar's text in the Philosophy and Religion section of this book.*

Reading Rhetorically

What you are about to read is over 2,000 years old and comes from a culture quite different from those of the Western world. As you would expect, Confucius had a different rhetorical sense of what was needed to persuade his audience about the value of his ideas than might be common today. As you read his writing, note especially how he is presented as "the Master" (*ethos*). This suggests that he lived in a world where people respected other people with titles much as we respect individuals today who have "Dr.," "President," or "Ph.D." associated with their names. Furthermore, although speaking of politics, he constantly makes reference to such things as "virtue," "propriety," "kindness," and "courtesy," which again tends to make us respect his ideas. When considering his actual message, note how his short, insightful sayings ("analects") are constantly organized into question/answer exchanges and conversations with others. Confucius's analects show him as a "master teacher" to those around him, some of whom are rather important people ("Duke" Ai). This unique use of the analect form not only underscores the importance of Confucius's overall message and how it was received even by elite members of society but also represents a valuable tool for spreading the message in a culture that would have communicated orally much more than in written form. Short narrations that lead up to key "punch lines" are considerably easier to remember and to share with other people than long, well-supported arguments. Limericks, proverbs, and jokes in the Western world follow this same pattern to this day, and, like Confucius's analects, they are popular with people largely because of the ways that they reinforce values, perspectives, and attitudes already present in the culture of day-to-day life. In the end, it is the day-to-day life and relationships between people that Confucius most sought to influence so as to restore harmony and peace in a land devastated by some 300 years of violent warfare.

The Sacred Books of Confucius: Paternal Government

Confucius, as a great humanist, looked at all political problems in terms of human relations. He based all his judgments on the moral codes, from which he evolved his ethical-political system of a paternal government. The good behavior of the ruler was a prerequisite for successful government. As taught by Confucius, a ruler had nine basic duties:

1. To cultivate his personal conduct
2. To honor men of worth

3. To cherish affection for his kinsmen
4. To show respect to great ministers
5. To have an interest in the welfare of all officials
6. To take paternal care of the common people
7. To promote all useful crafts
8. To be hospitable to strangers
9. To be friendly to the neighboring princes

It was especially important for a ruler to cultivate his own conduct, so that he could set a perfect moral example for his officials and for his people. The moral attributes of a ruler were the same as those of a *chün-tzu*. For a ruler, as well as for a *chün-tsu,* the cardinal virtues were *jen* [humanity], *li* [order], *yi* [understanding], and *hsin* [good faith], as illustrated in his teachings . . . .

244. The Master said: "To rule a state of a thousand chariots, there must be reverent attention to duties and sincerity, economy in expenditure, and love for the people, working them only at the proper seasons." [I–5]

245. The Master said: "One who governs by virtue is comparable to the polar star, which remains in its place while all the stars turn towards it." [II–1]

246. The Master said: "Govern the people by laws and regulate them by penalties, and the people will try to do no wrong, but they will lose the sense of shame. Govern the people by virtue and restrain them by rules of property, and the people will have a sense of shame and be reformed of themselves." [II–3]

247. Duke Ai asked: "What should I do to secure the submission of the people?" "Promote the upright and banish the crooked," said the Master; "then the people will be submissive. Promote the crooked and banish the upright; then the people will not be submissive." [II–19]

248. Chi Kang Tzu asked: "What should be done to make the people respectful and be encouraged to cultivate virtues?" "Approach the people with dignity," said the Master, "and they will be respectful. Show filial piety and kindness, and they will be loyal. Promote those who are worthy, and train those who are incompetent; and they will be encouraged to cultivate virtues." [II–20]

249. Duke Ting asked how a prince should employ his ministers and how ministers should serve their prince. Master K'ung said: "A prince should employ his ministers with propriety; ministers should serve their prince with loyalty." [III–19]

250. The Master said: "If a prince governs his state with propriety and courtesy, what difficulty will have? But if not, of what use are rituals?" [IV–13]

251. The Master said: "Yung would be a ruler." Then Chung Kung [Yung] asked about Tzu-sang Po-tzu. "He would be, too," said the Master, "but he is lax." "Such a man might be a ruler," said Chung Kung, "if he were scrupulous in his own conduct and lax only in his dealing with the people. But a man who was lax in his own conduct as well as in government would be too lax." The Master said: "What Young says is true." [VI–1]

252. [Alluding to the States of Ch'i and Lu], the Master said: "Ch'i, by one change, might attain to the level of Lu; and Lu, by one change, might attain to the *Tao!*" [VI–22]

253. The Master said: "A cornered vessel that has no corners. What a cornered vessel! What a cornered vessel!" [VI-23]

254. The Master said: "The people may be made to follow but not to understand." [VIII-9]

255. Tzu Kung asked about government, and the Master said: "The essentials of good government] are sufficient food, sufficient arms, and the confidence of the people." "But," asked Tzu Kung, "if you have to part with one of the three, which would you give up?" "Arms," said the Master. "But suppose," said Tzu Kung, "one of the remaining two has to be relinquished, which would it be?" "Food," said the Master. "From time immemorial, death has been the lot of all men, but a people without confidence is lost indeed." [XII-7]

256. Duke Ching asked Master K'ung about government, and Master K'ung said: "Let the ruler be ruler; the minister, minister; the father, father; and the son, son." "Good!" said the Duke. "For truly if the ruler be not ruler, the minister not minister; if the father be not father, and the son not son, then with all the grain in my possession, should I be able to relish it?" [XII-11]

257. The Master said: "In hearing lawsuits, I am no better than other men, but my aim is to bring about the end of lawsuits." [XII-13]

258. Tzu Chang asked about government, and the Master said: "Attend to its affairs untiringly, and carry it out loyally," [XII-14]

259. Chi Kang Tzu asked Master K'ung about government, and Master K'ung said: "To govern means to rectify. If you, Sir, lead the people in rectitude, who dares not be rectified?" [XII-17]

260. Chi Kang Tzu, being troubled by burglars, asked Master K'ung what he should do, and Master K'ung said: "If only you, Sir, are free from desire [for wealth], they will not steal even though you pay them." [XII-18]

261. Chi Kang Tzu asked Master K'ung about government, saying: "Suppose I kill the *Tao*-less for the good of the *Tao*-abiding, what do you think of it?" "What need, Sir," said Master K'ung, "is there of killing in your administration? Let you desire good, and the people will be good. The virtue of the prince [*chün-tzu*] is the wind, and that of the common people [*hsiao-jen*] the grass. The grass bends in the direction of the wind." [XII-19]

262. Tzu Lu asked about government, and the Master said: "Go before the people and be diligent in their affairs." When asked for further instruction, the Master said: "Be not weary." [XIII-1]

263. Chung Kung, chief minister of the Chi family, asked about government, and the Master said: "Employ first the services of your men, overlook minor faults, and then promote men of worth and talents." "How do I know a man of worth and talents in order to promote him?" said Chung Kung. "Promote those whom you know," said the Master. "Those whom you do not know others will certainly not neglect." [XIII-2]

264. Tzu Lu said: "The prince of Wei is awaiting you, Sir, to join his government. What will you do first, Sir?"

The Master said: "The first thing needed is the rectification of names."

"So, indeed!" said Tzu Lu. "How pedantic it sounds! Why must there be such rectification?" "Yu! How rude you are!" said the Master. "*Chün-tzu* abstains from what he does not know. If names are not correct, then words are inappropriate; when the words are inappropriate, then things cannot be accomplished. Then rites and music will not flourish, punishments will not be properly administered, and the people have nowhere to put hand or foot. Therefore *chün-tzu* designates what can be properly stated, and only speaks of what can be properly carried into effect. *Chün-tzu*, in what he says, leaves nothing that is remiss." [XIII–3]

265. The Master said: "If a prince himself is upright, all will go well without orders. But if he himself is not upright, even though he gives orders, they will not be obeyed." [XIII–6]

266. The Master said: "In their governments, Lu and Wei are still brothers." [XIII–7]

267. When the Master went to Wei, Jan Yu acted as driver of his carriage. The master said: "How thriving is the population here!" "Since it is so thriving," asked Jan Yu, "what more shall be done for the people?" "Enrich them!" was the Master's reply. "And when they are enriched, what more shall be done?" "Educate them!" said the Master. [XIII–9]

268. The Master said: "Were any prince to employ me, in a year something could be done; in three years, the work could be completed." [XIII–10]

269. The Master said: " 'Only if good men were to govern a country for one hundred years, would it be really possible to transform the evil and do away with killings.' How true is the saying!" [XIII–11]

270. The Master said: "If a prince has rendered himself upright, he will have no difficulty in governing the people. But if he cannot rectify himself, how can he hope to rectify the people?" [XIII–13]

271. The Master said: "If a sage-king were to arise, *jen*[1] would prevail within one generation." [XIII–12] . . .

281. Yen Yuen asked how to rule a state, and the Master said: "Follow the calendar of Hsia; ride in the carriage of Yin; wear the cap of Chou. Adopt the music of *Shao*, with its pantomime; banish the songs of *Cheng*; and keep away from glib talkers. For the song of *Cheng* is licentious and glib talkers are dangerous." [XV–10]

282. The Master said: "Suppose a prince has sufficient wisdom to attain power, but he has no *jen* to secure it. Though he gets it, he will certainly lose it. Suppose his wisdom brings him to power, and he has *jen* to secure it; if there is no dignity in his rule, the people will not show respect. Suppose his wisdom has brought him into power, he has *jen* to secure it and rules with dignity. However, if he acts contrary to the code of rituals, he is still not a good ruler." [XV–32]

283. Master K'ung said: "When the *Tao*[2] prevails in the world, ceremonies, music, and punitive expeditions proceed from the Emperor. When the

---

[1] *jen* Humanity or human heartedness. [Ed. note.]

[2] *Tao* In Confucianism: "the right way of life; the path of virtuous conduct." [Ed. note.]

Tao fails in the world, ceremonies, music, and military expeditions proceed from the feudal princes. When they proceed from a feudal prince, his power can seldom survive for ten generations. When they proceed from a state minister, his power can seldom survive for five generations. When a subordinate officer holds power in the kingdom, his power can seldom survive for three generations. When there is *Tao* in the world, the power is not in the hands of ministers. And when there is *Tao* in the world, the people do not even discuss government affairs." [XVI–2]

284. Master K'ung said: "For five generations the revenue has departed from the Ducal House [of Lu], and for four generations the government has been in the hands of ministers. That is why the descendants of the three Huan [the three powerful families] are so losing their powers!" [XVI–3]

285. Tzu Chang asked Master K'ung: "What must a man do to qualify himself for government position?" "Let him honor the five merits and banish the four demerits," said the Master, "then may he serve in the government." "What are the five merits?" asked Tzu Chang. "A *chün-tzu* is bounteous without extravagance; he works the people without causing their resentment; he has desires, but he is not covetous; he is dignified but not arrogant; he is majestic but not ferocious." "What do you mean by 'being bounteous without extravagance'?" said Tzu Chang. "Let him spend on what the people find advantageous; is this not being bounteous without extravagance? Let him work the people during the proper seasons; who will resent? Let him long for *jen* and become *fen*-minded; how can he be covetous? Whether he deals with many people or few, with the small or with the great, he never presumes to be arrogant; is this not being dignified but not arrogant? When he is properly dressed, with dignified manners, he will inspire awe on the onlookers; is this not being majestic but not ferocious?" Then Tzu Chang asked again: "What are the four demerits?" "To put the people to death without giving instruction," said the Master; "this is cruelty. To require accomplishment without previous warning; this is tyranny. To delay orders and hasten its execution; this is oppression. And to make offers but grudge to carry them out; this is the way of the petty officials." [XX–2]

Questions for Discussion and Your Reading Journal

1. What does Confucius value in a ruler? What are his assumptions?
2. How does this compare with Kautilya's and Machiavelli's (p. 35 and p. 43) versions of the ideal ruler?
3. Do you agree with Confucius's statements about the essentials of good government? Discuss.
4. Confucius based his ethical-political system on the family unit as it was known then, a paternal system. Could there be such a thing as "maternal government"? Would the "nine basic duties" of a ruler change if the ruler were female?

PLATO

Plato (428–348 BCE) turned to philosophy to temper raw political action after the democratically elected leaders of Athens voted for the death of his mentor, Socrates. In The Republic, *he assumes the persona of his teacher Socrates to argue that to rule wisely, statesmen need to become philosophers. Because the goal of the "true" philosopher is to seek wisdom rather than riches, fame, or self-gratification, he argued that an aristocracy of the most talented citizens would be the best way to create an "ideal state." The view that Amaury de Riencourt gives of the oppression and degradation of women in Athens during the very time of Plato's writing (see "Women of Athens" later in this chapter) suggests that the Greek world was far from being ideal for many of its inhabitants. Plato's ideas echo a belief in the power and goodness of ethical leadership not unlike the one expressed by Confucius in the previous reading. His ideas also foreshadow concerns with the excesses of democracy similar to those of Alexis de Tocqueville in* Democracy in America, *who examines the problem of "the tyranny of the majority" (reading later in this chapter). This view of the negative dimensions of democracy is perhaps an outgrowth of the fact that Plato's cherished teacher, Socrates, lost his life because of a democratic but highly politicized vote by the senators of Athens against him.*

Reading Rhetorically

As Plato lived at the very place and time that Western rhetoric was born, it is not surprising that his writing is profoundly imbued with a self-conscious sense of its own rhetorical nature. At the heart of his use of rhetoric is the "dialogue" form, a conversational genre of writing in which his main character, Socrates, asks questions and elicits reasoned and reasonable answers from his listeners. These answers lead, step by step, to a deeper understanding of an issue in an approach that is known to this day as the *Socratic Method.* This method is based upon a philosophy of education (see *The Allegory of the Cave* in the Religion and Philosophy chapter) that assumes as a basic principle that the ability to generate insight and knowledge already resides within each student. Plato (and, according to Plato, his mentor Socrates) was among the first thinkers of record to insist that "true education" was *not* a matter of wise teachers simply pouring knowledge and truth into the minds of their pupils. Rather, a good teacher was one who could lead students to their own insights into the truth of things through the use of the right questions. Because of this educational philosophy, a carefully structured and logically supported message (*logos*) was an essential piece of Plato's rhetorical approach. The message had to lead students in a logical and irrefutable manner to certain insights upon which all involved could agree. Equally important was Plato's appeal to the credibility of his main character, Socrates. As you read, note how Plato brings Glaucon and other characters into conversation with Socrates in a manner that constantly builds our respect for Socrates and our willingness to "trust" his *ethos,* even as Glaucon does. As you read, note also how Plato surprisingly has Socrates regularly point out the shortcomings of his own ideas. This represents another particularly effective way to get readers to respect the main character in his writing; in the same moment that he is claiming to be really nothing more than a "fool," Socrates impresses us with some of his wisest insights. In the end, we paradoxically find ourselves admiring and trusting this man's wisdom and insight despite his own protests that he is not terribly wise nor insightful. The logical implication of this is that he sees and knows far more than we are able to see and to know and therefore holds himself to a higher standard of learning than that embraced by more common minds. Finally, in your reading, note how much more speaking time is given to Socrates, the teacher, than that given to Glaucon, the student. Like us, Glaucon seems focused upon following Socrates' line of reasoning as best he can. In this manner, Plato is better able to get his readers to see and to feel what he has to say. As we read, it is easy for us mentally to join in the conversation to the point of analyzing whether the questions and concerns that Glaucon raises are either valid or not, and to accepting or to challenging Socrates' answers even as Glaucon does so. In short, Plato finds ways to entice his audience to join in the dialogue with Socrates through the role of the student/listener/questioner, Glaucon. In this manner, Plato rhetorically compels us to follow his questions step by step into our own deeper insights and knowledge of what might constitute ideal political leaders in an ideal republic. The fact that his work is still being read in universities around the world nearly 2,400 years after his death suggests that rhetorically Plato's writing did exceptionally well what it was intended to do.

The Republic

Now we must try to find out what it is that causes our cities to be so badly   1
governed and what prevents them from being governed well. What might be the least change that would transform bad government into good government? It would surely be preferable to manage this with a single change. If not one change then two; if not two, then the fewest and most moderate changes possible.

Proceed.   2

I think there is one change that could bring about the transformation we   3
desire. It is no small change, nor would it be easy to implement. But it is possible.

What is it?   4

So. At last I come face to face with what I have called the greatest of the   5
waves. But I will speak even if it break over my head and drown me in a flood of laughter and derision. Mark my words.

I am all attention.   6

Unless philosophers become kings in our cities, or unless those who now   7
are kings and rulers become true philosophers, so that political power and

philosophic intelligence converge, and unless those lesser natures who run after one without the other are excluded from governing, I believe there can be no end to troubles, my dear Glaucon, in our cities or for all mankind. Only then will our theory of the state spring to life and see the light of day, at least to the degree possible. Now you see why I held back so long from speaking out about so troublesome a proposition. For it points to a vexing lesson: whether in private or public life there is no other way to achieve happiness.

8   Socrates, after launching such an assault you must expect to be attacked by hordes of our leading men of learning. They will at once cast off their garments and strip for action—metaphorically speaking, of course. Snatching the first handy weapon, they will rush at you full tilt, fully prepared to do dreadful deeds. If you can't find arguments to fend them off and make your escape, you will learn what it means to be scorned and despised.

9   It was you who got me into this.

10   A good thing, too. But I won't desert you; I'll help defend you as best I can. My good will and encouragement may be of use, and perhaps I shall be able to offer more suitable answers than others. With such a helpmate at your side you should be able to be at your best in convincing the unbelievers that you are right.

11   Your invaluable offer of assistance obliges me to try. If we are going to find some way to elude our assailants, I think we must explain what we mean by our daring suggestion that philosophers ought to be rulers. First, we must make clear what it is to be a philosopher. Then, we should be able to vindicate ourselves by explaining that philosophy and political leadership are inherent qualities of the philosopher's nature, so that it behooves the others to let philosophy alone and to follow the leaders.

BOOK III: SELECTION AND PROBATION OF THE GUARDIANS

1   And as we are to have the best of guardians for our city, must they not be those who have most the character of guardians?

2   Yes.

3   And to this end they ought to be wise and efficient, and to have a special care of the State?

4   True.

5   And a man will be most likely to care about that which he loves?

6   To be sure.

7   And he will be most likely to love that which he regards as having the same interests with himself, and that of which the good or evil fortune is supposed by him at any time most to affect his own?

8   Very true, he replied.

9   Then there must be a selection. Let us note among the guardians those who in their whole life show the greatest eagerness to do what is for the good of their country, and the greatest repugnance to do what is against her interests.

10   Those are the right men.

And they will have to be watched at every age, in order that we may see 11
whether they preserve their resolution, and never, under the influence either of
force or enhancement, forget or cast off their sense of duty to the State.

How cast off? he said. 12

I will explain to you, I replied. A resolution may go out of a man's mind 13
either with his will or against his will; with his will when he gets rid of a falsehood and learns better, against his will whenever he is deprived of a truth.

I understand, he said, the willing loss of a resolution; the meaning of the 14
unwilling I have yet to learn.

Why, I said, do you not see that men are unwillingly deprived of good, and 15
willingly of evil? Is not to have lost the truth an evil, and to possess the truth
a good? and you would agree that to conceive things as they are is to possess
the truth?

Yes, he replied; I agree with you in thinking that mankind are deprived of 16
truth against their will.

And is not this involuntary deprivation caused either by theft, or force, or 17
enchantment?

Still, he replied, I do not understand you. 18

I fear that I must have been talking darkly, like the tragedians. I only mean 19
that some men are changed by persuasion and that others forget; argument
steals away the hearts of one class, and time of the other; and this I call theft.
Now you understand me?

Yes. 20

Those again who are forced are those whom the violence of some pain or 21
grief compels to change their opinion.

I understand, he said, and you are quite right. 22

And you would also acknowledge that the enchanted are those who 23
change their minds either under the softer influence of pleasure, or the sterner
influence of fear?

Yes, he said; everything that deceives may be said to enchant. 24

Therefore, as I was just now saying, we must enquire who are the best 25
guardians of their own conviction that what they think the interest of the State
is to be the rule of their lives. We must watch them from their youth upwards,
and make them perform actions in which they are most likely to forget or to
be deceived, and he who remembers and is not deceived is to be selected, and
he who fails in the trial is to be rejected. That will be the way?

Yes. 26

And there should also be toils and pains and conflicts prescribed for them, 27
in which they will be made to give further proof of the same qualities.

Very right, he replied. 28

And then, I said, we must try them with enchantments—that is the third 29
sort of test—and see what will be their behaviour: like those who take colts
amid noise and tumult to see if they are of a timid nature, so must we take our
youth amid terrors of some kind, and again pass them into pleasures, and
prove them more thoroughly than gold is proved in the furnace, that we may
discover whether they are armed against all enchantments, and of a noble

bearing always, good guardians of themselves and of the music which they have learned, and retaining under all circumstances a rhythmical and harmonious nature, such as will be most serviceable to the individual and to the State. And he who at every age, as boy and youth and in mature life, has come out of the trial victorious and pure, shall be appointed a ruler and guardian of the State; he shall be honoured in life and death, and shall received sepulture and other memorials of honour, the greatest that we have to give. But him who fails, we must reject. I am inclined to think that this is the sort of way in which our rulers and guardians should be chosen and appointed. I speak generally, and not with any pretension to exactness.

30 And, speaking generally, I agree with you, he said.

31 And perhaps the word 'guardian' in the fullest sense ought to be applied to this higher class only who preserve us against foreign enemies and maintain peace among our citizens at home, that the one may not have the will, or the others the power, to harm us. The young men whom we before called guardians may be more properly designated auxiliaries and supporters of the principles of the rulers.

32 I agree with you, he said.

33 How then may we devise one of those needful falsehoods of which we lately spoke—just one royal lie which may deceive the rulers, if that be possible, and at any rate the rest of the city?

34 What sort of lie? he said.

35 Nothing new, I replied; only an old Phoenician[1] tale of what has often occurred before now in other places, (as the poets say, and have made the world believe), though not in our time, and I do not know whether such an event could ever happen again, or could now even be made probable, if it did.

36 How your words seem to hesitate on your lips!

37 You will not wonder, I replied, at my hesitation when you have heard.

38 Speak, he said, and fear not.

39 Well then, I will speak, although I really know not how to look you in the face, or in what words to utter the audacious fiction, which I propose to communicate gradually, first to the rulers, then to the soldiers, and lastly to the people. They are to be told that their youth was a dream, and the education and training which they received from us, an appearance only; in reality during all that time they were being formed and fed in the womb of the earth, where they themselves and their arms and appurtenances were manufactured; when they were completed, the earth, their mother, sent them up; and so, their country being their mother and also their nurse, they are bound to advise for her good, and to defend her against attacks, and her citizens they are to regard as children of the earth and their own brothers.

40 You had good reasons, he said, to be ashamed of the lie which you were going to tell.

41 True, I replied, but there is more coming; I have only told you half. Citizens, we shall say to them in our tale, you are brothers, yet God has framed you differently. Some of you have the power of command, and in the composition of these he has mingled gold, wherefore also they have the greatest hon-

---

[1] Cp. Laws, 663 E.

our; others he has made of silver, to be auxiliaries; others again who are to be husbandmen and craftsmen he has composed of brass and iron; and the species will generally be preserved in the children. But as all are of the same original stock, a golden parent will sometimes have a silver son, or a silver parent a golden son. And God proclaims as a first principle to the rulers, and above all else, that there is nothing which they should so anxiously guard, or of which they are to be such good guardians, as of the purity of the race. They should observe what elements mingle in their offspring; for if the son of a golden or silver parent has an admixture of brass and iron, then nature orders a transposition of ranks, and the eye of the ruler must not be pitiful towards the child because he has to descend in the scale and become a husbandman or artisan, just as there may be sons of artisans who having an admixture of gold or silver in them are raised to honour, and become guardians or auxiliaries. For an oracle says that when a man of brass or iron guards the State, it will be destroyed. Such is the tale; is there any possibility of making our citizens believe in it?

Not in the present generation, he replied; there is no way of accomplish- 42 ing this; but their sons may be made to believe in the tale, and their sons' sons, and posterity after them.

I see the difficulty, I replied; yet the fostering of such a belief will make 43 them care more for the city and for one another. Enough, however, of the fiction which may now fly abroad upon the wings of rumour, while we arm our earth-born heroes, and lead them forth under the command of their rulers. Let them look round and select a spot whence they can best suppress insurrection, if any prove refractory within, and also defend themselves against enemies, who like wolves may come down on the fold from without; there let them encamp, and when they have encamped, let them sacrifice to the proper Gods and prepare their dwellings.

Republic III
Socrates, Glaucon. The selection of a site for the warriors' camp.

Just so, he said. 44

And their dwellings must be such as will shield them against the cold of 45 winter and the heat of summer.

I suppose that you mean houses, he replied. 46

Yes, I said; but they must be the houses of soldiers, and not of shop-keepers. 47

What is the difference? he said. 48

That I will endeavour to explain, I replied. To keep watch-dogs, who, 49 from want of discipline or hunger, or some evil habit or other, would turn upon the sheep and worry them, and behave not like dogs but wolves, would be a foul and monstrous thing in a shepherd?

The warriors must be humanized by education.

Truly monstrous, he said. 50

And therefore every care must be taken that our auxiliaries, being stronger 51 than our citizens, may not grow to be too much for them and become savage tyrants instead of friends and allies?

Yes, great care should be taken. 52

And would not a really good education furnish the best safeguard? 53

But they are well-educated already, he replied. 54

I cannot be so confident, my dear Glaucon, I said; I am much more cer- 55 tain that they ought to be, and that true education, whatever that may be, will have the greatest tendency to civilize and humanize them in their relations to one another, and to those who are under their protection.

60   Very true, he replied.

61   And not only their education, but their habitations, and all that belongs to them, should be such as will neither impair their virtue as guardians, nor tempt them to prey upon the other citizens. Any man of sense must acknowledge that.

Republic III Socrates, Glaucon.

62   He must.

63   Then let us consider what will be their way of life, if they are to realize our idea of them. In the first place, none of them should have any property of his own beyond what is absolutely necessary; neither should they have a private hour or store closed against any one who has a mind to enter; their provisions should be only such as are required by trained warriors, who are men of temperance and courage; they should agree to receive from the citizens a fixed rate of pay, enough to meet the expenses of the year and no more; and they will go to mess and live together like soldiers in a camp. Gold and silver we will tell them that they have from God; the diviner metal is within them, and they have therefore no need of the dross which is current among men, and ought not to pollute the divine by any such earthly admixture; for that commoner metal has been the source of many unholy deeds, but their own is undefiled. And they alone of all the citizens may not touch or handle silver or gold, or be under the same roof with them, or wear them, or drink from them. And this will be their salvation, and they will be the saviours of the State. But should they ever acquire homes or lands or moneys of their own, they will become housekeepers and husbandmen instead of guardians, enemies and tyrants instead of allies of the other citizens; hating and being hated, plotting and being plotted against, they will past their whole life in much greater terror of internal than of external enemies, and the hour of ruin, both to themselves and to the rest of the State, will be at hand. For all which reasons may we not say that thus shall our State be ordered, and that these shall be the regulations appointed by us for our guardians concerning their houses and all other matters?

Their way of life will be that of a camp.

They must have no homes or property of their own.

Republic III Socrates, Glaucon.

64   Yes, said Glaucon.

Questions for Discussion and Your Reading Journal

1. What is the problem that Socrates and his friend Glaucon are trying to solve in this dialogue?
2. Sum up Socrates' solution to the problem. Why does he call his solution "a troublesome proposition"?
3. In good, classical Greek argumentation style, Socrates gives a "thesis statement" early on that organizes the rest of his address. Write this thesis.
4. According to Socrates, what are the ways that people change their minds about ideas? How does he propose to test potential guardians to see if they will change their minds about good governing principles?
5. To whom does Socrates suggest the word "guardian" ought to be applied?
6. Sum up the "needful falsehood," the "audacious fiction" that Socrates proposes to teach "first to the rulers, then to the soldiers, and lastly to the people."

Does Glaucon think that the people can be made to believe this great lie? Explain.

7. Socrates argues that the guardians should be kept poor in material wealth. What reasons does he give for this? Do you find his argument convincing? Explain.

8. What effect does it have overall on you as reader that Plato has written this philosophical treatise in a conversational, dialogue style?

KAUTILYA

Kautilya, a minister to King Chandragupta Maurya who ruled in India from 322 BCE to 298 BCE, has been given credit for writing The Arthashastra. *The full title of this political manual translates to "A Treatise on Wealth and Power," and in it Kautilya offers his best advice to a despotic king about how the king can best maintain his own wealth and power while assuring the "contentment" of key groups of the citizenry. Kautilya's writing is in a vein similar to the work of Niccoló Machiavelli, who wrote his political treatise* The Prince *in Italy some 1,800 years later (next article in this chapter). Like Machiavelli, Kautilya presents an ideal form of government that is an autocratic and yet well-organized bureaucracy that effectively controls the day-to-day workings of the state. What distinguishes Kautilya's work from that of Machiavelli is his Indian emphasis upon the ruler's ability to balance ethical behavior, self-control, and wisdom with authoritarian and often forceful governing practices. In this, he is perhaps closer to Plato's philosopher/king (see previous reading) than Machiavelli's ideal prince. Of special note is his emphasis upon the proper use of spies (including "special spies parading as fortune tellers"). What he proposes in terms of "spies" is not entirely unlike the use of pollsters today who help politicians stay on top of what the people are thinking and feeling as they go about their daily lives.*

Reading Rhetorically

As you read, think about the purpose of what Kautilya wrote. His book was intended as a textbook of sorts for helping government employees of his time carry out the day-to-day decision making of the state, as well as for training future leaders. In a textbook, the purpose is rarely to convince a given audience of the validity of the ideas that are being communicated. Rather, the author takes a more authoritative voice and presents ideas as guidelines and even outright "truths" about what should be done to deal with this or that aspect of governing. Such an approach, of course, requires readers to accept for one reason or another that the writer should be respected and believed. In an autocratic state ruled by a powerful king, Kautilya could rely upon the power of his king to give his immediate readers reason to take his ideas seriously. Obviously this appeal to *ethos* has its limitations. If you are a student in a college classroom thousands of years and thousands of miles removed from King Chandragupta Maurya's influence, you may feel less compelled to respect and to trust Kautilya's advice. As you read, note the appeals to audience values and to reason that Kautilya uses to transcend this limitation as a writer in a distant kingdom long ago. In the opening segment of the reading, we see the author emphasizing the need for rulers to conquer six negative values "lust, anger, greed," and so on—and to acquire one important positive value, "balanced wisdom." The more that Kautilya is able to appeal to such universal values, the more his use of *pathos* is likely to appeal to a universal audience that lives on long after he is no longer around. In the last two lines of the same segment, Kautilya makes an appeal to reason that likewise breaks beyond a rhetorical appeal limited to his own narrow world of readers. After making the claim, "Authority is possible only with assistance," he quickly supplies a metaphorical example to support his point: "A single wheel cannot move by itself." The logic of the wheel metaphor sets up another and even bolder claim with, "The ruler, therefore, shall employ ministers and hear their advice." Had he simply stated this last sentence without the metaphorical reasoning, it is not inconceivable that his king could have taken personal offense at his audacity to give orders to the ruler, this in a world where people lost their heads for being so bold. Such use of logical reasoning and appeals to universal audience values rhetorically lifts the nature and quality of Kautilya's writing beyond a limited appeal to his place and time and helps to make it compelling reading to our day. We still look for political leaders who have conquered their own lust, anger, and greed and who are able to lead us with wisdom. We, like citizens in Kautilya's state, are likewise frustrated and angered when our leaders do not live up to such expectations.

The Arthashastra

CHAPTER 6: CONTROL OF SENSES

1 By conquering the six enemies of living (lust, anger, greed, vanity, haughtiness and exuberance) he (the ruler) shall acquire balanced wisdom. He shall keep company with the learned. He shall get information through his spies. By his actions, he shall set up safety and security. By enforcing his authority, he shall keep his subjects observing their duties and obligations. He shall exercise control over himself by learning sciences. He shall help his subjects to acquire wealth and do good to them.

2 In this manner, with control over his impulses, he shall abstain from hurting the women and the property of others. He shall avoid lust, falsehood, hauteur and evil inclinations. He shall keep away from wrong and wasteful transactions.

3 He shall enjoy his lawful desires in conformity with the right and the economic. He shall pursue the three merits of living: charity, wealth and desire.[1] Any one of these merits carried to excess not only hurts the other two, but itself.

4 Wealth is the foundation of the other two because charity and desire depend upon it for their fulfilment.

---

[1] I.e., *dharma, artha, kama.*

Teachers and ministers should keep the ruler away from dangers and warn 5 him of time-schedules even in private.[2] Such teachers and ministers are always respected.

Authority is possible only with assistance. A single wheel cannot move by 6 itself. The ruler, therefore, shall employ ministers and hear their advice.

CHAPTER 10: ON SPIES

Advised and assisted by a tried council of officers, the ruler should proceed to 7 institute spies.

Spies are in the guise of pseudo-student, priest, householder, trader, saint 8 practising renunciation, classmate or colleague, desperado, poisoner and woman mendicant.

An artful person, capable of reading human nature, is a pseudo-student. 9 Such a person should be encouraged with presents and purse and be told by the officer: "Sworn to the ruler and myself you shall inform us what wickedness you find in others."

One initiated in scripture and of pure character is a priest-spy. This spy 10 should carry on farming, cattle culture and commerce with resources given to him. Out of the produce and profit accrued, he should encourage other priests to live with him and send them on espionage work. The other priests also should send their followers on similar errands.

A householder-spy is a farmer fallen in his profession but pure in charac- 11 ter. This spy should do as the priest.[3]

A trader-spy is a merchant in distress but generally trustworthy. This spy 12 should carry on espionage, in addition to his profession.

A person with proper appearance and accomplishments as an ascetic is a 13 saint-spy. He surrounds himself with followers and may settle down in the suburb of a big city and may pretend prayer and fasting in public. Trader-spies may associate with this class of spies. He may practice fortune-telling, palmistry, and pretend supernatural and magical power by predictions. The followers will adduce proof for the predictions of their saint. He may even foretell official rewards and official changes, which the officers concerned may substantiate by reciprocating.

Rewarded by the rulers with money and titles, these five institutions of 14 espionage should maintain the integrity of the country's officers.

CHAPTER 12: HOME AND OPPOSITION PARTIES

Having instituted spies over his chief officers, the ruler should spread his intel- 15 ligence network over the citizens and the country folk.

---

[2]This refers to a later chapter which directs the ruler to set an example of energy and activity and assign his various functions to specific parts of the day. Here he is directed to maintain his schedule even when unobserved by others.

[3]I.e., carry on farming, as in the previous paragraph.

16   Social spies, forming into opposite camps, should carry propaganda into places of confluence of people, tourist centres, associations and general congregations. . . .

17   Spies should also know all news current in the state. Special spies should collect news of joy or distress among those who professionalise in grains, cattle and gold of the ruler, among those who supply them to the ruler (or administration); among those who harbour a relative or restrain a troubled area and those who check a wild tribe or an invading enemy. The greater the contentment of such groups of people, the greater the rewards given to them. Those who demur should be propitiated by presents or conciliation, or disputes may be created to break their alliance with each other, as from a neighbouring enemy, a wild tribe or a disputant to the ruler's position.

18   Failing this measure, they must be commissioned to collect unpopular fines and taxes. Those in severe opposition may be quelled by punishment in secret, or by exposing them to the wrath of the people of the land. Or having hostaged their families, they may be sent to the mines to break contact with the enemies [of the state].

19   The enemies [of the state] employ as instruments those who are incensed, those who are ambitious, as well as those who despise the ruler. Special spies, parading as fortune tellers, should be instituted to spy on such persons in their relation with each other and with foreigners.

20   Thus, in his own state, the ruler should preserve parties and factions among the people, friendly or opposed, powerful or puerile, against the intrigues and machinations of the foreigners.

CHAPTER 14: ADMINISTRATIVE COUNCILS

21   After consolidating the attitude of both internal and external parties, both within and abroad, the ruler should consider administrative affairs.

22   Deliberation in well-constituted councils precedes administrative measures. The proceedings of a council should be in camera and deliberations made top secret so that not even a bird can whisper. The ruler should be guarded against disclosure.

23   Whoever divulges secret deliberations should be destroyed. Such guilt can be detected by physical and attitudinal changes of ambassadors, ministers and heads.

24   Secrecy of proceedings in the council and guarding of officers participating in the council must be organised.

25   The causes of divulgence of counsels are recklessness, drink, talking in one's sleep and infatuation with women which assail councillors.

26   He of secretive nature or who is not regarded well will divulge council matters. Disclosure of council secrets is of advantage to persons other than the ruler and his high officers. Steps should be taken to safeguard deliberations. . . .

CHAPTER 16: PROTECTION OF PRINCES

27   . . . The prince should be protected from wicked influences. He should be taught properly, since he is at an age of trust. He should be told about right,

but not of non-right; he should be told of wealth, but not of non-wealth. He should be scared of drink and women by a process of making him drunk and of confronting him with blackmailing women. If fond of gambling, he should be blackmailed by tricksters. If fond of hunting, by forest brigands. If he shows proclivities[4] for rebelling, he should be scared by narration of hardships and even ignominious death attending such ventures.

When a prince is of commendable disposition, he should be made commander-in-chief or nominated successor. 28

Princes are of three categories: those of dynamic intelligence; those of stagnant intelligence; and those who are mentally deficient. 29

He who carries out mandates of right and leading to wealth is of dynamic intelligence. He who never carries out good instructions is of stagnant intelligence. He who entangles himself in avoidable dangers leading to wickedness and poverty is mentally incompetent. 30

If a ruler has a deficient son, attempt should be made to beget a grandson by him. Or to get sons from his daughters. 31

If a ruler is too old or diseased to beget children, he may mandate a close relation or any neighbouring ruler of high qualities to beget a son for him through his queen. 32

Never should a mentally deficient son be made to sit on the seat of power. 33

Unless in times of grave danger, the eldest son should succeed the ruler. Sometimes sovereignty may reside in a corporation. Corporate sovereignty is the most invincible form of authority in the world.[5] 34

CHAPTER 20: PERSONAL SECURITY

. . . The ruler should employ as his security staff only such persons as have noble and proven ancestry and are closely related to him and are well trained and loyal. No foreigners, or anonymous persons, or persons with clouded antecedents are to be employed as security staff for the ruler. 35

In a securely guarded chamber, the chief should supervise the ruler's food arrangements. 36

Special precautions are to be taken against contaminated and poisoned food. The following reveal poison: rice sending out deep blue vapour; unnaturally coloured and artificially dried-up and hard vegetables; unusually bright and dull vessels; foamy vessels; streaky soups, milk and liquor; white streaked honey; strange-tempered food; carpets and curtains stained with dark spots and threadbare; polishless and lustreless metallic vessels and gems. 37

The poisoner reveals himself by parched and dry mouth, hesitating talk, perspiration, tremour, yawning, evasive demeanour and nervous behavior. 38

Experts in poison detection should be in attendance on the ruler. The physicians attending the ruler should satisfy themselves personally as to the purity of the drugs which they administer to the ruler. The same precaution is indicated for liquor and beverages which the ruler uses. Scrupulous cleanliness 39

---

[4]**proclivities** Inclinations or predispositions toward something. [Ed. note.]

[5]Because each member acts as a check on the others.

should be insisted on in persons in charge of the ruler's dress and toilet requisites. This should be ensured by seals . . . .

40   In any entertainment meant for the amusement of the ruler, the actors should not use weapons, fire and poison. Musical instruments and accoutrements for horses, elephants and vehicles should be secured in the palace.

41   The ruler should mount beasts and vehicles only after the traditional rider or driver has done so. If he has to travel in a boat, the pilot should be trustworthy and the boat itself secured to another boat. There should be a proper convoy on land or water guarding the ruler. He should swim only in rivers which are free of larger fishes and crocodiles and hunt in forests free from snakes, man-eaters and brigands.

42   He should give private audience only attended by his security guards. He should receive foreign ambassadors in his full ministerial council. While reviewing his militia, the ruler should also attend in full battle uniform and be on horseback or on the back of an elephant. When he enters or exits from the capital city, the path of the ruler should be guarded by staffed officers and cleared of armed men, mendicants and the suspicious. He should attend public performances, festivals, processions or religious gatherings accompanied by trained bodyguards. The ruler should guard his own person with the same care with which he secures the safety of those around him through espionage arrangements.

CHAPTER 41: DECAY, STABILISATION, AND PROGRESS OF STATES

43 Every state can be said to have a sixfold policy as against any other state.

44   Ancient thinkers hold that armistice, war, neutrality, invasion, alliance and peace are the six principal policy-relations. Sixfold policy can be reduced into peace, which means concord supported by pacts; war, implying armed aggression; neutrality involving nonchalance; armed invasion against another power; alliance involving appeal for assistance to another power; bilateral policy involving making war with one and suing for peace with another.

45   Any power inferior to another should sue for peace; any power superior in might to another should launch into war; any power which fears no external attack and which has no strength to wage war should remain neutral; any power with high war-potential should indulge in invasion; any debilitated power should seek new alliances; any power which tries to play for time in mounting an offensive should indulge in a bilateral policy of making war with one and suing for peace with another.

46   A state should always observe such a policy as will help it strengthen its defensive fortifications and life-lines of communications, build plantations, construct villages, and exploit the mineral and forest wealth of the country, while at the same time preventing fulfillment of similar programmes in the rival state.

47   Whoever estimates that the rate of growth of the state's potential is higher than that of the enemy can afford to ignore such an enemy.

Any two states hostile to each other, finding that neither has an advantage 48
over the other in fulfilment of their respective programmes, should make peace
with each other.

No state should pursue a policy which, while not enabling it to have 49
means to fulfil its own programmes, does not impose a similar handicap on its
neighbour: This is the path to reversion.

When any state evaluates that its loss over time would be much less than 50
its acquisition as compared with its rivals, it can afford to ignore its present
recession.

When any two states which are rivals expect to acquire equal possessions 51
over the same span of time, they should keep peace with each other.

Stagnation occurs when there is neither progression nor regression. When 52
a temporary stagnation is expected to lead to greater rate of growth than that
of the rival, the stagnation can be ignored.

A state can augment its resources by observing peaceful pacts with an 53
enemy in the following situations:

Where, maintaining, peace, productive operations of strategic importance can 54
    be planned and executed, preventing the rival state at the same time from
    fulfilling similar programmes;

When under the terms of the peace pact, the state can enjoy the resources cre- 55
    ated by the productive projects of its enemy in addition to its own resources;

When the state can plan works of sabotage through espionage on the plans 56
    and projects of its enemy;

Where under powerful incentives of happy settlements, immigration conces- 57
    sions, tax exemptions, pleasant work-conditions, large profits and high
    wages, immigration can be induced of strategic workers from an enemy state;

Where because of a prior pact, the enemy can harass another state which is 58
    also hostile;

Where because of invasion of the enemy state by another power, the workers 59
    of the enemy state immigrate and settle down in the state;

Where because of damage to the productive sectors of the enemy, his potential 60
    for offensive is reduced;

Where the state can, by pacts with other states, increase its own resources; 61

Where a sphere of alliance is formed of which an enemy state is a member, the 62
    alliance can be broken by forming fresh alliances.

A state can increase its own resources by preserving hostility with another 63
state in the following situations:

Where the state is composed of military races and war-like corporations; 64

Where the state has natural defensive fortifications like mountains, woods, 65
    rivers and forts and is capable of liquidating the enemy's offensive;

Where harassing operations can be launched on an attacking enemy from 66
    powerful fortifications in the states;

Where internal disorders sabotage the war potential of the enemy; 67

Where invasion of the enemy by another hostile power can be expected to cre- 68
    ate strategic immigration of skilled workers into the state.

69   A policy of neutrality can be sustained in the following situations:

70 Where the balance of power between states is even: as when neither state can immobilise the other;

71 Where, in the event of an attack, the state can intensify the tribulations of the enemy without loss of its own strategic power.

72   A state can indulge in armed invasion only:

73 Where, by invasion, it can reduce the power of an enemy without in any way reducing its own potential, by making suitable arrangements for protection of its own strategic works.

74   A state should form an alliance with a powerful power where its potential is strong neither to harass its enemy nor to withstand its offensive. It should also attempt reconstruction of its potential from the stage of regression to that of stabilisation and from that of stabilisation to that of progress.

75   A state can pursue a bilateral policy where it can benefit in resources by maintaining peace with one enemy, and waging war with another.

76   The central aim of inter-state sixfold policy is to enable a state to advance from a condition of regression to progress through the intermediary state of stabilisation or balance of the forces of advance.

CHAPTER 54: RESTORATION OF LOST BALANCE OF POWER

77 When an invader is assailed by an alliance of his enemies, he should try to purchase the leader of the alliance with offers of gold and his own alliance and by diplomatic camouflage of the threat of treachery from the alliance of powers. He should instigate the leader of the allied enemies to break up his alliance.

78   The invader should also attempt to break the allied enemies' formation by setting up the leader of the alliance against the weaker of his enemies, or attempt to forge a combination of the weaker allies against their leader. He may also form a pact with the leader through intrigue, or offer of resources. When the confederation is shattered, he may form alliances with any of his former enemies.

79   If the allied enemies have no leader, the invader can form a pact with the most influential member of the confederated allies. Or with a powerful member, or with a popular member or with a designing member or with a transient ally, bent on protecting and advancing his own self-interest.

80   If a state is weak in treasury or in striking power, attention should be directed to strengthen both through stabilisation of authority. Irrigational projects are a source of agricultural prosperity. Good highways should be constructed to facilitate movements of armed might and merchandise. Mines should be developed, as they supply ammunition. Forests should be conserved, as they supply material for defence, communication and vehicles. Pasture lands are the source of cattle wealth.

Thus, a state should build up its striking power through development of 81 the exchequer, the army and wise counsel; and, till the proper time, should conduct itself as a weak power towards its neighbours, to evade conflict or envy from enemy or allied states. If the state is deficient in resources, it should acquire them from related or allied states. It should attract to itself capable men from corporations, from wild and ferocious tribes, and foreigners, and organise espionage that will damage hostile powers.

Questions for Discussion and Your Reading Journal

1. How does Kautilya define the wise ruler? What qualities should a ruler have? Why must *be* control *his* impulses? Why should the ruler not overindulge the merits of "charity, wealth, and desire"?
2. Do modern political candidates need to conquer the "six enemies"? Explain.
3. What roles do ministers and spies play according to Kautilya? How did spies disguise themselves? How might contemporary spies disguise themselves? Could there be a country that does not need spies? When, if ever, is it ethical or just to use spies? Explain, using your imagination or recent news stories.
4. Kautilya states that "those in severe opposition may be quelled by punishment in secret." What does this mean? What ethical principles, if any, can justify torture?
5. Discuss Kautilya's illustrations supporting his claim that "the prince [unlike Machiavelli's usage, this refers to a future ruler] should be protected from wicked influences." How effective do you think this education would be?

NICCOLÒ MACHIAVELLI

The ideas of Niccolò Machiavelli (1469–1527) retain a great deal of influence in the Western world today, 500 years after he wrote them down. A statesman turned political theorist who lived in Florence, Italy, during a time of great power struggles between Italian city states, Machiavelli was a pragmatic advocate of using whatever means necessary to obtain one's political ends. Machiavelli knew what it was to be on the good side and the bad side of the use of power. He wrote much of The Prince *while in prison as a suspected conspirator against Giuliano de Medici, the prince of Florence from 1512 to 1513. He was set free and returned to a position of authority at the end of Giuliano's short reign, but he retained a cynical view of power and the masses of people for the remainder of his days. As he summed up in one of his more blunt assessments of human existence, "the world consists only of the vulgar." Unlike Kautilya who wrote nearly 18 centuries before in a similar vein about getting and keeping political power over the masses (see previous*

*reading), Machiavelli was not concerned with the ruler's ability to bal-
ance ethical behavior with ugly governing practices. Rather, he made a
point of breaking with writers like Plato and Kautilya who were concerned about the "goodness" of political rulers, arguing explicitly that
"it is necessary for a prince, who wishes to maintain himself,* to learn
how not to be good" [editor's emphasis]. Machiavelli did not actually
advocate that his ideal prince be evil, only that he know how to use both
scandalous tactics and praiseworthy tactics to keep himself in power.
Political Science and History majors in Western universities continue to
study and to debate Machiavelli's writings heatedly to this day.*

Reading Rhetorically

In a rhetorical sense, Machiavelli faced a daunting challenge. He set out to
present a pragmatic message about getting and keeping power in a Christian
world. This meant that he needed to justify the brutal use of force, torture,
murder, and other un-Christian behaviors to an audience that would normally
have seen such things as evil. To do so, he began by stating explicitly that he
was writing for a highly select audience of those who "understand" the "real
truth of the matter" rather than for those who value ruling in kingdoms of the
"imagination." It is this pragmatic, real-world approach to the use of political
power that he used to justify breaking with idealists who had written about
the topic in the past. Throughout his treatise, he maintained this connection to
the base, vulgar "real world," with constant examples of the successes and
failures of various leaders of the past who had used both virtuous and unvir-
tuous approaches to ruling. As long as Machiavelli was able to get his readers
to accept his cynical and unflattering assumptions about the nature of the
"real world," his overall argument was compelling. In this undertaking, the
culture of his audience in 16th-century Italy actually supported him rather
well. His portrayal of the world as a place of vulgarity and evil fit smoothly
with Christian teachings of the fallen nature of humanity and the wickedness
of a world that had separated itself from the goodness of God. What is unique
about Machiavelli's work is that, rather than taking Jesus as a model of how
to rule in a wicked world, he encouraged the shrewd use of both virtue and
vice by princes who were noticeably "unchristian" in the ways that they ruled.
This works effectively as long as his readers accept that he was encouraging
princes to fight fire with fire or, more specifically, to use good and evil to rule
in a world that contained both good and evil. This underlying logic gives an
element of common sense and consistency to his message that makes it both
troubling and compelling for readers in the 21st century.

The Prince

CHAPTER XV

Of the Things for Which Men, and Especially Princes, Are Praised or Blamed

It now remains to be seen what are the methods and rules for a prince as 1 regards his subjects and friends. And as I know that many have written of this, I fear that my writing about it may be deemed presumptuous, differing as I do, especially in this matter, from the opinions of others. But my intention being to write something of use to those who understand, it appears to me more proper to go to the real truth of the matter than to its imagination; and many have imagined republics and principalities which have never been seen or known to exist in reality; for how we live is so far removed from how we ought to live, that he who abandons what is done for what ought to be done, will rather learn to bring about his own ruin than his preservation. A man who wishes to make a profession of goodness in everything must necessarily come to grief among so many who are not good. Therefore it is necessary for a prince, who wishes to maintain himself, to learn how not to be good, and to use this knowledge and not use it, according to the necessity of the case.

Leaving on one side, then, those things which concern only an imaginary 2 prince, and speaking of those that are real, I state that all men, and especially princes, who are placed at a greater height, are reputed for certain qualities which bring them either praise or blame. Thus one is considered liberal, another *misero* or miserly (using a Tuscan term, seeing that *avaro* with us still means one who is rapaciously acquisitive and *misero* one who makes grudging use of his own); one a free giver, another rapacious; one cruel, another merciful; one a breaker of his word, another trustworthy; one effeminate and pusillanimous, another fierce and high-spirited; one humane, another haughty; one lascivious, another chaste; one frank, another astute; one hard, another easy; one serious, another frivolous; one religious, another an unbeliever, and so on. I know that every one will admit that it would be highly praiseworthy in a prince to possess all the above-named qualities that are reputed good, but as they cannot all be possessed or observed, human conditions not permitting of it, it is necessary that he should be prudent enough to avoid the scandal of those vices which would lose him the state, and guard himself if possible against those which will not lose it him, but if not able to, he can indulge them with less scruple. And yet he must not mind incurring the scandal of those vices, without which it would be difficult to save the state, for if one considers well, it will be found that some things which seem virtues would, if followed, lead to one's ruin, and some others which appear vices result in one's greater security and well-being.

CHAPTER XVI

Of Liberality and Niggardliness

3   Beginning now with the first qualities above named, I say that it would be well to be considered liberal; nevertheless liberality such as the world understands it will injure you, because if used virtuously and in the proper way, it will not be known, and you will incur the disgrace of the contrary vice. But one who wishes to obtain the reputation of liberality among men, must not omit every kind of sumptuous display, and to such an extent that a prince of this character will consume by such means all his resources, and will be at last compelled, if he wishes to maintain his name for liberality, to impose heavy taxes on his people, become extortionate, and do everything possible to obtain money. This will make his subjects begin to hate him, and he will be little esteemed being poor, so that having by this liberality injured many and benefited but few, he will feel the first little disturbance and be endangered by every peril. If he recognises this and wishes to change his system, he incurs at once the charge of niggardliness.

4   A prince, therefore, not being able to exercise this virtue of liberality without risk if it be known, must not, if he be prudent, object to be called miserly. In course of time he will be thought more liberal, when it is seen that by his parsimony his revenue is sufficient, that he can defend himself against those who make war on him, and undertake enterprises without burdening his people, so that he is really liberal to all those from whom he does not take, who are infinite in number, and niggardly to all to whom he does not give, who are few. In our times we have seen nothing great done except by those who have been esteemed niggardly; the others have all been ruined. Pope Julius II, although he had made use of a reputation for liberality in order to attain the papacy, did not seek to retain it afterwards, so that he might be able to wage war. The present King of France has carried on so many wars without imposing an extraordinary tax, because his extra expenses were covered by the parsimony he had so long practised. The present King of Spain, if he had been thought liberal, would not have engaged in and been successful in so many enterprises.

5   For these reasons a prince must care little for the reputation of being a miser, if he wishes to avoid robbing his subjects, if he wishes to be able to defend himself, to avoid becoming poor and contemptible, and not to be forced to become rapacious; this niggardliness is one of those vices which enable him to reign. If it is said that Cæsar attained the empire through liberality, and that many others have reached the highest positions through being liberal or being thought so, I would reply that you are either a prince already or else on the way to become one. In the first case, this liberality is harmful; in the second, it is certainly necessary to be considered liberal. Cæsar was one of those who wished to attain the mastery over Rome, but if after attaining it he had lived and had not moderated his expenses, he would have destroyed that empire. And should any one reply that there have been many princes, who have done great things with their armies, who have been thought extremely liberal, I would answer by saying that the prince may either spend his own

wealth and that of his subjects or the wealth of others. In the first case he must be sparing, but for the rest he must not neglect to be very liberal. The liberality is very necessary to a prince who marches with his armies, and lives by plunder, sack and ransom, and is dealing with the wealth of others, for without it he would not be followed by his soldiers. And you may be very generous indeed with what is not the property of yourself or your subjects, as were Cyrus, Cæsar, and Alexander; for spending the wealth of others will not diminish your reputation, but increase it, only spending your own resources will injure you. There is nothing which destroys itself so much as liberality, for by using it you lose the power of using it, and become either poor and despicable, or, to escape poverty, rapacious and hated. And of all things that a prince must guard against, the most important are being despicable or hated, and liberality will lead you to one or other of these conditions. It is, therefore, wiser to have the name of a miser, which produces disgrace without hatred, than to incur of necessity the name of being rapacious, which produces both disgrace and hatred.

CHAPTER XVII

Of Cruelty and Clemency, and Whether
It Is Better to be Loved or Feared

Proceeding to the other qualities before named, I say that every prince must 6
desire to be considered merciful and not cruel. He must, however, take care not to misuse this mercifulness. Cesare Borgia was considered cruel, but his cruelty had brought order to the Romagna, united it, and reduced it to peace and fealty. If this is considered well, it will be seen that he was really much more merciful than the Florentine people, who, to avoid the name of cruelty, allowed Pistoia to be destroyed. A prince, therefore, must not mind incurring the charge of cruelty for the purpose of keeping his subjects united and faithful; for, with a very few examples, he will be more merciful than those who, from excess of tenderness, allow disorders to arise, from whence spring bloodshed and rapine; for these as a rule injure the whole community, while the executions carried out by the prince injure only individuals. And of all princes, it is impossible for a new prince to escape the reputation of cruelty, new states being always full of dangers. Wherefore Virgil through the mouth of Dido says:

> Res dura, et regni novitas me talia cogunt 7
> Moliri, et late fines custode tueri.[1]

Nevertheless, he must be cautious in believing and acting, and must not be 8
afraid of his own shadow, and must proceed in a temperate manner with prudence and humanity, so that too much confidence does not render him incautious, and too much diffidence does not render him intolerant.

---

[1]Hard times, and the newness of my reign, have forced me to post guards far and wide along our borders for our own safety. [Ed. trans.]

9   From this arises the question whether it is better to be loved more than feared, or feared more than loved. The reply is, that one ought to be both feared and loved, but as it is difficult for the two to go together, it is much safer to be feared than loved, if one of the two has to be wanting. For it may be said of men in general that they are ungrateful, voluble, dissemblers, anxious to avoid danger, and covetous of gain; as long as you benefit them, they are entirely yours; they offer you their blood, their goods, their life, and their children, as I have before said, when the necessity is remote; but when it approaches, they revolt. And the prince who has relied solely on their words, without making other preparations, is ruined; for the friendship which is gained by purchase and not through grandeur and nobility of spirit is bought but not secured, and at a pinch is not to be expended in your service. And men have less scruple in offending one who makes himself loved than one who makes himself feared; for love is held by a chain of obligation which, men being selfish, is broken whenever it serves their purpose; but fear is maintained by a dread of punishment which never fails.

10   Still, a prince should make himself feared in such a way that if he does not gain love, he at any rate avoids hatred; for fear and the absence of hatred may well go together, and will be always attained by one who abstains from interfering with the property of his citizens and subjects or with their women. And when he is obliged to take the life of any one, let him do so when there is a proper justification and manifest reason for it; but above all he must abstain from taking the property of others, for men forget more easily the death of their father than the loss of their patrimony. Then also pretexts for seizing property are never wanting, and one who begins to live by rapine will always find some reason for taking the goods of others, whereas causes for taking life are rarer and more fleeting.

11   But when the prince is with his army and has a large number of soldiers under his control, then it is extremely necessary that he should not mind being thought cruel; for without this reputation he could not keep an army united or disposed to any duty. Among the noteworthy actions of Hannibal is numbered this, that although he had an enormous army, composed of men of all nations and fighting in foreign countries, there never arose any dissension either among them or against the prince, either in good fortune or in bad. This could not be due to anything but his inhuman cruelty, which together with his infinite other virtues, made him always venetated and terrible in the sight of his soldiers, and without it his other virtues would not have sufficed to produce that effect. Thoughtless writers admire on the one hand his actions, and on the other blame the principal cause of them.

12   And that it is true that his other virtues would not have sufficed may be seen from the case of Scipio (famous not only in regard to his own times, but all times of which memory remains), whose armies rebelled against him in Spain, which arose from nothing but his excessive kindness, which allowed more license to the soldiers than was consonant with military discipline. He was reproached with this in the senate by Fabius Maximus, who called him a corrupter of the Roman militia. Locri having been destroyed by one of Scipio's officers was not revenged by him, nor was the insolence of that officer punished, simply by reason of his

easy nature; so much so, that some one wishing to excuse him in the senate, said that there were many men who knew rather how not to err, than how to correct the errors of others. This disposition would in time have tarnished the fame and glory of Scipio had he persevered in it under the empire, but living under the rule of the senate this harmful quality was not only concealed but became a glory to him.

I conclude, therefore, with regard to being feared and loved, that men love   13
at their own free will, but fear at the will of the prince, and that a wise prince must rely on what is in his power and not on what is in the power of others, and he must only contrive to avoid incurring hatred, as has been explained.

CHAPTER XVIII

In What Way Princes Must Keep Faith

How laudable it is for a prince to keep good faith and live with integrity, and   14
not with astuteness, every one knows. Still the experience of our times shows those princes to have done great things who have had little regard for good faith, and have been able by astuteness to confuse men's brains, and who have ultimately overcome those who have made loyalty their foundation.

You must know, then, that there are two methods of fighting, the one by   15
law, the other by force: The first method is that of men, the second of beasts; but as the first method is often insufficient, one must have recourse to the second. It is therefore necessary for a prince to know well how to use both the beast and the man. This was covertly taught to rulers by ancient writers, who relate how Achilles and many others of those ancient princes were given to Chiron the centaur to be brought up and educated under his discipline. The parable of this semi-animal, semi-human teacher is meant to indicate that a prince must know how to use both natures, and that the one without the other is not durable.

A prince being thus obliged to know well how to act as a beast must imi-   16
tate the fox and the lion, for the lion cannot protect himself from traps, and the fox cannot defend himself from wolves. One must therefore be a fox to recognise traps, and a lion to frighten wolves. Those that wish to be only lions do not understand this. Therefore, a prudent ruler ought not to keep faith when by so doing it would be against his interest, and when the reasons which made him bind himself no longer exist. If men were all good, this precept would not be a good one; but as they are bad, and would not observe their faith with you, so you are not bound to keep faith with them. Nor have legitimate grounds ever failed a prince who wished to show colourable excuse for the non-fulfilment of his promise. Of this one could furnish an infinite number of modern examples, and show how many times peace has been broken, and how many promises rendered worthless, by the faithlessness of princes, and those that have been best able to imitate the fox have succeeded best. But it is necessary to be able to disguise this character well, and to be a great feigner and dissembler; and men are so simple and so ready to obey present necessities, that one who deceives will always find those who allow themselves to be deceived.

17   I will only mention one modern instance. Alexander VI did nothing else but deceive men, he thought of nothing else, and found the occasion for it; no man was ever more able to give assurances, or affirmed things with stronger oaths, and no man observed them less; however, he always succeeded in his deceptions, as he well knew this aspect of things.

18   It is not, therefore, necessary for a prince to have all the above-named qualities, but it is very necessary to seem to have them. I would even be bold to say that to possess them and always to observe them is dangerous, but to appear to possess them is useful. Thus it is well to seem merciful, faithful, humane, sincere, religious, and also to be so; but you must have the mind so disposed that when it is needful to be otherwise you may be able to change to the opposite qualities. And it must be understood that a prince, and especially a new prince, cannot observe all those things which are considered good in men, being often obliged, in order to maintain the state, to act against faith, against charity, against humanity, and against religion. And, therefore, he must have a mind disposed to adapt itself according to the wind, and as the variations of fortune dictate, and, as I said before, not deviate from what is good, if possible, but be able to do evil if constrained.

19   A prince must take great care that nothing goes out of his mouth which is not full of the above-named five qualities, and, to see and hear him, he should seem to be all mercy, faith, integrity, humanity, and religion. And nothing is more necessary than to seem to have this last quality, for men in general judge more by the eyes than by the hands, for every one can see, but very few have to feel. Everybody sees what you appear to be, few feel what you are, and those few will not dare to oppose themselves to the many, who have the majesty of the state to defend them; and in the actions of men, and especially of princes, from which there is no appeal, the end justifies the means. Let a prince therefore aim at conquering and maintaining the state, and the means will always be judged honourable and praised by every one, for the vulgar is always taken by appearances and the issue of the event; and the world consists only of the vulgar, and the few who are not vulgar are isolated when the many have a rallying point in the prince. A certain prince of the present time, whom it is well not to name, never does anything but preach peace and good faith, but he is really a great enemy to both, and either of them, had he observed them, would have lost him state or reputation on many occasions.

CHAPTER XXIII

How Flatterers Must Be Shunned

20 I must not omit an important subject, and mention of a mistake which princes can with difficulty avoid, if they are not very prudent, or if they do not make a good choice. And this is with regard to flatterers, of which courts are full, because men take such pleasure in their own things and deceive themselves about them that they can with difficulty guard against this plague; and by wishing to guard against if they run the risk of becoming contemptible. Because there is no other way of guarding one's self against flattery than by

letting men understand that they will not offend you by speaking the truth; but when every one can tell you the truth, you lose their respect. A prudent prince must therefore take a third course, by choosing for his council wise men, and giving these alone full liberty to speak the truth to him, but only of those things that he asks and of nothing else; but he must ask them about everything and hear their opinion, and afterwards deliberate by himself in his own way, and in these councils and with each of these men comport himself so that every one may see that the more freely he speaks, the more he will be acceptable. Beyond these he should listen to no one, go about the matter deliberately, and be determined in his decisions. Whoever acts otherwise either acts precipitately through flattery or else changes often through the variety of opinions, from which it follows that he will be little esteemed.

I will give a modern instance of this. Pre' Luca, a follower of Maximilian, 21 the present emperor, speaking of his majesty said that he never took counsel with anybody, and yet that he never did anything as he wished; this arose from his following the contrary method of the aforesaid. As the emperor is a secret man he does not communicate his designs to any one or take any advice, but as on putting them into effect they begin to be known and discovered, they begin to be opposed by those he has about him, and he is easily diverted from his purpose. Hence it comes to pass that what he does one day he undoes the next, no one ever understands what he wishes or intends to do, and no reliance is to be placed on his deliberations.

A prince, therefore, ought always to take counsel, but only when he wishes, 22 not when others wish; on the contrary he ought to discourage absolutely attempts to advise him unless he asks it, but he ought to be a great asker, and a patient hearer of the truth about those things of which he has inquired; indeed, if he finds that any one has scruples in telling him the truth he should be angry. And since some think that a prince who gains the reputation of being prudent is so considered, not by his nature but by the good counsellors he has about him, they are undoubtedly deceived. It is an infallible rule that a prince who is not wise himself cannot be well advised, unless by chance he leaves himself entirely in the hands of one man who rules him in everything, and happens to be a very prudent man. In this case he may doubtless be well governed, but it would not last long, for that governor would in a short time deprive him of the state; but by taking counsel with many, a prince who is not wise will never have united councils and will not be able to bring them to unanimity for himself. The counsellors will all think of their own interests, and he will be unable either to correct or to understand them. And it cannot be otherwise, for men will always be false to you unless they are compelled by necessity to be true. Therefore it must be concluded that wise counsels from whoever they come, must necessarily be due to the prudence of the prince, and not the prudence of the prince to the good counsels received.

Questions for Discussion and Your Reading Journal

1. Outline Machiavelli's argument in each chapter and note the rhetorical purpose of each paragraph in his argument. What assumptions does he make

about power and human nature? Do you agree with these assumptions? Are they convincing? Which of Machiavelli's assumptions might you consider realistic? Cynical? Cite specific passages.

2. Use a Machiavellian interpretation to analyze the behavior of a current political figure or of one of the political thinkers about whom you have read. Do you agree or disagree with a Machiavellian view of this person's motives and program?

3. What is the rhetorical purpose of Machiavelli's opening line in Chapter XV?

4. Compare and contrast the means and ends of Kautilya's (p. 35) advice with Machiavelli's advice. What means are justified for what ends in both of these readings?

5. What ways can a ruler use to control the opposition? What is the value of appearing to have the "five good qualities" according to Machiavelli?

6. What does Machiavelli's analogy of the fox and the lion seek to prove? Explain.

7. Machiavelli states a prince must "learn how not to be good." Do you agree? Why or why not?

8. Discuss Machiavelli's opinion of advisors. In your own opinion, why might flattery be an effective means of persuasion? Illustrate, using your own examples.

9. Compare the attitudes of Machiavelli and Kautilya on the issue of power and its proper use.

THOMAS JEFFERSON

Thomas Jefferson (1743–1826), political philosopher and third president of the United States, wrote the Declaration of Independence in June 1776 to persuade some of the more reluctant members of the Continental Congress to break away from Britain and its colonial rule. In addition, the Declaration was aimed at persuading France to supply arms and aid to the colonies. In writing the Declaration, Jefferson drew upon the political theories of John Locke, a social philosopher whose concept of "social contract" argued that those who govern have obligations to the governed. Jefferson completed the Declaration in 17 days, redrafting it several times after he submitted it to a committee that included himself, John Adams, and Benjamin Franklin, among others.

Reading Rhetorically

Jefferson's Declaration of Independence is considered one of the most masterful pieces of written argumentation in U.S. history. It is concerned not only with "declaring" the separation of the 13 young colonies from political rule by Great Britain but more importantly with justifying such a monumental change in human events. Note Jefferson's explicit appeal to (and respect for) "the opinions of mankind" in his opening paragraph. Note also in his first paragraph the clear reference to "the laws of nature and of nature's God" as the source of authority that justified the Americans taking the bold step of breaking away from a parliamentary kingship to experiment with a more democratic form of government. In the next paragraphs, Jefferson lists of King George III's abuses of the colonies as evidence to further justify the main point of his argument. Equally important to his persuasive appeal is the way he presented his efforts and those of other colonial leaders to petition the British government "for redress in the most humble terms." This is what Aristotle would refer to as using *ethos* effectively to present yourself and other people on your side of an issue as trustworthy, believable, and of good character. Finally, note Jefferson's return again to a divine appeal for the rightness of the colonial separation from Great Britain in his closing paragraphs. This time, however, the divine authority for declaring independence is reinforced by another highly audience-sensitive source of authority, the authority of "the good people of these Colonies." The emerging concept that the people themselves had the right and authority to decide how they would be governed was something that Jefferson must have known would be highly popular with the independent-minded colonists and frontiersmen who were most essential to the success of the revolution that his Declaration of Independence set in motion. This rhetorical appeal to the masses as independent and empowered members of society helped to set the stage for one of the most innovative and successful experiments in government and politics in the human story.

The Declaration of Independence

A DECLARATION BY THE REPRESENTATIVES OF THE UNITED STATES OF AMERICA, IN GENERAL CONGRESS ASSEMBLED[1] JULY 4, 1776

When, in the course of human events, it becomes necessary for one people to dissolve the political bands which have connected them with another, and to assume among the powers of the earth the separate and equal station to which the laws of nature and of nature's God entitle them, a decent respect to the opinions of mankind requires that they should declare the causes which impel them to the separation.   1

We hold these truths to be self-evident; that all men are created equal; that they are endowed by their creator with [*inherent and*] inalienable rights; that among these are life, liberty, and the pursuit of happiness; that to secure these rights, governments are instituted among men, deriving their just powers from   2 certain

---

[1]This was Jefferson's original title. Congress changed it, on July 19, 1776, to "The Unanimous Declaration of the thirteen united States of America."

Since this is Jefferson's most famous paper, the text is given here as he first wrote it and as it was finally corrected. The parts stricken out by Congress are shown in brackets and in italics, and insertions are given in the margin or in a parallel column.

the consent of the governed; that whenever any form of government becomes destructive of these ends, it is the right of the people to alter or to abolish it, and to institute new government, laying its foundation on such principles, and organizing its powers in such form, as to them shall seem most likely to effect their safety and happiness. Prudence, indeed, will dictate that governments long established should not be changed for light and transient causes; and accordingly all experience hath shown that mankind are more disposed to suffer while evils are sufferable, than to right themselves by abolishing the forms to which they are accustomed. But when a long train of abuses and usurpations [*begun at a distinguished period and*] pursuing invariably the same object, evinces a design to reduce them under absolute despotism, it is their right, it is their duty to throw off such government, and to provide new guards for their future security. Such has been the patient sufferance of these Colonies;

alter and such is now the necessity which constrains them to [*expunge*] their former systems of government. The history of the present King of Great Britain is a

repeated history of [*unremitting*] injuries and usurpations, [*among which appears no*

all having *solitary fact to contradict the uniform tenor of the rest, but all have*] in direct object the establishment of an absolute tyranny over these States. To prove this, let facts be submitted to a candid world [*for the truth of which we pledge a faith yet unsullied by falsehood*].

3   He has refused his assent to laws the most wholesome and necessary for the public good.

4   He has forbidden his governors to pass laws of immediate and pressing importance, unless suspended in their operation till his assent should be obtained; and, when so suspended, he has utterly neglected to attend to them.

5   He has refused to pass other laws for the accommodation of large districts of people, unless those people would relinquish the right of representation in the Legislature, a right inestimable to them, and formidable to tyrants only.

6   He has called together legislative bodies at places unusual, uncomfortable, and distant from the depository of their public records, for the sole purpose of fatiguing them into compliance with his measures.

7   He has dissolved representative houses repeatedly [*and continually*] for opposing with manly firmness his invasions on the rights of the people.

8   He has refused for a long time after such dissolutions to cause others to be elected, whereby the legislative powers, incapable of annihilation, have returned to the people at large for their exercise, theState remaining, in the meantime, exposed to all the dangers of invasion from without and convulsions within.

9   He has endeavored to prevent the population of these States; for that purpose obstructing the laws for naturalization of foreigners, refusing to pass others to encourage their migrations hither, and raising the conditions of new appropriations of lands.

obstructed 10   He has [*suffered*] the administration of justice [*totally to cease in some of*

by   *these States*] refusing his assent to laws for establishing judiciary powers.

11   He has made [*our*] judges dependent on his will alone for the tenure of their offices, and the amount and payment of their salaries.

He has erected a multitude of new offices, [*by a self-assumed power*] and sent 12 hither swarms of new officers to harass our people and eat out their substance.

He has kept among us in times of peace standing armies [*and ships of war*] 13 without the consent of our Legislatures.

He has affected to render the military independent of, and superior to, the 14 civil power.

He has combined with others to subject us to a jurisdiction foreign to our 15 constitutions and unacknowledged by our laws, giving his assent to their acts of pretended legislation for quartering large bodies of armed troops among us; for protecting them by a mock trial from punishment for any murders which they should commit on the inhabitants of these States; for cutting off our trade with all parts of the world; for imposing taxes on us without our consent; for *in many cases* depriving us [ ] of the benefits of trial by jury; for transporting us beyond seas to be tried for pretended offences; for abolishing the free system of English laws in a neighboring province, establishing therein an arbitrary government, and enlarging its boundaries, so as to render it at once an example and fit instrument for introducing the same absolute rule into these [*States*]; for taking away *colonies* our charters, abolishing our most valuable laws, and altering fundamentally the forms of our governments; for suspending our own Legislatures, and declaring themselves invested with power to legislate for us in all cases whatsoever.

He has abdicated government here [*withdrawing his governors, and* 16 *by declaring us out of his protection,* *declaring us out of his allegiance and protection*].

He has plundered our seas, ravaged our coasts, burnt our towns, and 17 *and waging war against us* destroyed the lives of our people.

He is at this time transporting large armies of foreign mercenaries to com- 18 plete the works of death, desolation, and tyranny already begun with circum- stances of cruelty and perfidy [ ] unworthy the head of a civilized nation. *scarcely paralleled in the most*

He has constrained our fellow-citizens taken captive on the high seas to 19 *barbarous ages, and* bear arms against their country, to become the executioners of their friends *totally* and brethren, or to fall themselves by their hands. *excited domestic*

He has [ ] endeavored to bring on the inhabitants of our frontiers the mer- 20 *insurrection among us,* ciless Indian savages, whose known rule of warfare is an undistinguished *and has* destruction of all ages, sexes, and conditions [*of existence*].

[*He has incited treasonable insurrections of our fellow-citizens, with the* 21 *allurements of forfeiture and confiscation of our property.*

He has waged cruel war against human nature itself, violating its most 22 *sacred rights of life and liberty in the persons of a distant people who never offended him, captivating and carrying them into slavery in another hemi- sphere, or to incur miserable death in their transportation thither. This pirati- cal warfare, the opprobrium[2] of* INFIDEL *powers, is the warfare of the* CHRIS- TIAN *King of Great Britain. Determined to keep open a market where* MEN *should be bought and sold, he has prostituted his negative for suppressing every legislative attempt to prohibit or to restrain this execrable commerce. And that this assemblage of horrors might want no fact of distinguished die, he is now exciting those very people to rise in arms among us, and to purchase*

---

[2]**opprobrium** An action or behavior considered to be disgraceful. [Ed. note.]

that liberty of which he has deprived them, by murdering the people on whom he also obtruded them: thus paying off former crimes committed against the LIBERTIES *of one people with crimes which he urges them to commit against the* LIVES *of another.]*

23   In every stage of these oppressions we have petitioned for redress in the most humble terms: our repeated petitions have been answered only by repeated injuries.

24   A Prince whose character is thus marked by every act which may define a
free   tyrant is unfit to be the ruler of a [ ] people [*who mean to be free. Further ages will scarcely believe that the hardiness of one man adventured, within the short compass of twelve years only, to lay a foundation so broad and so undisguised for tyranny over a people fostered and fixed in principles of freedom.*]

25   Nor have we been wanting in attentions to our British brethren. We have
an unwar-   warned them from time to time of attempts by their legislature to extend [*a*]
rantable   jurisdiction over [*these our States*]. We have reminded them of the circum-
us   stances of our emigration and settlement here, [*no one of which could warrant so strange a pretension: that these were effected at the expense of our own blood and treasure, unassisted by the wealth or the strength of Great Britain: that in constituting indeed our several forms of government, we had adopted one common king, thereby laying a foundation for perpetual league and amity with them: but that submission to their parliament was no part of our Con-*
have   *stitution, nor ever in idea, if history may be credited: and,*] we [ ] appealed to
and we   their native justice and magnanimity[3] [*as well as to*] the ties of our common
have con-   kindred to disavow these usurpations which [*were likely to*] interrupt our con-
jured them   nection and correspondence. They too have been deaf to the voice of justice
by would   and of consanguinity,[4] [*and when occasions have been given them, by the reg-*
inevitably   *ular course of their laws, of removing from their councils the disturbers of our harmony, they have, by their free election, reestablished them in power. At this very time too, they are permitting their chief magistrate to send over not only soldiers of our common blood, but Scotch and foreign mercenaries to invade and destroy us. These facts have given the last stab to agonizing affection, and*
We must   *manly spirit bids us to renounce forever these unfeeling brethren. We must*
therefore   *endeavor to forget our former love for them, and hold them as we hold the*
and hold   *rest of mankind, enemies in war, in peace friends. We might have been a free*
them as   *and a great people together; but a communication of grandeur and of freedom,*
we hold   *it seems, is below their dignity. Be it so, since they will have it. The road to*
the rest   *happiness and to glory is open to us too. We will tread it apart from them,*
of   *and*] acquiesce in the necessity which denounces our [*eternal*] separation [ ]!
mankind,
enemies
in war,
in peace
friends.

26   We therefore the representatives of the United States of America in General Congress assembled, appealing to the supreme judge of the world for the rectitude of our intentions, do in the name, and by the authority of the good people of these Colonies, solemnity publish and declare, that these united Colonies are, and of right ought to be, free and independent States; that they are absolved from all allegiance to the British crown, and that all political con-

---

[3]**magnanimity** A generosity that suggests a noble action. [Ed. note.]

[4]**consanguinity** The state of being related by blood. [Ed. note.]

nection between them and the state of Great Britain is, and ought to be, totally dissolved; and that as free and independent States, they have full power to levy war, conclude peace, contract alliances, establish commerce, and to do all other acts and things which independent States may of right do.

And for the support of this declaration, with a firm reliance on the pro- 27 tection of divine providence, we mutually pledge to each other our lives, our fortunes, and our sacred honor.

We therefore the representatives of the United States of America in Gen- 28 eral Congress assembled, do in the name, and by the authority of the good people of these [*States reject and renounce all allegiance and subjection to the kings of Great Britain and all others who may hereafter claim by, through, or under them; we utterly dissolve all political connection which may heretofore have subsisted between us and the people or parliament of Great Britain: and finally we do assert and declare these Colonies to be free and independent States,*] and that as free and independent States, they have full power to levy war, conclude peace, contract alliances, establish commerce, and to do all other acts and things which independent States may of right do.

And for the support of this declaration, we mutually pledge to each other 29 our lives, our fortunes, and our sacred honor.

Questions for Discussion and Your Reading Journal

1. What are the various purposes and audiences for *The Declaration of Independence?* How might the second-to-last paragraph be an appeal to aid?
2. Why might the long passage on slavery have been taken out?
3. Read selected portions of this aloud and notice Jefferson's word choices. If you were a loyalist, an American supporter of the king, how might you react to the declaration?
4. What is the tone (the apparent attitude) of this declaration? How is this effective for the purposes suggested in the introduction?
5. Compare *The Declaration of Independence* to *The Arusha Declaration* (p. 91). How are their purposes similar? How are they different?
6. Choose one of the revisions made in *The Declaration of Independence* and speculate why the change might have been made.

ALEXIS DE TOCQUEVILLE

The French political theorist, historian, and politician Alexis de Tocqueville (1805–1859) did one of the earliest studies of the American experiment with democracy. It is also one of the best. De Tocqueville spent nine months traveling through the United States from the largest cities to the most distant frontier outposts in Indian country during 1831–1832 and then returned to France to write up his experiences, reflections, and insights into a balanced critique of the young nation. He was impressed by the quality of local self-government, the high degree of equal opportunity for whites in the political and social realm, and the general self-reliance he found among the hardworking citizens. However, he held grave reservations about the institution of slavery that was thriving in a nation built upon freedom, and he recognized the tragedy that was unfolding for the Native Americans whose lives, societies, and heritages were being devastated by the appetites of Euro-Americans for land, wealth, and power. Some of his greatest insights into the emerging American character focused upon the paradoxical "tyranny of the majority" in the United States that he found more powerful than the actual physical tyranny of kings and rulers in Europe of his time. This power, he argued, derived from the fact that the majority exercised an influence that was both "physical and moral at the same time." Once the majority decided upon a course of action to take, peer pressure and conformity became powerful tools in the hands of the citizens to silence further thought on the issue, debate, or dissent. De Tocqueville argued that no king or despot in all of Europe could be so effective at controlling people's minds as democracy in America was able to do when he traveled through the young nation in the 1830s.

Reading Rhetorically

Like many original thinkers throughout history, de Tocqueville was faced with a particularly difficult rhetorical challenge. His message was far ahead of the thinking of his audience and held elements that many of his readers would not like nor easily accept. Take this excerpt from the following reading, for example: "I know of no country in which there is so little independence of mind and real freedom of discussion as in America." This is a bold claim to make, one that is likely to make many Americans angry to this day. Note how much effort de Tocqueville took immediately after the claim, however, to provide logical evidence, comparisons to other societies, and extended theoretical examples to buttress his bold assertion. This is where de Tocqueville excelled. Although his readers may not want to accept his ideas, the weight and power of his evidence are hard to withstand. Even if one does not end up agreeing with him, it is difficult not to respect him and to admire the amount of careful thought that went into his insights into what he observed in America at the end of the first generation of the new nation.

Democracy in America

POWER EXERCISED BY THE MAJORITY IN AMERICA UPON OPINION

1   In America, when the Majority has once irrevocably decided a Question, all Discussion ceases.—Reason of this.—Moral Power exercised by the Majority upon Opinion.—Democratic Republics have applied Despotism to the Minds of Men.

It is in the examination of the exercise of thought in the United States, that 2
we clearly perceive how far the power of the majority surpasses all the powers with which we are acquainted in Europe. Thought is an invisible and sub-
tile power, that mocks all the efforts of tyranny. At the present time, the most
absolute monarchs in Europe cannot prevent certain opinions hostile to their
authority from circulating in secret through their dominions, and even in their
courts. It is not so in America; as long a the majority is still undecided, discussion is carried on; but as soon as its decision is irrevocably pronounced,
every one is silent, and the friends as well as the opponents of the measure
unite in assenting to its propriety. The reason of this is perfectly clear: no
monarch is so absolute as to combine all the powers of society in his own
hands, and to conquer all opposition, as a majority is able to do, which has
the right both of making and of executing the laws.

The authority of a king is physical, and controls the actions of men with- 3
out subduing their will. But the majority possesses a power which is physical
and moral at the same time, which acts upon the will as much as upon the
actions, and represses not only all contest, but all controversy.

I know of no country in which there is so little independence of mind and 4
real freedom of discussion as in America. In any constitutional state in Europe,
every sort of religious and political theory may be freely preached and dis-
seminated; for there is no country in Europe so subdued by any single authority, as not to protect the man who raises his voice in the cause of truth from
the consequences of his hardihood. If he is unfortunate enough to live under
an absolute government, the people are often upon his side; if he inhabits a
free country, he can, if necessary, find a shelter behind the throne. The aristocratic part of society supports him in some countries, and the democracy in
others. But in a nation where democratic institutions exist, organized like
those of the United States, there is but one authority, one element of strength
and success, with nothing beyond it.

In America, the majority raises formidable barriers around the liberty of 5
opinion: within these barriers, an author may write what he pleases; but woe
to him if he goes beyond them. Not that he is in danger of an *auto-da-fé*,[1] but
he is exposed to continued obloquy and persecution. His political career is
closed forever, since he has offended the only authority which is able to open
it. Every sort of compensation, even that of celebrity, is refused to him. Before
publishing his opinions, he imagined that he held them in common with others; but no sooner has he declared them, than he is loudly censured by his
opponents, whilst those who think like him, without having the courage to
speak out, abandon him in silence. He yields at length, overcome by the daily
effort which he has to make, and subsides into silence, as if he felt remorse for
having spoken the truth.

Fetters and headsmen were the coarse instruments which tyranny formerly 6
employed; but the civilization of our age has perfected despotism itself, though

---

[1] *auto-da-fé* Literally, "act of faith" in Portuguese. During the inquisition it referred to the act of
burning heretics. [Ed. note.]

it seemed to have nothing to learn. Monarchs had, so to speak, materialized oppression: The democratic republics of the present day have rendered it as entirely an affair of the mind, as the will which it is intended to coerce. Under the absolute sway of one man, the body was attacked in order to subdue the soul; but the soul escaped the blows which were directed against it, and rose proudly superior. Such is not the course adopted by tyranny in democratic republics; there the body is left free, and the soul is enslaved. The master no longer says, "You shall think as I do, or you shall die"; but he says, "You are free to think differently from me, and to retain your life, your property, and all that you possess; but you are henceforth a stranger among your people. You may retain your civil rights, but they will be useless to you, for you will never be chosen by your fellow-citizens, if you solicit their votes; and they will affect to scorn you, if you ask for their esteem. You will remain among men, but you will be deprived of the rights of mankind. Your fellow-creatures will shun you like an impure being; and even those who believe in your innocence will abandon you, lest they should be shunned in their turn. Go in peace! I have given you your life, but it is an existence worse than death."

7   Absolute monarchies had dishonored despotism; let us beware lest democratic republics should reinstate it, and render it less odious and degrading in the eyes of the many, by making it still more onerous to the few.

8   Works have been published in the proudest nations of the Old World, expressly intended to censure the vices and the follies of the times: Labruyère inhabited the palace of Louis XIV when he composed his chapter upon the Great, and Molière criticised the courtiers in the pieces which were acted before the court. But the ruling power in the United States is not to be made game of. The smallest reproach irritates its sensibility, and the slightest joke which has any foundation in truth renders it indignant; from the forms of its language up to the solid virtues of its character, everything must be made the subject of encomium. No writer, whatever be his eminence, can escape paying this tribute of adulation to his fellow-citizens. The majority lives in the perpetual utterance of self-applause; and there are certain truths which the Americans can only learn from strangers or from experience.

9   If America has not as yet had any great writers, the reason is given in these facts; there can be no literary genius without freedom of opinion, and freedom of opinion does not exist in America. The Inquisition has never been able to prevent a vast number of anti-religious books from circulating in Spain. The empire of the majority succeeds much better in the United States, since it actually removes any wish to publish them. Unbelievers are to be met with in America, but there is no public organ of infidelity. Attempts have been made by some governments to protect morality by prohibiting licentious books. In the United States, no one is punished for this sort of books, but no one is induced to write them; not because all the citizens are immaculate in conduct, but because the majority of the community is decent and orderly.

In this case the use of the power is unquestionably good; and I am dis- 10
cussing the nature of the power itself. This irresistible authority is a constant
fact, and its judicious exercise is only an accident.[2]

EFFECTS OF THE TYRANNY OF THE MAJORITY
UPON THE NATIONAL CHARACTER OF THE AMERICANS—
THE COURTIER-SPIRIT IN THE UNITED STATES

Effects of the Tyranny of the Majority more sensibly felt hitherto on the 11
Manners than on the Conduct of Society.—They check the Development
of great Characters.—Democratic Republics, organized like the United
States, infuse the Courtier-spirit into the Mass of the People.—Proofs of
this Spirit in the United States,—Why there is more Patriotism in the People than in those who govern in their Name.

The tendencies which I have just mentioned are as yet but slightly percep- 12
tible in political society; but they already exercise an unfavourable influence
upon the national character of the Americans. I attribute the small number of
distinguished men in political life to the ever-increasing despotism of the
majority in the United States.

When the American Revolution broke out, they arose in great numbers; 13
for public opinion then served, not to tyrannize over, but to direct the exertions of individuals. Those celebrated men, sharing the agitation of mind common at that period, had a grandeur peculiar to themselves, which was reflected
back upon the nation, but was by no means borrowed from it.

In absolute governments, the great nobles who are nearest to the throne 14
flatter the passions of the sovereign, and voluntarily truckle[3] to his caprices.
But the mass of the nation does not degrade itself by servitude; it often submits from weakness, from habit, or from ignorance, and sometimes from loyalty. Some nations have been known to sacrifice their own desires to those of
the sovereign with pleasure and pride, thus exhibiting a sort of independence
of mind in the very act of submission. These nations are miserable, but they
are not degraded. There is a great difference between doing what one does not
approve, and feigning to approve what one does; the one is the weakness of a
feeble person, the other befits the temper of a lackey.

In free countries, where every one is more or less called upon to give his 15
opinion on affairs of state,—in democratic republics, where public life is
incessantly mingled with domestic affairs, where the sovereign authority is

---

[2]De Tocqueville's remarks on this subject are rhetorical, and altogether too highly colored. It is
notorious, that, in politics, morality, and religion, the most offensive opinions are preached and
printed every week here in America, apparently for no other purpose than that of shocking the
sentiments of the great bulk of the community. Instead of complaining of the bondage of thought,
the judicious observer will rather grieve at the extreme licentiousness of the rostrum and the press.

[3]**truckle** Submit. [Ed. note.]

accessible on every side, and where its attention can always be attracted by vociferation,[4]—more persons are to be met with who speculate upon its weaknesses, and live upon ministering to its passions, than in absolute monarchies. Not because men are naturally worse in these states than elsewhere, but the temptation is stronger and of easier access at the same time. The result is a more extensive debasement of character.

16   Democratic republics extend the practice of currying favor with the many, and introduce it into all classes at once: This is the most serious reproach that can be addressed to them. This is especially true in democratic states organized like the American republics, where the power of the majority is so absolute and irresistible that one must give up his rights as a citizen, and almost abjure[5] his qualities as a man, if he intends to stray from the track which it prescribes.

17   In that immense crowd which throngs the avenues to power in the United States, I found very few men who displayed that manly candor and masculine independence of opinion which frequently distinguished the Americans in former times, and which constitutes the leading feature in distinguished characters wheresoever they may be found. It seems, at first sight, as if all the minds of the Americans were formed upon one model, so accurately do they follow the same route. A stranger does, indeed, sometimes meet with Americans who dissent from the rigor of these formularies,—with men who deplore the defects of the laws, the mutability and the ignorance of democracy,—who even go so far as to observe the evil tendencies which impair the national character, and to point out such remedies as it might be possible to apply; but no one is there to hear them except yourself, and you, to whom these secret reflections are confided, are a stranger and a bird of passage. They are very ready to communicate truths which are useless to you, but they hold a different language in public.

18   If ever these lines are read in America, I am well assured of two things;— in the first place, that all who peruse them will raise their voices to condemn me; and, in the second place, that many of them will acquit me at the bottom of their conscience.

19   I have heard of patriotism in the United States, and I have found true patriotism among the people, but never among the leaders of the people. This may be explained by analogy: Despotism debases the oppressed much more than the oppressor: In absolute monarchies, the king often has great virtues, but the courtiers are invariably servile. It is true that American courtiers do not say "Sire," or "Your Majesty,"—a distinction without a difference. They are forever talking of the natural intelligence of the people whom they serve: They do not debate the question which of the virtues of their master is pre-eminently worthy of admiration, for they assure him that he possesses all the virtues without having acquired them, or without caring to acquire them; they do not give him their daughters and their wives to be raised at his pleasure to the rank of his concubines; but, by sacrificing their opinions, they prostitute themselves. Moralists and philosophers in America are not obliged to conceal their opinions under the

---

[4]**vociferation** Shouting: [Ed. note.]

[5]**abjure** Reject. [Ed. note.]

veil of allegory; but before they venture upon a harsh truth, they say, "We are aware that the people whom we are addressing are too superior to the weaknesses of human nature to lose the command of their temper for an instant. We should not hold this language if we were not speaking to men whom their virtues and their intelligence render more worthy of freedom than all the rest of the world." The sycophants of Louis XIV could not flatter more dexterously.

For my part, I am persuaded that, in all governments, whatever their [20] nature may be, servility will cower to force, and adulation[6] will follow power. The only means of preventing men from degrading themselves is to invest no one with that unlimited authority which is the sure method of debasing them.

THE GREATEST DANGERS OF THE AMERICAN REPUBLICS PROCEED FROM THE OMNIPOTENCE OF THE MAJORITY

Democratic Republics liable to perish from a Misuse of their Power, and [21] not from Impotence.—The Governments of the American Republics are more Centralized and more Energetic than those of the Monarchies of Europe.—Dangers resulting from this.—Opinions of Madison and Jefferson upon this Point.

Governments usually perish from impotence or from tyranny. In the for- [22] mer case, their power escapes from them; it is wrested from their grasp in the latter. Many observers who have witnessed the anarchy of democratic states, have imagined that the government of those states was naturally weak and impotent. The truth is, that, when war is once begun between parties, the government loses its control over society. But I do not think that a democratic power is naturally without force or resources; say, rather, that it is almost always by the abuse of its force, and the misemployment of its resources, that it becomes a failure. Anarchy is almost always produced by its tyranny or its mistakes, but not by its want of strength.

It is important not to confound stability with force, or the greatness of a [23] thing with its duration. In democratic republics, the power which directs[7] society is not stable; for it often changes hands, and assumes a new direction. But, whichever way it turns, its force is almost irresistible. The governments of the American republics appear to me to be as much centralized as those of the absolute monarchies of Europe, and more energetic than they are. I do not, therefore, imagine that they will perish from weakness.[8]

If ever the free institutions of America are destroyed, that event may be [24] attributed to the omnipotence of the majority, which may at some future time urge the minorities to desperation, and oblige them to have recourse to physical

---

[6]adulation Excessive praise. [Ed. note.]

[7]This power may be centralized in an assembly, in which case it will be strong without being stable; or it may be centralized in an individual, in which case it will be less strong, but more stable.

[8]I presume that it is scarcely necessary to remind the reader here, as well as throughout this chapter, that I am speaking, not of the Federal government, but of the several governments of each State, which the majority controls at its pleasure.

force. Anarchy will then be the result, but it will have been brought about by despotism.

25 Mr. Madison expresses the same opinion in the Federalist, No. 51. "It is of great importance in a republic, not only to guard the society against the oppression of its rulers, but to guard one part of the society against the injustice of the other part. Justice is the end of government. It is the end of civil society. It ever has been, and ever will be, pursued until it be obtained, or until liberty be lost in the pursuit. In a society, under the forms of which the stronger faction can readily unite and oppress the weaker, anarchy may as truly be said to reign as in a state of nature, where the weaker individual is not secured against the violence of the stronger: And as, in the latter state, even the stronger individuals are prompted by the uncertainty of their condition to submit to a government which may protect the weak as well as themselves, so, in the former state, will the more powerful factions be gradually induced by a like motive to wish for a government which will protect all parties, the weaker as well as the more powerful. It can be little doubted, that, if the State of Rhode Island was separated from the Confederacy and left to itself, the insecurity of right under the popular form of government within such narrow limits would be displayed by such reiterated oppressions of the factious majorities, that some power altogether independent of the people would soon be called for by the voice of the very factions whose misrule had proved the necessity of it."

26 Jefferson also said: "The executive power in our government is not the only, perhaps not even the principal, object of my solicitude. The tyranny of the legislature is really the danger most to be feared, and will continue to be so for many years to come. The tyranny of the executive power will come in its turn, but at a more distant period."

27 I am glad to cite the opinion of Jefferson upon this subject rather than that of any other, because I consider him the most powerful advocate democracy has ever had.

Questions for Discussion and Your Reading Journal

1. What seems to be the purpose of this piece? Who is the audience?
2. What is the "tyranny of the majority"? How does it threaten democracy according to de Tocqueville?
3. Do you agree or disagree with de Tocqueville's analysis of democracy? Cite examples to support your position.
4. How does de Tocqueville view European monarchy? American republican government? How is oppression different in these forms of government?
5. How is the final quote from Jefferson relevant today?
6. De Tocqueville states that Americans tend to conform to the majority opinion. To what extent are Americans conformists? Explain.

KARL MARX AND FRIEDRICH ENGELS

In 1848, with revolutions arising throughout Europe, the Communist League, a group of organized tailors in London, asked the political organizer and philosopher Karl Marx (1818–1883) to write a declaration of principles, which he named The Communist Manifesto. *While his life-long friend and supporter Friedrich Engels contributed some of his ideas to the* Manifesto, *Marx did all of the writing. Part of its purpose was to create a communist party and to capitalize on conservative rhetoric that labeled almost any opposition group "communist." The* Manifesto *addresses these fears in the famous opening line, "A specter is haunting Europe." A student of the philosopher Hegel, Marx rejected Hegel's idealism—a philosophy in which ideas precede and form reality—in favor of a materialist of history.* Materialism *asserts that economic causes, and not ideas, create social and political systems. Having observed the textile factories in the north of England, Marx concluded that the class that controls the means of production can also control the state. This first chapter of the Manifesto can be compared to the writings of Jefferson (p. 52) and Nyerere (p. 83).*

Reading Rhetorically

In his first lines, Marx made it quite clear to whom he was writing with the words "all the powers of old Europe." These powers were united in their opposition to the emerging force of communism. In short, Marx was writing a declaration to his enemies, which is about as difficult a rhetorical task as one might wish to undertake. To pull it off effectively, he took a highly organized approach. Note how his introductory section sets out in very clear language the two guiding points of the rest of his manifesto. He continued this organization in the body of the reading, using logical claims buttressed by great amounts of evidence to move his position forward, much as de Tocqueville did in the previous reading. It is not surprising that both writers took this approach, as both were educated in Western societies strongly influenced by the rhetoricians of classical Greece who stressed the use of objective logic (and compelling evidence) for persuading people to accept a given position. Writers in non-Western societies such as the Chinese leader Mao Tse-tung (next reading) used other strategies to persuade such as literary eloquence or forceful language. Some writers use appeals to God or other divine powers. In his Declaration of Independence, Jefferson brought together all of these persuasive techniques (appeals to God, natural human rights, and logic). As an atheist, Marx did not attempt to present God as being in support of his ideas. Rather, he turned to human history as the source of evidence to show the rightness of his thinking.

What makes his writing particularly noteworthy in a rhetorical sense is how he quickly divided his overview of human history into "good" forces and "bad" forces, resulting in modern times in "two great hostile camps," which he labeled the *bourgeoisie* (capitalists/owners) and the *proletariat* (workers). The division of groups in his text allowed him to divide his audience as well. His wealthy readers were likely to identify with his bourgeoisie class and his poor readers with his proletariat class. At this point, he was in a position to use the negative rhetorical appeal of demonizing one group (the bourgeoisie) while simultaneously championing the virtues of the other (the proletariat). Out of this simple "good and evil" pairing, Marx then fashioned a morality tale of human history replete with good characters and bad characters and a clear message about what good, ethical readers should do to move the story forward in their own lives. The effectiveness of Marx's argument hinges upon one critical element; readers must accept his main claim at the beginning that "the history of all hitherto existing society is the history of class struggle." He expended a great deal of time and effort to bring together evidence to support this view of history. For readers interested in history, his argument is likely to be more engaging. For readers who are more future-oriented, this history-based approach to reasoning can be a major flaw in Marx's persuasive appeal. In general, U.S. readers belong to a future-orientated culture that tends to become impatient with extended appeals to historical knowledge, facts, and interpretations. However, people around the world continue to find Marx's ideas and arguments profoundly relevant to the world today. In China alone, 1.3 billion people live out their daily lives under a political system based upon culturally adapted elements of Marxism. (See next reading by Mao Tse-tung.)

Bourgeois and Proletarians[1]

1   A specter is haunting Europe—the specter of Communism. All the powers of old Europe have entered into a holy alliance to exorcise this specter: Pope and Czar, Metternich and Guizot, French Radicals[2] and German police-spies.

2   Where is the party in opposition that has not been decried as communistic by its opponents in power? Where is the Opposition that has not hurled back the branding reproach of Communism, against the more advanced opposition parties, as well as against its reactionary adversaries?

---

[1]By bourgeoisie is meant the class of modern capitalists, owners of the means of social production and employers of wage-labor; by proletariat, the class of modern wage-laborers who, having no means of production of their own, are reduced to selling their labor power in order to live.

[2]**Metternich** (1773–1859) Chancellor of the Austrian empire and acknowledged leader of the European reaction. **Guizot** (1787–1874) French intellectual protagonist of high finance and of the industrial bourgeoisie and the irreconcilable foe of the proletariat. **French Radicals** Marrast (1802–1852), Carnot (1801–1888), and Marie (1795–1870) waged polemic warfare against the Socialists and Communists. [Ed. note.]

Two things result from this fact: 3

I. Communism is already acknowledged by all European powers to be itself a power.
II. It is high time that Communists should openly, in the face of the whole world, publish their views, their aims, their tendencies, and meet this nursery tale of the specter of Communism with a manifesto of the party itself.

To this end, Communists of various nationalities have assembled in London, and sketched the following manifesto, to be published in the English, French, German, Italian, Flemish, and Danish languages. 4

The history of all hitherto existing society[3] is the history of class struggles. 5

Freeman and slave, patrician and plebeian, lord and serf, guild-master[4] and journeyman, in a word, oppressor and oppressed, stood in constant opposition to one another, carried on an uninterrupted, now hidden, now open fight, a fight that each time ended, either in a revolutionary reconstitution of society at large, or in the common ruin of the contending classes. 6

In the earlier epochs of history, we find almost everywhere a complicated arrangement of society into various orders, a manifold gradation of social rank. In ancient Rome we have patricians, knights, plebeians, slaves; in the Middle Ages, feudal lords, vassals guild-masters, journeymen, apprentices, serfs; in almost all of these classes, again, subordinate gradations. 7

The modern bourgeois society that has sprouted from the ruins of feudal society, has not done away with class antagonisms. It has but established new classes, new conditions of oppression, new forms of struggle in place of the old ones. 8

Our epoch, the epoch of the bourgeoisie, possesses, however, this distinctive feature: It has simplified the class antagonisms. Society as a whole is more and more splitting up into two great hostile camps, into two great classes directly facing each other—bourgeoisie and proletariat. 9

From the serfs of the Middle Ages sprang the chartered burghers[5] of the earliest towns. From these burgesses the first elements of the bourgeoisie were developed. 10

The discovery of America, the rounding of the Cape, opened up fresh ground for the rising bourgeoisie. The East Indian and Chinese markets, the 11

---

[3]That is, all *written* history. In 1837, the pre-history of society, the social organization existing previous to recorded history, was all but unknown. Since then Haxthausen [August von, 1792–1866] discovered common ownership of land in Russia, Maurer [Georg Ludwig von] proved it to be the social foundation from which all Teutonic races started in history, and, by and by, village communities were found to be, or to have been, the primitive form of society every where from India to Ireland. The inner organization of this primitive communistic society was laid bare, in its typical form, by Morgan's [Lewis H., 1818–1881] crowning discovery of the true nature of the *gens* and its relation to the *tribe*. With the dissolution of these primeval communities, society begins to be differentiated into separate and finally antagonistic classes. I have attempted to retrace this process of dissolution in *The Origin of the Family, Private Property and the State*.

[4]Guild-master, that is a full member of a guild, a master within, not a head of a guild.

[5]**Chartered burghers** Freemen who had been admitted to the privileges of a chartered borough thus possessing full political rights. [Ed. note.]

colonization of America, trade with the colonies, the increase in the means of exchange and in commodities generally, gave to commerce, to navigation, to industry, an impulse never before known, and thereby, to the revolutionary element in the tottering feudal society, a rapid development.

12   The feudal system of industry in which industrial production was monopolized by closed guilds,[6] now no longer sufficed for the growing wants of the new markets. The manufacturing system took its place. The guild-masters were pushed aside by the manufacturing middle class; division of labor between the different corporate guilds vanished in the face of division of labor in each single workshop.

13   Meantime the markets kept ever growing, the demand ever rising. Even manufacture no longer sufficed. Thereupon, steam and machinery revolutionized industrial production. The place of manufacture was taken by the giant, modern industry, the place of the industrial middle class, by industrial millionaires—the leaders of whole industrial armies, the modern bourgeois.

14   Modern industry has established the world market, for which the discovery of America paved the way. This market has given an immense development to commerce, to navigation, to communication by land. This development has, in its turn, reacted on the extension of industry; and in proportion as industry, commerce, navigation, railways extended, in the same proportion the bourgeoisie developed, increased its capital, and pushed into the background every class handed down from the Middle Ages.

15   We see, therefore, how the modern bourgeoisie is itself the product of a long course of development, of a series of revolutions in the modes of production and of exchange.

16   Each step in the development of the bourgeoisie was accompanied by a corresponding political advance of that class. An oppressed class under the sway of the feudal nobility, it became an armed and self-governing association in the medieval commune;[7] here independent urban republic (as in Italy and Germany), there taxable "third estate" of the monarchy (as in France); afterwards, in the period of manufacture proper, serving either the semi-feudal or the absolute monarchy as a counterpoise against the nobility, and, in fact, cornerstone of the great monarchies in general—the bourgeoisie has at last, since the establishment of modern industry and of the world market, conquered for itself, in the modern representative state, exclusive political sway. The executive of the modern state is but a committee for managing the common affairs of the whole bourgeoisie.

17   The bourgeoisie has played a most revolutionary role in history.

18   The bourgeoisie, wherever it has got the upper hand, has put an end to all feudal, patriarchal, idyllic relations. It has pitilessly torn asunder the motley

---

[6]**Craft guilds** Made up of exclusive and privileged groups of artisans during the feudal period, guilds granted monopoly rights to markets by municipal authorities. The guilds imposed minute regulations on their members controlling such matters as working hours, wages, prices, tools, and the hiring of workers. [Ed. note.]

[7]"Commune" was the name taken in France by the nascent towns even before they had conquered from their feudal lords and masters local self-government and political rights as the "Third Estate." Generally speaking, for the economic development of the bourgeoisie, England is here taken as the typical country, for its political development, France.

feudal ties that bound man to his "natural superiors," and has left no other bond between man and man than naked self-interest, than callous "cash payment." It has drowned the most heavenly ecstasies of religious fervor, of chivalrous enthusiasm, of philistine sentimentalism, in the icy water of egotistical calculation. It has resolved personal worth into exchange value, and in place of the numberless indefeasible chartered freedoms, has set up that single, unconscionable freedom—Free Trade. In one word, for exploitation, veiled by religious and political illusions, it has substituted naked, shameless, direct, brutal exploitation.

The bourgeoisie has stripped of its halo every occupation hitherto honored and looked up to with reverent awe. It has converted the physician, the lawyer, the priest, the poet, the man of science, into its paid wage-laborers. **19**

The bourgeoisie has torn away from the family its sentimental veil, and has reduced the family relation to a mere money relation. **20**

The bourgeoisie has disclosed how it came to pass that the brutal display of vigor in the Middle Ages, which reactionaries so much admire, found its fitting complement in the most slothful indolence. It has been the first to show what man's activity can bring about. It has accomplished wonders far surpassing Egyptian pyramids, Roman aqueducts, and Gothic cathedrals; it has conducted expeditions that put in the shade all former migrations of nations and crusades. **21**

The bourgeoisie cannot exist without constantly revolutionizing the instruments of production, and thereby the relations of production, and with them the whole relations of society. Conservation of the old modes of production in unaltered form, was, on the contrary, the first condition of existence for all earlier industrial classes. Constant revolutionizing of production, uninterrupted disturbance of all social conditions, everlasting uncertainty and agitation distinguish the bourgeois epoch from all earlier ones. All fixed, fast-frozen relations, with their train of ancient and venerable prejudices and opinions, are swept away, all new-formed ones become antiquated before they can ossify. All that is solid melts into air, all that is holy is profaned, and man is at last compelled to face with sober senses his real conditions of life and his relations with his kind. **22**

The need of a constantly expanding market for its products chases the bourgeoisie over the whole surface of the globe. It must nestle everywhere, settle everywhere, establish connections everywhere. **23**

The bourgeoisie has through its exploitation of the world market given a cosmopolitan character to production and consumption in every country. To the great chagrin of reactionaries, it has drawn from under the feet of industry the national ground on which it stood. All old-established national industries have been destroyed or are daily being destroyed. They are dislodged by new industries, whose introduction becomes a life and death question for all civilized nations, by industries that no longer work up indigenous raw material, but raw material drawn from the remotest zones; industries whose products are consumed, not only at home, but in every quarter of the globe. In place of the old wants, satisfied by the production of the country, we find new wants, requiring for their satisfaction the products of distant lands and climes. In place **24** of the old local and national seclusion and self-sufficiency, we have intercourse in every direction, universal inter-dependence of nations. And as in material, so also in intellectual production. The intellectual creations of individual nations become common property. National one-sidedness and narrow-mindedness become more and more impossible, and from the numerous national and local literatures there arises a world literature.

25   The bourgeoisie, by the rapid improvement of all instruments of production, by the immensely facilitated means of communication, draws all nations, even the most barbarian, into civilization. The cheap prices of its commodities are the heavy artillery with which it batters down all Chinese walls, with which it forces the barbarians' intensely obstinate hatred of foreigners to capitulate. It compels all nations, on pain of extinction, to adopt the bourgeois mode of production; it compels them to introduce what it calls civilization into their midst, i.e., to become bourgeois themselves. In a word, it creates a world after its own image.

26   The bourgeoisie has subjected the country to the rule of the towns. It has created enormous cities, has greatly increased the urban population as compared with the rural, and has thus rescued a considerable part of the population from the idiocy of rural life. Just as it has made the country dependent on the towns, so it has made barbarian and semi-barbarian countries dependent on the civilized ones, nations of peasants on nations of bourgeois, the East on the West.

27   More and more the bourgeoisie keeps doing away with the scattered state of the population, of the means of production, and of property. It has agglomerated population, centralized means of production, and has concentrated property in a few hands. The necessary consequence of this was political centralization. Independent, or but loosely connected provinces, with separate interests, laws, governments, and systems of taxation, became lumped together into one nation, with one government, one code of laws, one national class interest, one frontier, and one customs tariff.

28   The bourgeoisie, during its rule of scarce one hundred years, has created more massive and more colossal productive forces than have all preceding generations together. Subjection of nature's forces to man, machinery, application of chemistry to industry and agriculture, steam-navigation, railways, electric telegraphs, clearing of whole continents for cultivation, canalisation of rivers, whole populations conjured out of the ground—what earlier century had even a presentiment that such productive forces slumbered in the lap of social labour?

29   We see then that the means of production and of exchange, which served as the foundation for the growth of the bourgeoisie, were generated in feudal society. At a certain stage in the development of these means of production and of exchange, the conditions under which feudal society produced and exchanged, the feudal organisation of agriculture and manufacturing industry, in a word, the feudal relations of property became no longer compatible with the already developed productive forces; they became so many fetters. They had to be burst asunder; they were burst asunder.

Into their place stepped free competition, accompanied by a social and 30 political constitution adapted to it, and by the economic and political sway of the bourgeois class.

A similar movement is going on before our own eyes. Modern bourgeois 31 society with its relations of production, of exchange and of property, a society that has conjured up such gigantic means of production and of exchange, is like the sorcerer who is no longer able to control the powers of the nether world whom he has called up by his spells. For many a decade past the history of industry and commerce is but the history of the revolt of modern productive forces against modern conditions of production, against the property relations that are the conditions for the existence of the bourgeoisie and of its rule. It is enough to mention the commercial crises that by their periodical return put the existence of the entire bourgeois society on trial, each time more threateningly. In these crises a great part not only of the existing products, but also of the previously created productive forces, are periodically destroyed. In these crises there breaks out an epidemic that, in all earlier epochs, would have seemed an absurdity—the epidemic of over-production. Society suddenly finds itself put back into a state of momentary barbarism; it appears as if a famine, a universal war of devastation had cut off the supply of every means of subsistence; industry and commerce seem to be destroyed. And why? Because there is too much civilization, too much means of subsistence, too much industry, too much commerce. The productive forces at the disposal of society no longer tend to further the development of the conditions of bourgeois property; on the contrary, they have become too powerful for these conditions, by which they are fettered, and no sooner do they overcome these fetters than they bring disorder into the whole of bourgeois society, endanger the existence of bourgeois property. The conditions of bourgeois society are too narrow to comprise the wealth created by them. And how does the bourgeoisie get over these crises? On the one hand, by enforced destruction of a mass of productive forces; on the other, by the conquest of new markets, and by the more thorough exploitation of the old ones. That is to say, by paving the way for more extensive and more destructive crises, and by diminishing the means whereby crises are prevented.

The weapons with which the bourgeoisie felled feudalism to the ground 32 are now turned against the bourgeoisie itself.

But not only has the bourgeoisie forged the weapons that bring death to 33 itself; it has also called into existence the men who are to wield those weapons—the modern working class—the proletarians.

In proportion as the bourgeoisie, i.e., capital, is developed, in the same 34 proportion is the proletariat, the modern working class, developed—a class of laborers, who live only so long as they find work, and who find work only so long as their labor increases capital. These laborers, who must sell themselves piecemeal, are a commodity, like every other article of commerce, and are consequently exposed to all the vicissitudes of competition, to all the fluctuations of the market.

Owing to the extensive use of machinery and to division of labor, the work 35 of the proletarians has lost all individual character, and, consequently, all charm for the workman. He becomes an appendage of the machine, and it is only the most simple, most monotonous, and most easily acquired knack, that is required of him. Hence, the cost of production of a workman is restricted, almost entirely, to the means of subsistence that he requires for his maintenance, and for the propagation of his race. But the price of a commodity, and therefore also of labor, is equal to its cost of production. In proportion, therefore, as the repulsiveness of the work increases, the wage decreases. Nay more, in proportion as the use of machinery and division of labor increases, in the same proportion the burden of toil also increases, whether by prolongation of the working hours, by increase of the work exacted in a given time, or by increased speed of the machinery, etc.

36   Modern industry has converted the little workshop of the patriarchal master into the great factory of the industrial capitalist. Masses of laborers, crowded into the factory, are organized like soldiers. As privates of the industrial army they are placed under the command of a perfect hierarchy of officers and sergeants. Not only are they slaves of the bourgeois class, and of the bourgeois state; they are daily and hourly enslaved by the machine, by the over-looker, and, above all, by the individual bourgeois manufacturer himself. The more openly this despotism proclaims gain to be its end and aim, the more petty, the more hateful and the more embittering it is.

37   The less the skill and exertion of strength implied in manual labor, in other words, the more modern industry develops, the more is the labor of men superseded by that of women. Differences of age and sex have no longer any distinctive social validity for the working class. All are instruments of labor, more or less expensive to use, according to their age and sex.

38   No sooner has the laborer received his wages in cash, for the moment escaping exploitation by the manufacturer, than he is set upon by the other portions of the bourgeoisie, the landlord, the shopkeeper, the pawnbroker, etc.

39   The lower strata of the middle class—the small tradespeople, shopkeepers, and retired tradesmen generally, the handicraftsmen and peasants—all these sink gradually into the proletariat, partly because their diminutive capital does not suffice for the scale on which modern industry is carried on, and is swamped in the competition with the large capitalists, partly because their specialized skill is rendered worthless by new methods of production. Thus the proletariat is recruited from all classes of the population.

40   The proletariat goes through various stages of development. With its birth begins its struggle with the bourgeoisie. At first the contest is carried on by individual laborers, then by the work people of a factory, then by the operatives of one trade, in one locality, against the individual bourgeois who directly exploits them. They direct their attacks not against the bourgeois conditions of production, but against the instruments of production themselves; they destroy imported wares that compete with their labor, they smash machinery to pieces, they set factories ablaze, they seek to restore by force the vanished status of the workman of the Middle Ages.

41   At this stage the laborers still form an incoherent mass scattered over the whole country, and broken up by their mutual competition. If anywhere they unite to form more compact bodies, this is not yet the consequence of their

own active union, but of the union of the bourgeoisie, which class, in order to attain its own political ends, is compelled to set the whole proletariat in motion, and is moreover still able to do so for a time. At this stage, therefore, the proletarians do not fight their enemies, but the enemies of their enemies, the remnants of absolute monarchy, the landowners, the nonindustrial bourgeois, the petty bourgeoisie. Thus the whole historical movement is concentrated in the hands of the bourgeoisie; every victory so obtained is a victory for the bourgeoisie.

But with the development of industry the proletariat not only increases in   42
number; it becomes concentrated in greater masses, its strength grows, and it feels that strength more. The various interests and conditions of life within the ranks of the proletariat are more and more equalized, in proportion as machinery obliterates all distinctions of labor and nearly everywhere reduces wages to the same low level. The growing competition among the bourgeois, and the resulting commercial crises, make the wages of the workers ever more fluctuating. The unceasing improvement of machinery, ever more rapidly developing, makes their livelihood more and more precarious; the collisions between individual workmen and individual bourgeois take more and more the character of collisions between two classes. Thereupon the workers begin to form combinations (trade unions) against the bourgeoisie; they club together in order to keep up the rate of wages; they found permanent associations in order to make provision beforehand for these occasional revolts. Here and there the contest breaks out into riots.

Now and then the workers are victorious, but only for a time. The real   43
fruit of their battles lies, not in the immediate result, but in the ever expanding union of the workers. This union is furthered by the improved means of communication which are created by modern industry, and which place the workers of different localities in contact with one another. It was just this contact that was needed to centralize the numerous local struggles, all of the same character, into one national struggle between classes. But every class struggle is a political struggle. And that union, to attain which the burghers of the Middle Ages, with their miserable highways, required centuries, the modern proletarians, thanks to railways, achieve in a few years.

This organization of the proletarians into a class, and consequently into a   44
political party, is continually being upset again by the competition between the workers themselves. But it ever rises up again, stronger, firmer, mightier. It compels legislative recognition of particular interests of the workers, by taking advantage of the divisions among the bourgeoisie itself. Thus the ten-hour bill[8] in England was carried.

Altogether, collisions between the classes of the old society further the   45
course of development of the proletariat in many ways. The bourgeoisie finds itself involved in a constant battle. At first with the aristocracy; later on, with those portions of the bourgeoisie itself whose interests have become antagonistic to the progress of industry; at all times with the bourgeoisie of foreign

---

[8] **10-Hour Bill** Legislation for which the English workers had been fighting for 30 years; it was made law in 1847. [Ed. note.]

countries. In all these battles it sees itself compelled to appeal to the proletariat, to ask for its help, and thus, to drag it into the political arena. The bourgeoisie itself, therefore, supplies the proletariat with its own elements of political and general education, in other words, it furnishes the proletariat with weapons for fighting the bourgeoisie.

46   Further, as we have already seen, entire sections of the ruling classes are, by the advance of industry, precipitated into the proletariat, or are at least threatened in their conditions of existence. These also supply the proletariat with fresh elements of enlightenment and progress.

47   Finally, in times when the class struggle nears the decisive hour, the process of dissolution going on within the ruling class, in fact within the whole range of old society, assumes such a violent, glaring character, that a small section of the ruling class cuts itself adrift, and joins the revolutionary class, the class that holds the future in its hands. Just as, therefore, at an earlier period, a section of the nobility went over to the bourgeoisie, so now a portion of the bourgeoisie goes over to the proletariat, and in particular, a portion of the bourgeois ideologists, who have raised themselves to the level of comprehending theoretically the historical movement as a whole.

48   Of all the classes that stand face to face with the bourgeoisie today, the proletariat alone is a really revolutionary class. The other classes decay and finally disappear in the face of modern industry; the proletariat is its special and essential product.

49   The lower middle class, the small manufacturer, the shopkeeper, the artisan, the peasant, all these fight against the bourgeoisie, to save from extinction their existence as fractions of the middle class. They are therefore not revolutionary, but conservative. Nay more, they are reactionary, for they try to roll back the wheel of history. If by chance they are revolutionary, they are so only in view of their impending transfer into the proletariat; they thus defend not their present, but their future interests; they desert their own standpoint to adopt that of the proletariat.

50   The "dangerous class," the social scum (*Lumpenproletariat*), that passively rotting mass thrown off by the lowest layers of old society, may, here and there, be swept into the movement by a proletarian revolution; its conditions of life, however, prepare it far more for the part of a bribed tool of reactionary intrigue.

51   The social conditions of the old society no longer exist for the proletariat. The proletarian is without property; his relation to his wife and children has no longer anything in common with bourgeois family relations; modern industrial labor, modern subjection to capital, the same in England as in France, in America as in Germany, has stripped him of every trace of national character. Law, morality, religion, are to him so many bourgeois prejudices, behind which lurk in ambush just as many bourgeois interests.

52   All the preceding classes that got the upper hand, sought to fortify their already acquired status by subjecting society at large to their conditions of appropriation. The proletarians cannot become masters of the productive forces of society, except by abolishing their own previous mode of appropriation, and thereby also every other previous mode of appropriation. They have

nothing of their own to secure and to fortify; their mission is to destroy all previous securities for, and insurances of, individual property.

All previous historical movements were movements of minorities, or in the 53 interest of minorities. The proletarian movement is the self-conscious, independent movement of the immense majority, in the interest of the immense majority. The proletariat, the lowest stratum of our present society, cannot stir, cannot raise itself up, without the whole superincumbent strata of official society being sprung into the air.

Though not in substance, yet in form, the struggle of the proletariat with 54 the bourgeoisie is at first a national struggle. The proletariat of each country must, of course, first of all settle matters with its own bourgeoisie.

In depicting the most general phases of the development of the proletariat, 55 we traced the more or less veiled civil war, raging within existing society, up to the point where that war breaks out into open revolution, and where the violent overthrow of the bourgeoisie lays the foundation for the sway of the proletariat.

Hitherto, every form of society has been based, as we have already seen, 56 on the antagonism of oppressing and oppressed classes. But in order to oppress a class, certain conditions must be assured to it under which it can, at least, continue its slavish existence. The serf, in the period of serfdom, raised himself to membership in the commune, just as the petty bourgeois, under the yoke of feudal absolutism, managed to develop into a bourgeois. The modern laborer, on the contrary, instead of rising with the progress of industry, sinks deeper and deeper below the conditions of existence of his own class. He becomes a pauper, and pauperism develops more rapidly than population and wealth. And here it becomes evident, that the bourgeoisie is unfit any longer to be the ruling class in society, and to impose its conditions of existence upon society as an overriding law. It is unfit to rule because it is incompetent to assure an existence to its slave within his slavery, because it cannot help letting him sink into such a state, that it has to feed him, instead of being fed by him. Society can no longer live under this bourgeoisie, in other words, its existence is no longer compatible with society.

The essential condition for the existence and sway of the bourgeois class, 57 is the formation and augmentation of capital; the condition for capital is wage-labor. Wage-labor rests exclusively on competition between the laborers. The advance of industry, whose involuntary promoter is the bourgeoisie, replaces the isolation of the laborers, due to competition, by their revolutionary combination, due to association. The development of modern industry, therefore, cuts from under its feet the very foundation on which the bourgeoisie produces and appropriates products. What the bourgeoisie therefore produces, above all, are its own grave-diggers. Its fall and the victory of the proletariat are equally inevitable.

Questions for Discussion and Your Reading Journal

1. As an in-class activity, survey the reading by quickly reading the main points. Start with Marx's thesis and outline his argument. Where does

Marx's selection shift from an analysis of the past to a prediction of the future?

2. According to Marx, what will cause a class struggle between the bourgeoisie and the proletariat? What is the function of the bourgeoisie and the proletariat according to his view? What seems to be Marx's attitude (tone) toward the bourgeois and the proletariat?

3. Explain the crisis that will bring the proletariat to power.

4. What are Marx's Western biases? How does he refer to other countries and to the expansion of bourgeois industrial society to those countries?

5. Do you agree or disagree with Marx's analysis and predictions? Explain.

6. In-class essay question: Compare and contrast Marx's communism and Nyerere's "Ujamaa—The Basis of African Socialism" (p. 83). In particular, look at the notions of class and class struggle that are at the heart of Marx's argument and look at the assumptions of ujamaa that are central to Nyerere's argument.

MAO TSE-TUNG

Mao Tse-tung (1893–1976) rose to power in China during troubled times not unlike those faced by Confucius over 2,000 years before. Warlords and people of the wealthy upper classes were engaged in constant struggles for power and for resources, while the nation's poorer citizens suffered terribly from starvation and destitution. Mao became a popular leader with the poor masses by showing incredible self-discipline and commitment to the good of the common people. He is especially known for leading the "long march" of 1934–35, a 6,000-mile journey on foot leading 90,000 members of the revolutionary Red Army to safety from deadly attacks by the main government army. Half of the marchers died during the difficult journey. Those who survived led the communist forces to success against corrupt government forces over a decade later in 1948. Since the fall of the Berlin Wall in 1988, many Westerners assume that communism is defunct as a political system. And yet 1.3 billion Chinese citizens (20 percent of the entire world population) currently live under a thriving communist governing system that is finding successful ways to coexist with capitalistic and democratic systems around the world. The following text, taken from Chairman Mao's Little Red Book, gives a view of some of the key ideas, goals, and approaches to social action that underlie Mao's adaptations of Marxism and Leninism to China. Compiled in the 1960s, the Little Red Book brought together the teachings of Mao in a collection of readings that continues to be one of the most widely read and influential books in China.

Reading Rhetorically

China is almost exactly the same size as the United States in geographical terms. This means that in the same amount of space as the United Stats occupies, *1 billion more people* are living out their day-to-day lives. This leaves much less room for the free-wheeling individualism that is a primary social value in North America. Mao's use of rhetoric seems to confirm this point. Notice how he began the following message with an emphasis upon the role the vast population of China (600 million in 1957; 1.3 billion today) should hold as the focal point of political and social policy making. With so many people to be concerned about, it is not surprising that Mao's rhetorical appeal drew upon common values of unity, cooperation, and what he labeled "overall consideration," which is concerned with the good of "the whole people." Note also how the richness of the Chinese language emerged in his teachings through such slogans as, "Let a hundred flowers blossom, let a hundred schools of thought contend." He used many nature and farming-related metaphors in his political speech. The strong rhetorical appeal of these metaphors ("fragrant flowers," poisonous weeds," etc.) derive from the constant links they made back to the conceptual worlds of peasants and farmers, the people who swept Mao into power in the first place. Further reinforcing the primary role of simple farmers and poor people in his teachings is the constant split of society into good citizens (the proletariat, i.e., poor people, farmers, laborers, etc.) and bad citizens (the bourgeoisie, i.e., owners, intellectuals, elites who earn money from the labor of others). It is valuable to note how this two-dimensional thinking (good versus bad) shows up in other areas of Mao's thought. For example, he speaks of "right and wrong" in the fields of culture, art, and science. Although science may lend itself to some degree to the separation of ideas into categories of right or wrong, most people outside of China would find it more difficult to characterize elements of culture and art in terms of right or wrong. This may be, once again, an indicator of the need for conformity and social unity to which leaders of a nation of 1.3 billion are especially sensitive.

From "On the Correct Handling of Contradictions Among the People"

February 27, 1957

[Speech at the Eleventh Session (Enlarged) of the Supreme State Conference. Comrade Mao Tse-tung went over the verbatim record and made certain additions before its publication in the *People's Daily* on June 19, 1957.]

VII. OVER-ALL CONSIDERATION AND PROPER ARRANGEMENT

1   By over-all consideration we mean consideration that embraces the 600 million people of our country. In drawing up plans, handling affairs or thinking over problems, we must proceed from the fact that China has a population of 600 million, and we must never forget this fact. Why do we make a point of this? Is it possible that there are people who are still unaware that we have a population of 600 million? Of course, everyone knows this, but when it comes to actual practice, some people forget all about it and act as though the fewer the people, the smaller the circle, the better. Those who have this "small circle" mentality abhor the idea of bringing every positive factor into play, of uniting with everyone who can be united with, and of doing everything possible to turn negative factors into positive ones so as to serve the great cause of building a socialist society. I hope these people will take a wider view and fully recognize that we have a population of 600 million, that this is an objective fact, and that it is an asset for us. Our large population is a good thing, but of course it also involves certain difficulties. Construction is going ahead vigorously on all fronts and very successfully too, but in the present transition period of tremendous social change there are still many difficult problems. Progress and at the same time difficulties—this is a contradiction. However, not only should all such contradictions be resolved, but they definitely can be. Our guiding principle is over-all consideration and proper arrangement. Whatever the problem—whether it concerns food, natural calamities, employment, education, the intellectuals, the united front of all patriotic forces, the minority nationalities, or anything else—we must always proceed from the standpoint of over-all consideration, which embraces the whole people, and must make the proper arrangement, after consultation with all the circles concerned, in the light of what is feasible at a particular time and place. On no account should we complain that there are too many people, that others are backward, that things are troublesome and hard to handle, and close the door on them. Do I mean to say that the government alone must take care of everyone and everything? Of course not. In many cases, they can be left to the direct care of the public organizations or the masses—both are quite capable of devising many good ways of handling them. This also comes within the scope of the principle of over-all consideration and proper arrangement. We should give guidance on this to the public organizations and the people everywhere.

VIII. ON "LET A HUNDRED FLOWERS BLOSSOM, LET A HUNDRED SCHOOLS OF THOUGHT CONTEND" AND "LONG-TERM COEXISTENCE AND MUTUAL SUPERVISION"

2   "Let a hundred flowers blossom, let a hundred schools of thought contend" and "long-term coexistence and mutual supervision"—how did these slogans come to be put forward? They were put forward in the light of China's specific conditions, in recognition of the continued existence of various kinds of contradictions in socialist society and in response to the country's urgent need

to spend up its economic and cultural development. Letting a hundred flowers blossom and a hundred schools of thought contend is the policy for promoting progress in the arts and sciences and a flourishing socialist culture in our land. Different forms and styles in art should develop freely and different schools in science should contend freely. We think that it is harmful to the growth of art and science if administrative measures are used to impose one particular style of art or school of thought and to ban another. Questions of right and wrong in the arts and science should be settled through free discussion in artistic and scientific circles and through practical work in these fields. They should not be settled in an over-simple manner. A period of trial is often needed to determine whether something is right or wrong. Throughout history at the outset new and correct things often failed to win recognition from the majority of people and had to develop by twists and turns through struggle. Often, correct and good things were first regarded not as fragrant flowers but as poisonous weeds. Copernicus' theory of the solar system and Darwin's theory of evolution were once dismissed as erroneous and had to win out over bitter opposition. Chinese history offers many similar examples. In a socialist society, the conditions for the growth of the new are radically different from and far superior to those in the old society. Nevertheless, it often happens that new, rising forces are held back and sound ideas stifled. Besides even in the absence of their deliberate suppression, the growth of new things may be hindered simply through lack of discernment. It is therefore necessary to be careful about questions of right and wrong in the arts and sciences, to encourage free discussion and avoid hasty conclusions. We believe that such an attitude will help ensure a relatively smooth development of the arts and sciences.

Marxism, too, has developed through struggle. At the beginning, Marxism was subjected to all kinds of attack and regarded as a poisonous weed. This is still the case in many parts of the world. In the socialist countries, it enjoys a different position. But non-Marxist and, what is more, anti-Marxist ideologies exist even in these countries. In China, although socialist transformation has in the main been completed as regards the system of ownership, and although the large-scale, turbulent class struggles of the masses characteristic of times of revolution have in the main come to an end, there are still remnants of the overthrown landlord and comprador classes, there is still a bourgeoisie, and the remoulding of the petty bourgeoisie has only just started. Class struggle is by no means over. The class struggle between the proletariat and the bourgeoisie, the class struggle between the various political forces, and the class struggle between the proletariat and the bourgeoisie in the ideological field will still be protracted and tortuous and at times even very sharp. The proletariat seeks to transform the world according to its own world outlook, and so does the bourgeoisie. In this respect, the question of which will win out, socialism or capitalism, is not really settled yet. Marxists remain a minority among the entire population as well as among the intellectuals. Therefore, Marxism must continue to develop through struggle. Marxism can develop only through struggle, and this is not only true of the past and the present, it is necessarily true of the future as well. What is correct invariably develops in the course of struggle with what is wrong. The true, the good and the beautiful always exist by contrast with the false, the evil and the ugly, and grow in struggle with them. As soon as something erroneous is rejected and a particular truth accepted by mankind, new truths begin to struggle with new errors. Such struggles will never end. This is the law of development of truth and, naturally, of Marxism.

4   It will take a fairly long period of time to decide the issue in the ideological struggle between socialism and capitalism in our country. The reason is that the influence of the bourgeoisie and of the intellectuals who come from the old society, the very influence which constitutes their class ideology, will persist in our country for a long time. If this is not understood at all or is insufficiently understood, the gravest of mistakes will be made and the necessity of waging struggle in the ideological field will be ignored. Ideological struggle differs from other forms of struggle, since the only method used is painstaking reasoning, and not crude coercion. Today, socialism is in an advantageous position in the ideological struggle. The basic power of the state is in the hands of the working people led by the proletariat. The Communist Party is strong and its prestige high. Although there are defects and mistakes in our work, every fair-minded person can see that we are loyal to the people, that we are both determined and able to build up our motherland together with them, and that we have already achieved great successes and will achieve still greater ones. The vast majority of the bourgeoisie and the intellectuals who come from the old society are patriotic and are willing to serve their flourishing socialist motherland; they know they will have nothing to fall back on and their future cannot possibly be bright if they turn away from the socialist cause and from the working people led by the Communist Party.

5   People may ask, since Marxism is accepted as the guiding ideology by the majority of the people in our country, can it be criticized? Certainly it can. Marxism is scientific truth and fears no criticism. If it did, and if it could be overthrown by criticism, it would be worthless. In fact, aren't the idealists criticizing Marxism every day and in every way? And those who harbour bourgeois and petty-bourgeois ideas and do not wish to change—aren't they also criticizing Marxism in every way? Marxists should be not be afraid of criticism from any quarter. Quite the contrary, they need to temper and develop themselves and win new positions in the teeth of criticism and in the storm and stress of struggle. Fighting against wrong ideas is like being vaccinated—a man develops greater immunity from disease as a result of vaccination. Plants raised in hothouses are unlikely to be hardy. Carrying out the policy of letting a hundred flowers blossom and a hundred schools of thought contend will not weaken, but strengthen, the leading position of Marxism in the ideological field.

6   What should our policy be towards non-Marxist ideas? As far as unmistakable counter-revolutionaries and saboteurs of the socialist cause are concerned, the matter is easy, we simply deprive them of their freedom of speech. But incorrect ideas among the people are quite a different matter. Will it do to ban such ideas and deny them any opportunity for expression? Certainly not. It is not only futile but very harmful to use crude methods in dealing with ideological questions among the people, with questions about man's mental world. You may ban the expression of wrong ideas, but the ideas will still be

there. On the other hand, if correct ideas are pampered in hothouses and never exposed to the elements and immunized against disease, they will not win out against erroneous ones. Therefore, it is only by employing the method of discussion, criticism and reasoning that we can really foster correct ideas and overcome wrong ones, and that we can really settle issues.

It is inevitable that the bourgeoisie and petty bourgeoisie will give expression to their own ideologies. It is inevitable that they will stubbornly assert themselves on political and ideological questions by every possible means. You cannot expect them to do otherwise. We should not use the method of suppression and prevent them from expressing themselves, but should allow them to do so and at the same time argue with them and direct appropriate criticism at them. Undoubtedly, we must criticize wrong ideas of every description. It certainly would not be right to refrain from criticism, look on while wrong ideas spread unchecked and allow them to dominate the field. Mistakes must be criticized and poisonous weeds fought wherever they crop up. However, such criticism should not be dogmatic, and the metaphysical method should not be used, but instead the effort should be made to apply the dialectical method. What is needed is scientific analysis and convincing argument. Dogmatic criticism settles nothing. We are against poisonous weeds of whatever kind, but eve must carefully distinguish between what is really a poisonous weed and what is really a fragrant flower. Together with the masses of the people, we must learn to differentiate carefully between the two and use correct methods to fight the poisonous weeds.

At the same time as we criticize dogmatism, we must direct our attention to criticizing revisionism. Revisionism, or Right opportunism, is a bourgeois trend of thought that is even more dangerous than dogmatism. The revisionists, the Right opportunists, pay lip-service to Marxism; they too attack "dogmatism." But what they are really attacking is the quintessence of Marxism. They oppose or distort materialism and dialectics, oppose or try to weaken the people's democratic dictatorship and the leading role of the Communist Party, and oppose or try to weaken socialist transformation and socialist construction. Even after the basic victory of our socialist revolution, there will still be a number of people in our society who vainly hope to restore the capitalist system and are sure to fight the working class on every front, including the ideological one. And their right-hand men in this struggle are the revisionists.

Literally the two slogans—let a hundred flowers blossom and let a hundred schools of thought contend—have no class character; the proletariat can turn them to account, and so can the bourgeoisie or others.

Different classes, strata and social groups each have their own views on what are fragrant flowers and what are poisonous weeds. Then, from the point of view of the masses, what should be the criteria today for distinguishing fragrant flowers from poisonous weeds? In their political activities, how should our people judge whether a person's words and deeds are right or wrong? On the basis of the principles of our Constitution, the will of the overwhelming majority of our people and the common political positions which have been proclaimed on various occasions by our political parties, we consider that, broadly speaking, the criteria should be as follows:

1. Words and deeds should help to unite, and not divide, the people of all our nationalities.
2. They should be beneficial, and not harmful, to socialist transformation and socialist construction.
3. They should help to consolidate, and not undermine or weaken, the people's democratic dictatorship.
4. They should help to consolidate, and not undermine or weaken, democratic centralism.
5. They should help to strengthen, and not shake off or weaken, the leadership of the Communist Party.
6. They should be beneficial, and not harmful, to international socialist unity and the unity of the peace-loving people of the world.

11   Of these six criteria, the most important are the two about the socialist path and the leadership of the Party. These criteria are put forward not to hinder but to foster the free discussion of questions among the people. Those who disapprove these criteria can still state their own views and argue their case. However, so long as the majority of the people have clear-cut criteria to go by, criticism and self-criticism can be conducted along proper lines, and these criteria can be applied to people's words and deeds to determine whether they are right or wrong, whether they are fragrant flowers or poisonous weeds. These are political criteria. Naturally, to judge the validity of scientific theories or assess the aesthetic value of works of art, other relevant criteria are needed. But these six political criteria are applicable to all activities in the arts and sciences. In a socialist country like ours, can there possibly be any useful scientific or artistic activity which runs counter to these political criteria?

12   The views set out above are based on China's specific historical conditions. Conditions vary in different socialist countries and with different Communist Parties. Therefore, we do not maintain that they should or must adopt the Chinese way.

Questions for Discussion and Your Reading Journal

1. The difference between a communist/socialistic society and a capitalistic one has been summed up as the difference between having "equality" or "freedom" as the primary value of the people. Which value seems most evident in Chairman Mao's opening paragraph? Explain.
2. To what is Mao referring with the slogan "Let a hundred flowers blossom, let a hundred schools of thought contend"?
3. According to Mao, why will it "take a fairly long period of time" (Paragraph 4) for the struggle between socialism and capitalism to be decided in China?
4. Does Mao support the suppression of freedom of speech for all people in China who hold non-Marxist ideas?
5. Near the end of the speech, Mao writes, "In a socialist country like ours, can there possibly be any useful scientific or artistic activity which runs counter to these political criteria?" Can you think of examples where science and art have "run counter" to political concerns in the Western world?

JULIUS K. NYERERE

The orator and statesman Julius Nyerere (1922–) became president of the Tanganyikan African National Union (TANU) in the 1950s, when his country was still a British colony. TANU advocated replacing tribal and racial discrimination with the goals of a peaceful society that promoted greater social and economic equality and racial harmony. In 1961 Nyerere became the first prime minister of an independent Tanganyika. In 1964 Tanganyika was renamed Tanzania; and between 1964 and 1985 the TANU party, the backbone of Tanzania's single-party democracy, reelected Nyerere to the presidency for four consecutive terms before he stepped down from the office. Nyerere's definition of African socialism "Ujamaa" or "familyhood"—sets itself apart from the European definitions of socialism by claiming to be indigenous to Africa and by rejecting the notion of class struggle. In its opposition to class division, exploitation, and corruption, Ujamaa draws upon the cooperative work ethic and life of the traditional extended family in Tanzania. These ideals shaped the famous Arusha Declaration, which the TANU party adopted in 1967.

Reading Rhetorically

Nyerere comes from a very different society and a different world from those in which people in most developed, Western nations live. These differences are nowhere more evident than in the basic values that underlie Nyerere's writing. In his world, the primary value is to build an egalitarian society in which "the people care for each other's welfare." This gives him a negative view of capitalistic societies where the primary value tends toward individuals competing to see who can amass the most resources and riches for themselves. This perspective allows him to equate millionaires in a society with "parasites." To support such bold statements, Nyerere went to great pains to construct a logical argument buttressed by convincing support. Clearly he anticipated that others besides socialist-minded Africans might read his work. Note as you read how he depicts the world of "traditional African society" in terms of people caring for the welfare of other people (i.e., "African Socialism"). Nyerere's use of eloquent language intends to build an image of a world in which safety, security, and cooperation are the essential qualities. To this end, he equates the traditional tribal relations and hospitality codes of his native land with a pronounced sense of "familyhood." Rhetorically, such an appeal is most likely to resonate positively with any audience—whether at home in Tanzania or around the world—where the closeness of family is valued.

Ujamaa—The Basis of African Socialism

Socialism—like democracy—is an attitude of mind. In a socialist society it is   1
the socialist attitude of mind, and not the rigid adherence to a standard

political pattern, which is needed to ensure that the people care for each other's welfare.

2   The purpose of this paper is to examine that attitude. It is not intended to define the institutions which may be required to embody it in a modern society.

3   In the individual, as in the society, it is an attitude of mind which distinguishes the socialist from the non-socialist. It has nothing to do with the possession or non-possession of wealth. Destitute people can be potential capitalists—exploiters of their fellow human beings. A millionaire can equally well be a socialist; he may value his wealth only because it can be used in the service of his fellow men. But the man who uses wealth for the purpose of dominating any of his fellows is a capitalist. So is the man who would if he could!

4   I have said that a millionaire can be a good socialist. But a socialist millionaire is a rare phenomenon. Indeed he is almost a contradiction in terms. The appearance of millionaires in any society is no proof of its affluence; they can be produced by very poor countries like Tanganyika just as well as by rich countries like the United States of America. For it is not efficiency of production, nor the amount of wealth in a country, which make millionaires; it is the uneven distribution of what is produced. The basic difference between a socialist society and a capitalist society does not lie in their methods of producing wealth, but in the way that wealth is distributed. While, therefore, a millionaire could be a good socialist, he could hardly be the product of a socialist society.

5   Since the appearance of millionaires in a society does not depend on its affluence, sociologists may find it interesting to try and find out why our societies in Africa did not, in fact, produce any millionaires—for we certainly had enough wealth to create a few. I think they would discover that it was because the organization of traditional African society—its distribution of the wealth it produced—was such that there was hardly any room for parasitism. They might also say, of course, that as a result of this Africa could not produce a leisured class of landowners, and therefore there was nobody to produce the works of art or science which capitalist societies can boast. But works of art and the achievements of science are products of the intellect—which, like land, is one of God's gifts to man. And I cannot believe that God is so careless as to have made the use of one of His gifts depend on the *misuse* of another!

6   Defenders of capitalism claim that the millionaire's wealth is the just reward for his ability or enterprise. But this claim is not borne out by the facts. The wealth of the millionaire depends as little on the enterprise or abilities of the millionaire himself as the power of a feudal monarch depended on his own efforts, enterprise or brain. Both are users, exploiters, of the abilities and enterprise of other people. Even when you have an exceptionally intelligent and hard-working millionaire, the difference between his intelligence, his enterprise, his hard work, and those of other members of society, cannot possibly be proportionate to the difference between their "rewards." There must be something wrong in a society where one man, however hardworking or clever he may be, can acquire as great a "reward" as a thousand of his fellows can acquire between them.

Acquisitiveness for the purpose of gaining power and prestige is unsocial- 7
ist. In an acquisitive society wealth tends to corrupt those who posses it. It
tends to breed in them a desire to live more comfortably than their fellows, to
dress better, and in every way to outdo them. They begin to feel they must
climb as far above their neighbours as they can. The visible contrast between
their own comfort and the comparative discomfort of the rest of society
becomes almost essential to the enjoyment of their wealth, and this sets off the
spiral of personal competition—which is then anti-social.

Apart from the anti-social effects of the accumulation of personal wealth, 8
the very desire to accumulate it must be interpreted as a vote of "no confidence" in the social system. For when a society is so organized that it cares
about its individuals, then, provided he is willing to work, no individual
within that society should worry about what will happen to him tomorrow if
he does not hoard wealth today. Society itself should look after him, or his
widow, or his orphans. This is exactly what traditional African society succeeded in doing. Both the "rich" and the "poor" individual were completely
secure in African society. Natural catastrophe brought famine, but it brought
famine to everybody"poor" or "rich." Nobody starved, either of food or of
human dignity, because he lacked personal wealth; he could depend on the
wealth possessed by the community of which he was a member. That was
socialism. That *is* socialism. There can be no such thing as acquisitive socialism, for that would be another contradiction in terms. Socialism is essentially
distributive. Its concern is to see that those who sow reap a fair share of what
they sow.

The production of wealth, whether by primitive or modern methods, 9
requires three things. First, land. God has given us the land, and it is from the
land that we get the raw materials which we reshape to meet our needs. Secondly, tools. We have found by simple experience that tools do help! So we
make the hoe, the axe, or the modern factory or tractor, to help us to produce
wealth—the goods we need. And, thirdly, human exertion—or labour. We
don't need to read Karl Marx or Adam Smith to find out that neither the land
nor the hoe actually produces wealth. And we don't need to take degrees in
Economics to know that neither the worker nor the landlord produces land.
Land is God's gift to man—it is always there. But we do know, still without
degrees in Economics, that the axe and the plough were produced by the
labourer. Some of our more sophisticated friends apparently have to undergo
the most rigorous intellectual training simply in order to discover that stone
axes were produced by that ancient gentleman "Early Man" to make it easier
for him to skin the impala he had just killed with a club, which he had also
made for himself?

In traditional African society *everybody* was a worker. There was no other 10
way of earning a living for the community. Even the Elder, who appeared to
be enjoying himself without doing any work and for whom everybody else
appeared to be working, had, in fact, worked hard all his younger days. The
wealth he now appeared to possess was not *his*, personally; it was only "his"
as the Elder of the group which had produced it. He was its guardian. The

wealth itself gave him neither power nor prestige. The respect paid to him by the young was his because he was older than they, and had served his community longer; and the "poor" Elder enjoyed as much respect in our society as the "rich" Elder.

11   When I say that in traditional African society everybody was a worker, I do not use the word "worker" simply as opposed to "employer" but also as opposed to "loiterer" or "idler." One of the most socialistic achievements of our society was the sense of security it gave to its members, and the universal hospitality on which they could rely. But it is too often forgotten, nowadays, that the basis of this great socialistic achievement was this: that it was taken for granted that every member of society—barring only the children and the infirm—contributed his fair share of effort towards the production of its wealth. Not only was the capitalist, or the landed exploiter, unknown to traditional African society, but we did not have that other form of modern parasite—the loiterer, or idler, who accepts the hospitality of society as his "right" but gives nothing in return! Capitalistic exploitation was impossible. Loitering was an unthinkable disgrace.

12   Those of us who talk about the African way of life and, quite rightly, take a pride in maintaining the tradition of hospitality which is so great a part of it, might do well to remember the Swahili saying: "*Mgeni siku mbili; siku ya tatu mpe jembe*"—or in English, "Treat your guest as a guest for two days; on the third day give him a hoe!" In actual fact, the guest was likely to ask for the hoe even before his host had to give him one—for he knew what was expected of him, and would have been ashamed to remain idle any longer. Thus, working was part and parcel, was indeed the very basis and justification of this socialist achievement of which we are so justly proud.

13   There is no such thing as socialism without work. A society which fails to give its individuals the means to work, or, having given them the means to work, prevents them from getting a fair share of the products of their own sweat and toil, needs putting right. Similarly, an individual who can work—and is provided by society with the means to work—but does not do so, is equally wrong. He has no right to expect anything from society because he contributes nothing to society.

14   The other use of the word "worker," in its specialized sense of "employee" as opposed to "employer," reflects a capitalist attitude of mind which was introduced into Africa with the coming of colonialism and is totally foreign to our own way of thinking. In the old days the African had never aspired to the possession of personal wealth for the purpose of dominating any of his fellows. He had never had labourers or "factory hands" to do his work for him. But then came the foreign capitalists. They were wealthy. They were powerful. And the African naturally started wanting to be wealthy too. There is nothing wrong in our wanting to be wealthy; nor is it a bad thing for us to want to acquire the power which wealth brings with it. But it most certainly is wrong if we want the wealth and the power so that we can dominate somebody else. Unfortunately there are some of us who have already learnt to covet wealth for that purpose—and who would like to use the methods which the capitalist uses in acquiring it. That is to say, some of us would like to use, or exploit,

our brothers for the purpose of building up our own personal power and prestige. This is completely foreign to us, and it is incompatible with the socialist society we want to build here.

Our first step, therefore, must be to re-educate ourselves; to regain our   15
former attitude of mind. In our traditional African society we were individuals within a community. We took care of the community, and the community took care of us. We neither needed nor wished to exploit our fellow men.

And in rejecting the capitalist attitude of mind which colonialism   16
brought into Africa, we must reject also the capitalist methods which go with it. One of these is the individual ownership of land. To us in Africa land was always recognized as belonging to the community. Each individual within our society had a right to the use of land, because otherwise he could not earn his living and one cannot have the right to life without also having the right to some means of maintaining life. But the African's right to land was simply the right to use it; he had no other right to it, nor did it occur to him to try and claim one.

The foreigner introduced a completely different concept—the concept of   17
land as a marketable commodity. According to this system, a person could claim a piece of land as his own private property whether he intended to use it or not. I could take a few square miles of land, call them "mine," and then go off to the moon. All I had to do to gain a living from "my" land was to charge a rent to the people who wanted to use it. If this piece of land was in an urban area I had no need to develop it at all; I could leave it to the fools who were prepared to develop all the other pieces of land surrounding "my" piece, and in doing so automatically to raise the market value of mine. Then I could come down from the moon and demand that these fools pay me through their noses for the high value of "my" land—a value which they themselves had created for me while I was enjoying myself on the moon! Such a system is not only foreign to us, it is completely wrong. Landlords, in a society which recognizes individual ownership of land, can be, and usually are, in the same class as the loiterers I was talking about: the class of parasites.

We must not allow the growth of parasites here in Tanganyika. The TANU   18
Government must go back to the traditional African custom of land-holding. That is to say a member of society will be entitled to a piece of land *on condition that he uses it.* Unconditional, or "freehold," ownership of land (which leads to speculation and parasitism) must be abolished. We must, as I have said, regain our former attitude of mind—our traditional African socialism— and apply it to the new societies we are building today. TANU has pledged itself to make socialism the basis of its policy in every field. The people of Tanganyika have given us their mandate to carry out that policy, by electing a TANU Government to lead them. So the Government can be relied upon to introduce only legislation which is in harmony with socialist principles.

But, as I said at the beginning, true socialism is an attitude of mind. It is   19
therefore up to the people of Tanganyika—the peasants, the wage-earners, the students, the leaders, all of us—to make sure that this socialist attitude of mind is not lost through the temptations to personal gain (or to the abuse of positions of authority) which may come our way as individuals, or through the

temptation to look on the good of the whole community as of secondary importance to the interests of our own particular group.

20   Just as the Elder, in our former society, was respected for his age and his service to the community, so, in our modern society, this respect for age and service will be preserved. And in the same way as the "rich" Elder's apparent wealth was really only held by him in trust for his people, so, today, the apparent extra wealth which certain positions of leadership may bring to the individuals who fill them, can be theirs only in so far as it is a necessary aid to the carrying out of their duties. It is a "tool" entrusted to them for the benefit of the people they serve. It is not "theirs" personally; and they may not use any part of it as a means of accumulating more for their own benefit, nor as an "insurance" against the day when they no longer hold the same positions. That would be to betray the people who entrusted it to them. If they serve the community while they can, the community must look after them when they are no longer able to do so.

21   In tribal society, the individuals or the families within a tribe were "rich" or "poor" according to whether the whole tribe was rich or poor. If the tribe prospered all the members of the tribe shared in its prosperity. Tanganyika, today, is a poor country. The standard of living of the masses of our people is shamefully low. But if every man and woman in the country takes up the challenge and works to the limit of his or her ability for the good of the whole society, Tanganyika will prosper; and that prosperity will be shared by all her people.

22   But it must be shared. The true socialist may not exploit his fellows. So that if the members of any group within our society are going to argue that, because they happen to be contributing more to the national income than some other groups, they must therefore take for themselves a greater share of the profits of their own industry than they actually need, and if they insist on this in spite of the fact that it would mean reducing their group's contribution to the general income and thus slowing down the rate at which the whole community can benefit, then that group is exploiting (or trying to exploit) its fellow human beings. It is displaying a capitalist attitude of mind.

23   There are bound to be certain groups which, by virtue of the "market value" of their particular industry's products, will contribute more to the nation's income than others. But the others may actually be producing goods or services which are of equal, or greater, intrinsic value although they do not happen to command such a high artificial value. For example, the food produced by the peasant farmer is of greater social value than the diamonds mined at Mwadui. But the mine-workers of Mwadui could claim, quite correctly, that their labour was yielding greater financial profits to the community than that of the farmers. If, however, they went on to demand that they should therefore be given most of that extra profit for themselves, and that no share of it should be spent on helping the farmers, they would be potential capitalists!

24   This is exactly where the attitude of mind comes in. It is one of the purposes of trade unions to ensure for the workers a fair share of the profits of their labour. But a "fair" share must be fair in relation to the whole society. If it is greater than the country can afford without having to penalize some other section of society, then it is not a fair share. Trade union leaders and their

followers, as long as they are true socialists, will not need to be coerced by the Government into keeping their demands within the limits imposed by the needs of society as a whole. Only if there are potential capitalists amongst them will the socialist government have to step in and prevent them from putting their capitalist ideas into practice!

As with groups, so with individuals. There are certain skills, certain qualifications, which, for good reasons, command a higher rate of salary for their possessors than others. But, here again, the true socialist will demand only that return for his skilled work which he knows to be a fair one in proportion to the wealth or poverty of the whole society to which he belongs. He will not, unless he is a would-be capitalist, attempt to blackmail the community by demanding a salary equal to that paid to his counterpart in some far wealthier society. 25

European socialism was born of the Agrarian Revolution and the Industrial Revolution which followed it. The former created the "landed" and the "landless" classes in society; the latter produced the modern capitalist and the industrial proletariat. 26

These two revolutions planted the seeds of conflict within society, and not only was European socialism born of that conflict, but its apostles sanctified the conflict itself into a philosophy. Civil war was no longer looked upon as something evil, or something unfortunate, but as something good and necessary. As prayer is to Christianity or to Islam, so civil war (which they call "class war") is to the European version of socialism—a means inseparable from the end. Each becomes the basis of a whole way of life. The European socialist cannot think of his socialism without its father—capitalism! 27

Brought up in tribal socialism, I must say I find this contradiction quite intolerable. It gives capitalism a philosophical status which capitalism neither claims nor deserves. For it virtually says, "Without capitalism, and the conflict which capitalism creates within society, there can be no socialism"! This glorification of capitalism by the doctrinaire European socialists, I repeat, I find intolerable. 28

African socialism, on the other hand, did not have the "benefit" of the Agrarian Revolution or the Industrial Revolution. It did not start from the existence of conflicting "classes" in society. Indeed I doubt if the equivalent for the word "class" exists in any indigenous African language; for language describes the ideas of those who speak it, and the idea of "class" or "caste" was nonexistent in African society. 29

The foundation, and the objective, of African socialism is the extended family. The true African socialist does not look on one class of men as his brethren and another as his natural enemies. He does not form an alliance with the "brethren" for the extermination of the "non-brethren." He rather regards *all* men as his brethren—as members of his ever extending family. That is why the first article of TANU's Creed is: *"Binadamu wote ni ndugu zangu, na Afrika ni moja."* If this had been originally put in English, it could have been: "I believe in Human Brotherhood and the Unity of Africa." 30

"Ujamaa," then, or "Familyhood," describes our socialism. It is opposed to capitalism, which seeks to build a happy society on the basis of the exploitation 31 of man by man; and it is equally opposed to doctrinaire socialism which seeks to build its happy society on a philosophy of inevitable conflict between man and man.

32 We, in Africa, have no more need of being "converted" to socialism than we have of being "taught" democracy. Both are rooted in our own past—in the traditional society which produced us. Modern African socialism can draw from its traditional heritage the recognition of "society" as an extension of the basic family unit. But it can no longer confine the idea of the social family within the limits of the tribe, nor, indeed, of the nation. For no true African socialist can look at a line drawn on a map and say, "The people on this side of that line are my brothers, but those who happen to live on the other side of it can have no claim on me"; every individual on this continent is his brother.

33 It was in the struggle to break the grip of colonialism that we learnt the need for unity. We came to recognize that the same socialist attitude of mind which, in the tribal days, gave to every individual the security that comes of belonging to a widely extended family, must be preserved within the still wider society of the nation. But we should not stop there. Our recognition of the family to which we all belong must be extended yet further—beyond the tribe, the community, the nation, or even the continent—to embrace the whole society of mankind. This is the only logical conclusion for true socialism.

Questions for Discussion and Your Reading Journal

1. How does Nyerere define "ujamaa"?
2. Who does Nyerere's audience seem to be? What might be Nyerere's purposes in describing and arguing for ujamaa?
3. List the characteristics of ujamaa. How does Nyerere's socialism compare to Marx's communism? What African traditions does Nyerere appeal to?
4. How effective are Nyerere's arguments about the millionaire and the African worker? What analogies does he use? Are they clear? Are they convincing?

JULIUS K. NYERERE

Julius Nyerere wrote The Arusha Declaration and made it public in the town of Arusha, Tanzania. This declaration embodies Nyerere's ideals of ujamaa as expressed in "Ujamaa—The Basis of African Socialism." It was adopted by the Tanzanian African National Union (TANU), the official party in Tanzania's single-party democracy. A primary goal of The Arusha Declaration was to set forth the principles that would establish a democratic socialist government in Tanzania. This declaration calls for self-reliance (as opposed to dependence on foreign aid), collective farms, and literacy programs. Following TANU's adoption of the declaration, the Tanzanian government nationalized banks, insurance companies, grain mills, and the assets of multinational corporations.

The Arusha Declaration[1] and TANU's Policy on Socialism and Self-Reliance 5 February 1967

PART ONE

The Tanu Creed

The policy of TANU is to build a socialist state. The principles of socialism are laid down in the TANU Constitution and they are as follows: WHEREAS TANU believes:

a. That all human beings are equal;

b. That every individual has a right to dignity and respect;

c. That every citizen is an integral part of the nation and has the right to take an equal part in Government at local, regional and national levels;

d. That every citizen has the right to freedom of expression, of movement, of religious belief and of association within the context of the law;

e. That every individual has the right to receive from society protection of his life and of property held according to law;

f. That every individual has the right to receive a just return for his labour;

g. That all citizens together possess all the natural resources of the country in trust for their descendants;

h. That in order to ensure economic justice the state must have effective control over the principal means of production; and

i. That it is the responsibility of the state to intervene actively in the economic life of the nation so as to ensure the well-being of all citizens, and so as to prevent the exploitation of one person by another or one group by another, and so as to prevent the accumulation of wealth to an extent which is inconsistent with the existence of a classless society.

NOW, THEREFORE, the principal aims and objects of TANU shall be as follows:

a. To consolidate and maintain the independence of this country and the freedom of its people;

b. To safeguard the inherent dignity of the individual in accordance with the Universal Declaration of Human Rights;

c. To ensure that this country shall be governed by a democratic socialist government of the people;

d. To co-operate with all political parties in Africa engaged in the liberation of all Africa;

e. To see that the Government mobilizes all the resources of this country towards the elimination of poverty, ignorance and disease;

---

[1]The Declaration was discussed and then published in Swahili. This revised English translation clarifies ambiguities which existed in the translation originally issued.

f. To see that the Government actively assists in the formation and maintenance of co-operative organizations;

g. To see that wherever possible the Government itself directly participates in
the economic development of this country;

h. To see that the Government gives equal opportunity to all men and women
irrespective of race, religion or status;

i. To see that the Government eradicates all types of exploitation, intimida-
tion, discrimination, bribery and corruption;

j. To see that the Government exercises effective control over the principal
means of production and pursues policies which facilitate the way to collective ownership of the resources of this country;

k. To see that the Government co-operates with other states in Africa in bringing about African unity;

l. To see that Government works tirelessly towards world peace and security
through the United Nations Organization.

PART TWO

The Policy of Socialism

3   **A**bsence of Exploitation   A truly socialist state is one in which all people
are workers and in which neither capitalism nor feudalism exists. It does
not have two classes of people, a lower class composed of people who work
for their living, and an upper class of people who live on the work of others.
In a really socialist country no person exploits another; everyone who is physically able to work does so; every worker obtains a just return for the labour
he performs; and the incomes derived from different types of work are not
grossly divergent.

4   In a socialist country, the only people who live on the work of others, and
who have the right to be dependent upon their fellows, are small children,
people who are too old to support themselves, the crippled, and those whom
the state at any one time cannot provide with an opportunity to work for
their living.

5   Tanzania is a nation of peasants and workers, but it is not yet a socialist
society. It still contains elements of feudalism and capitalism—with their temptations. These feudalistic and capitalistic features of our society could spread
and entrench themselves.

6   **The Major Means of Production and Exchange Are Under the Control of
the Peasants and Workers**   To build and maintain socialism it is essential that
all the major means of production and exchange in the nation are controlled
and owned by the peasants through the machinery of their Government and
their co-operatives. Further, it is essential that the ruling Party should be a
Party of peasants and workers.

7   The major means of production and exchange are such things as: land;
forests; minerals; water; oil and electricity; news media; communications;
banks, insurance, import and export trade, wholesale trade; iron and steel,

machine-tool, arms, motor-car, cement, fertilizer, and textile industries; and any big factory on which a large section of the people depend for their living, or which provides essential components of other industries; large plantations, and especially those which provide raw materials essential to important industries.

Some of the instruments of production and exchange which have been 8 listed here are already owned or controlled by the people's Government of Tanzania.

The Existence of Democracy A state is not socialist simply because its 9 means of production and exchange are controlled or owned by the government, either wholly or in large part. For a country to be socialist, it is essential that its government is chosen and led by the peasants and workers themselves. If the minority governments of Rhodesia or South Africa controlled or owned the entire economies of these respective countries, the result would be a strengthening of oppression, not the building of socialism. True socialism cannot exist without democracy also existing in the society.

Socialism Is a Belief Socialism is a way of life, and a socialist society can- 10 not simply come into existence. A socialist society can only be built by those who believe in, and who themselves practise, the principles of socialism. A committed member of TANU will be a socialist, and his fellow socialists—that is, his fellow believers in this political and economic system—are all those in Africa or elsewhere in the world who fight for the rights of peasants and workers. The first duty of a TANU member, and especially of a TANU leader, is to accept these socialist principles, and to live his own life in accordance with them. In particular, a genuine TANU leader will not live off the sweat of another man, nor commit any feudalistic or capitalistic actions.

The successful implementation of socialist objectives depends very much 11 upon the leaders, because socialism is a belief in a particular system of living, and it is difficult for leaders to promote its growth if they do not themselves accept it.

Questions for Discussion and Your Reading Journal

1. What is the purpose of this declaration and who might be the audience(s) for it?
2. Summarize the key ideas of this declaration. Discuss the relationship between the state and the people according to Nyerere.
3. Compare the idea of the peasants and workers owning the means of production to the idea of a manager or entrepreneur as the owner. In what ways would society be affected if the peasants and workers owned the means of production?
4. Discuss some key similarities and differences between The Arusha Declaration and one of the following: The United Nations' Universal Declaration of Human Rights (p. 96) or the United States' Declaration of Independence (p. 53). What are some of the factors that might account for the differences? (Consider the context of each piece.)

UNITED NATIONS

U.S. President Franklin D. Roosevelt first coined the term United Nations *in 1942 to describe the joint efforts of a group of 26 nations who were united in their effort to fight against the axis powers in World War II. With the end of the war in 1945, this group grew to 50 nations, which came together with the broader purposes of ending the horrors of war, championing human rights, establishing justice and respect for international law, and working for social progress around the world. Currently, some 190 nations belong to the United Nations.*

Reading Rhetorically

Writing a document to simultaneously represent the views of 50 nations (and 191 nations today) was no easy task. The success of the U.N. Preamble comes from the clarity and simplicity of its language. It is an unambiguous and direct piece of writing that sums up the values and purposes for which the organization has stood for over six decades since its inception. Rhetorically, it is also a surprisingly positive expression of human character, given that it was penned before the guns had yet cooled in the aftermath of World War II, a conflict in which an estimated 30 million people were killed around the world. Note the constant appeal to the best qualities in human nature. The framers of the U.N. Charter knew that millions, even billions, of people from all nations around the world would one day read what they wrote. Therefore they wrote with words and language that would be the most inclusive as possible of all peoples, without sacrificing the aims and vision that they shared. And yet their vision of global society was controversial at the time and remains controversial today. Many people around the world still struggle with the notion that men and women should have equal rights. Equally difficult to accept by the most powerful nations today is that nations themselves, "large and small," should likewise have equal rights and equal votes in world affairs. Because of this, it is perhaps best to think of the U.N. Charter as a visionary document that looks ahead of people's attitudes and behaviors to a time when they will be more ready to live in peace, much as did the Declaration of Independence in 1776, when "all men" in the United States were far from equal.

Preamble to the Charter of the United Nations

WE THE PEOPLES OF THE UNITED NATIONS DETERMINED

- to save succeeding generations from the scourge of war, which twice in our lifetime has brought untold sorrow to mankind, and
- to reaffirm faith in fundamental human rights, in the dignity and worth of the human person, in the equal rights of men and women and of nations large and small, and

- to establish conditions under which justice and respect for the obligations arising from treaties and other sources of international law can be maintained, and
- to promote social progress and better standards of life in larger freedom,

AND FOR THESE ENDS

- to practice tolerance and live together in peace with one another as good neighbours, and
- to unite our strength to maintain international peace and security, and
- to ensure, by the acceptance of principles and the institution of methods, that armed force shall not be used, save in the common interest, and
- to employ international machinery for the promotion of the economic and social advancement of all peoples,

HAVE RESOLVED TO COMBINE OUR EFFORTS TO ACCOMPLISH THESE AIMS

Accordingly, our respective Governments, through representatives assembled in the city of San Francisco, who have exhibited their full powers found to be in good and due form, have agreed to the present Charter of the United Nations and do hereby establish an international organization to be known as the United Nations.

Questions for Discussion and Your Reading Journal

1. Based upon your current knowledge of world affairs and happenings, in which of the first four objectives does the United Nations seem to have made the most progress? The least progress? Explain your positions.
2. What kinds of behaviors does the United Nations suggest are the qualities of "good neighbors" in the second four goals of the organization?

UNITED NATIONS

Eleanor Roosevelt served as the first chairperson of the United Nations Human Rights Commission (1946–1951) and played a major role in drafting the Universal Declaration of Human Rights, which was adopted by the U.N. General Assembly in 1948. The Declaration serves as an international standard to judge the actions of governments. It offers moral and political authority for ending such human rights abuses as torture and detaining people without charge, and is often cited by human rights organizations such as Amnesty International when reporting on human rights violations.

Reading Rhetorically

As you read the long list of human rights outlined in the Declaration, you may begin to realize that in many places and in many cultures, including in the

United States, these human rights are not all fully realized or have been put aside for what leaders consider their national interests. As with other "charter" documents, such as the Constitution of the United States, the Universal Declaration of Human Rights rhetorically points to a world of the future as much as to current reality. Imbedded in it, then, is an argument about the way the world *should* be rather than a statement about the way the world actually is. Note the placement of logical support for this extended argument. It comes in the Preamble, giving readers justification from the outset for what follows. This is a deductive approach to the logic of the argument. If readers accept the conceptual evidence presented up front, it is likely that they will accept the long list of claims that follow. Hence the Preamble is the most essential element of the persuasive power of the rest of the document.

Universal Declaration of Human Rights

PREAMBLE

1 *Whereas* recognition of the inherent dignity and of the equal and inalienable rights of all members of the human family is the foundation of freedom, justice and peace in the world,

2 *Whereas* disregard and contempt for human rights have resulted in barbarous acts which have outraged the conscience of mankind, and the advent of a world in which human beings shall enjoy freedom of speech and belief and freedom from fear and want has been proclaimed as the highest aspiration of the common people,

3 *Whereas* it is essential, if man is not to be compelled to have recourse, as a last resort, to rebellion against tyranny and oppression, that human rights should be protected by the rule of law,

4 *Whereas* it is essential to promote the development of friendly relations between nations,

5 *Whereas* the peoples of the United Nations have in the Charter reaffirmed their faith in fundamental human rights, in the dignity and worth of the human person and in the equal rights of men and women and have determined to promote social progress and better standards of life in larger freedom,

6 *Whereas* Member States have pledged themselves to achieve, in cooperation with the United Nations, the promotion of universal respect for and observance of human rights and fundamental freedoms,

7 *Whereas* a common understanding of these rights and freedoms is of the greatest importance for the full realization of this pledge,

8 *Now, Therefore,*

9 *The General Assembly*

10 *Proclaims* this Universal Declaration of Human Rights as a common standard of achievement for all peoples and all nations, to the end that every individual and every organ of society, keeping this Declaration constantly in mind, shall strive by

teaching and education to promote respect for these rights and freedoms and by progressive measures, national and international to secure their universal and effective recognition and observance, both among the peoples of Member States themselves and among the peoples of territories under their jurisdiction.

ARTICLE 1

All human beings are born free and equal in dignity and rights. They are 11 endowed with reason and conscience and should act towards one another in a spirit of brotherhood.

ARTICLE 2

Everyone is entitled to all the rights and freedoms set forth in this Declaration, 12 without distinction of any kind, such as race, colour, sex, language, religion, political or other opinion, national or social origin, property, birth or other status.

Furthermore, no distinction shall be made on the basis of the political, 13 jurisdictional or international status of the country or territory to which a person belongs, whether it be independent, trust, non-self-governing or under any other limitation of sovereignty.

ARTICLE 3

Everyone has the right to life, liberty and the security of person. 14

ARTICLE 4

No one shall be held in slavery or servitude; slavery and the slave trade shall 15 be prohibited in all their forms.

ARTICLE 5

No one shall be subjected to torture or to cruel, inhuman or degrading treatment or punishment. 16

ARTICLE 6

Everyone has the right to recognition everywhere as a person before the law. 17

ARTICLE 7

All are equal before the law and are entitled without any discrimination to 18 equal protection of the law. All are entitled to equal protection against any discrimination in violation of this Declaration and against any incitement to such discrimination.

ARTICLE 8

19 Everyone has the right to an effective remedy by the competent national tribunals for acts violating the fundamental rights granted him by the constitution or by law.

ARTICLE 9

20 No one shall be subjected to arbitrary arrest, detention or exile.

ARTICLE 10

21 Everyone is entitled in full equality to a fair and public hearing by an independent and impartial tribunal, in the determination of his rights and obligations and of any criminal charge against him.

ARTICLE 11

22 1. Everyone charged with a penal offence has the right to be presumed innocent until proved guilty according to law in a public trial at which he has had all the guarantees necessary for his defence.
23 2. No one shall be held guilty of any penal offence on account of any act or omission which did not constitute a penal offence, under national or international law, at the time when it was committed. Nor shall a heavier penalty be imposed than the one that was applicable at the time the penal offence was committed.

ARTICLE 12

24 No one shall be subjected to arbitrary interference with his privacy, family, home or correspondence, nor to attacks upon his honour and reputation. Everyone has the right to the protection of the law against such interference or attacks.

ARTICLE 13

25 1. Everyone has the right to freedom of movement and residence within the borders of each State.
26 2. Everyone has the right to leave any country, including his own, and to return to his country.

ARTICLE 14

27 1. Everyone has the right to seek and to enjoy in other countries asylum from persecution.

2. This right may not be invoked in the case of prosecutions genuinely arising   28
from non-political crimes or from acts contrary to the purposes and principles of the United Nations.

ARTICLE 15

1. Everyone has the right to a nationality.   29
2. No one shall be arbitrarily deprived of his nationality nor denied the right   30
to change his nationality.

ARTICLE 16

1. Men and women of full age, without any limitation due to race, nationality   31
or religion, have the right to marry and to found a family. They are entitled
to equal rights as to marriage, during marriage and at its dissolution.
2. Marriage shall be entered into only with the free and full consent of the in-   32
tending spouses.
3. The family is the natural and fundamental group unit of society and is enti-   33
tled to protection by society and the State.

ARTICLE 17

1. Everyone has the right to own property alone as well as in association with   34
others.
2. No one shall be arbitrarily deprived of his property.   35

ARTICLE 18

Everyone has the right to freedom of thought, conscience and religion; this   36
right includes freedom to change his religion or belief, and freedom, either
alone or in community with others and in public or private, to manifest his
religion or belief in teaching, practice, worship and observance.

ARTICLE 19

Everyone has the right to freedom of opinion and expression; this right includes   37
freedom to hold opinions without interference and to seek, receive and impart
information and ideas through any media and regardless of frontiers.

ARTICLE 20

1. Everyone has the right to freedom of peaceful assembly and association.   38
2. No one may be compelled to belong to an association.   39

ARTICLE 21

40 1. Everyone has the right to take part in the government of his country, directly or through freely chosen representatives.

41 2. Everyone has the right of equal access to public service in his country.

42 3. The will of the people shall be the basis of the authority of government; this will shall be expressed in periodic and genuine elections which shall be by universal and equal suffrage and shall be held by secret vote or by equivalent free voting procedures.

ARTICLE 22

43 Everyone, as a member of society, has the right to social security and is entitled to realization, through national effort and international co-operation and in accordance with the organization and resources of each State, of the economic, social and cultural rights indispensable for his dignity and the free development of his personality.

ARTICLE 23

44 1. Everyone has the right to work, to free choice of employment, to just and favourable conditions of work and to protection against unemployment.

45 2. Everyone, without any discrimination, has the right to equal pay for equal work.

46 3. Everyone who works has the right to just and favourable remuneration ensuring for himself and his family an existence worthy of human dignity, and supplemented, if necessary, by other means of social protection.

47 4. Everyone has the right to form and to join trade unions for the protection of his interests.

ARTICLE 24

48 Everyone has the right to rest and leisure, including reasonable limitation of working hours and periodic holidays with pay.

ARTICLE 25

49 1. Everyone has the right to a standard of living adequate for the health and well-being of himself and of his family, including food, clothing, housing and medical care and necessary social services, and the right to security in the event of unemployment, sickness, disability, widowhood, old age or other lack of livelihood in circumstances beyond his control.

50 2. Motherhood and childhood are entitled to special care and assistance. All children, whether born in or out of wedlock, shall enjoy the same social protection.

ARTICLE 26

1. Everyone has the right to education. Education shall be free, at least in the   51
   elementary and fundamental stages. Elementary education shall be compulsory. Technical and professional education shall be made generally available and higher education shall be equally accessible to all on the basis of merit.
2. Education shall be directed to the full development of the human personal-   52
   ity and to the strengthening of respect for human rights and fundamental freedoms. It shall promote understanding, tolerance and friendship among all nations, racial or religious groups, and shall further the activities of the United Nations for the maintenance of peace.
3. Parents have a prior right to choose the kind of education that shall be   53
   given to their children.

ARTICLE 27

1. Everyone has the right freely to participate in the cultural life of the com-   54
   munity, to enjoy the arts and to share in scientific advancement and its benefits,
2. Everyone has the right to the protection of the moral and material interests   55
   resulting from any scientific, literary or artistic production of which he is the author.

ARTICLE 28

Everyone is entitled to a social and international order in which the rights and   56
freedoms set forth in this Declaration can be fully realized.

ARTICLE 29

1. Everyone has duties to the community in which alone the free and full de-   57
   velopment of his personality is possible.
2. In the exercise of his rights and freedoms, everyone shall be subject only to   58
   such limitations as are determined by law solely for the purpose of securing due recognition and respect for the rights and freedoms of others and of meeting the just requirements of morality, public order and the general welfare in a democratic society.
3. These rights and freedoms may in no case be exercised contrary to the pur-   59
   poses and principles of the United Nations.

ARTICLE 30

Nothing in this Declaration may be interpreted as implying for any State,   60
group or person any right to engage in any activity or to perform any act aimed at the destruction of any of the rights and freedoms set forth herein.

Questions for Discussion and Your Reading Journal

1. What purpose do the seven "whereas" clauses seem to serve in the rhetorical flow of ideas in this document?
2. What does the Declaration indicate will be the means of promoting respect and observance of the human rights guidelines presented here?
3. In what ways is the wording of Article 3 different from a similar and well-known statement in the second paragraph of the U.S. Declaration of Independence? What underlying American and global values seem to differ in these two statements of human rights?
4. Can you think of historical incidents in the past or present where the United States has been in violation of Article 7 to Article 11? Explain.
5. Why might Article 25 be titled "Family Human Rights"?
6. Which one of the 30 articles of the Declaration seems most important to you? Why?

JOHN RAWLS

John Rawls (1921–2002) has been hailed by many in the Western world as the most important political philosopher of the 20th century. A professor at Harvard University, he was one of the first to argue that democratic and culturally pluralistic governments can and should provide their peoples both with basic rights and with relatively equal opportunities. His focus from the beginning was upon "social justice." His goal in earlier writings was to show convincingly that it is possible to set up a social order that every citizen can find legitimate and just, despite large differences between cultural groups and social values. In The Law of Peoples *(1999), he turned his attention to showing how very different nations (which he prefers to call "peoples") could likewise guarantee social justice and stability on a global level. His core argument is that good relations between various peoples of the world must be based upon principles of freedom, respect for human rights, and nonintervention (particularly in military fashion) in each other's affairs.*

Reading Rhetorically

As you read Rawls's work, you will note that he has much of the same political and social optimism as is evident in the U.N. readings that precede this selection. His arguments for social justice and fairness are based upon assumptions that many people value and long for such things. The major challenge to his ideas comes from followers of the *realpolitik* philosophy, who argue that his ideas are not realistic and that nations with power can and should use that power to get what they want in the world. Note the pains Rawls went through to build a convincing counterargument to this "might makes right" argument based upon appeals to the best in human nature. Key in the process is his use of the word *reasonable*. As he distinguished between the "character of a people" and the "character of a state," we see the skill with which he translated the need for just government into "reasonable" human terms. He argued that states rarely limit their behaviors through a reasonable sense of treating others as they wish to be treated (the "reciprocity" principle: "Do unto others as you would have them do unto you"). However, he continued, peoples often do limit their interests and behaviors based upon how they would want others to treat them. This elevation of the goodness of people above the goodness of the state is a rhetorical move that his readers are apt to find compelling. With this kind of language and line of thinking. Rawls himself constantly modeled the best and most reasonable side of human character, displaying what Aristotle referred to as good *ethos*. The more that readers come to trust and to admire the values that they see in Rawls's character, the more likely they are to accept his arguments more generally.

The Law of Peoples

. . . *2.3. Basic Features of States.* The following remarks show that the character of a people in the Law of Peoples is different from the character of what I refer to as states. States are the actors in many theories of international politics about the causes of war and the preservation of peace.[1] They are often seen as rational, anxiously concerned with their power—their capacity (military, economic, diplomatic) to influence other states—and always guided by their basic interests.[2] The typical view of international relations is fundamentally the same as it was in Thucydides' day and has not been transcended in modern times, when world politics is still marked by the struggles of states for power, prestige, and wealth in a condition of global anarchy.[3] How far states differ from peoples rests on how rationality, the concern with power, and a state's basic interests are filled in. If *rationality* excludes the *reasonable* (that is, if a state is moved by the aims it has and ignores the criterion of reciprocity in dealing with other societies); if a state's concern with power is predominant; and if its interests include such things as converting other societies to the state's religion, enlarging its empire and winning territory, gaining dynastic or

---

[1]See Robert Gilpin's *War and Change in World Politics* (Cambridge: Cambridge University Press, 1981), chap. 1, pp. 9–25. See also Robert Axelrod's *The Complexity of Cooperation* (Princeton: Princeton University Press, 1997), chap. 4, "Choosing Sides," with its account of the alignments of countries in World War II.

[2]Lord Palmerston said: "England has no eternal friends, and no eternal enemies; only eternal interests." See Donald Kagan, *Origins of War and the Preservation of Peace* (New York: Doubleday, 1995), p. 144.

[3]Gilpin's main thesis is that "the fundamental nature of international relations has not changed over the millennia. International relations continue to be a recurring struggle for wealth and power among independent actors in a state of anarchy. The history of Thucydides is as meaningful a guide to the behavior of states today as when it was written in the fifth century B.C." See Gilpin, *War and Change in World Politics*, p. 7. He presents his reasons for this thesis in chapter 6.

imperial or national prestige and glory, and increasing its relative economic strength—then the difference between states and peoples is enormous.[4] Such interests as these tend to put a state at odds with other states and peoples, and to threaten their safety and security, whether they are expansionist or nor. The background conditions also threaten hegemonic war.[5]

2   A difference between liberal peoples and states is that just liberal peoples limit their basic interests as required by the reasonable. In contrast, the content of the interests of states does not allow them to be stable for the right reasons: that is, from firmly accepting and acting upon a just Law of Peoples. Liberal peoples do, however, have their fundamental interests as permitted by their conceptions of right and justice. They seek to protect their territory, to ensure the security and safety of their citizens, and to preserve their free political institutions and the liberties and free culture of their civil society. Beyond these interests, a liberal people tries to assure reasonable justice for all its citizens and for all peoples; a liberal people can live with other peoples of like character in upholding justice and preserving peace. Any hope we have of reaching a realistic utopia rests on there being reasonable liberal constitutional (and decent) regimes sufficiently established and effective to yield a viable Society of Peoples.

---

[4]In his great *History of the Peloponnesian War.* trans. Rex Warner (London: Penguin Books, 1954), Thucydides tells the story of the fated self-destruction of the Greek city-states in the long war between Athens and Sparta. The history ends in midstream, as if it is broken off. Did Thucydides stop, or was he unable to finish? It is as if he said: "and so on . . ." The tale of folly has gone on long enough. What moves the city-states is what makes the increasing self-destruction inevitable. Listen to the Athenians' first speech to the Spartans: "We have done nothing extraordinary, contrary to human nature in accepting empire when it was offered to us, then refusing to give it up. Very powerful motives prevent us from doing so—security, honor and self-interest. And we were not the first to act this way, far from it. It was always the rule that the weaker should be subject to the stronger, and, besides, we consider that we are worthy of our power. Up to the present moment you too used to think that we were; but now, after calculating your interests, you are beginning to talk in terms of right and wrong. Considerations of this kind have never turned people aside from opportunities of aggrandizement offered by superior strength. Those who really deserve praise are those who, while human enough to enjoy power, nevertheless pay more attention to justice than compelled to by their situation. Certainly we think that if anyone were in our position, it would be evident whether we act in moderation or not" (Book I: 76).

It is clear enough how the cycle of self-destruction goes. Thucydides thinks that, if the Athenians had followed Pericles' advice not to expand their empire as long as the war with Sparta and its allies lasted, they might well have won. But with the invasion of Melos and the folly of the Sicilian adventure urged on by Alcibiades' advice and persuasion, they were doomed to self-destruction. Napoleon is reputed to have said, commenting on his invasion of Russia: "Empires die of indigestion." But he wasn't candid with himself. Empires die of gluttony, of the ever-expanding craving for power. What makes peace among liberal democratic peoples possible is the internal nature of peoples as constitutional democracies and the resulting change of the motives of citizens. For the purposes of our story of the possibility of realistic utopia it is important to recognize that Athens was not a liberal democracy, though it may have thought of itself as such. It was an autocracy of the 35,000 male members of the assembly over the total population of about 300,000.

[5]Gilpin, *War and Change in World Politics*, esp. chap. 5, discusses the features of hegemonic war.

. . . *3.3. Fundamental Interests of Peoples.* In thinking of themselves as 3
free and equal, how do peoples (in contrast to states) see themselves and their
fundamental interests? These interests of liberal peoples are specified, I said
(§2.3), by their reasonable conception of political justice. Thus, they strive to
protect their political independence and their free culture with its civil liberties, to guarantee their security, territory, and the well-being of their citizens.
Yet a further interest is also significant: applied to peoples, it falls under what
Rousseau calls *amour-propre.*[6] This interest is a people's proper self-respect of
themselves as a people, resting on their common awareness of their trials during their history and of their culture with its accomplishments. Altogether distinct from their self-concern for their security and the safety of their territory,
this interest shows itself in a people's insisting on receiving from other peoples
a proper respect and recognition of their equality. What distinguishes peoples
from states—and this is crucial—is that just peoples are fully prepared to grant
the very same proper respect and recognition to other peoples as equals. Their
equality doesn't mean, however, that inequalities of certain kinds are not
agreed to in various cooperative institutions among peoples, such as the
United Nations, ideally conceived. This recognition of inequalities, rather, parallels citizens' accepting functional social and economic inequalities in their
liberal society.

It is, therefore, part of a people's being reasonable and rational that they 4
are ready to offer to other peoples fair terms of political and social cooperation. These fair terms are those that a people sincerely believes other equal
peoples might accept also; and should they do so, a people will honor the
terms it has proposed even in those cases where that people might profit by
violating them. Thus, the criterion of reciprocity applies to the Law of Peoples
in the same way it does to the principles of justice for a constitutional regime.
This reasonable sense of due respect, willingly accorded to other reasonable
peoples, is an essential element of the idea of peoples who are satisfied with
the status quo for the right reasons. It is compatible with ongoing cooperation
among them over time and the mutual acceptance and adherence to the Law
of Peoples. Part of the answer to political realism is that this reasonable sense
of proper respect is not unrealistic, but is itself the outcome of democratic
domestic institutions. I will come back to this argument later.

§4. THE PRINCIPLES OF THE LAW OF PEOPLES

4.1. Statement of the Principles. Initially, we may assume that the outcome of 5
working out the law of Peoples only for liberal democratic societies will be the

---

[6]My account here follows N. J. H. Dent in his *Rousseau* (Oxford: Basil Blackwell, 1988) and
Frederick Neuhouser's essay "Freedom and the General Will," *Philosophical Review,* July 1993.
Donald Kagan in his *Origins of War and the Preservation of Peace* notes two meanings of honor.
As I describe them in the text (above and in the next section), one is compatible with satisfied peo-
ples and their stable peace, whereas the other is not, setting the stage for conflict. I believe Kagan
underestimates the great difference between the two meanings of honor.

adoption of certain familiar principles of equality among peoples. These principles will also, I assume, make room for various forms of cooperative associations and federations among peoples, but will not affirm a world-state. Here I follow Kant's lead in *Perpetual Peace* (1795) in thinking that a world government—by which I mean a unified political regime with the legal powers normally exercised by central governments—would either be a global despotism or else would rule over a fragile empire torn by frequent civil strife as various regions and peoples tried to gain their political freedom and autonomy.[7] As I discuss below, it may turn out that there will be many different kinds of organizations subject to the judgment of the Law of Peoples and charged with regulating cooperation among them and meeting certain recognized duties. Some of these organizations (such as the United Nations ideally conceived) may have the authority to express for the society of well-ordered peoples their condemnation of unjust domestic institutions in other countries and clear cases of the violation of human rights. In grave cases they may try to correct them by economic sanctions, or even by military intervention. The scope of these powers covers all peoples and reaches their domestic affairs.

6　　These large conclusions call for some discussion. Proceeding in a way analogous to the procedure in *A Theory of Justice*,[8] let's look first at familiar and traditional principles of justice among free and democratic peoples.[9]

7　1. Peoples are free and independent, and their freedom and independence are to be respected by other peoples.

8　2. Peoples are to observe treaties and undertakings.

9　3. Peoples are equal and are parties to the agreements that bind them.

---

[7]Kant says in Ak:VIII:367: "The idea of international law presupposes the separate existence of independent neighboring states. Although this condition is itself a state of war (unless federative union prevents the outbreak of hostilities), this is rationally preferable to the amalgamation of states under one superior power, as this would end in one universal monarchy, and laws always lose in vigor what government gains in extent; hence a condition of soulless despotism falls into anarchy after stifling seeds of good." Kant's attitude to universal monarchy was shared by other writers of the eighteenth century. See, for example, Hume's "Of the Balance of Power" (1752), in *Political Essays*, ed. K. Haakonssen (Cambridge: Cambridge University Press, 1994). F. H. Hinsley, *Power and the Pursuit of Peace* (Cambridge: Cambridge University Press, 1966), also mentions Montesquieu, Voltaire, and Gibbon, pp. 162ff., and he has an instructive discussion of Kant's ideas in chapter 4. See also Patrick Riley, *Kant's Political Philosophy* (Totowa, N. J.: Rowman and Littlefield, 1983), chaps. 5 and 6.

[8]See *A Theory of Justice*, where chapter 2 discusses the principles of justice and chapter 3 gives the reasoning from the original position concerning the selection of principles. All references to *A Theory of Justice* are to the original edition (Harvard University Press, 1971).

[9]See J. L. Brierly, *The Law of Nations: An Introduction to the Law of Peace*, 6th ed. (Oxford: Clarendon Press, 1963), and Terry Nardin, *Law, Morality, and the Relations of States* (Princeton: Princeton University Press, 1983). Both Brierly and Nardin give similar lists as principles of international law.

4. Peoples are to observe a duty of non-intervention.   10

5. Peoples have the right of self-defense but no right to instigate war for rea-   11
sons other than self-defense.

6. Peoples are to honor human rights.   12

7. Peoples are to observe certain specified restrictions in the conduct of war.   13

8. Peoples have a duty to assist other peoples living under unfavorable condi-   14
tions that prevent their having a just or decent political and social regime.

. . . I contend that the eight principles of the Law of Peoples (see §4.1)   15
are superior to any others. Much as in examining the distributive principles in
justice as fairness, we begin with the baseline of equality—in the case of justice as fairness the equality of social and economic primary goods, in this case
the equality of and the equal rights of all peoples. In the first case we asked
whether any departure from the baseline of equality would be agreed to provided that it is to the benefit of all citizens of society and, in particular, the least
advantaged. (I only hint here at the reasoning.) With the Law of Peoples, however, persons are not under one but many governments, and the representatives
of peoples will want to preserve the equality and independence of their own
society. In the working of organizations and loose[10] confederations of peoples
inequalities are designed to serve the many ends that peoples share. In this case
the larger and smaller peoples will be ready to make larger and smaller contributions and to accept proportionately larger and smaller returns.

Questions for Discussion and Your Reading Journal

1. Sum up what Rawls tells us are the differences between the "character of
peoples" and the "character of states." Which of these "characters" does
Rawls argue gives us the best hope of achieving a "realistic utopia" in the
world?

2. What key point does Rawls make through reference to Jean-Jacques
Rousseau's concept of *amour-propre*?

3. What reasons does Rawls offer for his position against forming a "world
government"?

4. Based upon Rawls's eight principles of *The Law of Peoples,* would he be in
favor or against nations adopting a pre-emptive approach to making war
upon other nations? Explain.

5. Rawls contends that his eight principles of *The Law of Peoples* "are superior to any others." This is a bold statement. Sum up what you see as the
strengths and the weaknesses of his proposed principles.

---

[10]I use this adjective to emphasize that confederations are much less tight than federations and
do not involve the powers of federal governments.

THE GLOBALIZATION OF WEALTH AND POVERTY

OXFAM

Oxfam is an independent charity organization based in Britain with offices and programs that reach around the world. The organization describes itself on its Web site as "a development, relief, and campaigning organisation dedicated to finding lasting solutions to poverty and suffering around the world. We believe that every human being is entitled to a life of dignity and opportunity; and we work with poor communities, local partners, volunteers, and supporters to help this become a reality" (http://www.oxfam.org.uk/about_us/index.htm). The Oxfam report included here is addressed to leaders of the British government responsible for overseeing the nation's policies and objectives guiding a wide variety of globalization programs and projects. The Oxfam writers look at this issue from the perspective of how the lives of the world's poor people are being affected by the policies of the wealthier nations. Their findings challenge the current direction of globalization as "morally indefensible, economically inefficient, and socially unsustainable."

Reading Rhetorically

The writers of this Oxfam report face a difficult rhetorical challenge. They must try to convince leaders of one of the world's wealthiest nations of two things: (1) that globalization policies are going in exactly the opposite direction than they should be; and (2) that the people in wealthy nations who are benefiting a great deal from the current flow of goods and resources should reverse these policies. The Oxfam writers follow the classical Greek formula for developing a persuasive argument (*logos*) very closely in this paper. They begin by attempting to get everyone on the same page. This they do by reviewing prior commitments the British government has made to ending poverty around the world. They remind their readers of Britain's history of "championing the interests of the world's poorest countries and poorest peoples." Then they bridge to the issue of "winners and losers" in the globalization movement, emphasizing how this division affects some groups negatively right at home in England. Only after preparing their readers carefully with an extended introduction do the writers finally drop the hammer blow of their thesis, a thesis that is not likely to be immediately popular with their government audience. The remainder of the report is then devoted to the developing and supporting the main points they have made in the introduction. As you read the report, note such rhetorical moves as how and what kinds of evidence is brought in, how counterarguments are introduced and dealt with, and how solutions to the issue are brought into view. (Note that we have retained British spelling in this selection.)

Globalisation

SECTION 1: AN OVERVIEW OF GLOBALISATION

Introduction

Oxfam welcomes the Government's decision to prepare a White Paper on 1
the theme of globalisation. In 1997, the White Paper on International Development helped to define a new course for national policy. It made poverty reduction and achievement of the key 2015 development targets the centrepiece of development co-operation. It also recognised that, in an increasingly complex and integrated international economy, international trade, capital flows and global governance are far more important than aid in defining prospects for poverty reduction. The new White Paper provides an opportunity to assess whether current policies in these areas are consistent with the international community's commitment to the 2015 targets. More importantly, it provides an opportunity to define a new role for Britain in championing the interests of the world's poorest countries and poorest people. As a member of one of the world's most powerful trading blocs, as a major source of private capital, and as an important player in institutions such as the UN, IMF and the World Bank, Britain has special responsibilities and it has the capacity to make a difference.

Inevitably, perspectives on globalisation are shaped by the vantage point 2
of those viewing the phenomenon. Globalisation has opened new markets and investment opportunities for British companies, but British citizens have not been immune to the insecurity created by capital mobility—a fact underlined by the recent vicissitudes of the car industry. The same theme of "winners" and "losers" pervades the experience of poor countries. Women textile workers in Bangladesh, workers in the hi-technology industries of Bangalore, and millions of workers in countries as diverse as China, the Dominican Republic and Malaysia have benefited from export opportunities and foreign investment. At the other end of the spectrum, poor farmers in Mexico and the Philippines have seen their livelihoods destroyed by competition from imports, and millions of Indonesians have seen the human development gains made over a generation wiped out by instability of capital markets.

Northern governments, including the British Government, have tended to 3
stress the enormous potential inherent in globalisation. They have also promoted the spread of global markets, not least through the World Trade Organisation, the World Bank and the IMF. The potential gains are real, but they are not automatic—and in many cases the policies promoted in the name of globalisation have not addressed human development problems. As Joseph Stiglitz, the former Chief Economist at the World Bank has commented, the received wisdom took "privatisation and trade liberalisation as ends in themselves, rather than means to more sustainable, equitable and democratic growth." It is precisely this approach, and a failure to develop more equitable strategies for global governance, that is failing the poor. The end result is a process of globalisation that is redistributing wealth and opportunity in the wrong direction,

from the poor to the rich. This is morally indefensible, economically inefficient, and socially unsustainable. Left unattended, extreme inequalities
between countries will generate political instability and undermine the very
foundations of multilateralism. What is needed is a system of global governance capable of managing a process of globalisation with redistribution in
favour of the poor.

4   Global integration is proceeding at breakneck speed as barriers to trade
and capital come down and new technologies come on stream. The benefits
are obvious: faster growth, more choice, higher average incomes, and new
opportunities. But the process is uneven and unbalanced, as is the distribution
of opportunity. As the UN Secretary General has put it: "How can we say that
the half of the human race which has yet to make or receive a telephone call,
let alone use a computer, is taking part in globalisation? We cannot without
insulting their poverty." Poor countries and poor people are being left behind
in increasingly marginalised enclaves of deprivation within an ever more prosperous global economy. The rules of globalisation have neglected the needs of
those least equipped to benefit from new opportunities. In fact, they have been
written by rich countries and powerful transnational companies, primarily
with a view to their own advantage.

5   The consequences are reflected in the ever more obscene income gap separating rich and poor countries—and in growing income inequalities within
countries. While the benefits of globalisation have been disproportionately
captured by the rich, the poor bear the costs of increased vulnerability. Failure
to change this picture through a major redistribution in favour of the poor will
undermine national and international efforts to reduce poverty, restrict opportunities for economic growth, and—ultimately—generate instability. But globalisation with redistribution will require new approaches to multilateralism.
Global markets, like national markets, must be underpinned by rules based on
shared ideas about social justice, rather than the unrelenting pursuit of corporate profit and national self-interest.

Globalisation and Poverty?

6 Current debates suffer from three widespread globalisation myths. The first is
that there is nothing new or distinctive about globalisation at all. The second
is that globalisation is an inherently benign motor driving increased prosperity and accelerated poverty reduction—a view that remains widespread among
governments and international financial institutions. The third myth is the flip-
side of the second. It holds that globalisation is inherently bad, and that it will
necessarily increase poverty, aggravate inequalities and jeopardise social
rights.

7   Contrary to the first myth, Globalisation does in fact represent a new era
in international economic relations. Global integration has a chequered history
over the past century. Trade and investment flows expanded rapidly before the
First World War, but declined in the 1920s and 1930s in the face of trade barriers and national controls. For three decades after the 1950s, global integration and liberalisation in trade proceeded slowly (and even more slowly in

investment), before taking off in the 1980s. What has happened since then represents a qualitative break with the past.

Broadly defined, globalisation is a process of rapid economic integration 8 driven by the liberalisation of trade, investment and capital flows, as well as by rapid technological change and the "Information Revolution." International trade growth has consistently outstripped global GDP growth for almost two decades, so that almost all countries are now more dependent on trade. World financial markets and capital flows have expanded rapidly, further integrating national economies. The growth of money markets has been even more spectacular, with over one trillion dollars a day traded in currency transactions. Today, we are all more immediately affected by distant economic events than ever before. At the same time, new technologies have led to the development of increasingly knowledge-based systems of trade and production. In the future, national wealth, and the distribution of income, will increasingly reflect the distribution of human capital and the ability of populations to absorb and assimilate knowledge.

The second myth, which holds that globalisation has unleashed a new era 9 of rising prosperity and accelerating poverty reduction, is increasingly difficult to square with the facts. Economic growth in the world economy was modest in the 1990s, and while the "growth gap" between rich and poor countries narrowed this was almost entirely due to the dynamism of pre-crisis economies in East Asia. The income gap between the world's poorest region, sub-Saharan Africa, and the industrial countries continued to widen, albeit at a reduced pace.

What do current growth trends mean for the 2015 target of halving 10 income poverty? Recent estimates from the World Bank suggest that the proportion of people living on less than $1 a day declined from 32 per cent in 1987 to 26 per cent in 1998. Projecting this trend forward to 2015 produces a headcount index of 17 per cent, which is broadly in line with the 2015 target. However, almost the entire gain is due to East Asia, where growth estimates have been revised downwards following the 1997 financial crisis. If this region is excluded, the incidence of income poverty has declined by less than 2 per cent in the 1990s, from 35 per cent to 33 per cent.

If current trends continue there will be a massive shortfall in relation to 11 the 2015 goals, with the incidence of poverty in non-East Asian countries declining by 20 per cent, compared to the target rate of 50 per cent. In terms of overall numbers, the population affected by poverty declined only marginally during the 1990s, with 1.2 billion living below the poverty line. Excluding China, the number of poor people increased by 70 million in the 1990s. If current growth trends continue, this number is projected to increase over the next decade.

Overall trends obscure important regional variations. During the 1990s per 12 capita incomes in sub-Saharan Africa have increased by only 0.1 per cent per annum, following a decade of declining real incomes. The incidence of poverty has remained static, while the headcount has increased by almost 50 million. Latin America has integrated into the global economy more rapidly than any other developing region. Trade barriers have fallen and foreign investment regimes have been liberalised. Yet despite a strong economic recovery, the incidence of poverty remained the same, with another 5 million joining the ranks of those living on less than $1 a day. In South Asia average incomes increased by almost one third, while the incidence of poverty fell by only 4 per cent. At the end of the 1990s, the region had around 27 million more people living on less than $1 a day than at the start of the decade. There are also worrying signs for the future. In India, home to almost half of the world's poor, the rate of poverty reduction has slowed in the 1990s, suggesting that the linkage between growth and poverty reduction is weakening.

13   But if globalisation has failed to generate the automatic benefits predicted by some, it would be wrong to caricature it, as in the third myth, as an inherently destructive force. It is true that international trade creates winners and losers, and that the losers are often poor, but the poor also figure in the ranks of the winners. In Bangladesh, textile exports have created jobs for hundreds of thousands of desperately poor women. Access to northern markets has generated income needed to raise nutritional standards, meet health needs, and educate children. East Asia has recorded the most rapid reduction in poverty in history, partly as a result of rapid export growth. In China, that growth has been supported through sustained increases in foreign investment. The new technologies associated with globalisation also have the potential to improve the lives of the poor. In Latin America and South Asia, Oxfam is working with groups of producers using simple computer software to improve access to market information. All this suggests that the view that globalisation is inherently bad for the poor is wrong, what matters is that globalisation is managed in a way that extends opportunities for poor people by overcoming the disadvantages linked to their poverty.

Growth with Equity: The Missing Link

14   Widening inequalities are at the heart of the failure of globalisation to usher in a new phase of rapid human development. Inequalities matter for poverty reduction for an obvious reason: the larger the share of the economic cake and increments to growth captured by the poor, the faster the rate of poverty reduction. But extreme inequality is not just bad for poverty reduction—it is also bad for growth. This is because it restricts the size of markets and the potential for investment and innovation. Unfortunately, current patterns of globalisation are reinforcing already wide income inequalities, both at the global level and at the national level. These trends must be addressed by a redistribution of opportunity both within and between countries.

15   Inequalities are most pronounced at the global level. Today, the ratio of average GNP of the richest countries with one fifth of the world's population to the GNP per capita of countries with the poorest fifth, is 74:1. In 1990 it was 60:1, which was twice the ratio in 1960. While some countries in East Asia have closed the income gap, the poorest countries in particular have lost out. At the end of the 1990s, seen by some as the first decade of globalisation, the richest fifth of the world's population accounted for:

• 86 per cent of GDP (compared to 1 per cent for the poorest)

- 80 per cent of exports (compared to less than 1 per cent for the poorest)
- 70 per cent of foreign investment (compared to 0.8 per cent for the poorest)

Three decades ago an International Commission chaired by the former   16
Canadian Prime Minister Lester Pearson concluded that: "the widening gap
between the developed and the developing countries has become the central problem of our time." As the above facts suggest that problem remains unresolved.

The distribution of benefits from integrating into global markets within   17
countries has also been increasingly skewed in favour of the wealthy. The
widening income gaps between rich and poor states in India, between coastal
and inland areas in China, between the educated and the uneducated in Latin
America, and between commercial and food staple crop producing areas in
Africa are all testament to this problem. This includes countries that were
already highly unequal (such as Mexico), countries that were previously more
egalitarian (such as China and Thailand), poor countries (like Ethiopia) and rich
countries (including the US and Britain). The most comprehensive recent review
of national income inequality trends (the WIDER database) covers 77 countries,
in 45 of which inequality is increasing. This calls into question previous—and
current—World Bank research, which claims that growth during globalisation
has been distribution neutral. National income distribution trends have profound implications for poverty reduction. For instance, highly unequal countries such as Brazil have to grow at three times the rate of more equal countries such as Indonesia to increase average income of the poorest 20 per cent
by a similar amount.

It is sometimes argued that increasing inequality is a natural corollary of   18
market-led growth. This conveniently ignores the role of governments in shaping distributional outcomes. The process of globalisation has often been presented as a triumph for free markets, both in the international economy and
in national economies. In fact, markets have been carefully managed in a way
that has produced anti-poor distributional outcomes.

Nowhere is this more apparent than in matters of international trade and   19
finance. International trade is far more important to developing countries than
aid, not least because it can provide the foundations for more self-reliant
development. Yet protectionist barriers maintained by northern governments
cost developing countries an estimated $700bn a year—fourteen times the
amount they receive in aid.

While northern governments preach free trade, they practice protection-   20
ism. The double standards are reflected in WTO rules. These allow northern
governments to subsidise farmers on an epic scale, while demanding that poor
countries liberalise their markets. This helps to explain why two decades of
liberalisation by poor countries has produced disappointing results, with average trade deficits increasing by 3 per cent of GDP.

Trade policy is not the only problem. International aid could play an impor-   21
tant role in supporting more equitable patterns of globalisation. Yet the past
decade has witnessed unparalleled cuts in aid budgets, now at their lowest levels
in real terms for over twenty years. Similarly, failure to resolve the debt crisis in
poor countries has crippled prospects for growth and poverty reduction. The

management of private capital markets has also been highly disadvantageous for poor countries. Inadequate market regulation has left powerful financial conglomerates controlling vast sums in institutional savings free to move capital into high-risk developing country environments. When the East Asian crisis erupted in 1997, the same corporations were bailed-out by the IMF, which in turn imposed stringent austerity measures responsible for a massive increase in poverty.

22   At a national level, globalisation has been accompanied by a familiar mix of policies: trade liberalisation, privatisation and financial market deregulation. While market reforms have often been long overdue, the pace, sequencing and design of reform has frequently widened the gap between rich and poor. For example, rapid trade liberalisation and economic growth in Mexico has been accompanied by an increase in poverty, with 12 million more people living below the poverty line. Much of the growth has been concentrated among large-scale manufacturing industry and commercial farming, linked in both cases to export opportunities in the US economy. The increase in poverty has been concentrated in the "poverty-belt" states of the South, where the livelihoods of rural households have been undefined by subsidised agricultural imports.

Making Globalisation Work for the Poor

23 The White Paper on globalisation needs to start from a recognition that current patterns of globalisation are inconsistent with the 2015 targets for human development—targets to which the British Government is committed. This is not to suggest withdrawal from global markets is an option for poor countries, even if it were possible. As Amartya Sen has written: "to be generically against markets would be almost as odd as being generically against conversations between people." This applies per force to global markets. But acceptance of the reality of globalisation does not imply that global markets can be allowed to operate as they are at present. Principles of social justice and human development must be brought to the centre of the multilateral system, from where they are currently conspicuous by their absence. This is not just in the interests of poverty reduction and the world's poorest people. Ultimately, the concentration of power and wealth produced by the past ten years of global economic integration, coupled with the instability of the global financial system, makes present arrangements unsustainable.

24   What is needed is a reinvigorated system of global governance through which opportunities are more widely distributed. The survival of multilateralism is vital both to contain the systemic risks associated with globalisation, and to produce more equitable outcomes. But what currently passes for multilateralism, especially in the WTO and the International Monetary Fund, is unacceptable. Indeed, it is little more than a smokescreen for the pursuit of national and corporate self-interest.

25   The British Government is well placed to take the lead. It has championed the interests of the poorest countries in debt relief and trade, and it has a good record on aid. In other areas it is under-performing. Britain should be doing

far more to reform the international financial system, pressing for new rules to protect the interests of poor countries against private creditors, to regulate institutional investors, and to reform the IMF. Similarly, there are areas in which more joined-up government is needed. In seeking to advance the interests and investment rights of British companies through the Multilateral Agreement on Investment, Britain directly threatened the development of national poverty reduction strategies. Similarly, the benefits associated with increased aid may be much smaller than the potential costs of the WTO's intellectual property regime, for which the UK has been a powerful advocate.

Fifty years ago, at the end of the Second World War, the founding fathers 26 of the Bretton Woods institutions sought to create a system of global governance that would provide the foundations for future peace and stability. Their vision was extraordinarily ambitious. It was shaped by the experience of the 1920s, when the collapse of the international economic order ushered in a period of instability and depression that, in the eyes of many, had led to war. Above all, they recognised the destructive power of markets that were not underpinned by institutions and rules prioritising the public good over the pursuit of corporate profit and narrowly-defined national advantage. The global economy of the 21st century is urgently in need of precisely such institutions and rules.

Questions for Discussion and Your Reading Journal

1. According to the Oxfam writers, why does Britain have "special responsibilities" as well as "the capacity to make a difference" for the world's poorest peoples?
2. Oxfam observers argue that current globalization (U.S. spelling of the word) policies are "failing the poor." Who is responsible for this failure? How serious is the failure? And what do they suggest will happen if this problem is not resolved?
3. What are the three globalization myths that are currently hampering debate around this issue?
4. What kinds of evidence do the writers use to support their claim that poor people are getting poorer around the world? Is this evidence convincing?
5. What do the authors mean by "Growth with equity," and is this happening?
6. The writers point out that northern countries "preach free trade." Do these countries also practice free trade? Explain.
7. Sum up in three or four sentences what the Oxfam writers offer as ways to make globalization "work for the poor."

KOFI ANNAN

Kofi Annan (1938–) is the first secretary-general of the United Nations to rise up through the ranks of the U.N. staff to this prestigious position.

Born in Kumasi, Ghana (West Africa), and educated in Ghana, Switzerland, and the United States, he is fluent in the Twi language of Ghana, several other African languages, plus French and English. Since joining the United Nations in 1962, he has held positions with the World Health Organization, the High Commission for Human Rights in Geneva, the U.N. Economic Commission for Africa, and at U.N. headquarters in New York. He gained worldwide attention in 1990 by leading a special U.N. task force that helped 900 international staff members and citizens of Western nations leave Iraq safely in the face of war. From 1993 to 1995, and again in 1996, he headed the United Nation's Peacekeeping Department, coordinating the efforts of nearly 70,000 peacekeeping troops from 77 nations to reestablish peace during the breakup of the former Yugoslavia. In 1997, he replaced Boutros Boutros-Ghali to become the seventh secretary-general of the United Nations.

Reading Rhetorically

Kofi Annan faced two major rhetorical challenges to the successful delivery of his Nobel Peace Prize acceptance speech. First, he was speaking less than 2 months after the terrorist attacks on the United States of September 11, 2001, to a world still dazed by the horrors of these events. Second, he was calling for peaceful solutions to complex international issues at a time when other global leaders were turning to violent measures, as the United States had just done in its war on the Taliban and Al Qaida terrorists in Afghanistan the month before. Rather than confront the warring nations, Annan turns our attention to the plight of a typical baby girl born in Afghanistan (pathos). Through such concrete examples, he addressed the deeper issues that plagued the world before terrorism raised its head and that are likely to be with us long after terrorism fades. He spoke of issues that will require us to unite and to work together toward solutions, issues such as increasing poverty in the third world, discrimination against women and minorities, genocide, lack of education, inadequate health care, lack of democracy, and human rights violations. He also presented the three priorities of the United Nations for addressing these issues, followed by an appeal to the best in global religious and cultural traditions as his speech neared its close. He paid tribute to those creeds and cultural practices valued by different populations around the world in a manner that illustrates the possibilities for unity, goodwill, and productive action among the earth's diverse peoples. Finally, note how his two closing paragraphs return again to the "girl born in Afghanistan today" with which he opened his speech, driving home in sobering terms the ultimate responsibility that we all share in giving her a chance to live and to thrive in the 21st century.

Nobel Peace Prize Lecture, December 10, 2001

Your Majesties, Your Royal Highnesses, Excellencies, Members of the Norwegian Nobel Committee, Ladies and Gentlemen, 1

Today, in Afghanistan, a girl will be born. Her mother will hold her and 2 feed her, comfort her and care for her—just as any mother would anywhere in the world. In these most basic acts of human nature, humanity knows no divisions. But to be born a girl in today's Afghanistan is to begin life centuries away from the prosperity that one small part of humanity has achieved. It is to live under conditions that many of us in this hall would consider inhuman.

I speak of a girl in Afghanistan, but I might equally well have mentioned a 3 baby boy or girl in Sierra Leone. No one today is unaware of this divide between the world's rich and poor. No one today can claim ignorance of the cost that this divide imposes on the poor and dispossessed who are no less deserving of human dignity, fundamental freedoms, security, food and education than any of us. The cost, however, is not borne by them alone. Ultimately, it is borne by all of us—North and South, rich and poor, men and women of all races and religions.

Today's real borders are not between nations, but between powerful and 4 powerless, free and fettered, privileged and humiliated. Today, no walls can separate humanitarian or human rights crises in one part of the world from national security crises in another.

Scientists tell us that the 5 world of nature is so small and interdependent that a butterfly flapping its wings in the Amazon rainforest can generate a violent storm on the other side of the earth. This principle is known as the "Butterfly Effect." Today, we realize, perhaps more than ever, that the world of human activity also has its own "Butterfly Effect"—for better or for worse.

Ladies and Gentlemen, 6

We have entered the third 7 millennium through a gate of fire. If today, after the horror of 11 September, we see better, and we see further—we will realize

© Reuters NewMedia, Inc./CORBIS

that humanity is indivisible. New threats make no distinction between races, nations or regions. A new insecurity has entered every mind, regardless of wealth or status. A deeper awareness of the bonds that bind us all—in pain as in prosperity—has gripped young and old.

8   In the early beginnings of the 21st century—a century already violently disabused of any hopes that progress towards global peace and prosperity is inevitable—this new reality can no longer be ignored. It must be confronted.

9   The 20th century was perhaps the deadliest in human history, devastated by innumerable conflicts, untold suffering, and unimaginable crimes. Time after time, a group or a nation inflicted extreme violence on another, often driven by irrational hatred and suspicion, or unbounded arrogance and thirst for power and resources. In response to these cataclysms, the leaders of the world came together at mid-century to unite the nations as never before.

10   A forum was created—the United Nations—where all nations could join forces to affirm the dignity and worth of every person, and to secure peace and development for all peoples. Here States could unite to strengthen the rule of law, recognize and address the needs of the poor, restrain man's brutality and greed, conserve the resources and beauty of nature, sustain the equal rights of men *and* women, and provide for the safety of future generations.

11   We thus inherit from the 20th century the political, as well as the scientific and technological power, which—if only we have the will to use them—give us the chance to vanquish poverty, ignorance and disease.

12   In the 21st Century I believe the mission of the United Nations will be defined by a new, more profound, awareness of the sanctity and dignity of every human life, regardless of race or religion. This will require us to look beyond the framework of States, and beneath the surface of nations or communities. We must focus, as never before, on improving the conditions of the individual men and women who give the state or nation its richness and character. We must begin with the young Afghan girl, recognizing that saving that one life is to save humanity itself.

13   Over the past five years, I have often recalled that the United Nations' Charter begins with the words: "We the peoples." What is not always recognized is that "we the peoples" are made up of individuals whose claims to the most fundamental rights have too often been sacrificed in the supposed interests of the state or the nation.

14   A genocide begins with the killing of one man—not for what he has done, but because of who he is. A campaign of "ethnic cleansing" begins with one neighbour turning on another. Poverty begins when even one child is denied his or her fundamental right to education. What begins with the failure to uphold the dignity of one life, all too often ends with a calamity for entire nations.

15   In this new century, we must start from the understanding that peace belongs not only to states or peoples, but to each and every member of those communities. The sovereignty of States must no longer be used as a shield for gross violations of human rights. Peace must be made real and tangible in the daily existence of every individual in need. Peace must be sought, above all, because it is the condition for every member of the human family to live a life of dignity and security.

The rights of the individual are of no less importance to immigrants and 16
minorities in Europe and the Americas than to women in Afghanistan or children
in Africa. They are as fundamental to the poor as to the rich; they are as necessary to the security of the developed world as to that of the developing world.

From this vision of the role of the United Nations in the next century flow 17
three key priorities for the future: eradicating poverty, preventing conflict, and
promoting democracy. Only in a world that is rid of poverty can all men and
women make the most of their abilities. Only where individual rights are
respected can differences be channelled politically and resolved peacefully.
Only in a democratic environment, based on respect for diversity and dialogue, can individual self-expression and self-government be secured, and freedom of association be upheld.

Throughout my term as Secretary-General, I have sought to place human 18
beings at the centre of everything we do—from conflict prevention to development to human rights. Securing real and lasting improvement in the lives of
individual men and women is the measure of all we do at the United Nations.

It is in this spirit that I humbly accept the Centennial Nobel Peace Prize. 19
Forty years ago today, the Prize for 1961 was awarded for the first time to a
Secretary-General of the United Nations—posthumously, because Dag Ham-
marskjöld had already given his life for peace in Central Africa. And on the
same day, the Prize for 1960 was awarded for the first time to an African—
Albert Luthuli, one of the earliest leaders of the struggle against apartheid in
South Africa. For me, as a young African beginning his career in the United
Nations a few months later, those two men set a standard that I have sought
to follow throughout my working life.

This award belongs not just to me. I do not stand here alone. On behalf 20
of all my colleagues in every part of the United Nations, in every corner of the
globe, who have devoted their lives—and in many instances risked or given
their lives in the cause of peace—I thank the Members of the Nobel Committee for this high honour. My own path to service at the United Nations was
made possible by the sacrifice and commitment of my family and many friends
from all continents—some of whom have passed away—who taught me and
guided me. To them, I offer my most profound gratitude.

In a world filled with weapons of war and all too often words of war, the 21
Nobel Committee has become a vital agent for peace. Sadly, a prize for peace
is a rarity in this world. Most nations have monuments or memorials to war,
bronze salutations to heroic battles, archways of triumph. But peace has no
parade, no pantheon of victory.

What it does have is the Nobel Price—a statement of hope and courage 22
with unique resonance and authority. Only by understanding and addressing
the needs of individuals for peace, for dignity, and for security can we at the
United Nations hope to live up to the honour conferred today, and fulfil the
vision of our founders. This is the broad mission of peace that United Nations
staff members carry out every day in every part of the world.

A few of them, women and men, are with us in this hall today. Among 23
them, for instance, are a Military Observer from Senegal who is helping to provide basic security in the Democratic Republic of the Congo; a Civilian Police

Adviser from the United States who is helping to improve the rule of law in Kosovo; a UNICEF Child Protection Officer from Ecuador who is helping to secure the rights of Colombia's most vulnerable citizens; and a World Food Programme Officer from China who is helping to feed the people of North Korea.

24 Distinguished guests,

25   The idea that there is one people in possession of the truth, one answer to the world's ills, or one solution to humanity's needs, has done untold harm throughout history—especially in the last century. Today, however, even amidst continuing ethnic conflict around the world, there is a growing understanding that human diversity is both the reality that makes dialogue necessary, and the very basis for that dialogue.

26   We understand, as never before, that each of us is fully worthy of the respect and dignity essential to our common humanity. We recognize that we are the products of many cultures, traditions and memories; that mutual respect allows us to study and learn from other cultures; and that we gain strength by combining the foreign with the familiar.

27   In every great faith and tradition one can find the values of tolerance and mutual understanding. The Qur'an, for example, tells us that "We created you from a single pair of male and female and made you into nations and tribes, that you may know each other." Confucius urged his followers: "when the good way prevails in the state, speak boldly and act boldly. When the state has lost the way, act boldly and speak softly." In the Jewish tradition, the injunction to "love thy neighbour as thyself," is considered to be the very essence of the Torah.

28   This thought is reflected in the Christian Gospel, which also teaches us to love our enemies and pray for those who wish to persecute us. Hindus are taught that "truth is one, the sages give it various names." And in the Buddhist tradition, individuals are urged to act with compassion in every facet of life.

29   Each of us has the right to take pride in our particular faith or heritage. But the notion that what is ours is necessarily in conflict with what is theirs is both false and dangerous. It has resulted in endless enmity and conflict, leading men to commit the greatest of crimes in the name of a higher power.

30   It need not be so. People of different religions and cultures live side by side in almost every part of the world, and most of us have overlapping identities which unite us with very different groups. We *can* love what we are, without hating what—and who—we are *not*. We can thrive in our own tradition, even as we learn from others, and come to respect their teachings.

31   This will not be possible, however, without freedom of religion, of expression, of assembly, and basic equality under the law. Indeed, the lesson of the past century has been that where the dignity of the individual has been trampled or threatened—where citizens have not enjoyed the basic right to choose their government, or the right to change it regularly—conflict has too often followed, with innocent civilians paying the price, in lives cut short and communities destroyed.

32   The obstacles to democracy have little to do with culture or religion, and much more to do with the desire of those in power to maintain their position

at any cost. This is neither a new phenomenon nor one confined to any particular part of the world. People of all cultures value their freedom of choice, and feel the need to have a say in decisions affecting their lives.

The United Nations, whose membership comprises almost all the States in 33 the world, is founded on the principle of the equal worth of every human being. It is the nearest thing we have to a representative institution that can address the interests of all states, and all peoples. Through this universal, indispensable instrument of human progress, States can serve the interests of their citizens by recognizing common interests and pursuing them in unity. No doubt, that is why the Nobel Committee says that it "wishes, in its centenary year, to proclaim that the only negotiable route to global peace and cooperation goes by way of the United Nations."

I believe the Committee also recognized that this era of global challenges 34 leaves no choice but cooperation at the global level. When States undermine the rule of law and violate the rights of their individual citizens, they become a menace not only to their own people, but also to their neighbours, and indeed the world. What we need today is better governance—legitimate, democratic governance that allows each individual to flourish, and each State to thrive.

Your Majesties, 35
Excellencies,
Ladies and Gentlemen,

You will recall that I began my address with a reference to the girl born in 36 Afghanistan today. Even though her mother will do all in her power to protect and sustain her, there is a one-in-four risk that she will not live to see her fifth birthday. Whether she does is just one test of our common humanity—of our belief in our individual responsibility for our fellow men and women. But it is the only test that matters.

Remember this girl and then our larger aims—to fight poverty, prevent 37 conflict, or cure disease—will not seem distant, or impossible. Indeed, those aims will seem very near, and very achievable—as they should. Because beneath the surface of states and nations, ideas and language, lies the fate of individual human beings in need. Answering their needs will be the mission of the United Nations in the century to come.

Thank you very much.

Questions for Discussion and Your Reading Journal

1. What is the "Butterfly Effect" and for what purpose does Annan bring it up in his speech?
2. Sum up Annan's description of the purpose of the United Nations.
3. According to Annan, why is it important to "uphold the dignity of one life"? Do you find the examples he uses to support this point convincing? Explain.

4. What are Annan's "three key priorities for the future" in his work at the United Nations and why are these priorities important?
5. In your opinion, why do societies around the world build monuments to war and to soldiers and to battles but, as Annan points out, these societies rarely offer prizes for or awards to peace or to those who make peace?
6. What effect does it have when Annan brings in specific examples from a variety of religions when he talks of cultural diversity?
7. Does Annan believe that the "obstacles to democracy" come from cultural differences, or from the desire for power? Do you agree? Explain.
8. What effect does Annan achieve by closing his speech with a return to the same example as his opening paragraphs? Explain.

ROBERT REICH

The following reading comes from Robert B. Reich's book, The Work of Nations *(1991), in which he analyzes major economic trends of our time and offers explanations for why some Americans are getting richer while others are seeing their earnings diminish significantly from decade to decade. Reich is perhaps best known for showing how the future belongs economically to "symbolic analysts," not to routine factory workers of the past, or to "in-person servers" such as restaurant employees, cashiers, customer service employees, and so on, who are in high demand at present. Reich's symbolic analysts are educated innovators and problem solvers who sell ideas and solutions rather than manufactured goods or personal services. They include engineers, scientists, public relations people, marketing experts, management specialists, people in entertainment, and people in many other fields who market creative thinking, specialized skills, and valuable insights. The aim of Reich's work is to show why "the salaries and benefits of America's top executives, and many of their advisors and consultants, have soared to what years before would have been unimaginable heights, even as those of other Americans have declined" (Paragraph 44).*

Reading Rhetorically

A lot of people in America are angry and frustrated by current economic trends that seem to favor corporate executives and certain well-educated employees, while punishing the average worker. People who work in factories across the nation are seeing their jobs transferred to foreign countries where labor is far cheaper than in the United States. Service workers are in high demand by fast-food restaurants, hotels, convenience marts, and retail stores but are often paid less than enough to support a family and have few benefits. To avoid falling prey to the anger and negative rhetoric surrounding this highly personal issue, Reich uses a metaphor common in the fields of philosophy and ethics. He writes of boats "rising" or "sinking" for various constituencies of the labor market. This allows him to place some distance between the emotion of the issue and the pragmatic explanations of the historical trends unfolding in our generation. He uses facts, statistics, economic analysis, and other forms of evidence *(loops)* to illustrate why the boat of routine workers is sinking quickly, the boat of in-person servers is sinking more slowly, and the boat of the symbolic analysts is rising at a rate that would have been unimaginable a couple of decades ago.

Why the Rich Are Getting Richer and the Poor, Poorer

"The division of labour is limited by the extent of the market."
—ADAM SMITH, *An Inquiry into the Nature and Causes of the Wealth of Nations* (1776)

Regardless of how your job is officially classified (manufacturing, service, 1 managerial, technical, secretarial, and so on), or the industry in which you work (automotive, steel, computer, advertising, finance, food processing), your real competitive position in the world economy is coming to depend on the function you perform in it. Herein lies the basic reason why incomes are diverging. The fortunes of routine producers are declining. In-person servers are also becoming poorer, although their fates are less clear-cut. But symbolic analysts—who solve, identify, and broker new problems—are, by and large, succeeding in the world economy.

All Americans used to be in roughly the same economic boat. Most rose 2 or fell together as the corporations in which they were employed, the industries comprising such corporations, and the national economy as a whole became more productive—or languished. But national borders no longer define our economic fates. We are now in different boats, one sinking rapidly, one sinking more slowly, and the third rising steadily.

The boat containing routine producers is sinking rapidly. Recall that by 3 midcentury routine production workers in the United States were paid relatively well. The giant pyramidlike organizations at the core of each major industry coordinated their prices and investments—avoiding the harsh winds of competition and thus maintaining healthy earnings. Some of these earnings, in turn, were reinvested in new plant and equipment (yielding ever-larger-scale economies); another portion went to top managers and investors. But a large and increasing portion went to middle managers and production workers. Work stoppages posed such a threat to high-volume production that organized labor was able to exact an ever-larger premium for its cooperation. And the pattern of wages established within the core corporations influenced the pattern throughout the national economy. Thus the growth of a relatively affluent middle class, able to purchase all the wondrous things produced in high volume by the core corporations.

4   But, as has been observed, the core is rapidly breaking down into global webs which earn their largest profits from clever problem-solving, -identifying, and brokering. As the costs of transporting standard things and of communicating information about them continue to drop, profit margins on high-volume, standardized production are thinning, because there are few barriers to entry. Modern factories and state-of-the-art machinery can be installed almost anywhere on the globe. Routine producers in the United States, then, are in direct competition with millions of routine producers in other nations. Twelve thousand people are added to the world's population every hour, most of whom, eventually, will happily work for a small fraction of the wages of routine producers in America.[1]

5   The consequence is clearest in older, heavy industries, where high-volume, standardized production continues its ineluctable move to where labor is cheapest and most accessible around the world. Thus, for example, the Maquiladora factories cluttered along the Mexican side of the U.S. border in the sprawling shanty towns of Tijuana, Mexicali, Nogales, Agua Prieta, and Ciudad Juárez—factories owned mostly by Americans, but increasingly by Japanese—in which more than a half million routine producers assemble parts into finished goods to be shipped into the United States.

6   The same story is unfolding worldwide. Until the late 1970s, AT&T had depended on routine producers in Shreveport, Louisiana, to assemble standard telephones. It then discovered that routine producers in Singapore would perform the same tasks at a far lower cost. Facing intense competition from other global webs, AT&T's strategic brokers felt compelled to switch. So in the early 1980s they stopped hiring routine producers in Shreveport and began hiring cheaper routine producers in Singapore. But under this kind of pressure for ever-lower high-volume production costs, today's Singaporean can easily end up as yesterday's Louisianan. By the late 1980s, AT&T's strategic brokers found that routine producers in Thailand were eager to assemble telephones for a small fraction of the wages of routine producers in Singapore. Thus, in 1989, AT&T stopped hiring Singaporeans to make telephones and began hiring even cheaper routine producers in Thailand.

7   The search for ever-lower wages has not been confined to heavy industry. Routine data processing is equally footloose. Keypunch operators located anywhere around the world can enter data into computers, linked by satellite or transoceanic fiber-optic cable, and take it out again. As the rates charged by satellite networks continue to drop, and as more satellites and fiber-optic cables become available (reducing communication costs still further), routine data processors in the United States find themselves in ever more direct competition with their counterparts abroad, who are often eager to work for far less.

---

[1]The reader should note, of course, that lower wages in other areas of the world are of no particular attraction to global capital unless workers there are sufficiently productive to make the labor cost of producing *each unit* lower there than in higher-wage regions. Productivity in many low-wage areas of the world has improved due to the ease with which state-of-the-art factories and equipment can be installed there.

By 1990, keypunch operators in the United States were earning, at most, 8
$6.50 per hour. But keypunch operators throughout the rest of the world were
willing to work for a fraction of this. Thus, many potential American
data-processing jobs were disappearing, and the wages and benefits of
the remaining ones were in decline. Typical was Saztec International, a
$20-million-a-year data-processing firm headquartered in Kansas City, whose
American strategic brokers contracted with routine data processors in Manila
and with American-owned firms that needed such data-processing services.
Compared with the average Philippine income of $1,700 per year, data-entry
operators working for Saztec earn the princely sum of $2,650. The remainder
of Saztec's employees were American problem-solvers and -identifiers, searching for ways to improve the worldwide system and find new uses to which it
could be put.[2]

By 1990, American Airlines was employing over 1,000 data processors in 9
Barbados and the Dominican Republic to enter names and flight numbers
from used airline tickets (flown daily to Barbados from airports around the
United States) into a giant computer bank located in Dallas. Chicago publisher
R. R. Donnelley was sending entire manuscripts to Barbados for entry into
computers in preparation for printing. The New York Life Insurance Company was dispatching insurance claims to Castleisland, Ireland, where routine
producers, guided by simple directions, entered the claims and determined the
amounts due, then instantly transmitted the computations back to the United
States. (When the firm advertised in Ireland for twenty-five data-processing
jobs, it received six hundred applications.) And McGraw-Hill was processing
subscription renewal and marketing information for its magazines in nearby
Galway. Indeed, literally millions of routine workers around the world were
receiving information, converting it into computer-readable form, and then
sending it back—at the speed of electronic impulses—whence it came.

The simple coding of computer software has also entered into world 10
commerce. India, with a large English-speaking population of technicians
happy to do routine programming cheaply, is proving to be particularly attractive to global webs in need of this service. By 1990, Texas Instruments maintained a software development facility in Bangalore, linking fifty Indian pro-
grammers by satellite to TI's Dallas headquarters. Spurred by this and similar
ventures, the Indian government was building a teleport in Poona, intended to
make it easier and less expensive for many other firms to send their routine
software design specifications for coding.[3]

This shift of routine production jobs from advanced to developing nations 11
is a great boon to many workers in such nations who otherwise would be jobless or working for much lower wages. These workers, in turn, now have more
money with which to purchase symbolic-analytic services from advanced
nations (often embedded within all sorts of complex products). The trend is

---

[2]John Maxwell Hamilton, "A Bit Player Buys into the Computer Age," *New York Times Business World,* December 3, 1989, p. 14.

[3]Udayan Gupta, "U.S.-Indian Satellite Link Stands to Cut Software Costs," *Wall Street Journal,*
March 6, 1989, p. B2.

also beneficial to everyone around the world who can now obtain high-volume, standardized products (including information and software) more cheaply than before.

12   But these benefits do not come without certain costs. In particular the burden is borne by those who no longer have good-paying routine production jobs within advanced economies like the United States. Many of these people used to belong to unions or at least benefited from prevailing wage rates established in collective bargaining agreements. But as the old corporate bureaucracies have flattened into global webs, bargaining leverage has been lost. Indeed, the tacit national bargain is no more.

13   Despite the growth in the number of new jobs in the United States, union membership has withered. In 1960, 35 percent of all nonagricultural workers in America belonged to a union. But by 1980 that portion had fallen to just under a quarter, and by 1989 to about 17 percent. Excluding government employees, union membership was down to 13.4 percent.[4] This was a smaller proportion even than in the early 1930s, before the National Labor Relations Act created a legally protected right to labor representation. The drop in membership has been accompanied by a growing number of collective bargaining agreements to freeze wages at current levels, reduce wage levels of entering workers, or reduce wages overall. This is an important reason why the long economic recovery that began in 1982 produced a smaller rise in unit labor costs than any of the eight recoveries since World War II—the low rate of unemployment during its course notwithstanding.

14   Routine production jobs have vanished fastest in traditional unionized industries (autos, steel, and rubber, for example), where average wages have kept up with inflation. This is because the jobs of older workers in such industries are protected by seniority; the youngest workers are the first to be laid off. Faced with a choice of cutting wages or cutting the number of jobs, a majority of union members (secure in the knowledge that there are many who are junior to them who will be laid off first) often have voted for the latter.

15   Thus the decline in union membership has been most striking among young men entering the work force without a college education. In the early 1950s, more than 40 percent of this group joined unions; by the late 1980s, less than 20 percent (if public employees are excluded, less than 10 percent).[5] In steelmaking, for example, although many older workers remained employed, almost half of all routine steelmaking jobs in America vanished between 1974 and 1988 (from 480,000 to 260,000). Similarly with automobiles: During the 1980s, the United Auto Workers lost 500,000 members— one-third of their total at the start of the decade. General Motors alone cut 150,000 American production jobs during the 1980s (even as it added employ-

---

[4]*Statistical Abstract of the United States* (Washington, D.C.: U.S. Government Printing Office, 1989), p. 416, table 684.

[5]Calculations from Current Population Surveys by L. Katz and A. Revenga, "Changes in the Structure of Wages: U.S. and Japan," National Bureau of Economic Research, September 1989.

ment abroad). Another consequence of the same phenomenon: the gap between the average wages of unionized and nonunionized workers widened dramatically—from 14.6 percent in 1973 to 20.4 percent by end of the 1980s.[6] The lesson is clear. If you drop out of high school or have no more than a high school diploma, do not expect a good routine production job to be awaiting you.

Also vanishing are lower- and middle-level management jobs involving routine production. Between 1981 and 1986, more than 780,000 foremen, supervisors, and section chiefs lost their jobs through plant closings and lay-offs.[7] Large numbers of assistant division heads, assistant directors, assistant managers, and vice presidents also found themselves jobless. GM shed more than 40,000 white-collar employees and planned to eliminate another 25,000 by the mid-1990s.[8] As America's core pyramids metamorphosed into global webs, many middle-level routine producers were as obsolete as routine workers on the line.

As has been noted, foreign-owned webs are hiring some Americans to do routine production in the United States. Philips, Sony, and Toyota factories are popping up all over—to the self-congratulatory applause of the nation's governors and mayors, who have lured them with promises of tax abatements and new sewers, among other amenities. But as these ebullient politicians will soon discover, the foreign-owned factories are highly automated and will become far more so in years to come. Routine production jobs account for a small fraction of the cost of producing most items in the United States and other advanced nations, and this fraction will continue to decline sharply as computer-integrated robots take over. In 1977 it took routine producers thirty-five hours to assemble an automobile in the United States; it is estimated that by the mid-1990s, Japanese-owned factories in America will be producing finished automobiles using only eight hours of a routine producer's time.[9]

The productivity and resulting wages of American workers who run such robotic machinery may be relatively high, but there may not be many such jobs to go around. A case in point: in the late 1980s, Nippon Steel joined with America's ailing Inland Steel to build a new $400 million cold-rolling mill fifty miles west of Gary, Indiana. The mill was celebrated for its state-of-the-art technology, which cut the time to produce a coil of steel from twelve days to about one hour. In fact, the entire plant could be run by a small team of technicians, which became clear when Inland subsequently closed two of its old cold-rolling mills, laying off hundreds of routine workers. Governors and mayors take note: your much-ballyhooed foreign factories may end up employing distressingly few of your constituents.

---

[6]U.S. Department of Commerce, Bureau of Labor Statistics, "Wages of Unionized and Non-Unionized Workers," various issues.

[7]U.S. Department of Labor, Bureau of Labor Statistics, "Reemployment Increases Among Displaced Workers," *BLS News*, USDL 86-414, October 14, 1986, table 6.

[8]*Wall Street Journal*, February 16, 1990, p. A5.

[9]Figures from the International Motor Vehicles Program, Massachusetts Institute of Technology, 1989.

19   Overall, the decline in routine jobs has hurt men more than women. This is because the routine production jobs held by men in high-volume metal-bending manufacturing industries had paid higher wages than the routine production jobs held by women in textiles and data processing. As both sets of jobs have been lost, American women in routine production have gained more equal footing with American men—equally poor footing, that is. This is a major reason why the gender gap between male and female wages began to close during the 1980s.

20   The second of the three boats, carrying in-person servers, is sinking as well, but somewhat more slowly and unevenly. Most in-person servers are paid at or just slightly above the minimum wage and many work only part-time, with the result that their take-home pay is modest, to say the least. Nor do they typically receive all the benefits (health care, life insurance, disability, and so forth) garnered by routine producers in large manufacturing corporations or by symbolic analysts affiliated with the more affluent threads of global webs.[10] In-person servers are sheltered from the direct effects of global competition and, like everyone else, benefit from access to lower-cost products from around the world. But they are not immune to its indirect effects.

21   For one thing, in-person servers increasingly compete with former routine production workers, who, no longer able to find well-paying routine production jobs, have few alternatives but to seek in-person service jobs. The Bureau of Labor Statistics estimates that of the 2.8 million manufacturing workers who lost their jobs during the early 1980s, fully one-third were rehired in service jobs paying at least 20 percent less.[11] In-person servers must also compete with high school graduates and dropouts who years before had moved easily into routine production jobs but no longer can. And if demographic predictions about the American work force in the first decades of the twenty-first century are correct (and they are likely to be, since most of the people who will comprise the work force are already identifiable), most new entrants into the job market will be black or Hispanic men, or women—groups that in years past have possessed relatively weak technical skills. This will result in an even larger number of people crowding into in-person services. Finally, in-person servers will be competing with growing numbers of immigrants, both legal and illegal, for whom in-person services will comprise the most accessible jobs. (It is estimated that between the mid-1980s and the end of the century, about a quarter of all workers entering the American labor force will be immigrants.[12])

22   Perhaps the fiercest competition that in-person servers face comes from labor-saving machinery (much of it invented, designed, fabricated, or assembled in other nations, of course). Automated tellers, computerized cashiers,

---

[10]The growing portion of the American labor force engaged in in-person services, relative to routine production, thus helps explain why the number of Americans lacking health insurance increased by at least 6 million during the 1980s.

[11]U.S. Department of Labor, Bureau of Labor Statistics, "Reemployment Increases Among Disabled Workers," October 14, 1986.

[12]Federal Immigration and Naturalization Service, *Statistical Yearbook* (Washington, D.C.: U.S. Government Printing Office, 1986, 1987).

automatic car washes, robotized vending machines, self-service gasoline pumps, and all similar gadgets substitute for the human beings that customers once encountered. Even telephone operators are fast disappearing, as electronic sensors and voice simulators become capable of carrying on conversations that are reasonably intelligent and always polite. Retail sales workers— among the largest groups of in-person servers—are similarly imperiled. Through personal computers linked to television screens, tomorrow's consumers will be able to buy furniture, appliances, and all sorts of electronic toys from their living rooms—examining the merchandise from all angles, selecting whatever color, size, special features, and price seem most appealing, and then transmitting the order instantly to warehouses from which the selections will be shipped directly to their homes. So, too, with financial transactions, airline and hotel reservations, rental car agreements, and similar contracts, which will be executed between consumers in their homes and computer banks somewhere else on the globe.[13]

Advanced economies like the United States will continue to generate sizable numbers of new in-person service jobs, of course, the automation of older ones notwithstanding. For every bank teller who loses her job to an automated teller, three new jobs open for aerobics instructors. Human beings, it seems, have an almost insatiable desire for personal attention. But the intense competition nevertheless ensures that the wages of in-person servers will remain relatively low. In-person servers—working on their own, or else dispersed widely amid many small establishments, filling all sorts of personal-care niches—cannot readily organize themselves into labor unions or create powerful lobbies to limit the impact of such competition. 23

In two respects, demographics will work in favor of in-person servers, buoying their collective boat slightly. First, as has been noted, the rate of growth of the American work force is slowing. In particular, the number of young workers is shrinking. Between 1985 and 1995, the number of the eighteen- to twenty-four-year-olds will have declined by 17.5 percent. Thus, employers will have more incentive to hire and train in-person servers whom they might previously have avoided. But this demographic relief from the competitive pressures will be only temporary. The cumulative procreative energies of the postwar baby-boomers (born between 1946 and 1964) will result in a new surge of workers by 2010 or thereabouts.[14] And immigration—both legal and illegal—shows every sign of increasing in years to come. 24

Next, by the second decade of the twenty-first century, the number of Americans aged sixty-five and over will be rising precipitously, as the baby-boomers reach retirement age and live longer. Their life expectancies will lengthen not just because fewer of them will have smoked their way to their graves and more will have eaten better than their parents, but also because they 25

[13]See Claudia H. Deutsch, "The Powerful Push for Self-Service," *New York Times,* April 9, 1989, section 3, p. 1.

[14]U.S. Bureau of the Census, Current Population Reports, Series P-23, no. 138, tables 2-1, 4-6. See W. Johnson, A. Packer, et al., *Workforce 2000: Work and Workers for the 21st Century* (Indianapolis: Hudson Institute, 1987).

will receive all sorts of expensive drugs and therapies designed to keep them alive—barely. By 2035, twice as many Americans will be elderly as in 1988, and the number of octogenarians is expected to triple. As these decaying baby-boomers ingest all the chemicals and receive all the treatments, they will need a great deal of personal attention. Millions of deteriorating bodies will require nurses, nursing-home operators, hospital administrators, orderlies, home-care providers, hospice aides, and technicians to operate and maintain all the expensive machinery that will monitor and temporarily stave off final disintegration. There might even be a booming market for euthanasia specialists. In-person servers catering to the old and ailing will be in strong demand.[15]

26   One small problem: the decaying baby-boomers will not have enough money to pay for these services. They will have used up their personal savings years before. Their Social Security payments will, of course, have been used by the government to pay for the previous generation's retirement and to finance much of the budget deficits of the 1980s. Moreover, with relatively fewer young Americans in the population, the supply of housing will likely exceed the demand, with the result that the boomers' major investments—their homes—will be worth less (in inflation-adjusted dollars) when they retire than they planned for. In consequence, the huge cost of caring for the graying boomers will fall on many of the same people who will be paid to care for them. It will be like a great sump pump: in-person servers of the twenty-first century will have an abundance of health-care jobs, but a large portion of their earnings will be devoted to Social Security payments and income taxes, which will in turn be used to pay their salaries. The net result: no real improvement in their standard of living.

27   The standard of living of in-person servers also depends, indirectly, on the standard of living of the Americans they serve who are engaged in world commerce. To the extent that *these* Americans are richly rewarded by the rest of the world for what they contribute, they will have more money to lavish upon in-person services. Here we find the only form of "trickle-down" economics that has a basis in reality. A waitress in a town whose major factory has just been closed is unlikely to earn a high wage or enjoy much job security; in a swank resort populated by film producers and banking moguls, she is apt to do reasonably well. So, too, with nations. In-person servers in Bangladesh may spend their days performing roughly the same tasks as in-person servers in the United States, but have a far lower standard of living for their efforts. The difference comes in the value that their customers add to the world economy.

28   Unlike the boats of routine producers and in-person servers, however, the vessel containing America's symbolic analysts is rising. Worldwide demand for their insights is growing as the ease and speed of communicating them steadily increases. Not every symbolic analyst is rising as quickly or as dramatically as every other, of course; symbolic analysts at the low end are barely holding their own in the world economy. But symbolic analysts at the top are in such

---

[15]The Census Bureau estimates that by the year 2000, at least 12 million Americans will work in health services—well over 6 percent of the total work force.

great demand worldwide that they have difficulty keeping track of all their earnings. Never before in history has opulence on such a scale been gained by people who have earned it, and done so legally.

Among symbolic analysts in the middle range are American scientists and researchers who are busily selling their discoveries to global enterprise webs. They are not limited to American customers. If the strategic brokers in General Motors' headquarters refuse to pay a high price for a new means of making high-strength ceramic engines dreamed up by a team of engineers affiliated with Carnegie Mellon University in Pittsburgh, the strategic brokers of Honda or Mercedes-Benz are likely to be more than willing.

So, too, with the insights of America's ubiquitous management consultants, which are being sold for large sums to eager entrepreneurs in Europe and Latin America. Also, the insights of America's energy consultants, sold for even larger sums to Arab sheikhs. American design engineers are providing insights to Olivetti, Mazda, Siemens, and other global webs; American marketers, techniques for learning what worldwide consumers will buy; American advertisers, ploys for ensuring that they actually do. American architects are issuing designs and blueprints for opera houses, art galleries, museums, luxury hotels, and residential complexes in the world's major cities; American commercial property developers, marketing these properties to worldwide investors and purchasers.

Americans who specialize in the gentle art of public relations are in demand by corporations, governments, and politicians in virtually every nation. So, too, are American political consultants, some of whom, at this writing, are advising the Hungarian Socialist Party, the remnant of Hungary's ruling Communists, on how to salvage a few parliamentary seats in the nation's first free election in more than forty years. Also at this writing, a team of American agricultural consultants is advising the managers of a Soviet farm collective employing 1,700 Russians eighty miles outside Moscow. As noted, American investment bankers and lawyers specializing in financial circumnavigations are selling their insights to Asians and Europeans who are eager to discover how to make large amounts of money by moving large amounts of money.

Developing nations, meanwhile, are hiring American civil engineers to advise on building roads and dams. The present thaw in the Cold War will no doubt expand these opportunities. American engineers from Bechtel (a global firm notable for having employed both Caspar Weinberger and George Shultz for much larger sums than either earned in the Reagan administration) have begun helping the Soviets design and install a new generation of nuclear reactors. Nations also are hiring American bankers and lawyers to help them renegotiate the terms of their loans with global banks, and Washington lobbyists to help them with Congress, the Treasury, the World Bank, the IMF, and other politically sensitive institutions. In fits of obvious desperation, several nations emerging from communism have even hired American economists to teach them about capitalism.

Almost everyone around the world is buying the skills and insights of Americans who manipulate oral and visual symbols—musicians, sound engineers, film producers, makeup artists, directors, cinematographers, actors and actresses, boxers, scriptwriters, song-writers, and set designers. Among the wealthiest of symbolic analysts are Steven Spielberg, Bill Cosby, Charles Schulz, Eddie Murphy, Sylvester Stallone, Madonna, and other star directors and performers—who are almost as well known on the streets of Dresden and Tokyo as in the Back Bay of Boston. Less well rewarded but no less renowned are the unctuous anchors on Turner Broadcasting's Cable News, who appear daily, via satellite, in places ranging from Vietnam to Nigeria. Vanna White is the world's most-watched game-show hostess. Behind each of these familiar faces is a collection of American problem-solvers, -identifiers, and brokers who train, coach, advise, promote, amplify, direct, groom, represent, and otherwise add value to their talents.[16]

34   There are also the insights of senior American executives who occupy the world headquarters of global "American" corporations and the national or regional headquarters of global "foreign" corporations. Their insights are duly exported to the rest of the world through the webs of global enterprise. IBM does not export many machines from the United States, for example. Big Blue makes machines all over the globe and services them on the spot. Its prime American exports are symbolic and analytic. From IBM's world headquarters in Armonk, New York, emanate strategic brokerage and related management services bound for the rest of the world. In return, IBM's top executives are generously rewarded.

35   The most important reason for this expanding world market and increasing global demand for the symbolic and analytic insights of Americans has been the dramatic improvement in worldwide communication and transportation technologies. Designs, instructions, advice, and visual and audio symbols can be communicated more and more rapidly around the globe, with ever-greater precision and at ever-lower cost. Madonna's voice can be transported to billions of listeners, with perfect clarity, on digital compact discs. A new invention emanating from engineers in Battelle's laboratory in Columbus, Ohio, can be sent almost anywhere via modem, in a form that will allow others to examine it in three dimensions through enhanced computer graphics. When face-to-face meetings are still required—and videoconferencing will not suffice—it is relatively easy for designers, consultants, advisers, artists, and executives to board supersonic jets and, in a matter of hours, meet directly with their worldwide clients, customers, audiences, and employees.

36   With rising demand comes rising compensation. Whether in the form of licensing fees, fees for service, salaries, or shares in final profits, the economic result is much the same. There are also nonpecuniary rewards. One of the best-kept secrets among symbolic analysts is that so many of them enjoy their work. In fact, much of it does not count as work at all, in the traditional sense. The work of routine producers and in-person servers is typically monotonous; it causes muscles to tire or weaken and involves little independence or discre-

---

[16]In 1989, the entertainment business summoned to the United States $5.5 billion in foreign earnings—making it among the nation's largest export industries, just behind aerospace. U.S. Department of Commerce, International Trade Commission, "Composition of U.S. Exports," various issues.

tion. The "work" of symbolic analysts, by contrast, often involves puzzles, experiments, games, a significant amount of chatter, and substantial discretion over what to do next. Few routine producers or in-person servers would "work" if they did not need to earn the money. Many symbolic analysts would "work" even if money were no object.

At midcentury, when America was a national market dominated by core 37 pyramid-shaped corporations, there were constraints on the earnings of people at the highest rungs. First and most obviously, the market for their services was largely limited to the borders of the nation. In addition, whatever conceptual value they might contribute was small relative to the value gleaned from large scale—and it was dependent on large scale for whatever income it was to summon. Most of the problems to be identified and solved had to do with enhancing the efficiency of production and improving the flow of materials, parts, assembly, and distribution. Inventors searched for the rare breakthrough revealing an entirely new product to be made in high volume; management consultants, executives, and engineers thereafter tried to speed and synchronize its manufacture, to better achieve scale efficiencies; advertisers and marketers sought then to whet the public's appetite for the standard item that emerged. Since white-collar earnings increased with larger scale, there was considerable incentive to expand the firm; indeed, many of America's core corporations grew far larger than scale economies would appear to have justified.

By the 1990s, in contrast, the earnings of symbolic analysts were limited 38 neither by the size of the national market nor by the volume of production of the firms with which they were affiliated. The marketplace was worldwide, and conceptual value was high relative to value added from scale efficiencies.

There had been another constraint on high earnings, which also gave way by 39 the 1990s. At midcentury, the compensation awarded to top executives and advisers of the largest of America's core corporations could not be grossly out of proportion to that of low-level production workers. It would be unseemly for executives who engaged in highly visible rounds of bargaining with labor unions, and who routinely responded to government requests to moderate prices, to take home wages and benefits wildly in excess of what other Americans earned. Unless white-collar executives restrained themselves, moreover, blue-collar production workers could not be expected to restrain their own demands for higher wages. Unless both groups exercised restraint, the government could not be expected to forbear from imposing direct controls and regulations.

At the same time, the wages of production workers could not be allowed 40 to sink too low, lest there be insufficient purchasing power in the economy. After all, who would buy all the goods flowing out of American factories if not American workers? This, too, was part of the tacit bargain struck between American managers and their workers.

Recall the oft-repeated corporate platitude of the era about the chief exec- 41 utive's responsibility to carefully weigh and balance the interests of the corporation's disparate stakeholders. Under the stewardship of the corporate statesman, no set of stakeholders—least of all white-collar executives—was to gain a disproportionately large share of the benefits of corporate activity; nor was any stakeholder—especially the average worker—to be left with a share that was disproportionately small. Banal though it was, this idea helped to maintain the legitimacy of the core American corporation in the eyes of most Americans, and to ensure continued economic growth.

42   But by the 1990s, these informal norms were evaporating, just as (and largely because) the core American corporation was vanishing. The links between top executives and the American production worker were fading: an ever-increasing number of subordinates and contractees were foreign, and a steadily growing number of American routine producers were working for foreign-owned firms. An entire cohort of middle-level managers, who had once been deemed "white collar," had disappeared; and, increasingly, American executives were exporting their insights to global enterprise webs.

43   As the American corporation itself became a global web almost indistinguishable from any other, its stakeholders were turning into a large and diffuse group, spread over the world. Such global stakeholders were less visible, and far less noisy, than national stakeholders. And as the American corporation sold its goods and services all over the world, the purchasing power of American workers became far less relevant to its economic survival.

44   Thus have the inhibitions been removed. The salaries and benefits of America's top executives, and many of their advisers and consultants, have soared to what years before would have been unimaginable heights, even as those of other Americans have declined.

Questions for Discussion and Your Reading Journal

1. According to Reich, what are the three work "functions in the world economy" and how are workers in these categories faring overall?
2. Sum up Reich's views about why the "boat" containing routine workers is "sinking rapidly," in Reich's view?
3. Give at least four examples of "in-person server" jobs referred to in the text. Then sum up Reich's main points about why "in-person" servers are also losing out in today's global economy.
4. What impact will ageing baby-boomers have on younger generations of in-person server jobs and salaries, according to the reading?
5. Give at least four examples of "symbolic analyst" jobs and sum up the reasons Reich gives for the significant rise in job opportunities and salaries for these workers around the world.
6. What does the work of symbolic analysts involve, exactly?
7. According to Reich, why have the salaries of top executives in the United States risen to "unimaginable heights" at the same time that salaries of other Americans have gone down?
8. Sum up the kinds of evidence that Reich uses throughout the reading to support his points. Do you find his insights convincing? Explain.

WAR AND PEACE

GEORGE W. BUSH

George Walker Bush (1946–) was sworn in as the 43rd president of the United States in January 2001 after one of the closest and most contested elections in U.S. history. A sharply divided Supreme Court decision (5–4) finally awarded him the victory nearly a month after the actual voting process had ended. Bush's journey to the presidency was likewise unusual. After graduating from Yale University with a B.A. in 1968, he served in the Texas National Guard during the Vietnam War. He went on to earn a Master's of Business Administration degree at Harvard in 1975 and then followed the example of his father, President George H. W. Bush, by going into the Texas oil business. Although his father had made a fortune in oil, George W. Bush did not do nearly so well. In 1987–88, he took a leave from the corporate world to work as an advisor and speechwriter for his father's successful election to the presidency. After his father's victory, Bush turned to major league baseball for a career. From 1989 to 1994, he served as managing general partner for a group of investors who purchased the Texas Rangers baseball team. In 1994, he changed career paths again, entering the world of politics as his father had done. After a term as governor of Texas, Bush ran for and, ultimately, was declared the winner of the U.S. presidential elections of 2000. During his early days in office, Bush won approval from many conservative Americans for his unilateral approach to global issues in which he withdrew U.S. cooperation with other nations on a variety of fronts. Many observers around the world have since expressed shock and surprise that the United States would turn its back on the very multilateral relationships, international organizations, and global treaties that it spent over 50 years constructing in the aftermath of World War II. The following reading carries this unilateralism one step further, extending it to U.S. willingness to wage "preemptive war" against nations that are perceived as threatening to its security and its global interests. This policy reverses a more defensive U.S. policy throughout the nation's history that justified war only in response to foreign attack.

Reading Rhetorically

George Bush is sensitive to potential criticisms of U.S. unilateralism as he introduces the following National Security Strategy of the United States of America. To deflect these criticisms, he opens with an appeal to a common set of values that people in the United States share with many other peoples around the world. These include freedom, democracy, free enterprise, and basic human rights. Then he insists explicitly that the United States does not "use our strength to press for unilateral advantage" and outlines instead a more benevolent view of U.S. purposes and goals. Because he is writing a policy "statement" and not a formal argument, it is not requisite that he provide evidence to convince his audience of the validity of his position. Instead he moves on to a different kind of evidence to justify the main point of the new U.S. security strategy that has since become known as The Bush Doctrine. He turns to emotional concerns held by his readers surrounding the urgent issue in the United States of combating terrorism *(pathos)*. Here he outlines his administration's strategy for how best to deal with "shadowy networks" of new enemies requiring new approaches to warfare. One of the most significant and successful rhetorical moves made by the president is his effort to set up a classic "good" versus "evil" dichotomy that breaks the world into two groups. On one side are "the world's greatest powers," and on the other are the "dangers of terrorist violence and chaos." This two-part model is similar to the one used throughout the Cold War era to sim-plify the complex variations of capitalistic and communistic ideas that were present in nearly 200 nations around the globe. The simplification of com-plex issues into two parts allows Bush to reduce the world to a simple con-flict that people everywhere can understand and, ultimately, a conflict in which the world can be divided up again into two camps, as during the Cold War. By emphasizing this familiar model of "us" versus "them" and by por-traying "them" as negatively as possible, Bush offers a more compelling argument to his U.S. audience for a new doctrine of unilateral and preemp-tive warfare that significantly departs from the long tradition of defensive warfare in U.S. foreign policy. Throughout the rest of the policy statement, quotes from the president are used at the head of each new section to return readers to the basic rhetorical framework of "right" and "wrong" and to assure them that the U.S. government is in the "right" to implement its new security strategy.

The National Security Strategy of the United States of America (The Bush Doctrine)

INTRODUCTION

1   The great struggles of the twentieth century between liberty and totalitari-anism ended with a decisive victory for the forces of freedom—and a single sustainable model for national success: freedom, democracy, and free enterprise. In the twenty-first century, only nations that share a commitment to protecting basic human rights and guaranteeing political and economic free-dom will be able to unleash the potential of their people and assure their future

prosperity. People everywhere want to be able to speak freely; choose who will govern them; worship as they please; educate their children—male and female; own property; and enjoy the benefits of their labor. These values of freedom are right and true for every person, in every society—and the duty of protecting these values against their enemies is the common calling of freedom-loving people across the globe and across the ages.

Today, the United States enjoys a position of unparalleled military strength   2 and great economic and political influence. In keeping with our heritage and principles, we do not use our strength to press for unilateral advantage. We seek instead to create a balance of power that favors human freedom: conditions in which all nations and all societies can choose for themselves the rewards and challenges of political and economic liberty. In a world that is safe, people will be able to make their own lives better. We will defend the peace by fighting terrorists and tyrants. We will preserve the peace by building good relations among the great powers. We will extend the peace by encouraging free and open societies on every continent.

Defending our Nation against its enemies is the first and fundamental   3 commitment of the Federal Government. Today, that task has changed dramatically. Enemies in the past needed great armies and great industrial capabilities to endanger America. Now, shadowy networks of individuals can bring great chaos and suffering to our shores for less than it costs to purchase a single tank. Terrorists are organized to penetrate open societies and to turn the power of modern technologies against us.

To defeat this threat we must make use of every tool in our arsenal—   4 military power, better homeland defenses, law enforcement, intelligence, and vigorous efforts to cut off terrorist financing. The war against terrorists of global reach is a global enterprise of uncertain duration. America will help nations that need our assistance in combating terror. And America will hold to account nations that are compromised by terror, including those who harbor terrorists—because the allies of terror are the enemies of civilization. The United States and countries cooperating with us must not allow the terrorists to develop new home bases. Together, we will seek to deny them sanctuary at every turn.

The gravest danger our Nation faces lies at the crossroads of radicalism   5 and technology. Our enemies have openly declared that they are seeking weapons of mass destruction, and evidence indicates that they are doing so with determination. The United States will not allow these efforts to succeed. We will build defenses against ballistic missiles and other means of delivery. We will cooperate with other nations to deny, contain, and curtail our enemies' efforts to acquire dangerous technologies. And, as a matter of common sense and self-defense, America will act against such emerging threats before they are fully formed. We cannot defend America and our friends by hoping for the best. So we must be prepared to defeat our enemies' plans, using the best intelligence and proceeding with deliberation. History will judge harshly those who saw this coming danger but failed to act. In the new world we have entered, the only path to peace and security is the path of action.

As we defend the peace, we will also take advantage of an historic opportunity to preserve the peace. Today, the international community has the best   6 chance since the rise of the nation-state in the seventeenth century to build a world where great powers compete in peace instead of continually prepare for war. Today, the world's great powers find ourselves on the same side—united by common dangers of terrorist violence and chaos. The United States will build on these common interests to promote global security. We are also increasingly united by common values. Russia is in the midst of a hopeful transition, reaching for its democratic future and a partner in the war on terror. Chinese leaders are discovering that economic freedom is the only source of national wealth. In time, they will find that social and political freedom is the only source of national greatness. America will encourage the advancement of democracy and economic openness in both nations, because these are the best foundations for domestic stability and international order. We will strongly resist aggression from other great powers—even as we welcome their peaceful pursuit of prosperity, trade, and cultural advancement.

7   Finally, the United States will use this moment of opportunity to extend the benefits of freedom across the globe. We will actively work to bring the hope of democracy, development, free markets, and free trade to every corner of the world. The events of September 11, 2001, taught us that weak states, like Afghanistan, can pose as great a danger to our national interests as strong states. Poverty does not make poor people into terrorists and murderers. Yet poverty, weak institutions, and corruption can make weak states vulnerable to terrorist networks and drug cartels within their borders.

8   The United States will stand beside any nation determined to build a better future by seeking the rewards of liberty for its people. Free trade and free markets have proven their ability to lift whole societies out of poverty—so the United States will work with individual nations, entire regions, and the entire global trading community to build a world that trades in freedom and therefore grows in prosperity. The United States will deliver greater development assistance through the New Millennium Challenge Account to nations that govern justly, invest in their people, and encourage economic freedom. We will also continue to lead the world in efforts to reduce the terrible toll of HIV/AIDS and other infectious diseases.

9   In building a balance of power that favors freedom, the United States is guided by the conviction that all nations have important responsibilities. Nations that enjoy freedom must actively fight terror. Nations that depend on international stability must help prevent the spread of weapons of mass destruction. Nations that seek international aid must govern themselves wisely, so that aid is well spent. For freedom to thrive, accountability must be expected and required.

10   We are also guided by the conviction that no nation can build a safer, better world alone. Alliances and multilateral institutions can multiply the strength of freedom-loving nations. The United States is committed to lasting institutions like the United Nations, the World Trade Organization, the Organization of American States, and NATO as well as other long-standing alliances. Coalitions of the willing can augment these permanent institutions. In all cases, international obligations are to be taken seriously. They are not to be undertaken symbolically to rally support for an ideal without furthering its attainment.

Freedom is the non-negotiable demand of human dignity; the birthright of 11 every person—in every civilization. Throughout history, freedom has been threatened by war and terror; it has been challenged by the clashing wills of powerful states and the evil designs of tyrants; and it has been tested by widespread poverty and disease. Today, humanity holds in its hands the opportunity to further freedom's triumph over all these foes. The United States welcomes our responsibility to lead in this great mission.

George W. Bush
The White House,
September 17, 2002

I. OVERVIEW OF AMERICA'S INTERNATIONAL STRATEGY

"Our Nation's cause has always been larger than our Nation's defense. We 12 fight, as we always fight, for a just peace—a peace that favors liberty. We will defend the peace against the threats from terrorists and tyrants. We will preserve the peace by building good relations among the great powers. And we will extend the peace by encouraging free and open societies on every continent."

PRESIDENT BUSH
West Point, New York
June 1, 2002

The United States possesses unprecedented—and unequaled—strength and 13 influence in the world. Sustained by faith in the principles of liberty, and the value of a free society, this position comes with unparalleled responsibilities, obligations, and opportunity. The great strength of this nation must be used to promote a balance of power that favors freedom.

For most of the twentieth century, the world was divided by a great strug- 14 gle over ideas: destructive totalitarian visions versus freedom and equality.

That great struggle is over. The militant visions of class, nation, and race 15 which promised utopia and delivered misery have been defeated and discredited. America is now threatened less by conquering states than we are by failing ones. We are menaced less by fleets and armies than by catastrophic technologies in the hands of the embittered few. We must defeat these threats to our Nation, allies, and friends.

This is also a time of opportunity for America. We will work to translate 16 this moment of influence into decades of peace, prosperity, and liberty. The U.S. national security strategy will be based on a distinctly American internationalism that reflects the union of our values and our national interests. The aim of this strategy is to help make the world not just safer but better. Our goals on the path to progress are clear: political and economic freedom, peaceful relations with other states, and respect for human dignity.

And this path is not America's alone. It is open to all. To achieve these 17 goals, the United States will:

- champion aspirations for human dignity;
- strengthen alliances to defeat global terrorism and work to prevent attacks against us and our friends;
- work with others to defuse regional conflicts;
- prevent our enemies from threatening us, our allies, and our friends, with weapons of mass destruction;
- ignite a new era of global economic growth through free markets and free trade;
- expand the circle of development by opening societies and building the infrastructure of democracy;
- develop agendas for cooperative action with other main centers of global power; and
- transform America's national security institutions to meet the challenges and opportunities of the twenty-first century.

II. CHAMPION ASPIRATIONS FOR HUMAN DIGNITY

18   "Some worry that it is somehow undiplomatic or impolite to speak the language of right and wrong. I disagree. Different circumstances require different methods, but not different moralities."

PRESIDENT BUSH
West Point, New York
June 1, 2002

19   In pursuit of our goals, our first imperative is to clarify what we stand for: the United States must defend liberty and justice because these principles are right and true for all people everywhere. No nation owns these aspirations, and no nation is exempt from them. Fathers and mothers in all societies want their children to be educated and to live free from poverty and violence. No people on earth yearn to be oppressed, aspire to servitude, or eagerly await the midnight knock of the secret police.

20   America must stand firmly for the nonnegotiable demands of human dignity: the rule of law; limits on the absolute power of the state; free speech; freedom of worship; equal justice; respect for women; religious and ethnic tolerance; and respect for private property.

21   These demands can be met in many ways. America's constitution has served us well. Many other nations, with different histories and cultures, facing different circumstances, have successfully incorporated these core principles into their own systems of governance. History has not been kind to those nations which ignored or flouted the rights and aspirations of their people.

22   America's experience as a great multi-ethnic democracy affirms our conviction that people of many heritages and faiths can live and prosper in peace. Our own history is a long struggle to live up to our ideals. But even in our worst moments, the principles enshrined in the Declaration of Independence were there to guide us. As a result, America is not just a stronger, but is a freer and more just society.

23   Today, these ideals are a lifeline to lonely defenders of liberty. And when openings arrive, we can encourage change—as we did in central and eastern

Europe between 1989 and 1991, or in Belgrade in 2000. When we see democratic processes take hold among our friends in Taiwan or in the Republic of Korea, and see elected leaders replace generals in Latin America and Africa, we see examples of how authoritarian systems can evolve, marrying local history and traditions with the principles we all cherish.

Embodying lessons from our past and using the opportunity we have 24 today, the national security strategy of the United States must start from these core beliefs and look outward for possibilities to expand liberty.

Our principles will guide our government's decisions about international 25 cooperation, the character of our foreign assistance, and the allocation of resources. They will guide our actions and our words in international bodies.

We will: 26

- speak out honestly about violations of the nonnegotiable demands of human dignity using our voice and vote in international institutions to advance freedom;
- use our foreign aid to promote freedom and support those who struggle nonviolently for it, ensuring that nations moving toward democracy are rewarded for the steps they take;
- make freedom and the development of democratic institutions key themes in our bilateral relations, seeking solidarity and cooperation from other democracies while we press governments that deny human rights to move toward a better future; and
- take special efforts to promote freedom of religion and conscience and defend it from encroachment by repressive governments.

We will champion the cause of human dignity and oppose those who resist it.

III. STRENGTHEN ALLIANCES TO DEFEAT GLOBAL TERRORISM AND WORK TO PREVENT ATTACKS AGAINST US AND OUR FRIENDS

"Just three days removed from these events, Americans do not yet have the dis- 27 tance of history. But our responsibility to history is already clear: to answer these attacks and rid the world of evil. War has been waged against us by stealth and deceit and murder. This nation is peaceful, but fierce when stirred to anger. The conflict was begun on the timing and terms of others. It will end in a way, and at an hour, of our choosing."

PRESIDENT BUSH
Washington, D.C. (The National Cathedral)
September 14, 2001

The United States of America is fighting a war against terrorists of global 28 reach. The enemy is not a single political regime or person or religion or ideology. The enemy is terrorism—premeditated, politically motivated violence perpetrated against innocents.

29   In many regions, legitimate grievances prevent the emergence of a lasting peace. Such grievances deserve to be, and must be, addressed within a political process. But no cause justifies terror. The United States will make no concessions to terrorist demands and strike no deals with them. We make no distinction between terrorists and those who knowingly harbor or provide aid to them.

30   The struggle against global terrorism is different from any other war in our history. It will be fought on many fronts against a particularly elusive enemy over an extended period of time. Progress will come through the persistent accumulation of successes—some seen, some unseen.

31   Today our enemies have seen the results of what civilized nations can, and will, do against regimes that harbor, support, and use terrorism to achieve their political goals. Afghanistan has been liberated; coalition forces continue to hunt down the Taliban and al-Qaida. But it is not only this battlefield on which we will engage terrorists. Thousands of trained terrorists remain at large with cells in North America, South America, Europe, Africa, the Middle East, and across Asia.

32   Our priority will be first to disrupt and destroy terrorist organizations of global reach and attack their leadership; command, control, and communications; material support; and finances. This will have a disabling effect upon the terrorists' ability to plan and operate.

33   We will continue to encourage our regional partners to take up a coordinated effort that isolates the terrorists. Once the regional campaign localizes the threat to a particular state, we will help ensure the state has the military, law enforcement, political, and financial tools necessary to finish the task.

34   The United States will continue to work with our allies to disrupt the financing of terrorism. We will identify and block the sources of funding for terrorism, freeze the assets of terrorists and those who support them, deny terrorists access to the international financial system, protect legitimate charities from being abused by terrorists, and prevent the movement of terrorists' assets through alternative financial networks.

35   However, this campaign need not be sequential to be effective, the cumulative effect across all regions will help achieve the results we seek. We will disrupt and destroy terrorist organizations by:

36   • direct and continuous action using all the elements of national and international power. Our immediate focus will be those terrorist organizations of global reach and any terrorist or state sponsor of terrorism which attempts to gain or use weapons of mass destruction (WMD) or their precursors;

37   • defending the United States, the American people, and our interests at home and abroad by identifying and destroying the threat before it reaches our borders. While the United States will constantly strive to enlist the support of the international community, we will not hesitate to act alone, if necessary, to exercise our right of selfdefense by acting preemptively against such terrorists, to prevent them from doing harm against our people and our country; and

38   • denying further sponsorship, support, and sanctuary to terrorists by convincing or compelling states to accept their sovereign responsibilities. We will also wage a war of ideas to win the battle against international terrorism. This includes:

- using the full influence of the United States, and working closely with allies 39 and friends, to make clear that all acts of terrorism are illegitimate so that terrorism will be viewed in the same light as slavery, piracy, or genocide: behavior that no respectable government can condone or support and all must oppose;
- supporting moderate and modern government, especially in the Muslim 40 world, to ensure that the conditions and ideologies that promote terrorism do not find fertile ground in any nation;
- diminishing the underlying conditions that spawn terrorism by enlisting the 41 international community to focus its efforts and resources on areas most at risk; and
- using effective public diplomacy to promote the free flow of information 42 and ideas to kindle the hopes and aspirations of freedom of those in societies ruled by the sponsors of global terrorism.

While we recognize that our best defense is a good offense, we are also 43 strengthening America's homeland security to protect against and deter attack. This Administration has proposed the largest government reorganization since the Truman Administration created the National Security Council and the Department of Defense. Centered on a new Department of Homeland Security and including a new unified military command and a fundamental reordering of the FBI, our comprehensive plan to secure the homeland encompasses every level of government and the cooperation of the public and the private sector.

This strategy will turn adversity into opportunity. For example, emergency 44 management systems will be better able to cope not just with terrorism but with all hazards. Our medical system will be strengthened to manage not just bioterror, but all infectious diseases and mass-casualty dangers. Our border controls will not just stop terrorists, but improve the efficient movement of legitimate traffic.

While our focus is protecting America, we know that to defeat terrorism in 45 today's globalized world we need support from our allies and friends. Wherever possible, the United States will rely on regional organizations and state powers to meet their obligations to fight terrorism. Where governments find the fight against terrorism beyond their capacities, we will match their willpower and their resources with whatever help we and our allies can provide.

As we pursue the terrorists in Afghanistan, we will continue to work with 46 international organizations such as the United Nations, as well as non-governmental organizations, and other countries to provide the humanitarian, political, economic, and security assistance necessary to rebuild Afghanistan so that it will never again abuse its people, threaten its neighbors, and provide a haven for terrorists.

In the war against global terrorism, we will never forget that we are ulti- 47 mately fighting for our democratic values and way of life. Freedom and fear are at war, and there will be no quick or easy end to this conflict. In leading the campaign against terrorism, we are forging new, productive international relationships and redefining existing ones in ways that meet the challenges of the twenty-first century.

Questions for Discussion and Your Reading Journal

1. Bush argues in his introduction that "freedom, democracy, and free enterprise" represent the "single sustainable model for national success." How might the 1.3 billion people in China or citizens in other socialist nations around the world respond to this claim? (See Mao Tse-tung and Julius K. Nyerere readings earlier in this chapter.)

2. In your opinion, why does Bush bring up "values" (Paragraph 1) in this document that is actually about national defense?

3. Explain what Bush sees as "the gravest danger our Nation faces" (Paragraph 5) at this time? Do you agree?

4. How does poverty link to terrorism, in Bush's view?

5. If Bush's call for ongoing efforts to "prevent the spread of weapons of mass destruction" (Paragraph 9) are successful, who will be left possessing these weapons? How might nations without these weapons feel about this policy?

6. Sum up in one short paragraph the main points that Bush Administration writers make in Section I. Overview of America's International Strategy.

7. Sum up in one short paragraph the main points that Bush Administration writers make in Section II. Champion Aspirations for Human Dignity.

8. In Section III, the Bush writers define terrorism as "premeditated, politically motivated violence penetrated against innocents." Can you think of historical examples of free nations conducting "state-sponsored terrorism" if we apply this definition to their actions?

9. The bulleted items in Section III present the most criticized principles of the Bush Doctrine. Which policies outlined there do you think might cause concern among other nations of the world and even among our best allies?

10. The Bush Administration and mainstream Americans have often been criticized for assuming that most peoples living in other lands ultimately want to be "more like us" in terms of social values and institutions. Do you find any evidence of this attitude in the reading overall?

11. Compare the tone and the attitude of this reading toward global cultural diversity with the tone of Kofi Annan's or Jimmy Carter's speeches (also included in this chapter). In what ways are they similar? In what ways are they different?

CHARLES COLSON

Charles Colson (1931–) was voted the "Outstanding Young Man of 1960" by the Chamber of Commerce in his hometown of Boston. In 1969, he joined the Nixon Administration as a special counsel to the *president, where he soon became known as the "evil genius" behind many of President Nixon's efforts to cover up his illegal actions in the Watergate case. In 1974, Colson pled guilty to charges of obstruction of justice in the Watergate scandal and went to prison for 7 months. During this troubled period in his life, he became a born-again Christian and began to turn his "genius" to legal causes. In 1976, he founded the Prison Fellowship Ministries, a volunteer organization that offers Christian Bible study to prison inmates and to their families. Seven years later, he founded Justice Fellowship, a related organization that pushes for prison reform based upon biblical notions of criminal justice. In 1993, Colson won the Templeton Prize for Progress in Religion and donated the $1 million award to Prison Fellowship Ministries, as he has done with the money from some 20 books that he has written over the years. He has become a sought-after guest speaker by conservative groups in the United States and elsewhere and currently hosts his own syndicated radio talk show, "Breakpoint." In his article, Colson defends the first use of the Bush Doctrine of preemptive war against Iraq.*

Reading Rhetorically

Colson's position supporting the Bush Administration's attack upon Iraq is valuable to consider because, according to surveys at the time, a large majority of American citizens likewise supported an attack on Iraq. Some 70 percent of Americans continued to believe that Iraq had played a role in the terrorist attacks of 9/11 long after the CIA and other global intelligence organizations had insisted repeatedly in news articles throughout America that there was no evidence to support this. Because of this popular misconception, Colson could generally count upon a favorable response to his pro-war position by his American, and largely Christian, audience. With this audience in mind, Colson opens by challenging the position of another major Christian group, the Conference of Catholic Bishops, who held that a preemptive attack on Iraq would be difficult to justify under the Christian "just war" tradition. He uses evidence from the teachings of St. Augustine, a Christian teacher and saint, to argue that preemptive attacks can be "just." He supports this with his assertion that "the Christian wields the sword in fulfillment of the command to love our neighbors because we are protecting the innocent from the aggressor." He does not need to spell out who, precisely, is the "aggressor" and who is the "innocent" in this case as he could count on his audience to assume that Iraq had aggressively attacked the United States on 9/11, or, for those who knew this was not so, that Iraq at least might do so at some time in the future. The attendant assumption thereby follows that U.S. citizens were the innocent ones who were fighting a just war to protect themselves against the aggression of the Iraqis. This is a good example of the effective use of rhetoric grounded in popular assumptions and public fear (pathos) more than in established facts and concrete evidence (logos).

Just War, Preemption, and Iraq

1   Earlier this week, the U.S. Conference of Catholic Bishops expressed what it called "grave reservations" about a possible preemptive attack on Iraq. Bishop Wilton Gregory, the conference's president, said that it would be difficult to justify such an attack under the just war tradition.

2   With all due respect, I believe the bishops to be wrong.

3   The issue of whether a preemptive strike could be justified under the just war doctrine came up during a meeting I attended at the Pentagon last fall. Secretary of Defense Donald Rumsfeld asked religious leaders to come and give him advice on whether the just war tradition was being applied to the war in Afghanistan.

4   During the meeting, I asked the secretary, "How would you justify a preemptive strike against Iraq?" That led to a fascinating discussion about the administration's options in its prosecution of the war against terrorism. Rumsfeld argued that the 1981 Israeli bombing of an Iraqi nuclear power plant suspected of producing material for nuclear weapons set a precedent that the U.S. was prepared to follow.

5   Less than a year later, the question about preemptive strikes against Iraq is no longer hypothetical. As the administration makes it case, it's imperative that Christians be heard on this issue.

6   The just war tradition, most famously articulated by St. Augustine, requires that both the cause for which a war is fought and the means by which it is fought be just. Historically, this has meant that military force must be used only in response to an attack already underway.

7   But in some cases, waiting for the other side to shoot first is tantamount to committing national suicide. This led to the idea known as "preemption." As theologian George Weigel has written, preemption recognizes that sometimes "preemptive military action is not only morally justifiable but morally imperative."

8   During the Cold War, some argued that to keep the Soviets from having a "first-strike" capability, the U.S. should attack first. But Christians and our government realized that the U.S. could not do that. It meant targeting civilians, since under the mutually assured destruction policy, both sides were holding the other's cities hostage, and that kept a war from breaking out.

9   But the situation in Iraq is different. An attack would not—as in the Cold War—mean an attack on civilians. And whether preemption can be justified in the case of Iraq is a prudential judgment depending on the facts. And it's a case that the administration is obligated to make. If they can show that Iraq has weapons of mass destruction, and that it is preparing to use them or put them in the hands of those who will, then a preemptive strike would be morally justified. Of course, that strike must honor just war principles like protection of noncombatants.

10   One thing often forgotten in discussions of just war is why we fight these wars. As Augustine wrote, it's not out of a desire for revenge or even a desire to punish wrongdoers. Rather, the Christian wields the sword in fulfillment of

the command to love our neighbors because we are protecting the innocent from the aggressor.

This love of neighbor is what impels us to take an active role in the debates over the possible use of military force—because the Christian perspective needs to be heard as Congress debates the grave question of carrying this war to Baghdad.

11

Questions for Discussion and Your Reading Journal

1. Colson makes clear early on that he does not agree with the Conference of Catholic Bishops. At what point in the reading do you learn what his actual position is on the moral justification of a preemptive attack on Iraq?
2. What evidence does Colson offer to support his main claim convincingly? Do you find his evidence convincing? Explain.
3. In the second-to-last paragraph, Colson attempts to reconcile killing people in war with the Christian "command to love our neighbors." Do you find that he does so successfully? Explain.

JIMMY CARTER

James Earl Carter (1924–) became the 39th president of the United States in January of 1976. As a young man, he graduated in the top 10 percent of his class from the U.S. Naval Academy in 1946 and, 2 years later, was among an elite group of officers who were selected to pioneer the development of nuclear submarines for his country. Carter left the Navy upon his father's death in 1953 to return to his hometown of Plains, Georgia, and to run the family peanut farm. He had turned this small farm into a thriving business with a million dollars in assets by the time he left Georgia to serve as president 23 years later. As president, Carter made human rights a basic tenet of his foreign policy at a time when major nations of the world had yet to fully embrace such principles. He also proved himself an adept peacemaker by successfully persuading Israeli Premier Menahem Begin and Egyptian President Anwar el-Sadat to sign the Camp David accord in 1979. Carter's peacemaking skills were further challenged in 1979 when the people of Iran revolted against the repressive reign of the U.S.-supported Shah and took members of the American embassy staff prisoners for nearly 15 months. The Iranian hostage crisis overseas and a dismal economy at home combined to weaken Carter's bid for a second term as president, and he lost the 1980 elections to Ronald Reagan. Since leaving office, Carter has worked as a champion for human rights, for just and fair elections in troubled nations, for better health care, and for peace around the world. His success in international human rights efforts, as a monitor of fair elections in a variety of foreign nations, as an international mediator of conflicts in North Korea, Haiti, and Bosnia, plus his work to end epidemics in

Africa through his Carter Center, and his support of Habitat for Humanity all combined to earn him the Nobel Peace Prize in 2002. The following reading is his Nobel Prize acceptance speech. In this speech Carter responds to The Bush Doctrine articulated in the previous reading.

Reading Rhetorically

When Carter presented the following speech in December 2002, the world was in a state of high tension with the United States. The Bush Administration was on the brink of implementing its new "preemptive war" strategy against Iraq. Although most of the rest of the world accepted the earlier U.S. invasion of Afghanistan as a justified defensive action against the Taliban and Al Qaida in response to the terrorist attacks of 9/11, few nations supported an unprovoked attack upon Iraq. Countries like France and Germany were arguing convincingly to fellow member states of the United Nations that Iraq had been decimated by over 10 years of U.N. sanctions and that it posed little threat to its immediate neighbors, let alone to the United States, which was thousands of miles away. As a recipient of the Nobel Peace Prize, Carter found himself in a position to influence global opinion on this political standoff, and yet his role as a peacemaker was out of harmony with the decision making of his own current president, George W. Bush. At the time of his speech, Bush and his advisors were lobbying the U.N. Security Council to pass a resolution authorizing immediate attack on Iraq as part of an ambitious U.S. plan to create a more democratic and more Western-friendly nation in the Middle East. Carter used the opening of the speech to overview the sacrifices he and others have made for peace. He chose to speak of peace from the perspective of a "submarine officer," showing that he was personally aware that war and self-sacrifice are required "to defend our nation and its principles" at times. To this he added mention of his former role as "Commander-in-Chief of our armed forces" and the "sobering responsibility" that he felt to maintain peace during the height of the Cold War. Such references build what Aristotle called *ethos*, the credibility and believability of the person speaking to us. In order to effectively challenge the policies and actions of President Bush on the world stage, Carter had to argue in a manner that was fair, reasonable, and extremely well grounded. Note how he links "great American power" with a sense of great "responsibility" in a historical review of American democracy and respect for international law as demonstrated by other American presidents and political leaders before him. Finally, near the middle of his speech, Carter offered his position on the issue of an American preemptive war in Iraq. As many listeners might have expected, it is in opposition to the Bush position. He stated, "For powerful countries to adopt a principle of preventative war may well set an example that can have catastrophic consequences." In the place of preemptive war, Carter urged collaboration and cooperation with the U.N. Security Council, things that the Bush Administration was resisting. The remainder of Carter's speech pulled together support and evidence from a wide variety of personal experiences and examples in U.S. and world history to drive home his main points. Carter ended with an eloquent restatement of his main point that rhetorically leaves his listeners and readers with something to think about after his speech has ended: "War may sometimes be a necessary evil. But no matter how necessary, it is always an evil, never a good. We will not learn how to live together in peace by killing each other's children."

Nobel Peace Prize Lecture

Your Majesties, Members of the Norwegian Nobel Committee, Excellencies, Ladies and Gentlemen, 1

It is with a deep sense of gratitude that I accept this prize. I am grateful to my wife Rosalynn, to my colleagues at The Carter Center, and to many others who continue to seek an end to violence and suffering throughout the world. The scope and character of our Center's activities are perhaps unique, but in many other ways they are typical of the work being done by many hundreds of nongovernmental organizations that strive for human rights and peace. 2

Most Nobel Laureates have carried out our work in safety, but there are others who have acted with great personal courage. None has provided more vivid reminders of the dangers of peacemaking than two of my friends, Anwar Sadat and Yitzak Rabin, who gave their lives for the cause of peace in the Middle East. 3

Like these two heroes, my first chosen career was in the military, as a submarine officer. My shipmates and I realized that we had to be ready to fight if combat was forced upon us, and we were prepared to give our lives to defend our nation and its principles. At the same time, we always prayed fervently that our readiness would ensure that there would be no war. 4

Later, as President and as Commander-in-Chief of our armed forces, I was one of those who bore the sobering responsibility of maintaining global stability during the height of the Cold War, as the world's two superpowers confronted each other. Both sides understood that an unresolved political altercation or a serious misjudgment could lead to a nuclear holocaust. In Washington and in Moscow, we knew that we would have less than a half hour to respond after we learned that intercontinental missiles had been launched against us. There had to be a constant and delicate balancing of our great military strength with aggressive diplomacy, always seeking to build friendships with other nations, large and small, that shared a common cause. 5

In those days, the nuclear and conventional armaments of the United States and the Soviet Union were almost equal, but democracy ultimately prevailed because of commitments to freedom and human rights, not only by people in my country and those of our allies, but in the former Soviet empire as well. As president, I extended my public support and encouragement to Andrei Sakharov, who, although denied the right to attend the ceremony, was honored here for his personal commitments to these same ideals. 6

The world has changed greatly since I left the White House. Now there is only one superpower, with unprecedented military and economic strength. The coming budget for American armaments will be greater than those of the next 7 fifteen nations combined, and there are troops from the United States in many countries throughout the world. Our gross national economy exceeds that of the three countries that follow us, and our nation's voice most often prevails as decisions are made concerning trade, humanitarian assistance, and the allocation of global wealth. This dominant status is unlikely to change in our lifetimes.

8   Great American power and responsibility are not unprecedented, and have been used with restraint and great benefit in the past. We have not assumed that super strength guarantees super wisdom, and we have consistently reached out to the international community to ensure that our own power and influence are tempered by the best common judgment.

9   Within our country, ultimate decisions are made through democratic means, which tend to moderate radical or ill-advised proposals. Constrained and inspired by historic constitutional principles, our nation has endeavored for more than two hundred years to follow the now almost universal ideals of freedom, human rights, and justice for all.

10   Our president, Woodrow Wilson, was honored here for promoting the League of Nations, whose two basic concepts were profoundly important; "collective security" and "self-determination." Now they are embedded in international law. Violations of these premises during the last half-century have been tragic failures, as was vividly demonstrated when the Soviet Union attempted to conquer Afghanistan and when Iraq invaded Kuwait.

11   After the second world war, American Secretary of State Cordell Hull received this prize for his role in founding the United Nations. His successor, General George C. Marshall, was recognized because of his efforts to help rebuild Europe, without excluding the vanquished nations of Italy and Germany. This was a historic example of respecting human rights at the international level.

12   Ladies and gentlemen:

13   Twelve years ago, President Mikhail Gorbachev received your recognition for his preeminent role in ending the Cold War that had lasted fifty years.

14   But instead of entering a millennium of peace, the world is now, in many ways, a more dangerous place. The greater ease of travel and communication has not been matched by equal understanding and mutual respect. There is a plethora of civil wars, unrestrained by rules of the Geneva Convention, within which an overwhelming portion of the casualties are unarmed civilians who have no ability to defend themselves. And recent appalling acts of terrorism have reminded us that no nations, even superpowers, are invulnerable.

15   It is clear that global challenges must be met with an emphasis on peace, in harmony with others, with strong alliances and international consensus. Imperfect as it may be, there is no doubt that this can best be done through the United Nations, which Ralph Bunche described here in this same forum as exhibiting a "fortunate flexibility"—not merely to preserve peace but also to make change, even radical change, without violence.

16   He went on to say: "To suggest that war can prevent war is a base play on words and a despicable form of warmongering. The objective of any who sin-

cerely believe in peace clearly must be to exhaust every honorable recourse in the effort to save the peace. The world has had ample evidence that war begets only conditions that beget further war."

We must remember that today there are at least eight nuclear powers on   17 earth, and three of them are threatening to their neighbors in areas of great international tension. For powerful countries to adopt a principle of preventive war may well set an example that can have catastrophic consequences.

If we accept the premise that the United Nations is the best avenue for the   18 maintenance of peace, then the carefully considered decisions of the United Nations Security Council must be enforced. All too often, the alternative has proven to be uncontrollable violence and expanding spheres of hostility.

For more than half a century, following the founding of the State of Israel   19 in 1948, the Middle East conflict has been a source of worldwide tension. At Camp David in 1978 and in Oslo in 1993, Israelis, Egyptians, and Palestinians have endorsed the only reasonable prescription for peace: United Nations Resolution 242. It condemns the acquisition of territory by force, calls for withdrawal of Israel from the occupied territories, and provides for Israelis to live securely and in harmony with their neighbors. There is no other mandate whose implementation could more profoundly improve international relationships.

Perhaps of more immediate concern is the necessity for Iraq to comply   20 fully with the unanimous decision of the Security Council that it eliminate all weapons of mass destruction and permit unimpeded access by inspectors to confirm that this commitment has been honored. The world insists that this be done.

I thought often during my years in the White House of an admonition that   21 we received in our small school in Plains, Georgia, from a beloved teacher, Miss Julia Coleman. She often said: "We must adjust to changing times and still hold to unchanging principles."

When I was a young boy, this same teacher also introduced me to Leo Tol-   22 stoy's novel, "War and Peace." She interpreted that powerful narrative as a reminder that the simple human attributes of goodness and truth can overcome great power. She also taught us that an individual is not swept along on a tide of inevitability but can influence even the greatest human events.

These premises have been proven by the lives of many heroes, some of   23 whose names were little known outside their own regions until they became Nobel laureates: Albert John Lutuli, Norman Borlaug, Desmond Tutu, Elle Wiesel, Aung San Suu Kyi, Jody Williams and even Albert Schweitzer and Mother Teresa. All of these and others have proven that even without government power—and often in opposition to it—individuals can enhance human rights and wage peace, actively and effectively.

The Nobel prize also profoundly magnified the inspiring global influence   24 of Martin Luther King, Jr., the greatest leader that my native state has ever produced. On a personal note, it is unlikely that my political career beyond Georgia would have been possible without the changes brought about by the civil rights movement in the American south and throughout our nation.

25   On the steps of our memorial to Abraham Lincoln, Dr. King said: "I have a dream that on the red hills of Georgia the sons of former slaves and the sons of former slaveowners will be able to sit down together at a table of brotherhood."

26   The scourge of racism has not been vanquished, either in the red hills of our state or around the world. And yet we see ever more frequent manifestations of his dream of racial healing. In a symbolic but very genuine way, at least involving two Georgians, it is coming true in Oslo today.

27   I am not here as a public official, but as a citizen of a troubled world who finds hope in a growing consensus that the generally accepted goals of society are peace, freedom, human rights, environmental quality, the alleviation of suffering, and the rule of law.

28   During the past decades, the international community, usually under the auspices of the United Nations, has struggled to negotiate global standards that can help us achieve these essential goals. They include: the abolition of land mines and chemical weapons; an end to the testing, proliferation, and further deployment of nuclear warheads; constraints on global warming; prohibition of the death penalty, at least for children; and an international criminal court to deter and to punish war crimes and genocide. Those agreements already adopted must be fully implemented, and others should be pursued aggressively.

29   We must also strive to correct the injustice of economic sanctions that seek to penalize abusive leaders but all too often inflict punishment on those who are already suffering from the abuse.

30   The unchanging principles of life predate modern times. I worship Jesus Christ, whom we Christians consider to be the Prince of Peace. As a Jew, he taught us to cross religious boundaries, in service and in love. He repeatedly reached out and embraced Roman conquerors, other Gentiles, and even the more despised Samaritans.

31   Despite theological differences, all great religions share common commitments that define our ideal secular relationships. I am convinced that Christians, Muslims, Buddhists, Hindus, Jews, and others can embrace each other in a common effort to alleviate human suffering and to espouse peace.

32   But the present era is a challenging and disturbing time for those whose lives are shaped by religious faith based on kindness toward each other. We have been reminded that cruel and inhuman acts can be derived from distorted theological beliefs, as suicide bombers take the lives of innocent human beings, draped falsely in the cloak of God's will. With horrible brutality, neighbors have massacred neighbors in Europe, Asia, and Africa.

33   In order for us human beings to commit ourselves personally to the inhumanity of war, we find it necessary first to dehumanize our opponents, which is in itself a violation of the beliefs of all religions. Once we characterize our adversaries as beyond the scope of God's mercy and grace, their lives lose all value. We deny personal responsibility when we plant landmines and, days or years later, a stranger to us—often a child—is crippled or killed. From a great distance, we launch bombs or missiles with almost total impunity, and never want to know the number or identity of the victims.

34   At the beginning of this new millennium I was asked to discuss, here in Oslo, the greatest challenge that the world faces. Among all the possible

choices, I decided that the most serious and universal problem is the growing chasm between the richest and poorest people on earth. Citizens of the ten wealthiest countries are now seventy-five times richer than those who live in the ten poorest ones, and the separation is increasing every year, not only between nations but also within them. The results of this disparity are root causes of most of the world's unresolved problems, including starvation, illiteracy, environmental degradation, violent conflict, and unnecessary illnesses that range from Guinea worm to HIV/AIDS.

Most work of The Carter Center is in remove villages in the poorest 35 nations of Africa, and there I have witnessed the capacity of destitute people to persevere under heartbreaking conditions. I have come to admire their judgment and wisdom, their courage and faith, and their awesome accomplishments when given a chance to use their innate abilities.

But tragically, in the industrialized world there is a terrible absence of 36 understanding or concern about those who are enduring lives of despair and hopelessness. We have not yet made the commitment to share with others an appreciable part of our excessive wealth. This is a potentially rewarding burden that we should all be willing to assume.

Ladies and gentlemen: 37

War may sometimes be a necessary evil. But no matter how necessary, it is 38 always an evil, never a good. We will not learn how to live together in peace by killing each other's children.

The bond of our common humanity is stronger than the divisiveness of 39 our fears and prejudices. God gives us the capacity for choice. We can choose to alleviate suffering. We can choose to work together for peace. We can make these changes—and we must.

Thank you.

Questions for Discussion and Your Reading Journal

1. Early in his speech, Carter touches upon his background as a submarine officer in the Navy and his role as Commander-in-Chief of the U.S. military. In your opinion, how do these statements prepare his audience for his later position on launching a preemptive war in Iraq?
2. What is Carter's response to the policy of powerful nations adopting the principle of "preventative war"? To whom and to what nation can you assume he was referring?
3. What does Carter argue is the one action that could be taken to "profoundly improve international relationships"?
4. As you read Paragraph 28, how does it affect your understanding of Carter's rhetorical purpose to know that the Bush Administration had withdrawn from or refused to respect the precise initiatives he lists?
5. What point does Carter make after he proclaims "I worship Jesus Christ . . . ." How is this point different from the one made by fellow Christian Charles Colson in the previous reading?

6. What does Carter identify as "the greatest challenge that the world faces"? How does he support this claim? Does he convince you?
7. As you think back over Carter's speech, which lines do you find most thought-provoking and memorable? Why?

ARUNDHATI ROY

Arundhati Roy (1961–) is an Indian novelist, screenwriter, and peace activist who offers a third-world perspective and position on the major global issues of our time. In 1997, she won Britain's top literary prize, the Booker McConnell award, for her novel The God of Small Things. *She has also written screenplays for a number of highly acclaimed films, including* Massey Sahib, In Which Annie Gives It Those Ones, *and* Electric Moon. *She has used her wealth and fame to champion the rights of poor people around the globe and to give a voice to their concerns. In 2002 at home in India, the Indian Supreme Court found her in contempt for accusing the justices of trying to silence citizen protests against the Narmada dam building project, a highly ambitious project to build over 3,000 dams on India's Narmada River. The project was popular with government leaders but unpopular with millions of villagers who were being asked to abandon homes, villages, and thousands of years of their heritage to make way for the dams. In the end, the Court only sentenced her to a symbolic single day in jail for fear of a popular uprising if they gave more severe punishment. Roy has also taken stands against India's nuclear war policy and other regional issues. On a more global scale, some of her most eloquent, and most criticized, positions have been in opposition to the effects of U.S. and Western economic, political, and military policies on the lives of third-world peoples. She has spoken against U.S. bombing in Afghanistan, against the U.S.-led war on Iraq, and against a variety of European and American foreign policies that negatively affect third-world peoples.*

Reading Rhetorically

Roy writes and speaks from the perspective of a third-world person looking at first-world policies and actions. As one might expect, her perspective is often at odds with those perspectives that Americans and citizens of other first-world nations have of themselves. The first rhetorical challenge she faces, therefore, is that many members of her audience simply may not want to listen to her. Her approach to getting people to listen was to make what might seem like shocking statements (at least to first-world readers) and then to back up these statements with great amounts of factual evidence. Note how she dealt in her opening lines with the assumption that the Second World War was a "war for peace," underscoring with a sobering list of historical examples that there was not "an outbreak of peace" at the end of that war as it may have seemed to Americans and Europeans. Ultimately, however, Roy's primary audience is not first-world readers. As she made clear farther along in the reading, her audience is rather those other-world citizens who wish to oppose what she labels "this obscene accumulation of power, this greatly increased distance between those who make the decisions and those who have to suffer them." The expression "obscene accumulation of power" is how she defined "empire," which is a broad collection of first-world organizations and political bodies that she explicitly set out to "confront" throughout the essay. One of the key things she confronted is the "good" and "evil" dichotomy set up by George W. Bush in his introduction to The National Strategy of the United States of America. She quoted one of Bush's popular public statements, "You're either with us, or you are with the terrorists," and then called on her readers to respond with "No thank you." For Roy, there is a great deal of middle ground between what she satirically labels the "Malevolent Mickey Mouse" and the "Mad Mullahs" of Islam. It is in this middle ground that she places the majority of the people of the world and particularly the billions of people in the third world. In her closing, Roy addressed these people, individuals like herself, who would prefer to live their own lives and shape their own identities rather than accept artificial roles imposed by outside powers. In good rhetorical style, she offered them a solution to the problems that she had raised of "empire" and the increasing distance between "those who make the decisions and those who have to suffer them." This solution, delayed to the end of her essay to have more force, served as the thesis statement for all that came before it in her excerpt.

Excerpts from *War Talk*

How has the United States survived its terrible past and emerged smelling so   1
sweet? Not by owning up to it, not by making reparations, not by apologizing to black Americans or native Americans, and certainly not by changing its ways (it exports its cruelties now). Like most other countries, the United States has rewritten its history. But what sets the United States apart from other countries, and puts it way ahead in the race, is that it has enlisted the services of the most powerful, most successful publicity firm in the world: Hollywood. In the best-selling version of popular myth as history, U.S. "goodness" peaked during World War II (aka America's War Against Fascism). Lost in the din of trumpet sound and angel song is the fact that when fascism was in full stride in Europe, the U.S. government actually looked away. When Hitler was carrying out his genocidal pogrom against Jews, U.S. officials refused entry to Jewish refugees fleeing Germany. The United States entered the war only after the Japanese bombed Pearl Harbor. Drowned out by the noisy hosannas is its most barbaric act, in fact the single most savage act the world has ever witnessed: the dropping of the atomic bomb on civilian populations in Hiroshima and Nagasaki. The war was nearly over. The hundreds of thousands of Japanese people who were killed, the countless others who were crippled by cancers for generations to come, were not a threat to world peace. They were civilians. Just

as the victims of the World Trade Center and Pentagon bombings were civilians. Just as the hundreds of thousands of people who died in Iraq because of the U.S.-led sanctions were civilians. The bombing of Hiroshima and Nagasaki was a cold, calculated experiment carried out to demonstrate America's power. At the time, President Truman described it as "the greatest thing in history."

2   The Second World War, we're told, was a "war for peace." The atomic bomb was a "weapon of peace." We're invited to believe that nuclear deterrence prevented World War III. (That was before President George Bush Jr. came up with the "preemptive strike doctrine.") Was there an outbreak of peace after the Second World War? Certainly there was (relative) peace in Europe and America—but does that count as world peace? Not unless savage, proxy wars fought in lands where the colored races live (chinks, niggers, dinks, wogs, gooks) don't count as wars at all.

3   Since the Second World War, the United States has been at war with or has attacked, among other countries, Korea, Guatemala, Cuba, Laos, Vietnam, Cambodia, Grenada, Libya, El Salvador, Nicaragua, Panama, Iraq, Somalia, Sudan, Yugoslavia, and Afghanistan. This list should also include the U.S. government's covert operations in Africa, Asia, and Latin America, the coups it has engineered, and the dictators it has armed and supported. It should include Israel's U.S.-backed war on Lebanon, in which thousands were killed. It should include the key role America has played in the conflict in the Middle East, in which thousands have died fighting Israel's illegal occupation of Palestinian territory. It should include America's role in the civil war in Afghanistan in the 1980s, in which more than one million people were killed. It should include the embargos and sanctions that have led directly and indirectly to the death of hundreds of thousands of people, most visibly in Iraq. Put it all together, and it sounds very much as though there has been a World War III, and that the U.S. government was (or is) one of its chief protagonists.

4   . . . I've been asked to speak about "How to confront Empire?" It's a huge question, and I have no easy answers.

5   When we speak of confronting Empire, we need to identify what Empire means. Does it mean the U.S. government (and its European satellites), the World Bank. the International Monetary Fund, the World Trade Organization (WTO), and multinational corporations? Or is it something more than that?

6   In many countries, Empire has sprouted other subsidiary heads, some dangerous byproducts—nationalism, religious bigotry, fascism and, of course, terrorism. All these march arm in arm with the project of corporate globalization.

7   Let me illustrate what I mean. India—the world's biggest democracy—is currently at the forefront of the corporate globalization project. Its "market" of one billion people is being pried open by the WTO. Corporatization and privatization are being welcomed by the government and the Indian elite.

8   It is not a coincidence that the Prime Minister, the Home Minister, the Disinvestment Minister—the men who signed the deal with Enron in India, the men who are selling the country's infrastructure to corporate multinationals, the men who want to privatize water, electricity, oil, coal, steel, health, educa-

tion, and telecommunication—are all members or admirers of the Rashtriya Swayamsevak Sangh (RSS), a right wing, ultra-nationalist Hindu guild which has openly admired Hitler and his methods.

The dismantling of democracy is proceeding with the speed and efficiency 9 of a Structural Adjustment Program. While the project of corporate globalization rips through people's lives in India, massive privatization and labor "reforms" are pushing people off their land and out of their jobs. Hundreds of impoverished farmers are committing suicide by consuming pesticide.

Reports of starvation deaths are coming in from all over the country. 10

While the elite journeys to its imaginary destination somewhere near the 11 top of the world, the dispossessed are spiraling downwards into crime and chaos. This climate of frustration and national disillusionment is the perfect breeding ground, history tells us, for fascism.

The two arms of the Indian government have evolved the perfect pincer 12 action. While one arm is busy selling India off in chunks, the other, to divert attention, is orchestrating a howling, baying chorus of Hindu nationalism and religious fascism. It is conducting nuclear tests, rewriting history books, burning churches, and demolishing mosques. Censorship, surveillance, the suspension of civil liberties and human rights, the questioning of who is an Indian citizen and who is not, particularly with regard to religious minorities, are all becoming common practice now.

Last March, in the state of Gujarat, two thousand Muslims were 13 butchered in a state-sponsored pogrom. Muslim women were specially targeted. They were stripped, and gang-raped, before being burned alive. Arsonists burned and looted shops, homes, textiles mills, and mosques.

More than a hundred and fifty thousand Muslims have been driven from 14 their homes. The economic base of the Muslim community has been devastated.

While Gujarat burned, the Indian Prime Minister was on MTV promoting 15 his new poems. In December 2002, the government that orchestrated the killing was voted back into office with a comfortable majority. Nobody has been punished for the genocide. Narendra Modi, architect of the pogrom, proud member of the RSS, has embarked on his second term as the Chief Minister of Gujarat. If he were Saddam Hussein, of course each atrocity would have been on CNN. But since he's not—and since the Indian "market" is open to global investors—the massacre is not even an embarrassing inconvenience.

There are more than one hundred million Muslims in India. A time bomb 16 is ticking in our ancient land.

All this to say that it is a myth that the free market breaks down national 17 barriers. The free market does not threaten national sovereignty, it undermines democracy.

As the disparity between the rich and the poor grows, the fight to corner 18 resources is intensifying. To push through their "sweetheart deals," to corporatize the crops we grow, the water we drink, the air we breathe, and the dreams we dream, corporate globalization needs an international confederation of loyal, corrupt, authoritarian governments in poorer countries to push through unpopular reforms and quell the mutinies.

19   Corporate globalization—or shall we call it by its name?—Imperialism—needs a press that pretends to be free. It needs courts that pretend to dispense justice.

20   Meanwhile, the countries of the North harden their borders and stockpile weapons of mass destruction. After all they have to make sure that it's only money, goods, patents, and services that are globalized. Not the free movement of people. Not a respect for human rights. Not international treaties on racial discrimination or chemical and nuclear weapons or greenhouse gas emissions or climate change or—god forbid—justice.

21   So this—all this—is Empire. This loyal confederation, this obscene accumulation of power, this greatly increased distance between those who make the decisions and those who have to suffer them.

22   Our fight, our goal, our vision of another world must be to eliminate that distance.

23   So how do we resist Empire?

24   The good news is that we're not doing too badly. There have been major victories. Here in Latin America you have had so many—in Bolivia, you have Cochabamba. In Peru, there was the uprising in Arequipa. In Venezuela, President Hugo Chavez is holding on, despite the U.S. government's best efforts.

25   And the world's gaze is on the people of Argentina, who are trying to refashion a country from the ashes of the havoc wrought by the IMF.

26   In India the movement against corporate globalization is gathering momentum and is poised to become the only real political force to counter religious fascism.

27   As for corporate globalization's glittering ambassadors—Enron, Bechtel, WorldCom, Arthur Andersen—where were they last year, and where are they now?

28   And of course here in Brazil we must ask: who was the president last year, and who is it now?

29   Still, many of us have dark moments of hopelessness and despair. We know that under the spreading canopy of the War Against Terrorism, the men in suits are hard at work.

30   While bombs rain down on us and cruise missiles skid across the skies, we know that contracts are being signed, patents are being registered, oil pipelines are being laid, natural resources are being plundered, water is being privatized, and George Bush is planning to go to war against Iraq.

31   If we look at this conflict as a straightforward eye-ball to eye-ball confrontation between Empire and those of us who are resisting it, it might seem that we are losing.

32   But there is another way of looking at it. We, all of us gathered here, have, each in our own way, laid siege to Empire.

33   We may not have stopped it in its tracks—yet—but we have stripped it down. We have made it drop its mask. We have forced it into the open. It now stands before us on the world's stage in all its brutish, iniquitous nakedness.

34   Empire may well go to war, but it's out in the open now—too ugly to behold its own reflection. Too ugly even to rally its own people. It won't be long before the majority of American people become our allies.

In Washington, a quarter of a million people marched against the war on Iraq. Each month, the protest is gathering momentum.

Before September 11, 2001 America had a secret history. Secret especially from its own people. But now America's secrets are history, and its history is public knowledge. It's street talk.

Today, we know that every argument that is being used to escalate the war against Iraq is a lie. The most ludicrous of them being the U.S. government's deep commitment to bring democracy to Iraq.

Killing people to save them from dictatorship or ideological corruption is, of course, an old U.S. government sport. Here in Latin America, you know that better than most.

Nobody doubts that Saddam Hussein is a ruthless dictator, a murderer (whose worst excesses were supported by the governments of the United States and Great Britain). There's no doubt that Iraqis would be better off without him.

But, then, the whole world would be better off without a certain Mr. Bush. In fact, he is far more dangerous than Saddam Hussein.

So, should we bomb Bush out of the White House?

It's more than clear that Bush is determined to go to war against Iraq, regardless of the facts—and regardless of international public opinion.

In its recruitment drive for allies, the United States is prepared to invent facts.

The charade with weapons inspectors is the U.S. government's offensive, insulting concession to some twisted form of international etiquette. It's like leaving the "doggie door" open for last minute "allies" or maybe the United Nations to crawl through.

But for all intents and purposes, the new war against Iraq has begun.

What can we do?

We can hone our memory, we can learn from our history. We can continue to build public opinion until it becomes a deafening roar.

We can turn the war on Iraq into a fishbowl of the U.S. government's excesses.

We can expose George Bush and Tony Blair—and their allies—for the cowardly baby killers, water poisoners, and pusillanimous long-distance bombers that they are.

We can re-invent civil disobedience in a million different ways. In other words, we can come up with a million ways of becoming a collective pain in the ass.

When George Bush says "You're either with us, or you are with the terrorists," we can say "No thank you." We can let him know that the people of the world do not need to choose between a Malevolent Mickey Mouse and the Mad Mullahs.

Our strategy should be not only to confront Empire, but to lay siege to it. To deprive it of oxygen. To shame it. To mock it. With our art, our music, our literature, our stubbornness, our joy, our brilliance, our sheer relentlessness— and our ability to tell our own stories. Stories that are different from the ones we're being brainwashed to believe.

53   The corporate revolution will collapse if we refuse to buy what they are selling—their ideas, their version of history, their wars, their weapons, their notion of inevitability.

54   Remember this: We be many and they be few. They need us more than we need them.

Questions for Discussion and Your Reading Journal

1. Roy's two opening paragraphs might surprise American readers. Do you think that they would surprise people living in Korea, Guatemala, Cuba, Vietnam, Cambodia, Grenada, and so on? Explain.

2. Roy writes about efforts to "privatize water, electricity, oil, coal, steel, health, education, and telecommunication" in India. What dangers do citizens, especially in very poor nations, face when private, profit-making companies are allowed to buy and sell such things?

3. Roy mentions hundreds of suicides by poor farmers, 2,000 "butchered" Muslims, Muslim women who were gang-raped and burned alive, and 150,000 Muslims who were forced to leave their homes. All of this happened in India. Most people living in America at the time (2000–2002) were not at all aware, or only vaguely aware, of these events. In your opinion, how is it that citizens of the nation with the most television and radio stations, newspapers, and news magazines in the world could remain so ill informed about important events in India?

4. Do you agree or disagree with Roy that, had Saddam Hussein done the crimes listed in Question 3, "each atrocity would have been on CNN"? Explain.

5. Roy brings up the same issue of "the disparity between the rich and the poor" (Paragraph 18) that Jimmy Carter described as the greatest problem that the world faces today (see previous reading). What does her perspective as someone who lives among the poor add to our insight into this problem?

6. Sum up in your own words what Roy means by "So this—all this—is empire" (Paragraph 21).

7. What do you think Roy is referring to when she writes: "Before September 11, 2001 America had a secret history. Secret especially from its own people" (Paragraph 36)? Do you agree with her?

8. Does Roy call for the use of violence to "confront empire"? Explain.

9. Do you find that Roy's last two sentences add anything of value to her overall argument? Explain.

WENDELL BERRY

Wendell Berry (1943–) is a Kentucky farmer. He lives and works land that has been in his family since the early 1800s in Henry County, Kentucky. He is also an award-winning writer and a distinguished faculty member at the University of Kentucky. His writings constantly return to themes of close-knit communities, taking care of the land, and the moral and ethical responsibilities of community members toward each other and toward the world in which they live. Berry was recently given the Thomas Merton Award in recognition of his efforts to change the world for the better through his visionary writing, his philosophy of communities living in harmony with nature, and his personal efforts to put his ideas into practice on his Kentucky farm. In the following essay, Berry responds as an ethical and thoughtful citizen to the Bush Administration's National Security Strategy of the United States of America from 2002.

Reading Rhetorically

Berry established quickly in his essay that he was writing from the perspective of a "democratic citizen" who used his democratic independence to challenge the "royal 'we'" of the president of the United States. This challenge is like the proverbial David taking on Goliath in battle. To win this battle, Berry needed to convince us that the small voice of one citizen deserves as much to be heard and to be taken into consideration as the powerful voice of a president. Therefore, he set out first to recall to his readers' minds that, since the era of the Declaration of Independence and the Constitution, we have built a nation that is in direct opposition to the "royal 'we.'" With the voice of a common citizen, he argued that the American people have built a nation that stands against leaders who "act alone" using "secret information" to execute plans "without forewarning" and without the "consent of the governed," thereby making the people into "a public kept fearful and ignorant" (Paragraph 4). Immediately following this challenge to the presidency as a source of near absolute war power, Berry gave his main point, arguing that "participating citizens of a democratic nation . . . have no choice but to remove themselves from the illegitimate constraints of this 'we' in as immediate and public way as possible" (Paragraph 5). This is, of course, similar language to that used in the Declaration of Independence itself. By steeping his argument in the ideas and in the language of the very protest that gave birth to American democracy, Berry's small voice tapped into a powerful tradition of American resistance that has successfully challenged the voices of kings, emperors, foreign dictators, and even presidents since the founding of the nation. Berry held to this moderate but unyielding voice throughout the essay to call into question Bush Administration decisions and policies that he saw as "the ready products of the fear and hasty thought" (Paragraph 18) that enshrouded the nation immediately after the September 11 bombings.

A Citizen's Response to the National Security Strategy of the United States of America

"America! America!
God mend thine every flaw,
Confirm thy soul in self control,
Thy liberty in law."

KATHERINE LEE BATES, "America the Beautiful"

I.

1 The new national security strategy published by the White House in September 2002, if carried out, would amount to a radical revision of the political character of our nation. Its central and most significant statement is this:

2 While the United States will constantly strive to enlist the support of the international community, we will not hesitate to act alone, if necessary; to exercise our right of self defense by acting preemptively against such terrorists . . . (p. 6)

3 A democratic citizen must deal here first of all with the question, Who is this "we"? It is not the "we" of the Declaration of Independence, which referred to a small group of signatories bound by the conviction that "governments [derive] their just powers from the consent of the governed." And it is not the "we" of the Constitution, which refers to "*the people* [my emphasis] of the United States."

4 This "we" of the new strategy can refer only to the president. It is a royal "we". A head of state, preparing to act alone in starting a preemptive war, will need to justify his intention by secret information, and will need to plan in secret and execute his plan without forewarning. The idea of a government acting alone in preemptive war is inherently undemocratic, for it does not require or even permit the president to obtain the consent of the governed. As a policy, this new strategy depends on the acquiescence of a public kept fearful and ignorant, subject to manipulation by the executive power, and on the compliance of an intimidated and office dependent legislature. To the extent that a government is secret, it cannot be democratic or its people free. By this new doctrine, the president alone may start a war against any nation at any time, and with no more forewarning than preceded the Japanese attack on Pearl Harbor.

5 Would-be participating citizens of a democratic nation, unwilling to have their consent coerced or taken for granted, therefore have no choice but to remove themselves from the illegitimate constraints of this "we" in as immediate and public a way as possible.

6 The alleged justification for this new strategy is the recent emergence in the United States of international terrorism. But why the events of September 11,

2001, horrifying as they were, should have called for a radical new investiture of power in the executive branch is not clear.

The National Security Strategy defines terrorism as *"premeditated, politi-* 7 *cally motivated violence perpetrated against innocents" (p. 5).* This is truly a distinct kind of violence, but to imply by the word "terrorism" that this sort of terror is the work exclusively of "terrorists" is misleading. The "legitimate" warfare of technologically advanced nations likewise is premeditated, politically motivated violence perpetrated against innocents. The distinction between the intention to perpetrate violence against innocents, as in "terrorism," and the willingness to do so, as in "war," is not a source of comfort.

Supposedly, if a nation perpetrates violence officially—whether to bomb an 8 enemy airfield or a hospital it is not guilty of "terrorism." But there is no need to hesitate over the difference between "terrorism" and any violence or threat of violence that is terrifying. The National Security Strategy wishes to cause "terrorism" to be seen *"in the same light as slavery, piracy, or genocide" (p. 6)* but not in the same light as war. It accepts and affirms the legitimacy of war.

The war against terrorism is not, strictly speaking, a war against nations, 9 even though it has already involved international war in Afghanistan and presidential threats against other nations. This is a war against *"the embittered few" "thousands of trained terrorists"*—who are *"at large" (p. 5)* among many millions of others who are, in the language of this document, *"innocents,"* and thus are deserving of our protection.

Unless we are willing to kill innocents in order to kill the guilty, the need 10 to be lethal will be impeded constantly by the need to be careful. Because we must suppose a new supply of villains to be always in the making, we can expect the war on terrorism to be more or less endless, endlessly costly and endlessly supportive of a thriving bureaucracy.

Unless, that is, we should become willing to ask why, and to do some- 11 thing about the causes. Why do people become terrorists? Such questions arise from the recognition that problems have causes. There is, however, no acknowledgement in The National Security Strategy that terrorism might have a cause that could possibly be discovered and possibly remedied. *"The embittered few,"* it seems, are merely *"evil."*

II.

Much of the obscurity of our effort so far against terrorism originates in this 12 now official idea that the enemy is evil and that we are (therefore) good, which is the precise mirror image of the official idea of the terrorists.

The epigraph of Part III of The National Security Strategy contains this 13 sentence from President Bush's speech at the National Cathedral on September 14, 2001: *"But our responsibility to history is already clear: to answer these attacks and rid the world of evil."* A government, committing its nation to rid the world of evil, is assuming necessarily that it and its nation are good.

But the proposition that anything so multiple and large as a nation can be 14 "good" is an insult to common sense. It is also dangerous, because it precludes any attempt at self criticism or self correction; it precludes public dialogue. It leads us far indeed from the traditions of religion and democracy that are intended to measure and so to sustain our efforts to be good. Christ said, "He that is without sin among you, let him first cast a stone at her." And Thomas Jefferson justified general education by the obligation of citizens to be critical of their government: "for nothing can keep it right but their own vigilant and *distrustful* [my emphasis] superintendence." An inescapable requirement of true patriotism, love for one's land, is a vigilant distrust of any determinative power, elected or unelected, that may preside over it.

15   And so it is not without reason or precedent that a citizen should point out that, in addition to evils originating abroad and supposedly correctable by catastrophic technologies in "legitimate" hands, we have an agenda of domestic evils, not only those that properly self aware humans can find in their own hearts, but also several that are indigenous to our history as a nation: issues of economic and social justice, and issues related to the continuing and worsening maladjustment between our economy and our land.

16   There are kinds of violence that have nothing directly to do with unofficial or official warfare. I mean such things as toxic pollution, land destruction, soil erosion, the destruction of biological diversity and of the ecological supports of agriculture. To anybody with a normal concern for health and sanity, these "externalized costs" are terrible and are terrifying.

17   I don't wish to make light of the threats and dangers that now confront us. But frightening as these are, they do not relieve us of the responsibility to be as intelligent, principled, and practical as we can be. To rouse the public's anxiety about foreign terror while ignoring domestic terror, and to fail to ask if these terrors are in any way related, is wrong.

18   It is understandable that we should have reacted to the attacks of September 11, 2001, by curtailment of civil rights, by defiance of laws, and by resort to overwhelming force, for those things are the ready products of fear and hasty thought. But they cannot protect us against the destruction of our own land by ourselves. They cannot protect us against the selfishness, wastefulness, and greed that we have legitimized here as economic virtues, and have taught to the world. They cannot protect us against our government's long standing disdain for any form of self sufficiency or thrift, or against the consequent dependence, which for the present at least is inescapable, on foreign supplies, such as oil from the Middle East.

19   It is no wonder that the National Security Strategy, growing as it does out of unresolved contradictions in our domestic life, should attempt to compound a foreign policy out of contradictory principles.

20   There is, first of all, the contradiction of peace and war, or of war as the means of achieving and preserving peace This document affirms peace; it also affirms peace as the justification of war and war as the means of peace and thus perpetuates a hallowed absurdity. But implicit in its assertion of this (and, by implication, any other) nation's right to act alone in its own interest is an acceptance of war as a permanent condition. Either way, it is cynical to invoke the ideas of cooperation, community, peace, freedom, justice, dignity, and the

rule of law (as this document repeatedly does), and then proceed to assert one's intention to act alone in making war. One cannot reduce terror by holding over the world the threat of what it most fears.

This is a contradiction not reconcilable except by a self righteousness 21 almost inconceivably naive. The authors of the strategy seem now and then to be glimmeringly conscious of the difficulty. Their implicit definition of *"rogue state"* for example, is any nation pursuing national greatness by advanced military capabilities that can threaten its neighbors—except *our* nation.

If you think our displeasure with "rogue states" might have any under- 22 pinning in international law, then you will be disappointed to learn on page 31 that

> We will take the actions necessary to ensure that our efforts to meet our 23 global security commitments and protect Americans are not impaired by the potential for investigations, inquiry, or prosecution by the International Criminal Court (ICC), whose jurisdiction does not extend to Americans and which we do not accept.

The rule of law in the world, then, is to be upheld by a nation that has 24 declared itself to be above the law. A childish hypocrisy here assumes the dignity of a nation's foreign policy.

III.

A further contradiction is that between war and commerce. This issue arises 25 first of all in the war economy, which unsurprisingly regards war as a business and weapons as merchandise. However nationalistic may be the doctrine of the National Security Strategy, the fact is that the internationalization of the weapons trade is a result inherent in international trade itself. It is a part of globalization. Mr. Bush's addition of this Security Strategy to the previous bipartisan commitment to globalization exposes an American dementia that has not been so plainly displayed before.

The America Whose Business is Business has been internationalizing its 26 economy in haste (for bad reasons, and with little foresight), looking everywhere for "trading partners," cheap labor, and tax shelters. Meanwhile, the America Whose Business is National Defense is withdrawing from the world in haste (for bad reasons, with little foresight), threatening left and right, repudiating agreements, and angering friends. The problem of participating in the Global Economy for the benefit of Washington's corporate sponsors while maintaining a nationalist belligerence and an isolationist morality calls for superhuman intelligence in the secretary of commerce. The problem of "acting alone" in an international war while maintaining simultaneously our ability to import the foreign goods (for instance, oil) on which we have become dependent even militarily will call, likewise, for overtopping genius in the secretary of defense.

27   After World War II, we hoped the world might be united for the sake of peacemaking. Now the world is being "globalized" for the sake of trade and the so-called free market—for the sake, that is, of plundering the world for cheap labor, cheap energy, and cheap materials. How nations, let alone regions and communities, are to shape and protect themselves within this "global economy" is far from clear. Nor is it clear how the global economy can hope to survive the wars of nations.

28   For a nation to be, in the truest sense, patriotic, its citizens must love their land with a knowing, intelligent, sustaining, and protective love. They must not, for any price, destroy its health, its beauty, or its productivity. And they must not allow their patriotism to be degraded to a mere loyalty to symbols or any present set of officials.

29   One might reasonably assume, therefore, that a policy of national security would advocate from the start various practical measures to conserve and to use frugally the nation's resources, the objects of this husbandry being a reduction in the nation's dependence on imports and a reduction in the competition between nations for necessary goods.

30   Agriculture, which is the economic activity most clearly and directly related to national security—if one grants that we all must eat—receives such scant and superficial treatment as to amount to a dismissal. The document proposes only:

31   1. "*a global effort to address new technology, science, and health regulations that needlessly impede farm exports and improved agriculture*" *(p. 19).* This refers, without saying so, to the growing consumer resistance to genetically modified food. A global effort to overcome this resistance would help, not farmers and not consumers, but global agribusiness corporations.

32   2. "*transitional safeguards which we have used in the agricultural sector*" *(p. 19).* This refers to government subsidies, which ultimately help the agribusiness corporations, not farmers.

33   3. Promotion of "*new technologies, including biotechnology, [which] have enormous potential to improve crop yields in developing countries while using fewer pesticides and less water*" *(p. 23).* This is offered (as usual and questionably) as the solution to hunger, but its immediate benefit would be to the corporate suppliers.

34   This is not an agriculture policy, let alone a national security strategy. It has the blindness, arrogance, and foolishness that are characteristic of top down thinking by politicians and academic experts, assuming that "improved agriculture" would inevitably be the result of catering to the agribusiness corporations, and that national food security can be achieved merely by going on as before. It does not address any agricultural problem as such, and it ignores the vulnerability of our present food system dependent as it is on genetically impoverished monocultures, cheap petroleum, cheap long-distance transportation, and cheap farm labor to many kinds of disruption by "the embittered few," who, in the

event of such disruption, would quickly become the embittered many. On erod-ing, ecologically degraded, increasingly toxic landscapes, worked by failing or subsidy dependent farmers and by the cheap labor of migrants, we have erected the tottering tower of "agribusiness," which prospers and "feeds the world" (incompletely and temporarily) by undermining its own foundations.

IV.

Since the end of World War II, when the terrors of industrial warfare had been   35
fully revealed, many people and, by fits and starts, many governments have recognized that peace is not just a desirable condition, as was thought before, but a practical necessity. But we have not yet learned to think of peace apart from war. We wait, still, until we face terrifying dangers and the necessity to choose among bad alternatives, and then we think again of peace, and again we fight a war to secure it. At the end of the war, if we have won it, we declare peace; we congratulate ourselves on our victory; we marvel at the newly-proved efficiency of our latest weapons; we ignore the cost in lives, materials, and property, in suffering and disease, in damage to the natural world; we ignore the inevitable residue of resentment and hatred; and we go on as before, having, as we think, successfully defended our way of life.

That is pretty much the story of our victory in the Gulf War of 1991. In   36
the years between that victory and September 11, 2001, we did not alter our thinking about peace and war—that is, we thought much about war and little about peace; we continued to punish the defeated people of Iraq and their chil-dren; we made no effort to reduce our dependence on the oil we import from other, potentially belligerent countries; we made no improvement in our char-ity toward the rest of the world; we made no motion toward greater economic self-reliance; and we continued our extensive and often irreversible damages to our own land. We appear to have assumed merely that our victory confirmed our manifest destiny to be the richest, most powerful, most wasteful nation in the world. After the catastrophe of September 11, it again became clear to us how good it would be to be at peace, to have no enemies, to have no more needless deaths to mourn. And then, our need for war following with the cus-tomary swift and deadly logic our need for peace, we took up the customary obsession with the evil of other people.

It is useless to try to adjudicate a long-standing animosity by asking who   37
started it or who is the most wrong. The only sufficient answer is to give up the animosity and try forgiveness, to try to love our enemies and to talk to them and (if we pray) to pray for them. If we can't do any of that, then we must begin again by trying to imagine our enemies' children who, like our chil-dren, are in mortal danger because of enmity that they did not cause.

We can no longer afford to confuse peaceability with passivity. Authen-   38
tic peace is no more passive than war. Like war, it calls for discipline and intelligence and strength of character, though it calls also for higher principles and aims. If we are serious about peace, then we must work for it as ardently, seriously, continuously, carefully, and bravely as we now prepare for war.

Questions for Discussion and Your Reading Journal

1. With his title and his opening paragraphs, Berry sets up a clear confrontation in his essay. At the root, whom is this confrontation between?
2. Berry calls the very notion of a government declaring preemptive war as "inherently undemocratic." What reasoning does he use to support this claim? Are you convinced?
3. What is the basic hypocrisy surrounding the definition of terrorism and the common use of violence by nations such as the United States that Berry treats in Paragraph 7?
4. In Paragraph 11, what point does Berry bring up that was entirely overlooked in the Bush Administration's National Security Strategy document? Do you find this a relevant point to raise? Explain.
5. In Paragraph 12, Berry identifies an attitude in the United States that is "the precise mirror image of the official idea of the terrorists." To what is he referring and what are the implications of this insight, in your opinion?
6. In Paragraph 20, Berry brings up the same "hallowed absurdity" of making war in order to bring about peace that Jimmy Carter treated in his address earlier in this chapter. List the additional contradictions in the National Security document that Berry adds to this original absurdity in Paragraph 20 through Paragraph 23.
7. How does knowing that Berry is a devoted farmer who grows his own food on his family farm in Kentucky help you to understand his main points in Part III of the essay?
8. Do you agree with Berry's final statement? Do you think that most Americans agree with the ideas in it? Explain.

DANIELE ARCHIBUGI
AND IRIS MARION YOUNG

Daniele Archibugi lives in Italy and serves as director of the Italian National Research Council. An academic and advocate of a just system of global democracy, Archibugi has worked at some of the most respected institutions of learning in the Western world, including the Universities of Cambridge and Sussex in England, and the Universities of Rome and Naples in Italy. He has pushed for reform of the United Nations and has written extensively on the history of peace. Some of his more important works include Cosmopolitan Democracy: An Agenda for a New World Order *(Polity Press, 1995),* Re-imagining Political Community *(Polity Press, 1998), and* Innovation Policy in a Global Economy *(Cambridge University Press, 1999).*

Iris Marion Young lives in the United States and is a professor of political science at the University of Chicago. Like Archibugi, she is an advocate for global justice and democratic principles. At the University of Chicago, she is affiliated with the Human Rights Program. Her thought and positions in these areas are treated in detail in her books Inclusion and Democracy *(Oxford University Press, 2000) and* Intersecting Voices: Dilemmas of Gender, Political Philosophy, and Policy *(Princeton University Press, 1997).*

Reading Rhetorically

Archibugi and Young wrote of the terrorist attacks of 9/11 from a global perspective. They underscored that this is different from the "state" perspective taken by the Bush Administration that led quickly to the U.S. policy of declaring war on "another state or states." The authors set up their argumentative approach by offering their thesis at the outset of the reading (Paragraph 2) and developing their ideas and support from there. As scholars, Archibugi and Young did not proceed in their argument in a manner that depended upon knowledge of the popular assumptions and public fears of their audience, as Charles Colson did in "Just War, Preemption, and Iraq" (see earlier in this section). Rather, they proceeded with piece after piece of documented evidence detailing historical policies and actions of the Bush Administration since the events of 9/11. Their analysis of these political actions and their own more globally focused "Alternate Vision" of other possible courses of action grew out of a grounding in historical fact more than out of an effort to appeal to their readers' emotions and sympathies.

Envisioning a Global Rule of Law

The attacks on the World Trade Center and the Pentagon in September 2001 can appear within two different frames of interpretation. The first sees them as attacks on the United States as a state and its people. The second views them as crimes against humanity. The difference in interpretation is not technical, but political, and each implies different strategies of reaction. Shortly after the attack some public leaders, such as Mary Robinson, director of the United Nations Commission on Human Rights, recommended that the United States and the rest of the world adopt the second interpretation. It seemed that there might be some open discussion of how to interpret the attacks as an event in international affairs, and what sort of response was called for. In a few weeks, however, the United States solidified its interpretation as an attack on a state for which the appropriate response would be war on another state or states.

In this essay we question this statist response to the terrorist attacks and offer some vision of how the United States and other global actors might have conceived and can still conceive of their possibilities for action under a cosmopolitan vision of political responsibility. We argue that a different response to these attacks, based on the rule of law and international cooperation, could have been equally effective to combat terrorism in the long run and, in our view, could have also opened the way to a more just and stable world order.

THE STATIST INTERPRETATION

3   The Bush administration framed the attacks as an act of war on America, for which military retaliation was judged to be the appropriate response. This frame meant finding a state or states to engage in war, and the United States chose Afghanistan on the grounds that the Taliban government harbored and supported Al Qaeda. It has singled out Iraq, Syria, Somalia, and other countries as additional states toward which military action may be taken, although they have not been attacked so far. The construction of a response to the attacks as a state-to-state military conflict, however, has been difficult to sustain. Even within a traditional state-centered world politics, the fact that the government of Afghanistan allowed Al Qaeda leaders to run camps in its territory provides an uncertain justification for making war on the state. Aware of that shakiness, the United States shifted its reasons for the war against the Taliban from a rationale of self-defense to a humanitarian defense of freeing the Afghan people, especially its women, from oppression. We find this rationale cynical and opportunistic, since neither Bush nor the Clinton administration had previously articulated any concern with the plight of the Afghan people. Not surprisingly, this concern has almost disappeared from the agenda for reconstruction in Afghanistan. Responding to the terrorist attacks through the conduct of a war against a state neither fits the case nor is likely to be effective in making a safer world. Although the war has destroyed some Al Qaeda bases and the United States has captured some members of that group, there is no direct connection between the casualties and the nineteen suicidal attackers of September 11. Widely circulating estimates of civilian deaths in Afghanistan give a minimum of one thousand, some as many as thirty-seven hundred, and hundreds are likely to die from unexploded bombs.[1] It is still unknown the number of soldiers and armed men who have been killed, but some of the information, among it the massacre of hundreds of Taliban prisoners in the prison of Mazar-i-Sharif, has raised serious concerns about the legality in which the war operations have been conducted.[2] The number of refugees suffering hunger and frost because of the war is impossible to calculate, while civilian casualties attributed to military errors still continue despite the fact that the war formally ended many months ago.

4   There is no reason to think that the war has deterred other would-be terrorists around the world. After many months from the beginning of the war, there is little sign of political stability in Afghanistan or that the current government is genuinely respectful of human rights. The war may have contributed to destabilizing the region of central Asia with unforeseen consequences.

5   Although the United States did not act alone in prosecuting the war, it called the shots. The United States decided with whom to cooperate and assigned the role of other actors. It is difficult not to interpret U.S. policy in recent months as an effort to consolidate even more firmly its position as sovereign of the world. While many Americans no doubt think that this is a good thing, we believe that the existence of a single world military power that aims to enforce its will both is an anathema to democratic culture and impedes efforts to promote peace.[3]

In the last decade, the United States has used its military force in the Per- 6
sian Gulf, Somalia, Panama, the Balkans, and many other places. In every
case, the U.S. interventions have had victims, but few have been Americans.
The magnitude of U.S. military and economic power and the willingness of the
United States to wield it asymmetrically and with only the thinnest veneer of
multilateralism elicit hostile reactions all over the world, even from people
thought to be allies. A survey conducted by the Pew Research Center and the
International Herald Tribune in December 2001 found that most of the non-
Americans among the 275 political and business leaders polled believe that the
United States wrongly uses its power and that some of its policies are responsible for growing global disparities in well-being.[4] In response to such hegemony, it seems to us imperative that leaders and citizens all over the world
should envision a global rule of law and should try to shame and pressure the
United States to act more in conformity with such a vision.

AN ALTERNATIVE VISION

Aspirations to a global society governed by fair rules should be counted 7
among the casualties of September 11. The fall of the Berlin Wall brought with
it hope of constituting a world order founded on international legality and
with strengthened institutions of international cooperation. Recent debates
and demonstrations about the policies and procedures of international trade
and financial organizations have assumed the emergence of more global level
governance. The question has been whether global regulatory regimes will represent solely the interests of the world's most powerful actors or can include
the voices and interests of the global majority in transparent and accountable
institutions.

We base a vision of an alternative response to terrorism on these aspira- 8
tions for just and democratic global governance. Hitherto, discussions of an
international rule of law and global regulatory systems have paid less attention to the prevention and investigation of crimes and their prosecution in an
international system than to matters like international trade, investment, or
environmental protection. We propose two premises for reasoning about what
an alternative response to the terrorist attacks of September 11 might have
been and still can be. First, the situation should be conceptualized in people-
to-people, rather than state-to-state, terms.[5] The attackers were not representatives of a state, but members of private organizations, and those whom they
killed were, for the most part, private individuals from at least seventy different countries. Thus, second, the events should be conceptualized as crimes, not
acts of war, to which the proper response is criminal investigation and prosecution within a rule of law and legally mandated measures for preventing and
deterring similar crimes. For this reason, we disagree with those who think
that the concept of just war can be applied to the U.S. military reaction.[6]

Democratic states do not usually, and ought never, respond arbitrarily and 9
with military power to terrorist attacks committed inside their borders. Spain
in response to threats from the Basque separatist group ETA, Italy in dealing

with the Red Brigades, the United States in response to the bombing in Oklahoma City—all mobilized the instruments of law and police power. Stepping out of legal bounds, as did the Spanish government for a while when it authorized some state agents to use extrajudicial methods to combat terrorism, seems to have the effect of increasing the risk of attack. The enemies of peace point to illegal actions by states to justify their own illegal actions.[7]

10 The world ought to respond to international terrorist organizations, we suggest, according to the same principles of the rule of law that these governments use in responding to domestic terrorist organizations. Responding to acts and threats of terrorism and to transnational terrorist networks under a global rule of law need not imply being "softer" on terrorists than using a state-to-state response led by a hegemonic state. On the contrary, a genuinely global cooperative law enforcement response would be more effective in identifying and apprehending culprits, as well as preventing future attacks, while at the same time harming fewer people and destroying fewer goods, than has the war against Afghanistan.

11 We offer five principles to guide international policy to respond to threats and problems of violence. They each point to ideals and institutions of global cooperation that do not now exist. In that sense we intend them as visionary. At the same time, we believe that all five principles can serve to guide action now in the following way. As they consider options for actions now to respond to threats of terrorism, political actors and citizens can and should ask which courses of action have the potential to help realize the ideals the principles express and which actions are more likely to move the world away from them.

LEGITIMIZE AND STRENGTHEN INTERNATIONAL INSTITUTIONS

12 Actions and policies that treat terrorism and threats of terrorism as involving all the world's peoples within a rule of law should utilize international organizations and legal instruments. The United Nations system is most important here. Although there are many flaws in its design and operations, which should be changed, the United Nations is the only transnational institution with representation of nearly all the world's peoples. Institutions, policies, and conventions of the United Nations, moreover, cover many of the most urgent world problems.

13 Currently the UN is in an impossible position. On the one hand, it is called on the scene to restore peace, build governments and infrastructure, aid refugees, conduct health campaigns, and pursue many other activities, in dozens of regions of the world simultaneously. On the other hand, member states routinely deny the UN the means for carrying out such missions, not only by failing to provide funds, but also by limiting its authority. When the UN's efforts prove inadequate to solve problems, as often happens, world leaders regularly heap abuse on the organization for being unresponsive and inept. The United States and other world powers cannot continue to dump the consequences of its wars and economic decisions on the United Nations while at the same time encouraging people to disdain the organization.

The present organization of the UN Security Council, with its five perma- 14
nent members reflecting global politics in 1945, needs serious reform. That
Security Council, however, passed three Resolutions after the attacks of September 11 (resolutions no. 1368, September 12, 2001; no. 1373, September 28,
2001; and no. 1377, November 12, 2001), which call for transnational cooperation among all member states to deter and investigate terrorist and other
transnational criminal activity. If government leaders allied with social movements, the United States could be pressed to enter more genuinely multilateral
efforts to transnational criminal networks, efforts that give more decision-
making participation to the less developed world. The tragic paralysis of the
international community in response to the worst killing in Palestine and Israel
in two decades signals even more urgently the need to strengthen and reform
the United Nations as a peacemaking institution.

Coordinate Law Enforcement and Intelligence-Gathering Institutions Across the World

The United States Congress apparently has little interest in investigating how 15
two of the most sophisticated investigative and intelligence organizations in the
world, the CIA and the FBI, could have been caught so unaware by a crime of
such huge proportions. We suggest that one explanation is the state-centered-
ness of both agencies, along with the investigative and intelligence-gathering
agencies of most states. Simultaneous with increased transnational organization and movement of capital, labor, technology, and culture is the transnational organization and movement of crime. Intelligence and law enforcement
institutions, however, lag terribly behind this reality. Intelligence continues to
be principally an instrument of individual states against their enemies; in a spy
culture the agencies of one state engage in secret activities in relation to other
states, explicitly not trusting one another. Domestic law enforcement agencies,
furthermore, each have their own systems that make communication and
cooperation across borders difficult. The September 11 attacks should serve as
a siren call for reversing these structures of intelligence and law enforcement
enable greater cooperation among agencies to protect *citizens* of the world,
not states.

There are some international instruments on which to build for such a 16
purpose. INTERPOL, the international police organization with 179 member
nations, has worked against terrorism, drug trafficking, money laundering,
white collar crime, computer crime, counterfeit money, organized crime, and
traffic in women and children for decades. Even though its budget is minus-
cule compared to the task, it maintains extensive databases of known and suspected terrorists and criminals. It organizes data on counterfeit passports and
stolen credit card accounts that can be useful to law enforcement agents in
nearly any country. Yet state-based intelligence agencies infrequently work
with the organization to access its data.[8]

At its millennium meeting in November 2000, the UN General Assembly 17
adopted the Convention Against Transnational Organized Crime, which 140
countries, including the United States, have already signed. This convention
requires states to strengthen domestic laws aimed to control organized crime

and encourages states to enhance systems of transnational cooperation in legal expertise, extradition, and criminal investigation. It specifically calls for providing technical assistance to less developed countries to upgrade their capacities for dealing with organized crime. Although at the moment this Convention may be little more than a piece of paper, like some other UN negotiated treaties and conventions, it can be used by political leaders and social movements to demand institutions and resources that put its principles into action. The United States, along with any other states, can act to advance international cooperation in law enforcement, both domestic and transnational, as well as to create and strengthen global law enforcement agencies. A collective effort to combat terrorism with a greater involvement of the UN will certainly be beneficial to the United States, but this would imply that the United States commit itself to a greater loyalty toward the organization. As the president of the United Nations Association of the USA has rightly stressed, "to sustain the commitment of UN member states in this new war (against terrorism), and to dispel resistance stemming from resentment of American 'double standards,' Washington needs to affirm what the American public has long acknowledged—the rule of law applies to the great as well as the small."[9] A greater collaboration against organized political crime implies breaking down the statist distinction between domestic oriented police and internationally oriented spy agencies. Current policy in the United States and in many Western countries blurs this distinction, however, in just the wrong direction. By allowing the CIA and FBI to cooperate inside the United States, the government fosters a more repressive internal state at the same time that it becomes more defensive and suspicious externally. Increased transnational law enforcement cooperation should come with procedures of accountability and transparency in order to protect the rights of individuals.

Increase Financial Regulation

18 One of the most efficient ways to strike at terrorist networks, and organized crime more generally, is to hit their money. It is surprising that although Osama bin Laden has been known to head and fund terrorist operations for years, Al Qaeda has had the liberty to move the capital necessary. Why has no one until now succeeded at attacking the finances? We believe the answer lies partly in the fact that world business leaders resist financial regulation. Corporations regularly move their money around the world, for example, in order to avoid paying taxes. Tracking and regulating the movement of funds can dry up their flow to support criminal activities. A war on the free flow of money does not produce "collateral damage," create refugees, or pollute the air. The United States has indeed enhanced its capacity to investigate and regulate money flows. In this area it is obvious that even the most awesome military power of the world must depend on the cooperation of other governments, especially governments that dislike U.S. foreign policy. Such necessary cooperation is difficult to maintain when the same governments or their allies face military threats or covert intelligence operations from the United States.[10]

Use International Courts

The United States has put its response to attacks and threats of terrorism in a   19
state-to-state frame only for as long as it suits its goals. By refusing to treat
those captured in the war against Afghanistan as prisoners of war, the United
States takes the picture out of the statist frame. The Bush administration
argues that the prisoners are illegal combatants not covered by international
law as stated in the Geneva Convention. At the same time, it has decreed that
it will not apply its domestic principles of due process to noncitizen suspects
apprehended in the United States or elsewhere. Thus the United States declares
before the world that any non-Americans whom it apprehends and claims to
connect with terrorism will not be given the protection of the law.[11] This
stance is so outrageous that it has fomented dissent even within the Bush
administration and from within its most loyal ally, Britain. In response the
administration has slightly altered its stated position, but not its treatment of
prisoners.

When the United States began putting into place its plan for military tri-   20
bunals for those captured, Vice President Cheney said, "Terrorists don't
deserve the same guarantees and safeguards that would be used for an American citizens going through the normal judicial process."[12] This statement
reveals Cheney's scorn for the most elementary principles of due process:
Presumably it is up to judicial procedure to determine who is and who is not
a criminal.

If the September 11 attacks are seen as crimes against humanity rather   21
than against only the United States, an international tribunal instituted by the
United Nations, based on the model of those for the former Yugoslavia and
Rwanda, with the processing judges coming from Western and Islamic countries, would be appropriate. This would also have the advantage of not
appearing as a conflict between America and Islam, but rather between the
entire international community and a limited group of criminals. In the end ad
hoc tribunals should be handed over to a permanent International Criminal
Court, which was approved by treaty in Rome in July 1998 and started to be
implemented on April 12, 2002. (The United States has withdrawn its signa-
ture from this treaty, an unprecedented act.) "Had the International Criminal
Court been in existence," noted international lawyer Christopher Greenwood,
and had the relevant States been parties to its Statute, the perpetrators of the
11 September atrocities could have been tried by that Court for crimes against
humanity."[13]

We have heard several arguments against using international courts to   22
prosecute persons suspected of performing or materially contributing to terrorist acts. It's too slow, too expensive, and would wrongly give terrorists a
forum in which to air their ideas. We find all these reasons disingenuous. It
should not be any slower to pursue due process on an international level than
at a state level; the speed the United States seeks seems to be at the expense of
due process. Likewise, it should not be much more expensive to pay for an

international trial than a state-level trial, if both are fair. Finally, any public court proceeding, at any level, offers opportunities for actors to express their point of view on the alleged crimes; that is what they are for, and that is, of course, why the military tribunals the Bush administration plans will not be open to public view.

Narrow Global Inequalities

23   Since September 2001 many commentators have suggested that the vast disparities in wealth and well-being between Northern Hemisphere societies such as the United States, the European Union, or Japan, on the one hand, and the Middle East and South Asia, on the other hand, be taken into account in understanding what causes and motivates individuals to join or form terrorist groups. We agree with those who respond that these structural injustices neither justify nor excuse criminal acts. Nor do these circumstances even explain terrorist acts, for there are many poor places that do not provide recruits for international terrorist organizations.

24   Still, a huge portion of the world's population lives in horrible poverty.[14] We believe, as do many others in both the less developed and more developed parts of the world, that this poverty persists at least partly because of policies of the rich states, private corporations based in those countries, and international organizations in which those states and corporations have disproportionate power. Even those skeptical of this claim, however, should condemn the apparent unwillingness of the people and government of the United States, Europe, and Japan to effect significant transfer of capital, technological capacity, and goods to raise the quality of life of the world's poorest people. There is no doubt that such indifference amidst affluence fosters resentment in many corners of the world and endangers peace and prosperity for many outside the shantytowns.

25   At another tragic moment of history, with the defeat of fascism at the end of World War II, the United States understood that its security and prosperity depended on the rebirth of Europe. To enable this rebirth, the United States dedicated a huge amount of resources to the Marshall Plan to rebuild the infrastructure of devastated European societies. No development aid program since that time has been as large in scale and as effective. That this was done once should give hope that having the will opens the way to invest in poor societies to enable them to flourish. For decades social movements and governments in the less developed world have demanded that the powerful economic actors of the world stop exploiting their resources and workers and start programs of real investment in the infrastructure and human beings of poor countries. The developed world remains largely unresponsive to this calamity. Official development assistance of the OECD countries in 1998 was 0.24 percent of their combined gross national products, and private funding is also paltry. The many attempts made by global civil society to increase the resources devoted to development have so far not been matched by concrete action.[15]

Even the Bush administration cannot avoid acknowledging this moral 26
imperative. It could not stay away from the UN-sponsored conference on
rebuilding Afghanistan in January 2002 as it walked out on the Conference
on Racism in August 2001 and the Climate Change Conference in December.
At the January 2002 conference the United States pledged a mere $300 mil-
lion for the first year, and Japan and Europe each pledged $500 million for
the first two and one-half years.[16] Before the earthquake of March 2002, the
World Bank estimated that at least $4.9 *billion* was required for the two and
one-half years to help rebuilt Afghanistan at the most minimal level.[17] What
is certainly scandalous is that the majority of countries have not yet made
available the resources promised in February 2002. Up to June 21, 2002, the
United States has contributed to the Afghanistan Reconstruction Trust Fund
$5 million only.[18] Even at this moment of crisis, the rich countries of the
world remain unbelievably stingy, and the poor people of the world are
watching.

The world will not be able to move toward fair, inclusive, and effective 27
global governance without major reallocation of economic, technological, and
organizational capacities to reduce existing global disparities in the quality of
life and institutional order. For such ends we need new and strengthened international institutions that better represent the voices and perspectives of all the
world's peoples moreso than existing international finance and development
institutions such as the World Bank, with more ability to promote global redistribution. Without the global equivalent of the Marshall Plan, even the best
designed cooperative efforts to respond to transnational organized crime can
only be defensive and intermittent in their effectiveness.

CONCLUSION

The terrorist attacks of September 11, 2001, were a major challenge for the 28
United States, its European allies, and the rest of the world. The Bush administration and its allies decided to retaliate against a country rather than individually punishing the culprits. Those who opposed to the recourse to war
were often asked what the United States should have done. In this chapter we
have addressed this question by arguing that there was an alternative way to
combat terrorism. We do not argue that all culprits would have been taken
and processed, and we do not believe that the implementation of the policies
we have suggested would have been sufficient to destroy transnationally
organized networks of killers. Certainly, the war undertaken has achieved neither of these goals. But we are sure that the number of "collateral casualties"
would have been much lower if such an alternative strategy were followed.
And, perhaps more importantly, the alternative reaction here recommended
would have shown to the peoples of the world that the world's powerful leaders are able to support the rule of law and the instruments of justice also
beyond its own borders.

Our suggestions should be conceived for the long term, and they have not 29
lost their value after the bloodiest part of the military operations against

Afghanistan has passed. They derive from a general perspective on world politics that dates much before the tragic events of September 11. The vision upon which we draw considers that it is both possible and necessary to develop global democratic institutions.[19] A major new global threat, such as terrorism on the scale of September 11, should provide the chance for democratic countries of the world to nurture a global rule of law rather than a clash of fundamentalisms.

Notes

This is a revised version of "Toward a Global Rule of Law," *Dissent* (Spring 2002): pp. 27–32. We wish to thank Marc Herold, Mathias Koenig-Archibugi, Duncan Snidal, Michael Walzer, and Alexander Wendt for their criticism and suggestions. Thanks to Anne Harrington for research assistance.

1. The lower and upper estimations are reported from, respectively, the Project on Defense Alternatives and Marc Herold, University of New Hampshire. The latter report is available at http://www.cursor.org/stories/civilian_deaths.htm.
2. See Richard Falk, "In Defense of 'Just War' Thinking," *The Nation*, December 24, 2001, pp. 23–25.
3. See Robin Blackburn, "The Imperial Presidency, the War on Terrorism, and the Revolutions of Modernity," *Constellations*, 9.1 (2002): 3–33.
4. Brian Knowlton, "How the World Sees the U.S. and Sept. 11," *International Herald Tribune*, December 20, 2001.
5. See David Held, "Violence, Law and Justice, in a Global Age," *Debating Cosmopolitcs*, ed. Daniele Archibugi (London: Verso, 2002) Mary Kaldor, *Terror in the US: The Murky Road to War?* http://www.fathom.com/feature/ 122358.
6. It is not surprising that the petition supporting the conflict as a just war and signed by a number of important American intellectuals never mentions Afghanistan. Not even this document could establish a clear link between the action (the terrorist attacks) and the reaction (the war against Afghanistan). *What We're Fighting For,* Institute for American Values, released February 2002 and available at http://www.propositionsonline.com/Fighting_for.html. Signatories include Amitai Etzioni, Francis Fukuyama, Samuel Huntington, Robert Putnam and Michael Walzer.
7. See Montserrat Guibernau, *Nations Without States* Cambridge: Polity Press, 1999) especially pp. 145–148, "State Terrorism."
8. See David Zweshimo and Sbastian Rotella, "INTERPOL Hopes Terror Investigators Keep in Touch," *Los Angeles Times*, December 23, 2001.
9. In William H. Luers, ed., *Combating Terrorism: Does the U.N. Matter . . . and How* (New York: UNA-USA, 2002), p. 5.
10. See Phil Williams, "Crime, Illicit Markets, and Money Laundering," in *Managing Global Issues: Lessons Learned*, P. J. Simmons and Chantal de Jonge Oudraat, ed. (Washington, DC: Carnegie Endowment for International Peace, 2001), pp. 106–150.
11. The case is considered in Christopher Greenwood, "International Law and the 'War Against Terrorism,' " *International Affairs* 78.2 (2002): 301–317.

12. Reported in the *International Herald Tribune,* November 16, 2001, p. 5.

13. Greenwood, p. 317.

14. Data on world inequalities are scrutinized in the United Nations Development Program, *Human Development Report 2001* (New York: Oxford University Press, 2002). The ethical implications are addressed in an increasing vast literature, including Thomas Pogge, ed., *Global Justice* (Oxford: Blackwell, 2001).

15. Helmut Anheir, Marlies Glasius, and Mary Kaldor, eds., *Global Civil Society 2001* (Oxford: Oxford University Press, 2001).

16. The World Bank, *Afghanistan: Update on World Bank Activities,* note to update the Board of Executive Directors on a number of developments relating to World Bank activities in Afghanistan, Washington, DC, February 7, 2002.

17. World Bank, *Afghanistan.*

18. See The World Bank Group, *Afghanistan Reconstruction Fund. Contributions,* http://www.worldbank.org/artf. Figures reported are updated to June 21, 2002.

19. See, for example, David Held, *Democracy and the Global Order* (Cambridge: Polity Press, 1995); Richard Falk, *Law in an Emerging Global Village. A Post-Westphalian Perspective* (Ardsley: Transnational Publishers, 1998).

Questions for Discussion and Your Reading Journal

1. According to the authors, what were the two possible interpretations of the 9/11 terrorist attacks? Which interpretation did the U.S. Government adopt? In your opinion, why didn't the United States take the other interpretation?

2. How do the authors respond to the U.S. shift of reasons for launching war in Afghanistan from one of "self-defense" to "freeing the Afghan people, especially its women, from oppression"?

3. What do the authors think of having the United States as the "single world military power"? Do other peoples of the world share their position? Explain.

4. In their vision of a more effective global response to the 9/11 terrorist attacks, what do the authors mean when they propose that the attacks should be seen in "people-to-people" terms?

5. If we conceptualize the attacks of 9/11 as "crimes" instead of "acts of war," how does that change the appropriate course of action in response to these events, according to the authors? Are there examples of nations that have taken this approach?

6. Sum up the five principles of a visionary international policy that the writers give for responding more effectively to "threats and problems of violence." In your opinion, which of these would be most important for the long-term success of the effort to end terrorism? Explain.

7. What is the position of the Bush Administration concerning the legal rights of anyone arrested on charges of terrorism?

8. Other writers in this chapter have pointed to the huge disparities of wealth between rich nations and poor nations as the underlying cause of global

instability (see readings by Oxfam, Bygrave, Carter, and Roy). What is the position of Archibugi and Young on this issue?
9. Overall, what do you find most convincing and least convincing about Archibugi and Young's argument? Did it give you new ideas to consider? Did it leave out any key points that you can think of? Explain.

RACE, GENDER, AND OPPRESSION

ALBERT MEMMI

*The persistence of racism is not unique to America; it is a global prob-
lem. Drawing upon his experience in Tunisia in North Africa, the French
author Albert Memmi (1920–) looks at both economic and psychological factors that account for the continued survival of racism. Racism
appears to feed upon a circular logic in which social, political, and economic factors all reinforce racist stereotypes. Thus, according to Memmi,
people often interpret poverty and powerlessness as signs of inferiority
and incompetence; this rationalization then serves to justify discrimination and to perpetuate racism by excluding the oppressed from social,
economic, and political power. In* Dominated Man, *the book from which
this selection is taken, Memmi sees this process of racism as a symbol for
other kinds of oppression that discriminate against the colonized, Jews,
workers, women, and domestic servants.*

Reading Rhetorically

Memmi reversed the usual arrangement of the argument in this reading about racism. Rather than present a thesis statement early in the piece and proceed to develop and support it, he saved his most important points until the end. The delayed-thesis approach is often used when a writer is working with a particularly sensitive or potentially personal topic. Racism fits both of these categories. A delayed thesis is especially appropriate when the writer wishes to take a bold position on the topic in a manner that might shock or offend readers who are not prepared for it. By saving the main position until the end, the writer is able to lead readers more gently and convincingly to his or her points. Thus Memmi started out in harmless fashion with the purpose of informing us about "a number of characteristics of racism," hardly something that is likely to cause personal affront. As you read, think about the nature of the 14 points that Memmi then made, and consider the monumental challenge he had put before us by the time he reached his concluding paragraphs. When he finally got to his major point, he proposed that we would need to "uproot the entire cultural tradition" of the worlds in which we live if we really wanted to end racism. Memmi wisely judged that starting out with such a weighty pronouncement could have been off-putting to many readers. However, after he had spent several pages carefully leading up to this point, it came across as a rather logical conclusion to the many lesser points he elected to give before it.

Racism and Oppression

Everyone seems to be against racism. At least no one says openly that he 1 himself is a racist. Even those who practice discrimination, in both words and actions, do not defend it as a philosophy. They are almost unanimous in explaining those words and those actions in a way which, they insist, has nothing to do with racism.

Of course we could accept this at face value. Or we could try to under- 2 stand the phenomenon of racism, even if comprehension is likely to prove more disturbing than general indignation, in the long run. In this approach racism is taken as a topic for study; for the time being any moral issues must be left aside, and so, to some extent, must any concern with taking action.

Having chosen the second approach, we have discovered a certain num- 3 ber of characteristics of racism; they seem fairly decisive and, as we suspected, not so reassuring:

1. *Everyone, or nearly everyone, is an unconscious racist,* or a semi- 4 conscious one, or even a conscious one. The degrees range from the man who starts out, "I don't have any prejudice against any race, but . . ." to the one who claims the black man has a peculiar smell or the Jew a "concentration camp" look. From the man who professes to be anti-racist and yet cannot help feeling uncomfortably hesitant, to the defiant attitude of the nearly-avowed racist, who embraces everything about racism except the label. From the European who criticizes segregation in America but would avoid renting a room to a black student, to the Frenchman who upholds the methods of the Ku Klux Klan and would apply them in his own country if he could. All of these people offer ways to interpret and rationalize the attitudes they take and the speeches they make, but all of them, in the last analysis, share a *common denominator.* The man who speaks up for the Ku Klux Klan asserts that the hooded Americans want to defend their country, the virtue of their women and the color of their children's skin. Similarly, the man who merely refuses to rent a room to a black man and admits that he feels uneasy—even if he admits that he shouldn't—at seeing a black man walking with a white woman is also thinking, in a confused way, of the purity of women and the color of his country's children yet unborn.

   While from one to the other the interpretation differs, becoming an ex- 5 planation, a travesty, or an alibi, it always refers back to the same fact. It may be more or less out in the open, or more or less disguised, but it is always discernible.

2. In short, *racism is one of the most widespread attitudes in the world.* 6 Racial prejudice is a *social fact.* This in itself is enough to explain why it is

so important, so varied, so extensive, so deep and so general. This also means that it pre-exists, imposing itself on the individual.

7   In still other words, before taking root in the individual, racism has taken root in the institutions and ideologies all around him, in the education he receives and the culture he acquires.

8   It would be interesting to film one of these cultural circuits: the way the ideologists create ideologies from relations between forces and institutions; the way journalists vulgarize those ideologies and the newspaper reader swallows their diluted poison in such repeated doses that it soaks into him completely. Never has it been adequately pointed out that writers and literature of even the highest sort play an insidious role in propagating racist themes and images.[1] Religions themselves are not sinless in this respect. And lastly, the family circle is an extraordinary *culture medium* for prejudices, fears and resentments from which few children emerge wholly uncontaminated. First and foremost, racism is as intimate a part of the child's familial and social upbringing as the milk he sucks in infancy.

9   3. Why is this? Why is an attitude so negative and so obviously detrimental to the communal life of men so universal?

10   We promised that we would try to understand, instead of trying to reassure ourselves at all costs or merely waxing indignant over some people's unexpected wickedness. The truth is that the *racist explanation is convenient.* That is why it is so easily and so commonly used both by individuals and by the group: It is too tempting to be resisted.

11   Because it corresponds somehow to what is evident and is somehow confirmed, the racist accusation is a widespread and persuasive social fact. *It is a psycho-social fact, because racism is an institutional fact.*

12   The colonized was not only accused of being a second-class man. *He was in fact just that:* He did not have the same rights as the colonizer himself. The black American is not only described as a misfit: Far too often he *is just that.* The Jew *is* genuinely separate and is placed under a more or less discreet form of quarantine.

13   Since it is a matter for observation that the *object of racism* is inferior and is ground down, isn't it tempting to look on the *racist ideology as an adequate expression of that objective situation?* To say that if the Jew is separate, it is probably because something in him naturally alienates others and deserves to be kept separate? To explain that if the fate of the colonized is so overwhelming and so miserable, it is because he was ripe to become the target of colonialism?

14   Of course one could stand up and say the situation is the other way around: it is the ideology, the accusation inflated to mythical proportions which explains and legitimizes the iniquitous situation of the *person discriminated against.* But whoever spoke out so boldly would immediately have to blame himself, his family and his entire universe for having made the victim such a *victim*—and who would have strength enough to do that? It would take lucidity, honesty and courage such as even so-called

---

[1]See *Portrait of a Jew,* chapter 6, part I.

highly cultured men are scarcely capable of. It is more "natural," more spontaneous, and so much more *convenient* to look for an explanation which soothes the deep-lying guilt felt by both individual and group toward the *victim of racism.*

4. The racist explanation is, after all, the most *effective.* "Euphoria-inducing," 15 as the psychologists put it, it is a great help to the anxious and avid Narcissus[2] concealed in each one of us. It reassures and flatters the racist, excuses and strengthens him by reinforcing his individual and collective ego.

And so economically too! By making the other people pay! The racist 16 finds joy, solace and vindication at the expense of others. He doesn't even have to boast; he merely belittles the others to set off his own qualities. His superiority does not have to be proven, since it is implied in the other man's inferiority.

The racist temptation is certainly the one least resisted—such an inex- 17 pensive vice, that does not even appear to be bad for the sinner's health, since it is practiced to *other* people's detriment. Why not give in to a craving so easy to satisfy and so common, for that matter?

5. *To be big, all the racist need do is climb on someone else's back.* 18

It is easy to understand why he chooses for this purpose the most obvi- 19 ous and resigned of victims, the one who submits to blows in silence, the victim who is already the most victimized: the most convenient step in the whole very convenient process.

You never hear of anti-American or anti-British, or even anti-German 20 racism: These are men who are historically strong, backed up by powerful nations. Whereas the racist wrings his triumph only out of men whom history has already defeated, the weaker links in the chain of humanity. *The racist instinctively chooses the oppressed,* heaping more misfortune on the unfortunate.

6. For this reason the foreigner is choice prey for the racist, a promising and 21 unhoped-for rung on which the posturing victor can place his foot to climb higher. *Which explains the obvious, intimate relationship between racism and xenophobia.* The vulnerability of the foreigner arouses racism, just as infirmity arouses sarcasm and scorn.

7. This accounts for the surprising *racism practiced by the oppressed man* 22 *himself.* Sure enough, the proletarian, the colonized, the Negro, the black man—all can turn around and be racists too. How can one victim attack another? Simply enough: by the same process and in response to the same temptation. If the French proletarian wants to feel a little taller, whom is he to step on if not on the immigrant worker, who has been North African so far but might also be Italian, Spanish or Polish—in other words, of the same so-called race as himself? Proof, if proof were needed, that racism is not always directly connected with race. If the modest colonizer, himself so taken advantage of and so disinherited, wanted to take revenge, what other target was there than the colonized, whom he could look down

---

[2]**Narcissus** A young man in Greek and Roman mythology who fell in love with his own reflection in a pool of water. [Ed. note.]

upon from the limited height of those meager privileges which the colonial system gave him? So it is that the American Jew may be tempted to scorn the American black, who reciprocates heartily.

23   Everyone looks for an inferior rank compared to which he appears relatively lofty and grand. Racism offers everyone the solution that suits him best; he need only find someone smaller, more humiliated than himself, and there he has his victim, the target for his scorn and prejudice. *Racism is a pleasure within everyone's reach.*

24   8. But do men really have such a terrible urge to reassure and reassert themselves, even at the cost of humiliating others, to justify themselves even by accusing others? Once we realize how extensive this compulsion is, how often this solution is adopted, then we are forced to realize that the answer is yes.

25   Certainly the solution is false, the compensation vain, small and above all unjust, distorting criteria and warping perspectives, self-deceiving, destroying one man's dignity to give another the illusion of dignity. But it must be admitted that it *is a sort of a solution to genuine problems,* a tranquilizer for disturbances so manifest and so common that we would be surprised if we did not find them.

26   The sick man consoles himself with the thought that others are even more sick than he; he has a vague idea that there are still several degrees between himself and death and that, compared to so-and-so, he is not so badly off after all. It is a fact that misery consoles misery. Is it surprising then that the racist takes a rest from his own misery by looking at the next man's? He even goes one step further, claiming that the next man is more miserable, unfortunate and perverse than he really is.

27   This is made all the easier by the fact that the next man is virtually never neutral. Not enough emphasis has been placed on a particular ingredient of racism, which is the uneasiness and *fear aroused by differentness.* The foreigner, or even merely a man of another social class, is always somewhat strange and frightening. It is only a few short steps from fear to hostility, and from hostility to aggression. Loving means relaxing, yielding, forgetting oneself in the other person, identifying with him more or less. You do not forgive a foreigner until you have managed to adopt him. Otherwise he continues to be inscrutable, to resist, as it were, and your reaction is one of anxiety and irritation. How can you help resenting people who force you to remain on the defensive? And now affective logic, that misnamed upside-down reasoning, comes into play: How can these people you suspect and sentence beforehand help but turn around and resent you?

28   9. From this point on, the passions whirl around in a vicious circle of "reasoning" like this: Since these people probably detest us, they certainly deserve to have us hate them, and mustn't we take precautions against their possible acts of aggression by acting aggressively against them if necessary, etc., etc. . . . ? Any number of battles, both individual and collective, grow chiefly out of such mean and devious arguments, designed to exorcise fear of the next man and soothe a troubled conscience.

Guilt feelings constitute one of the most powerful driving forces in the 29 *racist mechanism.* Why do privilege and oppression arouse such a strong racist reaction? Because racism is undoubtedly one way of combating that inner misery which is remorse. If there is oppression it must be because someone is guilty, and if the oppressor himself does not plead guilty—a situation which would soon become intolerable—then it must be the oppressed man who is guilty. *In short, by means of racism, the victim is blamed for the real or imaginary crimes of the racist.*

10. In that case, what can be done? What indeed, if the evil is so deeply 30 rooted and so widespread, so much a part of our institutions and our collective thoughts, so tempting and seemingly so inexpensive? But I don't believe it really is inexpensive; I maintain that like any other oppression, racism deforms the racist himself, both his appearance and his behavior, just as imperialism transformed even Europeans of good will into imperialists. But here again, tremendous lucidity would be required to realize the harm done to oneself by fear, authority and privileges. What can actually be done to wipe out the creeping infection?

It seems that we must *bring our sympathy into action,*[3] that we must 31 make the painstaking effort *to put ourselves in the other man's place.* This sort of wisdom is as old as time; it is the best way of understanding how someone else suffers, how insults and blows humiliate and pain him. Through our thoughts, at least, we achieve a kind of empathy. The ultimate effort is to try to live certain situations ourselves—to live in the black man's skin, as in the astounding experiment carried out by the white American, Griffith, or actually to share the daily existence of the working man, as certain political militants or the worker-priests compel themselves to do. There can be no doubt, in such a case, that when led by the body and the mind, the imagination, usually so lazy where others are concerned, is made to participate. No doubt either that this is the most effective form of mental hygiene to prevent racism from setting in.

11. But precisely because this process is so noble and demands so much of the 32 individual, it should be completed by more *collective measures. Education* will certainly continue to be the best technique for training and liberating mankind. Because it is a slow process, and a preventive one, because it reaches out to the young, because it acts continuously on the individual and at the same time influences great masses, education (which should be accompanied by a campaign for *adult enlightenment*) must always aim to discover what needs to be done so that men will cease to carry arms against one another and their natural aggressiveness can be put to a different use.

12. But the main point, I think, is this. *The fight against racism coincides, at* 33 *least partly, with the fight against oppression.* For fight there will be, necessarily. Racism is not only a perverted feeling; it is also the result, the expression, and the adjunct of a *de facto* situation which must be changed if

---

[3]Or we must "empathize," to borrow the precise expression of my friend and colleague, the French sociologist P. H. Maucorps.

racism is to be defeated. This means that the *oppressed man must cease to be oppressed,* to be the easily victimized embodiment of the oppressor's guilt feelings. The counterpart is that *the oppressor must stop being an oppressor,* stop having a convenient victim, needing to have one and needing to find an excuse for that need.

34   Of course the idea is not to strip man entirely of his aggressiveness, as some racists sarcastically claim it is. They hide behind a poor excuse for philosophy, allegedly virile but actually based on disdain for the human being and his possible destruction. A man needs a certain amount of aggressiveness. It would be unhealthful and even dangerous if a man were never able to hate and even, on occasion, to strike.

35   But his quasi-normal hesitation in the face of differentness must not become the instrument and the alibi for his injustice. Prejudice must not turn into myth. He must not feel entitled to bully any individual because that person belongs to a group covered by a blanket accusation of depravity.

36   Many anti-racists, swept away by an oversimplifying generosity, maintain that every real difference between men must be denied. But this is not necessary. On the contrary, *the differences must be luckily acknowledged,* admitted and respected as such. Once the other man is recognized as another man, such differences can even become a source of self-enrichment, as recognition encourages dialogue and brings it about. Whereas denying the differences, closing one's eyes to an undeniable aspect of human reality is liable to result in dangerous astonishment and a spectacular about-face the day those differences are finally brought home to even the most generous of humanists: a painful experience to which many of them, and many teachers in the colonies, can already testify.[4]

37   When face to face with differentness, and the problems it inevitably creates, there are two possible reactions: war, or dialogue. The temptation to defeat someone else, reduce him to servitude, and find some ideological pretext for doing so is certainly very common, and seems more worthwhile than beginning a dialogue and deciding on measures of equitable reciprocity.

38   13. Here is where an ethical and political *option* comes into play. Until now we have deliberately left it aside. A choice must be made between an atti-

---

[4]I take this opportunity to clarify a point concerning humanism: In recent decades, humanism has been the object of a great many attacks, and I myself have mocked the humanists. But a distinction must be made among different sorts of attack. The fascists too violently condemned the humanists and sneered at them, because the humanists fought against the image of man which the fascists had drawn.

Our own impatience had a different meaning, of course. We simply regretted that the humanists were so carried away by their generous impulse towards universal man, towards brotherhood based on reason and on a denominator common to all men that they neglected the concrete, specific problems of such-and-such individual man. Not to mention that the man involved was often a man in a difficult historical situation, such as the colonized or the Jew. A serious oversight, since humanism was in danger of becoming the philosophy of an alibi.

This is not to say, by any means, that I deny the humanist ideal. It should be furthered. It leads the way.

tude and a type of behavior which crush and humiliate certain men in order to exalt others, and an attitude and behavior which originate in the belief that all men are of equal dignity. Here is the dividing line between racists and anti-racists. The racist accepts this type of primitive violence and claims to justify it; the end result is undeniably a certain philosophy of man and of human relationships. The anti-racist rejects such a rupture between men and refuses to place them in two categories from which there is no appeal: the inferior and the superior. He believes dialogue is possible and is willing to reconsider existing situations and privileges. *In the last analysis, the dividing line runs between two views of man and two philosophies.*

14. One final word: *There is no denying the difficulty of the fight against* 39
racism.

It is not easy to put oneself in the place of the oppressed man, whoever 40
he may be; the difficulty of "taking part" in someone else becomes greater as the oppressed man becomes more oppressed, i.e., as the social and psychological *distance* between himself and other men increases. Often the gap between the colonized and even the best-intentioned colonizer was so wide that the white European had no notion of what was going on within the soul of his "impenetrable" native servant. Moreover, the victim of oppression feels that there is no way out; no man who is not oppressed has experienced despair and anguish to this degree. The non-oppressed man who tries to put himself in the victim's place can, by definition, call a halt to his experiment. No matter how sincere Griffith, the white American, was in dyeing his skin and living as a black among blacks in the South, he knew that whenever he wanted to he could go back up North, announce "I'm white," and bring his voluntary nightmare to an end. No one can ever put himself completely in the place of a black man nor in that of a Jew whose family has been exterminated in a crematory.

At the same time, what is taught in the schools must overcome what 41
is taught in the home and the street. It will have to uproot the entire cultural tradition which, being vague and incoherent, offers that much more resistance.

Only by transforming the objective conditions of existence can an end 42
be put to the various forms of oppression, and this transformation will not happen overnight. It does not depend on the strength of the anti-racists alone. Nor is there any guarantee that once a much-fought-for political order has been established, it will not, during some social crisis, turn around and use the time-tested racist alibi itself.

The struggle to combat racism is long and arduous, an attack to be 43
launched again and again, a campaign that will probably never be ended.

Yet for that very reason it is a fight which should be fought without 44
respite and without concession. We cannot be indulgent towards racism any more than we would deliberately bring a monster into our house even—still less—if the monster were disguised. Doing that would mean giving it a chance, putting the animal and the humane sides of ourselves and other men into the scales, and finding that they came down on the

side of the animal. What would it mean to accept the racist's way of thinking, even just slightly? It would mean endorsing fear, injustice and violence. Agreeing that no light is to pierce the dimness and obscurity in which we are still largely accustomed to living. Agreeing that the foreigner is to remain a potential victim. (But what man is not a foreigner—to someone else?) In short, racism illustrates the totally negative condition of subjugated man and in a certain way sheds light on the entire human condition. While the fight against racism is demanding and its outcome always uncertain, it is one of the indispensable preliminaries to the progress from animality to humanity. *We cannot afford not to take up the racist challenge.*

Questions for Discussion and Your Reading Journal

1. Why is almost everyone a racist according to Memmi? What types of racists exist?
2. How is the racist explanation psychologically "convenient" and "effective"? (See Numbers 3 and 4.)
3. Explain how victims of racism can also be racists themselves. How might racism perpetuate itself?
4. How can people's reactions to "differentness" contribute to racism?
5. What is the psychological process that leads to racism? What is the relationship between guilt and racism? (See Numbers 8 and 9.)
6. List the solutions needed according to Memmi. Why does the author say that oppressive "conditions of existence" must change? What are the relationships between racism, poverty, and oppression?
7. What ethical and political alternatives to racism exist? Why are these alternatives and solutions discussed at the end of this reading? Is this effective? Why or why not?
8. Because of the date of this selection, the language does not reflect the guidelines most publishers now use for inclusive language (e.g., pronouns that include women). Find three examples of noninclusive pronouns in this reading and suggest inclusive pronouns to replace these examples.
9. What racist stereotypes have you seen on television or in the movies? List examples.
10. Discuss examples of racism in your community. What do you think are the causes and consequences of this?

GEORGE ORWELL

The English author George Orwell (the pseudonym for Eric Arthur Blair, 1903–1950) is well known for Animal Farm, *a satire on Stalinism, and* 1984, *a warning against the growing totalitarianism in both the East and the West. Orwell's political development began in the 1920s when he spent five years in Burma as a member of the Indian imperial police.*

As recorded in this well-known essay, his experience gave him an insider's view of British colonialism, the occupation of another people's land, and imperialism, the use of cultural, political, and economic domination to control another country.

Reading Rhetorically

Although Orwell wrote about a time nearly a century past, his narrative essay included here presents a set of circumstances strikingly similar to what many young Americans are currently experiencing as they are sent to far-off lands in the service of their country. Like U.S. soldiers who find themselves acting as local leaders and decision makers in nations where they do not know the cultures and do not speak the languages, young Orwell found himself in Burma (now Myanmar) working as a police officer for England in the 1920s. The experience allowed him to write about racism, oppression, and the difficulties of running an empire in storytelling fashion, which makes his essay more entertaining and in certain ways more insightful than an argument paper brimming with facts. The "facts" in this reading are simply the things that happened to him one day in a village when an elephant went on a rampage and killed a man. Although he interprets these facts for us, there is also a good deal of room for us to see, to feel, and to interpret on our own as we follow his story. The argument he thereby makes against oppression is less structured than in the classical approach to persuasion, but it is no less effective, relying as it does upon stimulating our emotions, feelings, and personal connections (*pathos*) more than logic and reason.

Shooting an Elephant

In Moulmein, in lower Burma, I was hated by large numbers of people—the   1
only time in my life that I have been important enough for this to happen to me. I was subdivisional police officer of the town, and in an aimless, petty kind of way anti-European feeling was very bitter. No one had the guts to raise a riot, but if a European woman went through the bazaars alone somebody would probably spit betel juice over her dress. As a police officer I was an obvious target and was baited whenever it seemed safe to do so. When a nimble Burman tripped me up on the football field and the referee (another Burman) looked the other way, the crowd yelled with hideous laughter. This happened more than once. In the end the sneering yellow faces of young men that met me everywhere, the insults hooted after me when I was at a safe distance, got badly on my nerves. The young Buddhist priests were the worst of all. There were several thousands of them in the town and none of them seemed to have anything to do except stand on street corners and jeer at Europeans.

All this was perplexing and upsetting. For at that time I had already made   2
up my mind that imperialism was an evil thing and the sooner I chucked up my job and got out of it the better. Theoretically—and secretly, of course—I

was all for the Burmese and all against their oppressors, the British. As for the job I was doing, I hated it more bitterly than I can perhaps make clear. In a job like that you see the dirty work of Empire at close quarters. The wretched prisoners huddling in the stinking cages of the lock-ups, the grey, cowed faces of the long-term convicts, the scarred buttocks of the men who had been flogged with bamboos—all these oppressed me with an intolerable sense of guilt. But I could get nothing into perspective. I was young and ill-educated and I had had to think out my problems in the utter silence that is imposed on every Englishman in the East. I did not even know that the British Empire is dying, still less did I know that it is a great deal better than the younger empires that are going to supplant it. All I knew was that I was stuck between my hatred of the empire I served and my rage against the evil-spirited little beasts who tried to make my job impossible. With one part of my mind I thought of the British Raj as an unbreakable tyranny, as something clamped down, in *saecula saeculorum*,[1] upon the will of prostrate peoples; with another part I thought that the greatest joy in the world would be to drive a bayonet into a Buddhist priest's guts. Feelings like these are the normal by-products of imperialism; ask any Anglo-Indian official, if you can catch him off duty.

3   One day something happened which in a roundabout way was enlightening. It was a tiny incident in itself, but it gave me a better glimpse than I had had before of the real nature of imperialism—the real motives for which despotic governments act. Early one morning the sub-inspector at a police station the other end of the town rang me up on the phone and said that an elephant was ravaging the bazaar. Would I please come and do something about it? I did not know what I could do, but I wanted to see what was happening and I got on to a pony and started out. I took my rifle, an old .44 Winchester and much too small to kill an elephant, but I thought the noise might be useful *in terrorem*. Various Burmans stopped me on the way and told me about the elephant's doings. It was not, of course, a wild elephant, but a tame one which had gone "must." It had been chained up, as tame elephants always are when their attack of "must" is due, but on the previous night it had broken its chain and escaped. Its mahout, the only person who could manage it when it was in that state, had set out in pursuit, but had taken the wrong direction and was now twelve hours' journey away, and in the morning the elephant had suddenly reappeared in the town. The Burmese population had no weapons and were quite helpless against it. It had already destroyed somebody's bamboo hut, killed a cow and raided some fruit-stalls and devoured the stock; also it had met the municipal rubbish van and, when the driver jumped out and took to his heels, had turned the van over and inflicted violences upon it.

4   The Burmese sub-inspector and some Indian constables were waiting for me in the quarter where the elephant had been seen. It was a very poor quarter, a labyrinth of squalid bamboo huts, thatched with palm-leaf, winding all over a steep hillside. I remember that it was a cloudy, stuffy morning at the beginning of the rains. We began questioning the people as to where the elephant had gone and, as usual, failed to get any definite information. That is

---

[1] *saecula saeculorum* For ever and ever. [Ed. note.]

invariably the case in the East; a story always sounds clear enough at a distance, but the nearer you get to the scene of events the vaguer it becomes. Some of the people said that the elephant had gone in one direction, some said that he had gone in another, some professed not even to have heard of any elephant. I had almost made up my mind that the whole story was a pack of lies, when we heard yells a little distance away. There was a loud, scandalized cry of "Go away, child! Go away this instant!" and an old woman with a switch in her hand came round the corner of a hut, violently shooing away a crowd of naked children. Some more women followed, clicking their tongues and exclaiming; evidently there was something that the children ought not to have seen. I rounded the hut and saw a man's dead body sprawling in the mud. He was an Indian, a black Dravidian coolie, almost naked, and he could not have been dead many minutes. The people said that the elephant had come suddenly upon him round the corner of the hut, caught him with its trunk, put its foot on his back and ground him into the earth. This was the rainy season and the ground was soft, and his face had scored a trench a foot deep and a couple of yards long. He was lying on his belly with arms crucified and head sharply twisted to one side. His face was coated with mud, the eyes wide open, the teeth bared and grinning with an expression of unendurable agony. (Never tell me, by the way, that the dead look peaceful. Most of the corpses I have seen looked devilish.) The friction of the great beast's foot had stripped the skin from his back as neatly as one skins a rabbit. As soon as I saw the dead man I sent an orderly to a friend's house nearby to borrow an elephant rifle. I had already sent back the pony, not wanting it to go mad with fright and throw me if it smelt the elephant.

The orderly came back in a few minutes with a rifle and five cartridges, 5
and meanwhile some Burmans had arrived and told us that the elephant was in the paddy fields below, only a few hundred yards away. As I started forward practically the whole population of the quarter flocked out of the houses and followed me. They had seen the rifle and were all shouting excitedly that I was going to shoot the elephant. They had not shown much interest in the elephant when he was merely ravaging their homes, but it was different now that he was going to be shot. It was a bit of fun to them, as it would be to an English crowd; besides they wanted the meat. It made me vaguely uneasy. I had no intention of shooting the elephant—I had merely sent for the rifle to defend myself if necessary—and it is always unnerving to have a crowd following you. I marched down the hill, looking and feeling a fool, with the rifle over my shoulder and an ever-growing army of people jostling at my heels. At the bottom, when you got away from the huts, there was a metalled road and beyond that a miry waste of paddy fields a thousand yards across, not yet ploughed but soggy from the first rains and dotted with coarse grass. The elephant was standing eight yards from the road, his left side towards us. He took not the slightest notice of the crowd's approach. He was tearing up bunches of grass, beating them against his knees to clean them and stuffing them into his mouth.

I had halted on the road. As soon as I saw the elephant I knew with per- 6
fect certainty that I ought not to shoot him. It is a serious matter to shoot a working elephant—it is comparable to destroying a huge and costly piece of

machinery—and obviously one ought not to do it if it can possibly be avoided. And at that distance, peacefully eating, the elephant looked no more dangerous than a cow. I thought then and I think now that his attack of "must" was already passing off; in which case he would merely wander harmlessly about until the mahout came back and caught him. Moreover, I did not in the least want to shoot him. I decided that I would watch him for a little while to make sure that he did not turn savage again, and then go home.

7   But at that moment I glanced round at the crowd that had followed me. It was an immense crowd, two thousand at the least and growing every minute. It blocked the road for a long distance on either side. I looked at the sea of yellow faces above the garish clothes—faces all happy and excited over this bit of fun, all certain that the elephant was going to be shot. They were watching me as they would watch a conjurer about to perform a trick. They did not like me, but with the magical rifle in my hands I was momentarily worth watching. And suddenly I realized that I should have to shoot the elephant after all. The people expected it of me and I had got to do it; I could feel their two thousand wills pressing me forward, irresistibly. And it was at this moment, as I stood there with the rifle in my hands, that I first grasped the hollowness, the futility of the white man's dominion in the East. Here was I, the white man with his gun, standing in front of the unarmed native crowd—seemingly the leading actor of the piece; but in reality I was only an absurd puppet pushed to and fro by the will of those yellow faces behind. I perceived in this moment that when the white man turns tyrant it is his own freedom that he destroys. He becomes a sort of hollow, posing dummy, the conventionalized figure of a sahib. For it is the condition of his rule that he shall spend his life in trying to impress the "natives," and so in every crisis he has got to do what the "natives" expect of him. He wears a mask, and his face grows to fit it. I had got to shoot the elephant. I had committed myself to doing it when I sent for the rifle. A sahib has got to act like a sahib; he has got to appear resolute, to know his own mind and do definite things. To come all that way, rifle in hand, with two thousand people marching at my heels, and then to trail feebly away, having done nothing—no, that was impossible. The crowd would laugh at me. And my whole life, every white man's life in the East, was one long struggle not to be laughed at.

8   But I did not want to shoot the elephant. I watched him beating his bunch of grass against his knees, with that preoccupied grandmotherly air that elephants have. It seemed to me that it would be murder to shoot him. At that age I was not squeamish about killing animals, but I had never shot an elephant and never wanted to. (Somehow it always seems worse to kill a *large* animal.) Besides, there was the beast's owner to be considered. Alive, the elephant was worth at least a hundred pounds; dead, he would only be worth the value of his tusks, five pounds, possibly. But I had got to act quickly. I turned to some experienced-looking Burmans who had been there when we arrived, and asked them how the elephant had been behaving. They all said the same thing: he took no notice of you if you left him alone, but he might charge if you went too close to him.

It was perfectly clear to me what I ought to do. I ought to walk up to 9 within, say, twenty-five yards of the elephant and test his behavior. If he charged, I could shoot; if he took no notice of me, it would be safe to leave him until the mahout came back. But also I knew that I was going to do no such thing. I was a poor shot with a rifle and the ground was soft mud into which one would sink at every step. If the elephant charged and I missed him, I should have about as much chance as a toad under a steamroller. But even then I was not thinking particularly of my own skin, only of the watchful yellow faces behind. For at that moment, with the crowd watching me, I was not afraid in the ordinary sense, as I would have been if I had been alone. A white man mustn't be frightened in front of "natives"; and so, in general, he isn't frightened. The sole thought in my mind was that if anything went wrong those two thousand Burmans would see me pursued, caught, trampled on and reduced to a grinning corpse like that Indian up the hill. And if that happened it was quite probable that some of them would laugh. That would never do. There was only one alternative. I shoved the cartridges into the magazine and lay down on the road to get a better aim.

The crowd grew very still, and a deep, low, happy sigh, as of people who 10 see the theatre curtain go up at last, breathed from innumerable throats. They were going to have their bit of fun after all. The rifle was a beautiful German thing with cross-hair sights. I did not then know that in shooting an elephant one would shoot to cut an imaginary bar running from ear-hole to ear-hole. I ought, therefore, as the elephant was sideways on, to have aimed straight at his ear-hole; actually I aimed several inches in front of this, thinking the brain would be further forward.

When I pulled the trigger I did not hear the bang or feel the kick—one 11 never does when a shot goes home—but I heard the devilish roar of glee that went up from the crowd. In that instant, in too short a time, one would have thought, even for the bullet to get there, a mysterious, terrible change had come over the elephant. He neither stirred nor fell, but every line of his body had altered. He looked suddenly stricken, shrunken, immensely old, as though the frightful impact of the bullet had paralysed him without knocking him down. At last, after what seemed a long time—it might have been five seconds, I dare say—he sagged flabbily to his knees. His mouth slobbered. An enormous senility seemed to have settled upon him. One could have imagined him thousands of years old. I fired again into the same spot. At the second shot he did not collapse but climbed with desperate slowness to his feet and stood weakly upright, with legs sagging and head drooping. I fired a third time. That was the shot that did for him. You could see the agony of it jolt his whole body and knock the last remnant of strength from his legs. But in falling he seemed for a moment to rise, for as his hind legs collapsed beneath him he seemed to tower upward like a huge rock toppling, his trunk reaching skywards like a tree. He trumpeted, for the first and only time. And then down he came, his belly towards me, with a crash that seemed to shake the ground even where I lay.

I got up. The Burmans were already racing past me across the mud. It was 12 obvious that the elephant would never rise again, but he was not dead. He was breathing very rhythmically with long rattling gasps, his great mound of a side painfully rising and falling. His mouth was wide open—I could see far down into caverns of pale pink throat. I waited a long time for him to die, but his breathing did not weaken. Finally I fired my two remaining shots into the spot where I thought his heart must be. The thick blood welled out of him like red velvet, but still he did not die. His body did not even jerk when the shots hit him, the tortured breathing continued without a pause. He was dying, very slowly and in great agony, but in some world remote from me where not even a bullet could damage him further. I felt that I had got to put an end to that dreadful noise. It seemed dreadful to see the great beast lying there, powerless to move and yet powerless to die, and not even to be able to finish him. I sent back for my small rifle and poured shot after shot into his heart and down his throat. They seemed to make no impression. The tortured gasps continued as steadily as the ticking of a clock.

13   In the end I could not stand it any longer and went away. I heard later that it took him half an hour to die. Burmans were bringing dahs and baskets even before I left, and I was told they had stripped his body almost to the bones by the afternoon.

14   Afterwards, of course, there were endless discussions about the shooting of the elephant. The owner was furious, but he was only an Indian and could do nothing. Besides, legally I had done the right thing, for a mad elephant has to be killed, like a mad dog, if its owner fails to control it. Among the Europeans opinion was divided. The older men said I was right, the younger men said it was a damn shame to shoot an elephant for killing a coolie, because an elephant was worth more than any damn Coringhee coolie. And afterwards I was very glad that the coolie had been killed; it put me legally in the right and it gave me a sufficient pretext for shooting the elephant. I often wondered whether any of the others grasped that I had done it solely to avoid looking a fool.

Questions for Discussion and Your Reading Journal

1. What is the purpose of this reading and who is the audience?
2. Why is the Burmese citizens' behavior toward the narrator "perplexing and upsetting" to him? Look up the definition of imperialism in a dictionary or encyclopedia. How might the narrator's desire to drive "a bayonet into a Buddhist priest's guts" (Paragraph 2) be caused by imperialism?
3. The narrator refers to his own role as master. How is the narrator both a master and a slave? How might this comment on the British presence in Burma?
4. How is the psychology of imperialism and of ethnocentrism similar to that of racism (see Memmi, p. 180) and/or sexism (de Beauvoir, p. 195)?
5. What might the elephant's slow death symbolize?
6. How is the final paragraph ironic?
7. Choose a descriptive passage. What purpose does it serve in Orwell's narrative? What is your reaction to it?
8. Narration is the telling of a story. How does Orwell's use of narrative persuade?

9. This is a historical event, but many historians would not consider this essay to be history. Why?

SIMONE DE BEAUVOIR

The French author and feminist Simone de Beauvoir (1908–1986) wrote the influential feminist classic The Second Sex *(1949), from which this portion of the introduction is excerpted. De Beauvoir studied philosophy at the Sorbonne and wrote several novels; the most well-known of these works,* The Mandarins *(1954), won the prestigious Prix Goncourt. She wrote* The Second Sex *after a visit to the United States, where she was struck by the diminishing opportunities for women after World War II (when working women were fired so that returning soldiers would have jobs). The notion that "femininity" is a social construct—that, in de Beauvoir's words "one is not born, but rather becomes, a woman"—is familiar today, but was at that time original and, to some, scandalous. In the selection given here, de Beauvoir compares the oppression of blacks and Jews to the oppression of women, and explains how the attitudes of men and women define women only in relation to men. As the "Other," a woman is of secondary importance. Ironically enough, de Beauvoir herself is often defined by those who write about her solely in terms of her long relationship with existentialist philosopher Jean-Paul Sartre.*

Reading Rhetorically

When she wrote the following excerpt (late 1940s), de Beauvoir was one of very few women who had succeeded in entering the male world of French university scholars and intellectuals. To gain access to that world, she had to learn to think and to write in a style similar to the way male intellectuals of her time wrote. This may make her writing seem stuffy, distant, and hard to penetrate for college-level readers who live in a different time and in very different cultures from de Beauvoir's world. Of necessity, she proceeded carefully, in a rhetorical question-and-answer mode with constant and detailed support of her points through scholarly references to philosophers and great thinkers (Aristotle, St. Thomas, Claude Lévi-Strauss) that her male, intellectual audience would know and respect. As she wrote these lines, she could be certain that her ideas would be debated, challenged, and attacked by her friends, colleagues, and by educated people in faculty rooms, cafés, and salons throughout all of France (indeed, the world). She could especially count upon males to respond negatively to her ideas about inequalities between the sexes and the secondary/inferior status of women. Hence she often used neutral-seeming language for situations and experiences that must have been quite painful to her personally. For example, women are described as "other" in her title rather than as "inferior" or "oppressed." In short, she was making a philosophical argument about the status of women in history and in her own time and she did so in a manner most likely to be understandable and compelling to men. Only near the end of the piece did she begin to move beyond objective, philosophical language to more emotionally charged words and statements where women were compared to "slaves" and were described as "dependent" and "heavily handicapped" by "man-the-sovereign" who rules over "woman-the-liege." However, rather than getting lost in this kind of language, de Beauvoir closed the excerpt with a compelling explanation for *why* women accept and often choose this secondary role to men.

Women as Other

1   We must face the question: What is a woman?

2   To state the question is, to me, to suggest, at once, a preliminary answer. The fact that I ask it is in itself significant. A man would never get the notion of writing a book on the peculiar situation of the human male.[1] But if I wish to define myself, I must first of all say: "I am a woman"; on this truth must be based all further discussion. A man never begins by presenting himself as an individual of a certain sex; it goes without saying that he is a man. The terms *masculine* and *feminine* are used symmetrically only as a matter of form, as on legal papers. In actuality the relation of the two sexes is not quite like that of two electrical poles, for man represents both the positive and the neutral, as is indicated by the common use of *man* to designate human beings in general; whereas woman represents only the negative, defined by limiting criteria, without reciprocity. In the midst of an abstract discussion it is vexing to hear a man say: "You think thus and so because you are a woman"; but I know that my only defense is to reply: "I think thus and so because it is true," thereby removing my subjective self from the argument. It would be out of the question to reply: "And you think the contrary because you are a man," for it is understood that the fact of being a man is no peculiarity. A man is in the right in being a man; it is the woman who is in the wrong. It amounts to this: Just as for the ancients there was an absolute vertical with reference to which the oblique was defined, so there is an absolute human type, the masculine. Woman has ovaries, a uterus; these peculiarities imprison her in her subjectivity, circumscribe her within the limits of her own nature. It is often said that she thinks with her glands. Man superbly ignores the fact that his anatomy also includes glands, such as the testicles, and that they secrete hormones. He thinks of his body as a direct and normal connection with the world, which he believes he apprehends objectively, whereas he regards the body of woman as a hindrance, a prison, weighed down by everything peculiar to it. "The female is a female by virtue of a certain *lack* of qualities," said Aristotle; "we should regard the female nature as afflicted with a natural defectiveness." And St. Thomas for his part pro-

---

[1]The Kinsey Report (Alfred C. Kinsey and others: *Sexual Behavior in the Human Male* [Philadelphia: W. B. Saunders Co., 1948]) is no exception, for it is limited to describing the sexual characteristics of American men, which is quite a different matter.

nounced woman to be an "imperfect man," an "incidental" being. This is symbolized in Genesis where Eve is depicted as made from what Bossuet called "a supernumerary bone" of Adam.

Thus humanity is male and man defines woman not in herself but as relative to him; she is not regarded as an autonomous being. Michelet writes: "Woman, the relative being. . . ." And Benda is most positive in his *Rapport d'Uriel:* "The body of man makes sense in itself quite apart from that of woman, whereas the latter seems wanting in significance by itself. . . . Man can think of himself without woman. She cannot think of herself without man." And she is simply what man decrees; thus she is called "the sex," by which is meant that she appears essentially to the male as a sexual being. For him she is sex—absolute sex, no less. She is defined and differentiated with reference to man and not he with reference to her; she is the incidental, the inessential as opposed to the essential. He is the Subject, he is the Absolute— she is the Other.[2]

The category of the *Other* is as primordial as consciousness itself. In the most primitive societies, in the most ancient mythologies, one finds the expression of a duality—that of the Self and the Other. This duality was not originally attached to the division of the sexes; it was not dependent upon any empirical facts. It is revealed in such works as that of Granet on Chinese thought and those of Dumezil on the East Indies and Rome. The feminine element was at first no more involved in such pairs as Varuna-Mitra, Uranus-Zeus, Sun-Moon, and Day-Night than it was in the contrasts between Good and Evil, lucky and unlucky auspices, right and left, God and Lucifer. Otherness is a fundamental category of human thought.

Thus it is that no group ever sets itself up as the One without at once setting up the Other over against itself. If three travelers chance to occupy the same compartment, that is enough to make vaguely hostile "others" out of all the rest of the passengers on the train. In small-town eyes all persons not belonging to the village are "strangers" and suspect; to the native of a country all who inhabit other countries are "foreigners"; Jews are "different" for the anti-Semite, Negroes are "inferior" for American racists, aborigines are "natives" for colonists, proletarians are the "lower class" for the privileged.

3

4

5

---

[2]E. Lévinas expresses this idea most explicitly in his essay *Temps et l'Autre.* "Is there not a case in which otherness, alterity [*altérité*], unquestionably marks the nature of a being, as its essence, an instance of otherness not consisting purely and simply in the opposition of two species of the same genus? I think that the feminine represents the contrary in its absolute sense, this contrariness being in no wise affected by any relation between it and its correlative and thus remaining absolutely other. Sex is not a certain specific difference . . . no more is the sexual difference a mere contradiction. . . . Nor does this difference lie in the duality of two complementary terms, for two complementary terms imply a pre-existing whole. . . . Otherness reaches its full flowering in the feminine, a term of the same rank as consciousness but of opposite meaning."

I suppose that Lévinas does not forget that woman, too, is aware of her own consciousness, or ego. But it is striking that he deliberately takes a man's point of view, disregarding the reciprocity of subject and object. When he writes that woman is mystery, he implies that she is mystery for man. Thus his description, which is intended to be objective, is in fact an assertion of masculine privilege.

6   Lévi-Strauss, at the end of a profound work on the various forms of primitive societies, reaches the following conclusion: "Passage from the state of Nature to the state of Culture is marked by man's ability to view biological relations as a series of contrasts; duality, alternation, opposition, and symmetry, whether under definite or vague forms, constitute not so much phenomena to be explained as fundamental and immediately given data of social reality."[3] These phenomena would be incomprehensible if in fact human society were simply a *Mitsein* or fellowship based on solidarity and friendliness. Things become clear, on the contrary, if, following Hegel, we find in consciousness itself a fundamental hostility toward every other consciousness; the subject can be posed only in being opposed—he sets himself up as the essential, as opposed to the other, the inessential, the object.

7   But the other consciousness, the other ego, sets up a reciprocal claim. The native traveling abroad is shocked to find himself in turn regarded as a "stranger" by the natives of neighboring countries. As a matter of fact, wars, festivals, trading, treaties, and contests among tribes, nations, and classes tend to deprive the concept *Other* of its absolute sense and to make manifest its relativity; willy-nilly, individuals and groups are forced to realize the reciprocity of their relations. How is it, then, that this reciprocity has not been recognized between the sexes, that one of the contrasting terms is set up as the sole essential, denying any relativity in regard to its correlative and defining the latter as pure otherness? Why is it that women do not dispute male sovereignty? No subject will readily volunteer to become the object, the inessential; it is not the Other who, in defining himself as the Other, establishes the One. The Other is posed as such by the One in defining himself as the One. But if the Other is not to regain the status of being the One, he must be submissive enough to accept this alien point of view. Whence comes this submission in the case of woman?

8   There are, to be sure, other cases in which a certain category has been able to dominate another completely for a time. Very often this privilege depends upon inequality of numbers—the majority imposes its rule upon the minority or persecutes it. But women are not a minority, like the American Negroes or the Jews; there are as many women as men on earth. Again, the two groups concerned have often been originally independent; they may have been formerly unaware of each other's existence, or perhaps they recognized each other's autonomy. But a historical event has resulted in the subjugation of the weaker by the stronger. The scattering of the Jews, the introduction of slavery into America, the conquests of imperialism are examples in point. In these cases the oppressed retained at least the memory of former days; they possessed in common a past, a tradition, sometimes a religion or a culture.

9   The parallel drawn by Bebel between women and the proletariat is valid in that neither ever formed a minority or a separate collective unit of mankind. And instead of a single historical event it is in both cases a historical develop-

---

[3]See C. Lévi-Strauss: *Les Structures élémentaires de la parenté.* My thanks are due to C. Lévi-Strauss for his kindness in furnishing me with the proofs of his work, which, among others, I have used liberally in Part II.

ment that explains their status as a class and accounts for the membership of *particular individuals* in that class. But proletarians have not always existed, whereas there have always been women. They are women in virtue of their anatomy and physiology. Throughout history they have always been subordinated to men,[4] and hence their dependency is not the result of a historical event or a social change—it was not something that *occurred*. The reason why otherness in this case seems to be an absolute is in part that it lacks the contingent or incidental nature of historical facts. A condition brought about at a certain time can be abolished at some other time, as the Negroes of Haiti and others have proved; but it might seem that a natural condition is beyond the possibility of change. In truth, however, the nature of things is no more immutably given, once for all, than is historical reality. If woman seems to be the inessential which never becomes the essential, it is because she herself fails to bring about this change. Proletarians say "We"; Negroes also. Regarding themselves as subjects, they transform the bourgeois, the whites, into "others." But women do not say "We," except at some congress of feminists or similar formal demonstration; men say "women," and women use the same word in referring to themselves. They do not authentically assume a subjective attitude. The proletarians have accomplished the revolution in Russia, the Negroes in Haiti, the Indo-Chinese are battling for it in Indo-China; but the women's effort has never been anything more than a symbolic agitation. They have gained only what men have been willing to grant; they have taken nothing, they have only received.

The reason for this is that women lack concrete means for organizing   10
themselves into a unit which can stand face to face with the correlative unit. They have no past, no history, no religion of their own; and they have no such solidarity of work and interest as that of the proletariat. They are not even promiscuously herded together in the way that creates community feeling among the American Negroes, the ghetto Jews, the workers of Saint-Denis, or the factory hands of Renault. They live dispersed among the males, attached through residence, housework, economic condition, and social standing to certain men—fathers or husbands—more firmly than they are to other women. If they belong to the bourgeoisie, they feel solidarity with men of that class, not with proletarian women; if they are white, their allegiance is to white men, not to Negro women. The proletariat can propose to massacre the ruling class, and a sufficiently fanatical Jew or Negro might dream of getting sole possession of the atomic bomb and making humanity wholly Jewish or black; but woman cannot even dream of exterminating the males. The bond that unites her to her oppressors is not comparable to any other. The division of the sexes is a biological fact, not an event in human history. Male and female stand opposed within a primordial *Mitsein*, and woman has not broken it. The couple is a fundamental unity with its two halves riveted together, and the cleavage of society along the line of sex is impossible. Here is to be found the basic trait of woman: she is the Other in a totality of which the two components are necessary to one another.

---

[4]With rare exceptions, perhaps, like certain matriarchal rulers, queens, and the like. [Ed. note.]

11   One could suppose that this reciprocity might have facilitated the liberation of woman. When Hercules sat at the feet of Omphale and helped with her spinning, his desire for her held him captive; but why did she fail to gain a lasting power? To revenge herself on Jason, Medea killed their children; and this grim legend would seem to suggest that she might have obtained a formidable influence over him through his love for his offspring. In *Lysistrata* Aristophanes gaily depicts a band of women who joined forces to gain social ends through the sexual needs of their men; but this is only a play. In the legend of the Sabine women, the latter soon abandoned their plan of remaining sterile to punish their ravishers. In truth woman has not been socially emancipated through man's need—sexual desire and the desire for offspring—which makes the male dependent for satisfaction upon the female.

12   Master and slave, also, are united by a reciprocal need, in this case economic, which does not liberate the slave. In the relation of master to slave the master does not make a point of the need that he has for the other; he has in his grasp the power of satisfying this need through his own action; whereas the slave, in his dependent condition, his hope and fear, is quite conscious of the need he has for his master. Even if the need is at bottom equally urgent for both, it always works in favor of the oppressor and against the oppressed. That is why the liberation of the working class, for example, has been slow.

13   Now, woman has always been man's dependent, if not his slave; the two sexes have never shared the world in equality. And even today woman is heavily handicapped, though her situation is beginning to change. Almost nowhere is her legal status the same as man's, and frequently it is much to her disadvantage. Even when her rights are legally recognized in the abstract, longstanding custom prevents their full expression in the mores. In the economic sphere men and women can almost be said to make up two castes; other things being equal, the former hold the better jobs, get higher wages, and have more opportunity for success than their new competitors. In industry and politics men have a great many more positions and they monopolize the most important posts. In addition to all this, they enjoy a traditional prestige that the education of children tends in every way to support, for the present enshrines the past—and in the past all history has been made by men. At the present time, when women are beginning to take part in the affairs of the world, it is still a world that belongs to men—they have no doubt of it at all and women have scarcely any. To decline to be the Other, to refuse to be a party to the deal—this would be for women to renounce all the advantages conferred upon them by their alliance with the superior caste. Man-the-sovereign will provide woman-the-liege with material protection and will undertake the moral justification of her existence; thus she can evade at once both economic risk and the metaphysical risk of a liberty in which ends and aims must be contrived without assistance. Indeed, along with the ethical urge of each individual to affirm his subjective existence, there is also the temptation to forgo liberty and become a thing. This is an inauspicious road, for he who takes it—passive, lost, ruined—becomes henceforth the creature of another's will, frustrated in his transcendence and deprived of every value. But it is an easy road; on it one avoids the strain involved in undertaking an authentic existence. When man

makes of woman the *Other,* he may, then, expect her to manifest deep-seated tendencies toward complicity. Thus, woman may fail to lay claim to the status of subject because she lacks definite resources, because she feels the necessary bond that ties her to man regardless of reciprocity, and because she is often very well pleased with her role as the *Other.* . . .

Questions for Discussion and Your Reading Journal

1. In your own words, discuss the idea of women as the Other. What does the author mean by calling the concept of the Other "primordial" (Paragraph 4)? When thinking about gender, de Beauvoir states that we create the categories of "Self" and "Other." In what other cases might we divide the world into Self versus Other? Illustrate with examples.
2. What might be the psychological and social consequences of this status of the Other for women?
3. According to de Beauvoir, why is recognizing the legal rights of women not enough for women to achieve equality?
4. How does de Beauvoir compare and contrast sexism to racism and to anti-Semitism? Also compare this selection to Albert Memmi's "Racism and Oppression" (p. 181). How might the categories of Self versus Other be useful for understanding racism and xenophobia?

AMAURY DE RIENCOURT

In his introduction to Sex and Power in History, *de Riencourt (1918–) argues that the conflict between the sexes is "the most significant element in the overall crisis of contemporary civilization." He states that, unlike Indian and Chinese civilizations that respected the differences between the sexes, Greek rational thought held women to be "inferior or incomplete males." Arguing that the devaluing of women provoked a feminist revolt that weakened Roman ethical values and family structure, de Riencourt fears that contemporary Western society could be similarly destroyed. He condemns those in the women's liberation movement who favor unisexual or androgynous values because these values imply "a social and cultural death-wish and the end of the civilization that endorses it." He rejects patriarchal values and calls for the creation of a new set of values "based on respect for the different specificities of the sexes and the same reverence for the creation of Life as for the creations of the Mind." In the chapter on Greece from which this selection is chosen, de Riencourt argues that, despite being patriarchal, the aristocracy of Greece's Homeric Age (10th–9th century BCE) still held some respect for women and granted them considerable liberties. This was not the case in the democratic Periclean period (5th century BCE), however, due in part to the Greek attitude toward love and to the discovery that males too had a part in procreation. Unlike contemporary forms of democracy, ancient Athens accepted inequality and so found no contradiction in practicing slavery and in oppressing women. This essay might be compared to Simone de Beauvoir's "Women as Other" (p. 196) and Albert Memmi's psychological analysis of racism and oppression (p. 181).*

Reading Rhetorically

The French author de Riencourt followed in the same vein as Simon de Beauvoir (previous reading) in his criticism of the long tradition of male privilege between the sexes in the Western world. However, where de Beauvoir wrote about the issue in a general sense, de Riencourt focused upon one historical case study: women in Athens around 500 BCE. Also like de Beauvoir, he delayed his main point until the end of the reading, a second testament to the highly sensitive nature of this topic for readers, particularly male readers, in the 20th century. De Reincourt started out as if he were simply seeking to inform readers of the facts of women's lives in classical Greece (expository writing). He wrote with the same detached, objective air that had long characterized male-dominated scholarship and writing in the West. He seemed to have no argumentative position as he presented quote after quote from long-revered male thinkers and writers from the time of classical Greece to present times. But, instead of celebrating their profound thinking and big ideas in the long-established tradition of other male (and occasionally female) writers, he quoted then often-shocking and puzzlingly negative views on the female sex of these "great minds." Only when we reach the last line of the piece do we see that he finally moved from offering us the "facts" to reveal his position. By that point, he has built such a compelling case for his position statement that it seems less the idea of a single writer and more an indisputable fact similar to the many lesser facts that have led up to it. With this "delayed-thesis" approach, de Riencourt skillfully anticipates and disarms most counterarguments that his readers (male readers in particular) might make to his position before they have a chance to make them.

Women in Athens

1   With the development of Greek culture came a steady regression of woman's status; from Herodotus to Thucydides, she gradually faded into the home, and Plutarch takes pleasure in quoting Thucydides to the effect that "the name of a decent woman, like her person, should be shut up in the house." Greek literature was suddenly full of disparaging remarks about woman and her innumerable faults—witness the writings of Hesiod, Lucian, Aristophanes, and Semonides of Amorgos.[1] Her legal status deteriorated: Inheritance through the mother disappeared; she could not make contracts or incur large debts or bring actions at law. Solon even went so far as to legislate

---

[1] W. Jaeger, *Paideia: The Ideals of Greek Culture*, 3 vols., trans. by G. Highet (Oxford: B. Blackwell, 1954), 122.

that anything done under the influence of woman could not be legally binding. Furthermore, she did not even inherit her husband's property after his death. She retreated to a virtual purdah, locked in her home and advised not to be seen near a window; she spent most of her life in the women's quarters and never appeared when male friends visited her husband.

Such downgrading at the height of Greek cultural achievements is strik- 2 ing, especially in Periclean Athens. But Pericles himself approved; in his famous Funeral Speech, he summed up his views: "If I must also speak a word to those who are in widowhood on the powers and duties of women, I will cast all my advice in one brief sentence. Great will be your glory if you do not lower the nature which is within you—hers most of all whose praise or blame is least bruited on the lips of men."[2]

The strongly masculine character of Greek culture may in part account for 3 this, but it is also a weird reversal of the basic concepts of sexual creativity. In the old days men were suitably ignorant about their creative role in life. Athenian lore claimed that before Cecrops, the legendary founder of Athens, "children did not know their own fathers."[3] The discovery of their role as sexual inseminators gave them a new pride and stimulated the patriarchal revolution. Now the Greeks went a step further. They fancied that *men alone* were endowed with generative power, women being merely empty vessels or, at best, sort of incubators designed to carry *their* child and nurse it in life's early stages. Like the Persians' divine Ohrmazd, more than one Greek sighed and uttered the famous "If only we could have children without having recourse to women!" This recurring theme of extreme misogynists was echoed again, some two thousand years later, by Thomas Browne: "I could be content that we might procreate like trees, without conjunction, or that there were any way to perpetuate the World without this trivial and vulgar way of union."[4] We shall see what Aeschylus did with this theme in his Oresteian trilogy.

Athenian women were hardly educated, in accord with Euripides' view 4 that women were harmed by an overly developed intellect. In the sixth century B.C., women still contributed somewhat to Greek literature; by the fifth century B.C., they were culturally barren. Having turned their respectable women into bores, men then searched elsewhere for entertainment and inspiration— in the extraordinary development of homosexuality and in the company of the only free women in Athens, the *hetairai*, the "companions," the most accomplished courtesans of the times. Demosthenes summed up the Athenian view of woman's uses in the following statement: "We have courtesans for the sake of pleasure, concubines for the daily health of our bodies, and wives to bear us lawful offspring and be the faithful guardians of our homes."

The only attractive—and therefore influential—women were the *hetairai*, 5 women of some social standing, endowed with a veneer of culture, and capable

[2]A. Zimmern, *The Greek Commonwealth* (Oxford: The Clarendon Press, 1924), 338.

[3]J. E. Harrison, *Prolegomena to the Study of Greek Religion* (Cambridge: Cambridge UP, 1922), 260–62.

[4]Browne, in *Harvard Classics*, 50 vols, ed. by C. W. Eliot (New York: P. F. Collier and Son, 1937), 3:323.

of witty and learned conversation. They were denied civil rights but were entitled to the protection of their special goddess, Aphrodite Pandemos. Many of
them left some mark on Greek history and literature—Aspasia, one of the precursors, who seduced Pericles and opened a school of rhetoric and philosophy;
the famous Clepsydra, who timed her lovers' visits with an hourglass;
Thargelia, the great spy for the account of the Persians; Danae, who influenced
Epicurus in his philosophic views; Archeanassa and Theoris, who amused
respectively Plato and Sophocles; and countless others. Some, whose plastic
beauty was breathtaking, inspired artists and served as models—Phryne, who
appeared stark naked at the Eleusinian festival and posed for Praxiteles'
"Aphrodite"; and also Lais of Corinth, one of the great beauties of all time,
whose eccentric adventures stunned her contemporaries. In fact, nothing symbolizes more aptly the Greek view of the female sex's social role and value as
Praxiteles' two antipodal statues, "The Weeping Wife" and "The Laughing
Hetairai."[5]

6   Greek men held a contemptuous view of the opposite sex; even the best-
endowed *hetairai* had a difficult time competing with their clients' male lovers.
Even in Sparta, where women enjoyed more prestige and influence than in the
rest of Greece. Alcman could pay no greater compliment to his women companions than to call them his "female boy-friends!"[6] The poet-politician
Critias stated that girls were charming only to the extent that they were
slightly boyish—and vice versa.[7] Homosexuality was both a cause and a consequence of this steady downgrading of the female of the species; and rave
against it as they might, the *hetairai* proved unable to curb it. At any rate, the
Greek example makes it plain that the prevalence of male homosexuality in
any given society is tightly linked with increasing misogyny and the social
repression of woman; a kind of *horror feminae* pervades the social atmosphere, springing from the fact that the typical feminine attributes—maternal
procreativity and sexual-libidinal endowments—are no longer appreciated.
Havelock Ellis quite rightly pointed out the close connection between infanticide (birth control) and homosexuality, a connection that is stamped by an
incipient death-wish on the part of any society where they prevail.[8] When the
point is reached that woman is rejected, even as a sex object, this society is,
psychologically, committing suicide—as the Greek example made plain a few
generations after Pericles.

7   If we dig further, it becomes clear that one main reason for this degradation of the female sex is that, whereas we put the emphasis of love on its object
and think of it in terms of the worthiness of the object, the ancient Greeks put
it on the urge itself, honoring the feeling even if it happened to focus on an
unworthy recipient. This made it easier for the Greeks to restrict their eroti-

---

[5]C. C. Zimmerman and S. J. Cervantes. *Marriage and the Family* (Chicago: H. Regnery Co.,
1956), 450.

[6]H. Ellis. *Studies in the Psychology of Sex,* 6 vols. (Philadelphia: F. A. Davis Co., 1911), 6:134.

[7]Jaeger, *Paideia,* 1:346.

[8]Zimmerman and Cervantes, *Marriage and the Family,* 451.

cism largely to homosexual relations. Its prevalence was such that it became part of public education in Sparta and Crete; it became the essential element in Greek military formations where pairs of lovers and male beloved ones formed the basic tactical unit, fighting side by side—the Sacred Band at Thebes, presumed to be the finest fighting force in the Hellenic world, was made up entirely of homosexuals.

Most Greeks had only pity for those few men who could fall in love with women with the same passion as with members of their own sex. Even the famous Platonic love is, in fact, sublimated love of an exclusively homosexual nature. In the *Symposium*, Pausanias states: 8

> There are two goddesses of love, and therefore, also two forms of Eros. 9
> The Eros of the earthly Aphrodite is earthly, universal, common and casual. And everything common worships her. Both sexes, man and woman, had part in the creation and birth of the earthly Aphrodite. The higher love comes from the heavenly Aphrodite and she is the creation of man. Therefore all youths and men who are seized with this love strive after their own sex, full of longing for the manly; they love the stronger nature and the higher mind.[9]

Such an outlook was devastating to feminine status, dignity, and influence. 10

Questions for Discussion and your Reading Journal

1. What is the purpose of this article? Who might be the audience?
2. How did ancient Athens view the role of women in procreation and sexual relations? How might this have been used to justify Athenian patriarchy (male rule)?
3. What sources of evidence does this article use to justify its claims? What other kinds of evidence could a historian use?
4. One of de Riencourt's claims is that women's loss of status is both a cause and a consequence of the rise of homosexuality in Athenian society. What evidence does de Riencourt use to support this claim? Is it convincing? Explain.
5. Review de Beauvoir's concept of the Other (p. 196). How were women treated as the Other in ancient Athens? What were the consequences of this? Are women in contemporary America also the Other? In what ways? What are the consequences of this?
6. Review the concept of the Other in de Beauvoir. How might de Riencourt treat homosexuals as the Other? In what ways does our society view homosexuals as the Other?

---

[9]E. Friedell, *A Cultural History of the Modern Age*, 3 vols., (New York: Knopf, 1953), 2:348–49.

MOHANDAS K. GANDHI

Mohandas K. Gandhi (1869–1948), the Indian leader of nonviolent resistance in South Africa and against British colonial ride in India, was influenced by a variety of traditions and writers. Hindu religion, Henry David Thoreau's classic essay "Civil Disobedience," Tolstoy's writings and letters to Gandhi, and Jesus' "Sermon on the Mount" are some of the sources that contributed to Gandhi's thought. He first applied "Satyagraha" (literally, "insistence on truth") before World War I in South Africa when the government began to legislate against the Indian minority there. This strategy included strikes, boycotts, mass demonstrations, peaceful picketing, noncooperation, and civil disobedience. Upon his return to India, Gandhi organized another wave of civil disobedience. In 1919, he fasted to protest the British imprisonment of Indians without trial. In Satyagraha, religion, truth, and politics are inseparable. According to Gandhi, living by eternal "Truth" (that which he calls "truly real" as opposed to the material world) requires people to develop their selflessness, their independence from material possessions, and their courage to resist using violence even when their opponents use it. Gandhi's nonviolent means are intended to achieve justice by appealing to the conscience of the oppressor. Since Martin Luther King Jr. was greatly influenced by Gandhi's ideas, this reading can be compared to King's "Letter from Birmingham Jail" (p. 212). Likewise, Gandhi's nonviolent protest can be contrasted to Nelson Mandela's justification of using sabotage (p. 227), a form of violence that is not directed against people.

Reading Rhetorically

In the following piece, Gandhi expounded the core of those ideas that made him known and celebrated throughout the world in his time. To pull this off successfully, he faced a daunting challenge: How does one present new and potentially unpopular ideas in a manner that both encourages an audience to hear the writer out and then to give weight to what he has said? Gandhi chose a rhetorical approach that parallels that used by Plato nearly 25 centuries before. After offering an introduction that defined his key terms, he set up a "dialogue" between his readers and himself. The "reader" in the following text offered questions and challenges to Gandhi. Gandhi then took the role of "editor" and responded point by point in a philosophical exposition of his ideas that interwove history, poetry, spirituality, argument, and pithy counter-argument to create his *ethos* as a writer.

Satyagraha

SECTION FIRST: WHAT SATYAGRAHA IS

1 Satyagraha, Civil Disobedience, Passive Resistance, Non-Co-operation

Satyagraha is literally holding on to Truth and it means, therefore, Truth-   1
force. Truth is soul or spirit. It is, therefore, known as soul-force. It
excludes the use of violence because man is not capable of knowing the
absolute truth and, therefore, not competent to punish. The word was coined
in South Africa to distinguish the non-violent resistance of the Indians of
South Africa from the contemporary "passive resistance" of the suffragettes
and others. It is not conceived as a weapon of the weak.

Passive resistance is used in the orthodox English sense and covers the suf-   2
fragette movement as well as the resistance of the Non-conformists. Passive
resistance has been conceived and is regarded as a weapon of the weak. Whilst
it avoids violence, being not open to the weak, it does not exclude its use if, in
the opinion of a passive resister, the occasion demands it. However, it has
always been distinguished from armed resistance and its application was at
one time confined to Christian martyrs.

Civil Disobedience is civil breach of unmoral statutory enactments. The   3
expression was, so far as I am aware, coined by Thoreau to signify his own
resistance to the laws of a slave State. He has left a masterly treatise on the
duty of Civil Disobedience. But Thoreau was not perhaps an out and out
champion of non-violence. Probably, also, Thoreau limited his breach of statutory laws to the revenue law, i.e., payment of taxes. Whereas the term Civil
Disobedience as practised in 1919 covered a breach of any statutory and
unmoral law. It signified the resister's outlawry in a civil, i.e., non-violent manner. He invoked the sanctions of the law and cheerfully suffered imprisonment.
It is a branch of Satyagraha.

Non-co-operation predominantly implies withdrawing of co-operation   4
from the State that in the non-co-operator's view has become corrupt and
excludes Civil Disobedience of the fierce type described above. By its very
nature, non-co-operation is even open to children of understanding and can be
safely practised by the masses. Civil Disobedience presupposes the habit of
willing obedience to laws without fear of their sanctions. It can, therefore, be
practised only as a last resort and by a select few in the first instance at any
rate. Non-co-operation, too, like Civil Disobedience is a branch of Satyagraha
which includes all non-violent resistance for the vindication of Truth.

5 Satyagraha or Passive Resistance[1]

Reader: Is there any historical evidence as to the success of what you have   5
called soul-force or truth-force? No instance seems to have happened of any

---

[1]In this section Gandhi as editor answers questions he thinks a reader might raise. [Ed. note.]

nation having risen through soul-force. I still think that the evil-doers will not cease doing evil without physical punishment.

6   **Editor:** The poet Tulsidas has said: "Of religion, pity, or love, is the root, as egotism of the body. Therefore, we should not abandon pity so long as we are alive." This appears to me to be a scientific truth. I believe in it as much as I believe in two and two being four. The force of love is the same as the force of the soul or truth. We have evidence of its working at every step. The universe would disappear without the existence of that force. But you ask for historical evidence. It is, therefore, necessary to know what history means. The Gujarati equivalent means: "It so happened." If that is the meaning of history, it is possible to give copious evidence. But, if it means the doings of kings and emperors, there can be no evidence of soul-force or passive resistance in such history. You cannot expect silver ore in a tin mine. History, as we know it, is a record of the wars of the world, and so there is a proverb among Englishmen that a nation which has no history, that is, no wars, is a happy nation. How kings played, how they became enemies of one another, how they murdered one another, is found accurately recorded in history, and if this were all that had happened in the world, it would have been ended long ago. If the story of the universe had commenced with wars, not a man would have been found alive today. Those people who have been warred against have disappeared as, for instance, the natives of Australia of whom hardly a man was left alive by the intruders. Mark, please, that these natives did not use soul-force in self-defence, and it does not require much foresight to know that the Australians will share the same fate as their victims. "Those that take the sword shall perish by the Sword." With us the proverb is that professional swimmers will find a watery grave.

7   The fact that there are so many men still alive in the world shows that it is based not on the force of arms but on the force of truth or love. Therefore, the greatest and most unimpeachable evidence of the success of this force is to be found in the fact that, in spite of the wars of the world, it still lives on.

8   Thousands, indeed tens of thousands, depend for their existence on a very active working of this force. Little quarrels of millions of families in their daily lives disappear before the exercise of this force. Hundreds of nations live in peace. History does not and cannot take note of this fact. History is really a record of every interruption of the even working of the force of love or of the soul. Two brothers quarrel; one of them repents and re-awakens the love that was lying dormant in him; the two again begin to live in peace; nobody takes note of this. But if the two brothers, through the intervention of solicitors or some other reason, take up arms or go to law—which is another form of the exhibition of brute force—their doing would be immediately noticed in the press, they would be the talk of their neighbours and would probably go down to history. And what is true of families and communities is true of nations. There is no reason to believe that there is one law for families and another for nations. History, then, is a record of an interruption of the course of nature. Soul-force, being natural, is not noted in history.

9   **Reader:** According to what you say, it is plain that instances of this kind of passive resistance are not to be found in history. It is necessary to understand

this passive resistance more fully. It will be better, therefore, if you enlarge upon it.

Editor: Passive resistance is a method of securing rights by personal suffering; 10 it is the reverse of resistance by arms. When I refuse to do a thing that is repugnant to my conscience, I use soul-force. For instance, the Government of the day has passed a law which is applicable to me. I do not like it. If by using violence I force the Government to repeal the law, I am employing what may be termed body-force. If I do not obey the law and accept the penalty for its breach, I use soul-force. It involves sacrifice of self.

Everybody admits that sacrifice of self is infinitely superior to sacrifice of 11 others. Moreover, if this kind of force is used in a cause that is unjust, only the person using it suffers. He does not make others suffer for his mistakes. Men have before now done many things which were subsequently found to have been wrong. No man can claim that he is absolutely in the right or that a particular thing is wrong because he thinks so, but it is wrong for him so long as that is his deliberate judgment. It is therefore meet that he should not do that which he knows to be wrong, and suffer the consequence whatever it may be. This is the key to the use of soul-force.

Reader: You would then disregard laws—this is rank disloyalty. We have always 12 been considered a law-abiding nation. You seem to be going even beyond the extremists. They say that we must obey the laws that have been passed, but that if the laws be bad, we must drive out the law-givers even by force.

Editor: Whether I go beyond them or whether I do not is a matter of no con- 13 sequence to either of us. We simply want to find out what is right and to act accordingly. The real meaning of the statement that we are a law-abiding nation is that we are passive resisters. When we do not like certain laws, we do not break the heads of law-givers but we suffer and do not submit to the laws. That we should obey laws whether good or bad is a newfangled notion. There was no such thing in former days. The people disregarded those laws they did not like and suffered the penalties for their breach. It is contrary to our manhood if we obey laws repugnant to our conscience. Such teaching is opposed to religion and means slavery. If the Government were to ask us to go about without any clothing, should we do so? If I were a passive resister, I would say to them that I would have nothing to do with their law. But we have so forgotten ourselves and become so compliant that we do not mind any degrading law.

A man who has realized his manhood, who fears only God, will fear no 14 one else. Man-made laws are not necessarily binding on him. Even the Government does not expect any such thing from us. They do not say: "You must do such and such a thing," but they say: "If you do not do it, we will punish you." We are sunk so low that we fancy that it is our duty and our religion to do what the law lays down. If man will only realize that it is unmanly to obey laws that are unjust, no man's tyranny will enslave him. This is the key to self-rule or home-rule.

It is a superstition and ungodly thing to believe that an act of a majority 15 binds a minority. Many examples can be given in which acts of majorities will be found to have been wrong and those of minorities to have been right. All reforms owe their origin to the initiation of minorities in opposition to majorities. If among a band of robbers a knowledge of robbing is obligatory, is a pious man to accept the obligation? So long as the superstition that men should obey unjust laws exists, so long will their slavery exist. And a passive resister alone can remove such a superstition.

16   To use brute-force, to use gunpowder, is contrary to passive resistance, for it means that we want our opponent to do by force that which we desire but he does not. And, if such a use of force is justifiable, surely he is entitled to do likewise by us. And so we should never come to an agreement. We may simply fancy, like the blind horse moving in a circle round a mill, that we are making progress. Those who believe that they are not bound to obey laws which are repugnant to their conscience have only the remedy of passive resistance open to them. Any other must lead to disaster.

12 Conditions for Successful Satyagraha

17 There can be no Satyagraha in an unjust cause. Satyagraha in a just cause is vain, if the men espousing it are not determined and capable of fighting and suffering to the end; and the slightest use of violence often defeats a just cause. Satyagraha excludes the use of violence in any shape or form, whether in thought, speech, or deed. Given a just cause, capacity for endless suffering and avoidance of violence, victory is a certainty.

13 Non-retaliation

18 Victory is impossible until we are able to keep our temper under the gravest provocation. Calmness under fire is a soldier's indispensable quality. A non-co-operator is nothing if he cannot remain calm and unperturbed under a fierce fire of provocation.

19   There should be no mistake. There is no civil disobedience possible, until the crowds behave like disciplined soldiers. And we cannot resort to civil disobedience, unless we can assure every Englishman that he is as safe in India as he is in his own home. It is not enough that we give the assurance. Every Englishman and Englishwoman must feel safe, not by reason of the bayonet at their disposal but by reason of our living creed of non-violence. That is the condition not only of success but our own ability to carry on the movement in its present form. There is no other way of conducting the campaign of non-co-operation.

14 Courage and Discipline Necessary

20 The pledge of non-violence does not require us to cooperate in our humiliation. It, therefore, does not require us to crawl on our bellies or to draw lines with our noses or to walk to salute the Union Jack or to do anything degrading at the dictation of officials. On the contrary our creed requires us to refuse to do any of these things even though we should be shot. It was, therefore, for instance, no part of the duty of the Jalianwala Bagh people to run away or

even to turn their backs when they were fired upon. If the message of non-violence had reached them, they would have been expected when fire was opened on them to march towards it with bare breasts and die rejoicing in the belief that it meant the freedom of their country. Non-violence laughs at the might of the tyrant and stultifies him by non-retaliation and non-retiral. We played into General Dyer's[1] hands because we acted as he had expected. He wanted us to run away from his fire, he wanted us to crawl on our bellies and to draw lines with our noses. That was a part of the game of "frightfulness." When we face it with eyes front, it vanishes like an apparition. We may not all evolve that type of courage. But I am certain that Swaraj[2] is unattainable this year if some of us have not the courage which enables us to stand firm like a rock without retaliating. The might of the tyrant recoils upon himself when it meets with no response, even as an arm violently waved in the air suffers dislocation.

And just as we need the cool courage described above, we need perfect discipline and training in voluntary obedience to be able to offer civil disobedience. Civil disobedience is the active expression of non-violence. Civil disobedience distinguishes the non-violence of the strong from the passive, i.e., negative non-violence of the weak. And as weakness cannot lead to Swaraj, negative non-violence must fail to achieve our purpose. 21

Have we then the requisite discipline? Have we, a friend asked me, evolved the spirit of obedience to our own rules and resolutions? Whilst we have made tremendous headway during the past twelve months, we have certainly not made enough to warrant us in embarking upon civil disobedience with easy confidence. Rules voluntarily passed by us and rules which carry no sanction save the disapproval of our own conscience must be like debts of honour held far more binding than rules superimposed upon us or rules whose breach we can purge by paying the penalty thereof. It follows that if we have not learnt the discipline of obeying our own rules, in other words carrying out our own promises, we are ill adapted for disobedience that can be at all described as civil. I do, therefore, suggest to every Congressman, every non-cooperator, and above all to every member of the All India Congress Committee to set himself or herself right with the Congress and his or her creed by carrying on the strictest self-examination and by correcting himself or herself wherever he or she might have failed. 22

Questions for Discussion and Your Reading Journal

1. Summarize the key characteristics of Gandhi's "Satyagraha" and the concept of "soul-force." What are his definitions of these ideas?

---

[1]In this passage Gandhi is referring to the Massacre at Amritsar. He had organized a Satyagraha in 1919 to protest British laws that imprisoned, without trial, those Indians suspected of sedition. At a public rally in Amritsar, British soldiers, under General Dyer, opened fire and killed nearly 400 Indians. [Ed. note.]

[2]**Swaraj** Self-government or home rule. [Ed. note.]

2. Compare the role of religion in Gandhi's and King's (p. 215) beliefs. How does each use religion to distinguish between just and unjust laws?
3. Discuss Gandhi's different definitions of history. How does his definition differ from a history of wars and the "doings of kings and emperors" (Paragraph 6)? How does this contribute to his argument?
4. Using current examples, discuss Gandhi's statement that "All reforms owe their origin to the initiation of minorities in opposition to majorities" (Paragraph 15).
5. Discuss why you would or would not apply Satyagraha in your own life.

MARTIN LUTHER KING JR.

Martin Luther King Jr. (1929–1968), winner of the Nobel Peace Prize, clergyman, and civil rights leader, organized the 1956 boycott of public buses in Montgomery, Alabama, that led the Supreme Court to outlaw segregation on intrastate and interstate transportation. He also organized the Southern Christian Leadership Conference (SCLC) as a means of creating a mass civil rights movement. In the spring of 1963, he campaigned to end segregation at lunch counters in Birmingham, Alabama, and wrote "Letter from Birmingham Jail" after he was arrested in this campaign. "Letter from Birmingham Jail," written in the epistolary tradition of St. Paul, is King's response to black and white clergymen who argued, in "Public Statement by Eight Alabama Clergymen," against public demonstrations. Influenced by Gandhi, King justifies the need for nonviolent direct action as a last resort in challenging unjust laws. King's efforts contributed to the passage of the Civil Rights Acts of 1964, which legally desegregated public housing and the workplace. But, despite legal changes, the persistence of social, political and economic discrimination against blacks frustrated King and many others in the civil rights movement. Since nonviolent methods often did not solve more deeply entrenched forms of racism, after 1965 Malcolm X, Stokely Carmichael, and others advocated a separatist black nationalism and the use of violence to combat the violence leveled against blacks.

Reading Rhetorically

The following reading is one of the most celebrated statements growing out of the American Civil Rights Movement of the mid-20th century. In it, King revealed the rhetorical skill that made him a top student at Boston University and that sustained him through the fray of one of the most troubled times of change in American history. What King presented in his "Letter" was a compelling blend of the best in two rhetorical traditions, the Christian "epistle" from the early days of the Church and the argument/counterargument of classical Greece. By first presenting to his readers the argument of eight white Alabama clergymen against his nonviolent protest movement in Birmingham,

Alabama, King set up a context in which he could lead readers more deeply into his own position in the extended counterargument that followed. This is a rhetorical model perfected by the Greeks in the courtrooms of classical antiquity. However, by adding to this the language and letter-writing style of the Christian epistle, King tapped into another rhetorical tradition growing directly out of a parallel time of injustice and persecution when the spiritual ancestors of his white audience were themselves the victims of discrimination and persecution in the Roman world, as recorded in the Bible's *New Testament*. With these rhetorical tools at his disposal, King rose to one of his most eloquent and persuasive moments in an impressive career of public discourse devoted to moral social action. Under his skillful pen, he paralleled the work of Paul the Apostle to spread the "gospel of Jesus Christ to the far corners of the Greco-Roman world" to his own efforts to "carry the gospel of freedom beyond my own home town" and across America. He wrote phrases that have since echoed throughout the world, such as "Injustice anywhere is a threat to justice everywhere." He also put into words the concrete conceptual steps that formed his philosophical approach to social change as much as "Satyagraha" represents the approach of Mohandas Gandhi.

Letter from Birmingham Jail

PUBLIC STATEMENT BY EIGHT ALABAMA CLERGYMEN

(April 12, 1963)

We the undersigned clergymen are among those who, in January, issued "An Appeal for Law and Order and Common Sense," in dealing with racial problems in Alabama. We expressed understanding that honest convictions in racial matters could properly be pursued in the courts, but urged that decisions of those courts should in the meantime be peacefully obeyed. 1

Since that time there has been some evidence of increased forbearance and a willingness to face facts. Responsible citizens have undertaken to work on various problems which cause racial friction and unrest. In Birmingham, recent public events have given indication that we all have opportunity for a new constructive and realistic approach to racial problems. 2

However, we are now confronted by a series of demonstrations by some of our Negro citizens, directed and led in part by outsiders. We recognize the natural impatience of people who feel that their hopes are slow in being realized. But we are convinced that these demonstrations are unwise and untimely. 3

We agree rather with certain local Negro leadership which has called for honest and open negotiation of racial issues in our area. And we believe this kind of facing of issues can best be accomplished by citizens of our own metropolitan area, white and Negro, meeting with their knowledge and experience of the local situation. All of us need to face that responsibility and find proper channels for its accomplishment. 4

5   Just as we formerly pointed out that "hatred and violence have no sanction in our religious and political traditions," we also point out that such actions as incite to hatred and violence, however technically peaceful those actions may be, have not contributed to the resolution of our local problems. We do not believe that these days of new hope are days when extreme measures are justified in Birmingham.

6   We commend the community as a whole, and the local news media and law enforcement officials in particular, on the calm manner in which these demonstrations have been handled. We urge the public to continue to show restraint should the demonstrations continue, and the law enforcement officials to remain calm and continue to protect our city from violence.

7   We further strongly urge our own Negro community to withdraw support from these demonstrations, and to unite locally in working peacefully for a better Birmingham. When rights are consistently denied, a cause should be pressed in the courts and in negotiations among local leaders, and not in the streets. We appeal to both our white and Negro citizenry to observe the principles of law and order and common sense.

Signed by:
C. C. J. CARPENTER, D. D., LL.D., *Bishop of Alabama*
JOSEPH A. DURICK, D. D., *Auxiliary Bishop, Diocese of Mobile, Birmingham*
Rabbi MILTON L. GRAFMAN, *Temple Emanu-El, Birmingham, Alabama*
Bishop PAUL HARDIN, *Bishop of the Alabama-West Florida Conference of the Methodist Church*
Bishop NOLAN B. HARMON, *Bishop of the North Alabama Conference of the Methodist Church*
GEORGE M. MURRAY, D. D., LL.D., *Bishop Coadjutor, Episcopal Diocese of Alabama*
EDWARD V. RAMAGE, *Moderator, Synod of the Alabama Presbyterian Church in the United States*
EARL STALLINGS, *Pastor, First Baptist Church, Birmingham, Alabama*

LETTER FROM BIRMINGHAM JAIL

MARTIN LUTHER KING, JR.
Birmingham City Jail
April 16, 1963

Bishop C. C. J. CARPENTER
Bishop JOSEPH A. DURICK
Rabbi MILTON L. GRAFMAN
Bishop PAUL HARDIN
Bishop NOLAN B. HARMON
The Rev. GEORGE M. MURRAY
The Rev. EDWARD V. RAMAGE
The Rev. EARL STALLINGS

My Dear Fellow Clergymen:[1]   8

    While confined here in the Birmingham city jail, I came across your recent   9
statement calling my present activities "unwise and untimely." Seldom do I
pause to answer criticism of my work and ideas. If I sought to answer all the
criticisms that cross my desk, my secretaries would have little time for anything other than such correspondence in the course of the day, and I would
have no time for constructive work. But since I feel that you are men of genuine good will and that your criticisms are sincerely set forth, I want to try to
answer your statement in what I hope will be patient and reasonable terms.

    I think I should indicate why I am here in Birmingham, since you have   10
been influenced by the view which argues against "outsiders coming in." I
have the honor of serving as president of the Southern Christian Leadership
Conference, an organization operating in every southern state, with headquarters in Atlanta, Georgia. We have some eighty-five affiliated organizations
across the South, and one of them is the Alabama Christian Movement for
Human Rights Frequently we share staff, educational, and financial resources
with our affiliates. Several months ago the affiliate here in Birmingham asked
us to be on call to engage in a nonviolent direct-action program if such were
deemed necessary. We readily consented, and when the hour came we lived up
to our promise. So I, along with several members of my staff, am here because
I was invited here. I am here because I have organizational ties here. . . .

    But more basically, I am in Birmingham because injustice is here. Just as   11
the prophets of the eighth century B.C. left their villages and carried their "thus
saith the Lord" far beyond the boundaries of their home towns, and just as the
Apostle Paul left his village of Tarsus and carried the gospel of Jesus Christ to
the far corners of the Greco-Roman world, so am I compelled to carry the
gospel of freedom beyond my own home town. Like Paul, I must constantly
respond to the Macedonian call for aid.

    Moreover, I am cognizant of the interrelatedness of all communities and   12
states. I cannot sit idly by in Atlanta and not be concerned about what happens in Birmingham. Injustice anywhere is a threat to justice everywhere. We
are caught in an inescapable network of mutuality, tied in a single garment of
destiny. Whatever affects one directly, affects all indirectly. Never again can we
afford to live with the narrow, provincial "outside agitator" idea. Anyone who
lives inside the United States can never be considered an outsider anywhere
within its bounds.

    You deplore the demonstrations taking place in Birmingham. But your   13
statement, I am sorry to say, fails to express a similar concern for the conditions

---

[1]This response to a published statement by eight fellow clergymen from Alabama . . . was composed under somewhat constricting circumstances. Begun on the margins of the newspaper in
which the statement appeared while I was in jail, the letter was continued on scraps of writing paper supplied by a friendly Negro trusty, and concluded on a pad my attorneys were eventually
permitted to leave me. Although the text remains in substance unaltered, I have indulged in the
author's prerogative of polishing it for publication.

that brought about the demonstrations. I am sure that none of you would want to rest content with the superficial kind of social analysis that deals merely with effects and does not grapple with underlying causes. It is unfortunate that demonstrations are taking place in Birmingham, but it is even more unfortunate that the city's white power structure left the Negro community with no alternative.

14   In any nonviolent campaign there are four basic steps: collection of the facts to determine whether injustices exist; negotiation; self-purification; and direct action. We have gone through all these steps in Birmingham. There can be no gainsaying the fact that racial injustice engulfs this community. Birmingham is probably the most thoroughly segregated city in the United States. Its ugly record of brutality is widely known. Negroes have experienced grossly unjust treatment in the courts. There have been more unsolved bombings of Negro homes and churches in Birmingham than in any other city in the nation. These are the hard, brutal facts of the case. On the basis of these conditions, Negro leaders sought to negotiate with the city fathers. But the latter consistently refused to engage in good-faith negotiation.

15   Then, last September, came the opportunity to talk with leaders of Birmingham's economic community. In the course of the negotiations, certain promises were made by the merchants—for example, to remove the stores' humiliating racial signs. On the basis of these promises, the Reverend Fred Shuttlesworth and the leaders of the Alabama Christian Movement for Human Rights agreed to a moratorium on all demonstrations. As the weeks and months went by, we realized that we were the victims of a broken promise. A few signs, briefly removed, returned; the others remained.

16   As in so many past experiences, our hopes had been blasted, and the shadow of deep disappointment settled upon us. We had no alternative except to prepare for direct action, whereby we would present our very bodies as a means of laying our case before the conscience of the local and the national community. Mindful of the difficulties involved, we decided to undertake a process of self-purification. We began a series of workshops on nonviolence, and we repeatedly asked ourselves: "Are you able to accept blows without retaliating?" "Are you able to endure the ordeal of jail?" We decided to schedule our direct-action program for the Easter season, realizing that except for Christmas, this is the main shopping period of the year. Knowing that a strong economic-withdrawal program would be the by-product of direct action, we felt that this would be the best time to bring pressure to bear on the merchants for the needed change.

17   Then it occurred to us that Birmingham's mayoral election was coming up in March, and we speedily decided to postpone action until after election day. When we discovered that the Commissioner of Public Safety, Eugene "Bull" Connor, had piled up enough votes to be in the run-off, we decided again to postpone action until the day after the run-off so that the demonstrations could not be used to cloud the issues. Like many others, we waited to see Mr. Connor defeated, and to this end we endured postponement after postponement. Having aided in this community need, we felt that our direct-action program could be delayed no longer.

You may well ask: "Why direct action? Why sit-ins, marches and so forth?   18
Isn't negotiation a better path?" You are quite right in calling for negotiation.
Indeed, this is the very purpose of direct action. Nonviolent direct action seeks
to create such a crisis and foster such a tension that a community which has constantly refused to negotiate is forced to confront the issue. It seeks so to drama-
tize the issue that it can no longer be ignored. My citing the creation of tension
as part of the work of the nonviolent-resister may sound rather shocking. But I
must confess that I am not afraid of the word "tension." I have earnestly
opposed violent tension, but there is a type of constructive, nonviolent tension
which is necessary for growth. Just as Socrates felt that it was necessary to create a tension in the mind so that individuals could rise from the bondage of
myths and half-truths to the unfettered realm of creative analysis and objective
appraisal, so must we see the need for nonviolent gadflies to create the kind of
tension in society that will help men rise from the dark depths of prejudice and
racism to the majestic heights of understanding and brotherhood.

The purpose of our direct-action program is to create a situation so cri-   19
sispacked that it will inevitably open the door to negotiation. I therefore con-
cur with you in your call for negotiation. Too long has our beloved Southland
been bogged down in a tragic effort to live in monologue rather than dialogue.

One of the basic points in your statement is that the action that I and my   20
associates have taken in Birmingham is untimely. Some have asked: "Why
didn't you give the new city administration time to act?" The only answer that
I can give to this query is that the new Birmingham administration must be
prodded about as much as the outgoing one, before it will act. We are sadly
mistaken if we feel that the election of Albert Boutwell as mayor will bring the
millennium to Birmingham. While Mr. Boutwell is a much more gentle person
than Mr. Connor, they are both segregationists, dedicated to maintenance of
the status quo. I have hope that Mr. Boutwell will be reasonable enough to see
the futility of massive resistance to desegregation. But he will not see this without pressure from devotees of civil rights. My friends, I must say to you that
we have not made a single gain in civil rights without determined legal and
nonviolent pressure. Lamentably, it is an historical fact that privileged groups
seldom give up their privileges voluntarily. Individuals may see the moral light
and voluntarily give up their unjust posture; but, as Reinhold Niebuhr has
reminded us, groups tend to be more immoral than individuals.

We know through painful experience that freedom is never voluntarily   21
given by the oppressor; it must be demanded by the oppressed. Frankly, I have
yet to engage in a direct-action campaign that was "well timed" in the view of
those who have not suffered unduly from the disease of segregation. For years
now I have heard the word "Wait!" It rings in the ear of every Negro with
piercing familiarity. This "Wait" has almost always meant "Never." We must
come to see, with one of our distinguished jurists, that "justice too long
delayed is justice denied."

We have waited for more than 340 years for our constitutional and God-   22
given rights. The nations of Asia and Africa are moving with jetlike speed
toward gaining political independence, but we still creep at horse-and-buggy
pace toward gaining a cup of coffee at a lunch counter. Perhaps it is easy for

those who have never felt the stinging darts of segregation to say, "Wait." But when you have seen vicious mobs lynch your mothers and fathers at will and drown your sisters and brothers at whim; when you have seen hate-filled policemen curse, kick and even kill your black brothers and sisters; when you see the vast majority of your twenty million Negro brothers smothering in an airtight cage of poverty in the midst of an affluent society; when you suddenly find your tongue twisted and your speech stammering as you seek to explain to your six-year-old daughter why she can't go to the public amusement park that has just been advertised on television, and see tears welling up in her eyes when she is told that Funtown is closed to colored children, and see ominous clouds of inferiority beginning to form in her little mental sky, and see her beginning to distort her personality by developing an unconscious bitterness toward white people; when you have to concoct an answer for a five-year-old son who is asking: "Daddy, why do white people treat colored people so mean?"; when you take a cross-country drive and find it necessary to sleep night after night in the uncomfortable corners of your automobile because no motel will accept you; when you are humiliated day in and day out by nagging signs reading "white" and "colored"; when your first name becomes "nigger," your middle name becomes "boy" (however old you are) and your last name becomes "John," and your wife and mother are never given the respected title "Mrs."; when you are harried by day and haunted by night by the fact that you are a Negro, living constantly at tiptoe stance, never quite knowing what to expect next, and are plagued with inner fears and outer resentments; when you are forever fighting a degenerating sense of "nobodiness"—then you will understand why we find it difficult to wait. There comes a time when the cup of endurance runs over, and men are no longer willing to be plunged into the abyss of despair. I hope, sirs, you can understand our legitimate and unavoidable impatience.

23   You express a great deal of anxiety over our willingness to break laws. This is certainly a legitimate concern. Since we so diligently urge people to obey the Supreme Court's decision of 1954 outlawing segregation in the public schools, at first glance it may seem rather paradoxical for us consciously to break laws. One may well ask: "How can you advocate breaking some laws and obeying others?" The answer lies in the fact that there are two types of laws: just and unjust. I would be the first to advocate obeying just laws. One has not only a legal but a moral responsibility to obey just laws. Conversely, one has a moral responsibility to disobey unjust laws. I would agree with St. Augustine that "an unjust law is no law at all."

24   Now, what is the difference between the two? How does one determine whether a law is just or unjust? A just law is a man-made code that squares with the moral law or the law of God. An unjust law is a code that is out of harmony with the moral law. To put it in the terms of St. Thomas Aquinas: An unjust law is a human law that is not rooted in eternal law and natural law. Any law that uplifts human personality is just. Any law that degrades human personality is unjust. All segregation statutes are unjust because segregation distorts the soul and damages the personality. It gives the segregator a false sense of superiority and the segregated a false sense of inferiority. Segregation,

to use the terminology of the Jewish philosopher Martin Buber, substitutes an "I-it" relationship for an "I-thou" relationship and ends up relegating persons to the status of things. Hence segregation is not only politically, economically and sociologically unsound, it is morally wrong and sinful. Paul Tillich has said that sin is separation. Is not segregation an existential expression of man's tragic separation, his awful estrangement, his terrible sinfulness? Thus it is that I can urge men to obey the 1954 decision of the Supreme Court, for it is morally right; and I can urge them to disobey segregation ordinances, for they are morally wrong.

Let us consider a more concrete example of just and unjust laws. An unjust   25
law is a code that a numerical or power majority group compels a minority group to obey but does not make binding on itself. This is *difference* made legal. By the same token, a just law is a code that a majority compels a minority to follow and that it is willing to follow itself. This is *sameness* made legal.

Let me give another explanation. A law is unjust if it is inflicted on a   26
minority that, as a result of being denied the right to vote, had no part in enacting or devising the law. Who can say that the legislature of Alabama which set up that state's segregation laws was democratically elected? Throughout Alabama all sorts of devious methods are used to prevent Negroes from becoming registered voters, and there are some counties in which, even though Negroes constitute a majority of the population, not a single Negro is registered. Can any law enacted under such circumstances be considered democratically structured?

Sometimes a law is just on its face and unjust in its application. For   27
instance, I have been arrested on a charge of parading without a permit. Now, there is nothing wrong in having an ordinance which requires a permit for a parade. But such an ordinance becomes unjust when it is used to maintain segregation and to deny citizens the First-Amendment privilege of peaceful assembly and protest.

I hope you are able to see the distinction I am trying to point out. In no sense   28
do I advocate evading or defying the law, as would the rabid segregationist. That would lead to anarchy. One who breaks an unjust law must do so openly, lovingly, and with a willingness to accept the penalty. I submit that an individual who breaks a law that conscience tells him is unjust, and who willingly accepts the penalty of imprisonment in order to arouse the conscience of the community over its injustice, is in reality expressing the highest respect for law.

Of course, there is nothing new about this kind of civil disobedience. It   29
was evidenced sublimely in the refusal of Shadrach, Meshach and Abednego to obey the laws of Nebuchadnezzar, on the ground that a higher moral law was at stake. It was practiced superbly by the Early Christians, who were willing to face hungry lions and the excruciating pain of chopping blocks rather than submit to certain unjust laws of the Roman Empire. To a degree, academic freedom is a reality today because Socrates practiced civil disobedience. In our own nation, the Boston Tea Party represented a massive act of civil disobedience.

We should never forget that everything Adolf Hitler did in Germany was   30
"legal" and everything the Hungarian freedom fighters did in Hungary was

"illegal." It was "illegal" to aid and comfort a Jew in Hitler's Germany. Even so, I am sure that, had I lived in Germany at the time, I would have aided and comforted my Jewish brothers. If today I lived in a Communist country where certain principles dear to the Christian faith are suppressed, I would openly advocate disobeying that country's antireligious laws.

31   I must make two honest confessions to you, my Christian and Jewish brothers. First, I must confess that over the past few years I have been gravely disappointed with the white moderate. I have almost reached the regrettable conclusion that the Negro's great stumbling block in his stride toward freedom is not the White Citizen's Counciler or the Ku Klux Klanner, but the white moderate, who is more devoted to "order" than to justice; who prefers a negative peace which is the absence of tension to a positive peace which is the presence of justice; who constantly says: "I agree with you in the goal you seek, but I cannot agree with your methods of direct action"; who paternalistically believes he can set the timetable for another man's freedom; who lives by a mythical concept of time and who constantly advises the Negro to wait for a "more convenient season." Shallow understanding from people of good will is more frustrating than absolute misunderstanding from people of ill will. Lukewarm acceptance is much more bewildering than outright rejection.

32   I had hoped that the white moderate would understand that law and order exist for the purpose of establishing justice and that when they fail in this purpose they become the dangerously structured dams that block the flow of social progress. I had hoped that the white moderate would understand that the present tension in the South is a necessary phase of the transition from an obnoxious negative peace, in which the Negro passively accepted his unjust plight, to a substantive and positive peace, in which all men will respect the dignity and worth of human personality. Actually, we who engage in nonviolent direct action are not the creators of tension. We merely bring to the surface the hidden tension that is already alive. We bring it out in the open, where it can be seen and dealt with. Like a boil that can never be cured so long as it is covered up but must be opened with all its ugliness to the natural medicines of air and light, injustice must be exposed, with all the tension its exposure creates, to the light of human conscience and the air of national opinion before it can be cured.

33   In your statement you assert that our actions, even though peaceful, must be condemned because they precipitate violence. But is this a logical assertion? Isn't this like condemning a robbed man because his possession of money precipitated the evil act of robbery? Isn't this like condemning Socrates because his unswerving commitment to truth and his philosophical inquiries precipitated the act by the misguided populace in which they made him drink hemlock? Isn't this like condemning Jesus because his unique God-consciousness and never-ceasing devotion to God's will precipitated the evil act of crucifixion? We must come to see that, as the federal courts have consistently affirmed, it is wrong to urge an individual to cease his efforts to gain his basic constitutional rights because the quest may precipitate violence. Society must protect the robbed and punish the robber.

I had also hoped that the white moderate would reject the myth concern- 34
ing time in relation to the struggle for freedom. I have just received a letter
from a white brother in Texas. He writes: "All Christians know that the colored people will receive equal rights eventually, but it is possible that you are
in too great a religious hurry. It has taken Christianity almost two thousand
years to accomplish what it has. The teachings of Christ take time to come to
earth." Such an attitude stems from a tragic misconception of time, from the
strangely irrational notion that there is something in the very flow of time that
will inevitably cure all ills. Actually, time itself is neutral; it can be used either
destructively or constructively. More and more I feel that the people of ill will
have used time much more effectively than have the people of good will. We
will have to repent in this generation not merely for the hateful words and
actions of the bad people but for the appalling silence of the good people.
Human progress never rolls in on wheels of inevitability; it comes through the
tireless efforts of men willing to be coworkers with God, and without this hard
work, time itself becomes an ally of the forces of social stagnation. We must
use time creatively, in the knowledge that the time is always ripe to do right.
Now is the time to make real the promise of democracy and transform our
pending national elegy into a creative psalm of brotherhood. Now is the time
to lift our national policy from the quicksand of racial injustice to the solid
rock of human dignity.

You speak of our activity in Birmingham as extreme. At first I was rather 35
disappointed that fellow clergymen would see my nonviolent efforts as those
of an extremist. I began thinking about the fact that I stand in the middle of
two opposing forces in the Negro community. One is a force of complacency,
made up in part of Negroes who, as a result of long years of oppression, are
so drained of self-respect and a sense of "somebodiness" that they have
adjusted to segregation; and in part of a few middle-class Negroes who,
because of a degree of academic and economic security and because in some
ways they profit by segregation, have become insensitive to the problems of
the masses. The other force is one of bitterness and hatred, and it comes per-
ilously close to advocating violence. It is expressed in the various black nationalist groups that are springing up across the nation, the largest and best-
known being Elijah Muhammad's Muslim movement. Nourished by the
Negro's frustration over the continued existence of racial discrimination, this
movement is made up of people who have lost faith in America, who have
absolutely repudiated Christianity, and who have concluded that the white
man is an incorrigible "devil."

I have tried to stand between these two forces, saying that we need emu- 36
late neither the "do-nothingism" of the complacent nor the hatred and despair
of the black nationalist. For there is the more excellent way of love and nonviolent protest. I am grateful to God that, through the influence of the Negro
church, the way of nonviolence became an integral part of our struggle.

If this philosophy had not emerged, by now many streets of the South 37
would, I am convinced, be flowing with blood. And I am further convinced
that if our white brothers dismiss as "rabble-rousers" and "outside agitators"
those of us who employ nonviolent direct action, and if they refuse to support

our nonviolent efforts, millions of Negroes will, out of frustration and despair, seek solace and security in black-nationalist ideologies—a development that would inevitably lead to a frightening racial nightmare.

38   Oppressed people cannot remain oppressed forever. The yearning for freedom eventually manifests itself, and that is what has happened to the American Negro. Something within has reminded him of his birthright of freedom, and something without has reminded him that it can be gained. Consciously or unconsciously, he has been caught up by the *Zeitgeist*,[2] and with his black brothers of Africa and his brown and yellow brothers of Asia, South America and the Caribbean, the United States Negro is moving with a sense of great urgency toward the promised land of racial justice. If one recognizes this vital urge that has engulfed the Negro community, one should readily understand why public demonstrations are taking place. The Negro has many pent-up resentments and latent frustrations, and he must release them. So let him march; let him make prayer pilgrimages to the city hall; let him go on freedom rides—and try to understand why he must do so. If his repressed emotions are not released in nonviolent ways, they will seek expression through violence; this is not a threat but a fact of history. So I have not said to my people: "Get rid of your discontent." Rather, I have tried to say that this normal and healthy discontent can be channeled into the creative outlet of nonviolent direct action. And now this approach is being termed extremist.

39   But though I was initially disappointed at being categorized as an extremist, as I continued to think about the matter I gradually gained a measure of satisfaction from the label. Was not Jesus an extremist for love: "Love your enemies, bless them that curse you, do good to them that hate you, and pray for them which despitefully use you, and persecute you." Was not Amos an extremist for justice: "Let justice roll down like waters and righteousness like an ever-flowing stream." Was not Paul an extremist for the Christian gospel: "I bear in my body the marks of the Lord Jesus." Was not Martin Luther an extremist: "Here I stand; I cannot do otherwise, so help me God." And John Bunyan: "I will stay in jail to the end of my days before I make a butchery of my conscience." And Abraham Lincoln: "This nation cannot survive half slave and half free." And Thomas Jefferson: "We hold these truths to be self-evident, that all men are created equal. . . ." So the question is not whether we will be extremists, but what kind of extremists we will be. Will we be extremists for hate or for love? Will we be extremists for the preservation of injustice or for the extension of justice? In that dramatic scene on Calvary's hill three men were crucified. We must never forget that all three were crucified for the same crime—the crime of extremism. Two were extremists for immorality, and thus fell below their environment. The other, Jesus Christ, was an extremist for love, truth and goodness, and thereby rose above his environment. Perhaps the South, the nation and the world are in dire need of creative extremists.

40   I had hoped that the white moderate would see this need. Perhaps I was too optimistic; perhaps I expected too much. I suppose I should have realized that few members of the oppressor race can understand the deep groans and

---

[2]*Zeitgeist* Spirit of the age. [Ed. note.]

passionate yearnings of the oppressed race, and still fewer have the vision to see that injustice must be rooted out by strong, persistent and determined action. I am thankful, however, that some of our white brothers in the South have grasped the meaning of this social revolution and committed themselves to it. They are still all too few in quantity, but they are big in quality. Some—such as Ralph McGill, Lillian Smith, Harry Golden, James McBride Dabbs, Ann Braden and Sarah Patton Boyle—have written about our struggle in eloquent and prophetic terms. Others have marched with us down nameless streets of the South. They have languished in filthy, roach-infested jails, suffering the abuse and brutality of policemen who view them as "dirty niggerlovers." Unlike so many of their moderate brothers and sisters, they have recognized the urgency of the moment and sensed the need for powerful "action" antidotes to combat the disease of segregation.

Let me take note of my other major disappointment. I have been so greatly 41
disappointed with the white church and its leadership. Of course, there are some notable exceptions. I am not unmindful of the fact that each of you has taken some significant stands on this issue. I commend you, Reverend Stallings, for your Christian stand on this past Sunday, in welcoming Negroes to your worship service on a nonsegregated basis. I commend the Catholic leaders of this state for integrating Spring Hill College several years ago.

But despite these notable exceptions, I must honestly reiterate that I have 42
been disappointed with the church. I do not say this as one of those negative critics who can always find something wrong with the church. I say this as a minister of the gospel, who loves the church; who was nurtured in its bosom; who has been sustained by its spiritual blessings and who will remain true to it as long as the cord of life shall lengthen.

When I was suddenly catapulted into the leadership of the bus protest in 43
Montgomery, Alabama, a few years ago, I felt we would be supported by the white church. I felt that the white ministers, priests and rabbis of the South would be among our strongest allies. Instead, some have been outright opponents, refusing to understand the freedom movement and misrepresenting its leaders; all too many others have been more cautious than courageous and have remained silent behind the anesthetizing security of stained-glass windows.

In spite of my shattered dreams, I came to Birmingham with the hope that 44
the white religious leadership of this community would see the justice of our cause and, with deep moral concern, would serve as the channel through which our just grievances could reach the power structure. I had hoped that each of you would understand. But again I have been disappointed.

I have heard numerous southern religious leaders admonish their wor- 45
shipers to comply with a desegregation decision because it is the law, but I have longed to hear white ministers declare: "Follow this decree because integration is morally right and because the Negro is your brother." In the midst of blatant injustices inflicted upon the Negro, I have watched white churchmen stand on the sideline and mouth pious irrelevancies and sanctimonious trivialities. In the midst of a mighty struggle to rid our nation of racial and economic injustice, I have heard many ministers say: "Those are social issues, with which the gospel has no real concern." And I have watched many

churches commit themselves to a completely otherworldly religion which makes a strange, un-Biblical distinction between body and soul, between the sacred and the secular.

46   I have traveled the length and breadth of Alabama, Mississippi and all the other southern states. On sweltering summer days and crisp autumn mornings I have looked at the South's beautiful churches with their lofty spires pointing heavenward. I have beheld the impressive outlines of her massive religious-education buildings. Over and over I have found myself asking: "What kind of people worship here? Who is their God? Where were their voices when the lips of Governor Barnett dripped with words of interposition and nullification? Where were they when Governor Wallace gave a clarion call for defiance and hatred? Where were their voices of support when bruised and weary Negro men and women decided to rise from the dark dungeons of complacency to the bright hills of creative protest?

47   Yes, these questions are still in my mind. In deep disappointment I have wept over the laxity of the church. But be assured that my tears have been tears of love. There can be no deep disappointment where there is not deep love. Yes, I love the church. How could I do otherwise? I am in the rather unique position of being the son, the grandson and the great-grandson of preachers. Yes, I see the church as the body of Christ. But, oh! How we have blemished and scarred that body through social neglect and through fear of being nonconformists.

48   There was a time when the church was very powerful—in the time when the early Christians rejoiced at being deemed worthy to suffer for what they believed. In those days the church was not merely a thermometer that recorded the ideas and principles of popular opinion; it was a thermostat that transformed the mores of society. Whenever the early Christians entered a town, the people in power became disturbed and immediately sought to convict the Christians for being "disturbers of the peace" and "outside agitators." But the Christians pressed on, in the conviction that they were "a colony of heaven," called to obey God rather than man. Small in number, they were big in commitment. They were too God-intoxicated to be "astronomically intimidated." By their effort and example they brought an end to such ancient evils as infanticide and gladiatorial contests.

49   Things are different now. So often the contemporary church is a weak, ineffectual voice with an uncertain sound. So often it is an archdefender of the status quo. Far from being disturbed by the presence of the church, the power structure of the average community is consoled by the church's silent—and often even vocal—sanction of things as they are.

50   But the judgment of God is upon the church as never before. If today's church does not recapture the sacrificial spirit of the early church, it will lose its authenticity, forfeit the loyalty of millions, and be dismissed as an irrelevant social club with no meaning for the twentieth century. Every day I meet young people whose disappointment with the church has turned into outright disgust.

51   Perhaps I have once again been too optimistic. Is organized religion too inextricably bound to the status quo to save our nation and the world? Perhaps I must turn my faith to the inner spiritual church, the church within the

church, as the true *ekklesia* and the hope of the world. But again I am thankful to God that some noble souls from the ranks of organized religion have broken loose from the paralyzing chains of conformity and joined us as active partners in the struggle for freedom. They have left their secure congregations and walked the streets of Albany, Georgia, with us. They have gone down the highways of the South on tortuous rides for freedom. Yes, they have gone to jail with us. Some have been dismissed from their churches, have lost the support of their bishops and fellow ministers. But they have acted in the faith that right defeated is stronger than evil triumphant. Their witness has been the spiritual salt that has preserved the true meaning of the gospel in these troubled times. They have carved a tunnel of hope through the dark mountain of disappointment.

I hope the church as a whole will meet the challenge of this decisive hour. 52 But even if the church does not come to the aid of justice, I have no despair about the future. I have no fear about the outcome of our struggle in Birmingham, even if our motives are at present misunderstood. We will reach the goal of freedom in Birmingham and all over the nation, because the goal of America is freedom. Abused and scorned though we may be, our destiny is tied up with America's destiny. Before the pilgrims landed at Plymouth, we were here. Before the pen of Jefferson etched the majestic words of the Declaration of Independence across the pages of history, we were here. For more than two centuries our forebears labored in this country without wages; they made cotton king; they built the homes of their masters while suffering gross injustice and shameful humiliation—and yet out of a bottomless vitality they continued to thrive and develop. If the inexpressible cruelties of slavery could not stop us, the opposition we now face will surely fail. We will win our freedom because the sacred heritage of our nation and the eternal will of God are embodied in our echoing demands.

Before closing I feel impelled to mention one other point in your statement 53 that has troubled me profoundly. You warmly commended the Birmingham police force for keeping "order" and "preventing violence." I doubt that you would have so warmly commended the police force if you had seen its dogs sinking their teeth into unarmed, nonviolent Negroes. I doubt that you would so quickly commend the policemen if you were to observe their ugly and inhumane treatment of Negroes here in the city jail; if you were to watch them push and curse old Negro women and young Negro girls; if you were to see them slap and kick old Negro men and young boys; if you were to observe them, as they did on two occasions, refuse to give us food because we wanted to sing our grace together. I cannot join you in your praise of the Birmingham police department.

It is true that the police have exercised a degree of discipline in handling 54 the demonstrators. In this sense they have conducted themselves rather "nonviolently" in public. But for what purpose? To preserve the evil system of segregation. Over the past few years I have consistently preached that nonviolence demands that the means we use must be as pure as the ends we seek. I have tried to make clear that it is wrong to use immoral means to attain moral ends. But now I must affirm that it is just as wrong, or perhaps even more so, to use moral means to preserve immoral ends. Perhaps Mr. Connor and his policemen have been rather nonviolent in public, as was Chief Pritchett in Albany, Georgia, but they have used the moral means of nonviolence to maintain the immoral end of racial injustice. As T. S. Eliot has said: "The last temptation is the greatest treason: To do the right deed for the wrong reason."

55   I wish you had commended the Negro sit-inners and demonstrators of Birmingham for their sublime courage, their willingness to suffer and their amazing discipline in the midst of great provocation. One day the South will recognize its real heroes. They will be the James Merediths, with the noble sense of purpose that enables them to face jeering and hostile mobs, and with the agonizing loneliness that characterizes the life of the pioneer. They will be old, oppressed, battered Negro women, symbolized in a seventy-two-year-old woman in Montgomery, Alabama, who rose up with a sense of dignity and with her people decided not to ride segregated buses, and who responded with ungrammatical profundity to one who inquired about her weariness: "My feets is tired, but my soul is at rest." They will be the young high school and college students, the young ministers of the gospel and a host of their elders, courageously and nonviolently sitting in at lunch counters and willingly going to jail for conscience sake. One day the South will know that when these disinherited children of God sat down at lunch counters, they were in reality standing up for what is best in the American dream and for the most sacred values in our Judaeo-Christian heritage, thereby bringing our nation back to those great wells of democracy which were dug deep by the founding fathers in their formulation of the Constitution and the Declaration of Independence.

56   Never before have I written so long a letter. I'm afraid it is much too long to take your precious time. I can assure you that it would have been much shorter if I had been writing from a comfortable desk, but what else can one do when he is alone in a narrow jail cell, other than write long letters, think long thoughts and pray long prayers?

57   If I have said anything in this letter that overstates the truth and indicates an unreasonable impatience, I beg you to forgive me. If I have said anything that understates the truth and indicates my having a patience that allows me to settle for anything less than brotherhood, I beg God to forgive me.

58   I hope this letter finds you strong in the faith. I also hope that circumstances will soon make it possible for me to meet each of you, not as an integrationist or a civil rights leader but as a fellow clergyman and a Christian brother. Let us all hope that the dark clouds of racial prejudice will soon pass away and the deep fog of misunderstanding will be lifted from our fear-drenched communities, and in some not too distant tomorrow the radiant stars of love and brotherhood will shine over our great nation with all their scintillating beauty.

—Yours for the cause of Peace and Brotherhood,
MARTIN LUTHER KING, JR.

Questions for Discussion and Your Reading Journal

1. Martin Luther King Jr. by choosing a letter format for his communication from jail, places this essay in the tradition of St. Paul writing to various Christian communities from jail. How does this choice of form add strength to his argument?
2. Who is King's audience? How does King justify his nonviolent protest to them? What type of authority does he appeal to? How is this appropriate?
3. What are the strategies and goals of a nonviolent campaign? Considering King's argument, why is the order of the four steps important?
4. How does King justify breaking some laws and not others? How does he support the distinction between just and unjust laws? Is it convincing? Why or why not?
5. Outline King's argument. How does the argument build?
6. Martin Luther King was a practicing minister. What elements of the text are like an oral delivery of a sermon? Are these devices effective? Why or why not?
7. How does he make use of what is called a rhetorical question (a question that is asked and is then answered)?
8. King states, "Anyone who lives inside the United States can never be considered an outsider anywhere within its bounds" (Paragraph 12). Do you agree? Why or why not?
9. Compare this piece to the ones by Gandhi and Mandela. How are they alike? How are they different?

NELSON MANDELA

Considered by black South Africans to be their leader, the black nationalist Nelson R. Mandela (1918–), until February 11, 1990, had been serving a life sentence imposed in 1964 for forming Umkonto We Sizwe (Spear of the Nation), a group that advocated violence as a means to topple apartheid. While in prison he was elected the president-general of the African National Congress (ANC) and later refused President P. W. Botha's offer to release him if he renounced the use of violence against the apartheid system. Apartheid, a policy of segregating people based on race, is a recent phenomenon in South African history. In 1948 the Nationalist Party of South Africa passed the Mixed Marriage Act of 1949 and the Immorality Amendment Act of 1950, which outlawed marriage and sexual relations between different races. The Reservation of Separate Amenities Act in 1953 segregated transportation and public places, such as restrooms, theaters, and parks. The white-controlled national government then created separate local administrations according to the government's definitions of the following racial groups: Whites, Coloureds, Asians, and Africans. To keep "Africans" away from white centers of power, the Bantu Self-Government Act of 1959 allowed the white-ruled government to move "Africans," depending upon government classifications of their "tribes," to one of ten different areas, called "Bantu Homelands." While these homelands were independent on paper, South Africa retained military and economic control over them and no other government recognized their independence.

In 1994, the era of apartheid ended when Mandela won the South African presidency in the country's first multiracial democratic elections. The new constitution abolished the Bantu Homelands and set up one central government with nine provincial legislatures.

Reading Rhetorically

It is difficult to think of a more intense rhetorical challenge than when attempting to write a statement declaring one is "prepared to die" in the service of an action or a cause. Like Martin Luther King (see previous text), Mandela wrote the following selection while in jail. He was awaiting trial for the serious charges of inciting violent resistance to sabotage the white government in South Africa. This text represents the defense he offered the white court in the case presented against him. As a lawyer himself, Mandela was well qualified to make such a defense. But what follows is more than a legal defense. Here Mandela rose above his training as a lawyer to speak with the voice of 23 million black South Africans who had suffered for generations under one of the most overtly racist white regimes in the Western world. Mandela gave expression to these voices in manner that foreshadowed the pivotal role he would later play in changing the course of his nation by becoming the first black president in its troubled history. His defense sheds light upon the detailed history and the moral nature of the black struggle for freedom in South Africa. It also reveals what happens when a government systematically uses its legal system and the threat of police violence to block the desires of a group of its citizens for freedom, justice, and equality. These desires do not simply melt away in the face of oppression. Rather, as Mandela illustrated, they find new and increasingly determined ways to fight back. What Mandela was most concerned to show in his text was the justification for his actions and the actions of his fellow leaders in the anti-apartheid movement. He used a historical defense to do this, one that resorted constantly to the flow of facts and evidence supporting the increasingly violent responses of his movement to an increasingly violent government. At the same time, it is perhaps the moderate, reasonable, fair and balanced voice with which he wrote that is most compelling rhetorically. He admitted much of what the government has charged against him, a tribute to his own personal honesty and integrity. With these admissions in mind, his audience would have great difficulty not to likewise believe him when he denies, with solid evidence, other charges brought against his movement. Rhetorically, it is as much his *ethos*, his own goodness of character, that makes "I Am Prepared to Die" not only a powerful defense of his actions but a foreshadowing of the kind of man who would emerge from prison 26 long years later. Rather than seek revenge upon the people who had caused so much suffering, he chose to lead all of South Africa toward the resolution and reconciliation of its ugly and painful past, a task that he accomplished peacefully.

I Am Prepared to Die

SECOND COURT STATEMENT, 1964

Mandela's statement from the dock in Pretoria Supreme Court, 20 April 1
1964, at the opening of the defence case.

I am the First Accused. 2

I hold a Bachelor's Degree in Arts and practised as an attorney in Johan- 3
nesburg for a number of years in partnership with Oliver Tambo. I am a convicted prisoner serving five years for leaving the country without a permit and for inciting people to go on strike at the end of May 1961.

At the outset, I want to say that the suggestion made by the State in its 4
opening that the struggle in South Africa is under the influence of foreigners or communists is wholly incorrect. I have done whatever I did, both as an individual and as a leader of my people, because of my experience in South Africa and my own proudly felt African background, and not because of what any outsider might have said.

In my youth in the Transkei I listened to the elders of my tribe telling sto- 5
ries of the old days. Amongst the tales they related to me were those of wars fought by our ancestors in defence of the fatherland. The names of Dingane and Bambata, Hintsa and Makana, Squngthi and Dalasile, Moshoeshoe and Sekhukhuni, were praised as the glory of the entire African nation. I hoped then that life might offer me the opportunity to serve my people and make my own humble contribution to their freedom struggle. This is what has motivated me in all that I have done in relation to the charges made against me in this case.

Having said this, I must deal immediately and at some length with the 6
question of violence. Some of the things so far told to the Court are true and some are untrue. I do not, however, deny that I planned sabotage. I did not plan it in a spirit of recklessness, nor because I have any love of violence. I planned it as a result of a calm and sober assessment of the political situation that had arisen after many years of tyranny, exploitation, and oppression of my people by the Whites.

I admit immediately that I was one of the persons who helped to form 7
Umkhonto we Sizwe, and that I played a prominent role in its affairs until I was arrested in August 1962.

In the statement which I am about to make I shall correct certain false 8
impressions which have been created by State witnesses. Amongst other things, I will demonstrate that certain of the acts referred to in the evidence

were not and could not have been committed by Umkhonto. I will also deal with the relationship between the African National Congress and Umkhonto, and with the part which I personally have played in the affairs of both organizations. I shall deal also with the part played by the Communist Party. In order to explain these matters properly, I will have to explain what Umkhonto set out to achieve; what methods it prescribed for the achievement of these objects, and why these methods were chosen. I will also have to explain how I became involved in the activities of these organizations.

9   I deny that Umkhonto was responsible for a number of acts which clearly fell outside the policy of the organization, and which have been charged in the indictment against us. I do not know what justification there was for these acts, but to demonstrate that they could not have been authorized by Umkhonto, I want to refer briefly to the roots and policy of the organization.

10   I have already mentioned that I was one of the persons who helped to form Umkhonto. I, and the others who started the organization, did so for two reasons. Firstly, we believed that as a result of Government policy, violence by the African people had become inevitable, and that unless responsible leadership was given to canalize and control the feelings of our people, there would be outbreaks of terrorism which would produce an intensity of bitterness and hostility between the various races of this country which is not produced even by war. Secondly, we felt that without violence there would be no way open to the African people to succeed in their struggle against the principle of white supremacy. All lawful modes of expressing opposition to this principle had been closed by legislation, and we were placed in a position in which we had either to accept a permanent state of inferiority, or to defy the Government. We chose to defy the law. We first broke the law in a way which avoided any recourse to violence; when this form was legislated against, and then the Government resorted to a show of force to crush opposition to its policies, only then did we decide to answer violence with violence.

11   But the violence which we chose to adopt was not terrorism. We who formed Umkhonto were all members of the African National Congress, and had behind us the ANC tradition of non-violence and negotiation as a means of solving political disputes. We believe that South Africa belongs to all the people who live in it, and not to one group, be it black or white. We did not want an interracial war, and tried to avoid it to the last minute. If the Court is in doubt about this, it will be seen that the whole history of our organization bears out what I have said, and what I will subsequently say, when I describe the tactics which Umkhonto decided to adopt. I want, therefore, to say something about the African National Congress.

12   The African National Congress was formed in 1912 to defend the rights of the African people which had been seriously curtailed by the South Africa Act, and which were then being threatened by the Native Land Act. For thirty-seven years—that is until 1949—it adhered strictly to a constitutional struggle. It put forward demands and resolutions; it sent delegations to the Government in the belief that African grievances could be settled through peaceful discussion and that Africans could advance gradually to full political rights. But White Governments remained unmoved, and the rights of Africans

became less instead of becoming greater. In the words of my leader, Chief Lutuli, who became President of the ANC in 1952, and who was later awarded the Nobel Peace Prize:

> Who will deny that thirty years of my life have been spent knocking in 13
> vain, patiently, moderately, and modestly at a closed and barred door?
> What have been the fruits of moderation? The past thirty years have seen
> the greatest number of laws restricting our rights and progress, until today
> we have reached a stage where we have almost no rights at all.

Even after 1949, the ANC remained determined to avoid violence. At this 14 time, however, there was a change from the strictly constitutional means of protest which had been employed in the past. The change was embodied in a decision which was taken to protest against apartheid legislation by peaceful, but unlawful, demonstrations against certain laws. Pursuant to this policy the ANC launched the Defiance Campaign, in which I was placed in charge of volunteers. This campaign was based on the principles of passive resistance. More than 8,500 people defied apartheid laws and went to jail. Yet there was not a single instance of violence in the course of this campaign on the part of any defier. I and nineteen colleagues were convicted for the role which we played in organizing the campaign, but our sentences were suspended mainly because the Judge found that discipline and non-violence had been stressed throughout. This was the time when the volunteer section of the ANC was established, and when the word "Amadelakufa"[1] was first used: This was the time when the volunteers were asked to take a pledge to uphold certain principles. Evidence dealing with volunteers and their pledges has been introduced into this case, but completely out of context. The volunteers were not, and are not, the soldiers of a black army pledged to fight a civil war against the whites. They were, and are, dedicated workers who are prepared to lead campaigns initiated by the ANC to distribute leaflets, to organize strikes, or do whatever the particular campaign required. They are called volunteers because they volunteer to face the penalties of imprisonment and whipping which are now prescribed by the legislature for such acts.

During the Defiance Campaign, the Public Safety Act and the Criminal 15 Law Amendment Act were passed. These Statutes provided harsher penalties for offences committed by way of protests against laws. Despite this, the protests continued and the ANC adhered to its policy of non-violence. In 1956, 156 leading members of the Congress Alliance, including myself, were arrested on a charge of high treason and charges under the Suppression of Communism Act. The non-violent policy of the ANC was put in issue by the State, but when the Court gave judgement some five years later, it found that the ANC did not have a policy of violence. We were acquitted on all counts, which included a count that the ANC sought to set up a communist state in place of the existing regime. The Government has always sought to label all its opponents as communists. This allegation has been repeated in the present case, but as I will show, the ANC is not, and never has been, a communist organization.

---

[1]**Amadelakufa** Those who are prepared to make sacrifices.

16   In 1960 there was the shooting at Sharpeville,[2] which resulted in the proclamation of a state of emergency and the declaration of the ANC as an unlawful organization. My colleagues and I, after careful consideration, decided that we would not obey this decree. The African people were not part of the Government and did not make the laws by which they were governed. We believed in the words of the Universal Declaration of Human Rights, that "the will of the people shall be the basis of authority of the Government," and for us to accept the banning was equivalent to accepting the silencing of the Africans for all time. The ANC refused to dissolve, but instead went underground. We believed it was our duty to preserve this organization which had been built up with almost fifty years of unremitting toil. I have no doubt that no self-respecting White political organization would disband itself if declared illegal by a government in which it had no say.

17   In 1960 the Government held a referendum which led to the establishment of the Republic. Africans, who constituted approximately 70 per cent of the population of South Africa, were not entitled to vote, and were not even consulted about the proposed constitutional change. All of us were apprehensive of our future under the proposed White Republic, and a resolution was taken to hold an All-In African Conference to call for a National Convention, and to organize mass demonstrations on the eve of the unwanted Republic, if the Government failed to call the Convention. The conference was attended by Africans of various political persuasions. I was the Secretary of the conference and undertook to be responsible for organizing the national stay-at-home which was subsequently called to coincide with the declaration of the Republic. As all strikes by Africans are illegal, the person organizing such a strike must avoid arrest. I was chosen to be this person, and consequently I had to leave my home and family and my practice and go into hiding to avoid arrest.

18   The stay-at-home, in accordance with ANC policy, was to be a peaceful demonstration. Careful instructions were given to organizers and members to avoid any recourse to violence. The Government's answer was to introduce new and harsher laws, to mobilize its armed forces, and to send Saracens,[3] armed vehicles, and soldiers into the townships in a massive show of force designed to intimidate the people. This was an indication that the Government had decided to rule by force alone, and this decision was a milestone on the road to Umkhonto.

19   Some of this may appear irrelevant to this trial. In fact, I believe none of it is irrelevant because it will, I hope, enable the Court to appreciate the attitude eventually adopted by the various persons and bodies concerned in the National Liberation Movement. When I went to jail in 1962, the dominant idea was that loss of life should be avoided. I now know that this was still so in 1963.

---

[2]**Sharpeville** The location where South African police killed 69 and wounded 178 demonstrators who were protesting South Africa's pass laws. [Ed. note.]

[3]**Saracens** British-made military troop carriers.

I must return to June 1961. What were we, the leaders of our people, to 20
do? Were we to give in to the show of force and the implied threat against
future action, or were we to fight it and, if so, how?

We had no doubt that we had to continue the fight. Anything else would 21
have been abject surrender. Our problem was not whether to fight, but was
how to continue the fight. We of the ANC had always stood for a non-racial
democracy, and we shrank from any action which might drive the races further apart than they already were. But the hard facts were that fifty years of
non-violence had brought the African people nothing but more and more
repressive legislation, and fewer and fewer rights. It may not be easy for this
Court to understand, but it is a fact that for a long time the people had been
talking of violence—of the day when they would fight the White man and win
back their country—and we, the leaders of the ANC, had nevertheless always
prevailed upon them to avoid violence and to pursue peaceful methods. When
some of us discussed this in May and June of 1961, it could not be denied that
our policy to achieve a nonracial State by non-violence had achieved nothing,
and that our followers were beginning to lose confidence in this policy and
were developing disturbing ideas of terrorism.

It must not be forgotten that by this time violence had, in fact, become a 22
feature of the South African political scene. There had been violence in 1957
when the women of Zeerust were ordered to carry passes; there was violence
in 1958 with the enforcement of cattle culling in Sekhukhuniland; there was
violence in 1959 when the people of Cato Manor protested against pass raids;
there was violence in 1960 when the Government attempted to impose Bantu
Authorities in Pondoland. Thirty-nine Africans died in these disturbances. In
1961 there had been riots in Warmbaths, and all this time the Transkei had
been a seething mass of unrest. Each disturbance pointed clearly to the
inevitable growth among Africans of the belief that violence was the only way
out—it showed that a Government which uses force to maintain its rule teaches
the oppressed to use force to oppose it. Already small groups had arisen in the
urban areas and were spontaneously making plans for violent forms of political
struggle. There now arose a danger that these groups would adopt terrorism
against Africans, as well as Whites, if not properly directed. Particularly disturbing was the type of violence engendered in places such as Zeerust,
Sekhukhuniland, and Pondoland amongst Africans. It was increasingly taking
the form, not of struggle against the Government—though this is what
prompted it—but of civil strife amongst themselves, conducted in such a way
that it could not hope to achieve anything other than a loss of life and bitterness.

At the beginning of June 1961, after a long and anxious assessment of the 23
South African situation, I, and some colleagues, came to the conclusion that as
violence in this country was inevitable, it would be unrealistic and wrong for
African leaders to continue preaching peace and non-violence at a time when
the Government met our peaceful demands with force.

This conclusion was not easily arrived at. It was only when all else had 24
failed, when all channels of peaceful protest had been barred to us, that the
decision was made to embark on violent forms of political struggle, and to
form Umkhonto we Sizwe. We did so not because we desired such a course,

but solely because the Government had left us with no other choice. In the Manifesto of Umkhonto published on 16 December 1961, which is Exhibit AD, we said:

25 The time comes in the life of any nation when there remain only two choices—submit or fight. That time has now come to South Africa. We shall not submit and we have no choice but to hit back by all means in our power in defence of our people, our future, and our freedom.

26 This was our feeling in June of 1961 when we decided to press for a change in the policy of the National Liberation Movement. I can only say that I felt morally obliged to do what I did.

27 We who had taken this decision started to consult leaders of various organizations, including the ANC. I will not say whom we spoke to, or what they said, but I wish to deal with the role of the African National Congress in this phase of the struggle, and with the policy and objectives of Umkhonto we Sizwe.

28 As far as the ANC was concerned, it formed a clear view which can be summarized as follows:

a. It was a mass political organization with a political function to fulfill. Its members had joined on the express policy of non-violence.

b. Because of all this, it could not and would not undertake violence. This must be stressed. One cannot turn such a body into the small, closely knit organization required for sabotage. Nor would this be politically correct, because it would result in members ceasing to carry out this essential activity: political propaganda and organization. Nor was it permissible to change the whole nature of the organization.

c. On the other hand, in view of this situation I have described, the ANC was prepared to depart from its fifty-year-old policy of non-violence to this extent that it would no longer disapprove of properly controlled violence. Hence members who undertook such activity would not be subject to disciplinary action by the ANC.

29 I say "properly controlled violence" because I made it clear that if I formed the organization I would at all times subject it to the political guidance of the ANC and would not undertake any different form of activity from that contemplated without the consent of the ANC. And I shall now tell the Court how that form of violence came to be determined.

30 As a result of this decision, Umkhonto was formed in November 1961. When we took this decision, and subsequently formulated our plans, the ANC heritage of non-violence and racial harmony was very much with us. We felt that the country was drifting towards a civil war in which Blacks and Whites would fight each other. We viewed the situation with alarm. Civil war could mean the destruction of what the ANC stood for; with civil war, racial peace would be more difficult than ever to achieve. We already have examples in South African history of the results of war. It has taken more than fifty years for the scars of the South African War to disappear. How much longer would it take to eradicate the scars of inter-racial civil war, which could not be fought without a great loss of life on both sides?

The avoidance of civil war had dominated our thinking for many years,   31
but when we decided to adopt violence as part of our policy, we realized that
we might one day have to face the prospect of such a war. This had to be taken
into account in formulating our plans. We required a plan which was flexible
and which permitted us to act in accordance with the needs of the times; above
all, the plan had to be one which recognized civil war as the last resort, and
left the decision on this question to the future. We did not want to be committed to civil war, but we wanted to be ready if it became inevitable.

Four forms of violence were possible. There is sabotage, there is guerrilla   32
warfare, there is terrorism, and there is open revolution. We chose to adopt the
first method and to exhaust it before taking any other decision.

In the light of our political background the choice was a logical one. Sab-   33
otage did not involve loss of life, and it offered the best hope for future race
relations. Bitterness would be kept to a minimum and, if the policy bore fruit,
democratic government could become a reality. This is what we felt at the
time, and this is what we said in our Manifesto (Exhibit AD):

> We of Umkhonto We Sizwe have always sought to achieve liberation with-   34
> out bloodshed and civil clash. We hope, even at this late hour, that our first
> actions will awaken everyone to a realization of the disastrous situation to
> which the Nationalist policy is leading. We hope that we will bring the
> Government and its supporters to their senses before it is too late, so that
> both the Government and its policies can be changed before matters reach
> the desperate stage of civil war.

The initial plan was based on a careful analysis of the political and eco-   35
nomic situation of our country. We believed that South Africa depended to a
large extent on foreign capital and foreign trade. We felt that planned destruction of power plants, and interference with rail and telephone communications,
would tend to scare away capital from the country, make it more difficult for
goods from the industrial areas to reach the seaports on schedule, and would
in the long run be a heavy drain on the economic life of the country, thus compelling the voters of the country to reconsider their position.

Attacks on the economic life lines of the country were to be linked with sab-   36
otage on Government buildings and other symbols of apartheid. These attacks
would serve as a source of inspiration to our people. In addition, they would provide an outlet for those people who were urging the adoption of violent methods
and would enable us to give concrete proof to our followers that we had adopted
a stronger line and were fighting back against Government violence.

In addition, if mass action were successfully organized, and mass reprisals   37
taken, we felt that sympathy for our cause would be roused in other countries, and
that greater pressure would be brought to bear on the South African Government.

This then was the plan. Umkhonto was to perform sabotage, and strict   38
instructions were given to its members right from the start, that on no account
were they to injure or kill people in planning or carrying out operations. These
instructions have been referred to in the evidence of "Mr. X" and "Mr. Z."[4]

---

[4]State witnesses in the trial whose names were withheld for their protection.

39   The affairs of the Umkhonto were controlled and directed by a National High Command, which had powers of co-option and which could, and did, appoint Regional Commands. The High Command was the body which determined tactics and targets and was in charge of training and finance. Under the High Command there were Regional Commands which were responsible for the direction of the local sabotage groups. Within the framework of the policy laid down by the National High Command, the Regional Commands had authority to select the targets to be attacked. They had no authority to go beyond the prescribed framework and thus had no authority to embark upon acts which endangered life, or which did not fit into the overall plan of sabotage. For instance, Umkhonto members were forbidden ever to go armed into operation. Incidentally, the terms High Command and Regional Command were an importation from the Jewish national underground organization Irgun Zvai Leumi, which operated in Israel between 1944 and 1948.

40   Umkhonto had its first operation on 16 December 1961, when Government buildings in Johannesburg, Port Elizabeth and Durban were attacked. The selection of targets is proof of the policy to which I have referred. Had we intended to attack life we would have selected targets where people congregated and not empty buildings and power stations. The sabotage which was committed before 16 December 1961 was the work of isolated groups and had no connection whatever with Umkhonto. In fact, some of these and a number of later acts were claimed by other organizations.

41   The Manifesto of Umkhonto was issued on the day that operations commenced. The response to our actions and Manifesto among the white population was characteristically violent. The Government threatened to take strong action, and called upon its supporters to stand firm and to ignore the demands of the Africans. The Whites failed to respond by suggesting change; they responded to our call by suggesting the laager.

42   In contrast, the response of the Africans was one of encouragement. Suddenly there was hope again. Things were happening. People in the townships became eager for political news. A great deal of enthusiasm was generated by the initial successes, and people began to speculate on how soon freedom would be obtained.

43   But we in Umkhonto weighed up the white response with anxiety. The lines were being drawn. The whites and blacks were moving into separate camps, and the prospects of avoiding a civil war were made less. The white newspapers carried reports that sabotage would be punished by death. If this was so, how could we continue to keep Africans away from terrorism?

44   Already scores of Africans had died as a result of racial friction. In 1920 when the famous leader, Masabala, was held in Port Elizabeth jail, twenty-four of a group of Africans who had gathered to demand his release were killed by the police and white civilians. In 1921, more than one hundred Africans died in the Bulhoek affair. In 1924 over two hundred Africans were killed when the Administrator of South-West Africa led a force against a group which had rebelled against the imposition of dog tax. On 1 May 1950, eighteen Africans died as a result of police shootings during the strike. On 21 March 1960, sixty-nine unarmed Africans died at Sharpeville.

How many more Sharpevilles would there be in the history of our country? 45
And how many more Sharpevilles could the country stand without violence and
terror becoming the order of the day? And what would happen to our people
when that stage was reached? In the long run we felt certain we must succeed,
but at what cost to ourselves and the rest of the country? And if this happened,
how could black and white ever live together again in peace and harmony?
These were the problems that faced us, and these were our decisions.

Experience convinced us that rebellion would offer the Government lim- 46
itless opportunities for the indiscriminate slaughter of our people. But it was
precisely because the soil of South Africa is already drenched with the blood
of innocent Africans that we felt it our duty to make preparations as a long-
term undertaking to use force in order to defend ourselves against force. If
war were inevitable, we wanted the fight to be conducted on terms most
favourable to our people. The fight which held out prospects best for us and
the least risk of life to both sides was guerrilla warfare. We decided, therefore,
in our preparations for the future, to make provision for the possibility of
guerrilla warfare.

All whites undergo compulsory military training, but no such training was 47
given to Africans. It was in our view essential to build up a nucleus of trained
men who would be able to provide the leadership which would be required if
guerrilla warfare started. We had to prepare for such a situation before it
became too late to make proper preparations. It was also necessary to build
up a nucleus of men trained in civil administration and other professions, so
that Africans would be equipped to participate in the government of this country as soon as they were allowed to do so.

At this stage it was decided that I should attend the Conference of the Pan- 48
African Freedom Movement for Central, East, and Southern Africa, which
was to be held early in 1962 in Addis Ababa, and, because of our need for
preparation, it was also decided that, after the conference, I would undertake
a tour of the African States with a view to obtaining facilities for the training
of soldiers, and that I would also solicit scholarships for the higher education
of matriculated Africans. Training in both fields would be necessary, even if
changes came about by peaceful means. Administrators would be necessary
who would be willing and able to administer a non-racial State and so would
men be necessary to control the army and police force of such a State.

It was on this note that I left South Africa to proceed to Addis Ababa as a 49
delegate of the ANC. My tour was a success. Wherever I went I met sympathy
for our cause and promises to help. All Africa was united against the stand of
White South Africa, and even in London I was received with great sympathy by
political leaders, such as Mr. Gaitskell and Mr. Grimond. In Africa I was promised support by such men as Julius Nyerere, now President of Tanganyika; Mr.
Kawawa, then Prime Minister of Tanganyika; Emperor Haile Selassie of
Ethiopia; General Abboud, President of the Sudan; Habib Bourguiba, President
of Tunisia; Ben Bella, now President of Algeria; Modibo Keita, President of
Mali; Leopold Senghor, President of Senegal; Sékou Touré, President of Guinea;
President Tubman of Liberia; and Milton Obote, Prime Minister of Uganda. It
was Ben Bella who invited me to visit Oujda, the Headquarters of the Algerian

Army of National Liberation, the visit which is described in my diary, one of the Exhibits.

50   I started to make a study of the art of war and revolution and, whilst abroad, underwent a course in military training. If there was to be guerrilla warfare, I wanted to be able to stand and fight with my people and to share the hazards of war with them. Notes of lectures which I received in Algeria are contained in Exhibit 16, produced in evidence. Summaries of books on guerrilla warfare and military strategy have also been produced. I have already admitted that these documents are in my writing, and I acknowledge that I made these studies to equip myself for the role which I might have to play if the struggle drifted into guerrilla warfare. I approached this question as every African Nationalist should do. I was completely objective. The Court will see that I attempted to examine all types of authority on the subject—from the East and from the West, going back to the classic work of Clausewitz, and covering such a variety as Mao Tse Tung and Che Guevara on the one hand, and the writings on the Anglo-Boer War on the other. Of course, these notes are merely summaries of the books I read and do not contain my personal views.

51   I also made arrangements for our recruits to undergo military training. But here it was impossible to organize any scheme without the co-operation of the ANC offices in Africa. I consequently obtained the permission of the ANC in South Africa to do this. To this extent then there was a departure from the original decision of the ANC, but it applied outside South Africa only. The first batch of recruits actually arrived in Tanganyika when I was passing through that country on my way back to South Africa.

52   I returned to South Africa and reported to my colleagues on the results of my trip. On my return I found that there had been little alteration in the political scene save that the threat of a death penalty for sabotage had now become a fact. The attitude of my colleagues in Umkhonto was much the same as it had been before I left. They were feeling their way cautiously and felt that it would be a long time before the possibilities of sabotage were exhausted. In fact, the view was expressed by some that the training of recruits was premature. This is recorded by me in the document which is Exhibit R.14. After a full discussion, however, it was decided to go ahead with the plans for military training because of the fact that it would take many years to build up a sufficient nucleus of trained soldiers to start a guerrilla campaign, and whatever happened the training would be of value.

53   I wish to turn now to certain general allegations made in this case by the State. . . .

54   [One] of the allegations made by the State is that the aims and objects of the ANC and the Communist Party are the same. I wish to deal with this and with my own political position, because I must assume that the State may try to argue from certain Exhibits that I tried to introduce Marxism into the ANC. The allegation as to the ANC is false. This is an old allegation which was disproved at the Treason Trial and which has again reared its head. But since the allegation has been made again, I shall deal with it as well as with the relationship between the ANC and the Communist Party and Umkhonto and that party.

The ideological creed of the ANC is, and always has been, the creed of African Nationalism. It is not the concept of African Nationalism expressed in the cry, "Drive the White man into the sea." The African Nationalism for which the ANC stands is the concept of freedom and fulfilment for the African people in their own land. The most important political document ever adopted by the ANC is the "Freedom Charter." It is by no means a blueprint for a socialist state. It calls for redistribution, but not nationalization, of land; it provides for nationalization of mines, banks, and monopoly industry, because big monopolies are owned by one race only, and without such nationalization racial domination would be perpetuated despite the spread of political power. It would be a hollow gesture to repeal the Gold Law prohibitions against Africans when all gold mines are owned by European companies. In this respect the ANC's policy corresponds with the old policy of the present Nationalist Party which, for many years, had as part of its programme the nationalization of the gold mines which, at that time, were controlled by foreign capital. Under the Freedom Charter, nationalization would take place in an economy based on private enterprise. The realization of the Freedom Charter would open up fresh fields for a prosperous African population of all classes, including the middle class. The ANC has never at any period of its history advocated a revolutionary change in the economic structure of the country, nor has it, to the best of my recollection, ever condemned capitalist society. 55

As far as the Communist Party is concerned, and if I understand its policy correctly, it stands for the establishment of a State based on the principles of Marxism. Although it is prepared to work for the Freedom Charter, as a short-term solution to the problems created by white supremacy, it regards the Freedom Charter as the beginning, and not the end, of its programme. 56

The ANC, unlike the Communist Party, admitted Africans only as members. Its chief goal was, and is, for the African people to win unity and full political rights. The Communist Party's main aim, on the other hand, was to remove the capitalists and to replace them with a working-class government. The Communist Party sought to emphasize class distinctions whilst the ANC seeks to harmonize them. This is a vital distinction. 57

It is true that there has often been close co-operation between the ANC and the Communist Party. But co-operation is merely proof of a common goal—in this case the removal of white supremacy—and is not proof of a complete community of interests. 58

The history of the world is full of similar examples. Perhaps the most striking illustration is to be found in the co-operation between Great Britain, the United States of America, and the Soviet Union in the fight against Hitler. Nobody but Hitler would have dared to suggest that such cooperation turned Churchill or Roosevelt into communists or communist tools, or that Britain and America were working to bring about a communist world. 59

Another instance of such co-operation is to be found precisely in Umkhonto. Shortly after Umkhonto was constituted, I was informed by some of its members that the Communist Party would support Umkhonto, and this then occurred. At a later stage the support was made openly. 60

61   I believe that communists have always played an active role in the fight by colonial countries for their freedom, because the short-term objects of communism would always correspond with the long-term objects of freedom movements. Thus communists have played an important role in the freedom struggles fought in countries such as Malaya, Algeria, and Indonesia, yet none of these States today are communist countries. Similarly in the underground resistance movements which sprung up in Europe during the last World War, communists played an important role. Even General Chiang Kai-Shek, today one of the bitterest enemies of communism, fought together with the communists against the ruling class in the struggle which led to his assumption of power in China in the 1930s.

62   This pattern of co-operation between communists and non-communists has been repeated in the National Liberation Movement of South Africa. Prior to the banning of the Communist Party, joint campaigns involving the Communist Party and the Congress movements were accepted practice. African communists could, and did, become members of the ANC, and some served on the National, Provincial, and local committees. Amongst those who served on the National Executive are Albert Nzula, a former secretary of the Communist Party; Moses Kotane, another former Secretary; and J. B. Marks, a former member of the Central Committee.

63   I joined the ANC in 1944, and in my younger days I held the view that the policy of admitting communists to the ANC, and the close co-operation which existed at times on specific issues between the ANC and the Communist Party, would lead to a watering down of the concept of African Nationalism. At that stage I was a member of the African National Congress Youth League, and was one of a group which moved for the expulsion of communists from the ANC. This proposal was heavily defeated. Amongst those who voted against the proposal were some of the most conservative sections of African political opinion. They defended the policy on the ground that from its inception the ANC was formed and built up, not as a political party with one school of political thought, but as a Parliament of the African people, accommodating people of various political convictions, all united by the common goal of national liberation. I was eventually won over to this point of view and I have upheld it ever since.

64   It is perhaps difficult for white South Africans, with an ingrained prejudice against communism, to understand why experienced African politicians so readily accept communists as their friends. But to us the reason is obvious. Theoretical differences amongst those fighting against oppression is a luxury we cannot afford at this stage. What is more, for many decades communists were the only political group in South Africa who were prepared to treat Africans as human beings and their equals; who were prepared to eat with us; talk with us, live with us, and work with us. They were the only political group which was prepared to work with the Africans for the attainment of political rights and a stake in society. Because of this, there are many Africans who, today, tend to equate freedom with communism. They are supported in this belief by a legislature which brands all exponents of democratic government and African freedom as communists and bans many of them (who are not

communists) under the Suppression of Communism Act. Although I have never been a member of the Communist Party, I myself have been named under that pernicious Act because of the role I played in the Defiance Campaign. I have also been banned and imprisoned under that Act.

It is not only in internal politics that we count communists as amongst 65 those who support our cause. In the international field, communist countries have always come to our aid. In the United Nations and other Councils of the world the communist *bloc* has supported the Afro-Asian struggle against colonialism and often seems to be more sympathetic to our plight than some of the Western powers. Although there is a universal condemnation of apartheid, the communist *bloc* speaks out against it with a louder voice than most of the white world. In these circumstances, it would take a brash young politician, such as I was in 1949, to proclaim that the Communists are our enemies.

I turn now to my own position. I have denied that I am a communist, and 66 I think that in the circumstances I am obliged to state exactly what my political beliefs are.

I have always regarded myself, in the first place, as an African patriot. 67 After all, I was born in Umtata, forty-six years ago. My guardian was my cousin, who was the acting paramount chief of Tembuland, and I am related both to the present paramount chief of Tembuland, Sabata Dalindyebo, and to Kaizer Matanzima, the Chief Minister of the Transkei.

Today I am attracted by the idea of a classless society, an attraction which 68 springs in part from Marxist reading and, in part, from my admiration of the structure and organization of early African societies in this country. The land, then the main means of production, belonged to the tribe. There were no rich or poor and there was no exploitation.

It is true, as I have already stated, that I have been influenced by Marxist 69 thought. But this is also true of many of the leaders of the new independent States. Such widely different persons as Gandhi, Nehru, Nkrumah, and Nasser all acknowledge this fact. We all accept the need for some form of socialism to enable our people to catch up with the advanced countries of this world and to overcome their legacy of extreme poverty. But this does not mean we are Marxists.

Indeed, for my own part, I believe that it is open to debate whether the 70 Communist Party has any specific role to play at this particular stage of our political struggle. The basic task at the present moment is the removal of race discrimination and the attainment of democratic rights on the basis of the Freedom Charter. In so far as that Party furthers this task, I welcome its assistance. I realize that it is one of the means by which people of all races can be drawn into our struggle.

From my reading of Marxist literature and from conversations with 71 Marxists, I have gained the impression that communists regard the parliamentary system of the West as undemocratic and reactionary. But, on the contrary, I am an admirer of such a system.

The Magna Charta, the Petition of Rights, and the Bill of Rights are doc- 72 uments which are held in veneration by democrats throughout the world.

I have great respect for British political institutions, and for the country's sys- 73 tem of justice. I regard the British Parliament as the most democratic institution in the world, and the independence and impartiality of its judiciary never fail to arouse my admiration.

74 The American Congress, that country's doctrine of separation of powers, as well as the independence of its judiciary, arouses in me similar sentiments.

75 I have been influenced in my thinking by both West and East. All this has led me to feel that in my search for a political formula, I should be absolutely impartial and objective. I should tie myself to no particular system of society other than of socialism. I must leave myself free to borrow the best from the West and from the East. . . .

76 There are certain Exhibits which suggest that we received financial support from abroad, and I wish to deal with this question.

77 Our political struggle has always been financed from internal sources— from funds raised by our own people and by our own supporters. Whenever we had a special campaign or an important political case—for example, the Treason Trial—we received financial assistance from sympathetic individuals and organizations in the Western countries. We had never felt it necessary to go beyond these sources.

78 But when in 1961 the Umkhonto was formed, and a new phase of struggle introduced, we realized that these events would make a heavy call on our slender resources, and that the scale of our activities would be hampered by the lack of funds. One of my instructions, as I went abroad in January 1962, was to raise funds from the African states.

79 I must add that, whilst abroad, I had discussions with leaders of political movements in Africa and discovered that almost every single one of them, in areas which had still not attained independence, had received all forms of assistance from the socialist countries, as well as from the West, including that of financial support. I also discovered that some well-known African states, all of them non-communists, and even anti-communists, had received similar assistance.

80 On my return to the Republic, I made a strong recommendation to the ANC that we should not confine ourselves to Africa and the Western countries, but that we should also send a mission to the socialist countries to raise the funds which we so urgently needed.

81 I have been told that after I was convicted such a mission was sent, but I am not prepared to name any countries to which it went, nor am I at liberty to disclose the names of the organizations and countries which gave us support or promised to do so.

82 As I understand the State case, and in particular the evidence of "Mr. X," the suggestion is that Umkhonto was the inspiration of the Communist Party which sought by playing upon imaginary grievances to enrol the African people into an army which ostensibly was to fight for African freedom, but in reality was fighting for a communist state. Nothing could be further from the truth. In fact the suggestion is preposterous. Umkhonto was formed by Africans to further their struggle for freedom in their own land. Communists and others supported the movement, and we only wish that more sections of the community would join us.

83 Our fight is against real, and not imaginary, hardships or, to use the language of the State Prosecutor, "so-called hardships." Basically, we fight against

two features which are the hallmarks of African life in South Africa and which are entrenched by legislation which we seek to have repealed. These features are poverty and lack of human dignity, and we do not need communists or so-called "agitators" to teach us about these things.

South Africa is the richest country in Africa, and could be one of the richest countries in the world. But it is a land of extremes and remarkable contrasts. The whites enjoy what may well be the highest standard of living in the world, whilst Africans live in poverty and misery. Forty per cent of the Africans live in hopelessly overcrowded and, in some cases, drought-stricken Reserves, where soil erosion and the overworking of the soil makes it impossible for them to live properly off the land. Thirty per cent are labourers, labour tenants, and squatters on white farms and work and live under conditions similar to those of the serfs of the Middle Ages. The other 30 per cent live in towns where they have developed economic and social habits which bring them closer in many respects to white standards. Yet most Africans, even in this group, are impoverished by low incomes and high cost of living.

The highest-paid and the most prosperous section of urban African life is in Johannesburg. Yet their actual position is desperate. The latest figures were given on 25 March 1964 by Mr. Carr, Manager of the Johannesburg Non-European Affairs Department. The poverty datum line for the average African family in Johannesburg (according to Mr. Carr's department) is R42.84 per month. He showed that the average monthly wage is R32.24 and that 46 per cent of all African families in Johannesburg do not earn enough to keep them going.

Poverty goes hand in hand with malnutrition and disease. The incidence of malnutrition and deficiency diseases is very high amongst Africans. Tuberculosis, pellagra, kwashiorkor, gastro-enteritis, and scurvy bring death and destruction of health. The incidence of infant mortality is one of the highest in the world. According to the Medical Officer of Health for Pretoria, tuberculosis kills forty people a day (almost all Africans), and in 1961 there were 58,491 new cases reported. These diseases not only destroy the vital organs of the body, but they result in retarded mental conditions and lack of initiative, and reduce powers of concentration. The secondary results of such conditions affect the whole community and the standard of work performed by African labourers.

The complaint of Africans, however, is not only that they are poor and the whites are rich, but that the laws which are made by the whites are designed to preserve this situation. There are two ways to break out of poverty. The first is by formal education, and the second is by the worker acquiring a greater skill at his work and thus higher wages. As far as Africans are concerned, both these avenues of advancement are deliberately curtailed by legislation.

The present Government has always sought to hamper Africans in their search for education. One of their early acts, after coming into power, was to stop subsidies for African school feeding. Many African children who attended schools depended on this supplement to their diet. This was a cruel act.

There is compulsory education for all white children at virtually no cost to their parents, be they rich or poor. Similar facilities are not provided for the African children, though there are some who receive such assistance. African children, however, generally have to pay more for their schooling than whites. According to figures quoted by the South African Institute of Race Relations in its 1963 journal, approximately 40 per cent of African children in the age group between seven to fourteen do not attend school. For those who do attend school, the standards are vastly different from those afforded to white children. In 1960–61 the *per capita* Government spending on African students at State-aided schools was estimated at R12.46. In the same years, the *per capita* spending on white children in the Cape Province (which are the only figures available to me) was R144.57. Although there are no figures available to me, it can be stated, without doubt, that the white children on whom R144.57 per head was being spent all came from wealthier homes than African children on whom R12.46 per head was being spent.

90   The quality of education is also different. According to the Bantu Educational Journal, only 5,660 African children in the whole of South Africa passed their Junior Certificate in 1962, and in that year only 362 passed matric.[5] This is presumably consistent with the policy of Bantu education about which the present Prime Minister said, during the debate on the Bantu Education Bill in 1953:

91   When I have control of Native education I will reform it so that Natives will be taught from childhood to realize that equality with Europeans is not for them. . . . People who believe in equality are not desirable teachers for Natives. When my Department controls Native education it will know for what class of higher education a Native is fitted, and whether he will have a chance in life to use his knowledge.

92   The other main obstacle to the economic advancement of the African is the industrial colour-bar under which all the better jobs of industry are reserved for Whites only. Moreover, Africans who do obtain employment in the unskilled and semi-skilled occupations which are open to them are not allowed to form trade unions which have recognition under the Industrial Conciliation Act. This means that strikes of African workers are illegal, and that they are denied the right of collective bargaining which is permitted to the better-paid White workers. The discrimination in the policy of successive South African Governments towards African workers is demonstrated by the so-called "civilized labour policy" under which sheltered, unskilled Government jobs are found for those white workers who cannot make the grade in industry, at wages which far exceed the earnings of the average African employee in industry.

93   The Government often answers its critics by saying that Africans in South Africa are economically better off than the inhabitants of the other countries in Africa. I do not know whether this statement is true and doubt whether any comparison can be made without having regard to the cost-of-living index in

---

[5]The Junior Certificate examination was generally taken by white children at the age of 15, and they cannot normally leave school before this. Matriculation is taken two years later and qualifies students for higher education. The educational system, however, ensures that very few Africans reach Junior Certificate level, so that what represents a basic standard for whites is one of achievement for Africans. Even fewer attain matriculation level.

such countries. But even if it is true, as far as the African people are concerned it is irrelevant. Our complaint is not that we are poor by comparison with people in other countries, but that we are poor by comparison with the white people in our own country, and that we are prevented by legislation from altering this imbalance.

The lack of human dignity experienced by Africans is the direct result of 94 the policy of white supremacy. White supremacy implies black inferiority. Legislation designed to preserve white supremacy entrenches this notion. Menial tasks in South Africa are invariably performed by Africans. When anything has to be carried or cleaned the white man will look around for an African to do it for him, whether the African is employed by him or not. Because of this sort of attitude, whites tend to regard Africans as a separate breed. They do not look upon them as people with families of their own; they do not realize that they have emotions—that they fall in love like white people do; that they want to be with their wives and children like white people want to be with theirs; that they want to earn enough money to support their families properly, to feed and clothe them and send them to school. And what "house-boy" or "garden-boy" or labourer can ever hope to do this?

Pass laws, which to the Africans are among the most hated bits of legisla- 95 tion in South Africa, render any African liable to police surveillance at any time. I doubt whether there is a single African male in South Africa who has not at some stage had a brush with the police over his pass. Hundreds and thousands of Africans are thrown into jail each year under pass laws. Even worse than this is the fact that pass laws keep husband and wife apart and lead to the breakdown of family life.

Poverty and the breakdown of family life have secondary effects. Children 96 wander about the streets of the townships because they have no schools to go to, or no money to enable them to go to school, or no parents at home to see that they go to school, because both parents (if there be two) have to work to keep the family alive. This leads to a breakdown in moral standards, to an alarming rise in illegitimacy, and to growing violence which erupts not only politically, but everywhere. Life in the townships is dangerous. There is not a day that goes by without somebody being stabbed or assaulted. And violence is carried out of the townships in the white living areas. People are afraid to walk alone in the streets after dark. Housebreakings and robberies are increasing, despite the fact that the death sentence can now be imposed for such offences. Death sentences cannot cure the festering sore.

Africans want to be paid a living wage. Africans want to perform work 97 which they are capable of doing, and not work which the Government declares them to be capable of. Africans want to be allowed to live where they obtain work, and not be endorsed out of an area because they were not born there. Africans want to be allowed to own land in places where they work, and not to be obliged to live in rented houses which they can never call their own. Africans want to be part of the general population, and not confined to living in their own ghettoes. African men want to have their wives and children to live with them where they work, and not be forced into an unnatural existence in men's hostels. African women want to be with their menfolk and not be left permanently widowed in the Reserves. Africans want to be allowed out after eleven o'clock at night and not to be confined to their rooms like little children. Africans want to be allowed to travel in their own country and to seek work where they want to and not where the Labour Bureau tells them to. Africans want a just share in the whole of South Africa; they want security and a stake in society.

98   Above all, we want equal political rights, because without them our disabilities will be permanent. I know this sounds revolutionary to the whites in this country, because the majority of voters will be Africans. This makes the white man fear democracy.

99   But this fear cannot be allowed to stand in the way of the only solution which will guarantee racial harmony and freedom for all. It is not true that the enfranchisement of all will result in racial domination. Political division, based on colour, is entirely artificial and, when it disappears, so will the domination of one colour group by another. The ANC has spent half a century fighting against racialism. When it triumphs it will not change that policy.

100   This then is what the ANC is fighting. Their struggle is a truly national one. It is a struggle of the African people, inspired by their own suffering and their own experience. It is a struggle for the right to live.

101   During my lifetime I have dedicated myself to this struggle of the African people. I have fought against white domination and I have fought against black domination. I have cherished the ideal of a democratic and free society in which all persons live together in harmony and with equal opportunities. It is an ideal which I hope to live for and to achieve. But if needs be, it is an ideal for which I am prepared to die.

102   *On 11 June 1964, at the conclusion of the trial, Mandela and seven others— Walter Sisulu, Govan Mbeki, Raymond Mhlaba, Elias Motsoaledi, Andrew Mlangeni, Ahmed Kathrada and Denis Goldberg—were convicted. Mandela was found guilty on four charges of sabotage and, like the others, was sentenced to life imprisonment. On 11 February 1990, after intense international pressure, he was released from prison.*

Questions for Discussion and Your Reading Journal

1. Nelson Mandela's piece was also written in jail. Look at the style, purpose, and audience. How are these different from King's (p. 214)?
2. Why did the African National Congress (ANC), after using nonviolent methods, choose violent protest?
3. What types of violence does Mandela list? Which did the ANC choose and why?
4. What is the ideology of the ANC? What does the South African government claim about it? How can it cooperate with the communists in South Africa and yet not be communist? How did Mandela's views on communism change?
5. Compare the social and political conditions of Mandela and King. How might this account for their different means to achieve similar ends?
6. Examine the solutions suggested for racism given in Memmi's essay (p. 181)? Which of these solutions could be applied to the situations described by Gandhi, King, and Mandela?

DAW AUNG SAN SUU KYI

Daw Aung San Suu Kyi (1945–) has become an internationally respected figure for her unwavering efforts to bring democracy and respect for human rights to Myanmar (Burma). Her father, General Aung San, was a leading force in Burmese politics and government until his assassination in 1947, shortly after his daughter turned 2 years old. Her mother, Daw Khin Kyi, later served as Burma's ambassador to India. In 1988 Daw Aung San Suu Kyi helped found and became the general secretary of the Burmese political party, The National League for Democracy (NLD). The NLD was immediately and violently opposed by Burma's military leadership junta, which formed the State Law and Order Restoration Council (SLORC) to give legitimacy to their dictatorial rule in the face of nationwide calls for greater democracy. Hundreds of Suu Kyi's supporters were killed in the ensuing military crackdown, and she was placed under indefinite house arrest through hastily passed laws that allowed for detention without charge or trial for up to 5 years. Despite the limitations of her confinement, in 1990 Daw Aung San Suu Kyi and her party won an overwhelming 82 percent of the seats in the national elections. The military leadership immediately annulled the election results and refused to acknowledge the victory. Later in 1990 Daw Aung San Suu Kyi was awarded the Sakharov Prize for Human Rights by the European Parliament. Then, in 1991 she won the Nobel Peace Prize and worldwide recognition as "one of the most extraordinary examples of civil courage in Asia in recent decades" and as "an important symbol in the struggle against oppression" (Aung San Suu Kyi, Freedom from Fear, New York: Penguin, 1991: 236.) She used the $1.3 million in prize money to establish a health and education trust for the Burmese people. All of this she accomplished from her home, where she remained under arrest until July of 1995. After her release, the military government continued to make her life difficult. Military patrols repeatedly blocked her car from moving forward as she attempted to drive to major meetings of her political party. On one occasion she spent 6 days blocked in her car because she refused to turn back and go home. In 1997 the military government refused to grant her ailing British husband of 25 years a visa so that they could be together before he died. He died in London that same year. She was not able to go to him for fear that the government would never let her return to her homeland. Throughout her standoffs with police and soldiers, Daw Aung San Suu Kyi continues to call for nonviolent resistance to political and social injustice and for the orderly transition to democracy in her homeland.

Reading Rhetorically

One of the unique rhetorical features of Aung San Suu Kyi's Beijing address is that she was a woman political figure speaking to other women at what was the largest global gathering of women in the history of the world to that point in time (1995). As a woman speaking to other women, she was free to talk on a more personal level than she might wish to do in a mixed audience. Indeed, she began on a personal note, explaining the conditions that required her to send a videotaped message to the conference rather than to attend in person. As she turned to her main topic, "peace, security, human rights, and democracy," one item was conspicuously absent. She never explicitly mentioned the word "freedom," a word that male writers on democracy often placed in the foreground as the most important value in their speeches and writings (see especially George W. Bush's Introduction to the National Security Strategy document earlier in this chapter). In contrast, Suu Kyi focused upon values such as tolerance, compassion, self-sacrifice, courage, perseverance, dignity, and security. The examples she used to illustrate her points upon these topics likewise turned to the dimensions of life usually associated with women through connections to "home" and "family." Such use of words and examples is likely to appeal effectively to the women of the world and to echo the day-to-day concerns that they face (pathos). Suu Kyi did not leave men out of the issues that she addressed, however. She articulated a conception of the proper relationship between men and women as they work together for a better world and explicitly challenged patterns of "patriarchal domination and degradation." One of the most complex rhetorical moves that Suu Kyi made came near the end of her speech where she proposed a more positive and productive way of looking at the world than as "opposing camps of good and evil." By rephrasing this traditional division with the concept of "those who are capable of learning and those who are incapable of doing so," she replaced a more traditional and confrontational view of the world with one that was more inclusive of all of humanity—what she portrays as the ongoing project of removing "the impediments to human development everywhere."

Keynote Address, Beijing Forum on Women, 1995

1 Aung San Suu Kyi,
Nobel Prize Laureate
31 August 1995

2 It is a wonderful but daunting task that has fallen on me to say a few words by way of opening this Forum, the greatest concourse of women (joined by a few brave men!) that has ever gathered on our planet. I want to try and voice some of the common hopes which firmly unite us in all our splendid diversity.

3   But first I would like to explain why I cannot be with you in person today. Last month I was released from almost six years of house arrest. The regaining of my freedom has in turn imposed a duty on me to work for the freedom of other women and men in my country who have suffered far more - and who continue to suffer far more - than I have. It is this duty which prevents me from

joining you today. Even sending this message to you has not been without difficulties. But the help of those who believe in international cooperation and freedom of expression has enabled me to overcome the obstacles. They made it possible for me to make a small contribution to this great celebration of the struggle of women to mould their own destiny and to influence the fate of our global village.

The opening plenary of this Forum will be presenting an overview of the global forces affecting the quality of life of the human community and the challenges they pose for the global community as a whole and for women in particular as we approach the twenty-first century. However, with true womanly understanding the Convener of this Forum suggested that among these global forces and challenges, I might wish to concentrate on those matters which occupy all my waking thoughts these days: peace, security, human rights and democracy. I would like to discuss these issues particularly in the context of the participation of women in politics and governance.

For millenia women have dedicated themselves almost exclusively to the task of nurturing, protecting and caring for the young and the old, striving for the conditions of peace that favour life as a whole. To this can be added the fact that, to the best of my knowledge, no war was ever started by women. But it is women and children who have always suffered most in situations of conflict. Now that we are gaining control of the primary historical role imposed on us of sustaining life in the context of the home and family, it is time to apply in the arena of the world the wisdom and experience thus gained in activities of peace over so many thousands of years. The education and empowerment of women throughout the world cannot fail to result in a more caring, tolerant, just and peaceful life for all.

If to these universal benefits of the growing emancipation of women can be added the "peace dividend" for human development offered by the end of the Cold War, spending less on the war toys of grown men and much more on the urgent needs of humanity as a whole, then truly the next millenia will be an age the like to which has never been seen in human history. But there still remain many obstacles to be overcome before we can achieve this goal. And not least among these obstacles are intolerance and insecurity.

This year is the International Year for Tolerance. The United Nations has recognised that "tolerance, human rights, democracy and peace are closely related. Without tolerance, the foundations for democracy and respect for human rights cannot be strengthened, and the achievements of peace will remain elusive". My own experience during the years I have been engaged in the democracy movement in Burma has convinced me of the need to emphasize the positive aspects of tolerance. It is not enough simply to "live and let live": genuine tolerance requires an active effort to try to understand the point of view of others; it implies broad- mindedness and vision, as well as confidence in one's own ability to meet new challenges without resorting to intransigence or violence. In societies where men are truly confident of their own worth women are not merely "tolerated", they are valued. Their opinions are listened to with respect, they are given their rightful place in shaping the society in which they live.

© Pelletier Micheline/CORBIS SYGMA

8   There is an outmoded Burmese proverb still recited by men, who wish to deny that women too can play a part in bringing necessary change and progress to their society: "The dawn rises only when the rooster crows". But Burmese people today are well aware of the scientific reason behind the rising of dawn and the falling of dusk. And the intelligent rooster surely realizes that it is because dawn comes that it crows and not the other way round. It crows to welcome the light that has come to relieve the darkness of night. It is not the prerogative of men alone to bring light to this world: women with their capacity for compassion and self-sacrifice, their courage and perseverence, have done much to dissipate the darkness of intolerance and hate, suffering and despair.

9   Often the other side of the coin of intolerance is insecurity. Insecure people tend to be intolerant, and their intolerance unleashes forces that threaten the security of others. And where there is no security there can be no lasting peace. In its Human Development Report for last year, the UNDP noted that human security "is not a concern with weapons—it is a concern with human life and dignity." The struggle for democracy and human rights in Burma is a struggle for life and dignity. It is a struggle that encompasses our political, social and economic aspirations. The people of my country want the two freedoms that spell security: freedom from want and freedom from war. It is want that has driven so many of our young girls across our borders to a life of sexual slavery where they are subject to constant humiliation and ill-treatment. It is fear of persecution for their political beliefs that has made so many of our people feel that even in their own homes they cannot live in dignity and security.

Traditionally the home is the domain of the woman. But there has never 10
been a guarantee that she can live out her life there safe and unmolested. There
are countless women who are subjected to severe cruelty within the heart of
the family which should be their haven. And in times of crisis when their menfolk are unable to give them protection, women have to face the harsh challenges of the world outside while continuing to discharge their duties within
the home.

Many of my male colleagues who have suffered imprisonment for their 11
part in the democracy movement have spoken of the great debt of gratitude
they owe their womenfolk, particularly their wives, who stood by them firmly,
tender as mothers nursing their newly born, brave as lionesses defending their
young. These magnificent human beings who have done so much to aid their
men in the struggle for justice and peace - how much more could they not
achieve if given the opportunity to work in their own right for the good of
their country and of the world?

Our endeavours have also been sustained by the activities of strong and 12
principled women all over the world who have campaigned not only for my
own release but, more importantly, for our cause. I cannot let this opportunity pass without speaking of the gratitude we feel towards our sisters everywhere, from heads of governments to busy housewives. Their efforts have
been a triumphant demonstration of female solidarity and of the power of an
ideal to cross all frontiers.

In my country at present, women have no participation in the higher lev- 13
els of government and none whatsoever in the judiciary. Even within the democratic movement only 14 out of the 485 MPs elected in 1990 were women -
all from my own party, the National League for Democracy. These 14 women
represent less than 3 percent of the total number of successful candidates.
They, like their male colleagues, have not been permitted to take office since
the outcome of those elections has been totally ignored. Yet the very high performance of women in our educational system and in the managment of commercial enterprises proves their enormous potential to contribute to the bet-
terment of society in general. Meanwhile our women have yet to achieve those
fundamental rights of free expression, association and security of life denied
also to their menfolk.

The adversities that we have had to face together have taught all of us 14
involved in the struggle to build a truly democratic political system in Burma
that there are no gender barriers that cannot be overcome. The relationship
between men and women should, and can be, characterized not by patroniz-
ing behavior or exploitation, but by metta (that is to say loving kindness),
partnership and trust. We need mutual respect and understanding between
men and women, instead of patriarchal domination and degradation, which
are expressions of violence and engender counter-violence. We can learn from
each other and help one another to moderate the "gender weaknesses"
imposed on us by traditional or biological factors.

There is an age old prejudice the world over to the effect that women talk 15
too much. But is this really a weakness? Could it not in fact be a strength?
Recent scientific research on the human brain has revealed that women are

better at verbal skills while men tend towards physical action. Psychological research has shown on the other hand that disinformation engendered by men has far more damaging effect on its victims than feminine gossip. Surely these discoveries indicate that women have a most valuable contribution to make in situations of conflict, by leading the way to solutions based on dialogue rather than on viciousness or violence?

16   The Buddhist paravana ceremony at the end of the rainy season retreat was instituted by the Lord Buddha, who did not want human beings to live in silence [I quote] "like dumb animals". This ceremony, during which monks ask mutual forgiveness for any offence given during the retreat, can be said to be a council of truth and reconciliation. It might also be considered a fore-runner of that most democratic of institutions, the parliament, a meeting of peoples gathered together to talk over their shared problems. All the world's great religions are dedicated to the generation of happiness and harmony. This demonstrates the fact that together with the combative instincts of man there co-exists a spiritual aspiration for mutual understanding and peace.

17   This forum of non-governmental organizations represents the belief in the ability of intelligent human beings to resolve conflicting interests through exchange and dialogue. It also represents the conviction that governments alone cannot resolve all the problems of their countries. The watchfulness and active cooperation of organizations outside the spheres of officialdom are nec-essary to ensure the four essential components of the human development par-adigm as identified by the UNDP: productivity, equity, sustainability and empowerment. The last is particularly relevant: it requires that "development must be by people, not only for them. People must participate fully in the deci-sions and processes that shape their lives." In other words people must be allowed to play a significant role in the governance of the country. And "peo-ple" include women who make up at least half of the world's population.

18   The last six years afforded me much time and food for thought. I came to the conclusion that the human race is not divided into two opposing camps of good and evil. It is made up of those who are capable of learning and those who are incapable of doing so. Here I am not talking of learning in the nar-row sense of acquiring an academic education, but of learning as the process of absorbing those lessons of life that enable us to increase peace and happi-ness in our world. Women in their roles as mothers have traditionally assumed the responsibility of teaching children values that will guide them throughout their lives. It is time we were given the full opportunity to use our natural teaching skills to contribute towards building a modern world that can with-stand the tremendous challenges of the technological revolution which has in turn brought revolutionary changes in social values.

19   As we strive to teach others we must have the humility to acknowledge that we too still have much to learn. And we must have the flexibility to adapt to the changing needs of the world around us. Women who have been taught

that modesty and pliancy are among the prized virtues of our gender are marvelously equipped for the learning process. But they must be given the opportunity to turn these often merely passive virtues into positive assets for the society in which they live.

These, then, are our common hopes that unite us—that as the shackles of 20 prejudice and intolerance fall from our own limbs we can together strive to identify and remove the impediments to human development everywhere. The mechanisms by which this great task is to be achieved provided the proper focus of this great Forum. I feel sure that women throughout the world who, like me, cannot be with you join me now in sending you all our prayers and good wishes for a joyful and productive meeting.

I thank you.

Questions for Discussion and Your Reading Journal

1. Upon what five topics does Suu Kyi choose to focus? In your own opinion, are these topics about which women might have valuable insights to offer? Explain.

2. What statements does the author make in Paragraphs 3 and 4 that she might choose not to make if she were speaking to a predominantly male audience? Explain.

3. Explain what Suu Kyi means by "tolerance."

4. In Paragraph 7, what Burmese proverb does she bring in and what point does she make with it?

5. According to the United Nations Human Development Report, is human security "a concern with weapons" as many people automatically assume? Explain.

6. What is Suu Kyi's ultimate point when she brings up the "debt of gratitude" many men in the democracy movement in Burma have expressed for the support their wives have given them in their darkest hours of suffering?

7. What was the situation for representation of women in government in Burma at the time of this speech? How does this compare to the numbers of women represented in government in your home country at present?

8. According to Suu Kyi, what should be the characteristics of the relationship between men and women? Do you agree?

9. Does the author see it as a problem that women tend to be more verbal than men? Explain.

10. What alternative does Suu Kyi offer to the common view of the human race as divided between "good and evil"? Do you find her view persuasive? Why or why not?

WRITING ASSIGNMENTS

A Summary and Response Essay: Exploring Major Political Ideas in Human History

TASK: Write a two- to three-page paper in standard MLA format that summarizes the political ideas in *one* of the following readings. Include in your essay a personal response that assesses the most important ideas that you feel we can learn today from this model of government or politics.

READINGS: Summarize and respond to *one* of the following readings.

> Confucius, *The Sacred Books of Confucius: Paternal Government* (China)
> Plato, *The Republic* (Greece)
> Kautilya, *The Arthashastra* (India)
> Niccolo Machiavelli, *The Prince* (Italy)
> Thomas Jefferson, The Declaration of Independence (U.S.A.)
> Karl Marx and Friedrich Engels, *Bourgeois and Proletarians* (Germany)
> Mao Tse-tung, from *On the Correct Handling of Contradictions Among the People* (China)
> Julius K. Nyerere, Ujamaa—The Basis of African Socialism (Africa)
> United Nations: Universal Declaration of Human Rights
> John Rawls, *The Law of Peoples* (U.S.A.)

Thinking Rhetorically about Your Audience and Purpose

Take as your audience a group of high-school sophomores who are in their first World History class. You have been invited by their teacher (one of your own favorite former teachers) to give an example of the kinds of things college students learn about the world in college classes. Your purpose should be to inform these students about the key thing(s) to be learned about good government (or about bad government) from the reading that you summarize.

(*Note to Instructor:* This is an ideal assignment for establishing links between your school and local high schools. Often high-school teachers are supportive of having your students share their work with high-school audiences either in group settings or through e-mail connections with younger students. We encourage you to consider these options for expanding the audience for student work in your classroom.)

Writing Objectives

- You will gain deeper understanding of political ideas different from those in your home culture.
- You will practice integrating summary writing into a larger piece of writing.

- You will practice organizing ideas (of others and your own) into essay format with an Introduction/Thesis, Body, and Conclusion.
- You will be expected to use Standard American English grammar and punctuation effectively to communicate your ideas.

Evaluative Criteria

- Does the essay open with a clear introduction to the reading with enough background to help the audience follow the ideas being presented?
- Does the introduction contain a coherent thesis statement that presents your thoughtful response about what we have to learn from the reading?
- Does the body of the paper support and develop the main ideas in the introduction through an effective summary of the reading text and a presentation of your own insights?
- Does a concluding paragraph sum up effectively your summary and response?
- Does the writing demonstrate mastery of Standard American English grammar and punctuation throughout?

Notes to the Student

1. Your first impulse when writing this essay might be to sum up the ideas of the chosen reading and then to tack on a couple of paragraphs about what is to be learned from it. This is a good way to begin the writing process but not a good way to end it. Think of your audience: high-school students. These are people who tend to go to sleep rather quickly. Especially when being lectured to. Even when they are being lectured to by other students only slightly older than themselves. It will be harder for them to do so if they understand from the beginning what you are talking about and what main points you wish to make. Here's how you make sure that happens.
2. Once you have your ideas about the summary and about your own response figured out, go back and organize your writing into a coherent "essay." This means:
   a. Start with a clear introductory paragraph or two that give a little background to the ideas in your summary *and* that include a thesis statement presenting your own ideas about what we have to learn from the reading. *Important Tip:* Do not put more than one to three main ideas in your thesis statement. Focus on the most important ideas in the reading, or you will probably overwhelm your audience with unnecessary information. If they like what they hear from you, they can go and read the entire reading for themselves.
   b. Next, use the body of the paper to summarize the reading in an organized manner that helps the audience understand the key points and ideas of the reading. There may be a number of less important points that you simply leave out. Also in the body, come back to your own main points from your thesis and develop them more fully with examples.

c. Finally, conclude with a final paragraph that pulls the summary of someone else's ideas and your own insights together in a manner that closes the essay.

An Annotated Bibliography (Summary) Paper: Issues in Government and Politics

Note to the Student

An annotated bibliography is simply a bibliography with a succinct, one-paragraph summary of the main points and subpoints of each source. An annotated bibliography is an excellent way to demonstrate your understanding of texts that treat complex issues and themes. It is especially useful as the first step in writing a complete research paper and your instructor may ask you to use this assignment as the beginning point of the research paper assignment that comes later in this chapter. (See Persuasive Writing—Research Paper: Issues in Government and Politics.)

TASK: Use the model provided at the end of this assignment sheet to set up the proper MLA format of an annotated bibliography and to annotate (summarize) three readings on one of the following issues. Be sure to label each sentence in your annotation (main point, subpoint, example) as is done in the model. Labeling sentences will help you to organize your annotation in a clear and understandable manner. (The reading itself may have a rather different organizational pattern.) Once you have completed annotations of three sources from this textbook, conduct outside research (in the library or electronically) to find two more sources on your topic. Your final annotated bibliography must have five total sources.

READINGS: Select any three readings that treat *one* of the issues in this chapter. (Refer to the Table of Contents to see the choices most clearly.) Annotate those three texts.

Thinking Rhetorically about Your Audience and Purpose

It actually works out best to make yourself the audience for this assignment. Annotated bibliographies are most useful as a tool for mastering big ideas that you will dig into more deeply later as you write a research paper on the same topic, or as you continue on in a major field of study more generally. Having yourself as the audience means putting ideas down clearly and succinctly enough that when you review them later they will still make sense to you. Note how the model annotated bibliography at the end of this assignment is structured so that you put the main point of a given article first, followed by supporting points and specific examples. Often articles themselves may not be organized so neatly. In some cases the main point may come somewhere in the middle or even at the end. This may work best for them as they develop big ideas in an extended article, but in your succinct annotation, you should focus on simply grasping and writing down in an organized manner the one to four biggest ideas of the reading.

Writing Objectives

- You will practice reading critically for main ideas, supporting points, and examples.
- You will practice synthesizing full articles in succinct annotation format.
- You will practice using MLA source citation format.
- You are expected to use Standard American English grammar and punctuation effectively to communicate your ideas.

Evaluative Criteria

- Do annotations show coherent understanding of main ideas, supporting points, and examples?
- Are annotations succinct and understandable?
- Is MLA source citation format used properly?
- Does the writing demonstrate mastery of Standard American English grammar and punctuation throughout?

MODEL ANNOTATED BIBLIOGRAPHY

Joanne Cadieux
Dr. Jarvis
CIT 200
Current Date

**Annotated Bibliography
of
The Social Impact of Popular Culture**

Malkin, Amy R., Kimberlie Wornian, and Joan C. Chrisler. "Women and Weight: Gendered Messages on Magazine Covers." <u>Writing Arguments: A Rhetoric with Readings</u>. Eds. John D. Ramage, John C. Bean, and June Johnson. 5th ed. Boston: Allyn and Bacon, 2001. 514–520.

The authors of the article "Women and Weight" argue that, unlike men's magazines, women's magazines send unrealistic messages to women on the "ideal beauty" that result in unhealthy behavior (main point). It was found that women's magazines emphasize weight loss through diet, which if not done right, can be damaging, whereas for men it is on bulking up (subpoint #1). For example, an examination was performed by Anderson and DiDomenico (1992) on 20 most popular magazines read by women and men and the results showed "the ratio of diet articles in men's and women's magazines was 1:10, which is identical to the actual ratio of eating disorders in men and women in the general population" (example #1). To make the goal of weight loss even harder for women, the magazines have conflicting messages (subpoint #2). For example, you will find a picture of a delectable ice cream cake with the heading "Ice-cream Extravaganza!" next to the exercise message that says "Trim your thighs in 3 weeks" (example #2).

Medved, Michael. From *A Sickness in the Soul. Writing Arguments: A Rhetoric with Readings.* Eds. John D. Ramage, John C. Bean, and June Johnson. 5th ed. Boston: Allyn and Bacon, 2001. 488–493.

In "A Sickness in the Soul," Medved argues that Hollywood has a negative impact on the minds of our youth and the increasing violence in our country (main point). Hollywood dismisses the concerns of the majority of Americans who have concerns over the destructive messages sent out in movies, television and popular music despite the results of many recent studies that reveal the public's disapproval of movies made nowadays (subpoint #1). For example, the results of a 1989 Time/CNN survey showed that 67% of those polled believe that violent images in movies are "mainly to blame" for the national epidemic of teenage violence (example #1). Medved also argues that Americans need to realize that with persistence they can make a difference and force changes in the show business industry (subpoint #2). After the showing of a Michael Jackson music video "Black or White" from his album Dangerous, viewers called in to the networks complaining of scenes of violence and sexuality and within 24 hours, "the chagrined superstar agreed to delete the controversial four-minute epilogue from all future versions of the video and issued an elaborate apology to his fans" (example #2).

Shulvitz, Judith. "Modern Makeup: Two Cheers for the Beauty Industry." Writing Arguments: A Rhetoric with Readings. Eds. John D. Ramage, John C. Bean, and June Johnson. 5th ed. Boston: Allyn and Bacon, 2001. 521–523.

Shulvitz argues that the makeup industry opened up a market whereby women are able to become successful entrepreneurs because of their "edge" despite controversial opinions on the use of makeup (main point). All in all it goes on to say that makeup is as complicated an issue as it ever has been (subpoint #1). Famous cosmetics company entrepreneurs such as Helena Rubinstein, Elizabeth Arden, Madame C. J. Walker and Annie Turnbo Malone, to name a few, had great success but not without obstacles such as obtaining capital and store shelves. Both bankers and distributors did not care to do business with the weaker sex (example #1). Over time, makeup has gone from being discouraged in society to mandatory, back to being discouraged by today's women's movement (subpoint #2). Today's feminist movements accuse makeup companies of being perpetrators to women having no self worth without makeup (example #2).

(*Note to Student:* To complete this assignment, you will need to follow the preceding examples to annotate two more sources from research beyond the textbook. Be sure to add these two additional sources into your annotated bibliography in alphabetical order by author's last name.)

A Comparison/Contrast Essay: Two Different Philosophies of Governing

TASK: Read two of the following articles that seem most interesting to you (focus upon readings under one topic or the other) and then write a two- to three-page comparison of the major ideas that they present. Use your own insights to point out areas where the two writers think alike, as well as areas where their ideas are different. Organize your points and insights into a standard essay in MLA format.

READINGS

Topic 1: Differing Philosophies of Governing

> Confucius, *The Sacred Books of Confucius: Paternal Government* (China)
> Plato, *The Republic* (Greece)
> Kautilya, *The Arthashastra* (India)
> Niccolo Machiavelli, *The Prince* (Italy)
> Thomas Jefferson, The Declaration of Independence (U.S.A.)
> Karl Marx and Friedrich Engels, *Bourgeois and Proletarians* (Germany)
> Mao Tse-tung, "On the Correct Handling of Contradictions Among the People (China)"
> Julius K. Nyerere, Ujamaa—The Basis of African Socialism (Tanzania, Africa)
> United Nations: Universal Declaration of Human Rights (Global)
> John Rawls, *The Law of Peoples* (Western World)

Topic 2: Dealing with Global Terrorism

> George W. Bush, The National Security Strategy of the United States of America (The Bush Doctrine)
> Jimmy Carter, Nobel Peace Prize Lecture, December 10, 2002
> Arundhati Roy, "Excerpts from *War Talk*"
> Wendell Berry, "A Citizen's Response to The National Security Strategy of the United States of America"

Charles Colson, "Just War, Preempton, and Iraq"
Daniele Archibugi and Iris Marion Young, "Envisioning a Global Rule of Law"

Thinking Rhetorically about Your Audience and Purpose

For this assignment, consider that your audience is rather evenly split between supporters of each of the authors that you treat. This means that you should try to be fair in your treatment of the authors as you point out the major similarities that they might have, as well as significant differences. As with all good essay writing, you will need to organize your writing into a coherent introduction, body, and conclusion. Your audience members will also expect some sort of main idea statement (thesis statement) from you that tells them *why* they ought to read your essay. Do we learn something valuable, insightful, surprising, or useful from comparing the two authors? Be sure to spell this out to your audience early on in your essay.

Writing Objectives

- You will practice comparing and contrasting the ideas of two authors.
- You will incorporate your own insights into a reflective essay.
- You are expected to use Standard American English grammar and punctuation effectively to communicate your ideas.

Evaluative Criteria

- Have you understood the main ideas from two readings?
- Are your own insights into the readings incorporated effectively into a comparison/contrast essay (containing an introduction with thesis statement/body/conclusion)?
- Does the essay demonstrate mastery of Standard American English grammar and punctuation throughout?

An Analysis Essay: The Globalization of Wealth and Poverty

TASK: Read the following articles on globalization and then write a three- to four-page analysis of the one to three key forces that seem to you to be the root causes of the growing gap between the rich people and the poor people of the world. Use standard MLA essay format to organize and to express your ideas. This is not intended to be a research paper. However, you will need to include a Works Cited page if you use quotes or specific ideas that come directly from your reading sources.

READINGS

> Oxfam "Globalisation" (United Kingdom),
> Kofi Annan, Nobel Peace Prize Lecture, December 10, 2001
> Arundhati Roy, "Excerpts from *War Talk*"
> Robert Reich, "Why the Rich Are Getting Richer and the Poor, Poorer"

Thinking Rhetorically about Your Audience and Purpose

For this assignment, imagine that you are writing for poor people who live in third-world nations but who are studying at the university level like yourself and who are anxious to improve the lives of people in their country one day. In order to do so, they need to hear from other people such as yourself who are likewise grappling with this issue. Use the insights that you gain about global economic trends and human relations from the four readings to give your own best analysis of the root causes of economic inequalities in our time.

Writing Objectives

- You will analyze the root causes of a major global issue, the growing gap between wealthy nations and poor nations.
- You will present your ideas in a well-organized analytical essay.
- You are expected to use Standard American English grammar and punctuation effectively to communicate your ideas.

Evaluative Criteria

- Does the essay demonstrate thoughtful analysis of the issue?
- Are your insights organized into a coherent and insightful essay that presents, develops, and supports your main ideas?
- Does the essay demonstrate mastery of Standard American English grammar and punctuation throughout?

A Synthesis of Sources Paper: Differing Positions on Terrorism

TASK: Read the following articles on global terrorism and then write a three- to five-page synthesis of the differing approaches to dealing with terrorism that the various authors offer. Organize your paper into separate paragraphs that use quotes and examples from each of your sources to show the ideas of each author. Include an introductory paragraph and a concluding paragraph that present the overall issue to your readers and that give your own assessment of which authors offer the most compelling approaches to grappling with terrorism around the globe. Use APA paper format to cite and to document your sources. Note that your references page will contain only sources from this textbook. You are not expected to do outside library research for this paper.

READINGS

> George W. Bush, The National Security Strategy of the United States of America (The Bush Doctrine)
> Charles Colson "Just War, Preemption, and Iraq"
> Jimmy Carter, Nobel Peace Prize Lecture, December 10, 2002
> Arundhati Roy, "Excerpts from *War Talk*"
> Daniele Archibugi and Iris Marion Young, "Envisioning a Global Rule of Law"

Thinking Rhetorically about Your Audience and Purpose

The readings for this assignment present different and often opposing positions on the appropriate response to global terrorism. This is, of course, an issue that inflames and angers people. Write your paper for an audience of concerned people in your country and around the world who genuinely want to understand more about why global terrorism has become so explosive in our time and what ought to be done about it (particularly by the world's remaining superpower, the United States of America). Use your sources to give these readers valuable insights from a variety of perspectives in the United States and beyond it.

Writing Objectives

- You will synthesize the ideas and quotes from a variety of different viewpoints into a single essay.
- You will present your ideas in a well-organized, coherent, and informative paper.
- You will use APA format and style to cite and to document your paper properly.
- You are expected to use Standard American English grammar and punctuation effectively to communicate your ideas.

Evaluative Criteria

- Have you effectively synthesized the ideas of a variety of writers into a single paper?
- Does the paper have an introduction that sets up the overall flow of the paper?
- Does the body of the paper develop the main point(s) of the introduction with quotes, examples, and ideas from individual authors?
- Does the conclusion sum up and close the key points of the paper effectively?
- Is APA format and style used properly to cite and to document sources?

- Does the essay demonstrate mastery of Standard American English grammar and punctuation throughout?

Critique of an Argument Paper: Differing Positions on Fighting Terrorism

TASK: Choose *one* of the following topics and read the two arguments presented. Then write a two- to three- page critique of the argument that you find most (or least) persuasive of the two presented. Organize your writing to systematically analyze the key aspects of the article that make it persuasive or not persuasive. Do not try to analyze every single element of the essay. Rather, focus upon the two to four major points that make it a convincing or not a convincing argument. The main point of your essay should be to answer the questions, *Is this argument convincing, and why, or why not?* Use the other source in the pair as evidence to clarify, strengthen, and support your points. Use standard MLA style to format your paper and to cite and document sources.

READINGS

Option 1

> George W. Bush, From The National Security Strategy of the United States of America (The Bush Doctrine)
> Daniele Archibugi and Iris Marion Young, "Envisioning a Global Rule of Law"

Option 2

> Charles Colson, "Just War, Preemption, and Iraq"
> Wendell Berry, "A Citizen's Response to The National Security Strategy of the United States of America"

Option 3

> George W. Bush, From The National Security Strategy of the United States of America (The Bush Doctrine)
> Arundhati Roy, "Excerpts from *War Talk*"

Thinking Rhetorically about Your Audience and Purpose

As you begin this assignment, you may soon realize that you are, in effect, writing an "argument about an argument." Your task is to persuade your readers that one of the readings is a particularly good or a particularly bad argument, and why. Do not get lost in the argument itself. For example, do not jump on board with any one writer because you personally agree with the author's position. Rather, critique the way the author argues. Does the author have sound reasons for his/her position? Does the author provide reliable and relevant evidence? Does the author consider alternative views or is the argument one-sided? Whom, exactly, does the author seem to be writing for? Is the author likely to be effective with that audience but not with other audiences? As you draft your critique, it might help to think of the *author* as your best audience. Use your critique to point out the strengths and/or the weaknesses of the author's argument in a systematic manner that even the author might find useful and informative.

Writing Objectives

- You will critique the argument of one author.
- You will present your ideas in a well-organized, coherent, and informative paper (i.e., contains an introduction with a main idea/thesis statement, a body, and a conclusion).
- You will use standard MLA style to format the paper and to document sources.
- You are expected to use Standard American English grammar and punctuation effectively to communicate your ideas.

Evaluative Criteria

- Do you effectively critique one argument?
- Does the paper have an opening paragraph that introduces the topic and sets up the critique?
- Does the body of the paper develop the main point(s) of the critique with convincing reasons, appropriate quotes, and specific evidence from the readings?
- Does the conclusion sum up and close the key points of the paper effectively?
- Is MLA format and style used properly?
- Does the essay demonstrate mastery of Standard American English grammar and punctuation throughout?

Persuasive Writing—Essay: Combating Racism and Oppression

Task: Select one of the following topics and read the articles listed on that topic. Then write a persuasive essay that presents what you think is the best way to combat whichever form of racism or oppression is the main focus of the readings. Use evidence from your own experience and from the readings to support your points. Use standard MLA paper format and documentation style to cite and to document any of the sources that you use.

Readings

Option 1

Albert Memmi, "Racism and Oppression"
Martin Luther King Jr., "Letter from Birmingham Jail"
Nelson Mandela, "I Am Prepared to Die"

Option 2

> Simone de Beauvior, "Women as Other"
> Amaury de Riencourt, "Women in Athens"
> Aung San Suu Kyi, Keynote Address, NGO Forum on Women, Beijing '95

Option 3

> Mohandas K. Gandhi, "Satyagraha"
> George Orwell, "Shooting an Elephant"
> Zayn Kassam, "Can a Muslim Be a Terrorist?" (from Chapter 5, Philosophy and Religion)

Thinking Rhetorically about Your Audience and Purpose

The attitudes that people have concerning racial and social equality generally are deeply held and highly personal. To persuade others to think differently about racist and oppressive attitudes that may have been handed down to them from generation to generation will not be an easy task. The ideal audience for this paper is not likely to be people who have strong racial and social prejudices. You should think more in terms of an audience of reasonable people who may not have seriously questioned their own attitudes and behaviors toward people of other races and religions or toward women. A manageable goal in this paper is to try to persuade reasonable people, such as many of your peers in the class you are taking, to reflect more deeply upon their own attitudes. If you can get them to begin thinking about their own attitudes, they will be more open to taking seriously your proposals for ways to combat the prejudices they may have toward your specific topic.

Writing Objectives

- You will write a thought-provoking and persuasive essay.
- You will organize your ideas around a specific issue that involves racism and/or oppression and will support your proposals for combating this issue with reading sources and/or personal experiences.
- You will use standard MLA style to format the paper and to document sources.
- You are expected to use Standard American English grammar and punctuation effectively to communicate your ideas.

Evaluative Criteria

- Does the paper present a clear argument for what should be done to combat racism and/or oppression in the world today?
- Does the body of the paper develop the main point(s) of the argument with convincing reasons, appropriate quotes, and specific evidence from the readings and/or from personal experience?
- Is MLA format and style used properly?

- Does the essay demonstrate mastery of Standard American English grammar and punctuation throughout?

Persuasive Writing—Research Paper: Issues In Government and Politics

TASK: Review the topics and readings contained in the Government and Politics chapter of this book. Select an issue from among these readings that interests you and conduct further research both by reading other articles in this book and through library and/or electronic research. Early on in your research, formulate a research question that you would like to find a good answer to on this topic, and then use your research paper both to answer your question and to convince your readers that your answer is a good one. Be careful that your research question is not simply a fact-based question (i.e., What are the basic principles of the Bush Doctrine?). Rather, formulate an *issue-oriented* question (i.e., How likely is the Bush Doctrine to bring about a more peaceful world?). (*Note:* This would be an ideal assignment with which to build upon the Annotated Bibliography assignment given earlier in this chapter.)

Paper Length

Seven to ten pages

Required Number of Sources

Use a minimum of 10 sources in this paper, including articles from this book, database sources, and Web sources. (*Caution:* Many Web sources are not very reliable or by reputable authors; be sure to base your research upon sources that are credible.)

Format and Style

Use APA format and style to format the paper and to document your use of sources.

Thinking Rhetorically about Your Audience and Purpose

Often when students begin a research project, their primary concern is to learn more about a specific topic. This is a great place to begin . . . and a bad place to end. You need to do more than come up with a lot of facts about your topic. Encyclopedias and dictionaries give us the facts. The purpose of a good academic research paper is to offer your readers some clear and compelling idea of *what they should do with or about the facts you offer*. In short, it is not enough in a good research paper to tell your audience in great detail that one group or another is being oppressed, or that one form of government or another works a certain way. Rather, you should persuade your audience members that they have something important to learn, or something that they ought to do, based upon looking at how a group is being oppressed or how a government is conducting itself. For an audience favorable to this task, imagine a group of fellow students who are open and idealistic about having some sort of positive influence in the world. Use this research paper to persuade them that there is something valuable that they can learn, or even that they can do, to improve a situation that needs to be improved.

Writing Objectives

- You will write a persuasive research paper on a topic in government and politics.
- You will use a minimum of 10 credible sources to support and develop your main points upon the research topic.
- You will use standard APA style to format the paper and to document sources.
- You are expected to use Standard American English grammar and punctuation effectively to communicate your ideas.

Evaluative Criteria

- Does the paper present a well-researched and persuasive argument upon a specific issue in government and/or politics?
- Does the body of the paper develop the main point(s) of the argument with convincing reasons, appropriate quotes, and specific evidence from the readings and/or from personal experience?
- Are a minimum of 10 credible sources used and are they documented properly in APA style?
- Does the essay demonstrate mastery of Standard American English grammar and punctuation throughout?

Persuasive Writing—Letter of Concern: Issues in Government and Politics

TASK: Draw upon what you have learned from any of the readings in this chapter to write a persuasive letter to a local newspaper or to a member of your state or national government similar to the one in the model at the end of this assignment. (*Teacher's Note:* This is an ideal assignment to use as a follow-up to the research paper. It allows students to share the insights that they have learned in their research work with a real-world audience in a meaningful context.)

Proper Format

See standard letter model at the end of this assignment.

Thinking Rhetorically about Your Audience and Purpose

As you begin the first draft of your letter, keep in mind that a persuasive letter will have a well supported message *(logos)*, it will present you as a reasonable and trustworthy letter writer *(ethos)*; and it will use language that gets your audience to see and to feel the importance of what you have to say *(pathos)*. Many letters to the editor of local newspapers or to representatives in government are what are commonly called "crank" letters. In these kinds of letters, the writer vents his/her anger on a given issue, treats anyone with opposing ideas as either foolish or downright evil, and generally misbehaves in various other ways right there on paper. Few people are swayed by such an outburst. Do not write a crank letter. Even if it makes you feel good to vent, you will just feel bad again when you receive your grade on this assignment. Rather, think of the specific audience who would really be reading this letter, should you decide actually to send it. Support your key points with good examples and evidence. Treat opposing positions with respect and consideration. Talk in terms that will help your audience feel the importance of your message. One last piece of advice: Send the letter and see how your audience responds.

Writing Objectives

- You will write a persuasive letter on a topic in government and politics.
- You will use *logos, ethos,* and *pathos* effectively in your writing.
- You will use standard letter format properly.
- You are expected to use Standard American English grammar and punctuation effectively to communicate your ideas.

Evaluative Criteria

- Does the letter show awareness of *logos, ethos,* and *pathos* in presenting a persuasive argument upon a specific issue?
- Does the letter demonstrate proper use of standard letter format?
- Does the letter demonstrate mastery of Standard American English grammar and punctuation throughout?

MODEL LETTER TO THE EDITOR

Joan B. Kagan, Regional Administrator
Massachusetts Society for the Prevention of Cruelty to Children
Springfield, MA 01101

April 23, 2001

Letters to the Editor
Union-News
P.O. Box 2350
Springfield, MA 01101-2350

Dear Editor:

April is Child Abuse Prevention Month. Statistics on child abuse are shocking and sobering, indeed. Nationally, more than 3 million children are victims of physical abuse and neglect each year. In Massachusetts, there were over 103,000 cases of abuse and neglect reported to the state Department of Social Services last year, including about 12,000 from Western Massachusetts.

How do we address the problem of child abuse? Prevention services can and do work and are at the heart of keeping children and families safe. They are cost-effective, and they decrease the toll on human misery and tragedy.

Compare $3,500 of prevention services to a family for a year with $17,000 per year per child in foster care, or with $80,000 for a children's residential treatment program for one year. If we help families in the first years of their child's life, we can have the greatest impact and make a difference.

What can you do? Wear a blue ribbon. The Massachusetts Society for the Prevention of Cruelty to Children is distributing 103,000 blue ribbons, one ribbon for every child reported for abuse and neglect in Massachusetts last year. By wearing a blue ribbon through April, you will represent a child that is in need of help.

Get involved! Support your child welfare agencies and advocate with your legislators to support prevention programs. Our community is fortunate to have many fine, high-quality child welfare, social service, and mental health agencies and organizations that provide an array of professional services to children and families at risk.

As a community, we need to work together to stop violence against children and to strengthen families by supporting prevention programs.

Sincerely,

Joan B. Kagan

CHAPTER 3
Art and Literature

©Royalty Free/CORBIS

Humans are characterized by curiosity about the world and what it means to be alive. While science is one path toward satisfying this curiosity, it does not answer some of the fundamental questions about who we are and why we are here. Likewise, although religion is a means of answering cosmic questions, it does not fulfill a mysterious and uniquely human impulse: the desire to create. Art and literature—while they cannot satiate hunger or provide protective shelter—do satisfy a compulsion to construct meaning, to grapple with abstract ideas, or to create beauty. They are the means by which creation is achieved.

For many artists, creation is a personal process that has no guaranteed significance beyond the individual artist. It is a means of personal exploration. However, the creation of art and literature—and, more important, their exposure in the world—can have profound social and cultural significance. Art, which in its broadest sense includes literature as a subcategory, can be a shared social experience that has meaning and purpose beyond the individual artist. When art is presented to an audience, it becomes a shared event; although the reception is unique to each member of the audience. Art influences culture by proposing alternative perspectives about what constitutes society, as well as by exploring abstract ideas that find no other expression. It both mirrors social reality and invites audience members to see beyond reflections of their world.

While finding a definition of art that would satisfy contemporary theorists would be impossible, contrasting the ways various parts of the world have looked at art is possible. The Western world has taken a great deal of its perspective on art from the ancient Greeks. Plato discussed art as a reflection (a "mirror") of reality inspired by intuition. Aristotle extended this Platonic view by introducing aesthetic principles, "rules" intended to delineate, define, and guide artistic creation, as well as to improve the understanding of the audience.[1] Aristotle contends that art has the ability to teach us about "truth" more effectively than a narration of actual experience. For example, a play about the concept of "greed" is more edifying than a factual account of a greedy person's life. Beyond its pedagogical value, art also has the power to promote the psychological well-being of the audience by giving potentially disturbing emotions a harmless release or, as he calls it, "catharsis."

Eastern art, on the other hand, has been defined in a different way. Hsieh Ho, a Buddhist artist of the fifth century, wrote "Six Principles of Painting."[2] The

---

[1] Aristotle, *Poetics*, trans. Malcolm Heath (New York: Penguin, 1997).

[2] Hsieh Ho, "Six Principles of Painting," in *The Chinese Theory of Art*, ed. Lin Yutang (New York: Putnam, 1937), 34.

first principle describes how art is infused with "Chi," which means "vital essence." In the East, art is "sacred" in that it has the power to communicate transcendent meaning. While the Greeks might have used the metaphor of the mirror to explain the function of art, the ancient Chinese would likely have construed art as a sacred vessel.

Taoist philosophy has also played a fundamental role in the development of Chinese art. The concepts of *yin* and *yang*, central to this philosophy, are evident in the emphasis on the balance of color and space. The conflict between these opposites is also represented in natural cycles of change; and the subject of a great deal of the art of China is the processes of nature: the eternal cycles of birth, growth, and death.

Another way in which people in diverse parts of the world have viewed art differently relates to the method by which it is categorized. In Western culture in the last few centuries, visual art has come to mean the "fine arts" (painting and sculpture) while "crafts" referred to other objects created to be functional or decorative. Part of the reason arts have been held in higher regard in the Western world than crafts is that the artist was generally a privileged white male with the leisure to pursue the arts, while craft was more often the product of men or women who were from the working class; it was the means by which they made a living.

In the 19th century European travelers visited the many places Europeans had colonized, like Africa, South America, and Australia, and collected a vast array of objects that they categorized as crafts, more interesting for what they seemed to tell about the culture from which they came than for their aesthetic value. Their creators, the people who were indigenous to the colonies, were considered racially inferior in much the same way as their creations were regarded as aesthetically inferior. The products were put on display in museums and elsewhere for primarily ethnographic reasons.

Over the last several decades, however, political change and increasing awareness of the cultural values from which aesthetic judgments have been made have greatly changed the ways that crafted products are considered. Today many of these objects are purchased at prices as high as or even higher than well-regarded paintings or sculpture. Definitions of "art" continue to evolve as aesthetic values change and cultural biases are recognized.

Like visual art, the subcategory of "literature" has been defined differently in various times and diverse places. Aristotle viewed literature as "an imitation of a sequence of events."[3] He believed literature could best be understood by categorizing it according to "the method of operation and execution of each category." In simple terms, literature could be identified by its function and form. Texts whose only function was artistic expression were considered "literature," while those with other applications were not. Later, as texts that had previously been functional became historical "artifacts," those also began to be seen as "literature" and the distinctions became increasingly blurred.

In the last several decades the distinction between what is literature and what is not has become hotly contested in much the same way as distinctions

---

[3]*Poetics,* 48.

about visual art. Traditionalists, like E. D. Hirsch in his book *Cultural Literacy,* assert that important literature has come primarily from the Western world and that students should study works that can be identified as "great" by a consensus of literary scholars. In recent years this traditional view has become widely unpopular; and most scholars would agree that there are great works of literature from all over the world, that many of these works would not be identified by consensus, and that a central pursuit of education should be "multicultural literacy."

A critic of the concept of "cultural literacy," Paulo Freire, in *Pedagogy of the Oppressed,* calls the teaching method supported by traditionalists such as E. D. Hirsch the "banking concept" of education,[4] a method by which literature "that has stood the test of time" is deposited into the minds of students. The problem with this method, according to Freire, is threefold: students are seen as passive containers; the literature they read represents only a small fraction of what the world has to offer; and the process of education promotes a continued cycle of oppression.

This chapter on art and literature is organized in a general way by beginning with definitions of visual art and continuing with a discussion of the visual art of various parts of the world. Then it moves to literature, opening with definitions and descriptions of the term "poetry", and continuing with thematically organized groupings of literature from around the world.

The first two readings present somewhat traditional Western perspectives on art. Readings from The Royal Bank of Canada and Susanne K. Langer ask the questions: "What use is art?" and "What is its cultural importance?" What follow are a number of definitions of art and descriptions of approaches to art that foreground the issue of privileging various arts and artists. Specifically, such articles as Roy Sieber's "Traditional Arts of Black Africa" and Philip Rawson's "Islamic Art: Calligraphy" question the initial definitions and expand beyond their categories. The illustrations that accompany many of these readings provide concrete points of reference for the concepts being discussed.

The literature section of the chapter opens with five poems about poetry itself. They offer definitions and descriptions of poetry, as well as discussions of poetry's purpose. Billy Collins's "Introduction to Poetry" begins the discussion in a setting very familiar to most students: an English class in the process of analyzing a poem. The rest of the poems take up this subject in a variety of ways, from academic abstraction to concrete demonstration.

The second group of literary readings explores the issue of oppression and its appearance in many forms all over the world. This relatively large section begins with a poem by the Nobel Prize winner Pablo Neruda, "The United Fruit Co." By describing the ways in which outside economic interests have "ravished" the country of Chile and destroyed its people, this poem conveys a message that is extended by the next nine texts. From describing racial discrimination and its effects, as in Paul Laurence Dunbar's "We Wear the Mask" and June Jordan's "A Poem about Intelligence for My Brothers and

---

[4]Paulo Freire, *Pedagogy of the Oppressed,* trans. Myra Bergman Ramos (New York: Continuum, 2001), 60–70.

Sisters," to the subjugation of women, as in Marzieh Ahmadi Oksooii's "I'm a Woman" and Maxine Hong Kingston's "No Name Woman," these texts evoke images of individuals and groups of people oppressed because of race, gender, socioeconomic class, and ethnicity.

Reflections about and descriptions of war are the focus of the next group of poems. Thomas Hardy imagines the ways in which his enemy is like himself in "The Man He Killed," while Anthony Hecht and Muriel Rukeyser describe and reflect on the Holocaust of World War II in "More Light! More Light!" and "Letter to the Front." This section ends with a poem by another Nobel Prize winner, William Butler Yeats, whose "Easter 1916" pays tribute to soldiers who fought for Irish independence.

The final section of this chapter on art and literature blends the two categories by presenting literature about artistic expression in nature. The section begins with a reading that combines lyrical prose with evocative poetry in its exploration of a woman's connection to her mother and all her ancestors, and the expression of that connection in her mother's garden. While the creation of gardens as works of art is the subject of such essays as Julia Smith Berrall's "The Garden: In the Time of the Pharaohs" and John Brookes's "The Concept of the Paradise Garden," Annie Dillard looks at raw natural phenomena in the excerpt from *Pilgrim at Tinker Creek*. In the last reading of the chapter, Dillard muses about God as the ultimate artist, the creator of the universe.

STUDENT ESSAY

NICOLE GOTTUSO The Greatest of Pleasures

Nicole Gottuso was raised in southern California and graduated from the University of California, Santa Barbara, with a degree in literature from the College of Creative Studies. She spent the fall semester of her junior year studying abroad in London, England. The experience gave her a visual context for the study of works by such authors as Charles Dickens, Arthur Conan Doyle, W. H. Auden, and Virginia Woolf. While in England, Nicole traced the footsteps of Virginia Woolf, whose detailed observations of London in both her essays and diaries are full of energy and intrigue.

Reading Rhetorically

The travel journal is a genre of writing that was very popular in the late 19th and early 20th centuries. Virginia Woolf, who lived during that time, is the subject of this student essay, which is based on writings from the student's travel journal. Because journals allow the writer a freedom of expression that more formal kinds of writing do not, they are very popular among travelers. As you read, think about why travelers are so eager to record their experiences.

There is no better way to understand the world than to explore it. Ever since I 1 discovered that travelling could provide me with academic credit as an undergraduate, I knew I had to go—somewhere. As a literature major, I chose to travel to London. It seemed an appropriate choice since I would be able to study British writers in the elements that inspired them. During a warm California day in August, I left for the United Kingdom with a journal, passport, and excitement for the months ahead.

In London I walked several miles a day without recognizing the distance. I 2 was consumed by the smell of Panini sandwiches roasting in a nearby café, or the headlines in the *Evening Standard.* During my months abroad I read several essays by Virginia Woolf, and encountered Bloomsbury and Oxford Street much as she had decades before. I looked at everything: vendors selling postcards for 10 p. each, a homeless man in front of the Dominion Theatre, sitting on a blue duffel bag, and the Italian silk ties hidden in arcades along Regent Street.

Woolf had a very specific time she preferred to wander the streets of London: 3 "Between four and six, we shed the self our friends know us by, and become part of that vast republican army of anonymous trampers" (155). In her essay "Street Haunting" she cites rambling the streets as "the greatest pleasure of town life" (155) and makes any excuse to experience it. Stepping outside, she leaves the comfortable world of her possessions to 'tramp' with other city dwellers.

Slowly I began to form my own attachment to London and its daily hustle. 4 From the top of a bus during morning traffic people spilled like water over stones, rushing through taxicabs. I was fortunate to rarely be in a hurry, and was able to observe these sights and record them in my journal.

On one particular afternoon a walk through Covent Garden allowed me to 5 enjoy an encounter with a young boy. Freckle-faced and no more than ten, he had the boldness to begin a conversation with me as I read *Mrs. Dalloway* outside a café.

"You live in London then?" He waited for my answer. 6

"For now," I said, surprised. 7

"This is my first time. Came down from Manchester for an audition. Did all 8 right I guess. Where you come from?"

"California," I said, and he offered a quick smile, a lift of the eyebrow. I 9 learned to expect this kind of reaction, the absolute awe.

"I thought ya had an American accent. Watch'a doin' here then? If I lived in 10 California I think I'd like to stay there."

"Well, I've lived in California all my life, so I wanted a change. I'm sure you'll 11 feel that way." But how impossible, at ten or eleven, to leave home with that kind of freedom—without having to realize that you must, eventually, return.

"What have you heard about California?" I wondered. 12

"It's hot, lots of people. Great beaches. What's the most posh place in the 13 states?"

I mentioned something about Beverly Hills, Hollywood, New York. 14

"New York! Is that where all the murderers and gangsters live?" 15

My first instinct was to burst with laughter. I knew the truth—that there are 16 other inhabitants besides criminals, but in his innocence and probable love for American films, he could have no other impression.

17   We parted just as the conversation became no longer fit for words. Without looking back I walked quickly towards New Oxford Street to catch the 38 bus back to my flat in Clerkenwell. As soon as I turned the corner I pulled a notebook and pen from my purse and scribbled everything I could remember. I could not forget this encounter.

18   The bus came just as the sun was setting. Heading north, I recalled Woolf's essay and enthusiasm for these particular moments. There are often incidents among complete strangers that offer considerable amounts of pleasure. And like her finishing a walk, I was on my way back to the possessions that comforted me: a copy of *Time Out* magazine left open on my living room table, pictures of my friends and family in the states, and fresh orange juice from Sainsbury's.

19   At the end of her essay Woolf returns home with a lead pencil that was her excuse for the outing. But even after a pleasant walk she felt that little was captured, that it could not all be recalled. Yet she decided to write, as I have, about the intangible moments of being that occur in city life.

20   I trampled down the street towards my door. The street, with its "long groves of darkness" (156), was quiet. Slipping my key into its lock, I realized I never asked the freckle-faced boy his name, or thought to. We shall remain unintroduced.

21   These are the experiences I remember most. Time spent with strangers, looking up at balconies on Carnaby Street with pink and yellow flags hanging from the metal railing. Browsing through used books on Charing Cross Road. Handing the homeless man in front of the Dominion Theatre a raspberry NutriGrain bar. What seemed like only rambling to pass the afternoon hours became something extraordinary. It happened quite frequently while I lived in London, and like Virginia Woolf I learned the single, greatest pleasure of a London walk: there is always something to be discovered.

Work Cited

Woolf, Virginia. *The Crowded Dance of Modern Life, Selected Essays: Volume Two.* London: Penguin Books, 1993.

Questions for Discussion and Your Reading Journal

1. Have you ever traveled outside the United States? If so, describe some of the cultural differences you noticed between the United States and the country to which you traveled. If not, think about the most distant place within the United States to which you have traveled. What cultural differences did you observe between that place and your home community?

2. In paragraph three the student quotes a passage by Virginia Woolf about tourists: she calls them a "vast republican army of anonymous trampers." What do you suppose Woolf means by this phrase? Have you ever felt like an "anonymous tramper"? If so, describe the situation in which you felt this way.

3. The middle section of the student's essay illustrates an encounter between the writer and a local child. What are the child's assumptions about America? To what degree are the child's assumptions accurate?

4. If you could travel anywhere, where would you go? Why would you go there? What assumptions about this place have you drawn from reading, television, and the movies? How accurate do you think your assumptions are?

5. How often do you take a walk just for its own sake? How is your attitude different at these times than it might be otherwise?

DEFINITIONS AND CULTURAL CONTEXTS

ROYAL BANK OF CANADA NEWSLETTER

Many people think of art as something that is useless and difficult to understand, something only "artistic types" can really take pleasure in. But "What Use Is Art?" discusses some of the ways art can help each of us enjoy the human experience more fully. The author claims that understanding and appreciating art give us the opportunity to rise above everyday life; to experience the world from many perspectives instead of just one; and to become more complex, more complete, and perhaps even more satisfied human beings.

The text of the article answers the question posed in its title. The author presents a series of reasons for considering art useful, not only to the individual who creates it or the one who perceives it but to the community as a whole.

Reading Rhetorically

The title of this essay is a question. A few other readings in this book also use a question as a title. This kind of title works particularly well when the topic being addressed is a common controversy about which people are likely to already have an opinion. As you read this article, look for reasons why the title is appropriate for the intended audience and well suited to its purpose.

This article, like many of the readings that follow, is concerned with definitions. Before you read it, think about how you would define the term "art." You may even want to jot your definition down on paper. What are the separate parts of your definition? Do you distinguish art from other fields in the humanities? Do you distinguish between visual and other kinds of art (like music and literature)? As you think about your own definition, try to determine the things that need to be included in a definition to make it useful.

What Use Is Art?

Some people will say that art is real when it shows sound knowledge, mastered craft, vivid imagination, strong common sense, truth, and wise meaning. Others will say that the distinguishing characteristic of a work of art is 1 that it serves no practical end, but is an end in itself. The human test of worth is: Does it give pleasure? To arouse the powers of enjoyment, of yielding to beauty, is the legitimate end of art.

2   Tolstoy said in his essay on art: "Art is a human activity consisting in this, that one man consciously, by means of certain external signs, hands on to others feelings he has lived through, and that others are infected by these feelings and also experience them." If one does not feel deeply stirred in the presence of great pictures, great sculpture or great music, he can be certain that he is living a vastly lower and more restricted life than he could be living. The mechanical world is of our own making, but the real world is one of deep emotional experience.

3   The term "Fine Arts" is conventionally used to designate those arts which are concerned with line, colour and form (painting, sculpture and architecture); with sound (music) and with the exploitation of words for both their musical and expressive values (prose and poetry). Architecture, sculpture, painting, music and poetry are by common consent the five principal or greater fine arts.

4   Fine art addresses itself not only to the eye but also to the imagination. The eye takes notice of ten different qualities of objects: light and darkness, colour and substance, form and position, distance and nearness, movement and rest. It is through his depiction of these in his work that the artist reaches our minds and animates our thoughts.

5   Art changes its outlook, just as so many other parts of life do. It is the expression of an age, perhaps even a revolt against the civilization of the age. One generation despises what its predecessor applauded, yet it would be a great mistake to suppose that the latest is always the best.

6   We should not approach our adventure into art without some preparation. The acuteness of our perception and of our judgment depends on the wealth of our knowledge. The more comparisons we are able to make, the more qualified we are to enjoy art and to express our opinions.

7   In addition to being open-minded when appraising art, you need to be independent. "To know what you prefer," said Robert Louis Stevenson, "instead of humbly saying 'Amen' to what the world tells you you ought to prefer, is to have kept your soul alive."

8   Appreciation of an art releases us from our claustrophobia and gives us a wider outlook. It helps us to rise above life's trivialities and to subdue its turbulence. Its purpose is not to help us escape from life but to enter into a larger life.

9   Art is useful because it raises men's minds to a level higher than merely existing. Here are activities that men and women put forth not because they need but because they like. In an age when material things have such prominence and such a deep influence on people's minds, it is increasingly important to be able to seek the relief to be found in aesthetic activity. It releases us from the arbitrariness of life.

Questions for Discussion and Your Reading Journal

1. What are the purpose and the audience for this piece?
2. Look at the definition of art given. How does it differ from Tolstoy's definition?
3. Outline the argument for the usefulness of art. Do you agree that art is useful? Why or why not?
4. According to the definition given here, is television art? Movies? Tattoos? Jewelry?
5. Do you agree that you need to know a lot about art in order to enjoy it?

SUSANNE K. LANGER

Susanne K. Langer (1895–1985) was educated at Radcliff and Harvard Universities and the University of Vienna. During her long career as a philosopher and teacher, she taught at such institutions as Columbia University, Connecticut College, Northwestern University, Ohio University, the University of Washington, and the University of Michigan. She wrote extensively on linguistic analysis and on aesthetics.

Langer's best-known work, "The Cultural Importance of the Arts" (1942), argues that art is a form of expression that symbolizes intuitive knowledge of certain feelings or emotions that language by itself cannot express. An accomplished cellist, Langer was particularly interested in music as such a form of expression.

In this essay, which was first given as a lecture in 1958, Langer defines art and explains her view of its importance. Because art can give us insight into our feelings in a way that logic and reason cannot, those societies in which art flourishes, she argues, tend to develop vital and creative ways of understanding this inward experience. This, Langer states, "is the beginning of a cultural age."

Reading Rhetorically

As you read this essay, try to determine its intended audience and probable purpose. What kind of reader is likely to tackle a book on this subject, do you suppose? The title suggests that the article will demonstrate art's "cultural importance"—what does this indicate about its purpose and the writer's *ethos*? Look specifically at the second sentence of the first paragraph and what it tells you about the intended audience.

Although Langer's article presents a lot of useful information about art and culture, its tone has been perceived by some readers to be "elitist." Look back to the introduction of this chapter and reread its discussion of the distinction between "arts" and "crafts." As you are reading and studying Langer's definition of the word "art," try to determine if Langer's definition would be likely to exclude work by the marginalized and oppressed people referred to in the chapter introduction. Look, also, for other indications of a particular cultural bias.

The Cultural Importance of the Arts

1   Every culture develops some kind of art as surely as it develops language. Some primitive cultures have no real mythology or religion, but all have some art—dance, song, design (sometimes only on tools or on the human body). Dance, above all, seems to be the oldest elaborated art.

2   The ancient ubiquitous character of art contrasts sharply with the prevalent idea that art is a luxury product of civilization, a cultural frill, a piece of social veneer.

3   It fits better with the conviction held by most artists, that art is the epitome of human life, the truest record of insight and feeling, and that the strongest military or economic society without art is poor in comparison with the most primitive tribe of savage painters, dancers, or idol-carvers. Wherever a society has really achieved culture (in the ethnological sense, not the popular sense of "social form") it has begotten art, not late in its career, but at the very inception of it.

4   Art is, indeed, the spearhead of human development, social and individual. The vulgarization of art is the surest symptom of ethnic decline. The growth of a new art or even a great and radically new style always bespeaks a young and vigorous mind, whether collective or single.

5   What sort of thing is art, that it should play such a leading role in human development? It is not an intellectual pursuit, but is necessary to intellectual life; it is not religion, but grows up with religion, serves it and in large measure determines it.

6   We cannot enter here on a long discussion of what has been claimed as the essence of art, the true nature of art, or its defining function; in a single lecture dealing with one aspect of art, namely its cultural influence, I can only give you by way of preamble my own definition of art, with categorical brevity. This does not mean that I set up this definition in a categorical spirit, but only that we have no time to debate it, so you are asked to accept it as an assumption underlying these reflections.

7   Art, in the sense here intended—that is, the generic term subsuming painting, sculpture, architecture, music, dance, literature, drama, and film—may be defined as the practice of creating perceptible forms expressive of human feeling. I say "perceptible" rather than "sensuous" forms because some works of art are given to imagination rather than to the outward senses. A novel, for instance, usually is read silently with the eye, but is not made for vision, as a painting is; and though sound plays a vital part in poetry, words even in poetry

are not essentially sonorous structures like music. Dance requires to be seen, but its appeal is to deeper centers of sensation. The difference between dance and mobile sculpture makes this immediately apparent. But all works of art are purely perceptible forms that seem to embody some sort of feeling.

"Feeling" as I am using it here covers much more than it does in the tech- 8
nical vocabulary of psychology, where it denotes only pleasure and pain, or even in the shifting limits of ordinary discourse, where it sometimes means sensation (as when one says a paralyzed limb has no feeling in it), sometimes sensibility (as we speak of hurting someone's feelings), sometimes emotion (e.g., as a situation is said to harrow your feelings, or to evoke tender feeling), or a directed emotional attitude (we say we feel strongly *about* something), or even our general mental or physical condition, feeling well or ill, blue, or a bit above ourselves. As I use the word, in defining art as the creation of percepti-ble forms expressive of human feeling, it takes in all those meanings; it applies to everything that may be felt.

Another word in the definition that might be questioned is "creation." I 9
think it is justified, not pretentious, as perhaps it sounds; but that issue is slightly beside the point here, so let us shelve it. If anyone prefers to speak of the "mak-ing" or "construction" of expressive forms that will do here just as well.

What does have to be understood is the meaning of "form," and more 10
particularly "expressive form"; for that involves the very nature of art and therefore the question of its cultural importance.

The word "form" has several current uses; most of them have some rela- 11
tion to the sense in which I am using it here, though a few, such as: "a form to be filled in for tax purposes" or "a mere matter of form" are fairly remote, being quite specialized. Since we are speaking of art, it might be good to point out that the meaning of stylistic pattern—"the sonata form," "the sonnet form"—is not the one I am assuming here.

I am using the word in a simpler sense, which it has when you say, on a 12
foggy night, that you see dimly moving forms in the mist; one of them emerges clearly, and is the form of a man. The trees are gigantic forms; the rills of rain trace sinuous forms on the window pane. The rills are not fixed things; they are forms of motion. When you watch gnats weaving in the air, or flocks of birds wheeling overhead, you see dynamic forms—forms made by motion.

It is in this sense of an apparition given to our perception, that a work of 13
art is a form. It may be a permanent form like a building or a vase or a pic-ture, or a transient, dynamic form like a melody or a dance, or even a form given to imagination, like the passage of purely imaginary, apparent events that constitutes a literary work. But it is always a perceptible, self-identical whole; like a natural being, it has a character of organic unity, self-sufficiency, individual reality. And it is thus, as an appearance, that a work of art is good or bad or perhaps only rather poor; as an appearance, not as a comment on things beyond it in the world, nor as a reminder of them.

This, then, is what I mean by "form"; but what is meant by calling such 14
forms "expressive of human feeling"? How do apparitions "express" any-thing—feeling or anything else? First of all, let us ask just what is meant here by "express"; what sort of "expression" we are talking about.

15   The word "expression" has two principal meanings: in one sense it means self-expression—giving vent to our feelings. In this sense it refers to a symptom of what we feel. Self-expression is a spontaneous reaction to an actual, present situation, an event, the company we are in, things people say, or what the weather does to us; it bespeaks the physical and mental state we are in and the emotions that stir us.

16   In another sense, however, "expression" means the presentation of an idea, usually by the proper and apt use of words. But a device for presenting an idea is what we call a symbol, not a symptom. Thus a word is a symbol, and so is a meaningful combination of words.

17   A sentence, which is a special combination of words, expresses the idea of some state of affairs, real or imagined. Sentences are complicated symbols. Language will formulate new ideas as well as communicate old ones, so that all people know a lot of things that they have merely heard or read about. Symbolic expression, therefore, extends our knowledge beyond the scope of our actual experience.

18   If an idea is clearly conveyed by means of symbols we say it is well expressed. A person may work for a long time to give his statement the best possible form, to find the exact words for what he means to say, and to carry his account or his argument most directly from one point to another. But a discourse so worked out is certainly not a spontaneous reaction. Giving expression to an idea is obviously a different thing from giving expression to feelings. You do not say of a man in a rage that his anger is well expressed. The symptoms just are what they are, there is no critical standard for symptoms. If, on the other hand, the angry man tries to tell you what he is fuming about, he will have to collect himself, curtail his emotional expression, and find words to express his ideas. For to tell a story coherently involves "expression" in quite a different sense: This sort of expression is not "self-expression," but may be called "conceptual expression."

19   Language, of course, is our prime instrument of conceptual expression. The things we can say are in effect the things we can think. Words are the terms of our thinking as well as the terms in which we present our thoughts, because they present the objects of thought to the thinker himself. Before language communicates ideas, it gives them form, makes them clear, and in fact makes them what they are. Whatever has a name is an object for thought. Without words, sense experience is only a flow of impressions, as subjective as our feelings; words make it objective, and carve it up into *things* and *facts* that we can note, remember, and think about. Language gives outward experience its form, and makes it definite and clear.

20   There is, however, an important part of reality that is quite inaccessible to the formative influence of language: that is the realm of so-called "inner experience," the life of feeling and emotion. The reason why language is so powerless here is not, as many people suppose, that feeling and emotion are irrational; on the contrary, they seem irrational because language does not help to make them conceivable, and most people cannot conceive anything without the logical scaffolding of words. The unfitness of language to convey subjective experience is a somewhat technical subject, easier for logicians to understand than for artists; but the gist of it is that the form of language does not reflect

the natural form of feeling, so we cannot shape any extensive concepts of feeling with the help of ordinary, discursive language. Therefore the words whereby we refer to feeling only name very general kinds of inner experience— excitement, calm, joy, sorrow, love, hate, etc. But there is no language to describe just how one joy differs, sometimes radically, from another. The real nature of feeling is something language as such—as discursive symbolism— cannot render.

For this reason, the phenomena of feeling and emotion are usually treated   21 by philosophers as irrational. The only pattern discursive thought can find in them is the pattern of outward events that occasion them. There are different degrees of fear, but they are thought of as so many degrees of the same simple feeling.

But human feeling is a fabric, not a vague mass. It has an intricate dynamic   22 pattern, possible combinations and new emergent phenomena. It is a pattern of organically interdependent and interdetermined tensions and resolutions; a pattern of almost infinitely complex activation and cadence. To it belongs the whole gamut of our sensibility, the sense of straining thought, all mental attitude and motor set. Those are the deeper reaches that underlie the surface waves of our emotion, and make human life a life of feeling instead of an unconscious metabolic existence interrupted by feelings.

It is, I think, this dynamic pattern that finds its formal expression in the arts.   23 The expressiveness of art is like that of a symbol, not that of an emotional symptom; it is as a formulation of feeling for our conception that a work of art is properly said to be expressive. It may serve somebody's need of self-expression besides; but that is not what makes it good or bad art. In a special sense one may call a work of art a symbol of feeling, for, like a symbol, it formulates our ideas of inward experience, as discourse formulates our ideas of things and facts in the outside world. A work of art differs from a genuine symbol—that is, a symbol in the full and usual sense—in that it does not point beyond itself to something else. Its relation to feeling is a rather special one that we cannot undertake to analyze here; in effect, the feeling it expresses appears to be directly given with it—as the sense of a true metaphor, or the value of a religious myth—and is not separable from its expression. We speak of the feeling *of*, or the feeling *in*, a work of art, not the feeling it means. And we speak truly; a work of art presents something like a direct vision of vitality, emotion, subjective reality.

The primary function of art is to objectify feeling so we can contemplate   24 and understand it. It is the formulation of so-called "inward experience," the "inner life," that is impossible to achieve by discursive thought, because its forms are incommensurable with the forms of language and all its derivatives (e.g., mathematics, symbolic logic). Art objectifies the sentience and desire, self-consciousness and world-consciousness, emotions and moods that are generally regarded as irrational because words cannot give us clear ideas of them. But the premise tacitly assumed in such a judgment—namely, that anything language cannot express is formless and irrational—seems to me to be an error. I believe the life of feeling is not irrational; its logical forms are merely very different from the structures of discourse. But they are so much like the dynamic forms of art that art is their natural symbol. Through plastic works, music, fiction, dance, or dramatic forms we can conceive what vitality and emotion feel like.

25   This brings us, at last, to the question of the cultural importance of the arts. Why is art so apt to be the vanguard of cultural advance, as it was in Egypt, in Greece, in Christian Europe (think of Gregorian music and Gothic architecture), in Renaissance Italy—not to speculate about ancient cavemen, whose art is all that we know of them? One thinks of culture as economic increase, social organization, the gradual ascendancy of rational thinking and scientific control of nature over superstitious imagination and magical practices. But art is not practical; it is neither philosophy nor science; it is not religion, morality, nor even social comment (as many drama critics take comedy to be). What does it contribute to culture that could be of major importance?

26   It merely presents forms—sometimes intangible forms—to imagination. Its direct appeal is to that faculty, or function, that Lord Bacon considered the chief stumbling block in the way of reason, that enlightened writers like Stuart Chase never tire of condemning as the source of all nonsense and bizarre erroneous beliefs. And so it is; but it is also the source of all insight and true beliefs. Imagination is probably the oldest mental trait that is typically human—older than discursive reason; it is probably the common source of dream, reason, religion, and all true general observation. It is this primitive human power—imagination—that engenders the arts and is in turn directly affected by their products.

27   Somewhere at the animalian starting line of human evolution lie the beginnings of that supreme instrument of the mind—language. We think of it as a device for communication among the members of a society. But communication is only one, and perhaps not even the first, of its functions. The first thing it does is to break up what William James called the "blooming, buzzing confusion" of sense perception into units and groups, events and chains of events—things and relations, causes and effects. All these patterns are imposed on our experience by language. We think, as we speak, in terms of objects and their relations.

28   But the process of breaking up our sense experience in this way, making reality conceivable, memorable, sometimes even predictable, is a process of imagination. Primitive conception is imagination. Language and imagination grow up together in a reciprocal tutelage.

29   What discursive symbolism—language in its literal use—does for our awareness of things about us and our own relation to them, the arts do for our awareness of subjective reality, feeling and emotion; they give form to inward experiences and thus make them conceivable. The only way we can really envisage vital movement, the stirring and growth and passage of emotion, and ultimately the whole direct sense of human life, is in artistic terms. A musical person thinks of emotions musically. They cannot be discursively talked about above a very general level. But they may nonetheless be known—objectively set forth, publicly known—and there is nothing necessarily confused or formless about emotions.

30   As soon as the natural forms of subjective experience are abstracted to the point of symbolic presentation, we can use those forms to imagine feeling and understand its nature. Self-knowledge, insight into all phases of life and mind, springs from artistic imagination. That is the cognitive value of the arts.

But their influence on human life goes deeper than the intellectual level. As 31 language actually gives form to our sense-experience, grouping our impressions around those things which have names, and fitting sensations to the qualities that have adjectival names, and so on, the arts we live with—our picture books and stories and the music we hear—actually form our emotive experience. Every generation has its styles of feeling. One age shudders and blushes and faints, another swaggers, still another is godlike in a universal indifference. These styles in actual emotion are not insincere. They are largely unconscious—determined by many social causes, but *shaped* by artists, usually popular artists of the screen, the juke-box, the shop window, and the picture magazine. (That, rather than incitement to crime, is my objection to the comics.) Irwin Edman remarks in one of his books that our emotions are largely Shakespeare's poetry.

This influence of art on life gives us an indication why a period of efflo- 32 rescence in the arts is apt to lead a cultural advance: it formulates a new way of feeling, and that is the beginning of a cultural age. It suggests another matter for reflection, too: That a wide neglect of artistic education is a neglect in the education of feeling. Most people are so imbued with the idea that feeling is a formless total organic excitement in men as in animals, that the idea of educating feeling, developing its scope and quality, seems odd to them, if not absurd. It is really, I think, at the very heart of personal education.

There is one other function of the arts that benefits not so much the 33 advance of culture as its stabilization; an influence on individual lives. This function is the converse and complement of the objectification of feeling, the driving force of creation in art: It is the education of vision that we receive in seeing, hearing, reading works of art—the development of the artist's eye, that assimilates ordinary sights (or sounds, motions, or events) to inward vision, and lends expressiveness and emotional import to the world. Wherever art takes a motif from actuality—a flowering branch, a bit of landscape, a historic event or a personal memory, any model or theme from life—it transforms it into a piece of imagination, and imbues its image with artistic vitality. The result is an impregnation of ordinary reality with the significance of created form. This is the subjectification of nature, that makes reality itself a symbol of life and feeling.

The arts objectify subjective reality, and subjectify outward experience of 34 nature. Art education is the education of feeling, and a society that neglects it gives itself up to formless emotion. Bad art is corruption of feeling. This is a large factor in the irrationalism which dictators and demagogues exploit.

Questions for Discussion and Your Reading Journal

1. What are the audience and the purpose of this piece? What specific words or phrases tell you this? How would a cultural anthropologist react to the second sentence of the first paragraph?
2. How does Langer define art? Compare her definition to that in "What Use Is Art?" What does Langer believe to be art's function?

3. Why does Langer believe art is important? Outline her argument as she develops it in her essay.

4. Taking Langer's definition, what is the difference between an art and a craft? For example, would she define quilting as an art? Pottery making? Why or why not?

5. List as many things as you can from your own life that you would consider "art." Do the definitions you have read apply to these things? How would strangers describe you if they could see only the art in your room (posters, music, and so on)?

6. How would you define art? How do you judge art? In your opinion, what makes a piece of art good or bad?

E. H. GOMBRICH

Art historian Sir Ernst Hans Gombrich (1909–2001) was born in Vienna, Austria, and died in London. He was educated in Vienna and received honorary degrees from institutions all over the world, including Oxford, Cambridge, and Harvard. During World War II, Gombrich was employed by the BBC as a radio monitor. After the war he worked for the Warburg Institute, eventually becoming its director in 1959. At the same time he was a professor of history at the University of London. His major publications include The Story of Art *(1950) and* Art and Illusion: A Study in the Psychology of Pictorial Representation *(1960).*

In his writings Gombrich has tried to take the study of art out of isolation and to look at it in the context of cultural history, asking questions about how culture influences artistic expression. His introduction to art history, The Story of Art, *is one of the most popular art textbooks ever written. In this selection, Gombrich explains the theory behind the unique forms of painting, relief, and sculpture.*

Reading Rhetorically

Unlike many of the other readings in this chapter, "Art for Eternity" analyzes the art of various parts of the world in its historical context. Like the first essay in the chapter ("What Use Is Art?"), however, this essay explains the function of art. As you read the essay, look for clues about the writer's purpose and his *ethos*.

In addition, Gombrich uses a pattern of development that is common to texts that explain. He begins with a description and follows with an interpretation of the elements he has described. Many times student writers want to jump right into interpretation without first laying a foundation in description. However, without concrete details and specific examples, interpretation does not work very well. Look for this pattern in the essay that follows, and examine the way in which interpretation is set up by description.

Art for Eternity: Egypt, Mesopotamia, and Crete

Some form of art exists everywhere on the globe, but the story of art as a 1
continuous effort does not begin in the caves of southern France or among
the North American Indians. There is no direct tradition which links these
strange beginnings with our own days, but there is a direct tradition, handed
down from master to pupil, and from pupil to admirer or copyist, which links
the art of our own days, any house or any poster, with the art of the Nile Valley of some five thousand years ago. For we shall see that the Greek masters
went to school with the Egyptians, and we are all the pupils of the Greeks.
Thus the art of Egypt has a tremendous importance for us.

Everyone knows that Egypt is the land of the pyramids, those mountains 2
of stone which stand like weathered landmarks on the distant horizon of history. However remote and mysterious they seem, they tell us much of their
own story. They tell us of a land which was so thoroughly organized that it
was possible to pile up these gigantic mounds in the lifetime of a single king,
and they tell us of kings who were so rich and powerful that they could force
thousands and thousands of workers or slaves to toil for them year in, year
out, to quarry the stones, to drag them to the building site, and to shift them
with the most primitive means till the tomb was ready to receive the king. No
king and no people would have gone to such expense, and taken so much trouble, for the creation of a mere monument. In fact, we know that the pyramids
had their practical importance in the eyes of the kings and their subjects. The
king was considered a divine being who held sway over them, and on his
departure from this earth he would again ascend to the gods whence he had
come. The pyramids soaring up to the sky would probably help him to make
his ascent. In any case they would preserve his sacred body from decay. For
the Egyptians believed that the body must be preserved if the soul is to live on
in the beyond. That is why they prevented the corpse from decaying by an
elaborate method of embalming it, and binding it up in strips of cloth. It was
for the mummy of the king that the pyramid had been piled up, and his body
was laid right in the centre of the huge mountain of stone in a stone coffin.
Everywhere round the burial chamber, spells and incantations were written to
help him on his journey to the other world.

But it is not only these oldest relics of human architecture which tell of the 3
role played by age-old beliefs in the story of art. The Egyptians held the belief
that the preservation of the body was not enough. If the likeness of the king
was also preserved, it was doubly sure that he would continue to exist for ever.
So they ordered sculptors to chisel the king's head out of hard, imperishable
granite, and put it in the tomb where no one saw it, there to work its spell and
to help his soul to keep alive in and through the image. One Egyptian word
for sculptor was actually "He-who-keeps-alive."

At first these rites were reserved for kings, but soon the nobles of the royal 4
household had their minor tombs grouped in neat rows round the king's
mound; and gradually every self-respecting person had to make provision for
his after-life by ordering a costly grave which would house his mummy and his

likeness, and where his soul could dwell and receive the offerings of food and drink which were given to the dead. Some of these early portraits from the pyramid age, the fourth "dynasty" of the "Old Kingdom," are among the most beautiful works of Egyptian art. . . . There is a solemnity and simplicity about them which one does not easily forget. One sees that the sculptor was not trying to flatter his sitter, or to preserve a fleeting expression. He was concerned only with essentials. Every lesser detail he left out. Perhaps it is just because of this strict concentration on the basic forms of the human head that these portraits remain so impressive. For, despite their almost geometrical rigidity, they are not primitive. . . . Nor are they as lifelike as the naturalistic portraits of the artists of Nigeria. . . . The observation of nature, and the regularity of the whole, are so evenly balanced that they impress us as being lifelike and yet remote and enduring.

5   This combination of geometric regularity and keen observation of nature is characteristic of all Egyptian art. We can study it best in the reliefs and paintings that adorned the walls of the tombs. The word "adorned," it is true, may hardly fit an art which was meant to be seen by no one but the dead man's soul. In fact, these works were not intended to be enjoyed. They, too, were meant to "keep alive." Once, in a grim distant past, it had been the custom when a powerful man died to let his servants and slaves accompany him into the grave. They were sacrificed so that he should arrive in the beyond with a suitable train. Later, these horrors were considered either too cruel or too costly, and art came to the rescue. Instead of real servants, the great ones of this earth were given images as substitutes. The pictures and models found in Egyptian tombs were connected with the idea of providing the soul with helpmates in the other world.

6   To us these reliefs and wall-paintings provide an extraordinarily vivid picture of life as it was lived in Egypt thousands of years ago. And yet, looking at them for the first time, one may find them rather bewildering. The reason is that the Egyptian painters had quite a different way from ours of representing real life. Perhaps this is connected with the different purpose their paintings had to serve. What mattered most was not prettiness but completeness. It was the artists' task to preserve everything as clearly and permanently as possible. So they did not set out to sketch nature as it appeared to them from any fortuitous angle. They drew from memory, according to strict rules which ensured that everything that had to go into the picture would stand out in perfect clarity. Their method, in fact, resembled that of the mapmaker rather than that of the painter. . . . If we had to draw . . . a [garden (see Fig. 1)] we might wonder from which angle to approach it. The shape and character of the trees could be seen clearly only from the sides, the shape of the pond would be visible only if seen from above. The Egyptians had no compunction about this problem. They would simply draw the pond as if it were seen from above, and the trees from the side. The fishes and birds in the pond, on the other hand, would hardly look recognizable as seen from above, so they were drawn in profile.

7   In such a simple picture, we can easily understand the artist's procedure. A similar method is often used by children. But the Egyptians were much more

Figure 1   This painting of a garden with a pond illustrates how Egyptian artists strove to represent their art as clearly as possible. From a tomb in Thebes, ca. 1400 B.C.E. Courtesy of the Egyptian Museum, Cairo.

consistent in their application of these methods than children ever are. Everything had to be represented from its most characteristic angle. . . . The head was most easily seen in profile so they drew it sideways. But if we think of the human eye we think of it as seen from the front. Accordingly, a full-face eye was planted into the side view of the face. The top half of the body, the shoulders and chest, are best seen from the front, for then we see how the arms are hinged to the body. But arms and legs in movement are much more clearly seen sideways. That is the reason why Egyptians in these pictures look so strangely flat and contorted. Moreover the Egyptian artists found it hard to visualize either foot seen from the outside. They preferred the clear outline from the big toe upwards. So both feet are seen from the inside, and the man on the relief looks as if he had two left feet. It must not be supposed that Egyptian artists thought that human beings looked like that. They merely followed a rule which allowed them to include everything in the human form that they considered important. Perhaps this strict adherence to the rule had something to do with their magic purpose. For how could a man with his arm "foreshortened" or "cut off" bring or receive the required offerings to the dead?

8   Here as always, Egyptian art is not based on what the artist could see at a given moment, but rather on what he knew belonged to a person or a scene. It was out of these forms which he had learned, and which he knew, that he built his representations, much as the tribal artist builds his figures out of the forms he can master. It is not only his knowledge of forms and shapes that the artist embodies in his picture, but also his knowledge of their significance. We sometimes call a man a "big boss." The Egyptian drew the boss bigger than his servants or even his wife. . . .

9   It is one of the greatest things in Egyptian art that all the statues, paintings and architectural forms seem to fall into place as if they obeyed one law. We call such a law, which all creations of a people seem to obey, a "style." It is very difficult to explain in words what makes a style, but it is far less difficult to see. The rules which govern all Egyptian art give every individual work the effect of poise and austere harmony.

10   The Egyptian style comprised a set of very strict laws, which every artist had to learn from his earliest youth. Seated statues had to have their hands on their knees; men had to be painted with darker skin than women; the appearance of every Egyptian god was strictly laid down: Horus, the sun-god, had to be shown as a falcon or with a falcon's head, Anubis, the god of death, as a jackal or with a jackal's head. Every artist also had to learn the art of beautiful script. He had to cut the images and symbols of the hieroglyphs clearly and accurately in stone. But once he had mastered all these rules he had finished his apprenticeship. No one wanted anything different, no one asked him to be "original." On the contrary, he was probably considered the best artist who could make his statues most like the admired monuments of the past. So it happened that in the course of three thousand years or more Egyptian art changed very little. Everything that was considered good and beautiful in the age of the pyramids was held to be just as excellent a thousand years later. True, new fashions appeared, and new subjects were demanded of the artists, but their mode of representing man and nature remained essentially the same.

11   Only one man ever shook the iron bars of the Egyptian style. He was a king of the Eighteenth Dynasty, in the period known as the "New Kingdom," which was founded after a catastrophic invasion of Egypt. This king, called Amenophis IV, was a heretic. He broke with many of the customs hallowed by age-old tradition. He did not wish to pay homage to the many strangely shaped gods of his people. For him only one god was supreme, Aton, whom he worshipped and whom he had represented in the shape of the sun. He called himself Akhnaton, after his god, and he moved his court out of reach of the priests of the other gods, to a place which is now called El-Amarna.

12   The pictures which he commissioned must have shocked the Egyptians of his day by their novelty. In them none of the solemn and rigid dignity of the earlier Pharohs was to be found. Instead, he had himself depicted lifting his daughter on to his knees, walking with his wife in the garden, leaning on his stick. Some of his portraits show him as an ugly man . . .—perhaps he wanted the artists to portray him in all his human frailty or, perhaps, he was so convinced of his unique importance as a prophet that he insisted on a true likeness. Akhnaton's successor was Tutankhamen, whose tomb with its treasures

was discovered in 1922. Some of these works are still in the modern style of the Aton religion—particularly the back of the king's throne . . ., which shows the king and queen in a homely idyll. He is sitting on his chair in an attitude which might have scandalized the strict Egyptian conservative—almost lolling, by Egyptian standards. His wife is no smaller than he is, and gently puts her hand on his shoulder while the Sun-god, represented as a golden orb, is stretching his hands in blessing down to them.

It is not impossible that this reform of art in the Eighteenth Dynasty was 13 made easier for the king because he could point to foreign works that were much less strict and rigid than the Egyptian products. On an island overseas, in Crete, there dwelt a gifted people whose artists delighted in the representation of swift movement. When the palace of their king at Knossos was excavated at the end of the nineteenth century, people could hardly believe that such a free and graceful style could have been developed in the second millennium before our era. Works in this style were also found on the Greek mainland. . . .

But this opening of Egyptian art did not last long. Already during the reign 14 of Tutankhamen the old beliefs were restored, and the window to the outside world was shut again. The Egyptian style, as it had existed for more than a thousand years before his time, continued to exist for another thousand years or more, and the Egyptians doubtless believed it would continue for all eternity. Many Egyptian works in our museums date from this later period, and so do nearly all Egyptian buildings such as temples and palaces. New themes were introduced, new tasks performed, but nothing essentially new was added to the achievement of art.

Egypt, of course, was only one of the great and powerful empires which 15 existed in the Near East for many a thousand years. We all know from the Bible that little Palestine lay between the Egyptian kingdom of the Nile and the Babylonian and Assyrian empires, which had developed in the valley of the two rivers Euphrates and Tigris. The art of Mesopotamia, as the valley of the two rivers was called in Greek, is less well known to us than the art of Egypt. This is at least partly due to accident. There were no stone quarries in these valleys, and most buildings were made of baked brick which, in course of time, weathered away and fell to dust. Even sculpture in stone was comparatively rare. But this is not the only explanation of the fact that relatively few early works of that art have come down to us. The main reason is probably that these people did not share the religious belief of the Egyptians that the human body and its likeness must be preserved if the soul is to continue. In the very early times, when a people called the Sumerians ruled in the capital of Ur, kings were still buried with their whole household, slaves and all, so that they should not lack a following in the world beyond. Graves of this period have been discovered, and we can admire some of the household goods of these ancient, barbarous kings in the British Museum. We see how much refinement and artistic skill can go together with primitive superstition and cruelty. There was, for instance, a harp in one of the tombs, decorated with fabulous animals. . . . They look rather like our heraldic beasts, not only in their general appearance but also in their arrangement, for the Sumerians had a taste for symmetry and precision. We do not know exactly what these fabulous animals were meant to signify, but it is almost certain that they were figures from the mythology of these early days, and that the scenes which look to us like pages from a children's book had a very solemn and serious meaning.

16　　Though artists in Mesopotamia were not called upon to decorate the walls of tombs, they, too, had to ensure, in a different way, that the image helped to keep the mighty alive. From early times onwards it was the custom of Mesopotamian kings to commission monuments to their victories in war, which told of the tribes that had been defeated, and the booty that had been taken. . . . Perhaps the idea behind these monuments was not only to keep the memory of these victories alive. In early times, at least, the ancient beliefs in the power of the image may still have influenced those who ordered them. Perhaps they thought that, as long as the picture of their king with his foot on the neck of the prostrate enemy stood there, the defeated tribe would not be able to rise again.

17　　In later times such monuments developed into complete picture-chronicles of the king's campaign. The best preserved of these chronicles date from a relatively late period, the reign of King Asurnasirpal II of Assyria, who lived in the ninth century BC, a little later than the biblical King Solomon. They are kept in the British Museum. There we see all the episodes of a well-organized campaign; we see the army crossing rivers and attacking fortresses . . ., their camps and their meals. The way in which these scenes are represented is rather similar to Egyptian methods, but perhaps a little less tidy and rigid. As one looks at them, one feels as if one were watching a newsreel of 2,000 years ago. It all looks so real and convincing. But as we look more carefully we discover a curious fact: There are plenty of dead and wounded in these gruesome wars—but not one of them is an Assyrian. The art of boasting and propaganda was well advanced in these early days. But perhaps we can take a slightly more charitable view of these Assyrians. Perhaps even they were still ruled by the old superstition which has come into this story so often: the superstition that there is more in a picture than a mere picture. Perhaps they did not want to represent wounded Assyrians for some such reason. In any case, the tradition which then began had a very long life. On all the monuments which glorify the war-lords of the past, war is no trouble at all. You just appear, and the enemy is scattered like chaff in the wind.

Questions for Discussion and Your Reading Journal

1. As an art historian, Gombrich must interpret as well as narrate the past. Examine the text for words and phrases that show interpretation as well as description of Egyptian art. What is his interpretation?

2. What is the purpose of art in ancient Egypt, according to Gombrich? Compare Gombrich's interpretation to the purpose of art according to some of the other readings in this section, such as "The Cultural Importance of the Arts," "Understanding Indian Art," "Traditional Arts of Black Africa," and "Islamic Art."

3. What are some of the "rules" of ancient Egyptian art? Why was it important for the artist to strictly follow a traditional style?

4. Using the definition of "naturalism" from the list of art terms (in the Instructor's Manual), explain how the forms and shapes of Egyptian art differ from naturalistic art.

5. Examine the illustration of the garden, and then read the essay on the garden in the time of the pharaohs. Can you consider the Egyptian garden "art" as defined in this part of the book?

6. Which Egyptians are the subjects of ancient Egyptian art? What might we infer about their lives?

7. Why was Amenophis IV (Akhnaton) considered a heretic? How was art during his rule different from previous periods? How might art from outside of Egypt have influenced this period?

8. What functions did art serve in the Mesopotamian empires? How is this similar to and different from the Egyptian art Gombrich describes?

ANANDA K. COOMARASWAMY

Ananda K. Coomaraswamy (1877–1947) was born in Ceylon (now Sri Lanka) and attended the University of London, where he received a doctoral degree in geology. His interest in Indian art, at first incidental to his work as a scientist, soon became the focus of his career, and he spent the last 30 years of his life as Keeper of Indian and Mohammedan Art in the Museum of Fine Arts, Boston. When Coomaraswamy first began to study Indian art, it was still viewed by most art critics as primitive, savage, and worthy only of anthropological study. His many books (Medieval Singhalese Art, The Indian Craftsman, History of Indian and Indonesian Art, Indian Drawings, The Arts and Crafts of India and Ceylon, The Dance of Shiva, Bronzes of Ceylon, to name just a few) helped to change that view of Indian aesthetics. His writings display an encyclopedic knowledge of his subject, a deep understanding of the religious traditions behind the art under discussion, and objectivity born of his scientific training.

In the following selection, Coomaraswamy compares and contrasts European and Indian artistic theories to show that the two cultures hold very different philosophies of art. A brief history of Indian art follows, concluding with an examination of the impact of European influences on that art.

Reading Rhetorically

Like Langer and Gombrich, Coomaraswamy defines "art" in his essay. When a term has many connotations and has been interpreted in a number of different ways, providing a definition can be an essential first step in writing about the term's subject. Compare Coomaraswamy's definition with those of the other authors and with your own.

The middle section of the article presents a history of art in this part of the world. These kinds of expositional texts can be dry and technical. Coomaraswamy, however, finds ways to make his historical account interesting and relevant. As you read this section, look for ways the author makes his subject interesting to his audience, as well as how he presents his *ethos*.

The article ends with a discussion of artistic influence among various parts of the world. Think about the author's purpose here. Why might it be important to determine how cultures have affected each other in relation to artistic expression? Think, also, about why the author might have chosen to end with this discussion.

Understanding Indian Art

1   Works of art have been thought of in two very different ways. According to the modern view the artist is a special or even abnormal kind of man, endowed with a peculiar emotional sensibility which enables him to see what we call beauty; moved by a mysterious aesthetic urge he produces paintings, sculpture, poetry or music. These are regarded as a spectacle for the eyes or a gratification for the ear; they can only be enjoyed by those who are called lovers of art and these are understood to be temperamentally related to the artist but without his technical ability. Other men are called workmen and make things which everyone needs for use; these workmen are expected to enjoy art, if they are able, only in their spare time.

2   In ideal art, the artist tries to improve upon nature. For the rest, the truth of the work of art is held to be its truth to an external world which we call nature, and expect the artist to observe. In this kind of art there is always a demand for novelty. The artist is an individual, expressing himself, and so it has become necessary to have books written about every artist individually, for since each makes use of an individual language, each requires explanation. Very often a biography is substituted for the explanation. Great importance is attached to what we call genius, and less to training. Art history is chiefly a matter of finding out the names of artists and considering their relation to one another. The work of art itself is an arrangement of colours or sounds, adjudged good or bad according to whether these arrangements are pleasing or otherwise. The meaning of the work of art is of no significance; those who are interested in such merely human matters are called Philistines.

3   This point of view belongs only to the last few centuries in Europe, and to the decadence of classical civilization in the Mediterranean. It has not been endorsed by humanity at large, and may be quite a false view. According to another and quite different assumption, which prevailed throughout the Middle Ages in Europe and is in fact proper to the Christian as well as the Hindu philosophy of life, art is primarily an intellectual act; it is the conception of form, corresponding to an idea in the mind of the artist. It is not when he observes nature with curiosity, but when the intellect is self-poised, that the forms of art are conceived. The artist is not a special kind of man, but every man is a special

kind of artist or else is something less than a man. The engineer and the cook, the mathematician and the surgeon are also artists. Everything made by man or done skilfully is a work of art, a thing made by art, artificial.

The things to be made by art in imitation of the imagined forms in the 4 mind of the artist are called true when these imagined forms are really embodied and reproduced in the wood or stone or in the sounds which are the artist's material. He has always in view to make some definite thing, not merely something beautiful, no matter what; what he loves is the particular thing he is making; he knows that anything well and truly made will be beautiful. Just what is to be made is a matter for the patron to decide; the artist himself if he is building his own house, or another person who needs a house, or in the broadest sense the patron, is the artist's whole human environment, for example when he is building a temple or laying out a city. In unanimous societies, as in India, there is general agreement as to what is most needed; the artist's work is therefore generally understood; where everyone makes daily use of works of art there is little occasion for museums, books or lectures on the appreciation of art.

The thing to be made, then, is always something humanly useful. No 5 rational being works for indefinite ends. If the artist makes a table, it is to put things on; if he makes an image, it is as a support for contemplation. There is no division of fine or useless from decorative and useful arts; the table is made to give intellectual pleasure as well as to support a weight, the image gives sensual, or as some prefer to call it, aesthetic pleasure at the same time that it provides a support for contemplation. There is no caste division of the artist from the workman such as we are inured to in industrial societies where, as Ruskin so well expressed it, "Industry without art is brutality."

In this kind of art there is no demand for novelty, because the fundamen- 6 tal needs of humanity are always and everywhere the same. What is required is originality, or vitality. What we mean by "original" is "coming from its source within," like water from a spring. The artist can only express what is in him, what he is. It makes no difference whether or not the same thing has been expressed a thousand times before. There can be no property in ideas. The individual does not make them, but finds them; let him only see to it that he really takes possession of them, and his work will be original in the same sense that the recurrent seasons, sunrise and sunset are ever new although in name the same. The highest purpose of Christian and Eastern art alike is to reveal that one and the same principle of life that is manifested in all variety. Only modern art, reflecting modern interests, pursues variety for its own sake and ignores the sameness on which it depends.

Finally, the Indian artist, although a person, is not a personality; his per- 7 sonal idiosyncrasy is at the most a part of his equipment, and never the occasion of his art. All of the greatest Indian works are anonymous, and all that we know of the lives of Indian artists in any field could be printed in a tract of a dozen pages.

Let us now consider for a short time the history of Indian art. Our knowl- 8 edge of it begins about 3000 B.C. with what is known as the Indus Valley culture. Extensive cities with well-built houses and an elaborate drainage system have been excavated and studied. The highest degree of artistic ability can be recognized in the engraved seals, sculptured figures in the round, finely wrought jewellery, silver and bronze vessels and painted pottery. From the *Rgveda*, the Bible of India, datable in its present form about 1000 B.C., we learn a good deal about the arts of the carpenter, weaver and jeweller.

9   The more familiar Indian art of the historical period has been preserved abundantly from the third century B.C. onwards. The greater part of what has survived consists of religious architecture and sculpture, together with some paintings, coins, and engraved seals. The sculptures have been executed in the hardest stone with steel tools. From the sculptures and paintings themselves we can gather a more detailed knowledge of the other arts. The temples are often as large as European cathedrals. Almost peculiar to India has been the practice of carving out such churches in the living rock, the monolithic forms repeating those of the structural buildings. Amongst notable principles developed early in India which have had a marked influence on the development of architecture in the world at large are those of the horse-shoe arch and transverse vault.

10   An increasing use is made of sculpture. As in other countries, there is a stylistic sequence of primitive, classical, and baroque types. The primitive style of Bhārhut and Sāñcī can hardly be surpassed in significance and may well be preferred for the very reason that it restricts itself to the statement of absolute essentials and is content to point out a direction which the spectator must follow for himself. Nevertheless, in many ways, the Gupta period, from the fourth to the sixth centuries A.D., may be said to represent the zenith of Indian art. By this time the artist is in full and facile command of all his resources. The paintings of Ajantā, approximately comparable to those of the very early Renaissance in Europe, depict with irresistible enchantment a civilization in which the conflict of spirit and matter has been resolved in an accord such as has hardly been realised anywhere else, unless perhaps in the Far East and in Egypt. Spirituality and sensuality are here inseparably linked and seem to be merely the inner and outer aspects of one and the same expanding life. The art of this age is classical, not merely within the geographical limits of India proper, but for the whole of the Far East, where all the types of Buddhist art are of Indian origin.

11   There follows a mediaeval period which was essentially an age of devotion, learning and chivalry; the patronage of art and literature moving together as a matter of course.

12   From the twelfth century onwards, the situation is profoundly modified so far as the North of India is concerned by the impact of Muhammadan invasions of Persian and Central Asian origin. But while the effects of these invasions were to an appalling extent destructive, the Islamic art added something real and valuable to that of India; and finally, though only for a short time, under the Great Mughals in the 16th and 17th centuries, there developed in India a new kind of life which found expression in a magnificent architecture and a great school of painting. Just because of its more humanistic and worldly preoccupations, this art is better known to and better appreciated by

Europeans at the present day than is the more profound art of Hindu India. Everyone has heard of the Taj Mahal, a wonder of inlaid marble built by Shāh Jahān to be the tomb of a beloved wife; everyone can easily understand and therefore admire the Mughal paintings that provide us with a faithful portrait gallery of all the great men of Northern India during a period of two centuries. This is a kind of art that really corresponds to that of the late Renaissance, with all its personal, historic and romantic interests.

In the meantime, Hindu culture persisted almost unchanged in the South. 13 In the great temple cities of the South both the reality and the outward aspects of the ancient world have survived until now and the world has no more wonderful spectacle to offer than can be seen here. In the North, Hindu culture survived too in Rajputana and the Punjab Himalayas and here, in direct continuity with ancient tradition, there developed the two schools of Rajput painting that are the last great expressions of the Indian spirit in painting or sculpture. Modern developments in Bengal and Bombay represent attempts either to recover a lost tradition or for the development of an eclectic style, neither wholly Indian nor wholly European. At the present day the Indian genius is finding expression rather in the field of conduct than in art.

European influence on Indian art has been almost purely destructive: in 14 the first place, by undermining the bases of patronage, removing by default the traditional responsibilities of wealth to learning. Secondly, the impact of industrialism, similarly undermining the status of the responsible craftsman, has left the consumer at the mercy of the profiteer and no better off than he is in Europe. Thirdly, by the introduction of new styles and fashions, imposed by the prestige of power, which the Indian people have not been in a position to resist. A reaction against these influences is taking place at the present day, but can never replace what has been lost; India has been profoundly impoverished, intellectually as well as economically, within the last hundred years.

Even in India, an understanding of the art of India has to be rewon; and 15 for this, just as in Europe where the modern man is as far from understanding the art of the Middle Ages as he is from that of the East, a veritable intellectual rectification is required. What is needed in either case is to place oneself in the position of the artist by whom the unfamiliar work was actually made and in the position of the patron for whom the work was made: to think their thoughts and to see with their eyes. For so long as the work of art appears to us in any way exotic, bizarre, quaint or arbitrary, we cannot pretend to have understood it. It is not to enlarge our collection of bric-a-brac that we ought to study ancient or foreign arts, but to enlarge our own consciousness of being.

As regards India, it has been said that "East is East and West is West and 16 never the twain shall meet." This is a counsel of despair that can only have been born of the most profound disillusion and the deepest conviction of impotence. I say on the contrary that human nature is an unchanging and everlasting principle; and that whoever possesses such a nature—and not merely the outward form and habits of the human animal—is endowed with the power of understanding all that belongs to that nature, without respect to time or place.

Questions for Discussion and Your Reading Journal

1. How does the author define art? How does the definition differ from that of Gombrich in "Art for Eternity"?
2. What are the two contrasting views of art described by Coomaraswamy?
3. Which view does he endorse? What are his reasons? Outline his argument.
4. How have other cultures influenced Indian art?
5. Of what use is art, according to this author?
6. Why, according to the author, is the identity of the artist unimportant in Indian art? How important is the identity of the artist in the Western world?

ROY SIEBER

Roy Sieber, professor emeritus of art history at Indiana University, spent considerable time in Africa. He was a Ford Foundation Fellow in Nigeria, then visiting professor at the University of Ghana and visiting research professor at the University of Ife in Nigeria. He was instrumental in developing his own university's museum collection of African, Pacific, and pre-Columbian art.

Sieber's writing is focused not only on masterpieces but also on art from which one can learn the significance of the objects to the people who created and used them. He has written widely on African art. In this selection he explains some of the general styles and the cultural importance of the African art he has studied, showing that it is more complex and sophisticated than we might at first realize, given our orientation toward Western European art.

Reading Rhetorically

In the first paragraph of the essay, Sieber writes, "To understand the traditional arts of Africa . . . it is necessary to set aside several popularly held misconceptions." From this sentence, the reader can infer that people from other parts of the world have conceived African art in ways that are not consistent with its nature and essence. After digesting this sentence, the reader can predict that the essay will go on to list the misconceptions. Sieber does give the reader the expected list, and he goes on to explain why each conception is false (*logos*). This organizational strategy is a logical means to achieve the author's intended aim, which is to counter faulty perceptions of African art. As you read the rest of the essay think about the reasons why Sieber might have begun the text in this way.

A picture of a statue of a king accompanies this article. The picture's caption explains that the head-to-body ratio of the statue is 1:3, meaning that the size of the head is out of realistic proportion to the body. Think about why Sieber included this information in the caption. When you come to the end of the article, pay particular attention to the picture and caption and speculate about the author's purpose in including them.

Traditional Arts of Black Africa

To understand the traditional arts of Africa south of the Sahara it is neces- 1
sary to set aside several popularly held assumptions. First, African arts are
not primitive, if by primitive is meant simple, crude, or original in the sense of
being without a history. The arts of Africa are, in fact, sophisticated and possess a long history. Second, African art is not produced solely for aesthetic
ends—that is, it is not art for art's sake, as is so much of recent Western art;
rather, it is deeply embedded in the belief patterns of the society. Third, and
this refers to more than the arts, Africa's history, although difficult to recon-
struct at times, is certainly as long and as rich in texture and fabric as is that
of any other world area.

STYLE AND FORM

African art may be characterized as conservative, for it lay at the core of com- 2
monly held traditional belief patterns and strongly reflected those shared
values, at the same time reinforcing and symbolizing them. It was radical in the
sense that it was at the root of all beliefs and values. It was symbolic or representative rather than abstract or representational. Viewed from Western traditions of realism or naturalism, African sculpture seems not to be "correct."
The human body is presented most frequently in a 1:3 or 1:4 proportion of
head to body, whereas accurate measurement would be approximately 1:5 and
Hellenistic and Mannerist proportions edged past 1:6. Thus, to Western eyes,
African figure carvings tend to appear head-heavy, and this tendency is combined with an emphasis on balance and symmetry (see Fig. 1). There is no easy
explanation for the style characteristics of African art, or indeed for the arts of
any other culture. The proportions appear and become accepted; once accepted
they become required and expected. The result for Africa is a norm that is
frontal and symmetrical and that gives an impression of fixed austerity, which
is reinforced by the absence of transitory facial expression. Masks and figures,
for the most part, present expressionless, cool countenances; facial twitches of
rage, pleasure, or horror are absent. Bodies exhibit long torsos and short legs,
bent at hip and knee; arms, often bent at the elbow, are usually placed calmly
against the belly or side and only rarely indulge in emphatic gestures. Stance,
gesture, and expression combine to lend a strong sense of calm and austere
power to most African figurative sculpture.

Despite these abstract and often simplified forms, details are accurate: 3
Characteristic hair styles, body ornaments, or scarification patterns are
depicted with clarity and correctness, probably because they describe lineage
affiliation or social condition as well as local fashion.

This "basic" style is combined with a limited number of figure . . . types. 4
Like the basic style, the types appear broadly in sub-Saharan African. Essentially, figure types are limited to standing, seated, occasionally equestrian, and
more rarely kneeling postures. Women with children are frequently depicted,
expressing the great emphasis on continuity of the family and of the group. . . .

5   To survey African figure carving across West and Central Africa, the area where figurative art appeared most frequently, is to experience more than a single style and a limited number of types, however. Rather, a rich and amazing diversity of area, tribal, and sub-tribal styles can be discerned.

6   This complex body of styles and types amazed Western artists and critics early in this century and aroused their often extravagant admiration, but it also proved a snare and a delusion. Artists, seeking to break with the conventionalities of Western art, classicism and idealism, naturalism and materialism, assumed, quite inaccurately, that African art was highly inventive and innovative, whereas it was in fact extremely conservative in style as well as in meaning. An example of this conservatism is the continuity of the "basic" style over centuries: Over-size head, short legs, detailed coiffure, expressionless and calm balance describe equally well the art of the Nok culture of two thousand years ago . . . or that of the Dogon of a few centuries ago . . ., as it does Lulua . . . or Yoruba . . . figures made in the last century.

7   Recent scholarship has tended to emphasize the differences of styles and forms and the multiplicity of uses of African art; in short, it has tended to dwell on a rich variety of trees while ignoring the forest. In the broadest sense there does seem to be an

Figure 1 African art presents the human body in a head to body ratio of 1:3 or 1:4. *Oni (King) of Ife, Southwestern Nigeria, Classic phase.* Courtesy of the National Commission for Museums and Monuments.

African figure style, quite possibly developed in perishable materials, usually wood. Grafted on this general style is the particular style of an area. For example, figure carving from the western Sudan tends to be tall, vertical, spare, and austere. . . . The body and arms become vertical cylinders. At the same time, the surfaces are carefully, often delicately worked with reference to scar patterns and bangles. Other variations of the basic African style can be found in other geographical areas. The forms of the sculptures of the Yoruba of the rain forest of southwestern Nigeria, for example . . ., tend to be rounder and fuller than the more spare forms of the arid western Sudan. Such large geographic area styles are discernible not only for the western Sudan and the Guinea coast, but also for the equatorial rain forest and for the northern and southern Congo River basins.

Within these larger geographic areas, "tribal" styles have also developed. 8 The term *tribe* in African art studies refers to an ethnic and cultural base for a discrete style. In a sense, these tribal styles are the most visible because they are the most easily identifiable, and indeed, most survey books of African sculpture emphasize the styles of "tribal" groups.

In addition to the larger style areas and the tribal styles, still smaller units 9 may be found. In fact, if one examines African sculptural forms closely, it is possible to determine "subtribal" styles, village styles, and even the styles of individual carvers. Thus the style of the Dogon or the Yoruba reflects both the larger style area and the increasingly smaller, specific style areas to which it belongs, and ultimately it is possible to identify the "hand" of the particular sculptor. Unfortunately the names of these artists are too often lost. At times they have been forgotten by the owners and users of the carvings, but more frequently the scholars who collected the pieces neglected to establish the identity of the artists, for they assumed, incorrectly, that the sculptors were anonymous. The opposite of this assumption is far more often true. Where we do have evidence, it becomes clear that the individual sculptors were known, their works were admired, and their genius was celebrated.

Questions for Discussion and Your Reading Journal

1. Explain the distinction the authors make between "primitive" and sophisticated art. How would Susanne K. Langer view this distinction?
2. How, according to this essay, is African art different from much Western European art?
3. How do the authors support their claim that African art is "conservative"?
4. How does the figure of the Nigerian king (Figure 1) exemplify the principles of African art as Sieber explains them? What is your reaction to this piece?

PHILIP RAWSON

Author, academic, and artist Philip Rawson (1924–) provides a description of the underlying principles and structural techniques of Islamic calligraphy in the following text. Geometric art was part of the Roman and Byzantine traditions. Islamic art built upon this tradition, in part because of the prohibition against the portrayal of human figures in Islamic art as a way of preventing the worship of idols.

This preference for geometric design in art coincided with the Islamic reverence for the written word in the form of the Koran (sometimes spelled Quran), the holy book of Islam. Because the Koran was considered to be holy only when written in Arabic, the language itself took on great importance, and calligraphy became the highest art form; some of the most important artists in the Islamic world have devoted themselves to the art of calligraphy. The following piece describes the art of calligraphy in the Islamic world, along with some of the religious ideas behind the art.

Reading Rhetorically

Do you consider any text to be "holy" or "sacred"? If so, how does your belief influence your perception of the writing itself? The idea that words can have transcendent importance (beyond their communicated meaning) is common to many cultures. As you read, think about the reasons many world cultures have endowed writing with this kind of importance.

This article is accompanied by an illustration, a calligraphic manuscript page from the Koran. In some cases, particularly in relation to exposition about art, concepts are far more clearly made when they are represented in both visual and textual mediums. As you read the article, look back to the illustration to see how the text is supported by the manuscript page itself.

Islamic Art: Calligraphy

1   The doctrines of Islam, rigidly governing every aspect of religious and secular life, are enshrined chiefly in the Koran, the word of Allah dictated through Muhammad, and also in a large collection of maxims and sermons, the *Traditions,* supposedly spoken by the Prophet. The Arabic text of the Koran was probably established in definitive, edited form by the middle of the ninth century. Its text was always written with a slant-cut reed-pen, in a calligraphy intended not only to convey His message but also, in its beauty, to reflect the glory of God. Calligraphy, the art of writing the sacred book, was regarded as the highest of all the arts, and the calligraphic forms of Arabic letters were soon used as ornament on textiles, metalwork, ceramics, furnishings and architecture (Fig. 1). As the art of the scribe developed, other forms of decoration, chiefly arabesque and geometric, were introduced to provide elaborate frames for chapter headings and "rubrics"—emphasized phrases.

2   The earliest scripts used to transcribe the Koran were the Kufic group, developed in the seventh century. They stress the horizontal and vertical strokes, but use loops sparingly. Then the ends of the horizontals and verticals

Figure 1 A manuscript page from a Koran (1691–1692) of the Hilyah, a description of Muhammad the Prophet. Reproduced courtesy of the Trustees of the Chester Beatty Library, Dublin.

were greatly extended, and even "foliated" with elaborate serifs—a mode probably invented in Egypt in the eighth century. During the tenth century the use of the more curvilinear Naskh script became widespread, and by the fifteenth century six other kinds of script had been developed. To write any of these scripts well demands, according to Islamic tradition, special qualities of personal purity, concentration and even divine inspiration. In its developed form the calligraphy corresponded to the rhythms and cadences of chanted speech, so that the lengths and proportions of the letters were altered, not only to enrich the visual pattern, but also to embody the musical phrasing in which the words were sung. Though much less individual than Chinese calligraphy, written with the brush, Islamic calligraphy permits the writer some freedom of expression, by allowing him to follow the promptings of his inner ear—within the recognized canons of perfection for each type of script. It was perhaps the scribe's personal urge to express praise and reverence for the sacred book that carried him beyond the forms of the letters themselves into abstract decoration, usually developed out of the calligraphic forms, but also incorporating the geometric and arabesque patterns originating in other arts; once they had been introduced, it was chiefly in manuscripts that these patterns were developed and transmitted.

3   The arabesque is essentially an S curve, composed of opposing spirals. The relative proportions of the spirals may vary considerably, and the foliage and flowers forming its original basis are usually stylized out of recognition. As in calligraphy, the Islamic aesthetic demands that the hand be schooled to execute the arabesque without any of those tremors or linear faults which indicate a failure of concentration. Beside, or instead of, the arabesque, which was used as a background linking together the sequences of lines, a repeating geometric pattern—interwoven combinations of circles, squares, pentagons, hexagons, octagons or stars—was used for the frontispieces, especially of Korans of the thirteenth and fourteenth centuries. These are often strikingly reminiscent of masterpieces of Christian Celtic art. . . .

4   Geometrical shapes have a profoundly important role to play in Islamic art, since they are considered as the archetypes of all form, symbolizing the divinely ordained pattern of the universe. A generalized, "all-over" geometric design was even felt to be superior to the idiosyncratic variations of calligraphy or arabesque, and to represent the closest approach of the human understanding to God's Nature. Though the educated Muslim recognizes that geometrical forms are not in themselves divine, but merely symbols of divinity, nevertheless a kind of geometrical complacency has been the particular disease to which Muslim art has sometimes succumbed. Islam, however, seems to have preserved a continuing consciousness of the sacred function of ornament which other decorative traditions once possessed, but usually have lost.

Questions for Discussion and Your Reading Journal

1. Why did calligraphy become the highest art form in the Islamic world?
2. Discuss how Islam views the artist.
3. Discuss the relationship of art and religion as described in this text compared to the same relationship as described in "Art for Eternity" (p. 287), "Understanding Indian Art" (p. 294), and "The Window of Our Cultural Soul" (p. 364).
4. How does the illustration at the end of the article support what the text says about Islamic calligraphy? To what degree would the text be effective without the illustration?

BILLY COLLINS

Billy Collins (1941–) was born in New York City. An American Poet Laureate inaugurated in 2001, he teaches English at the City University of New York. His poems have been published in a number of prestigious journals, from The New Yorker *to* Paris Review; *and Collins has produced five books of poetry to date, the most recent being* The Art of Drowning, *from which this poem is taken.*

First in this chapter's series of poems about poetry, "Introduction to Poetry" is written from the perspective of an English teacher. Because it discusses precisely the situation you are now in, as a student studying poetry, this poem is a good place to start an exploration of the definitions of poetry and the practices involved in reading it.

Collins's poetry is written in a distinctive style that imbeds subtle and serious ideas in simple language and everyday situations. His work is characterized by gentle irony and sometimes-offbeat humor.

Reading Rhetorically

Have you ever been in an English class where you felt that a work of literature was being over-examined or that the class's analysis was ruining your enjoyment of the work? Typically, students are the ones who feel this way, but this poem shows the classroom situation from the teacher's perspective. As you read this poem, think about that perspective (the teacher's *ethos*) and look for places where your expectations are overturned.

The poem is loaded with unusual images. Trying to envision these images as you read and reread it can be a way of enjoying the poem without talking about it.

Introduction to Poetry

I ask them to take a poem
and hold it up to the light
like a color slide

or press an ear against its hive.

I say drop a mouse into a poem   5
and watch him probe his way out,

or walk inside the poem's room
and feel the walls for a light switch.

I want them to water-ski
across the surface of a poem   10
waving at the author's name on the shore.

But all they want to do
is tie the poem to a chair with rope
and torture a confession out of it.

15 They begin beating it with a hose
to find out what it really means.

Questions for Discussion and Your Reading Journal

1. Do you enjoy reading poetry? Explain the reasons for your enjoyment or lack of enjoyment.
2. What are some of the purposes of reading poetry? In what ways have English classes, in your experience, supported and/or subverted those purposes?
3. What did you like best about this poem? What did you like least?
4. The last two lines talk about finding out "what [the poem] really means." Do you feel like you understand what this poem means? Would it be appropriate to dissect the meaning of this poem? Explain why or why not.

JON STALLWORTHY

Jon Stallworthy (1935–) is a poet and scholar/professor at Oxford University. His work includes two critical studies of Yeats's poetry, The Oxford Book of War Poetry, *and biographies of Wilfred Owen and Louis MacNeice. Most recently he published his autobiography,* The Singing School, *and* Rounding the Horn: Collected Poems. *While he has been a professor of English literature at Cornell and Oxford, he is currently Senior Research Fellow of Wolfson College, Oxford University.*

Stallworthy expresses in his work a fascination with the power of the creative imagination and the poet's ability to project a personal vision and affect the life of the reader. Unlike many modern poets, Stallworthy does not always directly address pressing social and political issues; in "Letter to a Friend," he justifies his own poetic themes. He claims that he wants his poetry to do more than just mirror the pain and misery of the world; instead, he strives to expand the reader's imaginative understanding of the world to create a perspective from which the world's beauty can be seen.

Reading Rhetorically

Each of the three stanzas of this poem begins with the same phrase: "You blame me. . . ." Repetition in poetry can do a number of things: it can set up a structure; it can provide emphasis of an idea; it can contribute to cadence and rhythm. Look at this poem and think about the function of repetition here.

The poem also is interesting in relation to its "speaker." The speaker in a poem is the voice from which the words emerge. Even though a poem may use the words "I" or "me," the speaker is not necessarily the poet. Often the poet invents a separate character. In this poem the speaker appears to be very closely related to the poet himself. Think about the characteristics of this speaker (his or her *ethos*) as you read the poem.

Letter to a Friend

You blame me that I do not write
With the accent of the age:
The eunuch voice of scholarship,
Or the reformer's rage
(Blurred by a fag-end[1] in the twisted lip).   5
You blame me that I do not call
Truculent nations to unite.
I answer that my poems all
Are woven out of love's loose ends;
For myself and for my friends.   10

You blame me that I do not face
The banner-headline fact
Of rape and death in bungalows,
Cities and workmen sacked.
Tomorrow's time enough to rant of those,   15
When the whirlpool sucks us in.
Turn away from the bitter farce,
Or have you now forgotten
That cloud, star, leaf, and water's dance
Are facts of life, and worth your glance?   20

You blame me that I do not look
At cities, swivelled, from
The eye of the crazy gunman, or
The man who drops the bomb.
Twenty years watching from an ivory tower,   25
Taller than your chimney-stack,
I have seen fields beyond the smoke:
And think it better that I make
In the sloganed wall the people pass,
A window—not a looking-glass.   30

1961

Questions for Discussion and Your Reading Journal

1. According to the speaker of the poem, what do others say he should write about?

---

[1]**fag-end** The end of a cigarette: a worthless remnant. [Ed. note.]

2. Does he feel that his own poems, which often treat subjects such as love and nature, are less valuable? Why or why not? (Cite specific passages from the poem.)
3. Does art have a social purpose? Would Langer in "The Cultural Importance of the Arts" agree with the speaker in this poem?
4. Restate the theme of this poem in your own words.

ARCHIBALD MACLEISH

Archibald MacLeish (1892–1982) was born in Illinois and graduated from Yale and Harvard Law School. Always possessed of a strong social conscience, he volunteered as an ambulance driver and captain of field artillery during World War I; after the war he practiced law in Boston. His interests, however, lay in writing rather than law, so in 1923 he took his family to France where he could concentrate fully on his poetry. He published several volumes of poems while in France and moved back to America a few years later. He worked for Fortune *magazine during the Depression and, as World War II approached, he devoted much of his time to writing and speaking on the dangers of fascism and the possibility of war. President Roosevelt named him Librarian of Congress in 1939; he was appointed director of the Office of Facts and Figures (a wartime department that dealt in part with propaganda) in 1941; and, from 1944 to 1945, Assistant Secretary of State. He retired from teaching in 1962 but continued to write poetry and drama, often centering his works on the theme of the creation of beauty and meaning in the face of death and nothingness. "Ars Poetica" ("Art of Poetry"), like the other poems about poetry in this section, seeks to define poetry, to examine and express its unique qualities and powers.*

Reading Rhetorically

Like the first poem in this series (Stallworthy's "Letter to a Friend"), this poem appears to be made up of three stanzas, often broken up into two-line sections (couplets). However, you may notice that in two places, between one section and the next, three asterisks are centered on a line. This notation is sometimes used by an editor of a work to show that part of the poem has been omitted. Here, however, the notation was included by the poet himself. Think about why he put the asterisks between the groups of lines.

After you have read the poem, go back and look at the lines again. Which ones seems most meaningful to you? When you read works of literature, either poetry or prose, they can become more meaningful if you can find something that specifically connects with you and your experience. Think about whether or not you are persuaded by the last line of the poem.

Ars Poetica

A POEM should be palpable and mute
As a globed fruit

Dumb
As old medallions to the thumb

Silent as the sleeve-worn stone   5
Of casement ledges where the moss has grown—
A poem should be wordless
As the flight of birds
                        * * *

A poem should be motionless in time
As the moon climbs   10

Leaving, as the moon releases
Twig by twig the night-entangled trees,

Leaving, as the moon behind the winter leaves,
Memory by memory the mind—

A poem should be motionless in time   15
As the moon climbs
                        * * *

A poem should be equal to:
Not true

For all the history of grief
An empty doorway and a maple leaf   20

For love
The leaning grasses and two lights above the sea—
A poem should not mean
But be

                                                    1926

Questions for Discussion and Your Reading Journal

1. How would you describe MacLeish's attitude toward poetry, his opinion of the value and usefulness of poetry?
2. In your own words, explain what MacLeish means by the line, "A poem should be equal to: / Not true."
3. Compare and contrast this poem with Marianne Moore's "Poetry" (p. 312) Where do you think the two poets would agree and disagree about the nature and definition of poetry?

4. Carefully examine MacLeish's extensive use of figurative language in this poem. How do you respond to the imagery he uses? What do you feel gives the poetic symbol its power?
5. What do you see as the theme, important imagery, and purpose of each of the three sections of the poem? How do they work together?

JAVIER HERAUD

Javier Heraud (1942–1963) was born in Lima, Peru. At 16 he began studying at the Catholic University of Lima, and later he attended the National University of San Marcos. After a brief period of teaching literature and English, he returned his attention to poetry, and in 1960 he was awarded the title of Young Poet of Peru. The next year he traveled to Cuba to continue his studies but quickly became involved in the Revolution and joined the Peruvian Army of National Liberation. In 1963, while trying secretly to cross the Rio Maranon back into Peru, he was killed by government troops.

While much of Heraud's poetry was centered on political and social themes, the one that follows is a poem mainly about poetry itself. Having the same title as the last poem, this "Ars Poetica" seems to speak much more directly to the reader. Heraud's style is characterized by this direct, almost conversational approach.

Reading Rhetorically

Examine the speaker's voice in this poem. Although the speaker may sound casual, there is some evidence, particularly toward the end, that he is quite serious about the importance of his subject. Think about how the speaker's voice and *ethos* seems to change as you read.

The last stanza of this poem serves the same function as do many conclusions of essays. Examine the last stanza and think about its purpose. Then look back at the poem to see if the assertion made in the conclusion is borne out by the earlier parts of the poem.

Ars Poetica

In truth, and frankly speaking,
poetry is a difficult job
that's won or lost
to the rhythm of the autumnal years.

5 (When one is young
and the flowers that fall are never gathered up,
one writes on and on at night,

at times filling hundreds and hundreds
of useless sheets of paper.
One can boast and say: 10
"I write without revising,
poems leave my hand
like Spring discarded
by the cypresses on my street.")
But as time passes   15
and the years filter in between the temples,
poetry becomes
the potter's art:
clay fired in the hands,
clay shaped by the quick flames.   20

And poetry is a marvelous lightning,
a rain of silent words,
a forest of throbbings and hopes,
the song of oppressed peoples,
the new song of liberated peoples.   25

So poetry, then,
is love, is death,
is man's redemption.

Madrid, 1961   *Havana, 1962*

Questions for Discussion and Your Reading Journal

1. Trace the images of nature throughout the poem. How does the imagery affect your response to this piece?
2. Discuss the distinction Heraud makes between the young poet and the older, more experienced poet. What are the motivations and contributions of each?
3. What connection does Heraud make in this poem between poetry and politics? What does he mean when he says poetry "is love, is death,/is man's redemption"?
4. Contrast this poem to MacLeish's poem on poetry and its function. What are the differences?

MARIANNE MOORE

Marianne Moore (1887–1972) received numerous awards for her poetry. She was born in St. Louis in 1887 and received her degree from Bryn Mawr in 1909. She was subsequently a teacher of stenography for several years at the U.S. Indian School in Carlisle, Pennsylvania, after which she moved to New York and worked as a secretary, a tutor, and an assistant at the New York Public Library. She was editor of the Dial, *a respected journal that focused mainly on literary reviews, from 1926 to 1929, and continued to write and give readings of her poems throughout the rest of her life.*

Moore's work is witty, ironic, and insightful; it is a unique blend of prose and poetry, filled with animal imagery and sprinkled with seemingly unpoetic facts and quotations. The following poem is characterized by a concern for the "genuineness" of true poetry.

Reading Rhetorically

Some terms are applied to poetry and other kinds of literature to facilitate discussion; one of those terms is "tone." The "tone" of a poem is related to the mood it creates in the reader—this mood is affected by the attitude of the poet toward the subject of the poem. The tone may be affected by a number of other conventions that the poem uses, such as meter or rhythm. If you find a poem exciting, it is because something about that poem affects your mood or emotions *(pathos)*. That "something" is less definable than the feeling it creates. As you read this poem, think about the mood it creates and the emotions it brings out. "Tone" can be an effective means of influencing the way a reader interprets a poem.

One specific poetic element that affects the tone of this poem is its imagery. As you read, you might want to mark the images that are particularly noticeable to you. Later you can go back and examine why these images grabbed your attention.

Poetry

I, too, dislike it: there are things that are important beyond all this fiddle.
    Reading it, however, with a perfect contempt for it, one discovers in
        it, after all, a place for the genuine.
           Hands that can grasp, eyes
5   that can dilate, hair that can rise
              if it must, these things are important not because a

high-sounding interpretation can be put upon them but because they are
    useful. When they become so derivative as to become unintelligible,
    the same thing may be said for all of us, that we
10   do not admire what
        we cannot understand: the bat
           holding on upside down or in quest of something to

eat, elephants pushing, a wild horse taking a roll, a tireless wolf under
    a tree, the immovable critic twitching his skin like a horse that feels a flea,
    the base-
15   ball fan, the statistician—

nor is it valid
    to discriminate against "business documents and

school-books"; all these phenomena are important. One must make a distinction
however: when dragged into prominence by half poets, the result is not poetry,
nor till the poets among us can be   20
    "literalists of
the imagination"—above
    insolence and triviality and can present

for inspection, imaginary gardens with real toads in them, shall we have
    it. In the meantime, if you demand on the one hand,   25
    the raw material of poetry in
        all its rawness and
        that which is on the other hand
            genuine, then you are interested in poetry.

1921

Questions for Discussion and Your Reading Journal

1. Marianne Moore's tone in the piece is complex. How would you describe
   it? What are her feelings about poetry? Discuss the words, phrases, and images that give you this impression.
2. Compare and contrast the tone of Moore's piece with the tone of the two
   "Ars Poetica" poems and Stallworthy's "Letter to a Friend."
3. What is it, according to Moore, that distinguishes good poetry from bad
   poetry, "half poets" from genuine poets?
4. What does Moore feel is the proper subject matter for poetry? Which of the
   other poets you have studied in this section of the chapter would agree with
   this claim? Which would disagree? Use specific examples from their poems
   to support your opinion.

RACE, GENDER, AND OPPRESSION

PABLO NERUDA

*Pablo Neruda (1904–1973) was actually named Neftalí Ricardo Reyes
Basoalto. He was born on July 12, 1904, in the town of Parral, Chile.
Pablo Neruda was a pen name he adopted at the age of 16 to honor an
admired Czechoslovakian poet. Although his mother, who was a teacher,
died shortly after his birth, Neruda had a strong relationship with his
father, who was a railway employee. At the age of 13, Neruda began to
write poems for publication.*

As an adult, Neruda became very active in politics. Around 1930 he wrote his most famous work, his Canto General de Chile, *an epic poem about the whole South American continent. This work consists of approximately 250 poems brought together into 15 literary cycles. In 1945 Neruda was elected senator of the Republic of Chile, and he joined the Communist Party. Because of his public criticism of the country's president, Neruda had to live in hiding for several years.*

Neruda won the Nobel Peace Prize for literature in 1971. He was admired for his innovative style and the thematic variety of his work, which ranges from sensuous love poems to odes in praise of everyday objects (such as "Ode to an Onion" and "Ode to Socks") to passionate and forceful political poetry. The following poem, "The United Fruit Co.," illustrates Neruda's social concerns: his sympathy for the exploited and oppressed laboring class and his anger at the foreign powers that he feels are primarily responsible for this exploitation. The poem is unified by the imagery of ripe fruit symbolizing the wealth, the people, and the dignity of his land, resources that are appropriated or discarded at will by outsiders like the United Fruit Co.

Reading Rhetorically

This poem begins a new thematic section of the chapter. It deals with the oppression of a specific group of people, as will a number of poems and prose works that follow. In this case the oppressed individuals are farm workers whose labor does more to support the economic gain of large corporations than it does to sustain the laborers. The term "theme" involves the larger message set out in a work of literature. By focusing on the theme of this poem as you read, you can have a clearer understanding of the images and ideas that support it. As you read, think about the use of *pathos* in the poem.

The United Fruit Co.

Cuando sonó la trompeta, estuvo
todo preparado en la tierra,
y Jehová repartió el mundo
a Coca-Cola Inc., Anaconda,
5 Ford Motors, y otras entidades:
la Compañía Frutera Inc.
se reservó lo más jugoso,
la costa central de mi tierra,
la dulce cintura de América.
10 Bautizó de nuevo sus tierras
como "Repúblicas Bananas,"
y sobre los muertos dormidos,
sobre los héroes inquietos

que conquistaron la grandeza, 15
la libertad y las banderas,
estableció la ópera bufa:
enajenó los albedríos,
regaló coronas de César,
desenvainó la envidia, atrajo
la dictadura de las moscas, 20
moscas Trujillos, moscas Tachos,
moscas Carías, moscas Martínez,
moscas Ubico, moscas húmedas
de sangre humilde y mermelada,
moscas borrachas que zumban 25
sobre las tumbas populares,
moscas de circo, sabias moscas
entendidas en tirania.

Entre las moscas sanguinarias
la Frutera desembarca, 30
arrasando el café y las frutas,
en sus barcos que deslizaron
como bandejas el tesoro
de nuestras tierras sumergidas.

Mientras tanto, por los abismos 35
azucarados de los puertos,
caían indios sepultados
en el vapor de la mañana:
un cuerpo rueda, una cosa
sin nombre, un número caído, 40
un racimo de fruta muerta
derramada en el pudridero.

When the trumpets had sounded and all
was in readiness on the face of the earth,
Jehovah divided his universe:
Anaconda, Ford Motors,
Coca-Cola Inc., and similar entities: 5
the most succulent item of all,
The United Fruit Company Incorporated
reserved for itself: the heartland
and coasts of my country,
the delectable waist of America. 10
They rechristened their properties:
the "Banana Republics"—
and over the languishing dead,
the uneasy repose of the heroes
who harried that greatness, 15
their flags and their freedoms,

they established an *opéra bouffe:*
they ravished all enterprise,
awarded the laurels like Caesars,
20 unleashed all the covetous, and contrived
the tyrannical Reign of the Flies—
Trujillo the fly, and Tacho the fly,
the flies called Carias, Martinez,
Ubico[1]—all of them flies, flies
25 dank with the blood of their marmalade
vassalage, flies buzzing drunkenly
on the populous middens;
the fly-circus fly and the scholarly
kind, case-hardened in tyranny.

30 Then in the bloody domain of the flies
The United Fruit Company Incorporated
unloaded with a booty of coffee and fruits
brimming its cargo boats, gliding
like trays with the spoils
35 of our drowning dominions.

And all the while, somewhere, in the sugary
hells of our seaports,
smothered by gases, an Indian
fell in the morning:
40 a body spun off, an anonymous
chattel, some numeral tumbling,
a branch with its death running out of it
in the vat of the carrion, fruit laden and foul.

Questions for Discussion and Your Reading Journal

1. What is the theme of this poem?
2. What effective metaphors and similes does Neruda use? Discuss how this imagery unifies the poem.
3. What does Neruda see as the threat of foreign powers in Chile?

PAUL LAURENCE DUNBAR

Paul Laurence Dunbar (1872–1906) was one of the best-known African-American writers of his century. He was class poet and editor of his high-school paper in Dayton, Ohio, and his interest in fiction and poetry

---

[1]Names of dictators who were closely associated with U.S. Business interests. [Ed. Note.]

continued after his graduation. With the encouragement and public praise of writer William Dean Howells, Dunbar and his poetry soon achieved fame. Unlike most African-American poets of this time, Dunbar was able to support himself financially with his writing. His dialect poems were especially popular, though he felt constrained by their popularity and would rather have written more of his serious (but less lucrative) poetry. Dunbar has received some criticism for not dealing more extensively in his writings with racial problems; but, as the following poem reveals, he was not unaware of the injustices faced by African Americans in the United States.

Reading Rhetorically

Although metaphors are used in all literary genres, they are especially important in poetry. Metaphors identify one object or idea with another. The meaning of a poem frequently depends on the success of a metaphor. Some poetry is characterized by elaborate *conceits,* or extended metaphors. Poets in Shakespeare's time extended their comparisons to great lengths with impressive results. Contemporary poets, however, tend to favor fewer and simpler metaphors. Dunbar, who wrote this poem at the end of the 19th century, fits somewhere in between.

This poem depends on a central metaphor: the mask. Before reading the poem, think about situations in your own life for which a "mask" metaphor may be appropriate. Then, as you read the poem, examine the way Dunbar uses it.

We Wear the Mask

We wear the mask that grins and lies,
It hides our cheeks and shades our eyes,—
This debt we pay to human guile;
With torn and bleeding hearts we smile,
And mouth with myriad subtleties.   5

Why should the world be overwise,
In counting all our tears and sighs?
Nay, let them only see us, while
    We wear the mask.

We smile, but, O great Christ, our cries   10
To thee from tortured souls arise.
We sing, but oh the clay is vile
Beneath our feet, and long the mile;
But let the world dream otherwise,
    We wear the mask!   15

1895

Questions for Discussion and Your Reading Journal

1. Discuss Dunbar's metaphor of the mask. What kinds of associations do you think he wants us to make with the mask he and his people wear?
2. The poet says the souls of his people are "tortured." Why would he want the world to "dream otherwise"?
3. Describe the tone of this poem. Who is its audience?
4. How would you summarize its theme? What other pieces in this section are similar in terms of theme and purpose?

JUNE JORDAN

June Jordan (1936–) was born in Harlem. She attended private schools and, in 1953, entered Barnard College. She married Michael Meyer, a white student, in 1955; her own education was interrupted so that he could continue his studies. This interracial marriage was not well accepted by society (in fact, it was illegal in 43 states), and Jordan experienced a great deal of verbal abuse when she and her husband were together in public. They were divorced in 1965. In 1967 she began her teaching career, which led to a tenured professorship at the State University of New York, Stony Brook. In 1969 she published her first book, Who Look at Me, *and since then her many volumes of poems and essays have earned her an honored place among African-American writers.*

The schools Jordan attended and the writers she studied there were predominately white. The language and themes of these poets and essayists seemed remote from her own, weakening Jordan's faith in the value of her own young poetic voice. But her deep feelings of responsibility toward her race led Jordan to develop a literary style that has become a powerful and significant expression of her activism.

The poem reprinted here is Jordan's indictment of the labels society often imposes on minorities and the effects of such labeling. It contains the diction and syntax of the people in the Harlem area where the poet grew up. (Note: The intelligence tests referred to in the poem have been highly criticized since that time and, as a result, have been revised to reduce discrimination against marginalized groups.)

Reading Rhetorically

This poem incorporates dialogue between the poet persona (the "I" who tells the story) and her neighbor. While dialogue is used frequently in fiction, it is not so common in poetry. As you read the poem, think about why the poet might have chosen to include dialogue rather than to simply tell what happened.

In addition, examine the "diction" employed in the poem. "Diction" is the literary term for word choice, which is an important element of this poem. As you read, you may want to mark words or phrases that you find particularly interesting or effective. Then, after you have finished reading, you can go back and examine them to get a better understanding of how and why they affected you in the way they did *(pathos)*.

A Poem about Intelligence for My Brothers and Sisters

A few year back and they told me Black
means a hole where other folks
got brain/it was like the cells in the heads
of Black children was out to every hour on the hour naps
Scientists called the phenomenon the Notorious   5
Jensen Lapse, remember?[1]
Anyway I was thinking
about how to devise
a test for the wise
like a Stanford-Binet   10
for the C.I.A.
you know?
Take Einstein
being the most the unquestionable the outstanding
the maximal mind of the century   15
right?

And I'm struggling against this lapse leftover
from my Black childhood to fathom why
anybody should say so:
$E = mc \ squared?$ 20
I try that on this old lady live on my block:
She sweeping away Saturday night from the stoop
and mad as can be because some absolute
jackass have left a kingsize mattress where
she have to sweep around it stains and all she   25
don't want to know nothing about in the first place
"Mrs. Johnson!" I say, leaning on the gate
between us: "What you think about somebody come up with an E equals $M \ C \ 2$?"

"How you doin," she answer me, sideways, like she don't
want to let on she know I ain   30
combed my hair yet and here it is
Sunday morning but still I have the nerve
to be bothering serious work with these crazy
questions about

---

[1]Arthur Robert Jensen is a psychologist who has argued that the poor scholastic achievement of blacks is due to genetic inferiority rather than to cultural factors [Ed. note.]

35   "*E* equals what say again, dear?"
Then I tell her, "Well
also this same guy? I think
he was undisputed Father of the Atom Bomb!"
"That right." She mumbles or grumbles, not too politely
40   "And dint remember to wear socks when he put on
his shoes!" I add on (getting desperate)
at which point Mrs. Johnson take herself and her broom
a very big step down the stoop away from me
"And never did nothing for nobody in particular
45   lessen it was a committee
and
used to say, "What time is it"
and
you'd say, 'Six o'clock.'
50   and
he'd say, 'Day or night'
and
and he never made nobody a cup of tea
in his whole brilliant life!"
55   "and
(my voice rises slightly)
and
he dint never boogie neither: never!"

"Well," say Mrs. Johnson, "Well, honey,
60   I do guess
that's genius for you"

1980

Questions for Discussion and Your Reading Journal

1. Jordan is often admired for her skilled use of voice. How is the voice of this poem essential to its subject matter and theme?
2. What is the significance of the group of facts about Einstein the speaker relates to Mrs. Johnson? How would you describe the speaker's attitude toward Einstein? Toward her own intelligence?
3. What exactly does Jordan seem to be criticizing in this piece? Support your answer with specific passages from the poem.

MARZIEH AHMADI OSKOOII

Marzieh Ahmadi Oskooii (1945–1973) was born in Oskooi (Iran). Throughout her life, she was involved in fighting against social injustices in Iran. She was imprisoned for her antigovernment involvement, and was shot and killed by government forces. She was only 28 years old.

The social and political poems she left behind were an inspiration to the people to continue to fight for justice. The following poem is, in a sense, a definition poem in which Oskooii claims that the reality of being a woman in society is much greater and more complex than the mere word "woman" implies—"woman" can, in fact, mean anything from mother to Iranian revolutionary.

Reading Rhetorically

Like Nawal El Saadawi in the autobiographical reading *Growing Up Female in Egypt,* which appears later in this chapter, Oskooii was persecuted for her actions in support of social justice in an Islamic culture. The angry tone of this poem, which is directed at an enemy she refers to anonymously as "you," emerges from a litany of complaints about injustice in relation to women's treatment. Look for specific words and phrases in the poem that project this tone.

Another interesting aspect of the poem involves the poet persona (the speaker). Although she refers to herself as the first person singular "I," she appears to represent more than one person. As you read, take notice of the "I" and determine whom the first person singular pronoun represents.

Finally, examine this poem as an exercise in the process of definition. The word "woman" as it is defined in a standard dictionary involves a comparison between one human gender and the other. Here, however, the definition is a lot more complicated. Look for elements of Oskooii's definition of "woman" as you read this poem.

I'm a Woman

I'm a mother,
I'm a sister,
faithful spouse,
woman—
a woman, who, from the beginning   5
with bare feet,
has run hither and thither over the steaming hot sands
of the deserts.

I'm from the small villages of the North,
a woman, who from the beginning,   10
has worked to the limits of her power
in the price paddies and tea plantations, who
along with my skinny cow in the
threshing field, from dawn to dusk,
has felt the weight of pain,   15
A woman who gives birth to her babe
in the mountains,
loses her goat in the expanse of

the plains,
20   to sit mourning.

I'm a woman,
worker whose hands turn
the great machines of the factory,
which each day,
25   tear to bits my strength,
in the threads of the wheels,
in front of my eyes,

A woman from whose life's blood,
the carcass of the blood-sucker bloats
30   and from the loss of whose blood,
the profit of the usurer increases.

A woman, for whom, in your shameless lexicon,
there is no word
corresponding to her significance.
35   Your vocabulary speaks only of woman,
whose hands are white,
whose body is supple,
whose skin soft,
the hair perfumed.

40   I'm a woman,
a woman whose skin is the mirror of the deserts
and whose hair smells of factory smoke.
I'm a woman—
hands full of wounds,
45   from the cutting blades of giant pain.

How shameless of you to announce
that my hunger is an illusion,
my nakedness
a make-believe.

50   A woman for whom
in your shameless lexicon,
is no word
corresponding to her significance.
A woman in whose chest
55   is a heart
full of the festering
wounds of wrath,
in whose eyes
the red
60   reflection of the arrows
of liberty is flying.
It is she whose hands have

been trained
through all her sorrows, to also man
the gun.   65

Questions for Discussion and Your Reading Journal

1. Who seems to be the intended audience for this poem?
2. What is the poem's purpose?
3. According to Oskooii, what does the word "woman" mean to her reader?
4. What is her definition of the word "woman"?
5. Discuss what she means by the phrase "shameless lexicon" (Line 32).
6. How would an American rewrite this poem to fit American culture? How much would change?

JOY HARJO

Joy Harjo (1951–) is of the Muskogee Tribe; she was born in Tulsa, Oklahoma. Harjo attended the University of New Mexico, where she received a B.A. in 1976; she then studied at the University of Iowa, from which she was awarded an M.F.A. Harjo has taught at Arizona State University, Santa Fe Community College, the University of Colorado, the University of Arizona, and the University of New Mexico. She is currently teaching at the University of California at Los Angeles. She is also on the board of directors for the National Association of Third World Writers and the policy panel of the National Endowment for the Arts.

Harjo began writing poetry as a young adult. Her poetry is often focused on the topic of Native-American social issues and the political changes that need to take place to better her people's lives. Harjo's poetry collections include The Last Song, What Moon Drove Me to This, *and* She Had Some Horses, *from which the following poem is taken. Her most recent book of poetry is* How We Became Human: New and Selected Poems. *The poem that follows deals literally with the subject implied in its title, although the reader may speculate that the title is metaphorical.*

Reading Rhetorically

Unlike the last poem in which the enemy was "you" and the central figure was "I," the antagonist in this poem is "they" and the central figure is "she." By referring to them in the third person, the poet puts distance between the subjects of the poem and the speaker, distancing the speaker from the misery and tragedy she describes.

This poem uses repetition as an effective means of bringing the reader back to the poem's theme and of creating suspense about what will happen at the end of the poem. As you read, consider reasons for the repetition of the title phrase and try to predict what will happen at the end. Then, after you have finished reading, determine the degree to which your prediction was accurate and assess the evidence on which your prediction was based.

The Woman Hanging from the 13th Floor Window

She is the woman hanging from the 13th floor
window. Her hands are pressed white against the
concrete moulding of the tenement building. She
hangs from the 13th floor window in east Chicago,
5 with a swirl of birds over her head. They could
be a halo, or a storm of glass waiting to crush her.

She thinks she will be set free.

The woman hanging from the 13th floor window
on the east side of Chicago is not alone.
10 She is a woman of children, of the baby, Carlos,
and of Margaret, and of Jimmy who is the oldest.
She is her mother's daughter and her father's son.
She is several pieces between the two husbands
she has had. She is all the women of the apartment
15 building who stand watching her, watching themselves.

When she was young she ate wild rice on scraped down
plates in warm wood rooms. It was in the farther
north and she was the baby then. They rocked her.

She sees Lake Michigan lapping at the shores of
20 herself. It is a dizzy hole of water and the rich
live in tall glass houses at the edge of it. In some
places Lake Michigan speaks softly, here, it just sputters
and butts itself against the asphalt. She sees
other buildings just like hers. She sees other
25 women hanging from many-floored windows
counting their lives in the palms of their hands
and in the palms of their children's hands.

She is the woman hanging from the 13th floor window
on the Indian side of town. Her belly is soft from
30 her children's births, her worn levis swing down below
her waist, and then her feet, and then her heart.
She is dangling.

The woman hanging from the 13th floor hears voices.
They come to her in the night when the lights have gone

dim. Sometimes they are little cats mewling and scratching   35
at the door, sometimes they are her grandmother's voice,
and sometimes they are gigantic men of light whispering
to her to get up, to get up, to get up. That's when she wants
to have another child to hold onto in the night, to be able
to fall back into dreams.   40

And the woman hanging from the 13th floor window
hears other voices. Some of them scream out from below
for her to jump, they would push her over. Others cry softly
from the sidewalks, pull their children up like flowers and gather
them into their arms. They would help her, like themselves.   45

But she is the woman hanging from the 13th floor window,
and she knows she is hanging by her own fingers, her
own skin, her own thread of indecision.

She thinks of Carlos, of Margaret, of Jimmy.
She thinks of her father, and of her mother.   50
She thinks of all the women she has been, of all
the men. She thinks of the color of her skin, and
of Chicago streets, and of waterfalls and pines.
She thinks of moonlight nights, and of cool spring storms.
Her mind chatters like neon and northside bars.   55
She thinks of the 4 a.m. lonelinesses that have folded
her up like death, discordant, without logical and
beautiful conclusion. Her teeth break off at the edges.
She would speak.

The woman hangs from the 13th floor window crying for   60
the lost beauty of her own life. She sees the
sun falling west over the grey plane of Chicago.
She thinks she remembers listening to her own life
break loose, as she falls from the 13th floor
window on the east side of Chicago, or as she   65
climbs back up to claim herself again.

Questions for Discussion and Your Reading Journal

1. Describe the woman in the poem—who is she? Describe the effect the last
   two lines have on your understanding of who this woman is.
2. What do the specific details about the setting tell you about the woman's
   life? Why is it the 13th floor window the woman is hanging from?
3. Compare this poem to Oskooii's "I'm a Woman." What are the likenesses?
   The differences?
4. Is this a hopeful poem? Why or why not?

NAWAL EL SAADAWI

Nawal El Saadawi is a novelist, a psychiatrist, and a writer. Her books about the situation of women in Egyptian and Arab society have profoundly affected women of three different generations, and her courageous efforts have put her life in danger. Indeed, she was imprisoned by Sadat until the time of his death. Saadawi has been awarded several international literary prizes, and her works have been translated into over 30 languages.

The reading excerpted here is the first chapter of Saadawi's novel entitled Woman at Point Zero. *The novel is based on the life story of a woman imprisoned in the Qanatir prison in Egypt and executed in 1973. (You may remember that the poet Marzieh Ahmadi Oskooii, author of the poem "I'm a Woman," which appeared earlier in the chapter, was shot and killed by government forces in Iran in 1973.) First published in English in 1983, the novel tells the story of a prostitute who has killed her pimp. As she is waiting to be executed, she tells her story to a female medical researcher and writer who is visiting the prison (a character very much like the author herself). The prostitute's story reveals the horrors that can await an unprotected woman trying to survive on her own.*

Reading Rhetorically

Sadaawi's story is told in a style reminiscent of the technique pioneered by Truman Capote in his book *In Cold Blood,* in which a writer interviews two murderers waiting to be executed. The technique combines journalistic reportage with novelistic speculation. As you read about the murderess in this story, examine the style in which her story is told, and think about why the writer has chosen to combine fictional license with biographical narrative.

In addition, pay particular attention to the characterization of the prostitute. How realistic does she seem? What elements of her characterization might have been exaggerated, and why might that exaggeration have been employed? Compare and contrast the characterization of the narrator (and her *ethos*) with that of the prostitute and think about the author's possible purposes in presenting them this way.

Growing Up Female in Egypt

1　This is the story of a real woman. I met her in the Qanatir Prison a few years ago. I was doing research on the personalities of a group of women prisoners and detainees convicted or accused of various offences.

2　The prison doctor told me that this woman had been sentenced to death for killing a man. Yet she was not like the other female murderers held in the prison.

'You will never meet anyone like her in or out of prison. She refuses all 3
visitors, and won't speak to anyone. She usually leaves her food untouched,
and remains wide awake until dawn. Sometimes the prison warder observes
her as she sits staring vacantly into space for hours. One day she asked for pen
and paper, then spent hours hunched over them without moving. The warder
could not tell whether she was writing a letter or something else. Perhaps she
was not writing anything at all.'

I asked the prison doctor, 'Will she see me?' 4

'I shall try to persuade her to speak to you for a while,' he said. 'She might 5
agree if I explain you are a psychiatrist, and not one of the Public Prosecutor's
assistants. She refuses to answer my questions. She even refused to sign an appeal
to the President so that her sentence be commuted to imprisonment for life.'

'Who made out the appeal for her?' I asked. 6

'I did,' he said. 'To be quite honest, I do not really feel she is a murderer. 7
If you look into her face, her eyes, you will never believe that so gentle a
woman can commit murder.'

'Who says murder does not require that a person be gentle?' 8

He stared at me in surprise for a brief moment, and then laughed nervously. 9

'Have you ever killed anybody?' 10

'Am I a gentle woman?' I replied. 11

He turned his head to one side, pointed to a tiny window, and said, 'That's 12
her cell. I'll go and persuade her to come down and meet you.'

After a while he came back without her. Firdaus had refused to see me. 13

I was supposed to examine some other women prisoners that day, but 14
instead I got into my car and drove away.

Back home I could not do anything. I had to revise the draft of my latest 15
book, but I was incapable of concentrating. I could think of nothing but the
woman called Firdaus who, in ten days' time, would be led to the gallows.

Early next morning I found myself at the prison gates again. I asked the 16
warder to let me see Firdaus, but she said: 'It's no use, Doctor. She will never
agree to see you.'

'Why?' 17

'They're going to hang her in a few days' time. What use are you, or any- 18
body else to her? Leave her alone!'

There was a note of anger in her voice. She gave me a look charged with 19
wrath, as though I was the one who would hang Firdaus in a few days' time.

'I have nothing to do with the authorities either here or any other place,' 20
I said.

'That's what they all say,' she said angrily. 21

'Why are you so worked up?' I asked. 'Do you think Firdaus is innocent, 22
that she didn't kill him?'

She replied with an added fury, 'Murderer or not, she's an innocent 23
woman and does not deserve to be hanged. They are the ones that ought to
hang.'

'They? Who are *they*?' 24

She looked at me with suspicion and said, 'Tell me rather, who are you? 25
Did they send you to her?'

26 'Whom do you mean by "they"?' I asked again.

27 She looked around cautiously, almost with fear, and stepped back away from me.

28 ' "They". . .You mean to say you don't know them?'

29 'No,' I said.

30 She emitted a short, sarcastic laugh and walked off. I heard her muttering to herself:

31 'How can she be the only one who does not know them?'

32 I returned to the prison several times, but all my attempts to see Firdaus were of no avail. I felt somehow that my research was now in jeopardy. As a matter of fact, my whole life seemed to be threatened with failure. My self-confidence began to be badly shaken, and I went through difficult moments. It looked to me as though this woman who had killed a human being, and was shortly to be killed herself, was a much better person than I. Compared to her, I was nothing but a small insect crawling upon the land amidst millions of other insects.

33 Whenever I remembered the expression in the eyes of the warder, or the prison doctor, as they spoke of her complete indifference to everything, her attitude of total rejection, and above all her refusal to see me, the feeling that I was helpless, and of no significance grew on me. A question kept turning round and round in my mind increasingly: 'What sort of woman was she? Since she had rejected me, did that mean she was a better person than me? But then, she had also refused to send an appeal to the President asking him to protect her from the gallows. Could that signify that she was better than the Head of State?'

34 I was seized by a feeling very close to certainty, yet difficult to explain, that she was, in fact, better than all the men and women we normally hear about, or see, or know.

35 I tried to overcome my inability to sleep, but another thought started to occupy my mind and keep me awake. When she refused to see me did she know who I was, or had she rejected me without knowing?

36 The following morning, I found myself back once more in the prison. I had no intention of trying to meet Firdaus, for I had given up all hope. I was looking for the warder, or the prison doctor. The doctor had not yet arrived but I found the warder.

37 'Did Firdaus tell you she knew me?' I asked her.

38 'No, she did not tell me anything,' the warder replied. 'But she does know you.'

39 'How do you know that she knows me?'

40 'I can sense her.'

41 I just stood there as though turned to stone. The warder left me to get on with her work. I tried to move, to go towards my car and leave, but in vain. A strange feeling of heaviness weighed down my heart, my body, drained my legs of their power. A feeling heavier than the weight of the whole earth, as though instead of standing above its surface, I was now lying somewhere beneath it. The sky also had undergone a change; its colour had turned to black, like that of the earth, and it was pressing down upon me with its added load.

It was a feeling I had known only once before, many years ago. I had 42
fallen in love with a man who did not love me. I felt rejected, not only by him,
not only by one person amongst the millions that peopled the vast world, but
by every living being or thing on earth, by the vast world itself.

I straightened my shoulders, stood as upright as I could, and took a deep 43
breath. The weight on my head lifted a little. I began to look around me and
to feel amazed at finding myself in the prison at this early hour. The warder
was bent double, scrubbing the tiled floor of the corridor. I was overcome by
an unusual contempt towards her. She was no more than a woman cleaning
the prison floor. She could not read or write and knew nothing about psychology, so how was it that I had so easily believed her feelings could be
true?

Firdaus did not actually say she knew me. The warder merely sensed it. 44
Why should that indicate that Firdaus really knew me? If she had rejected me
without knowing who I was there was no reason for me to feel hurt. Her
refusal to see me was not directed against me personally, but against the world
and everybody in it.

I started to walk towards my car with the intention of leaving. Subjective 45
feelings such as those that had taken hold of me were not worthy of a
researcher in science. I almost smiled at myself as I opened the door of the car.
The touch of its surface helped to restore my identity, my self-esteem as a doctor. Whatever the circumstances, a doctor was surely to be preferred to a
woman condemned to death for murder. My normal attitude towards myself
(an attitude which rarely deserts me) gradually returned. I turned the ignition
key and pressed my foot down on the accelerator, firmly stamping out the sudden feeling (which occasionally haunts me in moments of failure) of merely
being an insignificant insect, crawling on the earth amidst myriads of other
similar insects. I heard a voice behind me, rising over the sound of the engine.

'Doctor! Doctor!' 46

It was the warder. She ran up to me panting heavily. Her gasping voice 47
reminded me of the voices I often heard in my dreams. Her mouth had grown
bigger, and so had her lips, which kept opening and closing with a mechanical
movement, like a swing door.

I heard her say, 'Firdaus, Doctor! Firdaus wants to see you!' 48

Her breast was heaving up and down, her breathing had become a series 49
of rapid gasps, and her eyes and face reflected a violent emotion. If the President of the Republic in person had asked to see me, she could not have been
swept by such an overpowering emotion.

My breathing in turn quickened, as though by infection, or to be more pre- 50
cise, I felt out of breath, for my heart was beating more strongly than it had
ever done before. I do not know how I climbed out of the car, nor how I followed so closely behind the warder that I sometimes overtook her, or moved
ahead. I walked with a rapid, effortless pace, as though my legs were no longer
carrying a body. I was full of a wonderful feeling, proud, elated, happy. The sky
was blue with a blueness I could capture in my eyes. I held the whole world in
my hands; it was mine. It was a feeling I had known only once before, many
years ago. I was on my way to meet the first man I loved for the first time.

51   I stopped for a moment in front of Firdaus' cell to catch my breath and adjust the collar of my dress. But I was trying to regain my composure, to return to my normal state, to the realization that I was a researcher in science, a psychiatrist, or something of the kind. I heard the key grind in the lock, brutal, screeching. The sound restored me to myself. My hand tightened its grasp on the leather bag, and a voice within me said, 'Who is this woman called Firdaus? She is only . . .'

52   But the words within me stopped short. Suddenly we were face to face. I stood rooted to the ground, silent, motionless. I did not hear the beat of my heart, nor the key as it turned in the lock, closing the heavy door behind me. It was as though I died the moment her eyes looked into mine. They were eyes that killed, like a knife, probing, cutting deep down inside, their look steady, unwavering. Not the slightest movement of a lid. Not the smallest twitch of a muscle in the face.

53   I was brought back suddenly by a voice. The voice was hers, steady, cutting deep down inside, cold as a knife. Not the slightest wavering in its tone. Not the smallest shiver of a note. I heard her say:

54   'Close the window.'

55   I moved up to the window blindly and closed it, then cast a bemused look around. There was nothing in the cell. Not a bed, or a chair, or anything on which I could sit down. I heard her say:

56   'Sit down on the ground.'

57   My body bent down and sat on the ground. It was January and the ground was bare, but I felt no cold. Like walking in one's sleep. The ground under me was cold. The same touch, the same consistency, the same naked cold. Yet the cold did not touch me, did not reach me. It was the cold of the sea in a dream. I swam through its waters. I was naked and knew not how to swim. But I neither felt its cold, nor drowned in its waters. Her voice too was like the voices one hears in a dream. It was close to me, yet seemed to come from afar, spoke from a distance and seemed to arise from nearby. For we do not know from where these voices arise: from above or below, to our left or our right. We might even think they come from the depths of the earth, drop from the rooftops, or fall from the heavens. Or they might even flow from all directions, like air moving in space reaches the ears.

58   But this was no dream. This was not air flowing into my ears. The woman sitting on the ground in front of me was a real woman, and the voice filling my ears with its sound, echoing in a cell where the window and door were tightly shut, could only be her voice, the voice of Firdaus.

Questions for Discussion and Your Reading Journal

1. Describe the narrator. What do you know about her? Why is she telling this story?

2. Describe the main character. What is her crime and why is she being executed for it?

3. Discuss the style in which the story is told. What are the advantages of combining actual experience with fiction? What may be some disadvantages?

4. To what degree does the writer sympathize with the murderess? To what degree do you sympathize with her? Why do her captors appear to have so little sympathy?

5. In what ways is the main character of this story different from American prostitutes? Do you think an American prostitute who murdered a pimp would be likely to be punished in the same way? Why or why not?

YU HSUAN-CHI

The Chinese poet Yu Hsuan-Chi (ca. 843–868), a well-educated and highly sophisticated woman, was taken as a concubine by an official, Li Yi, to whom many of her poems are addressed. He later abandoned her at the insistence of his wife, and Yu Hsuan-Chi became a Taoist nun. In great poverty, she began to take lovers once more and was finally charged (probably falsely) with killing her maid. Although her poet friends tried to intervene, she was executed.

Yu Hsuan-Chi's intense, symbolic, and subtly passionate poetry conveys a keen awareness of the fact that, as a woman, she is considered inferior and dependent upon men. In the following poem, she expresses her resentment that only men were allowed to take the imperial examinations.

Reading Rhetorically

The author of this poem, the author of a previous poem (Marzieh Ahmadi Oskooii), and the subject of the previous excerpt from the novel *Woman at Point Zero* were all executed, two for the crime of murder and one for political activism. Read this poem with the awareness that the poet would subsequently be put to death by the government of her country, and think about how this knowledge affects your reading of the poem. To what degree do you think the poet's gender affected her ultimate fate? Think about how what you know about the life of the poet supports the message of her poem.

Note that this poem was written well over a thousand years ago. Its subject appears to be timeless, however. As you read and think about this very short poem, examine the degree to which it is meaningful to a contemporary audience.

On a Visit to Ch'ung Chen Taoist Temple

Cloud capped peaks fill the eyes
In the Spring sunshine.
Their names are written in beautiful characters
And posted in order of merit.
How I hate this silk dress   5
That conceals a poet.
I lift my head and read their names
In powerless envy.

Questions for Discussion and Your Reading Journal

1. The imperial examinations were, in a sense, entrance exams. By doing well on these exams, a young man could be chosen for a coveted government position. Even if he was not chosen for government service, he became part of the powerful intellectual elite of the culture. Part of the examination had to do with writing poetry. How does this fact relate to the lines "How I hate this silk dress/That conceals a poet"?
2. What does the first image of the poem, the "cloud capped peaks" in the spring sunshine, have to do with the rest of the poem?
3. Contrast this poem with "I'm a Woman." What are the main differences?
4. Both the woman who wrote this poem and the main character of the story that precedes it were executed for murder. In both cases the women were almost certainly punished unjustly, and injustice is a theme in both works. How is the injustice represented in this poem different from and similar to that in the story that precedes it?

SOR JUANA DE LA CRUZ

Mexican poet Sor (Sister) Juana Ines de la Cruz (1648 or 1651–1695) was one of the earliest writers of the Americas; she was also among the earliest champions of women's rights. Her intellectual curiosity was exceptional: she learned to read as a child by secretly following her sister to school, and by the age of 13 she was famed for her extensive learning (both in the arts and the sciences) and her intellectual capacity. Church records indicate that Sor Juana was an illegitimate child—apparently the reason for the controversy surrounding her date of birth—born in the small village of Nepantla. She was raised with her mother's family under the eye of her learned and appreciative grandfather. Soon after his death, she went to Mexico City to live with wealthy relatives. She became a favorite of nobility there and spent 2 years in the Mexican court before entering a convent.

From the convent, Sor Juana continued her correspondence with members of the court, often writing poems for important courtly events. She also continued to study fervently until 1691, when the church demanded that she give up her writing, her studies, and her other worldly attachments. It is very likely that church officials were motivated by envy rather than spiritual concerns, for Sor Juana's beauty and accomplishments were legendary. She wrote an eloquent response to their demands, the "Respuesta a Sor Filotea," which is the New World's first affirmation of the right of women to learn and to write; but in the end she obeyed the church's orders and, in documents signed with her own blood, reaffirmed her vows. She died in 1695 while helping the sick during a plague.

Reading Rhetorically

Each of the stanzas of this poem asserts a single judgment, critical of the "foolish men" who "accuse women," measured into four lines. Each stanza also follows a pattern of rhyming (or nearly rhyming) the first and last lines and the second and third lines. This rigid structure might have been intended to create a certain mood and to affect the reader in a particular way *(pathos)*. As you read, decide how the form of the poetry affects your reception of it.

She Proves the Inconsistency of the Desires and Criticism of Men Who Accuse Women of What They Themselves Cause

Foolish men who accuse
women unreasonably,
you blame yet never see
you cause what you abuse.

You crawl before her, sad,   5
begging for a quick cure;
why ask her to be pure
when you have made her bad?

You combat her resistance
and then with gravity,   10
you call frivolity
the fruit of your intents.

In one heroic breath
your reason fails, like a wild
bogeyman made up by a child   15
who then is scared to death.

With idiotic pride
you hope to find your prize:
a regal whore like Thaïs
and Lucretia for a bride.   20

Has anyone ever seen
a stranger moral fervor:
you who dirty the mirror
regret it is not clean?

You treat favor and disdain   25
with the same shallow mocking
voice: love you and you squawk,
demur and you complain.

No answer at her door
30 will be a proper part:
say no—she has no heart,
say yes—and she's a whore.

Two levels to your game
in which *you* are the fool:
35 one you blame as cruel,
one who yields, you shame.

How can one not be bad
the way you love pretends
to be? Say no and she offends
40 Consent and you are mad.

With all the fury and pain
your whims cause her, it's good
for her who has withstood
you. Now go and complain!

45 You let her grief take flight
and free her with new wings.
Then after sordid things
you say she's not upright.

Who is at fault in all
50 this errant passion? She
who falls for his pleas, or he
who pleads for her to fall?

Whose guilt is greater in
this raw erotic play?
55 The girl who sins for pay
or man who pays for sin?

So why be shocked or taunt
her for the steps you take?
Care for her as you make
60 her, or shape her as you want,

but do not come with pleas
and later throw them in
her face, screaming of sin
when you were at her knees.

65 You fight us from birth
with weapons of arrogance.
Between promise and pleading stance,
you are devil, flesh, and earth.

Questions for Discussion and Your Reading Journal

1. What is the theme of this poem? What audience do you imagine Sor Juana
   had in mind when she wrote it?

2. What is the speaker's attitude toward men at the beginning of the poem? Does her opinion undergo any changes by the end?

3. Compare the poem to Hsuan-Chi's "On a Visit to Ch'ung . . ." and Alice Walker's "In Search of Our Mother's Gardens" (later in the chapter). These three women wrote in very different times and cultures; how are their experiences and responses to these experiences similar?

4. Do you agree with Sor Juana's accusations? Do you feel that her poem is still relevant today? Think of examples from your own experiences and culture (television, film, advertising) that in your opinion confirm or disprove Sor Juana's argument.

SAPPHO

Sappho was born around 630 BCE on the island of Lesbos. Her lyric poetry was famous among the ancients, and she was often referred to as the 10th muse. Unfortunately, of the thousands of lines she wrote, only one or two short poems and various fragments have survived; but these are clearly worthy of the praise they received from the classical critics, and they have established Sappho's poetic genius for modern readers.

Sappho wrote most often of the life of women in Greece: of youth, marriage, and love, especially love between young women. (In Sappho's time, this love was considered a natural stage in a girl's life between her childhood and her role as wife or mother.) In the following poem, the speaker prays to Aphrodite, the goddess of love; like Yu Hsuan-Chi in her lyric poem "On a Visit to Ch'ung Chen . . . ," Sappho expresses an intense moment of feeling.

Reading Rhetorically

The poem is made up of a conversation (of sorts) between a woman and the goddess of love. The woman's thoughts, feelings, and desires frame the goddess's words to her. In particular, look at Aphrodite's speech in the fifth and sixth stanzas. The poem follows a narrowing path from detailed description, to a request, to a response, to a reflection on the response. As you read the poem, examine its organization and think about why the poem is structured in this way.

In addition, examine the dialogue between the woman and the goddess. What does each speaker's voice reveal about her character or personality? How would you represent the speech of a goddess? The unique subject of this poem allows you to imagine a humanized version of a divine figure.

Invocation to Aphrodite

Throned in splendor, deathless, O Aphrodite,
child of Zeus, charm-fashioner, I entreat you

not with griefs and bitterness to break my
   spirit, O goddess;

5 standing by me rather, if once before now
far away you heard, when I called upon you,
left your father's dwelling place and descended,
   yoking the golden

chariot to sparrows, who fairly drew you
10 down in speed aslant the black world, the bright air
trembling at the heart to the pulse of countless
   fluttering wingbeats.

Swiftly then they came, and you, blessed lady,
smiling on me out of immortal beauty,
15 asked me what affliction was on me, why I
   called thus upon you,

what beyond all else I would have befall my
tortured heart: "Whom then would you have Persuasion
force to serve desire in your heart? Who is it,
20 Sappho, that hurt you?

Though she now escape you, she soon will follow;
though she take not gifts from you, she will give them:
though she love not, yet she will surely love you
   even unwilling."

25 In such guise come even again and set me
free from doubt and sorrow; accomplish all those
things my heart desires to be done; appear and
stand at my shoulder.

Questions for Discussion and Your Reading Journal

1. What is the speaker of the poem asking of Aphrodite?
2. This poem implies a relationship between love and pain. What is that relationship? To what degree is the relationship represented here consistent with your experience of love?
3. How does this poem fit the definitions of art in the essays earlier in this chapter, "What Use Is Art?" and "The Cultural Importance of the Arts"?
4. Contrast the attitude toward women expressed in this poem with that explained in "Women in Athens" (found in Chapter 2).

MAXINE HONG KINGSTON

*Maxine Hong Kingston (1940–) was born in Stockton, California. Her
mother had been a midwife in Canton, China, and her father had been a*

scholar who taught near there. After immigrating to America, her father worked in a gambling house and Maxine was named after a lucky gambler who frequented the casino. Kingston grew up surrounded by other immigrants from her father's village, whose storytelling about their native land influenced her writing in her later life. An extremely bright student, Kingston won 11 scholarships to the University of California at Berkeley; and, although she began as an engineering major, she eventually switched to English literature. She received a B.A. in 1962 and a teaching certificate in 1965. Kingston became a teacher and worked at a number of schools in California and Hawaii. In 1976 she published her first book, The Woman Warrior: Memoirs of a Girlhood Among Ghosts, *which was an enormous success.*

The following chapter from The Woman Warrior *illustrates Kingston's highly acclaimed ability to weave together myth, history, and legend. This selection tells the story of the tragic fate of the narrator's Chinese aunt while at the same time emphasizing the narrator's own struggle to come to terms with both her Chinese and her American cultures, particularly their respective treatment of women. At the end of* The Woman Warrior, *the introverted main character breaks the traditional silence of women and carries forward her culture's oral tradition in written form. Like Neruda and others in this chapter, Kingston deals with the complexities that result when two very different cultures meet.*

Reading Rhetorically

In this reading, a story is told within a story. A contemporary situation enfolds a historical tale within. In both cases the main character is a young woman struggling with the constraints her gender imposes on her. This narrative technique can be an effective way of contrasting the past and present and also of having the present reflect on the past and the past shed light on the present. Being aware of this complex narrative structure as well as the narrator's *ethos* as you read may help you to understand and appreciate the story.

No Name Woman

"You must not tell anyone," my mother said, "what I am about to tell you. In China your father had a sister who killed herself. She jumped into the family well. We say that your father has all brothers because it is as if she had never been born.

"In 1924 just a few days after our village celebrated seventeen hurry-up weddings—to make sure that every young man who went 'out on the road' would responsibly come home—your father and his brothers and your grandfather and his brothers and your aunt's new husband sailed for America, the Gold Mountain. It was your grandfather's last trip. Those lucky enough to get contracts waved goodbye from the decks. They fed and guarded the stowaways and helped them off in Cuba, New York, Bali, Hawaii. 'We'll meet in California next year,' they said. All of them sent money home.

3   "I remember looking at your aunt one day when she and I were dressing; I had not noticed before that she had such a protruding melon of a stomach. But I did not think, 'She's pregnant,' until she began to look like other pregnant women, her shirt pulling and the white tops of her black pants showing. She could not have been pregnant, you see, because her husband had been gone for years. No one said anything. We did not discuss it. In early summer she was ready to have the child, long after the time when it could have been possible.

4   "The village had also been counting. On the night the baby was to be born the villagers raided our house. Some were crying. Like a great saw, teeth strung with lights, files of people walked zigzag across our land, tearing the rice. Their lanterns doubled in the disturbed black water, which drained away through the broken bunds. As the villagers closed in, we could see that some of them, probably men and women we knew well, wore white masks. The people with long hair hung it over their faces. Women with short hair made it stand up on end. Some had tied white bands around their foreheads, arms, and legs.

5   "At first they threw mud and rocks at the house. Then they threw eggs and began slaughtering our stock. We could hear the animals scream their deaths— the roosters, the pigs, a last great roar from the ox. Familiar wild heads flared in our night windows; the villagers encircled us. Some of the faces stopped to peer at us, their eyes rushing like searchlights. The hands flattened against the panes, framed heads, and left red prints.

6   "The villagers broke in the front and the back doors at the same time, even though we had not locked the doors against them. Their knives dripped with the blood of our animals. They smeared blood on the doors and walls. One woman swung a chicken, whose throat she had slit, splattering blood in red arcs about her. We stood together in the middle of our house, in the family hall with the pictures and tables of the ancestors around us, and looked straight ahead.

7   "At that time the house had only two wings. When the men came back, we would build two more to enclose our courtyard and a third one to begin a second courtyard. The villagers pushed through both wings, even your grandparents' rooms, to find your aunt's, which was also mine until the men returned. From this room a new wing for one of the younger families would grow. They ripped up her clothes and shoes and broke her combs, grinding them underfoot. They tore her work from the loom. They scattered the cooking fire and rolled the new weaving in it. We could hear them in the kitchen breaking our bowls and banging the pots. They overturned the great waist-high earthenware jugs; duck eggs, pickled fruits, vegetables burst out and mixed in acrid torrents. The old woman from the next field swept a broom through the air and loosed the spirits-of-the-broom over our heads. 'Pig.' 'Ghost.' 'Pig,' they sobbed and scolded while they ruined our house.

8   "When they left, they took sugar and oranges to bless themselves. They cut pieces from the dead animals. Some of them took bowls that were not broken and clothes that were not torn. Afterward we swept up the rice and sewed it back up into sacks. But the smells from the spilled preserves lasted. Your

aunt gave birth in the pigsty that night. The next morning when I went for the water, I found her and the baby plugging up the family well.

"Don't let your father know that I told you. He denies her. Now that you 9
have started to menstruate, what happened to her could happen to you. Don't humiliate us. You wouldn't like to be forgotten as if you had never been born. The villagers are watchful."

Whenever she had to warn us about life, my mother told stories that ran 10
like this one, a story to grow up on. She tested our strength to establish realities. Those in the emigrant generations who could not reassert brute survival died young and far from home. Those of us in the first American generations have had to figure out how the invisible world the emigrants built around our childhoods fits in solid America.

The emigrants confused the gods by diverting their curses, misleading 11
them with crooked streets and false names. They must try to confuse their offspring as well, who, I suppose, threaten them in similar ways—always trying to get things straight, always trying to name the unspeakable. The Chinese I know hide their names; sojourners take new names when their lives change and guard their real names with silence.

Chinese-Americans, when you try to understand what things in you are 12
Chinese, how do you separate what is peculiar to childhood, to poverty, insanities, one family, your mother who marked your growing with stories, from what is Chinese? What is Chinese tradition and what is the movies?

If I want to learn what clothes my aunt wore, whether flashy or ordinary, 13
I would have to begin, "Remember Father's drowned-in-the-well sister?" I cannot ask that. My mother has told me once and for all the useful parts. She will add nothing unless powered by Necessity, a riverbank that guides her life. She plants vegetable gardens rather than lawns; she carries the odd-shaped tomatoes home from the fields and eats food left for the gods.

Whenever we did frivolous things, we used up energy; we flew high kites. 14
We children came up off the ground over the melting cones our parents brought home from work and the American movie on New Year's Day—*Oh, You Beautiful Doll* with Betty Grable one year, and *She Wore a Yellow Ribbon* with John Wayne another year. After the one carnival ride each, we paid in guilt; our tired father counted his change on the dark walk home.

Adultery is extravagance. Could people who hatch their own chicks and 15
eat the embryos and the heads for delicacies and boil the feet in vinegar for party food, leaving only the gravel, eating even the gizzard lining—could such people engender a prodigal aunt? To be a woman, to have a daughter in starvation time was a waste enough. My aunt could not have been the lone romantic who gave up everything for sex. Women in the old China did not choose. Some man had commanded her to lie with him and be his secret evil. I wonder whether he masked himself when he joined the raid on her family.

Perhaps she had encountered him in the fields or on the mountain where 16
the daughters-in-law collected fuel. Or perhaps he first noticed her in the marketplace. He was not a stranger because the village housed no strangers. She had to have dealings with him other than sex. Perhaps he worked an adjoining

field, or he sold her the cloth for the dress she sewed and wore. His demand must have surprised, then terrified her. She obeyed him; she always did as she was told.

17 When the family found a young man in the next village to be her husband, she had stood tractably beside the best rooster, his proxy, and promised before they met that she would be his forever. She was lucky that he was her age and she would be the first wife, an advantage secure now. The night she first saw him, he had sex with her. Then he left for America. She had almost forgotten what he looked like. When she tried to envision him, she only saw the black and white face in the group photograph the men had had taken before leaving.

18 The other man was not, after all, much different from her husband. They both gave orders: She followed. "If you tell your family, I'll beat you. I'll kill you. Be here again next week." No one talked sex, ever. And she might have separated the rapes from the rest of living if only she did not have to buy her oil from him or gather wood in the same forest. I want her fear to have lasted just as long as rape lasted so that the fear could have been contained. No drawn-out fear. But women at sex hazarded birth and hence lifetimes. The fear did not stop but permeated everywhere. She told the man, "I think I'm pregnant." He organized the raid against her.

19 On nights when my mother and father talked about their life back home, sometimes they mentioned an "outcast table" whose business they still seemed to be settling, their voices tight. In a commensal tradition, where food is precious, the powerful older people made wrongdoers eat alone. Instead of letting them start separate new lives like the Japanese, who could become samurais and geishas, the Chinese family, faces averted but eyes glowering sideways, hung on to the offenders and fed them leftovers. My aunt must have lived in the same house as my parents and eaten at an outcast table. My mother spoke about the raid as if she had seen it, when she and my aunt, a daughter-in-law to a different household, should not have been living together at all. Daughters-in-law lived with their husbands' parents, not their own; a synonym for marriage in Chinese is "taking a daughter-in-law." Her husband's parents could have sold her, mortgaged her, stoned her. But they had sent her back to her own mother and father, a mysterious act hinting at disgraces not told me. Perhaps they had thrown her out to deflect the avengers.

20 She was the only daughter; her four brothers went with her father, husband, and uncles "out on the road" and for some years became western men. When the goods were divided among the family, three of the brothers took land, and the youngest, my father, chose an education. After my grandparents gave their daughter away to her husband's family, they had dispensed all the adventure and all the property. They expected her alone to keep the traditional ways, which her brothers, now among the barbarians, could fumble without detection. The heavy, deep-rooted women were to maintain the past against the flood, safe for returning. But the rare urge west had fixed upon our family, and so my aunt crossed boundaries not delineated in space.

21 The work of preservation demands that the feelings playing about in one's guts not be turned into action. Just watch their passing like cherry blossoms. But perhaps my aunt, my forerunner, caught in a slow life, let dreams grow and fade and after some months or years went toward what persisted. Fear at

the enormities of the forbidden kept her desires delicate, wire and bone. She looked at a man because she liked the way the hair was tucked behind his ears, or she liked the question-mark line of a long torso curving at the shoulder and straight at the hip. For warm eyes or a soft voice or a slow walk—that's all— a few hairs, a line, a brightness, a sound, a pace, she gave up family. She offered us up for a charm that vanished with tiredness, a pigtail that didn't toss when the wind died. Why, the wrong lighting could erase the dearest thing about him.

It could very well have been, however, that my aunt did not take subtle   22 enjoyment of her friend, but, a wild woman, kept rollicking company. Imagining her free with sex doesn't fit, though. I don't know any women like that, or men either. Unless I see her life branching into mine, she gives me no ancestral help.

To sustain her being in love, she often worked at herself in the mirror,   23 guessing at the colors and shapes that would interest him, changing them frequently in order to hit on the right combination. She wanted him to look back.

On a farm near the sea, a woman who tended her appearance reaped a   24 reputation for eccentricity. All the married women blunt-cut their hair in flaps about their ears or pulled it back in tight buns. No nonsense. Neither style blew easily into heart-catching tangles. And at their weddings they displayed themselves in their long hair for the last time. "It brushed the backs of my knees," my mother tells me. "It was braided, and even so, it brushed the backs of my knees."

At the mirror my aunt combed individuality into her bob. A bun could   25 have been contrived to escape into black streamers blowing in the wind or in quiet wisps about her face, but only the older women in our picture album wear buns. She brushed her hair back from her forehead, tucking the flaps behind her ears. She looped a piece of thread, knotted into a circle between her index fingers and thumbs, and ran the double strand across her forehead. When she closed her fingers as if she were making a pair of shadow geese bite, the string twisted together catching the little hairs. Then she pulled the thread away from her skin, ripping the hairs out neatly, her eyes watering from the needles of pain. Opening her fingers, she cleaned the thread, then rolled it along her hairline and the tops of her eyebrows. My mother did the same to me and my sisters and herself. I used to believe that the expression "caught by the short hairs" meant a captive held with a depilatory string. It especially hurt at the temples, but my mother said we were lucky we didn't have to have our feet bound when we were seven. Sisters used to sit on their beds and cry together, she said, as their mothers or their slave removed the bandages for a few minutes each night and let the blood gush back into their veins. I hope that the man my aunt loved appreciated a smooth brow, that he wasn't just a tits-and-ass man.

Once my aunt found a freckle on her chin, at a spot that the almanac said   26 predestined her for unhappiness. She dug it out with a hot needle and washed the wound with peroxide.

More attention to her looks than these pullings of hairs and pickings at   27 spots would have caused gossip among the villagers. They owned work clothes and good clothes, and they wore good clothes for feasting the new seasons. But since a woman combing her hair hexes beginnings, my aunt rarely found an occasion to look her best. Women looked like great sea snails—the corded wood, babies, and laundry they carried were the whorls on their backs. The Chinese did not admire a bent back; goddesses and warriors stood straight. Still there must have been a marvelous freeing of beauty when a worker laid down her burden and stretched and arched.

28   Such commonplace loveliness, however, was not enough for my aunt. She dreamed of a lover for the fifteen days of New Year's, the time for families to exchange visits, money, and food. She plied her secret comb. And sure enough she cursed the year, the family, the village, and herself.

29   Even as her hair lured her imminent lover, many other men looked at her. Uncles, cousins, nephews, brothers would have looked, too, had they been home between journeys. Perhaps they had already been restraining their curiosity, and they left, fearful that their glances, like a field of nesting birds, might be startled and caught. Poverty hurt, and that was their first reason for leaving. But another, final reason for leaving the crowded house was the never-said.

30   She may have been unusually beloved, the precious only daughter, spoiled and mirror gazing because of the affection the family lavished on her. When her husband left, they welcomed the chance to take her back from the in-laws; she could live like the little daughter for just a while longer. There are stories that my grandfather was different from other people, "crazy ever since the little Jap bayoneted him in the head." He used to put his naked penis on the dinner table, laughing. And one day he brought home a baby girl, wrapped up inside his brown western-style greatcoat. He had traded one of his sons, probably my father, the youngest, for her. My grandmother made him trade back. When he finally got a daughter of his own, he doted on her. They must have all loved her, except perhaps my father, the only brother who never went back to China, having once been traded for a girl.

31   Brothers and sisters, newly men and women, had to efface their sexual color and present plain miens. Disturbing hair and eyes, a smile like no other, threatened the ideal of five generations living under one roof. To focus blurs, people shouted face to face and yelled from room to room. The immigrants I know have loud voices, unmodulated to American tones even after years away from the village where they called their friendships out across the fields. I have not been able to stop my mother's screams in public libraries or over telephones. Walking erect (knees straight, toes pointed forward, not pigeon-toed, which is Chinese feminine) and speaking in an inaudible voice, I have tried to turn myself American-feminine. Chinese communication was loud, public. Only sick people had to whisper. But at the dinner table, where the family members came nearest one another, no one could talk, not the outcasts nor any eaters. Every word that falls from the mouth is a coin lost. Silently they gave and accepted food with both hands. A preoccupied child who took his bowl with one hand got a sideways glare. A complete moment of total attention is due everyone alike. Children and lovers have no singularity here, but my aunt used a secret voice, a separate attentiveness.

She kept the man's name to herself throughout her labor and dying; she 32
did not accuse him that he be punished with her. To save her inseminator's
name she gave silent birth.

He may have been somebody in her own household, but intercourse with 33
a man outside the family would have been no less abhorrent. All the village
were kinsmen, and the titles shouted in loud country voices never let kinship
be forgotten. Any man within visiting distance would have been neutralized as
a lover—"brother," "younger brother," "older brother"—one hundred and
fifteen relationship titles. Parents researched birth charts probably not so much
to assure good fortune as to circumvent incest in a population that has but one
hundred surnames. Everybody has eight million relatives. How useless then
sexual mannerisms, how dangerous.

As if it came from an atavism deeper than fear, I used to add "brother" 34
silently to boys' names. It hexed the boys, who would or would not ask me to
dance, and made them less scary and as familiar and deserving of benevolence
as girls.

But, of course, I hexed myself also—no dates. I should have stood up, both 35
arms waving, and shouted out across libraries, "Hey, you! Love me back." I
had no idea, though, how to make attraction selective, how to control its
direction and magnitude. If I made myself American-pretty so that the five or
six Chinese boys in the class fell in love with me, everyone else—the Caucasian, Negro, and Japanese boys—would too. Sisterliness, dignified and honorable, made much more sense.

Attraction eludes control so stubbornly that whole societies designed to 36
organize relationships among people cannot keep order, not even when they
bind people to one another from childhood and raise them together. Among
the very poor and the wealthy, brothers married their adopted sisters, like
doves. Our family allowed some romance, paying adult brides' prices and providing dowries so that their sons and daughters could marry strangers. Marriage promises to turn strangers into friendly relatives—a nation of siblings.

In the village structure, spirits shimmered among the live creatures, bal- 37
anced and held in equilibrium by time and land. But one human being flaring
up into violence could open up a black hole, a maelstrom that pulled in the
sky. The frightened villagers, who depended on one another to maintain the
real, went to my aunt to show her a personal, physical representation of
the break she had made in the "roundness." Misallying couples snapped off
the future, which was to be embodied in true offspring. The villagers punished
her for acting as if she could have a private life, secret and apart from them.

If my aunt had betrayed the family at a time of large grain yields and 38
peace, when many boys were born, and wings were being built on many
houses, perhaps she might have escaped such severe punishment. But the
men—hungry, greedy, tired of planting in dry soil—had been forced to leave
the village in order to send food-money home. There were ghost plagues, ban-
dit plagues, wars with the Japanese, floods. My Chinese brother and sister had
died of an unknown sickness. Adultery, perhaps only a mistake during good
times, became a crime when the village needed food.

39   The round moon cakes and round doorways, the round tables of graduated size that fit one roundness inside another, round windows and rice
bowls—these talismans had lost their power to warn this family of the law: A
family must be whole, faithfully keeping the descent line by having sons to
feed the old and the dead, who in turn look after the family. The villagers came
to show my aunt and her lover-in-hiding a broken house. The villagers were
speeding up the circling of events because she was too shortsighted to see that
her infidelity had already harmed the village, that waves of consequences
would return unpredictably, sometimes in disguise, as now, to hurt her. This
roundness had to be made coin-sized so that she would see its circumference:
punish her at the birth of her baby. Awaken her to the inexorable. People who
refused fatalism because they could invent small resources insisted on culpa-
bility. Deny accidents and wrest fault from the stars.

40   After the villagers left, their lanterns now scattering in various directions
toward home, the family broke their silence and cursed her, "Aiaa, we're going
to die. Death is coming. Death is coming. Look what you've done. You've
killed us. Ghost! Dead ghost! Ghost! You've never been born." She ran out
into the fields, far enough from the house so that she could no longer hear their
voices, and pressed herself against the earth, her own land no more. When she
felt the birth coming, she thought that she had been hurt. Her body seized
together. "They've hurt me too much," she thought. "This is gall, and it will
kill me." With forehead and knees against the earth, her body convulsed and
then relaxed. She turned on her back, lay on the ground. The black well of sky
and stars went out and out and out forever; her body and her complexity
seemed to disappear. She was one of the stars, a bright dot in blackness, without home, without a companion, in eternal cold and silence. An agoraphobia
rose in her, speeding higher and higher, bigger and bigger; she would not be
able to contain it; there would be no end to fear.

41   Flayed, unprotected against space, she felt pain return, focusing her body.
This pain chilled her—a cold, steady kind of surface pain. Inside, spasmodi-
cally, the other pain, the pain of the child, heated her. For hours she lay on the
ground, alternately body and space. Sometimes a vision of normal comfort
obliterated reality; She saw the family in the evening gambling at the dinner
table, the young people massaging their elders' backs. She saw them congrat-
ulating one another, high joy on the mornings the rice shoots came up. When
these pictures burst, the stars drew yet further apart. Black space opened.

42   She got to her feet to fight better and remembered that old-fashioned
women gave birth in their pigsties to fool the jealous, pain-dealing gods, who
do not snatch piglets. Before the next spasms could stop her, she ran to the
pigsty, each step a rushing out into emptiness. She climbed over the fence and
knelt in the dirt. It was good to have a fence enclosing her, a tribal person alone.

43   Laboring, this woman who had carried her child as a foreign growth that
sickened her every day, expelled it at last. She reached down to touch the hot,
wet, moving mass, surely smaller than anything human, and could feel that it
was human after all—fingers, toes, nails, nose. She pulled it up on to her belly,
and it lay curled there, butt in the air, feet precisely tucked one under the other.
She opened her loose shirt and buttoned the child inside. After resting, it

squirmed and thrashed and she pushed it up to her breast. It turned its head this way and that until it found her nipple. There, it made little snuffling noises. She clenched her teeth at its preciousness, lovely as a young calf, a piglet, a little dog.

She may have gone to the pigsty as a last act of responsibility. She would 44 protect this child as she had protected its father. It would look after her soul, leaving supplies on her grave. But how would this tiny child without family find her grave when there would be no marker for her anywhere, neither in the earth nor the family hall? No one would give her a family hall name. She had taken the child with her into the wastes. At its birth the two of them had felt the same raw pain of separation, a wound that only the family pressing tight could close. A child with no descent line would not soften her life but only trail after her, ghostlike, begging her to give it purpose. At dawn the villagers on their way to the fields would stand around the fence and look.

Full of milk, the little ghost slept. When it awoke, she hardened her breasts 45 against the milk that crying loosens. Toward morning she picked up the baby and walked to the well.

Carrying the baby to the well shows loving. Otherwise abandon it. Turn 46 its face into the mud. Mothers who love their children take them along. It was probably a girl; there is some hope of forgiveness for boys.

"Don't tell anyone you had an aunt. Your father does not want to hear her 47 name. She has never been born." I have believed that sex was unspeakable and words so strong and fathers so frail that "aunt" would do my father mysterious harm. I have thought that my family, having settled among immigrants who had also been their neighbors in the ancestral land, needed to clean their name, and a wrong word would incite the kinspeople even here. But there is more to this silence: They want me to participate in her punishment. And I have.

In the twenty years since I heard this story I have not asked for details nor 48 said my aunt's name; I do not know it. People who can comfort the dead can also chase after them to hurt them further—a reverse ancestor worship. The real punishment was not the raid swiftly inflicted by the villagers, but the family's deliberately forgetting her. Her betrayal so maddened them, they saw to it that she would suffer forever, even after death. Always hungry, always needing, she would have to beg food from other ghosts, snatch and steal it from those whose living descendants give them gifts. She would have to fight the ghosts massed at crossroads for the buns a few thoughtful citizens leave to decoy her away from village and home so that the ancestral spirits could feast unharassed. At peace, they could act like gods, not ghosts, their descent lines providing them with paper suits and dresses, spirit money, paper houses, paper automobiles, chicken, meat, and rice into eternity—essences delivered up in smoke and flames, steam and incense rising from each rice bowl. In an attempt to make the Chinese care for people outside the family, Chairman Mao encourages us now to give our paper replicas to the spirits of outstanding soldiers and workers, no matter whose ancestors they may be. My aunt remains forever hungry. Goods are not distributed evenly among the dead.

My aunt haunts me—her ghost drawn to me because now, after fifty years 49 of neglect, I alone devote pages of paper to her, though not origamied into houses and clothes. I do not think she always means me well. I am telling on her, and she was a spite suicide, drowning herself in the drinking water. The Chinese are always very frightened of the drowned one, whose weeping ghost, wet hair hanging and skin bloated, waits silently by the water to pull down a substitute.

Questions for Discussion and Your Reading Journal

1. The narrator says her mother told stories to "warn us about life." What might the mother have been trying to teach her daughter with this story? What clues are there that the mother has interpreted events to fit her purpose?
2. How does the daughter reinterpret the story her mother tells? Why? How does this change the meaning?
3. One of the central themes of ethnic literature in America is the quest for identity. What difficulties does the narrator face in coming to terms with her Chinese-American heritage?
4. Where does the daughter receive her information about China? How reliable are these sources?
5. How does this fictional text illustrate the concept of woman as "Other," as discussed in the selection by Simone de Beauvoir (found in Chapter 2)?
6. The publishers originally called this piece autobiography, but the author calls it fiction. What makes it fiction? What is the difference between fiction and autobiography?

WAR AND PEACE

THOMAS HARDY

Thomas Hardy (1840–1928) was one of the most famous and influential literary figures of the late Victorian era. A novelist and poet, he questioned many cultural institutions and social conventions. In the following poem, "The Man He Killed," Hardy ruminates on the topic of war.

Thomas Hardy was born in the English countryside of Dorset on June 2, 1840. As a young adult, Hardy moved to London to work for a prominent architect. There he wrote poetry for the first time, but he soon turned his attention to fiction. For most of his life, Hardy was a novelist.

Late in his life, Hardy wrote his most famous novels, including Tess of the D'Urbervilles *and* Jude the Obscure. *This last novel created the one of the most infamous controversies of that time.* Jude the Obscure *(1895) flouted Victorian morality by depicting marriage as a destructive institution. The controversy did not discourage book sales, but readers tended to hide the novel from public view and clergymen all over the country publicly denounced it. Hardy himself was very disappointed by the reaction his book caused, and he stopped writing fiction altogether. He turned his attention to poetry.*

In "The Man He Killed," the poet persona (the speaker in the poem) grapples with a realization that his enemy in other circumstances might easily have been his friend. The poem was written during World War I, a time when many artists and intellectuals expressed moral outrage at the consequences of war.

Reading Rhetorically

When readers encounter the word "I" in a poem, they tend to equate the "I" with the poet. While sometimes the speaker may be the poet, other times the speaker is a kind of character created by the poet. Because readers generally are not certain about the identity of the speaker, the safest course is to use the term "poet persona" when referring to the speaker in a poem.

Another area of difficulty in reading this poem involves the vocabulary of the poet. Although words like "nipperkin" and " 'list" would be familiar to readers in Hardy's time, they are alien to contemporary readers. In the first case, the phrase "wet right many a nipperkin" can be translated as "drink some beers." In the second, " 'list" is simply a contraction of the word "enlist."

Although the distinctions in vocabulary and circumstances between the early 20th and the early 21st centuries are important and should be considered, the similarities between the two eras are perhaps more significant. As you read this poem, think about the ways in which the thoughts expressed by this soldier in World War I could be those of a contemporary soldier.

The Man He Killed

"Had he and I but met
        By some old ancient inn,
We should have sat us down to wet
        Right many a nipperkin!

"But ranged as infantry,   5
        And staring face to face,
I shot at him and he at me,
        And killed him in his place.

"I shot him dead because—
        Because he was my foe,   10
Just so—my foe of course he was;
        That's clear enough; although

"He thought he'd 'list perhaps,
        Off-hand like—just as I—

15   Was out of work—had sold his traps—
  No other reason why.

  "Yes; quaint and curious war is!
  You shoot a fellow down
You'd treat if met where any bar is,
20   Or help to half-a-crown."

Questions for Discussion and Your Reading Journal

1. Why did the two soldiers (on opposite sides) enlist in the infantry? In what ways are they similar to one another? In what ways are they similar to soldiers of today? How are they different from soldiers of today? Explain the significance of these similarities and differences.
2. In what places were you startled or surprised as you read the poem? How is the poem constructed to cause your reaction of surprise? Why do you think it is constructed that way?
3. Describe the tone of the poem. Does the tone seem appropriate to the subject? How does the tone affect the way you interpret the poem's message?

ANTHONY HECHT

Anthony Hecht was born in New York City in 1923. Hecht attended Bard College, from which he received a B.A. in 1944. After 3 years in the U.S. Army, serving in Europe and Japan, he continued his education at Columbia University, earning an M.A. in 1950. Hecht has taught at several universities, including the University of Rochester, and is currently a professor in the graduate school of Georgetown University. He was awarded the Pulitzer Prize for The Hard Hours *(1967). His most recent books of poetry are* The Transparent Man *(1990) and* Collected Earlier Poems *(1990). A Chancellor Emeritus of The Academy of American Poets, he lives in Washington, D.C.*

Hecht's early poetry is acclaimed for its technical brilliance and inventiveness, but it is in his later poems, such as "More Light! More Light!" that Hecht begins seriously to examine the themes and subjects he finds moving and important He was appalled by what he witnessed during World War II, and the following poem expresses his horror at the atrocities of the Holocaust.

Reading Rhetorically

This poem is the first in a series of readings about the horrors of war. War is the subject of a great deal of the world's greatest art and literature. As you read this poem, look for ideas about war with which you are familiar, as well as those that are new to you. Mark any words or phrases that stick out as you read them. Later you may want to go back to those marked sections and think about the reasons for their effect on you *(pathos)*.

Darkness and light have traditionally symbolized evil and good, as well as the power that shields evil and the force that brings truth from hiding. As you examine this poem, take note of (you may want to mark with underlining) the images of darkness and those of light to see how they correspond with the evil perpetrated during the Holocaust.

More Light! More Light!¹

For Heinrich Blücher and Hannah Arendt²

Composed in the Tower before his execution
These moving verses, and being brought at that time
Painfully to the stake, submitted, declaring thus:
"I implore my God to witness that I have made no crime."

Nor was he forsaken of courage, but the death was horrible,   5
The sack of gunpowder failing to ignite.
His legs were blistered sticks on which the black sap
Bubbled and burst as he howled for the Kindly Light.³

And that was but one, and by no means one of the worst;
Permitted at least his pitiful dignity;   10
And such as were by made prayers in the name of Christ,
That shall judge all men, for his soul's tranquility.

We move now to outside a German wood⁴
Three men are there commanded to dig a hole
In which the two Jews are ordered to lie down   15
And be buried alive by the third, who is a Pole.

---

¹The last words of the German poet Goethe (1749–1832).

²Hannah Arendt, author of a number of books on anti-Semitism and totalitarianism (including *Eichmann in Jerusalem: A Report of the Banality of Evil*) emigrated from Germany to the United States with her husband Heinrich Blücher in 1941. [Ed. note.]

³The details are conflated from several executions, including Latimer and Ridley [Bishops of the Anglican Church who were executed in 1555 for their religious beliefs] whose deaths at the stake are described by Foxe in *Acts and Monuments*. But neither of them wrote poems just before their deaths, as others did. [Hecht's note].

⁴The place described is the Nazi concentration camp Buchenwald. The incident described took place in 1944 and is documented in Eugen Kogon's *The Theory and Practice of Hell* (New York, 1958). [Ed. note.]

Not light from the shrine at Weimar[5] beyond the hill
Nor light from heaven appeared. But he did refuse.
A Lüger settled back deeply in its glove.
20 He was ordered to change places with the Jews.

Much casual death had drained away their souls.
The thick dirt mounted toward the quivering chin.
When only the head was exposed the order came
To dig him out again and to get back in.

25 No light, no light in the blue Polish eye.
When he finished a riding boot packed down the earth.
The Lüger hovered lightly in its glove.
He was shot in the belly and in three hours bled to death.

No prayers or incense rose up in those hours
30 Which grew to be years, and every day came mute
Ghosts from the ovens, sifting through crisp air,
And settled upon his eyes in a black soot.

1967

Questions for Discussion and Your Reading Journal

1. Discuss Hecht's use of the word "light" in this poem. What different meanings and connotations does it have with each use?
2. Describe the two different executions Hecht presents. What similarities and differences do you see? Does he seem to think one of the executions is worse than the other? If so, why?
3. In Line 21, Hecht says of the Jews: "Much casual death had drained away their souls." Do you think he feels this excuses their actions?
4. Describe the change the Pole undergoes. How would you characterize Hecht's attitude toward him?
5. In your own words, explain the metaphor of the final stanza.

MURIEL RUKEYSER

Muriel Rukeyser (1913–1980) was born in New York to wealthy parents; she attended prestigious schools in her childhood and as a young adult. Although she went to Vassar College for 2 years, she was frustrated by the passivity involved in being a student, and she moved back to New York to lead a more active life. After college Rukeyser worked as an editor, and during this time she witnessed a number of violent and

---

[5]Weimar is the city where Goethe lived most of his life. The German government between the two world wars was called the Weimar Republic; it was so named because the national assembly drawing up the new constitution after World War I met in the town identified with Goethe to symbolize the break with Prussian militarism. [Ed. note.]

unjust events that led her to use poetry as a vehicle for social protest. Rukeyser's sense of responsibility in relation to social justice was often focused on issues of race, class, and gender.

Rukeyser experimented with language and structure, extending to her poetry the same kind of intellectual fervor that characterized her journalism. The range of Rukeyser's work is clearly evident in her Collected Poems (1979). *Many women poets, including Anne Sexton, have remarked that Rukeyser's poetry influenced their own. Rukeyser died in New York City in 1980.*

Among Rukeyser's many poetic subjects are women's rights, religious oppression, and the injustices of Western capitalism. In the following excerpt from "Letter to the Front," Rukeyser examines her Jewish heritage, especially in light of the horrors of the holocaust.

Reading Rhetorically

This poem strikes many readers as being both intellectual and emotionally moving. It requires careful reading and interpretation. As you read you may want to mark words and phrases that are particularly difficult to decipher. After you have read the poem once, you can go back and examine these difficult parts and then read the poem again with more understanding.

Sometimes words and ideas that appear to be opposites are actually connected in unexpected ways. In this poem, the concept of "gift" is equated with the idea of "torment." How can torment be a gift? As you read this poem, follow the connections between the ideas connoted by the words "gift," "torment," and "freedom." The logic that connects these ideas goes beyond simple oppositions and dichotomies.

Letter to the Front

To be a Jew in the twentieth century
Is to be offered a gift. If you refuse,
Wishing to be invisible, you choose
Death of the spirit, the stone insanity.
Accepting, take full life. Full agonies: 5
Your evening deep in labyrinthine blood
Of those who resist, fail, and resist; and God
Reduced to a hostage among hostages.

The gift is torment. Not alone the still
Torture, isolation; or torture of the flesh.   10
That may come also. But the accepting wish,
The whole and fertile spirit as guarantee
For every human freedom, suffering to be free,
Daring to live for the impossible.

1944

Questions for Discussion and Your Reading Journal

1. What, according to Rukeyser, are the rewards and difficulties for a Jew of accepting the Jewish heritage? Of rejecting Judaism? Which choice is portrayed more positively?
2. Explain, using examples from the poem.
3. What is "the impossible" of the last line of the poem?
4. What do you think was Rukeyser's purpose in writing this poem? Who is her audience? What is her relationship to this audience?
5. Discuss this poem in relation to Anthony Hecht's "More, Light! More, Light!" (p. 349). What themes are common to both? What are the similarities and differences in image, tone, and purpose?

WILLIAM BUTLER YEATS

Irish poet William Butler Yeats (1865–1939) is one of the more important poets of the 20th century. He also has remained one of the more controversial, accused of fascism and ridiculed for his preoccupation with the occult. His writings display a body of knowledge that is impressively large and eclectic, a combination of Eastern and Western culture, ancient and modern thought; yet he always remains an Irish poet.

Yeats was born in Dublin, Ireland, in 1865, the son of a well-known Irish painter, John Butler Yeats. He spent his childhood in Ireland and much of his adolescence in London. Yeats returned to Dublin at the age of 15 to study painting but quickly changed his course of study to poetry. During this time he became involved with the Celtic Revival, a movement against the cultural and political influence of England, and his poetry is often grounded in Irish mythology and folklore. He was awarded the Nobel Prize in 1923 and died in 1939 at the age of 73.

The following poem is Yeats's tribute to the Easter Rebellion of April 24, 1916, in which a group of Irish nationalists briefly took control of a post office and some other buildings in Dublin. The rebels, some of whom are named in Lines 75 and 76 of the poem, were captured and executed by authorities. Yeats was acquainted with several of these people before the rebellion, and in his poem he traces the "transformation" they have achieved by their actions.

Reading Rhetorically

Although many poems are easy to read and understand using their language alone, others come out of a particular historical and literary context that needs to be explained in order for the poem to be fully understood. The footnotes that accompany this poem provide the historical and literary context that will allow you to more fully appreciate it. Pay particular attention to this poem's footnotes as you read and study it.

Easter 1916

I have met them at close of day
Coming with vivid faces
From counter or desk among grey
Eighteenth-century houses.
I have passed with a nod of the head   5
Or polite meaningless words,
Or have lingered awhile and said
Polite meaningless words,
And thought before I had done
Of a mocking tale or a gibe   10
To please a companion
Around the fire at the club,
Being certain that they and I
But lived where motley is worn:
All changed, changed utterly: 15
A terrible beauty is born.[1]

That woman's days were spent
In ignorant good-will,
Her nights in argument
Until her voice grew shrill.   20
What voice more sweet than hers
When, young and beautiful,
She rode to harriers?[2]
This man had kept a school
And rode our winged horse;[3]   25
This other his helper and friend[4]
Was coming into his force;
He might have won fame in the end,
So sensitive his nature seemed,
So daring and sweet his thought.   30
This other man I had dreamed
A drunken, vainglorious lout.[5]
He had done most bitter wrong

---

[1]The "terrible beauty" refers to the sacrifice of the rebel leaders as it coincides with the day celebrating Christ's resurrection.

[2]Countess Markiewicz (Constance Gore-Booth, 1868–1927), who took part in the rebellion. A harrier is a hound used for hunting rabbits.

[3]Patrick Pearse (1879–1916) founded a school for boys near Dublin and wrote poetry (Pegasus is the winged horse of Greek mythology, a symbol of immortality). He was the leader of the rebellion.

[4]Thomas MacDonagh (1878–1916) was Pearse's friend and also a poet.

[5]Major John MacBride, the estranged husband of Maud Gonne (the Irish nationalist and actress, with whom Yeats was in love).

To some who are near my heart,
35 Yet I number him in the song;
He, too, has resigned his part
In the casual comedy;
He, too, has been changed in his turn,
Transformed utterly:
40 A terrible beauty is born.

Hearts with one purpose alone
Through summer and winter seem
Enchanted to a stone
To trouble the living stream.
45 The horse that comes from the road,
The rider, the birds that range
From cloud to tumbling cloud,
Minute by minute they change;
A shadow of cloud on the stream
50 Changes minute by minute;
A horse-hoof slides on the brim,
And a horse plashes within it;
The long-legged moor-hens dive,
And hens to moor-cocks call;
55 Minute by minute they live:
The stone's in the midst of all.

Too long a sacrifice
Can make a stone of the heart.
O when may it suffice?
60 That is Heaven's part, our part
To murmur name upon name,
As a mother names her child
When sleep at last has come
On limbs that had run wild.
65 What is it but nightfall?
No, no, not night but death;
Was it needless death after all?
For England may keep faith

For all that is done and said.[6]
70 We know their dream; enough
To know they dreamed and are dead;
And what if excess of love
Bewildered[7] them till they died?
I write it out in a verse—
75 MacDonagh and MacBride

---

[6]England had promised Ireland home rule.

[7]This word can mean "made wild" as well as "confused."

And Connolly and Pearse
Now and in time to be,
Wherever green is worn,
Are changed, changed utterly:
A terrible beauty is born.   80

Questions for Discussion and Your Reading Journal

1. Describe the progress of Yeats's attitude toward the leaders of the Easter Rebellion, as related in this poem. How does he feel about each of them before the demonstration? Afterward?
2. Given the fate of these Irish Nationalists (Line 66), what is the significance of the refrain, "A terrible beauty is born"? How does Yeats connect Dublin's Easter Rebellion with the events of the first Easter?
3. Although the title of this poem is "Easter 1916," the poem barely touches on the actual events that occurred on this day. What might have been Yeats's purpose in focusing on the leaders of the rebellion rather than on the event itself?
4. Compare and contrast the theme of change and transformation in this poem with the imagery of stones. What does Yeats associate with each of these ideas? What connotations are they given?

THE ENVIRONMENT/THE GARDEN IN GLOBAL CONTEXTS

ALICE WALKER

Alice Walker (1944–), probably best known as the author of The Color Purple, *has created a body of fiction, nonfiction, and poetry that has done much to restore to African-Americans the history of their experiences here—a history that previously had been lost, forgotten, or relegated to library basements.*

Walker was born in Eatonton, Georgia, the youngest child in a large sharecropping family. In 1965 she graduated from Sarah Lawrence College and went on to teach at several schools, among them Wellesley College; Yale University; and the University of California, Berkeley. She also worked as an editor of Ms. *magazine. Her writings have earned her the highest respect, as well as a Guggenheim Fellowship and a fellowship from the National Endowment for the Arts. The essay reprinted here touches upon many important issues raised elsewhere in this anthology; the experience of African-Americans (especially women) in America, the power and value of art, the oppression of women and their struggle for self-expression, and the significance of the family and its transmission of cultural heritage.*

Reading Rhetorically

This essay is the first in a series of texts about gardens and what they represent in various cultures. Although most people think of a garden as a source of food and a place where workers sweat and toil, they are also a source of beauty and inspiration to both the people who grow them and those who observe them.

This essay about gardens combines prose and poetry. The poetry functions in a particular way to support the prose. As you read, look for the ways in which the poetry complements the prose. You may even want to write your ideas in the margins of the textbook. After you have finished reading, go back to examine the poetry again. In particular, look at the last poem. It uses powerfully moving images to bring together all the pieces woven into the essay.

In Search of Our Mothers' Gardens

"I described her own nature and temperament. Told how they needed a larger life for their expression. . . . I pointed out that in lieu of proper channels, her emotions had overflowed into paths that dissipated them. I talked, beautifully I thought, about an art that would be born, an art that would open the way for women the likes of her. I asked her to hope, and build up an inner life against the coming of that day. . . . I sang, with a strange quiver in my voice, a promise song."

"Avey," JEAN TOOMER, *Cane*
The poet speaking to a prostitute
who falls asleep while he's talking

1   When the poet Jean Toomer walked through the South in the early twenties, he discovered a curious thing: Black women whose spirituality was so intense, so deep, so *unconscious,* they were themselves unaware of the richness they held. They stumbled blindly through their lives: creatures so abused and mutilated in body, so dimmed and confused by pain, that they considered themselves unworthy even of hope. In the selfless abstractions their bodies became to the men who used them, they became more than "sexual objects," more even than mere women: They became "Saints." Instead of being perceived as whole persons, their bodies became shrines: What was thought to be their minds became temples suitable for worship. These crazy Saints stared out at the world, wildly, like lunatics—or quietly, like suicides; and the "God" that was in their gaze was as mute as a great stone.

2   Who were these Saints? These crazy, loony, pitiful women?

3   Some of them, without a doubt, were our mothers and grandmothers.

4   In the still heat of the post-Reconstruction South, this is how they seemed to Jean Toomer: exquisite butterflies trapped in an evil honey, toiling away their lives in an era, a century, that did not acknowledge them, except as "the *mule* of the world." They dreamed dreams that no one knew—not even them-

selves, in any coherent fashion—and saw visions no one could understand. They wandered or sat about the countryside crooning lullabies to ghosts, and drawing the mother of Christ in charcoal on courthouse walls.

They forced their minds to desert their bodies and their striving spirits 5 sought to rise, like frail whirlwinds from the hard red clay. And when those frail whirlwinds fell, in scattered particles, upon the ground, no one mourned. Instead, men lit candles to celebrate the emptiness that remained, as people do who enter a beautiful but vacant space to resurrect a God.

Our mothers and grandmothers, some of them: moving to music not yet 6 written. And they waited.

They waited for a day when the unknown thing that was in them would 7 be made known; but guessed, somehow in their darkness, that on the day of their revelation they would be long dead. Therefore to Toomer they walked, and even ran, in slow motion. For they were going nowhere immediate, and the future was not yet within their grasp. And men took our mothers and grandmothers, "but got no pleasure from it." So complex was their passion and their calm.

To Toomer, they lay vacant and fallow as autumn fields, with harvest time 8 never in sight: And he saw them enter loveless marriages, without joy; and become prostitutes, without resistance; and become mothers of children, without fulfillment.

For these grandmothers and mothers of ours were not Saints, but Artists; 9 driven to a numb and bleeding madness by the springs of creativity in them for which there was no release. They were Creators, who lived lives of spiritual waste, because they were so rich in spirituality—which is the basis of Art—that the strain of enduring their unused and unwanted talent drove them insane. Throwing away this spirituality was their pathetic attempt to lighten the soul to a weight their workworn, sexually abused bodies could bear.

What did it mean for a black woman to be an artist in our grandmothers' 10 time? In our great-grandmothers' day? It is a question with an answer cruel enough to stop the blood.

Did you have a genius of a great-great-grandmother who died under some 11 ignorant and depraved white overseer's lash? Or was she required to bake biscuits for a lazy backwater tramp, when she cried out in her soul to paint watercolors of sunsets, or the rain falling on the green and peaceful pasturelands? Or was her body broken and forced to bear children (who were more often than not sold away from her)—eight, ten, fifteen, twenty children—when her one joy was the thought of modeling heroic figures of rebellion, in stone or clay?

How was the creativity of the black woman kept alive, year after year and 12 century after century, when for most of the years black people have been in America, it was a punishable crime for a black person to read or write? And the freedom to paint, to sculpt, to expand the mind with action did not exist. Consider, if you can bear to imagine it, what might have been the result if singing, too, had been forbidden by law. Listen to the voices of Bessie Smith, Billie Holiday, Nina Simone, Roberta Flack, and Aretha Franklin, among others, and imagine those voices muzzled for life. Then you may begin to comprehend the lives of our "crazy," "Sainted" mothers and grandmothers. The agony of the lives of women who might have been Poets, Novelists, Essayists, and Short-Story Writers (over a period of centuries), who died with their real gifts stifled within them.

13   And, if this were the end of the story, we would have cause to cry out in my paraphrase of Okot p'Bitek's great poem:

O, my clanswomen
Let us all cry together!
Come,
Let us mourn the death of our mother,
The death of a Queen
The ash that was produced
By a great fire!
O, this homestead is utterly dead
Close the gates
With *lacari* thorns,
For our mother
The creator of the Stool is lost!
And all the young men
Have perished in the wilderness!

14   But this is not the end of the story, for all the young women—our mothers and grandmothers, *ourselves*—have not perished in the wilderness. And if we ask ourselves why, and search for and find the answer, we will know beyond all efforts to erase it from our minds, just exactly who, and of what, we black American women are.

15   One example, perhaps the most pathetic, most misunderstood one, can provide a backdrop for our mothers' work: Phillis Wheatley, a slave in the 1700s.

16   Virginia Woolf, in her book *A Room of One's Own,* wrote that in order for a woman to write fiction she must have two things, certainly: a room of her own (with key and lock) and enough money to support herself.

17   What then are we to make of Phillis Wheatley, a slave, who owned not even herself? This sickly, frail black girl who required a servant of her own at times—her health was so precarious—and who, had she been white, would have been easily considered the intellectual superior of all the women and most of the men in the society of her day.

18   Virginia Woolf wrote further, speaking of course not of our Phillis, that "any woman born with a great gift in the sixteenth century [insert "eighteenth century," insert "black woman," insert "born or made a slave"] would certainly have gone crazed, shot herself, or ended her days in some lonely cottage outside the village, half witch, half wizard [insert "Saint"], feared and mocked at. For it needs little skill and psychology to be sure that a highly gifted girl who had tried to use her gift of poetry would have been so thwarted and hindered by contrary instincts [add "chains, guns, the lash, the ownership of one's body by someone else, submission to an alien religion"], that she must have lost her health and sanity to a certainty."

19   The key words, as they relate to Phillis, are "contrary instincts." For when we read the poetry of Phillis Wheatley—as when we read the novels of Nella

Larsen or the oddly false-sounding autobiography of that freest of all black women writers, Zora Hurston—evidence of "contrary instincts" is everywhere. Her loyalties were completely divided, as was, without question, her mind.

But how could this be otherwise? Captured at seven, a slave of wealthy,   20
doting whites who instilled in her the "savagery" of the Africa they "rescued" her from . . . one wonders if she was even able to remember her homeland as she had known it, or as it really was.

Yet, because she did try to use her gift for poetry in a world that made her   21
a slave, she was "so thwarted and hindered by . . . contrary instincts, that she . . . lost her health. . . ." In the last years of her brief life, burdened not only with the need to express her gift but also with a penniless, friendless "freedom" and several small children for whom she was forced to do strenuous work to feed, she lost her health, certainly. Suffering from malnutrition and neglect and who knows what mental agonies, Phillis Wheatley died.

So torn by "contrary instincts" was black, kidnapped, enslaved Phillis that   22
her description of "the Goddess"—as she poetically called the Liberty she did not have—is ironically, cruelly humorous. And, in fact, has held Phillis up to ridicule for more than a century. It is usually read prior to hanging Phillis's memory as that of a fool. She wrote:

The Goddess comes, she moves divinely fair,   23
Olive and laurel binds her *golden* hair.
Wherever shines this native of the skies,
Unnumber'd charms and recent graces rise. [My italics]

It is obvious that Phillis, the slave, combed the "Goddess's" hair every   23
morning; prior, perhaps, to bringing in the milk, or fixing her mistress's lunch. She took her imagery from the one thing she saw elevated above all others.

With the benefit of hindsight we ask, "How could she?"   24

But at last, Phillis, we understand. No more snickering when your stiff,   25
struggling, ambivalent lines are forced on us. We know now that you were not an idiot or a traitor; only a sickly little black girl, snatched from your home and country and made a slave; a woman who still struggled to sing the song that was your gift, although in a land of barbarians who praised you for your bewildered tongue. It is not so much what you sang, as that you kept alive, in so many of our ancestors, *the notion of song.*

Black women are called, in the folklore that so aptly identified one's status   26
society, "the *mule* of the world," because we have been handed the burdens that everyone else—*everyone* else—refused to carry. We have also been called "Matriarchs," " Superwomen," and "Mean and Evil Bitches." Not to mention "Castraters" and "Sapphire's Mama." When we have pleaded for understanding, our character has been distorted; when we have asked for simple caring, we have been handed empty inspirational appellations, then stuck in the farthest corner. When we have asked for love, we have been given children. In short, even our plainer gifts, our labors of fidelity and love, have been knocked down our throats. To be an artist and a black woman, even today, lowers our status in many respects, rather than raises it: And yet, artists we will be.

27   Therefore we must fearlessly pull out of ourselves and look at and identify with our lives the living creativity some of our great-grandmothers were not allowed to know. I stress *some* of them because it is well known that the majority of our great-grandmothers knew, even without "knowing" it, the reality of their spirituality, even if they didn't recognize it beyond what happened in the singing at church—and they never had any intention of giving it up.

28   How they did it—those millions of black women who were not Phillis Wheatley, or Lucy Terry or Frances Harper or Zora Hurston or Nella Larsen or Bessie Smith; or Elizabeth Catlett, or Katherine Dunham, either—brings me to the title of this essay, "In Search of Our Mothers' Gardens," which is a personal account that is yet shared, in its theme and its meaning, by all of us. I found, while thinking about the far-reaching world of the creative black woman, that often the truest answer to a question that really matters can be found very close.

29   In the late 1920s my mother ran away from home to marry my father. Marriage, if not running away, was expected of seventeen-year-old girls. By the time she was twenty, she had two children and was pregnant with a third. Five children later, I was born. And this is how I came to know my mother: She seemed a large, soft, loving-eyed woman who was rarely impatient in our home. Her quick, violent temper was on view only a few times a year, when she battled with the white landlord who had the misfortune to suggest to her that her children did not need to go to school.

30   She made all the clothes we wore, even my brothers' overalls. She made all the towels and sheets we used. She spent the summers canning vegetables and fruits. She spent the winter evenings making quilts enough to cover all our beds.

31   During the "working" day, she labored beside—not behind—my father in the fields. Her day began before sunup, and did not end until late at night. There was never a moment for her to sit down, undisturbed, to unravel her own private thoughts; never a time free from interruption—by work or the noisy inquiries of her many children. And yet, it is to my mother—and all our mothers who were not famous—that I went in search of the secret of what has fed that muzzled and often mutilated, but vibrant, creative spirit that the black woman has inherited, and that pops out in wild and unlikely places to this day.

32   But when, you will ask, did my overworked mother have time to know or care about feeding the creative spirit?

33   The answer is so simple that many of us have spent years discovering it. We have constantly looked high, when we should have looked high—and low.

34   For example: In the Smithsonian Institution in Washington, D.C., there hangs a quilt unlike any other in the world. In fanciful, inspired, and yet simple and identifiable figures, it portrays the story of the Crucifixion. It is considered rare, beyond price. Though it follows no known pattern of quilt-making, and though it is made of bits and pieces of worthless rags, it is obviously the work of a person of powerful imagination and deep spiritual feeling. Below this quilt I saw a note that says it was made by "an anonymous Black woman in Alabama, a hundred years ago."

If we could locate this "anonymous" black woman from Alabama, she   35
would turn out to be one of our grandmothers—an artist who left her mark in
the only materials she could afford, and in the only medium her position in
society allowed her to use.

As Virginia Woolf wrote further, in *A Room of One's Own:*   36

> Yet genius of a sort must have existed among women as it must have existed   37
> among the working class. [Change this to "slaves" and "the wives and
> daughters of sharecroppers."] Now and again an Emily Brontë or a Robert
> Burns [change this to "a Zora Hurston or a Richard Wright"] blazes out
> and proves its presence. But certainly it never got itself on to paper. When,
> however, one reads of a witch being ducked, of a woman possessed by dev-
> ils [or "Sainthood"], of a wise woman selling herbs [our root workers], or
> even a very remarkable man who had a mother, then I think we are on the
> track of a lost novelist, a suppressed poet, or some mute and inglorious Jane
> Austen. . . . Indeed, I would venture to guess that Anon, who wrote so
> many poems without signing them, was often a woman. . . .

And so our mothers and grandmothers have, more often than not anony-   38
mously, handed on the creative spark, the seed of the flower they themselves
never hoped to see: or like a sealed letter they could not plainly read.

And so it is, certainly, with my own mother. Unlike "Ma" Rainey's songs,   39
which retained their creator's name even while blasting forth from Bessie
Smith's mouth, no song or poem will bear my mother's name. Yet so many of
the stories that I write, that we all write, are my mother's stories. Only recently
did I fully realize this: that through years of listening to my mother's stories of
her life, I have absorbed not only the stories themselves, but something of the
manner in which she spoke, something of the urgency that involves the knowledge that her stories—like her life—must be recorded. It is probably for this
reason that so much of what I have written is about characters whose counterparts in real life are so much older than I am.

But the telling of these stories, which came from my mother's lips as nat-   40
urally as breathing, was not the only way my mother showed herself as an
artist. For stories, too, were subject to being distracted, to dying without conclusion. Dinners must be started, and cotton must be gathered before the big
rains. The artist that was and is my mother showed itself to me only after
many years. This is what I finally noticed:

Like Mem, a character in *The Third Life of Grange Copeland,* my mother   41
adorned with flowers whatever shabby house we were forced to live in. And
not just your typical straggly country stand of zinnias, either. She planted
ambitious gardens—and still does—with over fifty different varieties of plants
that bloom profusely from early March until late November. Before she left
home for the fields, she watered her flowers, chopped up the grass, and laid
out new beds. When she returned from the fields she might divide clumps of
bulbs, dig a cold pit, uproot and replant roses, or prune branches from her
taller bushes or trees—until night came and it was too dark to see.

Whatever she planted grew as if by magic, and her fame as a grower of flow-   42
ers spread over three counties. Because of her creativity with her flowers, even

my memories of poverty are seen through a screen of blooms—sunflowers, petunias, roses, dahlias, forsythia, spirea, delphiniums, verbena . . . and on and on.

43   And I remember people coming to my mother's yard to be given cuttings from her flowers; I hear again the praise showered on her because whatever rocky soil she landed on, she turned into a garden. A garden so brilliant with colors, so original in its design, so magnificent with life and creativity, that to this day people drive by our house in Georgia—perfect strangers and imperfect strangers—and ask to stand or walk among my mother's art.

44   I notice that it is only when my mother is working in her flowers that she is radiant, almost to the point of being invisible—except as Creator: hand and eye. She is involved in work her soul must have. Ordering the universe in the image of her personal conception of Beauty.

45   Her face, as she prepares the Art that is her gift, is a legacy of respect she leaves to me, for all that illuminates and cherishes life. She has handed down respect for the possibilities—and the will to grasp them.

46   For her, so hindered and intruded upon in so many ways, being an artist has still been a daily part of her life. This ability to hold on, even in very simple ways, is work black women have done for a very long time.

47   This poem is not enough, but it is something, for the woman who literally covered the holes in our walls with sunflowers:

They were women then
My mama's generation
Husky of voice—Stout of
Step
With fists as well as
Hands
How they battered down
Doors
And ironed
Starched white
Shirts
How they led
Armies
Headragged Generals
Across mined
Fields
Booby-trapped
Kitchens
To discover books
Desks
A place for us
How they knew that we
Must know
Without knowing a page
Of it
Themselves

Guided by my heritage of a love of beauty and a respect for strength—in 48
search of my mother's garden, I found my own.

And perhaps in Africa over two hundred years ago, there was just such a 49
mother; perhaps she painted vivid and daring decorations in oranges and yel-
lows and greens on the walls of her hut; perhaps she sang—in a voice like
Roberta Flack's—*sweetly* over the compounds of her village; perhaps she wove
the most stunning mats or told the most ingenious stories of all the village storytellers. Perhaps she was herself a poet—though only her daughter's name is
signed to the poems that we know.

Perhaps Phillis Wheatley's mother was also an artist. 50

Perhaps in more than Phillis Wheatley's biological life is her mother's sig- 51
nature made clear.

Questions for Discussion and Your Reading Journal

1. What does Walker mean when she says spirituality "is the basis of Art" (Paragraph 8)?
2. What role does the story of Phillis Wheatley play in this essay? How do her experiences illustrate the "contrary instincts" faced by African-American women in their struggle for freedom and self-expression?
3. Describe the "Goddess" Phillis Wheatley esteemed so highly. How is this Goddess different from Alice Walker's heroines?
4. How did Walker's mother teach her about art? How might Walker define art? Support your answer with examples from her essay.
5. How would Walker agree or disagree with the definitions of poetry represented by Jon Stallworthy's "Letter to a Friend," Marianne Moore's "Poetry," and Javier Heraud's "Ars Poetica"?

CHRIS MASER

Chris Maser is a research scientist in forest ecology and a consultant to government agencies around the world. In his work he advocates bringing sacred appreciation of nature into both large-scale resource management and the average person's life. In his book Global Imperative: Harmonizing Culture and Nature, *from which the following essay is taken, he argues for a change in our attitude toward nature from one of control to one of cooperation; we need, he says, to work out a balance between our culture's needs and the capacity of nature to sustain its equilibrium. In the section of his book just preceding this excerpt, Maser states that we need to focus on caring for the environment, integrating such things as agricultural and livestock-grazing needs with the need for protecting biodiversity. We must, he says, stop trying to "manage" nature through technology and move toward "connectivity" of the landscape, working within nature's evolved patterns.*

Reading Rhetorically

The author of this essay, Chris Maser, is a research scientist, but here he focuses not on the scientific aspects of ecological preservation but on developing a spiritual connection with the natural world. If you compare this essay about environmentalism with those in the science chapter (Chapter 4), you will see that a writer's attitude toward a subject, not the subject itself, is more salient in determining the genre of his writing. At the same time, it is important to remember that genres are not discreet categories—they often have overlapping commonalities.

Assuming that this text belongs in the same genre as the one that precedes it, Alice Walker's "In Search of Our Mothers' Gardens," you might call it a "literary essay." Look for the literary characteristics of this essay that distinguish it from the scientific articles in the chapter on Science and Technology.

The Window of Our Cultural Soul

The shift from attempting to "manage" Nature through economics, science, and technology (which all too often assumes the attitude of pillaging) to the sacred act of gardening with Nature through spirituality and art is a shift from the intellectual pursuit of arrogance through coercion and control to the spiritual pursuit of humility through cooperation and coordination. To understand this shift, however, we must first have some concept of the meaning embodied in the words "spirituality" and "art."

SPIRITUALITY

1   " 'Spiritual' refers to the experience of being related to or in touch with an 'other' that transcends one's individual sense of self and gives meaning to one's life at a deeper than intellectual level."[1] In a spiritual experience, therefore, one encounters something larger or greater than oneself. We need not conceptualize the "other" that we encounter in any traditionally religious terms.

2   The transcendent other may be seen as a supernatural deity, such as God, or as a natural entity, such as the Earth. It may be something existing objectively "out there," like the process of evolution, or it may be a subjective inner phenomenon like creative inspiration. It may originate independently of the human sphere, like wilderness, or it may be a product of human culture, like a community. For some people, the "other" may not even be a specific, definable entity but might instead be an undefinable sense of being "grounded" or "centered," a feeling that gives meaning to existence.

3   Regardless of the way this sense of the transcendent "other" is encountered and experienced, it is more than just a passing, casual occurrence. It gives meaning to one's life in some important way and helps define one's life in the greater context of the Universe. The experience is felt at some undefinable level of "knowing" that is far deeper than that of intellectual knowledge. It is usually

difficult if not impossible for us to put such an experience into words, but we feel it in our hearts, and it may stir powerful emotions in us. Although we encounter experiences of this kind in many contexts and settings, we may find their primary setting to be Nature.

Nature is often more than a setting for a spiritual experience. She can con- 4
jure other images in our personal and social psyches. According to psychologist Carl Jung, our human psyche has different levels or layers, much as an onion has a number of different layers. Immediately below the level of our conscious awareness lies the personal unconscious, including our personal feelings, attitudes, and memories, which we have repressed and "cut off" from our conscious awareness. At a deeper level lies what Jung called the "collective unconscious," which contains the basic, intuitive patterns of behavior, emotions, and imagery common to all humans through time. These intuitive patterns, or "archetypes," not only guide but also give meaning to our interactions with other human beings and with the Universe as a whole.

Archetypes function like templates in the unconscious mind, where they give 5
rise to the symbolic images that enter conscious expression through dreams, myths, religious experiences, and spontaneous fantasies. One of the most important ways in which archetypes express themselves is through both positive and negative "projection," a psychological phenomenon through which we experience the contents of the unconscious mind outside of ourselves as if they belonged to someone or something else. This is analogous to an image on film being projected or cast outward through the lens of the projector and viewed at some distance on a screen: A person sitting in the audience is unaware of the projector and perceives only the "independent" image on the screen.

A classic example of a negative projection with which I think we can all 6
identify is that of an "enemy." If I can identify an enemy, I can project (through my lens) the unconscious, repressed traits that I detest about myself and with which I refuse to deal (the film) onto someone or something else (the neutral, unaware screen). I can thus hate what I think my enemy stands for without having to acknowledge and deal with the fact that what I "see" in my enemy is my own repressed self-loathing. I think I can avoid dealing with my repressed self-loathing by projecting it onto the screen of an innocent person. In so doing, I think the unwanted reflection I see belongs to the other person rather than to my own inner self.

What, you might ask, has this got to do with spirituality and Nature? 7
Consider that Nature is viewed by some as an enemy to be conquered, by others as a commodity to be converted into money, and by still others as a representation of spirituality. All of these perceptions can be thought of as projections of unconscious archetypes onto various elements of the environment or onto Nature as a whole. Here, one might ask what is being projected onto Nature, why it is being projected, and what implications these projections may have both for the individual and for the collective psyche.

Today people turn to the literature of mythology in order to understand 8
the symbolic portrayals of the archetypes that are active in the collective psyche of human culture. . . .

9   The most compelling example is the archetype of the Great Mother, a powerful psychological complex that can have either a positive, nurturing effect or a negative, destructive effect on the psychological development of an individual. The concept of "Mother Nature" or "Mother Earth" in her benevolent and malevolent moods is a personification of this archetype, which is a recurrent and increasing projection onto Nature.

10   Unconscious archetypes have powerful effects on the way people experience, relate to, and behave in the world. It is therefore important for the conscious mind to be able to relate in a constructive way to the material of the unconscious archetypes. This conscious relation to the archetypes has traditionally been the function of mythological symbols, rites, and rituals of a religious nature. . . .

11   So long as the archetypal projections remain unconscious, there will be severe problems in our society, because we do not realize that our experiences come from within our psyches, and we will instead believe that they are due entirely to something "out there." Thus a person who is projecting an archetype tends to perceive the world in terms of subjective opposites, ideals, and absolutes, a projection that blinds the person to the objective nature of the "other" onto which the archetype is being projected. This blindness causes people to disregard objective information, to hold unrealistic expectations, and to behave in rigid, even fanatical ways. . . .

12   As we become aware of the way we project archetypes onto Nature, we acquire a sort of "double vision," and experiencing Nature becomes like peering out of a house through a pane of window glass. Through the window we see objects that lie outside the house, and simultaneously we see reflections of things that lie inside the house. Similarly, we can observe the workings of the outer world of Nature through physics and biology while at the same time Nature reflects back to us the inner workings and images of our own psychological world. This phenomenon is perhaps most clearly illustrated in the night sky, where stars and constellations bear names and images of our mythological heritage while concurrently serving as an entry into the scientific understanding of the physical universe. And it is through art that this "double vision" of the inner and the outer are expressed simultaneously.

ART

13   Art is not only the expression of this "double vision" but also a window to our souls. In this sense, art and mythology are one. They embody an inner experience expressed in an outer, symbolic manner through the conscious production or arrangement of sounds, colors, forms, movements, or other elements in a way that affects the sense of beauty, the sense of Self. Although most people probably think of art specifically as the production of beauty in a graphic or plastic medium, art also encompasses the sheer enjoyment of beauty for its own sake.

14   The historic foundations of much of our contemporary American sense of aesthetics in landscapes are found in European and American art and litera-

ture. The works of seventeenth-, eighteenth-, and nineteenth-century painters and critics concerned with the beauty of the fine arts both depicted and evoked images of neat, tidy landscapes. Although they bore a resemblance to Nature's landscapes, they had been cleansed of Nature's seemingly untidy aspects. . . .

During the eighteenth century, however, writers and painters began to see beauty in the apparently chaotic, clearly wild images of a continent with greater physical and biological diversity than that of Europe. Baron Fredrich von Humboldt of Germany was one of these people. As a founding father of modern geography, he was acutely aware of the effect beautiful landscapes had on the human imagination and of the relationship landscapes forged between our inner world of ideas and feelings and our outer world of physical things. Humboldt recognized the different quality of enjoyment and feelings evoked by viewing a forest or a meadow as opposed to those conjured by dissecting a plant. . . .

15

Despite advances in viewing landscapes with an eye toward their artistic beauty, Americans needed to evolve a landscape myth of place in time, a myth that would be unique to North America. Americans became increasingly convinced that transferring a sense of European landscape myth to the North American continent was no longer tenable. But it wasn't until the 1930s and 1940s that Aldo Leopold, the father of American ecology, gave voice to the need for a conscious "land aesthetic." Such an aesthetic, wrote Leopold, must deal not only with Nature's landscapes but also with humanity's cultural landscapes. It must be a land aesthetic grounded in ecological awareness and sensitivity as well as in sound landscape husbandry. . . .

16

Today there are two approaches to landscape, the objective and the subjective. The objective approach focuses on the visual aspects, which are composed of form and elements, and views human beings as separate from the landscape. The landscape can affect people and people can affect it through manipulation, but there is no "communication" between them—something that makes irrelevant a search for meaning in a landscape. This view allows for the concentration on specific elements of a landscape as commodities at the expense of the long-term health of the whole.

17

The subjective approach, on the other hand, offers insight into values and meanings. It attends to the structural and functional characteristics of a particular place as well as human responses to them. It can be thought of as the result of people projecting their archetypal emotions, feelings, and ideas onto their surroundings in such a way that a knowledge of the landscape is gained through personal interaction with it.

18

People "communicate" with the landscape. In so doing they change the landscape and are changed by it, because conversation is not limited to a discourse between humans or even to the present. And to converse with any part of Nature is to be in unity with it, whatever it is—even with the stars. So our communication with our respective landscapes is not only relevant but also critical both to the well-being of human society and to the long-term health of the landscapes themselves. That sort of communication brings us to the notion of gardening.

19

AND A SENSE OF GARDENING

20 Gardening is the act in which spirituality and art merge into the context of Nature's landscape. It is where we use the form and function of Universal Laws to transpose in graphic form the cultural beauty and spiritual harmony of our inner landscape to the fluid medium of Nature's outer landscape. Gardening is the conscious marriage of cultural myth and Universal Laws of Being. To garden is to bring Nature, art, and our souls into harmony with one another in such a way that one cannot tell where Nature ends and art begins, and vice versa. . . .

21 Only when we have the discipline to garden the inner landscape of our minds and our souls, weeding out all inharmonious thoughts, will our inner harmony be consummated in the outer landscape. Whether we wish to admit it or not, says ecological restorationist William Jordan, the world really is a garden that invites, even requires, our constant participation and habitation. In this sense, gardening the Earth means to negotiate a new reality with Nature, one that is based on Universal Laws and on our spiritual evolution, because the patterns created on the landscape by a society are a true "pictorial" reflection of its collective spiritual attainment and ecological understanding as well as the economics of its "management." Note that the root word for both *ecology* and *economics* is based on the Greek word for *house*. Ecology is the study of the house, and economics is its management.

22 I say "spiritual attainment," because gardening is an act born out of our love for the Earth. Love creates an openness to experience, an unfolding without judgment. It expands awareness of and compassion for oneself and others in relationship, and its intimacy permits connectivity of distance—even unto the generations of the future. Love personalizes the Universe while keeping it intrinsically free unto itself.

23 It was from this sense of a personalized, loving relationship with the Earth that Aldo Leopold wrote: "The average dolled-up estate merely proves what we will some day learn to acknowledge: that bread and beauty grow best together. Their harmonious integration can make farming not only a business but an art; the land not only a food-factory but an instrument for self-expression, on which each can play music of his own choosing." It is hard for us, said Leopold, to visualize that creating an artistically beautiful landscape is not the prerogative of "esthetic priests" but of "dirt farmers." A farmer designs fields with plowshare and seed; a farmer not only wields spade and pruning shears but also determines the presence or absence of plants and animals in a particular place and time. In this sweep of human thought are the seeds of change, "including, perhaps, a rebirth of that social dignity which ought to inhere in land-ownership."[2]

24 I would today change the notion of "land-*ownership*" to land-*trusteeship,* because we "own" nothing but our thoughts and our behavior. Everything else we merely borrow both from Nature and from our children, and their children, and theirs into the blue haze of the future's horizon. In addition, ownership connotes the present in the present for the present, but trusteeship connotes the maintenance and protection of the principle, held in trust by adults in the present for the benefit of the future—the children, the trustees.

I feel a sense of trusteeship when nature writer Wendell Berry writes about 25
farming, which, he says, "cannot take place except in nature; therefore, if
nature does not thrive, farming cannot thrive.". . . .

Farming is . . . "gardening" when it is done by Nature's measure, which 26
is predicated on the answers Nature has given to a farmer's questions about
his or her particular place. This means that "farmers must tend farms that they
know and love, farms small enough to know and love, using tools and methods that they know and love, in the company of neighbors that they know and
love."[3]

Gardening is giving to the Earth and all its inhabitants, including our- 27
selves, the only things of value that we each have to give: our love, our trust,
and our respect. The very process of gardening is thus the process through
which we become attuned with Nature and, through Nature, with ourselves.
To engage in the act of gardening is to commune with and to know the God
in ourselves, in one another, and in all of Nature. To treat the Earth in the
sacred manner of gardening as a vehicle to know God is our global imperative
if we want to coexist as truly equitable and peaceful human societies. To garden the earth is to love Nature.

Notes

1. Herbert W. Schroeder, "The Spiritual Aspect of Nature: A Perspective from
   Depth Psychology." *Proceedings of Northeastern Recreation Research
   Conference*, Saratoga Springs, NY, April 8, 1991 (in press).
2. Aldo Leopold, "The Conservation Ethic," *Journal of Forestry* 31 (1933):
   634–643.
3. Wendell Berry, "Taking Nature's Measure." *Harper's Magazine* March
   1990: 20–22.

Questions for Discussion and Your Reading Journal

1. How does Maser define spirituality? Art? What does he see as the link between the two? Compare his view of the connection between art and spirituality with Walker's. How are they alike? Where do they differ?
2. Note that Maser capitalizes the word "nature" throughout. What rhetorical effect does this have?
3. Compare Maser's discussion of the experience of the "other" to that of Simone de Beauvoir's "Women as Other" (found in Chapter 2). In what ways
   is nature treated as "other" in Western society?
4. Maser asserts that "Americans need to evolve a landscape myth of place
   and time" unique to North America. What do you think he means by this
   statement?
5. The essay outlines two approaches to landscape, objective and subjective.
   Explain in your own words what those approaches are. Then read the selections that follow this essay on the Chinese garden and the Islamic garden. Which approach is embodied in each of these two gardens?

MARGE PIERCY

Marge Piercy (1936–) was born, in Detroit, Michigan, into a family that had been affected very adversely by the Depression. Athough she was poor, Piercy's childhood was happy, partly because of her relation-ship with her maternal grandmother, a great storyteller. Piercy credits her mother, a highly imaginative woman, with influencing her to become a poet. Although she left home at 17, Piercy was able to attend the University of Michigan on scholarship. She was the first person in her family to go to college. She continued her education by earning an M.A. from Northwestern, where she had a fellowship.

Piercy's first years as a writer were very hard. She wrote several novels but could not get them published, partly, she believed, because she was a woman and partly because her work was so concerned with political issues. Like Simone de Beauvoir, she wanted to write about working-class people, women in particular, who were more complex and interesting than many other writers gave them credit for being. Although a great deal of her early career was spent in New York City, Piercy found the environment of the city unhealthful. She moved to Cape Cod in 1971. There she began gardening almost immediately. She loved working in the dirt—growing fruit and vegetables, as well as flowers. Piercy's poetic voice is characterized by a deep connection to nature.

Piercy has written a number of novels, among them Woman on the Edge of Time; *several volumes of poetry; and a collection of essays, reviews, and interviews entitled* Parti-Colored Blocks for a Quilt. *This poem, from* Stone, Paper, Knife *(1983), is one of a set of four having to do with the four ancient elements—earth, air, fire, and water. The poem celebrates the ecological side of feminism.*

Reading Rhetorically

Have you ever felt a special connection to a plot of earth, the yard of your childhood home, for instance, or your grandparents' garden? If so, you might have felt as though you wanted to talk to it, as a person might talk to the earth that makes up the burying place of a loved one.

In this poem, the poet persona speaks to a piece of land, which at times appears to be a simple garden and at other times seems to be Nature itself. In poetry the device of giving human qualities to nonhuman things (like gardens) is called "personification." When personification is used gracefully and intelli-gently, as it is here, it can arouse a powerful emotional response *(pathos)*. As you read and study this poem, notice the ways in which the garden is por-trayed in human terms and the response that portrayal evokes in you.

The Common Living Dirt

The small ears prick on the bushes,
furry buds, shoots tender and pale.
The swamp maples blow scarlet.
Color teases the corner of the eye,
delicate gold, chartreuse, crimson,   5
mauve speckled, just dashed on.

The soil stretches naked. All winter
hidden under the down comforter of snow,
delicious now, rich in the hand
as chocolate cake: the fragrant busy   10
soil the worm passes through her gut
and the beetle swims in like a lake.

As I kneel to put the seeds in
careful as stitching, I am in love.
You are the bed we all sleep on.   15
You are the food we eat, the food
we ate, the food we will become.
We are walking trees rooted in you.

You can live thousands of years
undressing in the spring your black   20
body, your red body, your brown body
penetrated by the rain. Here
is the goddess unveiled,
the earth opening her strong thighs.

Yet you grow exhausted with bearing   25
too much, too soon, too often, just
as a woman wears through like an old rug.
We have contempt for what we spring
from. Dirt, we say, you're dirt
as if we were not all your children.   30

We have lost the simplest gratitude.
We lack the knowledge we showed ten
thousand years past, that you live
a goddess but mortal, that what we take
must be returned; that the poison we drop   35
in you will stunt our children's growth.

Tending a plot of your flesh binds
me as nothing ever could, to the seasons,
to the will of the plants, clamorous

40 in their green tenderness. What
calls louder than the cry of a field
of corn ready, or trees of ripe peaches?

I worship on my knees, laying
the seeds in you, that worship rooted
45 in need, in hunger, in kinship,
flesh of the planet with my own flesh,
a ritual of compost, a litany of manure.
My garden's a chapel, but a meadow

gone wild in grass and flower
50 is a cathedral. How you seethe
with little quick ones, vole, field
mouse, shrew and mole in their thousands,
rabbit and woodchuck. In you rest
the jewels of the genes wrapped in seed.

55 Power warps because it involves joy
in domination; also because it means
forgetting how we too starve, break
like a corn stalk in the wind, how we
die like the spinach of drought,
60 how what slays the vole slays us.

Because you can die of overwork, because
you can die of the fire that melts
rock, because you can die of the poison
that kills the beetle and the slug,
65 we must come again to worship you
on our knees, the common living dirt.

Questions for Discussion and Your Reading Journal

1. The speaker addresses the poem to "you." Who or what is that "you"?
2. Discuss the various images the speaker uses to describe the earth in the first three stanzas. What effect do these images create?
3. Maser refers to the spiritual nature of gardening, as does Piercy in this poem. How does Piercy differ from Maser in the discussion of deity?
4. Paraphrase the second-to-last stanza of the poem as it relates to the essay by Maser.

SUSAN GRIFFIN

Susan Griffin is a writer who lives in Berkeley, California. Her books include Pornography and Silence: Culture's Revenge Against Nature *and a collection of poetry,* Unremembered Country. *She is currently working on a book about women and war. In the preface to* Women and Nature: The Roaring Inside Her, *from which the following selection is taken, Griffin states that the book began when she was asked to deliver a lecture on women and ecology: "I said in that lecture that women were always being asked to clean up, and to this I added the observation that men consider women to be more material than themselves, or more a part of nature. The fact that man does not consider himself a part of nature, but indeed considers himself superior to matter, seemed to me to gain significance when placed against man's attitude that woman is both inferior to him and closer to nature." The following selection draws an analogy between managing nature and managing an office.*

Reading Rhetorically

An analogy is a comparison between two things that are different in many ways but that have certain specific characteristics in common—understanding the characteristics of one will help to shed light on the similar characteristics of the other. In simpler terms, an analogy uses one thing to explain another. In this selection, Griffin uses an extended analogy that equates management of nature with management of an office. As you read the essay, isolate the characteristics that the two things have in common and think about how understanding one increases your understanding of the other.

How the Forest Should Look

"There is but one way in which the office manager can control scientifically; that is by standardization . . . The office manager should, therefore, continually direct his efforts to having each operation . . . always done in exact accordance with the manner he has prescribed."

—LEFFINGWELL and ROBINSON,
Textbook of Office Management

"Proper regrowth and efficient forest management of our present and prospective forested areas will assure sufficient lumber for domestic requirements and a profitable export trade."

—NELSON C. BROWN, *Lumber*

"Foresters will have worked out more precisely the types of forest to establish on different soils to give the greatest sustained yield, and species of trees used will have been bred for this purpose."

—E. M. NICHOLSON, "Orchestrating the Use of Land,"
The World in 1984, vol. 1 (1964)

The trees in the forest should be tall and free from knot-causing limbs for most of their height. They should not taper too much between the butt

and the top last saw log. They should be straight. (Among applicants, a person with high intelligence should be sought. She should be an expert typist. A
5   stenographer. She should be diplomatic, neat and well dressed.)

Trees growing in the forest should be
useful trees.
For each tree ask if
it is worth the space it grows in.
10   Aspen, Scrub Pine, Chokeberry, Black Gum, Scrub Oak,
Dogwood, Hemlock, Beech are weed trees
which should be
eliminated. A thousand
cubic feet of one species can be
15   worth more than the same
quantity of another. (Standard
procedures for clerical work
should be initiated. Find out
the purpose of each kind of
20   work, ask, "Is this
work necessary?") Find out
which species are of
highest value
to the consumer, and
25   plant these.
    For harvesting trees, it is desirable that a stand be all of the same
    variety and age. Nothing should grow on the forest floor, not seedling
    trees, not grass not shrubbery. (In one case,
nineteen girls all
30   working on the same operation
were using ten
different methods.) Clearcutting
the virgin stand and replanting
the desired
35   species is
recommended.
    In the well-managed forest poor and surplus trees have been thinned
    to make room for good trees. In such a forest there is no room for
    overripe trees, past their best growing years, for diseased trees or
40   damaged trees, branchy or badly shaped trees.
(Is she accurate? Neat in her work and personal habits?
Is she loyal? Can she be trusted? Is she courteous?
Does she have a pleasing telephone personality?)
The forest
45   is more easily
managed if
it is large and the
trees should be planted close together

so they will grow straight and
tall to reach the light. (There   50
should be one central stenographic
pool to render
service for the entire
office instead of
small groups of uncontrolled   55
stenographers throughout
the office.)
  Is she emotionally stable? Is she responsible? Versatile? Creative?
  Consistent? Confident? Does she have a good memory? Is she alert to
  the needs of others? Does she   60
try her best? Can she spell?
Does she learn from) The
forest should be close to
a sawmill. (When the
work is centralized each   65
stenographer will
produce more than
would otherwise be the) Trees
bred to grow more
rapidly, to be more   70
healthy, sounder,
taller, thicker, straighter and
of more
use to the
consumer should   75
gradually replace their
inferiors. (The study
of human aptitudes, the selection
of the human element best
fitted to perform any   80
task) in this
way the forest
will yield, and
yield again what is
desired.   85

Questions for Discussion and Your Reading Journal

1. Griffin's work has been described as a "collage." Discuss how the collage
   works artistically and how this piece is like a collage.
2. The juxtaposition of the quotations from the textbook for office management and a book on the management of the forest implies that managing
   trees is like managing office workers (most of whom are women). Discuss
   the likenesses that are implied in each section of this piece. How do these
   juxtapositions help to establish the tone?

3. Reread the essays by Maser and by de Beauvoir. Discuss how this selection implies some of the ideas raised in those two pieces, particularly the notion of both women and nature as "other," something to be feared and to exert one's power over.

4. Reread the poem by Marge Piercy; what are the points of similarity between these two pieces?

5. Paraphrase the last few lines of this selection. What are the various meanings of the word "yield"? How do the various meanings connect with the rest of the selection?

JULIA SMITH BERRALL

Julia Smith Berrall, a freelance lecturer and writer, is an expert in the history of gardens and flowers. She has received a number of awards and citations for her work in the field from such organizations as the National Council of State Garden Clubs, the American Horticultural Society, and the International Federation of Landscape Architects. She also worked for a time in art museums. Her books include A History of Flower Arrangement, Flowers in Glass, *and* The Garden—An Illustrated History, *from which this selection is taken.*

Reading Rhetorically

Look carefully at the first paragraph of this essay. While the rest of the essay is narrowly focused on the subject of Egyptian gardens in the time of the pharaohs, the introduction goes back to the earliest biblical time, that of Adam and Eve in the Garden of Eden. When you are writing in relation to a very specific topic, one about which your reader is likely to know little or nothing, it can be enormously helpful to wade into the subject by placing it within the context of something the reader knows very well, as Berrall does in this essay.

The Garden: In the Time of the Pharaohs

1   Man's earliest cultures developed beside the mighty rivers of the Near East—the Nile, the Tigris, and the Euphrates—where the two life-giving factors of water and hot sunshine enabled man's first civilizations to grow, as seeds grow. Here, we are taught, the first garden was created—the Garden of Eden. Eden, Paradise, Park: The words were synonymous to the old translators. The Old Testament story tells how the Lord planted trees of all kinds, including the Tree of Life and the Tree of Knowledge of Good and Evil, and of how "a river went out of Eden to water the garden." This was the very essence of ancient gardening: shade for comfort and water for irrigation.

We know more about Egyptian gardens than about any others in the $\quad$ 2
ancient world, for they were pictured in the tombs, either in sculptural relief
or in painting, and there are many references to gardening, trees, and flowers
in hieroglyphics carved on the walls and written on papyri. No ancient home
or palace is extant today, as their bricks and timbers have not survived, but the
stone temples and the tombs, built as eternal dwellings for the dead, reveal to
us the full story of life in ancient Egypt.

Not only the gardens but the whole of Egyptian life and economy were $\quad$ 3
dependent on the great river running the length of the country from its
cataracts to the Mediterranean. The Nile has always overflowed with predictable regularity and gentleness, gradually depositing over the land a broad
layer of dark, fertile soil which is easy to work and full of nutrients. Its flooding, from mid-July to mid-October, has insured dependable crops for centuries. The Nile Valley is a long casually winding ribbon of greenery, sometimes bordered by the dull brown of arid land and sometimes rimmed with
shimmering deserts or rocky cliffs.

Many prosperous Egyptians built their villas outside the limits of towns $\quad$ 4
and cities, and their extensive landholdings supported large households,
including slaves. Huge walls were constructed around these country estates to
protect them from marauders and wild animals and from the searing desert
winds. The estates above the flood lines of the Nile needed irrigation to sustain orchards and vineyards as well as vegetable and flower beds. To achieve
this, canals were dug from the river, some deep enough for river boats, others
designed as ditches from which water could be carried to the crops or to storage wells and pools. The latter, either T-shaped or rectangular, often became
decorative elements in the garden. A simple water hoist was devised, consisting of a pole weighted at one end by a stone and a leather bucket suspended
from the other end. Called a *shaduf,* it is still used in Egypt today. Water was
also transported by serfs carrying water skins or wearing shoulder yokes from
which clay pots were suspended. With constant evaporation under the hot sun,
it must have been a continuous chore to keep plants watered and the reservoirs
full. Some paintings show trees surrounded with built-up rims of earth to conserve the moisture.

All plans and delineations of Egyptian gardens indicate that they were for- $\quad$ 5
mal and geometrical and therefore, in design, the prototype of all gardens
throughout Europe and the Near East for over three thousand years.

The most complete plan of a villa and its surroundings was discovered in $\quad$ 6
a Theban tomb during the last century by the Italian Egyptologist Ippolito
Rosellini. The estate may have belonged to a high official of the reign of Amen-
hotep III (circa 1411–1375 B.C.), for its mile-long canal, imposing entrance
gate, numerous trees, and large vineyard all suggest great wealth. One can
imagine arriving there by boat, stepping immediately into the cool protection
of the gate, and then walking to the villa under the shelter of the grape arbor.
The roof of the villa is shaded by awnings, and small garden pavilions overlooking the storage pools invite relaxation. One is impressed not only by the
architectural details, the orderly symmetry, and the loveliness of growing
things, but also by the functionalism of the whole plan. The shade-giving trees

all bore fruit. We recognize the date palm and the forked doum palm, sometimes called the gingerbread palm. Probably the darker trees are sycamore figs *(Ficus sycomorus),* which, because of their dense, almost evergreen foliage, were desirable as shade trees. The smaller trees beneath the palms were probably the common fig *(Ficus carica)* or pomegranate. The large vineyard of long, trellised arbors gave a bounteous wine harvest and the rectangular, papyrus-bordered pools containing lotus and water fowl also became storage tanks for fish, which were fed and kept for eating.

7   The wall painting of Neb-Amun's gratitude for his wealth dating from the Eighteenth Dynasty (circa 1415 B.C.), has the same features of shade and water. It shows a T-shaped pool bordered with sycamores and terminated by a gate opening to a vine-covered pergola* where servants are gathering grapes. The posts of the pergola were probably painted, and the columns have conventionalized papyrus capitals. A funeral scene found in another tomb of the same period contains a detail of a large garden in which a small summerhouse and a large pond are depicted. The corpse of the owner is being rowed across as a priest offers prayers. On shore, men are burning incense and waiting to honor the dead man with flowers. We see wine jars for the burial feast, covered with vine leaves to keep them cool, and bread and cakes prepared as votive offerings.

8   Besides the large garden estates there were small city gardens belonging to the middle classes in which a tree-shaded well was probably the most important single feature, with checkerboard vegetable plots and straggling grapevines. Sometimes there may have been a few flowers such as red poppies or blue cornflowers *(Centaurea cyanus),* for we know from their art that the Egyptians loved pure, bright color. These utilitarian gardens were pleasurable only insofar as they also provided restful shade and a few colorful flowers. It also seems possible that acacia and tamarisk trees were sometimes planted, for their blossoms attract bees, and honey was the only known sweetener in those days.

9   The gardens belonging to the temples and the royal gardens were naturally the largest of all. A wonderfully complete plan of a royal villa and its grounds, including an orchard of trees surrounding a very large pool, was found in the tomb of a high priest at Tell el 'Amarna, the site of the city built by Ikhnaton in the fourteenth century B.C. Outdoor living space shaded by trees is indicated in the complex of colonnaded courtyards, at the center of which is a high altar reached by ramps. The plan also indicates living quarters for a large number of people, horse stables, and many store rooms.

10   A temple garden represented in an early scene is believed to be that of Karnak. Large boats on the Nile approach the canal and pool in front of the temple. Inside the temple the high priest is presenting King Neferhotep with a bouquet for his queen, Meryet-Re, who has been awaiting him outside. If this is the Karnak temple, as, from the obelisk standing near the entrance pylon, it appears to be, it was depicted before King Thutmose III (who reigned from circa 1501 to 1496 B.C. and circa 1493 to 1447 B.C.) built the vast hall with its rows of heavy columns. At one time fine gardens spanned the two-mile dis-

---

*Pergola An arbor or trellis. [Ed. note.]

tance between the temple at Karnak and the one at Luxor. Excavation is still going on along the stone roadway connecting them, where probably as many as fourteen hundred sphinxes, at fifteen-foot intervals, line the sides. A revealing inscription on the base of one of them tells of the Thirteenth Dynasty pharaoh who started the road: "He built this road in honor of his father and lined it with trees and flowers."

Questions for Discussion and Your Reading Journal

1. Read some of the selections in this part of the book that define the term "art" (for example, Maser and Langer). Can gardens be considered "art"? Why or why not?
2. Read the selection by Gombrich at the beginning of this chapter. Discuss how the garden pictured in that essay embodies some of the characteristics described in this one.
3. Note that the author uses the Latin names of the trees and plants she describes. What might this tell you about the audience she thinks will read her book?
4. Both Walker and Maser talk about the link between art, spirituality, and gardens. After reading this selection and the next two, discuss the relationship of the spiritual to gardens in Egypt, Ancient China, and early Islamic society.

JOHN BROOKES

John Brookes has a degree in landscape design from the University of London and is the founder of the Clockhouse School of Garden Design in West Sussex, England. He lectures and holds workshops on garden design around the world; his books include Room Outside, Gardens for Small Places, Improve Your Lot, The Book of Garden Design, *and* Gardens of Paradise, *from which the following selection is taken.*

In an interview for the publication Contemporary Authors, *Brookes said that one of his writing interests is "to draw attention to the place of the garden within the landscape: how it should relate to the landscape in both its layout and the use of its plant material. At its crudest, how do we relate twentieth-century knowledge of art forms and design experience to native plant material and where does Harry Homeowner fit in? I haven't found the answer yet." This essay represents part of Brookes's effort to make sense of the relationship between gardens, culture, and individual people.*

Reading Rhetorically

In this essay, Brookes writes, "[The Quran] is believed to be the actual Word of God. So what it relates about the garden, its form and content, is not merely descriptive: God has actually defined paradise as a garden, and it is up to the individual not only to aspire to it in the after-life, but also to try to create its image here on earth." The distinction between the words "descriptive" and "prescriptive" is very important to an understanding of the paradise garden. Whereas the creation of a garden, for most of us in America, is the product of an individual's imagination, the creation of a paradise garden is the replication of a prescribed form. After you have read the essay, examine the illustration at the end. It shows the complexity, symmetry, and exquisitely beautiful detail of the garden's pattern, which can only be hinted at in the words of the text. Think about the degree to which, in your opinion, the garden's prescribed form adds to its beauty or detracts from its artistic merit.

The Concept of the Paradise Garden

1   The diversity of peoples, of temperature ranges and climates, of social conditions, and of those regions which Islam encompasses is enormous. A great concentration of its disciples lies in the Middle East, but it extends eastwards into India, South-East Asia, Malaysia and Indonesia and even into China. Northwards, it stretches from its holy centre at Mecca in Saudi Arabia through Iran, Turkey and what is now the southern Soviet Union. Southwards, Islam reaches into the heart of Africa, from where (until the fifteenth century) it reached through Spain into central France.

2   Islam, then, is not a single place or just a religion; it is a way of life for the vast numbers of people in those areas. The rules of Islam are set out in the Holy Book, the Quran. . . .

3   The Quran dictates how those of Islam should live their lives; it outlines a series of laws circumscribing what they may and may not do, and constantly draws similes and analogies to make its points more clear, very much in the way the Christian prophets told parables. The garden is constantly cited as a symbol for paradise, with shade and water as its ideal elements. "Gardens underneath which rivers flow" is a frequently used expression for the bliss of the faithful, and occurs more than thirty times throughout the Quran. Four main rivers of paradise are also specified, one of water, one of milk, one of wine and one of purified honey. This is the origin of the quartered garden, known in Persian as the *chahar bagh,* or four gardens, which were divided by means of four water-channels and all contained within a private, walled enclosure.

4   Also frequently mentioned are the abundant fruit trees in the paradise garden and the rich pavilions set among them, wherein the owners of the gardens and their friends might relax. Thus, within this concept of paradise is a clear indication as to what the garden should contain: fruit trees, water and rich pavilions, intended as places for pleasure and cool enjoyment. To a desert people, this concept was desirable as an ultimate perfection which contrasted sharply with the stark reality of the desert in which they lived. Descriptions of gardens in the Quran may have been inspired by the actual gardens of Damascus, a town which would have been seen and appreciated by merchants from Mecca at the end of their long caravan-route and which must have seemed a veritable paradise in contrast to the arid wilderness of their homeland.

Other civilizations, such as those of the ancient Egyptians or the Vikings, 5
imagined paradise as a continuation of life on earth, but with none of its
disadvantages. The early Muslims, however, living in one of the most inhos-
pitable parts of the world, saw paradise as a complete contrast. After spreading out of the Arabian peninsula, they proceeded to create in their conquered
lands the closest possible version of paradise on earth in superb gardens which
spanned the Islamic world.

To the Muslim the beauty of the garden, and indeed of the whole of cre- 6
ation, was held to be a reflection of God. Some of the greatest outpourings of
Islamic poetry glorify this, and poets constantly used the image of the garden
to describe their feelings towards a beloved. The great mystic Sufi poet Rumi
used much garden imagery:

The trees are engaged in ritual prayer and the birds in 7
singing the litany,
the violet is bent down in prostration.

or again

See the upright position form the Syrian rose, 8
and the violet the genuflection,
the leaf has attained prostration: refresh the Call to Prayer!

So all-pervasive was this idea of the garden, that not only poets but all 9
artists included references to gardens in their repertoire; not only were houses
and palaces set in gardens, but their interiors glowed with representations of
them, too—in mosaics, paintings and ceramics, and even on carpets. On these
can be seen quite clearly the arrangement of the *chahar bagh*, with either an
octagonal pool placed in it or perhaps a tomb or pavilion at its centre, or the
great landscaped garden with pavilions providing a series of beautiful perspectives. A third type was to appear in India, where the form of the garden
became that of a palace itself.

The Quran, therefore, is not, like the New Testament, a record of the 10
prophet's activities and teachings on earth; it is believed to be the actual Word
of God. So what it relates about the garden, its form and content, is not merely
descriptive: God has actually defined paradise as a garden, and it is up to the
individual not only to aspire to it in the after-life, but also to try to create its
image here on earth. The way in which this Word of God was, and is, presented
to man was also important, giving the Arabic script in which it was written far
greater significance than that possessed by mere printed records of events.
When you consider, too, that an early Islamic concept equated the depiction of
a human image with idolatry, it is not hard to understand why the art of calligraphy should reach such a supremely high standard of artistic expression.

At another level, calligraphic pattern is used as pure decoration, together 11
with abstract or geometric design, to cover, on the grandest scale, both the
interior and exterior of a building, or on a much smaller scale to decorate a
plate or vase. The mystical and universal equality of value which is placed on
each element of a design, on whatever scale, establishes the unity of style
which is so significant in all the artistic outpourings of Islam. . . .

Figure 1   The pattern and motifs of a Persian garden carpet, which here include fish and deer as well as trees and plants, reflect both the formal divisions and the content of a *chahar bagh* or a paradise garden. From Weidenfeld Nicholson Limited.

Questions for Discussion and Your Reading Journal

1. What are the origins of the "quartered garden" Brookes describes? Reread the essay by Rawson on Islamic art; what relationship do you see between patterns of calligraphy described in that essay and patterns of Islamic gardens?
2. Compare the idea of the afterlife embodied in Islamic gardens with that of Egyptian gardens. What are the likenesses and what are the differences?
3. What is the link between the Islamic religion and Islamic gardens?
4. Compare this essay to the one on Chinese gardens that follows. What are the likenesses between the two concepts of how to use space in landscape? What are the differences?

MITCHELL BRING
AND JOSSE WAYEMBERGH

Mitchell Bring and Josse Wayembergh spent 4 years in Japan as graduate researchers at Kyoto University's Department of Architecture: together they published Japanese Gardens: Design and Meaning, *from which the following selection is taken. In the introduction to the book, they point out that while the Chinese and Japanese garden is natural looking compared with the geometric gardens of Europe and the Middle East, "the tremendous amount of labor needed to maintain one certainly precludes any notions of its being a balanced ecosystem." The garden as it developed in these cultures was "more than a simple ornament, for it embodied not only religious traditions but an understanding of the mechanics of the environment as well."*

Reading Rhetorically

In this essay the garden is demonstrated via *logos* to be a living metaphor for harmony and balance, two of the most cherished ideals of Eastern culture. Think of ways in which the values that you hold are expressed in metaphors outside language. For example, the architecture of a church, with its high ceilings, arched doorways, and soaring steeple, may be a metaphor for a spirit reaching toward heaven. Language may be the primary expression of metaphor in most of our experience, but it may not be the most powerfully affecting. As you read about the metaphorical Chinese garden, think about "gardens" in your own experience that represent some of your highest ideals.

Chinese Gardens

By the time Chinese teachings reached Japan in earnest in the sixth century, the Chinese had already developed a comprehensive and sophisticated understanding of the physical universe. To the literate Chinese, who had developed knowledge in the areas of astronomy, mathmatics, civil engineering, and other fields, the landscape had meanings beyond the animistic* sacredness attributed to it by the Japanese. In landscape the Chinese saw the working of great universal forces and laws. Observation of nature not only provided spiritual inspiration but offered a key to cosmic understanding. 1

Unlike the Japanese of the time, the Chinese were great builders, and their cities, temples, tombs, and homes were modeled after their conceptions of the universal order. In addition, the arts of landscape gardening and painting were meant to exemplify the action of cosmic design. 2

LANDSCAPE PHILOSOPHY: THE HARMONIC IDEAL

Certain ideas run like main currents throughout the course of Chinese philosophy. There is a central assumption that the universe is in constant change, a continuing process of growth and decay, creation and destruction, life and death. Everything is subject to this process, and nothing remains static: Just as the clouds change shape in the wind and the stars move in the heavens, so too do the mountains and valleys change, though they move too slowly for human 3

---

*animistic From animism, the belief that nature and natural objects have souls. [Ed. note.]

observation. Two great opposing forces are revealed in this constant process, and since time immemorial they have been called yin and yang.

4 Yin is female, mother, negative, dark, damp, deep, and destructive. Yang is male, father, positive, bright, hard, high, penetrating, and constructive. Between these opposite poles, the great oscillations of the universe take place. Neither can exist independently, for all things yang contain some small element of yin and vice versa. In the extreme of one we see the creation of the other in a pattern much like a sinusoidal wave: Strong activity results in rest, as extreme winter coldness gives way to spring warmth. Thus creation is seen as a multitude of cyclic processes represented by black-and-white diagrams that express these whirling patterns of change.

5 A goal in life, as well as in art, for many was to achieve harmony: harmony of forces within an individual and of those without. Internally, various practices (yoga) were used to manipulate and balance breathing and sexual energy, which were considered direct human manifestations of yin and yang forces. Externally, people sought to integrate their homes and ancestral tombs with the energy in the environment. Landscape was invested with sexual attributes, and every element could be classified, depending on shape and quality, into yin or yang. The very word for landscape, a combination of the Chinese characters for mountain (yang) and water (yin), implies this dualism. Landscape art, both painting and gardening, sought to represent ideal harmony. The "opening and closing" relationships of hills and valleys, positive and negative shapes, horizontal and vertical, were invoked as evidence of balanced yin and yang.

6 Other symbols were also used to express the workings of yin and yang. A primary idea of Chinese culture was the division of the universe into three parts: heaven, earth, and man. The problems of human existence could be solved by reconciling the claims of heaven (yang) and earth (yin). Heaven, represented by a circle, was seen as the source of the various energies that worked through the passive earth (represented by a square) where people labored to effect favorable changes for themselves in their present life and after death. The old-fashioned Chinese coin—a circle pierced by a square with an Imperial inscription between the two forms—represents this fundamental relationship. A chief function of the Emperor was to serve as an intermediary between the two realms.[1] By performing rites in his palace and city, which were specifically designed for this purpose, he attempted to reconcile the claims of each. A major natural disaster was an almost certain sign that the Emperor was unsuccessful in fulfilling his duties.

7 Chinese landscape art always depicted elements of heaven, earth, and people, or something man-made (such as a path or bridge), implying that no matter how small the human element seemed in comparison to the majestic mountains and seas, the scene was not complete without some indication of human presence. Landscape painting tried to show the harmonic ideal, and great engineering feats—which imply the subjugation of nature—are usually not pictured. Conversely, ruins or wrecks such as those painted in romantic European landscapes, suggesting the domination of nature over people, never appear in East Asian landscape paintings.

Such paintings instead pictured a person in complete harmony with the   8
environment: hence the recurring figure in painting and literature of the
scholar hermit in his retreat. Freed from the petty concerns and intrigues of an
official career, the hermit scholar was able to find inspiration, insight, and fulfillment amid the mountains and rivers of the countryside. Most often pictured
alone—or with a single attendant—living in a simple thatched hut, the recluse
represented an ultimate in tranquility and harmony.[2]. . .

LANDSCAPE PRACTICE: GEOMANCY

Given this expressed goal of harmony, these questions must be asked: How did   9
the Chinese, and later the Japanese, conceive of nature (heaven and earth) and
how did they try to harmonize with it when building cities, homes, and gardens? Analysis of Chinese geomancy provides answers to both questions in
summary form. Defined as "the art of adapting the residences of the living and
the dead so as to cooperate and harmonize with the local currents of the cosmic breath,"[3] geomancy has been the subject of considerable interest and controversy. Ernest Eitel,[4] writing in 1873, called geomancy (*feng-shui*, Chinese,
and *fusui*, Japanese—literally meaning wind and water) the "rudiments of
Chinese natural science," and he recorded the strong objections voiced by the
Chinese of Hong Kong to British planned improvements such as telegraphs,
railroads, and even church spires because they violated geomantic principles.
Joseph Needham called geomancy a "far reaching pseudo science" and
acknowledged its contributions to modern science, such as the invention of the
magnetic compass and the attention to landscape that resulted in topographi-
cal mapping.[5] . . . It is now thought to be a principal foundation of urban
planning in the Chinese realm[6] with geomantic ideas closely incorporated into
early garden making practice.

The concern of geomancy for integrating structures of human origin with   10
the great forces of nature made it the "ecology" of its day. The "wind and
waters" of Chinese geomancy refer to the cosmic breath or energy *(ch'i)* of
heaven and earth, which had to be determined for a particular site before anything could be built. Earth here means the living biological earth where
seasonal cycles of plant and animal life seemed to demonstrate the fixed mathematical laws seen in the motions of the heavenly bodies. The fundamental
energy of *ch'i*, which flows through the heavens, was similarly perceived to be
flowing through the bodies of all living things, including the "body" of earth.
Just as humans have veins and acupuncture sites where *ch'i* can be stimulated
and adjusted, the earth too had veins (surface and subterranean watercourses)
and centers of *ch'i*. This is graphically described by a fourteenth-century Chinese scientist:

> The body of the earth is like that of a human being. . . . Ordinary people,   11
> not being able to see the veins and vessels which are disposed in order within
> the body of man, think that it is no more than a lump of solid flesh. Like-
> wise, not being able to see the veins and vessels which are disposed in order
> under the ground, they think that the earth is just a homogeneous mass.[7]

12   Just as a person should be judged for signs of sickness or health by physical appearance, so could a prospective building site. This was extremely
important, for the health of human beings was seen to be directly interrelated
with the health of their environment:

13   Now if the ch'i of the earth can get through the veins, then the water and
the earth above will be fragrant and flourishing; and all men and things
will be pure and wise . . . but if the ch'i of the earth is stopped up, then
the water and earth and natural products will be bitter, cold and withered
. . . and all men and things will be evil and foolish.[8]

14   This relationship between people and the earth was considered very delicate and easily damaged or repaired:

15   When Hideyoshi's [d. 1598] soldiers of Japan invaded Korea, they set up
camp in Sonsan for a time. A Japanese geomancer of the army unit
observed the form of the mountains and realized that the place would
produce many great men and that Korea would be prosperous.

   For this reason, the Japanese geomancer advised the soldiers to burn an
important place on the mountain in the back of Sonsan town and to drive
in a great iron piling. In this way he killed the vital energy for the mountain.

   After that time, strangely, no great men were born in Sonsan or even
in the neighbouring counties.

   Thus, until a few decades ago it is said that people were roaming
around in the mountains of Sonsan County in order to find the iron bar.[9]

16   The key factor affecting the energy of a site was its orientation, and the
magnetic compass was first developed in service to geomancy. It was used by
the Chinese for site reading and planning centuries before they used it for navigation. The original compass consisted of a square plate (representing the
earth) marked with the main compass points beneath a polished circular disk
(representing heaven); a magnetic spoon made from lodestone modeled after
the shape of the Big Dipper was placed on the disk to indicate direction. Subsequent developments saw the spoon replaced by the familiar dry pivot compass, which was surrounded by numerous concentric rings pertaining to both
the positions of the heavens and the conditions of the landscape. One ring, for
example, is based on the twelve-year cycle of Jupiter, with each year represented
by an animal. On the compass dial, each of the twelve divisions also pertains
to a month, a direction, and a two-hour period of the day. Time and direction
were thus inseparably linked in the Chinese classification, and the compass, like
the calendar year, was divided into 365¼ units. The geomantic compass embodied large portions of the Chinese understanding of natural processes.[10]

17   In building site selection, ideally the geomancer would be free to choose
the most auspicious spot in the landscape. Often, however, such selection was
not possible and, in these cases, the geomancer was called upon to evaluate
and provide instructions for site improvements. The compass was aligned and
calculations were made regarding positions of the heavens. Next, important
landscape features were observed and their relative position noted. A tally was
kept of all these important celestial and terrestrial factors, and the final com-

putations resulted in a formula for building: Perhaps a pond had to be dug or an artificial mountain built; a too-yang angular hill might have to be rounded by bushes or a too-yin site might need some prominent trees or stones. Like a giant acupuncture needle, a pagoda might be erected to stimulate the local currents of *ch'i.*

When reading the actual landscape, geomancers found significance in many things. Mountains, often called "dragons" in the geomantic literature, were the most powerful determinants of *ch'i.* In general, geomancers sought to avoid disturbing the sleeping dragons. Just before his death, a builder of the Great Wall remarked, "I could not make the Great Wall without cutting through the veins of the earth."[11] Stones (and dinosaur bones) were often called the bones of the dragons and were considered to harbor great concentrations of energy.

The origin and flow of watercourses was next in importance in determining the *ch'i* of a site. Water could block the flow of *ch'i* and thus could be harmful if it prevented *ch'i* from entering a site, or good if it helped concentrate the *ch'i* by slowing its exit. Underground watercourses were also carefully noted, as were wind and soil conditions. This attention to natural phenomena resulted in some practical benefits.

The first thing recommended by a geomancer was a south-facing site, preferably protected by a horseshoe-shaped mountain closed on all sides except the south. In terms of sun exposure and protection from bad weather, this makes sound sense environmentally, as does the predilection for flowing water near dwellings. Geomantic practice placed the dwelling in the "belly of the dragon," i.e., inside the bend of a river, where it was not prone to the eroding action that cuts away the outside bank. A strong aversion to underground seepage led to careful observation of terrain and soil, which was examined for "inauspicious" insects at the same time. This careful site selection was practical, as was the planting of trees to form a windbreak in accord with the geomantic preference for a calm site. Trees were also often planted simply to balance the energy of a site.

A large part of geomancy—its less functional side—was concerned with allegorical readings of meaning in the landscape. Land forms were given descriptive poetic names such as the "sitting general" or "horses standing still," and the needs and functions of landscape were assessed in allegorical terms as illustrated by this story from Korea, where Chinese geomancy was also practiced:

The Kim family of Sangchon lived in Mokchon village with great prosperity and power. Whenever a new governor of Andong County arrived, he had to visit the family first and greet them. When Maeng Sasong came to Andong as the governor of the county, he thought that this visit was not the right thing to do for a person who was in the position of governor. Therefore, he changed the direction of a stream to Sangchon village in order to suppress the auspiciousness of Mokchon. This was done because the landscape of the Kim village was the type of a silkworm's head, and therefore the silkworm could not cross the stream to reach the mulberry grove. In addition, he removed the mulberry trees and planted lacquer trees in order to kill the silkworm. After that, the Kim family lost its fortune and declined.[12]

23   This allegorical understanding of landscape was also an aesthetic evaluation. Geomancers saw "beauty" as a clear indication of auspiciousness, and often modifications were made to the landscape principally to improve its appearance and thus one's fortune. Indeed, Needham credits geomancy with responsibility for the "exceptional beauty of the positioning of farmhouses, manors, villages and cities throughout the realm of the Chinese culture."[13]

24   Because the garden was built within the context of a greater landscape, its siting had to be integrated with the macropatterns of the region. And because it used the real substances of earth—stones, trees, and water—the micropatterns of *ch'i* had to be coordinated within the garden. The garden artist had to discern the veins of energy contained within the stones and harmonize the currents between them. Paths, river courses, and other shapes generated their own currents which also had to be fully harmonized with each other.

25   Thus seen through the eyes of a geomancer, the artificially constructed environment which we today call a garden had many different levels of meaning. It was made to be the most ideal of landscapes, designed to bring the best possible luck. It was both beautiful, for beauty is a sign of good fortune, and functional, as it manipulated the local currents of *ch'i* for maximum benefit. The beautiful landscape was the geomantically correct landscape. . . .

Notes

1. Philip Rawson and Laszlo Legeza, *Tao: The Chinese Philosophy of Time and Change.* (London: Thames and Hudson, 1973), 13.
2. Andrew Boyd, *Chinese Architecture 1500 B.C.–A.D. 1911.* (London: Alec Tiranti, 1962) 111–112.
3. H. Chatley, *"Feng-shui,"* Encyclopedia Sinica. Shanghai: Kelly and Walsh, 1917.
4. E. J. Eitel, *Feng-shui; Principles of the Natural Science of the Chinese.* Hong Kong: Lane, Crawford, 1873.
5. Joseph Needham, *Science and Civilization in China, vol. 2.* (Cambridge: Cambridge UP, 1959) 359.
6. Paul Wheatley, *The Pivot of the Four Corners.* (Edinburgh: Edinburgh UP, 1971) 419.
7. Cheng Ssu-Hsiao, *So-Nun Wen Chi* (Collected Writings of Cheng Ssu-Hsiao, 1340), trans. Joseph Needham. *Science and Civilization in China,* vol. 3, (Cambridge: Cambridge UP, 1959) 650.
8. Ibid.
9. Choi Sangsu, *Hankuk Mingan Chonsoljip,* trans. Hong-Key Yoon. *Geomantic Relationships between Culture and Nature in Korea.* (Taipei: Orient Cultural Service, 1976) 214.

10. For a complete description of how the compass is used, see Stephan D. R. Feuchtwang, *An Anthropological Analysis of Chinese Geomancy.* (Vientiane, Laos: Editions Vithogna, 1974).

11. Meng T'ien (d. 210)., *Shih Chi,* trans. Joseph Needham, *Science and Civilization in China,* vol. 4, part 1. (Cambridge: Cambridge UP, 1962) 240.

12. Hong-Key Yoon, *Geomantic Relationship between Culture and Nature in Korea,* (Taipei: Orient Cultural Service, 1976) 142.

13. Needham, op. cit., vol. 2, p. 361.

Questions for Discussion and Your Reading Journal

1. Define *yin* and *yang* in your own words. According to the authors, how are these philosophical concepts part of the design of Chinese gardens? How are these concepts part of Chinese art?

2. What is geomancy? In what way is it, in the authors' words, "the ecology of its day"?

3. Describe the relationship of humans to the environment in Chinese philosophy. How did this relationship influence the design of gardens?

4. Maser, in the earlier reading, also discusses the links between art, spirituality, and gardens. Explain those links with regard to these two rather different kinds of gardens.

5. Discuss the concepts of yin and yang in light of de Beauvoir's notion of woman as "other."

ANNIE DILLARD

Writer and poet Annie Dillard was born in 1945 in Pittsburgh, Pennsylvania. Dillard's parents encouraged her from a very young age to explore the natural world; they also supported her writing talent.

Dillard went to post-secondary school in Virginia at Hollins College, where she studied theology and English. Although she attended the Presbyterian Church as a child, Dillard developed her own belief system over the course of her life, a blend of Christianity, Sufism, Buddhism, and Hasidic Judaism, among other things. Most recently, she has converted to the Catholic Church. Her writing has appeared in many magazines from The Christian Science Monitor *to* Cosmopolitan. *She has received numerous grants and awards including the New York Press Club Award and, most notably, the Pulitzer Prize for the work that is excerpted here,* Pilgrim at Tinker Creek.

Annie Dillard has been called a modern-day mystic because her writing expresses a deep appreciation for inexplicable mysteries in the natural world. At the same time, she observes nature's phenomena with scientific exactitude. In Pilgrim at Tinker Creek, *which began as a personal journal, Dillard tells stories of her experiences after suffering a near fatal attack of pneumonia. During her recovery, Dillard decided to take up residence near Tinker Creek, an isolated area surrounded by creeks, forests, and a myriad of plant and animal life.*

Reading Rhetorically

Dillard observes natural events meticulously, bringing into her descriptions a broad base of scientific knowledge and infusing them with profound philosophical implications. Think about the *ethos* she projects as you read. Much of the power of the story told here lies in the element of surprise, so you should know as little as possible before reading it. As you read and after you have finished reading, reflect on larger meanings or truths that are implied in this observation of cruelty in nature.

Excerpt from *Pilgrim at Tinker Creek*

1   A couple of summers ago I was walking along the edge of the island to see what I could see in the water, and mainly to scare frogs. Frogs have an inelegant way of taking off from invisible positions on the bank just ahead of your feet, in dire panic, emitting a froggy "Yike!" and splashing into the water. Incredibly, this amused me, and, incredibly, it amuses me still. As I walked along the grassy edge of the island, I got better and better at seeing frogs both in and out of the water. I learned to recognize, slowing down, the difference in texture of the light reflected from mudbank, water, grass, or frog. Frogs were flying all around me. At the end of the island I noticed a small green frog. He was exactly half in and half out of the water, looking like a schematic diagram of an amphibian, and he didn't jump.

2   He didn't jump; I crept closer. At last I knelt on the island's winterkilled grass, lost, dumbstruck, staring at the frog in the creek just four feet away. He was a very small frog with wide, dull eyes. And just as I looked at him, he slowly crumpled and began to sag. The spirit vanished from his eyes as if snuffed. His skin emptied and drooped; his very skull seemed to collapse and settle like a kicked tent. He was shrinking before my eyes like a deflating football. I watched the taut, glistening skin on his shoulders ruck, and rumple, and fall. Soon, part of his skin, formless as a pricked balloon, lay in floating folds like bright scum on top of the water: it was a monstrous and terrifying thing. I gaped bewildered, appalled. An oval shadow hung in the water behind the drained frog; then the shadow glided away. The frog skin bag started to sink.

3   I had read about the giant water bug, but never seen one. "Giant water bug" is really the name of the creature, which is an enormous, heavy-bodied brown beetle. It eats insects, tadpoles, fish, and frogs. Its grasping forelegs are mighty and hooked inward. It seizes a victim with these legs, hugs it tight, and paralyzes it with enzymes injected during a vicious bite. That one bite is the only bite it ever takes. Through the puncture shoot the poisons that dissolve

the victim's muscles and bones and organs—all but the skin—and through it the giant water bug sucks out the victim's body, reduced to a juice. This event is quite common in warm fresh water. The frog I saw was being sucked by a giant water bug. I had been kneeling on the island grass; when the unrecognizable flap of frog skin settled on the creek bottom, swaying, I stood up and brushed the knees of my pants. I couldn't catch my breath.

Of course, many carnivorous animals devour their prey alive. The usual method seems to be to subdue the victim by downing or grasping it so it can't flee, then eating it whole or in a series of bloody bites. Frogs eat everything whole, stuffing prey into their mouths with their thumbs. People have seen frogs with their wide jaws so full of live dragonflies they couldn't close them. Ants don't even have to catch their prey: in the spring they swarm over newly hatched, featherless birds in the nest and eat them tiny bite by bite. 4

That it's rough out there and chancy is no surprise. Every live thing is a survivor on a kind of extended emergency bivouac. But at the same time we are also created. In the Koran, Allah asks, "The heaven and the earth and all in between, thinkest thou I made them *in jest?*" It's a good question. What do we think of the created universe, spanning an unthinkable void with an unthinkable profusion of forms? Or what do we think of nothingness, those sickening reaches of time in either direction? If the giant water bug was not made in jest, was it then made in earnest? Pascal uses a nice term to describe the notion of the creator's, once having called forth the universe, turning his back to it: *Deus Absconditus*. Is this what we think happened? Was the sense of it there, and God absconded with it, ate it, like a wolf who disappears round the edge of the house with the Thanksgiving turkey? "God is subtle," Einstein said, "but not malicious." Again, Einstein said that "nature conceals her mystery by means of her essential grandeur, not by her cunning." It could be that God has not absconded but spread, as our vision and understanding of the universe have spread, to a fabric of spirit and sense so grand and subtle, so powerful in a new way, that we can only feel blindly of its hem. In making the thick darkness a swaddling band for the sea, God "set bars and doors" and said, "Hitherto shalt thou come, but no further." But have we come even that far? Have we rowed out to the thick darkness, or are we all playing pinochle in the bottom of the boat? 5

Cruelty is a mystery, and the waste of pain. But if we describe a world to compass these things, a world that is a long, brute game, then we bump against another mystery: the inrush of power and light, the canary that sings on the skull. Unless all ages and races of men have been deluded by the same mass hypnotist (who?), there seems to be such a thing as beauty, a grace wholly gratuitous. About five years ago I saw a mockingbird make a straight vertical descent from the roof gutter of a four-story building. It was an act as careless and spontaneous as the curl of a stem or the kindling of a star. 6

The mockingbird took a single step into the air and dropped. His wings were still folded against his sides as though he were singing from a limb and not falling, accelerating thirty-two feet per second per second, through empty air. Just a breath before he would have been dashed to the ground, he unfurled his wings with exact, deliberate care, revealing the broad bars of white, spread 7 his elegant, white-banded tail, and so floated onto the grass. I had just rounded a corner when his insouciant step caught my eye; there was no one else in sight. The fact of his free fall was like the old philosophical conundrum about the tree that falls in the forest. The answer must be, I think, that beauty and grace are performed whether or not we will or sense them. The least we can do is try to be there.

8   Another time I saw another wonder: sharks off the Atlantic coast of Florida. There is a way a wave rises above the ocean horizon, a triangular wedge against the sky. If you stand where the ocean breaks on a shallow beach, you see the raised water in a wave is translucent, shot with lights. One late afternoon at low tide a hundred big sharks passed the beach near the mouth of a tidal river in a feeding frenzy. As each green wave rose from the churning water, it illuminated within itself the six- or eight-foot-long bodies of twisting sharks. The sharks disappeared as each wave rolled toward me; then a new wave would swell above the horizon, containing in it, like scorpions in amber, sharks that roiled and heaved. The sight held awesome wonders: power and beauty, grace tangled in a rapture with violence.

Questions for Discussion and Your Reading Journal

1. Point to a specific place in the story where you were startled or shocked. At what point did you begin to understand what was really happening?
2. After the story of the frog, two paragraphs are devoted to a philosophical discussion. Locate those paragraphs and summarize the points that are made there.
3. The aforementioned paragraphs are followed by a second example that focuses on sharks. What philosophical questions arise from these two examples of cruelty in nature? Why might Dillard have brought in the second example?
4. Make a list of some of the verbs in the passage. What do you notice about these verbs? Try to characterize or categorize them in some way. Explain your reasons for characterizing or categorizing them in that way.

WRITING ASSIGNMENTS

A Summary Essay

READINGS: Choose one of the following.

Royal Bank of Canada Newsletter, "What Use Is Art?"

Susanne K. Langer, "The Cultural Importance of the Arts"

E. H. Gombrich, "Art for Eternity" Alice Walker, "In Search of Our Mothers' Gardens"

Chris Maser, "The Window of Our Cultural Soul" Julia Smith Berrall, "The Garden: In the Time of the Pharaohs"

John Brookes, "The Concept of the Paradise Garden"

Mitchell Bring and Josse Wayem Bergh, "Chinese Gardens"

Annie Dillard, Excerpt from *Pilgrim at Tinker Creek*

TASK: Compose a two-page summary of a chosen article.

Audience and Purpose

You will be writing this paper for your peers and instructor.

Thinking Rhetorically about Audience and Purpose

Because writing summaries is the most common kind of writing assigned in the university, writing this paper will give you an opportunity to strengthen your skills in this area. Think back over your last year of school: on what occasions were you asked to summarize something? Why do you think you were assigned this task? Was composing the summary related to a larger assignment? If so, what was the assignment and why was the summary a part of it?

Objectives

- You will be able to summarize the central idea of an article in a thesis statement.
- You will practice reading an article to elicit the main ideas.
- You will practice restating the main ideas of an article in a summary form.

Evaluative Criteria

- Does the thesis of the summary recapitulate the central idea of the article?
- Are the other main ideas in the article represented (in your own words) in the summary?
- Does the summary show a careful reading of the article?
- Is the summary free from major errors in mechanics?

Notes to the Student

Since summarizing a text is a crucial skill to master before many other types of thinking and writing assignments can be done, we begin with this assignment. You must read the article carefully and critically before you can write a good summary of it. I suggest the following strategy:

1. Scan the article quickly. See if you can discover the topic and central focus.
2. Read the article carefully once without underlining anything or making any notes in the margins. Beginning university students often have difficulty deciding which ideas are really important; sometimes they mark a lot more than is really helpful. (As you gain practice in critical reading, you will be able to discriminate much more readily between more- and less-important ideas during a first reading.)
3. Reread, dividing the passage into sections as you go. These sections will be clusters of paragraphs (or sentences) having to do with particular ideas. Finally, label in the margins of the text each section or stage of thought. Underline key ideas and terms.
4. Write one-sentence summaries on a separate sheet of paper of each stage of thought.
5. Write a thesis statement: a one-sentence summary of the entire article. The thesis should express the central idea of the passage. Think of the questions journalists ask when they compose a "lead" for a story: the who, what, when, where, why, and how of the matter.
6. Write a first draft of the summary by combining the thesis with the one-sentence summaries, adding significant details from the passage. Eliminate less-important ideas.
7. Check your summary against the article and make any adjustments necessary for accuracy and completeness.
8. Revise your summary, inserting transitional words and phrases improve coherence. Try to avoid a series of short, choppy sentences; combine sentences for a smooth flow.
9. Proofread for grammatical correctness, punctuation, and spelling.

An Annotated Bibliography

TASK: Write an annotated bibliography about the art of a particular nation or region of the world. Include at least 10 entries in two categories: general sources and academic sources.

READINGS

> Royal Bank of Canada Newsletter, "What Use Is Art?"
> Sussane K. Langer, "The Cultural Importance of the Arts"
> E. H. Gombrich, "Art for Eternity"
> Ananda K. Coomaraswamy, "Understanding Indian Art"
> Roy Sieber, "Traditional Arts of Black Africa"
> Philip Rawson, "Islamic Art: Calligraphy"

Audience and Purpose

Think of the audience for this paper as your instructor and peers in the classroom.

Thinking Rhetorically about Your Audience and Purpose

Internet research is a tricky business. Many different kinds of resources are available on the Internet, and each kind is intended for a specific audience and purpose. While some sources may be meant to entertain, others may be intended to inform or persuade a general audience, and still others are meant for a specialized academic or professional audience. In what situations do you look for sources with entertainment value? What method do you use to find these sources? When do you look for sources of general interest? How do you find these kinds of sources? In what circumstances do you look for sources written by professionals in a particular field? What is your approach when looking for these more academic sources?

Objectives

- You will distinguish between the kinds of sources available on the Internet.
- You will practice Internet research based on the kind of source being sought.
- You will include the kinds and the number of sources required.
- You will present your bibliography using the MLA style, and the conventions of that style will be followed carefully.

Evaluative Criteria

- Are the sources in the bibliography of the right kind and number?
- Have the sources been carefully chosen based on an understanding of the differences between sources on the Internet?
- Does the bibliography follow the MLA style?

Notes to the Student

1. This assignment is fairly straightforward, but the aspect that may give you the most trouble is distinguishing between kinds of sources available. Remember that a lot of the information on the Internet is basically rubbish. By itself, your computer cannot sort information according to quality, so your search strategy will have to be carefully thought out. Many handbooks that describe Internet research strategies are available. A wise first step may be to look at such a handbook.
2. After you have found your sources, you will need to summarize them in a way that gets quickly to the point. *Note:* Never take word-for-word text from the Internet and represent it as your own—this is the easiest kind of plagiarism for your instructor to discover.

3. Use a handbook to make sure your bibliography follows the MLA format. Even the most experienced writers use a writer's handbook as a reference when they write bibliographical entries.

Definition and Analysis of Poetry

TASK: Write a three- to four-page essay that defines the term "poetry" and analyzes a particular poem in relation to the definition.

READINGS

Billy Collins, "Introduction to Poetry"
Jon Stallworthy, "Letter to a Friend"
Archibald MacLeish, "Ars Poetica"
Javier Heraud, "Ars Poetica"
Marianne Moore, "Poetry"

Audience and Purpose

In this paper you will be writing to learn—so your audience is yourself, but you will also share your learning with your peers in class and your instructor.

READINGS

Maxine Hong Kingston, "No Name Woman"
Nawal El Saadawi, "Growing Up Female in Egypt"
Alice Walker, "In Search of Our Mothers' Gardens"
Marge Piercy, "The Common Living Dirt"

Audience and Purpose

Consider that you are writing this story to be read by your children and grandchildren (when they are over the age of 13 or so) to tell them about something you have learned from your own experience.

Thinking Rhetorically about Your Audience and Purpose

The "theme" of a work of fiction can be seen in simple terms as the lesson learned over the course of the story. Think about an experience you had that made a lasting impression on you and from which you learned something important. What images come to your mind when you think about that experience? How do you feel now and what do you remember feeling at the time in relation to the experience? What did you learn from the experience at the time it happened? What have you learned over time?

Objectives

- You will read autobiographical, biographical, or fictional stories to examine their themes and rhetorical strategies.
- You will reflect on your personal experience as a source for writing.
- You will write autobiographical essays that clearly describe a personal experience.
- You will organize your stories to demonstrate a lesson learned.

Evaluative Criteria

- Is the personal experience used effectively as a source for describing a lesson learned?
- Is the message/theme/lesson clearly demonstrated in the essay?
- Is the essay mechanically sound?

Notes to the Student

1. As you read the essays, think about the themes that are described and how the writers have used personal experience to demonstrate those themes.
2. Use the essays as loose models for your own.
3. Brainstorm about experiences that may make a good focus for your essay; try to come up with at least two or three. Freewrite about each one for a couple of minutes, and then choose the one that seems most promising.
4. Write a rough draft of your essay, focusing mainly on telling your story clearly and describing the events/people/images in it vividly.
5. If necessary, rewrite your essay to frame the lesson you learned from the experience. That lesson may be explained in the introduction and the conclusion in the conclusion only, in the introduction only, or in some other way.
6. Revise your paper to make it flow logically and smoothly. You may need to insert transitions and/or topic sentences.
7. Proofread your essay for grammatical correctness, punctuation, spelling, and other mechanical issues.

A Thematic Synthesis

TASK: Write a four- to five-page essay that discusses a theme from the perspective of a number of sources, including readings from this book and personal narrative.

READINGS: Choose one of the following groups.

Poets on Poetry

> Billy Collins, "Introduction to Poetry"
> Jon Stallworthy, "Letter to a Friend"
> Archibald MacLeish, "Ars Poetica"

Javier Heraud, "Ars Poetica"
Mariane Moore, "Poetry"

Poems and Texts on Women and Feminism

June Jordan, "A Poem about Intelligence for My Brothers and Sisters"
Marzieh Ahmadi Oskooii, "I'm a Woman"
Joy Harjo, "The Woman Hanging from the 13th Floor Window"
Nawal El Saadawi, "Growing Up Female in Egypt"
Yu Hsuan-Chi, "On a Visit to Ch'ung Chen Taoist Temple"
Sor Juana De La Cruz, "She Proves the Inconsistency . . ."
Sappho, "Invocation to Aphrodite"
Maxine Hong Kingston, "No Name Woman"

Poems and Texts on War

Thomas Hardy, "The Man He Killed"
Anthony Hecht, "More Light! More Light!"
Muriel Rukeyser, "Letter to the Front"
William Butler Yeats, "Easter 1916"

Audience and Purpose

In this paper you will be writing to learn—so your audience is yourself. However, you will also share your learning with your peers in class and your instructor.

Thinking Rhetorically About Your Audience and Purpose

The term "synthesis" indicates making connections, sometimes between rather disparate things. You may connect a personal experience to a story you hear in the news and a book you've read. All three sources focus, to some degree, on an idea or ideas in common with each other. By making these connections, people make sense of the world and their place in it.

Think of a recent news event about which you have strong feelings. In what ways did you connect the outside event with your own life? Did it also connect with something else you had seen, heard about, or read? If so, how?

Objectives

- You will make connections between ideas from disparate sources.
- You will discuss the idea/s in relation to each source, as well as in relation to each other.
- You will organize your exploration of the idea/s in a clear, logical manner.
- You will come to some conclusion about the overall significance of the idea/s in relation to yourself and to the larger world.

Evaluative Criteria

- Does the essay have a thesis that sets out a clear idea and indicates its representation in various sources?
- Is the idea presented in relation to each source separately and in relation to the other sources?
- Does the essay come to a conclusion about the overall significance of the idea?
- Is the essay clearly organized and mechanically sound?

Notes to the Student

1. Because the purpose of this paper is to help you learn and to demonstrate your learning, the paper itself may follow the pattern of your learning experience. It may begin with a description of your discovery of the idea, followed by explanations of your identification of the same idea in other places. Or it may show how you picked the idea from a source and then made the connection to other sources and your own experience.
2. If you are having trouble getting started, pick a reading from the list provided that seems to be about something in which you are personally interested. Then identify an important idea in that reading on which you can focus your essay.
3. After you have identified your idea, look for other sources in which that idea is discussed. You may want to start with the "Art and Literature" chapter, and then find one or more sources in the other chapters that focus, at least to some degree, on the same idea.
4. Either before or after you read the texts, think carefully about the idea in relation to your own experience. You do not have to write about something that has happened to you personally—you can write about someone you know or something you have witnessed; the important thing is that you talk about the idea from your own perspective and connect it to your own life in some way.
5. Make a rough outline of your essay, indicating the thesis, how the idea is represented in each separate source, the connections between the sources, and a statement of the possible significance of the idea.
6. Write a rough draft of the essay, and then see if you can get some feedback about it from your peers or instructor.
7. Revise the rough draft, inserting transitions where necessary.
8. Write a final draft and then proofread it carefully.

A Comparison and Contrast Essay: Cultural Conceptions of Gardening

TASK: Write a four-page paper that compares and contrasts the process and conception of gardening in the context of two particular cultures.

Readings

> Alice Walker, "In Search of Our Mothers' Gardens"
> Chris Maser, "The Window of Our Cultural Soul"
> Marge Piercy, "The Common Living Dirt"
> Susan Griffin, "How the Forest Should Look"
> Julia Smith Berrall, "The Garden: In the Time of the Pharaohs"
> John Brookes, "The Concept of the Paradise Garden"
> Mitchell Bring and Josse Wayem Bergh, "Chinese Gardens"
> Annie Dillard, Excerpt from *Pilgrim at Tinker Creek*

Audience and Purpose

Think of the audience for this paper as a group of people your own age who have little or no experience with gardening. Demonstrate to them how gardening is significant to a particular cultural group.

Thinking Rhetorically about Your Audience and Purpose

Using comparison and contrast as a method of development can suit a number of purposes: to persuade, to describe, and to explain, for example. In this paper you will use comparison and contrast to describe gardening in its cultural context and to explain its significance to members of that culture.

For many people, gardening can be a particularly fulfilling activity. Watching something grow from the seeds they planted and caring for the plant as it grows to maturity provide a satisfaction unlike any other. And the work itself can feel purposeful and valuable. Think of someone you know who enjoys gardening (it may be you). Find out why it gives them satisfaction and enjoyment.

Objectives

- You will practice the comparison-and-contrast method of development.
- You will use comparison and contrast to describe and to demonstrate significance.
- You will organize your essay clearly and logically.
- You will draw on at least two of the readings listed to support the points in your essay.

Evaluative Criteria

- Does the essay have a thesis that indicates that comparison and contrast will be used to describe and explain the significance of something?
- Is the idea presented in relation to each culture separately and in relation to common areas between cultures?
- Does the essay come to a conclusion about overall significance?
- Is the essay clearly organized and mechanically sound?

Notes to the Student

1. If you are having trouble getting started, pick a reading from the list that is about a culture you are personally interested in. Then think carefully about the idea in relation to your own experience—connect it to your own life in some way.

2. After you have identified your topic and the cultures to be compared and contrasted, look through the readings to find their main ideas. List each reading's ideas and find out which are similar and which are different. Use these lists to form the basis for your comparison and contrast.

3. Comparison-and-contrast essays generally use either the "block" or the "point-by-point" method, or some combination of the two. The block method tells all about one thing and then all about the other. The point-by-point method focuses on an idea and then tells about each topic in relation to that idea, then moves on to the next idea, and so on. Decide which method better suits your thesis and write an outline for your essay.

4. After you make a rough outline of your essay, see if you can get some feedback about it from your peers or instructor.

5. Revise the rough draft, inserting transitions where necessary.

6. Write a final draft and then proofread it carefully.

CHAPTER 4

Science and Technology

Science is most often described as the observation, investigation, and explanation of the various phenomena on Earth and in the universe. Individuals from all over the world have conducted scientific study using a number of different methods. The dominant scientific model can be called Western due to its origins in Ancient Greek and European culture.

Aristotle, whose philosophy has been a fundamental influence on Western science, held that since "nature makes nothing without some end in view, nothing to no purpose, it must be that nature has made (animals and plants) for the sake of man."[1] Some aspects of the Judeo-Christian tradition have strongly reinforced this assumption, including the common interpretation of God's message to Adam in the Old Testament: "Increase and multiply and dominate the Earth."[2] In the Western scientific model the natural world is separate from humans and subject to their control, while in most world cultures humans are viewed as inseparable from the environment and dependent on its harmony.

The method of inquiry used by the Western world is commonly called the "scientific method." While the scientific method attempts to minimize the impact of the subjective experience of the scientist, most scientists agree that absolute objectivity is not possible to achieve.

The scientific method includes the following steps:

- Observation and description of a phenomenon
- Formulation of a hypothesis to explain the phenomenon
- Conducting of experimental tests in relation to the hypothesis
- Explanation of the results of the tests and evaluation of the accuracy of the hypothesis

The range of phenomena that can be studied using the preceding method is limited. It works best when the variables related to the phenomenon can be isolated from other factors and when experiments can be conducted repeatedly. However, isolation is frequently not possible and sometimes it can be prohibitively difficult, time-consuming, and expensive to repeatedly conduct experiments.

European exploration and imperialism around the world brought Western science and the "scientific method" to other lands, leaving lasting influences on the cultures they encountered. According to M. Adams, in *Machines as the Measure of Man,*

In the late eighteenth and nineteenth centuries, most European thinkers concluded that the unprecedented control over nature made possible by

---

[1]Aristotle, *Politics* (Hammondworth, England: Penguin, 1985).

[2]Genesis 1: 26–28.

Western science and technology proved that European modes of thought and social organization corresponded much more closely to the underlying realities of the universe than did those of any other people or society, past or present.[3]

In cases where there were supernatural explanations of phenomena like birth and death that were not accepted in the Western world, Western scientific explanations were promoted and indigenous explanations were denigrated. In an article about science as it is practiced by the Yupiaq people of northern Alaska, A. Kawagley asserts, "[A] narrow view of science not only diminishes the legitimacy of knowledge derived through generations of naturalistic observation and insight, it simultaneously devalues those cultures which traditionally rely heavily on naturalistic observation and insight."[4]

In a multicultural world there are competing scientific models of observing, investigating, and explaining natural phenomena. While Western scientists of the past tended to assume that their work was objective and free from the influence of the values of the larger culture, current scientists generally agree that science is a socially constructed discipline and therefore inherently based around the values, attitudes, and desires of the broader community.

Recently many scientists and scholars from all over the world have begun to question the idea that Western science is superior to other scientific approaches. For example, if science is fundamentally an understanding of nature, Native-Americans have had a very sound science of their own based on centuries of observation and experimentation, but their scientific methods are premised on a values system with different assumptions than those of Western science. Following is a list of Native-American values, taken from a bulletin at the Smithsonian Institution:

1. Nature is viewed as sacred.
2. Humans are part of the web of life.
3. Humans should live in harmony with nature.
4. The entire world is viewed as being alive.
5. Technology should be low impact.[5]

Most non-Western cultures, including Native-American, Maori, Buddhist, Hindu, and many others, promote conservative use of natural resources. The differences between the values inherent in different approaches to science are becoming increasingly important as the resources of the earth are being consumed at an accelerating rate.

This chapter, "Science and Technology," is intended to present a multicultural view of science, the role of scientists in society, and a number of scientific issues. The readings in the chapter are arranged into four groups, with each group focusing on a separate theme.

---

[3]M. Adams, *Machines Are the Measure of Man: Science, Technology and Ideologies of Western Man* (Ithaca, N.Y.: Cornell University Press, 1989), 7.

[4]William W. Cobern, "Defining 'Science' in a Multicultural World"; available from http://www.wmich.edu/slcsp/148.html

[5]"Native American Views about Nature" (Smithsonian Institution, 1996).

Following the student essay by Ellen Salud is the "Definitions and Cultural Contexts" group. It begins with an introductory essay by Edward T. Hall called "The Anthropology of Manners." Anthropology is a social science concerned with the entirety of human experience, all over the world, both historically and currently. This essay takes a social-scientific look at global cultures and continues the discussion from earlier in the textbook of the need to understand the context of behaviors and beliefs, since these can be vastly different from one culture to the next.

Included with the introductory essay is a group of essays that deal with definitions of the terms "science" and "scientist." Then definitions of a specific kind of science and scientist are presented—chemistry and chemists—so that the general ideas in the initial essays can be applied specifically. This grouping shows how science and religion, although both fundamentally premised on the search for "truth," can be understood in contrast to each other: they are two different ways of knowing or modes of inquiry about existence. Science attempts to explain the processes that govern the natural world and, as a result, tends to provide a mechanistic description of reality. Religion attempts to provide meaning to existence, generally expressing a transcendent view of reality.

The subsequent essays in this group explore global differences and connections in relation to the historical development of scientific principles and their evolution. Before the 17th century when travel between continents was relatively uncommon, developments in science tended to be geographically localized. The mathematics of Western Europe, for example, evolved in a much different way from the mathematics of the Arab world, as is demonstrated by the differences between the Latin and the Arabic numeral systems. However, for the last three centuries, natural and physical sciences have been conducted in an international community.

This part of the chapter lays out the history and advancements of science in China and the Middle East and looks at differences and similarities between Eastern and Western science. Finally, the exchange of scientific ideas and inventions between nations is explored in an article by Fritjof Capra called "The Tao of Physics," which makes connections between the principles of Taoism and those of the science of Physics.

The second group of readings, "The Environment in Global Contexts," explores the consequences of globalization in relation to ecology. Capitalism and policies regarding the development of poorer nations are discussed in the context of processes of social transformation in non-Western nations. In the past the Western world has depended on using the natural resources and, in many cases, the labor force of less-developed nations. These readings suggest that by increasing the access of those nations to current tools in science and technology, not only can their poverty and dependence on the West be reduced, but their ability to protect their natural environment can be enhanced as well.

One of the most important factors influencing the ecological health of the planet is war inside and among nations. Technology in support of war has made ecological devastation a reality all over the world. Therefore, the third group of readings, "War and Peace," focuses on the science and technology of

war, not only in terms of its environmental impact but also in relation to issues important in the social sciences. The first essay of this section asks questions about human nature, extending Charles Darwin's theory of evolution to
the realm of human behavior. Then, George Simpson's "Early Social Darwinism" asserts that humans are warlike by nature. Margaret Mead refutes this
claim in the essay that follows, in which she theorizes that war is a human invention and is not biologically hardwired into human behavior. As an example
of science in relation to a specific war, the next several essays discuss World
War II and, in particular, the use of the atomic bomb.

The last group of readings in the chapter, "Race, Gender, and Oppression," examines connections between science and gender. Although feminist
scientists are concerned about the impact of scientific development on all subordinated social groups in relation to race, class, and other bases of inequality,
their central focus is on gender. Essays in this section show how science can be
used to confront gender discrimination. They also posit theories about psychological conceptions of masculinity and femininity. Finally, this section examines the cultural phenomenon of a third gender role, the *xanith* of Omani
culture.

STUDENT ESSAY

ELLEN SALUD Sixty Feet Deep

*Ellen Salud was inspired to write "Sixty Feet Deep" by her time as a
research assistant for the Barbados Sea Turtle Project. Along with Ellen's
growing passion for scuba diving and ocean environments, she enjoys
traveling. In addition to her adventures in the Caribbean, she has ventured through Europe and explored the Philippine Islands. Ellen currently resides in the diverse Northern California Bay Area until her next
adventure abroad.*

*While she worked both above and below the ocean surface to pre-
serve the Hawksbill, a magnificent species of sea turtle, Ellen discovered
that cultural differences can be far more complex than she had thought.
In the following essay, she asks herself about the relativity of ethical principles and moral beliefs.*

Reading Rhetorically

Ellen Salud's essay "Sixty Feet Deep" is a first-person narrative about an emotional experience that changed the author's perspective about culture and differences among cultures. Stories from the first-person perspective can be the
most engaging and powerfully moving kinds of writing. As you read this essay,
think about an experience you have had that changed your perspective about
cultural differences.

Sixty feet deep beneath the surface of the Caribbean Sea is where I've left an abyss full of fond memories, deep secrets, and unanswered questions that only the ocean and I know. During many of my dives I had wished I had a pen and paper to record the perceptions and sensations stimulated by the ocean life and environment around me. I would then be able to share them with others and recollect the events later for my own amusement. Without pen and paper to record them, I can only express those perceptions and sensations as a secondhand memory.

Sixty feet beneath the sea I was synchronously human and machine; my scuba tank served as an extension of my own lungs, breathing highly compressed air, while my BCD (Buoyancy Control Device) served as an inflatable vest for flotation that allowed me to glide through the water into neutral buoyancy. I remember feeling free in the unfamiliar water world in a meditative and supremely calm state, which lasted until my return to the familiar world above. This amazing scuba diving apparatus conceived in the imaginations of artists, like Leonardo da Vinci, and evolved into reality by the contributions of many brilliant scientists, like Haley and Boyle, kept me adrift in the belly of the ocean. This was a place where my imagination twisted, twirled, and tickled my perception of the liquid world, as well as the world above. There I marveled at the magnificent Hawksbill turtles.

In the water, on the water, or by the water is where I spent most of my days and nights during my time in Barbados. I traveled through the Caribbean in an effort to gain new perspectives, as well as to challenge my own, through immersion in foreign cultures; I chose the tropical island of Barbados particularly

The Barbados Sea Turtle Project (BSTP) was started in 1987 by Dr. Julia Horrocks from the University of the West Indies, Cave Hill. My interest in working on the project stemmed from seeing the creatures during recreational scuba dives. The mission of BSTP is to work towards conservation of endangered Hawksbill sea turtles by providing 24-hour beach surveillance along the coasts of the 155 square mile tropical island, Barbados. © Stephen Frink/CORBIS

because of my passion for ocean environments. While I was abroad scuba diving became a Sunday ritual with my dive crew (B.A.D.A.S.S. also know Barbados-American Diver's Association), and beach patrol became a nightly sacrament during my time as a field research assistant with the Barbados Sea Turtle Project (BSTP).

I recall a Sunday morning dive off the south coast of Barbados after a night beach patrol with BSTP. After my sixty-foot descent down to Caribb Reef off the island's south coast, I witnessed a Hawksbill turtle gracefully glide through the water like a bird in the sky. The creature hovered as an underwater astronaut over the colorful reef made of black sponge, orange and purple coral, sea eel, and angelfish. When I surfaced from the dive, feeling the warm seawater ooze from my ears, I gazed towards shore looking forward to that night's coming patrol with BSTP.

On that night the BSTP crew came across an area of sand spotted with blood. The crimson tainted sand made a quarter-mile trail that led to a cold alley where we found the remains of a poached turtle. A mildly sour smell permeated the area where the turtle had been gutted and stripped of her eggs. Her carapace and body were taken, and only her inside remains along with a clutch of seventy-five eggs were left behind. A mound of sand sparsely covered the eggs, as if the culprits had a sudden attack of compassion for the unborn hatchlings and tried to preserve the eggs by burying them; their compassion was a waste. For us, it was a tragic sight.

The following day it was back in the water for me. Back down at sixty feet I listened to the bubbles gurgle from my regulator, watching another beautiful Hawksbill serenely glide through the water in her natural habitat. Recalling the night before, I thought about how the poachers stripped the Hawksbill of her life and the life she was to bear in exchange for a profit to be made from her meat and beautiful shell. The sight was such a shame. In the back of my head I heard the voices of my island friends telling me, "Turtle meat is a delicious delicacy, and the eggs—they make for a smooth cake. You ought to try." Of course, working with BSTP toward conserving the life of the endangered species, I couldn't think of cake made from turtle eggs on my plate. Aiding these creatures to sustain their population is what we worked towards. Even though upset by the turtle poaching because such incidences deterred our goals, I began to question if it was really so wrong.

At sixty feet deep, I contemplated the value and importance of my effort with BSTP. I was in this foreign country, working towards conserving the Hawksbill and against acts that deterred this. I supported a group that enforced punishment on anyone caught poaching turtle. However, was what I supported truly right? If it wasn't, how could conserving life be wrong? It was simple to reason that conserving endangered life couldn't be wrong. The deeper question remained: was it right to come into a foreign land and impose these beliefs and support punishment for those who didn't follow them? I wondered if I had a right to claim the wrongness and cruelty in killing the Hawksbill turtle, or instead, was I wrong to impose this moral judgment on a culture that had traditionally accepted the animal as a delicacy for many years. While watching the Hawksbill go about her peaceful swim and recalling the events of the previous night, I wondered who were the real protagonists and antagonists in this story.

Gazing at the light shimmering through the water onto the green and brownish-gold colors of the turtle's shell, I felt a sudden detachment from the animals that I had once felt so connected to after watching them nest night after night in the field. I could not reason an absolute answer to my questions. Perhaps there was none. I floated in the liquid womb of mother earth, humbled by her greatness, and thought perhaps only she knew the answers, if there were any. Floating deep underwater, attached to my scuba apparatus, I wondered if Leonardo da Vinci or the scientists who contributed to this awesome scuba invention ever felt detached from their work and passions as artists and scientists, as I suddenly did with the Hawksbill.

As I made my ascent back to the surface I thought of my upcoming night to follow out in the field. I would look at things differently. I would still be amused by the miracle of life while watching the turtles nest. I would help preserve the endangered Hawksbill, deter poachers, and probably disappoint someone out of using the tradition of turtle eggs to bake a cake. One or two poachers might get by and do things that I thought they shouldn't, but of course they would believe they should, and have every right to. All along the question would remain—who is right? Perhaps it's all culturally relative, and absolute right and wrong don't exist.

I finally completed my ascent to the surface, again feeling the sensation of warm ocean water oozing from my ear holes. I inflated my BCD, spit out my regulator, and looked toward the shores I would be patrolling in a few hours. For the time being I left my dilemma of cultural relativism and absolute right behind in the abyss of secrets shared with the ocean, thinking perhaps I'll come across an answer on my next dive.

Questions for Discussion and Your Reading Journal

1. The student repeats the title phrase "sixty feet deep" a number of times in the essay. What purposes might the repetition serve?
2. In the second paragraph the student writes that she was "synchronously human and machine." If you have ever used scuba gear, describe the sensation that the above phrase evokes. If you have never used scuba gear, describe how you imagine it would feel to rely on a machine to breathe.
3. To what extent do you think scientists should work to save endangered species? Are some species more important to save than others? Why or why not?
4. Should indigenous people have the right to determine whether native animals should be protected or harvested? Explain your reasoning.
5. What does the student mean when she uses the phrase "cultural relativism" in the last paragraph? How does that phrase apply to the student's situation? Think of other examples of issues involving cultural relativism and describe their context.

DEFINITIONS AND CULTURAL CONTEXTS

EDWARD T. HALL

Edward T. Hall (1914–) was born in Webster Groves, Missouri. He attended Columbia University, where he received his Ph.D. in anthropology in 1942. As an anthropologist, Hall is interested in the nature of human communication and other aspects of human behavior.

Anthropology is concerned with everything that is human in all parts of the world, both present and past. It is unique among the social sciences in the breadth of its scope. Most disciplines focus only on modern civilization or concentrate on single aspects of life, such as government or the economy. Anthropology is interested in all human societies and views life as a complexly integrated whole that is more than the sum of its parts. It is the human experience as a whole that this social science seeks to understand.

Anthropology is divided into four subcategories. Cultural anthropology studies the enormous diversity in contemporary cultures throughout the world. Linguistic anthropology explores language and its part in the development of human thinking and behavior. Physical anthropology studies biological evolution and examines how heredity affects behavior. Archaeology explores the human past, from a few hundred to many thousands of years ago. The commonality between the subcategories is the study of "culture."

Culture in relation to etiquette is the subject of the following essay, "The Anthropology of Manners," which was written in 1955 for the journal Scientific American. *In this essay Hall, who served as a director of a government program for training international diplomats, discusses the importance of manners in successful intercultural communication. He provides several examples of different standards of etiquette across cultures and discusses the problems that these differences can cause. Hall demonstrates that an awareness of cultural diversity will provide substantial benefits in communication between the various people of the world.*

Reading Rhetorically

Developing the skilled use of transitions in writing is one of the central objectives of college composition courses. In the following essay, Hall uses transitions to show the logical connections between somewhat disparate ideas, helping the reader to follow the smooth flow of his argument in favor of intercultural understanding.

Using appeals to *logos*, Hall sets out a series of examples of situations in which cultural differences have been mistakenly interpreted as bad manners. Examine the movement from one example to the next and note how Hall makes connections between them. The persuasive power of the essay exists not only in the number and clarity of examples but also in the logical transitions between them.

The Anthropology of Manners

The Goops they lick their fingers
   and the Goops they lick their knives;
They spill their broth on the table cloth—
   Oh, they lead disgusting lives.
The Goops they talk while eating,
   and loud and fast they chew;
And that is why I'm glad that I
   am not a Goop—are you?

In Gelett Burgess[1] classic on the Goops we have an example of what anthropologists call "an enculturating device"—a means of conditioning the young to life in our society. Having been taught the lesson of the goops from childhood (with or without the aid of Mr. Burgess) Americans are shocked when they go abroad and discover whole groups of people behaving like goops—eating with their fingers, making noises and talking while eating. When this happens, we may (1) remark on the barbarousness or quaintness of the "natives" (a term cordially disliked all over the world) or (2) try to discover the nature and meaning of the differences in behavior. One rather quickly discovers that what is good manners in one context may be bad in the next. It is to this point that I would like to address myself.

The subject of manners is complex; if it were not, there would not be so many injured feelings and so much misunderstanding in international circles everywhere. In any society the code of manners tends to sum up the culture—to be a frame of reference for all behavior. Emily Post[2] goes so far as to say: "There is not a single thing that we do, or say, or choose, or use, or even think, that does not follow or break one of the exactions of taste, or tact, or ethics of good manners, or etiquette—call it what you will." Unfortunately many of the most important standards of acceptable behavior in different cultures are elusive: They are intangible, undefined and unwritten.

An Arab diplomat who recently arrived in the U.S. from the Middle East attended a banquet which lasted several hours. When it was over, he met a fellow countryman outside and suggested they go get something to eat, as he was starving. His friend, who had been in this country for some time, laughed and said; "But, Habib, didn't you know that if you say, 'No, thank you,' they think you really don't want any?" In an Arab country etiquette dictates that the

---

[1] **Gelett Burgess (1866–1947)** American writer; the above stanza is taken from *Goops and How to Be Them* (1900). [Ed. note.]

[2] **Emily Post (1872–1960)** American expert on manners. [Ed. note.]

person being served must refuse the proffered dish several times, while his host urges him repeatedly to partake. The other side of the coin is that Americans in the Middle East, until they learn better, stagger away from banquets having eaten more than they want or is good for them.

4 When a public-health movie of a baby being bathed in a bathinette was shown in India recently, the Indian women who saw it were visibly offended. They wondered how people could be so inhuman as to bathe a child in stagnant (not running) water. Americans in Iran soon learn not to indulge themselves in their penchant for chucking infants under the chin and remarking on the color of their eyes, for the mother has to pay to have the "evil eye" removed. We also learn that in the Middle East you don't hand people things with your left hand, because it is unclean. In India we learn not to touch another person, and in Southeast Asia we learn that the head is sacred.

5 In the interest of intercultural understanding various U.S. Government agencies have hired anthropologists from time to time as technical experts. The State Department especially has pioneered in the attempt to bring science to bear on this difficult and complex problem. It began by offering at the Foreign Service Institute an intensive four-week course for Point 4 technicians. Later these facilities were expanded to include other foreign service personnel.

6 The anthropologist's job here is not merely to call attention to obvious taboos or to coach people about types of thoughtless behavior that have very little to do with culture. One should not need an anthropologist to point out, for instance, that it is insulting to ask a foreigner. "How much is this in real money?" Where technical advice is most needed is in the interpretation of the unconscious aspects of a culture—the things people do automatically without being aware of the full implications of what they have done. For example, an ambassador who has been kept waiting for more than half an hour by a foreign visitor needs to understand that if his visitor "just mutters an apology" this is not necessarily an insult. The time system in the foreign country may be composed of different basic units, so that the visitor is not as late as he may appear to us. You must know the time system of the country to know at what point apologies are really due.

7 Twenty years of experience in working with Americans in foreign lands convinces me that the real problem in preparing them to work overseas is not with taboos, which they catch on to rather quickly, but rather with whole congeries of habits and attitudes which anthropologists have only recently begun to describe systematically.

8 Can you remember tying your shoes this morning? Could you give the rules for when it is proper to call another person by his first name? Could you describe the gestures you make in conversation? These examples illustrate how much of our behavior is "out of awareness," and how easy it is to get into trouble in another culture.

9 Nobody is continually aware of the quality of his own voice, the subtleties of stress and intonation that color the meaning of his words or the posture and distance he assumes in talking to another person. Yet all these are taken as cues to the real nature of an utterance, regardless of what the words say. A simple illustration is the meaning in the tone of voice. In the U.S. we raise our

voices not only when we are angry but also when we want to emphasize a point, when we are more than a certain distance from another person, when we are concluding a meeting and so on. But to the Chinese, for instance, over-loudness of the voice is most characteristically associated with anger and loss of self-control. Whenever we become really interested in something, they are apt to have the feeling we are angry, in spite of many years' experience with us. Very likely most of their interviews with us, however cordial, seem to end on a sour note when we exclaim heartily: "WELL, I'M CERTAINLY GLAD YOU DROPPED IN, MR. WONG."

The Latin Americans, who as a rule take business seriously, do not under-   10
stand our mixing business with informality and recreation. We like to put our feet up on the desk. If a stranger enters the office, we take our feet down. If it turns out that the stranger and we have a lot in common, up go the feet again—a cue to the other fellow that we feel at ease. If the office boy enters, the feet stay up; if the boss enters and our relationship with him is a little strained at the moment, they go down. To a Latin American this whole behavior is shocking. All he sees in it is insult or just plain rudeness.

Differences in attitudes toward space—what would be territoriality in   11
lower forms of life—raise a number of other interesting points. U.S. women who go to live in Latin America all complain about the "waste" of space in the houses. On the other hand, U.S. visitors to the Middle East complain about crowding, in the houses and on the streetcars and buses. Everywhere we go space seems to be distorted. When we see a gardener in the mountains of Italy planting a single row on each of six separate terraces, we wonder why he spreads out his crop so that he has to spend half his time climbing up and down. We overlook the complex chain of communication that would be broken if he didn't cultivate alongside his brothers and his cousin and if he didn't pass his neighbors and talk to them as he moves from one terrace to the next.

A colleague of mine was caught in a snowstorm while traveling with com-   12
panies in the mountains of Lebanon. They stopped at the next house and asked to be put up for the night. The house had only one room. Instead of distributing the guests around the room, their host placed them next to the pallet where he slept with his wife—so close that they almost touched the couple. To have done otherwise in that country would have been unnatural and unfriendly. In the U.S. we distribute ourselves more evenly than many other people. We have strong feelings about touching and being crowded; in a streetcar, bus or elevator we draw ourselves in. Toward a person who relaxes and lets himself come into full contact with others in a crowded place we usually feel reactions that could not be printed on this page. It takes years for us to train our children not to crowd and lean on us. We tell them to stand up, that it is rude to slouch, not to sit so close or not to "breathe down our necks." After a while they get the point. By the time we Americans are in our teens we can tell what relationship exists between a man and woman by how they walk or sit together.

In Latin America, where touching is more common and the basic units of   13
space seem to be smaller, the wide automobiles made in the U.S. pose problems. People don't know where to sit. North Americans are disturbed by how

close the Latin Americans stand when they converse. "Why do they have to get so close when they talk to you?" "They're so pushy." "I don't know what it is, but it's something in the way they stand next to you." And so on. The Latin Americans, for their part, complain that people in the U.S. are distant and cold—*retraidos* (withdrawing and uncommunicative).

14   An analysis of the handling of space during conversations shows the following: A U.S. male brought up in the Northeast stands 18 to 20 inches away when talking face to face to a man he does not know very well; talking to a woman under similar circumstances, he increases the distance about four inches. A distance of only eight to 13 inches between males is considered either very aggressive or indicative of a closeness of a type we do not ordinarily want to think about. Yet in many parts of Latin America and the Middle East distances which are almost sexual in connotation are the only ones at which people can talk comfortably. In Cuba, for instance, there is nothing suggestive in a man's talking to an educated woman at a distance of 13 inches. If you are a Latin American, talking to a North American at the distance he insists on maintaining is like trying to talk across a room.

15   To get a more vivid idea of this problem of the comfortable distance, try starting a conversation with a person eight or 10 feet away or one separated from you by a wide obstruction in a store or other public place. Any normally enculturated person can't help trying to close up the space, even to the extent of climbing over benches or walking around tables to arrive within comfortable distance. U.S. businessmen working in Latin America try to prevent people from getting uncomfortably close by barricading themselves behind desks, typewriters or the like, but their Latin American office visitors will often climb up on desks or over chairs and put up with loss of dignity in order to establish a spatial context in which interaction can take place for them.

16   The interesting thing is that neither party is specifically aware of what is wrong when the distance is not right. They merely have vague feelings of discomfort or anxiety. As the Latin American approaches and the North American backs away, both parties take offense without knowing why. When a North American, having had the problem pointed out to him, permits the Latin American to get close enough, he will immediately notice that the latter seems much more at ease.

17   My own studies of space and time have engendered considerable cooperation and interest on the part of friends and colleagues. One case recently reported to me had to do with a group of seven-year-olds in a crowded Sunday school classroom. The children kept fighting. Without knowing quite what was involved, the teacher had them moved to a larger room. The fighting stopped. It is interesting to speculate as to what would have happened had the children been moved to a smaller room.

18   The embarrassment about intimacy in space applies also to the matter of addressing people by name. Finding the proper distance in the use of names is even more difficult than in space, because the rules for first-naming are unbelievably complex. As a rule we tend to stay on the "mister" level too long with Latins and some others, but very often we swing into first-naming too quickly, which amounts to talking down to them. Whereas in the U.S. we use Mr. with

the surname, in Latin America the first and last names are used together and señor (Sr.) is a title. Thus when one says, "My name is Sr. So-and-So," is it interpreted to mean, "I am the Honorable, his Excellency So-and-So." It is no wonder that when we stand away, barricade ourselves behind our desks (usually a reflection of status) and call ourselves mister, our friends to the south wonder about our so-called "good-neighbor" policy and think of us as either high-hat or unbelievably rude. Fortunately most North Americans learn some of these things after living in Latin America for a while, but the aversion to being touched and to touching sometimes persists after 15 or more years of residence and even under such conditions as intermarriage.

The difference in sense of time is another thing of which we are not aware. An Iranian, for instance, is not taught that it is rude to be late in the same way that we in the U.S. are. In a general way we are conscious of this, but we fail to realize that their time system is structured differently from ours. The different cultures simply place different values on the time units. 19

Thus let us take as a typical case of the North European time system (which has regional variations) the situation in the urban eastern U.S. A middle-class businessman meeting another of equivalent rank will ordinarily be aware of being two minutes early or late. If he is three minutes late, it will be noted as significant but usually neither will say anything. If four minutes late, he will mutter something by way of apology; at five minutes he will utter a full sentence of apology. In other words, the major unit is a five-minute block. Fifteen minutes is the smallest significant period for all sorts of arrangements and it is used very commonly. A half hour of course is very significant, and if you spend three quarters of an hour or an hour, either the business you transact or the relationship must be important. Normally it is an insult to keep a public figure or a person of significantly higher status than yourself waiting even two or three minutes, though the person of higher position can keep you waiting or even break an appointment. 20

Now among urban Arabs in the Eastern Mediterranean, to take an illustrative case of another time system, the unit that corresponds to our five-minute period is 15 minutes. Thus when an Arab arrives nearly 30 minutes after the set time, by his reckoning he isn't even "10 minutes" late yet (in our time units). Stated differently, the Arab's tardiness will not amount to one significant period (15 minutes in our system). An American normally will wait no longer than 30 minutes (two significant periods) for another person to turn up in the middle of the day. Thereby he often unwittingly insults people in the Middle East who want to be his friends. 21

How long is one expected to stay when making a duty call at a friend's house in the U.S.? While there are regional variations, I have observed that the minimum is very close to 45 minutes, even in the race of pressing commitments elsewhere, such as a roast in the oven. We may think we can get away in 30 minutes by saying something about only stopping for "a minute," but usually we discover that we don't feel comfortable about leaving until 45 minutes have elapsed. I am referring to afternoon social calls; evening calls last much longer and operate according to a different system. In Arab countries an American paying a duty call at the house of a desert sheik causes consternation if he gets 22 up to leave after half a day. There a duty call lasts three days—the first day to prepare the feast, the second for the feast itself and the third to taper off and say farewell. In the first half day the sheik has barely had time to slaughter the sheep for the feast. The guest's departure would leave the host frustrated.

23   There is a well-known story of a tribesman who came to Kabul, the capital of Afghanistan, to meet his brother. Failing to find him, he asked the merchants in the market place to tell his brother where he could be found if the brother showed up. A year later the tribesman returned and looked again. It developed that he and his brother had agreed to meet in Kabul but had failed to specify what year! If the Afghan time system were structured similarly to our own, which it apparently is not, the brother would not offer a full sentence of apology until he was five years late.

24   Informal units of time such as "just a minute," "a while," "later," "a long time," "a spell," "a long, long time," "years" and so on provide us with the culturological equivalent of Evil-Eye Fleegle's "double-whammy" (in *Li'l Abner*). Yet these expressions are not as imprecise as they seem. Any American who has worked in an office with someone else for six months can usually tell within five minutes when that person will be back if he says, "I'll be gone for a while." It is simply a matter of learning from experience the individual's system of time indicators. A reader who is interested in communications theory can fruitfully speculate for a while on the very wonderful way in which culture provides the means whereby the receiver puts back all the redundant material that was stripped from such a message. Spelled out, the message might go somewhat as follows: "I am going downtown to see So-and-So about the Such-and-Such contract, but I don't know what the traffic conditions will be like or how long it will take me to get a place to park nor do I know what shape So-and-So will be in today, but taking all this into account I think I will be out of the office about an hour but don't like to commit myself, so if anyone calls you can say I'm not sure how long I will be; in any event I expect to be back before 4 o'clock."

25   Few of us realize how much we rely on built-in patterns to interpret messages of this sort. An Iranian friend of mine who came to live in the U.S. was hurt and puzzled for the first few years. The new friends he met and liked would say on parting: "Well, I'll see you later." He mournfully complained: "I kept expecting to see them, but the 'later' never came." Strangely enough we ourselves are exasperated when a Mexican can't tell us precisely what he means when he uses the expression *mañana*.[3]

26   The role of the anthropologist in preparing people for service overseas is to open their eyes and sensitize them to the subtle qualities of behavior—tone of voice, gestures, space and time relationships—that so often build up feelings of frustration and hostility in other people with a different culture. Whether we are going to live in a particular foreign country or travel in many, we need a frame of reference that will enable us to observe and learn the significance of differences in manners. Progress is being made in this anthropological study, but it is also showing us how little is known about human behavior.

---

[3]*mañana* Spanish for "tomorrow."

Questions for Discussion and Your Reading Journal

1. For what audience is Hall writing this piece? What is the purpose of the essay?
2. List synonyms for the word "Goop." What is the difference between a klutz and a Goop?
3. Pick out a sentence in the first paragraph that you would consider to encompass the main idea. How are manners related to context?
4. What is a cultural anthropologist? Why would such a person be an asset to a government's state department?
5. Discuss or freewrite about any encounters with people from other cultures that you have had. Have you had any experiences similar to the ones described in this article?
6. What is ethnocentrism? What causes an attitude of ethnocentrism to develop?

JULIUS ROBERT OPPENHEIMER

Julius Robert Oppenheimer (1904–1967) presented the following speech, "The Scientist in Society," to alumni of Princeton University in 1953. Oppenheimer, a physicist, is most famous for his work contributing to the development of the atomic bomb. Oppenheimer describes scientists not as disinterested manipulators of the physical environment but as individuals who must take personal responsibility for their experiments and discoveries in the laboratory. Scientists, he asserts, must evaluate the social consequences of their work as a part of the scientific process. Oppenheimer also notes the modern tendency of nonscientists to ignore scientific and technological advances. Questioning the notion that all scientific discovery is progressive, Oppenheimer urges people to recognize the importance of understanding and evaluating issues in science that have global repercussions.

Reading Rhetorically

Julius Robert Oppenheimer was among the first scientists to recognize that the work he had done had repercussions beyond his intentions. As you read this article think about scientific discoveries, not only in the field of nuclear warfare and warfare in general but in every field, that have turned out to have implications more far-reaching than the scientists involved had imagined. The first scientists to examine DNA, for example, could not have been aware that only decades later their work would be put to use to clone animals, even humans. Like Einstein and Russell in the subsequent essays on science and religion, Oppenheimer does not sanction the argument that scientific discovery should take place in a moral vacuum and that others should make decisions about the ethical questions arising from the work of scientists. It is important to note that he is addressing not a general audience but an audience made up of scientists like himself.

In order to better understand it, read this essay as an extended argument aimed at other scientists and try to determine as early on as possible the subject and nature of the argument. Then you can follow the points Oppenheimer makes one by one, examining them for their persuasive impact. Imagine also the arguments that would be made against those of Oppenheimer and determine if the essay addresses those arguments effectively.

By the time you have finishing reading, try to make a determination of your overall response: did Oppenheimer persuade you? If so, was this persuasion accomplished primarily by *logos, pathos,* or *ethos?*

The Scientist in Society

1 There is something inherently comforting about a panel of experts. One knows that the partial and inadequate and slanted and personal views that he expresses will be corrected by the less partial, less personal views of everyone else on the panel; it is not unlike the experience of the professor who always is glad that he has to meet his class again because he can correct the mistakes that he made the last time. It is with such tentativeness that I am going to talk to you.

2 This is a vast terrain—one full of strange precipices, chasms and terrors. What I thought I would do first is to run over in a quite synoptic way a few general opinions, almost words only, which seem to me involved in the relations between science and man's life. It is my hope that I will do this with enough baldness so that you will pick up some of these words and deal with them more fully and more wisely than in this summary. I will then devote a little time to one problem which seems to me singularly fit in this hall and in this company, which worries me a great deal, and as to a resolution for which I have only the most rudimentary notions.

3 For one thing, we have changed the face of the earth; we have changed the way men live. We may not change the condition of man's life, but we have changed all modes in which that condition occurs. I do not by this mean to say that from the existence of science, from the discovery, knowledge, technique and power of science the particularities of the present time follow. But we all know that if life today is very different from what it was two hundred years ago, if we meet our human and political problems in a quite new form, that has much to do with the fact that we know how to do a great many things, and that there are people who are eager to do them, not typically scientists, but people who are glad to use the knowledge and with it the control which science has made available.

4 I need not belittle two points. One is that the effect of science on the condition of man's life is also in part a cultural and intellectual one. I shall return to that because it is my persuasion that this is largely a happy symbiosis of the past; today we have very little of it. The ideas which have changed the think-

ing caps of men and which derived from experience in science are really not contemporary ideas but go back a century or two centuries or more.

The second, of course, is not to try to give to scientific life an autonomy 5 of society. It is possible, manifestly, for society so to arrange things that there is no science. The Nazis made a good start in that direction; maybe the Communists will achieve it; and there is not one of us free of the worry that this flourishing tree may someday not be alive any more.

But nonetheless we *have* changed the face of the earth; any beginning of a 6 talk about science and society must take that as a fact.

There is another theme. This is a time that tends to believe in progress. 7 Our ways of thought, our ways of arranging our personal lives, our political forms, point to the future, point not merely to change, to decay, to alteration, but point with a hopeful note of improvement that our progress is inevitable. In the acquisition of knowledge, in the very notion of a cumulative discipline, tomorrow in a certain sense comprises today and yesterday. How much this built-in sense of progress in man's life—which is, I think, not a religious notion, not a Christian notion—how much this derives from the effects of science on philosophical and political thought I would leave to historians of ideas. It is probably not wholly trivial.

A third theme is that science in a certain sense is universal. It is not uni- 8 versal in the sense that all men participate in it. It is universal in the sense that all men can participate in it. It is nonnational, nonlocal and, although one would not say noncultural, singularly independent of the form of government, the immediate tradition, or the affective life of a people. It has to do with *humanitas*. This universality is not a trivial thing at a time when forms of unity, large forms of unity in the world, appear to be for other reasons rather necessary. This has been very much in all our minds in the years since the last war. I remember that on one occasion when I was in this hall, at the Bicentennial of the University, we were talking about the universality of science; and at that very moment the Soviet delegate to the United Nations Atomic Energy Commission was imploring his government for permission to accept the scientific and technical report of the subcommittee of this commission. This, I think, is the last time—the last time I remember—that the Soviet government has said *yes* to anything, has said *yes* to an agreement of fact. I know how bitterly disappointing the experiences of these years have been as to universality of science, but we all know that this is bad politics but not bad science. We all know that there is no such thing as German physics or Soviet genetics or American astronomy. These fields can open themselves to all reasonable men willing to take the trouble to inquire.

There is also what may first seem like the opposite of universality; I hope 9 you will bear that in mind when I talk of science as a great and beautiful word. There *is* a unity to it; but there is also an even more striking and immense diversity. Both of your speakers this morning are physicists, and I think we are very different from our brothers the chemists and our brothers the mathematicians. In our values, in our style, we are different. Physics is perhaps the branch of science which has been most concerned to keep itself one. The Physical Society splits off divisions from time to time but is reluctant to do so; and the divisions largely have to do with semiapplied science. Physics has a history of close association with mathematics, with astronomy, with epistemology and cosmology too. And yet we do not know very much about the rest of the scientists. I know that it is a very happy occasion at the Institute when some piece of work turns up which is of interest to both the mathematicians and the physicists. It is a very rare occasion and we tend to ring bells when a small bit of cement can be found between their interests. I would stress especially that there is no systematic unity of techniques, of appreciation, of values, of style between the many things that we call science. There is a lot of difference between the nuclear physicist and the agricultural scientist exploring the possibility of improving crops in some poor island in the Caribbean. They are scientists, and they understand each other, and we hope love each other. But they are not very much alike.

10 There are perhaps two or three other general things. One I believe may be of more importance to some of the other panels than to this. This is one of the by-products of the great flowering of science that dates back to the time when science did have an effect on culture and on ideas. We have been impressed, and I must say I never stop being impressed, by the great sweep of general order in which particulars are recognized as united. You know the examples: Electricity and light, the quantum theory and the theory of valence, places where things that appeared to be separate, and each having its own order, appear as illustrations of a more general order. And one may say, I suppose, that science is a search for regularity and order in those domains of experience which have proven accessible to it.

11 I am not sure that the effect of the impressive victory of man's mind in this enterprise has not been to make us a little obtuse to the role of the contingent and the particular in life. It is true that many particulars can be understood and subsumed by a general order. But it is probably no less a great truth that elements of abstractly irreconcilable general orders can be subsumed by a particular. And this notion might be more useful to our friends who study man and his life than an insistence on following the lines which in natural science have been so overwhelmingly successful.

12 There is another great complex of questions. These I feel reassured to mention hardly at all because my friend and successor Dr. Waterman has thought so deeply about them; he is perhaps as well informed as any man in the world. This has to do with the great variety of means whereby society patronizes science, whereby it is possible for the scientist to operate and live and eat and do his work, get in some sense a bit of encouragement and in some sense a bit of nourishment. The problem of patronage is a complex one; it is changing; it has changed enormously in the last decade in this country. I leave it with a good conscience to Alan Waterman that he may deal with it wisely.

13 What is it, then, that bothers me especially, that I want not merely to mention but to worry about here? I think that in this matter perhaps this panel is not so different than the panel on the role of the artist, or the panel on the role of the philosopher. To put it with great brutality, the point is that the scientist is not in society today, any more than is the artist or the philosopher.

Of course, he does get paid, he does get patronized and even, for odd rea- 14
sons that he sometimes does not understand, respected. But he is not in society,
in the sense that the ideas he has, the work he is doing, stop really rather short
with the limits of his profession. They are not part of the intellectual and cultural
life of the times. I am over and over again appalled by how ignorant, how incredibly ignorant of the most rudimentary things about my subject are my fellows the
historians, my acquaintances the statesmen, my friends the men of affairs. They
have no notion of what cooks in physics; I think that they have very little notion
of what cooks in any other science. And I know that only by good luck and some
hard work do I have even a rudimentary notion of what cooks in other parts of
the house called science than the one that I live in. I read the *Physical Review* and
work very hard to catch up with it every two weeks; and I think maybe I have
some notion of what is going on in some parts of physics; but by and large we
know little about one another, and the world outside knows nothing about us. I
think this may vary a little from place to place. Perhaps it is tradition in Britain,
where there is a sort of delicate tendency, a national tendency, to refuse to let
things become obscure and recondite, that there is a little more effort to see that
civilized men have a notion of what the mathematicians and astronomers and
physicists are doing—not merely to know the by-products of their works, the
practical products, but what they are thinking.

This is in very sharp contrast, this startling general ignorance of scientific 15
ideas and discoveries at the edge of the technical disciplines, in very sharp contrast to the state of affairs two or three centuries ago; and some of the reasons
for this are manifest. But I believe that the science of today is subtler, richer,
more relevant to man's life and more useful to man's dignity than the science
which had such a great effect on the age of the enlightenment, had such a great
effect, among other things, on the forms and patterns, traditions and hopes—
reflected in our Constitution—of human society. Science is not retrograde; and
there is no doubt that the quantum mechanics represents a more interesting,
more instructive, richer analogy of human life than Newtonian mechanics
could conceivably be. There is no doubt that even the theory of relativity,
which was been so much vulgarized and so little understood, that even the theory of relativity is a matter which would be of real interest to people at large.
There is no doubt that the findings of biology and astronomy and chemistry
are discoveries that would enrich our whole culture if they were understood.
And what is perhaps more troublesome, there is a gulf between the life of the
scientist and the life of a man who isn't actively a scientist, dangerously deep.
The experience of science—to stub your toe hard and then notice that it was
really a rock on which you stubbed it—this experience is something that is
hard to communicate by popularization, by education, or by talk. It is almost
as hard to tell a man what it is like to find out something new about the world
as it is to describe a mystical experience to a chap who has never had any hint
of such an experience.

The enlightenment was a peculiar time; it was hopeful, and superficial, 16
and humane; and how much of the ideas of the enlightenment derived from an
appreciation of science, it is perhaps not right for anyone but careful historian

to say. But we know that the same men who wrote about politics and philosophy—not very good philosophy, and not too good politics—also wrote about natural science, about physics, and astronomy, and mathematics. We know that on two very different planes Franklin and Jefferson managed to span the whole way from a living, and in some cases even practicing, interest in science to the world of affairs. And we know how full their writings are of the illumination which one sheds on the other.

17   Science in those days was connected with the practical arts; it was very close to common sense. Yet always there is in science little more than the infinitely diligent and patient and unremitting application of the practical arts and common sense. By now it has come to be a long chain. The mere process of carrying a boy through the elementary steps of this chain consumes so much of his life and is such an exhausting operation, to the teacher and student alike, that the simple means of communication and understanding, which sufficed in the seventeenth and eighteenth centuries, are clearly not good enough.

18   This is a problem that has had the thought of many wise people; I do not pretend to be talking of anything new or strange. I suppose the notion of having laboratory courses was an attempt to bring the young man and woman into this experience of really discovering something; yet my fear is that by the time it gets into the laboratory and the professor knows the answer, the whole operation is different; it is an imitation and not the real thing. I suppose all of you have read the eloquent pleas which a number of scientists, of whom perhaps President Conant is the best known, have made for attempting to communicate some understanding of science by what is essentially the historical method. These do, I think, establish the fact that science as a human activity is treatable by the historical method. They do not, I think, establish that a scientific method, or a scientific discovery, is communicable by these means. I have a great anxiety that our educational directions, far from making us a part of the world we live in, in this very special sense that we share ideas and some bit of experience with our fellow men, may even be moving rather in the opposite direction.

19   This is odd: We live in the world very much affected by science, and even our thinking caps, and our ideas and the terms in which we tend to talk about things, the notion of progress, the notion of a fraternity of scholars and scientists which is so familiar to a Christian life and which has a new twist because of the spread of science—all of these we can see originally at a time when science was understood by men of affairs, by artists, by poets. We live today in a world in which poets and historians and men of affairs are proud that they wouldn't even begin to consider thinking about learning anything of science, regarding it as the far end of a tunnel too long for any wise man to put his head into. We therefore have, in so far as we have at all, a philosophy that is quite anachronistic and, I am convinced, quite inadequate to our times. I think that whatever may have been thought of Cartesian[1] and Newtonian[2] reforms

---

[1]Cartesian Pertaining to the science and philosophy on René Descartes (1596–1650), a religious skeptic, author of the famous kernel, "I think; therefore I am." [Ed. note.]

[2]Newtonian Relating to Sir Isaac Newton (1642–1727), whose work included the theories of gravitation and differential calculus. [Ed. note.]

in the intellectual life of Europe, the time when these were what the doctor ordered—all that the doctor ordered—is long past. Far more subtle recognition of the nature of man's knowledge and of his relations to the universe is certainly long overdue, if we are to do justice to the wisdom which our tradition has in it and to the brilliant and ever-changing flower of discovery which is modern science.

Research is action, and the question I want to leave in a very raw and   20
uncomfortable form with you is how to communicate this sense of action to our fellow men who are not destined to devote their lives to the professional pursuit of new knowledge.

Questions for Discussion and Your Reading Journal

1. Look at the introduction to the article. Who is the audience that Oppenheimer is addressing? What might be some unique characteristics of such an audience?
2. What are the implications of the tentative nature of science?
3. What is Oppenheimer's concern about the relationship between the general population and the scientific community? Considering this concern, what might be the purpose of the article?
4. What does Oppenheimer mean by describing science as "cumulative" (Paragraph 7)?
5. Why should/shouldn't science be universal, nonnational, and nonlocal?
6. Examine the final statement: "Research is action." What might this mean?

ANNE WALTON

Anne Walton is a contemporary scientist and science writer in Great Britain. She frequently speaks on the topic of women in science. The following essay, "Women Scientists: Are They Really Different?" discusses the question of whether women are by nature unsuited (or less suited than men) to scientific study. Walton traces the prejudice against women scientists through the centuries and focuses on the barriers keeping women out of the sciences in the contemporary world. The article, which includes a number of interesting quotations from prominent scientists of the past and the present, attempts to persuade the reader that the misogynistic attitudes toward women in science have no basis in empirical data.

Reading Rhetorically

If you look at the last essay (by Oppenheimer), you will notice that he uses the pronoun "he" throughout the essay to refer to scientists in general. Think about this convention before reading the Walton essay. You may or may not consider that the tendency to use the male pronoun to refer to scientists is one social convention that discourages girls from entering the field even before they have considered doing so.

Walton appears to have intended this article for a particular audience in much the same way that Oppenheimer did in the last essay. Think about the difference between the two audiences and how that difference may affect the substance of each author's argument. Before you begin reading, you may also try to predict some of the things Walton will say. It may be helpful to make a brief list of your expectations, so that you can compare them with the points she actually makes. Writing this list will give you an idea of some of your own preconceptions about women in science.

As you read, take notice of the quotations from various scientists that Walton uses in the essay. Think about the reasons she may have for quoting so many different individuals, and the impact of the number and variety of quotations on the reader. Does this contribute to her own *ethos* or not?

Women Scientists: Are They Really Different?

INTRODUCTION

1   For most of my working life I have been a practising scientist. I have worked in industrial and academic laboratories—as a laboratory assistant—and as a consultant. I have also taught chemistry from "O" level to the supervision of PhD students. But it is only in recent years that I have begun to look seriously beyond my own personal experience to the role of women in science in a wider context.

2   To my dismay, it seemed that there had been little improvement since I had embarked on my own career. The dice are *still* so heavily loaded against girls and women choosing a scientific career that I was astonished that so *many* had succeeded, against all the odds, rather than that there were so few.

3   Many factors deter girls from choosing a scientific career and one of these is undoubtedly the attitudes adopted by parents, teachers, friends and society in general. It was this area which I decided to investigate and my studies so far have indicated that negative attitudes towards women scientists have always existed and still prevail. These attitudes need to be demonstrated and combated because they adversely affect women's careers, role models for girls and boy's expectations of women.

4   Science is dominated by men, most of its practitioners are men and it is said to have a masculine image. Society does not expect women to become scientists so those that do, know that they are "stepping out of line." This, in itself, makes them 'special' in some way because the men, in a male dominated profession are not, in any sense, rebels. In an attempt to discover whether women scientists have any other characteristics in common, I have been gathering information about their lives, the way they work, the nature of that work and what they say about themselves.

If one includes both past and present women scientists one finds, superfi- 5
cially at least, a great diversity, particularly in their backgrounds, which range
from poor, working-class to rich aristocracy. Some are married, with children,
while some are unmarried and childless. However, it is evident that most of
them developed habits of independent thought at an early age. Often these
seem to have been fostered by parents who, in some cases, were subsequently
dismayed when their daughters insisted on following their own inclinations
and rejected traditional roles. Perhaps the parents *inadvertently* sowed the
seeds of rebellion. Not all of the women scientists had to struggle against
adversity as we normally think of it. The privileged ones who could have led
idle, comfortable lives, chose not to, but all were quietly confident that what
they were doing was *right for them.*

On the whole, I have limited my investigations so far mainly to women 6
working in the physical and applied sciences because they represent a much
smaller minority than women in the biological sciences. A consideration of the
type of work which these women do may be significant. Interestingly, while
most of them began by studying *pure* science and mathematics, as their careers
developed, many of them seem to have been drawn to research areas with
applications in everyday life, particularly in medicine. Their chosen fields of
research, as intellectually tough as any in science, yet had strong humanitarian
connotations.

This suggested to me that possibly science as constructed by males might 7
prove to be a "bad fit" for females. Certainly many girls seem to be ill at ease
when confronted by science. Perhaps those women who had forged a career
for themselves on the "inside" of the scientific edifice were consciously or
unconsciously, adjusting and adapting their own function within that framework so as to derive more satisfaction from their work by relating it to a social
context.

ATTITUDES TO WOMEN IN SCIENCE

It seemed to me that the fairest way to discuss attitudes would be to illustrate 8
them using direct quotations by the women's contemporaries wherever possible. These fall into a number of categories each of which exemplifies a particular group of attitudes, although there is considerable overlap.

The idea that there might be innate differences between the intellectual 9
powers of men and women has been bandied about for hundreds, if not thousands, of years. Indeed, a great deal of effort has been put into the search for
differences, so far with limited success. At one time, brain size was thought to
be an indicator of mental capacity. After the death of the eminent mathematician, Sonya (or Soña) Kovalevskaia in 1891, her brain, which had been preserved in alcohol, was weighed and the weight compared with that of the brain
of the scientist Herman van Helmholtz (Osen, 1974). Given the difference in
body weight, her brain was proportionately larger. This practice was dropped
when the brains of some idiots turned out to be heavier than those of the brilliant! More recently, there has been an interest in the functions of the left and
right hemispheres of the brain and attempts have been made to relate these to

---

Box 1—Inherent Differences

The female . . . seldom reach any farther than to a sleight superficial smattering in any deep science. (*The Compleat Midwifes Practice Enlarged,* 1659)

Women have no share in sciences and employments, because that they are not capable thereof. (Poulain de la Barre, 1673 [English translation, 1677])

Women are cast in too soft a mould, are made of too fine, too delicate a composure to endure the severity of study, the drudgery of contemplation, the fatigue of profound speculation. (*The British Apollo,* 1708)

The principal feature which appears to me to characterize the caucasian . . . is the power that many of its *male* members have of advancing the horizon of science. (Bennett, 1870)

There can be no real question that the female mind stands considerably below the male . . . the ready firmness of decision which belongs by nature to the truly masculine mind is very rarely to be met with in the feminine (Romanes, 1887)

When we come to science we find women are simply nowhere. The feminine mind is quite unscientific . . . (Swinburne, 1902)

We must put a stop to this, or we shall have Mary [Somerville] in a straight-jacket one of these days. (Mary Somerville's father about 1800 [Osen, 1974])

The reporter suggested to Irène (Joliot-Curie) that perhaps the career she had chosen would be too punishing for a woman. (Reid, 1978)

Nature herself prescribed to the woman her function as mother and housewife and that laws of nature cannot be ignored . . . without grave damage, which . . . would especially manifest itself in the following generation. (Max Planck, about 1897 [Krafft, 1978])

---

gender stereotypes. In a book published in 1982 by Richter the question is asked "Are there then some types of scientific work that women on the whole can do better than men?" And later "It may be concluded that women are not lacking in the abilities required for scientific research." Then in the same paragraph "The different fields of science offer a wide range of opportunities for people with many different kinds of abilities and so long as they do not expect too much, they offer a life that many find rewarding and enjoyable." This is hardly encouraging to the budding female scientist.

10   Some further examples of these attitudes are shown in Box 1.

11   The notion that intense intellectual activity was damaging to women and particularly to their reproductive function and possible offspring, flourished towards the end of the nineteenth century. Rosenberg's *Beyond Separate Spheres* (Rosenberg, 1982) includes an interesting discussion on this issue and its significance for women then entering higher education in the United States.

12   It follows from the arguments outlined above that if women *do* become scientists they are only fit for work at the lower levels or under the direction of a man, or both. I recently talked to a woman chemist who was employed in industry in the 1920s and 1930s, she said, "I was expected to do all the bor-

---

Box 2—What Women Can Do

[Women] make excellent assistants, and they could probably do the work of the assay, or city analyst's office, or of an observatory, better than most men. Ladies' names often appear as authors of papers, generally in organic chemistry, or in subjects involving tedious but accurate readings of instruments—. (Swinburne, 1902)

[Caroline Herschel] took care of all the laborious numerical calculations and reductions, all the record keeping, and the other tedious minutiae that required a trained mind but would have consumed too much of Sir William's time. (Osen, 1974)

All [woman's] perceptions of minute details, all her delicate observation of color, of form, of shape, of change, and her capability of patient routine, would be of immense value in the collection of scientific facts. (Professor Maria Mitchell, Vassar, 1876 [*Science,* 1979])

Even Professor A. accords me his sanction when I sew his papers or tie up a sore finger or dust the table etc. . . . they can't say study spoils me for anything else . . . Professor Ordway trusts me to do his work for him . . . I am only too happy to do anything for him. (Ellen Swallow [became a founder of the American Home Economics Association] 1870–1873 at MIT [Bernard, 1964])

In the case of Pierre and Marie Curie, Pierre Curie was the creator, who with his genius established new laws of physics. Marie was outstanding for other qualities such as character, exceptional tenacity, precision and patience. (Leprince-Ringuet [Richter, 1982])

Some teachers encouraged me by saying that [anthropology] would be nice for a woman because there are . . . domestic aspects such as cooking and clothing. I did not like such remarks. (Chie Nakane, Tokyo—contemporary [Richter, 1982])

---

ing jobs that came into the laboratory, while anything interesting was handed out to one of the men." Later she said, "I was second in command in my own, now large department, and, as the head enjoyed rather poor health, I often had to run things for weeks or months on end." When she left in 1935, she says "they had difficulty in finding my successor, finally paying me the supreme compliment of replacing me by a young man to whom they paid a salary £100 greater than the figure I was receiving after ten years."

Information on the type of work available to women scientists in America 13 up to 1940 may be found in Rossiter's (1982) *Women Scientists in America* where she points out that promotion to senior positions was virtually confined to the women's colleges unless women were willing to move out of "mainstream" science into such areas as home economics or nutrition which attracted relatively few men.

Some further examples are given in Box 2. There are many more. 14

If a woman does manage to succeed in science, against all the odds, the 15 commonest allegation made is that it is because she is collaborating with a man. Because most scientists are men and because in the experimental sciences most people work in a team, the chance of a woman collaborating with a man is very high. Certainly the support of a powerful male sponsor (Rossiter, 1982) can sometimes ensure that a woman is not overlooked, but receives the

---

Box 3—Helped by a Man or "Exceptional"

Such work is either done in conjunction with men, or is obviously under their guidance and supervision, and much is made about it out of gallantry. (Swinburne, 1902)

There existed a vocal group very ready to revive the view that Marie Curie had ridden to success on her husband's coat-tails. (Reid, 1978)

Errors are notoriously hard to kill, but an error that ascribes to a man what was actually the work of a woman, has more lives than a cat. (Hertha Ayrton, of Marie Curie, approx. 1909 [Reid, 1978])

All the eminent women scientists have achieved their best work when collaborating with a male colleague. (Sir William Ramsay, approx. 1910, [*ibid*])

There he [her husband] stood waiting while the President conferred the PhD degree . . . yet I could not help feeling that he was suggesting something: He was there when it all happened, a woman could never do it alone. (W. Muta Maathai, Nairobi, Kenya—contemporary [Richter, 1982])

If a woman has a special gift—which does not happen often—I do not think it right to refuse her the chance and means of studying . . . [but] such a case must always be regarded just as an exception. (Max Planck, approx. 1897 [Krafft, 1978])

But when a person of the sex which . . . must encounter infinitely more difficulties than men . . . succeeds nevertheless . . . then without doubt she must have the noblest courage, quite extraordinary talents and a superior genius. (Gauss to Sophie Germain, 1807 [Ernest, 1976])

---

promotion she deserves. There is no doubt that women scientists have been helped in this way. Mary Fieser, for example, would not have been allowed to practise chemistry at Harvard (Pramer, 1985) had she not been married to Louis Fieser. She became his graduate student and continued as a research associate while other women were not taken on because the professors would not have women in their research teams. Agnes Pockels's work would probably never have been published unless she had received the support of Lord Rayleigh (Giles and Forrester, 1971) who submitted her work for publication. It seems to me that there is nothing unfair or unreasonable in young persons of either sex being helped and encouraged by those who have already achieved success.

16   Another misleading allegation frequently levelled at successful women scientists is that they are "exceptional" and therefore that there is no need to bother about any women who are less than outstanding. In a sense, men scientists are "let off the hook" if they can point to a few women Nobel Prize winners and say "Ah, but *they* are exceptional." True, but the majority of men practising science are doing no more than useful, competent jobs and why should women be excluded from making similar contributions?

17   Some quotations related to these themes are given in Box 3.

18   Because of the way that society is organized, I believe that it is still true to say that most women have greater social and domestic responsibilities than men. Experimental scientists cannot work at, or from, home for a lot of the time because they have to be in the laboratory. A family crisis often involves

---

Box 4—Social and Domestic Responsibilities

A man can always command his time under the plea of business; a woman is not allowed any such excuse. At Chelsea I was always supposed to be at home when friends and acquaintances came out to see me. (Mary Somerville, 1780–1872 [Osen, 1974]

I wonder you let Mary waste her time in reading; she never sews more than if she were a man. [She hoped she] would give up her foolish manner of life and make a respectable and useful wife. (Mary Somerville's family [Osen, 1974])

I cannot emphasize too much the importance of his [her husband's] emotional support as well as his actual help with the tasks often considered to be "women's work." (Marian W. Kies, Bethesda, USA [Richter, 1982])

It was not very easy for me to take care of my child, his father and the house, together with my scientific work. (Liana Bolis, Messina, Sicily [*ibid*])

My parents became seriously ill when I was about to leave [for college]. I had to stay home and care for them. (R. Rajalakshmi, Baroda, India, [*ibid*])

But nobody knows the sense of guilt in having to leave the children to be looked after by somebody else for long periods. (Liana Bolis, Messina, Sicily [*ibid*])

I have never neglected any essential aspects of their upbringing, but I do not feel that I have done them any harm by delegating the washing of nappies and their supervision in playgrounds to others. (Tahereh M. Z. Ralumani, Tehran, Iran [*ibid*])

---

time off from work for the woman of the family rather than the man. It is still assumed that child rearing and care for the sick and elderly is primarily a woman's job, and many a promising career has been damaged or even abandoned as a result.

19   Some quotations to illustrate these points are given in Box 4. All except the first two are by contemporary women.

20   Many married women scientists are strongly supported in their career aspirations by their husbands. Nevertheless, if a conflict of interests arises between husband's and wife's career, it is nearly always the husband's career that wins. Examples abound but the two long quotations in Box 5 give a clear picture of a common situation. This was reinforced for me recently on hearing from an ex-student of mine—a woman chemist—who writes "When my husband was moved to a new job, it was the economically most sensible thing for me to move too—and of course, while he got more money for moving, I would have to make do with anything I could get, so the salary differential just widened at each move."

21   If it is difficult to get a job when you move to further your husband's career, it is often even worse if you stop altogether to raise children and then try to reenter your profession. The problems are exemplified in the last quotation in Box 5.

22   Many women scientists have had to endure some form of unpleasant sexual innuendo at some time in their lives. Anne Briscoe, an American biochemist, wrote in 1981, "I ignored my stepmother who said if I got a PhD, I

Box 5—Marriage and Husband's Career

A married woman in science must therefore be very strongly motivated to enable her to overcome all kinds of difficulties. (Inga Pischer-Hjalmars, Stockholm, Sweden—contemporary [Ritcher, 1982])

I was under-ranked and underpaid, but "they" told me I should not be ambitious for myself—only for my husband. I justified my career and my ambitions by being the "best wife" I could. I did all the household chores and errands and all the entertaining. It seemed right and natural for us to organize our lives around his career . . . it did not occur to either of us to make choices based on the opportunities for *both* of us. Twice we chose the best opportunity for him and each time I changed direction, adapted and took a professional step backwards. We left Penn in August because my husband was lured back to Columbia University . . . But what of the wife who had relocated again? (Anne Briscoe, 1981—contemporary American)

I protected my husband against all the daily annoyances of running a home and rearing four children. During the years when he left us promptly after dinner to return to the laboratory . . . or down to his study to work at home, I again took over all the family problems. In this way he was free to devote himself to his work and he was extremely successful, . . . when our last child was finally away at school . . . I returned to my husband's university. I was given a section of the introductory course to teach and a lab section. After a while I was being shunted in whatever direction current registration or absent personnel indicated need. (Anon—contemporary American [Bernard, 1964])

---

would never get a rich husband." Later in the same article, "At times it was difficult not to feel the stigma of the spinster status. After I married, it seemed as if my male colleagues had more respect for me." One infers from this that a clever girl is unattractive and an unmarried one is a failure or a freak. Other examples, some of which are given in Box 6, bear out these ideas. The woman scientist, because of her choice of a male-dominated profession is at best "unfeminine" and at worst, "masculine." This attitude, however, does not prevent her from being appraised as a sex object in spite of the fact that such a practice is totally inappropriate in the context of her work. When objections were made to the appointment of the distinguished mathematician, Emmy Noether, on the grounds of her sex, one of her supporters, David Hilbert, retorted "the Senate is not a bathhouse."

23   Sonja Kovalevskaia was supposed to be pleased when a man said she was "the first handsome mathematical lady I have ever seen" and Strindberg called her a "monstrosity" (Koblitz, 1984). One of her recent biographers referred to her "masculine energy" (Kennedy, 1983). In a discussion on the technology of thin films, a pioneer in this field, Katherine Blodgett, is described, as "small, unassuming, bright-eyed and very sharp" (Tucker, 1982). A physics student, talking about her schooldays said, only last year, "All the girls thought I wasn't really a girl. The boys told me I was mad. 'You'll fail your exams,' they scoffed, 'Physics is a boy's subject' " (Couper, 1984).

24   It has been shown that women frequently overqualify themselves in order to compensate for the prejudice against their sex. This so-called "Madame

---

Box 6—Masculine, Feminine or Neuter?

Such affectation never was part of her character, which was masculine and just. (Voltaire of Emille de Breteuil, Marquise du Chatâlet [Osen, 1974])

What will our soldiers think when they return to the University and find that they are expected to learn at the feet of a woman? (Faculty of the University of Göttingen, of Emmy Noether [Osen, 1974])

She was heavy of build and loud of voice . . . no one could contend that the graces had stood by her cradle, but if we in Göttingen often chaffingly referred to her as "Der Noether," it was also done with a respectful recognition of her power as a creative thinker who seemed to have broken through the barrier of sex. (Hermann Weyl, 1935 [Ernest, 1976])

By choice she did not emphasize her feminine qualities, though her features were strong, she was not unattractive and might have been quite stunning had she taken even a mild interest in clothes. This she did not. There was never lipstick to contrast with her straight black hair, while at the age of thirty-one her dresses showed all the imagination of English blue-stocking adolescents. (Watson [1968], of Rosalind Franklin)

If such a girl studies science and becomes successful, she will find it difficult to act as shy, inferior and apologetic. If she does not do so however, she may be accused of behaving "like a man." (W. Muta Maathal, Nairobi—contemporary [Ritchter, 1982])

Many people on hearing the words "female mathematician" conjure up an image of a six-foot, grey-haired, tweed suited Oxford clad woman . . . this image, of course, doesn't attract the young woman who is continually being bombarded with messages . . . to be beautiful, "feminine," and to catch a man. (Professor Martha Smith—contemporary American [Ernest, 1976])

I wondered how she would look if she took off her glasses and did something novel with her hair. (Watson [1968], of Rosalind Franklin)

Curie Effect" (Rossiter, 1982) may account for what seems to be fear of competition on the part of male colleagues. Various strategies have been used by men to prevent women becoming dominant and some examples are given in Box 7. Presumably it is this fear which accounts for the apparently irrational prejudice which is not uncommon. The second quotation and the three quotations from Richter in Box 7 are all by contemporary scientists so the problem has not disappeared.

Other examples exist showing the reluctance of some professors to let 25 women work in the same laboratory as men. May Fieser (Pramer, 1985) was made to work "in the deserted basement of an adjoining building where he [the professor] had no intention of supervising activity." Otto Hahn says of Lise Meitner (Hahn, 1966) "with the condition that she was not to enter the laboratories where male students were working, she was permitted to work with me in the wood shop."

The fact that most European and American universities were closed to 26 women for so long and that Cambridge University did not award degrees to women until 1948 cannot be justified on rational grounds. Neither can a company justify the statement "We do not employ women chemists" nor another

---

Box 7—Male Prejudice

Clearly Rosy had to go or be put in her place. The former was obviously preferable because . . . it would be very difficult for Maurice to maintain a dominant position. (Watson [1968], of Rosalind Franklin)

My Record was good but they did not want to hire a woman. One of them was a third-rate biochemist from a tenth rate medical school. It did not matter that I had a first-rate record from a top drawer university, they preferred men of their own calibre. (Anne Briscoe [1981])

I was mostly left to myself because my colleagues were not accustomed to working with women. [However] when the post of director fell vacant, a man with inferior qualifications to mine was appointed. (Kamala Sohonie, Bombay [Richter, 1982])

Attacks on women colleagues come always from men who are lacking in self-confidence and distinguished achievement. Strong support for women comes from elderly men of distinction. (Chie Nakane, Tokyo [*ibid*])

Mistakes made by women are still *women's* mistakes, while much more serious mistakes made by a man are always the mistakes of a concrete Ivan or Piotr. (Natalie P. Bechtereva, Leningrad [*ibid*])

Women cannot be part of the Institute of France. (M. Amagat, quoted by Eve Curie [Curie, 1939])

Emil Fischer cherished a strong aversion to women in the laboratories . . . this dislike stemmed from his constant worry with a Russian student lest her rather exotic hairstyle result in its catching fire on the bunsen burner. (Kraft [1978])

---

paying a woman 80 per cent of the man's rate of pay and also having a scale for women which rose much more slowly than that for men. In 1960 the same company offered me a job doing fundamental long-term research on the grounds that there was no chance of me moving into sales or management and so I would remain "at the bench." I suppose one could regard this as an example of "positive discrimination"!

27   If I were to pick out one theme which has constantly recurred during my studies on women scientists it would be that of "invisibility." By that I mean that their work has been discounted, underrated, unacknowledged and ignored and they themselves have been belittled. Inevitably this theme has been implicit in much of what has been said already. There is a mass of evidence and, thanks particularly to some recent work, many sources of information are now available. Reference has already been made to *Women Scientists in America* (Rossiter, 1982). Cole's careful analysis (1979) in *Fair Science: Women in the Scientific Community* includes an important chapter on the marginality of women scientists and in *Machina ex Dea* (Rothschild, 1983) the contributors show that women's achievements in technology have been far greater than has generally been supposed. (The book also examines many of the issues surrounding the relationship between women and technology.) These works go a long way to redress the balance.

Turning now to some specific examples, Agnes Pockels invented the slide   28
trough for the investigation of surface films on water in 1882. Fortunately, she
sent an account of her work to Lord Rayleigh who arranged for it to be published in *Nature* in 1891. An improved version of the Pockels trough became
known as the Langmuir trough and is described in Langmuir's paper of 1917.
All this is well documented and accessible (Giles and Forrester, 1971; Derrick,
1982) but I doubt whether one could claim that Pockels was a household word
in most surface science circles.

Interestingly, another woman made a major contribution in surface sci-   29
ence. She was Katharine Blodgett, born in 1898. After receiving her master's
degree in 1918 she went to work at the General Electric Laboratory with
Langmuir on the transfer of thin films from water to a solid surface. In his
paper of 1919, Langmuir acknowledged Blodgett's contribution saying that
she had carried out "most of the experimental work." Langmuir-Blodgett
films, or LB films as they are now called, have many applications such as the
manufacture of antiglare glass, in integrated optics and lasers and in creating
new types of semiconductor (Tucker, 1982; Davis, 1984). But again, Blodgett's
name is not a familiar one.

A number of women have made important contributions to the earth sci-   30
ences but it has been pointed out (Arnold, 1975) that these are ignored in earth
science curriculum materials for American schools. The case of Florence Bas-
com is cited. She was the first woman to be awarded a PhD by Johns Hopkins
and this was the first geology doctorate in the United States (in 1983). She was
the first woman Fellow of the Geological Society of America and became a
vice-president in 1930.

Among biologists, two outstanding examples of women whose work has   31
been unappreciated for too long or underestimated are Barbara McClintock who
discovered genetic transposition (Keller, 1983) and Nettie Stevens who played a
major role in the discovery of chromosomal sex determination (Brush, 1978).

Some quotations illustrating the "belittlement" theme particularly, are   32
given in Box 8.

The allegation of noncitation is quite common. It is very discouraging and   33
depressing to *know* that you have made a significant contribution in a particular field and then to find that no one acknowledges it.

A woman chemist wrote to me of her experiences in World War II.   34
"Although it was so often publicly stated that industry was short of scientists,
the Appointments Board were not able to tell me of a single opening for which
a woman would be considered. Well-qualified women were not wanted, only
quite inexperienced women as handmaidens." And "I was set to serve a former
wages clerk . . . He was good enough to show me how to work percentages."

Another of my correspondents has, I think, managed to identify one   35
aspect of the problem. She says, "There is a real, and usually unspoken, set of
attitudes . . . unfortunately not uncommon . . . which come into play when
a woman's work, or personality, is at issue. I see it as a *fundamental lack of
seriousness,* as if these matters can be dealt with negligently because they are
never of real consequence" (my emphasis).

Box 8—The Invisible Woman

You must have been amused at all the furor created by the visit of Madame Curie to this country . . . I was quite pleasantly surprised to find that she was quite keen about scientific matters and in an unusually amiable mood . . . I felt sorry for the old girl, she was a distinctly pathetic figure. (Boltwood, on Marie Curie's visit to the USA in 1921 [Reid, 1978])

Perhaps you have seen that Monsieur Ramsay has published some work on the atomic weight of radium. He arrives at exactly the same result as I did and his measurements are less consistent than mine. In spite of that he concludes that his work is the first good work on this subject. (Marie Curie in a letter to Rutherford [*ibid*])

My husband suggested to Hahn . . . that he should at least make some reference, in his lectures and publications, to my criticism of Fermi's experiments. Hahn answered that he did not wish to make me look ridiculous as my assumption . . . was really absurd. (Ida Noddack, 1935 [Jungk, 1960])

When the assistants of the Chemical Institute met her [Lise Meltner] and Hahn they somewhat obviously greeted them with "Guten Tag, Herr Hahn." (Kraft, 1978)

All a male competitor has to say of a female scientist is that her work is not very original. When such a remark is made to a grants review panel immeasurable harm is done. (Marian W. Kies, USA—contemporary [Richter, 1982])

When the question is asked "Who are the top ten in your field?" the woman is not likely to be among those named. (Bernard, 1964)

My former students often write to me appreciatively of my work but they do not find it necessary to cite it in their own. (Anon,—contemporary quoted in Bernard [1964])

---

36   I know I used to wonder how old I had to be before I would be taken seriously as a scientist. I hoped it would be 30, but this was not the case, and it seemed to me that I was well past 40 before I felt that I had been accepted as a member of the scientific community.

37   In an article in the *New Scientist* last year Koblitz comments, "It is sobering to think that the achievements of nineteenth century women scientists had so little impact on the attitude of scientists, educationalists and women themselves that now a century later, we still need special initiatives such as WISE (Women into Science and Engineering) to increase the numbers of women practising science" (Koblitz, 1984).

38   The variety of attitudes which women scientists have expressed about themselves, their work and their colleagues has already been demonstrated to some extent and some others are shown in Box 9.

39   Some women even give men credit for their own ideas. According to Kitteringham (1982), "Margaret Bryan writing on natural philosophy in 1806, offered herself 'merely as a reflector of the intrinsic light of superior genius and erudition. . . .'"

40   Elizabeth Fulhame, however, in her *Essay on Combustion,* published in 1794, went in appropriately, with all guns blazing:

Box 9—Women Scientists' Own Attitudes

I objected to myself that it was not the profession of a lady to teach, that she should remain silent, listen and learn, without displaying her own knowledge. That it is above her station to offer a work to the public and that a reputation gained thereby is not ordinarily to her advantage since men always scorn and blame the products of a woman's wit. (Marie Meurdrac, 1666 [Bishop and Deloach, 1970])

In writing these pages, the author was more than once checked in her progress by the apprehension that such an attempt might be considered by some, either as unsuited to the ordinary pursuits of her sex, or ill-justified by her own imperfect knowledge of the subject. (Jane Marcet, *Conversations on Chemistry,* 10th ed. 1825 [Marcet, 1825])

I believe that men and women's scientific aptitudes are exactly the same—a woman of science should renounce worldly obligations. I consider science to be the primordial interest of my life. (Irène Joliot-Curie [Reid, 1978])

I do not like being made conscious of being a woman, and particularly I don't like having to take account of sex in matters concerned with research. (Chie Nakane, Tokyo—contemporary [Richter, 1982])

Two X chromosomes have . . . spelled the destiny for endless generations of individuals, irrespective of their natural talents and inclinations. (Rita Levi, Montalcini, Rome—contemporary [*ibid*])

But censure is perhaps inevitable, for some are so ignorant, that they grow sullen and silent, and are chilled with horror at the sight of anything, that bears the resemblance of learning, in whatever shape it may appear; and should the spectre appear in the shape of a woman, the pangs which they suffer are truly dismal. (Rayner-Canham, 1983)

MEN OF GOODWILL

Those of us who did manage to become women scientists owe a great debt to those men who were willing to teach, train and encourage us. Negative attitudes abound, as we have seen, but it is important to acknowledge the existence also of positive ones. Naming names can be invidious but mention must be made in this context of the Braggs and Bernal who encouraged women crystallographers and of the biochemist Gowland Hopkins who took on women research students. Katharine Blodgett worked with Rutherford at the Cavendish Laboratory and was the first woman to be awarded a PhD in Physics from Cambridge (Tucker, 1982). Agnes Pockels's work would have been unknown without Rayleigh's help (Giles and Forrester, 1971) and Weierstrass gave private tuition to Sonja Kovalevskaia (Koblitz, 1983). Gauss was very encouraging to Sophie Germain and he wrote an appreciative letter of thanks to Caroline Herschel on receipt of her edited and updated version of Flamsteed's catalogue (Osen, 1974). Evelyn Wilson said of Louis Fieser that "he was one of the few professors who treated female students as seriously as male students" (Pramer, 1985). Perhaps I should end this necessarily selective section by paying tribute to Professor William Klyne, the first head of the chemistry department at Westfield College, University of London, who declared "other things being equal" he wanted women on his staff and, as a result, appointed me and one other woman among the founder members of the department in 1961.

CONCLUDING REMARKS

42   There are obvious practical reasons why it is important that the prejudices outlined in this paper should be exposed and combated. More scientists and technologists are needed; industry is increasingly based on these disciplines. Girls and women need jobs and can fulfill these requirements if they are appropriately trained.

43   There has been much discussion of late about whether there is such a thing as feminist science. I believe that women do have a different perspective to offer which would enrich science and that they could contribute to the process of change which seems to me to be necessary.

44   I would like to close with a quotation on the subject of change from the eminent astronomer, Cecilia Payne-Gaposchkin written in 1979, the year of her death, at the age of 79.

> For we spend our lives in trying to overthrow obsolete ideas and to replace them with something that represents Nature better. There is no joy more intense than that of coming upon a fact that cannot be understood in terms of currently accepted ideas . . . Only those who have shared this activity can understand the joy of it. Science is a living thing, not a dead dogma. (Haramundanis, 1984)

APPENDIX

45   Some women scientists and mathematicians of the past, mentioned in this chapter.

Name	Dates	Discipline(s)
Emile de Breteuil	1706–1749	Mathematics/theoretical physics
Marie Curie	1867–1934	Chemistry/physics
Rosalind Franklin	1920–1958	Chemistry/crystallography
Sophie Germain	1776–1831	Mathematics/physics
Caroline Herschel	1750–1848	Mathematics/astronomy
Irène Jolit-Curie	1897–1956	Physics
Sonja Kovalevskaia	1850–1891	Mathematics
Jane Marcet	1769–1858	Chemistry
Lise Meitner	1878–1968	Physics
Ida Noddack	1896–1979	Chemistry
Emmy Noether	1882–1935	Mathematics
Mary Somerville	1780–1872	Mathematics/astronomy

References

Arnold, L. (1975). *Journal of Geological Education, 23,* 110.

Bennett, J. H. (1870). *The Lancet, 2,* 887 (see Easlea, p. 139).

Bernard, J. (1964). *Academic women.* New York: Meridian.

Bishop, L. O., & De Loach, W. S. (1970). *Journal of Chemical Education, 47,* 448.

Briscoe, A. (1981). *International Journal of Women's Studies, 4,* 420.

British Apollo, The, (1708). (see Easlea, p. 69).

Brush, S. G. (1978). *Isis, 69,* 163.

Cole, J. R. (1979). *Fair science: Women in the scientific community.* New York and London: Macmillan.

Compleat midwifes practice enlarged, The, (1659). (see Easlea, p. 69).

Couper, H. (1984, March). *SHE,* p. 78.

Curie, E. (1939). *Madame Curie.* London: Readers Union/Heinemann.

Davis, K. A. (1984). *Journal of Chemical Education, 61,* 437.

Derrick, M. E. (1982). *Journal of Chemical Education, 59,* 1030.

Easlea, B. (1981). *Science and sexual oppression.* London: Weidenfeld and Nicolson.

Ernest, J. (1976). *American Mathematics Monthly, 83,* 595.

Giles, C. H., & Forrester, S. D. (1971, 9 January). *Chemistry and Industry.*

Hahn, O. (1966). *Otto Hahn: A scientific autobiography.* New York: Charles Scribner & Sons.

Haramundanis, K. (Ed.) (1984). *Cecilia Payne-Gaposchkin.* Cambridge: Cambridge University Press.

Jungk, R. (1960). *Brighter than a thousand suns.* Harmondsworth, England: Penguin.

Keller, E. F. (1983). *A Feeling for the organism: The life and work of Barbara McClintock.* New York: W. E. Freeman.

Kennedy, D. H. (1983). *Little sparrow: A portrait of Sophia Kovalevsky.* Athens, OH: Ohio University Press.

Kitteringham, G. (1982, 21 May). *Times Higher Educational Supplement.*

Koblitz, A. H. (1983). *A convergence of lives, Sofia Kovalevskaia: Scientist, writer and revolutionary.* Boston: Birkhäuser.

Koblitz, A. H. (1984, 16 February). *Sofia Kovalevskaia: "Muse of the heavens," New Scientist.*

Krafft, F. (1978). *Angewandte Chemie, International Edition in English, 17,* 826.

Langmuir, I. (1917). *Journal of the American Chemical Society, 39,* 1848.

Marcet, J. (1825). *Conversations on chemistry . . .,* (10th ed.). London: Longman, Hurst, Rees and Orme.

Osen, L. M. (1974). *Women in mathematics.* Cambridge, MA, and London: MIT Press.

Poulain de la Barre (1673). English translation, (1677) (see Easlea, p. 71).

Pramer, S. (1985). *Journal of Chemical Education, 62,* 186.

Rayner-Canham, G. W. (1983). *Education in Chemistry, 20,* 140.

Reid, R. (1978). *Marie Curie,* St. Albans, England: Paladin.

Richter, D. (1982). *Women scientists: The road to liberation.* England: London and Basingstoke, England: Macmillan.

Romanes, G. J. (1887). *The nineteenth century, 21,* 189 (see Easlea, p. 146).

Rosenberg, R. (1982). *Beyond separate spheres: Intellectual roots of modern feminism,* New Haven, CT, and London: Yale University Press.

Rossiter, M. W. (1982). *Women Scientists in America: Struggles and strategies to 1940.* Baltimore: Johns Hopkins University Press.

Rothschild, J. (Ed.). (1983). *Machina es dea.* New York and Oxford: Pergamon Press. *Science,* (1979). *203,* 150.

Swinburne, J. (1902). *Westminster Review, 158,* 189.

Tucker, A. (1982, 8 March). *The Guardian.*

Watson, J. D. (1968). *The double helix.* London: Weidenfeld and Nicolson.

Questions for Discussion and Your Reading Journal

1. Why do you think Walton has written this article? For whom is the article intended?
2. Walton begins the essay with a brief description of her experience as a woman scientist. Why does she begin in this way?
3. What cultural factors contribute to the low percentage of women in the scientific professions? Discuss your own experience with these aspects of your culture.
4. Are there any physical differences between men and women that account for the paucity of women scientists? Explain.
5. Discuss the organization of the essay. How does the organization contribute to the method of argument? How does the information in the boxes contribute to Walton's argument? Why do you think the quotes are presented in lists?
6. What can women do to help remove the prejudices against women in science? What can men do? Why would she separate these two in the essay?
7. Summarize the main idea in Walton's conclusion. To what degree is the conclusion persuasive to persons of either gender?

ROALD HOFFMANN

Roald Hoffmann (1937–) was born in Zloczow, Poland. As a child he lived through the Nazi occupation of Poland during World War II, and afterward he emigrated to America. He graduated from Columbia University and got a Ph.D. in 1962 from Harvard University. Hoffmann continued on at Harvard from 1962 to 1965 and then went to Cornell, where he is now the Frank H. T. Rhodes Professor of Humane Letters and Professor of Chemistry. He has received numerous honors, including over 25 honorary degrees. In 1981 he shared the Nobel Prize in Chemistry with Kenichi Fukui.

"Applied theoretical chemistry" is the term Roald Hoffmann uses to describe the construction of generalized models that is his contribution to chemistry. In numerous articles and two books he explores new and useful ways to look at the geometry and reactivity of molecules, from organic through inorganic to infinitely extended structures. Hoffman also sees a connection between science and the artistic sublime that he explores in his poetry, which has appeared in various literary magazines and in two collections.

Hoffmann's recent publications point to the dualities that lie under the surface of chemistry. Like Einstein and Russell in their essays that follow, Hoffmann looks at how science and religion are both about eternal and important questions of the natural and the unnatural, the human and the divine.

Reading Rhetorically

Although the rhetorical method of development most broadly used in this article is description, the article also includes an element of persuasion. As you read the article, think about the ways in which description might be focused in order to set up an argument. Think also about the author's use of *logos*.

This article was published by *Scientific American* in 1993. The audience for this journal is a general readership with no particular expertise in a scientific field. However, the readers of *Scientific American* can be considered to have some things in common. They are clearly curious about science and interested in scientific developments. Think about other characteristics the readers might share.

Finally, think about some of the issues in science that are of particular concern to you and your friends. The way these issues are discussed in various kinds of publications can be very different. As you read the article, examine its tone and decide to what degree the article is suited to your particular reading tastes.

How Should Chemists Think?

Chemists can create natural molecules by unnatural means. Or they can make beautiful structures never seen before. Which should be their grail?

The Vatican holds a fresco by Raphael entitled *The School of Athens*. Plato   1 and Aristotle stride toward us. Plato's hand points to the heavens, Aristotle's outward, along the plane of the earth. The message is consistent with their philosophies—whereas Plato had a geometric prototheory of the chemistry of matter, Aristotle described in reliable detail how Tyrian purple (now known to be a precursor of indigo) was extracted from rock murex snails. Plato searched for the ideal; Aristotle looked to nature.

2   Remarkably, modern chemistry faces the quandary that Raphael's fresco epitomized. Should it follow the hand sign of Aristotle or that of Plato? Is nature as fertile a source for new materials as some assert it to be? Can we, for example, hope to make better composites by mimicking the microstructure of a feather or of a strand of spider's silk? Are chemists better advised to seek their inspiration in ideal mathematical forms. In icosahedra and in soccer balls? Or should we hazard chance?

Plato and Aristotle in a detail of Raphael's fresco *The School of Athens* are depicted in a way that symbolizes their approach to knowledge. Aristotle gestures toward the earth; Plato points his finger to the heavens. Aristotle looked to nature for answers; Plato searched for the ideal. Should chemists follow the hand sign of Aristotle or that of Plato? © Scala/Art Resource, NY

3   To some, the division between natural and unnatural is arbitrary; they would argue that man and woman are patently natural, and so are all their transformations. Such a view is understandable and has a venerable history, but it does away with a distinction that troubles ordinary and thoughtful people. So I will not adopt it and instead will distinguish between the actions, mostly intended, of human beings and those of animals, plants and the inanimate world around us. A sunset is natural, a sulfuric acid factory is not. The 1.3 billion head of cattle in this world pose an interesting problem for any definition. Most of them are both natural and unnatural—the product of breeding controlled by humans.

4   The molecules that exist naturally on the earth emerged over billions of years as rocks cooled, oceans formed, gases escaped and life evolved. The number of natural molecules is immense; perhaps a few hundred thousand have been separated, purified and identified. The vast majority of the compounds that fit into the unnatural category were created during the past three centuries. Chemists have added some 15 million well-characterized molecules to nature's bounty.

5   To every thing of this world, be it living or not, there is structure. Deep down are molecules, persistent groupings of atoms associated with other atoms. There is water in the distilled form in the laboratory, in slightly dirty and acid snow, in the waters associated with our protein molecules. All are H_2O. When chemistry was groping for understanding, there was a reasonable reluctance to merge the animate and inanimate worlds. Friedrich Wöhler convinced many people that the worlds were not separate by synthesizing, in 1828, organic urea from inorganic silver cyanate and ammonium chloride.

How are molecules made in nature—penicillin in a mold or a precursor of 6 indigo in a rock murex snail? How are they made in glass-glittery laboratories— those acres of food wrap, those billion pills of aspirin? By a common process— synthesis.

Chemistry is the science of molecules and their transformations. Be it nat- 7 ural or human steered, the outcome of transformation, A → B, is a new substance. Chemical synthesis, the making of the new, is patently a creative act. It is as much an affirmation of humanity as a new poem by A. R. Ammons or the construction of democracy in Russia. Yet creation is always risky. A new sedative may be effective, but it also may induce fetal malformation. A Heberto Padilla poem may be "counterrevolutionary" to a Cuban apparatchik. Some people in Russia still don't like democracy.

Wöhler mixed together two substances, heated them and obtained an 8 unexpected result. Much has happened since 1828. To convey what the making of molecules is like today and to relate how the natural intermingles with the unnatural in this creative activity, let me tell you about the synthesis of two substances. Primaxin and the ferric wheel.

Primaxin is one of the most effective antibiotics on the market, a prime 9 money-maker for Merck & Co. The pharmaceutical is not a single molecule but a designed mixture of two compounds, imipenem and cilastin [see box]. These are their "trivial" names. The "systematic" names are a bit longer: for instance, Imipenem is

|5R-|5α.   6α(R*)||-6-(1-hydroxyethyl)-3-||2-[(iminomethyl)amino] 10 ethyl[thio]-7-oxo-l-azabicyclo |3.2.0 |hept-2-ene-2-carboxylic acid

Primaxin was created by a bit of unnatural tinkering, emulating the natu- 11 ral tinkering of evolution. Imipenem by itself is a fine antibiotic. But it is degraded rapidly in the kidney by an enzyme. This would give the drug limited use for urinary tract infections. The Merck chemists found in their sample collection a promising compound, synthesized in the 1940s, that inhibited that orney enzyme. Modified for greater activity, this became cilastatin. It was obvious to try the combination of the antibiotic and the enzyme inhibitor, and the mix worked.

Imipenem derives from a natural product, cilastatin does not. Both are 12 made synthetically in the commercial process. I will return to this after tracing further the history of one of the components.

Imipenem was developed in the 1970s by a team of Merck chemists led by 13 Burton G. Christensen. It is a slightly modified form of another antibiotic, thienamycin. That, in turn, was discovered while screening soil samples from New Jersey. It is produced by a mold, *Streptomyces cattleya,* so named because its lavender color resembles that of the cattleya orchid. The mold is a veritable drug factory, producing thienamycin and several other varieties of antibiotics.

Unfortunately, thienamycin was not chemically stable at high concentrations. 14 And, to quote one of the Merck crew, "The lovely orchid-colored organism was too stingy." The usual fermentation processes, perfected by the pharmaceutical industry over the past 50 years, did not produce enough of the molecule. So the workers decided to produce greater quantities of thienamycin in the laboratory.

The Making of an Antibiotic

The anbitiotic Primaxin is a mixture of two compounds known as Imipenem (ball-and-stick model at right) and cilastatin (model at left). Imipenem is a slightly modified form of thienamycin, which is produced naturally by a mold. Chemists developed a procedure (summarized below) that produces thienamycin more efficiently than any known natural process. The stick figures shown are the chemist's typical notation; not all atoms are identified. Those vertices that do not have atomic labels represent carbon atoms. Most of the hydrogen atoms have been left out. It is possible to deduce the location of the missing hydrogen atoms because every carbon atom should form four bonds. An arrow represents each chemical transformation in the process. The percent figure near each arrow is the experimental yield. . . . Wedges indicate details of geometry, atoms above or below the plane.

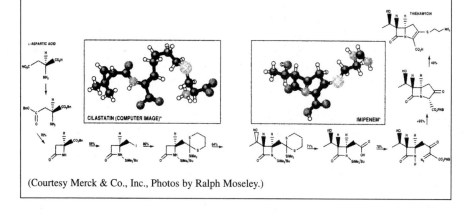

(Courtesy Merck & Co., Inc., Photos by Ralph Moseley.)

15   The production of thienamycin required 21 major steps, each involving several physical operations: dissolution, heating, filtration, crystallization. Between the starting material—a common amino acid, L-aspartic acid—and the desired product—thienamycin—20 other molecules were isolated and purified. Of these, only eight are shown in the condensed "reaction scheme."

16   The first impression that one gets is of complexity. That intricacy is essential, a laboratory counterpoint to the biochemical complexity of bacteria and us. We would like there to be "magic bullets" of abiding simplicity. The real world is complicated and beautiful. We had better come to terms with that richness.

17   To get a feeling for the sweat, if not the blood and tears, of the process, we need to turn to the experimental section of the paper reporting the synthesis. Here is an excerpt of that experimental protocol, describing a critical, inventive step in the synthesis—the transformation from compound 8 to 9:

A suspension of diazo keto ester 8 (3.98 g, 10.58 mmol) and rhodium(II) acetate dimer (0.04 g, 0.09 mmol) in anhydrous toluene (250 mL) was thoroughly purged with nitrogen, and then heated with stirring in an oil bath maintained at 80° C. After heating for two hours, the reaction mixture was removed from the bath and filtered while warm through a pad of anhydrous magnesium sulfate. The filtrate was evaporated under vacuum to afford the bicyclic keto ester 9 (3.27 g, 89%) as an off-white solid. . . .

You can be sure that this jargon-laden account of an experimental procedure is a sanitized, too linear narrative; it is the way things were at the end: neat, optimized. Not the way it first happened. Putting that aside, you feel work, a sequence of operations that take time and effort. Sometimes, just as in our romantic notions of words springing from the brow of inspired poets, we forget the sheer labor of creation. Even the Creator rested on the seventh day. 18

You might be interested to see the way these experimental procedures change when the very same process is scaled up. You can't make hundreds of millions of dollars' worth of thienamycin the same way you make a few grams in the laboratory. Here is the description of the industrial synthesis, for the very same step: 19

> The solids containing 200 kg of 8 are dropped into 476 gallons of $MeCl_2$ in tank TA-1432. Meanwhile, the reactor ST-1510 is cleaned out by a 200-gallon $MeCl_2$ boilout. The slurry is transferred to ST-1510, followed by a 50 gallon $MeCl_2$ line flush. An additional 400 gallons of dry $MeCl_2$ are added to ST-1510, and hot water (65° C) is applied to the jackets to concentrate the batch to 545 gallons where the slurry KF (Karl Fischer) is approximately 0.5 g/l H_2O. Distillates are condensed and collected in another tank.

Making a veal stroganoff for a thousand people is not the same as cooking at home for four. 20

The synthesis of thienamycin is a building process, proceeding from simple pieces to the complex goal. It shares many features with architecture. For instance, a necessary intermediate structure may be more complicated than either the beginning or end; think of scaffolding. Chemical synthesis is a local defeat of entropy, just as our buildings and cities are. The analogy to architecture is so strong that one forgets how different, how marvelous, this kind of construction is, in a flask there may be 10^{23} molecules, moving rapidly, colliding often. Hands off, following only the strong dictates of thermodynamics, they proceed to shuffle their electrons, break and make bonds, do our bidding. If we're lucky, 99 percent of them do. 21

Chemists can easily calculate, given a certain number of grams of starting material, how much product one should get. That is the theoretical yield. The actual amount obtained is the experimental yield. There is no way to get something out of nothing but many ways to get less than you theoretically could. One way to achieve a 50-percent yield is to spill half the solution on the floor. This will impress no one. But even if you perform each transfer as neatly as possible, nature may not give you what you desire but instead transform 70 percent into black gunk. This is also not impressive, for it does not demonstrate control of mind over matter. Experimental yields are criteria not only of efficiency, essential to the industrial enterprise, but also of elegance and control. 22

There is more, much more, to say about the planned organic synthesis. But let me go on to my second case study: the ferric wheel. Stephen J. Lippard and 23

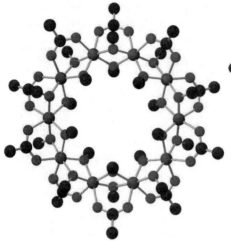

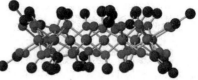

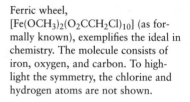

Ferric wheel, $[Fe(OCH_3)_2(O_2CCH_2Cl)_{10}]$ (as formally known), exemplifies the ideal in chemistry. The molecule consists of iron, oxygen, and carbon. To highlight the symmetry, the chlorine and hydrogen atoms are not shown.

Kingsley L. Taft of the Massachusetts Institute of Technology synthesized the ferric wheel, also known as $[Fe(OCH_3)_2(O_2CCH_2Cl)]_{10}$. They discovered this exquisite molecule while studying model molecules for inorganic reactions that occur in biological systems. For instance, a cluster of iron and oxygen atoms is at the core of several important proteins, such as hemerythrin, ribonucleotide reductase, methane monooxygenase and ferritin (not household words these, but essential to life).

24　　In the course of their broad attack on such compounds, Lippard and Taft performed a deceptively simple reaction. Just how simple it seems may be seen from the experimental section, reproduced in its entirety:

> Compound 1 was prepared by allowing the monochloroacetate analogue of basic iron acetate, $[Fe_3O(O_2CCH_2Cl)_6(H_2O)_3](NO_3)$ (0.315 g, 0.366 mmol), to react with 3 equiv of $Fe(NO_3)_3 \lozenge 9H_2O$ (0.444 g, 1.10 mmol) in 65 mL of methanol. Diffusion of ether into the green-brown solution gave a yellow solution, from which both gold-brown crystals of 1 and a yellow precipitate deposited after several days.

25　　Using x-ray diffraction on the gold-brown crsytals, Lippard and Taft determined the arrangement of atoms in the molecule. The structure consists of 10 ferric ions [iron in oxidation state three] in a near circular array. Each iron atom is joined to its neighbors by methoxide and carboxylate bridges, "forming a molecular ferric wheel," to quote its makers.

26　　No one will deny the visual beauty of this molecule. It does not have the annual sales of Primaxin, estimated to be $500 million. On the contrary, it probably cost the U.S. taxpayer several thousand dollars to make it. But I do not know a single curmudgeonly chemist who would not respond positively to this lovely creation. Perhaps some day the ferric wheel will find a use: perhaps it will form a link in explaining the function of iron-containing proteins. I do not really care—for me, this molecule provides a spiritual high akin to hearing a Haydn piano trio I like.

Why is this molecule beautiful? Because its symmetry reaches directly into   27
the soul. It plays a note on a Platonic ideal. Perhaps I should have compared
it to Judy Collins singing "Amazing Grace" rather than the Haydn trio. The
melodic lines of the trio indeed sing, but the piece works its effect through
counterpoint, the tools of complexity. The ferric wheel is pure melody.

Were we to write out the synthesis of the ferric wheel, there would be but   28
a single arrow, from the iron chloroacetate and ferric nitrate to the product.
This is a very different type of synthesis—the product essentially self-
assembles to its final glory. When I see such a process, much more typical of
inorganic systems than organic ones, I immediately wonder what I'm missing.
The Swedish chemist Sture Forsén has aptly expressed the frustration in not
being able to observe the intermediate stages of a reaction:

> The problem facing the scientist has been compared with that of a specta-
> tor of a drastically shortened version of a classical drama "Hamlet," say—
> where he or she is only shown the opening scenes of the first act and the
> last scene of the finale. The main characters are introduced, then the cur-
> tain falls for change of scenery, and as it rises again we see on the scene
> floor a considerable number of "dead" bodies and a few survivors. Not an
> easy task for the inexperienced to unravel what actually took place in
> between.

Wheels, ferric or ferris, don't really self-assemble in one fell swoop. It   29
remains for us to learn in the future how those bridges and irons come
together.

Some chemists, especially those who practice the mentally demanding,   30
intellectually exhilarating many-step, planned synthesis of the thienamycin type
look askance at one-step self-assembly. Such one-fell-swoop syntheses are especially common in solid-state chemistry, in the formation of materials extended
infinitely in one, two or three dimensions. The high-temperature superconduc-
tors are a good example of molecules made just this way. Their synthesis does
not appear to show control of mind over matter. It looks like magic.

I exaggerate, but this is one strand of thought in the community. If I could   31
corner my straw-man scoffer at self-assembly, typically an organic chemist,
and engage him or her in a Socratic dialogue, I would begin with the question
"When have you made any diamond for me lately?" Diamond is a beautifully
simple three dimensional structure (natural!) It contains in it six membered
rings, the bread-and-butter of organic chemistry. Such rings of carbon atoms
are easy to make in a discrete molecule. But diamond can be made only by
techniques organic chemists find unsporting, by discharges forming a plasma
in methane or by pressing graphite.

Organic chemists are masterful at exercising control in zero dimensions.   32
To one piece of carbon, perhaps asymmetric, they add another piece. Slowly,
painstakingly, a complex edifice emerges. (Thienamycin is pretty simple compared to what you can do today.) One subculture of organic chemists has
learned to exercise control in one dimension. These are polymer chemists, the
chain builders. Although they may not have as much honor in organic chemistry as they should, they do earn a good bit of money.

33   But in two or three dimensions, it's a synthetic wasteland. The methodology for exercising control so that one can make unstable but persistent extended structures on demand is nearly absent. Or to put it in a positive way—this is a certain growth point of the chemistry of the future.

34   Syntheses, like human beings, do not lend themselves to typology. Each one is different; each has virtues and shortcomings. From each we learn, I will stop, however reluctantly, with primaxin and the ferric wheel and turn to some general questions they pose, especially about the natural and the unnatural.

35   Two paradoxes are hidden in the art of synthesis. The first is that the act of synthesis is explicitly human and therefore unnatural, even if one is trying to make a product of nature. The second is that in the synthesis of ideal molecules, where doing what comes unnaturally might seem just the thing, one sometimes has to give in to nature. Let me explain in the context of the two syntheses I have just discussed.

36   Imipenem, one component of the successful Merck antibiotic, is made from thienamycin. The thienamycin is natural, to be sure, but an economic and chemical decision dictated that in its commercial production thienamycin be made synthetically.

37   There is no doubt in this case that the natural molecule served as an inspiration for the synthetic chemists. But, of course, they did not make thienamycin in the laboratory the way it is made by the mold. The organism has its own intricate chemical factories, enzymes shaped by evolution. Only recently have we learned to use genetic engineering to harness those factories, even whole organisms, for our own purposes.

38   We have grown proficient at simpler, laboratory chemistries than those evolved by biological organisms. There is no way that Christensen and his team would set out to mimic a mold enzyme in detail. They did have confidence that they could carry out a very limited piece of what the lowly mold does, to make thienamycin, by doing it differently in the laboratory. Their goal was natural, but their process was not.

39   To make thienamycin, Christensen and his co-workers used a multitude of natural and synthetic reagents. For instance, one of their transformations—the synthesis of compound 3 [*see box*]—uses a magnesium compound, $(CH_3)_3CMgCl$, known as a Grignard reagent. Magnesium compounds are abundant in nature (witness Epsom salt and chlorophyll). But the reagent in question, a ubiquitous tool of the synthetic chemist, was concocted by Victor Grignard some time around the turn of the century. The creation of compound 3 also requires treatment with hydrochloric acid and ammonium chloride, both natural products. (Your stomach has a marginally lower concentration of hydrochloric acid than that used in this reaction, and ammonium chloride is the alchemist's sal ammoniac.) But even though these molecules occur in nature, they are far easier to make in a chemical plant.

40   Because everything in the end does come from the earth, air or water, every unnatural reagent used in the synthesis ultimately derives from natural organic or inorganic precursors. The very starting material in the synthesis of imipenem is an amino acid, aspartic acid.

Now consider the most unnatural and beautiful ferric wheel. It was made 41
simply by reacting two synthetic molecules, the iron monochloroacetate and
ferric nitrate, in methanol, a natural solvent. The methanol was probably
made synthetically; the two iron-containing reagents derive from reactions of
iron metal, which in turn is extracted from iron ores. And the final wrinkle is
the method of assembly: the pieces of the molecule seem to just fall into place
(self-assembly). What could be more natural than letting things happen spontaneously, giving in to the strong dictates of entropy?

It is clear that in the unnatural making of a natural molecule (thienamycin) 42
or of an unnatural one (the ferric wheel), natural and synthetic reagents and
solvents are used in a complex, intertwined theater of letting things be and of
helping them along. About the only constant is change, transformation.

We may still wonder about the psychology of chemical creation. Which 43
molecules should we expend our energies in making? Isn't there something
inherently better in trying to make the absolutely new?

Four beautiful polyhedra of carbon have piqued the interest of synthetic 44
organic chemists during the past 40 years: tetrahedrane (C_4H_4), cubane
(C_8H_8), dodecahedrane ($C_{20}H_{20}$) and buckminsterfullerene (C_{60}). Cubane is
quite unstable because of the strain imposed at each carbon. (In cubane the
angle between any three carbon atoms is 90 degrees, but each carbon would
"prefer" to form angles of 109.5 degrees with its neighbors.) C_{60} is also somewhat strained because of both its nonplanarity and its five-membered rings.
Tetrahedrane is particularly unstable. One has to create special conditions of
temperature and solvent to see it; even then, the parent molecule has not yet
been made, only a "substituted derivative," in which hydrogen is replaced by
a bulky organic group.

As far as we know, tetrahedrane, cubane and dodecahedrane do not exist 45
naturally on the earth. C_{60} has been found in old soot and a carbon-rich
ancient rock, shungite. It may turn up elsewhere. Be that as it may, all four
molecules were recognized as synthetic targets at least 20 years, in some cases
50 years, before they were made. Some of the best chemists in the world tried
to make them and failed. The syntheses of cubane and especially dodecahedrane were monumental achievements in unnatural product chemistry.

C_{60} was different. The pleasing polyhedral shape was first noted by some 46
theoreticians. Their calculations indicated some stability; such indications as
the theoreticians had at their command were sometimes unreliable. These theoreticians' dreams were ignored by the experimentalists and by other theoreticians. It is sometimes difficult to see the shoulders of the giants we stand on
when we are looking so intently ahead. I myself have suggested a still unsyn-
thesized metallic modification of carbon, different from diamond or graphite,
and even though I have substantially more visibility among chemists than the
proposers of buckminsterfullerene, no one has paid much attention to my pipe
dream either, probably for good reason. We see what we want to see.

One organic chemist I know, a very good one, Orville L. Chapman of the 47
University of California at Los Angeles, independently thought up the structure and devoted much time to the planned, systematic making of C_{60}. After
all, this was a "simple" molecule, not an extended material like the repeating

Tetrahedrane

Cubane

Dodecahedrane

Buckminsterfullerene

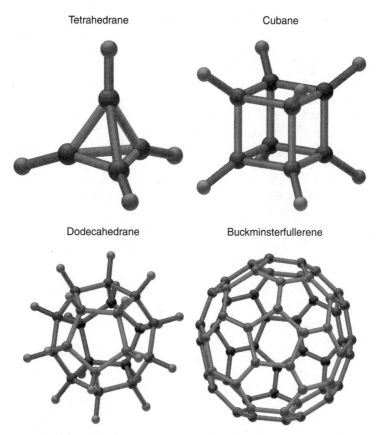

Four polyhedra based on carbon were recognized decades ago as targets for chemists to synthesize. Buckminsterfullerenes were discovered in 1985 and were then found to occur naturally on the earth. Tetrahedrane, the simplest of the structures, has not yet been synthesized. Tetrahedrane, cubane and dodecahedrane consist of carbon atoms and hydrogen atoms. Buckminsterfullerenes are made solely from carbon.

lattice of carbon atoms that make up a diamond. So it should be possible to make it. Despite persistent efforts over a 10-year period, Chapman and his students failed in their effort.

48   The first evidence, indirect but definitive, for C_{60} was obtained from a very different branch of our science, physical chemistry. The credit for the discovery belongs properly to Richard E. Smalley and Robert F. Curl of Rice University and Harold W. Kroto of the University of Sussex. They obtained hard evidence for tiny amounts of C_{60} in the gas phase, assigned the molecule its name and, more important, deduced its structure. Did they make it? Absolutely. It did not matter to me or to other believers in their evidence that they had made "just" 10^{10} molecules instead of the 10^{20} we need to see in a tiny crystal. But there were doubters, many I suspect, in the organic community. One wanted to see the stuff.

Grams of buckminsterfullerene were provided by a synthesis by Donald R. 49
Huffman of the University of Arizona and Wolfgang Krätschmer and Konstantinos Postiropoulos of the Max Planck Institute for Nuclear Physics in Heidelberg. Striking a carbon arc in a helium atmosphere (which is what they did) is about as unsporting as firing a laser at graphite (the Smalley-Kroto-Curl synthesis). But it certainly makes plenty of C_{60}, enough of the molecule to determine its structure by typical organic methods, enough to convince any chemist that it has the soccer-ball structure ["Fullerenes," by Robert F. Curl and Richard E. Smalley; SCIENTIFIC AMERICAN, October 1991].

I think many chemists wished C_{60} had been made in a planned, unnatural 50
way. I am happy that—just to make the world slightly less rational than we would like it to be—it was made in a serendipitous way.

Serendipity—a word invented by Horace Walpole—has come to mean "a 51
discovery by chance" Yet whether it is a chemical synthesis of a Japanese master potter piling organic matter around the ceramic objects in his Bizen kiln, chance favors the prepared mind. You need to have the knowledge (some call it intuition) to vary the conditions of striking the arc or the arrangement of the leaves in the kiln just so. You need to have the instruments and intuition to deduce structure from a few fuzzy lines in a spectrum and to reject false leads. And you need to have the courage to shatter a vase that didn't come out right and to learn from one firing what to do in the next.

Many chemical syntheses, even if part of a grand design, proceed by steps 52
that are serendipitous. One wants to link up a bond here, but it doesn't work. So one follows a hunch, anything but the codified scientific method. One knows that if a reaction works, one can construct a rationalization for it—an argument spiffy clean enough to make an impression on one's colleagues. Eventually one can make the damned reaction work if it is a necessarily step in the design.

Because chance also operates to foil every design, it is almost certain that 53
in the course of any planned synthesis there will be a step that will not work by any known process. So a new one will be invented, adding to the store of the chemists, aiding others around the world facing the same problem. Some synthetic chemists—for instance, E. J. Corey of Harvard University, a grand master of the art—have a special talent for not only making interesting molecules but also using the opportunity of the synthesis to introduce a brilliant, unprecedented methodology, applicable to other syntheses.

When the synthesis is planned, be its aim a natural or unnatural molecule, 54
we suppress the aleatory nature of the enterprise. We want to project an image of mind over matter, of total control. When the molecule made is unanticipated, as the ferric wheel was, we find it very difficult to hide the workings of chance. But hazard—to use the meaning that is dominant in the French root of our word, and secondary in ours—plays an unrecognized and enlivening role in all synthesis.

Let us return to nature and our struggles to emulate it. Or surpass it. Can 55
we make substances that have properties superior to those found in nature? I say "yes" while recognizing that the phrase "superior to nature" is patently

value laden and anthropocentric and should immediately evoke ecological concerns.

56   There is nylon instead of cotton in fishing nets, nylon instead of silk in women's stockings. No one, least of all Third World fishermen, will go back to the old nets. Some people may go back to silk stockings, but they will only be the rich, out to impress. There are new chemical materials and new combinations of old materials for dental restorations. They make a world of difference to older people in this world, and their benefit cannot be dismissed.

57   Yet the thought that we can do better than nature is provocatively arrogant. As we have attempted to improve on nature (while failing to control the most natural thing about us, our drive to procreate), we have introduced so many transformations and in such measure that we have fouled our nest and intruded into the great cycles of this planet. We must face the reality that natural evolution proceeds far too slowly to cope with our changes. This is a concern that, just as much as utility, should guide the industrial-scale synthesis of the future.

58   I want to touch on another kind of human arrogance implicit in the intellectual drama of synthesis. A French chemist, Alain Sevin, has put it well.

> The incredible richness and fantasy of Nature is an act of defiance to Man, as if he had to do better in any domain. Flying faster than birds, diving deeper than whales. . . . We are Promethean characters in an endless play which now is in its molecular act.

59   We are driven to transform. We have learned to do it very well. But this play is not a comedy.

60   Were chemical synthesis in search of a single icon, the out-stretched hand of Prometheus bringing fire to humanity would serve well. Prometheus, a name meaning "forethought," represents the element of design, the process of fruitfully taking advantage of chance creation. Fire is appropriate because it drives transformation. The hand of Prometheus is the symbol of creation—the hand of God reaching to Adam in Michelangelo's fresco, the hands in contentious debate in Dürer's *Christ among the Doctors*, the infinite variety of hands that Rodin sculpted. Hands bless, caress and hide, but most of all, they shape.

61   The sculptor's art itself mimics the complexity of motion of a chemist across the interface between natural and unnatural. Rodin, in his human act of creation, sketches, then shapes by hand (with tools) an out-of-scale yet "realistic" artifact, a sculpture of a hand, out of materials that are synthetic (bronze) but that have natural origins (copper and tin ores). He uses a building process (maquettes, a cast) that is complex in its intermediate stages. The sculptor creates something very real, whose virtue may reside in calling to our minds the ideal.

62   Margaret Drabble has written that Prometheus is "firmly rooted in the real world of effort, danger and pain." Without chemical synthesis, there would be no aspirin, no cortisone, no birth-control pills, no anesthetics, no dynamite. The achievements of chemical synthesis are firmly bound to our attempt to break the shackles of disease and poverty. In search of an ideal, making real things, the mind and hands engage.

Questions for Discussion and Your Reading Journal

1. This article is accompanied by an illustration of Raphael's fresco "The School of Athens," which shows Aristotle and Plato walking, talking, and gesturing, and indicates a difference in the way the two are focused. How would you describe this difference? How might this fresco illustrate what you already know about Aristotle and/or Plato?

2. In the first part of the article, Hoffmann discusses the division between "natural and unnatural" (Paragraph 3). Explain this division in your own words. Can you think of any examples to illustrate your explanation?

3. Hoffmann believes that chemistry is both highly complex and deeply beautiful. How might it be beneficial for a chemist to think in both analytical and aesthetic ways about the things s/he studies?

4. The kind of chemistry that Hoffmann describes is a fundamentally creative process. How is the creativity involved in chemistry different from and similar to artistic creativity?

5. The article concludes with a number of statements about chemical synthesis that are intended to be persuasive. Of what is Hoffmann trying to persuade the reader? Why might he think it important for others to see chemistry in this way?

ALBERT EINSTEIN

Albert Einstein (1879–1955) was the most influential scientist of the 20th century. His quantum theory and the famous theory of relativity (which includes the equation $E = mc^2$) revolutionized contemporary physics, making possible such inventions as the atomic bomb and the space shuttle.

Einstein was born in Ulm, Germany. Einstein's parents had little education in the areas of math and science, but they supported their son's scholarship and research. As a young scientist Einstein developed theories in relation to quantum law and the emission and absorption of light, the inertia of energy, and the electrodynamics of moving bodies. His research on quantum law and the emission and absorption of light won him the Nobel Prize in Physics in 1921.

Although he did his scientific research in solitude, Einstein was a public figure who frequently spoke out about issues that concerned him. While his theories form the basis for the way the scientific community currently views time and space, his speeches and writings were also influential in shaping public opinion about cultural issues related to scientific development.

Einstein, a German Jew, was ousted from his native country during the Nazi regime; at that time, fearing that the Germans would develop the atomic bomb first, a group of American scientists asked Einstein to sign a letter to President Roosevelt requesting that he expedite research

in that area. Although he signed the letter, Einstein was later deeply dis-
mayed by the destruction caused by America's use of the bomb against
Japan. (For a description of that destruction, see the excerpt from Ibuse's
Black Rain *later in the chapter.) In the essay here, "Religion and Science"*
(1934), Einstein poses philosophical questions in response to issues in
science. Compare this essay with the subsequent reading from Bertrand
Russell.

Reading Rhetorically

Albert Einstein and Bertrand Russell (the author of the next essay in the chapter) co-wrote the "Russell-Einstein Manifesto," which was published in July of 1955. In this document they refer to "weapons of mass destruction" and plead with the scientific community and the world at large to carefully control the technology that can eradicate cities within seconds. Today we are as concerned with weapons of mass destruction as were the people of the 1950s. As you read this essay by Einstein, look for other issues of contemporary concern and examine the ways in which Einstein's points are relevant to current concerns.

Einstein tries to influence his audience by choosing a particular kind of language and a distinct style of writing. Examine the word choices he makes, for example, or the ways he structures his sentences. Assuming that Einstein's diction and style are deliberate choices, speculate about his reasons for making these writerly choices. Think also about how his own *ethos* as one of the world's most famous scientists contributes to the argument.

Religion and Science

1   Everything that the human race has done and thought is concerned with the satisfaction of deeply felt needs and the assuagement of pain. One has to keep this constantly in mind if one wishes to understand spiritual movements and their development. Feeling and desire are the motive force behind all human endeavour and human creation, in however exalted a guise the latter may present itself to us. Now what are the feelings and needs that have led men to religious thought and belief in the widest sense of the words? A little consideration will suffice to show us that the most varying emotions preside over the birth of religious thought and experience. With primitive man it is above all fear that evokes religious notions—fear of hunger, wild beasts, sickness, death. Since at this stage of existence understanding of causal connexions is usually poorly developed, the human mind creates for itself more or less analogous beings on whose wills and actions these fearful happenings depend. Thus one tries to secure the favour of these beings by carrying out actions and offering sacrifices which, according to the tradition handed down from generation to generation, propitiate them or make them well disposed towards a

mortal. I am speaking now of the religion of fear. This, though not created, is in an important degree stabilised by the formation of a special priestly caste which sets itself up as a mediator between the people and the beings they fear, and erects a hegemony on this basis. In many cases a leader or ruler whose position depends on other factors, or a privileged class, combines priestly functions with its secular authority in order to make the latter more secure; or the political rulers and the priestly caste make common cause in their own interests.

The social impulses are another source of the crystallisation of religion. Fathers and mothers and the leaders of larger human communities are mortal and fallible. The desire for guidance, love and support prompts men to form the social or moral conception of God. This is the God of Providence, who protects, disposes, rewards and punishes; the God who, according to the width of the believer's outlook, loves and cherishes the life of the tribe or of the human race, or even life itself; the comforter in sorrow and unsatisfied longing; he who preserves the souls of the dead. This is the social or moral conception of God. 2

The Jewish scriptures admirably illustrate the development from the religion of fear to moral religion, a development continued in the New Testament. The religions of all civilised peoples, especially the peoples of the Orient, are primarily moral religions. The development from a religion of fear to moral religion is a great step in a nation's life. And yet, that primitive religions are based entirely on fear and the religions of civilised peoples purely on morality is a prejudice against which we must be on our guard. The truth is that all religions are a varying blend of both types, with this differentiation: that on the higher levels of social life the religion of morality predominates. 3

Common to all these types is the anthropomorphic character of their conception of God. Only individuals of exceptional endowments and exceptionally high-minded communities, as a general rule, get in any real sense beyond this level. But there is a third stage of religious experience which belongs to all of them, even though it is rarely found in a pure form, and which I will call cosmic religious feeling. It is very difficult to explain this feeling to any one who is entirely without it, especially as there is no anthropomorphic conception of God corresponding to it. 4

The individual feels the nothingness of human desires and aims and the sublimity and marvellous order which reveal themselves both in Nature and in the world of thought. He looks upon individual existence as a sort of prison and wants to experience the universe as a single significant whole. The beginnings of cosmic religious feeling already appear in earlier stages of development, e.g., in many of the Psalms of David and in some of the Prophets. Buddhism, as we have learnt from the wonderful writings of Schopenhauer[1] especially, contains a much stronger element of this. 5

The religious geniuses of all ages have been distinguished by this kind of religious feeling, which knows no dogma and no God conceived in man's image; so that there can be no church whose central teachings are based on it. 6

---

[1]**Arthur Schopenhauer (1788–1860)** Author of *The World as Will and Representation* (1819), a philosophical treatise in which God, freewill, and immortality are seen as illusions. [Ed. note.]

Hence it is precisely among the heretics of every age that we find men who were filled with the highest kind of religious feeling and were in many cases regarded by their contemporaries as atheists, sometimes also as saints. Looked at in this light, men like Democritus,[2] Francis of Assisi,[3] and Spinoza[4] are closely akin to one another.

7   How can cosmic religious feeling be communicated from one person to another, if it can give rise to no definite notion of a God and no theology? In my view, it is the most important function of art and science to awaken this feeling and keep it alive in those who are capable of it.

8   We thus arrive at a conception of the relation of science to religion very different from the usual one. When one views the matter historically one is inclined to look upon science and religion as irreconcilable antagonists, and for a very obvious reason. The man who is thoroughly convinced of the universal operation of the law of causation cannot for a moment entertain the idea of a being who interferes in the course of events—provided, of course, that he takes the hypothesis of causality really seriously. He has no use for the religion of fear and equally little for social or moral religion. A God who rewards and punishes is inconceivable to him for the simple reason that a man's actions are determined by necessity, external and internal, so that in God's eyes he cannot be responsible, any more than an inanimate object is responsible for the motions it undergoes. Hence science has been charged with undermining morality, but the charge is unjust. A man's ethical behaviour should be based effectually on sympathy, education, and social ties; no religious basis is necessary. Man would indeed be in a poor way if he had to be restrained by fear and punishment and hope of reward after death.

9   It is therefore easy to see why the churches have always fought science and persecuted its devotees. On the other hand I maintain that the cosmic religious feeling is the strongest and noblest incitement to scientific research. Only those who realise the immense efforts and, above all, the devotion which pioneer work in theoretical science demands can grasp the strength of the emotion out of which alone such work, remote as it is from the immediate realities of life, can issue. What a deep conviction of the rationality of the universe and what a yearning to understand, were it but a feeble reflection of the mind revealed in this world, Kepler and Newton must have had to enable them to spend years of solitary labour in disentangling the principles of the celestial sphere! Those whose acquaintance with scientific research is derived chiefly from its practical results easily develop a completely false notion of the mentality of the men who, surrounded by a sceptical world, have shown the way to those fel-

---

[2]**Democritus (b. 460 B.C.E.)** Greek philosopher who wrote on the natural sciences, mathematics, morals, and music, and who advanced a theory that the world was formed by the interaction of atoms. [Ed. note.]

[3]**Saint Francis of Assisi (1181?–1226)** Founded the Franciscan order based on joyousness and love of nature, devoted to relief of those in need. [Ed. note.]

[4]**Benedict de Spinoza (1632–1677)** Philosopher who viewed God as immanent, that is, existing within all the elements of nature; Spinoza denied personal immorality and believed in determinism. [Ed. note.]

low spirits scattered wide through the world and the centuries. Only one who has devoted his life to similar ends can have a vivid realisation of what has inspired these men and given them the strength to remain true to their purpose in spite of countless failures. It is cosmic religious feeling that gives a man strength of this sort. A contemporary has said, not unjustly, that in this materialistic age of ours the serious scientific workers are the only profoundly religious people.

THE RELIGIOUSNESS OF SCIENCE

You will hardly find one among the profounder sort of scientific minds with-   10
out a peculiar religious feeling of his own. But it is different from the religion of the naive man. For the latter, God is a being from whose care one hopes to benefit and whose punishment one fears; a sublimation of a feeling similar to that of a child for its father, a being to whom one stands to some extent in a personal relation, however deeply it may be tinged with awe.

But the scientist is possessed by the sense of universal causation. The future,   11
to him, is every whit as necessary and determined as the past. There is nothing divine about morality; it is a purely human affair. His religious feeling takes the form of a rapturous amazement at the harmony of natural law, which reveals an intelligence of such superiority that, compared with it, all the systematic thinking and acting of human beings is an utterly insignificant reflection. This feeling is the guiding principle of his life and work, insofar as he succeeds in keeping himself from the shackles of selfish desire. It is beyond question closely akin to that which has possessed the religious geniuses of all ages.

Questions for Discussion and Your Reading Journal

1. Outline the organizational pattern of this essay. How does Einstein build his argument?
2. Define the words *religion* and *science* in your own words. How does Einstein define religion and science? How are these definitions different from your own?
3. What are the two motivating factors, according to Einstein, of all human behavior? What other factors might he have left out?
4. Einstein remarks, "With primitive man it is above all fear that evokes religious notions" (Paragraph 1). Explain this statement. What does he mean by "primitive"? Examine the possible cultural bias in this remark. Is modern religious belief in developed countries ever motivated by fear? Explain.
5. According to Einstein, the "most important function of art and science" is to awaken a "cosmic religious feeling" (Paragraph 7). What does this statement mean? How is the statement related to the author's purpose in writing the article? Who is the intended audience?
6. For what reason has science been "charged with undermining morality" (Paragraph 8)? Why does Einstein say the charge is "unjust"? Do you agree with his argument? Why or why not?
7. Explain what you think "the religiousness of science" might entail.

BERTRAND RUSSELL

Bertrand Russell (1872–1970) was a mathematician and philosopher. Born in Trelleck, Wales, he was an orphan from the age of 3. He went to Cambridge University where he studied mathematics and philosophy. Russell was an outspoken moralist. His greatest literary achievement was his History of Western Philosophy *(1946). Russell was an honored member of the English aristocracy, although he sometimes wrote and said controversial and unpopular things in criticism of the government. He became an Earl in 1931 and received the British Order of Merit in 1949. An English lord and a Nobel Laureate, Russell applied mathematical thinking processes to questions of ethics, religion, and politics. In* Religion and Science *(1960), Russell explores the controversies that have arisen between the two fields over the centuries. Russell claims that religion has waged a war "against scientific discovery" that has been generally unsuccessful until recent times. His introductory chapter, reproduced here, explains the "grounds and history" of that war. Interesting similarities can be seen between Russell's message and the essay of the same title by Albert Einstein.*

Reading Rhetorically

Russell's style is significantly different from that of Albert Einstein. Where one is erudite and displays a wide knowledge of history and culture, the other is plainspoken and focused on the present. Think about which of the two styles you prefer; and, as you study this reading, examine the effect of Russell's style on his message.

　　Think also about the reasons definitions are so important to writers of many kinds and scholars in all fields. Both Russell and Einstein (in the previous essay) are concerned with definitions of the words "religion" and "science." Examine Russell's definitions to see how they support his arguments. Then decide to what degree your own definitions of these words would be similar to those of Russell. Also examine his use of *logos*.

Religion and Science

1　Religion and Science are two aspects of social life, of which the former has been important as far back as we know anything of man's mental history, while the latter, after a fitful flickering existence among the Greeks and Arabs, suddenly sprang into importance in the sixteenth century, and has ever since increasingly moulded both the ideas and the institutions among which we live. Between religion and science there has been a profound conflict, in which, until the last few years, science has invariably proved victorious. But the rise of new religions in Russia and Germany, equipped with new means of missionary activity provided by science, has again put the issue in doubt, as it was at the beginning of the scientific epoch, and has made it again important to examine the grounds and the history of the warfare waged by traditional religion against scientific knowledge.

Science is the attempt to discover, by means of observation, and reasoning 2 based upon it, first, particular facts about the world, and then laws connecting facts with one another and (in fortunate cases) making it possible to predict future occurrences. Connected with this theoretical aspect of science there is scientific technique, which utilizes scientific knowledge to produce comforts and luxuries that were impossible, or at least much more expensive, in a prescientific era. It is this latter aspect that gives such great importance to science even for those who are not scientists.

Religion, considered socially, is a more complex phenomenon than science. 3 Each of the great historical religions has three aspects: (1) a Church, (2) a creed, and (3) a code of personal morals. The relative importance of these three elements has varied greatly in different times and places. The ancient religions of Greece and Rome, until they were made ethical by the Stoics,[1] had not very much to say about personal morals; in Islam the Church has been unimportant in comparison with the temporal monarch; in modern Protestantism there is a tendency to relax the rigors of the creed. Nevertheless, all three elements, though in varying proportions, are essential to religion as a social phenomenon, which is what is chiefly concerned in the conflict with science. A purely personal religion, so long as it is content to avoid assertions which science can disprove, may survive undisturbed in the most scientific age.

Creeds are the intellectual source of the conflict between religion and sci- 4 ence, but the bitterness of the opposition has been due to the connection of creeds with Churches and with moral codes. Those who questioned creeds weakened the authority, and might diminish the incomes, of Churchmen; moreover, they were thought to be undermining morality, since moral duties were deduced by Churchmen from creeds. Secular rulers, therefore, as well as Churchmen, felt that they had good reason to fear the revolutionary teaching of the men of science.

In what follows, we shall not be concerned with science in general, nor yet 5 with religion in general, but with those points where they have come into conflict in the past, or still do so at the present time. So far as Christendom is concerned, these conflicts have been of two kinds. Sometimes there happens to be a text in the Bible making some assertion as to a matter of fact, for example, that the hare chews the cud. Such assertions, when they are refuted by scientific observation, cause difficulties for those who believe, as most Christians did until science forced them to think otherwise, that every word of the Bible is divinely inspired. But when the Biblical assertions concerned have no inherent religious importance, it is not difficult to explain them away, or to avoid controversy by deciding that the Bible is only authoritative on matters of religion

---

[1]**Stoics** A group of Greek philosophers founded by Zeno of Citium about 310 B.C.E.; Stoics held that happiness is achieved through freeing oneself from the passions and appetites, and that virtue is the highest good while suffering is a necessary part of experience. [Ed. note]

and morals. There is, however, a deeper conflict when science controverts some important Christian dogma, or some philosophical doctrine which theologians believe essential to orthodoxy. Broadly speaking, the disagreements between religion and science were, at first, of the former sort, but have gradually become more and more concerned with matters which are, or were, considered a vital part of Christian teaching.

6 Religious men and women, in the present day, have come to feel that most of the creed of Christendom, as it existed in the Middle Ages, is unnecessary, and indeed a mere hindrance to the religious life. But if we are to understand the opposition which science encountered, we must enter imaginatively into the system of ideas which made such opposition seem reasonable. Suppose a man were to ask a priest why he should not commit murder. The answer "because you would be hanged" was felt to be inadequate, both because the hanging would need justification, and because police methods were so uncertain that a large proportion of murderers escaped. There was, however, an answer which, before the rise of science, appeared satisfactory to almost everyone, namely, that murder is forbidden by the Ten Commandments, which were revealed by God to Moses on Mount Sinai. The criminal who eluded earthly justice could not escape from the Divine wrath, which had decreed for impenitent murderers a punishment infinitely more terrible than hanging. This argument, however, rests upon the authority of the Bible, which can only be maintained intact if the Bible is accepted as a whole. When the Bible seems to say that the earth does not move, we must adhere to this statement in spite of the arguments of Galileo,[2] since otherwise we shall be giving encouragement to murderers and all other kinds of malefactors. Although few would now accept this argument, it cannot be regarded as absurd, nor should those who acted upon it be viewed with moral reprobation.

7 The mediaeval outlook of educated men had a logical unity which has now been lost. We may take Thomas Aquinas[3] as the authoritative exponent of the creed which science was compelled to attack. He maintained—and his view is still that of the Roman Catholic Church—that some of the fundamental truths of the Christian religion could be proved by the unaided reason, without the help of revelation. Among these was the existence of an omnipotent and benevolent Creator. From His omnipotence and benevolence it followed that He would not leave His creatures without knowledge of His decrees, to the extent that might be necessary for obeying His will. There must therefore be a Divine revelation, which, obviously, is contained in the Bible and the decisions of the Church. This point being established, the rest of what we need to know can be inferred from the Scriptures and the pronouncements of ecumenical Councils. The whole argument proceeds deductively from premisses formerly accepted by almost the whole population of Christian coun-

---

[2]**Galileo Galilei (1564–1642)** Italian astronomer and physicist who observed laws of gravity; Galileo was forced to repudiate the Copernican view of the universe by the inquisition (1633). [Ed. note.]

[3]**Saint Thomas Aquinas (1225–1274)** Italian philosopher and theologian whose Christian philosophy is based on Aristotle. [Ed. note]

tries, and if the argument is, to the modern reader, at times faulty, its fallacies were not apparent to the majority of learned contemporaries.

Now logical unity is at once a strength and a weakness. It is a strength 8 because it insures that whoever accepts one stage of the argument must accept all later stages; it is a weakness because whoever rejects any of the later stages must also reject some, at least, of the earlier stages. The Church, in its conflict with science, exhibited both the strength and the weakness resulting from the logical coherence of its dogmas.

The way in which science arrives at its beliefs is quite different from that 9 of mediaeval theology. Experience has shown that it is dangerous to start from general principles and proceed deductively, both because the principles may be untrue and because the reasoning based upon them may be fallacious. Sciences starts, not from large assumptions, but from particular facts discovered by observation or experiment. From a number of such facts a general rule is arrived at, of which, if it is true, the facts in question are instances. This rule is not positively asserted, but is accepted, to begin with, as a working hypothesis. If it is correct, certain hitherto unobserved phenomena will take place in certain circumstances. If it is found that they do take place, that so far confirms the hypothesis; if they do not, the hypothesis must be discarded and a new one must be invented. However many facts are found to fit the hypothesis, that does not make it certain, although in the end it may come to be thought in a high degree probable; in that case, it is called a theory rather than a hypothesis. A number of different theories, each built directly upon facts, may become the basis for a new and more general hypothesis from which, if true, they all follow; and to this process of generalization no limit can be set. But whereas, in mediaeval thinking, the most general principles were the starting point, in science they are the final conclusion—final, that is to say, at a given moment, though liable to become instances of some still wider law at a later stage.

A religious creed differs from a scientific theory in claiming to embody 10 eternal and absolutely certain truth, whereas science is always tentative, expecting that modifications in its present theories will sooner or later be found necessary, and aware that its method is one which is logically incapable of arriving at a complete and final demonstration. But in an advanced science the changes needed are generally only such as serve to give slightly greater accuracy; the old theories remain serviceable where only rough approximations are concerned, but are found to fail when some new minuteness of observation becomes possible. Moreover, the technical inventions suggested by the old theories remain as evidence that they had a kind of practical truth up to a point. Science thus encourages abandonment of the search for absolute truth, and the substitution of what may be called "technical" truth, which belongs to any theory that can be successfully employed in inventions or in predicting the future. "Technical" truth is a matter of degree: A theory from which more successful inventions and predictions spring is truer than one which gives rise to fewer. "Knowledge" ceases to be a mental mirror of the universe, and becomes merely a practical tool in the manipulation of matter. But these implications of scientific method were not visible to the pioneers of science, who, though they practised a new method of pursuing truth, still conceived truth itself as absolutely as did their theological opponents.

11   An important difference between the medieval outlook and that of modern science is in regard to authority. To the schoolmen, the Bible, the dogmas of the Catholic faith, and (almost equally) the teachings of Aristotle,[4] were above question; original thought and even investigation of facts, must not overstep the limits set by these immutable boundaries of speculative daring. Whether there are people at the antipodes, whether Jupiter has satellites, and whether bodies fall at a rate proportional to their mass were questions to be decided, not by observation, but by deduction from Aristotle or the Scriptures. The conflict between theology and science was quite as much a conflict between authority and observation. The men of science did not ask that propositions should be believed because some important authority had said they were true; on the contrary, they appealed to the evidence of the senses, and maintained only such doctrines as they believed to be based upon facts which were patent to all who chose to make the necessary observations. The new method achieved such immense successes, both theoretical and practical, that theology was gradually forced to accommodate itself to science. Inconvenient Bible texts were interpreted allegorically or figuratively; Protestants transferred the seat of authority in religion, first from the Church and the Bible to the Bible alone, and then to the individual soul. It came gradually to be recognized that the religious life does not depend upon pronouncements as to matters of fact, for instance, the historical existence of Adam and Eve. Thus, religion, by surrendering the outworks, has sought to preserve the citadel intact—whether successfully or not remains to be seen.

12   There is, however, one aspect of the religious life, and that perhaps the most desirable, which is independent of the discoveries of science, and may survive whatever we may come to believe as to the nature of the universe. Religion has been associated, not only with creeds and churches, but with the personal life of those who felt its importance. In the best of the saints and mystics, there existed in combination the belief in certain dogmas and a certain way of feeling about the purposes of human life. The man who feels deeply the problems of human destiny, the desire to diminish the sufferings of mankind, and the hope that the future will realize the best possibilities of our species, is nowadays often said to have a religious outlook, however little he may accept of traditional Christianity. In so far as religion consists in a way of feeling, rather than in a set of beliefs, science cannot touch it. Perhaps the decay of dogma may, psychologically, make such a way of feeling temporarily more difficult, because it has been so intimately associated with theological belief. But this difficulty need not endure for ever; in fact, many freethinkers have shown in their lives that this way of feeling has no essential connection with a creed. No real excellence can be inextricably bound up with unfounded beliefs; and if theological beliefs are unfounded, they cannot be necessary for the preser-

---

[4]**Aristotle (384–322 B.C.E.)** Greek philosopher who studied under Plato; Aristotle's works cover logic, moral philosophy, metaphysics, poetry, physics, zoology, politics, and rhetoric; he created "logic," the science of reasoning. [Ed note.]

vation of what is good in the religious outlook. To think otherwise is to be filled with fears as to what we may discover, which will interfere with our attempts to understand the world; but it is only in the measure in which we achieve such understanding that true wisdom becomes possible.

Questions for Discussion and Your Reading Journal

1. What is the purpose of this reading? Who might the intended audience be?
2. How does Russell define science? Religion? Compare and contrast Russell's definitions with those of Einstein. Then compare and contrast them with your own.
3. What is a "purely personal religion" (Paragraph 3)? Give an example from your own experience.
4. What are creeds and how are they "the source of the conflict between religion and science" (Paragraph 4)
5. Describe the conflict between scientific inquiry and religious assertions as to matters of "fact." How has religion resolved the conflict?
6. Analyze the method for ascertaining truths in science. Then contrast that method with the practices of religion in proving its beliefs.
7. Discuss the differences between the "tentative" nature of scientific hypotheses and the "absolute" nature of religious truth.
8. Outline Russell's pattern of organization. How does he build his argument? Compare and contrast the structure with that of Einstein's essay.

RAYMOND DAWSON

Raymond Dawson (1923–2002), a professor of political science and one of the world's foremost authorities on Chinese history, has written extensively about the art, literature, and history of China and, specifically, about the history of science in relation to its influence on the Western world.

In The Legacy of China *(1984), Raymond Dawson describes Chinese science in its historical context. "Science and China's Influence on the World" discusses the prominence of Chinese scientific achievements before and after the European Renaissance. Pointing out that Chinese scientists were responsible for such world-shattering developments as the production of gunpowder and the making of clocks, Dawson emphasizes the international connections between scientific inventions and discoveries and subsequent development. Read this excerpt in conjunction with the text on Islamic science and the excerpt from Fritjof Capra's* The Tao of Physics. *In this comparative context, this reading provides insight into the weblike interrelationship that has developed in the area of science between the many cultures of the world.*

An interesting cultural difference between nations in their approaches to science and scientific discovery involves their relative emphasis on the identity of individual scientists. In this essay Dawson contends "independent invention" is "unlikely" (Paragraph 3). In China and many other nations of the world, individual scientists are not focused on to the degree that they are in America, for example. While their discoveries were extremely important to the development of science in their nations, their names have many times not even been recorded. Speculate about the kinds of cultural differences that might lead to an extreme emphasis on the identity of a scientist as compared to a total lack of emphasis.

Reading Rhetorically

Although this is a very short text, it packs together a great deal of information. Think about a strategy for reading a text that is densely packed with information. It might involve making notes in the margin or a notebook, as well as other techniques for noting and organizing information. As you read Dawson's historical exposition, try to consciously use your strategy. Also notice how the exposition includes some persuasive elements. Think about what Dawson is trying to persuade you of, and how.

Science and China's Influence on the World

1   In technological influences before and during the Renaissance China occupies a quite dominating position. In the body of this contribution we shall mention among other things the efficient equine harness, the technology of iron and steel, the inventions of gunpowder and paper, the mechanical clock, and basic engineering devices such as the driving-belt, the chain-drive, and the standard method of converting rotary to rectilinear motion, together with segmental arch bridges and nautical techniques such as the stern-post rudder. The world owes far more to the relatively silent craftsmen of ancient and medieval China than to the Alexandrian mechanics, articulate theoreticians though they were.

2   We have next to think of those achievements of Asian and Chinese science which, though not genetically connected with the first rise of modern science, yet deserve close attention. They may or may not be directly related genetically to their corresponding developments in post-Renaissance modern science. Perhaps the most outstanding Chinese discovery which was so related, even though it influenced the West relatively late (the end of the eighteenth and the beginning of the nineteenth centuries), was that of the first successful immunization technique. Variolation, the forerunner of Jennerian vaccination, had been in use in China certainly since the beginning of the sixteenth century, and if tradition is right since the eleventh; it consisted in the inoculation of a minute amount of the contents of the smallpox pustule itself into the nostril of the patient to be immunized, and Chinese physicians had gradually worked out methods of attenuating the virus so as to give greater safety. The origins of the whole science of immunology lie in a practice based on medieval

Chinese medical thought. A case of direct theoretical influence which springs to mind concerns cosmology—the old Chinese doctrine of infinite empty space as opposed to the solid crystalline celestial spheres of medieval Europe, but again it did not exert its full effect towards their dissolution until after Galileo's time. Examples of later incorporation would be the development of undulatory theory in eighteenth-century physics, which immensely elaborated characteristically Chinese ideas without knowing anything of them; or the use of ancient and medieval Chinese records of novae and supernovae by modern radio-astronomers. A good case of the probable absence of any stimulus would be the seismograph as used in China from the second to the seventh centuries A.D.; though an outstanding achievement as a permanent legacy to the history of geology, it was almost certainly unknown to any of the scientific men who developed seismographs again in post-Renaissance Europe. Chinese biological and pathological classification systems occupy the same position; they were clearly unknown to Linnaeus and Sydenham, but none the less worthy of study, for only by drawing up the balance-sheet in full shall we ever ascertain what each civilization has contributed to human advancement. Similarly, it is now becoming clear that medieval Chinese anatomy was far more advanced than has generally been thought, for judgments have been based by Western anatomists only on the few remaining block-print illustrations, since they were unable to read the texts themselves and to pursue the complex and elaborate nomenclature. But it exerted no influence on the revival and development of anatomy in Renaissance Europe. Nor did the outstandingly good iconographic tradition of the pharmaceutical compendia of the *Pen-ts'ao* genre, centuries ahead of the West in accurate botanical illustration, which has gained appreciation only in our own time.

Lastly we have to think of technical inventions which only became incorporated, whether or not by reinvention, into the corpus of modern technology after the Renaissance period. A case in point might be the paddle-wheel boat, but it is uncertain, for we do not know whether the first European successes were based on a Byzantine idea never executed, or on a vast fund of practical Chinese achievement during the preceding millennium, or on neither. A clearer example is the iron-chain suspension bridge, for while the first European description came towards the end of the sixteenth century, the first realization occurred only in the eighteenth, and in knowledge of the Chinese antecedents, going back, as we know, for more than a thousand years previously. Independent invention occurred, no doubt, with the differential gear, for though this was present in the south-pointing carriages of ancient China, their construction has been revealed only by modern historical research and could hardly have inspired the later mechanics of the West who fitted up again this important form of enmeshing wheel-work. So also the Chinese methods of steelmaking by the co-fusion process and by the direct oxygenation of cast iron, though of great seniority to the siderurgy of Europe, were not able to exert any influence upon it, if indeed they did, which is still uncertain, until long after the Renaissance. At the same time one must always refrain from being too positive about the absence of influence. In human intercourse there have been innumerable capillary channels which we cannot see, and especially for earlier

3

times we should never be tempted to dogmatism in the denial of transmissions. Sometimes one wonders whether humanity ever forgets anything. The sailing-carriage of early seventeenth-century Europe was consciously modelled on supposed Chinese prototypes which had in fact been rather different, but it is possible that they in their turn derived from the model boats with sails outspread which, supported upon low wooden wagons, conveyed the coffins of ancient Egyptian gods or kings across the deserts to their tombs. Broadly speaking, experience shows that the further one goes back in history the more unlikely independent invention was; we cannot infer it from the conditions of modern science today, where it frequently occurs.

Questions for Discussion and Your Reading Journal

1. Why might it be important to understand the history of science, especially in relation to how one country's scientific developments affected the rest of the world?
2. What does the phrase "attenuating a virus" (Paragraph 2) mean? Why was the invention of immunization so important at this point in time?
3. Explain Dawson's contention that "independent invention" is "unlikely" (Paragraph 3). What does this imply about the tendency of our society to point to inventors as absolute creators?
4. List the scientific achievements of China during the Renaissance. Which items surprise you? Which did you know about? How did the rest of the world continue to develop some of these discoveries? Gunpowder? Clocks? Others?

JOHN B. CHRISTOPHER

John B. Christopher, a former member of the Department of History at the University of Rochester, co-authored A History of Civilization *(1955), which displayed his wide-ranging expertise in modern art, French and German literature, Islamic culture, and world history.*

In The Islamic Tradition *(1972), Christopher discusses the science of the Islamic empire of the Middle Ages. Muslim, Christian, and Jewish scientists living in the geographical area dominated by Islam made substantial contributions to some of the major fields of scientific inquiry, including medicine, mathematics, and the physical sciences. Physicians such as Avicenna received acclaim and respect for their work, while mathematicians developed the Arabic numeral system, a far more practically useful tool than the system of Roman numerals. Mathematical developments contributed to the rise of the physical sciences, particularly astronomy. The cross-cultural borrowing that characterized medieval Islamic science reflects that described by Raymond Dawson in "Science and China's Influence on the World."*

Reading Rhetorically

In some ways, this selection reads like a "defense" of the Islamic world in relation to its contribution to the various fields of science. When you are reading a text that seems to be defending something, it is important to try to figure out the writer's motivation. Who or what is it being defended against? In this case Christopher seems to be directing his writing to "Modern Westerners." In the first paragraph under the heading "Astrology and Alchemy" (Paragraph 15), Christopher writes, "Modern Westerners . . . are amused by the talent expended on such fanciful gadgets." In the previous paragraph he has referred to these same devices as both "practical" and "ingenious." He seems to be implying, rather than stating outright, that Westerners tend to underestimate and devalue Islamic inventions. Think about why he does not state this directly. As you read, look for other clues that Christopher is writing a defense and think about why he might have been motivated to present his information in this way. Also look for his use of *logos*.

Science in Islam

Several of the great names in Islamic philosophy—ar-Razi, al-Farabi, 1 Avicenna—also figure prominently in the history of Islamic science. Scientists, too, built on the work of older civilizations, Greek, Persian, Hindu, and even Chinese (it is possible that the Arabic word *alchemy* is derived from the Chinese for *gold-extracting juice*). In science as in philosophy, many of the men responsible for transmitting older traditions were non-Muslims; Christians translated Greek works, and in Baghdad certain Christian and Jewish families, generation after generation, supplied the physicians and pharmacists who served the upper classes.

The extremely important contributions made by non-Muslims to Islamic 2 culture suggest that in this context the term *Islamic* has such broad and syncretistic implications that, unlike *Muslim,* it does not necessarily refer to participation in a particular religious faith. Some historians refer to the Abbasid caliphate as the *Islamic empire* to point up the contrast between its cosmopolitan and the more primitive, more soldierly, and predominantly Muslim qualities of the Umayyads' *Arab kingdom.* Medieval Spain furnished striking examples of a kind of cultural free trade between Muslims and non-Muslims. The Jew Maimonides (1134–1204) is a significant personage in the Islamic tradition because he was physician to Saladin, wrote in Arabic not Hebrew, and carried forward the philosophical inquiries of his master, Averroes. Jews and Christians participated significantly in the intellectual and scientific life of Toledo, which continued almost without interruption after the city passed permanently from Muslim to Christian control in 1085. In the twelfth and thirteenth centuries the archbishops of Toledo, the ranking prelates of Spain, made the city far and away the most important center for translating works by Muslim intellectuals into Latin.

3   The linguistic preeminence of Arabic and the relative case of travel across the length and breadth of the medieval Islamic world permitted the development of important scientific centers all the way from Spain and Morocco to Samarkand in Central Asia, capital of the conqueror Tamerlane, who established a great school there at the close of the Middle Ages. In the first two Muslim centuries the major scientific center was the city of Jundishapur in southwestern Persia, founded by the Sasanid emperor Shapur, who defeated the legions of Rome in the third century A.D. Renowned for its hospital and its medical and scientific academics, Jundishapur attracted many Nestorian refugees from Byzantine persecution. Under the early Abbasid caliphs leadership passed to Baghdad, where the caliphs' House of Wisdom established a vigorous intellectual tradition continued by the city's schools and hospitals. In the tenth and eleventh centuries the energy of the Ismaili movement and the patronage of the Fatimid caliphs, particularly in establishing a great library, brought Cairo to the first rank. It remained there during many later political vicissitudes thanks to the continuity provided by institutions such as its famous hospitals and the university of al-Azhar.

MEDICINE

4   In the medieval Islamic world the medical profession was established and recognized to a degree unknown in Catholic Europe. Reputable physicians were on the whole highly esteemed and well paid; an outstanding doctor such as Avicenna served Persian princes not only as a physician but also as a political counsellor. The starting point of Islamic medicine was the legacy of Hindu and Persian medical lore preserved at Jundishapur, supplemented by the Arabic translation of the Greek physician Galen, who had summarized the medical legacy of the ancient Mediterranean world in the second century A.D.

5   Past authorities did not necessarily command uncritical deference from Muslim physicians. For example, ar-Razi, who flourished about A.D. 900, cited Greek, Syriac, Persian, and Hindu opinions on a given question and then presented his own views. This independent attitude enabled ar-Razi to make some important discoveries, above all to distinguish for the first time the differences between smallpox and measles. Here is an excerpt from his monograph on these two diseases:

> The outbreak of small-pox is preceded by continuous fever, aching in the back, itching in the nose and shivering during sleep. The main symptoms of its presence are: back-ache with fever, stinging pain in the whole body, congestion of the face, sometimes shrinkage, violent redness of the cheeks and eyes, a sense of pressure in the body, creeping of the flesh, pain in the throat and breast accompanied by difficulty of respiration and coughing, dryness of the mouth, thick salivation, hoarseness of the voice, headache and pressure in the head, excitement, anxiety, nausea and unrest. Excitement, nausea and unrest are more pronounced in measles than in small-

pox, whilst the aching in the back is more severe in small-pox than in measles.[1]

Through careful detailed observation, ar-Razi added much to the store of clinical data about infectious diseases that had been accumulating since the pioneering work of Hippocrates 1300 years earlier. 6

Ar-Razi's contribution to Islamic medicine was the more remarkable because he only began his studies in middle age, when he already had many other intellectual irons in the fire. He directed a hospital in his native Rayy, then another at Baghdad, and wrote more than fifty clinical studies in addition to more ambitious general works. The latter included the *Comprehensive Book*, the longest medical work in the Arabic language (over eighteen volumes in an incomplete modern edition), which Renaissance Europeans much respected in its Latin translation. In the present century ar-Razi has attracted attention because of his *Spiritual Physick* (see pp. 109–110) and other original works on the psychological and sociological aspects of medicine. A few pertinent titles are: *On the Fact That Even Skillful Physicians Cannot Heal All Diseases; Why Frightened Patients Easily Forsake Even the Skilled Physician; Why People Prefer Quacks and Charlatans.* 7

A hundred years later, Avicenna also placed considerable stress on psychosomatic medicine and reportedly was able to cure a prince suffering from a severe depression. The patient imagined himself to be a cow, made lowing noises, and demanded to be butchered and converted into stew beef; Avicenna, posing as a cheerful butcher, refused to oblige, claiming that the intended victim was too scrawny and needed to be fattened up; whereupon the patient began eating heartily and eventually recovered his health. Avicenna compiled an encyclopedia, *The Canon of Medicine*, which was more systematic than Razi's *Comprehensive Book* and was widely consulted in the Arab world down to the last century and in Western Europe until the 1600s. Avicenna appears to have been the first doctor to describe and identify meningitis and the first to recommend alcohol as a disinfectant. 8

The more scholars examine the sources, the more "firsts" can be claimed for Islamic medicine. The work of Avicenna and others on eye diseases, very prevalent in the Middle East, and on the nature of vision helped to found the study of optics. These studies also made possible rather complicated operations on the eye. Muslim surgeons used opium for anesthesia and attempted experimental operations, including the extraction of teeth and their replacement by ones made from animal bones, the removal of kidney stones lodged in the bladder, and possibly even colostomy (opening of an artificial anus after removal of cancerous tissue). 9

However, it is important to keep a proper perspective on Islamic medical achievements and not to magnify them unduly. Mortality among surgical 10

---

[1]Quoted by Max Meyerhof, "Science and Medicine," in T. Arnold and A. Guillaume, eds., *The Legacy of Islam* (London: Oxford UP, 1931), 323–324.

patients appears to have been very high, because doctors knew little about either antiseptic measures or the details of anatomy. Muslim tradition forbade dissecting corpses, though a little clandestine dissection may have occurred, mainly in Spain. Some scholars, therefore, discount reports that a thirteenth century Egyptian physician discovered the existence of the pulmonary circulation, which accounts for the passage of the blood from one chamber of the heart to another via the lungs. He may have advanced this theory three centuries before it was confirmed by European scientists; but it was a purely speculative hypothesis, untested clinically or experimentally.

MATHEMATICS AND THE PHYSICAL SCIENCES

11   To describe certain procedures mathematicians borrowed from the vocabulary of surgery the term *al-jahr,* meaning restoration or reestablishment of something broken (Spaniards still call a bone-setter an *algebrista*). Islamic algebra was built on Greek and Hindu foundations and closely linked to geometry; its principal architects were the ninth-century Zoroastrian, al-Khuwarizmi, and the twelfth-century Persian, Omar Khayyam. Al-Khuwarizmi, who worked at the House of Wisdom in Baghdad, wrote a very influential book on algebra and also contributed to the development of trigonometry. He described an angle by an Arabic word meaning *pocket* or *pouch,* which was translated into the Latin *sinus*—whence our *sine.* Omar Khayyam, who was also a poet and a Sufi as well as an astronomer, is an excellent instance of the Muslim who sought both the rationalist and the gnostic paths to truth. Indeed, many Islamic mathematicians, like the Pythagoreans of ancient Greece, believed that through numbers men could ascend beyond the world of bewildering phenomena into a higher realm of abstractions and eternal verities. Because the science of numbers was regarded as "the tongue which speaks of unity and transcendence," it was appropriate to use as charms magic squares based on the numerical value of some of the ninety-nine names of God.

12   To the average Westerner, Arabic numbers have the merit of great simplicity, in contrast to the cumbersome Roman system based on letters. The simplicity of the Arabic system, however, is somewhat deceptive. The numerals used in the West, except for 1 and 9, do not look much like those used today by Arabs and Persians: Their numerals are derived from those used in medieval Iraq, whereas ours come through medieval Spain. All of them, except for zero, almost certainly go back ultimately to the Hindus. The most revolutionary innovation of Arabic numbers was not their greater convenience, valuable and time-saving though this was; it lay in the Arabs' use of a dot to indicate an empty column, ten, for example, being 1·, one hundred one 1·1, and one million and one 1 · · · · · 1. The dot was called *sifr* ("empty"), whence our *cipher* and, through an Italian translation, our *zero.* This system made possible a whole new world of arithmetical operations.

13   Islamic mathematicians opened new worlds to science, or at least freshened understanding of older worlds. Increased knowledge of geometry and algebra aided the development of optics. The tables compiled by observers systematically recording their findings were utilized by later astronomers both in

the Islamic world and in Europe. Islamic advances in trigonometry allowed computations that refined the picture of the earth-centered universe drawn by Ptolemy, the Greco-Egyptian astronomer of the second century A.D. One such refinement disclosed the eccentric behavior of Venus, which would have been easier to explain if the planet had been viewed as orbiting around the sun rather than around the earth. But, as in the medieval West, acceptance of the Ptolemaic system was too ingrained to countenance such a radical innovation as the heliocentric universe.

In certain instances theoretical science was turned to practical account. 14 Astronomical tables enabled the faithful to determine the direction of Mecca and to schedule the five daily prayers and fix the annual festivals and holy days of the lunar calendar. Astronomy and geography facilitated navigation of the monsoon-swept Indian ocean, and mathematics and physics encouraged improvement of water clocks and of water wheels and other irrigation apparatus. Mechanical devices were sometimes remarkably ingenious, as in this thirteenth-century clock consisting of an elephant and a fantastic contrivance mounted on its back:

> Every half-hour the bird on top of the cupola whistles and turns while the mahout hits the elephant with his pick-axe and sounds a tattoo with his drumstick. In addition, the little man who seems to be looking out of a window . . . moves his arms and legs to induce the falcon below to release a pellet. This moving downward, makes the dragon turn until it is finally ejected into the little vase on the elephant's back. From there it drops into the animal, hits a gong, and finally comes to rest in a little bowl where the observer can establish the half-hours passed by counting the number of little balls collected there.[2]

ASTROLOGY AND ALCHEMY

Modern Westerners, who are amused by the talent expended on such fanciful 15 gadgets, are uneasy when they learn that many Islamic astronomers were also astrologers and that a pioneer psychologist and physician such as ar-Razi could also be an alchemist. Astrology is based on the belief that the universe is, as the name suggests, a totality in which the stars do determine and indeed predestine activities on earth. Alchemy is based on the theory that there is a hierarchy of metals, from the base to the pure; if man can find the magical philosopher's stone or elixir, he will be able to change one to the other, iron to gold, or lead to silver, and perhaps also to make glass or quartz into emeralds or some other precious stone.

To us today all this seems an unfortunate confusion between true science 16 and occult or pseudo science; our medieval forebears accepted the occult as a matter of course. Ancient traditions, together with the gnostic elements present in both Christianity and Islam, nourished the widely held conviction that there were other pathways to truth beside the one that we call rationalist or

---

[2]Richard Ettinghausen, *Arab Painting* (Cleveland: World, 1962) 95.

scientific. The more radical Shiites, especially the Ismailis with their concern for discovering the hidden message of the Koran, endeavored to unlock the secrets of nature by esoteric means as well as by scientific ones. The Sufis strove to release themselves from the physical restraints of body and mind to enable the soul to penetrate the veils concealing God.

17   A modern Persian scholar, familiar both with the history of science and with the Shii and Sufi traditions, advances this explanation for the popularity of alchemy:

> We must remember that ancient and medieval man did not separate the material order from the psychological and spiritual in the categorical manner that has become customary today. There was a "naiveness" in the mentality of premodern man which made it possible for him . . . to see a deeper significance in physical phenomena than just plain facts. . . . The basic symbols and principles of alchemy stem from the earliest periods of history and convey through their very concreteness the primordial character of this point of view. Ancient man, during the millennia before recorded history, considered metals to be a special class of beings, which did not belong to the natural environment of the "Adamic race." The earliest iron probably came from meteorites which, in falling from the heavens, gave that metal special virtues and powers.[3]

18   Although this hypothesis is controversial, there seems little doubt that alchemy was regarded as a quasi-religious pursuit. It has been argued that, just as the alchemist sought to transmute baser metals into gold, so he also sought a kind of transmutation of the soul, which would release it from the sin imposed by the fall of Adam from Eden and allow it to reach a nobler state. The alchemist has likewise been compared to a Sufi sheik, guiding his disciples on their way to God, and to the Christian priest, celebrating the miracle of the mass, which transforms the bread and wine into the body and blood of Christ.

19   Astrology and alchemy were, in effect, the face and obverse of the same coin, the one turned toward the heavens and the other toward the earth. The seven metals of the alchemist were the earthly symbols of the astrologer's seven planets—gold symbolized the sun, silver the moon, quicksilver Mercury, copper Venus, iron Mars, tin Jupiter, and lead Saturn. From the ancient Greeks Islamic alchemists borrowed the concept of four fundamental elements—fire, air, earth, and water. Each of these, they argued, combined two of the four fundamental characteristics or qualities of nature, heat, cold, dryness, and wetness: Fire was hot and dry, air hot and wet, earth cold and dry, and water cold and wet.

20   Islamic physicians, also borrowing from the Greeks, put the four humors of the human body into this pattern, noting that each produced a characteristic temperament. Yellow bile, which was hot and dry, made a man fiery or choleric; blood, which was hot and wet, made him sanguine or cheerful; black bile, which was cold and dry, made him melancholy; and phlegm, cold and wet, made him phlegmatic. When the humors were reasonably balanced, the

---

[3]Seyyed Hossein Nasr, *Science and Civilization in Islam* (Cambridge: Harvard UP, 1968) 243.

individual was in good health. In illness, the balance was destroyed; and treatment consisted in prescribing for the patient drugs and a diet that would supply the humors in which he was deficient until his normal balance was restored.

The doctrines of astrology and alchemy did not win universal approval in   21
the medieval Islamic world. The ulema[4] proclaimed them contrary to the faith, and several distinguished philosophers rejected them as contrary to reason. Ibn-Khaldun concluded:

> The worthlessness of astrology from the point of view of the religious law, as well as the weakness of its achievements from the rational point of view, are evident. In addition, astrology does harm to human civilization. It hurts the faith of the common people when an astrological judgment occasionally happens to come true. . . . Ignorant people are taken in by that and suppose that all the other astrological judgments must be true.[5]

And Avicenna flatly denied the possibility of physical transmutation: 22

> As to the claims of the alchemists, it must be clearly understood that it is not in their power to bring about any true change of species. They can, however, produce excellent imitations, dyeing the red metal white so that it resembles silver, or dyeing it yellow so that it closely resembles gold. They can, too, dye the white metal with any colour they desire, until it bears a close resemblance to gold or copper; and they can free the leads from most of their defects and impurities. Yet in these dyed metals the essential nature remains unchanged.[6]

This last passage nevertheless suggests how the Arabic *al-kimiya* was to fur-   23
nish modern chemistry both with its name and with some of its techniques and apparatus. In addition to being expert dyers, the alchemists developed methods of refining metals and of applying varnish to protect iron or waterproof cloth. They employed such chemical processes as distillation, evaporation, sublimation, crystallization, and filtration. Ar-Razi, in his writings on alchemy, describes vials, beakers, mortars and pestles, flasks, smelters, and other items of equipment. A modern scholar has compared the power attributed to the elusive philosopher's stone with that actually present in a chemical catalyst.[7]

MUSIC

At first glance it seems strange that the quantitative sciences of the medieval   24
Islamic curriculum should have included arithmetic, geometry, astronomy, optics—and music, a discipline that we tend to bracket with the arts and

---

[4]**ulema** Doctors of Muslim religion and law; learned men. [Ed. note.]

[5]Ibn-Khaldun, *The Muqaddinah*, abridged (Princeton: Princeton UP, 1969) 408.

[6]Quoted in A. C. Crombie, "Avicenna's Influence on the Medieval Scientific Tradition," in G. M. Wickens, ed., *Avicenna: Scientist and Philosopher* (London: Luzac, 1952) 96.

[7]A. Mieli, *La Science Arabe et Son Rôle dans l'Evolution Scientifique Mondiale* (Leiden: Brill, 1938) 131–132.

humanities. Yet the same list of subjects, except for optics, formed the quadrivium (fourfold way to knowledge) in the schools of the medieval West. Many of the leading Islamic scientists wrote on music—ar-Razi, who was a talented lute-player; AVicenna, who was an expert in rhythm; and, above all, al-Farabi, who compiled the *Grand Book of Music,* considered the most important work on musical theory written in the Middle Ages.

25   In theory Islamic musicians relied heavily on Pythagoras and other ancient Greeks and also on Byzantine and Persian precedents and on rhythmical early Arab poetry. Their greatest innovation was technical, indeed quantitative: it was a system of measures that assigned each sound a time value, in contrast to the unmeasured plain song of the early medieval West. Measures endowed music with greater structure, encouraged new concepts of rhythm, and ultimately led to the full, half, quarter, and other notes we use today. Islamic musicians applied mathematics to stringed instruments by the device of frets, which allowed the player to tune a string to a desired note. These musicians provided the West with the lute (in Arabic, *aloud*), with the rebec, a pioneering two-stringed instrument played with a bow rather than plucked, and possibly with the guitar (*qitara* in Arabic), though the instrument, like its name, *kithara*, may have been of Greek origin. The tambourine ("little drum") is of Islamic origin, as is *fanfare*, a word derived from the Arabic for *trumpets* and reflecting Muslim enthusiasm for martial music.

26   Music had no recognized formal role in Islamic life. The chanting of Koranic passages and the intonation of prayers were not regarded as musical activities, and fundamentalists opposed free indulgence in music as conducive to debauchery and paganism. al-Ghazali once recommended that the best way to disarm the temptations of secular music was to break the instruments used and rout the singers. Yet the same al-Ghazali wrote *Music and Ecstasy,* praising the contribution of music to the Sufi dhikr; and visitors to Konya may still hear the strains of flute, rebec, and drum to which the Mevievi dervishes danced their way to a mystical trance.

27   In practice, then, music played an important informal role in Islamic life. It accompanied the recital of poetry, and it was recommended to relieve the distress of the ill or the depressed (musical therapy is not a twentieth-century invention). Music was a central ingredient in military and palace ceremonies; and it underscored the capers of jesters, which inspired those morris dances that sound so very English but were actually Moorish and performed by dancers with faces blackened to resemble Moors. Music illustrates once again the complexity of the Islamic tradition, the coexistence of the sacred and the profane, the gnostic and the scientific.

Questions for Discussion and Your Reading Journal

1. Describe the kinds of sharing between cultures that contributes to the science of Islam.
2. What does the writer's purpose seem to be in this article? Who is the audience?

3. What does "linguistic preeminence" (Paragraph 3) mean? Give an example of linguistic preeminence in another context.
4. List the developments in medicine mentioned by Christopher. Evaluate their significance.
5. Why was the invention of Arabic numerals such a great contribution to the field of mathematics?
6. How have the inventions and developments mentioned in this article been developed by or influenced by other cultures?

FRITJOF CAPRA

Fritjof Capra (1939–) is a professor at Schumacher College in England, where he specializes in ecological studies. Capra also directs the Center for Ecoliteracy in Berkeley, California, which promotes ecological awareness in primary and secondary education.

In his book entitled The Tao of Physics *(1975), Capra discusses the connections between modern physics and concepts in the Eastern philosophy of mysticism. He views the world as an integrated whole. Drawing from Gestalt psychology and quantum physics, Capra sees all organisms as networks of cells and ecosystems as networks of organisms and biological systems. Capra asserts that the revolutionary ideas uncovered in the study of atomic and subatomic physics have their roots in the ancient philosophy of the Far East. Capra's thesis reinforces that of Raymond Dawson in "Science and China's Influence on the World": scientific learning involves a complex web of influence and interrelationships between cultures.*

Reading Rhetorically

In this essay Capra sets up a dialectic between Eastern and Western ways of understanding the world. He then contrasts "classical physics" with "modern physics." At this point he begins to focus on similarities between the physics that explains the "submicroscopic realm" (Paragraph 4) of scientific inquiry and Eastern mysticism, again, in contrast to "classical physics." As you read this epilogue, try to follow its complex structure of comparison and contrast. Understanding the structure will help you see the connections Capra is making between science and mysticism, particularly the similarities between their ways of understanding the world.

You have probably encountered the terms "yin" and "yang." The symbol that represents them is a divided circle in which each side not only contrasts the other, but also seems to invade it. As a result the circle's halves are not simply opposites. Think about how this article discusses things in the ways they oppose each other, as well as in the ways they are interconnected. Finally, examine his use of *logos*.

Excerpt from *The Tao of Physics*

EPILOGUE

1   The Eastern religious philosophies are concerned with timeless mystical knowledge which lies beyond reasoning and cannot be adequately expressed in words. The relation of this knowledge to modern physics is but one of its many aspects and, like all the others, it cannot be demonstrated conclusively but has to be experienced in a direct intuitive way. What I hope to have achieved, to some extent, therefore, is not a rigorous demonstration, but rather to have given the reader an opportunity to relive, every now and then, an experience which has become for me a source of continuing joy and inspiration; that the principal theories and models of modern physics lead to a view of the world which is internally consistent and in perfect harmony with the views of Eastern mysticism.

2   For those who have experienced this harmony, the significance of the parallels between the world views of physicists and mystics is beyond any doubt. The interesting question, then, is not *whether* these parallels exist, but *why*; and, furthermore, what their existence implies.

3   In trying to understand the mystery of Life, man has followed many different approaches. Among them, there are the ways of the scientist and mystic, but there are many more; the ways of poets, children, clowns, shamans, to name but a few. These ways have resulted in different descriptions of the world, both verbal and nonverbal, which emphasize different aspects. All are valid and useful in the context in which they arose. All of them, however, are only descriptions, or representations, of reality and are therefore limited. None can give a complete picture of the world.

4   The mechanistic world view of classical physics is useful for the description of the kind of physical phenomena we encounter in our everyday life and thus appropriate for dealing with our daily environment, and it has also proved extremely successful as a basis for technology. It is inadequate, however, for the description of physical phenomena in the submicroscopic realm. Opposed to the mechanistic conception of the world is the view of the mystics which may be epitomized by the word "organic," as it regards all phenomena in the universe as integral parts of an inseparable harmonious whole. This world view emerges in the mystical traditions from meditative states of consciousness. In their description of the world, the mystics use concepts which are derived from these non-ordinary experiences and are, in general, inappropriate for a scientific description of macroscopic phenomena. The organic world view is not advantageous for constructing machines, nor for coping with the technical problems in an overpopulated world.

5   In everyday life, then, both the mechanistic and the organic views of the universe are valid and useful; the one for science and technology, the other for a balanced and fulfilled spiritual life. Beyond the dimensions of our everyday environment, however, the mechanistic concepts lose their validity and have to be replaced by organic concepts which are very similar to those used by the

mystics. This is the essential experience of modern physics which has been the subject of our discussion. Physics in the twentieth century has shown that the concepts of the organic world view, although of little value for science and technology on the human scale, become extremely useful at the atomic and subatomic level. The organic view, therefore, seems to be more fundamental than the mechanistic. Classical physics, which is based on the latter, can be derived from quantum theory, which implies the former, whereas the reverse is not possible. This seems to give a first indication why we might expect the world views of modern physics and Eastern mysticism to be similar. Both emerge when man enquires into the essential nature of things—into the deeper realms of matter in physics; into the deeper realms of consciousness in mysticism—when he discovers a different reality behind the superficial mechanistic appearance of everyday life.

The parallels between the views of physicists and mystics become even 6
more plausible when we recall the other similarities which exist in spite of their different approaches. To begin with, their method is thoroughly empirical. Physicists derive their knowledge from experiments; mystics from meditative insights. Both are observations, and in both fields these observations are acknowledged as the only source of knowledge. The object of observation is of course very different in the two cases. The mystic looks within and explores his or her consciousness at its various levels, which include the body as the physical manifestation of the mind. The experience of one's body is, in fact, emphasized in many Eastern traditions and is often seen as the key to the mystical experience of the world. When we are healthy, we do not feel any separate parts in our body but are aware of it as an integrated whole, and this awareness generates a feeling of well-being and happiness. In a similar way, the mystic is aware of the wholeness of the entire cosmos which is experienced as an extension of the body. In the words of Lama Govinda,

> To the enlightened man . . . whose consciousness embraces the universe, to him the universe becomes his "body," while his physical body becomes a manifestation of the Universal Mind, his inner vision an expression of the highest reality, and his speech an expression of eternal truth and mantric power.[1]

In contrast to the mystic, the physicist begins his enquiry into the essential 7
nature of things by studying the material world. Penetrating into ever deeper realms of matter, he has become aware of the essential unity of all things and events. More than that, he has also learnt that he himself and his consciousness are an integral part of this unity. Thus the mystic and the physicist arrive at the same conclusion; one starting from the inner realm, the other from the outer world. The harmony between their views confirms the ancient Indian wisdom that *Brahman*, the ultimate reality without, is identical to *Atman*, the reality within.

---

[1]Lama Anagarika Govinda, *Fountains of Tibetan Mysticism*. (New York: Samuel Weiser, 1974) 225.

8   A further similarity between the ways of the physicist and mystic is the fact that their observations take place in realms which are inaccessible to the ordinary senses. In modern physics, these are the realms of the atomic and subatomic world; in mysticism they are non-ordinary states of consciousness in which the sense world is transcended. Mystics often talk about the experiencing higher dimensions in which impressions of different centers of consciousness are integrated into a harmonious whole. A similar situation exists in modern physics where a four-dimensional "space-time" formalism has been developed which unifies concepts and observations belonging to different categories in the ordinary three-dimensional world. In both fields, the multidimensional experiences transcend the sensory world and are therefore almost impossible to express in ordinary language.

9   We see that the ways of the modern physicist and the Easter mystic, which seem at first totally unrelated, have, in fact, much in common. It should not be too surprising, therefore, that there are striking parallels in their descriptions of the world. Once these parallels between Western science and Eastern mysticism are accepted, a number of questions will arise concerning their implications. Is modern science, with all its sophisticated machinery, merely rediscovering ancient wisdom, known to the Eastern sages for thousands of years? Should physicists, therefore, abandon the scientific method and begin to meditate? Or can there be a mutual influence between science and mysticism; perhaps even a synthesis?

10   I think all these questions have to be answered in the negative. I see science and mysticism as two complementary manifestations of the human mind; of its rational and intuitive faculties. The modern physicist experiences the world through an extreme specialization of the rational mind; the mystic through an extreme specialization of the intuitive mind. The two approaches are entirely different and involve far more than a certain view of the physical world. However, they are complementary, as we have learned to say in physics. Neither is comprehended in the other, nor can either of them be reduced to the other, but both of them are necessary, supplementing one another for a fuller understanding of the world. To paraphrase an old Chinese saying, mystics understand the roots of the *Tao* but not its branches; scientists understand its branches but not its roots. Science does not need mysticism and mysticism does not need science; but man needs both. Mystical experience is necessary to understand the deepest nature of things, and science is essential for modern life. What we need, therefore, is not a synthesis but a dynamic interplay between mystical intuition and scientific analysis.

11   So far, this has not been achieved in our society. At present, our attitude is too *yang*—to use again Chinese phraseology—too rational, male and aggressive. Scientists themselves are a typical example. Although their theories are leading to a world view which is similar to that of the mystics, it is striking how little this has affected the attitudes of most scientists. In mysticism, knowledge cannot be separated from a certain way of life which becomes its living manifestation. To acquire mystical knowledge means to undergo a transformation; one could even say that the knowledge *is* the transformation. Scientific knowledge, on the other hand, can often stay abstract and theoretical.

Thus most of today's physicists do not seem to realize the philosophical, cultural and spiritual implications of their theories. Many of them actively support a society which is still based on the mechanistic, fragmented world view, without seeing that science points beyond such a view, towards a oneness of the universe which includes not only our natural environment but also our fellow human beings. I believe that the world view implied by modern physics is inconsistent with our present society, which does not reflect the harmonious interrelatedness we observe in nature. To achieve such a state of dynamic balance, a radically different social and economic structure will be needed: a cultural revolution in the true sense of the word. The survival of our whole civilization may depend on whether we can bring about such a change. It will depend, ultimately, on our ability to adopt some of the *yin* attitudes of Eastern mysticism; to experience the wholeness of nature and the art of living with it in harmony.

Questions for Discussion and Your Reading Journal

1. Define the term *Tao*. Why is this word used in the title?
2. Discuss the related concepts of *yin* and *yang*. How might such separations be universal?
3. Discuss the limitations of the Western worldview, as Capra represents them. How is the Eastern worldview different from the Western?
4. What is meant by the words "mystic" (Paragraph 2) and "mysticism" (Paragraph 5)? What is mysticism presented in opposition to? Discuss the cultural advantages and limitations of focusing exclusively on either one or the other.
5. How are the concepts of Tao interconnected with concepts of Western science?

THE ENVIRONMENT IN GLOBAL CONTEXTS

RACHEL CARSON

Rachel Carson (1907–1964) was an American biologist and writer known for her books about the sea and her writings concerning the use of pesticides. Beginning in 1947 she worked as editor in chief of the U.S. Fish and Wildlife Service publications. In her essay entitled "The Obligation to Endure" from Silent Spring *(1961), Carson describes the ways in which humankind, in its relatively short time on earth, has drastically altered the natural world. An ardent and eloquent environmentalist, Carson questions the value of the gains achieved by the sacrifice of natural resources. Most specifically, Carson indicts chemical insecticides as instruments that may well work the destruction of much plant and animal life. Like several of the other scientists represented here, Carson warns that "the obligation to endure" endows each person with a responsibility to be aware of scientific activities and to make sound decisions based on that awareness.*

Reading Rhetorically

This article introduces the topic of science and the environment, a topic that will be taken up by a number of articles that follow. It has been placed first in this group because it begins with a very general focus: "[t]he history of life on earth." Movement from the general to the specific is a common rhetorical strategy. By introducing readers to the breadth of a topic, the writer can help them develop a cognitive structure into which more specific information can be organized. If a text begins with a very specific focus and the reader has little understanding of the overall issue, the text can be less effective in achieving its purpose because the reader will lack a context for the information. However, if a text begins with a focus on a general topic about which the reader already has a clear understanding, the text can also be less effective because the redundant information will get in the way of the reader's interest in the topic.

As you read the first paragraphs of this essay, think about how Carson has set up the reader to understand the specific topic of the essay by talking first about pollution in general; then, more specifically, about chemical pollution; and, finally, about the particular chemical pollution that results from the use of pesticides. Look for her appeals to *logos* and *pathos*.

The Obligation to Endure

1   The history of life on earth has been a history of interaction between living things and their surroundings. To a large extent, the physical form and the habits of the earth's vegetation and its animal life have been molded by the environment. Considering the whole span of earthly time, the opposite effect, in which life actually modifies its surroundings, has been relatively slight. Only within the moment of time represented by the present century has one species—man—acquired significant power to alter the nature of his world.

2   During the past quarter century this power has not only increased to one of disturbing magnitude but it has changed in character. The most alarming of all man's assaults upon the environment is the contamination of air, earth, rivers, and sea with dangerous and even lethal materials. This pollution is for the most part irrecoverable; the chain of evil it initiates not only in the world that must support life but in living tissues is for the most part irreversible. In this now universal contamination of the environment, chemicals are the sinister and little-recognized partners of radiation in changing the very nature of the world—the very nature of its life. Strontium 90, released through nuclear explosions into the air, comes to earth in rain or drifts down as fallout, lodges in soil, enters into the grass or corn or wheat grown there, and in time takes

up its abode in the bones of a human being, there to remain until his death. Similarly, chemicals sprayed on croplands or forests or gardens lie long in soil, entering into living organisms, passing from one to another in a chain of poisoning and death. Or they pass mysteriously by underground streams until they emerge and, through the alchemy of air and sunlight, combine into new forms that kill vegetation, sicken cattle, and work unknown harm on those who drink from once pure wells. As Albert Schweitzer[1] has said, "Man can hardly even recognize the devils of his own creation."

It took hundreds of millions of years to produce the life that now inhabits the earth—eons of time in which that developing and evolving and diversifying life reached a state of adjustment and balance with its surroundings. The environment, rigorously shaping and directing the life it supported, contained elements that were hostile as well as supporting. Certain rocks gave out dangerous radiation; even within the light of the sun, from which all life draws its energy, there were short-wave radiations with power to injure. Given time—time not in years but in millennia—life adjusts, and a balance has been reached. For time is the essential ingredient; but in the modern world there is no time.

The rapidity of change and the speed with which new situations are created follow the impetuous and heedless pace of man rather than the deliberate pace of nature. Radiation is no longer merely the background radiation of rocks, the bombardment of cosmic rays, the ultraviolet of the sun that have existed before there was any life on earth; radiation is now the unnatural creation of man's tampering with the atom. The chemicals to which life is asked to make its adjustment are no longer merely the calcium and silica and copper and all the rest of the minerals washed out of the rocks and carried in rivers to the sea; they are the synthetic creations of man's inventive mind, brewed in his laboratories, and having no counterparts in nature.

To adjust to these chemicals would require time on the scale that is nature's; it would require not merely the years of man's life but the life of generations. And even this, were it by some miracle possible, would be futile, for the new chemicals come from our laboratories in an endless stream; almost five hundred annually find their way into actual use in the United States alone. The figure is staggering and its implications are not easily grasped—500 new chemicals to which the bodies of men and animals are required somehow to adapt each year, chemicals totally outside the limits of biologic experience.

Among them are many that are used in man's war against nature. Since the mid-1940s over 200 basic chemicals have been created for use in killing insects, weeds, rodents and other organisms described in the modern vernacular as "pests"; and they are sold under several thousand different brand names.

These sprays, dusts, and aerosols are now applied almost universally to farms, gardens, forests, and homes—nonselective chemicals that have the power to kill every insect, the "good" and the "bad," to still the song of birds and the leaping of fish in the streams, to coat the leaves with a deadly film, and

---

[1]Albert Schweitzer (1875–1965) Alsatian theologian, musician, and medical missionary. [Ed. note.]

to linger on in soil—all this though the intended target may be only a few weeds or insects. Can anyone believe it is possible to lay down such a barrage of poisons on the surface of the earth without making it unfit for life? They should not be called "insecticides," but "biocides."

8   The whole process of spraying seems caught up in an endless spiral. Since DDT was released for civilian use, a process of escalation has been going on in which ever more toxic materials must be found. This has happened because insects, in a triumphant vindication of Darwin's principle of the survival of the fittest, have evolved super races immune to the particular insecticide used, hence a deadlier one has always to be developed—and then a deadlier one than that. It has happened also because, for reasons to be described later, destructive insects often undergo a "flareback," or resurgence, after spraying, in numbers greater than before. Thus the chemical war is never won, and all life is caught in its violent crossfire.

9   Along with the possibility of the extinction of mankind by nuclear war, the central problem of our age has therefore become the contamination of man's total environment with such substances of incredible potential for harm—substances that accumulate in the tissues of plants and animals and even penetrate the germ cells to shatter or alter the very material of heredity upon which the shape of the future depends.

10   Some would-be architects of our future look toward a time when it will be possible to alter the human germ plasm by design. But we may be easily doing so now by inadvertence, for many chemicals, like radiation, bring about gene mutations. It is ironic to think that man might determine his own future by something so seemingly trivial as the choice of an insect spray.

11   All this has been risked—for what? Future historians may well be amazed by our distorted sense of proportion. How could intelligent beings seek to control a few unwanted species by a method that contaminated the entire environment and brought the threat of disease and death even to their own kind? Yet this is precisely what we have done. We have done it, moreover, for reasons that collapse the moment we examine them. We are told that the enormous and expanding use of pesticides is necessary to maintain farm production. Yet is our real problem not one of *overproduction?* Our farms, despite measures to remove acreages from production and to pay farmers *not* to produce, have yielded such a staggering excess of crops that the American taxpayer in 1962 is paying out more than one billion dollars a year as the total carrying cost of the surplus-food storage program. And is the situation helped when one branch of the Agriculture Department tries to reduce production while another states, as it did in 1958. "It is believed generally that reduction of crop acreages under provisions of the Soil Bank will stimulate interest in use of chemicals to obtain maximum production on the land retained in crops."

12   All this is not to say there is no insect problem and no need of control. I am saying, rather, that control must be geared to realities, not to mythical situations, and that the methods employed must be such that they do not destroy us along with the insects.

The problem whose attempted solution has brought such a train of disas- 13
ter in its wake is an accompaniment of our modern way of life. Long before
the age of man, insects inhabited the earth—a group of extraordinarily varied
and adaptable beings. Over the course of time since man's advent, a small percentage of the more than half a million species of insects have come into conflict with human welfare in two principal ways: as competitors for the food
supply and as carriers of human disease.

Disease-carrying insects become important where human beings are 14
crowded together, especially under conditions where sanitation is poor, as in
time of natural disaster or war or in situations of extreme poverty and deprivation. Then control of some sort becomes necessary. It is a sobering fact,
however, as we shall presently see, that the method of massive chemical control has had only limited success, and also threatens to worsen the very conditions it is intended to curb.

Under primitive agricultural conditions the farmer had few insect prob- 15
lems. These arose with the intensification of agriculture—the devotion of
immense acreages to a single crop. Such a system set the stage for explosive
increases in specific insect populations. Single-crop farming does not take
advantage of the principles by which nature works; it is agriculture as an engineer might conceive it to be. Nature has introduced great variety into the landscape, but man has displayed a passion for simplifying it. Thus he undoes the
built-in checks and balances by which nature holds the species within bounds.
One important natural check is a limit on the amount of suitable habitat for
each species. Obviously then, an insect that lives on wheat can build up its population to much higher levels on a farm devoted to wheat than on one in which
wheat is intermingled with other crops to which the insect is not adapted.

The same thing happens in other situations. A generation or more ago, the 16
towns of large areas of the United States lined their streets with the noble elm
tree. Now the beauty they hopefully created is threatened with complete
destruction as disease sweeps through the elms, carried by a beetle that would
have only limited chance to build up large populations and to spread from tree
to tree if the elms were only occasional trees in a richly diversified planting.

Another factor in the modern insect problem is one that must be viewed 17
against a background of geologic and human history: the spreading of thousands of different kinds of organisms from their native homes to invade new
territories. This worldwide migration has been studied and graphically
described by the British ecologist Charles Elton in his recent book *The Ecology of Invasions*. During the Cretaceous Period, some hundred million years
ago, flooding seas cut many land bridges between continents and living things
found themselves confined in what Elton calls "colossal separate nature
reserves." There, isolated from others of their kind, they developed many new
species. When some of the land masses were joined again, about 15 million
years ago, these species began to move out into new territories—a movement
that is not only still in progress but is now receiving considerable assistance
from man.

18   The importation of plants is the primary agent in the modern spread of species, for animals have almost invariably gone along with the plants, quarantine being a comparatively recent and not completely effective innovation. The United States Office of Plant Introduction alone has introduced almost 200,000 species and varieties of plants from all over the world. Nearly half of the 180 or so major insect enemies of plants in the United States are accidental imports from abroad, and most of them have come as hitchhikers on plants.

19   In new territory, out of reach of the restraining hand of the natural enemies that kept down its numbers in its native land, an invading plant or animal is able to become enormously abundant. Thus it is no accident that our most troublesome insects are introduced species.

20   These invasions, both the naturally occurring and those dependent on human assistance, are likely to continue indefinitely. Quarantine and massive chemical campaigns are only extremely expensive ways of buying time. We are faced, according to Dr. Elton, "with a life-and-death need not just to find new technological means of suppressing this plant or that animal"; instead we need the basic knowledge of animal populations and their relations to their surroundings that will "promote an even balance and damp down the explosive power of outbreaks and new invasions."

21   Much of the necessary knowledge is now available but we do not use it. We train ecologists in our universities and even employ them in our governmental agencies but we seldom take their advice. We allow the chemical death rain to fall as though there were no alternative, whereas in fact there are many, and our ingenuity could soon discover many more if given opportunity.

22   Have we fallen into a mesmerized state that makes us accept as inevitable that which is inferior or detrimental, as though having lost the will or the vision to demand that which is good? Such thinking, in the words of the ecologist Paul Shepard, "idealizes life with only its head out of water, inches above the limits of toleration of the corruption of its own environment . . . Why should we tolerate a diet of weak poisons, a home in insipid surroundings, a circle of acquaintances who are not quite our enemies, the noise of motors with just enough relief to prevent insanity? Who would want to live in a world which is just not quite fatal?"

23   Yet such a world is pressed upon us. The crusade to create a chemically sterile, insect-free world seems to have engendered a fanatic zeal on the part of many specialists and most of the so-called control agencies. On every hand there is evidence that those engaged in spraying operations exercise a ruthless power. "The regulatory entomologists . . . function as prosecutor, judge and jury, tax assessor and collector and sheriff to enforce their own orders," said Connecticut entomologist Neely Turner. The most flagrant abuses go unchecked in both state and federal agencies.

24   It is not my contention that chemical insecticides must never be used. I do contend that we have put poisonous and biologically potent chemicals indiscriminately into the hands of persons largely or wholly ignorant of their potentials for harm. We have subjected enormous numbers of people to contact with these poisons, without their consent and often without their knowledge. If the

Bill of Rights contains no guarantee that a citizen shall be secure against lethal poisons distributed either by private individuals or by public officials, it is surely only because our forefathers, despite their considerable wisdom and foresight, could conceive of no such problem.

I contend, furthermore, that we have allowed these chemicals to be used 25 with little or no advance investigation of their effect on soil, water, wildlife, and man himself. Future generations are unlikely to condone our lack of prudent concern for the integrity of the natural world that supports all life.

There is still very limited awareness of the nature of the threat. This is an 26 era of specialists, each of whom sees his own problem and is unaware of or intolerant of the larger frame into which it fits. It is also an era dominated by industry, in which the right to make a dollar at whatever cost is seldom challenged. When the public protests, confronted with some obvious evidence of damaging results of pesticide applications, it is fed little tranquilizing pills of half truth. We urgently need an end to these false assurances, to the sugar coating of unpalatable facts. It is the public that is being asked to assume the risks that the insect controllers calculate. The public must decide whether it wishes to continue on the present road, and it can do so only when in full possession of the facts. In the words of Jean Rostand, "The obligation to endure gives us the right to know."

Questions for Discussion and Your Reading Journal

1. Who might be the intended audience of this text? Is the vocabulary suited to a general audience? List words that may be too specialized for the lay reader.
2. What is Carson's purpose in writing this essay? Look for a statement of purpose in the text.
3. What is meant by the phrase "the obligation to endure"?
4. Describe the ways in which the use of certain pesticides has endangered the environment.
5. What solution to the problem does Carson offer? Is it a viable one? Explain.
6. Is the conclusion persuasive? Analyze the language of the last paragraph to locate elements of persuasion.
7. Discuss other threats to the environment. Propose possible solutions to the problems.
8. Analyze Carson's practice of questioning the reader. In what ways is this an effective strategy for argument?

MERETE REITVELD

Merete Reitveld, a faculty member at Stanford University, is a book reviewer for the journal Genome News Network. *Genomics is the investigation of the structure and function of a large number of genes. The sequence of genes encodes information about an organism or species. Genetics is a fairly new field; it became established in the early 1960s. In the last two decades the study of genomics has become important, not only to scholars in biology but also to a number of interests in the public and private sectors. For example, criminologists use genomics as a way to conclusively identify many criminals (and to exonerate the innocent), and drug companies use it to develop new approaches to treating disease.*

In the context of this review, which focuses on a nonfiction book called The Killers Within: The Deadly Rise of Drug-Resistant Bacteria *by Michael Shnayerson and Mark J. Plotkin, genomics in relation to bacteria is the subject. In the same way that insects become resistant to pesticides, a phenomenon that is explained in the previous article by Rachel Carson, bacteria quickly mutate to lose their susceptibility to antibiotics. This puts many animals, including humans, at risk for developing infections that cannot be cured. For example, small doses of antibiotics are given to farm animals to improve their ability to grow so that the larger animals can bring in more profits. At the same time, physicians prescribe the newest and most powerful antibiotics to treat their patients' infections. The result is that the bacteria mutate and the drugs that used to kill them are no longer effective, so pharmaceutical companies and public agencies must scramble to find effective ways of dealing with the drug-resistant bacteria.*

Reading Rhetorically

Besides its topical importance, this reading is interesting because of its "genre": the review. Reviews, sometimes called "critiques," are articles that summarize something and then respond to it. Movie reviews are probably the most familiar kind of critiques to students, but the genre is used widely in academia as well as journalism. In fact, summary papers and summary and response papers are the most frequently given assignments for undergraduates.

Summary and response texts, like this book review, present the most salient information from and about the source, while commenting on the value of that information or the way in which it is presented. Sometimes reviews develop their subject by presenting a block of summary information and then a block of response. More commonly, however, they are organized around ideas from the text, summarizing one idea and responding to it, then moving to the next idea, and so on. Reviews may also employ both the "block" and "point-by-point" methods of development in tandem. For example, they may present a block of summary at the beginning, a point-by-point analysis of ideas in the middle, and a block of response at the end.

As you read this review, examine the way in which Rietveld structures her summary and response. Speculate about why she organizes it in that way. Does she persuade you that this is a book you should read? If so, what persuaded you?

Mutant Bacteria and the Failure of Antibiotics

Hospitals have germs. And germs have a remarkable ability to develop 1
resistance to the antibiotics we rely on to kill them. These facts are well
known to the medical community and have been a source of great concern for
years. A number of books and articles for both the lay reader and the professional have been written on the subject, each in its way raising a red flag that
says, in one way on another, we have to control the use of antibiotics less we
lose them to smart bacteria that learn to become immune to their toxic effects.

Michael Shnayerson and Mark J. Plotkin, authors of *The Killers Within:* 2
The Deadly Rise of Drug-Resistant Bacteria, have now joined the army of
alert writers who are concerned about the dangers of antibiotic resistance and
its implications for the return of infectious diseases that cannot be effectively
treated. The authors argue that today's hospitals are not only spreading bacteria from patient to patient, but are also harboring a tougher breed of bug—
one that is resistant to antibiotics.

Most infections are either bacterial or viral, and bacterial infections are 3
susceptible to antibiotics. These drugs are designed to attach to enzymes on
bacterial cell walls, either preventing the microbes from replicating or killing
them outright. Unless, that is, the bacteria mutate and change their enzymes,
thus preventing the drug from attaching.

Penicillin was greeted as a panacea when it was developed in the early- 4
20th century. In the decades since, the authors claim—as have others before
them that the overuse of antibiotics for every possible illness has "educated"
bacteria, creating opportunities for mutations to occur: "If misuse of antibiotics created drug resistance in the first place, poor infection control in hospitals allowed the bugs to spread."

Bacteria may be small, but these one-celled organisms can divide and 5
reproduce into more daughter cells that the human population of Earth in just
fourteen hours.

Plotkin, an ethnobiologist, and Shnayerson, a contributing editor to *Van-* 6
ity Fair, report what they have learned from interviews and the scientific literature about how bacteria develop resistance and the role genes play in this
process. They express admiration for bacteria's clever defense mechanisms,
including the evolution of enzymes that attack antibiotics and tiny pumps that
vomit the drug out of the cell.

In the first half of this book, the authors try to scare the general public into 7
recognizing the seriousness of the threat (chapter titles include "The Silent
War," "Nightmare Come True," "Flesheaters"). Yet despite the scare tactics,
the authors succeed in creating a suspenseful narrative.

Indeed, their claim that the medical industry has not taken growing drug- 8
resistance seriously enough and has failed to improve antibiotics suggests a
fatal conclusion fitting of Stephen King: People are dying of bacterial infections that were treatable a few years ago.

By shadowing scientists around the globe—including the "genetic detec- 9
tives" and "microbe hunters" who work with the world's most dangerous

pathogens, as well as epidemiologists investigating outbreaks of bacterial infection—the authors craft an informative thriller with vivid descriptions and tales of scientific sleuthing.

10   The book tells the story, for instance, of William Noble, a microbiologist at St. John's Hospital for Disease of the Skin in London, who, in the early 1990s, created a strain of *Staphylococcus aureus* that was resistant to the antibiotic vancomycin by exposing the microbe to another bacterium with resistant genes. A few years later, a vancomycin-resistant *S. aureus* was isolated from a lung-cancer patient in Japan, suggesting that Noble's laboratory experiment had happened in nature.

11   Like hospitals, the meat industry is a source of rising drug-resistance. Small doses of antibiotics (called "growth-promoters") added to animal feed contribute to the development of resistant strains by familiarizing bacteria with the drugs without actually threatening them. The authors argue that substantial research shows that these resistant bacteria are easily transferred to humans eating these animals.

12   Toward the end of the book, the authors leave behind the horrors of resistant bacteria and begin to describe the search for new antibiotics. Until recently, most natural antibiotics have been found in soil and fungi. Among the scientists trying novel approaches to discovering antibiotics are researchers who collect saliva from lizards in Indonesia and distill sewage water in the former Soviet Republic of Georgia.

13   These researchers are experimenting with animal peptides and miniscule viruses that act as natural antibiotics. Peptides punch their way through the bacterial cell membrane regardless of these enzymes.

14   Scientists in Georgia have been using viruses called "phages" for decades to puncture the bacterial membrane but with the purpose of injecting DNA. Phages take over the bacteria's genetic machinery in order to produce more phages, rather than bacteria. An interesting footnote in this passage is that phages are also the basis of genetic engineering: Geneticists insert certain genes into phages, prompting the bacteria to manufacture those genes.

15   The subject of resistant bacteria is not breaking news. The problem has been widely discussed in the medical community although the general public may not be as familiar with the issue. While the authors focus on the ignorance and blindness of the medical community towards this problem, they also reveal the obstacles preventing new antibiotics from being developed and problematic behaviors from being changed.

16   For readers interested in the topic, *The Killers Within* provides an overview of the biological, medical, policy-oriented and personal perspectives involved. And for those who have the stomach to digest the chilling dangers posed by resistant bacteria, this book will be a thrilling read.

Questions for Discussion and Your Reading Journal

1. The review begins with an assertion: "we have to control the use of antibiotics." Given that statement, what do you expect the rest of the review to focus on?

2. Describe the process by which bacteria become resistant.
3. The reviewer says that in places the book reads like a "thriller." What is a "thriller"? Why might the authors have borrowed from this genre in their writing of the nonfiction book?
4. The end of the book (and the review) is a discussion of the development of antibiotics. For what reasons might the authors and the reviewer have ended on this note?
5. This review examines a book by Michael Shnayerson and Mark J. Plotkin called *The Killers Within: The Deadly Rise of Drug-Resistant Bacteria*. How much of the review is about the book itself and how much is about the topic of the book? What might this tell you about the purpose of reviewing the book?
6. Examine the organizational pattern of the review itself. How much is summary? How much is response? How are they put together? Discuss the degree to which this organizational pattern is effective.

JOHN W. MELLOR

Like Fritjof Capra, John W. Mellor, director of the International Food Policy Research Institute and an expert in the field of economics and agriculture, is concerned with changing the way people think about the world in order to promote ecological preservation. Mellor points to the interdependence of all species, including humans, in the systems of nature. He pleads for a universal ethical approach to the maintenance of ecological balance, based on clearly documented scientific understanding.

John W. Mellor's "The Intertwining of Environmental Problems and Poverty" discusses the ways in which rural poverty contributes to environmental devastation and how environmental problems then cause even more hardship for the poor. He explains the interrelationships between population growth, mismanagement of natural resources, and continuance of extreme poverty in many developing countries in Asia, Africa, and Latin America. Mellor presents problem-solving strategies that will require the assistance of wealthier countries, arguing that solving the problems will benefit both the developing and the developed parts of the world.

Reading Rhetorically

This article contains a couple of illustrations. Writers employ illustrations for a number of reasons: as a means of emphasizing an important point; as a visual representation to reinforce the meaning of the words; as an artistic accompaniment to enhance the text; and as a method of exposition that cannot be accomplished by using only words, sentences, and paragraphs. This article uses illustrations mainly for the first and last reasons. After you have read it, glance through the article and look specifically at the illustrations. Examine the ways and the degree to which the illustrations support the text, or use visual imagery itself as a form of persuasion, as outlined in Chapter 1.

This article may contain several words and phrases with which you are unfamiliar. By examining the words in context, you can make reasonably sound assumptions about what they mean. Look, for example, at Paragraph 15. In this paragraph the phrase "rural infrastructure" appears. There are contextual clues that can combine with your understanding of what the root words mean to give you a fairly good idea of what the author is saying about rural infrastructure. Use this technique of examining context and looking at root words whenever you encounter an unfamiliar phrase.

Finally, think about the forms of persuasion Mellor uses to convince you of his thesis, which he states in the first sentence of the essay.

The Intertwining of Environmental Problems and Poverty

1   In developing countries, environmental problems and poverty are inseparable. At least three-quarters of a billion people in these countries cannot afford sufficient food to maintain minimum activity levels for healthy, productive lives. Such extreme poverty is especially prevalent in rural areas; in Asia and Africa, 80 to 90 percent of the poor live outside cities. Even in Latin America, the countryside is home to 60 percent of the poor. Half of these rural poor live on resources with the potential to increase substantially production and income in environmentally sustainable ways. Increasingly, however, as development raises incomes in these countries' more productive regions, rural poverty concentrates in environmentally fragile areas.

2   The rural poor largely depend directly or indirectly on agriculture and therefore on the environmental for their income. As a result, environmental problems are inextricably linked with the problems of growing populations. Increasing numbers of people survive by subsistence farming, growing just the crops they need to eat to survive. The growing population also forces land appropriate only to perennial crops, such as tree crops or grasses, to be farmed for annual crops, particularly food crops, which the soil cannot sustain indefinitely. Thus environmental preservation depends on a complex interaction of income and population pressures that contribute to both environmental and agricultural instability.

3   As leaders of developing countries work to preserve their environments and eliminate poverty, they face several difficult questions. First, they must determine what environmental damage is irreversible and how much damage they can afford to tolerate for their citizens' current well-being. They must also consider to what extent environmental destruction impedes their ability to ensure the well-being of future generations. In other words, people in developing countries are forced to decide how much of the future they can or must give up to ensure today's survival.

Meanwhile, the people of developed countries also must ask important 4
questions: How does environmental damage in developing countries affect the
quality of life? How much will it cost to contain the damage? What common
threads connect concerns about poverty and the environment? Should concerns
be focused locally, nationally, or internationally? Considering the unequal distribution of wealth around the globe, does not the universal concern for the
environment require payment not only commensurate with the damage done,
but also with the ability to pay? Should the richer nations provide financial
assistance to the poorest people of the poorest countries to assist their progress
toward sustainable, self-reliant growth to reduce environmental stress?

It is important to note that the environmental destruction in developed 5
countries is immensely more threatening and costly than that in developing
countries and has yet to be tackled adequately. Environmental destruction in
developing countries mostly affects the people of those countries, whereas the
destruction wrought by the rich countries—for example, destruction of the
ozone layer and air pollution that causes the greenhouse effect—has major
consequences for *all* the world. Nevertheless, developed countries must not
forget about the environmental problems of developing countries.

Many less developed countries are falling into the extreme poverty associ- 6
ated with rapid population growth, poor nutrition and hygiene, and low levels of education. All these trends make population control and environmental
programs less effective. As a result, environmental exploitation and abuse are
increasing in ever more damaging ways. Developed nations have a responsibility to help them break this cycle and replace it with an agenda that ensures
sustainable population patterns, improved education levels, and increased production and employment rates.[1]

POPULATION AND INCOME

The most pervasive manifestation of environmentally destructive poverty in 7
developing countries is the dangerous exploitation of fragile resources by bur-
geoning populations. Deforestation and cultivation of easily eroded land and
overgrazing of natural pastures are the most obvious examples. In South Asia
and other developing regions, half of the poor occupy one-quarter of the land
area that could most easily be developed with high-yield crop varieties. However, as the income of people raising high-yield crops on fertile land rise, rural
poverty is progressively concentrated in pockets of land less responsive to
high-yield crops. . . . Within growing populations, farmers are rarely able to
increase the sizes of their farms; even if they do, their incomes do not necessarily rise proportionally with the extra land and effort involved. For instance,
in Bangladesh the growing population has forced a decline in farm sizes,
shrinking opportunities to expand income (see Figure 1). As agricultural productivity declines, the land loses its ability to sustain a growing population,
and pressures on the forests increase. With shorter crop rotations and subsequent soil erosion, incomes decrease and destabilize. In bad years, incomes in
Bangladesh fall to the lowest level of poverty, which forces people to destroy
more of the physical environment to provide short-term survival. This year,

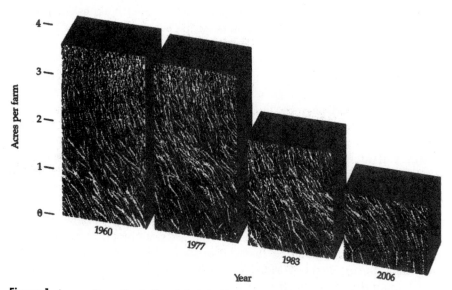

Figure 1 Average Farm Size In Bangladesh in 1960, 1977, 1983, and Projected to 2006. Source: R. Ahmed, "A Structural Perspective of Farm and Non-Farm Households in Bangladesh," *Bangladesh Development Studies* 55 (June 1987): 87–122.

distant, upstream deforestation greatly increased the ferocity of floods inundating highly productive soils.

8   The forces of population and poverty can also be seen dramatically at work in the hill regions of Nepal. With few advances in available agricultural technology for the relatively favorable lowland soils, Nepalese farmers cannot maintain their incomes as the population rises and farms become smaller.[2] Farmers are forced to clear and crop the hillsides. Cultivating this less productive land exacerbates soil erosion problems on the hillsides and may flood and pollute the lowlands. In fact, between the late 1960s and early 1980s, the forested area in Nepal's hills dropped from between 55 and 60 percent, depending on specific location, to 40 percent of total area. The tree cover shrank even more substantially when the remaining forest was thinned. In contrast, the area under agricultural production expanded from between 15 and 35 percent to far more than 40 percent during that same period.

9   Nepal's forests have been pushed so far back from rural populations that it takes, on average, 1.4 additional hours each day for women to collect firewood and fodder than it did just a decade ago. The extra hours are taken, in part, from women's work time in agricultural production, reducing total farm labor by as much as 24 percent per household and thus lowering household productivity. By lowering agricultural productivity, this deforestation has reduced food consumption on average more than 100 calories per capita per day. In addition, time for food preparation and child care have also been lost; this loss furthers the decline in nutrition, especially for children. Expanded planting on hillsides shifts cropping patterns away from rice and other high-quality calorie sources, reducing the nutritional content of the families' diets

even more. The combined effect is a downward spiral of incomes and health, as malnourished individuals are less and less able to overcome the problems caused by deforestation.

To relieve population pressure on the environment in developing coun- 10
tries, population control must be combined with increased intensity of land use in high-potential agricultural areas. Therefore, a long-term strategy for poverty abatement must be planned and should include an adequate agricultural research and extension system that can develop new, high-yield crop varieties for developing countries' flat valleys. This new technology will allow farmers to increase their productivity by intensifying production so that they can feed more people on less land and earn higher incomes. Larger incomes will also help create the social environment within which other measures can effectively reduce population growth.

Intensified agriculture on good land will also relieve population pressures 11
on more fragile lands. Increased farm incomes allow people to spend more on goods and services that are produced in labor-intensive ways in nonagricultural sectors and on labor-intensive agricultural commodities that are less harmful to the environment. As their incomes rise, farmers typically spend about 40 percent of their additional income on locally produced, labor-intensive, nonagricultural goods and services.[3] They spend another 20 percent on livestock and horticultural commodities. Therefore, in a country like Nepal, more land could be planted with perennial tree crops such as fruit orchards, which preserve the hillsides, and more land could be accorded to perennial grasses to feed more livestock. Thus, higher rural incomes are conducive to more environmentally sound land use.

Important environment tradeoffs occur under the pressures of population 12
growth and falling per capita incomes. For instance, to maintain their incomes, farmers must often clear more and more land. One way to overcome this kind of tradeoff is to increase fertilizer use on lowland areas, which boosts productivity and helps to prevent cultivation on hillsides. These efforts require cheap, reliable fertilizers and crop varieties that respond to increased fertilizer. Today, these fertilizers can be produced most cheaply from the vast quantities of gas that are going to waste in the Middle East and the Soviet Union. The question remains how those gas resources can best be mobilized to protect the even more easily exhaustible land resources.

The effects of poverty on the environment are endlessly complex. Thomas 13
Reardon of the International Food Policy Research Institute points out that in the Sahel of Burkina Faso, with highly variable crop production, households have developed complex mechanisms to lessen extreme variations of income. For instance, in economically good times, livestock numbers rise well above the range carrying capacity of the Sahel. In these circumstances, foreign assistance increases income, livestock numbers, and therefore environmental degradation. Thus incomes rise but people's food security problems are not properly addressed. Providing food security requires greater integration with the outside world and effort by the international community. In contrast, on Burkina Faso's somewhat rainier Mossi plateau, poverty is more intense than in the Sahel, and higher incomes often lead to investment in bunds and other

land-protecting devices. Even for such village-level cooperation, the investment structure needs to be reviewed and funds channeled effectively. Peter A. Oram in "Moving Toward Sustainability: Building the Agroecological Framework" treats the important issue of how to classify the agroecological conditions to facilitate those investment decisions. . . .

14   As the complex relationships between technology, input intensification, and environmental preservation are examined, the importance of commercialization and infrastructure to the environment becomes apparent. Land resources in developing countries are very diverse; optimal land use requires growing a wide variety of crops. However, marketing this variety of crops requires demand for those crops, which in turn requires higher incomes. To achieve higher incomes and the trade associated with diversity, low-cost transport is necessary. If people are to diversify their agricultural strategies enough to preserve the land, there must be broad demand for the products. Such demand cannot occur when incomes are at the minimal survival levels. For example, hill lands must generate income from perennial tree crops. The demand for these crops must come in part from local areas, but the income to buy the crops requires intensification of agriculture on other land. In part, the demand must also come from outside.

15   Increasing income and demand requires commercialization and development of the rural infrastructure. In Senegal, the introduction of cowpeas (legumes beneficial to the soil) to the rapidly degrading peanut basin is being delayed by lack of marketing infrastructure. Roads and communication systems also have a powerful impact on the environment. In Bangladesh, for example, in villages with good physical infrastructure (which generally means roads usable in all weather) only 12 percent of the population falls under the absolute poverty line, while 21 percent of the people are below the poverty line in villages without this infrastructure.[4] In villages with good infrastructure, employment per hectare of land is 4 percent higher; in nonagricultural sectors, employment is 30 percent higher; and wage rates are 12 percent higher than in villages without good infrastructure.[5] All those forces reduce the pressure to abuse the land for short-term survival.

16   A perennial problem for many developing countries is land tenure. The land often belongs to someone other than the people who are farming it. Since the farmers do not know how long they will be able to continue working on a parcel of land, they have little incentive to make long-term investments in it. In Africa, poorly defined land rights cause insecurity, and labor productivity is so low that farmers are preoccupied with wresting a minimum subsistence. Even with improved tenure conditions, only the research thrusts that E. T. York spells out in "Improving Sustainability with Agricultural Research" . . . can raise agricultural productivities.

POVERTY AND HEALTH

17 Much of the anxiety over environmental destruction in developed countries stems from health concerns. Pollution of cities, streams, and rivers cause serious illnesses. In developing countries, this concern is even greater because the

Table 1 Percentage of Time Preschoolers and Women in Southwestern Kenya are Sick with Any Illness and with Diarrhea, Measured by Per Capita Income Quartile, for 1984–1985.

Illness	Poorest Quartile	Poorer Than Average Quartile	Richer Than Average Quartile	Richest Quartile
Preschoolers				
All illness[a]	27.5%	26.0%	29.5%	26.5%
Diarrhea[a]	4.9	6.4	6.2	4.6
Women				
All illness[a]	30.2	26.8	29.8	26.6
Diarrhea[b]	1.2	1.4	2.2	3.7

Note: The quartiles are based on total household income per capita.

[a]There was no significant difference across income quartiles.

[b]Women in the poorest and poorer than average quartiles reported significantly shorter duration of diarrhea at the 0.05 level than woemn did in the richest quartile.

Source: Eileen Kennedy, International Food Policy Research Institute, "Survey 1984/85," South Nyanza, Kenya.

state of health is so poor. For example, a lack of sanitation facilities creates serious health threats in densely populated rural areas—a problem that rarely exists in developed countries. Without adequate disposal facilities, not only the streams but the land around small towns in developing countries is heavily polluted.

Although rising incomes lead to improved food intake, they do not necessarily improve health. For example, a study of women and children at different economic levels in southwestern Kenya found no significant differences in total illness (see Table 1). However, a significant relationship exists between illness and the presence of general health and sanitation services in Kenya.[6] These problems are particularly severe in areas with dense rural populations and limited sanitation and health facilities. These areas also may have poorly drained alluvial soils, which add to the problems of population density and sanitation. In deforested regions, the quality of drinking water has dropped as water sources shift from fresh forest streams to increasingly contaminated rivers and ponds. Poor health cuts labor productivity and income in this "Catch-22" cycle.

Solving these problems requires tremendous investments of resources. However, solutions to environmental problems do not necessarily compete for resources with efforts to alleviate poverty and vice versa. However, many forms of investment benefit both endeavors. In Bangladesh, for example, the quality of the water supply and sanitary conditions are strongly influenced by improved rural infrastructure.[7] Also, health problems such as river blindness in Africa, tsetse fly infestation, and malaria all lend themselves to solution through modern biological research. Solving these problems would make it possible to populate more densely areas that are not environmentally fragile, thus relieving pressure on the fragile areas.

EDUCATION'S ROLE

20 Education affects the environment in three ways. First, some environmental destruction occurs simply because people do not understand the harm of what they are doing. Education can bring understanding of the environmental impacts of certain actions and lead to acceptance of complex technologies such as the biological control of insects and diseases. However, there is not much correlation between education and acceptance of a simple technology like high-yield wheat. Thus, educational levels in rural areas of developing countries must be raised to permit environmental improvements. This educational expansion must occur at all levels. At the secondary level, farmers must be taught to work with more complex technologies. At the college level, people need to be trained to teach this knowledge to farmers.

21 Second, education influences population growth. With all else equal, including income, rural people with more education tend to have somewhat smaller families. Perhaps with educated children who can get better jobs, parents need fewer children to support them in their old age.

22 Third, education increases income. In an increasingly complex world, education is necessary to understand the technological changes and the institutional interactions that can be used to raise farmers' incomes. So educational opportunities must grow to increase incomes.

AGRICULTURE AND STABILITY

23 Agriculture is innately and notoriously unstable, and the instability of production and prices is increasing. In bad times, instability drives poor people below the line of minimum subsistence. This drop cuts their ability to plan for the long term and leads them (and their animals) to assault the environment for short-run gains in ways they would never do if their incomes were stable above the subsistence level.

24 Areas with fragile environmental resources often have either low rainfall or rainfall that fluctuates around the critical level for arable agriculture. These areas in particular need to be returned to grassland or other perennial crops such as trees to counter the destruction that occurs, especially during periods of low rainfall. People must be provided with some means of support to carry them through these bad periods so they will not destroy the environment. Agricultural instability causes greater problems in areas of excessive poverty and environmental fragility, but the damage also carries into the middle classes.

25 Food scarcity wreaks devastating consequences on the poorest of a population rather than on the wealthiest. In India, a 10 percent reduction in food supplies reduces the consumption of the wealthiest 5 percent of the people by 8 percent, whereas the poorest 20 percent of the people are forced to reduce their consumption by 40 percent.[8]

26 Thus, ways must be found to stabilize the incomes of the very poor in the face of agricultural instability. Modern mechanisms do exist for just this purpose. Food aid can be useful. The International Monetary Fund,* through its

*International Monetary Fund A specialized agency of the United Nations, established in 1945 to discharge international indebtedness and stabilize exchange rates. [Ed. note.]

cereal facility, loans money to countries so that they can stabilize their food supply with imports during periods of extreme stress. Still, the recipient governments must have the facilities and institutions to utilize grain imports.

To reduce instability, unviable areas must, in the long run, lose population 27 density through emigration to areas able to accept new technology and to realize rapid growth in nonagricultural employment. Those processes require infrastructure to facilitate specialization and trade.

A SHARED FUTURE

Unfortunately, income problems require solutions much more complex than 28 just alleviating the grinding poverty of one-third to one-half of the population of the Third World. Quite simply, reversing the downward spiral of poverty and environmental destruction requires financial resources. Problems will be solved only through substantial expenditure on public goods, including investments in research, infrastructure, services, and education. But the tax base is thin and shallow in developing countries. The combination of high proportions of populations living at subsistence levels, little administrative capacity, and inadequate commercialization shrinks the proportion of the gross national products spent in the public sector (to levels one-half to three-quarters of that spent in the United States, for example). Developing countries are constrained from generating resources because high taxation on those who live above the subsistence level and on the commercial sector discourages work and enterprise. Thus, a vital link in the poverty-environment nexus is to obtain adequate public resources for the physical and institutional infrastructure needed to raise incomes, reduce population growth, improve health, and increase education, as well as to undertake direct public action to protect and rehabilitate rural areas.

Given that people in poor countries often must sacrifice long-term envi- 29 ronmental stability for short-run survival, wealthy countries must put aside the common belief that the poor can solve these problems on their own without enhanced resources and face up to the reality that substantial financial assistance in the short run is crucial to saving the environment from irreversible damage. However, if that assistance concurrently enhances progress toward self-reliant growth, it will be necessary only for a short while and can be beneficial to the donors themselves.

Developed countries must recognize that environmental protection and 30 the growth of incomes of very poor people in developing countries will demand scientific and financial assistance to develop improved agricultural technologies. Investments in infrastructure and food aid will also help to dissolve poverty.

The leaders of developed countries need to understand how trade relation- 31 ships can accelerate processes, allowing developing countries to import some agricultural commodities that they would otherwise be forced to produce on very fragile land resources, and to export commodities that are more suitable to those resources. Perennial crops, for example, could help pay for the imported commodities. Developed countries need to work toward an ecologically optimal global allocation of production systems. Most important, the rich nations need to consider the environmental problems of developing countries in a positive way, looking for solutions rather than criticizing their attempts to struggle with such complex problems.

Notes

1. See J. W. Mellor, *The New Economics of Growth* (Ithaca, NY: Cornell UP, 1976), for a description of the role of agriculture and employment growth in development.
2. S. K. Kumar and D. Hotchkiss, *Energy and Nutrition Links to Agriculture in a Hill Region of Nepal* (Washington, DC: International Food Policy Research Institute, 1988).
3. P. B. R. Hazell and A. Roell, *Rural Growth Linkages: Household Expenditure Patterns in Malaysia and Nigeria,* Research Report 41 (Washington, DC: International Food Policy Research Institute, 1983) 28.
4. S. K. Kumar, *Rural Infrastructure in Bangladesh: Effects on Food Consumption and Nutrition of the Population* (Washington, DC: International Food Policy Research Institute, 1988). Poverty is defined here as the inability to secure more than 80 percent of the minimum requirement of daily calories.
5. R. Ahmed and M. Hossain, *Infrastructure and Development of a Rural Economy* (Washington, DC: International Food Policy Research Institute, 1987).
6. E. T. Kennedy and B. Cogill, *Income and Nutritional Effects of the Commercialization of Agriculture in Southwestern Kenya,* Research Report 63 (Washington, DC: International Food Policy Research Institute, 1987) 42–49.
7. Kumar, note 4 above.
8. J. W. Mellor and S. Gavian, "Famine: Causes, Prevention, and Relief," *Science* 235 (1987): 539–45.

Questions for Discussion and Your Reading Journal

1. Why is the author particularly qualified to write about the relationship between environmental problems and poverty? Why might he have written this article? For what audience is it intended?
2. What resources do the rural poor use to sustain life? Describe how the use of these resources contributes to environmental concerns.
3. What specific problems do developing countries most need to focus on? Consider the questions posed by Mellor in the third and fourth paragraphs.
4. Why should developed countries take an interest in the environmental concerns of developing countries?
5. Describe the problem of poverty and the environment in Bangladesh and Nepal. What factors contribute to the problem?
6. How is the issue of birth control related to environmental problems? How can the use of fertilizer help alleviate these problems? What other technological assistance might be used?

7. What is meant by the phrase "rural infrastructure" (Paragraph 15)? What contextual clues lead you to this meaning? What conclusions does the author make about rural infrastructure?
8. How does the environmental damage affect the health of the native population? What actions can be taken to reduce such health risks?
9. Discuss possible solutions to the problems in the article. Explain why a combination of actions must be taken.

PETER H. RAVEN

Peter H. Raven, (1936–), director of the Missouri Botanical Gardens in St. Louis and Englemann Professor of Botany at Washington University, discusses the ways in which "third-world" countries affect the more affluent nations of the world in "Third World in the Global Future." The article originally appeared in the Bulletin of the Atomic Scientists, *a newsmagazine about science, the practical applications of scientific discoveries, and the ethical consequences of employing new scientific technologies.*

This article focuses on the interconnectedness of the wealthiest and poorest countries in the world. According to Raven, the world's population is both booming (tripling in one lifetime) and redistributing from more-developed to less-developed countries. Raven warns that in order to survive, citizens all over the world must overcome the temptation to behave as though they are powerless in this "extraordinarily dangerous time."

Reading Rhetorically

This article was not originally intended for a general audience. It was written for a magazine that is read primarily by scientists in a wide variety of fields. As you read, think about the ways the writing of this article might have been influenced by an awareness of its intended audience, especially in the author's use of *logos* to persuade. At the same time take notice of how you, as a college undergraduate, have the ability to clearly understand it, in spite of the fact that you do not have a degree in science. When you are finished reading, examine the strategies you used as you were reading to unpack the meaning of the text. These are precisely the kinds of strategies you will need to use in advanced courses in the disciplines as you tackle difficult reading assignments.

One particular strategy you may employ as you read is to write in the margins of the textbook. Oftentimes beginning university students have difficulty making distinctions between more- and less-important ideas. One way to address this difficulty is to read a paragraph (or a series of short paragraphs) and to write the main idea of the paragraph in the margin; you need not write in complete sentences, but you should cover both the main subject and the main action being discussed. Using this technique allows you to keep your focus on the main ideas rather than the minor details. It also provides you with an easy means of reviewing the reading once you have finished.

Third World in the Global Future

1   The problems associated with the Third World affect us all. If we are wise enough or lucky enough to avoid nuclear war, how we deal with those problems will largely determine our future, and that of our children and grandchildren.

2   What was already, in 1950, a record human population tripled during the course of a single human lifetime. This represents an extraordinary and unprecedented situation. The challenge presented to the productivity capacity of the earth by this increase is neither "normal" nor a circumstance that we can expect to deal with by applying the standard behaviors of the past.

3   The worldwide distribution pattern of this population growth ought also to be a major cause of concern. During the past 34 years, well over two billion people have been added in the less developed countries alone. This number equals the entire world population as recently as 1932. During the same period "only" 300 million people were added in the developed countries, including those of the Near East and Korea which are not tropical. About 90 percent of such countries do lie wholly or partly in the tropics, a relationship that is important to understand.

4   During our single hypothetical lifetime, from 1950 to 2020, the proportion of people living in developed countries will fall from about a third of the total world population to about a sixth. Over the same period, the population of the mainly tropical, less developed countries will grow from approximately 45 percent of the total to more than 64 percent. In sum, the plurality of people live in the tropics, and their percentage of the world population is rapidly increasing, while ours is rapidly falling. Small wonder that we hear more and more about El Salvador, Nicaragua, the Philippines, Africa and other tropical regions and that we are steadily becoming more and more concerned with the development of appropriate policies to pursue in these hitherto unfamiliar parts of the world.

5   The worldwide rate of economic growth has fallen substantially from the 4 percent characteristic of the third quarter of the twentieth century. For the next two decades, many estimate that it may be no higher than 2 percent, as it has been for the past several years. This sort of economic environment, in the context of the much-discussed debts of countries like Brazil, Mexico, Nigeria and Kenya, makes it difficult to imagine how these countries will be able to meet the ordinary needs of their people, much less be able to improve conditions in the future.

6   The developed countries, with less than a quarter of the people in the world and an average per capita income of more than $9,000, control some 80 percent of the global economy. In stark contrast, the less developed countries, with an average per capita income of less than $1,000, control only

about 17.6 percent of that economy. Further, the developed countries consume about 80 percent of the total world supply of energy, the less developed countries about 12 percent. And, as a final index to the disproportionate distribution of wealth, the consumption of iron, copper and aluminum by developed countries ranges from 86 to 92 percent, by the less developed countries, even including China, from 8 to 14 percent.

A quarter of the world's population (a proportion that is rapidly dropping) controls more than four-fifths of the world's goods, while a majority of the population (rapidly increasing in size) have access to no more than a sixth of any commodity involved in the world's productivity. Can this relationship be sustained as the disproportionate distribution of people becomes ever more extreme? The consequences of population growth in Kenya today are absolutely different from those in Europe or the United States of a century ago, and a direct comparison between the two situations is invalid.   7

An associated global problem is that of the rapid destruction of the forests and other potentially renewable tropical resources. In 1981, the Tropical Forest Resources Assessment Project of the U.N. Food and Agriculture Organization (FAO) estimated that 44 percent of the tropical rain forests had already been disturbed. The study estimated that about 1.1 percent of the remainder was being logged each year at that time. The total area of the remaining forest amounted to approximately the size of the United States west of the Mississippi River, with an additional area about half the size of Iowa being logged each year. If the clearing were to continue at this rate, all of the tropical rain forests would be gone in 90 years—a minimum estimate of the time necessary for their disappearance.   8

This estimate only begins to suggest the gravity of the problem. First, clearcutting is merely the most extreme form of forest conversion. Norman Myers, in his outstanding book *The Primary Source* (Norton, 1984), estimates the overall rate to be two to three times as great as that suggested by the FAO figures, or more than 2 percent per year. At that rate, even with no acceleration, the forests will all have been converted in less than 50 years. And other kinds of forest conversion are also threatening the extinction of species.   9

In the next 36 years alone, the population of the tropical countries will approximately double from its present level to about five billion. The governments of these countries are already faced with staggering debts, a sluggish world economy and the rapid loss of the productive capacity of their lands. For these governments to be able to expand their economies rapidly enough to continue to care for the needs of their people at 1984 levels clearly would be an unprecedented economic miracle. But even if they were able to do so, the numbers of their people living in absolute poverty would continue to increase as rapidly as their populations as a whole. Poor people would obviously continue to destroy their forests more and more rapidly with each passing year.   10

The rate of destruction and deterioration of tropical forests is by no means uniform. Three large forest blocks—in the western Brazilian Amazon, in the interior of the Guyanas and in the Congo Basin—are larger, less densely populated, and therefore being exploited more slowly than the remainder. Some of the forests in these three regions might actually persist in a relatively undisturbed   11 condition for another 40 years or so, until the surging populations of their respective countries finally exhaust them. But all of the remaining forests in other parts of the tropics will surely be gone, or at least profoundly altered in nature and composition, much earlier. For the most part, these forests will not remain undisturbed beyond the end of the present century. This process of destruction is apparently irreversible, and it is accelerating rapidly. The tropical forests certainly will never recover from this onslaught.

12   The uneven distribution of wealth is one major factor in the destruction of tropical forests. The World Bank estimates that, of the 2.5 billion people now living in the tropics, one billion exist in absolute poverty. This term describes a condition in which a person is unable to count on being able to provide food, shelter and clothing for himself and his family from one day to the next. According to the World Health Organization, between 500 and 700 million people, approximately one out of every four living in the tropics, are malnourished. UNICEF has estimated that more than 10 million children in tropical countries starve to death unnecessarily each year. Worse, many millions more exist in a state of lethargy, their mental capacities often permanently impaired by lack of access to adequate amounts of food.

13   Shifting cultivation and other forms of agriculture generally fail quickly in most tropical regions. The reason lies in some of the characteristics of the soils and plant communities that occur in these areas. Although tropical soils are extremely varied, many are highly infertile. They are able to support lush forests, in spite of their infertility, because most of the meagre amounts of nutrients present actually are held within the trees and other vegetation. The roots of these trees spread only through the top inch or two of soil. Quickly and efficiently, the roots recover nutrients from the leaves that fall to the ground, transferring them directly back into the plants from which they have fallen.

14   Once the trees have been cut, they decay or are burned, releasing relatively large amounts of nutrients into the soil. It is then possible to grow crops on this land successfully for a few years, until the available nutrients are used up. If the cut-over areas are then left to recover for many years, and if there is undisturbed forest nearby, the original plant communities may eventually be restored. This process normally takes decades, even centuries, depending upon the type of forest involved. But rarely will it be allowed to reach completion anywhere in the world in the future. There are simply too many people and consequently too little time. The relentless search for firewood, the most important source of energy in many parts of the tropics, is one reason that the forests usually cannot recover.

15   Shifting cultivation, particularly under circumstances where the time of rotation must be short, virtually guarantees continued poverty for the people who practice it. Agricultural development in the tropics without proper management of the soil is not successful. Cultivation can be sustained on the better tropical soils under ideal conditions, involving fertilization, but such conditions lack meaning for the roughly 40 percent of the people who make up the rural poor—those who actually are destroying most of the forests. Trees generally make more productive crops in the humid tropics than do other

kinds of plants; and agroforestry, the combination of annual crops and pastures with trees, is probably the most suitable form of agriculture for many of these regions. Unfortunately, very little research is being done in this area, and the practical options are few.

The FAO estimates that a 60 percent increase in world food production   16
will be needed by the year 2000 if the world's population is to be fed. It does not appear that current efforts will lead to our even beginning to approach this goal, although some optimistic estimates have suggested that we might achieve half of it. In *World Indices of Agricultural and Food Production,* issued last year, the U.S. Department of Agriculture calculated that there has been little progress since 1973 in raising food consumption per capita for the world as a whole. Only greatly expanded efforts might offer the hope of improving this record significantly in the near future.

In sub-Saharan Africa, the problem is worse than elsewhere. There, per   17
capita food production has declined every year since at least 1961; the Department of Agriculture estimated that in 1982 it was 11 percent less than in 1970. Currently, food production in this region is growing at about 1.3 percent per year, the population at about 3 percent. Even worse, food production *per acre* has been declining in recent years, despite some $8 billion of international aid spent annually in Africa.

For tropical countries, only sustainable local agricultural productivity—   18
not food exports—will lead to stability. There are indications that other regions, including northeastern Brazil, the Andean countries, Central America and the Indian subcontinent, may soon face the same difficulties in food production that Africa does now, if their rapid population growth, soil erosion and underinvestment in agriculture continue unchecked. Only about 8 percent of the food eaten in tropical countries is imported, and it is highly improbable that this total could be increased significantly, especially in the face of these nations' staggering debts and their rapid population increases.

Unless we recognize and address these problems, we can expect the insta-   19
bility now characteristic of so many tropical countries to spread and to become increasingly serious. About two-thirds of the people in these countries are farmers, and this number includes most of the truly poor, many with very little land, or none at all. Only if we can find better ways to use tropical land productivity for human benefit, concentrating on the areas that will be most productive and on the rural poor, shall we be making a genuine contribution to peace and harmony for those who come after us.

The population of Central America is about 23 million. In concentrating   20
on that area, we are concerning ourselves with only one percent of all the people in the tropics—and their total number is projected to double in the next 30 years or so! To attain our political and economic goals throughout the world, we must find some way to help to alleviate the plight of the billion people in the tropics who are at the edge of starvation. If we cannot collectively find the means to eliminate rural poverty in these regions, as many experienced observers have concluded, these poor people will soon topple any government, be it friendly or unfriendly to us.

21   Yet despite these realities, the authors of the Kissinger Report on Central America pay very limited attention to the ecological problems that underlie the complex difficulties confronting that region. Although the Report explicitly recognizes the contribution of widespread poverty and population pressures to the difficulties of that area, it fails to connect them with their underlying ecological causes. Only by coping with all these factors can true regional stability be attained, and we can begin to secure U.S. interests there.

22   It is no coincidence that El Salvador is ecologically the most devastated of all the countries of Central America. For well over a decade, the relationship between its degraded environment, the lot of its people and its persistent internal conflicts has been stressed by virtually everyone concerned with that country's future. Throughout Central America and the other tropical regions, the best land is held by relatively few people; half of the farmland in El Salvador is owned by 2 percent of the population, for example. In practice, such a pattern tends to force the peasants to shifting cultivation in, and consequent permanent destruction of, the productivity of marginal lands.

23   Today, about a sixth of all American manufactured exports go to tropical countries, exports which support over 600,000 jobs in the United States alone. We also send nearly half of our agricultural exports to these areas and obtain many of our most important commodities from them. Such commerce will not be possible in the kind of world that is rapidly developing. The instability spreading throughout the tropics, including the constant threat of war, arises in many cases because of the prevalent extreme poverty and resource depletion. This poverty has brought about massive emigration. The U.S. Immigration and Naturalization Service in 1982–1983 apprehended over a million illegal immigrants at the Mexican border alone and estimates that 30 to 40 million more Latin Americans may enter the country illegally by the end of the 20th century, in addition to the number who enter legally. Such a pattern occurs precisely because after 40 years of sustained economic growth, fully half of the population of Mexico still lives in poverty.

24   Beyond the social and political consequences of the exhaustion of tropical resources, however, is a still more fundamental problem. It is the extinction of a major fraction of the plants, animals and microorganisms during the lifetime of a majority of people on earth today.

25   Approximately 1.5 million kinds of organisms have been named and classified, but these include only about 500,000 from the tropics. The total number of species of organisms in temperate regions is estimated to be approximately 1.5 million, but in relatively well-known groups of organisms—birds, mammals and plants—there are about twice as many species in the tropics as in the temperate regions. It may therefore be estimated that at least three million species exist in the tropics. Of these, we have named, and therefore registered, no more than one in six.

26   Many tropical organisms are very narrow in their geographical ranges and are highly specific in their ecological and related requirements. Thus, tropical organisms are unusually vulnerable to extinction through disturbance of their habitats. More than half of the species of tropical organisms are confined to

the lowland forests. In most areas, these forests will be substantially altered or gone within the next 20 years.

Nearly 20 percent of all the kinds of organisms in the world occur in the   27
forests of Latin America outside the Amazon Basin; another 20 percent occur in the forests of Asia and Africa outside the Congo Basin. All of the forests in which these organisms occur will have been destroyed by early in the next century. What would be a reasonable estimate of the loss of species that will accompany such destruction?

The loss of half of the species in these forests would amount to at least   28
750,000 species, about most of which we know nothing. This amounts to more than 50 species a day—fewer in the immediate future, more in the early part of the next century. And, because of the subsequent destruction of the remaining large forest blocks, there will be a continuing acceleration in the rate of extinction. The ultimate possibility is that of reaching stability after the human population does so, but only after many additional organisms have become extinct.

What we have in the tropics, therefore, is a record and explosively grow-   29
ing human population, already well over twice as large as it was in 1950 and projected to double again in size in the next 30 years or so. More than one out of every four of these people are malnourished, many of them actually living at the edge of starvation. These people are dealing with the natural resources of their countries largely without regard to their sustainability, since no other options are available to them.

A human population with these characteristics will certainly exterminate   30
a major proportion of the living species of plants, animals and microorganisms on earth before it begins to approach stability. For those unfamiliar with ecology and tropical biology to ignore or attempt to minimize the importance of events of this magnitude is to court disaster for themselves and for all the rest of us.

The extinction event projected within our lifetimes and those of our chil-   31
dren may be about as extensive as that which occurred at the end of the Cretaceous Period 65 million years ago. For that time, David Raup, professor of geology at the University of Chicago, has estimated very approximately that about 20 to 30 percent of the total number of species may have disappeared permanently. There has been no comparable event since.

With the loss of organisms, we give up not only the opportunity to study   32
and enjoy them, but also the chance to utilize them to better the human condition, both in the tropics and elsewhere. The economic importance of wild species, a tiny proportion of which we actually use, has been well documented elsewhere. Suffice it to say that the entire basis of our civilization rests on a few hundred species out of the millions that might have been selected, and we have just begun to explore the properties of most of the remaining ones.

The process of extinction cannot be reversed or completely halted. Its   33
effects can, however, be moderated by finding the most appropriate methods of utilizing the potentially sustainable resources of tropical countries for human benefit. The explicit relationship between conservation and development was

well outlined in the World Conservation Strategy, issued jointly in 1980 by the International Union for the Conservation of Nature and Natural Resources, the World Wildlife Fund and the United Nations Environmental Program.

34   Beyond the extinction of species, we are participating passively in the promotion of unstable world conditions in which it will no longer be possible to enjoy the benefits of civilization as we know them. It may seem comforting, temporarily, to use unwarranted scepticism and inadequate understanding of ecology as a basis for offering false reassurance to our leaders. To do so, however, is to offer them exceedingly bad advice at an extraordinarily dangerous time.

Questions for Discussion and Your Reading Journal

1. Who is the probable audience for this article? In what ways might it have been tailored to fit the audience? In what ways is it relevant to a general audience?
2. What have been the results of the recent population growth and of shifts in population from relatively rich to poor regions of the world? What does Raven seem to imply individuals should do about the consequences of the population changes?
3. Raven points out that "developed countries consume about 80 percent of the total world supply of energy, the less developed countries about 12 percent." How does the uneven distribution of wealth factor into global environmental problems in relation to forestlands? What are some possible solutions to these problems?
4. Why is it important for third-world countries to be agriculturally self-sufficient, according to the author? What barriers stand in the way of their self-sufficiency?
5. How does the political and economic instability of third-world countries affect more affluent nations? In what ways are affluent nations addressing the third world's problems? What policy changes might affluent nations make to improve stability in the third world?

JARED DIAMOND

Jared Diamond (1937–), professor of physiology at the UCLA School of Medicine, is the author of the award-winning The Third Chimpanzee. *Although he began his career in physiology, Diamond has extended his scholarship into the areas of evolutionary biology and biogeography. He has been elected to the American Academy of Arts and Sciences, the National Academy of Sciences, and the American Philosophical Society and has received a MacArthur Foundation fellowship and the Burr Award of the National Geographic Society.*

Diamond is accomplished in two scientific areas: physiology and evolutionary biology. In his new theories of human development he brings together history and biology in presenting a global account of the evolution of civilization.

In "The Erosion of Civilization: The Fertile Crescent's Fall Holds a Message for Today's Trouble Spots," Diamond explains how a part of the earth that was once known as one of its most fertile areas has become one of its most desolate. Diamond calls for attention to be paid not only to the Fertile Crescent but also to other areas of the world that are similarly vulnerable.

Reading Rhetorically

In this article Jared Diamond makes use of *logos;* he first sets up a problem: the erosion of fertile lands all over the world. Then he proposes a list of three responses, only one of which he recommends. The organizational pattern of presenting a problem and then a solution is very common in texts with the purpose of persuading the reader about something. In this case Diamond hopes to persuade the reader to support early intervention to help the countries in which erosion is taking place.

Less common, however, is the strategy of giving the reader a list of alternatives from which to choose. Diamond carefully leads the reader to his preferred choice. Examine the way he does this and decide whether you think he is persuasive.

The Erosion of Civilization

Iraq sits along a stretch of land once so productive that the whole region— 1 which included present-day Syria, Iran and Jordan—was known as the Fertile Crescent. In ancient times, the area led the world in agriculture and technology. It's hard to reconcile that history with the reality of today, when the term "Infertile Crescent" would seem more appropriate.

The Fertile Crescent's current desperation stands as testament to the steep- 2 est downturn of local fortunes since the end of the last Ice Age. For 8,000 years Iraq and its neighbors led the world as the source of most things embodied in the term "civilization." Technology, ideas and power flowed outward from Iraq to Europe and eventually to America. Iraq's decline holds lessons the world should heed.

The region's ancient dominance didn't arise from any biological superior- 3 ity of its people, just as America's dominance today has nothing to do with our own biology. Instead, Fertile Crescent, peoples profited from an accident of biogeography: They had the good fortune to occupy the world's largest zone of Mediterranean climate, home to the largest number of wild plant and animal species suitable for domestication. Until 8500 BC, all the world's peoples obtained their food by gathering wild plants and hunting wild animals. Then the ancient Iraqis and other Fertile Crescent peoples began to develop farming and herding, domesticating wild wheat, barley, peas, sheep, goat, pigs and cows. Even today, these species remain the world's staple crops and livestock. Agriculture fueled a population explosion, and also generated food surpluses that could be used to feed full-time professional specialists, who no longer had to devote time to procuring their own food.

4   These specialists fed by agriculture included smiths and metal workers, who developed the world's first copper tools around 5000 BC, bronze tools around 3000 BC and iron tools around 1500 BC. The specialists also included accountants and scribes, who developed the world's first writing system around 3400 BC. That was a huge head start: Writing didn't reach what is now the United States until 5,000 years later. It makes Iraq's current rate of illiteracy an especially cruel irony.

5   Agriculture also fed politicians, bureaucrats and judges. That's why the world's first states arose in Iraq around 3500 BC, and the first multiethnic empire arose there around 3000 BC. The Middle East continued to lead and dominate western Eurasia for several thousand more years, and its languages were spoken from Ireland to India. The English we speak today grew out of the Indo-European languages originally spoken by Middle Eastern peoples, and the fact that people in the United States speak it—as opposed to a language derived from ancient Algonquin or some other Native American language family—is a testament to the Middle East's ancient dominance.

6   So how did Fertile Crescent peoples lose that big lead? The short answer is ecological suicide: They inadvertently destroyed the environmental resources on which their society depended. Just as the region's rise wasn't due to any special virtue of its people, its fall wasn't due to any special blindness on their part. Instead, they had the misfortune to be living in an extremely fragile environment, which, because of its low rainfall, was particularly susceptible to deforestation.

7   When you clear a forest in a high-rainfall tropical area, new trees grow up to a height of 15 feet within a year; in a dry area like the Fertile Crescent, regeneration is much slower. And when you add to the equation grazing by sheep and goats, new trees stand little chance. Deforestation led to soil erosion, and irrigation agriculture led to salinization, both by releasing salt buried deep in the ground and by adding salt through irrigation water. After centuries of degradation, areas of Iraq that formerly supported productive irrigation agriculture are today salt pans where nothing grows.

8   Once the Fertile Crescent began to decline for those environmental reasons, hostile neighbors helped speed the process. The original flow of power westward from the Fertile Crescent reversed in 330 BC, when the Macedonian army of Alexander the Great advanced eastward to conquer the eastern Mediterranean. In the Middle Ages, Mongol invaders from Central Asia destroyed Iraq's irrigation systems. After World War I, England and France dismembered the Ottoman Empire and carved out Iraq and other states as pawns of European colonial interests. As the end product of this history, the former world center of wealth, power and civilization is now poor in everything except oil. Iraq's leaders ensured that few benefits of that oil reached their people.

9   Iraq's decline holds a broader significance. Many other countries today face similar crippling environmental problems, including the deforestation, over-

grazing, erosion and salinization that brought down the Fertile Crescent. Other countries already crippled or nearly so by such problems include Haiti, Somalia, Rwanda, Afghanistan, Pakistan, Nepal, the Philippines and Indonesia.

You may well detect a similarity between this list of looming environmen- 10
tal disasters and the CIA's list of overseas trouble spots, places prone to civil wars and violent regime changes—places to which we often end up dispatching U.S. troops. Those two lists are related by cause and effect. When environmental damage makes people economically desperate, they are likely to suffer from poor health and short life spans, blame their governments, kill each other, end up with crazy leaders and seek to immigrate illegally to more favored landscapes.

The First World can respond to these Third World problems in one of 11
three ways. It can provide humanitarian aid once a crisis has arisen. It can ignore the situation as long as possible and then intervene militarily once the crisis cannot be ignored (at a cost, in the case of Afghanistan and Iraq, of an estimated $100 billion per intervention when you add up all the potential costs of military action and rebuilding). Or it can intervene before a crisis to stave off looming problems.

There are lots of other countries teetering on the brink. We will be hear- 12
ing more from Bangladesh, Haiti, Nepal, Indonesia and others. Even for a country as wealthy as the United States, there is a limit to the number of $100-billion interventions we can afford, and there are many alternative uses at home for that money—improving our schools, say, or fixing Social Security or establishing universal health insurance.

The most effective and least expensive approach would be to help Third 13
World countries solve their basic environmental and public health problems before they cripple societies. The cost of a global program to combat AIDS, malaria and tuberculosis—the world's three most costly infectious diseases— is estimated by public health organizations at about $25 billion, or one-quarter the cost of a single military intervention.

Attacking problems before crises is a policy that differs in motivation 14
(though not in policies pursued) from a traditional humanitarian response that comes out of a moral commitment to address crises. Its motive is selfish. Preventing chaos abroad benefits the United States. Presidential Bush would be on the right track with his policy of preemption if he were aiming at preempting crises, rather than at preempting military aggression.

In today's globalized world, any country can pose a threat: Just took at 15
Somalia and Afghanistan, which rank among the poorest, weakest, most isolated countries on Earth. We can't take on the whole world militarily. Keeping weak countries from getting into the kind of trouble Iraq found itself in would ultimately save the U.S. money—and generate global political capital.

Questions for Discussion and Your Reading Journal

1. Describe the difference between the Iraq of ancient times and the Iraq of today. How did this change take place?

2. Diamond does not blame the Iraqi people for the destruction of fertile lands. Instead, how does he account for it? Why do you think he accounts for the responsibility in this way?

3. Toward the end of the article Diamond describes the similarities between what happened in Iraq and what is happening in other parts of the world. For what reasons might he have placed this point near the end?

4. Examine the list of three possible responses to the problem of erosion in various parts of the world. List the reasons Diamond prefers the third response. Do you find these reasons persuasive? Why or why not?

EDWARD O. WILSON

Edward O. Wilson (1929–) is a professor of biology at Harvard University. He has written two Pulitzer Prize–winning books, On Human Nature *(1978) and* The Ants *(1990).*

In the following excerpt from the book The Future of Life *(2002), Wilson lays out a number of concrete things that can be done to save the planet from ecological devastation. Two of the most important involve steps that will be very challenging for world leaders to take: disarmament and ideological change in relation to nationalism. This ideological change is necessary, according to Wilson, in order for nations to cooperate with one another for the greater good of all nations. The smaller steps, like making conservation more profitable, are also outlined and explained. In opposition to those who predict and expect Armageddon, Wilson offers optimistic strategies for change.*

Reading Rhetorically

Wilson writes, "Everyone is an avowed environmentalist. No one says flatly, 'To hell with nature.'" (Paragraph 10). Because the stated purpose of the book is changing people's attitudes and behaviors in order to preserve the environment, this point seems contradictory; why would a supporter of environmentalism need to persuade people who are already environmentalists to change their perspective? Persuasive writing often includes concessions like this. The sentence following the aforementioned one begins with the phrase "on the other hand." This use of *logos*, making a concession and then arguing against it, is a rhetorical strategy that can be highly effective. As you read this section of the text, determine the degree to which you think the strategy is successful.

Wilson also uses an illustration in this text. Although the illustration is simple, it makes a very important point. Think about why the author might have used this strategy to communicate his ideas and why illustrations are used in general in texts of this kind (see Chapter 1 on visual rhetoric).

The Solution

The human species is like the mythical giant Antaeus, who drew strength 1
from contact with his mother, Gaea, the goddess Earth, and used it to
challenge and defeat all comers. Hercules, learning his secret, lifted and held
Antaeus above the ground until the giant weakened—then crushed him. Mortal humans are also handicapped by our separation from Earth, but our
impairment is self-administered, and it has this added twist: our exertions also
weaken Earth.

What humanity is inflicting on itself and Earth is, to use a modern meta- 2
phor, the result of a mistake in capital investment. Having appropriated the
planet's natural resources, we chose to annuitize them with a short-term maturity reached by progressively increasing payouts. At the time it seemed a wise
decision. To many it still does. The result is rising per-capita production and
consumption, markets awash in consumer goods and grain, and a surplus of
optimistic economists. But there is a problem: the key elements of natural capital, Earth's arable land, ground water, forests, marine fisheries, and petroleum, are ultimately finite, and not subject to proportionate capital growth.
Moreover, they are being decapitalized by overharvesting and environmental
destruction. With population and consumption continuing to grow, the per-
capita resources left to be harvested are shrinking. The long-term prospects are
not promising. Awakened at last to this approaching difficulty, we have begun
a frantic search for substitutes.

Meanwhile, two collateral results of the annuitization of nature, as op- 3
posed to its stewardship, are settling in to beg our attention. The first is economic disparity: in relative terms the rich grow richer and the poor poorer.
According to the United Nations Human Development Report 1999, the
income differential between the fifth of the world's population in the wealthiest countries and the fifth in the poorest was 30 to 1 in 1960, 60 to 1 in 1990,
and 74 to 1 in 1995. Wealthy people are also by and large profligate consumers, and as a result the income differential has this disturbing consequence:
for the rest of the world to reach United States levels of consumption with
existing technology would require four more planet Earths.

Europe is only slightly behind, while the Asian economic tigers appear to 4
be pulling up at maximum possible speed. The income gap is the setting for
resentment and fanaticism that causes even the stronger nations, led by the
American colossus, to conduct their affairs with an uneasy conscience and a
growing fear of heaven-bound suicide bombers.

The second collateral result, and the principal concern of the present 5
work, is the accelerating extinction of natural ecosystems and species. The
damage already done cannot be repaired within any period of time that has
meaning for the human mind. The fossil record shows that new faunas and flo-
ras take millions of years to evolve to the richness of the prehuman world. The
more the losses are allowed to accumulate, the more future generations will

suffer for it, in some ways already felt and in others no doubt waiting to be painfully learned.

6   Why, our descendants will ask, by needlessly extinguishing the lives of other species, did we permanently impoverish our own? That hypothetical question is not the rhetoric of radical environmentalism. It expresses a growing concern among leaders in science, religion, business, and government, as well as the educated public.

7   What is the solution to biological impoverishment? The answer I will now pose is guardedly optimistic. In essence, it is that the problem is now well understood, we have a grip on its dimensions and magnitude, and a workable strategy has begun to take shape.

8   The new strategy to save the world's fauna and flora begins, as in all human affairs, with ethics. Moral reasoning is not a cultural artifact invented for convenience. It is and always has been the vital glue of society, the means by which transactions are made and honored to ensure survival. Every society is guided by ethical precepts, and every one of its members is expected to follow moral leadership and ethics-based tribal law. The propensity does not have to be beaten into us. Evidence exists instead of an instinct to behave ethically, or at least to insist on ethical behavior in others. Psychologists, for example, have discovered a hereditary tendency to detect cheaters and to respond to them with intense moral outrage. People by and large are natural geniuses at spotting deception in others, and equally brilliant to constructing deceptions of their own. We are daily soaked in self-righteous gossip. We pummel others with expostulation, and we hunger for sincerity in all our relationships. Even the tyrant is sterling in pose, invoking patriotism and economic necessity to justify his misdeeds. At the next level down, the convicted criminal is expected to show remorse, in the course of which he explains he was either insane at the time or redressing personal injustice.

9   And everyone has some kind of environmental ethic, even if it somehow makes a virtue of cutting the last ancient forests and damming the last wild rivers. Done, it is said, to grow the economy and save jobs. Done because we are tunning short of space and fuel. *Hey, listen, people come first!*—and most certainly before beach mice and louseworts. I recall vividly the conversation I had with a cab driver in Key West in 1968 when we touched on the Everglades burning to the north. Too bad, he said. The Everglades are a wonderful place. But wilderness always gives way to civilization, doesn't it? That is progress and the way of the world, and we can't do much about it.

10   Everyone is also an avowed environmentalist. No one says flatly, "To hell with nature." On the other hand, no one says, "Let's give it all back to nature." Rather, when invoking the social contract by which we all live, the typical people-first ethicist thinks about the environmental short-term and the typical environmental ethicist thinks about it long-term. Both are sincere and have something true and important to say. The people-first thinker says we need to take a little cut here and there; the environmentalist says nature is dying the death of a thousand cuts. So how do we combine the best of short-term and long-term goals? Perhaps, despite decades of bitter philosophical dis-

pute, an optimum mix on the goals might result in a consensus more satisfactory than either side thought possible from total victory alone. Down deep, I believe, no one wants a total victory. The people-firster likes parks, and the environmentalist rides petroleum-powered vehicles to get there.

The first step is to turn away from claims of inherent moral superiority 11 based on political ideology and religious dogma. The problems of the environment have become too complicated to be solved by piety and an unyielding clash of good intentions.

The next step is to disarm. The most destructive weapons to be stacked 12 are the stereotypes, the total-war portraits crafted for public consumption by extremists on both sides. I know them very well from years of experience on the boards of conservation organizations, as a participant in policy conferences, and during service on government advisory committees. To tell the truth, I am a little battle-fatigued. The stereotypes cannot be simply dismissed, since they are so often voiced and contain elements of real substance, like rocks in snowballs. But they can be understood clearly and sidestepped in the search for common ground. Let me illustrate a stereotype skirmish with imaginary opponents engaging in typical denunciations.

THE PEOPLE-FIRST CRITIC STEREOTYPES
THE ENVIRONMENTALISTS

Environmentalists or conservationists is what they usually call themselves. 13 Depending on how angry we are, we call the greens, enviros, environmental extremists, or environmental wackos. Mark my word, conservation pushed by these people always goes too far, because it is an instrument for gaining political power. The wackos have a broad and mostly hidden agenda that always comes from the left, usually far left. How to get power? is what they're thinking. Their aim is to expand government, especially the federal government. They want environmental laws and regulatory surveillance to create government-supported jobs for their kind of bureaucrats, lawyers, and consultants. The New Class, these professionals have been called. What's at stake as they busy themselves are your tax dollars and mine, and ultimately our freedom too. Relax your guard when these people are in power and your property rights go down the tube. Some Bennington College student with a summer job will find an endangered red spider on your property, and before you know what happened the Endangered Species Act will be used to shut you down. Can't sell to a developer, can't even harvest your woodlot. Business investors can't get at the oil and gas on federal lands this country badly needs. Mind you, I'm all for the environment, and I agree that species extinction is a bad thing, but conservation should be kept in perspective. It is best put in private hands. Property owners know what's good for their own land. They care about the plants and animals living there. Let them work out conservation. They are the real roots in this country. Let them be the stewards and handle conservation. A strong, growing free-market economy, not creeping socialism, is what's best for America—and it's best for the environment too.

THE ENVIRONMENTALIST STEREOTYPES
THE PEOPLE-FIRST CRITICS

14   "Critics" of the environmental movement? That may be what they call themselves, but we know them more accurately as anti-environmentalists and
brown lashers or, more locally out west, wise users (their own term, not
intended to be ironic) and sagebrush rebels. In claiming concern of any kind
for the natural environment, these people are the worst bunch of hypocrites
you'll ever not want to find. What they are really after, especially the corporate heads and big-time landowners, is unrestrained capitalism with land
development *über alles*. They keep their right-wing political agenda mostly
hidden when downgrading climate change and species extinction, but for them
economic growth is always the ultimate, and maybe the only, good. Their idea
of conservation is stocking trout streams and planting trees around golf
courses. Their conception of the public trust is a strong military establishment
and subsidies for loggers and ranchers. The anti-environmentalists would be
laughed out of court if they weren't tied so closely to the corporate power
structure. And notice how rarely international policy makers pay attention to
the environment. At the big conferences of the World Trade Organization and
other such gatherings of the rich and powerful, conservation almost never gets
so much as a hearing. The only recourse we have is to protest at their meetings. We hope to attract the attention of the media and at least get our
unelected rulers to look out the window. In America the right-wingers have
made the word "conservative" a mockery. What exactly are they trying to
conserve? Their own selfish interests, for sure, not the natural environment.

15   There are partisans on both sides who actually state their case in this manner, either in pieces or in entirety. And the accusations sting, because so many
people on either side believe them. The suspicion and anger they express par-
alyze further discussion. Worse, in an era when journalism feeds on controversy, its widely used gladiatorial approach divides people and pushes them
away from the center toward opposite extremes.

16   It is a contest that will not be settled by partisan victory. The truth is that
everyone wants a highly productive economy and lots of well-paying jobs. People almost all agree that private property is a sacred right. On the other hand,
everyone treasures a clean environment. In the United States at least, the preservation of nature has almost the status of a sacred trust. In a 1996 survey conducted by Belden & Russonello for the U.S. Consultative Group on Biological
Diversity, 79 percent rated a healthy and pleasant environment of the greatest
importance, giving it a 10 on a scale of 1 to 10. Seventy-one percent agreed at
the same high level with the statement. "Nature is God's creation and humans
should respect God's work." Only when these two obvious and admirable goals,
prosperity and saving the creation, are cast in opposition does the issue become
confused. And when the apparent conflict is in addition reinforced by opposing
political ideologies, as it frequently is, the problem becomes, intractable.

17   The ethical solution is to diagnose and disconnect extraneous political ideology, then shed it in order to move toward the common ground where economic progress and conservation are treated as one and the same goal.

The guiding principles of a united environmental movement must be, and   18
eventually will be, chiefly long-term. If two hundred years of history of environmentalism have taught us anything, it is that a change of heart occurs when
people look beyond themselves to others, and then to the rest of life. It is
strengthened when they also expand their view of landscape, from parish to
nation and beyond, and their sweep of time from their own life spans to multiple generations and finally to the extended future history of humankind.

The precepts of the people-firsters are foundationally just as ethical as   19
those of the traditional environmentalist, but their arguments are more about
method and short-term results. Further, their values are not, as often assumed,
merely a reflection of capitalist philosophy. Corporate CEOs are people too,
with families and the same desire for a healthy, biodiverse world. Many are
leaders in the environmental movement. It is time to recognize that their commitment is vital to success. The world economy is now propelled by venture
capital and technical innovation; it cannot be returned to a pastoral civilization.
Nor will socialism return in a second attempt to rescue us, at least in any form
resembling the Soviet model. Quite the contrary, its demise was a good thing
all around for nature. In most places the socialist experiment was tried, its
record was even worse than in capitalist countries. Totalitarianism, left or right,
is a devil's bargain: slavery purchased at the price of a ruined environment.

The juggernaut of technology-based capitalism will not be stopped. Its   20
momentum is reinforced by the billions of poor people in developing countries
anxious to participate in order to share the material wealth of the industrialized nations. But its direction can be changed by mandate of a generally shared
long-term environmental ethic. The choice is clear; the juggernaut will very
soon either chew up what remains of the living world, or it will be redirected
to save it.

Science and technology are themselves reason for optimism. They are   21
growing exponentially—in the case of computer capacity, superexponentially,
the doubling time having dropped to one year. The consequences are not predictable, but one is almost certainly to be an improvement of human self-
understanding. Within several decades, many neuroscientists believe, we will
have a much firmer grasp of the biological sources of mind and behavior. That
in turn will provide the basis for a more solid social science, and a better
capacity to anticipate and step away from political and economic disasters.

Also emerging swiftly is a sophisticated picture of changes in global envi-   22
ronment and available resources. Concrete measures such as the ecological
footprint and the Living Planet Index form the groundwork for wiser economic planning. Science and technology also promise the means for raising
per-capita food production while decreasing material and energy consumption, both of which are preconditions for successful long-term conservation
and a sustainable economy.

All this information is coming on-line worldwide. It will allow people   23
everywhere to see the planet as the astronauts see it, a little sphere with a
razor-thin coat of life too fragile to bear careless tampering. A growing cadre
of leaders in business, government, and religion now think in this foresighted
manner. They understand that humanity is in a bottleneck of overpopulation

and wasteful consumption. They agree, at least in principle, that we will have to maneuver carefully in order to pass through the bottleneck safely.

24   To lift a stabilized world population to a decent quality of life while salvaging and restoring the natural environment is a noble and attainable goal. This brings me to another source of cautious optimism, the growing prominence of the environment in religious thought. The trend is important not only for its moral content, but for the conservatism and authenticity of its nature. Religious leaders are by necessity very careful in the values they choose to promote. The sacred texts from which they draw authority tolerate few amendments. In modern times, as knowledge of the material world and the human predicament has soared, the leaders have followed rather than led the evolution of ethics. First into the new terrain venture saints and radical theologians. They are followed by growing numbers of the faithful and then, warily, by the bishops, patriarchs, and imams.

25   For the Abrahamic religions, Judaism, Christianity, and Islam, the environmental ethic is compatible with belief in the holiness of the Earth and the perception of nature as God's handiwork. In the thirteenth century Saint Francis of Assissi prayed for the welfare of God's creatures, his avowed "brothers and sisters," and extolled the "beautiful relationship" of humankind and nature. In Genesis 1:28, God instructs Adam and Eve to "fill the earth, and subdue it, and rule over the fishes of the sea, and the birds of the air, and all living, creatures that move upon the earth." Once in history the passage was construed to validate the conversion of nature to exclusively human needs. Now it is more commonly interpreted to mean the stewardship of nature. Thus Pope John Paul II has affirmed that "the ecological crisis is a moral issue." And Patriarch Bartholomew I, spiritual leader of the world's 250 million Orthodox Christians, has declared, in the clarion tones of an Old Testament prophet, that "for humans to cause species to become extinct and to destroy the biological diversity of God's creation, for humans to degrade the integrity of the earth by causing changes in its climate, by stripping the earth of its natural forests, or destroying its wetlands, for humans to contaminate the earth's waters, its land, its air and its life with poisonous substances, these are sins."

26   Some Protestant denominations are active in conservation. Among them are evangelical sects prone to literal interpretations of the Bible. In 1988 the Reverend Stan L. LeQuire, director of the Evangelical Environmental Network, stated the issue incisively: "We evangelicals are recognizing more and more that environmental issues are not Republican or Democratic, that they really come from the most wonderful teachings that we have in Scripture, which commend us to honor God by caring for creation." His network, organized into "Noah Congregations," proved its mettle: it contributed $1 million to the successful campaign against congressionnal efforts to weaken the Endangered Species Act.

27   In the evangelical culture God can still strike the wicked, even if only through the dire consequences of their own actions. Listen to the voice of Janisse Ray, a young poet from southern Georgia, who in her 1999 memoir *Ecology of a Cracker Childhood* decries the destruction of the region's long-

leaf pine forests. Her warning perfectly captures the cadence of an evangelical sermon:

> If you clear a forest, you'd better pray continuously. While you're pushing a road through and rigging the cables and moving between trees on the dozer, you'd better be talking to God. While you're cruising timber and marking trees with a blue slash, be praying, and pray while you're peddling the chips and logs and writing Friday's checks and paying the diesel bill—even if it's under your breath, a rustling at the lips. If you're manning the saw head or the scissors, snipping the trees off at the ground, going from one to another, approaching them brusquely and laying them down, I'd say, pray extra hard; and pray hard when you're hauling them away.
>
> God doesn't like a clearcut. It makes his heart turn cold, makes him wince and wonder what went wrong with his creation, and sets him to thinking about what spoils the child.

A scattering of Roman Catholic dioceses and Jewish synagogues have also 28 joined in environmental activism. The Religious Campaign for Forest Conservation, an interfaith group founded in 2000, aims at uniting Jewish and Christian efforts. Its members share a conviction that activities destroying the natural environment "foster injustice and gross economic inequities. Most grievously we declare them spiritually bankrupt because they deny God and foster the degradation of human society."

On one memorable occasion, in the fall of 1986, I was invited by the Com- 29 mittee on Human Values of the U.S. Roman Catholic Bishops to discuss the relation of science to religion. I was joined at their two-day retreat, held near Detroit, by three other scientists and a group of Catholic lay theologians. As one professor of theology expressed it, "Science went out the door with Aquinas and we never invited her back." The times were changing. At the end of our varied and frank discussions the bishops drew up a list of priorities for postconference study. Second from the top was environment and conservation. 30

On a later occasion, also symptomatic of the trend toward moral consensus, I was invited by my friend Bruce Babbitt, then secretary of the interior under President Clinton, to join him, another scientist, and several religious leaders for a discussion of the role of our respective callings in promoting conservation. The atmosphere was wholly congenial, even faintly conspiratorial. As we closed, Babbitt remarked that if the two most powerful forces in America, religion and science, could be united on the issue, the country's environmental problems would be quickly solved.

Such a collaboration is feasible. I like to think that the environmental val- 31 ues of secular and religious alike arise from the same innate attraction to nature. They express the same compassion for animals, aesthetic response to free-living flowers and birds, and wonder at the mysteries of wild environments. Of course, secular and religious thinkers differ as ever in their explanations of where these feelings originate. They argue about who, or Who, judges the stewardship that a common ethic commands. But these epistemological distinctions, so important in other spheres of public life, can be safely put aside in the case of the environment. Polls show that, in the United States at least, people of all socioeconomic groups and religious beliefs become conservationists when well informed, and primarily for moral reasons. Even despoilers pay tribute to virtue. They assure us that under certain conditions the logging of old trees reduces fire damage and helps wildlife. They protest that maybe global warming won't be so bad after all. They allow that protecting pandas and gorillas and eagles is a good idea.

32   The convergence in opinion is strong enough that the problem is no longer the reasons for conservation but the best method to achieve it. The challenge, while enormous, can be met. During the past two decades, scientists and conservation professionals have put together a strategy aimed at the protection of most of the remaining ecosystems and species. Its key elements are the following:

33 • Salvage immediately the world's hotspots, those habitats that are both at the greatest risk and shelter the largest concentrations of species found nowhere else. Among the most valuable hotspots on the land, for example, are the surviving remnants of rainforest in Hawaii, the West Indies, Ecuador, Atlantic Brazil, West Africa, Madagascar, the Philippines, Indo-Burma, and India, as well as the Mediterranean-climate scrublands of South Africa, southwestern Australia, and southern California. Twenty-five of these special ecosystems cover only 1.4 percent of Earth's land surface, about the same as Texas and Alaska combined. Yet they are the last remaining homes of an impressive 43.8 percent of all known species of vascular plants and 35.6 percent of the known mammals, birds, reptiles, and amphibians. The twenty-five hotspots have already been reduced 88 percent in area by clearing and development; some could be wiped out entirely within several decades by continued intrusion.

34 • Keep intact the five remaining frontier forests, which are the last true wildernesses on the land and home to an additional large fraction of Earth's biological diversity. They are the rainforests of the combined Amazon Basin and the Guianas; the Congo block of Central Africa; New Guinea; the temperate conifer forests of Canada and Alaska combined; and the temperate conifer forests of Russia, Finland, and Scandinavia combined.

35 • Cease all logging of old-growth forests everywhere. For every bit of this habitat lost or degraded, Earth pays a price in biodiversity. The cost is especially steep in tropical forests, and it is potentially catastrophic in the forested hotspots. At the same time, let secondary native forests recover. The time has come—rich opportunity shines forth—for the timber-extraction industry to shift to tree farming on already converted land. The cultivation of lumber and pulp should be conducted like the agribusiness it is, using high-quality, fast-growing species and strains for higher productivity and profit. To that end, it would be valuable to forge an international agreements, similar to the Montreal and Kyoto Protocols, that prohibits further destruction of old-growth forests and thereby provides the timber-extraction economy with a level playing field.

36 • Everywhere, not just in the hotspots and wilderness, concentrate on the lakes and river systems, which are the most threatened ecosystems of all. Those in tropical and warm-temperate regions in particular possess the highest ratio of endangered species to area of any kind of habitat.

- Define precisely the marine hotspots of the world, and assign them the 37 same action priority as for those on the land. Foremost are the coral reefs, which in their extremely high biological diversity rank as the rainforests of the sea. More than half around the world—including, for example, those of the Maldives and parts of the Caribbean and Philippines—have been savaged variously by overharvesting and rising temperatures, and are in critical condition. 38

- In order to render the conservation effort exact and cost-effective, complete the mapping of the world's biological diversity. Scientists have estimated that 10 percent or more of flowering plants, a majority of animals, and a huge majority of microorganisms remain undiscovered and unnamed, hence of unknown conservation status. As the map is filled in, it will evolve into a biological encyclopedia of value not only in conservation practice but also in science, industry, agriculture, and medicine. The expanded global biodiversity map will be the instrument that unites biology. 39

- Using recent advances in mapping the planet's terrestrial, fresh-water, and marine ecosystems, ensure that the full range of the world's ecosystems are included in a global conservation strategy. The scope of conservation must embrace not only the habitats, such as tropical forests and coral reefs, that harbor the richest assemblages of species, but also the deserts and arctic tundras whose beautiful and austere inhabitants are no less unique expressions of life. 40

- Make conservation profitable. Find ways to raise the income of those who live in and near the reserves. Give them a proprietary interest in the natural environment and engage them professionally in its protection. Help raise the productivity of land already converted to cropland and cattle ranches nearby, while tightening security around the reserves. Generate sources of revenue in the reserves themselves. Demonstrate to the governments, especially of developing countries, that ecotourism, bioprospecting, and (eventually) carbon credit trades of wild land can yield more income than logging and agricultural of the same land cleared and planted. 41

- Use biodiversity more effectively to benefit the world economy as a whole. Broaden field research and laboratory biotechnology to develop new crops, livestock, cultivated food fish, farmed timber, pharmaceuticals, and biomedical bacteria. Where genetically engineered crop strains prove nutritionally and environmentally safe upon careful research and regulation, as I outlined in chapter 5, they should be employed. In addition to feeding the hungry, they can help take the pressure off the wildlands and the biodiversity they contain.

- Initiate restoration projects to increase the share of Earth allotted to na- 42 ture. Today about 10 percent of the land surface is protected on paper. Even if rigorously conserved, this amount is not enough to save more than a modest fraction of wild species. Large numbers of plant and animal species are left with populations too small to persist. Every bit of space that can be added will pass more species through the bottleneck of over-population and development for the benefit of future generations. Eventually, and the sooner the better, a higher goal can and should be set. At the risk of being called an extremist, which on this topic I freely admit I am, let me suggest 50 percent. Half the world for humanity, half for the rest of life, to create a planet both self-sustaining and pleasant.

43 • Increase the capacity of zoos and botanical gardens to breed endangered species. Most are already working to fill that role. Prepare to clone species when all other preservation methods fail. Enlarge the existing seed and spore banks and create reserves of frozen embryos and tissue. But keep in mind that these methods are expensive and at best supplementary. Moreover, they are not feasible for the vast majority of species, especially the countless bacteria, archaeans, protistans, fungi, and insects and other invertebrates that make up the functioning base of the biosphere. And even if somehow, with enormous effort, all these species too could be stored artificially, it would be virtually impossible to reassemble them later into sustainably free-living ecosystems. The only secure way to save species, as well as the cheapest (and on the evidence the only sane way), is to preserve the natural ecosystems they now compose.

44 • Support population planning. Help guide humanity everywhere to a smaller biomass, a lighter footstep, and a more secure and enjoyable future with biodiversity flourishing around it.

45   Earth is still productive enough and human ingenuity creative enough not only to feed the world now but also to raise the standard of living of the population projected to at least the middle of the twenty-first century. The great majority of ecosystems and species still surviving can also be protected. Of the two objectives, humanitarian and environmental, the latter is by far the cheaper, and the best bargain humanity has ever been offered. For global conservation, only one-thousandth of the current annual world domestic product, or $30 billion out of approximately $30 trillion, would accomplish most of the task. One key element, the protection and management of the world's existing natural reserves, could be financed by a one-cent-per-cup tax on coffee.

46   Progress toward global conservation, acceptance of the bargain, will pick up or falter depending on cooperation among the three secular stanchions of civilized existence: government, the private sector, and science and technology.

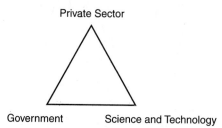

47   Governments devise laws and regulatory practices that, if ethically based, give long-term benefit to the governed. They treat the environment as a public trust. They are moreover party to treaties that protect the planetary environment as a whole, such as the 1982 United Nations Convention on the Law of the Sea, the 1987 Montreal Protocol on Substances That Deplete the Ozone, and the Convention on Biological Diversity of the 1992 Rio Earth Summit. The private sector, working within the public-trust constraints defined by government policy, is the engine of society. A strong economy

improves the material quality of life, allowing the populace to look and plan ahead in all venues important to them, including the environment. In the process it buoys science and technology, the means to improve knowledge of the material world, control our own lives, and secure the prerequisites of personal fulfillment.

The interlocking of the three key agents is vital to global conservation. The trends in their evolution are encouraging. A legion of private and government-supported institutions is pursuing environmental initiatives unimagined twenty years ago. Public support of conservation, once tenuous around the world, has begun to quicken. Mexico, Ecuador, Brazil, Papua New Guinea, and Madagascar are among the developing countries with national programs directed at the preservation of natural habitats that most need them. 48

The spearhead of the global conservation movement consists of the nongovernmental organizations (NGOs). They range in size from the relatively giant Conservation International, Wildlife Conservation Society, World Wide Fund for nature, World Wildlife Fund—U.S., and The Nature Conservancy to much smaller, specialized groups, of which the following is a representative sample: the Seacology Foundation (island environments and culture), Ecotrust (temperate rainforests of North America), Xerces Society (insects and other invertebrates), Bat Conservation International, and the Balikpapan Orangutan Society—USA. In 1956 there were, according to the Union of International Organizations, 985 NGOs devoted to humanitarian or environmental causes or both. By 1996 the number had increased to more than 20,000. Their membership and coordination has expanded throughout that period, a trend now enhanced by Internet advertising and communication. In the late 1990s there was one paid membership in some environmental organization or other for every twenty Americans, and more than one such membership for every citizen of Denmark. The governing boards and advisory committees bring together scientists, corporate executives, private investors, media stars, and other private citizens devoted to the cause. . . . 49

At the end of the day, in a more democratic world, it will be the ethics and desires of the people, not their leaders, who give power to government and the NGOs or take it away. They will decide if there are to be more or fewer reserves, and choose whether particular species live or die. That is why I am personally encouraged by the swift growth of nongovernmental organizations devoted to conservation. The ability of people to devise initiatives fitted to the occasion, from the protection of a local riverine woodland and endangered frog species to the support of rainforest wilderness reserves and international treaties, is strong and growing. There is also a reasonable expectation that the study of biodiversity and concern for its welfare will be an increasing focus of education from kindergarten to twelfth grade and college, and beyond. What better way to teach science than to present it as a friend of life rather than as an uncontrolled destructive force? 50

At the risk of seeming politically correct, I will now close with a tribute to protest groups. They gather like angry bees at meetings of the World Trade Organization, the World Bank, and the World Economic Forum. They boycott insufficiently green restaurant franchises. They mass on logging roads. In 51 response the executives and trustees they target ask, Who are these people? What are they really after? The answers to these questions are simple. They are people who feel excluded from the conference table by faceless power, and they distrust decisions secretly made that will affect their lives. They have a point. The CEOs and governing boards of the largest corporations, supported by government leaders committed to an expanding capital economy, are the commanders of the industrialized world. Like princes of old, they can, in the realm of economics at least, rule by fiat. The protesters say: Include us, and while you're at it, the rest of life.

52   The protest groups are the early warning system for the natural economy. They are the living world's immunological response. They ask us to listen. Julia (Butterfly) Hill, the young lady who lived 180 feet up in a California redwood tree for two years (December 1997–December 1999) in an attempt to save the redwoods of the surrounding forest, just wanted to express her opinion and change minds. Her argument was simple: it is morally wrong to cut down these ancient giants, even if you own them. She lost. She persuaded Pacific Lumber MAXXAM to save only her tree and three acres of land around it. But how many now know her name and the name of the tree (Luna), and how many know the names of the corporate executives who ordered the logging to continue around the tiny preserve?

53   Granted, some of the protest groups are tainted by the violent actions of a few. Rioters attacking police, burners of construction sites, and drivers of spikes into trees marked for logging deserve fines and jail terms. But the vast majority of the protesters, those honest, loud-shouting picketers dressed in turtle costumes and homeless-shelter couture, gather to demand equal time for the poor and for nature. I say bless them all. Their wisdom is deeper than their chants and tramping feet suggest, deeper than that of many of the power brokers they oppose. With the help of the media, which feeds on controversy, they keep open public discourse on crucial issues otherwise slighted. And if they are uniformly left-wing in ideology, so be it. Their youthful energies therapeutically disturb and counter the cynicism endemic to the conservative temperament.

54   The central problem of the new century, I have argued, is how to raise the poor to a decent standard of living worldwide while preserving as much of the rest of life as possible. Both the needy poor and vanishing biological diversity are concentrated in the developing countries. The poor, some 800 million of whom live without sanitation, clean water, and adequate food, have little chance to advance in a devastated environment. Conversely, the natural environments where most biodiversity hangs on cannot survive the press of land-hungry people with nowhere else to go.

55   I hope I have justified the conviction, shared by many thoughtful people from all walks of life, that the problem can be solved. Adequate resources exist. Those who control them have many reasons to achieve that goal, not least their own security. In the end, however, success or failure will come down to an ethical decision, one on which those now living will be defined and judged for all generations to come. I believe we will choose wisely. A civilization able to envision God and to embark on the colonization of space will surely find the way to save the integrity of this planet and the magnificent life it harbors.

Questions for Discussion and Your Reading Journal

1. What are some of the ecological consequences of current policies and practices in various parts of the world?
2. Why is the preservation of forests so important ?
3. The text is accompanied by a simple triangular illustration. What is the purpose of the illustration?
4. Make an abbreviated list (in your own words) of the bulleted steps necessary for ecological protection. What actions will be necessary to complete each of the steps?
5. What are "NGOs"? Why are they so important to Wilson's solution?

WAR AND PEACE

CHARLES DARWIN

Charles Darwin (1809–1882) was a geologist and biologist, born in Shrewsbury, England. His father was a physician; and his grandfather was a poet, philosopher, and naturalist. Darwin studied medicine at Edinburgh University but changed direction after a short time and prepared to be a clergyman instead. His interest in science did not diminish, however, and he left England to go on a 5-year scientific expedition to the Pacific coast.

Darwin's research as a naturalist on this expedition formed the basis for his treatise On the Origin of Species by Means of Natural Selection, *which was published in 1859. Although several European scientists were formulating similar theories at the same time, Darwin became known as the founder of the theory of evolution because his writings on the subject were the most widely read. This theory has been one of the most influential of the last two centuries, both for scientific and cultural reasons.*

When the book first came out, a large part of its readership was outraged; they believed his theory contradicted the biblical account of how God created life. The controversy continues to this day. Some schools have insisted that Darwin's theory be discounted or studied in conjunction with the biblical description of creation. Most contemporary science curriculum, however, presents Darwin's theory as a fundamental part of understanding how life on Earth has evolved over time.

Darwin posited that animals evolve over generations by a natural process of selection. The characteristics of the fittest members of a species, because these are the most likely to breed, are passed on to the next generation. In the following essay from Darwin's On the Origin of Species, *the process of natural selection is described.*

Reading Rhetorically

Before reading this article, consider what you already know about Darwin and the theory of evolution. Most students' understanding of this topic comes not from the original source, Darwin's book, but from interpretations of that source by textbook writers and teachers. As you read, determine how the information in the text connects with what you already know. Think about the benefits of learning directly from a source, and consider the drawbacks, as well. Think also about his use of *logos*.

The Action of Natural Selection

1   In order to make it clear how, as I believe, natural selection acts, I must beg permission to give one or two imaginary illustrations. Let us take the case of a wolf, which preys on various animals, securing some by craft, some by strength, and some by fleetness; and let us suppose that the fleetest prey, a deer for instance, had from any change in the country increased in numbers, or that other prey had decreased in numbers, during that season of the year when the wolf is hardest pressed for food. I can under such circumstances see no reason to doubt that the swiftest and slimmest wolves would have the best chance for surviving, and so be preserved or selected—provided always that they retained strength to master their prey at this or at some other period of the year, when they might be compelled to prey on other animals. I can see no more reason to doubt this, than that man can improve the fleetness of his greyhounds by careful and methodical selection, or by that unconscious selection which results from each man trying to keep the best dogs without any thought of modifying the breed.

2   Even without any change in the proportional numbers of the animals on which our wolf preyed, a cub might be born with an innate tendency to pursue certain kinds of prey. Nor can this be thought very improbable; for we often observe great differences in the natural tendencies of our domestic animals; one cat, for instance, taking to catch rats, another mice; one cat, according to Mr. St. John, bringing home winged game, another hares or rabbits, and another hunting on marshy ground and almost nightly catching woodcocks or snipes. The tendency to catch rats rather than mice is known to be inherited. Now, if any slight innate change of habit or of structure benefited an individual wolf, it would have the best chance of surviving and of leaving offspring. Some of its young would probably inherit the same habits or structure, and by the repetition of this process, a new variety might be formed which would either supplant or coexist with the parent-form of wolf. Or, again, the wolves inhabiting a mountainous district, and those frequenting the lowlands, would naturally be forced to hunt different prey; and from the continued preservation of the individuals best fitted for the two sites, two varieties might slowly be formed. These varieties would cross and blend where they met; but to this subject of intercrossing we shall soon have to return. I may add, that, accord-

ing to Mr. Pierce, there are two varieties of the wolf inhabiting the Catskill Mountains in the United States, one with a light greyhound-like form, which pursues deer, and the other more bulky, with shorter legs, which more frequently attacks the shepherd's flocks.

Let us now take a more complex case. Certain plants excrete a sweet juice, apparently for the sake of eliminating something injurious from their sap: This is effected by glands at the base of the stipules in some Leguminosac, and at the back of the leaf of the common laurel. This juice, though small in quantity, is greedily sought by insects. Let us now suppose a little sweet juice or nectar to be excreted by the inner bases of the petals of a flower. In this case insects in seeking the nectar would get dusted with pollen, and would certainly often transport the pollen from one flower to the stigma of another flower. The flowers of two distinct individuals of the same species would thus get crossed; and the act of crossing, we have good reason to believe (as will hereafter be more fully alluded to), would produce very vigorous seedlings, which consequently would have the best chance of flourishing and surviving. Some of these seedlings would probably inherit the nectar-excreting power. Those individual flowers which had the largest glands or nectaries, and which excreted most nectar, would be oftenest visited by insects, and would be oftenest crossed; and so in the long-run would gain the upper hand. Those flowers, also, which had their stamens and pistils placed, in relation to the size and habits of the particular insects which visited them, so as to favor in any degree the transportal of their pollen from flower to flower, would likewise be favored or selected. We might have taken the case of insects visiting flowers for the sake of collecting pollen instead of nectar; and as pollen is formed for the sole object of fertilization, its destruction appears a simple loss to the plant; yet if a little pollen were carried, at first occasionally and then habitually, by the pollen-devouring insects from flower to flower, and a cross thus effected, although nine-tenths of the pollen were destroyed, it might still be a great gain to the plant; and those individuals which by us, might profit a bee or other insect, so that an individual so characterized would be able to obtain its food more quickly, and so have a better chance of living and leaving descendants. Its descendants would probably inherit a tendency to a similar slight deviation of structure. The tubes of the corollas of the common red and incarnate clovers (Trifolium pratense and incarnatum) do not on a hasty glance appear to differ in length; yet the hive-bee can easily suck the nectar out of the incarnate clover, but not out of the common red clover, which is visited by humble-bees alone; so that whole fields of the red clover offer in vain an abundant supply of precious nectar to the hive-bee. Thus it might be a great advantage to the hive-bee to have a slightly longer or differently constructed proboscis. On the other hand, I have found by experiment that the fertility of clover greatly depends on bees visiting and moving parts of the corolla, so as to push the pollen on to the stigmatic surface. Hence, again, if humble-bees were to become rare in any country, it might be a great advantage to the red clover to have a shorter or more deeply divided tube to its corolla, so that the hive-bee could visit its flowers. Thus I can understand how a flower and a bee might slowly become, either simultaneously or one after the other, modified and adapted in the most perfect manner to each other, by the continued preservation of individuals presenting mutual and slightly favorable deviations of structure.

4   I am well aware that this doctrine of natural selection, exemplified in the above imaginary instances, is open to the same objections which were at first urged against Sir Charles Lyell's[1] noble views on "the modern changes of the earth, as illustrative of geology"; but we now very seldom hear the action, for instance, of the coast-waves, called a trifling and insignificant cause, when applied to the excavation of gigantic valleys or to the formation of the longest line of inland cliffs. Natural selection can act only by the preservation and accumulation of infinitesimally small inherited modifications, each profitable to the preserved being; and as modern geology has almost banished such views as the excavation of a great valley by a single diluvial wave, so will natural selection, if it be a true principle, banish the belief of the continued creation of new organic beings, or of any great and sudden modification in their structure.

---

[1]Sir Charles Lyell (1797–1875) English geologist who completely revolutionized the prevailing ideas about the age of the earth. [Ed. note.]

Questions for Discussion and Your Reading Journal

1. Two of the articles that appear earlier in the chapter discuss how insects and bacteria mutate and thus evolve within a very short span of time. The description of evolution presented here, however, deals with relatively large animals. Discuss the reasons for the difference between the evolution of bacteria and insects and that of larger animals.

2. What might be Darwin's purpose in writing this article? Who is the intended audience?

3. Outline the structure of the article. How does the organization of the article help to persuade the reader of the validity of Darwin's theory regarding natural selection?

4. What is "natural selection" (Paragraph 1)? How do the examples of the wolf and deer help to explain this concept? What other examples does Darwin use? How do those illustrations add to your understanding of the concept?

5. Explain the point Darwin is making in the last paragraph. How is this point supported?

GEORGE E. SIMPSON

George E. Simpson (1904–1998) was born in Knoxville, Iowa, on October 4, 1904. He received his Ph.D. from the University of Pennsylvania in 1934. After teaching at Temple University and at Pennsylvania State University, he went to Oberlin College and became a professor of sociology and anthropology. Simpson wrote over 60 books and articles, including Black Religion in the New World *(1978). He received numer-*

ous honors and awards for his work. Among these was the Honorary Doctor of Humane Letters from Oberlin College (1976).

In "Early Social Darwinism" (1959) George Simpson discusses the application of Darwin's theories to human culture. The idea of the "survival of the fittest" is applied to society to explain why some people attain power and wealth while others are the victims of poverty and hunger. The Social Darwinists use this application of Darwin's theories to argue in favor of unrestricted economic competition and imperialism. Margaret Mead, however, takes an opposing view in the reading that follows this one: "Warfare: An Invention—Not a Biological Necessity."

Reading Rhetorically

It is important to note that the author himself, George Simpson, is not explicitly identified from this text to be in support of Social Darwinism. Many times authors write about individuals and ideas with which they do not agree. The degree to which Simpson himself was a proponent of the ideology of Social Darwinism is a current subject of debate among scholars.

Distinguishing between the points of view of the writer and the person being written about is the job of the critical reader. As you read about Social Darwinists and Social Darwinism, look for clues to his *ethos,* and also clues that indicate how the writer's perspective might be different from or similar to that of his subjects. Pay particular attention to the introduction and conclusion, which are commonly places where writers express either a general or a personal response to their subjects. Do these parts of this text reveal anything important about Simpson's own views? When you are finished reading, decide how much you can infer about Simpson and his personal ideology.

Early Social Darwinism

The application of Darwin's principle of natural selection to human society, with special emphasis on competition and struggle, became known as "Social Darwinism." This doctrine, congenial to the intellectual climate of the end of the nineteenth century, was endorsed by the advocates of unrestricted competition in private enterprise, the colonial expansionists, and the opponents of voluntary social change. Among others, Ernest Haeckel[1] provided scientific sanction for this point of view:

> The theory of selection teaches that in human life, as in animal and plant life, everywhere and at all times, only a small and chosen minority can exist and flourish, while the enormous majority starve and perish miserably and more or less prematurely. . . . The cruel and merciless struggle

[1]Ernest Haeckel (1834–1919) German biologist and natural philosopher. [Ed. note.]

for existence which rages through living nature, and in the course of nature must rage, this unceasing and inexorable competition of all living creatures is an incontestable fact; only the picked minority of the qualified fittest is in a position to resist it successfully, while the great majority of the competitors must necessarily perish miserably. We may profoundly lament this tragical state of things, but we can neither controvert nor alter it. "Many are called, but few are chosen." This principle of selection is as far as possible from democratic, on the contrary it is aristocratic in the strictest sense of the word.

2   Herbert Spencer and William Graham Sumner were prominent in advancing the doctrine of the social Darwinists. Despite differences in their philosophies, both saw the poor as the "unfit." Because they are the result of the operations of the laws of evolution, they cannot be assisted and efforts to help them through legislation, public charity, and social reconstruction are evil. According to Spencer, "The whole effort of nature is to get rid of them, and make room for better . . . If they are sufficiently complete to live, they do live, and its is well they should live. If they are not sufficiently complete to live, they die, and it is best they should die."

3   Although Darwin pointed out that militarism and war occasion reverse selection by exposing the biologically soundest young men to early death or preventing them from marrying during the prime of life and, at the same time, by providing those with poorer constitutions with greater opportunity to marry and propagate their kind, many of the social Darwinists praised war as a means of furthering social progress. An English scientist, Karl Pearson, wrote: "History shows me one way and one way only, in which a high state of civilization has been produced, namely the struggle of race with race, and the survival of the physically and mentally fitter race. If men want to know whether the lower races of man can evolve a higher type, I fear the only course is to leave them to fight it out among themselves."

4   Nineteenth century imperialists, calling upon Darwinism in defense of the subjugation of "backward" races, could point to *The Origin of Species* which had referred in its sub-title to *The Preservation of Favored Races in the Struggle for Life.* Darwin had been talking about pigeons but they saw no reason why his theories should not apply to men, and the whole spirit of the naturalistic world view seemed to call for a vigorous and unrelenting thoroughness in the application of biological concepts. Darwinian theory was utilized to justify the conflicts of rival empires, the ententes and the alliances of the "balance of power." Bismarck in Germany, Chamberlain in England, and Theodore Roosevelt in the United States found in social Darwinism a sanction for their theories of force and expansion.

5   Another aspect of social Darwinism at the turn of the century was the eugenics movement. Like other early social Darwinists, the eugenicists equated the "fit" with the upper classes and the "unfit" with the poor. Believing that disease, poverty, and crime are due largely to heredity, they warned against the high reproductive rates of the lower classes.

SOCIAL DARWINISM IN RECENT YEARS

Adolf Hitler's racism and Nazism have been called perversions of Darwinism. 6
Hitler's virulent doctrines were the culmination of a half-century of social Darwinistic thinking in Germany. One of his most influential immediate predecessors was General Freidrich von Bernhardi, who said of the Germans that "no
nation on the face of the globe is so able to grasp and appropriate all the elements of culture, to add to them from the stores of its own spiritual endowment, and to give back to mankind richer gifts than it received." Bernhardi
glorified war as a biological necessity, as the greatest factor in the furtherance
of culture and power, and claimed that the Germans could fulfill their great
and urgent duty toward civilization only by the sword.

Hitler's doctrines are so well-known that extended reference to them here 7
is unnecessary. According to *Mein Kampf,* the "Aryan" alone "furnishes the
great building-stones and plans for all human progress." The Aryan had subjugated "lower races" and made them do his will, the Jew's "intellect is never
constructive," "the mingling, of blood . . . is the sole reason for the dying-out
of old cultures," and hyperindividualism had cheated Germany of world domination and a peace "founded on the victorious sword of a lordly people. . . ." Hitlerism represents the most extreme variety of social Darwinism
and the one which has had the most powerful effects on the destinies of modern peoples.

CONCLUSION

One hundred years after the publication of *The Origin of Species,* and eighty- 8
eight years after the appearance of *The Descent of Man,* natural selection
remains an important concept in biology, anthropology, sociology, even in
international relations. Modern man is subject to selection, natural and artificial. If this were not so, all human genotypes would produce surviving children
in the same ratio as the occurrence of these genotypes in existing populations.
Today the adaptive value of cooperation is more widely acknowledged and the
role of ruthless aggression as a factor in the evolution of man, society, and culture is given smaller significance. Social Darwinistic thinking has not disappeared, but increasingly the "nature, red in tooth and claw" version of natural selection is regarded as an outdated brand of Darwinism.

Questions for Discussion and Your Reading Journal

1. Who is the audience of this text? What is its purpose?
2. Outline the pattern of organization. How does the organization of the article reflect its purpose?
3. What is Social Darwinism? Who were its early proponents? Discuss their
   theories about human nature.

4. According to the Social Darwinist, why do humans compete with one another?

5. Do you agree with the Social Darwinists' view that human beings are naturally warlike? Defend your answer.

MARGARET MEAD

Margaret Mead (1901–1979) was a cultural anthropologist and a popularizer of cultural anthropology. She did much of her fieldwork in the South Pacific; her dissertation, "Coming of Age in Samoa" (1928), in which she demonstrates that adolescence is not a time of strife and difficulties in all cultures, made her famous.

Mead's "Warfare: An Invention—Not a Biological Necessity" (1940) was intended to educate the English-speaking world about nonaggressive cultures, questioning the assumption of Social Darwinists like those discussed in the previous article that war is an inevitable part of human experience.

Reading Rhetorically

This essay, as indicated by its title, implies a choice between two alternatives: either it is human nature to be warlike, or it is not. Ponder, as you read, if there are alternatives to this "one or the other" approach to the topic. Sometimes choices between two things can be called "false dichotomies" because they discount points of view beyond the two that are being contrasted. Other times, answering a question with a "yes" or a "no" is the most sensible approach. Determine whether you think the different points of view reflected in this article are the only two sensible alternatives.

As you read this essay, think about why Mead wants to persuade readers that war is an invention, and what political position such a belief would support. How does she make use of *logos* in her argument? Think about applications of this argument to current wars and politicians, and which current political figures might benefit from a public perception of war as an inevitable part of human nature.

Warfare: An Invention—
Not a Biological Necessity

1   Is war a biological necessity, a sociological inevitability or just a bad invention? Those who argue for the first view endow man with such pugnacious instincts that some outlet in aggressive behavior is necessary if man is to reach full human stature. It was this point of view which lay back of William

James's[1] famous essay, "The Moral Equivalent of War," in which he tried to retain the warlike virtues and channel them in new directions. A similar point of view has lain back of the Soviet Union's attempt to make competition between groups rather than between individuals. A basic, competitive, aggressive, warring human nature is assumed, and those who wish to outlaw war or outlaw competitiveness merely try to find new and less socially destructive ways in which these biologically given aspects of man's nature can find expression. Then there are those who take the second view: Warfare is the inevitable concomitant of the development of the state, the struggle for land and natural resources of class societies springing, not from the nature of man, but from the nature of history. War is nevertheless inevitable unless we change our social system and outlaw classes, the struggle for power, and possessions; and in the event of our success warfare would disappear, as a symptom vanishes when the disease is cured.

One may hold a compromise position between these two extremes; one may   2 claim that all aggression springs from the frustration of man's biologically determined drives and that, since all forms of culture are frustrating, it is certain each new generation will be aggressive and the aggression will find its natural and inevitable expression in race war, class war, nationalistic war, and so on.

All three positions are very popular today among those who think seriously   3 about the problems of war and its possible prevention, but I wish to urge another point of view, less defeatist perhaps than the first and third, and more accurate than the second: That is, that warfare, by which I mean organized conflict between two groups as *groups*, in which each group puts an army (even if the army is only fifteen Pygmies) into the field to fight and kill, if possible, some of the members of the army of the other group—that warfare of this sort is an invention like any other of the inventions in terms of which we order our lives, such as writing, marriage, cooking our food instead of eating it raw, trial by jury, or burial of the dead, and so on. Some of this list any one will grant are inventions: Trial by jury is confined to very limited portions of the globe; we know that there are tribes that do not bury their dead but instead expose or cremate them; and we know that only part of the human race has had a knowledge of writing as its cultural inheritance. But, whenever a way of doing things is found universally, such as the use of fire or the practice of some form of marriage, we tend to think at once that it is not an invention at all but an attribute of humanity itself. And yet even such universals as marriage and the use of fire are inventions like the rest, very basic ones, inventions which were perhaps necessary if human history was to take the turn it has taken, but nevertheless inventions. At some point in his social development man was undoubtedly without the institution of marriage or the knowledge of the use of fire.

The case of warfare is much clearer because there are peoples even today   4 who have no warfare. Of these the Eskimo are perhaps the most conspicuous example, but the Lepchas of Sikkim are an equally good one.[2] Neither of these

---

[1]William James (1842–1910) American philosopher and psychologist. [Ed. note.]

[2]Sikkim A small kingdom between India and Tibet that became an Indian state in 1975. [Ed. note.]

peoples understands war, not even defensive warfare. The idea of warfare is lacking, and this idea is as essential to carrying on war as an alphabet or a syllabary is to writing. But whereas the Lepchas are a gentle, unquarrelsome people, and the advocates of other points of view might argue that they are not full human beings or that they had never been frustrated and so had no aggression to expend in warfare, the Eskimo case gives no such possibility of interpretation. The Eskimo are not a mild and meek people; many of them are turbulent and troublesome. Fights, theft of wives, murder, cannibalism occur among them—all outbursts of passionate men goaded by desire or intolerable circumstance. Here are men faced with hunger, men faced with loss of their wives, men faced with the threat of extermination by other men, and here are orphan children, growing up miserably with no one to care for them, mocked and neglected by those about them. The personality necessary for war, the circumstances necessary to goad men to desperation are present, but there is no war. When a traveling Eskimo entered a settlement he might have to fight the strongest man in the settlement to establish his position among them, but this was a test of strength and bravery, not war. The idea of warfare, of one *group* organizing against another *group* to maim and wound and kill them was absent. And without that idea passions might rage but there was no war.

5   But, it may be argued, isn't this because the Eskimo have such a low and undeveloped form of social organization? They own no land, they move from place to place, camping, it is true, season after season on the same site, but this is not something to fight for as the modern nations of the world fight for land and raw materials. They have no permanent possessions that can be looted, no towns that can be burned. They have no social classes to produce stress and strains within the society which might force it to go to war outside. Doesn't the absence of war among the Eskimo, while disproving the biological necessity of war, just go to confirm the point that it is the state of development of the society which accounts for war, and nothing else?

6   We find the answer among the Pygmy peoples of the Andaman Islands in the Bay of Bengal. The Andamans also represent an exceedingly low level of society; they are a hunting and food-gathering people; they live in tiny hordes without any class stratification; their houses are simpler than the snow houses of the Eskimo. But they knew about warfare. The army might contain only fifteen determined pygmies marching in a straight line, but it was the real thing none the less. Tiny army met tiny army in open battle, blows were exchanged, casualties suffered, and the state of warfare could only be concluded by a peace-making ceremony.

7   Similarly, among the Australian aborigines, who built no permanent dwellings but wandered from water hole to water hole over their almost desert country, warfare—and rules of "international law"—were highly developed. The student of social evolution will seek in vain for his obvious causes of war, struggle for lands, struggle for power of one group over another, expansion of population, need to divert the minds of a populace restive under tyranny, or even the ambition of a successful leader to enhance his own prestige. All are absent, but warfare as a practice remained, and men engaged in it and killed one another in the course of a war because killing is what is done in wars.

From instances like these it becomes apparent that an inquiry into the   8
causes of war misses the fundamental point as completely as does an insistence
upon the biological necessity of war. If a people have an idea of going to war
and the idea that war is the way in which certain situations, defined within
their society, are to be handled, they will sometimes go to war. If they are a
mild and unaggressive people, like the Pueblo Indians, they may limit themselves to defensive warfare; but they will be forced to think in terms of war
because there are peoples near them who have warfare as a pattern, and offensive, raiding, pillaging warfare at that. When the pattern of warfare is known,
people like the Pueblo Indians will defend themselves, taking advantage of
their natural defenses, the *mesa* village site, and people like the Lepchas, having no natural defenses and no idea of warfare, will merely submit to the
invader. But the essential point remains the same. There is a way of behaving
which is known to a given people and labeled as an appropriate form of
behavior. A bold and warlike people like the Sioux or the Maori may label
warfare as desirable as well as possible;[3] a mild people like the Pueblo Indians
may label warfare as undesirable; but to the minds of both peoples the possibility of warfare is present. Their thoughts, their hopes, their plans are oriented about this idea, that warfare may be selected as the way to meet some
situation.

So simple peoples and civilized peoples, mild peoples and violent, assertive   9
peoples, will all go to war if they have the invention, just as those peoples who
have the custom of dueling will have duels and peoples who have the pattern
of vendetta will indulge in vendetta. And, conversely, peoples who do not
know of dueling will not fight duels, even though their wives are seduced and
their daughters ravished; they may on occasion commit murder but they will
not fight duels. Cultures which lack the idea of the vendetta will not meet
every quarrel in this way. A people can use only the forms it has. So the Balinese have their special way of dealing with a quarrel between two individuals:[4]
if the two feel that the causes of quarrel are heavy they may go and register
their quarrel in the temple before the gods, and, making offerings, they may
swear never to have anything to do with each other again. Under the Dutch
government they registered such mutual "not-speaking" with the Dutch government officials. But in other societies, although individuals might feel as full
of animosity and as unwilling to have any further contact as do the Balinese,
they cannot register their quarrel with the gods and go on quietly about their
business because registering quarrels with the gods is not an invention of
which they know.

Yet, if it be granted that warfare is after all an invention, it may neverthe-   10
less be an invention that lends itself to certain types of personality, to the exi-
gent needs of autocrats, to the expansionist desires of crowded peoples, to the
desire for plunder and rape and loot which is engendered by a dull and frustrating life. What, then, can we say of this congruence between warfare and its

---

[3]**Maori** The aboriginal people of New Zealand. [Ed. note.]
[4]**Balinese** The people of Bali, a province of Indonesia. [Ed. note.]

uses? If it is a form which fits so well, is not this congruence the essential point? But even here the primitive material causes us to wonder, because there are tribes who go to war merely for glory, having no quarrel with the enemy, suffering from no tyrant within their boundaries, anxious neither for land nor loot nor women, but merely anxious to win prestige which within that tribe has been declared obtainable only by war and without which no young man can hope to win his sweetheart's smile of approval. But if, as was the case with the Bush Negroes of Dutch Gulana,[5] it is artistic ability which is necessary to win a girl's approval, the same young man would have to be carving rather than going out on a war party.

11   In many parts of the world, war is a game in which the individual can win counters—counters which bring him prestige in the eyes of his own sex or of the opposite sex; he plays for these counters as he might, in our society, strive for a tennis championship. Warfare is a frame for such prestige-seeking merely because it calls for the display of certain skills and certain virtues; all of these skills—riding straight, shooting straight, dodging the missiles of the enemy and sending one's own straight to the mark—can be equally well exercised in some other framework and, equally, the virtues—endurance, bravery, loyalty, steadfastness—can be displayed in other contexts. The tie-up between proving oneself a man and proving this by a success in organized killing is due to a definition which many societies have made of manliness. And often, even in those societies which counted success in warfare a proof of human worth, strange turns were given to the idea, as when the Plains Indians gave their highest awards to the man who touched a live enemy rather than to the man who brought in a scalp—from a dead enemy—because killing a man was less risky. Warfare is just an invention known to the majority of human societies by which they permit their young men either to accumulate prestige or avenge their honor or acquire loot or wives or slaves or sago lands or cattle or appease the blood lust of their gods or the restless souls of the recently dead. It is just an invention, older and more widespread than the jury system, but none the less an invention.

12   But, once we have said this, have we said anything at all? Despite a few instances, dear to the hearts of controversialists, of the loss of the useful arts, once an invention is made which proves congruent with human needs or social forms, it tends to persist. Grant that war is an invention, that it is not a biological necessity nor the outcome of certain special types of social forms, still, once the invention is made, what are we to do about it? The Indian who had been subsisting on the buffalo for generations because with his primitive weapons he could slaughter only a limited number of buffalo did not return to his primitive weapons when he saw that the white man's more efficient weapons were exterminating the buffalo. A desire for the white man's cloth may mortgage the South Sea Islander to the white man's plantation, but he does not return to making bark cloth, which would have left him free. Once an invention is known and accepted, men do not easily relinquish it. The

---

[5]**Dutch Gulana** Formerly Surinam in northern South America. [Ed. note.]

skilled workers may smash the first steam looms which they feel are to be their undoing, but they accept them in the end, and no movement which has insisted upon the mere abandonment of usable inventions has ever had much success. Warfare is here, as part of our thought; the deeds of warriors are immortalized in the words of our poets; the toys of our children are modeled upon the weapons of the soldier; the frame of reference within which our statesmen and our diplomats work always contains war. If we know that it is not inevitable, that it is due to historical accident that warfare is one of the ways in which we think of behaving, are we given any hope by that? What hope is there of persuading nations to abandon war, nations so thoroughly imbued with the idea that resort to war is, if not actually desirable and noble, at least inevitable whenever certain defined circumstances arise?

In answer to this question I think we might turn to the history of other 13 social inventions, inventions which must once have seemed as firmly entrenched as warfare. Take the methods of trial which preceded the jury system: ordeal and trial by combat. Unfair, capricious, alien as they are to our feeling today, they were once the only methods open to individuals accused of some offense. The invention of trial by jury gradually replaced these methods until only witches, and finally not even witches, had to resort to the ordeal. And for a long time the jury system seemed the one best and finest method of settling legal disputes, but today new inventions, trial before judges only or before commissions, are replacing the jury system. In each case the old method was replaced by a new social invention; the ordeal did not go out because people thought it unjust or wrong, it went out because a method more congruent with the institutions and feelings of the period was invented. And, if we despair over the way in which war seems such an ingrained habit of most of the human race, we can take comfort from the fact that a poor invention will usually give place to a better invention.

For this, two conditions at least are necessary. The people must recognize 14 the defects of the old invention, and some one must make a new one. Propaganda against warfare, documentation of its terrible cost in human suffering and social waste, these prepare the ground by teaching people to feel that warfare is a defective social institution. There is further needed a belief that social invention is possible and the invention of new methods which will render warfare as out-of-date as the tractor is making the plow, or the motor car the horse and buggy. A form of behavior becomes out-of-date only when something else takes its place, and in order to invent forms of behavior which will make war obsolete, it is a first requirement to believe that an invention is possible.

Questions for Discussion and Your Reading Journal

1. Who is the audience for the essay? (Reread the headnote.) How might the author's awareness of her audience affect her content?
2. What do you consider to be the purpose of the essay? Outline the structure of the argument. Discuss how each point builds on the last.
3. The essay begins with a question. What is Mead's answer? How do you know?

4. Which peoples of the world have no warfare? Why is this important to Mead's thesis?

5. What points does Mead concede to her assumed opposition? Is her argument weakened by these concessions? Explain.

6. What other points does Mead present to prove that war is an invention?

7. If war is a bad invention, why does it persist?

8. Do you think it is possible or even desirable to end war? Why or why not?

JOHN CONNOR

The two short newspaper articles that follow, "The U.S. Was Right" by John Connor and "The U.S. Was Wrong" by Gar Alperovitz, appeared in the New York Times *in August 1985, 40 years after the atomic bomb was dropped on Hiroshima, Japan. Connor, who supports the U.S. military action, worked out of General Douglas MacArthur's headquarters in Tokyo during the period just after World War II. Alperovitz, who argues against the bombing, is an economist and the author of* Atomic Diplomacy: Hiroshima and Potsdam.

President Harry S. Truman's decision to drop the atomic bomb on the two Japanese cities continues to be one of the most controversial issues of the 20th century. Each year on the anniversary of the dropping of the bomb on Hiroshima, debates and discussions are held on the topic in universities all over the world. Although the bombing happened more than half a century ago, historians and researchers continue to delve into every aspect of its record.

The facts remain that on August 6, 1945, an atomic bomb was dropped on Hiroshima, killing at least 140,000 people. On August 9, a second bomb, which killed 70,000 people, was dropped on Nagasaki.

Reading Rhetorically

The arguments of both authors are written using a chronological account of the events interspersed with commentary that interprets the events. Examine the use of *logos*, especially the ways in which the factual details are presented in each essay. The way a fact is presented can affect how the reader reacts to it. Beyond that, the choice of facts that a writer includes or excludes can affect the reception of a text. Contrast the two articles in terms of which facts are included and how they are presented. Which facts included by Connor are left out by Alperovitz, and vice versa?

Another element of persuasion employed by both authors is careful word choice. "Diction" is the technical term for word choice. Examine the diction of each of the articles. Which words in each article provoke an emotional response? Asking these kinds of questions as you read will help you focus on the merit of the authors' arguments rather than being persuaded by the emotional impact (*pathos*) of their writerly choices.

The U.S. Was Right

Forty years ago this week in Hiroshima: the dreadful flash, the wrist watches 1
fused forever at 8:16 A.M. The question still persists: Should we have
dropped the atomic bomb?

History seldom gives decisive answers, but recently declassified documents 2
point to a clear judgment: Yes, it was necessary to drop the bomb. It was
needed to end the war. It saved countless American and Japanese lives.

In the early summer of 1945, Japan, under tight control of the militarists, 3
was an implacable, relentless adversary. The Japanese defended territory with
a philosophy we had seldom encountered: Soldiers were taught that surrender
was worse than death. There was savage resistance to the end in battle after
battle.

Of the 5,000-man Japanese force at Tarawa in November 1943, only 17 4
remained alive when the island was taken. When Kwajalein was invaded in
February 1944, Japanese officers slashed at American tanks with samurai
swords; their men held grenades against the sides of tanks in an effort to dis-
able them.

On Saipan, less than 1,000 of the 32,000 defending Japanese troops sur- 5
vived. Casualties among the Japanese-ruled civilians on the island numbered
10,000. Parents bashed their babies' brains out on rocky cliff sides, then
leaped to their deaths. Others cut each other's throats; children threw grenades
at each other. America suffered 17,000 casualties.

Just 660 miles southeast of Tokyo, Iwo Jima's garrison was told to defend 6
the island as if it were Tokyo itself. They did. In the first day of fighting, there
were more American casualties than during "D-Day" in Normandy. At Okinawa—only 350 miles south of Kyushu—more than 110,000 Japanese soldiers and 100,000 civilians were killed. Kamikaze attacks cost the Navy alone
some 10,000 casualties. The Army and Marines lost more than 50,000 men.

In the early summer of 1945, the invasion of Japan was imminent and 7
everyone in the Pacific was apprehensive. The apprehension was justified,
because our intelligence was good: With a system code named "Magic," it had
penetrated Japanese codes even before Pearl Harbor, "Magic" would play a
crucial role in the closing days of the war.

Many have maintained that the bomb was unnecessary because in the 8
closing days of the war intercepted Japanese diplomatic messages disclosed a
passionate desire for peace. While that is true, it is irrelevant. The Japanese
Government remained in the hands of the militarists: *Their* messages indicated
a willingness to fight to the death.

Japanese planes, gasoline and ammunition had been hoarded for the com- 9
ing invasion. More than 5,000 aircraft had been hidden everywhere to be used
as suicide weapons, with only enough gas in their tanks for a one-way trip to
the invasion beaches. More than two million men were moving into positions
to defend the home islands.

The object was to inflict such appalling losses that the Americans would 10
agree to a treaty more favorable than unconditional surrender. The Army

Chief of Staff, Gen. George C. Marshall, estimated potential American casualties as high as a million.

11   The willingness of the Japanese to die was more than empty bravado. Several of my colleagues at Kyushu University told me that as boys of 14 or 15, they were being trained to meet the Americans on the beaches with little more than sharpened bamboo spears. They had no illusions about their chances for survival.

12   The Potsdam declaration calling for unconditional surrender was beamed to Japan on July 27. On July 30, the Americans were informed that Japan would officially ignore the ultimatum. A week later, the bomb was dropped.

13   Could we not have warned the Japanese in advance, critics asked, and dropped a demonstration bomb? That alternative was vetoed on the grounds the bomb might not work, or that the plane carrying it might be shot down. Moreover, it is questionable how effective a demonstration bomb might have been. The militarists could have imposed a news blackout as complete as the one imposed after the disastrous battle of Midway and continued on their suicidal course. That is exactly what happened at Hiroshima. Within hours, the Japanese Government sent in a team of scientists to investigate the damage. Their report was immediately suppressed and was not made public until many years after the war.

14   After midnight on Aug. 10, a protracted debate took place in an air-raid shelter deep inside the Imperial Palace. The military insisted that Japan should hold out for terms far better than unconditional surrender. The peace faction favored accepting the Potsdam declaration, providing that the Emperor would be retained. The two factions remained at an impasse. At 2 A.M., Prime Minister Kantaro Suzuki asked the Emperor to decide. In a soft, deliberate voice, the Emperor expressed his great longing for peace. The war had ended.

15   It was impossible, in August 1945, to predict the awesome shadow the bomb would cast on humanity. The decision to drop it seemed both simple and obvious. Without it, the militarists might have prevailed, an invasion ordered. And the loss of both American and Japanese lives would have been awesome.

16   The atomic bomb accomplished what it had been designed to do. It ended the war.

GAR ALPEROVITZ

The U.S. Was Wrong

17   Though it has not yet received broad public attention, there exists overwhelming historical evidence that President Harry S Truman knew he could almost certainly end World War II without using the atomic bomb: The United States had cracked the Japanese code, and a stream of documents released over the last 40 years show that Mr. Truman had two other options.

The first option was to clarify America's surrender terms to assure the [18] Japanese we would not remove their Emperor. The second was simply to await the expected Soviet declaration of war—which, United States intelligence advised, appeared likely to end the conflict on its own.

Instead, Hiroshima was bombed on Aug. 6, 1945, and Nagasaki on Aug. 9. [19] The planned date for the Soviet Union's entry into the war against Japan was Aug. 8.

The big turning point was the Emperor's continuing June–July decision to [20] open surrender negotiations through Moscow. Top American officials—and, most critically, the President—understood the move was extraordinary: Mr. Truman's secret diaries, lost until 1978, call the key intercepted message "the telegram from Jap Emperor asking for peace."

Other documents—among them newly discovered secret memorandums [21] from William J. Donovan, director of the Office of Strategic Services—show that Mr. Truman was personally advised of Japanese peace initiatives through Swiss and Portuguese channels as early as three months before Hiroshima. Moreover, Mr. Truman told several officials he had no objection in principle to Japan's keeping the Emperor, which seemed the only sticking point.

American leaders were sure that if he so chose "the Mikado could stop the [22] war with a royal word"—as one top Presidential aide put it. Having decided to use the bomb, however, Mr. Truman was urged by Secretary of State James F. Byrnes not to give assurances to the Emperor before the weapon had been demonstrated.

Additional official records, including minutes of top-level White House [23] planning meetings, show the President was clearly advised of the importance of a Soviet declaration of war. It would pull the rug out from under Japanese military leaders who were desperately hoping the powerful Red Army would stay neutral.

Gen. George C. Marshall in mid-June told Mr. Truman that "the impact [24] of Russian entry on the already hopeless Japanese may well be the decisive action levering them into capitulation at that time or shortly thereafter if we land."

A month later, the American-British Combined Intelligence Staffs advised [25] their chiefs of the critical importance of a Red Army attack. As the top British general, Sir Hastings Ismay summarized the conclusions for Prime Minister Winston Churchill: "If and when Russia came into the war against Japan, the Japanese would probably wish to get out on almost any terms short of the dethronement of the Emperor."

Mr. Truman's private diaries also record his understanding of the signifi- [26] cance of this option. On July 17, 1945, when Stalin confirmed that the Red Army would march, Mr. Truman privately noted: "Fini Japs when that comes about."

There was plenty of time: The American invasion of Japan was not sched- [27] uled until the spring of 1946. Even a preliminary landing on the island Kyushu was still three months in the future.

Gen. Dwight D. Eisenhower, appalled that the bomb would be used in these [28] circumstances, urged Mr. Truman and Secretary of War Henry L. Stimson not to drop it. In his memoirs, he observed that weeks before Hiroshima, Japan had been seeking a way to surrender. "It wasn't necessary," he said in a later interview, "to hit them with that awful thing."

29   The one man who presided over the Joint Chiefs of Staff, Adm. William D. Leahy, was equally shocked: "The use of this barbarous weapon at Hiroshima and Nagasaki was of no material assistance in our war against Japan. The Japanese were already defeated and ready to surrender."

30   Why, then, was the bomb used?

31   American leaders rejected the most obvious option—simply waiting for the Red Army attack—out of political, not military, concerns.

32   As the diary of one official put it, they wanted to end the war before Moscow got "in so much on the kill." Secretary of the Navy James V. Forrestal's diaries record that Mr. Byrnes "was most anxious to get the Japanese affair over with before the Russians got in."

33   United States leaders had also begun to think of the atomic bomb as what Secretary Stimson termed the "master card" of diplomacy. President Truman postponed his Potsdam meeting with Stalin until July 17, 1945—one day after the first successful nuclear test—to be sure the atomic bomb would strengthen his hand before confronting the Soviet leader on the shape of a postwar settlement.

34   To this day, we do not know with absolute certainty Mr. Truman's personal attitudes on several key issues. Yet we do know that his most important adviser, Secretary of State Byrnes, was convinced that dropping the bomb would serve crucial long-range diplomatic purposes.

35   As one atomic scientist, Leo Szilard, observed: "Mr. Byrnes did not argue that it was necessary to use the bomb against the cities of Japan in order to win the war. Mr. Byrnes' . . . view [was] that our possessing and demonstrating the bomb would make Russia more manageable."

Questions for Discussion and Your Reading Journal

1. What was the purpose of each of the two articles? Who are the writers trying to persuade? (Reread the headnote.)
2. List the arguments made by Connor. Then list the arguments made by Alperovitz. Determine whether each argument is basically an appeal to reason or to emotion. Justify your categorization.
3. Which of the two articles do you find the more persuasive? Why?
4. What arguments might you add to Connor's essay? To Alperovitz's?

SIDNEY SHALETT

The following article by Sidney Shalett appeared in the New York Times *just after the first atomic bomb was dropped on Hiroshima, Japan, in August 1945. Shalett's celebratory, patriotic tone sharply contrasts that of Masuji Ibuse in his description of the event (found in the subsequent reading). The lack of details in Shalett's account results, at least in part, from U.S. government censorship of information regarding nuclear technology. Ibuse's description is a much more graphic rendering of the devastation that occurred. Those Americans alive during World War II who read accounts of the bombing written by journalists who were Shalett's contemporaries tend to see the use of the bomb as a necessary decision. Younger people, who have read more recently written accounts of the war, tend to be more skeptical and are more inclined to see other motivations at work.*

The issue has also set war veterans against scholars—the former are assumed to have an emotional investment in considering the act patriotic, while the latter are considered intellectuals who debate the event in the detachment of the ivory tower.

Reading Rhetorically

It is important for a reader to consider the time when a historical account of an event was written. A news story written right after the event occurred will undoubtedly be different in its emphasis and focus than one written many years later. Think about the advantages and disadvantages of reading an account written at the time of an event.

As you read this article, remember that it was written right after the bomb was dropped. A useful analogy for comparing Shalett's article with some of the others in this group may involve an examination of stories about the war in Iraq (in the year 2003). At the time it was begun, most news stories were uncritical of the war in Iraq and the motivations for starting it. Months later, however, news stories often tended to be critical of the decision to go to war.

It may also be useful to think about the particular style that characterizes newspaper stories. News stories tend to be organized in descending order of importance; that is, they start with the most important details and move on to less-important ones. The reason for using this organizational strategy is that newspaper readers often read only the beginning of a story, and they want the main ideas to be included there. Look at this article and determine the degree to which its organization is consistent with the pattern just described. Although the story is meant to convey factual information, look for any elements you might consider persuasive as well.

First Atomic Bomb Dropped on Japan

The White House and War Department announced today that an atomic [1] bomb, possessing more power than 20,000 tons of TNT, a destructive force equal to the load of 2,000 B-29s and more than 2,000 times the blast power of what previously was the world's most devastating bomb, had been dropped on Japan.

2   The announcement, first given to the world in utmost solemnity by President Truman, made it plain that one of the scientific landmarks of the century had been passed, and that the "age of atomic energy," which can be a tremendous force for the advancement of civilization as well as for destruction, was at hand.

3   At 10:45 o'clock this morning, a statement by the President was issued at the White House that sixteen hours earlier—about the time that citizens on the Eastern seaboard were sitting down to their Sunday suppers—an American plane had dropped the single atomic bomb on the Japanese city of Hiroshima, an important army center.

4   What happened at Hiroshima is not yet known. The War Department said it "as yet was unable to make an accurate report" because "an impenetrable cloud of dust and smoke" masked the target area from reconnaissance planes. The Secretary of War will release the story "as soon as accurate details of the results of the bombing become available."

5   But in a statement vividly describing the results of the first test of the atomic bomb in New Mexico, the War Department told how an immense steel tower had been "vaporized" by the tremendous explosion, how a 40,000-foot cloud rushed into the sky, and two observers were knocked down at a point 10,000 yards away. And President Truman solemnly warned:

> It was to spare the Japanese people from utter destruction that the ultimatum of July 26 was issued at Potsdam. Their leaders promptly rejected that ultimatum. If they do not now accept our terms, they may expect a ruin from the air the like of which has never been seen on this earth.

6   The President referred to the joint statement issued by the heads of the American, British and Chinese governments, in which terms of surrender were outlined to the Japanese and warning given that rejection would mean complete destruction of Japan's power to make war.

7   [The atomic bomb weighs about 400 pounds and is capable of utterly destroying a town, a representative of the British Ministry of Aircraft Production said in London, the United Press reported.]

8   What is this terrible new weapon, which the War Department also calls the "Cosmic Bomb"? It is the harnessing of the energy of the atom, which is the basic power of the universe. As President Truman said, "the force from which the sun draws its power has been loosed against those who brought war to the Far East."

9   The imagination-sweeping experiment in harnessing the power of the atom has been the most closely guarded secret of the war. America to date has spent nearly $2,000,000,000 in advancing its research. Since 1939, American, British and Canadian scientists have worked on it. The experiments have been conducted in the United States, both for reasons of achieving concentrated efficiency and for security; the consequences of having the material fall into the hands of the enemy, in case Great Britain should have been successfully invaded, were too awful for the Allies to risk.

10   All along, it has been a race with the enemy. Ironically enough, Germany started the experiments, but we finished them. Germany made the mistake of

expelling, because she was a "non-aryan," a woman scientist who held one of the keys to the mystery, and she made her knowledge available to those who brought it to the United States. Germany never quite mastered the riddle, and the United States, Secretary Stimson declared, is "convinced that Japan will not be in a position to use an atomic bomb in this war."

Not the slightest spirit of braggadocio is discernible either in the wording 11 of the official announcements or in the mien of the officials who gave out the news. There was an element of elation in the realization that we had perfected this devastating weapon for employment against an enemy who started the war and has told us she would rather be destroyed than surrender, but it was grim elation. There was sobering awareness of the tremendous responsibility involved.

Secretary Stimson said that this new weapon "should prove a tremendous 12 aid in the shortening of the war against Japan," and there were other responsible officials who privately thought that this was an extreme understatement and that Japan might find herself unable to stay in the war under the coming rain of atom bombs.

It was obvious that officials at the highest levels made the important deci- 13 sion to release news of the atomic bomb because of the psychological effect it may have in forcing Japan to surrender. However, there are some officials who feel privately it might have been well to keep this completely secret. Their opinion can be summed up in the comment by one spokesman: "Why bother with psychological warfare against an enemy that already is beaten and hasn't sense enough to quit and save herself from utter doom?"

No details were given on the plane that carried the bomb. Nor was it 14 stated whether the bomb was large or small. The President, however, said the explosive charge was "exceedingly small." It is known that tremendous force is packed into tiny quantities of the element that constitutes these bombs. Scientists, looking to the peacetime uses of atomic power envisage submarines, ocean liners and planes traveling around the world on a few pounds of the element. Yet, for various reasons, the bomb used against Japan could have been extremely large.

Hiroshima, first city on earth to be the target of the "Cosmic Bomb," is a 15 city of 318,000 which is—or was—a major quartermaster depot and port of embarkation for the Japanese. In addition to large military supply depots, it manufactured ordnance, mainly large guns and tanks, and machine tools and aircraft-ordnance parts.

President Truman grimly told the Japanese that "the end is not yet. In their 16 present form these bombs are now in production," he said, "and even more powerful forms are in development."

He sketched the story of how the late President Roosevelt and Prime Min- 17 ister Churchill agreed that it was wise to concentrate research in America, and how great secret cities sprang up in this country, where, at one time, 125,000 men and women labored to harness the atom. Even today more than 65,000 workers are employed.

"What has been done," he said, "is the greatest achievement of organized sci- 18 ence in history. We are now prepared to obliterate more rapidly and completely every productive enterprise the Japanese have above ground in any city. We shall destroy their docks, their factories and their communications. Let there be no mistake; we shall completely destroy Japan's power to make war."

19 The President emphasized that the atomic discoveries were so important, both for the war and for the peace, that he would recommend to Congress that it consider promptly establishing "an appropriate commission to control the production and use of atomic power within the United States."

20 "I shall give further consideration and make further recommendations to the Congress as to how atomic power can become a powerful and forceful influence toward the maintenance of world peace," he said.

21 Secretary Stimson called the atomic bomb "the culmination of years of herculean effort on the part of science and industry, working in cooperation with the military authorities." He promised that "improvements will be forthcoming shortly which will increase by several fold the present effectiveness."

22 "But more important for the long-range implications of this new weapon," he said, "is the possibility that another scale of magnitude will be developed after considerable research and development." The scientists are confident that over a period of many years atomic bombs may well be developed which will be very much more powerful than the atomic bombs now at hand.

23 (The plants which manufactured the atom bombs) were amazing phenomena in themselves. They grew into large, self-sustaining cities, employing, thousands upon thousands of workers. Yet, so close was the secrecy that not only were the citizens of the area kept in darkness about the nature of the project, but the workers themselves had only the sketchiest ideas—if any—as to what they were doing. This was accomplished, Mr. Stimson said, by "compartmentalizing" the work so "that no one had been given more information that was absolutely necessary to his particular job."

24 A special laboratory also has been set up near Santa Fe, N.M., under direction of Dr. J. Robert Oppenheimer of the University of California. Dr. Oppenheimer also supervised the first test of the atomic bomb on July 16, 1945. This took place in a remote section of the New Mexico desert lands, with a group of eminent scientists gathered, frankly fearful to witness the results of the invention which might turn out to be either the salvation or the Frankenstein's monster of the world.

25 "Atomic fission holds great promise for sweeping developments by which our civilization may be enriched when peace comes, but the overriding necessities of war have precluded the full exploration of peacetime applications of this new knowledge," Mr. Stimson said. "However, it appears inevitable that many useful contributions to the well-being of mankind will ultimately flow from these discoveries when the world situation makes it possible for science and industry to concentrate on these aspects."

26 Although warning that many economic factors will have to be considered "before we can say to what extent atomic energy will supplement coal, oil and water as fundamental sources of power," Mr. Stimson acknowledged that "we are at the threshold of a new industrial art which will take many years and much expenditure of money to develop."

The War Department gave this supplementary background on the development of the atomic bomb: 27

> The series of discoveries which led to the development of the atomic bomb started at the turn of the century when radioactivity became known to science. Prior to 1939, the scientific work in this field was world-wide, but more particularly so in the United States, the United Kingdom, Germany, France, Italy, and Denmark. One of Denmark's great scientists, Dr. Neils Bohr, a Nobel prize winner, was whisked from the grasp of the Nazis in his occupied homeland and later assisted in developing the atomic bomb.
>
> It is known that Germany worked desperately to solve the problem of controlling atomic energy.

Questions for Discussion and Your Reading Journal

1. Like the articles by Connor and Alperovitz, this article was written for a newspaper. Unlike those articles, which were "features" rather than news stories, this article was intended to report on a current event. Does the article answer the five Ws (who, what, when, where, and why) of journalistic writing? Describe those answers.
2. How might an article for a newspaper be organized differently from a magazine article? How do you account for the difference?
3. How does the solemnity of Truman's announcement contrast with the tone of the rest of the article?
4. Was the ultimatum offered for the sake of sparing the lives of Japanese citizens? What other motives might be involved?
5. No other nation besides the United States has ever used a nuclear weapon against another nation. How might this fact affect the attitudes of citizens of other nations toward the United States?
6. The author seems aware of the risk of a nuclear arms race and the possible annihilation of human life ("Frankenstein's monster"), as does Truman, who consequently sets up a commission. Are the benefits of nuclear technology worth the risks?
7. Discuss the anticipated positive outcomes of nuclear technology mentioned in the article. Remember that this article was written the day after the bomb was dropped.
8. What justifications do the President and the military officials offer for dropping the bomb?
9. Why isn't human destruction described? Consider Shalett's audience and purpose.

MASUJI IBUSE

Masuji Ibuse (1898–1993) was born into a family of farmers. He spent his childhood in the country near the city of Hiroshima. In 1917 Ibuse began studies at Waseda University in Tokyo, but he left without graduating.

Instead he started writing, and in the late 1920s his short stories began to gain public attention.

When Japan entered World War II, Ibuse was inducted into the military against his will and he served as a propaganda writer. Ibuse witnessed the annihilation of Hiroshima firsthand. While he did not write much during this period, his experiences became the subject of Black Rain *(1969), the novel from which the following excerpt was taken.*

Black Rain, *translated into English by John Bester in 1979, has become the world's best-known Japanese novel. It describes the experiences of a Japanese family in Hiroshima before, during, and after the dropping of the atomic bomb in 1945. This fictional account is based on Ibuse's own experience and his research of the stories of victims of the bombing. In the segment reprinted here, a couple, Shigematsu (husband) and Shigeko (wife), and their niece Yasuko are traveling through the atomic rubble in an absurd quest for normalcy. While Shigematsu and Shigeko have escaped extreme exposure to radiation, Yasuko, playing in the schoolyard during the bombing, was drenched by the "black rain" that fell on some areas of the city. Although some American officials at the time claimed that the black rain was harmless, Yasuko later in the novel becomes critically ill.*

This selection, with its first-person narrative description of the victims and the site of the bombing, presents a stark contrast to the news story by Shalett, as well as to the subsequent American high-school textbook representation of the event.

Reading Rhetorically

Some critics have asserted that Ibuse's novel is an attempt to humanize the inhuman. His fictional method combines sharp psychological insights with sympathetic descriptions of the thoughts and actions of ordinary people. Because of this method of development, the novel is distinct from newspaper and textbook accounts of the bombing. In his depiction of the most horrific act of violence the world has known, Ibuse weaves together destruction, humor, beauty, horror, and mild political critique.

As you read this excerpt, think of the limitations experienced by news and textbook writers that are not imposed on literary artists. In some ways a work of fiction may be truer than a nonfiction text. Also as you read, think about the issues raised in the section of Chapter 1 entitled "Reading and Writing About Literature and Art."

Excerpt from *Black Rain*

1   Still Shigematsu continued the transcription of his "Journal of the Bombing." This month, he reflected, was a succession of festivals. The Mass for Dead Insects had gone by already; the Rice-Planting Festival came on the

eleventh, and the Iris Festival, by the old lunar calendar, on the fourteenth. On the fifteenth there was the River Imp Festival, and on the twentieth the Bamboo-Cutting Festival. In all these countless little festivals he seemed to sense the affection that the peasants of the past, poor though they were, had lavished on each detail of their daily lives. And as he wrote on, and the horrors of that day came back to him ever more vividly, it seemed to him that in their very insignificance these farmers' festivals were something to be loved and cherished. . . .

We reached the streetcar stop at Kamiya-chō. The streetcar tracks crossed 2 each other here, and broken overhead wires and cables hung down in tangled profusion over the road. I had a terrifying feeling that one or the other of them must be live, since these were the same wires that one usually saw emitting fierce, bluish-white sparks. The occasional refugees who passed to and fro had the sense to crouch down as they passed beneath them.

I wanted to take the left-hand edge of the road across Aioi Bridge to 3 Sakan-chō, but the heat from the still-smoldering fires seemed likely to bar the way. I tried turning to the right, but a blast of hot air swept over me with an authority that would have made the bravest man waver, so I turned back again. Even so, as I approached a Western-style brick building, a great lump of glowing charcoal came hurtling down from what had been the window frames.

The only alternative was to go along the middle of the road. Since the 4 overhead wires were cut at various points, there was no likelihood of their being live, but the very fact that they were crossing and touching each other made one fear some display of the mysterious properties of electricity. Beneath one of the dangling wires lay the blackened bodies of a man and two women. We, too, numbered two women and one man.

"Come on, under the wires after me!" I called. "Whatever you do, don't 5 touch the wires. I'll hold them out of the way. If I get a shock don't touch anything except my clothes. Do you understand?—you get hold of the end of my trouser leg and drag me away." I followed the example of the other refugees, and pushed the wires away to either side with a piece of stick, crawling on all fours when necessary, crouching down when necessary.

"Look," I yelled back again. "Wrap a towel round your left elbow like 6 those people have done. Your left elbow goes on the ground."

Time and again it was necessary to crouch down beneath the wires, but at 7 last we were safely past. We stopped and took stock of each other. Shigeko was completely unscathed, but Yasuko, who had wound the towel round her arm in the wrong way, had a painful-looking graze on her elbow.

Shigeko sat down beside her on a stone by the roadside and attended to 8 her elbow with mentholatum and a triangular bandage. Suddenly, it occurred to me that we were directly in front of an entrance that I knew.

"Just a moment—" I said, "Surely that stone's one from Mr. Ōmuro's 9 garden?"

The Ōmuros in question were an old family, said to date back to the Edo 10 period, and the present head was engaged in chemical research on spinning thread. He was a man of property, owning mills in three different places, as well as dabbling in calligraphy, painting, and art-collecting. I had visited the house myself several times during the past year for the benefit of his advice on matters concerning textile products. It had been an imposing mansion, with a splendid old-style garden. Now, however, it was completely razed to the ground. Where the main building and clay-walled storehouse had once stood was an arid waste scattered with broken tiles. The stone on which Shigeko and Yasuko were sitting was almost certainly a rock from the garden inside the grounds. Rock though it was, a thin layer had been burned away all over it.

11   "That rock's granite, you know," I said. "I expect it was covered with moss only this morning."

12   "Do you think the whole household was wiped out, then?" said Shigeko.

13   I did not reply. It was a scene of cruel desolation. Where the ornamental pond had been was an uneven stretch of blackish mud, and at the foot of a rounded hillock of earth lay the blackened skeletons of three large pine trees. Beside the trunk of the thickest of the three stood a narrow, square pillar of stone. Why it alone should have remained standing was a mystery. Mr. Ōmuro had once told me that an ancestor of his, several generations back, had had it erected there. It was somewhat over ten feet tall, and instead of the usual long inscription it had the single character "Dream" carved on it, about two and a half feet from the top. Some high-ranking priest was said to have written the original, and the effect was doubtless considered stylish and rather sophisticated in its day, but at present, style and sophistication alike failed utterly.

14   Both Shigeko and Yasuko were deathly pale. My throat was so dry it felt as though it might close up entirely, and a slight tic affected my eye as I walked.

15   We reached the entrance to the West Parade Ground. The grass on the west side of the embankment had been burned away, leaving the earth smooth and bare. The trees seemed to have been carbonized where they stood, and retained their branches, but not a single leaf. The divisional commander's residence, the temporary army hospital, the Gokoku Shrine and, of course, the keep of Hiroshima Castle, were all gone.

16   My eyes began to hurt, so I massaged them as I walked by rubbing the eyelids with my fingers. They smarted, and at the same time felt as though there was grit in them. Shigeko and Yasuko had cheered up a little, and were talking about the now vanished mushroom cloud—its size, its shape, its color, the shape of its stalk, and the way it had moved. Concluding that my eyes hurt because I had too much blood in the head, I had Yasuko give me the treatment they used to give children who had nosebleed. It consisted of no more than pulling out three hairs from the back of the head, but it helped the pain a little.

17   The West Parade Ground was an unbroken expanse of sand. It reminded me of a vast desert I had seen in a movie called "Morocco." Even in the film, the desert had seemed to exhale a smell of sand, and it had been quite empty, with not a single footprint visible. The sandy waste of the parade ground, however, was rather different: the hot breath it gave off stank of smoke, and there were a number of human trails leading away in the direction of the hills. It must have been raining. The sand was fine enough for holes the size of broad beans to be visible all over its surface, and the newspapers scattered here and

there were covered with countless bean-sized black spots. The black rain had evidently fallen here. I had realized that the stalk of the mushroom cloud was a shower, but I had not imagined that the drops were as big as this.

At the western edge of the ground, we found a number of what looked like round black balls lying in the sand. At first I could not identify them, but as I got closer I realized they were lumps of what had been tin sheeting. They must have been torn away by the blast and have risen up into the sky, where they had been softened by the intense heat, then kneaded into balls by the wind before falling. To have gone quite round, like dumplings, they must have been sucked up into the great whirlwind of flame and have spun round and round furiously before finally descending to earth. 18

I glanced back across the sandy waste. A solitary figure—a boy wearing his underpants and an undershirt that flapped in the breeze at the front, exposing his naked belly—was walking rapidly in the direction of the hills. "Hi!" he called, turning in our direction and waving his hand at us. It seemed a peculiarly pointless gesture. 19

We walked on northwards. By the bank skirting the Gokoku Shrine a sentry stood with his rifle at order. Closer to, we found he was dead at his post, his back propped against the embankment, his eyes wide and staring. The badge on his collar showed him to be a private first-class in the army. He was about thirty-seven or eight, and old for a ranker, yet his features had an indefinable air of breeding. 20

"Why—just like the soldier with his bugle," said Shigeko. 21

"Come woman, mind your tongue," I said sternly, though if the truth be told I, too, had been reminded of the same story—of the bugler found dead at his post during the Sino-Japanese War, with his bugle still held to his lips. 22

The area was near the point where the bomb had been dropped. We saw another of them at the west corner of the grounds of Hiroshima Castle: a young man, still on his bicycle and carrying a wooden box as though on his way to deliver an order from a restaurant, propped dead against the stone ramparts. This one was a mere youth, and as skinny as a grasshopper. 23

We had often been taught during air raid drill that one must always breathe out steadily while a bomb was falling. Perhaps the sentry and the delivery boy had been breathing in at the moment the bomb burst? I did not understand the physiology of it, but it occurred to me that a blast just as one had filled one's lungs to capacity might well press on them and cause instant death. 24

We were taking a rest just this side of the embankment when we were hailed by an acquaintance, Police Sergeant Susumo Satō. 25

"Hello—I'm glad to see you safe," I said. 26

"Why, your face has caught it, hasn't it?" he said. 27

I spoke to him for a while before joining the others, and he told me that Superintendent-General Otsuka of the Chūgoku District Commissary had been trapped under his home and burned to death. 28

I had not known that Satō had been transferred from the police station to the Chūgoku District Commissary. I had not even known, in fact, that there existed a government office of that name. It was most remiss of me. I learned 29 for the first time from Satō that the enemy's attacks had grown so fierce recently that it had been decided that Japan must prepare to do battle on home territory. Local governing agencies known as "district commissaries" had been set up, so that the struggle could be continued in each region independently should the country be split up by enemy forces. With the same objective, war materials had been stored at factories and primary schools throughout the area in which Hiroshima stood.

30   "So that's what it meant—" I said, "the slogan about the war only just beginning."

31   "Yes," said Satō, "the idea is to go ahead with the grand policy of a wealthy and militarily powerful nation launched over half a century ago. It's not for you or me to assume that this is a kind of tragic finale. *This* is precisely what we've been brought up for. It's fate."

32   The Chūgoku Commissary, located in the Hiroshima University of Liberal Arts and Science, had had responsibility for the five prefectures of the Chūgoku district. The Superintendent-General himself—Isei Ōtsuka, a man with the bearing of an old-time samurai—had been in the Superintendent-General's official residence at Kami-Nagaregawa-machi when the bomb fell, and had been caught beneath the house. His wife had managed with great difficulty to crawl out of the wreckage, but the Superintendent-General had been hopelessly trapped. The good lady had been beside herself, but the Superintendent-General had insisted on her leaving him. "I'm ready for whatever comes," he had said, "Get yourself away, woman, as fast as you can." The flames were already close at hand, so she had had no choice but to flee.

33   "The Superintendent-General was cremated where he lay. A ghastly business," Satō said. "I myself didn't know which way to run from the flames." His eyes filled with tears. Normally, his manner of speech was cheerful and his face gave an immediate impression of openness and sunniness, but today his eyes were bloodshot and his face grim.

34   Arriving on the embankment, we found the middle section of Misasa Bridge missing. Changing my plan, I set off along the embankment downstream with the idea of crossing Aioi Bridge. Countless dead bodies were lying in the undergrowth at the foot of the embankment of our right. Other bodies came floating in steady succession along the river. Every so often, one of them would catch on the roots of a riverside willow, swing round with the current, and suddenly rear its face out of the water. Or one would come along rocking in the water, so that first its upper half then its lower half bobbed to the surface. Or another would swing round beneath a willow tree and raise its arms as though to grasp at a branch, so that it almost seemed, for a moment, to be alive.

35   We had sighted from some way off the body of a woman who lay stretched out dead across the path on top of the embankment. Suddenly Yasuko, who was walking ahead of us, came running back with a cry of "Uncle! Uncle!" and burst into tears. As I drew closer, I saw a baby girl of about three who had opened the corpse's dress at the top and was playing with the breasts. When we came up to her, she clutched tight at both breasts and gazed up at us with apprehensive eyes.

What could we possibly do for her? To ask ourselves this was our only 36
recourse. I stepped gently over the corpse's legs so as not to frighten the little
girl, and walked briskly on another ten yards or so downstream. Here I spotted another group of four or five women dead together in the undergrowth,
and a boy of five or six crouched on the ground as though caught between the
bodies.

"Come along," I called waving with both arms to the others, who were 37
still hesitating. "Just step over it as quietly as possible and come on." Shigeko
and Yasuko stepped over the body and joined me.

At the end of Aioi Bridge we found a carter and the ox harnessed to his 38
cart both seated, dead, on the electric car tracks. The ropes around the load
had come undone, and the goods had been rifled.

Here, too, the corpses came floating one after the other down the river, 39
and it was a sickening sight to see them butt their heads against the piers of
the bridge and swivel round in the water. Near its center, the bridge reared in
a hump about a yard high, and on what one might have called the crest of the
wave a young foreigner with fair hair lay dead with his arms clasped about his
head. The surface of the bridge was distorted and undulating.

Around Sakan chō and Sorazaya-chō, it was clear that the flames had 40
swept evenly across the whole area. The corpses lay scattered in every conceivable condition—one with only the upper half of the body burned to the
bone, one completely skeletonized save for one arm and one leg, another lying
face down, consumed from the knees down, yet another with the two legs
alone cremated—and an unspeakable stench hanging over all. Nauscating
though the odor was, there was no way to escape it.

In Tera-machi, the "temple quarter," not a single temple was standing. All 41
that remained was clay walls crumbled and collapsed till they were barely recognizable, and venerable trees with their limbs torn open to expose the naked
wood within. Even the branch of the Honganji temple, famed as the greatest
temple building in the whole quarter, had vanished without trace. The smoke
still rising from the embers drifted menacingly over the crumbling walls, then
crept low over the surface of the river till it vanished at the other bank.

On the other side of Yokogawa Bridge the flames were still rising. Fanned 42
by the wind, fires were swirling white-hot up to the skies from the whole area
on the opposite bank. To approach was out of the question.

We found the road ahead completely blocked on this side of the bridge. 43
The iron girders forming the bow-shaped framework of the bridge were discolored up to a height of some twelve to fifteen feet, and close to one of the
piers of the bridge that rested on a stretch of grass stood a horse badly burned
on its back and the back of its head. It was trembling violently and looked as
though it might collapse at any moment. Close by its side a corpse, the upper
half burned away, lay face downwards. The lower half, which was untouched,
wore army breeches and boots with spurs. The spurs actually gleamed gold. If
the owner had been an army man, then he had been an officer, for only an officer could wear boots with gold spurs like that. I pictured the scene to myself:
the officer running to the stables, mounting his horse barebacked, rushing outside. . . . The horse must have been a favorite of the soldier's. Though it was

on the verge of collapse, it still seemed—or was it my imagination?—to be yearning for some sign from the man in the spurred boots. How immeasurable the pain it must have felt, with the west-dipping sun beating down unmercifully on its burned flesh; how immeasurable its love for the man in the boots! But pity eluded me: I felt only a shudder of horror.

44　　Our only choice was to walk on through the river. Close to the bank there were grassy shoals, but in places they were too far apart for us to tread dry ground all the time. We stepped into the flowing water and set off walking upstream. Even at its deepest, the water only came up to our knees. The district we were passing through would have been Hirose Kitamachi or thereabouts. On the sandy parts, where the river had dried up, our shoes spouted water with a squelching sound. No sooner did the water empty out of them a little, and walking become a little pleasanter, than the sand would start getting in our shoes and almost lame us with the pain.

45　　We decided it was actually better to walk in the water, and splashed on regardless. On a pebbly shoal a man lay with both hands thrust in the water, drinking. We approached, thinking to join him, and found he was not drinking water but dead, with his face thrust down into the water.

46　　"I wonder if the water in this river is poisonous, then?" said Yasuko, voicing my own unspoken question.

47　　"There's no telling," I replied, setting off through the water again. "But perhaps we'd better not drink it."

48　　The smoke blowing across from the town gradually diminished, and paddy fields appeared on our right, so we clambered up a crumbling stone wall and onto the bank.

49　　We reached the rice fields. Walking along the raised paths between them in the direction of the electric car tracks, we came across a number of schoolgirls and schoolboys lying here and there in the field, dead. They must have fled in disorder from the factory where they had been doing war work. There were adults lying about too. One of them, an elderly man, had fallen across the path, and the front of his jacket was soaked with water. He had evidently drunk to bursting point from the paddy field water, then—either unable to care any more or in a fit of vertigo—subsided onto the ground and expired where he lay.

50　　We stepped over the body and wound our way, first left then right, along the paths between the fields, till finally they led us into a bamboo grove. The grove must have been kept for the purpose of gathering bamboo shoots, for the undergrowth was well cut back. Finding ourselves in cool, leafy shade at last, we sank to the ground without exchanging a word.

51　　I unfastened my first-aid kit, took off my air raid hood and my shoes, and sprawled out on my back. At once my body seemed to be dissolving into thin air, and before I knew it I had slipped into a deep slumber.

52　　I awoke, I knew not how long after, to a raging thirst and a pain in my throat. My wife and Yasuko were both lying with their heads pillowed on their arms. I rolled onto my belly, and, filching the quart bottle of water out of my wife's rucksack, drank. It was a heaven-sent nectar. I had had no idea that water was so good. The ecstasy was touched, almost, with a kind of pride. I must have drunk all of a third of a pint.

My wife and Yasuko awoke too. By now, the sun was sinking toward the 53 west. Without a word Shigeko took the bottle I handed her and, lifting it with both hands, drank greedily. She probably drank another third of a pint. Then she passed the bottle to Yasuko, also without a word. Yasuko in her turn raised it with both hands. She paused between each mouthful, but every time she upended the bottle a stream of bubbles ran up through it and the remaining water decreased visibly. I was almost despairing of her leaving any at all, when she finally put the bottle down with about one-third of a pint still in it.

From her rucksack, my wife took out the cucumbers she had brought 54 for want of anything better, and opened a packet of salt. The cucumbers were blackened and discolored on one side. "Where did you buy these?" I asked. "Mrs. Murakami from Midori-chō brought them for us this morning," she said.

Early that morning, apparently, Mrs. Murakami had brought us three 55 cucumbers and a dozen or so tiny dried fish, of the kind used in flavoring soup, in return for a share of some tomatoes that Shigeko's people in the country had sent us. Shigeko had left the cucumbers in a bucket of water by the pool in the garden, and the flash from the bomb had discolored them.

"It's funny," I said. "When I went back to the house from the university 56 sports ground, the basket worms were eating the leaves of the azalea. The cucumber was burned, but the insects were still alive."

I dipped the cucumber in the salt and turned the question over in my mind 57 as I ate. Some physical reaction had obviously taken place on the surface of the water in the bucket. Could it be that reflection inside the bucket had stepped up the amount of heat and light? Glancing at the pond as I went to sink the mosquito net in the water, I had noticed basket worms on the azalea that grew out over the water, busily eating the new summer buds. I shook the branch, and they drew back into their baskets, but when I got back from collecting pieces of brick to sink the net with, they were busily eating once more. The buds themselves were not discolored, nor were the worms' baskets burned, which suggested that light and heat had caused some chemical change when it came up against metal. Or had the basket worms and azalea been sheltered by the house, or by some other obstacle, when the bomb had burst? The rice plants in the open paddy fields seemed to have been affected by the flash. It seemed likely that they, too, would have turned black by the following morning.

I washed my small towel in a ditch at the end of the bamboo grove, wiped 58 my right cheek and the sinews of my neck, then rinsed the towel time and time again. I wrung it out and rinsed it, wrung it out and rinsed it, repeating the same seemingly pointless procedure over and over again. To wring out my towel was the one thing, it seemed to me, that I was free to do as I pleased at that moment. My left cheek smarted painfully. A shoal of minnows was swimming in the ditch, and in a patch of still water the flags were growing in profusion. Here is shadow, they seemed to say, here is safety. . . .

Smoke came drifting from deep within the bamboo grove. Going to investigate, I peered through the bamboos and saw a group of refugees who had 59 built a shelter of green bamboo and branches and were preparing a meal. They seemed to have been burned out of their homes and to be making ready to spend the night out.

60   I strained my ears to catch their conversation. It seemed from what they said that the houses along the main highway had all closed their shutters in order to keep out refugees. At one sundry goods store this side of Mitaki Station on the Kabe line, they had found a woman who had got in unnoticed and died in one of their closets. When the owner of the store dragged the body out, he found that the garment it was wearing was his own daughter's best summer kimono. Scandalized, he had torn the best kimono off the body, only to find that it had no underwear on underneath. She must have been burned out of her home and fled all the way there naked, yet still—being a young woman—sought something to hide her nakedness even before she sought water or food. The refugees were wondering whether bombs like today's would be dropped on other cities besides Hiroshima. What were Japan's battleships and land forces up to, they were asking each other. It would be a wonder if there weren't a civil war. . . .

61   I made my way back quietly through the bamboo, and with a "Come on" to the others started to get ready. I had a stabbing pain in my toes. "Come on," I urged them again, but neither Shigeko nor Yasuko made any reply. They seemed utterly exhausted. "Well, then, I'm off!" I said sharply, and this time they reluctantly got to their feet and started to get ready.

62   Walking made my toes hurt so that I nearly danced with the pain. The others were complaining of the pain too. I myself must have walked some ten or eleven miles already. My wife had walked five or six, and Yasuko about five. We ate parched rice as we walked. We would thrust a hand into the cloth bag my wife was carrying, take out a handful and, putting it in our mouths, chew on it as we walked. It gradually turned to sugar, and tasted sweet in the mouth; it was better than either the water or the cucumber. The most effective way seemed to be to chew as one walked, and I could understand why travelers in olden times took parched rice with them as rations for the journey. Finally, one gulped it down, then took another handful out of the cloth bag and put it in one's mouth. Parched rice may be very unappetizing-looking, but I gave thanks in my heart to my wife's folk for sending it.

63   The main highway was dotted with refugees. Just as I had overheard the people in the bamboo grove saying, the houses by the roadside all had their doors and shutters fastened. Where there was a roofed gateway, its doors were shut fast. Outside one of the gates with shut doors lay a bundle of straw scorched by fire. I wondered if passing refugees had set fire to it.

64   However far we went, still the houses along the road had their doors shut. Here the breeze was cool, unlike the hot breath of the town, and ripples were running over the rice plants in the paddy fields. The fathers from the Catholic church on the north side of Yamamoto Station went running past us at top speed, carrying a stretcher. With them was one father, a man past middle age, whom I had often seen on the Kabe-bound train on my way to work. He came panting along far behind the others carrying the stretcher, and as he passed me he glanced into my face and nodded briefly in recognition. "Good luck to you," I called after him.

At last, we reached Yamamoto Station. From here on, the trains were run- 65
ning. A train was standing in the station, every coach full, but we managed to
squeeze our way into the vestibule of one of them. Wedged tight, I tried to
make more room by nudging at a bundle directly in front of me. Wrapped in
a cloth, it rested on the shoulders of a woman of about thirty. Somehow, it felt
different from a bundle of belongings, so I tried touching it furtively with my
hand. I contacted what felt like a human ear: A child seemed to be in the bundle. To carry a child in such a fashion was outrageous. It was almost certain
to suffocate in such a crush.

"Excuse me Ma'am," I said softly. "Is it your child in here?" 66

"Yes," she said in a scarcely audible voice. "He's dead." 67

"I'm sorry," I said, taken aback. "I didn't know. . . . I really must apol- 68
ogize, to be pushing and. . . ."

"Not at all," she said gently. "None of us can help it in such a crowd." 69
She hitched the bundle up, bent her head, and was seized with a fit of weeping.

"It was when the bomb burst," she said through her sobs. "The sling of
his hammock broke, and he was dashed against the wall and killed. Then the
house started to burn, so I wrapped him in a quilt cover and brought him away
on my back. I'm taking him to my old home in Iimori, so I can bury him in
the cemetery there."

She stopped weeping, and ceased talking at the same time. I could not 70
bring myself to address her any further.

A kite was wheeling in the air above the wires. The cicadas were chirp- 71
ing, and a dabchick was bustling about the pond with waterlilies by the side
of the highway. A perfectly commonplace scene that somehow seemed quite
extraordinary. . . .

The conductor announced the train's imminent departure, and a fiercer 72
clamor arose from those who had not succeeded in getting on. The train
lurched forward and stopped, lurched and stopped again.

"What the hell're you up to? Are you starting or aren't you?" bellowed a 73
voice, to be followed by another voice that launched into a speech somewhere
inside the coach: "Ladies and gentlemen, you can see for yourselves how sadly
decadent the national Railways have become. Concerned only with carrying
black market goods, they have nothing but contempt for the ordinary passen-
ger. . . ." But this time the train glided smoothly into motion, and the rest of
the speech was lost forever in the clatter of its wheels.

Questions for Discussion and Your Reading Journal

1. This reading is a fictional account of the bombing based on the diaries of
   survivors. Contrast the impact of this style of writing with the journalistic
   style of Shalett. Discuss the effectiveness of such fictional techniques as dialogue, characterization, and irony.
2. How might the festivals mentioned in the first paragraph have been affected by the bombing?
3. What is the narrator of the story describing? What are the characters looking for? Their search for normalcy is clearly absurd: why do they continue?

4. What are some of the horrors the three encounter as they return through the wreckage to their home?
5. What surprises you about the way the victims react to the bombing?
6. Some scientists asserted that the "black rain" that fell after the bomb was dropped was completely harmless. What effects do you think the black rain will have on the niece?
7. How could the information presented in this fictionalized account of the bombing be synthesized into a historical account? How would the impact of the information be affected?

SUZANNE H. SANKOWSKY

The following excerpts from the American high-school textbook Mainstreams of World History, *published in the 1970s, and the Japanese textbook,* Progress of Japan, *published in the 1950s, describe the use of the atomic bomb by the United States on the Japanese cities of Hiroshima and Nagasaki.*

Textbooks from around the world tend to discuss World War II and the use of the atomic bomb in a much more complex and open-ended manner than do American books, although American textbooks, from the 1960s forward, attempt to look at the event from perspectives besides that of the American military of the time. The American high-school textbook here attempts to place the bombing in the context of the larger war effort, rather than discussing it in isolation.

The paragraphs from Progress of Japan *describe the bombing of Pearl Harbor by Japan and the dropping of the atomic bomb by the United States from the Japanese perspective. (Note: The date of the bombing of Pearl Harbor is labeled December 8th because of the 24-hour time difference between Japan and the United States.) The two perspectives are remarkable both in their differences and their similarities.*

Reading Rhetorically

Contrast these textbook excerpts with the account of the bombing presented in the Shalett story, which precedes them. In what ways does the hindsight of history seem to have influenced the telling of the story? Examine, also, the ways in which these excerpts from textbooks might have been geared to their particular audiences, American and Japanese high-school students, to persuade them of a certain view of historical events.

Some current Japanese textbooks criticize Truman's decision and emphasize the suffering of the Japanese people, while others discuss the larger context of the war and question Japan's ethics. This Japanese textbook does neither. Given that it was written in the late 1950s, think about the tone and content of this excerpt as you read and try to determine why there is so little criticism of the United States.

Excerpt from *Mainstreams of World History*

The Japanese are defeated Even while the main military effort was being 1
directed against Germany, the Allied offensive in the Pacific was making
progress. But after Germany's defeat the Americans and the British greatly
intensified their struggle against Japan. This was a war in which naval vessels,
especially aircraft carriers, and planes played major roles. In the fall of 1944,
U.S. forces retook the Philippines and Guam from Japan, while the British
drove the enemy out of Burma. In the following months, the British pushed
toward Malaya, while American forces continued the "island hopping" drive
toward the main islands of Japan. The fighting was especially severe on the
islands of Saipan, Iwo Jima, and Okinawa. Thousands of American lives were
lost before these places were taken.

In July, 1945, Japan received an official ultimatum from the United 2
Nations leaders: surrender unconditionally or be completely destroyed. The
military rulers of Japan ignored the ultimatum, and the country paid a most
terrible penalty. On August 6 and 9 two atomic bombs were dropped, the first
one on Hiroshima and the second on Nagasaki, destroying most of each city
and killing or injuring vast numbers of the inhabitants. Only then did the
Japanese leaders surrender and ask for peace.

The whole world was shocked and startled at the announcement of the 3
atomic bombs, which had been in utmost secrecy. (This spectacular accomplishment was made possible by the contributions of scientists of several countries who had been working on nuclear fission—the splitting of the atom.)
Never before had such a destructive force been known, and people were therefore greatly alarmed at the new possibilities of warfare.

On the day before the second atom bombing, Soviet Russia had declared war 4
against Japan and had sent troops into Manchuria and Korea. On August 14,
Japan surrendered. But formal surrender took place on the U.S.S. *Missouri*
September 2. General Douglas MacArthur was put in command of the occupation of the defeated country. The war was now over and the United Nations
celebrated V-J (Victory in Japan) Day.

KEIGO TAKARAZUKI
AND KAZUO KASAHARA

Excerpt from *Progress of Japan*

In Europe around this time [the 1930s] despotic governments had begun to 1
rule in Germany and Italy, military forces were expanded, and surrounding
countries were threatened.

2   Observing this situation, the [Japanese] government signed a pact with Germany and Italy, prepared for war, dissolved all political parties and unions, and planned to unify the country's power under strict military control. Delegates were sent to the United States to negotiate in an attempt to avoid war, but it did not work out as hoped.

THE FATEFUL DAY

3   Soon after, in the fall of 1941, the Tojo Cabinet, which represented the military faction, was formed. In spite of opposition within the country, the Tojo Cabinet decided upon war with the United States. And, on December 8th of the same year, the Japanese Armed Forces attacked Hawaii by surprise, and started the Pacific War. . . . Taking advantage of initial victories, the Japanese forces conquered a large area in the south, but after the United States regained her footing, the situation was reversed and we were unsparingly attacked by the allied forces. During the third year of war, the major cities of Japan proper were air-raided and were burned out.

4   The American forces finally landed on Okinawa, and in August of 1945 the United States dropped the horrible atom bomb on Hiroshima and Nagasaki. On top of this, the U.S.S.R. declared war on Japan; thus helpless, the Emperor ordered the cessation of war by a radio broadcast on August 15th. The harassing, long war came to an end, and the people felt rather relieved of an oppressed feeling despite their sorrow.

Questions for Discussion and Your Reading Journal

1. For whom are these textbooks written? In what ways do you think the information presented here is modified for its audience? What might be some purposes of history textbooks? How might the content have been modified to accommodate those purposes?
2. For each of the textbooks, answer the following questions: What information is given? What is left out? Why might this information have been omitted?
3. How is the Japanese textbook different from the American one? How do you account for the differences? How are the textbooks similar?
4. Describe the tone (the attitude of the author toward the subject) of each of the textbooks. How might you account for the tone of each? In what ways might the text have been adapted, in both tone and content, to suit an audience of school children?
5. Analyze Sankowsky's diction. (Why does she describe the bombing as a "spectacular accomplishment" [Paragraph 3], for example?) Compare and contrast Sankowsky's diction with that of Takarazuki.
6. What information about the use of the atomic bomb do you think should be included in American and Japanese high-school textbooks? Justify your changes to these books, if any.

BURTON BOLLAG

In the Winter 2001 issue of American Educator, *the journal published by the American Federation of Teachers, Burton Bollag (1952–) writes an analysis of textbooks like those represented in the last two readings. Bollag is an international correspondent for the* Chronicle of Higher Education, *and he also writes for a number of European newspapers and magazines. Having worked for the World Health Organization and National Public Radio, Bollag focuses his writing on issues of international concern.*

In this instance Bollag writes about current textbook depictions of the dropping of the atomic bomb during World War II. This article can be examined in reference to the American textbook excerpt written in the 1970s and the textbook excerpt from Japan written in the 1950s.

Reading Rhetorically

Bollag's article presents another perspective on the controversy, since he is neither American nor Japanese. Instead of diminishing over time, intellectual and emotional responses to representations of World War II seem to increase with every anniversary of the dropping of the bomb.

The controversy is frequently centered on textbooks, not only in Japan and America but also in China and other parts of the world. As you read this article by Bollag, compare his perspective with those of the American and Japanese textbook writers, and think about the reasons his writing may be perceived as more objective or more credible than theirs. Pay particular attention to issues presented by Bollag that were not discussed in any of the previous readings, and think about how this article, written in 2001, represents current social concerns. Think also about the persuasive elements in the essay.

A Confrontation with the Past: The Japanese Textbook Dispute

This past summer an unusual battle was fought out at school districts across Japan. At issue was whether to adopt a new history textbook for junior high school, which was written by nationalist historians. The text, its supporters say, is intended to promote self-pride and reverse the "masochist" approach to history education, which teaches Japanese schoolchildren their country was an evil aggressor during its recent history. 1

Nobukatsu Fujioka, a professor of education at the University of Tokyo, is the founder of the Japanese Society for History Textbook Reform, which is promoting the new textbook. An amiable, even charming, former Communist and later pacifist, he was reborn 10 years ago as a nationalist. 2

"Japanese children are only taught that their country has done bad things," he explained to me recently at the university's graduate school of education 3 where he works. "They are not taught anything they can be proud of. The current textbooks only teach them how to apologize."

4   The controversial book, entitled *New History Textbook,* was published by the small, recently founded Fuso publishing company. It presents Japan's military occupation of other Asian countries in the years before and during World War II in a more positive light than do other texts. The book justifies the colonization of Korea, from 1910 to 1945, as necessary to protect Japan's security and economic interests. It suggests that Japan's subjugation of other Asian peoples was at least in part positive because it helped hasten their liberation from Western colonial rule; and it ignores the sexual slavery forced on tens of thousands of young women, the germ warfare experiments on prisoners, and other atrocities committed by Japan's Imperial Army.

5   Japan's neighbors reacted angrily, especially to the fact that Japan's education ministry approved the Fuso textbook for use in public schools. The issue provoked strong, diplomatic protests from South Korea and China. In a compromise gesture in October 2001, Japanese Prime Minister Junichiro Koizumi agreed, during a summit meeting with his South Korean counterpart, to establish a joint committee to propose revisions to the controversial textbook.

6   The issue illustrates how painful and difficult it can be to confront the more shameful parts of a country's past, even in a nation where the rules of good behavior require the utterance of the phrase "I am sorry" many times a day.

AN UPROAR IN TOCHIGI

7   During the summer, Japan's 543 central textbook boards, each comprising on average six school districts, chose the textbooks they will use for the next four years. Normally, this is a rather routine affair. Each board examines texts from a list of titles approved by the education ministry. The boards make their choices according to the style and educational approach they consider best suited to their communities.

8   But this year was different, observes Kazuo Fujimura, executive director of the Japan Textbook Research Center, which represents the interests of many of the country's textbook publishers. "This time, political groups have been trying to influence the choice," Fujimura says, "They say we should rather use textbooks which give us more self-pride."

9   Well before the summer, support for Fuso's *New History Textbook* became a rallying cry of Japan's resurgent nationalistic right wing. School boards across the country were lobbied by the right wing of the ruling Liberal Democratic Party. Nationalist groups joined the campaign, as did the conservative Sankei media group, which includes a major national newspaper and several television stations.

10   Tochigi prefecture, a quiet, hilly agricultural area about 70 miles north of Tokyo, made news this summer when one of its central textbook boards first chose the controversial Fuso book, then reversed itself after a storm of local protest. The board, which chooses the textbooks for the public schools of the

Demonstrators at the city hall of Suginami, a ward in the city of Tokyo, protesting the adoption of a controversial nationalist history book. Copyright © 2001 Burton Bollag.

prefecture's 10 towns, divides the task according to subjects. The five members of the 23-member board who had the job of recommending social studies texts proposed one of the uncontroversial history books. But at a stormy meeting July 11, a majority of the entire board voted to overturn the recommendation and the pick the Fuso text instead. One member, a superintendent of education from one of the towns, who asked not to be identified, says the board was swayed both by the right-wing campaign in favor of the nationalist text and by several conservative senior board members.

The next day, all hell broke loose. Parents, representatives of the teacher's 11 union, journalists, and other local people began besieging the public education offices of the 10 towns, protesting the decision. They called, sent faxes, and showed up personally to complain. The superintendent, who requested anonymity, showed me several knee-high stacks of manila envelopes, piled up on the floor next to his desk, containing 1,800 faxes that had arrived at his office alone. Outraged residents staged a protest demonstration in the district's biggest town. Then the municipal school boards of each of the 10 towns voted individually to reject the Fuso book.

Clearly the 23-member board had not anticipated this groundswell of oppo- 12 sition. Two weeks after its original decision, the board met and voted to reverse itself, choosing one of the uncontroversial texts instead. "It was really confusing for two weeks," remarked the superintendent. "But in the end we got it right."

There were many small demonstration across Japan, in which people 13 demanded that their local authorities not choose the Fuso book. In Suginami, a ward of Tokyo, several hundred people staged a noisy demonstration at the local town hall, beating drums and cymbals and forming a human chain around the square, gray, seven-story building.

Naoko Tomita, who cares for residents of a state institution for mentally 14 handicapped people, was one of the protesters. She says that when her two

college-age children were in public
school, "they learned only part of the
truth" about Japan's role before and
during World War II. Japan's invasions
of its neighbor were coyly referred to
as "advances," and her children hadn't
learned about the "comfort women,"
the name Japanese authorities at the
time gave to the tens of thousands of
young women from Korea and other
occupied countries who were forced
into military-run brothels, where they
had to provide sex to large numbers of
Japanese soldiers daily.

15   "The Japanese government wants
to hide the truth about the comfort
women," she said. "They may want
another war."

16   Despite all the public anxiety,
almost no one chose the Fuso text.
When the deadline for choosing textbooks passed at the end of August,
only three of the 543 central textbook
boards had chosen it, and then only
for their schools for disabled children.

Professor Saburo Ienaga, the Japanese
teacher and historian who repeatedly sued
the Japanese government to protest its censorship of his history textbooks. © Itsuo
Inouye/Associated Press

Several private schools also picked the text. In the end, it appears that only
about 10 out of more than 10,000 junior high schools in Japan plan to use it.

17   The result was a setback for the nationalists. But their movement to trans-
form history education continues, and even received a boost, when Prime Min-
ister Koizumi made a controversial decision to end a taboo and visit Tokyo's
Yasukuni shrine in August. It is the most important Shinto shrine honoring
Japan's war dead, including the soldiers and commanders of the Imperial
Army. So what is behind this current resurgence of nationalist feelings?

18   In part, it appears to be a response to a loss of confidence due to almost a
decade of economic malaise, including record unemployment, bank failures,
and a stubborn recession. If the Japanese economic miracle is coming undone,
some people feel, this is a time for history lessons to teach children to be proud
of their country, not guilty about its past.

19   At the same time, many observers see support for the Fuso text as a back-
lash against gradual moves over the last two decades to make history textbooks—and the official government position—more open about the past.

TALKING ABOUT THE PAST

20 In the first years after Japan's defeat in World War II, the education authorities, then under the supervision of the American occupation forces, produced

a new history curriculum. It was very different from the prewar lessons, which had taught the Japan had an almost divine right to rule over its neighbors.

The Japanese were exhausted and sick of war, which had brought them not 21 the glory they were promised, but destruction, defeat, and humiliation. The country's new history curriculum branded Japan the aggressor during the just-ended war. But the curriculum was, above all, pacifist: It stressed the horrors of war in general and how much the Japanese people had suffered because of it.

By the mid-1950's, however, the approach to curriculum began to change. 22 Japan had become a key Cold-War ally of the United States; it was an important rear base for American forces during the Korean War; and in 1954 the two countries signed a mutual defense-assistance pact. History lessons that inculcated in young people too much of a sense of pacifism were no longer deemed appropriate. Often against the objections of teachers, who tended, then as now, to be left-leaning, the education ministry began screening textbooks, requiring them to tone down their criticisms of Japan's role during the war, and insisting they promote student's patriotic feelings.

A few textbook authors tried to include specific references to atrocities 23 Japan had committed during World War II. The education ministry invariably sent the texts back demanding that the references be deleted. Many writers censored themselves to avoid long negotiations with ministry officials or possible rejection of their books. It was not until the early 1980s that the policy changed again and the authorities gradually began allowing textbooks to address the unsavory aspects of Japan's foreign policy in the 1930s and 1940s.

The turning point came in 1982, when the ministry issued guidelines for text- 24 book publishers, saying texts now had to show "concern for neighboring countries." Those countries—for example, South Korea, China, and the Philippines—were growing stronger and becoming increasingly important export markets for Japanese goods. "The Japanese government couldn't help paying more attention to their interests," says Yutaka Yoshida, a professor of history at Hitotsubashi University in Tokyo and co-author of a junior high school history textbook that probably goes the furthest in speaking openly about Japan's war crimes.

This period was also marked by the start of a slow dance in which suc- 25 cessive Japanese leaders circled painfully round and round, moving ever closer to apologizing—though never quite managing to do so—for Japan's invasions and brutal occupations of its neighbors. In 1986, then-Prime Minister Yasuhiro Nakasone publicly admitted for the first time to "invasive aspects" in Japan's actions during World War II. Finally, in August 1995, with the whole world watching what Japan would say on the 50th anniversary of the end of the war, then-Prime Minister Tomiichi Murayama went further. He expressed deep regret—but still could not quite bring himself to apologize—for the "great damage and suffering" Japan had caused other Asian peoples through its "invasion" of their countries.

IENAGA'S BATTLE

While political leaders were grudgingly making it more permissible to talk 26 about the past, developments on several other fronts forced the authorities to

Taking Responsibility: Japan vs. Germany

Japan's efforts to deny or minimize war time atrocities contrast sharply with Germany's postwar behavior. Why did it take so long—a half century—for Japan to acknowledge its guilt? Part of the answer lies in the fact that Japan, which carried out such harsh subjugation of its neighbors, had nonetheless become a solid democracy after the war. As Manabu Sato, a professor in the University of Tokyo's Graduate School of Education, points out, until about a decade ago Korea, the Philippines, Indonesia, and other Asian countries were dictatorships that jailed people for publishing information unfavorable to their governments. This weakened the moral force of their demands that Japan come clean about its wartime conduct.

A defeated Germany, on the other hand—at least its western half—had as its neighbors the community of democratic Western European nations. There were several other significant differences in the fate of Japan and Germany after the war. These differences help explain why, while Japan still resists taking responsibility for its war crimes, and quibbles over what took place, Germany has long since acknowledged the full horrors committed by the Nazi regime, and made that information part of its standard school curriculum.

At the end of the war, the victorious allies set about to destroy Germany's ruling Nazi apparatus, which had been responsible for the war. The rest of society could then begin rebuilding a democratic system. But unlike Germany, prewar Japan had not been usurped by a Fascist party. On the contrary, the war had been prosecuted by the country's long-standing power structure: the emperor, the imperial government, and the army. The United States forces occupying a defeated Japan decided, in the name of a peaceful transition, to leave the emperor on his throne—at least as a figurehead—and concentrated on prosecuting a small number of army leaders. The result was that Japan did not make—indeed could not have made—as clean a break with its wartime past as did Germany.

Ian Buruma, author of a 1994 book, *The Wages of Guilt: Memories of War in Germany and Japan,* points to another factor. Germany was occupied by the United States, Britain, and France (with the Soviet Union occupying the eastern part of the country) and quickly began to finds its place among the Western European democracies. But Japan was occupied by the United States alone. "The trouble was that virtually all the changes were made on American orders," writes Buruma. "This was, of course, the victor's prerogative, and many of the changes were beneficial. But the systematic subservience of Japan meant that the country never really grew up." And never took full responsibility for confronting its past.

allow more of the truth into school textbooks. One factor was several lawsuits claiming it was unconstitutional for the education ministry to censor references to atrocities committed by the Imperial Army. The most famous court action was by Saburo Ienaga, a historian. He first filed suit in 1965 after the ministry ordered him to delete or rewrite passages about wartime atrocities in a textbook he had written.

27   His court battle continued for 32 years. Finally, in 1997, Ienaga won a major victory when Japan's Supreme Court ruled in his favor. While dozens of his supporters in the packed courtroom rose and applauded, Ienaga, then 83, smiled and bowed deeply. The court decided that the ministry had acted illegally when, in 1980 and 1983, it had removed from a textbook Ienaga was

writing a description of biological experiments Japan carried out on 3,000 soldiers and civilians taken prisoner in northern China during World War II. In the experiments, conducted by the army's infamous Unit 731, victims were allowed to die without treatment after being injected with diseases like typhoid, or dissected without anesthesia. However the victory was only partial. The court rejected Ienaga's claims that the ministry had illegally censored seven other portions of his textbook. During his long legal fight, Ienaga had at times required police protection from right-wing thugs who felt he had disgraced Japan and its old Imperial Army.

Another factor was the collapse of the Soviet Union and the end of the   28
Cold War. With many former Communist countries coming clean about their past misdeeds, it seemed increasingly incongruous for Japan to refuse to do the same. Even more so since, in the last few years, a number of old Japanese soldiers have come forward publicly and admitted to having taken part in massacres, rapes, and other crimes. Furthermore, some of the elderly surviving "comfort women" ended nearly a half century of silence and began speaking out about their painful ordeals as sexual slaves and the physical and emotional scars they carried for the rest of their lives. The first to speak publicly was a South Korean woman, Kim Hak-Son, in 1991. Others followed, from all over Asia and as far away as Holland. Tokyo long denied that the Imperial Army was responsible, claiming that prostitution was a private business. Then, a researcher in Japan unearthed documents proving the army's responsibility. In 1993, the prime minister's office admitted as much and apologized. But the government has refused to accept legal responsibility or pay compensation to survivors.

"The survivors feel insulted a second time," said Yayori Matsui, when I   29
met her in her small downtown office where one takes off one's shoes before entering. Matsui is a determined former journalist and author who now heads a group fighting against the rape and abuse of women during war. "The most important thing for them is to establish that this was a war crime against women."

These various pressures culminated in 1996 to produce a crop of seven   30
approved junior high school history textbooks that, for the first—and perhaps the last—time, all included information the nationalists had tried to keep out: the basic facts about Japan's actions toward its neighbors during the 1930s and 1940s, as understood by most historians around the world. All the books said, without equivocating, that Japan had been the aggressor. They all made note, for example, of the "comfort women," the cruel biological experiments, and the Nanking massacre. The latter refers to the slaughter of up to 300,000 people by the Imperial Army in that southern Chinese city in the winter of 1937–38.

THE UNSETTLED STORY

Even with the rejection of the Fuso book, the right-wing campaign has had a   31
definite impact on what children are taught. All textbooks used in public and private schools must be screened and approved by the education ministry

every four years. (This year's screening process came five years after the last one in order to coincide with the introduction of curriculum changes.) All of the seven junior high school history texts approved by the ministry in 1996 mentioned Japan's major war crimes. But this year, publishers "have tried to tone down" those references in response to the pressure for the Fuso book, says Fujimura, of the textbook research center. For example, each of the seven books mentioned the "comfort women" in 1996; this year only three do.

32   This backsliding was made possible by a lack of commitment on the part of the government to face up to the past, says Professor Yoshida, the historian and textbook author from Mitsubashi University in Tokyo. With their gradual and grudging acknowledgments of past war crimes, the Japanese authorities have often appeared to be giving in to pressure, rather than leading the nation with a principled stance, he says. "The Japanese government started expressing regret to Korea and China in the 1980s before getting consensus among the Japanese people. So people are confused."

33   The Fuso text, as nationalistic as it is, was even more so in the version submitted to the ministry for screening. For example, the text claimed the invasion and annexation of Korea "proceeded legally according to the basic rules of international relations of the days when it was carried out." The text raised serious doubts about whether the Nanking massacre took place: ". . .there could have been some killings, but the incident was nothing like the Holocaust."

34   Ministry officials demanded changes to these and 135 other passages before approving the text. The other seven textbooks each required between 13 and 41 changes. Keita Sasata, the education ministry official in charge of screening social sciences textbooks, says Fuso's text focused too much on the suffering of the Japanese people. He says he told Fuso: "You should try to understand; we were not the only victims."

35   I asked Professor Fujioka, head of the society promoting the Fuso book, for his reaction. "The U.S. dropped atomic bombs on Hiroshima and Nagasaki," he said. "Do American textbooks say the United States was evil for doing this? No. Yet the atomic bombings were the worst crime of World War II. All we are trying to do," argues Fujioka, "is to write a textbook with an interpretation of history that is similar to the way the United States, Great Britain, and other countries approach their own histories."

36   What about the fact that the Fuso book plays down or excludes mention of most of the war crimes widely accepted to have been committed by Japan? That is the "Tokyo trials perception of history," he told me. In other words, the version based on testimony at the trials of high-ranking Japanese military leaders during the American occupation, which he feels distorted history to suit the American victors.

37   Fujioka and his co-thinkers brush off Japan's responsibility by clinging to shreds of doubt. The Nanking massacre? There was heavy fighting, but there is no convincing proof that a massacre took place. Survivors were encouraged, even paid, to give false evidence against the Japanese. The testimony of scores of former "comfort women"? Their words are not backed up by documentary proof. The horrible biological experiments? There may be some truth to it, but nothing has been definitively proven yet.

One of the groups in the forefront of the fight to teach students more 38
about Japan's war crimes is the Japan Teachers' Union. With 400,000 members, it is the main association of teachers in the country. Its national headquarters in Tokyo occupies a large crowded floor with scores of people working in small cubicles. There, Hiroshi Higuchi, the union's vice president, told me the Fuso textbook "should never be put in the hands of children."

A survey of more than 2,000 adults carried out last year by Japan's large 39
state television broadcasting company, NHK, found that 51 percent agreed with the statement that during World War II, Japan had carried on a "war of aggression." That was exactly the same proportion who agreed in a similar survey in 1982. However, the polls found that young adults are increasingly unsure. In 1982, 11 percent of people in their 20s said they didn't know or gave no response; last year, 37 percent said they didn't know.

Higuchi says that as old people with firsthand experience of the horrors of 40
the last war die out, public education must ensure that younger generations don't forget what happened. "As Japanese, we don't even know the facts. How can people who don't know the past cooperate with the victims?"

During the decades of conquest and war that culminated in the atomic 41
bombing of Hiroshima and Nagasaki, Japan's school teachers played a central role in preparing young people to follow the orders to fight. In 1951, still living in the ruins of their bombed-out cities, and under American occupation, the teachers' union adopted a slogan that Higuchi says is still a guiding principle for the group today: "Never again send our children to the battlefield."

Questions for Discussion and Your Reading Journal

1. What does the content of textbooks, according to Bollag, tell us about how various nations interpret historical events?
2. In what ways does he show how historical accounts change over time?
3. Writing national history is more complicated than narrating facts and listing the dates on which events occurred. What are some of the factors that complicate writing about historical events?
4. Almost 60 years after the Japanese surrender during World War II, Americans, the Japanese, and others are still arguing about what happened. Why might it be so important to people, so long after the fact, to present events in a particular way?

CARL SANDBURG

The poet Carl Sandburg (1878–1967) was born in a three-room cottage in Galesburg, Illinois. Sandburg's experiences working at a variety of low-paying jobs and traveling as a hobo greatly influenced his writing and political views. He was struck by the sharp contrast between rich and poor, and as a young adult he was drawn to the ideology of socialism. After he was married and had a family to support, Sandburg worked as a reporter for the Chicago Daily News, *covering labor issues. He was eventually given his own politically oriented newspaper column.*

Although producing poetry and other literary works did not bring in much of an income, the young Sandburg was an enthusiastic writer. When he was 38, he began to attract literary fame. A biography called Abraham Lincoln: The Prairie Years, *published in 1926, brought Sandburg his first major financial success. The four additional volumes of biography,* Abraham Lincoln: The War Years, *won him a Pulitzer Prize in 1940. Sandburg's body of poetry, compiled in a volume called* Complete Poems, *was awarded a second Pulitzer Prize in 1951.*

In the poem "Men of Science Say Their Say," Sandburg reflects on the consequences of scientific discovery—a theme that is taken up earlier in this chapter. Specifically, Sandburg envisions what life would be like after a nuclear war.

Reading Rhetorically

One of the first things you may notice as you look at this poem is that there are few capital letters and punctuation marks. Poets often play with the mechanical conventions of writing to suit their artistic purposes. As you read this poem, think about how the presence or lack of capitals and punctuation might affect the meaning of the lines.

Beyond mechanics, the organization of the poem is notable. There are several separated sections (stanzas). Look for a division between sections as you read, and reflect on why the poem might have been divided this way. Think also about the issues raised on Chapter 1, "Reading and Writing About Literature and Art."

Men of Science Say Their Say

men of science say their say:
there will be people left over
enough inhabitants among the Eskimos
among jungle folk
5 denizens of plains and plateaus
cities and towns synthetic miasma missed
enough for a census
enough to call it still a world
though definitely my friends my good friends
10 definitely not the same old world
the vanquished saying, "What happened?"
the victors saying, "We planned it so."
if it should be at the end
in the smoke the mist the silence of the end
15 if it should be one side lost the other side won

the changes among those leftover people
the scattered ones the miasma missed
their programs of living their books and music
they will be simple and conclusive
in the ways and manners of early men and women   20
the children having playroom
rulers and diplomats finding affairs less complex
new types of cripples here and there
and indescribable babbling survivors
listening to plain scholars saying,   25
should a few plain scholars have come through,
"As after other wars the peace is something else again."

amid the devastated areas and the untouched
the historians will take an interest
finding amid the ruins and shambles   30
tokens of contrast and surprise
testimonies here curious there monstrous
nuclear fission corpses having one face
radioactivity cadavers another look
bacteriological victims not unfamiliar   35
scenes and outlooks nevertheless surpassing
       those of the First World War
       and those of the Second or Global War
       —the historians will take an interest
       fill their note-books pick their way   40
       amid burned and tattered documents
       and say to each other,
       "What the hell! it isn't worth writing,
       posterity won't give a damn what we write."

in the Dark Ages many there and then   45
had fun and took love and made visions
and listened when Voices came.
then as now were the Unafraid.
then as now, "What if I am dropped into levels
       of ambiguous dust and covered   50
       over and forgotten? Have I in my
       time taken worse?"
then as now, "What if I am poured into numbers
       of the multitudinous sea and sunk
       in massive swarming fathoms? Have   55
       I gone through this last year
and the year before?"
in either Dark Ages or Renascence have there
been ever the Immeasurable Men, the Incalculable
Women, their outlooks timeless?   60
of Rabelais, is it admissible he threw an excellent laughter and his flagons and

ovens made him a name?
of Piers Plowman, is it permissible he made sad
lovable songs out of stubborn land, straw and
hoe-handles, barefoot fold treading dirt floors?
65 should it be the Dark Ages recur, will there be
again the Immeasurable Men, the Incalculable
Women?

Questions for Discussion and Your Reading Journal

1. Make a list of the vocabulary words with which you are unfamiliar. Examine the context of each of the words. How much of each word's meaning can you learn from the context? Next, go to a dictionary and look up the words. How accurate were your inferences?
2. In the first section of the poem, which describes nuclear devastation, there are a number of images. To which ones do you react most strongly? Describe your reactions.
3. Break the poem into stanzas. What is the main idea in each stanza? How are the ideas related to each other?
4. Examine the use of punctuation and capitalization in the poem. What might be some reasons for using (or not using) capitalization and punctuation in this way?

RACE, GENDER, AND OPPRESSION

JEFFREY Z. RUBIN, FRANK J. PROVENZANO, AND ZELLA LURIA

The "battle of the sexes" is one type of cultural clash that seems to cut across differences in age, affluence, and even national and ethnic boundaries. Most people would agree that an individual's sex is a major influence on that individual's behavior, role in society, and even opportunities for fulfillment. But how much of our so-called sex differences are the result of our biological gender?

In the following article, "The Eye of the Beholder: Parents' View on Sex of Newborns," Jeffrey Rubin, Frank Provenzano, and Zella Luria illustrate that the cultural sex-role socialization defining much of what we mean by "masculine" and "feminine" begins almost at birth. This article, reprinted from the American Journal of Orthopsychiatry, *reports and discusses the results of a study in which parents are asked to describe a baby using adjectives commonly associated with gendered stereotypes.*

Reading Rhetorically

Written in a style typical of scientific journals that report the results of experiments, this article begins with an abstract (that summarizes the article as a whole), continues with a description of the subjects and methods, and ends by telling the results and discussing their significance. As you read, pay particular attention to the distinctive organization and style of the writing. What kind of material goes into each section? How are the sections divided? What transitions, if any, exist between sections? Because this organizational style is the standard of scientific journal articles, understanding it will give you a head start in completing reading assignments for university courses in scientific disciplines—like biology, psychology, and chemistry, to name a few.

Besides paying attention to the structure of the article, take notice of its intended audience. Readers of the *American Journal of Orthopsychiatry* are likely to be professionals in that field or in related disciplines. Reading this article may pose a more difficult challenge than reading many of the others in this chapter. Use contextual clues to interpret words and phrases unfamiliar to you, and keep a dictionary handy to look up those that defy contextual definition. Also notice the use of *logos*.

The Eye of the Beholder:
Parents' View on Sex of Newborns

ABSTRACT

Thirty pairs of primiparous parents, fifteen with sons and fifteen with daughters, were interviewed within the first 24 hours postpartum. Although male and female infants did not differ in birth length, weight, or Apgar scores, daughters were significantly more likely than sons to be described as little, beautiful, pretty, and cute, and as resembling their mothers. Fathers made more extreme and stereotyped rating judgments of their newborns than did mothers. Findings suggest that sex-typing and sex-role socialization have already begun at birth.

As Schaffer[10] has observed, the infant at birth is essentially an asocial, largely undifferentiated creature. It appears to be little more than a tiny ball of hair, fingers, toes, cries, gasps, and gurgles. However, while it may seem that "if you've seen one, you've seen them all," babies are *not* all alike—a fact that is of special importance to their parents, who want, and appear to need, to view their newborn child as a creature that is special. Hence, much of early parental interaction with the infant may be focused on a search for distinctive features. Once the fact that the baby is normal has been established, questions such as "Who does the baby look like?" and "How much does it weigh?" are asked.

Of all the questions parents ask themselves and each other about their infant, one seems to have priority: "Is it a boy or a girl?" The reasons for and consequences of posing this simple question are by no means trivial. The answer, "boy" or "girl," may result in the parents' organizing their perception of the infant with respect to a wide variety of attributes—ranging from its size to its activity, attractiveness, even its future potential. It is the purpose of the present study to examine the kind of verbal picture parents form of the newborn infant, as a function both of their own and their infant's gender.

4   As Asch[2] observed years ago, in forming our impressions of others, we each tend to develop a *Gestalt*—a global picture of what others are like, which permits us to organize our perceptions of the often discrepant, contradictory aspects of their behavior and manner into a unified whole. The awareness of another's status,[13] the belief that he is "warm" or "cold,"[2, 5] "extroverted" or "introverted,"[6] even the apparently trivial knowledge of another's name[4]—each of these cues predisposes us to develop a stereotypic view of that other, his underlying nature, and how he is likely to behave. How much more profound, then, may be the consequences of a cue as prominent in parents' minds as the gender of their own precious, newborn infant.

5   The study reported here is addressed to parental perceptions of their infants at the point when these infants first emerge into the world. If it can be demonstrated that parental sex-typing has already begun its course at this earliest of moments in the life of the child, it may be possible to understand better one of the important antecedents of the complex process by which the growing child comes to view itself as boy-ish or girl-ish.

6   Based on our review of the literature, two forms of parental sex-typing may be expected to occur at the time of the infant's birth. First, it appears likely that parents will view and label their newborn child differentially, as a simple function of the infant's gender. Aberle and Naegele[1] and Tasch,[12] using only fathers as subjects, found that they had different expectations for sons and daughters: Sons were expected to be aggressive and athletic, daughters were expected to be pretty, sweet, fragile, and delicate. Rebelsky and Hanks[9] found that fathers spent more time talking to their daughters than their sons during the first three months of life. While the sample size was too small for the finding to be significant, they suggest that the role of father-of-daughter may be perceived as requiring greater nurturance. Similarly, Pedersen and Robson[8] reported that the fathers of infant daughters exhibited more behavior labeled (by the authors) as "apprehension over well-being" than did the fathers of sons.

7   A comparable pattern emerges in research using mothers as subjects. Sears, Maccoby and Levin,[11] for example, found that the mothers of kindergartners reported tolerating more aggression from sons than daughters, when it was directed toward parents and peers. In addition, maternal nurturance was seen as more important for the daughter's than the son's development. Taken together, the findings in this body of research lead us to expect parents (regardless of their gender) to view their newborn infants differentially—labeling daughters as weaker, softer, and therefore in greater need of nurturance, than sons.

8   The second form of parental sex-typing we expect to occur at birth is a function both of the infant's gender *and* the parent's own gender. Goodenough[3]

interviewed the parents of nursery school children, and found that mothers were less concerned with sex-typing their child's behavior than were fathers. More recently, Meyer and Sobieszek[7] presented adults with videotapes of two seventeen-month-old children (each of whom was sometimes described as a boy and sometimes as a girl), and asked their subjects to describe and interpret the children's behavior. They found that male subjects, as well as those having little contact with small children, were more likely (although not always significantly so) to rate the children in sex-stereotypic fashion—attributing "male qualities" such as independence, aggressiveness, activity, and alertness to the child presented as a boy, and qualities such as cuddliness, passivity, and delicacy to the "girl." We expect, therefore, that sex of infant and sex of parent will interact, such that it is fathers, rather than mothers, who emerge as the greater sex-typers of their newborn

In order to investigate parental sex-typing of their newborn infants, and   9 in order, more specifically, to test the predictions that sex-typing is a function of the infant's gender, as well as the gender of both infant and parent, parents of newborn boys and girls were studied in the maternity ward of a hospital, within the first 24 hours postpartum, to uncover their perceptions of the characteristics of their newborn infants.

METHOD

Subjects

The subjects consisted of 30 pairs of primiparous [first-time] parents, fifteen of   10 whom had sons, and fifteen of whom had daughters. The subjects were drawn from the available population of expecting parents at a suburban Boston hospital serving local, predominantly lower-middle-class families. Using a list of primiparous expectant mothers obtained from the hospital, the experimenter made contact with families by mail several months prior to delivery, and requested the subjects' assistance in "a study of social relations among parents and their first child." Approximately one week after the initial contact by mail, the experimenter telephoned each family, in order to answer any questions the prospective parents might have about the study, and to obtain their consent. Of the 43 families reached by phone, eleven refused to take part in the study. In addition, one consenting mother subsequently gave birth to a low birth weight infant (a 74-ounce girl), while another delivered an unusually large son (166 ounces). Because these two infants were at the two ends of the distribution of birth weights, and because they might have biased the data in support of our hypotheses, the responses of their parents were eliminated from the sample.

All subjects participated in the study within the first 24 hours postpartum—the fathers almost immediately after delivery, and the mothers (who were often   11 under sedation at the time of delivery) up to but not later than 24 hours later. The mothers typically had spoken with their husbands at least once during this 24 hour period.

There were no reports of medical problems during any of the pregnancies   12 or deliveries, and all infants in the sample were full-term at time of birth.

Deliveries were made under general anesthesia, and the fathers were not allowed in the delivery room. The fathers were not permitted to handle their babies during the first 24 hours, but could view them through display windows in the hospital nursery. The mothers, on the other hand, were allowed to hold and feed their infants. The subjects participated individually in the study. The fathers were met in a small, quiet waiting room used exclusively by the maternity ward, while the mothers were met in their hospital rooms. Every precaution was taken not to upset the parents or interfere with hospital procedure.

Procedure

13   After introducing himself to the subjects, and after congratulatory amenities, the experimenter (FJP) asked the parents: "Describe your baby as you would be to a close friend or relative." The responses were tape-recorded and subsequently coded.

14   The experimenter then asked the subjects to take a few minutes to complete a short questionnaire. The instructions for completion of the questionnaire were as follows:

> On the following page there are 18 pairs of opposite words. You are asked to rate your baby in relation to these words, placing an "x" or a checkmark in the space that best describes your baby. The more a word describes your baby, the closer your "x" should be to that word.
>
> Example: Imagine you were asked to rate Trees.
>
> Good :____:____:____:____:____:____:____:____:____:____: Bad
>
> Strong :____:____:____:____:____:____:____:____:____:____: Weak
>
> If you cannot decide or your feelings are mixed, place your "x" in the center space. Remember, the more you think a word is a good description of your baby, the closer you should place your "x" to that word. If there are no questions, please begin. Remember, you are rating your baby. Don't spend too much time thinking about your answers. First impressions are usually the best.

Having been presented with these instructions, the subjects then proceeded to rate their baby on each of the eighteen following, eleven-point, bipolar adjective scales: firm-soft; large featured-fine featured; big-little; relaxed-nervous; cuddly-not cuddly; easy going-fussy; cheerful-cranky; good eater-poor eater; excirable-calm; active-inactive; beautiful-plain; sociable-unsociable; well coordinated-awkward; noisy-quiet; alert-inattentive; strong-weak; friendly-unfriendly; hardy-delicate.

15   Upon completion of the questionnaire, the subjects were thanked individually, and when both parents of an infant had completed their participation, the underlying purposes of the study were fully explained.

Hospital Data

In order to acquire a more objective picture of the infants whose characteris- 16
tics were being judged by the subjects, data were obtained from hospital
records concerning each infant's birth weight, birth length, and Apgar scores.
Apgar scores are typically assigned at five and ten minutes postpartum, and
represent the physician's ratings of the infant's color, muscle tonicity, reflex
irritability, and heart and respiratory rates. No significant differences between
the male and female infants were found for birth weight, birth length, or
Apgar scores at five and ten minutes postpartum.*

Results

In Table 1, the subjects' mean ratings of their infant, by condition, for each of 17
the eighteen bipolar adjective scales, are presented. The right-extreme column
of Table 1 shows means for each scale, which have been averaged across

---

*Birth weight ($\bar{X}_{Sons}$ = 114.43 ounces, $\bar{X}_{Daughters}$ = 110.00, t (28) = 1.04); Birth length ($\bar{X}_{Sons}$ = 19.80 inches, $\bar{X}_{Daughters}$ = 19.96, t (28) = 0.52); 5 minute Apgar score ($\bar{X}_{Sons}$ = 9.07, $\bar{X}_{Daughters}$ = 9.33, t (28) = 0.69); and 10 minute Apgar score ($\bar{X}_{Sons}$ = 10.00, $\bar{X}_{Daughters}$ = 10.00).

Table 1 **Mean Ratings on the 18 Adjective Scales, as a Function of Sex of Parent (Mother vs. Father) and Sex of Infant (Son vs. Daughter)[a].**

SCALE	EXPERIMENTAL CONDITION				
(I)–(II)	M-S	M-D	F-S	F-D	$\bar{X}$
Firm-Soft	7.47	7.40	3.60	8.93	6.85
Large featured-Fine featured	7.20	7.53	4.93	9.20	7.22
Big-Little	4.73	8.40	4.13	8.53	6.45
Relaxed-Nervous	3.20	4.07	3.80	4.47	3.88
Cuddly-Not cuddly	1.40	2.20	2.20	1.47	1.82
Easy going-Fussy	3.20	4.13	3.73	4.60	3.92
Cheerful-Cranky	3.93	3.73	4.27	3.60	3.88
Good eater-Poor eater	3.73	3.80	4.60	4.53	4.16
Excitable-Calm	6.20	6.53	5.47	6.40	6.15
Active-Inactive	2.80	2.73	3.33	4.60	3.36
Beautiful-Plain	2.13	2.93	1.87	2.87	2.45
Sociable-Unsociable	4.80	3.80	3.73	4.07	4.10
Well coordinated-Awkard	3.27	2.27	2.07	4.27	2.97
Noisy-Quiet	6.87	7.00	5.67	7.73	6.82
Alert-Inattentive	2.47	2.40	1.47	3.40	2.44
Strong-Weak	3.13	2.20	1.73	4.20	2.82
Friendly-Unfriendly	3.33	3.40	3.67	3.73	3.53
Hardy-Delicate	5.20	4.67	3.27	6.93	5.02

[a]The larger the mean, the greater the rated presence of the attribute denoted by the second (right-hand)
adjective to each pair.

conditions. Infant stimuli, overall, were characterized closer to the scale anchors of soft, fine featured, little, relaxed, cuddly, easy going, cheerful, good eater, calm, active, beautiful, sociable, well coordinated, quiet, alert, strong, friendly, and hardly. Our parent-subjects, in other words, appear to have felt on Day 1 of their babies' lives that their newborn infants represented delightful, competent new additions to the world!

18   Analysis of variance of the subjects' questionnaire responses (1 and 56 degrees of freedom) yielded a number of interesting findings. There were *no* rating differences on the eighteen scales as a simple function of Sex of Parent: Parents appear to agree with one another, on the average. As a function of Sex of Infant, however, several significantly softer ($F = 10.67$, $p < .005$), finer featured ($F = 9.27$, $p < .005$), littler ($F = 28.83$, $p < .001$), and more inattentive ($F = 4.44$, $p < .05$). In addition, significant interaction effects emerged for seven of the eighteen scales: firm-soft ($F = 11.22$, $p < .005$), large featured-fine featured ($F = 6.78$, $p < .025$), cuddly-not cuddly ($F = 4.18$, $p < .05$), well coordinated-awkward ($F = 12.52$, $p < .001$), alert-inattentive ($F = 5.10$, $p < .05$), strong-weak ($F = 10.67$, $p < .005$), and hardy-delicate ($F = 5.32$, $p < .025$).

19   The meaning of these interactions becomes clear in Table 1, in which it can be seen that six of these significant interactions display a comparable pattern; Fathers were more extreme in their ratings of *both* sons and daughters than were mothers. Thus, sons were rated as firmer, larger featured, better coordinated, more alert, stronger, and hardier—and daughters as softer, finer featured, more awkward, more inattentive, weaker, and more delicate—by their fathers than by their mothers. Finally, with respect to the other significant interaction effect (cuddly-not cuddly), a rather different pattern was found. In this case, mothers rated sons as cuddlier than daughters, while fathers rated daughters as cuddlier than sons—a finding we have dubbed the "oedipal" effect.

20   Responses to the interview question were coded in terms of adjectives used and references to resemblance. Given the open-ended nature of the question, many adjectives were used—healthy, for example, being a high frequency response cutting across sex of babies and parents. Parental responses were polled, and recurrent adjectives were analyzed by X^2 analysis for sex of child. Sons were described as big more frequently than were daughters (X^2 (1) = 4.26, $p < .05$); daughters were called little more often than were sons (X^2 (1) = 4.28, $p < .05$). The "feminine" cluster—beautiful, pretty, and cute—was used significantly more often to describe daughters than sons (X^2 (1) = 5.40, $p < .05$). Finally, daughters were said to resemble mothers more frequently than were sons (X^2 (1) = 3.87, $p < .05$).

Discussion

21 The data indicate that parents—especially fathers—differentially label their infants, as a function of the infant's gender. These results are particularly striking in light of the fact that our sample of male and female infants did *not* differ in birth length, weight, or Apgar scores. Thus, the results appear to be a pure case of parental labeling—what a colleague has described as "nature's first projective test" (personal communication, Leon Eisenberg). Given the

importance parents attach to the birth of their first child, it is not surprising that such ascriptions are made.

But why should posing the simple question, "Is it a boy or a girl?" be so 22 salient in parents' minds, and have such important consequences? For one thing, an infant's gender represents a truly *distinctive* characteristic. The baby is either a boy or a girl—there are no ifs, ands, or buts about it. A baby may be active sometimes, and quiet at others, for example, but it can always be assigned to one of two distinct classes: boy or girl. Secondly, an infant's gender tends to assume the properties of a *definitive* characteristic. It permits parents to organize their questions and answers about the infant's appearance and behavior into an integrated *Gestalt*. Finally, an infant's gender is often a *normative* characteristic. It is a property that seems to be of special importance not only to the infant's parents, but to relatives, friends, neighbors, and even casual passersby in the street. For each of these reasons, an infant's gender is a property of considerable importance to its parents, and is therefore one that is likely to lead to labeling and the investment of surplus meaning.

The results of the present study are, of course, not unequivocal. Although 23 it was found, as expected, that the sex-typing of infants varied as a function of the infant's gender, as well as the gender of both infant and parent, significant differences did not emerge for all eighteen of the adjective scales employed. Two explanations for this suggest themselves. First, it may simply be that we have overestimated the importance of sex-typing at birth. A second possibility, however, is that sex-typing is more likely to emerge with respect to certain classes of attributes—namely, those which denote physical or constitutional, rather than "internal," dispositional, factors. Of the eight different adjective pairs for which significant main or interaction effects emerged, six (75%) clearly refer to external attributes of the infant. Conversely, of the ten adjective pairs for which no significant differences were found, only three (30%) clearly denote external attributes. This suggests that it is physical and constitutional factors that specially lend themselves to sex-typing at birth, at least in our culture.

Another finding of interest is the lack of significant effects, as a simple 24 function of sex of parent. Although we predicted no such effects, and were therefore not particularly surprised by the emergence of "non-findings," the implication of these results is by no means trivial. If we had omitted the sex of the infant as a factor in the present study, we might have been led to conclude (on the basis of simply varying the sex of the parent) that *no* differences exist in parental descriptions of newborn infants—a patently erroneous conclusion! It is only when the infant's and the parent's gender are considered together, in interaction, that the lack of differences between overall parental mean ratings can be seen to reflect the true differences between the parents. Mothers rate both sexes closer together on the adjective pairs than do fathers (who are the stronger sex-typers), but *both* parents agree on the direction of sex differences.

An issue of considerable concern, in interpreting the findings of the present study appropriately, stems from the fact that fathers were not permitted to handle their babies, while mothers were. The question then becomes: Is it possible that the greater sex-typing by fathers is simply attributable to their lesser 25 exposure to their infants? This, indeed, may have been the case. However, it seems worthwhile to consider some of the alternative possibilities. Might not the lesser exposure of fathers to their infants have led not to greater sex-typing, but to a data "wash out"—with no differences emerging in paternal ratings? After all, given no opportunity to handle their babies, and therefore deprived of the opportunity to obtain certain first-hand information about them, the fathers might have been expected to make a series of neutral ratings—hovering around the middle of each adjective scale. The fact that they did not do this suggests that they brought with them a variety of sex stereotypes that they then imposed upon their infant. Moreover, the fact that mothers, who were allowed to hold and feed their babies, made distinctions between males and females that were in keeping with cultural sex-stereotypes (see Table 1), suggests that even if fathers had had the opportunity of holding their infants, similar results might have been obtained. We should also not lose sight of the fact that father-mother differences in exposure to infants continue well into layer years. Finally, one must question the very importance of the subjects' differential exposure on the grounds that none of the typical "exposure" effects reported in the social psychological literature[14] were observed. In particular, one might have expected mother to have come to rate their infants more favorably than fathers, simply as a result of greater exposure. Yet such was not the case.

26   The central implication of the study, then, is that sex-typing and sex-role socialization appear to have already begun their course at the time of the infant's birth, when information about the infant is minimal. The *Gestalt* parents develop, and the labels they ascribe to their newborn infant, may well affect subsequent expectations about the manner in which their infant ought to behave, as well as parental itself. This parental behavior, moreover, when considered in conjunction with the rapid unfolding of the infant's own behavioral repertoire, may well lead to a modification of the very labeling that affected parental behavior in the first place. What began as a one-way street now bears traffic in two directions. In order to understand the full importance and implications of our findings, therefore, research clearly needs to be conducted in which delivery room stereotypes are traced in the family during the first several months after birth, and their impact upon parental behavior is considered. In addition, further research is clearly in order if we are to understand fully the importance of early paternal sex-typing in the socialization of sex-roles.

References

1. Aberle, D., & Naegele, K. (1952). Middle-class fathers' occupational role and attitudes toward children. *American Journal of Orthopsychiatry, 22*(2), 366–378.
2. Asch, S. (1946). Forming impressions of personality. *Journal of Abnormal and Social Psychology, 41,* 258–290.
3. Goodenough, E. (1957). Interest in persons as an aspect of sex difference in the early years. *Genetic Psychology Monographs, 55,* 287–323.

4. Harari, H., & McDavid, J. Name stereotypes and teachers' expectations. *Journal of Educational Psychology.* (in press)

5. Kelley, H. (1950). The warm-cold variable in first impressions of persons. *Journal of Personality 18,* 431–439.

6. Luchins, A. (1957). Experimental attempts to minimize the impact of first impressions. In C. Hovland, (Ed.), *The order of presentation in persuasion.* New Haven.: Yale University Press.

7. Meyer, J., & Sobieszek, B. (1972). Effect of a child's sex on adult interpretations of its behavior. *Development Psychology, 6,* 42–48.

8. Pedersen, P., & Robson, K. (1969). Father participation in infancy. *American Journal of Orthopsychiatry, 39*(3), 466–472.

9. Rebelsky, F., & Hanks, C. (1971). Fathers' verbal interaction with infants in the first three months of life. *Child Development, 42,* 63–68.

10. Schaffer, H. (1971). *The growth of sociability.* Baltimore: *Penguin Books.*

11. Sears, R., Maccoby, E., & Levin, H. (1957). *Patterns of child rearing.* Evanston, IL: Row, Peterson.

12. Tasch, R. (1952). The role of the father in the family. *Journal of Experimental Education, 20,* 319–361.

13. Wilson, P. (1968). The perceptual distortion of height as a function of ascribed academic status. *Journal of Social Psychology, 74,* 97–102.

14. Zajonc, R. (1968). Attitudinal effects of mere exposure. *Journal of Personality and Social Psychology, Monograph Supplement 9,* 1–27.

Questions for Discussion and Your Reading Journal

1. Who is the audience for this article? How do the language and structure reflect that audience?

2. Why do parents focus so intensely on the gender of their newborn babies?

3. What are the two kinds of parental behavior that illustrate gender discrimination regarding newborns?

4. Do the differences that parents discriminate actually exist, according to the authors? What might account for the perceptual problems?

5. This text is structured according to a pattern typical of articles in scientific journals. Analyze the organization of the essay. Why are the sections separated? What function does each section serve?

ROBERT BRANNON

Both this essay and the following one take up where the last essay leaves off. What begins in infancy continues throughout adulthood—gender stereotyping is a lifelong process.

Robert Brannon, an associate professor of psychology at Brooklyn College, expounds his theory about the social construction of male roles in "Why Men Become Men, and Other Theories." The coeditor of The 49% Majority: The Male Sex, *Brannon desires to go beyond simply describing men's gendered behavior; he wants to change it. Brannon is the founder of the National Organization for Changing Men.*

Reading Rhetorically

As the headnote indicates, Brannon's article is about changing the way people think of men and their roles in society. Knowing this, what kinds of topics do you think the article is likely to cover? What strategies for persuasion is he likely to use? Examining the title of an article and the explanatory material that accompanies it (such as a headnote) can be an excellent pre-reading strategy, because these activities help to contextualize the information you read from the first word forward. Practice this strategy in relation to Brannon's article. When you are finished reading, evaluate the degree to which the exercise was worthwhile. This article has at least two purposes: explaining male roles and working toward changing them. As you read, look for stylistic differences in the parts of the article that are mainly intended to inform and the parts that are geared toward persuasion. What are some of the differences in word choice? What are the differences in sentence structure? What other differences do you see? A writer's style can be a powerful tool in achieving his or her purpose.

Why Men Become Men, and Other Theories

1   A revolution is taking place in scientific thinking today about why men and women act and behave somewhat differently. The revolution seeks to displace a theory in American social science that has been around since the late 1930s. Until recently the older theory or explanation for human differences was so universal, so completely without competition that people didn't really see it as a theory, they saw it as the only explanation. Let me step back and look at that time to show the context in which an important scientific theory appears.

2   In the late 1800s and early 1900s, there was a growing concern that American men were getting too soft, that they were not measuring up to the demands of manhood. Eighty percent of American men before the Civil War had been farmers or self-employed. But cities grew after that and many urban men became isolated from the traditional hunting and fishing activities that previously defined manhood. At the same time, the battle for the vote for women was reaching its climax, and articles began to appear in popular magazines with titles such as "The Effeminization of the American Man" or "Are We Raising A Nation of Sissies?"

3   Biographies written at the time began to move away from praising men who had qualities such as thrift and piety and to talk about forcefulness. City parents were concerned that their sons would grow up ignorant of how to tie knots and identify trees and tracks in the wilderness. A group of adults decided that what the country really needed was something to help boys develop into strong, manly men. They formed an organization called The Boy Scouts of America.

Then came the Depression, and record numbers of American men were   4
in the terrible situation of being unemployed. Their identities as providers
and heads of families were threatened as never before. A book called *Sex and
Personality* (1936) appeared by a famous Stanford psychologist, Louis Terman, and Catherine Cox Miles, his associate, who enunciated a new theory
of why the sexes were different and what the differences were. The theory
never really had a name, because it became so ubiquitous that people didn't
realize it was just one possible explanation. In retrospect, people are beginning to call it the "gender identity theory" or the "sex-role identity theory."
The word "identity" is what distinguishes it. For four decades it remained
the dominant theory in social science about women and men, and people
like Benjamin Spock put it into terms that parents and educators could
understand.

The theory says basically that boys and girls develop different patterns of   5
interests and behaviors because of something that happens to them when they're
quite young. Sometime around the age of two, something mysterious happens,
the child acquires something we can't measure or see but know to be vitally
important—the child forms a gender identity, learns what sex he or she is. This
interior event was thought to cause the development of sex-differentiated
behavior in which the little boy began to play with trucks and the little girl
began to play with dolls.

Although the theory postulated that this is the normal course of develop-   6
ment, it could, according to psychologists, easily go astray. Most of their concern was that boys would not adequately acquire the male identity (although
the theory applied to girls as well). If they didn't get this gender identity the
way they should at this young age, a variety of negative things could happen:
They might not fit into society, they might not be popular and well-adjusted,
or they might turn into homosexuals. This lurking fear in American social science was basic and pervasive.

The original book in which the theory was enunciated mentioned off-   7
handedly that there is the masculine man, the man who is less masculine, the
man who is almost feminine in his interests and behaviors, and the invert, or
homosexual man, "capable of attraction only to members of his own sex." We
can see now that there was a fundamental confusion in the minds of scientists
who were laying out ideas that would guide us through the next forty years.
They believed that sexual orientation (which sex one is attracted to) had something inexorably and automatically to do with the extent to which each of us
acts feminine or masculine, compared with others of our own sex. To learn if
their child was on the right track, adults looked at the child's behavior. Thus
the direction of causality was reversed, and we inferred that little Johnny had
a male identity because he had begun to play with boy's toys.

This led to a serious paradox. Science began to say that a polarity is essen-   8
tial to mental health, that the more masculine the little boy acts, the better, the
more feminine the little girl acts, the better. There are even examples of social
workers and educators telling teachers that little Johnny may be a problem in
the classroom—he might tear the wings off flies and set cats on fire—but at
least he's all boy. In this convoluted sense, behavior that was undesirable was

seen as good, because it meant that at least the boy wasn't going to become one of those unmentionable types of men.

9   Terman and Miles then developed the Masculinity/Femininity Test for measuring whether or not a child has acquired a gender identity appropriately. It's a paper and pencil instrument that was given to literally hundreds of thousands of American children, teenagers, and young adults. There have been many forms of it that have followed, and you will find smaller versions of it embedded in a large number of psychological tests still in use.

10   Let me give you a sample of a few questions from it. What is a marigold? If you know the answer, give yourself one point toward having a feminine identity. How many people are there on a baseball team? That gives you one point toward masculinity. Who were the Rough Riders? Masculine. What is a loom used for? Feminine. And here's an esthetic question: Does the color red go best with lavender, purple, pink, or black? If you think you know, you may have a feminine identity. A few other questions: Have you been expelled from school? If so, masculine. If you like to wear expensive clothing, feminine. Do you like to watch love scenes in the movies? Feminine. Do you dislike the opposite sex? Masculine. Would you like to visit Paris? Feminine. Would you like to visit a Chicago slaughterhouse? Masculine.

11   This scale and its variations obviously don't measure anything fundamental besides facts and preferences. Each of these items was included in this measure simply because in large use of the test more men than women answered "yes" to a question, so it was put on the masculine scale.

12   Although it was not based on any underlying psychological theory, the Masculinity/Feminity test has been used with tenacity and certainty by several generations of American scholars. The very first use to which it was put was as a screening device to find homosexuals in the general population. Male college students who scored a little less masculine than others and female students who scored a little less feminine were invited in for special counseling. It was not a successful measure, but any man interested in art and music would often end up being counseled, and a woman who took herself seriously and wanted to use her mind was suspected of lesbianism. In some cases, teenaged boys who had gotten feminine scores on this test were administered truth serum—without their consent or the knowledge of their parents—to see if they would admit to homosexual activities (Pleck, 1981).

13   As the years have gone by, more and more evidence has been piling up that simply does not fit this gender identity theory very well. Like certain other belief systems in the social sciences—notably Freudian thinking—it has proved remarkably lasting and able to explain anything by simply flip-flopping the assumptions—if men act too feminine, they don't have the right gender identity; if men become hypermasculine and get into delinquency, alcoholism, or antisocial aggression, they are overcompensating for a weak identity.

ENTER A NEW THEORY

14   The way theories change in science is that for a long time we keep saying that this doesn't quite fit, but we still believe the theory. Eventually the theory is

weighted down by all the exceptions and the stage is set for the emergence of a new explanation that does a better job.

The newer theory that has emerged in the social sciences and is beginning to make an appearance in textbooks can best be called the "sex-role theory." The key concept is that of a role, a set of behaviors a person plays under certain circumstances. It relies heavily on the analogy of the theater. If I play the role of Hamlet, I speak words that someone else wrote. Some play Hamlet better than others, but we all say the same words and go through much the same sequence of events. In the same sense there are many things we do every day as social roles. You become a customer in a store for a little while; that's a social role. When you drive a car your own personality is pretty much submerged to the demands of the situation and you act out a socially determined set of behaviors.

We are cast in our social roles at the moment of birth. When a baby is born, and if it has a penis they say, "Oh, it's a boy." As in a play, the baby has been assigned a male sex and will remain in that role for the rest of his life. Unfortunately, they don't hand him a script that tells him how to be a man; he has to spend the next twenty or so years of his life slowly, painfully learning that.

In the United States the male role defines masculinity and what a man is supposed to do, think, be interested in, and act like. These things make up a rather complex set of guidelines, not all equally important, but almost every American man has been affected, to one extent or another, by them. The guidelines include such traits as avoiding displays of emotional openness, vulnerability, or dependence. We men are not supposed to let others know when we feel scared or depressed or even when we feel happy or in love. At the emotional level we're supposed to even things out. We avoid anything that people think of as "sissy" or feminine: any color, any personal product, any mannerism, any type of food, any type of vocabulary. A man, for instance, should never use words like "sweet," "precious," or "darling."

As part of our masculinity, we are supposed to be looked up to and be admired. This has a variety of possible outlets, but the traditional one is financial. A man becomes the breadwinner, the head of his family, the king within his little castle, and he demands respect from his wife and children. Even better is if he can become a leader of other men, if he can achieve success, be visible with wealth, fame, power—all of these things count toward masculinity.

A man is supposed to be in control of things, be able to get things done. He is supposed to be confident, decisive, logical, tough, independent, self-reliant, serious, to have that whole range of characteristics we see in the Hollywood heroes: Paul Newman, Burt Reynolds, John Wayne, Clint Eastwood, all the familiar cowboys and detectives.

We have begun to recognize that the amazing, elusive phenomenon that so characterizes our social life—the great division into female and male—is in many ways a phenomenon of roles. Sex appears to be primarily and essentially a learned social role. Our bodies are somewhat different, there are different physical differences (men are somewhat bigger and more muscular, women bear children and nurse them), but these biological facts appear to have less to do with differences in personality, lifestyles, and interests than with the fact that we've been raised to learn how to be a man or how to be a woman.

21   The gender identity theory, which still underlies most of what is written in our area, is basically conservative. It believes that differences that characterize behavior somehow spring from some deep essence and has something unchangeable to do with mental health. To tamper with this—for women to want high-paying, leadership jobs, for example, or to exercise their intelligence—somehow tampers with the fundamental nature of things. For men to feel emotions of tenderness, love and caring, to not want to be competitive or aggressive, is to deviate from the nature of things.

22   The new sex-role theory, in contrast, is more or less agnostic toward social change. It does not actively advocate change. It says that while a society such as ours is divided into male and female, there's nothing intrinsically right about this division. If society is going to evolve in a different direction, and if the sex roles that have channeled male and female areas are evolving and changing, there is no fundamental reason why this should cause a problem.

References

Pleck, Joseph. *Myth of Masculinity.* Cambridge: MIT P, 1981.
Terman, Lewis, and Catherine Cox Miles. *Sex and Personality.* London: McGraw-Hill, 1936.

Questions for Discussion and Your Reading Journal

1. Brannon begins his article with a description of a traditional theory about the origin of gender roles. Summarize the theory. Why do you suppose Brannon begins with this traditional view?
2. What are the consequences of accepting the traditional theory in relation to child rearing? What paradox results, according to Brannon, from holding the traditional view?
3. Why did psychologists use tests to measure the relative "masculinity" or "femininity" of children? What kind of tests did they use? In what ways were the test results used? Evaluate the use of the test results.
4. What new theory does Brannon posit for the construction of gender roles? How are the assumptions that underlie Brannon's theory different from the assumptions that underlie the traditional theory?
5. List the characteristics of the male role as they are presented in the article. What other characteristics might you add? What might you subtract?
6. What are the social consequences of holding Brannon's theory? How are these consequences different from those that follow the traditional theory?

NAOMI WEISSTEIN

Naomi Weisstein, a psychologist in New York City, graduated from Harvard University in 1964. An active participant in the radical feminist movement, she has specialized in research about women. In "Psychology

Constructs the Female," Weisstein posits a theory of gender construction similar to that of Brannon in the previous article. Like Brannon, Weisstein begins by describing the assumptions and conceptions of opposing theories; then she explains the flaws that she discerns in those assumptions and conceptions.

Feminist scientists see scientific "knowledge" and "truth" as being subjective. They propose that science can serve different objectives and that those objectives have generally reflected the desires of a particular group of people. Thus, focusing on the experience of people outside that group can lead to different conceptions of "knowledge" and "truth."

On the other hand, dominant cultural conceptions of what is "feminine" can be constructed in such a way as to exclude women from certain pursuits, to deny the importance of women's activities and interests, and to promote the economic and social interests of men at the expense of women. These acts of discrimination are often legitimized by authorities in scientific fields because they have the power to construct the definitions involved in "science."

Reading Rhetorically

A pre-reading strategy that can be very helpful in getting a general sense of what a text is about is examining subheadings. There are several subheadings in this article, and reading them can indicate not only what the article is generally about but also the direction in which its development will proceed. Read quickly through the subheadings in "Psychology Constructs the Female" to give yourself a head start in understanding its content and structure.

Like the author of the previous article, Weisstein is writing to promote change. She intends to influence her audience in favor of changing traditional conceptions of what is masculine and what is feminine. As you read, compare and contrast Weisstein's persuasive strategies with those of Brannon in the previous article. Although there are some similarities, the differences between the two writers' styles and approaches are remarkable and instructive.

Psychology Constructs the Female

It is an implicit assumption that the area of psychology which concerns itself with personality has the onerous but necessary task of describing the limits of human possibility. Thus when we are about to consider the liberation of women, we naturally look to psychology to tell us what "true" liberation would mean: what would give women the freedom to fulfill their own intrinsic natures. Psychologists have set about describing the true natures of women with a certainty and a sense of their own infallibility rarely found in the secular world. Bruno Bettelheim, of the University of Chicago, tells us (1965) that "We must start with the realization that, as much as women want to be good scientists or engineers, they want first and foremost to be womanly companions of men and to be mothers." Erik Erikson of Harvard University (1964), upon noting that young women often ask whether they can "have an identity before they know whom they will marry, and for whom they will make a home," explains somewhat elegiacally that "Much of a young woman's identity is already defined in her kind of attractiveness and in the selectivity of her search for the man (or men) by whom she wishes to be sought. . . ." Mature womanly fulfillment, for Erikson, rests on the fact that a woman's ". . . somatic design harbors an "inner space" destined to bear the offspring of chosen men, and with it, a biological, psychological, and ethical commitment to take care of human infancy." Some psychiatrists even see the acceptance of woman's role by women as a solution to societal problems. "Woman is nurturance. . .," writes Joseph Rheingold (1964), a psychiatrist at Harvard Medical School, ". . . anatomy decrees the life of a woman . . . when women grow up without dread of their biological functions and without subversion by feminist doctrine, and therefore enter upon motherhood with a sense of fulfillment and altruistic sentiment, we shall attain the goal of a good life and a secure world in which we live it" (p. 714).

2   These views from men who are assumed to be experts reflect, in a surprisingly transparent way, the cultural consensus. They not only assert that a woman is defined by her ability to attract men, they see no alternative definitions. They think that the definition of a woman in terms of a man is the way it should be: And they back it up with psychosexual incantation and biological ritual curses. A woman has an identity if she is attractive enough to obtain a man, and thus, a home: For this will allow her to set about her life's task of "joyful altruism and nurturance." . . .

3   The central argument of my article, then, is this. Psychology has nothing to say about what women are really like, what they need and what they want, essentially because psychology does not know. I want to stress that this failure is not limited to women; rather, the kind of psychology which has addressed itself to how people act and who they are has failed to understand, in the first place, why people act the way they do, and certainly failed to understand what might make them act differently.

4   The kind of psychology which has addressed itself to these questions divides into two professional areas: academic personality research, and clinical psychology and psychiatry. The basic reason for failure is the same in both these areas: The central assumption for most psychologists of human personality has been that human behavior rests on an individual and inner dynamic, perhaps fixed in infancy, perhaps fixed by genitalia, perhaps simply arranged in a rather immovable cognitive network. But this assumption is rapidly losing ground as personality psychologists fail again and again to get consistency in the assumed personalities of their subjects (Block, 1968). Meanwhile, the evidence is collecting that what a person does, and who he believes himself to be, will in general be a function of what people around him expect him to be, and what the overall situation in which he is acting implies that he is. Compared to the influence of the social context within which a person lives, his or her history and "traits," as well as biological makeup, may simply be random variations, "noise" superimposed on the true signal which can predict behavior.

Some academic personality psychologists are at least looking at the 5
counter evidence and questioning their theories; no such corrective is occurring in clinical psychology and psychiatry. Freudians and neo-Freudians, Adle-
rians and neo-Adlerians, classicists and swingers, clinicians and psychiatrists,
simply refuse to look at the evidence against their theory and practice. And
they support their theory and their practice with stuff so transparently biased
as to have absolutely no standing as empirical evidence.

To summarize: The first reason for psychology's failure to understand 6
what people are and how they act is that psychology has looked for inner traits
when it should have been looking for social context; the second reason for psychology's failure is that the theoreticians of personality have generally been
clinicians and psychiatrists, and they have never considered it necessary to
have evidence in support of their theories.

THEORY WITHOUT EVIDENCE

Let us turn to this latter cause of failure first: the acceptance by psychiatrists 7
and clinical psychologists of theory without evidence. If we inspect the literature of personality, it is immediately obvious that the bulk of it is written by
clinicians and psychiatrists, and that the major support for their theories is
"years of intensive clinical experience." This is a tradition started by Freud.
His "insights" occurred during the course of his work with his patients. Now
there is nothing wrong with such an approach to theory *formulation:* A person is free to make up theories with any inspiration which works: divine revelation, intensive clinical practice, a random numbers table. But he is not free
to claim any validity for his theory until it has been tested and confirmed. But
theories are treated in no such tentative way in ordinary clinical practice. Consider Freud. What he thought constituted evidence violated the most minimal
conditions of scientific rigor. In *The Sexual Enlightenment of Children* (1963),
the classic document which is supposed to demonstrate empirically the existence of a castration complex and its connection to a phobia, Freud based his
analysis not on the little boy who had the phobia, but on the reports of the
father of the little boy, himself in therapy, and a devotee of Freudian theory. I
really don't have to comment further on the contamination in this kind of evidence. It is remarkable that only recently has Freud's classic theory on the
sexuality of women—the notion of the double orgasm—been actually tested
physiologically and found just plain wrong. Now those who claim that fifty
years of psychoanalytic experience constitute evidence enough of the essential
truths of Freud's theory should ponder the robust health of the double orgasm.
Did women, until Masters and Johnson (1966), believe they were having two
different kinds of orgasm? Did their psychiatrists intimidate them into reporting something that was not true? If so, were there other things they reported
that were also not true? Did psychiatrists ever learn anything different than
their theories had led them to believe? If clinical experience means anything at
all, surely we should have been done with the double orgasm myth long before
the Masters and Johnson studies.

8　　But certainly, you may object, "years of intensive clinical experience" is the only reliable measure in a discipline which rests for its findings on insight, sensitivity, and intuition. The problem with insight, sensitivity, and intuition is that they can confirm for all time the biases that one started out with. People used to be absolutely convinced of their ability to tell which of their number were engaging in witchcraft. All it required was some sensitivity to the workings of the devil.

9　　Years of intensive clinical experience is not the same thing as empirical evidence. The first thing an experimenter learns in any kind of experiment which involves humans is the concept of the "double blind." The term is taken from medical experiments, where one group is given a drug which is presumably supposed to change behavior in a certain way, and a control group is given a placebo. If the observers or the subjects know which group took which drug, the result invariably comes out on the positive side for the new drug. Only when it is not known which subject took which pill, is validity remotely approximated. In addition, with judgments of human behavior, it is so difficult to precisely tie down just what behavior is going on, let alone what behavior should be expected, that one must test again and again the reliability of judgments. How many judges, blind, will agree in their observations? Can they replicate their own judgments? Can they replicate their own judgments at some later time? When, in actual practice, these judgment criteria are tested for clinical judgments, then we find that the judges cannot judge reliably, nor can they judge consistently: They do no better than chance in identifying which of a certain set of stories were written by men and which by women; which of a whole battery of clinical test results are the products of homosexuals and which are the products of heterosexuals (Hooker, 1957); and which of a battery of clinical test results *and* interviews (where questions are asked such as "Do you have delusions?"—Little & Schneidman, 1959) are products of psychotics, neurotics, psychosomatics, or normals. Lest this summary escape your notice, let me stress the implications of these findings. The ability of judges, chosen for their clinical expertise, to distinguish male heterosexuals from male homosexuals on the basis of three widely used clinical projective tests—the Rorschach, the TAT, and the MAP—was *no better than chance.* The reason this is such devastating news, of course, is that sexuality is supposed to be of fundamental importance in the deep dynamic of personality; if what is considered gross sexual deviance cannot be caught, then what are psychologists talking about when they, for example, claim that at the basis of paranoid psychosis is "latent homosexual panic"? They can't even identify what homosexual anything is, let alone "latent homosexual panic."[1] More frightening,

---

[1] It should be noted that psychologists have been as quick to assert absolute truths about the nature of homosexuality as they have about the nature of women. The arguments presented in this article apply equally to the nature of homosexuality: Psychologists know nothing about it; there is no more evidence for the "naturalness" of heterosexuality than for the "naturalness" of homosexuality. Psychology has functioned as a pseudo-scientific buttress for our cultural sex-role notions, that is, as a buttress for patriarchal ideology and patriarchal social organization; women's liberation and gay liberation fight against a common victimization.

expert clinicians cannot be consistent on what diagnostic category to assign to a person, again on the basis of both tests and interviews; a number of normals in the Little & Schneidman study were described as psychotic, in such categories as "schizophrenic with homosexual tendencies" or "schizoid character with depressive trends." But most disheartening, when the judges were asked to rejudge the test protocols some weeks later, their diagnoses of the same subjects on the basis of the same protocol differed markedly from their initial judgments. It is obvious that even simple descriptive conventions in clinical psychology cannot be consistently applied; that these descriptive conventions have any explanatory significance is therefore, of course, out of the question. . . .

You may argue that the theory may be scientifically "unsound" but at least 10 it cures people. There is no evidence that it does. In 1952, Eysenck reported the results of what is called an "outcome of therapy" study of neurotics which showed that, of the patients who receive psychoanalysis the improvement rate was 44%; of the patients who received psychotherapy the improvement rate was 64%; and of the patients who received no treatment at all the improvement rate was 72%. These findings have never been refuted; subsequently, later studies have confirmed the negative results of the Eysenck study (Barron & Leary, 1955; Bergin, 1963; Cartwright and Vogel, 1960; Truax, 1963; Powers and Witmer, 1951). How can clinicians and psychiatrists, then, in all good conscience, continue to practice? Largely by ignoring these results and being careful not to do outcome-of-therapy studies. The attitude is nicely summarized by Rotter (1960) (quoted in Astin, 1961); "Research studies in psychotherapy tend to be concerned with psychotherapeutic procedure and less with outcome . . . to some extent, it reflects an interest in the psychotherapy situation as a kind of personality laboratory." Some laboratory.

THE SOCIAL CONTEXT

Thus, since clinical experience and tools can be shown to be worse than use- 11 less when tested for consistency, efficacy, agreement, and reliability, we can safely conclude that theories of a clinical nature advanced about women are also worse than useless. I want to turn now to the second major point in my article, which is that, even when psychological theory is constructed so that it may be tested, and rigorous standards of evidence are used, it has become increasingly clear that in order to understand why people do what they do, and certainly in order to change what people do, psychologists must turn away from the theory of the causal nature of the inner dynamic and look to the social context within which individuals live.

Before examining the relevance of this approach for the question of 12 women, let me first sketch the groundwork for this assertion.

In the first place, it is clear (Block, 1968) that personality tests never yield 13 consistent predictions; a rigid authoritarian on one measure will be an unauthoritarian on the next. But the reason for this inconsistency is only now becoming clear, and it seems overwhelmingly to have much more to do with the social situation in which the subject finds himself than with the subject himself.

14   In a series of brilliant experiments. Rosenthal and his co-workers (Rosenthal and Jacobson, 1968; Rosenthal, 1966) have shown that if one group of experimenters has one hypothesis about what it expects to find, and another group of experimenters has the opposite hypothesis, both groups will obtain results in accord with their hypotheses. The results obtained are not due to mishandling of data by biased experimenters; rather, somehow, the bias of the experimenter creates a changed environment in which subjects actually act differently. For instance, in one experiment, subjects were to assign numbers to pictures of men's faces, with high numbers representing the subject's judgment that the man in the picture was a successful person, and low numbers representing the subject's judgment that the man in the picture was an unsuccessful person. One group of experimenters was told that the subjects tended to rate the faces high; another group of experimenters was told that the subjects tended to rate the faces low. Each group of experimenters was instructed to follow precisely the same procedure: They were required to read to subjects a set of instructions, and to *say nothing else.* For the 375 subjects run, the results showed clearly that those subjects who performed the task with experimenters who expected high ratings gave high ratings, and those subjects who performed the task with experimenters who expected low ratings gave low ratings. How did this happen? The experimenters all used the same words: It was something in their conduct which made one group of subjects do one thing, and another group of subjects do another thing.[2]. . .

15   Thus, even in carefully controlled experiments, and with no outward or conscious difference in behavior, the hypotheses we start with will influence enormously the behavior of another organism. These studies are extremely important when assessing the validity of psychological studies of women. Since it is beyond doubt that most of us start with notions as to the nature of men and women, the validity of a number of observations of sex differences is questionable, even when these observations have been made under carefully controlled conditions. Second, and more important, the Rosenthal experiments point quite clearly to the influence of social expectation. In some extremely important ways, people are what you expect them to be or at least they behave as you expect them to behave. Thus, if women, according to Bettelheim, want first and foremost to be good wives and mothers, it is extremely likely that this is what Bruno Bettelheim, and the rest of society, want them to be. . . .

BIOLOGICALLY BASED THEORIES

16   Biologists also have at times assumed they could describe the limits of human potential from their observations of animal rather than human behavior. Here, as in psychology, there has been no end of theorizing about the sexes, again with a sense of absolute certainly. These theories fall into two major categories.

17   One biological theory of differences in nature argues that since females and males differ in their sex hormones, and sex hormones enter the brain

---

[2]I am indebted to Jesse Lemisch for his valuable suggestions in the interpretation of these studies.

(Hamburg & Lunde in Maccoby, 1966), there must be innate behavioral differences. But the only thing this argument tells us is that there are differences in physiological state. The problem is whether these differences are at all relevant to behavior.

Consider, for example, differences in testosterone levels. A man who calls himself Tiger[3] has recently argued (1970) that the greater quantities of testosterone found in human males as compared with human females (of a certain age group) determines innate differences in aggressiveness, competitiveness, dominance, ability to hunt, ability to told public office, and so forth. But Tiger demonstrates in this argument the same manly and courageous refusal to be intimidated by evidence which we have already seen in our consideration of the clinical and psychiatric tradition. The evidence does not support his argument, and in some cases, directly contradicts it. Testosterone level co-varies neither with hunting ability, nor with dominance, nor with aggression, nor with competitiveness. As Storch has pointed out (1970), all normal male mammals in the reproductive age group produce much greater quantities of testosterone than females; yet many of these males are neither hunters nor are they aggressive. Among some hunting mammals, such as the large cats, it turns out that more hunting is done by the female than the male. And there exist primate species where the female is clearly more aggressive, competitive, and dominant than the male (Mitchell, 1969; and see below). Thus, for some species, being female, and therefore, having less testosterone than the male of that species means hunting more, or being more aggressive, or being more dominant. Nor does having *more* testosterone preclude behavior commonly thought of as "female": There exist primate species where females do not touch infants except to feed them: the males care for the infants (Mitchell, 1969; see fuller discussion below). So it is not clear what testosterone or any other sex-hormonal difference means for differences in nature of sex-role behavior.

18

In other words, one can observe identical sex-role behavior (e.g., "mothering") in males and females despite known differences in physiological state, i.e., sex hormones. What about the converse to this? That is, can one obtain differences in behavior given a single physiological state? The answer is overwhelmingly yes, not only as regards non-sex-specific hormones . . . but also as regards gender itself. Studies of hermaphrodites with the same diagnosis (the genetic, gonadal, hormonal sex, the internal reproductive organs, and the ambiguous appearances of the external genitalia were identical) have shown that one will consider oneself male or female depending simply on whether one was defined and raised as male or female (Money, 1970; Hampton & Hampton, 1961):

19

> There is no more convincing evidence of the power of social interaction on gender-identity differentiation than in the case of congenital hermaphrodites who are of the same diagnosis and similar degree of hermaphroditism but are differently assigned and with a different postnatal medical and life history. (Money, 1970, p. 432.)

---

[3]Schwarz Belkin (1914) claims that the name was originally *Mouse,* but this may be a reference to an earlier L. Tiger (putative).

20   Thus, for example, if out of two individuals diagnosed as having the adrenogenital syndrome of female hermaphroditism, one is raised as a girl and one as a boy, each will act and identify her/himself accordingly. The one raised as a girl will consider herself a girl; the one raised as a boy will consider himself a boy; and each will conduct her/ himself successfully in accord with that self-definition.

21   So, identical behavior occurs given different physiological states; and different behavior occurs given an identical physiological starting point. So it is not clear that differences in sex hormones are at all relevant to behavior.

22   There is a second category of theory based on biology, a reductionist theory. It goes like this. Sex-role behavior in some primate species is described, and it is concluded that this is the "natural" behavior for humans. Putting aside the not insignificant problem of observer bias (for instance, Harlow, 1962, of the University of Wisconsin, after observing differences between male and female rhesus monkeys, quotes Lawrence Sterne to the effect that women are silly and trivial, and concludes that "men and women have differed in the past and they will differ in the future"), there are a number of problems with this approach.

23   The most general and serious problem is that there are no grounds to assume that anything primates do is necessary, natural, or desirable in humans, for the simple reason that humans are not non-humans. For instance, it is found that male chimpanzees placed alone with infants will not "mother" them. Jumping from hard data to ideological speculation researchers conclude from this information that *human* females are necessary for the safe growth of human infants. It would be as reasonable to conclude, following this logic, that it is quite useless to teach human infants to speak, since it has been tried with chimpanzees and it does not work. . . .

24   [E]ven for the limited function that primate arguments serve, the evidence has been misused. Invariably, only those primates have been cited which exhibit exactly the kind of behavior that the proponents of the biological basis of human female behavior wish were true for humans. Thus, baboons and rhesus monkeys are generally cited: Males in these groups exhibit some of the most irritable and aggressive behavior found in primates, and if one wishes to argue that females are naturally passive and submissive, these groups provide vivid examples. There are abundant counter examples, such as those mentioned above (Mitchell, 1969); in fact, in general, a counter example can be found for every sex-role behavior cited, including, as mentioned in the case of marmosets, male "mothers."

25   But the presence of counter examples has not stopped florid and overarching theories of the natural or biological basis of male privilege from proliferating. For instance, there have been a number of theories dealing with the innate incapacity in human males for monogamy. Here, as in most of this type of theorizing, baboons are a favorite example, probably because of their fantasy value: The family unit of the hamadryas baboon, for instance, consists of a highly constant pattern of one male and a number of females and their young. And again, the counter examples, such as the invariably monogamous gibbon, are ignored.

An extreme example of this maiming and selective truncation of the evidence in the service of a plea for the maintenance of male privilege is a recent book, *Men in Groups* (1969) by Tiger (see above and footnote 3). The central claim of this book is that females are incapable of honorable collective action because they are incapable of "bonding" as in "male bonding." What is "male bonding"? Its surface definition is simple: ". . . a particular relationship between two or more males such that they react differently to members of their bonding units as compared to individuals outside of it" (pp. 19–20). If one deletes the world male, the definition, on its face, would seem to include all organisms that have any kind of social organization. But this is not what Tiger means. For instance, Tiger asserts that females are incapable of bonding; and this alleged incapacity indicates to Tiger that females should be restricted from public life. Why is bonding an exclusively male behavior? Because, says Tiger, it is seen in male primates. All male primates? No, very few male primates. Tiger cites two examples where male bonding is seen: rhesus monkeys and baboons. Surprise, surprise. But not even all baboons: As mentioned above, the hamadry, as social organization consists of one-male units; so does that of the Gelada baboon (Mitchell, 1969). And the great apes do not go in for male bonding much either. The "male bond" is hardly a serious contribution to scholarship; one reviewer for *Science* has observed that the book ". . . shows basically more resemblance to a partisan political tract than to a work of objective social science," with male bonding being ". . . some kind of behavioral phlogiston" (Fried, 1969, p. 884). 26

In short, primate arguments have generally misused the evidence; primate studies themselves have, in any case, only the very limited function of describing some possible sex-role behavior; and at present, primate observations have been sufficiently limited so that even the range of possible sex-role behavior for non-human primates is not known. This range is not known since there is only minimal observation of what happens to behavior if the physical or social environment is change. . . . Thus, even if there were some way, which there isn't, to settle on the behavior of a particular primate species as being the "natural" way for humans, we would not know whether or not this were simply some function of the present social organization of that species. And finally, once again it must be stressed that even if non-human primate behavior turned out to be relatively fixed, this would say little about our behavior. More immediate and relevant evidence, i.e., the evidence from social psychology, points to the enormous plasticity in human behavior, not only from one culture to the next, but from one experimental group to the next. One of the most salient features of human social organization is its variety; there are a number of cultures where there is at least a rough equality between men and women (Mead, 1949). In summary, primate arguments can tell us very little about our "innate" sex-role behavior; if they tell us anything at all, they tell us that there is no one biologically "natural" female or male behavior, and that sex-role behavior in non-human primates is much more varied than has previously been thought. 27

CONCLUSION

28   In brief, the uselessness of present psychology (and biology) with regard to women is simply a special case of the general conclusion; one must understand the social conditions under which women live if one is going to attempt to explain the behavior of women. And to understand the social conditions under which women live, one must be cognizant of the social expectations about women.

29   How are women characterized in our culture, and in psychology? They are inconsistent, emotionally unstable, lacking in a strong conscience or superego, weaker, "nurturant" rather than productive, "intuitive" rather than intelligent, and, if they are at all "normal," suited to the home and the family. In short, the list adds up to a typical minority group stereotype of inferiority (Hacker, 1951): If they know their place, which is in the home, they are really quite lovable, happy, childlike, loving creatures. In a review of the intellectual differences between little boys and little girls. Eleanor Maccoby (1966) has shown that there are no intellectual differences until about high school, or, if there are, girls are slightly ahead of boys. At high school, girls begin to do worse on a few intellectual tasks, such as arithmetic reasoning, and beyond high school, the achievement of women now measured in terms of productivity and accomplishment drops off even more rapidly. There are a number of other, non-intellectual tests which show sex differences; I chose the intellectual differences since it is seen clearly that women start becoming inferior. It is no use to talk about women being different but equal; all of the tests I can think of have a "good" outcome and a "bad" outcome. Women usually end up at the "bad" outcome. In light of social expectations about women, what is surprising is not that women end up where society expects they will; what is surprising is that little girls don't get the message that they are supposed to be stupid until high school; and what is even more remarkable is that some women resist this message even after high school, college, and graduate school.

30   My article began with remarks on the task of the discovery of the limits of human potential. Psychologists realize that it is they who are limiting discovery of human potential. They refuse to accept evidence, if they are clinical psychologists, or, if they are rigorous, they assume that people move in a context-free ether, with only their innate dispositions and their individual traits determining what they will do. Until psychologists begin to respect evidence, and until they begin looking at the social contexts within which people move, psychology will have nothing of substance to offer in this task of discovery. I don't know what immutable differences exist between men and women apart from differences in their genitals; perhaps there are some other unchangeable differences; probably there are a number of irrelevant differences. But it is clear that until social expectations for men and women are equal, until we provide equal respect for both men and women, our answers to this question will simply reflect our prejudices.

References

Astin, A. W. (1961). The functional autonomy of psychotherapy. *American Psychologist 16,* 75–8.

Barron, F., & Leary, T. (1955) Changes in psychoneurotic patients with and without psychotherapy. *Journal of Consulting Psychology, 19,* 239–245.

Bergin, A. E. (1963). The effects of psychotherapy: Negative results revisited. *Journal of Consulting Psychology, 10,* 244–250.

Bettelheim, B. (1965). The commitment required of a woman entering a scientific profession in present-day American society. *Woman and the Scientific Profession,* the MIT Symposium on American Women in Science and Engineering.

Block, J. (1968). Some reasons for the apparent inconsistency of personality. *Psychological Bulletin, 70* 210–212.

Cartwright, R. D., & Vogel. J. L. (1960). A comparison of changes in psychoneurotic patients during matched periods of therapy and Xo-therapy. *Journal of Consulting Psychology, 24,* 121–127.

Erikson, E. (1964). Inner and outer space: Reflections on womanhood. *Daedalus, 93,* 582–606.

Eysenck, H. J. (1952). The effects of psychotherapy: An evaluation. *Journal of Consulting Psychology, 16,* 319–324.

Fried, M. H. (1969). Mankind excluding woman. [Review of Tiger's Men in Groups.] *Science, 165,* 883–884.

Freud, S. (1963). *The sexual enlightenment of children.* New York? Collier Books Edition.

Goldstein, A. P., & Dean. S. J. (1966). *The investigation of psychotherapy: Commentaries and readings.* New York: John Wiley & Sons.

Hacker, H. M. (1951). Women as a minority group. *Social Forces, 30,* 60–69.

Hamburg, D. A., & Lunde, D. T. (1966). Sex hormones in the development of sex differences in human behavior. In Maccoby (Ed.), *The development of sex differences* (pp. 1–24). Palo Alto: Stanford University Press.

Hampton, J. L., & Hampton, J. C. (1961). The Ontogenesis of Sexual Behavior in Man. In W. C. Young (Ed.), *Sex and internal secretions,* 1401–1432.

Harlow, H. F. (1962). The heterosexual affectional system in monkeys. *The American Psychologist, 17,* 1–9.

Hooker, E. (1957). Male homosexuality in the rorschach. *Journal of Projective Techniques, 21,* 18–31.

Itani, J. (1963). Paternal care in the wild Japanese monkeys, *Macaca Fuscata.* In C. H. Southwick (Ed.), *Primate Social Behavior.* Princeton: Van Nostrand.

Little, K. B, & Schneidman, E. S. (1959). Congruences among interpretations of psychological and anamnestic data. *Psychological Monographs, 73,* 1–42.

Maccoby, Eleanor E. (1966). Sex differences in intellectual functioning. In Maccoby (Ed.), *The development of sex differences* (pp. 25–55). Palo Alto: Stanford University Press.

Masters, W. H., & Johnson, V. E. (1966). *Human sexual response*. Boston: Little Brown.

Mead, M. (1949). *Male and female: A study of the sexes in a changing world*, New York: William Morrow.

Mitchell, G. D. (1969). Paternalistic behavior in primates. *Psychological Bulletin, 71* 339–417.

Money, J. (1970). Sexual dimorphism and homosexual gender identity. *Psychological Bulletin, 74*(6) 425–440.

Powers, E., & Witmer, H. (1951). *An experiment in the prevention of delinquency*. New York: Columbia University Press.

Rheingold, J. (1964). *The fear of being a woman*. New York: Grune & Stratton.

Rosenthal, R. (1963). On the social psychology of the psychological experiment: The experimenter's hypothesis as unintended determinant of experimental results. *American Scientist, 51*, 268–283.

Rosenthal, R. (1966). *Experimenter effects in behavioral research*. New York: Appleton-Century-Crofts.

Rosenthal, R., & Jacobson, L. (1968). *Pygmalion in the classroom: Teacher expectation and pupil's intellectual development*. New York: Holt, Rinehart & Winston.

Rotter, J. B. (1960). Psychotherapy. *Annual Review of Psychology, 11* 381–414.

Schwarz-Belkin, M. (1914). Les fleurs de mal. In *Festschrift for Gordon Piltdown*. New York: Ponzi Press.

Storch, M. (1970). Reply to Tiger. Unpublished manuscript.

Tiger, L. (1969). *Men in groups*. New York: Random House.

Tiger, L. (1970, October 25). Male dominance? Yes. Alas. A sexist plot? No. *New York Times Magazine*, Section N.

Truax, C. B. (1963). Effective ingredients in psychotherapy: An approach to unraveling the patient-therapist interaction. *Journal of Counseling Psychology, 10*, 256–263.

Questions for Discussion and Your Reading Journal

1. How does Weisstein begin the article? Why do you suppose she introduces her topic in this way?

2. What is "feminine" according to the psychologists Erikson and Bettelheim? According to the author? What are the social consequences of this definition of the female role?

3. How and why have practitioners in the field of psychology failed to understand gender constructions, according to the author?

4. What is Freud's theory about gender? What aspects of this theory does Weisstein refute? Evaluate the effectiveness of her refutation.

5. What is "double-blind" research? Discuss the problems involved in the application of "double-blind" research to the issue of gender construction.

6. What are "outcome-of-therapy studies"? For what reasons does the author suggest such studies have not been done in relation to gender socialization?
7. Weisstein argues that "a study of human behavior requires, first and foremost, a study of social contexts within which people move, the expectations as to how they will behave, and the authority which tells them who they are and what they are supposed to do." Explain your disagreement or agreement with this argument.
8. Describe "biologically based theories." What methods does Weisstein use to refute these theories? How effective is her refutation?
9. Like Brannon in the previous article, Weisstein concludes by implying that psychological theories and psychologists' practices should change. What changes do you suppose she supports? Find evidence in the article to support your interpretation of the author's intention.

UNNI WIKAN

This chapter from an anthropological book called Behind the Veil in Arabia: Women in Oman, *by Unni Wikan, discusses the ways in which culture constructs gender and, in particular, the possibility of extending distinctions to a third gender role. This "special kind of person," called a* xanith, *is neither male nor female; nor is such a person considered "aberrant or deviant."* Xaniths *exhibit traits characteristic of a unique third gender and fit within the gender continuum somewhere between female and male.*

In Arabian culture xaniths *make up more than 2 percent of the population. They fulfill a particular role in the culture and have a place in the day-to-day activities of the society. The author quotes the Quran: "Look how Allah made your hand, he gave you five fingers, but each a little bit different. . . . People are the same way, every one of them different." While* xaniths *are far fewer than males or females, they constitute a distinct gender category.*

Reading Rhetorically

Early on in the article the author identifies herself as a female anthropologist. The first article in this chapter is also written by an anthropologist but in that case a male. As you read this article, pay attention to the ways in which the author claims her gender influences her work (her use of *ethos*). Are there other ways, besides those mentioned by Wikan, that the article appears to come out of a female perspective? Think about how a reader's knowledge of an author's gender might influence his or her perception of a text (if at all). The headnote to the first article in this chapter explains: "Anthropology is interested in all human societies and views life as a complexly integrated whole that is more than the sum of its parts. It is the human experience as a whole that this social science seeks to understand." This description of anthropology is particularly well suited to the subject of this article. As you read, think about how the role of the *xanith* in Omani culture is part of a "complexly integrated whole that is more than the sum of its parts."

The *Xanith:* A Third Gender Role?

"Look how Allah made your hand, he gave you five fingers, but each a little bit different. . . . People are the same way, every one of them different."

1   Any discussion of the social roles of the sexes in Sohar would be incomplete without detailed attention also to a special kind of person, known locally as *xanith* and, for many purposes, regarded by Soharis as neither man nor woman. In English, one might call such persons male transvestites or transsexuals. The way they are conceptualized in Sohar and the way they function in that society, they cannot lightly be dismissed as aberrant or deviant individuals, but are better understood, as far as I can judge, as having a truly distinct, third gender role. The existence of such a triad of gender roles—woman, man, and *xanith*—provides an unusually productive opportunity to explore more thoroughly the basic properties and preconditions of male and female roles as they are conceptualized in Sohar. . . .[1]

2   The word *xanith* carries the sense of effeminate, impotent, soft. Although anatomically male, *xaniths* speak of themselves with emphasis and pride as "women." They are socially classified with women with respect to the strict rules of segregation. According to the estimates of informants, in 1976 there were about sixty *xaniths* in Sohar, as well as an unknown number of men who had been *xaniths* previously, but no longer were. In other words, well above one in every fifty males has a past or present history as a *xanith*. In the following I shall seek to develop a role analysis that does not see the *xanith* in artificial isolation, but confronts the role in the context of the reciprocal roles of man and woman, and the basic constitution of social persons and relationships in this society.

3   To perform such an analysis, I need to describe both how people classify and think about each other, and how they act and interact. I shall try to show how the conceptualization of each role in the triad reflects the existence of the other two, and how the realization of any one role in behavior presupposes, and is dependent on, the existence and activities of both the other roles. In this manner, I mean to use the role of the *xanith* as a key to answer the following questions: What is the basis for the Sohari conceptualization of sex and gender identity? What insight does this provide into the construction of male and female roles in Sohar, and into fundamental values and premises in Omani society?

---

[1]After I had completed this manuscript, Dr. Frank H. Stewart kindly alerted me to references in the anthropological literature to transvestism, both male and female, among the Marsh Arabs of Iraq. I acknowledge that other references may also have been made, but I have not been in a position to check the literature systematically.

Let me first describe some of the concrete behavior enacted by *xaniths* by   4
describing the process by which I myself discovered them. I had completed
four months of field work when one day a friend of mine asked me to go visiting with her. Observing the rules of decency, we made our way through the
back streets away from the market, where we met a man, dressed in a pink
dishdasha, with whom my friend stopped to talk. I was highly astonished, as
no decent woman—and I had every reason to believe my friend was one—
stops to talk with a man in the street. So I reasoned he must be her very close
male relative. But their interaction did not follow the pattern I had learned to
expect across sex lines, she was too lively and informal, their interaction too
intimate. I began to suspect my friend's virtue. Could the man be her secret
lover? No sooner had we left him than she identified him. "That one is a
xanith," she said. In the twenty-minute walk that followed, she pointed out
four more. They all wore pastel-colored *dishdashas,* walked with a swaying
gait, and reeked of perfume. I recognized one as a man who had been singing
with the women at a wedding I had recently attended. And my friend
explained that all men who join women singing at weddings are *xaniths.*
Another was identified as the brother of a man who had offered to be our
servant—an offer we turned down precisely because of this man's disturbingly
effeminate manners. And my friend explained that all male servants (except
for slaves), are *xaniths,* that all *xaniths* are homosexual prostitutes, and that
it is quite common for several brothers to partake of such an identity. Another
bizarre experience now became intelligible: at a wedding celebration, on the
wedding night, when no male other than the bridegroom himself may see the
bride's face, I was witness to a man casually making his way into the bride's
seclusion chamber and peeping behind her veil! But no one in the audience
took offense. Later that night, the same man ate with the women at the wedding meal, where men and women are strictly segregated. At the time, I took
him to be a half-wit; that was the only reason I could find for such deviant
behavior to be accepted. The man's strangely effeminate manners and high-
pitched voice, giving him a rather clownish appearance, lent further credence
to my interpretation. I then realized that he, as well as the five men we had met
that day, were transvestites or transsexuals.

This incident also serves to highlight problems of discovery and interpre-   5
tation in field work which are made acute in a strictly sex-segregated society
like Oman. I wonder whether persons corresponding to *xaniths* who have not
previously been reported in the anthropological literature on the Middle East
may not indeed be found some places there, but have escaped notice because
the vast majority of field workers have been men. Barred from informal contact with the women, the male anthropologist might miss the crucial clues to
the transvestite/transsexual phenomenon. He is likely to meet some effeminate men whom he will recognize as homosexuals (as we did our would-be
servant), and other who will strike him as half-wits (like some Omani male
singers). The fact that *xaniths* do not assume full female clothing would also
give credence to the above interpretations. But the essential feature of the
phenomenon—persons who are anatomically male, but act effeminately and
move freely amongst women behind purdah—would easily escape the male

anthropologist, for the forums and arenas where this interaction takes place are inaccessible to him.

6 A brief comparative perspective and clarification of terms is helpful at this point. The term *transvestite,* by which such phenomena have generally been known in the anthropological literature, means, etymologically, cross-dressing, and it has come to refer to the act of dressing in the clothes of the opposite sex. The classical anthropological case is the *berdache* of the Plains Indians—men who dressed like women, performed women's work, and married men (Lowie 1935). However, it is not easy to assess, in the anthropological record, the cross-cultural distribution of transvestites, for they are often simply referred to as homosexuals; and homosexuality again is usually equated with a high degree of effeminacy in males. But we know unequivocally that, in a few societies, a transvestite role was a fully institutionalized part of traditional life, as for example, the Koniag of Alaska, Tanala of Madagascar, Mesakin of Nuba, and Chukchee of Siberia. However, I have not been able to find evidence that these institutions are practiced today with their traditional vitality.

7 On the Batinah coast of Oman, on the contrary, *xaniths* are an integral part of the local social organization and very much in evidence. As we have seen, they cannot be said to wear either female or male clothing, but have a distinctive dress of their own. But Soharis believe that if *xaniths* had the option, they would choose to dress like women. In the event, they are forbidden to do so, as we shall soon see. Does this then mean that they are to be understood most truly as "transvestites"?

8 The term *transsexual* was first introduced by D. O. Cauldwell in 1949. It became well known after the publication of Harry Benjamin's book *The Transsexual Phenomenon* in 1966. Prior to 1949, transsexuals had always been labeled as transvestites—a term introduced sometime around the turn of the century (Dr. John Money, personal communication). Dr. Benjamin's significant discovery was that men who impersonate women can derive extremely different feelings of subjective identity from the act; For some, impersonating women is a way to bolster their subjectively cherished identity as a *male;* for others, it is the way to escape from an undesired male identity and *become* a woman. The transvestite achieves his purpose through the secret fetishistic sexual pleasure he derives from female clothing. There seems to be an emerging consensus in psychiatric and sociological literature today to regard this kind of person as a transvestite. An authority on the topic writes, for instances: "For these men, not only are their penises the source of the greatest erotic pleasure, but they also consider themselves men, not just males. Transsexuals, on the other hand, are *never* found to be fetishistic. They have no capacity for episodes of unremarkably masculine appearance. They do not grow out of their feminity. They do not work in masculine professions" (Stoller 1971, p. 231).

9 According to this usage, it is probable that the Omani *xaniths* are better classified as transsexuals rather than as transvestites in that they claim to be women, not men; they never truly grow out of their femininity; and they are assumed by women to resemble themselves in basic sexual attitudes. However, *xaniths* are also clearly analogues to the cases described in traditional anthropological literature as "transvestites" and should be seen in this comparative

perspective. Finally, the question remains whether a *xanith* can be illuminated by being classified as either a transvestite or a transsexual. As Dr. Money has lucidly observed (personal communication): "In an area of the world where there is no local vernacular or differential diagnostic terminology for men who impersonate women, one has the same problem as existed in Europe and America before the middle 19th century. The Omani *xaniths* have only one way of expressing themselves, and that is as *xaniths* and not as either transvestites or transsexuals." In the following, therefore, I shall stick to Omani terminology.

As I have pointed out, the population of Sohar contains not only approximately sixty *xaniths,* but also an unknown number of *former xaniths.* A male's career as a "woman" may have several alternative terminations: (1) the man may be a woman for some years, whereupon he reverts to being a man for the rest of his life; (2) he may live as a woman until old age; (3) he may become a woman, return to being a man, again become a woman, and so forth. To us it would appear obvious that the decisive criterion by which men and women are distinguished is anatomical, and that it is only through hormonal change and surgical modification that one's sex and gender role are changed. Omanis apparently hold a fundamentally different view. But it should be emphasized that this potential for change is a characteristic of males only. Omani females, on the contrary, retain female identity throughout life. I shall return to the reasons for this contrast between the possible careers of men and women.

Let me now turn to a description of the role that we seek to understand. Its character as an intermediate role is most clearly shown in counterpoint to male and female roles.

Women wear *burqas** before all marriageable males. They need not wear them before *xaniths* and slaves, because they, in their own words, do not feel shy before them. The *xanith,* on the other hand, is not allowed to wear the *burqa,* nor any other female clothing. His clothes are intermediate between male and female: He wears the *dishdasha,* the ankle-length shirt of the male, but with the swung waist of the female dress. Male clothing is white; females wear patterned cloth in bright colors; *xaniths* wear unpatterned cloth in pastel colors. Men cut their hair short, women wear theirs long, *xaniths* medium long. Men comb their hair backward away from the face, women comb theirs diagonally forward from a central part, *xaniths* comb theirs forward from a side part, and they oil it heavily in the style of women. Both men and women cover their head; *xaniths* go bareheaded. Men always have their arms covered; women may be uncovered from elbow to wrist in private, but never in public (the specific Koranic injunction on this point makes it clear that the arm above the wrist is regarded as erotic and intimate); *xaniths* characteristically expose their lower arms in public. Perfume is used by both sexes, especially at festive occasions and during intercourse. The *xanith* is generally heavily perfumed, and he uses much make-up to draw attention to himself. This is also achieved by his affected swaying gait, emphasized by the close-fitting garments. His

10

11

12

*****burqa** (or *abaya* in many places): a long garment with only a grid through which to see, used by Muslim women to cover their bodies. [Ed. note.]

sweet falseto voice and facial expressions and movements also closely mimic those of women. If *xaniths* wore female clothing, I doubt that it would in many instances be possible to see that they are, anatomically speaking, male and not female. The *xanith's* appearance is judged by the standards of female beauty; white skin, shiny black hair, large eyes, and full cheeks. Some *xaniths* fulfill these ideals so well that women may express great admiration for their physical beauty.

13   Eating cooked food together represents a degree of intimacy second only to intercourse and physical fondling. Only in the privacy of the elementary family do men and women eat together; and Omanis are so shy about eating that host and guest, even when they are of the same sex, normally do not eat major meals (as contrasted to coffee, sweets, and fruit) together. Whenever food is offered in public, for example, at weddings, *xaniths* eat with the women.

14   Women are secluded in their homes and must have the husband's permission to go visiting family or friends. The *xanith*, in contrast, moves about freely; but like women, he stays at home in the evenings, whereas men may spend their time in clubs and cafés.

15   Division of labor follows sex lines. Housework is women's work. The *xanith* does housework in his own home and is often complimented and flattered for excelling women in his cooking, home decoration, and neatness. He may also take employment as a domestic servant, which no woman or freeman can be induced to do.[2] By this employment he supports himself, as a man must. But wherever tasks are allocated by sex, the *xanith* goes with the women. At weddings, women sing, while the men are musicians; *xaniths* are praised as the best singers. By appearing together with the women singers at weddings, the *xanith* broadcasts his status to a wide public. These performances characteristically serve as occasions to announce in public a change of identity from man to *xanith*. Thus, during my field work, there was a sheikh's son—a married man and the father of three children—who suddenly appeared at a wedding singing with the women. The audience was in no doubt as to the meanings of this act, and one woman of my acquaintance later remarked: "Imagine, the son of a sheikh, married to a pretty woman with very white skin, and yet he turns *xanith!*"

16   Women are legally minors and must be represented by a guardian. *Xaniths* represent themselves, as do all sane men. Legally speaking, they retain male status.

17   What then does the *xanith* mean by saying, as he explicitly does, that he is a woman, and why is he socially classified and treated as a woman in situations where sex differences are important? He was born an ordinary boy and acted and was treated as a normal boy until he started his career as a prostitute, commonly at the age of twelve or thirteen. When then is he classified as a *xanith*—a person with a distinctive gender identity—and not merely as a male homosexual prostitute?

18   Let us observe closely the process by which the *xanith* returns to a male identity in order to search for an answer to this question. The change from

---

[2]In Oman domestic employment is taken only by young boys, *xaniths,* or ex-slaves—before all of whom women may discard their *burqas.*

xanith to man takes place in connection with marriage. But the critical criterion is more explicit than this: The *xanith* must demonstrate, as must every normal bridegroom, that he can perform intercourse in the male role. Among Sohari Arabs, the marriage celebration has a customary form so that consummation is publicly verified. Intercourse takes place between the spouses in private; but next morning, the groom must document his potency in one of two ways: by handing over a bloodstained handkerchief, which also serves as a proof of the bride's honor, to the bride's attendant *(mikobra),* or by raising an outcry, which spreads like wildfire, and lodging a complaint to the bride's father, and maybe also the Wali, because the bride was not a virgin, and he has been deceived.

If neither event takes place, the impotence of the groom is revealed by default. This will cause grave concern among the bride's family and nervous suspense among the wedding guests. . . . The essential point here is simply that such a groom's adequacy as a man is in doubt. Conversely, the *xanith* who does deflower the bride becomes, like every other successful bridegroom, a *man.*   19

From this moment, all women must observe the rules of modesty and segregation before him,[3] always wear the *burqa*, never speak to him, never let him step into the compound when the husband is absent. Women stress that this does not pose difficulties. The *xanith* himself changes overnight into a responsible man, maintaining the proper distance and, in turn, protecting his own wife as would any other man. In other words, the *xanith* has been transformed from a harmless friend to a compromising potential sexual partner.[4]   20

But in all his demeanor—facial expressions, voice, laughter, movements— a *xanith* will reveal his past: His femininity remains conspicuous. I consequently expressed pity to some female friends for the poor woman who has such a "woman" for a husband; I felt she could not possibly respect him.[5] "No-no," they corrected me—*of course* she would respect him and love him. He had proved his potency; so he is a *man.*   21

Here, then, may be the key to an understanding of the gender system in Sohar. It is the sexual *act,* not the sexual organs, which is fundamentally constitutive of gender. A man who acts as a woman sexually *is* a woman socially. And there is no confusion possible in this culture between the male and female role in intercourse: The man "enters," the woman "receives"; the man is active, the woman is passive. Behavior, and not anatomy, is the basis for the Omani conceptualization of gender identity.   22

---

[3]A *xanith* groom-to-be usually stops his prostitute activities a few weeks prior to marriage.

[4]As their motive for an eventual marriage, *xaniths* give the desire for security in sickness and old age. Only a wife can be expected to be a faithful nurse and companion. Significantly, however, our best *xanith* informant, a femininely beautiful seventeen-year-old boy, did not realize the full implications of marriage for his gender identity. He was definite that he would be able to continue his informal relationship with women after marriage, arguing that he was to women like both a father and a mother. This is out of the question in Omani society, but his belief may serve as a significant measure of the *xanith*'s own confused identity.

[5]*Xaniths* fetch their brides from far away, and marriages are negotiated by intermediaries, so the bride's family will be uninformed about the groom's irregular background.

23   Consequently, the man who enters into a homosexual relationship in the active role in no way endangers his male identity, whereas the passive, receiving homosexual partner cannot possibly be conceptualized as a man. Therefore, in Oman, all homosexual prostitutes are ascribed the status of *xanith*.

24   Such conceptualizations also imply that a person with female sexual organs is a *maiden (bint)* until she has intercourse. At that moment, she becomes a *woman (horma)*. A spinster, no matter how old, remains a girl, a maiden.

25   Yet Omanis recognize, as do all other peoples in the world, the fundamental, undeniable character of anatomical sex. Girl and boy, female and male, are identities ascribed at birth. This is one reason why the Omani homosexual prostitute becomes a *xanith,* treated *as if* he were a woman. Yet he is referred to in the masculine grammatical gender, and he is forbidden to dress in women's clothes, for reasons we shall return to shortly. Attempts by *xaniths* to appear dressed as women have taken place, but *xaniths* were punished by imprisonment and flogging. But because the *xanith* must be fitted in somewhere in a society based on a fundamental dichotomization of the sexes, he is placed with those whom he resembles most: in this society, with women.

26   It is consistent with these conceptualizations that, in the absence of sexual activity, anatomical sex reasserts itself as the basis for classification. When in old age a *xanith* loses his attraction and stops his trade, he is assimilated to the old-man *(agoz)* category. From the few cases I came across, my impression is that such men tend to avoid large public occasions, where the issue of their gender identity would arise.

27   Most societies regard sexual organs as the ultimate criterion for gender identity. It is fascinating to speculate over the origin of the *xanith* status in Oman. Did it emerge through a clarification of the male role, whereby Omani men declared, "You act like a woman; you do not belong among us"? Or was it the *xaniths* themselves who wished to be women and progressively transgressed the gender boundary? The fact that *xaniths* cluster in groups of brothers suggests the existence of developmental causes for their motivation. Or the motive may be, as I have suggested elsewhere (1975), a desire to escape from the exacting demands of the Omani male role. But, in either case, why is the *xanith* not seen as a threat to the virtue of women and thus constrained by the men? Physically, there is no denying that he has male organs. Yet, considering the lack of safeguards observed, it is true to say that he is treated as a eunuch. And, as far as I know, no documentary sources are available that might illuminate the origin of the Omani *xanith* status.

28   Every role, however, also has a sociological origin, which may be identified in synchronic and consequently potentially far more adequate data. That a role once was created does not explain its continued existence: It must be perpetuated, re-created anew every day in the sense that some persons must choose to realize it, and others acknowledge it, as part of their daily life—whether in admiration, disgust, contempt, or indifference. In how they relate to the role encumbent, they also reveal something of themselves and their values. The institutionalized role of the *xanith* in Oman in 1976 is therefore a clear expression of basic premises and values in that culture today.

As regards the question of what makes some males choose to become   29
xaniths, we may distinguish two kinds of data that can illuminate it: people's
own understanding of the nature of the *xanith* and his relationships, and why
he seeks such an identity, or, on the other hand, objective, distinctive features,
which an investigator may identify in the background, situation, or person of
acknowledged *xaniths.*

The folk understanding of why some young boys turn into *xaniths* is decep-   30
tively simple. Men say that when young boys at puberty start being curious and
exploring sexual matters, they may "come to do that thing" together, and then
the boy "who lies underneath" may discover that he likes it. If so, he "comes to
want it," and, as the Soharis say, "An egg that is once broken can never be put
back together," "Water that has been spilt can not be put back again."

Thus the homosexual activity of the *xanith* is seen by others as a compulsion: 31
degrading to the person, but springing from his inner nature. Although it is performed for payment of money, its cause is emphatically not seen as economic
need stemming from poverty. Indeed, informants insist that old *xaniths* who are
no longer able to attract customers will end up paying men to serve them.

In the limited material I have been able to obtain, I have been unable to   32
identify any clear social or economic factors effecting recruitment to the *xanith*
role. Cases are found in all ethnic groups; they show a considerable range of
class and wealth in family background. There is nothing remarkable, to the
outsider, about the homes in which they grow up. Closer investigations, however, might uncover some such factors.

Homosexual practices and relationships, of course, have a certain frequency   33
in most, if not all, societies. And, in that sense, there is nothing remarkable
about their occurrence in Sohar. Our interest focuses on the crystallization of
the distinctive category of *xanith* whereby the passive party to male homosexuality is institutionalized as a recognized role and, for general social purposes,
treated as if he constituted a third gender. Are there identifiable factors in the
Omani conceptualization of sexuality and sexual relations which give rise
to this?

We might go part of the way in answering this question by comparing the   34
role of the *xanith* with that of males practicing homosexuality elsewhere in the
Middle East. Homosexual practice is a common and recognized phenomenon
in many Middle Eastern cultures, often in the form of an institutionalized
practice whereby older men seek sexual satisfaction with younger boys. But
this homosexual relationship generally has two qualities that make it fundamentally different from that practiced in Oman. First, it is part of a deep
friendship or love relationship between two men, which has qualities, it is
often claimed, of being purer and more beautiful than love between man and
woman. Such relationships are also said to develop sometimes in Sohar, but
very infrequently, and those who enter into them will try to conceal them from
others. Neither party to such a relationship is regarded as a *xanith.* Second,
both parties play both the active and the passive sexual role—either simultaneously or through time. In contrast, there is nothing in the Omani *xanith's*
behavior which is represented as pure or beautiful; and he does not seek sexual release for himself. Indeed, till he has proved otherwise (most?) people

doubt that he is capable of having an erection.[6] Like a fallen woman, he simply sells his body to men in return for money: he is a common prostitute.

35   Herein lies the other component, I will argue, of the explanation why the *xanith* emerges as an intermediate gender role, rather than representing an irregular pattern of recruitment to the female role. The *xanith* is treated as if he were a woman, and, for, many critical purposes, he is classified with women, but he is not allowed to become completely assimiliated to the category by wearing female dress. This is not because he is anatomically a male, but because he is sociologically something that no Omani woman should be: a prostitute. For such a person to dress like a woman would be to dishonor womanhood. The woman's purity and virtue are an axiom. Officially, there is no such thing as female prostitution. (In practice it exists, but in a concealed form.) By his mere existence, the *xanith* defines the essence of womanhood; he moves as an ugly duckling among the beautiful and throws them into relief. Through him, the pure and virtuous character of women may be conceptualized. One may speculate whether this aspect of the female role would be so clarified, were it not for him.

36   According to this hypothesis, it would be difficult to maintain a conception of women as simultaneously pure and sexually active, if some among them were publicly acknowledged also to serve as prostitutes. If the public view, however, is that prostitution is an act of *xaniths,* whereas women are not associated with the moral decay that prostitution represents, then women may be conceptualized as pure and virtuous *in* their sexual role. *Womanhood* is thereby left uncontaminated by such vices, even though individual women may be involved. Indeed, the term by which women refer to the activities of female prostitutes (that is, women who are not merely unfaithful for love, but have sexual relations with several men) in *yitxannith,* the active verbal form of *xanith.*

37   The *xanith* thus illuminates major components of the female role in Sohar. But he can also serve us in a broader purpose, as a key to the understanding of basic features of Sohari culture and society, and the fundamental premises on which interaction in this society is based.

38   Homosexual prostitution is regarded as shameful in Oman; and all forms of sexual aberration and deviance are sinful according to religion. Boys who show homosexual tendencies in their early teens are severely punished by anguished parents and threatened with eviction from home. So far, reactions in Oman are as one might expect in our society. But the further course of development is so distinctly Omani that any feeling of similarity disappears.

39   If the deviant will not conform in our society, we tend to respond with moral indignation, but with no organizational adjustments. He is disgusting

---

[6]Women were definite that *xaniths* who were prostitutes on a large scale *(waegid xanith)* were incapable of performing intercourse in the male role. However, one popular *xanith* whom we interviewed was equally definite that he could, though he had never tried, arguing that he knew several men who had practiced on an even larger scale than himself, yet had been potent. When I reported this view to some female friends, they categorically rejected it. To their understanding, there is an antithesis between performance in the male and the female sexual role; true bisexuality cannot be imagined. Therefore, if an *ex-xanith* proved potent, the modest extent of his activities would thus be proved ex post facto.

and despicable, a violation of our sense of modesty and a threat to public morality. Strong sanctions force him to disguise his deviance and practice it covertly. But because we do not wish to face up to him, we also fail to take cognizance of his distinctive character. As a result, we construct a social order where men and women who are sexually attracted by members of their *own* sex nonetheless are enjoined to mix freely with them in situations where *we* observe rules of sexual modesty, such as public baths and toilets.

Omanis, on the other hand, draw the consequences of the fact that the   40
sexual deviant cannot be suppressed. He is acknowledged and reclassified as a *xanith* and left in peace to practice his deviance. The condition is simply that he establish his little brothel under a separate roof; he must rent a date-palm hut for himself. But this may be located anywhere in town, and it is not shameful to sublet to him.

This reaction to the sexual deviant is a natural consequence of the basic   41
Omani view of life: The world is imperfect; people are created with dissimilar natures and are likewise imperfect. It is up to every person to behave as correctly—that is, tactfully, politely, hospitably, morally, and amicably—as possible in all the different encounters in which he or she engages, rather than to demand such things of others. To blame, criticize, or sanction those who fall short of such ideals is to be tactless and leads to loss of esteem. The world contains mothers who do not love their children, children who do not honor their parents, wives who deceive their husbands, men who act sexually like women . . . and it is not for me to judge or sanction them, unless the person has offended me in the particular relationship I have to him. It is up to the husband to control and punish his wife, the parents, their children, the state—if it so chooses—the sexual deviant. The rest of us are not involved—on the contrary, we are under an obligation always to be tactful and hospitable to people. . . .

References

Lowie, R. H. *The Crow Indians.* New York: Rinehart & Co., 1935.

Stoller, Robert J. The term "Transvestism." *Arch. Gen. Psychiatry,* 24.3 (1971).

Wikan, Unni. "Hustyrann eller kanarifugl—Kvinnerollen i to arabiske samfunn." [Domestic Tyrant or Pet Canary—Women's Roles in Two Arab Societies]. *Tidsskrift for samfunnsforskning,* 16.4 (1975).

Questions for Discussion and Your Reading Journal

1. At the end of the third paragraph Wikan poses two questions. Why do you think these questions appear in the beginning of the article? As a reader, how are you affected by these questions?

2. How did the author discover *xaniths*? Why do you suppose she was so fascinated by their existence? What words or phrases indicate her own biases?

3. Why might male anthropologists have missed clues about the *xanith* subculture, according to the author?

4. In what ways are *xaniths* best understood as "transvestites"? In what ways are they "transsexuals"? Why does the author ultimately reject both terms?

5. How is the position of *xaniths* as prostitutes relevant to their role and status in Oman?

6. Discuss some of the role and status differences between men and women in Omani culture. How are religious beliefs related to these differences? Why are *xaniths* closer to women than men in social terms?

7. The author remarks, "Thus the homosexual activity of the *xanith* is seen by others as a compulsion: degrading to the person but springing from his inner nature." What does this remark reveal about attitudes toward homosexuality in Oman? How is the attitude toward *xaniths* similar to and distinct from the attitudes toward homosexual men in America?

WRITING ASSIGNMENTS

A Summary Essay: Gender Issues

TASK: Write a two-page summary of an article on gender issues.

READINGS: Choose one of the following articles.

> Jeffrey Z. Rubin, Frank J. Provenzano, and Zella Luria, "The Eye of the Beholder: Parents' View on Sex of Newborns"
> Robert Brannon, "Why Men Become Men, and Other Theories"
> Naomi Weisstein, "Psychology Constructs the Female"
> Unni Wikan, "The *Xanith*: A Third Gender Role?"

Thinking Rhetorically about Audience and Purpose

You will be writing this paper for your peers and instructor. Because writing summaries is the most common kind of writing assigned in the university, writing this paper will give you an opportunity to strengthen your skills in this area. Think back over your last year of school: on what occasions were you asked to summarize something? Why do you think you were assigned this task? Was composing the summary related to a larger assignment? If so, what was the assignment and why was the summary a part of it?

Objectives

* You will be able to summarize the central idea of an article in a thesis statement.
* You will practice reading an article to elicit the main ideas.
* You will practice restating the main ideas of an article in a summary form.

Evaluative Criteria

* Does the thesis of the summary recapitulate the central idea of the article?

- Are the other main ideas in the article represented (in your own words) in the summary?
- Does the summary show a careful reading of the article?
- Is the summary free from major errors in mechanics?

Notes to the Student

Since summarizing a text is a crucial skill to master before many other types of thinking and writing assignments can be done, this is the first assignment. You must read the article carefully and critically before you can write a good summary of it. I suggest the following strategy:

1. Scan the article quickly. See if you can discover the topic and central focus.
2. Read the article carefully once without underlining anything or making any notes in the margins. Beginning university students often have difficulty deciding which ideas are really important; sometimes they mark a lot more than is really helpful. (As you gain practice in critical reading, you will be able to discriminate much more readily between more- and less-important ideas during a first reading.)
3. Reread, dividing the passage into sections as you go. These sections are clusters of paragraphs (or sentences) having to do with particular ideas. Finally, label in the margins of the text each section or stage of thought. Underline key ideas and terms.
4. Write one-sentence summaries on a separate sheet of paper of each stage of thought.
5. Write a thesis statement: a one-sentence summary of the entire article. The thesis should express the central idea of the passage. Think of the questions journalists ask when they compose a "lead" for a story: the who, what, when, where, why, and how of the matter.
6. Write a first draft of the summary by combining the thesis with the one-sentence summaries, adding significant details from the passage. Eliminate less-important ideas.
7. Check your summary against the article and make any adjustments necessary for accuracy and completeness.
8. Revise your summary, inserting transitional words and phrases to improve coherence. Try to avoid a series of short, choppy sentences; combine sentences for a smooth flow.
9. Proofread for grammatical correctness, punctuation, and spelling.

A Summary and Response Essay: Scientists' Roles

TASK: Compose a three-page summary-and-response paper in relation to a chosen article on the topic of scientists and their roles in society.

READINGS: Choose one of the following articles.

Edward T. Hall, "The Anthropology of Manners"
Julius Robert Oppenheimer, "The Scientist in Society"

Anne Walton, "Women Scientists: Are They Really Different?"
Albert Einstein, "Religion and Science"
Bertrand Russell, Excerpt from *Religion and Science*

Thinking Rhetorically about Audience and Purpose

Imagine the audience for this essay to be undergraduates majoring in an area of the sciences. You will be writing to summarize and respond to a major issue of relevance to science. It may be the relevance of culture in science, the role of the scientist in society, the particular role of women in science, or the connections and contradictions between science and religion.

A summary-and-response paper is about setting out a subject clearly and making judgments about the subject. Most people make judgments about things every day: the quality of a meal, the entertainment value of a movie, the educational value of an article or book, for instance. How do you respond to the judgments of others when they are not accompanied by sensible reasons? When someone recommends a movie, for instance, what kinds of questions do you ask them to decide for yourself if you want to see it? Do you simply trust the judgment of some people? Why or why not? Does anyone you know trust your judgment implicitly? If so, who and why?

Objectives

- You will be able to summarize the central idea of an article in a thesis statement.
- You will practice reading an article to elicit main ideas.
- You will practice restating the main ideas of an article in a summary form.
- You will formulate thoughtful responses to the ideas in the article.
- You will reflect upon the meaning and significance of the ideas in the article.

Evaluative Criteria

- Does the thesis of the critique recapitulate the central idea of the article as well as your overall response to it?
- Are the other main ideas in the article represented (in your own words) in the critique?
- Does the critique demonstrate your careful reading of the article?
- Does the critique show critical thinking and insight into the meaning/significance/implications of the ideas summarized?
- Is the critique free from major errors in mechanics?

Notes to the Student

Like summaries, critiques (summary-and-response essays) are common assignments for students across the university's curriculum. In order to write a critique, you must understand the ideas in the article well enough to respond to them with critical thinking. After following the steps involved in writing a summary, I suggest the following strategy:

1. Read through the thesis and the main ideas of the summary to determine your overall response to the article: do you agree or disagree with the writer's points? Write a sentence to describe your position; this sentence may be incorporated into your thesis statement. Then look at the points individually and decide why you do or do not agree with each one. Write a sentence for each point; these sentences may become topic sentences for the paragraphs in your paper.

2. Ask yourself questions about the writer and the article. Who is the writer? What seems to be the writer's belief system or outlook on the world? How might these beliefs or this outlook have biased the writer's message? Write about your impressions of the writer's perspective. These impressions may become part of the body of your response.

3. Your critique must be organized clearly and logically, but there is no single organizational strategy. You may begin by discussing the writer's perspective and potential bias. Continue by writing a paragraph or two about what you agree with, providing enough support to allow your reader to understand your response. Then you may follow by discussing the parts of the article with which you disagree, clearly and fully explaining your unwillingness to accept those points. Another strategy is to follow the points of the summary one by one, responding to each one in a separate paragraph.

4. I highly recommend examining critiques professional writers have written. They appear regularly in newspapers and magazines. The easiest place to find a critique is the "review section," where books and movies are summarized and responded to. Notice the kinds of things the critique writer discusses, as well as the organizational strategy being used. You might take a look at a couple of these reviews.

5. As with the summary, when you have completed a solid rough draft, revise your critique, inserting transitional words and phrases to improve coherence. Try to combine short, choppy sentences for a smooth flow.

6. Proofread for grammatical correctness, punctuation, and spelling.

A Secondary Research Paper: Environmentalism

TASK: Write a seven- to eight-page secondary research paper exploring an issue involving environmentalism. The paper will cite sources of several different types: periodicals with a general audience, specialized periodicals (for example, professional journals), newspapers, book-length sources, and Internet sources.

READINGS

Rachel Carson, "The Obligation to Endure"
Merete Rietveld, "Mutant Bacteria and the Failure of Antibiotics"
John W. Mellor, "The Intertwining of Environmental Problems and Poverty"
Peter H. Raven, "Third World in the Global Future"
Edward O. Wilson, "The Solution"

Thinking Rhetorically about Audience and Purpose

Think of the audience for this essay as your peers and instructor. You will be writing to explore an issue in the area of environmentalism. The process of research writing involves developing a certain degree of expertise in an area by locating and reading texts from scholars and experts in the field you are researching. What are the characteristics of an "expert"? How does a person become an expert? Are you an expert on any subject? If so, how did you become one? On what occasions in your own life do you look to an expert for information or advice? What are your reasons for choosing this particular person?

Objectives

- You will be able to locate a number of useful sources.
- You will study and practice writing using sources of several different types.
- You will cite sources correctly.
- You will develop logical organizational strategies for papers.

Evaluative Criteria

- Is the paper clearly and logically structured?
- Does the paper use the required number and kinds of sources and cite them correctly?
- Does the essay draw on the sources for support?
- Is the essay mechanically sound?

Notes to the Student

1. Look through the suggested readings to find a topic you are interested in researching. Once you have found a topic, read all the essays in the textbook that deal with that topic. These sources can count toward those required for the paper.
2. Formulate a research plan. Think about all the places you can locate sources, decide which are appropriate for your topic, and prioritize them. The Internet may provide the easiest way to find sources, but the sources you find may not be very strong. Using a research-writing guide can be an enormous help. In addition, your university's library staff will be happy to help you formulate a research plan, so do not hesitate to ask, even if you have never set foot in the library before. Reference librarians are experts on finding information from experts.
3. After you have located a number of sources, scan their indexes to find where the information you want is most likely to be. Do not assume that you will need to read whole books, or even articles. You need to read only that information that best fits your purposes.
4. As you find passages and quotations you can use in your paper, you may want to use index cards to help organize the information. Put the quota-

tions and the source information on the cards. Then you can organize the cards in a logical order to develop a rough draft.

5. As you begin to write your rough draft, remember your audience and purpose. You are writing to explore an issue, so you may want to focus on describing and explaining as your method of development. You may choose to explore the issue in another way—if so, consult with your instructor to make sure your planned method of development is appropriate to the assignment.

6. Write a rough draft, inserting and discussing your sources as you describe and explain your topic. *Note:* Never use the words of a source without citing it. Plagiarism is not only unethical, it is remarkably easy to detect.

7. As you revise the rough draft of your paper, get as much feedback from your peers and instructor as possible. Another perspective can make a world of difference when it comes to revision.

8. Write a final draft and a list of works cited. Use the method of documentation your instructor recommends, and consult a handbook any time you have a question—even the most experienced writers use writing handbooks to reference documentation rules.

9. Proofread for grammatical correctness, punctuation, spelling, and so on. Pay particular attention to quotations and citations of sources, including the list of works cited at the end of the paper.

A Persuasive Essay: Racism, Oppression, and Human Nature

TASK: Write a three- to five-page persuasive essay dealing with the question of whether one of the following is an inevitable result of human nature: (a) war or (b) racism and oppression.

READINGS

George Simpson, "Early Social Darwinism"
Margaret Mead, "Warfare: An Invention—Not a Biological Necessity"
Robert Brannon, "Why Men Became Men, and Other Theories"
Naomi Weisstein, "Psychology Constructs the Female"
Unni Wikan, "The *Xanith:* A Third Gender Role?"

Thinking Rhetorically about Audience and Purpose

One of the most common reasons people write is to persuade others. Most people probably already have an opinion about this topic, so persuading them will require acknowledging both sides of the issue as you set out your arguments.

People frequently talk about "human nature," particularly in relation to behavior that is hard to understand. Why might people attribute such behavior to "human nature"? Why is it important to understand those aspects of behavior that are an inevitable part of universal human experience and those that are shaped by a person's individual or cultural experiences and circumstances?

Objectives

- You will study and practice writing to persuade others.
- You will be able to structure an argument logically.
- You will practice finding and using sources (at least four) to support an argument.
- You will use critical thinking skills to grapple with a specific but complex question about human nature.

Evaluative Criteria

- Is the paper persuasive?
- Is the argument logical and well structured?
- Does the essay draw on strong sources (at least four) for support?
- Is the essay mechanically sound?

Notes to the Student

1. Your first step might be to read the suggested essays, isolate their main ideas, and then determine your position on the question. Then organize the arguments in favor of and against your position. You might even list them in order of importance.
2. Examine the essay by Margaret Mead. It is an excellent example of writing to persuade. See how she structures her argument, and model the strategies that will suit your purpose.
3. The two predominant ways to structure persuasive essays are: (1) You can set out your arguments and develop them one by one. (2) You can set out your opponents' arguments, rebut them, and then develop your arguments further. The topic of this paper probably lends itself better to the second method. You may want to talk about your organization strategy with your instructor before you begin to write a rough draft.
4. Write a rough draft of your essay. Get feedback, if possible, from peers and your instructor.
5. Revise your persuasive essay, inserting transitional words and phrases to improve coherence.
6. Write a final draft. Proofread for grammatical correctness, punctuation, spelling, and so on. Pay particular attention to quotations and citations of sources, including the list of works cited at the end of the paper.

Textbook Proposal: Dropping the Bomb in WWII

TASK: Write a four- to five-page essay dealing with the question of the dropping of the atomic bomb on Japan in World War II and proposing textbook revisions based on your analysis of this subject.

READINGS

Margaret Mead, "Warfare: An Invention—Not a Biological Necessity"
John Connor, "The U.S. Was Right"

Gar Alperovitz, "The U.S. Was Wrong"
Sidney Shalett, "First Atomic Bomb Dropped on Japan"
Masuji Ibuse, Excerpt from *Black Rain*
Suzanne H. Sankowsky, Excerpt from *Mainstreams of World History*
Keigo Takarazuki and Kazuo Kasahara, Excerpt from *Progress of Japan*
Burton Bollag, "A Confrontation with the Past: The Japanese Textbook Dispute"
Carl Sandburg, "Men of Science Say Their Say"

Thinking Rhetorically about Audience and Purpose

Writing a proposal involves writing to persuade. In this case you will be persuading a high-school history textbook publisher to change the way that the dropping of the bomb on Japan is represented in a new edition of a textbook currently being used. You may decide it should be revised in any number of ways, but the point is to be persuasive about the reasons for making the revisions.

Objectives

- You will study and practice writing to persuade others.
- You will be able to structure an argument logically.
- You will practice using sources (from the textbook) to support an argument.
- You will use critical thinking skills to grapple with a specific but complex question about human nature.

Evaluative Criteria

- Is the paper persuasive?
- Is the argument logical and well structured?
- Does the essay draw on strong sources (at least four) for support?
- Is the essay mechanically sound?

Notes to the Student

1. You should definitely use sources from this textbook in your paper. You may also use the Internet and the library to find sources.
2. Complete a rough draft of the paper using the steps from prewriting through the rough draft stage of the writing process.
3. Revise your persuasive essay, inserting transitional words and phrases to improve coherence.
4. Proofread for grammatical correctness, punctuation, spelling, and so on. Pay particular attention to quotations and citations of sources, including the list of works cited at the end of the paper.

CHAPTER 5

Religion
and Philosophy

© Peter Guttman/CORBIS

Religion has surged to the forefront of global issues in recent years. The reassertion of the importance of religion has surprised and confused many nonreligious peoples by its intensity and ferocity. People who do not attach a great deal of personal importance to a religious belief system find it hard to understand why other human beings—in the name of their religion—would blow themselves up as human bombs in public places or fly airplanes into large buildings killing thousands of people. Many decry terrorism as a barbaric expression of religious belief, and yet it would be hard to argue that the response to terrorism by governments and armies around the world has somehow been more humane. This new cycle of human violence that has erupted onto the global stage at the opening of the 21st century underscores one important insight evident since the earliest days of human civilization: religious and philosophic ideas have tremendous power both to build and to destroy the worlds in which we live.

Religion and philosophy are, in a fundamental way, considerably more dangerous than the body of technical ideas that led humans to the development of the Colt revolver, nuclear weapons, or the Minuteman missile. The religion/philosophy (in the Eastern world, these two concepts are not separate) of a given people are what allows them actually to use the revolver, the nuclear weapon, or the missile on other human beings.

Conversely, this means that religion and philosophy are also the same influences that can "not allow" a given people to resort to violence and destruction, as the pacifist tradition in many cultures well illustrates. In religious philosophies such as Hinduism and Buddhism, not only do devout believers not kill their fellow humans but they abstain from killing and eating animals. Some count it a sin even to step or to sit on an unoffending insect. In the current world of constant media focus upon religion as a root of terrorism (and, less obviously, of "anti-terrorism"), it is easy to lose sight of these more common, day-to-day, life-sustaining dimensions of religion and philosophy.

"Religion" comes from Latin origins with a root that can mean both "to read over again" and "to bind."[1] Notions of "rereading" and of "binding" reflect the dual roles that religion has long played and continues to play in the human experience. Through the "rereading," "reflecting on," and constant "return to" a given body of other-worldly ideas, religious groups maintain their sense of both group and individual identities.

Philosophy fulfills a similar function, so similar in fact that religions such as Hinduism, Buddhism, Sikhism, and others are equally considered philosophies by their followers. Such Eastern philosophies as Confucianism and

---

[1]*Oxford English Dictionary.*

Taoism are likewise considered religions by their adherents. It was the Greeks in the Western world who developed the category of "philosophy." They defined the word as "The love, study, or pursuit of wisdom, or of knowledge of things and their causes."[2] The element noticeably absent from the Greek definition of philosophy is "god." Philosophy grew up in Greece in conjunction with the birth of Western science and gave rise to a scientific/secular approach to seeing and understanding the world. In order to coexist in a Western world that increasingly turned to Christianity after the fall of the Roman Empire, it became essential to distinguish between "religious" and "philosophical" ways of making sense of the world. This conceptual difference did not begin to take root in the Eastern world until the last century or two as the Western scientific tradition (and Communism in China) was introduced.

Humans generally want to make sense of their lives and their worlds. Religion and philosophy help them do so. It can be unnerving to see a human being who has been stripped of any religious or philosophical sense of identity. Anthropologists have studied such people in South America. They use the term "cultural castaways" to refer to millions of native people who have been forcibly "deculturated" as the forces of modernity have removed them from their traditional homelands, tribal customs, and religious beliefs and practices. In extreme cases, they lose all reason for existence and begin to wander the streets and highways in places like Lima, Peru; São Paolo, Brazil; and Bogota, Columbia. They stop wearing clothing and are too antisocial even to beg for food. Stripped of their religious beliefs in a world that no longer makes sense to them, they soon die from starvation or from exposure to the elements. They lose the will to live.[3]

The fear of such a chaotic state of meaninglessness is what motivates many peoples to respond violently in modern times to threats against their religious/philosophical identities. This chapter explores such deep-seated fear of human *anomie* (Latin for "namelessness") by first showing the great diversity and wealth of meaning that religious and philosophical ideas have brought to the human experience over time. The first reading comes from a young American college student who chose to leave America in her own personal quest to come to know how religion and philosophy shape life in Sri Lanka. This is followed by three overviews showing where various religions exist, how large they are, and the "bibles" that they have produced. Following these, an essay by religious expert Winston King examines the fundamental differences between Eastern and Western views of religion and philosophy. King's article is valuable not only for understanding the terms "religion" and "philosophy" but also for understanding profound differences in the ways that Eastern and Western peoples conceptualize the very world in which we live.

Then the chapter turns, appropriately, to the first beginnings of world religions through examination of six creation stories from various continents. Just as it is difficult to understand a good film when you walk into the theater midway through, so it is challenging to try to understand a religion or philosophy

---

[2]Ibid.

[3]Jack Weatherford, *Savages and Civilization* (New York: Fawcett Columbine, 1994), 264–66.

if you have no idea how the thing got started. After a representative view of creation, the chapter explores the "Foundations of Belief" from Eastern traditions through influential writings in the Hindu, Buddhist, Taoist, and Confucian traditions. The diversity of thought in the Western world is presented through writings by Plato and the Native-American Chief Seattle, an overview of the philosophical ideas of Friedrich Nietzsche, and an excerpt from a treatise on existentialism by Jean-Paul Sartre.

The final section of the chapter offers readers the opportunity to read about and to participate in a number of current religious and philosophical debates that are raging around the world. In the sections devoted to "Race, Gender, and Oppression" and "War and Peace," primary and secondary readings plunge students into the religious and philosophical tugs-of-war surrounding changing gender identities, religion and terrorism, and the increasing need for tolerance in an increasingly interconnected world community. The chapter ends with a variety of writing assignments that guide students into a deeper engagement with the ideas and issues covered by chapter readings.

Many readings in this section will be challenging for you, as students in the United States, to read. They come from peoples, cultures, and places very distant from our own. As in previous chapters, this final chapter again encourages you to use a unique set of conceptual tools for interpreting the writings of peoples across cultural, historical, and geographical borders. As outlined in Chapter 1, the toolkit consists of Aristotle's three primary rhetorical principles that teach us to focus upon (1) the specific message (2) that a specific writer is trying to communicate (3) to a specific audience. Each headnote before a reading includes essential background information and a "Reading Rhetorically" overview to help you better grasp: (1) what the message is, (2) who the writer is/was, and (3) who would have been the original audience. In the pages that follow, these headnotes and Aristotle's rhetoric offer valuable keys for unlocking the meanings of some of the most influential religious and philosophical writings in the human story. May they be as enriching to you as to millions—even to billions—of people before you.

<hr>

STUDENT ESSAY

<hr>

JILL JARVIS An Island Mosaic: Language, Religion, and Beauty in Sri Lanka

Jill Jarvis (1979–) currently resides in New York City where she is a high-school mathematics teacher in the Bronx for the children of newly arrived immigrants from around the world. While a student in Religious Studies at Whitman College in Walla Walla, Washington, Jarvis elected to spend her junior year abroad in Sri Lanka. The focus of her studies there was upon Buddhism, Hinduism, and Islam, as well as upon the language (Sinhalese) and the cultures of Sri Lanka. After graduation from Whitman College, Jarvis received a Fullbright Fellowship from the U.S.

government to return for an additional year of independent study in Sri Lanka. During this time, she devoted herself to working with Buddhist nuns and learning more about their lives. Her essay offers insight into what she learned not only about Buddhist nuns but also about "language, religion, and beauty" in this island nation.

Reading Rhetorically

In the following pages, Jarvis faces the difficult task of communicating the complexity of a world very different from her native culture in the United States to an audience that may have little familiarity with that world. She can anticipate that the way of life she finds in Sri Lanka is significantly different from the day-to-day worlds of her American readers. To bridge this cultural gap between reader and subject, she chooses the metaphor of a "mosaic," a picture or a design made up of small, often richly colored stones or tiles. In order to perceive the coherence of the larger picture thus created, one has to step back from a narrow focus upon any individual piece of it. The beauty of a mosaic is in the whole much more than in any one piece, and so it is with the essay that Jarvis has written. She brings together bits and pieces of experiences that revolve around relationships with people of different backgrounds, different languages, different cultures, different religions, and different values and attitudes. Amid this human diversity, however, she is able to find common ground. Note as you read how she does this. She closes her journey high on a remote mountaintop among "hundreds of strangers" who unite in a shared experience of wonder and awe at the simplest of daily rituals in the natural world—the rising of the sun bringing a new day. The overall coherence of her essay is reinforced by her closing piece about a religious pilgrimage with both friends and strangers to a distant mountaintop. As you read, think about the nature of the final image, an experience on a mountain, and how it is universal as well as personal.

"Beauty itself is the language to which we have no key; it is the mute cipher, the cryptogram, the uncracked, unbroken code. And it could be that for beauty, as it is for French, that there is no key, that *"oui"* will never make sense in our language but only in its own, and that we need to start all over again, on a new continent, learning the strange syllables one by one."

—ANNIE DILLARD, *Pilgrim at Tinker Creek*, p. 109.

1 Human religious experience isn't neat. It's not safe. It doesn't keep still. It's notoriously difficult to write about. When I deserted the sedate classrooms of my college for two years of study in Sri Lanka, I felt like I had leapt into an ocean of human relationships, a sea of convoluted and magnificent stories where any one thing is linked to every other. I found myself compelled to embrace ambiguity and complexity. It was either sink or swim, and, honestly, the textbooks contained little by way of preparation or instruction. I realized this: you must learn the language of another culture to even begin to understand it. You must listen to other people explain their beliefs in their own words and in their own tongues in order to begin

to understand their lives. And this: there is no final arrival point of understanding. Understanding is a journey, a perpetual process that will create relationships and revelations that alter your life forever.

As a college junior, I went to Sri Lanka to study language (Sinhala) and reli- 2 gion (primarily Buddhism). I lived in the country twice, for a total of two years. The second time I was fresh out of college and interested in the lives of Sri Lankan Buddhist nuns—women who choose to renounce lay life, shave their heads, take up orange robes, and dedicate themselves to ending their existential suffering. My research project hatched, sprouted wings, snatched me up by the scruff of the neck, and swept me off at top speed. I spent a lot of time with nuns. I spent long midnight hours crouched in dim temple kitchens slicing pounds of vegetables on curved, upturned machete knives with old women and young nuns to prepare ritual offering feasts. I spent long daylight hours poring over Sanskrit and Sinhala books with young student nuns, straying from the translations to tell stories and ask questions, and to laugh ourselves to distraction.

Once, I observed thirteen women receiving novice ordination at a marathon, 3 all-night ceremony. I had arrived at the ashram the day before the solemn ritual began and was quickly absorbed into a hive of women who dressed me in white clothes and put me to work. Preparations lasted all night (most Sri Lankan Buddhist rituals seem to involve high doses of sleeplessness). I snatched two hours of sleep on the stone floor and was awakened at about 2:30 A.M. by thirteen (nervous?) women stepping over and around me while dressing in white robes and brushing their long hair for the last time in their lives. I crawled out of deep sleep to drink a mug of hot tea in the dreamcloaked pre-dawn darkness while holding the hand of a sobbing mother as she related to me her grief over her daughter's unshakeable decision to leave home and family for monastic life.

Another time, I witnessed the initiation of one girl alone. Her entire family trav- 4 eled to the temple from their village hundreds of miles away. A few of this girl's relatives were jealously opposed to her decision to renounce and therefore conscripted the angry spirit of a dead grandmother to disrupt the renunciation by possessing the girl every night for a month before the ceremony. Be it grandmother-ghost or the complex psychological manifestation of cold feet, this possession caused quite a scene. I watched wide-eyed as this gentle girl writhed, stricken and tense, on the floor, swearing belligerently in her grandmother's raspy voice. Yet despite familial jealousies and grouchy grandmother-spirits, the ordination happened as planned and that girl is now a practicing Buddhist nun with a new name, new identity, and a new life.

I will never forget the moment that this twenty-three-year-old woman's hair was 5 cut by the elder nun, a wry, wiry, no-nonsense woman of forty. I stood quietly in a gathered circle of women beside the well to witness her initiation at the auspicious moment, about four A.M. The cement platform around the well became littered with locks of thick black hair as the elder nun cut it, reciting the appropriate gathas. The girl's mother stood silently, holding the first cut lock of hair in meditation. The other women present—sisters cradling infants, aunts, sisters in law—wept silently. So did I. The gravity of the moment a woman chooses to so dramatically alter her identity is deeply moving. In renouncing sexuality, marriage, and childbearing, she has willfully chosen to become the antithesis of what her culture expects of her. She has chosen a subversive path, difficult and lonely. The resolve in her eyes is quiet and powerful. Had I not seen this, I could never have understood it. Having seen it, I will never forget.

6   Sri Lanka is often described as a Buddhist country. It's not. Certainly, Sri Lankans preserved Buddhism when the tradition disappeared in India thousands of years ago; it was from Sri Lanka that the then tradition spread to the rest of Asia over time; it is to Sri Lanka that scholars and pilgrims turn to for the "original" Theravadin form of Buddhism. Sinhala Buddhists in Sri Lanka are the largest group within a remarkably diverse population. The island is home to Sinhala Buddhists and Sinhala Christians (Catholic and Protestant); Tamils who are Hindu and Christian; Muslims (many of whom speak Tamil) of Sunni, Shi'ia, Borah, and Malay origin; Burghers descended from Portuguese colonists, Zoroastrian Parsis, and the indigenous Vedda people. Sri Lanka's history is a history of exchange and hybridity; it presents a struggle to create a culture of tolerance within this fantastic plurality. After two raucous days on an archaeological field trip with a roving band of philosophy students from the University of Peradeniya, my cheeks aching from the stretch and strain of so much laughter and my mind a tired, jumbled babel of languages and impressions, I could never again speak of Sri Lanka as a Buddhist country. That's far too simplistic.

7   Imagine, if you will, a motley collection of Sri Lankan twenty-something-year-olds. One of them is a serene-faced, highly intelligent, somewhat radical, full-fledged Buddhist monk wrapped in a deep red robe and barefoot because he follows a strict monastic code which forbids the wearing of shoes. Five of them are Tamil-speaking Muslims, three of whom are girls veiled in the hijab. Two are Tamil girls from the war-devastated north, wearing the distinctive "pottu" mark between their eyes. The others are Sinhala Buddhists, who constitute the country's ethnic majority. Plus this random white girl of indeterminate origin—myself. Among us: multiple cultures, religions, languages, a constant banter and roar of translation and code-switching. *Imagine.* The renowned literary and cultural critic Edward Said says that the human cultures of this world are hybrid and heterogeneous, embroiled in a perpetual process of cross-pollination, exchange, and polemic. We are a complicated human ecosystem: Sri Lanka is a case in point. Do we not all live in some way or another with these sorts of categories? Race. Religion. Ethnicity. Class. Us-and-them.

8   Let me tell you, this odd band of philosophy students was certainly messing with everyone's categories. I could see surprise like a shadow in the wrinkled foreheads and double-takes of anyone watching our colorful troupe parade nonchalantly and haphazardly (as young people are wont to do) about the archaeological sites, museums, and tea stalls of North Central Sri Lanka. The gatekeepers of every Buddhist temple we visited harassed the Muslim girls as they moved toward stupas and altars, curious like the rest of us about this history carved in stone but halted by stalwarts shouting with the deepest disrespect that they either uncover their heads out of respect or stay out of the temple. They stayed out, patiently. The AK-47-armed guards at every checkpoint we passed through (a regular feature of the Lankan landscape, especially around Buddhist monuments) patted the Tamil girls down with anxious scrutiny and pried them with particularly probing questions, sus-

picious that they might be LTTE suicide bombers. Tired sighs; resignation; one of the Tamil girls whispered to me, "Can you believe what we put up with?"

Identity may be something that people inhabit daily, something worn on the outside: specific clothing, marks between the eyes, certain jewelry, veils. Ethnicity is buried in the accents that betray the languages that flow from people's tongues. Deep prejudices and violence in Sri Lanka (and, I'll be so bold as to advance, the world in general) fester in the voids between the borders of these identities, in the gaping lack of human-to-human communication. Interaction between these too-often crystallized identities is too-often troubled and rare to see happening openly in any positive way.

Yet our motley presence, the continual acts of communication within our group and the statement that the mere existence of such a group communicated to anyone watching us, implicitly and unassumingly challenged the supposed rigidity of Sri Lanka's ethnic boundaries. We laughed, loudly. We held hands. Peeked under veils. Tried on each others' languages. Argued about philosophy. Religion. Cultural habits. Made fun of each other. Made fun of ourselves. By the end of day, the Sinhala girls and I had stuck distinctly Tamil pottus to our foreheads, carefully centered there by the Tamil girls. Some of the boys even put them on, but only inside the bus, while the young monk, Venerable Maitri, laughed indulgently from his seat in the front. One of the Muslim girls offered to let me borrow her extra veil in order to cover my skin so that I could sneak, un-harassed, into the next museum to circumvent the separate (and much higher) price for white foreigners. In this manner we romped about, unlikely arm in arm, fumbling for words, singing songs, trying on identities, eliciting consternation, offering no easy solutions to peoples' perplexed and gaping stares.

I returned from that trip exhausted yet quietly exhilarated, my ears ringing from the songs and drumming in the bus on the rain-drenched ride home, eyes attuned to alternate dimensions of Sri Lankan experience. Our ability to shapeshift, to create and transform our identities, to allow our symbols to be malleable, to communicate in new words and in others' languages, to stretch ourselves outside our skins, to define ourselves despite what the louder and uglier voices of our cultures might insist—this is the very best of our humanity. What gives me hope is this capacity to question, to adapt, to share, to love, to play, to survive. And to reach laughing across boundaries. To never be completely, wholly defined.

Sri Pada is a Sri Lankan mountain destined by topography to become an object of obsession. It is a strange, jutting anomaly of a landform, poking up in a solitary nudge from surrounding softer-shouldered hills of central Sri Lanka, a likely target for human yearning to climb. As the Buddhists tell the story, this weird rock attracted attention from the Buddha himself, who left a decidedly super-human sized footprint on its peak during his long-ago visit to the island. It is this footprint, etched in stone and covered now by a shrine, that Buddhist pilgrims flock up the mountain to worship, under protection of the Butterfly God Saman Deviyo, who inhabited the mountain long before the Buddha came or was even born, and who'll likely as not be there until people forget why they continue to climb it. Saman Deviyo is recognized by Hindus as well, while Muslims and Christians believe the footprint to belong to Adam, the first man on earth. It is a mountain sacred to all Sri Lanka's people.

13   I climbed Sri Pada once with a pilgrimage group led by Buddhist nuns. The Sri Pada pilgrimage, if done right, is done at night (like any other Sri Lankan religious ritual!). After five hours' staggering up the mountainside in the darkness, we reached the temple at the summit by eleven o'clock in the evening. The glory of arrival was emphatically complemented by a cutting wind. Enormously fat gray night-moths clung desperately to the electric lights, the brittle carcasses of their dead littering the ground to be sent spiraling wildly in the pitiless gale. Nearly delirious, I found refuge on the stone floor of a jam-packed shelter that some generous and compassionate temple patron must have once constructed, and awakened a few hours later with the hundreds of other pilgrims to witness the sunrise.

14   The sunrise is the reason why any self-respecting pilgrim must hike the mountain at night. Cloaked in extra sheets and newspapers, with towels tied around heads to fend off the carnivorous cold, old people and sick people and young mothers with tiny bundled-up babies and everyone in between gathers at dawn on the eastern edge of the mountaintop temple to watch the shifting kaleidoscope of colors as the sun prepares to emerge. We watch the intimate celestial details of this daily cosmic ritual as if it is happening for us: we have endeavored to make this sweaty pilgrimage and now our attentive birds-eye gaze becomes the gravity that will yank the sun into the darkness to create a new day.

15   At five A.M. there is only a slender, bluish glow on the horizon, but this spreads slowly into pinks and oranges, peeling back the foggy layers of dark while five hundred sleepless faces watch with raw intensity, murmuring as they try to pinpoint the precise place from which the sun will appear. The ripening light fans out, the architecture of the clouds becomes ecstatic, but still no familiar fireball. People talk impatiently yet cheerfully to the strangers beside them, reminding me of Americans waiting anxiously for the fireworks on Fourth of July night.

16   "Maybe it won't rise today," someone teases anxiously. This seems like this is a real possibility, though everyone laughs. But at last, by the collective strength of our many wills, the sun peeks (once, twice, thrice) and AHH! blazes over the silhouetted backs of the eastern mountains in retina-scalding magnificence. People spontaneously gasp words of worship, "Sadhu, sadhu, saaaadhu!" words they use to honor a monk or a nun, a sacred relic, words used in religious ceremony. I feel it too, startled awe in the face of beauty.

17   Some say that the most simple of natural rituals, sunrises, sunsets, full moons, storms, are close to the source of all our profound religious impulses. I'm shy about sweeping claims, but I will admit that at that moment and others, in sickness and in health, in love and in war, despite our radical differences, we do as human beings seem to share one another's capacity for wonder. That day, hundreds of strangers stood together on a mountain we had climbed. We gasped together, sighed together, worshipped together, and finally tread our way together back down the mountain where we again took up our separate lives. Yet the shared experience, I believe, remains with us.

18   Living in Sri Lanka was a mountaintop experience for me, a form of personal pilgrimage toward deeper understanding of the complexities of this world and the people with whom I share it. By impulsively stretching across oceans, continents, and differences, I met people whose imprints will remain with me for the rest of

my life. I learned new syllables, new ways of relating, new ways of seeing. Moreover, through learning of others, I learn of myself; through having glimpsed and grappled with another culture on its own terms, I believe that I better understand my own.

> "We shall not cease from exploration
> And the end of all our exploring
> Will be to arrive where we started
> And know the place for the first time."
>
> —T. S. ELIOT, "Little Gidding,"
> from *The Four Quartets*

Questions for Discussion and Your Reading Journal

1. What role does Jarvis suggest learning a language plays in understanding another culture? How does learning the language (Sinhala) well seem to change the overall nature of her experience in Sri Lanka?
2. Jarvis states in her first paragraph that college textbooks "contained little by way of preparation" for what she experienced in Sri Lanka. Pick out a specific incident later in her narrative that illustrates this point effectively.
3. What deeper insight into the Buddhist nature of Sri Lanka did Jarvis learn from "two raucous days on an archaeological field trip with a roving band of philosophy students from the University of Peradeniya"?
4. Jarvis writes several times about young people "trying on identities" of other young people. In your opinion, what did immersing herself in a foreign culture seem to do to her self-identity?
5. Have you ever had an experience with nature similar to what Jarvis and hundreds of other pilgrims felt and saw as the sun rose to greet them on top of Sri Pada Mountain? Explain.

DEFINITIONS AND CULTURAL CONTEXTS

WHAT THE WORLD BELIEVES

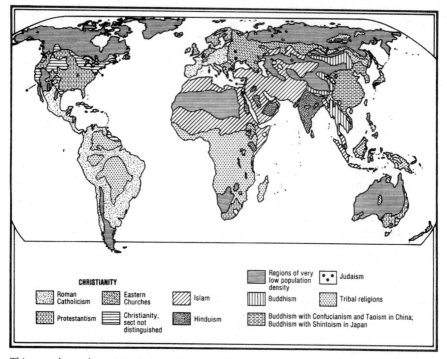

This map shows the major religions of the world by geographical area. As you read selections from and about various religious traditions, the map will help you place those traditions geographically.

MAJOR RELIGIONS OF THE WORLD RANKED BY NUMBER OF ADHERENTS

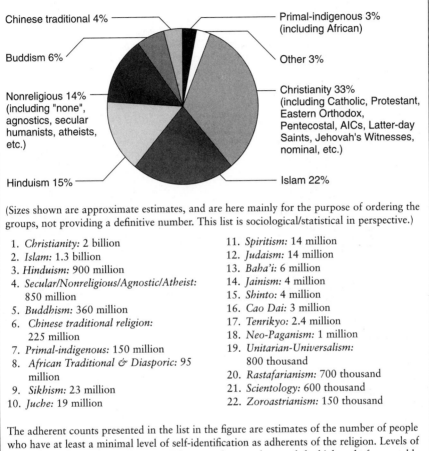

Chinese traditional 4%

Buddism 6%

Nonreligious 14%
(including "none",
agnostics, secular
humanists, atheists,
etc.)

Hinduism 15%

Primal-indigenous 3%
(including African)

Other 3%

Christianity 33%
(including Catholic, Protestant,
Eastern Orthodox,
Pentecostal, AICs, Latter-day
Saints, Jehovah's Witnesses,
nominal, etc.)

Islam 22%

(Sizes shown are approximate estimates, and are here mainly for the purpose of ordering the groups, not providing a definitive number. This list is sociological/statistical in perspective.)

1. *Christianity:* 2 billion
2. *Islam:* 1.3 billion
3. *Hinduism:* 900 million
4. *Secular/Nonreligious/Agnostic/Atheist:* 850 million
5. *Buddhism:* 360 million
6. *Chinese traditional religion:* 225 million
7. *Primal-indigenous:* 150 million
8. *African Traditional & Diasporic:* 95 million
9. *Sikhism:* 23 million
10. *Juche:* 19 million
11. *Spiritism:* 14 million
12. *Judaism:* 14 million
13. *Baha'i:* 6 million
14. *Jainism:* 4 million
15. *Shinto:* 4 million
16. *Cao Dai:* 3 million
17. *Tenrikyo:* 2.4 million
18. *Neo-Paganism:* 1 million
19. *Unitarian-Universalism:* 800 thousand
20. *Rastafarianism:* 700 thousand
21. *Scientology:* 600 thousand
22. *Zoroastrianism:* 150 thousand

The adherent counts presented in the list in the figure are estimates of the number of people who have at least a minimal level of self-identification as adherents of the religion. Levels of participation vary within all groups. These numbers **tend toward the high end** of reasonable worldwide estimates. Valid arguments can be made for different figures, but if the same criteria are used for all groups the relative order should be the same.

Source: www.adherents.com/Religions_By_Adherents.html. Courtesy Adherents.com.

OVERVIEW OF "BIBLES" OF THE WORLD

Peoples of the Western world are generally familiar with the Judeo-Christian Bible and, to a lesser degree, the "bible" of the Islamic faith, the Quran. However, according to the *Encyclopedia of World Scriptures* (Snodgrass, London: McFarland & Co. Publishers, 2001), there are a total of 27 identifiable collections of sacred writings in existence around the world. The oldest writings come from Egypt and Mesopotamia of some 6,000 years ago. The newest include *The Book of Mormon*, *White Roots of Peace* (Iroquois) and *Black Elk Speaks* (Lakota Sioux) in North America, which have been written down in the last two centuries.

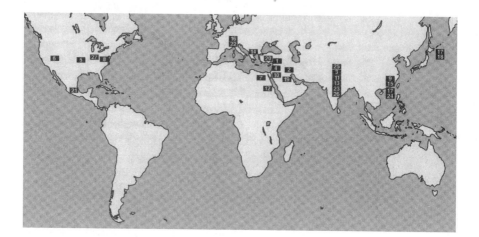

1—Apocrypha	10—Dead Sea Scrolls	19—Koran
2—Avesta	11—Dhammapada	20—Mathnawi
3—Bhagavad Gita	12—Ethiopian Book of the	21—Popol Vuh
4—Bible	Dead	22—Talmud
5—*Black Elk Speaks*	13—Granth	23—Tantra
6—Book of Mormon	14—Homeric Hymns	24—Tao-te Ching
7—Book of the Dead	15—I Ching	25—Tibetan Book of the
(Egyptian)	16—Kabbala	Dead
8—Christian Science writings	17—Koan	26—Vedas
9—Confucius's Analects	18—Kojiki	27—*White Roots of Peace*

Source: Map by Raymond Barrett, Jr.

WINSTON KING

In his foreword to Religion and Nothingness, *Winston King, emeritus professor at Vanderbilt University, discusses the problem of approaching Eastern religious systems with Western concepts of religion and philosophy. Westerners tend to see these as distinctly different entities. In the East, religions are often deeply philosophical and philosophies often are quite religious. King briefly explores the implications these differing approaches to knowledge have in terms of the ways the East and the West see the universe and the place of humans within it.*

Reading Rhetorically

King's rhetorical task is rather straightforward. He seeks to inform his audience about profound differences between Western and Eastern conceptions of the categories of knowledge that we call "religion" and "philosophy." Thus his writing is more expository (information-oriented) than argumentative (persuasion-oriented). He is not trying to persuade his readers that there is anything inherently superior either to the Western or the Eastern views in these areas. Rather, his goal is to inform us, as clearly as possible, about two very different knowledge systems. The challenge, then, is to make these culturally oppositional bodies of knowledge somehow clear and meaningful to adherents in both camps. Note how he does this through constant use of concrete examples, clarifying facts, and short narratives. Although King distinguishes carefully between Western ideas and Eastern ideas, some peoples in the West tend to share a more Eastern view of the "interconnectedness" of all of creation.

Religion and Nothingness

A basic difficult that stares us in the face immediately is the differing relation of philosophy and religion in East and West. And it is very important to keep this in mind from the beginning. For us in the West, religion and philosophy have been two ever since the time of the Greek philosophers. For though the Catholic theological tradition incorporated Aristotle into its theology and Platonism into its experience, philosophy never lost its independence, even in the Middle Ages. In the early modern period it asserted its independence anew under the impulse of humanism and the new empirical sciences. By the time of the Enlightenment it had come to qualify and question the basic foundations and assumptions of the Christian faith and ended up, as at present, occasionally in rational support of religious verities (always on the basis of its own rational foundations), more often in outright hostility toward all religion, but in any event always completely separate. And this separation has been institutionalized in the faculty structures of many universities, especially in the United States.

In the millennia-long traditions of the Hindu and Buddhist East, philosophy and religion have in effect and intent been branches of the same enterprise, that of seeking man's salvation. In India it is not uncommon for the professor of philosophy to spend the years of his retirement in personal religious quest, that is, in fully existentializing his intellectualism. In Japan since the Meiji Restoration, the Western pattern of separating the public (national and prefectural) universities from the religiously founded and supported ones has been faithfully followed, but the interchange of professors between the two systems and the similar content of the philosophico-religious courses taught in both bring them closer. After all, the Western pattern has been present in university learning for only a century, while the Buddhist cultural pattern has been dominant in all Japanese learning for fifteen centuries. Thus it is no anomaly in Japan that Nishitani should concurrently teach philosophy in Kyoto University (national) and religion in Ōtani University (a Jōdo Shinshū Buddhist institution). A Japanese friend says flatly that there would have been no difference in content between the way in which Nishitani would have taught a given course in the "philosophy" faculty of Kyoto University and in the department of "religion" in Ōtani University. . . .

3   There is yet another factor, Buddhist in general and Zen in particular, which is fully as central to the difficulty of East-West communication as any of the above: the differing East-West views of the universe and man's place in it. A comparison of the two by means of somewhat stereotypical models may illustrate this fundamental difference of cultural stance. The Western traditional model of the universe may be said to be a mechanical one, not too unlike an intricate piece of clockwork with the greater and lesser wheels and their movements meticulously geared to one another. The whole tends to be a more or less definite and limited system, both in time and space. The parts may be closely related to one another, but much of the causality is conceived in a somewhat mechanical single-line mode, item to item. (I recognize that modern physical theory greatly qualifies this picture; but this does not alter the general validity of the comparison here.) Relationships therein are genuine and important but tend to be discreet and external; there is no confusion of the being or individuality of any one part with that of any other.

4   Conjoint with this underlying conceptual model, part and parcel of the same cultural philosophical mode of awareness, are the basic building blocks of the Western thought structure—culturally inevitable, one might say. In Western religious thought there is God (prime mover, "watch" creator) who is transcendent of his creation, including man. (Judaism and all its derivates have been strongly averse to humanizing God or divinizing man.) But since man is more Godlike than any other creature, he in turn transcends them all, the little lord of creation under its Great Lord. The ultimate purpose of this subcreation, according to Christianity, is to serve man and in the end to be conductive to his eternal bliss. In post-Christian philosophy man as subject remains rather lordly in his relation to objects. Mind, soul, or consciousness alone "within" the citadel of individual selfhood looks "out" at everything else, whether human or nonhuman, as "other." As Nishitani often insists, this Cartesian division of reality into immaterial, invisible, subjective consciousness and material, visible objectivity is the epitome of Western thought, the creator of its cultures and civilization. Out of this climate has arisen the Western dichotomous type of logical assertion that A is *not, can*not be B. Nurtured in this atmosphere, deeply conditioned by the Christian world view, there has arisen the dualistic ethic of (absolute) good versus (absolute) evil, right versus wrong, selfishness versus unselfishness and similar sharp distinctions. On this same subject-object foundation, the human intellect, deliberately abstracting itself from all emotion and aesthetic sensibility (except perhaps the beauty of systematic order), can dispassionately and logically consider and analyze any *other*, be it man, animal, plant, rock, star, or component thereof, and thus create an immense and all-pervasive structure called science.

By contrast the Eastern and Buddhist model for conceiving the universe can 5
be termed a biological-organic one. The East speaks of the interdependency of
part upon part and of part and whole, of the internal relations of one entity to
another within the organism that is the universe. There is here the amorphous
unity of nondistinction, of the Taoist Great Primordial Nothingness (which is
prior, perhaps temporally, certainly structurally, to all individual being in the
universe) out of which beings flow in their diverse forms and to whose ocean-
like womb they return upon dissolution. Hua Yen Buddhism's philosophy of
totality placed all beings in what Van Bragt, using a Christian term for the inter-
relations within the Trinity, calls "circuminsessional interpenetration" of one
another. Fa Tsang illustrated it by his hall of mirrors in which each mirror (individual being) reflects (or "contains") the central Buddha image as well as every
other mirror in the hall (the universe). Thus the whole can be said to be *in* the
part as truly as the part is *in* the whole. These and many similar figures clearly
suggest a living body rather than an intricate machine.

It is then inevitable that a philosophy (Zen Buddhist) which had its origins 6
and nourishment in this thought complex will characteristically portray the universe in a way radically different from the Western manner. In place of one-on-
one causal sequences there will be holistic, contextual-causal interpretations. In
place of a straight-line historical causal "progress" of events to a climax of
some sort in a limited time-span there will be a historical "process" wherein
time is cyclical and infinite, and "purpose," "drive," and "direction" much
less obvious and important. Individual entities, including man, will not be seen
as so substantially separable from other entities as in Western thought, but
rather as a single flowing event in which the interdependent relationships are
as real as, or even more real than the related entities themselves. And man will
have none of that proud, unique difference and lordship over creation which
the Christian West has given him—and which he retains in post-Christian sec-
ularized form. In Eastern thought he is part and parcel of the universe in which
his existence is set, one little wavelet in a vast ocean of being/non-being. And
quite obviously his visceral values, existential concerns, and intuitional awareness will be fully as important in relating to and understanding the universe as
his sheerly rational knowledge—if not more so.

Questions for Discussion and Your Reading Journal

1. Who is the audience for this piece? From what standpoint does Winston
   King write?
2. How are philosophy and religion conceptualized in the Eastern world?
   Compare this to Western concepts of philosophy and religion.
3. According to King, how do people in the East view the universe and the
   place of human beings within it? How do Westerners view these?
4. Over the past centuries, Western nations have sent and continue to send
   thousands of Christian missionaries to convert Eastern peoples. Why
   would it be valuable for these missionaries to understand what "philosophy" and "religion" mean to Easterners?
5. What valuable contributions might Eastern and Western thought make to
   each other, according to this author?

DAVID BROOKS

Besides serving as a senior editor at the Weekly Standard, *David Brooks is also a regular contributor to the* New York Times, *the* Atlantic Monthly, *and* Newsweek. *He provides commentary upon current American politics for the "News Hour with Jim Lehrer" that airs weekdays on PBS. Brooks has also gained attention for his book-length analyses of American culture. His bestseller,* Bobos in Paradise: The New Upper Class and How They Got There, *is a comic cultural critique of the "bourgeois bohemians" ("hippie capitalists") created by the high-tech economic boom of the 1990s. Nearly 5 years of experience as a foreign correspondent for the* Wall Street Journal *in the Middle East, Russia, Europe, and South America allow him to see and to analyze cultural trends beyond the borders of the United States as well. In the following reading, Brooks explores the resurgence of traditional religions around the entire world. As he points out, religious conviction is neither fading nor dying in the modern, secular world. His reading introduces "secular fundamentalists" in a manner that adds a further dimension to Karen Armstrong's overview of religious fundamentalism in the reading "Fundamentalism and the Modern World" that comes later in this chapter.*

Reading Rhetorically

Brooks's article was published in the magazine the *Atlantic Monthly*. The audience who reads the *Atlantic* is composed mostly of educated and affluent Americans interested in politics, social trends, art, and literature. Brooks sets out to challenge ideas about the relationship between wealth, education, and religious belief that his readers commonly hold. As a self-proclaimed "recovering secularist," Brooks lays out a factual overview of the "religious boom" that is reasserting itself around the world. Then he lays out the "six steps in the recovery process" to help people suffering from the illusion that the whole world is turning away from religion to embrace science and progress. As you read, note how his use of humor contributes to his *ethos* in the argument he makes.

Kicking the Secularist Habit

1   Like a lot of people these days, I'm a recovering secularist. Until September 11 I accepted the notion that as the world becomes richer and better educated, it becomes less religious. Extrapolating from a tiny and unrepresentative sample of humanity (in Western Europe and parts of North America), this theory holds that as history moves forward, science displaces dogma and reason replaces unthinking obedience. A region that has not yet had a reformation and an enlightenment, such as the Arab world, sooner or later will.

It's now clear that the secularization theory is untrue. The human race   2
does not necessarily get less religious as it grows richer and better educated.
We are living through one of the great periods of scientific progress and the
creation of wealth. At the same time, we are in the midst of a religious boom.

Islam is surging. Orthodox Judaism is growing among young people, and   3
Israel has gotten more religious as it has become more affluent. The growth of
Christianity surpasses that of all other faiths. In 1942 this magazine published
an essay called *"Will the Christian Church Survive?"* Sixty years later there are
two billion Christians in the world; by 2050, according to some estimates, there
will be three billion. As Philip Jenkins, a Distinguished Professor of History and
Religious Studies at Pennsylvania State University, has observed, perhaps the
most successful social movement of our age is Pentecostalism (see *"The Next
Christianity,"* October *Atlantic*). Having gotten its start in Los Angeles about a
century ago, it now embraces 400 million people—a number that, according to
Jenkins, could reach a billion or more by the half-century mark.

Moreover, it is the denominations that refuse to adapt to secularism that   4
are growing the fastest, while those that try to be "modern" and "relevant"
are withering. Ecstatic forms of Christianity and "anti-modern" Islam are
thriving. The Christian population in Africa, which was about 10 million in
1900 and is currently about 360 million, is expected to grow to 633 million
by 2025, with conservative, evangelical, and syncretistic groups dominating.
In Africa churches are becoming more influential than many nations, with
both good and bad effects.

Secularism is not the future; it is yesterday's incorrect vision of the future.   5
This realization sends us recovering secularists to the bookstore or the library
in a desperate attempt to figure out what is going on in the world. I suspect I
am not the only one who since September 11 has found himself reading a
paperback edition of the Koran that was bought a few years ago in a fit of
high-mindedness but was never actually opened. I'm probably not the only one
boning up on the teachings of Ahmad ibn Taymiyya, Sayyid Qutb, and
Muhammad ibn Abd al-Wahhab.

There are six steps in the recovery process. First you have to accept the   6
fact that you are not the norm. Western foundations and universities send out
squads of researchers to study and explain religious movements. But as the
sociologist Peter Berger has pointed out, the phenomenon that really needs
explaining is the habits of the American professoriat: religious groups should
be sending out researchers to try to understand why there are pockets of people in the world who do not feel the constant presence of God in their lives,
who do not fill their days with rituals and prayers and garments that bring
them into contact with the divine, and who do not believe that God's will
should shape their public lives.

Once you accept this—which is like understanding that the earth revolves   7
around the sun, not vice-versa—you can begin to see things in a new way.

The second step toward recovery involves confronting fear. For a few   8
years it seemed that we were all heading toward a benign end of history, one
in which our biggest worry would be boredom. Liberal democracy had won
the day. Yes, we had to contend with globalization and inequality, but these

were material and measurable concepts. Now we are looking at fundamental clashes of belief and a truly scary situation—at least in the Southern Hemisphere—that brings to mind the Middle Ages, with weak governments, missionary armies, and rampant religious conflict.

9   The third step is getting angry. I now get extremely annoyed by the secular fundamentalists who are content to remain smugly ignorant of enormous shifts occurring all around them. They haven't learned anything about religion, at home or abroad. They don't know who Tim LaHaye and Jerry B. Jenkins are, even though those co-authors have sold 42 million copies of their books. They still don't know what makes a Pentecostal a Pentecostal (you could walk through an American newsroom and ask that question, and the only people who might be able to answer would be the secretaries and the janitorial staff). They still don't know about Michel Aflaq, the mystical Arab nationalist who served as a guru to Saddam Hussein. A great Niagara of religious fervor is cascading down around them while they stand obtuse and dry in the little cave of their own parochialism—and many of them are journalists and policy analysts, who are paid to keep up with these things.

10   The fourth step toward recovery is to resist the impulse to find a materialistic explanation for everything. During the centuries when secularism seemed the wave of the future, Western intellectuals developed social-science models of extraordinary persuasiveness. Marx explained history through class struggle, other economists explained it through profit maximization. Professors of international affairs used conflict-of-interest doctrines and game theory to predict the dynamics between nation-states.

11   All these models are seductive and partly true. This country has built powerful institutions, such as the State Department and the CIA, that use them to try to develop sound policies. But none of the models can adequately account for religious ideas, impulses, and actions, because religious fervor can't be quantified and standardized. Religious motivations can't be explained by cost-benefit analysis.

12   Over the past twenty years domestic-policy analysts have thought hard about the roles that religion and character play in public life. Our foreign-policy elites are at least two decades behind. They go for months ignoring the force of religion; then, when confronted with something inescapably religious, such as the Iranian revolution or the Taliban, they begin talking of religious zealotry and fanaticism, which suddenly explains everything. After a few days of shaking their heads over the fanatics, they revert to their usual secular analyses. We do not yet have, and sorely need, a mode of analysis that attempts to merge the spiritual and the material.

13   The recovering secularist has to resist the temptation to treat religion as a mere conduit for thwarted economic impulses. For example, we often say that young Arab men who have no decent prospects turn to radical Islam. There's obviously some truth to this observation. But it's not the whole story: neither Mohammed Atta nor Osama bin Laden, for example, was poor or oppressed. And although it's possible to construct theories that explain their radicalism as the result of alienation or some other secular factor, it makes more sense to acknowledge that faith is its own force, independent of and perhaps greater than economic resentment.

Human beings yearn for righteous rule, for a just world or a world that   14
reflects God's will—in many cases at least as strongly as they yearn for money
or success. Thinking about that yearning means moving away from scientific
analysis and into the realm of moral judgment. The crucial question is not
What incentives does this yearning respond to? but Do individuals pursue a
moral vision of righteous rule? And do they do so in virtuous ways, or are they,
like Saddam Hussein and Osama bin Laden, evil in their vision and methods?

Fifth, the recovering secularist must acknowledge that he has been too   15
easy on religion. Because he assumed that it was playing a diminishing role in
public affairs, he patronized it. He condescendingly decided not to judge other
creeds. They are all valid ways of approaching God, he told himself, and ultimately they fuse into one. After all, why stir up trouble by judging another's
beliefs? It's not polite. The better option, when confronted by some nasty practice performed in the name of religion, is simply to avert one's eyes. Is Wahhabism a vicious sect that perverts Islam? Don't talk about it.

But in a world in which religion plays an ever larger role, this approach is   16
no longer acceptable. One has to try to separate right from wrong. The problem is that once we start doing that, it's hard to say where we will end up.
Consider Pim Fortuyn, a left-leaning Dutch politician and gay-rights advocate
who criticized Muslim immigrants for their attitudes toward women and gays.
When he was assassinated, last year, the press described him, on the basis of
those criticisms, as a rightist in the manner of Jean-Marie Le Pen, which was
far from the truth. In the post-secular world today's categories of left and right
will become inapt and obsolete.

The sixth and final step for recovering secularists is to understand that this   17
country was never very secular anyway. We Americans long for righteous rule as
fervently as anybody else. We are inculcated with the notion that, in Abraham
Lincoln's words, we represent the "last, best hope of earth." Many Americans
have always sensed that we have a transcendent mission, although, fortunately,
it is not a theological one. We instinctively feel, in ways that people from other
places do not, that history is unfulfilled as long as there are nations in which
people are not free. It is this instinctive belief that has led George W. Bush to
respond so ambitiously to the events of September 11, and that has led most
Americans to support him.

Americans are as active as anyone else in the clash of eschatologies. Sad-   18
dam Hussein sees history as ending with a united Arab nation globally dominant and with himself revered as the creator of a just world order. Osama bin
Laden sees history as ending with the global imposition of sharia. Many Europeans see history as ending with the establishment of secular global institutions under which nationalism and religious passions will be quieted and
nation-states will give way to international law and multilateral cooperation.
Many Americans see history as ending in the triumph of freedom and consti-
tutionalism, with religion not abandoned or suppressed but enriching democratic life.

We are inescapably caught in a world of conflicting visions of historical   19
destiny. This is not the same as saying that we are caught in a world of conflicting religions. But understanding this world means beating the secularist
prejudices out of our minds every day.

Questions for Discussion and Your Reading Journal

1. What point is Brooks making when he refers to himself in the opening sentence as "a recovering secularist"?
2. Sum up in one to three sentences the main points of "the secularization theory."
3. Do you find Brooks's evidence about the current "religious boom" around the world convincing? Why or why not?
4. List the six steps in what Brooks labels "the recovery process" from belief in the secularization theory.
5. In your own life, do you personally feel that humans long for "righteous rule" as much as they long for "money or success," as Brooks claims? Explain.
6. What major world populations are left out of Brooks's summary of competing "eschatologies" in his second-to-last paragraph? (*Note: Eschatology* refers to ideas or doctrine of the final state of human existence.)

CONCEPTS OF CREATION

The six creation stories presented in this section give some idea of the rich variety of ideas that different cultures have developed to explain the beginning of the human story. It is important to understand that each of these narratives existed as oral traditions for thousands—in some cases, perhaps, tens of thousands—of years before they were written down. They were transmitted from generation to generation through fireside story telling, religious ritual and drama, and public discourse for far longer than they have existed as written texts. They are, in short, a collection of "ancestral memories" that brings to us through language the hopes and fears, spiritual longings, and social conceptualizations of who we are and who we have been over thousands of years.

Creation stories offer an obvious place to begin any serious examination of religion—and of philosophy as well, which was born in the Western world in opposition to some of the basic elements of religion. The following creation stories contain the seeds of much that follows later in the respective cultures and societies that have grown out of them. Notions of the divine, male/female roles, attitudes toward nature and the place of humans within it, social norms, group versus individual striving, the very meaning and point of human existence as defined by a certain people in a certain place—all of these are here in one form or another. Brief explanatory notes precede each selection.

Reading Rhetorically

All of these are narratives, but they do not all fit our Western notion of how a story should proceed. As you read, note the similarities and the differences not only among the stories themselves but also in the way they are told. Also note what you think might be the "oral" features of these texts—things that helped a nonliterate person remember them as they were told.

China: "Nu Kwa"

"Nu Kwa" comes from the ancient Manchu region of Northern China and is considered among the oldest of stories about human beginnings.

To the valleys of the wide flowing Hwang Ho, came the Goddess Nu Kwa 1
and there from the rich golden earth, She fashioned the race of golden people, carefully working the features of each with Her skillful fingers. But so arduous was Her task that She soon tired of making these individual creations and began to pull a string through the mud. In this way She made the others, though not as carefully formed, as She had made those of the golden earth, the ancestors of the Chinese people.

From the Kun Lun mountains, sweet western paradise whose summits reach 2
the heights of heaven, Nu Kwa sent the great winds and the life giving waters, making the earth good for planting, pouring the excess waters into the Chihli Po Hai Bay—and then She filled it with fish so that all might eat to satisfaction.

But there came a time when all the universe was in great chaos; fires raged 3
and waters brought floods. At this time, the pillar of the north, the pillar of the south, the pillar of the east, and the pillar of the west—all of these were destroyed. The nine provinces of the earth separated from each other and even heaven and earth were no longer suited to each other, for they had blown so far apart. Everything was wrong. Animals ate the people. Vultures seized and killed the elderly and weak.

Then Great Mother Nu Kwa saw what had happened and came to repair the 4
damage, using coloured stones to patch the heavens. Seeing the ruins of the pillars, those which had supported the four corners of heaven, She took the legs of the great turtle and used them as columns, placing them firmly at the four compass points of the world. With Her mighty arms She smothered the blazing fires and when the burning reeds had turned to ash, She piled the ashes high enough so that the wild flooding waters came to repose where they are today. When all was once again in place—only then was Mother Nu Kwa satisfied to rest.

It was then that She looked upon all that She had done. It was a time of 5
perfect harmony when all flowed in its course, each at its own pace. The stars followed their correct paths in the heavens. The rain came only when the rain should come. Each season followed the one before—in rightful order. Mother Nu Kwa had repaired the pattern for all that occurred in the universe, so that the crops were plentiful, the people were no longer the meal of the wild animal, vultures did not prey among the weak and old, nor were serpents harmful to them either.

Life was spent in nights of peace, undisturbed by anxious dream, and 6
waking time was carefree and untroubled. It was the time of Mother Nu Kwa, She who established the patterns of existence, the order and rhythm of the universe, the sacred way of harmony and balance.

Questions for Discussion and Your Reading Journal

1. What is unique about the kind of deity that is portrayed in this early creation story?
2. Why do you think the earliest peoples would conceive of human creation as the result of the work of a goddess rather than a god? What might this tell us about the relationship of early peoples to the world of nature?
3. Once they were created, humans soon faced a time of "great chaos." What long-term view of nature might we expect to result from this period of trouble?
4. Rather than give her creations a divine set of rules and commands, the divine figure (or force) Nu Kwa leaves them with a "sacred way." What does this sacred way seem to suggest in terms of the proper human relationship to the universe in which they live?

India: "Shakti"

"Shakti" is one of several creation stories from oral traditions in ancient India. The word shakti *means "power" or "life force."*

1   She who holds the Universe in Her womb,

source of all creative energies,
Maha Devi who conceives
and bears and nourishes
all that exists—
She is the ghanibuti,
the massed condensed power of energy;
She is the sphurana,
the power that burgeons forth into action;
She is purest consciousness and bliss,
inherent in the manifestation of all being.

2   Never can She be known
in Her perfect completeness,
for Her omnipotence is in all
that She continually does.
Do they not say
that even Shiva is unable to stir,
lies as a corpse,
until She grants him Her energies?
In the form of the coiled serpent,[1]
the Bhunjangi Kundalini,

---

[1]**serpent** In Kundalini yoga, energy lies coiled at the base of the spinal cord like a serpent, waiting to be awakened through yoga exercise. [Ed. note.]

She unwinds Herself through the chakras,[2]
through the lotuses[3] of the body,
as She creates Her cosmic serpent spiral
through the lotus chakras of the Universe.
At Her sacred shrine of Kamrupa,
they drink the kula nectar
that is the blood that passes from Her
as the moon passes from the sky,
while those who reach out to know Her
sit in Her circle of worshippers,
the sacred Shakti Cakra Pravartika,
knowing that if they worship Her with full devotion,
She will appear and give what is requested,
as She maintains the many beings of the world.

Some say that there are many worlds,   3
each ruled by a goddess or a god,
but that there is just the One Great Mother,
the Jagad Amba, the Makara,
Shakti of all existence,
She to whom even gods bow down
in reverent worship and respect,
anxious for even the dust of Her feet
to touch their waiting heads—
for it is Shakti who is the ultimate source,
the infinite Cosmic Energy of all that occurs,
Maha Devi[4] of the thousand petalled lotus.

Questions for Discussion and Your Reading Journal

1. What similarities does Shakti, from India, have with the goddess Nu Kwa from China? What are some of the differences?
2. Shiva is the supreme male deity in other Indian creation stories. According to this reading, what is Shakti's relationship to Shiva?
3. What evidence is there in the final stanza of the reading to suggest that the person(s) who wrote this creation story down existed in a rich and diverse world of ideas and beliefs?
4. Based upon the role model given by Shakti, what roles might you expect would bring the most respect to women in India today? Explain.

---

[2]chakras Literally, "circles." The points on the body serving mystical purposes in Tantric yoga exercises. [Ed. note.]

[3]lotuses Hindu religious symbols roughly equivalent to the cross in Christianity. As the lotus grows in a swamp but its beautiful flower blooms untouched above the mire, so is a Hindu in the world but not of it. [Ed. note.]

[4]Jagad Amba, the Makara . . . Maha Devi All names for the Great Mother. [Ed. note.]

Mesopotamia: Excerpt from *Enuma Elish*

The story of the god Marduk comes from the larger Mesopotamian epic called the Enuma Elish *(meaning "When on High") and represents the root creation story in the Middle East. It was written down on stone tablets in Akkadian, one of the oldest written languages developed in the Old Babylonian period (3000 BCE). In about 1800 BCE, near the end of the Babylonian civilization, the Hebrew patriarch Abraham left Mesopotamia to migrate with his clan into Palestine where his descendants later gave rise to the Jewish, Christian, and Islamic traditions. Many scholars see in Genesis 1–2 a refined version of the conflict between males and females, and the subsequent demotion of women to lower status, of the creation story that first appears in the* Enuma Elish. *The following reading opens with Marduk, a powerful, young male god ("the Son" of the gods) challenging to mortal combat Tiamat, a female deity who has taken control of the assembly of gods in heaven. Scholars suggest that the victory of the god Marduk over the goddess Tiamat represents the victory of ancient male warrior culture over female life-giving culture. This shift in human values in ancient Mesopotamia offers a glimpse into how the power of males to "take life" ascended to a higher social, political, and cultural place in society than the power of women to "give life."*

MARDUK CREATES THE WORLD: THE *ENUMA ELISH* TABLETS

Stand thou up, that I and thou meet in single combat!
When Tiamat heard this,
   She was like one possessed; she took leave of her senses.
In fury Tiamat cried out aloud.
To the roots her legs shook both together.
She recites a charm, keeps casting her spell,
   While the gods of battle sharpen their weapons.
Then joined issue Tiamat and Marduk, wisest of gods.
They strove in single combat, locked in battle.
The lord spread out his net to enfold her,
   The Evil Wind, which followed behind, he let loose in her face.
When Tiamat opened her mouth to consume him,
   He drove in the Evil Wind that she close not her lips.
As the fierce winds charged her belly,
   Her body was distended and her mouth was wide open.
He released the arrow, it tore her belly,
   It cut through her insides, splitting the heart.
Having thus subdued her, he extinguished her life.

He cast down her carcass to stand upon it.
After he had slain Tiamat, the leader,
    Her band was shattered, her troupe broken up;
    And the gods, her helpers who marched at her side,
    Trembling with terror, turned their backs about,
    In order to save and preserve their lives.
Tightly encircled, they could not escape.
He made them captives and he smashed their weapons.
Thrown into the net, they found themselves ensnared;
    Placed in cells, they were filled with wailing;
    Bearing his wrath, they were held imprisoned.
And the eleven creatures which she had charged with awe,
    The band of demons that marched . . . before her,
    He cast into fetters, their hands . . .
For all their resistance, he trampled them underfoot.
And Kingu, who had been made chief among them,
    He bound and accounted him to Uggae.
He took from him the Tablets of Fate, not rightfully his,
    Sealed them with a seal and fastened them on his breast.
When he had vanquished and subdued his adversaries,
        Had . . . the vainglorious foe,
    Had wholly established Anshar's triumph over the foe,
    Nudimmud's desire had achieved, valiant Marduk
        Strengthened his hold on the vanquished gods,
    And turned back to Tiamat whom he had bound.
The lord trod on the legs of Tiamat,
    With his unsparing mace he crushed her skull.
When the arteries of her blood he had severed,
    The North Wind bore it to places undisclosed.
On seeing this, his fathers were joyful and jubilant,
    They brought gifts of homage, they to him.
Then the lord paused to view her dead body,
    That he might divide the monster and do artful works.
He split her like a shellfish into two parts:
    Half of her he set up and ceiled it as sky,
    Pulled down the bar and posted guards.
    He bade them to allow not her waters to escape. . . .
In her belly he established the zenith.
The Moon he caused to shine, the night to him entrusting.
He appointed him a creature of the night to signify the days:
'Monthly, without cease, form designs with a crown.
At the month's very start, rising over the land,
    Thou shalt have luminous horns to signify six days,
    On the seventh day reaching a [half]crown.
At full moon stand in opposition in mid-month.

When the sun [overtakes] thee at the base of heaven,
  Diminish [thy crown] and retrogress in light.
[At the time of disappearance] approach thou the course of the sun,
  And [on the twenty-ninth] thou shalt again stand in opposition to the sun.'

[The remainder of this tablet is broken away or too fragmentary for
  translation.]

When Marduk hears the words of the gods,
  His heart prompts him to fashion artful works.
Opening his mouth, he addresses Ea
  To impart the plan he had conceived in his heart:
'Blood I will mass and cause bones to be,
I will establish a savage, "man" shall be his name.
Verily, savage-man I will create.
He shall be charged with the service of the gods that they might be at ease!
The ways of the gods I will artfully alter.
Though alike revered, into two [groups] they shall be divided.'
Ea answered him, speaking a word to him,
  Giving him another plan for the relief of the gods:
'Let but one of their brothers be handed over;
  He alone shall perish that mankind may be fashioned.
Let the great gods be here in Assembly,
Let the guilty be handed over that they may endure.'
Marduk summoned the great gods to Assembly;
  Presiding graciously, he issues instructions.
To his utterance the gods pay heed.
The king addresses a word to the Anunnaki:
'If your former statement was true,
  Do [now] the truth on oath by me declare!
Who was it that contrived the uprising,
  And made Tiamat rebel, and joined battle?
Let him be handed over who contrived the uprising.
His guilt I will make him bear. You shall dwell in peace!'
The Igigi, the great gods, replied to him,
To Lugaldimmerankia, counsellor of the gods, their lord:
'It was Kingu who contrived the uprising,
  And made Tiamat rebel, and joined battle.'
They bound him, holding him before Ea.
They imposed on him his guilt and severed his blood [vessels].
Out of his blood they fashioned mankind.
He imposed the service and let free the gods.
After Ea, the wise, had created mankind,
  Had imposed upon it the service of the gods
  That work was beyond comprehension;
  As artfully planned by Marduk, did Nudimmud create it—
  Marduk, the king of the gods divided
    All the Anunnaki above and below.

He assigned them to Anu to guard his instructions.
Three hundred in the heavens he stationed as a guard.
In like manner the ways of the earth he defined.
In heaven and on earth six hundred thus he settled.
After he had ordered all the instructions,
To the Anunnaki of heaven and earth had allotted their portions,
The Anunnaki opened their mouths
And said to Marduk, their lord:
'Now, O lord, thou who has caused our deliverance,
What shall be our homage to thee?
Let us build a shrine whose name shall be called 'Lo, a chamber for our
nightly rest';
Let us repose in it!
Let us build a throne, a recess for his abode!
On the day that we arrive we shall repose in it.'
When Marduk heard this,
Brightly glowed his features, like the day:
'Like that of lofty Babylon, whose building you have requested,
Let its brickwork be fashioned. You shall name it "The Sanctuary".'
The Anunnaki applied the implement;
For one whole year they moulded bricks.
When the second year arrived,
They raised high the head of Esagila equalling Apsu.
Having build a stage-tower as high as Apsu,
They set up in it an abode for Marduk, Enlil and Ea,
In their presence he adorned it in grandeur.
In the base of Esharra its horns look down.
After they had achieved the building of Esaglia,
The Anunnaki themselves erected their shrines.
[. . .] all of them gathered,
[. . .] they had built as his dwelling.
The gods, his fathers, at his banquet he seated:
'This is Babylon, the place that is your home!
Make merry in its precincts, occupy its broad [places].'
The great gods took their seats,
They set up festive drink, sat down to a banquet.
After they had made merry within it,
In Esaglia, the splendid, had performed their rites,
The norms had been fixed [and] all [their] portents,
All the gods apportioned the stations of heaven and earth.
The fifty great gods took their seats.
The seven gods of destiny set up the three hundred [in heaven].
Enlil raised the bow, his weapon, and laid it before them.
The gods, his fathers, saw the net he had made.
When they beheld the bow, how skillful its shape,
His fathers praised the work he had wrought.
Raising it, Anu spoke up in the Assembly of the gods,

As he kissed the bow: "This is my daughter!"
He named the names of the bow as follows:
'Longwood is the first, the second is [. . .];
   Its third name is Bow-Star, in heaven I have made it shine."
He fixed a place which the gods, its brothers [. . .]
After Anu had decreed the fate of the Bow,
   And had placed the exalted royal throne before the gods,
   Anu seated it in the Assembly of the gods.
When the great gods had assembled,
   And had [. . .] the fate which Marduk had exalted,
   They pronounced among themselves a curse,
   Swearing by water and oil to place life in jeopardy.
When they had granted him the exercise of kingship of the gods,
   They confirmed him in dominion over the gods of heaven and earth.
Anshar pronounced supreme his name Asaruluhi:
'Let us make humble obeisance at the mention of his name;
   When he speaks, the gods shall pay heed to him.
Let his utterance be supreme above and below!'

Most exalted be the Son, our avenger;
   Let his sovereignty be surpassing, having no rival.
May he shepherd the black-headed ones, his creatures.
To the end of days, without forgetting, let them acclaim his ways.
May he establish for his fathers the great food-offerings;
   Their support they shall furnish, shall tend their sanctuaries.
May he cause incense to be smelled, . . . their spells,
   A likeness on earth of what he has wrought in heaven.
May he order the black-headed to revere him,
   May the subjects ever bear in mind their god,
   And may they at his word pay heed to the goddess.
May food-offerings be borne for their gods and goddesses.
Without fail let them support their gods!
Their lands let them improve, build their shrines,
Let the black-headed wait on their gods.
As for us, by however many names we pronounce, he is our god!

Questions for Discussion and Your Reading Journal

1. What "weapons" does Tiamat use to fight against Marduk? What weapons does Marduk use against Tiamat? What can you see that might be symbolic about these different sets of "weapons"?
2. Older creation stories such as "Nu Kwa" and "Shakti" present female figures as creators of the world. How is this older concept preserved in the Marduk version of creation?
3. When Marduk plans the creation of "man," what kind of being is he to be and what do the gods see as his main function?
4. Who, exactly, is forced to "perish that mankind may be fashioned"?

5. Once Marduk has finished his work, how do the older gods, the "fathers" of Marduk, respond to the magnificent war bow that he has made?

6. Near the end of the reading, whose people do the "black-headed" (humans, who invariably had dark hair in the Mesopotamian region) become and what role are they given in the grand scheme of existence?

7. As you review the Mesopotamian story of Marduk, are there any themes, events, or figures that seem to be shared by the Jewish, Christian, and/or Muslim traditions as well? Explain.

Palestine: Genesis, Chapters 1–3

Genesis 1 through 3 contains the traditional Judeo-Christian and Muslim account of creation. Much of early Genesis is indebted to Mesopotamian traditions for its source material. This is not surprising as the patriarch Abraham and his people came from Babylon in Mesopotamia near the end of the Old Babylonian Empire around 1800 BCE. Among the cultural artifacts that the early Hebrews brought with them from Mesopotamia were their own versions of events recorded on the Enuma Elish tablets, events such as the creation and the flood story. Although the Hebrews evolved a strongly monotheistic religion, you will note echoes of the Mesopotamia past in Genesis 1:26, where the plural pronouns "us" and "our" are used when referring to "God." In many ways, Genesis continues the story of the gods contained in the previous reading where Marduk destroyed the goddess Tiamat and created the earth out of her body. Genesis shifts the focus of the creation story from a preoccupation with the interactions of many gods in a divine realm to the dealings of one specific god with humans (the "black-headed" in the Enuma Elish) in an earthly realm. Some of the major themes from "Marduk" are kept intact in the Genesis account. These include the references to the plurality of gods and the ascendancy of male culture over female culture in social status and authority.

CHAPTER 1

In the beginning God created the heaven and the earth.

2 And the earth was without form, and void; and darkness was upon the face of the deep. And the Spirit of God moved upon the face of the waters.

3 And God said, Let there be light: and there was light.

4 And God saw the light, that it was good: and God divided the light from the darkness.

5 And God called the light Day, and the darkness he called Night. And the evening and the morning were the first day.

6 And God said, Let there be a firmament in the midst of the waters, and let it divide the waters from the waters.

7 And God made the firmament, and divided the waters which were under the firmament from the waters which were above the firmament: and it was so.

8 And God called the firmament Heaven. And the evening and the morning were the second day.

9 And God said, Let the waters under the heaven be gathered together unto one place, and let the dry land appear: and it was so.

10 And God called the dry land Earth; and the gathering together of the waters called he Seas: and God saw that it was good.

11 And God said, Let the earth bring forth grass, the herb yielding seed, and the fruit tree yielding fruit after his kind, whose seed is in itself, upon the earth: and it was so.

12 And the earth brought forth grass, *and* herb yielding seed after his kind, and the tree yielding fruit, whose seed *was* in itself, after his kind: and God saw that *it was* good.

13 And the evening and the morning were the third day.

14 And God said, Let there be lights in the firmament of the heaven to divide the day from the night; and let them be for signs, and for seasons, and for days, and years:

15 And let them be for lights in the firmament of the heaven to give light upon the earth: and it was so.

16 And God made two great lights; the greater light to rule the day, and the lesser light to rule the night: *he made* the stars also.

17 And God set them in the firmament of the heaven to give light upon the earth,

18 And to rule over the day and over the night, and to divide the light from the darkness; and God saw that *it was* good.

19 And the evening and the morning were the fourth day.

20 And God said, Let the waters bring forth abundantly the moving creature that hath life, and fowl *that* may fly above the earth in the open firmament of heaven.

21 And God created great whales, and every living creature that moveth, which the waters brought forth abundantly, after their kind, and every winged fowl after his kind: and God saw that *it was* good.

22 And God blessed them, saying, Be fruitful, and multiply, and fill the waters in the seas, and let fowl multiply in the earth.

23 And the evening and the morning were the fifth day.

24 And God said, Let the earth bring forth the living creature after his kind, cattle, and creeping thing, and beast of the earth after his kind: and it was so.

25 And God made the beast of the earth after his kind, and cattle after their kind, and every thing that creepeth upon the earth after his kind: and God saw that *it was* good.

26 And God said, Let us make man in our image, after our likeness: and let them have dominion over the fish of the sea, and over the fowl of the air, and over the cattle, and over all the earth, and over every creeping thing that creepeth upon the earth.

27 So God created man in his *own* image, in the image of God created he him; male and female created he them.

28 And God blessed them, and God said unto them, Be fruitful, and multiply, and replenish the earth, and subdue it: and have dominion over the fish of the sea, and over the fowl of the air, and over every living thing that moveth upon the earth.

29 And God said, Behold, I have given you every herb bearing seed, which *is* upon the face of all the earth, and every tree, in which *is* the fruit of a tree yielding seed; to you it shall be for meat.

30 And to every beast of the earth, and to every fowl of the air, and to every thing that creepeth upon the earth, wherein *there is* life, *I have given* every green herb for meat: and it was so.

31 And God saw every thing that he had made, and behold, *it was* very good. And the evening and the morning were the sixth day.

CHAPTER 2

Thus the heavens and the earth were finished, and all the host of them.

2 And on the seventh day God ended his work which he had made; and he rested on the seventh day from all his work which he had made.

3 And God blessed the seventh day, and sanctified it: because that in it he had rested from all his work which God created and made.

4 These *are* the generations of the heavens and of the earth when they were created, in the day that the LORD God made the earth and the heavens,

5 And every plant of the field before it was in the earth, and every herb of the field before it grew: for the LORD God had not caused it to rain upon the earth, and *there was* not a man to till the ground.

6 But there went up a mist from the earth, and watered the whole face of the ground.

7 And the LORD God formed man *of* the dust of the ground, and breathed into his nostrils the breath of life; and man became a living soul.

8 And the LORD God planted a garden eastward in Eden; and there he put the man whom he had formed.

9 And out of the ground made the LORD God to grow every tree that is pleasant to the sight, and good for food; the tree of life also in the midst of the garden, and the tree of knowledge of good and evil.

10 And a river went out of Eden to water the garden; and from thence it was parted, and became into four heads.

11 The name of the first *is* Pī-sŏn; that *is* it which compasseth the whole land of Hăv′-ĭ-läh, where *there is* gold;

12 And the gold of that land *is* good: there *is* bdellium and the onyx stone.

13 And the name of the second river *is* Gī′-hŏn: the same *is* it that compasseth the whole land of Ē-thĭ-ŏ′-pĭ-ā

14 And the name of the third river *is* Hĭd′-dĕ-kēl: that *is* it which goeth toward the east of Assyria. And the fourth river *is* Eu-phrā′-tĕs.

15 And the LORD God took the man, and put him into the garden of Eden to dress it and to keep it.

16 And the LORD God commanded the man, saying, Of every tree of the garden thou mayest freely eat:

17 But of the tree of the knowledge of good and evil, thou shalt not eat of it: for in the day that thou eatest thereof thou shalt surely die.

18 And the LORD God said, *It is* not good that the man should be alone; I will make him an help meet for him.

19 And out of the ground the LORD God formed every beast of the field, and every fowl of the air; and brought *them* unto Adam to see what he would call them: and whatsoever Adam called every living creature, that *was* the name thereof.

20 And Adam gave names to all cattle, and to the fowl of the air, and to every beast of the field; but for Adam there was not found an help meet for him.

21 And the LORD God caused a deep sleep to fall upon Adam, and he slept: and he took one of his ribs, and closed up the flesh instead thereof;

22 And the rib, which the LORD God had taken from man, made he a woman, and brought her unto the man.

23 And Adam said, This *is* now bone of my bones, and flesh of my flesh: she shall be called Woman, because she was taken out of Man.

24 Therefore shall a man leave his father and his mother, and shall cleave unto his wife: and they shall be one flesh.

25 And they were both naked, the man and his wife, and were not ashamed.

CHAPTER 3

Now the serpent was more subtil than any beast of the field which the LORD God had made. And he said unto the woman. Yea, hath God said, Ye shall not eat of every tree of the garden?

2 And the woman said unto the serpent, We may eat of the fruit of the trees of the garden:

3 But of the fruit of the tree which *is* in the midst of the garden, God hath said, Ye shall not eat of it, neither shall ye touch it, lest ye die.

4 And the serpent said unto the woman, Ye shall not surely die:

5 For God doth know that in the day ye eat thereof, then your eyes shall be opened, and ye shall be as gods, knowing good and evil.

6 And when the woman saw that the tree *was* good for food, and that it *was* pleasant to the eyes, and a tree to be desired to make *one* wise, she took of the fruit thereof, and did eat, and gave also unto her husband with her; and he did eat.

7 And the eyes of them both were opened, and they knew that they *were* naked; and they sewed fig leaves together, and made themselves aprons.

8 And they heard the voice of the LORD God, walking in the garden in the cool of the day: and Adam and his wife hid themselves from the presence of the LORD God amongst the trees of the garden.

9 And the LORD God called unto Adam, and said unto him, Where *art* thou?

10 And he said, I heard thy voice in the garden, and I was afraid, because I *was* naked; and I hid myself.

11 And he said, Who told thee that thou *wast* naked? Hast thou eaten of the tree, whereof I commanded thee that thou shouldest not eat?

12 And the man said, The woman whom thou gavest *to be* with me, she gave me of the tree, and I did eat.

13 And the LORD God said unto the woman, What *is* this *that* thou hast done? And the woman said, The serpent beguiled me, and I did eat.

14 And the LORD God said unto the serpent, Because thou hast done this, thou *art* cursed above all cattle, and above every beast of the field; upon thy belly shalt thou go, and dust shalt thou eat all the days of thy life:

15 And I will put enmity between thee and the woman, and between thy seed and her seed; it shall bruise thy head, and thou shalt bruise his heel.

16 Unto the woman he said, I will greatly multiply thy sorrow and thy conception; in sorrow thou shalt bring forth children; and thy desire *shall* be ⁵to thy husband, and he shall rule over thee.

17 And unto Adam he said, Because thou hast hearkened unto the voice of thy wife, and hast eaten of the tree, of which I commanded thee, saying, Thou shalt not eat of it: cursed *is* the ground for thy sake; in sorrow shalt thou eat *of* it all the days of thy life;

18 Thorns also and thistles shall it bring forth to thee; and thou shalt eat the herb of the field;

19 In the sweat of thy face shalt thou eat bread, till thou return unto the ground; for out of it wast thou taken: for dust thou *art,* and unto dust shalt thou return.

20 And Adam called his wife's name Eve; because she was the mother of all living.

21 Unto Adam also and to his wife did the LORD God make coats of skins, and clothed them.

22 And the LORD God said, Behold, the man is become as one of us, to know good and evil; and now, lest he put forth his hand, and take also of the tree of life, and eat, and live for ever:

23 Therefore the LORD God sent him forth from the garden of Eden, to till the ground from whence he was taken.

24 So he drove out the man; and he placed at the east of the garden of Eden Chĕr'-ū-bīms, and a flaming sword which turned every way, to keep the way of the tree of life.

Questions for Discussion and Your Reading Journal

1. What effect does the use of the plural pronouns "us" and "our" in Genesis 1:26 have upon the common understanding of Judaism as a monotheistic faith?

2. Many modern environmentalists feel that attitudes permitting the misuse and exploitation of the earth's natural resources in the Western world stem from interpretations of Genesis 1, verses 26–27. Explain how these verses could be interpreted in such a way.

3. As you may note, there are actually two creation stories in this reading. In terms of when animals were created, when male humans were created, and

when female humans were created, how does the creation story in Genesis 2 differ from the creation as outlined in Genesis 1? Which creation seems more closely related to scientific accuracy and which seems to be more of a theological justification of differences in male and female social status and gender roles? Explain your response.

4. As you read closely the events in Genesis 3, do you see any benefits to Eve's decision to eat of the "tree of knowledge of good and evil"? Explain.

5. Some readers have suggested that the treatment of Eve in Genesis 3 parallels in some ways the treatment of the goddess Tiamat by Marduk in the *Enuma Elish* (see previous reading). Do you agree or disagree? Explain.

Africa (Yoruba): "The Descent from the Sky"

The Yoruba people who give us this African creation story constitute one of the major tribal cultures of Nigeria and Bénin. In this version of creation, both male and female deities participate. As is common with many other creation stories, the female deity moves down to the earthly realm and is associated with water, while the male deities remain in the sky as sky gods.

1 In ancient days, at the beginning of time, there was no solid land here where people now dwell. There was only outer space and the sky, and, far below, an endless stretch of water and wild marshes. Supreme in the domain of the sky was the orisha, or god, called Olorun, also known as Olodumare and designated by many praise names. Also living in that place were numerous other orishas, each having attributes of his own, but none of whom had knowledge or powers equal to those of Olorun. Among them was Orunmila, also called Ifa, the eldest son of Olorun. To this orisha Olorun had given the power to read the future, to understand the secret of existence and to divine the processes of fate. There was the orisha Obatala, King of the White Cloth, whom Olorun trusted as though he also were a son. There was the orisha Eshu, whose character was neither good nor bad. He was compounded out of the elements of chance and accident, and his nature was unpredictability. He understood the principles of speech and language, and because of this gift he was Olorun's linguist. These and the other orishas living in the domain of the sky acknowledged Olorun as the owner of everything and as the highest authority in all matters. Also living there was Agemo, the chameleon, who served Olorun as a trusted servant.

2 Down below, it was the female deity Olokun who ruled over the vast expanses of water and wild marshes, a grey region with no living things in it, either creatures of the bush or vegetation. This is the way it was, Olorun's living sky above and Olokun's domain of water below. Neither kingdom troubled the other. They were separate and apart. The orishas of the sky lived on, hardly noticing what lay below them.

3 All except Obatala, King of the White Cloth, He alone looked down on the domain of Olokun and pondered on it, saying to himself: "Everything

down there is great wet monotony. It does not have the mark of any inspira- 4
tion or living thing." And at last he went to Olorun and said: "The place ruled
by Olokun is nothing but sea, marsh and mist. If there were solid land in that
domain, fields and forests, hills and valleys, surely it could be populated by
orishas and other living things."

Olorun answered: "Yes, it would be a good thing to cover the water with 5
land. But it is an ambitious enterprise. Who is to do the work? And how
should it be done?"

Obatala said: "I will undertake it. I will do whatever is required." 6

He left Olorun and went to the house of Orunmila, who understood the 7
secrets of existence, and said to him: "Your father has instructed me to go
down below and make land where now there is nothing but marsh and sea, so
that living beings will have a place to build their towns and grow their crops.
You, Orunmila, who can divine the meanings of all things, instruct me further.
How may this work be begun?"

Orunmila brought out his divining tray and cast sixteen palm nuts on it. 8
He read their meanings by the way they fell. He gathered them up and cast
again, again reading their meanings. And when he had cast many times he
added meanings to meanings, and said: "These are the things you must do:
Descend to the watery wastes on a chain of gold, taking with you a snail shell
full of sand, a white hen to disperse the sand, a black cat to be your companion, and a palm nut. That is what the divining figures tell us."

Obatala went next to the goldsmith and asked for a chain of gold long 9
enough to reach from the sky to the surface of the water.

The goldsmith asked, "Is there enough gold in the sky to make such a 10
chain?"

Obatala answered: "Yes, begin your work. I will gather the gold." Depart- 11
ing from the forge of the goldsmith, Obatala went then to Orunmila, Eshu and
the other orishas, asking each of them for gold. They gave him whatever they
had. Some gave gold dust, some gave rings, bracelets or pendants. Obatala collected gold from everywhere and took it to the goldsmith.

The goldsmith said, "More gold is needed." 12

So Obatala continued seeking gold, and after that he again returned to the 13
goldsmith, saying, "Here is more metal for your chain."

The goldsmith said, "Still more is needed." 14

Obatala said, "There is no more gold in the sky." 15

The goldsmith said, "The chain will not reach to the water." 16

Obatala answered: "Nevertheless, make the chain. We shall see." 17

The goldsmith went to work. When the chain was finished he took it to 18
Obatala. Obatala said, "It must have a hook at the end."

"There is no gold remaining," the goldsmith said. 19

Obatala replied, "Take some of the links and melt them down." 20

The goldsmith removed some of the links, and out of them he fashioned a 21
hook for the chain. It was finished. He took the chain to Obatala.

Obatala said, "Now I am ready." He fastened the hook on the edge of the 22
sky and lowered the chain. Orunmila gave him the things that were needed—
a small shell of sand, a white hen, a black cat, and a palm nut. Then Obatala

gripped the chain with his hands and feet and began the descent. The chain was very long. When he had descended only half its length Obatala saw that he was leaving the realm of light and entering the region of greyness. A time came when he heard the wash of waves and felt the damp mists rising from Olokun's domain. He reached the end of the golden chain, but he was not yet at the bottom, and he clung there, thinking, "If I let go I will fall into the sea."

23   While he remained at the chain's end thinking such things, he heard Orunmila's voice from above, saying, "The sand."

24   So Obatala took the snail shell from the knapsack at his side and poured out the sand.

25   Again he heard Orunmila call to him, saying this time, "The hen."

26   Obatala dropped the hen where he had poured the sand. The hen began at once to scratch at the sand and scatter it in all directions. Wherever the sand was scattered it became dry land. Because it was scattered unevenly the sand formed hills and valleys. When this was accomplished, Obatala let go of the chain and came down and walked on the solid earth that had been created. The land extended in all directions, but still it was barren of life.

27   Obatala named the place where he had come down Ife. He built a house there. He planted his palm nut and a palm tree sprang out of the earth. It matured and dropped its palm seeds. More palm trees came into being. Thus there was vegetation at Ife. Obatala lived on, with only his black cat as a companion.

28   After some time had passed, Olorun the Sky God wanted to know how Obatala's expedition was progressing. He instructed Agemo the chameleon to descend the golden chain. Agemo went down. He found Obatala living in his house at Ife. He said: "Olorun instructed me this way: He said, 'Go down, discover for me how things are with Obatala.' That is why I am here."

29   Obatala answered, "As you can see, the land has been created, and palm groves are plentiful. But there is too much greyness. The land should be illuminated."

30   Agemo returned to the sky and reported to Olorun what he had seen and heard. Olorun agreed that there should be light down below. So he made the sun and set it moving. After that there was warmth and light in what had once been Olokun's exclusive domain.

31   Obatala lived on, with only his black cat for a companion. He thought, "Surely it would be better if many people were living here." He decided to create people. He dug clay from the ground, and out of the clay he shaped human figures which he then laid out to dry in the sun. He worked without resting. He became tired and thirsty. He said to himself, "There should be palm wine in this place to help a person go on working." So he put aside the making of humans and went to the palm trees to draw their inner fluid, out of which he made palm wine. When it was fermented he drank. He drank for a long while. When he felt everything around him softening he put aside his gourd cup and went back to modeling human figures. But because Obatala had drunk so much wine his fingers grew clumsy, and some of the figures were misshapen. Some had crooked backs or crooked legs, or arms that were too short. Some did not have enough fingers, some were bent instead of being straight. Because of the palm wine inside him, Obatala did not notice these things. And when

he had made enough figures to begin the populating of Ife he called out to Olorun the Sky God, saying, "I have made human beings to live with me here in Ife, but only you can give them the breath of life." Olorun heard Obatala's request, and he put breath in the clay figures. They were no longer clay, but people of blood, sinews and flesh. They arose and began to do the things that humans do. They built houses for themselves near Obatala's house, and in this way the place Obatala named Ife became the city of Ife.

But when the effects of the palm wine had worn off Obatala saw that some of the humans he had made were misshapen, and remorse filled his heart. He said: "Never again will I drink palm wine. From this time on I will be the special protector of all humans who have deformed limbs or who have otherwise been created imperfectly." Because of Obatala's pledge, humans who later came to serve him also avoided palm wine, and the lame, the blind and those who had no pigment in their skin invoked his help when they were in need. . . .

Questions for Discussion and Your Reading Journal

1. In what ways is the opening paragraph of the Yoruba creation story similar to the beginning of Genesis 1? In what ways is it different?
2. An unusual twist in this creation story is that while a male deity rules the realm of the sky, a female deity reigns over the natural world below. Are there any parallels to this division in the way people in the United States tend to think of "God" and "nature" today? Explain.
3. What aspects of the creation process seem to be uniquely African to you?
4. In many other creation stories, the first humans were imperfect creatures. In the Bible, these first people were killed off by floods as the gods tried to improve the human race. How does this text explain human imperfections? Are the humans punished for being imperfect?

North America: "The Iroquois Story of Creation"

The Iroquois are a confederation of six Native-American tribes: the Cayuga, the Mohawk, the Seneca, the Oneida, the Onondaga, and the Tuscarora. At the height of their civilization in the 15th century CE, they controlled land from New England to Ohio and northward into Ontario, Canada. Although each tribe has its own version of the following creation story, the major elements are similar among them.

Long before there were human beings, there were Sky People. They dwelled in the celestial world. In those days there was no sun. All light came from the large white blossoms on the celestial tree that stood in front of the Lodge of the Sky Chief. This Sky Chief had married a young wife. In time this wife, Sky Woman, began to show signs that she would soon bear a child.

Creations Battle 1980 by John Fadden, Mohawk, Onchiota, New York, shows the struggle between the Good Twin and the Evil Twin at the time of Creation. *Creations Battle* © 1980 by John McFadden.

2   There was a troublesome being, called Firedragon, in the Sky World. Firedragon was always spreading rumors. Now he whispered to Sky Chief that the child who was about to be born would not be his. In a fit of anger and jealousy, Sky Chief uprooted the great celestial tree in front of his lodge. He pushed his wife through the hole where the tree had once stood.

3   Sky Woman fell rapidly down toward the vast dark waters below. The birds, feeling sorry for her, flew underneath and gently supported her, breaking her fall and carrying her slowly downward. At the same time, the water animals hurried to make a place for her. Turtle said that he would support a world on his back. The sea animals plunged down into the water looking for some earth. Muskrat succeeded and came up with a large mouthful of earth, which he placed on Turtle's back. The light from the blossoms of the fallen celestial tree shone through the hole where it had stood and became the sun. When Sky Woman landed, everything was in readiness for her, with grass and trees beginning to grow.

4   Sky Woman gave birth to a daughter. When this daughter grew to womanhood, she began to be with child. No one knows whether her husband was Turtle or West Wind, but she gave birth to two remarkable twin boys—one good and one evil. The Good Twin was born in the usual way. But the Evil Twin was in a hurry and pushed through his mother's side to be born. In doing so, he killed his mother.

Sky Woman buried her daughter, and plants miraculously began to grow 5
from various parts of the daughter's body—a tobacco plant, a cornstalk, a
bean bush, and a squash vine. This was the origin of all the plants that would
be most important to the human beings who would come later.

The Good Twin and the Evil Twin quickly grew to manhood. As soon as 6
they were grown, they proved true to their names. The Good Twin began creating all sorts of good things: plants, animals, medicinal herbs, rivers, and
streams. The Evil Twin began to spoil his brother's work, putting rapids and
boulders in the rivers, creating poisonous plants, thorns and briars, diseases,
and monsters. The Good and Evil Twins fought against each other to see who
would predominate in creation, but the Evil could never overcome the Good.
Finally the Good Twin created human beings to enjoy all the good things he
had made for them. And that is how it all began.

Questions for Discussion and Your Reading Journal

1. What might be another name for "Sky People" that is commonly used in
   most other creation stories? What kinds of things do we learn about Iroquois concepts of the divine world and its beings from this story?
2. In other creation stories, deities hold total responsibility for making the
   world and everything in it. Who assists Sky Woman in her creation work,
   and what does this suggest about the way the Iroquois might view other
   creatures and living things in the natural world?
3. In "Marduk," the earth was made of a divine female's body. What similar
   creation happens in this story?
4. How does the Iroquois creation story explain the existence of both "good
   things" and "bad things" in nature?
5. The human beings are the very last things created in this story and appear
   almost as an afterthought in the next-to-last line. What does that suggest
   about the place and the level of importance the Iroquois might accord to
   humans in the larger picture of all that exists?

FOUNDATIONS OF BELIEF

THE EASTERN WORLD

HINDUISM

*The Upanishads represent the first recorded efforts of early Indian
philosophers and wise men to come to grips with "knowing" and
"being." Written in Sanskrit sometime after 600 BCE, the Upanishads's
purpose is summed up in the words of a chant in the "Brihad-Aranyaka
Upanishad":*

From the unreal lead me to the real!
From darkness lead me to light!
From death lead me to immortality!

This collection of metaphysical writings translated by Robert Ernest Hume shows the first systematic attempts of the Hindus to solve the mysteries of human origins and the purpose of existence. At the same time, Pythagoras among the Greeks, Confucius in China, and Buddha in both India and China were formulating their own responses to these mysteries. These writings are still very much in use today after some 25 centuries. They are to the Indian believer what the New Testament is to the Christian. Perhaps their major contribution to the world of ideas is the formulation of the concept of the ultimate unity and oneness of all that exists. Called the doctrine of universal immanence or intelligent monism, it teaches that not only did the supreme Person create all that exists but everything in existence is part of the creator. Deity is not viewed as an individual being separate from the rest of creation. Humans, animals, the wind, water, the earth, the planets, all are filled with the presence of the divine spirit, and all are part of the divine physical being. As one approaches this text or the other texts in this section on Buddhism, Taoism, Judaism, and Christianity, it is valuable to know that oral traditions were much more a part of the societies that produced these writings. The actual writing of the texts often came after traditions, beliefs, and ideas had been kept alive for centuries through oral histories and rituals. For this reason, many of the written forms reflect oral structures that could be easily memorized in short, rhythmic, sometimes even poetic language.

Reading Rhetorically

Religious writings like the *Upanishads* existed orally from generation to generation for hundreds or even thousands of years before they were written down. This helps to explain why they are organized into short, easily memorized statements. Priests and priestesses would chant them as part of religious rituals and ceremonies. Devotees could commit them to memory and regularly turn to them for insight and guidance in their lives. However, for modern readers not familiar with the religious, cultural, and social contexts of India in which these ideas were developed, it is a challenge to interpret the layers of meaning inherent in each statement. This is particularly true for Western readers who generally expect each sentence to have one explicit and coherent meaning, allowing different peoples to communicate specific meanings. This is not generally the intention and purpose of spiritual writings in either the West or the East. The purpose of the following reading is much more to inspire and to enlighten its audience in a limitless number of ways, each depending upon the individual reader. Ultimately, the rhetorical persuasiveness of this kind of writing is based not upon claims and evidence as is more common in Western traditions but upon each individual's personal response to the words and ideas offered.

Muṇḍaka Upanishad

SECOND MUṆḌAKA: THE DOCTRINE OF BRAHMA-ĀTMAN

First Khaṇḍa

The Imperishable, the source and the goal of all beings

1. This is the truth:—

As, from a well-blazing fire, sparks
By the thousand issue forth of like form,
So from the Imperishable, my friend, beings manifold
Are produced, and thither also go.

The supreme Person

2. Heavenly (divya), formless (a-mūrtta) is the Person (Purusha).

He is without and within, unborn,
Breathless (a-prāna), mindless (a-manas), pure (śubhra),
Higher than the high Imperishable.

The source of the human person and of the cosmic elements

3. From Him is produced breath (prāṇa),

Mind (manas), and all the senses (indriya),
Space (kha), wind, light, water,
And earth, the supporter of all.

The macrocosmic Person

4. Fire is His head; His eyes, the moon and sun;

The regions of space, His ears; His voice, the revealed Vedas;
Wind, His breath (prāṇa); His heart, the whole world. Out of His feet,
The earth. Truly, He is the Inner Soul (Ātman) of all.

Second Khaṇḍa

The all-inclusive Brahma

1. Manifest, [yet] hidden; called 'Moving-in-secret';

The great abode! Therein is placed that
Which moves and breathes and winks.
What that is, know as Being (sad) and Non-being (a-sad),
As the object of desire, higher than understanding,
As what is the best of creatures!

2. That which is flaming, which is subtler than the subtle,

On which the worlds are set, and their inhabitants—
That is the imperishable Brahma.
It is life (prāṇa), and It is speech and mind.
That is the real. It is immortal.
It is [a mark] to be penetrated. Penetrate It, my friend!

A target to be penetrated by meditation on 'Om'

3. Taking as a bow the great weapon of the Upanishad,

   One should put upon it an arrow sharpened by meditation.
   Stretching it with a thought directed to the essence of That,
   Penetrate that Imperishable as the mark, my friend.

4. The mystic syllable. *Om (praṇava)* is the bow. The arrow is the soul *(ātman)*.

   Brahma is said to be the mark *(lakṣya)*.
   By the undistracted main is It to be penetrated.
   One should come to be in It, as the arrow [in the mark].

The immortal Soul, the one warp of the world and of the individual

5. He on whom the sky, the earth, and the atmosphere

   Are woven, and the mind, together with all the life-breaths *(prāṇa)*,
   Him alone know as the one Soul (Ātman). Other
   Words dismiss. He is the bridge to immortality.

The great Soul to be found in the heart

6. Where the channels are brought together

   Like the spokes in the hub of a wheel—
   Therein he moves about,
   Becoming manifold.
   Om!—Thus meditate upon the Soul (Ātman).
   Success to you in crossing to the farther shore beyond darkness!

7. He who is all-knowing, all-wise,

   Whose is this greatness on the earth—
   He is in the divine Brahma city

The source of the world and of the individual

5. From Him [proceeds] fire, whose fuel is in the sun;

   From the moon (Soma), rain; herbs, on the earth.
   The male pours seed in the female.
   Many creatures are produced from the Person (Purusha).

The source of all religious rites

6. From Him the Rig Verses, the Sāman Chant, the sacrificial formulas *(yajus)*, the initiation rite *(dīkṣā)*.

   And all the sacrifices, ceremonies, and sacrificial gifts *(dakṣiṇā)*,
   The year too, and the sacrificer, the worlds
   Where the moon (Soma) shines brightly, and where the sun.[1]

The source of all forms of existence

7. From Him, too, gods are manifoldly produced,

   The celestials (Sādhyas), men, cattle, birds,

---

[1]That is, the world of the fathers, and the world of the gods, respectively.

The in-breath and the out-breath *(prāṇāpānau)*, rice and barley, austerity *(tapas)*,
Faith *(śraddhā)*, truth, chastity, and the law *(vidhi)*.

The source of the activity of the senses

8. Form Him come forth the seven life-breaths *(prāṇa)*,[2]

   The seven flames, their fuel, the seven oblations,
   These seven worlds, wherein do move
   The life-breaths that dwell in the secret place [of the heart] placed seven and seven.

The source of the world—the immanent Soul of the things

9. From Him, the seas and the mountains all.

   From Him roll rivers of every kind.
   And from Him all herbs, the essence, too,
   Whereby that Inner Soul *(antarātman)* dwells in beings.

The supreme Person found in the heart

10. The Person (Purusha) himself is everything here:

    Work *(karman)* and austerity *(tapas)* and Brahma, beyond death.
    He who knows That, set in the secret place [of the heart]—
    He here on earth, my friend, rends asunder the knot of ignorance.
    And in the heaven established! The Soul (Ātman)!
    Consisting of mind, leader of the life-breaths and of the body,
    He is established on food, controlling the heart.
    By this knowledge the wise perceive
    The blissful Immortal that gleams forth.

Deliverance gained through vision of Him

8. The knot of the heart is loosened,

   All doubts are cut off,
   And one's deeds *(karman)* cease
   When He is seen—both the higher and the lower.

The self-luminous light of the world

9. In the highest golden sheath

   Is Brahma, without stain, without parts.
   Brilliant is It, the light of lights—
   That which knowers of the Soul (Ātman) do know!

10. The sun shines not there, nor the moon and stars;

    These lightnings shine not, much less this [earthly] fire!

---

[2]Śankara explains these seven *prāṇa* as the seven organs of sense in the head (i.e. two eyes, two ears, two nostrils, and the mouth). They are compared to seven different sacrificial oblations. The enlightenments produced by their activity are the flames of the sacrifice; the objects which supply their action, the fuel. Each sense moves in an appropriate world of its own; but they are all co-ordinated by the mind *(manas)*, which is located in the heart.

After Him, as He shines, doth everything shine.
This whole world is illumined with His light.

The omnipresent Brahma

11. Brahma, indeed, is this immortal. Brahma before,

Brahma behind, to right and to left.
Stretched forth below and above,
Brahma, indeed, is this whole world, this widest extent.

THIRD MUNDAKA: THE WAY TO BRAHMA

First Khanda

Recognition of the Great Companion, the supreme salvation

1. Two birds, fast bound companions,

Clasp close the self-same tree.
Of these two, the one eats sweet fruit;
The other looks on without eating.

2. On the self-same tree a person, sunken,

Grieves for his impotence, deluded;
When he sees the other, the Lord (*īś*), contented,
And his greatness, he becomes freed from sorrow.

3. When a seer sees the brilliant

Maker, Lord, Person, the Brahma-source,
Then, being a knower, shaking off good and evil,
Stainless, he attains supreme identity *(sāmya)* [with Him].

Delight in the Soul, the life of all things

4. Truly, it is Life *(prāṇa)* that shines forth in all things!

Understanding this, one becomes a knower. There is no superior speaker.
Having delight in the Soul (Ātman), having pleasure in the Soul, doing the rites,
Such a one is the best of Brahma-knowers.

The pure Soul obtainable by true methods

5. This Soul (Ātman) is obtainable by truth, by austerity *(tapas)*,

By proper knowledge *(jñāna)*, by the student's life of chastity *(brahmacarya)* constantly [practised].
Within the body, consisting of light, pure is He
Whom the ascetics *(yati)*, with imperfections done away, behold.

6. Truth alone conquers, not falsehood.

By truth is laid out the path leading to the gods *(devayāna)*
By which the sages whose desire is satisfied ascend
To where is the highest repository of truth.

The universal inner Soul

7. Vast, heavenly, of unthinkable form,

   And more minute than the minute, It shines forth.
   It is farther than the far, yet here near at hand,
   Set down in the secret place [of the heart], even here among those who
   behold [It].

Obtainable by contemplation, purified from sense

8. Not by sight is It grasped, not even by speech,

   Not by any other sense-organs (deva), austerity, or work.
   By the peace of knowledge (jñāna-prasāda), one's nature purified—
   In that way, however, by mediating, one does behold Him who is with-
   out parts.

9. That subtle Soul (Ātman) is to be known by thought (cetas)

   Wherein the senses (prāṇa) fivefoldly have entered.
   The whole of men's thinking is interwoven with the senses.
   When that is purified, the Soul (Ātman) shines forth.

The acquiring power of thought

10. Whatever world a man of purified nature makes clear in mind,

    And whatever desires he desires for himself—
    That world he wins, those desires too.
    Therefore he who is desirous of welfare should praise the knower of the
    Soul (Ātman).

Second Khaṇḍa

Desires as the cause of rebirth

1. He knows that Supreme Brahma-abode,

   Founded on which the whole world shines radiantly,
   They who, being without desire, worship the Person (Purusha)
   And are wise, pass beyond the seed (śukra) [of rebirth] here.

2. He who in fancy forms desires,

   Because of his desires is born [again] here and there.
   But of him whose desire is satisfied, who is a perfected soul (kṛtātman),
   All desires even here on earth vanish away.

The Soul (Ātman) known only be revelation to His own elect

3. This Soul (Ātman) is not to be obtained by instruction,

   Nor by intellect, nor by much learning.
   He is to be obtained only by the one whom He chooses;
   To such a one that Soul (Ātman) reveals His own person (tanūm svām).

Certain indispensable conditions, pre-eminently knowledge

4. This Soul (Ātman) is not to be obtained by one destitute of fortitude,

   Nor through heedlessness, nor through a false notion of austerity *(tapas)*.
   But he who strives by these means, provided he knows—
   Into his Brahma-abode this Soul (Ātman) enters.

In tranquil union with the Soul of all is liberation from death and from all distinctions of individuality

5. Attaining Him, the seers *(ṛṣi)* who are satisfied with knowledge,

   Who are perfected souls *(kṛtātman)*, from passion free *(vītarāga)*, tranquil—
   Attaining Him who is the universally omnipresent, those wise,
   Devout souls *(yuktātman)* into the All itself do enter.

6. They who have ascertained the meaning of the Vedānta-knowledge,

   Ascetics *(yati)* with natures purified through the application of renunciation *(saṁnyāsa-yoga)*—
   They in the Brahma-worlds at the end of time
   Are all liberated beyond death.

7. Gone are the fifteen parts[3] according to their station,

   Even all the sense-organs *(deva)* in their corresponding divinities!
   One's deeds *(karman)* and the self that consists of understanding *(vijñāna-mayaātman)*—
   All become unified in the supreme Imperishable.

8. As the flowing rivers in the ocean

   Disappear, quitting name and form,[4]
   So the knower, being liberated from name and form,
   Goes unto the Heavenly Person, higher than the high.

The rewards and the requisite conditions of this knowledge of Brahma

9. He, verily, who knows that supreme Brahma, becomes very Brahma.[5] In his family no one ignorant of Brahma arises. He crosses over sorrow. He crosses over sin *(pāpman)*. Liberated from the knots of the heart, he becomes immortal.

10. This very [doctrine] has been declared in the verse:—

   They who do the rites, who are learned in the Vedas, who are intent on Brahma,

---

[3]That is, of the microcosm back into the macrocosm. Cf. Praśna, 6, 5.

[4]The Sanskrit idiom for 'individuality.'

[5]In the title to his Latin translation, 'Oupnekhat,' Anquetil Duperron set this sentence evidently as the summary of the contents of the Upanishads: 'Quisquis Deum intelligit, Deus fit,' 'whoever knows God, becomes God.'

They who, possessing faith *(śraddhayan),* make oblation of themselves, even of the one seer[6]—
To them indeed one may declare this knowledge of Brahma,
When, however, the Muṇḍaka-vow[7] has been performed by them according to rule.'

11. This is the truth. The seer *(ṛṣi)* Aṅgiras declared it in ancient time. One who has not performed the vow does not read this.

Adoration to the highest seers!
Adoration to the highest seers!

Questions for Discussion and Your Reading Journal

1. A text such as this often seems confusing and awkward to Westerners when they first encounter it. What problems can you think of that might make translating this kind of writing into English especially difficult?
2. Both Hinduism and Buddhism teach that all things that exist come from the same source. This principle of oneness is based upon the idea that all creations are made from the same basic matter and draw upon the same life-giving force, though each is a uniquely different expression of existence. What evidence of the principle of oneness can you find in the "Second Muṇḍaka"?
3. In the Foreword to *Religion and Nothingness* (p. 627), Winston King indicated that Eastern religions tend to view human beings as inseparably connected to a much larger, holistic, cyclical, and infinite process of being and nonbeing. In what ways does "The Doctrine of Brahma-Atman" place humans within a framework of connectedness to other parts of existence?
4. In your own words sum up a definition of "the all-inclusive Brahma."
5. The "Third Muṇḍaka" describes the way to reach one's supreme identity and perfect union with the Soul through knowledge of Brahma. In what ways is this similar to reaching "heaven" in Christianity? In what ways is it quite different?

---

[6]Identified with Prāna, 'Life,' in Praśna 2. II. The reference, then, is probably to the mystical Prānāgnihotra sacrifice, in which 'breath' is symbolically sacrificed for an Agnihotra ceremony.

[7]Śaṅkara explains this as 'carrying fire on the head—a well-known Vedic vow among followers of the Atharva-Veda.' But it is more likely to be 'shaving the head,' as Buddhist monks did later. This preliminary requisite to the study of the Upanishad doubtless gave it the title 'The Shaveling Upanishad,' or 'The Upanishad of the Tonsured.'

JOHN JARVIS

John Jarvis (1955–) is a Professor of Communication and Culture at Bay Path College in Longmeadow, Massachusetts, and is one of the editors of this textbook. In the following reading, he offers background information useful for understanding the historical, spiritual, and social contexts that gave rise to the Buddha (meaning "enlightened one") and his teachings. This text is intended as a companion to the one that follows it and that uses a narrative format to take readers more intimately into the enlightenment experience of the Buddha.

Reading Rhetorically

The following reading is a classic example of "expository writing." Its purpose is to inform readers of what we know about the Buddha as a historical and religious figure. It does not attempt to introduce new ideas or alternate hypotheses about the subject in a way that requires persuasion. Rather, the aim is to assure that readers have a foundation of knowledge on which to move into the more debatable ideas and issues that Buddha's thinking presents in the subsequent reading.

Introduction to Buddhism

1   The life story of Siddhartha Gautama (who became Buddha, or "the enlightened one") and the origins of the religion he founded occurred in a time and place quite different in many ways from the modern world, East or West. Most significantly for historical study of the period, it was a time when writing was not the primary means of preserving important events and ideas. Rather, the spoken word in the form of oral history and the memorization and recitation of religious doctrines served these functions. It was not until centuries after Buddha's death that his teachings began to be written down and gathered into the collections that we have today. As in the case of Jesus, we do not have the Buddha's own words about his life and ideas to draw upon, but the writings of the monks who followed the path he offered. Thus, many details in the story of this important figure remain obscure and uncertain.

2   The first full accounts of the life of Buddha, written some five hundred years after his death, indicate that he was born around 560 B.C.E. in Kapilavastu, a region that his now in Nepal. His father was a minor prince in the kingdom and legend tells us that he went to great lengths to raise his son, the future Buddha, in noble style, protected from the suffering and struggles of the common people outside of the court. Around the age of 29, a turning point came for the young prince as he took a series of chariot rides outside of the protected world that his father had maintained. For the first time, he saw peasants laboring in their fields for survival, and constantly facing old age, disease,

and death. This affected him profoundly, and he began to meditate on the true nature of human existence. When he saw a wandering religious man on another ride in the country, he decided to abandon the safety of household life (he was now married with an infant son) and to seek the true meaning of life. In his uncompromising quest for truth, Gautama's willingness to give up his father's kingdom, as well as a wife and small son, is called the Great Renunciation. This act has served as an example for countless devotees over the last twenty-five centuries who have likewise given up worldly ways to become Buddhist monks and nuns.

For a time, Gautama wandered on his own, learning from other spiritual   3
wise men and practicing extreme forms of vegetarianism, fasting, and meditation. He found that these practices left him too weak and confused to attain the state of philosophical insight that he sought, so he tried a "middle way" of seeking enlightenment that encouraged taking better care of the body. Then, legend has it that he seated himself under a Bodhi tree with the resolve of not rising until he had found the meaning of existence through meditation. After much effort, he succeeded on the night of a full moon, and, as the night wore on, he formulated the ideas that would become the foundation of Buddhism.

Buddha's purpose in seeking enlightenment was closely connected to the   4
world he had discovered outside of his father's protected court. He wanted to show people the path to free themselves from the misery and pain of human existence. Buddha and other religious thinkers of his time understood one's place of birth and good or bad fortune in this life as being the result of actions in a previous life. A person who had practiced noble deeds in a past life would be reincarnated into a good family and into less painful circumstances as a reward in this life. If one continued to do good here, even better circumstances could be anticipated in the next life. The reverse was also true: doing evil in this life would only lead to being reborn into worse suffering in the life to come. Buddha's goal was to find a way to escape this unending cycle of rebirth by achieving a state of existence no longer characterized by struggle and by some degree of pain at every level.

For Buddha, the key to reaching *nirvana,* or a state of complete peace   5
beyond human comprehension, was to take complete control of one's thoughts and actions and to cease to participate in behavior that had bad effects. He taught that, by overcoming all ignorance, low views, and inferior deeds, one could break out of the cycle of human rebirth and existence. His teachings, which offer a good example of the fine line between philosophy and religion in Eastern thought, are based upon what came to be called the Four Noble Truths; (1) life is suffering, (2) suffering comes from ignorance and low views, (3) the cycle of being reborn into human suffering can only be broken by overcoming the ignorance that causes it, and (4) there is a true path (the Noble or Holy Eightfold Path) that leads to the end of suffering.

The Noble Eightfold Path gives the devoted Buddhist a clear set of eight   6
behaviors to master in order to reach a state of enlightenment. These are: (1) holding right views (avoiding the illusion of happiness offered by greed or the sensual pleasures of life), (2) right intentions (being entirely devoted to the quest for complete happiness and letting go of the illusionary pleasures of this

world), (3) right speech (speaking only the truth), (4) right action (being honest, true and pure in all behavior), (5) right living (hurting no other creatures, human or otherwise, hence vegetarianism is often encouraged), (6) right effort (maintaining strict self-control), (7) right-mindedness (being disciplined in one's thoughts), and (8) right meditation (contemplating life deeply and using the principles employed by Buddha himself to reach enlightenment).

7   Buddha is said to have died at the age of eighty, which would have been around 480 B.C.E. Though Buddhism gradually faded in importance in India where Hinduism absorbed many of its major concepts, it became the major religion of China by the first century C.E., and from there spread to Japan. In both places it remains influential today. At the peak of its popularity, it attracted more followers than any other world religion, but in modern times, only about six percent of the world's population profess Buddhism as their religion. Despite its relative decline, the impact of this religion remains deeply imprinted in the cultures of the Eastern world, and it has increasingly found acceptance among Westerners in the twentieth century. Today, despite the passage of time and profound changes in the world, millions of people worldwide continue to find relevant and meaningful the view of the world and the place of human existence in that world as formulated by Siddhartha Gautama over twenty-five centuries ago. This is perhaps the truest test of the value of Buddha's contribution to the world of religion and philosophy.

Questions for Discussion and Your Reading Journal

1. How have the biography and teachings of Buddhism been preserved for more modern times? What effects do you think this way of preserving facts and ideas might have upon what we can really know about Buddhism and its founder?
2. What was Siddhartha Gautama's "Great Renunciation"?
3. According to this text, what seemed to be Buddha's main purpose in seeking enlightenment?
4. What aspects of Buddhism's Four Noble Truths seem philosophical? What elements seem more religious? Based upon these four principles and the Noble (or Holy) Eightfold Path, do you find Buddhism more a religion or a philosophy? Why?

NINIAN SMART
AND RICHARD D. HECHT, EDS.

This second-century CE *text is an account of Buddha's coming to awareness of the true nature and purpose of human existence. Buddha (his name in life was Siddhartha Gautama) died around 500 BCE, but he left a lasting religious tradition that sees life as a painful proving ground where living creatures are born, die, and are reborn (reincarnated) again and again until they learn to overcome ignorance, low views, inferior deeds, and violent passions. Buddhism teaches that complete joy and freedom from suffering (nirvana) are the result of a religious and philo-sophical journey toward "enlightenment," which is defined as under-standing the true nature of life. Note that in each of the watches of the night in the text, Buddha progressively comes to understand the princi-ples that will become the foundation of his teachings. The "watches of the night" were the means by which ancient cities kept time, with the first watch corresponding to our evening hours, the second watch to the hours just before and after midnight, the third watch to our early morn-ing hours, and the fourth watch to the time around dawn. It is from Bud-dha's insights in the third watch of the night that the key doctrines of the Four Noble Truths and the Noble Eightfold Path are derived.*

Reading Rhetorically

"Buddhacarita" or "enlightenment of the Buddha" is in narrative form. The aim of the text is to present Buddha's teachings in a more personal manner than could be accomplished through a doctrinal overview of points and sub-points. The narrative attempts to go beyond Buddhist doctrine to convey the stature and qualities of the man who went in search of "the ultimate reality of things and the final goal of existence." In this spiritual story, Buddha becomes the "hero" figure who triumphs over adversity and opposition to reach his goal of ultimate enlightenment. The followers of Buddha who wrote down the story some 300 years after his death interweave Buddhist doctrine into the plot of the narrative in a manner that allows readers both to see the exalted spirit of the Buddha-hero and, simultaneously, to learn his teachings. This would have made Buddhism much more accessible to large numbers of people who were illiterate and who depended upon oral storytelling to learn new ideas. Once a storyteller passed through a region and shared the story, it could there-after be passed on more easily in story form than as a list of memorized state-ments of Buddhist doctrine. As you read, note what might be "oral" elements of the text, cues to help a storyteller remember it.

The Enlightenment of the Buddha: Buddhacarita

Now that he had defeated Māra's[1] violence by his firmness and calm, the Bodhisattva,[2] possessed of great skill in Transic meditation,[3] put himself into trance, intent of discerning both the ultimate reality of things and the final goal of existence. After he had gained complete mastery over all the degrees and kinds of trance:

1

---

[1]**Māra** 'Death-dealer'; the Buddhist Evil One or Satan. [Ed. note.]

[2]**Bodhisattva** (i.e., a Being destined for Enlightenment) Until his Enlightenment the Buddha has the title of Bodhisattva. [Ed. note.]

[3]**Transic meditation** Disciplined progression through particular mental states, the climax of which is an experience of enhanced psychic vitality. There are usually four states: concentration of the mind on a single subject, mental and physical joy and ease, then a sense of ease only, then fi-nally a sense of perfect equanimity. [Ed. note.]

1. In the first watch of the night he recollected the successive series of his former births. "There was I so and so; that was my name; deceased from there I came here"—in this way he remembered thousands of births, as though living them over again. When he had recalled his own births and deaths in all these various lives of his, the Sage, full of pity, turned his compassionate mind towards other living beings, and he thought to himself: "Again and again they must leave the people they regard as their own, and must go on elsewhere, and that without ever stopping. Surely this world is unprotected and helpless, and like a wheel it turns round and round." As he continued steadily to recollect the past thus, he came to the definite conviction that this world of samsāra[4] is as unsubstantial as the pith of a plantain tree.

2. Second to none in valour, he then, in the second watch of the night, acquired the supreme heavenly eye, for he himself was the best of all those who have sight. Thereupon with the perfectly pure heavenly eye he looked upon the entire world, which appeared to him as though reflected in a spotless mirror. He saw that the decease and rebirth of beings depend on whether they have done superior or inferior deeds. And his compassionateness grew still further. It became clear to him that no security can be found in this flood of samsāric existence, and that the threat of death is ever-present. Beset on all sides, creatures can find no resting place. In this way he surveyed the five places of rebirth with his heavenly eye. And he found nothing substantial in the world of becoming, just as no core of heartwood is found in a plantain tree when its layers are peeled off one by one.

3. Then, as the third watch of that night drew on, the supreme master of trance turned his meditation to the real and essential nature of this world: "Alas, living beings wear themselves out in vain! Over and over again they are born, they age, die, pass on to a new life, and are reborn! What is more, greed and dark delusion obscure their sight, and they are blind from birth. Greatly apprehensive, they yet do not know how to get out of this great mass of ill." He then surveyed the twelve links of conditioned co-production,[5] and saw that, beginning with ignorance, they lead to old age and death, and, beginning with the cessation of ignorance, they lead to the cessation of birth, old age, death and all kinds of ill.

When the great seer had comprehended that where there is no ignorance whatever, there also the karma[6]-formations are stopped—then he had achieved a correct knowledge of all there is to be known, and he stood out in the world as a Buddha. He passed through the eight stages of Transit Insight, and quickly reached their highest point. From the summit of the world downwards he could detect no self anywhere. Like the fire, when its

---

[4]**samsāra** Changing, used to describe the unceasing round of birth, death, and rebirth. [Ed. note.]

[5]**conditioned co-production** These are described in full in Buddha's First Sermon, delivered to five monks who had been his companions in pursuit of the spiritual life. The word "ill" is a translation of "dukkha," which may also be translated as "suffering." [Ed. note.]

[6]**karma** In Hinduism and Buddhism, the whole ethical consequence of one's acts considered as fixing one's lot in the future existence. [Ed. note.]

fuel is burnt up, he became tranquil. He had reached perfection, and he thought to himself: "This is the authentic Way on which in the past so many great seers, who also knew all higher and all lower things, have travelled on to ultimate and real truth. And now I have obtained it!"

4. At that moment, in the fourth watch of the night, when dawn broke and all the ghosts that move and those that move not went to rest, the great seer took up the position which knows no more alteration, and the leader of all reached the state of all-knowledge. When, through his Buddhahood, he had cognized this fact, the earth swayed like a woman drunken with wine, the sky shone bright with the Siddhas[7] who appeared in crowds in all the directions, and the mighty drums of thunder resounded through the air. Pleasant breezes blew softly, rain fell from a cloudless sky, flowers and fruits dropped from the trees out of season—in an effort, as it were, to show reverence for him. Mandarava flowers and lotus blossoms, and also water lilies made of gold and beryl, feel from the sky on to the ground near the Shakya sage, so that it looked like a place in the world of the gods. At that moment no one anywhere was angry, ill, or sad; no one did evil, none was proud; the world became quite quiet, as though it had reached full perfection. Joy spread through the ranks of those gods who longed for salvation; joy also spread among those who lived in the regions below. Everywhere the virtuous were strengthened, the influence of Dharma[8] increased, and the world rose from the dirt of the passions and the darkness of ignorance. Filled with joy and wonder at the Sage's work, the seers of the solar race who had been protectors of men, who had been royal seers, who had been great seers, stood in their mansions in the heavens and showed him their reverence. The great seers among the hosts of invisible beings could be heard widely proclaiming his fame. All living things rejoiced and sensed that things went well. Māra alone felt deep displeasure, as though subjected to a sudden fall.

For seven days he dwelt there—his body gave him no trouble, his eyes never closed, and he looked into his own mind. He thought: "Here I have found freedom," and he knew that the longings of his heart had at last come to fulfilment. Now that he had understood the principle of causation and had become certain of the lack of self in all that is, he roused himself again from his deep trance, and in his great compassion he surveyed the world with his Buddha-eye, intent on giving it peace. When, however, he saw on the one side of the world lost in low views and confused efforts, thickly covered with the dirt of the passions, and saw on the other side the exceeding subtlety of the Dharma of emancipation, he felt inclined to take no action. But when he weighed up the significance of the pledge to enlighten all beings he had taken in the past, he became again more favourable to the idea of proclaiming the path to Peace. Reflecting in his mind on this question, he also considered that, while some people have a great deal of passion, others have but little. As soon as Indra and Brahmā,

---

[7]**Siddhas** Men who have obtained perfection. [Ed. note.]

[8]**Dharma** Teaching of Buddha. [Ed. note.]

the two chiefs of those who dwell in the heavens, had grasped the Sugata's[9] intention to proclaim the path to Peace, they shone brightly and came up to him, the weal of the world their concern. He remained there on his seat, free from all evil and successful in his aim. The most excellent Dharma which he had seen was his most excellent companion. His two visitors gently and reverently spoke to him these words, which were meant for the weal of the world: "Please do not condemn all those that live as unworthy of such treasure! Oh, please engender pity in your heart for beings in this world! So varied is their endowment, and while some have much passion, others have only very little. Now that you, O Sage, have yourself crossed the ocean of the world of becoming, please rescue also the other living beings who have sunk so deep into suffering! As a generous lord shares his wealth, so may also you bestow your own virtues on others! Most of those who know what for them is good in this world and the next, act only for their own advantage. In the world of men and in heaven it is hard to find anyone who is impelled by concern for the weal of the world." Having made this request to the great seer, the two gods returned to their celestial abode by the way they had come. And the sage pondered over their words. In consequence he was confirmed in his decision to set the world free.

Questions for Discussion and Your Reading Journal

1. In the first and second watches of the night, what did the Buddha learn about the "ultimate reality" of earthly existence?
2. In the second and third watches of the night, the Buddha contemplated the cycle of death and rebirth that is commonly called "reincarnation." What did he discover about the way to escape from this difficult cycle?
3. Many religions are concerned with an individual's outward actions toward others. Their commandments and rules focus upon doing good to fellow human beings and respecting deity. Buddhism does not have this focus. From this text, what does the focus of Buddhism seem to be?

LAO-TZU

The Chinese philosopher Lao-tzu was born around 600 BCE and lived contemporary to Confucius. "Lao-tzu" is not a name but, rather, at title given him and means "old person or old philosopher." Tradition and the first histories of his time give his original name as Li Erh and indicate that he served as librarian in the court of the Chou dynasty. At the heart of the philosophy/religion that grew out of his teachings is the concept of the "Tao." Tao is a broad, vague term meaning the way the universe functions. Literally, it means "path"; figuratively, it describes the path followed by the natural functioning of all aspects of the seen and unseen

---

[9]**Sugata** Another title of the Buddha, 'One who has gone well.' [Ed. note.]

universe. The planets move in their orbits; day is followed by night; and water runs downhill, wearing away the most rigid barriers that try to stop it. In the same way, Taoism teaches that humans can follow a natural path of harmony if they choose to do so. Lao-tzu was one of the first in China to teach that through a meditative quest for wisdom, human beings can find the Tao and exist in a perfectly peaceful state of being, free from unproductive desires such as lust, greed, anger, fear, sorrow, regret, and the meaningless human activity that grows out of these desires. The ideal state for the Taoist is to attain the purity and simplicity of a child or, to use another Taoist symbol, an "uncarved block."

Reading Rhetorically

Lao-tzu (and later writers who edited his work into book form) wrote in a genre that is known as "wisdom literature." The purpose of such literature is to persuade readers (and listeners through oral transmission) that certain ideas and courses of action are preferable to, or wiser than, others. The evidence given to support key ideas and points, however, is implicit in the statements of wisdom themselves. To support one statement of wisdom, such as "The world is sacred. It can't be improved," the text uses other statements of wisdom, such as "There is a time for being ahead, a time for being behind," and so on. The value of ideas presented in this manner is not to be judged upon an appeal to factual, systematic, or rational evidence. Rather, the text appeals to each reader's lived experience and own perceptions. The sayings of Lao-tzu become "persuasive" to the extent that they coincide with and build upon the experiences of the reader. As Lao-tzu puts it in Part 67:

> Some say that my teaching is nonsense.
> Others call it lofty but impractical.
> But to those who have looked inside themselves,
> This nonsense makes perfect sense.
> And to those who put it into practice,
> This loftiness has roots that go deep.

As you read, think about how some of these sayings may pertain to your own experience.

The Sayings of Lao-tzu

29

Do you want to improve the world?
I don't think it can be done.

The world is sacred.
It can't be improved.

If you tamper with it, you'll ruin it.
If you treat it like an object, you'll lose it.

There is a time for being ahead,
a time for being behind;
a time for being in motion,
a time for being at rest;
a time for being vigorous,
a time for being exhausted;
a time for being safe,
a time for being in danger.

The Master sees things as they are,
without trying to control them.
She lets them go their own way,
and resides at the center of the circle.

30

Whoever relies on the Tao in governing men
doesn't try to force issues
or defeat enemies by force of arms.
For every force there is a counterforce.
Violence, even well intentioned,
always rebounds upon oneself.

The master does his job
and then stops.
He understands that the universe
is forever out of control,
and that trying to dominate events
goes against the current of the Tao.
Because he believes in himself,
he doesn't try to convince others.
Because he is content with himself,
he doesn't need others' approval.
Because he accepts himself,
the whole world accepts him.

31

Weapons are the tools of violence;
all decent men detest them.

Weapons are the tools of fear;
a decent man will avoid them
except in the direst necessity
and, if compelled, will use them
only with the utmost restraint.

Peace is his highest value.
If the peace has been shattered,
how can he be content?
His enemies are not demons,
but human beings like himself.
He doesn't wish them personal harm.
Nor does he rejoice in victory.
How could he rejoice in victory
and delight in the slaughter of men?

He enters a battle gravely,
with sorrow and with great compassion,
as if he were attending a funeral.

37

The Tao never does anything,
yet through it all things are done.

If powerful men and women
could center themselves in it,
the whole world would be transformed
by itself, in its natural rhythms.
People would be content
with their simple, everyday lives,
in harmony, and free of desire.

When there is no desire,
all things are at peace.

38

The Master doesn't try to be powerful;
thus he is truly powerful.
The ordinary man keeps reaching for power;
thus he never has enough.

The master does nothing,
yet he leaves nothing undone.
The ordinary man is always doing things,
yet many more are left to be done.

The kind man does something,
yet something remains undone.
The just man does something,
and leaves many things to be done.
The moral man does something,
and when no one responds
he rolls up his sleeves and uses force.

When the Tao is lost, there is goodness.
When goodness is lost, there is morality.
When morality is lost, there is ritual.
Ritual is the husk of true faith,
the beginning of chaos.

Therefore the Master concerns himself
with the depths and not the surface,
with the fruit and not the flower.
He has no will of his own.
He dwells in reality,
and lets all illusions go.

46

When a country is in harmony with the Tao,
the factories make trucks and tractors.
When a country goes counter to the Tao,
warheads are stockpiled outside the cities.

There is no greater illusion than fear,
no greater wrong than preparing to defend yourself,
no greater misfortune than having an enemy.

Whoever can see through all fear
will always be safe.

53

The great Way is easy,
yet people prefer the side paths.
Be aware when things are out of balance.
Stay centered within the Tao.

When rich speculators prosper
while farmers lose their land;
when government officials spend money
on weapons instead of cures;
when the upper class is extravagant and irresponsible
while the poor have nowhere to turn—
all this is robbery and chaos.
It is not in keeping with the Tao.

57

If you want to be a great leader,
you must learn to follow the Tao.
Stop trying to control.
Let go of fixed plans and concepts,
and the world will govern itself.

The more prohibitions you have,
the less virtuous people will be.
The more weapons you have,
the less secure people will be.
The more subsidies you have,
the less self-reliant people will be.

Therefore the Master says:
I let go of the law,
and people become honest.
I let go of economics,
and people become prosperous.
I let go of religion,
and people become serene.
I let go of all desire for the common good,
and the good becomes common as grass.

58

If a country is governed with tolerance,
the people are comfortable and honest.
If a country is governed with repression,
the people are depressed and crafty.

When the will to power is in charge,
the higher the ideals, the lower the results.
Try to make people happy,
and you lay the groundwork for misery.
Try to make people moral,
and you lay the groundwork for vice.

Thus the Master is content
to serve as an example
and not to impose her will.
She is pointed, but doesn't pierce.
Straightforward, but supple.
Radiant, but easy on the eyes.

59

For governing a country well
there is nothing better than moderation.

The mark of a moderate man
is freedom from his own ideas.
Tolerant like the sky,
all-pervading like sunlight,
firm like a mountain,
supple like a tree in the wind,

he has no destination in view
and makes use of anything
life happens to bring his way.

Nothing is impossible for him.
Because he has let go,
he can care for the people's welfare
as a mother cares for her child.

60

Governing a large country
is like frying a small fish.
You spoil it with too much poking.

Center your country in the Tao
and evil will have no power.
Not that it isn't there,
but you'll be able to step out of its way.

Give evil nothing to oppose
and it will disappear by itself.

61

When a country obtains great power,
it becomes like the sea:
all streams run downward into it.
The more powerful it grows,
the greater the need for humility.
Humility means trusting the Tao,
thus never needing to be defensive.

A great nation is like a great man:
When he makes a mistake, he realizes it.
Having realized it, he admits it.
Having admitted it, he corrects it.
He considers those who point out his faults
as his most benevolent teachers.
He thinks of his enemy
as the shadow that he himself casts.

If a nation is centered in the Tao,
if it nourishes its own people
and doesn't meddle in the affairs of others,
it will be a light to all nations in the world.

65

The ancient Masters
didn't try to educate the people,
but kindly taught them to not-know.

When they think that they know the answers,
people are difficult to guide.
When they know that they don't know,
people can find their own way.

If you want to learn how to govern,
avoid being clever or rich.
The simplest pattern is the clearest.
Content with an ordinary life,
you can show all people the way
back to their own true nature.

66

All streams flow to the sea
because it is lower than they are.
Humility gives it its power.

If you want to govern the people,
you must place yourself below them.
If you want to lead the people,
you must learn how to follow them.

The Master is above the people,
and no one feels oppressed.
She goes ahead of the people,
and no one feels manipulated.
The whole world is grateful to her.
Because she competes with no one,
no one can compete with her.

67

Some say that my teaching is nonsense.
Others call it lofty but impractical.
But to those who have looked inside themselves,
this nonsense makes perfect sense.
And to those who put it into practice,
this loftiness has roots that go deep.

I have just three things to teach:
simplicity, patience, compassion.

These three are your greatest treasures.
Simple in actions and in thoughts,
you return to the source of being.
Patient with both friends and enemies,
you accord with the way things are.
Compassionate toward yourself,
you reconcile all beings in the world.

Questions for Discussion and Your Reading Journal

1. Earlier in this chapter, the Chinese creation story "Nu Kwa" introduces the concept of "the sacred way of harmony and balance." Give one example of how the "Tao" or the harmonious and balanced "way of the universe" shows up in Lao-tzu's reading.
2. What evidence does the text give that a good Taoist would tend to be a peaceful person rather than a conqueror?
3. Which saying do you find most interesting and/or wise in this small sampling of Lao-tzu's ideas? Why?
4. Once you have completed the reading, sum up in one or two sentences your own interpretation of the concept "the Tao."

WILLIAM H. MCNEILL
AND JEAN W. SEDLAR

In this overview of Confucianism, historians William H. McNeill and Jean W. Sedlar briefly outline the life of Confucius (550–479 BCE) as we know it and describe the main tenets of his philosophy. As with many philosophical and religious figures of ancient times (Socrates, Buddha, and Jesus, for example), Confucius wrote nothing himself; his sayings were passed on orally by his followers and written down much later. As McNeill and Sedlar point out, however, these sayings, or analects, are the best source for the original ideas and teachings of Confucius as well as for major themes in Chinese thought that were later included in the Confucian tradition.

Reading Rhetorically

McNeill and Sedlar offer a rich overview of the historical and cultural world of China in the fifth-century BCE that gave us Confucius and his teachings. Their reading is expository in nature, seeking to inform; as you read, note how they present unfamiliar material in a way that makes it understandable. Their final paragraph on *The Analects* (short, pithy sayings) of Confucius provides key background information on this unique genre of written and oral expression.

Introduction to Confucius

Until very recent times in China, Confucius (K'ung Fu Tzu,[1] or Master K'ung) was generally regarded as the greatest thinker who ever lived. The complex of ideas attached to his name—human-heartedness, decorum, respect for parents and ancestors—expresses the characteristic attitude of the traditional Chinese. From about the first century B.C. until the twentieth century A.D. Confucianism was recognized, with occasional interruptions, as the official philosophy of the Chinese empire. The Confucian Classics were the basic texts of Chinese education and the subject matter of the civil service examinations, virtually ensuring that the imperial bureaucracy would be imbued with Confucian principles. The all-pervasiveness of Confucian influence in social norms and private morals, the exalted status accorded to Confucius himself, and the general acceptance of his reputed opinions as almost unquestioned truths, gave to Confucianism many of the characteristics which in other civilizations have belonged to religion rather than philosophy.

Confucius himself was born in the small state of Lu on the northeast China plain, in what was then one of the oldest centers of Chinese culture. His traditional dates, 550–479 B.C., are approximately accurate, making him a contemporary of the Buddha, the pre-Socratic philosphers of Greece, and perhaps the Persian Zoroaster. Confucius himself tells us that his background was humble. But he was well educated by the standards of his century—a fact strongly suggesting that he belonged to the lower aristocracy. As a young man he apparently held minor official posts in his native state; his ambition was to gain a position of political influence, but this eluded him. Much of his life evidently was devoted to study and teaching; history does not record how he supported himself. He probably began to evolve his ideas in informal debates with friends, and gradually the force of his intellect and personality attracted others to his company. When nearly sixty years old, he began a series of wide-ranging travels to the various courts of China, seeking a prince who would make use of his talents. Preceded by his reputation for learning, he was everywhere received with honor. But no one offered him a position in which he could influence events; and after some ten years of wandering he returned home to Lu.

Confucius' reputation, then, rests upon his ideas rather than his statesmanship. He is said to have been the first independent teacher in China—as opposed to the tutors employed by noble houses—though this is hard to prove. Certainly teaching in his day was not recognized as a profession. The education which Confucius provided included politics, history, and literature, but ignored the aristocrats' traditional training in archery and charioteering. This emphasis on mental rather than physical prowess was undoubtedly an innovation at that time. Confucius' early followers were derided as *ju* ("weaklings"). Within a

---

[1]*Tzu* is a title of respect meaning "Master." It is affixed to the names of many eminent Chinese, e.g., Meng Tzu (Mencius), Mo Tzu, Hsün Tzu, etc.

century of his death, however, the word lost its pejorative significance; and it remains to this day the standard term for "Confucian" (or "literati") in the Chinese language.

4   Though Confucius described himself as a transmitter rather than a creator of ideas, there can be no doubt that he was both. Certainly he loved the traditional Chinese culture and revered the legendary sage-kings of antiquity, Yao, Shun, and Yü. He liked to speak in archaic formulas and proverbs, and often disparaged the present by comparison with the past. But reverence for antiquity—then as later—was a common trait in China, and Confucius spoke far less about it than most of his followers did. His primary concern was to improve contemporary society; and, without doubt, the conditions of his day left much to be desired. The titular emperor of China exercised a purely nominal authority over all but a small area around his capital; his functions were mainly ceremonial. His supposed vassals, the *de facto* rulers of the various Chinese states, were constantly at war both with one another and with the semi-barbarian states on their borders. The north China plain—the heartland of Chinese culture—had become a vast battleground. Confucius sought to discover the means of ending this chaos.

5   He said little about the methods he rejected, but it is clear what they were. Obviously, he did not believe that additional warfare could serve any good purpose. At the same time, he refused to look to supernatural beings for assistance. While not denying the existence of gods or spirits—who were supposed to inhabit trees, rocks, rivers, and many other natural phenomena—he preferred not to discuss them. Heaven *(T'ien)*, on the other hand, he treated as a remote, impersonal principle which did not intervene in human affairs. The positive basis of Confucius' thought was *Tao*, or the "Way." As used by the Taoist school of philosophy, the term meant something analogous to the course of Nature; Confucius regarded it as the standard of ethics in human affairs.

6   Conduct in harmony with Tao meant faithfulness and loyalty, reasonableness and moderation, respect for the feelings and rights of others. To the modern mind such precepts are in no way remarkable, but in China of the sixth century B.C. they represented a decided shift of emphasis. In pre-Confucian China, as in other early civilizations, the chief regulator of human behavior was the necessity of pleasing divine beings. The gods and spirits had to be provided with suitable offerings and expressions of devotion according to strictly prescribed formulae. Confucius' insistence upon an internal regulator of conduct—as opposed to the external demands of ritual—was a major innovation in his time. Confucius spoke not of propitiating the spirits, but of cultivating human character. Righteousness, in the broadest possible sense, was his standard for both private and public morals. While respecting the ancient religious ritual, he interpreted it as an aspect of propriety or decorum—a conventional form of social intercourse which directs human behavior into harmonious channels and prevents extremes of emotion.

7   In later centuries the followers of Confucius were known for their great devotion to book-learning, and similar habits were attributed to the Master as well. But it is unlikely that Confucius himself consulted many books, if only

because in his lifetime they were expensive, hard to obtain, and clumsy to use. Legend, nonetheless, has made of him a formidable scholar, and assigned him a role in the composition or editing of the Five Confucian classics. He is supposed to have selected the 305 poems of the *Book of Songs* from an existing collection of over three thousand, and to have put together the documents which now comprise the *Book of History.* He is similarly reputed to have inspired, if not actually composed, the *Book of Rites,* and to be the author of the *Spring and Autumn Annals* and the appendices to the *Book of Changes.* None of these assertions stands up under critical scrutiny. Most of the material in the Classics post-dates Confucius by at least several centuries; and even these portions of the *History* and the *Changes* which preceded him were arranged into the present Classics long after his death. Of the Five Classics, only the *Book of Songs* existed in approximately its present form in the sixth century B.C.; and Confucius probably had nothing to do with selecting its contents.

The one work which is accurately attributed to Confucius is the *Analects* 8 (*Lun Yü,* or "Selected Sayings"). But even this small book—a collection of pithy and discounted statements on a variety of subjects—did not come from the Master's own hand. It is rather a fourth-century B.C. compilation of his sayings as remembered and passed on by his followers. At one time there were probably several sets of *Analects* in existence, each the product of a different Confucian school. As we have it today, the collection consists of twenty chapters (or "books") of varying dates, of which the third through the ninth contain sayings which probably originated with Confucius himself. Other books are clearly later insertions, and in some cases they contain ideas of which he would scarcely have approved.

The *Analects* remains, nonetheless, the best extant source for the actual 9 opinions of Confucius. Within a few centuries of his death, various notions quite alien to what we know of him became attached to his name. As the Confucian school gained popularity and attracted the patronage of emperors under the Han dynasty (206 B.C.—A.D. 220), an increasing number of ideas that derived from the rival schools of Taoism, Legalism, and Yin-Yang came to be presented under the Confucian label. The Five Classics—supposedly authentic accounts of Confucius' own ideas—are in fact an eclectic mass of divergent and sometimes discordant elements. But in ceasing to be the system of a single and rather obscure individual, Confucianism became a vast intellectual edifice embodying all the major tendencies of Chinese thought. Accepted by ordinary people for its applicability to everyday human concerns and its insistence that government exists for the common welfare, revered by the educated classes for its stress on advancement through merit and its code of gentlemanly behavior, and supported by emperors for its inherent conservatism combined with a reputation for benevolence, Confucianism remained the dominant intellectual system of China until well into the twentieth century.

Questions for Discussion and Your Reading Journal

1. In what ways did the Chinese people traditionally view Confucius as more than merely a philosopher?

2. Why were Confucius' early followers considered "weaklings"? How did their identity change within the first century after their master's death?

3. What was Confucius' approach to ending the wars and social chaos of his time?

CONFUCIUS

For valuable background information upon the life of Confucius and upon his Analects, *see the previous reading.*

Reading Rhetorically

Like other examples of "wisdom literature" in this chapter, *The Analects* aim to persuade through an appeal to the inner wisdom and personal experience of their readers. They rely not upon facts, evidence, and reason for this but, rather, upon shared perceptions about what is good and what is not good in the human experience. The "analect" as a vehicle for communicating ideas was born in oral traditions. These succinct, pithy sayings are more easily memorized than long, doctrinal dissertations and could be readily passed on from person to person and from generation to generation.

The Analects

ON EDUCATION

The Master said, "At fifteen I set my heart on learning; at thirty I took my stand; at forty I came to be free from doubts; at fifty I understood the Decree of Heaven; at sixty my ear was attuned; at seventy I followed my heart's desire without overstepping the bounds." (II: 4)

The Master said, "He who learns but does not think, is lost. He who thinks but does not learn is in great danger." (II, 15)

The Master said, "Yu, shall I teach you what knowledge is? When you know a thing, to recognize that you know it, and when you do not know a thing, to recognize that you do not know it. That is knowledge." (II, 17)

The Master said, "I have 'transmitted what was taught to me without making up anything of my own. I have been faithful to and loved the Ancients. In these respects, I make bold to think, not even our old P'eng can have excelled me." (VII, 1)

The Master said, "I have listened in silence and noted what was said. I have never grown tired of learning nor wearied of teaching others what I have learnt. These at least are merits which I can confidently claim." (VII, 2)

In his leisure hours the Master's manner was very free and easy, and his expression alert and cheerful. (VII, 4)

The Master said, "Even when walking in the company of two other men, I am bound to be able to learn from them. The good points of the one I copy; the bad points of the other I correct in myself." (VII: 22)

The Master said, "I never enlighten anyone who has not been driven to distraction by trying to understand a difficulty or who has got into a frenzy trying to put his ideas into words." (VII: 8)

The Master instructs under four heads: culture, moral conduct, doing one's best, and being trustworthy in what one says (VII: 25).

Fan Ch'ih asked about benevolence. The Master said, "Love your fellow men." He asked about wisdom. The Master said, "Know your fellow men." (XII: 22)

Confucius said, "Those who are born with knowledge are the highest. Next come those who attain knowledge through study. Next again come those who turn to study after having been vexed by difficulties. The common people, in so far as they make no effort to study even after having been vexed by difficulties, are the lowest." (XVI: 9)

ON GOODNESS

[The word *jen* in Chinese is the generic term for "human being." Here rendered as "Goodness," it is most often translated into English as "humanity" or "human-heartedness." *Jen* is perhaps the most important single concept in *The Analects,* though Confucius nowhere defines it precisely. He speaks of it in a very broad sense as the sum of the qualities which the ideal human being ought to possess, i.e., humanness in the highest degree. Courtesy, loyalty, and unselfishness lie "in its direction," though they are not the whole of it. In Confucius' use of the term, *jen* is in fact a more than human quality. He conceded that the sage-kings of antiquity had possessed it, but refused to apply the word to any living person.]

The Master said, "Clever talk and a pretentious manner" are seldom found in the Good." (I, 3)

The Master said, "A young man's duty is to behave well to his parents at home and to his elders abroad, to be cautious in giving promises and punctual in keeping them, to have kindly feelings towards everyone, but seek the intimacy of the Good. If, when all that is done, he has any energy to spare, then let him study the polite arts." (I, 6)

The Master said, "Just as to sacrifice to ancestors other than one's own is presumption, so to see what is right and not do it is cowardice." (II, 24)

The Master said, "Without Goodness a man
Cannot for long endure adversity,
Cannot for long enjoy prosperity.
The Good Man rests content with Goodness; he that is merely wise pursues Goodness in the belief that it pays to do so." (IV, 2)

Of the adage "Only a Good Man knows how to like people, knows how to dislike them," the Master said, "He whose heart is in the smallest degree set upon Goodness will dislike no one." (IV, 3, 4)

Tzu-kung asked saying, "Is there any single saying that one can act upon all day and every day?" The Master said, "Perhaps the saying about consideration: 'Never do to others what you would not like them to do to you.'" (XV, 23)

ON THE IDEAL PERSON ("GENTLEMAN")

1 The Master said, "The gentleman seeks neither a full belly nor a comfortable home. He is quick in action but cautious in speech. He goes to men possessed of the Way to be put right. Such a man can be described as eager to learn." (I: 14)

2 The Master said, "In his dealings with the world the gentleman is not invariably for or against anything. He is on the side of what is moral." (IV: 10)

3 The Master said, "The gentleman helps others to realize what is good in them; he does not help them to realize what is bad in them. The small man does the opposite." (XII: 16)

4 The Master said, "There are nine things the gentleman turns his thought to: to seeing clearly when he uses his eyes, to hearing acutely when he uses his ears, to looking cordial when it comes to his countenance, to appearing respectful when it comes to his demeanor, to being conscientious when he speaks, to being reverent when he performs his duties, to seeking advice when he is in doubt, to the consequences when he is enraged, and to what is right at the sight of gain." (XVI: 10)

ON WOMEN

1 "The lord of a state uses the term 'lady' for his wife. She uses the term 'little boy' for herself. The people of the state refer to her by the term 'the lady of the lord,' but when abroad they use the term 'the little lord.' People of other states also refer to her by the term 'the lady of the lord.'" (XVI: 14)

2 The Master said, "I have yet to meet the man who is as fond of virtue as he is of beauty in women." (IX: 18)

3 The Master said, "In one's household, it is the women and the small men that are difficult to deal with. If you let them get too close, they become insolent. If you keep them at a distance, they complain." (XVII: 25)

ON ECONOMIC MATTERS

4 The Master said, "If one is guided by profit in one's actions, one will incur much ill will." (IV: 12)

5 The Master said, "The gentleman understands what is moral. The small man understands what is profitable." (IV: 16)

6 Tzu-kung said, "If you had a piece of beautiful jade here, would you put it away safely in a box or would you try to sell it for a good price?" The Master said, "Of course I would sell it. Of course I would sell it. All I am waiting for is the right offer." (IX: 13)

ON FILIAL PIETY (REVERENCE/RESPECT FOR PARENTS, ANCESTORS, ELDERS)

The Master said, "Observe what a man has in mind to do when his father is 7 living, and then observe what he does when his father is dead. If, for three years, he makes no changes to his father's ways, he can be said to be a good son." (I: 11)

The Master said, "In serving your father and mother you ought to dis- 8 suade them from doing wrong in the gentlest way. If you see your advice being ignored, you should not become disobedient but remain reverent. You should not complain even if in so doing you wear yourself out." (IV: 18)

The Master said, "With Yü I can find no fault. He ate and drank the 9 meanest fare while making offerings to ancestral spirits and gods with the utmost devotion proper to a descendant. . . ." (VII: 21)

Questions for Discussion and Your Reading Journal

1. To what extent do Confucius' teachings seem to be shaped by his conceptions of a god and a divine will? Explain.
2. Which of Confucius' analects concerning education appeals to you most? Why?
3. Which of the analects concerning goodness appeals to you most? Why?
4. Sum up in one sentence Confucius' portrayal of the "ideal person." what do his subsequent comments about women suggest about how females fit into his concept of the ideal person?
5. In present times, China resists adopting a capitalistic economic system similar to those in the West. What evidence exists in *The Analects* of an anti-capitalist spirit?
6. Confucius mentions the word "god" in his teachings on filial piety (reverence for our elders). What importance does he seem to give to "ancestral spirits" by putting them in the same sentence with the word "gods"?

THE WESTERN WORLD

PLATO

Though Socrates (470–399BCE) is considered one of the greatest thinkers and philosophers of the Western world, he wrote nothing. We know of him primarily through the writings of Plato (428–348 BCE), his pupil. Both lived and developed their ideas during the height of classical Greek civilization. The "Allegory of the Cave" comes from Plato's book The Republic, *an extended work in which he uses the personas of Socrates and Glaucon to present ideas for establishing an ideal government and a utopian society in ancient Greece. In this section of* The

Republic, *Plato presents his philosophy of learning and of education. (For more on Plato's background, see* The Republic *in Chapter 2.)*

Reading Rhetorically

As Plato lived at the very place and time that Western rhetoric was born, it is not surprising that his writing is profoundly imbued with a self-conscious sense of its own rhetorical nature. At the heart of his use of rhetoric is the "dialogue" form, a conversational genre of writing in which his main character, Socrates, asks questions and elicits reasoned and reasonable answers from his listeners. These answers lead, step by step, to a deeper understanding of an issue in an approach that is known and respected to this day as the "Socratic method." This method is based upon a philosophy of "education and ignorance" that is at the core of the reading that follows. Plato uses an extended allegory to express what was in his time and still is today a controversial understanding of how "true" education works. An allegory is a story with symbolic meaning reaching beyond the story itself. It is a sophisticated tool of persuasion that is particularly suited to convincing an audience of new ideas that, if stated succinctly and bluntly, may be immediately rejected. A symbolic story, such as that of the cave dwellers that follows, has a tendency to get readers to suspend negative judgments in the interest of following the story line. If successfully done, the allegory thus buys the writer enough time to develop ideas fully and persuasively so that, in the end, disagreement is dealt with before it fully has a chance to erupt. As you read, think about how successful this allegory is in persuading you as reader.

The Allegory of the Cave

1   "Next, then," I said, "take the following parable of education and ignorance as a picture of the condition of our nature. Imagine mankind as dwelling in an underground cave with a long entrance open to the light across the whole width of the cave; in this they have been from childhood, with necks and legs fettered, so they have to stay where they are. They cannot move their heads round because of the fetters, and they can only look forward, but light comes to them from fire burning behind them higher up at a distance. Between the fire and the prisoners is a road above their level, and along it imagine a low wall has been built, as puppet showmen have screens in front of their people over which they work their puppets."

2   "I see," he said.

3   "See, then, bearers carrying along this wall all sorts of articles which they hold projecting above the wall, statues of men and other living things,[1] made of stone or wood and all kinds of stuff, some of the bearers speaking and some silent, as you might expect."

---

[1]Including models of trees, etc.

"What a remarkable image," he said, "and what remarkable prisoners!" 4

"Just like ourselves," I said. "For, first of all, tell me this: What do you 5
think such people would have seen of themselves and each other except their
shadows, which the fire cast on the opposite wall of the cave?"

"I don't see how they could see anything else," said he, "if they were com- 6
pelled to keep their heads unmoving all their lives!"

"Very well, what of the things being carried along? Would not this be the 7
same?"

"Of course it would." 8

"Suppose the prisoners were able to talk together, don't you think that 9
when they named the shadows which they saw passing they would believe they
were naming things?"[2]

"Necessarily." 10

"Then if their prison had an echo from the opposite wall, whenever one 11
of the passing bearers uttered a sound, would they not suppose that the passing shadow must be making the sound? Don't you think so?"

"Indeed I do," he said. 12

"If so," said I, "such persons would certainly believe that there were no 13
realities except those shadows of handmade things."[3]

"So it must be," said he. 14

"Now consider," said I, "what their release would be like, and their cure 15
from these fetters and their folly; let us imagine whether it might naturally be
something like this. One might be released, and compelled suddenly to stand
up and turn his neck round, and to walk and look towards the firelight; all this
would hurt him, and he would be too much dazzled to see distinctly those
things whose shadows he had seen before. What do you think he would say,
if someone told him that what he saw before was foolery, but now he saw
more rightly, being a bit nearer reality and turned towards what was a little
more real? What if he were shown each of the passing things, and compelled
by questions to answer what each one was? Don't you think he would be puzzled, and believe what he saw before was more true than what was shown to
him now?"

"Far more," he said. 16

"Then suppose he were compelled to look towards the real light, it would 17
hurt his eyes, and he would escape by turning them away to the things which
he was able to look at, and these he would believe to be clearer than what was
being shown to him."

"Just so," said he. 18

"Suppose, now," said I, "that someone should drag him thence by force, 19
up the rough ascent, the steep way up, and never stop until he could drag him
out into the light of the sun, would he not be distressed and furious at being

---

[2]Which they had never seen. They would say "tree" when it was only a shadow of the model of
a tree.

[3]Shadows of artificial things, not even the shadow of a growing tree; another stage from reality.

Figure 1 Socrates' parable of our education and subsequent ignorance is illustrated in this drawing on the Cave. "Plato's Cave" from *The Great Dialogues of Plato* translated by J.C.G. Rouse. Copyright 1956, renewed copyright © 1984 by J.C.G. Rouse. Reprinted by permission of the publishers, New American Library, a division of Penguin Books USA, Inc.

dragged; and when he came into the light, the brilliance would fill his eyes and he would not be able to see even one of the things now called real?"[4]

20   "That he would not," said he, "all of a sudden."

21   "He would have to get used to it, surely, I think, if he is to see the things above. First he would most easily look at shadows, after that images of mankind and the rest in water, lastly the things themselves. After this he would find it easier to survey by night the heavens themselves and all that is in them, gazing at the light of the stars and moon, rather than by day the sun and the sun's light."

22   "Of course."

23   "Last of all, I suppose, the sun; he could look on the sun itself in its own place, and see what it is like, not reflections of it in water or as it appears in some alien setting."

24   "Necessarily," said he.

25   "And only after all this he might reason about it, how this is he who provides seasons and years, and is set over all there is in the visible region, and he is in a manner the cause of all things which they saw."

26   "Yes, it is clear," said he, "that after all that, he would come to this last."

27   "Very good. Let him be reminded of his first habitation, and what was wisdom in that place, and of his fellow-prisoners there; don't you think he would bless himself for the change, and pity them?"

28   "Yes, indeed."

29   "And if there were honours and praises among them and prizes for the one who saw the passing things most sharply and remembered best which of them

[4]To the next stage of knowledge: the real thing, not the artificial puppet.

used to come before and which after and which together, and from these was best able to prophesy accordingly what was going to come—do you believe he would set his desire on that, and envy those who were honoured men or potentates among them? Would he not feel as Homer says,[5] and heartily desire rather to be serf of some landless man on earth and to endure anything in the world, rather than to opine as they did and to live in that way?"

"Yes indeed," said he, "he would rather accept anything than live like that." 30

"Then again," I said, "just consider; if such a one should go down again and sit on his old seat, would he not get his eyes full of darkness coming in suddenly out of the sun?" 31

"Very much so," said he. 32

"And if he should have to compete with those who had been always prisoners, by laying down the law about those shadows while he was blinking before his eyes were settled down—and it would take a good long time to get used to things—wouldn't they all laugh at him and say he had spoiled his eyesight by going up there, and it was not worth-while so much as to try to go up? And would they not kill anyone who tried to release them and take them up, if they could somehow lay hands on him and kill him?"[6] 33

"That they would!" said he. 34

"Then we must apply this image, my dear Glaucon," said I, "to all we have been saying. The world of our sight is like the habitation in prison, the firelight there to the sunlight here, the ascent and the view of the upper world is the rising of the soul into the world of mind; put it so and you will not be far from my own surmise, since that is what you want to hear; but God knows if it is really true. At least, what appears to me is, that in the world of the known, last of all,[7] is the idea of the good, and with what toil to be seen! And seen, this must be inferred to be the cause of all right and beautiful things for all, which gives birth to light and the king of light in the world of sight, and, in the world of mind, herself the queen produces truth and reason; and she must be seen by one who is to act with reason publicly or privately." 35

"I believe as you do," he said, "in so far as I am able." 36

"Then believe also, as I do," said I, "and do not be surprised, that those who come thither are not willing to have part in the affairs of men, but their souls ever strive to remain above; for that surely may be expected if our parable fits the case." 37

"Quite so," he said. 38

"Well then," said I, "do you think it surprising if one leaving divine contemplations and passing to the evils of men is awkward and appears to be a great fool, while he is still blinking—not yet accustomed to the darkness around him, but compelled to struggle in law courts or elsewhere about shadows of justice, or the images which make the shadows, and to quarrel about notions of justice in those who have never seen justice itself?" 39

---

[5] *Odyssey* xi. 489.

[6] Plato probably alludes to the death of Socrates.

[7] The end of our search.

40   "Not surprising at all," said he.

41   "But any man of sense," I said, "would remember that the eyes are doubly confused from two different causes, both in passing from light to darkness and from darkness to light; and believing that the same things happen with regard to the soul also, whenever he sees a soul confused and unable to discern anything he would not just laugh carelessly; he would examine whether it had come out of a more brilliant life, and if it were darkened by the strangeness; or whether it had come out of greater ignorance into a more brilliant light, and if it were dazzled with the brighter illumination. Then only would he congratulate the one soul upon its happy experience and way of life, and pity the other; but if he must laugh, his laugh would be a less downright laugh than his laughter at the soul which came out of the light above."

42   "That is fairly put," said he.

43   "Then if this is true," I said, "our belief about these matters must be this, that the nature of education is not really such as some of its professors say it is; as you know, they say that there is not understanding in the soul, but they put it in, as if they were putting sight into blind eyes."

44   "They do say so," said he.

45   "But our reasoning indicates," I said, "that this power is already in the soul of each, and is the instrument by which each learns; thus if the eye could not see without being turned with the whole body from the dark towards the light, so this instrument must be turned round with the whole soul away from the world of becoming until it is able to endure the sight of being and the most brilliant light of being: And this we say is the good, don't we?"

46   "Yes."

47   "Then this instrument," said I, "must have its own art, for the circum-turning or conversion, to show how the turn can be most easily and successfully made; not an art of putting sight into an eye, which we say has it already, but since the instrument has not been turned aright and does not look where it ought to look—that's what must be managed."

48   "So it seems," he said.

49   "Now most of the virtues which are said to belong to the soul are really something near to those of the body; for in fact they are not already there, but they are put later into it by habits and practices; but the virtue of understanding everything really belongs to something certainly more divine, as it seems, for it never loses its power, but becomes useful and helpful or, again, useless and harmful, by the direction in which it is turned. Have you not noticed men who are called worthless but clever, and how keen and sharp is the sight of their petty soul, and how it sees through the things towards which it is turned? Its sight is clear enough, but it is compelled to be the servant of vice, so that the clearer it sees the more evil it does."

50   "Certainly," said he.

51   "Yet if this part of such a nature," said I, "had been hammered at from childhood, and all those leaden weights of the world of becoming knocked off—the weights, I mean, which grow into the soul from gorging and gluttony and such pleasures, and twist the soul's eye downwards—if, I say, it had shaken these off and been turned round towards what is real and true, that

same instrument of those same men would have seen those higher things most clearly, just as now it sees those towards which it is turned."

"Quite likely," said he.   52

"Very well," said I, "isn't it equally likely, indeed, necessary, after what   53 has been said, that men uneducated and without experience of truth could never properly supervise a city, nor can those who are allowed to spend all their lives in education right to the end? The first have no single object in life, which they must always aim at in doing everything they do, public or private; the second will never do anything if they can help it, believing that they have already found mansions abroad in the Islands of the Blest."[8]

"True," said he.   54

"Then it is the task of us founders," I said, "to compel the best natures to   55 attain that learning which we said was the greatest, both to see the good, and to ascend that ascent; and when they have ascended and properly seen, we must never allow them what is allowed now."

"What is that, pray?" he asked.   56

"To stay there," I said, "and not be willing to descend again to those pris-   57 oners, and to share their troubles and their honours, whether they are worth having or not."

"What!" said he, "are we to wrong them and make them live badly, when   58 they might live better?"

"You have forgotten again, my friend," said I, "that the law is not concerned   59 how any one class in a city is to prosper above the rest; it tries to contrive prosperity in the city as a whole, fitting the citizens into a pattern by persuasion and compulsion, making them give of their help to one another wherever each class is able to help the community. The law itself creates men like this in the city, not in order to allow each one to turn by any way he likes, but in order to use them itself to the full for binding the city together."

"True," said he, "I did forget."   60

"Notice then, Glaucon," I said, "we shall not wrong the philosophers who   61 grow up among us, but we shall treat them fairly when we compel them to add to their duties the care and guardianship of the other people. We shall tell them that those who grow up philosophers in other cities have reason in taking no part in public labours there; for they grow up there of themselves, though none of the city governments wants them; a wild growth has its rights, it owes nurture to no one, and need not trouble to pay anyone for its food. But you we have engendered, like king bees[9] in hives, as leaders and kings over yourselves and the rest of the city; you have been better and more perfectly educated than the others, and are better able to share in both ways of life. Down you must go then, in turn, to the habitation of the others, and accustom yourselves to their darkness; for when you have grown accustomed you will see a thousand times better than those who live there, and you will know what the images are and what they are images of, because you have seen the realities behind just

---

[8]Cf. *Banquet,* p. 77, n. 3.

[9]Both the Greeks and Romans spoke always of "king," not "queen," of a hive.

and beautiful and good things. And so our city will be managed wide awake for us and for you, not in a dream, as most are now, by people fighting together for shadows, and quarrelling to be rulers, as if that were a great good. But the truth is more or less that the city where those who are to rule are least anxious to be rulers is of necessity best managed and has least faction in it; while the city which gets rulers who want it most is worst managed."

62   "Certainly," said he.

63   "Then will our fosterlings disobey us when they hear this? Will they refuse to help, each group in its turn, in the labours of the city, and want to spend most of their time dwelling in the pure air?"

64   "Impossible," said he, "for we shall only be laying just commands on just men. No, but undoubtedly each man of them will go to the ruler's place as to a grim necessity, exactly the opposite of those who now rule in cities."

65   "For the truth is, my friend," I said, "that only if you can find for your future rulers a way of life better than ruling, is it possible for you to have a well-managed city; since in that city alone those will rule who are truly rich, not rich in gold, but in that which is necessary for a happy man, the riches of a good and wise life: But if beggared and hungry, for want of goods of their own, they hasten to public affairs, thinking that they must snatch goods for themselves from there, it is not possible. Then rule becomes a thing to be fought for; and a war of such a kind, being between citizens and within them, destroys both them and the rest of the city also."

66   "Most true," said he.

67   "Well, then," said I, "have you any other life despising political office except the life of true philosophy?"

68   "No, by heaven," said he.

69   "But again," said I, "they must not go awooing office like so many lovers! If they do, their rival lovers will fight them."

70   "Of course they will!"

71   "Then what persons will you compel to accept guardianship of the city other than those who are wisest in the things which enable a city to be best managed, who also have honours of another kind and a life better than the political life?"

72   "No others," he answered.

73   "Would you like us, then, to consider next how such men are to be produced in a city, and how they shall be brought up into the light, as you know some are said to go up from Hades to heaven?"

74   "Of course I should," said he. "Remember that this, as it seems, is no spinning of a shell,[10] it's more than a game; the turning of a soul round from a day which is like night to a true day—this is the ascent into real being, which we shall say is true philosophy."

75   "Undoubtedly."

76   "We must consider, then, which of the studies has a power like that."

77   "Of course."

---

[10]A game. Boys in two groups would spin a shell, black on one side and white on the other, and according as it fell, one party would run and the other chase. The one who tossed called out, "Night or Day!"

"Then, my dear Glaucon, what study could draw the soul from the world   78
of becoming to the world of being? But stay, I have just thought of something
while speaking—surely we said that these men must of necessity be athletes of
war in their youth."

"We did say so."   79

"Then the study we seek must have something else in addition."   80

"What?"   81

"Not to be useless for men of war."   82

"Oh yes, it must," he said, "if possible."   83

"Gymnastic and music[11] we used before to educate them."   84

"That is true," said he.   85

"Gymnastic, I take it, is devoted to what becomes and perishes, for it pre-   86
sides over bodily growth and decay."

"So it appears."   87

"Then this, I suppose, could not be the study we seek."   88

"No indeed."   90

"Is it music, then, as far as we described that?"   90

"But if you remember," said he, "music was the counter-balance of gymnas-   91
tic. Music educated the guardians by habits, and taught them no science, but a
fine concord by song and a fine rhythm by tune, and the words they used had in
them qualities akin to these, whether the words were fabulous tales or true. But
a study! There was nothing in it which led to any such good as you now seek."

"Thanks for reminding me," said I. "What you say is quite accurate; it had   92
nothing of that sort in it. But, my dear man, Glaucon, what study could there
be of that sort? For all the arts and crafts were vulgar, at least we thought so."

"Certainly we did, but what study is left apart from gymnastic and music   93
and the arts and crafts?"

"Look here," I said; "if we can't find anything more outside these, let us   94
take one that extends to them all."

"Which?" he asked.   95

"This, which they have in common, which is used in addition by all arts   96
and all sciences and ways of thinking, which is one of the first things every
man must learn of necessity."

"What's that?" he asked again.   97

"Just this trifle," I said—"to distinguish between one and two and three: 98
I mean, in short, number and calculation. Is it not always true that every art
and science is forced to partake of these?"

"Most certainly," he said.   99

"Even the art of war?"   100

"So it must," said he.   101

"At least," I said, "Palamedes[12] in the plays is always making out   102
Agamemnon to be a perfectly ridiculous general. Haven't you noticed that

---

[11]In their wide meanings, of course.

[12]A chief in the Grecian army before Troy and a proverbial master of inventions. All three tragedians brought him into their plays, and he was credited with the invention of number, among
other things. Plato is bored with Palamedes.

Palamedes claims to have invented number, and with this arranged the ranks in the encampment before Troy, and counted the ships and everything else, as if they had not been counted before and as if before this Agamemnon did not know how many feet he had, as it seems if he really could not count? Then what sort of general do you think he was?"

103   "Odd enough," said he "if that was true!"

104   "Then shall we not put down this," I said, "as a study necessary for a soldier, to be able to calculate and count?"

105   "Nothing more so," said he, "if he is to understand anything at all about his own ranks, or, rather, if he is to be even anything of a man."

106   "I wonder," said I, "if you notice what *I* do about this study."

107   "And what may that be?"

108   "It is really one of those we are looking for, those which lead naturally to thinking; but no one uses it rightly, although it draws wholly towards real being."

109   "What do you mean?" he asked.

110   "I will try to explain," said I, "what I, at least, believe. Whatever points I distinguish in my own mind as leading in favour of or against what we are speaking of, pray look at them with me and agree or disagree; then we shall see more clearly if this study is what I divine it to be."

111   "Do indicate them," said he.

112   "That is what I am doing," I said. "If you observe, some things which the senses perceive do not invite the intelligence to examine them, because they seem to be judged satisfactorily by the sense; but some altogether urge it to examine them because the sense appears to produce no sound result."

Questions for Discussion and Your Reading Journal

1. How does Plato's use of dialogue contribute to his purpose of instructing his audience?
2. How does Socrates characterize the world of physical sight in the text? To what does he compare "the world of the mind" (Paragraph 35)? Which of the two would this suggest is more real, true, and good?
3. Would Socrates agree that the process of education means putting education into souls like "putting sight into blind eyes" (Paragraph 43)?
4. Who are the philosophers Socrates speaks of? Why does he feel they would make good rulers?
5. Define what the text means by "true philosophy" (Paragraph 67).

CHIEF SEATTLE

Chief Seattle (1788–1866) reputedly delivered the speech presented here as an "Environmental Statement" in which he responded to a treaty proposed by the U.S. government to buy 2 million acres of land occupied by his people for $150,000. Seattle was a Native American who, late in life, *also became known as an antiwar activist. In this essay, Seattle questions the notion that people can own land, that the Earth is a material commodity. Presenting the lifestyle of his people—the Duwamish tribe of the Puget Sound region—as communal, Seattle argues in favor of a responsible, forward-looking perspective on land use. Seattle's concerns prefigure the ethical questions raised by contemporary ecologists such as Rachel Carson.*

Although this speech has been attributed to Chief Seattle, it has been altered by a number of translators and popularizers. According to Linda Marsa in an article called "Talk Is Chief: When Seattle Spoke, Were Environmentalists Listening?" (Omni, December 1992), the speech was first written down by Henry Smith, a frontier doctor, in 1887; in the 1930s it was updated by publishers; and in 1970 a television scriptwriter incorporated elements of the speech into a documentary. Although the text contains anachronistic references, the sentiments are essentially compatible with those expressed by Seattle. Nevertheless, some scholars complain about the attribution of the speech to the Chief: " 'Native American culture is constantly being exploited and appropriated as illustrations of whatever European theory is in fashion,' says Jack Forbes, a professor of Native American studies at the University of California at Davis" (Marsa 32). As you read the speech, consider the controversy surrounding it.

Reading Rhetorically

As the headnote states, this is a speech reputedly made by Seattle in 1855 to a gathering of whites and Native-Americans. The two groups were negotiating the "sale" of tribal land around the present city of Seattle, Washington, to the whites. Chief Seattle's speech was not written down in an English translation until many years after it was delivered, and what follows may not be at all close to what he actually said. Leaving aside the issue of actual authorship, the rhetoric of the speech is grounded in a nature-centered, holistic, and interconnected view of the universe similar to what Winston King found to be characteristic of Eastern religions (see the Foreword to *Religion and Nothingness* in this chapter). Figurative language is used to express a spiritual reverence for the earth and for the natural world; the persuasive power of the rhetoric flows from this language rather than from a carefully argued theological or philosophical statement, much as in a poem. As you read, note examples of the images evoked in the statement and how effective you think they are.

Environmental Statement

How can you buy or sell the sky, the warmth of the land? The idea is 1
strange to us.

2   If we do not own the freshness of the air and the sparkle of the water, how can you buy them?

3   Every part of this earth is sacred to my people. Every shining pine needle, every sandy shore, every mist in the dark woods, every clearing and humming insect is holy in the memory and experience of my people. The sap which courses through the trees carries the memories of the red man.

4   The white man's dead forget the country of their birth when they go to walk among the stars. Our dead never forget this beautiful earth, for it is the mother of the red man. We are part of the earth and it is part of us. The perfumed flowers are our sisters; the deer, the horse, the great eagle, these are our brothers. The rocky crests, the juices in the meadows, the body heat of the pony, and man—all belong to the same family.

5   So, when the Great Chief in Washington sends word that he wishes to buy our land, he asks much of us. The Great Chief sends word he will reserve us a place so that we can live comfortably to ourselves. He will be our father and we will be his children.

6   So we will consider your offer to buy our land. But it will not be easy. For this land is sacred to us. This shining water that moves in the streams and rivers is not just water but the blood of our ancestors. If we sell you land, you must remember that it is sacred, and you must teach your children that it is sacred and that each ghostly reflection in the clear water of the lakes tells of events and memories in the life of my people. The water's murmur is the voice of my father's father.

7   The rivers are our brothers, they quench our thirst. The rivers carry our canoes, and feed our children. If we sell you our land, you must remember, and teach your children, that the rivers are our brothers and yours, and you must henceforth give the rivers the kindness you would give any brother.

8   We know that the white man does not understand our ways. One portion of land is the same to him as the next, for he is a stranger who comes in the night and takes from the land whatever he needs. The earth is not his brother, but his enemy, and when he has conquered it, he moves on. He leaves his father's grave behind, and he does not care. He kidnaps the earth from his children, and he does not care. His father's grave, and his children's birthright are forgotten. He treats his mother, the earth, and his brother, the sky, as things to be bought, plundered, sold like sheep or bright beads. His appetite will devour the earth and leave behind only a desert.

9   I do not know. Our ways are different from your ways. The sight of your cities pains the eyes of the red man. There is no quiet place in the white man's cities. No place to hear the unfurling of leaves in spring or the rustle of the insect's wings. The clatter only seems to insult the ears. And what is there to life if a man cannot hear the lonely cry of the whippoorwill or the arguments of the frogs around the pond at night? I am a red man and do not understand. The Indian prefers the soft sound of the wind darting over the face of a pond and the smell of the wind itself, cleansed by a midday rain, or scented with piñon pine.

10   The air is precious to the red man for all things share the same breath, the beast, the tree, the man, they all share the same breath. The white man does

not seem to notice the air he breathes. Like a man dying for many days he is numb to the stench. But if we sell you our land, you must remember that the air is precious to us, that the air shares its spirit with all the life it supports.

The wind that gave our grandfather his first breath also receives his last 11 sigh. And if we sell you our land, you must keep it apart and sacred as a place where even the white man can go to taste the wind that is sweetened by the meadow's flowers.

You must teach your children that the ground beneath their feet is the ashes 12 of our grandfathers. So that they will respect the land, tell your children that the earth is rich with the lives of our kin. Teach your children that we have taught our children that the earth is our mother. Whatever befalls the earth befalls the sons of the earth. If men spit upon the ground, they spit upon themselves.

This we know: The earth does not belong to man; man belongs to the 13 earth. All things are connected. We may be brothers after all. We shall see. One thing we know which the white man may one day discover: Our God is the same God.

You may think now that you own Him as you wish to own our land; but 14 you cannot. He is the God of man, and His compassion is equal for the red man and the white. This earth is precious to Him, and to harm the earth is to heap contempt on its creator. The whites too shall pass; perhaps sooner than all other tribes. Contaminate your bed and you will one night suffocate in your own waste.

But in your perishing you will shine brightly fired by the strength of the 15 God who brought you to this land and for some special purpose gave you dominion over this land and over the red man.

That destiny is a mystery to us, for we do not understand when the buffalo 16 are all slaughtered, the wild horses are tame, the secret corners of the forest heavy with scent of many men and the view of the ripe hills blotted by talking wires.

Where is the thicket? Gone. Where is the eagle? Gone. 17

The end of living and the beginning of survival. 18

Questions for Discussion and Your Reading Journal

1. To whom is Seattle's statement addressed? Why did he give the speech?
2. Why is the idea of ownership of land alien to Seattle and his people? Why is it "natural" to the white settlers?
3. The belief that the land is sacred imposes certain responsibilities on those who use the land. What are those responsibilities? Why is it important to Seattle that the white people recognize those obligations?
4. How does Seattle's use of the analogy of the family help support his main idea?
5. In what ways do Seattle's concerns look forward to the problems that contemporary ecologists point out?
6. Compare and contrast the concerns of Seattle with those of Rachel Carson in her essay "The Obligation to Endure" on page 477.
7. Review the headnote at the beginning of the article. Speculate about possible reasons for altering the speech. Evaluate the degree to which alterations may or may not be justified.

FRIEDRICH NIETZSCHE

In Friedrich Nietzsche's (1844–1900) view, one of the core dilemmas in the modern world is the profound disconnect between ancient moral codes (the Judeo-Christian tradition and others) and the realities and needs of modern life. In some ways, he was a direct descendant of Plato in his ideas about power, leadership, and the nature of "reality." He believed that "philosophers" of superior intellect and insight, whom he labeled first as "free spirits" and later ubermensch (supermen), are the ones who are best suited to lead society. He had very little confidence in democracy, since the common man could not be depended upon to make intelligent choices. His ideas of the "will to power" and, ultimately, his concept of the ubermensch, the ultimate man or superman who rises above good and evil, build upon and refine Plato's concept of the "philosopher-king." Above all, Nietzsche argued that, in a view of the human condition based upon facing the truth, there is no god and humans do not have souls. Rather, all people have some degree of a "will to power." It is this will to power that determines the rightness or wrongness of their moral and ethical conduct. According to Nietzsche, stronger, more intelligent people with a great will to power should rule over and dominate weaker, less intelligent people. For him, this was the way and the truth of the universe. Nietzsche has been called the first "existentialist."

Reading Rhetorically

Although Nietzsche follows in the same philosophical tradition as Plato, his rhetorical approach is quite different. Rather than seeking to bring the reader's own wisdom and insight to the surface and then to lead the individual toward a higher level of understanding, Nietzsche takes a much more direct approach. In the manner of classical rhetoric, his writing moves constantly from claims to proof of the claims based upon reasons and evidence. The genre of his text is closest to the personal essay form, which allows him to express an idea, then to clarify, support, and develop it. The personal essay form allows Nietzsche to write first and foremost for himself, clarifying his thought as he goes. But he also has a second audience in mind. It consists of other philosophers who share his disdain for religion and who are eager to explore moral and ethical alternatives to a god-based universe and church-based societies where religious divisions lead to great human suffering. As you read, note how his arguments appeal to this particular audience.

Excerpt from *Beyond Good and Evil*

34

At whatever standpoint of philosophy one may place oneself nowadays, 1
seen from every position, the *erroneousness* of the world in which we
think we live is the surest and most certain thing our eyes can light upon: we
find proof after proof thereof, which would fain allure us into surmises concerning a deceptive principle in the "nature of things." He, however, who
makes thinking itself, and consequently "the spirit," responsible for the false-
ness of the world—an honourable exit, which every conscious or unconscious
advocatus dei avails himself of—he who regards this world, including space,
time, form, and movement, as falsely *deduced,* would have at least good reason
in the end to become distrustful also of all thinking; has it not hitherto been
playing upon us the worst of scurvy tricks? and what guarantee would it give
that it would not continue to do what it has always been doing? In all seriousness, the innocence of thinkers has something touching and respect-inspiring in
it, which even nowadays permits them to wait upon consciousness with the
request that it will give them *honest* answers: for example whether it be "real"
or not, and why it keeps the outer world so resolutely at a distance, and other
questions of the same description. The belief in "immediate certainties" is a
moral naïveté which does honour to us philosophers; but—we have now to
cease being *"merely* moral" men! Apart from morality, such belief is a folly
which does little honour to us! If in middle-class life an ever-ready distrust is
regarded as the sign of a "bad character," and consequently as an imprudence,
here amongst us, beyond the middle-class world and its Yeas and Nays, what
should prevent our being imprudent and saying: the philosopher has at length
a *right* to "bad character," as the being who has hitherto been most befooled
on earth—he is now under *obligation* to distrustfulness, to the wickedest
squinting out of every abyss of suspicion.—Forgive me the joke of this gloomy
grimace and turn of expression; for I myself have long ago learned to think and
estimate differently with regard to deceiving and being deceived, and I keep at
least a couple of pokes in the ribs ready for the blind rage with which philosophers struggle against being deceived? Why *not?* It is nothing more than a moral
prejudice that truth is worth more than semblance; it is, in fact, the worst proved
supposition in the world. *So* much must be conceded: there could have been no
life at all except upon the basis of perspective estimates and semblances; and if,
with the virtuous enthusiasm and stupidity of many philosophers, one wished to
do away altogether with the "seeming world"—well, granted that *you* could do
that,—at least nothing of your "truth" would thereby remain! Indeed, what is it

that forces us in general to the supposition that there is an essential opposition of "true" and "false"? Is it not enough to suppose degrees of seemingness, and as it were lighter and darker shades and tones of semblance—different *valeurs*, as the painters say? Why might not the world *which concerns us*—be a fiction? And to any one who suggested: "But to a fiction belongs an originator?"—might it not be bluntly replied" *Why?* May not this "belong" also belong to the fiction? It is not at length permitted to be a little ironical towards the subject, just as towards the predicate and object? Might not the philosopher elevate himself above faith in grammar? All respect to governesses, but is it not time that philosophy should renounce governess-faith?

35

O Voltaire! O humanity! O idiocy! There is something ticklish in "the truth," and in the *search* for the truth; and if man goes about it too humanely—"*il ne cherche le vrai que pour faire le bien*"—I wager he finds nothing!

42

A new order of philosophers is appearing; I shall venture to baptize them by a name not without danger. As far as I understand them, as far as they allow themselves to be understood—for it is their nature to *wish* to remain something of a puzzle—these philosophers of the future might rightly, perhaps also wrongly, claim to be designated as *"tempters."* This name itself is after all only an attempt, or, if it be preferred, a temptation.

43

Will they be new friends of "truth," these coming philosophers? Very probably, for all philosophers hitherto have loved their truths. But assuredly they will not be dogmatists. It must be contrary to their pride, and also contrary to their taste, that their truth should still be truth for every one—that which has hitherto been the secret wish and ultimate purpose of all dogmatic efforts. "My opinion is *my* opinion: another person has not easily a right to it"—such a philosopher of the future will say, perhaps. One must renounce that bad taste of wishing to agree with many people. "Good" is no longer good when one's neighbour takes it into his mouth. And how could there be a "common good"! The expression contradicts itself; that which can be common is always of small value. In the end things must be as they are and have always been—the great things remain for the great, the abysses for the profound, the delicacies and thrills for the refined, and, to sum up shortly, everything rare for the rare.

44

Need I say expressly after all this that they will be free, *very* free spirits, these philosophers of the future—as certainly also they will not be merely free spirits, but something more, higher, greater, and fundamentally different, which does not wish to be misunderstood and mistaken? But while I say this, I feel under *obligation* almost as much to them as to ourselves (we free spirits who are their heralds and forerunners), to sweep away from ourselves altogether a stupid old prejudice and misunderstanding, which, like a fog, has too long made the conception of "free spirit" obscure. In every country of Europe, and the same in America, there is at present something which makes an abuse of this name: a very narrow, prepossessed, enchained class of spirits, who desire almost the opposite of what our intentions and instincts prompt—not to mention that in respect to the *new* philosophers who are appearing, they must still more be closed windows and bolted doors. Briefly and regrettably, they belong to the *levellers,* these wrongly named "free spirits"—as glib-tongued and scribe-fingered slaves of the democratic taste and its "modern ideas": all of them men without solitude, without personal solitude, blunt, honest fellows to whom neither courage nor honourable conduct ought to be denied; only, they are not free, and are ludicrously superficial, especially in their innate partiality for seeing the cause of almost *all* human misery and failure in the old forms in which society has hitherto existed—a notion which happily inverts the truth entirely! What they would fain attain with all their strength, is the universal, green-meadow happiness of the herd, together with security, safety, comfort, and alleviation of life for every one; their two most frequently chanted songs and doctrines are called "Equality of Rights" and "Sympathy with all Sufferers"—and suffering itself is looked upon by them as something which must be *done away with.* We opposite ones, however, who have opened our eye and conscience to the question how and where the plant "man" has hitherto grown most vigorously, believe that this has always taken place under the opposite conditions, that for this end the dangerousness of his situation had to be increased enormously, his inventive faculty and dissembling power (his "spirit") had to develop into subtlety and daring under long oppression and compulsion, and his Will to Life had to be increased to the unconditioned Will to Power:—we believe that severity, violence, slavery, danger in the street and in the heart, secrecy, stoicism, tempter's art and devilry of every kind,—that everything wicked, terrible, tyrannical, predatory, and serpentine in man, serves as well for the elevation of the human species as its opposite:—we do not even say enough when we only say *this much*; and in any case we find ourselves here, both with our speech and our science, at the *other* extreme of all modern ideology and gregarious desirability, as their antipodes perhaps? What wonder that we "free spirits" are not exactly the most communicative spirits? that we do not wish to betray in every respect *what* a spirit can free itself from, and *where* perhaps it will then be driven? And as to the import of the dangerous formula, "Beyond Good and Evil," with which we at least avoid confusion, we *are* something else than *"libres-penseurs," "liberi pensatori,"* "freethinkers," and whatever these honest advocates of "modern ideas" like to call themselves. Having been at home, or at least guests, in many realms of the spirit; having escaped again and again from the gloomy, agreeable nooks in which preferences and prejudices, youth, origin, the accident of men and books, or even the weariness of travel seemed to confine us; full of malice against the seductions of dependency which lie concealed in honours, money, positions, or exaltation of the senses; grateful even for distress and the vicissitudes of illness, because they always free us from some rule, and its "prejudice," grateful to the God, devil, sheep, and worm in us; inquisitive to a fault, investigators to the point of cruelty, with unhesitating fingers for the intangible, with teeth and stomachs for the most indigestible, ready for any business that requires sagacity and acute senses, ready for every adventure, owing to an excess of "free will"; with anterior and posterior souls, into the ultimate intentions of which it is difficult to pry, with foregrounds and backgrounds to the end of which no foot may run; hidden ones under the mantles of light, appropriators, although we resemble heirs and spendthrifts, arrangers and collectors from morning till night, misers of our wealth and our full-crammed drawers, economical in learning and forgetting, inventive in scheming; sometimes proud of tables of categories, sometimes pedants, sometimes night-owls of work even in full day; yea, if necessary; even scarecrows—and it is necessary nowadays, that is to say, inasmuch as we are the born, sworn, jealous friends of *solitude,* of our own profoundest midnight and mid-day solitude:—such kind of men are we, we free spirits! And perhaps *ye* are also something of the same kind, ye coming ones, ye *new* philosophers?

Questions for Discussion and Your Reading Journal

1. What is the first major claim that Nietzsche makes in the opening paragraph of this reading? What evidence does he give in subsequent sentences to convince you of his claim? Are you convinced? Why or why not?
2. In Section 35, the French sentence means "He only seeks the truth to do good with it." Does Nietzsche seem to be in favor of this approach? Explain.
3. In Section 42, Nietzsche speaks of a "new order of philosophers" that is coming. In Section 44, what does he mean when he calls these philosophers of the future "free spirits"?
4. In one paragraph, sum up the qualities he suggests that the "free spirit" philosophers of the future will have.

JEAN-PAUL SARTRE

Jean-Paul Sartre (1905–1980) was a French novelist and playwright, also known as a proponent of the philosophy of existentialism. He described his childhood as lonely; be lost his father early and grew up in the home of his maternal grandfather, mocked by children his age because he was cross-eyed. He attended the prestigious École Normale Supérieure in Paris and taught for many years in French secondary schools. Rejecting what he called the "bourgeois" institution of marriage, he formed a long-lasting relationship with the writer Simone de Beauvoir; the two of them founded and edited Les Temps Modernes, *a monthly review. His philosophical work* Being and Nothingness *(1943) is one of his best-*

known, along with his plays (such as "No Exit," 1946) and his studies of French writer Jean Genet. He was awarded the Nobel Prize for literature in 1964 but declined it. It is important for non-European readers to understand that Sartre's ideas on existentialism were formulated amid the tremendous social chaos brought about by two world wars, which decimated the population and ruined the economies of entire nations. Like the nihilists of the late 19th century, many of whom lived through the suffering caused by such chaos, he came to doubt the existence of a divine being. But while existentialists agree with nihilists that there is no divine power guiding earthly matters, they choose a radically different path in assessing what humans must do as a result. Existentialists insist that individuals must assume the moral responsibility for shaping their own lives, as Sartre explains in the selection reprinted here.

Reading Rhetorically

Sartre follows in the tradition of Nietzsche in terms of ideas. Nietzsche was one of the first European philosophers to state that "God is dead." With this as a beginning point, Nietzsche and other European philosophers began to fashion a philosophy of human existence that came into full blossom with Sartre under the name of existentialism. Sartre's rhetorical approach is similar to that of Nietzsche, and both follow the model of the classical Greek philosophers and rhetoricians. Sartre takes this rhetorical form to a new high, however, combining the constant movement from claim to supporting reasons and evidence with the rhetorical questioning that is a common feature in Plato's work. Note how he pauses to ask the reader, "But what do we mean by this?" thereby pulling the reader into a larger conversation about ideas and the nature of human existence. His use of down-to-earth examples makes his work much more accessible to the common reader. Indeed, it is his appeal to such common readers that most distinguishes Sartre's writing from that of Nietzsche. Sartre seeks to communicate his ideas clearly and unambiguously to the very masses that Nietzsche despised and avoided. This appeal to average people made him one of the most popular and admired philosophers of the 20th century.

Existentialism

A theistic existentialism, which I represent, . . . states that if God does not   1
exist, there is at least one being in whom existence precedes essence, a being who exists before he can be defined by any concept, and that this being is man, or, as Heidegger says, human reality. What is meant here by saying that existence precedes essence? It means that, first of all, man exists, turns up, appears on the scene, and, only afterwards, defines himself. If man, as the existentialist conceives him, is indefinable, it is because at first he is nothing. Only afterward will he be something, and he himself will have made what he will

be. Thus, there is no human nature, since there is no God to conceive it. Not only is man what he conceives himself to be, but he is also only what he wills himself to be after this thrust toward existence.

2   Man is nothing else but what he makes of himself. Such is the first principle of existentialism. It is also what is called subjectivity. But what do we mean by this, if not that man has a greater dignity than a stone or table? For we mean that man first exists, that is, that man first of all is the being who hurls himself toward a future and who is conscious of imaging himself as being in the future. Man is at the start a plan which is aware of itself, rather than a patch of moss, a piece of garbage, or a cauliflower; nothing exists prior to this plan; there is nothing in heaven; man will be what he will have planned to be. Not what he will want to be. Because by the word "will" we generally mean a conscious decision, which is subsequent to what we have already made of ourselves. I may want to belong to a political party, write a book, get married; but all that is only a manifestation of an earlier, more spontaneous choice that is called "will." But if existence really does precede essence, man is responsible for what he is. Thus, existentialism's first move is to make every man aware of what he is and to make the full responsibility of his existence rest on him. And when we say that a man is responsible for himself, we do not only mean that he is responsible for his own individuality, but that he is responsible for all men.

3   The word "subjectivism" has two meanings. Subjectivism means, on the one hand, that an individual chooses and makes himself; and, on the other, that it is impossible for man to transcend human subjectivity. The second of these is the essential meaning of existentialism. When we say that man chooses his own self, we mean that every one of us does likewise; but we also mean by that that in making this choice he also chooses all men. In fact, in creating the man that we want to be, there is not a single one of our acts which does not at the same time create an image of man as we think he ought to be. To choose to be this or that is to affirm at the same time the value of what we choose, because we can never choose evil. We always choose the good, and nothing can be good for us without being good for all.

4   If, on the other hand, existence precedes essence, and if we grant that we exist and fashion our image at one and the same time, the image is valid for everybody and for our whole age. Thus, our responsibility is much greater than we might have supposed, because it involves all mankind. If I am workingman and choose to join a Christian trade union rather than be a Communist, and if by being a member, I want to show that the best thing for a man is resignation, that the kingdom of man is not of this world, I am not only involving my own case—I want to be resigned for everyone. As a result, my action has involved all humanity. To take a more individual matter, if I want to marry, to have children, even if this marriage depends solely on my own circumstances or passion or wish, I am involving all humanity in monogamy and not merely myself. Therefore, I am responsible for myself and for everyone else. I am creating a certain image of man of my own choosing. In choosing myself, I choose man.

5   The existentialist thinks it very distressing that God does not exist, because all possibility of finding values in a heaven of ideas disappears along

with Him; there can no longer be an a priori Good, since there is no infinite and perfect consciousness to think it. Nowhere is it written that the good exists, that we must be honest, that we must not lie; because the fact is we are on a plane where there are only men. Dostoievsky said, "If God didn't exist, everything would be possible." That is the very standing point of existentialism. Indeed, everything is permissible if God does not exist, and as a result man is forlorn, because neither within him or without does he find anything to cling to. He can't start making excuses for himself.

If existence really does precede essence, there is no explaining things away 6 by reference to a fixed and given nature. In other words, there is no determinism, man is free, man is freedom. On the other hand, if God does not exist, we find no values or commands to turn to which legitimize our conduct. So, in the bright realm of values, we have no excuse behind us, nor justification before us. We are alone, with no excuses.

That is the idea I shall try to convey when I say that man is condemned to 7 be free. Condemned, because he did not create himself, yet, in other respects is free; because, once thrown into the world, he is responsible for everything he does.

To give you an example which will enable you to understand forlornness 8 better, I shall cite the case of one of my students who came to see me under the following circumstances: His father was on bad terms with his mother, and, moreover, was inclined to be a collaborationist, his older brother had been killed in the German offensive of 1940, and the young man, with somewhat immature but generous feelings, wanted to avenge him. His mother lived alone with him, very much upset by the half-treason of her husband and the death of her older son; the boy was her only consolation.

The boy was faced with the choice of leaving for England and joining the 9 Free French forces—that is, leaving his mother behind—or remaining with his mother and helping her to carry on. He was fully aware that the woman lived only for him and that his going off—and perhaps his death—would plunge her into despair. He was also aware that every act that he did for his mother's sake was a sure thing, in the sense that it was helping her to carry on, whereas every effort he made toward going off and fighting was an uncertain move which might run aground and prove completely useless; for example, on his way to England he might, while passing through Spain, be detained indefinitely in a Spanish camp; he might reach England or Algiers and be stuck in an office at a desk job. As a result, he was faced with two very different kinds of action: one, concrete, immediate, but concerning only one individual; the other concerned an incomparably vaster group, a national collectivity, but for that very reason was dubious, and might be interrupted en route. And, at the same time, he was wavering between two kinds of ethics. On the one hand, an ethics of sympathy, of personal devotion; on the other, a broader ethics, but one whose efficacy was more dubious. He had to choose between the two.

Who could help him choose? Christian doctrine? No. Christian doctrine 10 says, "Be charitable, love your neighbor, take the more rugged path, etc., etc." But which is the more rugged path? Whom should he love as a brother? The fighting man or his mother? Which does the greater good, the vague act of fighting in a group, or the concrete one of helping a particular human being to go on living? Who can decide a priori? Nobody. No book of ethics can tell him. The Kantian ethics says, "Never treat any person as a means, but as an end." Very well, if I stay with my mother, I'll treat her as an end and not as a means; but by virtue of this very fact, I'm running the risk of treating the people around me who are fighting, as means; and conversely, if I go to join those who are fighting, I'll be treating them as an end, and, by doing that, I run the risk of treating my mother as a means.

11   If values are vague, and if they are always too broad for the concrete and specific case that we are considering, the only thing left for us is to trust our instincts. That's what this young man tried to do; and when I saw him, he said, "In the end, feeling is what counts. I ought to choose whichever pushes me in one direction. If I feel that I love my mother enough to sacrifice everything else for her—my desire for vengeance, for action, for adventure—then I'll stay with her. If, on the contrary, I feel that my love for my mother isn't enough, I'll leave."

12   But how is the value of a feeling determined? What gives his feeling for his mother value? Precisely the fact that he remained with her. I may say that I like so-and-so well enough to sacrifice a certain amount of money for him, but I may say so only if I've done it. I may say "I love my mother well enough to remain with her" if I have remained with her. The only way to determine the value of this affection is, precisely, to perform an act which confirms and defines it. But, since I require this affection to justify my act, I find myself caught in a vicious circle.

13   Given that men are free and that tomorrow they will freely decide what man will be, I cannot be sure that, after my death, fellow-fighters will carry on my work to bring it to its maximum perfection. Tomorrow, after my death, some men may decide to set up Fascism, and the others may be cowardly and muddled enough to let them do it. Fascism will then be the human reality, so much the worse for us.

14   Actually, things will be as man will have decided they are to be. Does that mean that I should abandon myself to quietism? No. first, I should involve myself; then, act on the old saw, "Nothing ventured, nothing gained." Nor does it mean that I shouldn't belong to a party, but rather that I shall have no illusions and shall do what I can. For example, suppose I ask myself, "Will socialization, as such, ever come about?" I know nothing about it. All I know is that I'm going to do everything in my power to bring it about. Beyond that, I can't count on anything. Quietism is the attitude of people who say, "Let others do what I can't do." The doctrine I am presenting is the very opposite of quietism, since it declares, "There is no reality except in action." Moreover, it goes further, since it adds, "Man is nothing else than his plan; he exists only to the extent that he fulfills himself; he is therefore nothing else than the ensemble of his acts, nothing else than his life."

15   Now, for the existentialist there is really no love other than one which manifests itself in a person's being in love. There is no genius other than one which is expressed in works of art; the genius of Proust is the sum of Proust's works; the genius of Racine is his series of tragedies. Outside of that, there is nothing. Why say that Racine could have written another tragedy, when he

didn't write it? A man is involved in life, leaves his impress on it, and outside of that there is nothing. To be sure, this may seem a harsh thought to someone whose life hasn't been a success. But, on the other hand, it prompts people to understand that reality alone is what counts, that dreams, expectations, and hopes warrant no more than to define a man as a disappointed dream, as miscarried hopes, as vain expectations. In other words, to define him negatively and not positively. However, when we say, "You are nothing else than your life," that does not imply that the artist will be judged solely on the basis of his works of art; a thousand other things will contribute toward summing him up. What we mean is that a man is nothing else than a series of undertakings, that he is the sum, the organization, the ensemble of the relationships which make up these undertakings.

When all is said and done, what we are accused of, at bottom, is not our 16 pessimism, but an optimistic toughness. If people throw up to us our works of fiction in which we write about people who are soft, weak, cowardly, and sometimes even downright bad, it's not because these people are soft, weak, cowardly, or bad; because if we were to say, as Zola did, that they are that way because of heredity, the workings of environment, society, because of biological or psychological determinism, people would be reassured. They would say, "Well, that's what we're like, no one can do anything about it." But when the existentialist writes about a coward, he says that this coward is responsible for his cowardice. He's not like that because he has a cowardly heart or lung or brain; he's not like that on account of his physiological make-up; but he's like that because he has made himself a coward by his acts. There's no such thing as a cowardly constitution; there are nervous constitutions; there is poor blood, as the common people say, or strong constitutions. But the man whose blood is poor is not a coward on that account, for what makes cowardice is the act of renouncing or yielding. A constitution is not an act; the coward is defined on the basis of the acts he performs. People feel, in a vague sort of way, that this coward we're talking about is guilty of being a coward, and the thought frightens them. What people would like is that a coward or a hero be born that way.

Existentialism is nothing else than an attempt to draw all the consequences 17 of a coherent atheistic position. It isn't trying to plunge man into despair at all. But if one calls every attitude of unbelief despair, like the Christians, then the word is not being used in its original sense. Existentialism isn't so atheistic that it wears itself out showing that God doesn't exist. Rather, it declares that even if God did exist, that would change nothing. There you've got our point of view. Not that we believe that God exists, but we think that the problem of His existence is not the issue. In this sense existentialism is optimistic, a doctrine of action, and it is plain dishonesty for Christians to make no distinction between their own despair and ours and then to call us despairing.

Questions for Discussion and Your Reading Journal

1. How does Sartre explain the concept "existence precedes essence" (Paragraph 1)?

2. Atheistic existentialism presupposes that there is no divine creator with a predetermined plan already established for the human race. Who, then, would Sartre say is responsible for what humans are and for what their purpose in existence is?

3. In your opinion, how might Sartre fit into Plato's "The Allegory of the Cave" (p. 684)?

4. Would you agree that this essay is in the form of an argument? If so, who might be the audience that Sartre wishes to persuade? Does he give any indications of who might be in opposition to his point of view?

PAUL DAVIES

Paul Davies (1946–) was born in London and currently holds concurrent teaching positions in physics and natural philosophy at Imperial College London; the University of Queensland, Australia; and Macquarie University, Australia. In addition to his work as a teacher, he is a prolific writer, a television presence, and a radio personality—all in his role as master scientist. Work in physics and astrobiology has brought him the honor of having an asteroid named after him (labeled 6870 Pauldavies). One of the most significant and unusual honors for a scientist came to him in 1995 when he was awarded the British Templeton Prize for progress in religion, the world's largest prize of intellectual achievement.

Reading Rhetorically

It quickly becomes clear in the following reading that Davies has long experience writing and speaking about science to nonscientists. As he seeks to clarify common ground between the scientific method and mysticism, he does so in a manner that is largely free of specialized jargon and complex terminology. When he brings in quotes from other authors, he warns us of their difficult language and then takes pains to clarify after each quote the key points that he draws from them. It is this constant use of expert sources as evidence for his own major points that most identifies Davies' approach as rooted in the scientific rhetoric and traditions of the Western world. He goes to great pains first to establish the main point or thesis of the reading and then to develop and support this thesis with a great deal of evidence. As you read, note how he builds his own *ethos* as a writer.

Excerpt from *The Mind of God*

MYSTICAL KNOWLEDGE

1 Most scientists have a deep mistrust of mysticism. This is not surprising, as mystical thought lies at the opposite extreme to rational thought,

which is the basis of the scientific method. Also, mysticism tends to be confused with the occult, the paranormal, and other fringe beliefs. In fact, many of the world's finest thinkers, including some notable scientists such as Einstein, Pauli, Schrödinger, Heisenberg, Eddington, and Jeans, have also espoused mysticism. My own feeling is that the scientific method should be pursued as far as it possibly can. Mysticism is no substitute for scientific inquiry and logical reasoning so long as this approach can be consistently applied. It is only in dealing with ultimate questions that science and logic may fail us. I am not saying that science and logic are likely to provide the wrong answers, but they may be incapable of addressing the sort of "why" (as opposed to "how") questions we want to ask.

The expression "mystical experience" is often used by religious people, or 2 those who practice meditation. These experiences, which are undoubtedly real enough for the person who experiences them, are said to be hard to convey in words. Mystics frequently speak of an overwhelming sense of being at one with the universe or with God, of glimpsing a holistic vision of reality, or of being in the presence of a powerful and loving influence. Most important, mystics claim that they can grasp *ultimate reality* in a single experience, in contrast to the long and tortuous deductive sequence (petering out in turtle trouble) of the logical-scientific method of inquiry. Sometimes the mystical path seems to involve little more than an inner sense of peace—"a compassionate, joyful stillness that lies beyond the activity of busy minds," was the way a physicist colleague once described it to me. Einstein spoke of a "cosmic religious feeling" that inspired his reflections on the order and harmony of nature. Some scientists, most notably the physicists Brian Josephson and David Bohm, believe that regular mystical insights achieved by quiet meditative practices can be a useful guide in the formulation of scientific theories.

In other cases mystical experiences seem to be more direct and revelatory. 3 Russell Stannard writes of the impression of facing an overpowering force of some kind, "of a nature to command respect and awe. . . . There is a sense of urgency about it; the power is volcanic, pent up, ready to be unleashed." Science writer David Peat describes "a remarkable feeling of intensity that seems to flood the whole world around us with meaning. . . . We sense that we are touching something universal and perhaps eternal, so that the particular moment in time takes on a numinous character and seems to expand in time without limit. We sense that all boundaries between ourselves and the outer world vanish, for what we are experiencing lies beyond all categories and all attempts to be captured in logical thought."

The language used to describe these experiences usually reflects the culture 4 of the individual concerned. Western mystics tend to emphasize the personal quality of the presence, often describing themselves as being with someone, usually God, who is different from themselves but with whom a deep bond is felt. There is, of course, a long tradition of such religious experiences in the Christian Church and among the other Western religions. Eastern mystics emphasize the wholeness of existence and tend to identify themselves more closely with the presence. Writer Ken Wilber describes the Eastern mystical experience in characteristically cryptic language:

5   In the mystical consciousness, Reality is apprehended directly and immediately, meaning without any mediation, any symbolic elaboration, any
conceptualization, or any abstractions; subject and object become one in
a timeless and spaceless act that is beyond any and all forms of mediation.
Mystics universally speak of contacting reality in its "suchness", its
"isness", its "thatness", without any intermediaries; beyond words, symbols, names, thoughts, images.

6   The essence of the mystical experience, then, is a type of shortcut to truth,
a direct and unmediated contact with a perceived ultimate reality. According
to Rudy Rucker:

7   The central teaching of mysticism is this: *Reality is One.* The practice of
mysticism consists in finding ways to experience this unity directly. The
One has variously been called the Good, God, the Cosmos, the Mind, the
Void, or (perhaps most neutrally) the Absolute. No door in the
labyrinthine castle of science opens directly onto the Absolute. But if one
understands the maze well enough, it is possible to jump out of the system
and experience the Absolute for oneself. . . . But, ultimately, mystical
knowledge is attained all at once or not at all. There is no gradual
path. . . .

8   In chapter 6 I described how some scientists and mathematicians claim to
have had sudden revelatory insights akin to such mystical experiences. Roger
Penrose describes mathematical inspiration as a sudden "breaking through"
into a Platonic realm. Rucker reports that Kurt Gödel also spoke of the "other
relation to reality," by which he could directly perceive mathematical objects,
such as infinity. Gödel himself was apparently able to achieve this by adopting
meditative practices, such as closing off the other senses and lying down in a
quiet place. For other scientists the revelatory experience happens spontaneously, in the midst of the daily clamor. Fred Hoyle relates such an incident
that occurred to him while he was driving through the North of England.
"Rather as the revelation occurred to Paul on the Road to Damascus, mine
occurred on the road over Bowes Moor." Hoyle and his collaborator Jayant
Narlikar had, in the late 1960s, been working on a cosmological theory of
electromagnetism that involved some daunting mathematics. One day, as they
were struggling over a particularly complicated integral, Hoyle decided to take
a vacation from Cambridge to join some colleagues hiking in the Scottish
Highlands.

9   As the miles slipped by I turned the quantum mechanical problem . . .
over in my mind, in the hazy way I normally have in thinking mathematics in my head. Normally, I have to write things down on paper, and then
fiddle with the equations and integrals as best I can. But somewhere on
Bowes Moor my awareness of the mathematics clarified, not a little, not
even a lot, but as if a huge brilliant light had suddenly been switched on.
How long did it take to become totally convinced that the problem was
solved? Less than five seconds. It only remained to make sure that before
the clarity faded I had enough of the essential steps stored safely in my

recallable memory. It is indicative of the measure of certainty I felt that in the ensuing days I didn't trouble to commit anything to paper. When ten days or so later I returned to Cambridge I found it possible to write out the thing without difficulty.

Hoyle also reports a conversation on the topic of revelation with Richard   10
Feynman:

> Some years ago I had a graphic description from Dick Feynman of what a   11
> moment of inspiration feels like, and of it being followed by an enormous
> sense of euphoria, lasting for maybe two or three days. I asked how often
> had it happened, to which Feynman replied 'four', at which we both
> agreed that twelve days of euphoria was not a great reward for a lifetime's
> work.

I have recounted Hoyle's experience here rather than in chapter 6 because   12
he himself describes it as a truly religious (as opposed to a merely Platonic)
event. Hoyle believes that the organization of the cosmos is controlled by a
"superintelligence" who guides its evolution through quantum processes, an
idea I mentioned briefly in chapter 7. Furthermore, Hoyle's is a teleological
God (somewhat like that of Aristotle or Teilhard de Chardin) directing the
world toward a final state in the infinite future. Hoyle believes that by acting
at the quantum level this superintelligence can implant thoughts or ideas from
the future, ready-made, into the human brain. This, he suggests, is the origin
of both mathematical and musical inspiration.

THE INFINITE

In our quest for ultimate answers it is hard not to be drawn, in one way or   13
another, to the infinite. Whether it is an infinite tower of turtles, an infinity of
parallel worlds, an infinite set of mathematical propositions, or an infinite Creator, physical existence surely cannot be rooted in anything finite. Western religions have a long tradition of identifying God with the Infinite, whereas Eastern philosophy seeks to eliminate the differences between the One and the
Many, and to identify the Void and the Infinite—zero and infinity.

When the early Christian thinkers such as Plotinus proclaimed that God is   14
infinite, they were primarily concerned to demonstrate that he is not limited in
any way. The mathematical concept of infinity was at that time still fairly
vague. It was generally believed that infinity is a limit toward which an enu-
meration may proceed, but which is unachievable in reality. Even Aquinas,
who conceded God's infinite nature, was not prepared to accept that infinity
had more than a potential, as opposed to an actual, existence. An omnipotent
God "cannot make an absolutely unlimited thing," he maintained.

The belief that infinity was paradoxical and self-contradictory persisted   15
until the nineteenth century. At this stage the mathematician Georg Cantor,
while investigating problems of trigonometry, finally succeeded in providing a
rigorous logical demonstration of the self-consistency of the actually infinite.
Cantor had a rough ride with his peers, and was dismissed by some eminent

mathematicians as a madman. In fact, he did suffer mental illness. But eventually the rules for the consistent manipulation of infinite numbers, though often strange and counterintuitive, came to be accepted. Indeed, much of twentieth-century mathematics is founded on the concept of the infinite (or infinitesimal).

16 If infinity can be grasped and manipulated using rational thought, does this open the way to an understanding of the ultimate explanation of things without the need for mysticism? No, it doesn't. To see why, we must take a look at the concept of infinity more closely.

17 One of the surprises of Cantor's work is that there is not just one infinity but a multiplicity of them. For example, the set of all integers and the set of all fractions are both infinite sets. One feels intuitively that there are more fractions than integers, but this is not so. On the other hand, the set of all decimals is bigger than the set of all fractions, or all integers. One can ask: is there a "biggest" infinity? Well, how about combining all infinite sets together into one superduperset. The class of all possible sets has been called Cantor's Absolute. There is one snag. This entity is not itself a set, for if it were it would by definition include itself. But self-referential sets run smack into Russell's paradox.

18 And here we encounter once more the Gödelian limits to rational thought—the mystery at the end of the universe. We cannot know Cantor's Absolute, or any other Absolute, by rational means, for any Absolute, being a Unity and hence complete within itself, must include itself. As Rucker remarks in connection with the Mindscape—the class of all sets of ideas—"If the Mindscape is a One, then it is a member of itself, and thus can only be known through a flash of mystical vision. No rational thought is a member of itself, so no rational thought could tie the Mindscape into a One."[11]

WHAT IS MAN?

"I do not feel like an alien in this universe."

—FREEMAN DYSON

19 Does the frank admission of hopelessness discussed in the previous section mean that all metaphysical reasoning is valueless? Should we adopt the approach of the pragmatic atheist who is content to take the universe as given, and get on with cataloguing its properties? There is no doubt that many scientists are opposed temperamentally to any form of metaphysical, let alone mystical arguments. They are scornful of the notion that there might exist a God, or even an impersonal creative principle or ground of being that would underpin reality and render its contingent aspects less starkly arbitrary. Personally I do not share their scorn. Although many metaphysical and theistic theories seem contrived or childish, they are not obviously more absurd than the belief that the universe exists, and exists in the form it does, reasonlessly.

It seems at least worth trying to construct a metaphysical theory that reduces some of the arbitrariness of the world. But in the end a rational explanation for the world in the sense of a closed and complete system of logical truths is almost certainly impossible. We are barred from ultimate knowledge, from ultimate explanation, by the very rules of reasoning that prompt us to seek such an explanation in the first place. If we wish to progress beyond, we have to embrace a different concept of "understanding" from that of rational explanation. Possibly the mystical path is a way to such an understanding. I have never had a mystical experience myself, but I keep an open mind about the value of such experiences. Maybe they provide the only route beyond the limits to which science and philosophy can take us, the only possible path to the Ultimate.

The central theme that I have explored in this book is that, through sci- 20 ence, we human beings are able to grasp at least some of nature's secrets. We have cracked part of the cosmic code. Why this should be, just why *Homo sapiens* should carry the spark of rationality that provides the key to the universe, is a deep enigma. We, who are children of the universe—animated stardust—can nevertheless reflect on the nature of the same universe, even to the extent of glimpsing the rules on which it runs. How we have become linked into this cosmic dimension is a mystery. Yet the linkage cannot be denied.

What does it mean? What is Man that we might be party to such privi- 21 lege? I cannot believe that our existence in this universe is a mere quirk of fate, an accident of history, an incidental blip in the great cosmic drama. Our involvement is too intimate. The physical species *Homo* may count for nothing, but the existence of mind in some organism on some planet in the universe is surely a fact of fundamental significance. Through conscious beings the universe has generated self-awareness. This can be no trivial detail, no minor byproduct of mindless, purposeless forces. We are truly meant to be here.

Questions for Discussion and Your Reading Journal

1. What is Davies' thesis in the first paragraph of the reading? Which approach does he indicate is best suited to addressing the "why" questions that scientists often want to ask?
2. Sum up in one or two sentences what Davies means by "mystical experience."
3. What example does Davies give to support his claim: "The language used to describe these experiences usually reflects the culture of the individual concerned"?
4. Give an example of how mysticism has helped a scientist solve a complex problem, according to Davies.
5. In the third paragraph from the end, Davies acknowledges that he has never personally had a mystical experience. What reasons does he give for taking an interest in such experiences?

THE MIDDLE EAST

SOLOMON

Solomon (970–930 BCE) was among the greatest of the Hebrew Kings, and a biblical account of his life is chronicled in Second Samuel and First and Second Kings in the sacred writings of the Tanak (called the Old Testament by Christians). His original name was Jedidiah and he was the son of the Hebrew King David, who slew the giant Goliath as a young man. His mother was the renowned Queen Bathsheba, a wise and articulate figure in the Tanak in her own right. Although Solomon was a despot whose heavy-handed rule alienated a large portion of his people, he was also shrewd enough to establish powerful alliances with the Egyptians to the south of his kingdom and with the Phoenicians to the north. Through valuable political alliances such as these and trade, his reign marks a high point in Jewish cultural heritage. Solomon extended the kingdom in size, built many new cities, and commissioned the construction of the first great temple in Jerusalem. He was also credited by his people and by generations afterward for his wisdom. The Proverbs that follow are ascribed to him. They are one of the earliest examples of the "wisdom literature" genre that includes other writings from this chapter, such as those of Buddha, Confucius, Lao-tzu, and Plato.

Reading Rhetorically

"Proverbs" are pithy, short sayings that communicate what a given people consider a basic truth of life. Proverbs are often moral in nature, but they are distinguished from statements of religious doctrine or theology by their earthy, practical nature. They are not spiritual laws or commandments but, rather, are intended to persuade us that certain ideas and courses of action are preferable to or wiser than others. The ancient Hebrew prophets and spiritual leaders produced one of the most voluminous collections of laws known to mankind. They gave their followers 613 laws covering everything from proper diet and eating to respect of the Sabbath, to dress and grooming, and to proper worship rituals. They cover so much territory that the 63 books of the *Talmud* are devoted simply to interpreting Jewish law. Because Solomon was a king, not a prophet, the work ascribed to him departs from the legalistic tradition. In the Proverbs, Solomon (and others who contributed after his death to the collection of wise sayings carrying his name) is seeking to advise us, not to convince us as Plato seeks to do. The Proverbs were developed orally and later written down for a clearly defined and narrow audience, the Jewish people. Because this audience could be counted upon to share a specific range of ideas and values concerning God, the meaning of life, and their human identities, it would have been assumed that "wise" people would naturally see the beneficial courses of action implied by each proverb. Anyone who was not convinced by the message of a proverb, or who simply did not understand it, risked being considered a fool. Ultimately, the purpose of this kind of wisdom literature is not so much to convince as it is to get listeners and readers to see the link between their own values and the life-shaping behaviors, positive or negative, that result from these values.

The Proverbs

ON EDUCATION

"The fear of the Lord is the beginning of knowledge: *but* fools despise wisdom and instruction." (1:7)

"The fear of the Lord is the beginning of wisdom: and the knowledge of the holy is understanding." (9:10)

"For the Lord giveth wisdom: out of his mouth cometh knowledge and understanding. He layeth up sound wisdom for the righteous: he is a buckler to them that walk uprightly." (2:6–7)

"The Lord by wisdom hath founded the earth; by understanding hath he established the heavens." (3:19)

"Wisdom is the principal thing; therefore get wisdom: and with all thy getting, get understanding." (4:7)

"The wise in heart will receive commandments: but a prating fool shall fall." (10:8)

"My son, forget not my law; but let thine heart keep my commandments. . . . Let not mercy and truth forsake thee: bind them about thy neck; write them upon the table of thine heart. . . . Trust in the Lord with all thine heart; and lean not unto thine own understanding. In all thy ways acknowledge him, and he shall direct thy paths. . . ." (3:1, 3, 5–6)

"Receive my instruction, and not silver; and knowledge rather than choice gold. For wisdom is better than rubies; and all the things that may be desired are not to be compared to it." (8:10–11)

ON ECONOMIC MATTERS

"Honor the Lord with thy substance, and with the first-fruits of all thine increase [make offerings]: So shall thy barns be filled with plenty, and thy presses shall burst out with new wine." (3:9–10)

"He becometh poor that dealeth with a slack hand: but the hand of the diligent maketh rich. He that gathereth in summer is a wise son: but he that sleepeth in harvest is a son that causeth shame." (10:4–5)

"A gracious woman retaineth honor: and strong men retain riches." (11:16)

"Riches profit not in the day of wrath: but righteousness delivereth from death." (11:4)

"Wealth gotten by vanity shall be diminished: but he that gathereth by labor shall increase." (13:11)

"A good name is rather to be chosen than great riches, and loving favour rather than silver and gold." (22:1)

"Labor not to be rich . . . for riches certainly make themselves wings; they fly away as an eagle toward heaven." (23:4–5)

ON FILIAL PIETY

"My son, hear the instruction of thy father, and forsake not the law of thy mother: for they shall be an ornament of grace unto thy head and chains about thy neck." (1:8–9)

"My son, despise not the chastening of the Lord; neither be weary of his correction: For whom the Lord loveth he correcteth: even as a father the son in whom he delighteth." (3:11–12)

"Hearken unto thy father that begat thee, and despise not thy mother when she is old." (23:22)

ON THE IDEAL PERSON ("WISE MAN")

". . . rebuke a wise man, and he will love thee. Give instruction to a wise man, and he will be yet wise: teach a just man, and he will increase in learning." (9:8–9)

"The wise in heart will receive commandments: but a prating fool shall fall." (10:8)

"A wise man is strong; yea a man of knowledge increaseth strength. For by wise counsel thou shalt make thy war: and in multitude of counsellers there is safety." (24:5–6)

ON VIRTUE

"My son, if sinners entice thee, consent thou not." (1:10)

"My son, attend unto my wisdom . . . that thou mayest regard discretion, and that thy lips may keep knowledge. For the lips of a strange woman drip as a honeycomb, and her mouth is smoother than oil: But her end is bitter as wormwood, sharp as a two-edged sword. Her feet go down to death; her steps take hold on hell." (5:1–5)

"My son, forget not my law; but let thine heart keep my commandments. . . . Let not mercy and truth forsake thee: bind them about thy neck; write them upon the table of thine heart. . . . Trust in the Lord with all thine heart; and lean not unto thine own understanding. In all thy ways acknowledge him, and he shall direct thy paths. . . ." (3:1, 3, 5–6)

"These six things doth the Lord hate: . . . A proud look, a lying tongue, and hands that shed innocent blood, a heart that deviseth wicked imaginations, feet that be swift in running to mischief, a false witness that speaketh lies, and he that soweth discord among brethren." (6:16–19)

ON WOMEN

"As a jewel of gold in a swine's snout, so is a fair woman which is without discretion." (11:22)

"A virtuous woman is a crown to her husband: but she that maketh ashamed is as the rottenness in his bones." (12:4)

". . . a virtuous woman . . . seeketh wool, and flax, and worketh willingly with her hands. She riseth also while it is yet night, and giveth meat to her household, and a portion to her maidens. She considereth a field, and buyeth it: with the fruit of her hands she planteth a vineyard. She girdeth her loins with strength, and strengtheneth her arms. . . . She layeth her hands to the spindle, and her hands hold the distaff. She stretcheth out her hand to the poor; yea, she reacheth forth her hands to the needy. . . . Strength and honour are her clothing; and she shall rejoice in time to come. She openeth her mouth with wisdom; and in her tongue is the law of kindness. She looketh well to the ways of her household; and catch not the bread of idleness. . . . Favour is deceitful, and beauty is vain; but a woman that feareth the Lord, she shall be praised. Give her of the fruit of her hands; and let her own works praise her in the gates." (31:10, 13, 15–17, 19–20, 25–27, 30–31)

Questions for Discussion and Your Reading Journal

1. In terms of education, how much do the Proverbs encourage each individual to look into himself or herself to find wisdom, as Plato encourages students to do? Explain.
2. When the Proverbs speak of economic matters, how is wealth considered differently for men and women? (See especially Proverbs 11:16.)
3. In what ways are parental roles similar in the Proverbs relating to "filial piety" (respect of children for parents)? In what ways are they different?
4. What force seems most deeply rooted at the center of notions of the ideal person and virtue?
5. Based upon the proverbs relating to women's roles, what do we mean when we say that Judaism is a "patriarchal religion." Give examples that illustrate this.

MATTHEW

The Gospel according to Matthew is the first book of the Christian New Testament. This book marks the fundamental cultural transition of the Judeo-Christian tradition from Judeo to Christian in theology, ritual, and daily practice. Although the events recorded here are entirely steeped in Jewish culture, the ideas about the mission of Jesus the Christ are very much Christian. Jesus is the Greek name for Yoshua ben Yosef, or

Joshua, son of Joseph, a Jewish prophet/savior who became the central figure of the new Christian religion. Christ is a Greek translation of the Hebrew word for messiah, meaning anointed. Jesus is considered by Christian believers to be the historical figure anointed by the Judeo-Christian God to save humankind from sin. The book of Matthew contains the most authoritative overview of the life of Jesus. Because the book was originally written in Greek rather than in Hebrew and because it appeared nearly 50 years after the death of the historical Jesus, most biblical scholars doubt that it was actually written by Matthew himself. The New Testament in which the book appears is a collection of 27 short books containing the four Gospels, the birth and early history of the Christian faith, and letters to new believers in Greece and Rome by early church leaders, particularly by the Apostle Paul. A group of Catholic bishops met at the Council of Carthage in AD *397 to confirm the official canon of the New Testament of the Bible.*

Reading Rhetorically

Matthew, or those individuals who later compiled the book that carries his name, had daunting purpose in mind for the words that appear in the following Gospel: speak as a god, or as the son of a god would speak to humankind. Rhetorically, the most obvious means of accomplishing this task is through direct quotation, which is what happens in Matthew 10: 34–39. Instead of trying to call others to the service of Jesus (and, by implication, God), the writer(s) of Matthew allow Jesus himself to make the call. Note how this approach appears again in Chapter 5 through Chapter 7 of St. Matthew. Here we see the narrator quickly set up the quoted material and then disappear from our view as Jesus preaches. Because Jesus never wrote down any of his teachings personally, all the writers of the New Testament have the flexibility of drawing upon oral traditions and remembered sayings of Jesus to bring together a broad view of his teachings and ideas not limited to entirely accurate accounts of precisely what was said at any given historical moment. Thus the Sermon on the Mount provides another excellent example of "wisdom literature" that embodies the best of what Jesus had to say overall during his life.

Mission of Jesus 10:34–39

34 Think not that I am come to send peace on earth: I came not to send peace, but a sword.

35 For I am come to set a man at variance against his father, and the daughter against her mother, and the daughter in law against her mother in law.

36 And a man's foes *shall be* they of his own household.

37 He that loveth father or mother more than me is not worthy of me: and he that loveth son or daughter more than me is not worthy of me.

38 And he that taketh not his cross, and followeth after me, is not worthy of me.

39 He that findeth his life shall lose it: and he that loseth his life for my sake shall find it.

Sermon on the Mount 5–7

Chapter 5

And seeing the multitudes, he went up into a "mountain: and when he was set, his disciples came unto him:

2 And he opened his mouth, and taught them, saying,

3 Blessed *are* the poor in spirit: for theirs is the kingdom of heaven.

4 Blessed *are* they that mourn: for they shall be comforted.

5 Blessed *are* the meek: for they shall inherit the earth.

6 Blessed *are* they which do hunger and thirst after righteousness: for they shall be filled.

7 Blessed *are* the merciful: for they shall obtain mercy.

8 Blessed *are* the pure in heart: for they shall see God.

9 Blessed *are* the peacemakers: for they shall be called the children of God.

10 Blessed *are* they which are persecuted for righteousness' sake: for theirs is the kingdom of heaven.

11 Blessed are ye, when *men* shall revile you, and persecute *you,* and shall say all manner of evil against you falsely, for my sake.

12 Rejoice, and be exceeding glad: for great *is* your reward in heaven: for so persecuted they the prophets which were before you.

13 Ye are the salt of the earth: but if the salt have lost his savour, where with shall it be salted? It is thenceforth good for nothing, but to be cast out, and to be trodden under foot of men.

14 Ye are the light of the world. A city that is set on an hill cannot be hid.

15 Neither do men. light a candle, and put it under a bushel, but on a candlestick; and it giveth light unto all that are in the house.

16 Let your light so shine before men, that they may see your good works, and glorify your Father which is in heaven.

17 Think not that I am come to destroy the law, or the prophets: I am not come to destroy, but to fulfill.

18 For verily I say unto you, Till heaven and earth pass, one jot or one tittle shall in no wise pass from the law, till all be fulfilled.

19 Whosoever therefore shall break one of these least commandments, and shall teach men so, he shall be called the least in the kingdom of heaven but whosoever shall do and teach *them,* the same shall be called great in the kingdom of heaven.

20 For I say unto you, That except your righteousness shall exceed *the righteousness* of the scribes and Pharisees, ye shall in no case enter into the kingdom of heaven.

21 Ye have heard that it was said by them of old time, Thou shalt not kill; and whosoever shall kill shall be in danger of the judgment:

22 But I say unto you, That whosoever is angry with his brother without a cause shall be in danger of the judgment: and whosoever shall say to his brother, Ra′-că, shall be in danger of the council: but whosoever shall say, Thou fool, shall be in danger of hell fire.

23 Therefore if thou bring thy gift to the altar, and there rememberest that thy brother hath ought against thee;

24 Leave there thy gift before the altar, and go thy way; first be reconciled to thy brother, and then come and offer thy gift.

25 Agree with thine adversary quickly, whiles thou art in the way with him; lest at any time the adversary deliver thee to the judge, and the judge deliver thee to the officer, and thou be cast into prison.

26 Verily I say unto thee, Thou shalt by no means come out thence, till thou hast paid the uttermost farthing.

27 Ye have heard that it was said by them of old time. Thou shalt not commit adultery:

28 But I say unto you, That whosoever looketh on a woman to lust after her hath committed adultery with her already in his heart.

29 And if thy right eye offend thee, pluck it out, and cast *it* from thee: for it is profitable for thee that one of thy members should perish, and not *that* thy whole body should be cast into hell.

30 And if thy right hand offend thee, cut it off, and cast *it* from thee: for it is profitable for thee that one of thy members should perish, and not *that* thy whole body should be cast into hell.

31 It hath been said, Whosoever shall put away his wife, let him give her a writing of divorcement:

32 But I say unto you, That whosoever shall put away his wife, saving for the cause of fornication, causeth her to commit adultery: and whosoever shall marry her that is divorced committeth adultery.

33 Again, ye have heard that it hath been said by them of old time, Thou shalt not forswear thyself, but shalt perform unto the Lord thine oaths:

34 But I say unto you, Swear not at all; neither by heaven; for it is God's throne:

35 Nor by the earth; for it is his footstool: neither by Jerusalem; for it is qthe city of the great King.

36 Neither shalt thou swear by thy head, because thou canst not make one hair white or black.

37 But let your communication be, Yea, yea; Nay, nay: for whatsoever is more than these cometh of evil.

38 Ye have heard that it hath been said, An eye for an eye, and a tooth for a tooth:

39 But I say unto you, That ye resist not evil: but whosoever shall smite thee on thy right cheek, turn to him the other also.

40 And if any man will sue thee at the law, and take away thy coat, let him have *thy* cloake also.

41 And whosoever shall compel thee to go a mile, go with him twain.

42 Give to him that asketh thee, and from him that would borrow of thee turn not thou away.

43 Ye have heard that it hath been said, Thou shalt love thy neighbour, and hate thine enemy.

44 But I say unto you, Love your enemies, bless them that curse you, do good to them that hate you, and pray for them which despitefully use you, and persecute you;

45 That ye may be the children of your Father which is in heaven: for he maketh his sun to rise on the evil and on the good, and sendeth rain on the just and on the unjust.

46 For if ye love them which love you, what reward have ye? do not even the publicans the same?

47 And if ye salute your brethren only, what do ye more *than others?* do not even the publicans so?

48 Be ye therefore perfect, even as your Father which is in heaven is perfect.

Chapter 6

Take heed that ye do not your alms before men, to be seen of them: otherwise ye have no reward of your Father which is in Heaven.

2 Therefore when thou doest *thine* alms, do not sound a trumpet before thee, as the hypocrites do in the synagogues and in the streets, that they may have glory of men. Verily I say unto you, They have their reward.

3 But when thou doest alms, let not thy left hand know what thy right hand doeth:

4 That thine alms may be in secret: and thy Father which seeth in secret himself shall reward thee openly.

5 And when thou prayest, thou shalt not be as the hypocrites *are:* for they love to pray standing in the synagogues and in the corners of the streets, that they may be seen of men. Verily I say unto you, They have their reward.

6 But thou, when thou prayest, enter into thy closet, and when thou hast shut thy door, pray to thy Father which is in secret; and thy Father which seeth in secret shall reward thee openly.

7 But when ye pray, use not vain repetitious, as the heathen *do:* for they think that they shall be heard for their much speaking.

8 Be not ye therefore like unto them: for your Father knoweth what things ye have need of, before ye ask him.

9 After this manner therefore pray ye: Our Father which art in heaven, Hallowed be thy name.

10 Thy kingdom come. They will be done in earth, as *it is* in heaven.

11 Give us this day our daily bread.

12 And forgive us our debts, as we forgive our debtors.

13 And lead us not into temptation, but deliver us from evil: For thine is the kingdom, and the power, and the glory, for ever. Ä'· měn.

14 For if ye forgive men their trespasses, your heavenly Father will also forgive you:

15 But if ye forgive not men their trespasses, neither will your Father forgive your trespasses.

16 Moreover when ye fast, be not, as the hypocrites, of a sad countenance; for they disfigure their faces, that they may appear unto men to fast. Verily I say unto you, They have their reward.

17 But thou, when thou fastest, anoint thine head, and wash thy face;

18 That thou appear not unto men to fast, but unto thy Father which is in secret: and thy Father, which seeth in secret, shall reward thee openly.

19 Lay not up for yourselves treasures upon earth, where moth and rust doth corrupt, and where thieves break through and steal:

20 But lay up for yourselves treasures in heaven, where neither moth nor rust doth corrupt, and where thieves do not break through nor steal:

21 For where your treasure is, there will your heart be also.

22 The light of the body is the eye: if therefore thine eye be single, thy whole body shall be full of light.

23 But if thine eye be evil, thy whole body shall be full of darkness. If therefore the light that is in thee be darkness, how great *is* that darkness!

24 No man can serve two masters: for either he will hate the one, and love the other; or else he will hold to the one, and despise the other. Ye cannot serve God and mammon.

25 Therefore I say unto you, Take no thought for your life, what ye shall eat, or what ye shall drink; nor yet for your body, what ye shall put on. Is not the life more than meat, and the body than raiment?

26 Behold the fowls of the air: for they sow not, neither do they reap, nor gather into barns; yet your heavenly Father feedeth them. Are ye not much better than they?

27 Which of you by taking thought can add one cubit unto his stature?

28 And why take ye thought for raiment? Consider the lilies of the field, how they grow; they toil not, neither do they spin:

29 And yet I say unto you. That even Solomon in all his glory was not arrayed like one of these.

30 Wherefore, if God so clothe the grass of the field, which to day is, and to morrow is cast into the oven, *shall he* not much more *clothe* you, O ye of little faith?

31 Therefore take no thought, saying, What shall we eat? or, What shall we drink? or, Wherewithal shall we be clothed?

32 (For after all these things do the Gentiles seek:) for your heavenly Father knoweth that ye have need of all these things.

33 But seek ye first the kingdom of God, and his righteousness; and all these things shall be added unto you.

34 Take therefore no thought for the morrow: for the morrow shall take thought for the things of itself. Sufficient unto the day *is* the evil thereof.

Chapter 7

1 Judge not, that ye be not judged.

2 For with what judgment ye judge, ye shall be judged: and with what measure ye mete, it shall be measured to you again.

3 And why beholdest thou the mote that is in thy brother's eye, but considerest not the beam that is in thine own eye?

4 Or how wilt thou say to thy brother, Let me pull out the mote out of thine eye: and, behold, a beam *is* in thine own eye?

5 Thou hypocrite, first cast out the beam out of thine own eye; and then shalt thou see clearly to cast out the mote out of thy brother's eye.

6 Give not that which is holy unto the dogs, neither cast ye your pearls before swine, lest they trample them under their feet, and turn again and rend you.

7 Ask, and it shall be given you; seek, and ye shall find: knock, and it shall be opened unto you:

8 For every one that asketh receiveth; and he that seeketh findeth; and to him that knocketh it shall be opened.

9 Or what man is there of you, whom if his son ask bread, will he give him a stone?

10 Or if he ask a fish, will he give him a serpent?

11 If ye then, being evil, know how to give good gifts unto your children, how much more shall your Father which is in heaven give good things to them that ask him?

12 Therefore all things whatsoever ye would that men should do to you, do ye even so to them: for this is the law and the prophets.

13 Enter ye in at the strait gate; for wide *is* the gate, and broad *is* the way, that leadeth to destruction, and many there be which go in thereat:

14 Because strait *is* the gate, and narrow *is* the way, which leadeth unto life, and few there be that find it.

15 Beware of false prophets, which come to you in sheep's clothing, but inwardly they are ravening wolves.

16 Ye shall know them by their fruits. Do men gather grapes of thorns, or figs of thistles?

17 Even so every good tree bringeth forth good fruit; but a corrupt tree bringeth forth evil fruit.

18 A good tree cannot bring forth evil fruit, neither *can* a corrupt tree bring forth good fruit.

19 Every tree that bringeth not forth good fruit is hewn down, and cast into the fire.

20 Wherefore by their fruits ye shall know them.

21 Not every one that saith unto me, Lord, Lord, shall enter into the kingdom of heaven; but he that doeth the will of my Father which is in heaven.

22 Many will say to me in that day, Lord, Lord, have we not prophesied in thy name? and in thy name have cast out devils? and in thy name done many wonderful works?

23 And then will I profess unto them, I never knew you: depart from me, ye that work iniquity.

24 Therefore whosoever heareth these sayings of mine, and doeth them, I will liken him unto a wise man, which built his house upon a rock:

25 And the rain descended, and the floods came, and the winds blew, and beat upon that house; and it fell not: for it was founded upon a rock.

26 And every one that heareth these sayings of mine, and doeth them not, shall be likened unto a foolish man, which built his house upon the sand:

27 And the rain descended, and the floods came, and the winds blew, and beat upon that house; and if fell: and great was the fall of it.

28 And it came to pass, when Jesus had ended these sayings, the people were astonished at his doctrine:

29 For he taught them as *one* having authority, and not as the scribes.

Questions for Discussion and Your Reading Journal

1. In Matthew 10:34, Jesus proclaims that he has not come to bring peace but, rather, "a sword." How do you interpret his meaning in the verses (35 to 39) that follow? Did he seem to support wars between armies and nations, as his followers have sometimes done in his name?

2. The eight statements that begin with the word "blessed" at the start of Chapter 5 are called the "beatitudes," meaning "state of supreme happiness." What is unique about what Jesus suggests should make his followers "supremely happy"? How does this compare to what normally seems to make people happy?

3. Beginning in Matthew 5:27, Jesus compares moral codes of "old time" (the Hebrew laws of the Old Testament) with his new moral code. What differences do you note in the two moral codes?

4. In Matthew 6, Jesus continues his moral teachings. What seems to be the primary emphasis of these teachings?

5. The focus of Chapter 7 is upon "hypocrites." Give at least three examples of what Jesus would consider hypocritical behavior.

6. In the overall perspective, in what ways does the wisdom literature of Jesus seem to differ from the wisdom literature of Solomon? In what ways are they similar?

JOHN B. CHRISTOPHER

The Prophet
The Teachings of Islam

John B. Christopher, emeritus professor of history at the University of Rochester, has published widely on Islamic culture. The following excerpts from The Islamic Tradition *demonstrate Émile Durkheim's definition of religion as a system of beliefs and practices that revolve around concepts of the sacred and the profane. Muhammad the Prophet*

(570–632 CE) brought a new system of beliefs to the clannish and violent societies of sixth- and seventh-century Arabia. These beliefs took active expression in what came to be called "the five pillars of the faith." Concepts of what is good (sacred) and of what is evil (profane) are tied directly to the Koran (sometimes spelled Quran), the sacred book of the Islamic faith compiled by 652 CE. People who accept its teachings are called "Muslims," meaning "those who have submitted." This book defines for Muslims what is proper belief and correct behavior and what is not. Many parallels have been drawn between Islam and the Jewish and Christian traditions, which are also religions that are founded upon a sacred book.

Reading Rhetorically

Christopher's treatment of Muhammad the Prophet and of the core teachings of Islam is expository in nature. He seeks to inform his readers of historical facts and ideas that one must know to better understand the Islamic religion. Because of the biographical nature of his topic, he uses a narrative of the life of Muhammad to present this influential man's ideas and teachings in a coherent manner. As you read Christopher's work, note how his writing style shifts at the end of the narrative of Muhammad's life. When overviewing the Koran and the major teachings of the Prophet, he moves back to pure exposition of facts and ideas without a storytelling voice to carry the information. This part of his reading is more academic in nature and resembles more closely the kinds of academic reading most common to university-level studies.

THE PROPHET

Muhammad was born, probably about the year A.D. 570, into a family of the Banu Hashim ("sons of Hashim"), a clan of Quraish that had played a prominent role in Meccan history, and from whom the Hashimite monarchs of twentieth-century Jordan and Iraq claim descent. The great Muslim biography of the Prophet, The *Sira*,[1] which dates from the eighth century, traced the ancestry of Muhammad back to Ishmael, son of Abraham in the Book of Genesis by the concubine Hagar. Muslims believe that Ishmael was the progenitor of the Arab people, whereas Isaac, the son born later to Abraham and his wife Sarah, was the progenitor of the Jewish people. Modern scholars reject the genealogy of Muhammad and many other details of the *Sira* as extravagant embellishments in the story-telling tradition of Arabic literature, but they accept its broad outlines as sound in the main. It is generally agreed that Muhammad's great-grandfather, for whom the Banu Hashim were named, pioneered in the caravan trade with Syria, and that Muhammad's grandfather had the important privilege of furnishing food and water to

[1] *Sirat Rasul Allah* ("Life of the Prophet of God"), written by ibn-Ishaq and edited by ibn-Hisham; there is an English translation by Alfred Guillaume, *The Life of Muhammad* (London: Oxford UP, 1955).

pilgrims visiting the Kaaba. His grandfather is also credited with having reconstructed the sacred well of Zamzam, the waters of which, according to legend, first appeared when the angel Gabriel intervened to slake the thirst of Hagar and Ishmael after Abraham had abandoned them at the insistence of Sarah.

2   Muhammad's father died on a caravan journey, probably before his son was born; and the boy was brought up by his grandfather and, after his death, by Muhammad's uncle abu-Talib, the head of the Banu Hashim. At this time the Banu Hashim, though still respected in Mecca, had been surpassed in riches and influence by other clans. Because Muhammad did not inherit wealth, he had to make his own way; he apparently served as business agent for Khadija, a well-to-do widow many years his senior, whom he eventually married. The couple had six children, and their marriage seems to have been outstandingly congenial; not until after Khadija's death, in A.D. 619, did Muhammad follow Arab custom and take other wives.

3   The *Sira* claims that Muhammad made a journey to Syria as Khadija's agent and also an earlier trip as a lad accompanying a caravan of his uncle. These claims have prompted much speculation and controversy as to whether Muhammad must therefore have had some kind of direct experience with Syrian Christianity. But it cannot be proved that Muhammad ever traveled to Syria, and it is the consensus of scholars that, although he was aware of Christianity and Judaism, his knowledge was general and vague, based on hearsay, on the second-hand reports circulating in Mecca. There is no evidence that he had any first-hand acquaintance with Jewish or Christian worship or with the Bible. Indeed, Muslim tradition holds that Muhammad was illiterate, in spite of the fact that one would expect a business agent to have had some ability to read and write.

4   It is conjectured that Muhammad's religious views may have been influenced to a considerable degree by the *hanifs,* who were very critical of the pagan practices and low moral tone of Meccan society. Recent scholarship, particularly Montgomery Watt's study, *Muhammad at Mecca* (Oxford University Press, 1953), stresses the significance of his personal concern over the city's increasing commercialism and materialism. Muhammad is thought to have participated in the League of the Virtuous, which linked the Banu Hashim and other less prosperous clans against attempts by the wealthy clans to exclude Yemenis from trade with Mecca. The issue here was partly economic, since the poorer clans depended on wares supplied by Yemenis for the conduct of their own little businesses. But a question of justice was also at stake, for the Yemeni merchants had a long-established and recognized position in Mecca.

The Call to Recite

5 As the years passed, Muhammad's sense of alienation from existing Meccan society evidently increased, and at times he retreated to a cave in a nearby mountain for meditation and power. During one retreat, probably about the year A.D. 610, when he was approximately 40 years old, he experienced the traumatic seizure or awakening that was to transform him into a prophet. In

a dream or vision Muhammad saw a heavenly being, who may have been the angel Gabriel, he later suggested, or possibly even Allah himself. The being commanded Muhammad to recite certain messages and, when Muhammad at first refused, struggled with him until he agreed to comply. And so Muhammad memorized and then repeated the messages to his family and some of his fellow citizens as divine revelations. Here is part of the first message:

Recite: In the name of thy Lord who created,
        created Man of a blood-clot.
Recite: And thy Lord is the Most Generous,
        who taught by the Pen,
        taught Man that he knew not.
        No indeed: surely Man waxes insolent,
        for he thinks himself self-sufficient.
        Surely unto thy Lord is the Returning.[2]

During the remaining years of his life Muhammad experienced a great 6 many additional seizures and received a host of additional revelations, usually, he believed, through the angel Gabriel. The complete roster of revelations comprises the *Koran*, a word which means *recital* and has in Arabic a sacred connotation very like that of *scripture* in English.

Until recently many non-Muslims dismissed Muhammad's alleged reli- 7 gious experiences as the convulsions of an epileptic, or the outbursts of a hysterical person, or the fraudulent, self-induced episodes of an opportunist. In the light of modern medical and psychological knowledge, such views no longer appear very tenable. Epileptics, for example, have no memory of what has occurred during their attacks, whereas Muhammad gave vivid reports of what happened to him. Moreover, the very symptoms which used to be thought indicative of Muhammad's epilepsy are now considered quite compatible with intense religious excitement—convulsive movements during his seizures, foam on his lips, profuse sweating even on a cold day, complaints of hearing the clanking of chains or the ringing of bells. Do these symptoms suggest the delusions of hysteria? Most scholars today think not. It is conjectured that Muhammad seldom had visions after his initial experience, nor did he necessarily hear an actual voice relaying to him the full text of a divine message. Many a revelation apparently came to Muhammad as a sudden intuition, a flash of inspiration, an idea implanted by the angel Gabriel rather than a word-by-word communication.

The accounts of Muhammad's prolonged and anguished doubts over the 8 source of his messages argue very strongly in favor of his sincerity. The perpetrator of a fraud could hardly have invented the crisis that engulfed Muhammad after his first revelation, when, fearing that an evil jinni had taken possession of him, he contemplated suicide. Sustained by the sympathy of Khadija, and gradually reassured by further revelations, he became convinced after many months had passed that he had indeed been chosen to be the Prophet or messenger of Allah.

---

[2]A. J. Arberry, *The Koran Interpreted*, II (New York: Macmillan, 1955), sura 96, 345.

THE TEACHINGS OF ISLAM

9   The primary source of Islamic teachings is the Koran. To Muslims it is no mere book but the word of God as revealed to Muhammad, supplementing and completing the revelations of the early prophets and of Jesus; it contains in its entirety a truth of which only a part may be found in the Old Testament or the New. It is, a sympathetic Western expert notes,

10   the holy of holies. It must never rest beneath other books, but always on top of them; one must never drink or smoke when it is being read aloud, and it must be listened to in silence. It is a talisman against disease and disaster. In many places children under ten years of age are required to learn by heart its 6200 odd verses. . . .

There is something impressive and touching in the sight of simple people murmuring the sacred text as they travel. . . . Some people never leave their homes without having a small copy . . . on their person. The bereaved find their great consolation in reading it. No event of consequence passes without the reading of an appropriate passage.[1]

11   Recitation or chanting of selected verses is the closest Islamic approach to liturgy or to hymn-singing; and Koranic passages are much favored for the decoration of mosques, where the depiction of human beings or other living creatures is forbidden. For Muslims the significance of the Koran is all-embracing, perhaps even surpassing that of the Bible for fundamentalist Christians.

12   The full text of the Koran, as we now have it, dates from about twenty years after Muhammad's death when it was pieced together, in the picturesque words of the traditional account, from "scraps of parchment and leather, tablets of stone, ribs of palm branches, camels' shoulder blades and ribs, pieces of board, and the breasts of men." By this time trained reciters had committed large portions of the Koran to memory, just as they were accustomed to do with the great poems of the sixth century. It is also probable that Muhammad himself had been so concerned with the accurate preservation of certain verses that he dictated them to secretaries.

13   Although there is little reason to suppose that the lag of twenty years before the completion of the Koran distorted the essence of Muhammad's message, the task of non-Muslim students of Islam has been complicated. The reasons why were admirably summarized more than a century ago by Thomas Carlyle, one of the first Western men of letters to attempt a fair-minded appraisal of Muhammad:

Nothing but a sense of duty could carry any European through the Koran. We read in it, as we might in the State-Paper Office, masses of lumber, that perhaps we may get some glimpses of a remarkable man. It is true we have it under disadvantages: the Arabs see more method in it that we. Mahomet's followers found the Koran lying all in fractions, . . . and they published it, without any discoverable order as to time or otherwise; merely trying. . . . and this not very strictly, to put the longest chapters

---

[1]Alfred Guillaume, *Islam* (Narmondsworth: Penguin, 1954) 74.

first. The real beginning of it, in that way, lies almost at the end: for the earliest portions were the shortest. Read in its historical sequence it perhaps would not be so bad. Much of it, too, they say is rhythmic; a kind of wild chanting song, in the original. This may be a great point; much perhaps has been lost in the Translation here. Yet with every allowance, one feels it difficult to see how any mortal ever could consider this Koran as a Book written in Heaven, too good for the Earth; as a well-written book, or indeed as a *book* at all; and nor a bewildered rhapsody.[2]

The 6200 verses of the Koran are grouped in 114 chapters or suras, which   14
vary enormously in length, from a very few lines to more than thirty pages. As Carlyle complained, the arrangement of chapters by order of decreasing length places near the end the brief, early Meccan suras, which contain the most dramatic verses of the Koran. Another source of difficulty lies in the titles assigned to the suras, some of which bear little relation to their content; a famous example is sura 2, the longest of all, called "The Cow." Four suras are titled by one or more letters of the Arabic alphabet—*Ta, Ha, Ya, Sin, Sad, Qaf*—and a few others are prefaced by groups of letters after the title—*Alif, Lam, Mim, Ra,* and so on. The reasons for this remain a mystery; perhaps the solution lies in the ingenious suggestion that the disjointed letters represent Muhammad's stammering and mumbling efforts to articulate immediately after the traumatic experience of receiving a revelation (M. Rodinson, *Mohammed* [Pantheon, 1971], pp. 75, 93).

Muslims justify the unique structure of the Koran on the ground that it   15
was prescribed by Muhammad himself. A leading Western convert to Islam finds a rationale for the placement of the early Meccan suras: "The inspiration of the Prophet progressed from inmost things to outward things, whereas most people find their way through outward things to things within."[3]

The early Meccan verses are indeed concerned with inmost things—the   16
relationship of man and God, the imminence of the Last Judgment—and are written in a crisp, rhyming prose that sounds like poetry. The verses from Medina are less poetic and more concerned with outward things, such as the administration of the *umma* and the day-to-day conduct of its members. The first Medinan suras, from the period immediately after the Hegira, include stories or parables from the Old and New Testaments, often in rather garbled form. As Muhammad's expectation of swift conversion of Jews and Christians faded, the later Medinan suras focused on Abraham, whom Muhammad called the "friend of God," because he was a pioneering *hanif* and preacher against the worship of idols. The Arabs and Jews, Muhammad believed, as descendants of Abraham through his sons Ishmael and Isaac, respectively, should fulfill their historic destiny by accepting Islam.

The Koran exemplifies in the highest degree the hypnotic qualities of early   17
Arabic literature. In Muslim devotions the Koran is not read, in the conven-

---

[2]Thomas Carlyle, "The Hero as Prophet," *On Heroes, Hero-Worship and the Heroic in History* (London: Oxford UP, 1946) 25–86.

[3]M. M. Pickthall, *The Meaning of the Glorious Koran: An Explanatory Translation* (New York: New American Library, 1953) xxviii–xxix.

tional sense of the term, but recited or intoned in a fashion that stresses its poetic quality and its power to stir or grip the listener. Muslims tend to hold that it is improper—indeed, sacrilegious—to tamper with the traditional order or original language of the Koran. In deference to Muslim sensibilities some English versions bear such titles as *The Koran Interpreted* or *The Meaning of the Glorious Koran: An Explanatory Translation* to indicate that they cannot presume to be the actual words of God.[4] Other translations, however, attempt to make what Carlyle termed "a bewildered rhapsody" more intelligible to non-Muslim readers by arranging the suras and even individual verses in their proper chronological sequence.[5]

Hadiths

18 The Koran is not the sole source of direct information about Muhammad and his teachings. Reports of statements he had made and actions he had taken in everyday life were passed along by word of mouth from his companions to later generations; these statements are called *hadiths* or traditions. Although not claimed by Muslims to be the words of God, the hadiths have been endowed with a special importance since even the details of Muhammad's daily routine could reflect divine guidance. Many hadiths were incorporated into the *Sira,* the early biography of the Prophet . . .; later, al-Bukhari (A.D. 810–870) issued a compendium of hadiths. Here is one of the thousands of traditions he included:

> Muhammad ibn Muqatil Abu'l-Hasan has related to me saying: Abdallah informed us on the authority of Humaid ibn Abd ar-Rahman, on the authority of Abu Huraira—with whom may Allah be pleased—that a man came to the Apostle of Allah—upon whom be Allah's blessing and peace—saying: "O Apostle of Allah, there is no hope for me . . . I had intercourse with my wife during Ramadan." The Prophet answered: "Then set free a slave." Said he: "I have none." The Prophet answered: "Then fast for two months on end." Said he: "But I could not." The Prophet answered: "Then feed sixty poor people." Said he: "I have not the wherewithall." Just then there was brought to the Prophet a basket of dates, so he said to the man: "Take this and distribute it as charitable alms in expiation of your sin." Said he: "O Apostle of Allah, am I to distribute it to other than my own family? when by Him in whose hands is my soul there is no one between the gateposts of the city more needy than I am." Thereat the Prophet laughed till his canine teeth showed, and he said: "Go along and take it."[6]

---

[4]Arberry, *The Koran Interpreted;* Pickthall, *The Meaning of the Glorious Koran.*

[5]Examples are J. M. Rodwell, *The Koran,* first published in 1861 (London: Everyman's Library, 1933); Richard Bell's scholarly dissection and reconstruction, *The Qur'an, Translated with a Critical Re-arrangement of the Surahs,* 2 vols. (Edinburgh: T. and T. Clark, 1937; rpt. 1960); and N. J. Dawood's more readable, *The Koran: A New Translation* (Harmondsworth: Penguin, 1956).

[6]Adapted with modified spelling and punctuation from Arthur Jeffery, ed., *A Reader on Islam* ('s-Gravenhage: Mouton, 1962) 86.

This text suggests the almost insoluble problems surrounding the authen- 19
ticity of hadiths transmitted orally over a span of more than two centuries.
Perhaps the authorities cited were not reliable, perhaps one of them might
have misquoted the Prophet, perhaps the whole hadith was forged by an interested party—no one could, or can, be entirely certain. Some alleged hadiths
were obviously borrowed from the Old Testament or the New; some were edifying precepts devised by good Muslims to attract errant brethren back to the
path of righteousness; and some were simply tall tales made up by storytellers
to elicit generous tips from their audiences. Al-Bukhari is said to have examined 600,000 hadiths (another source says 300,000) and classified each as
"sound," "good," "weak," or "unsound"; he judged fewer than 3,000 to be
sound, and excluded all the others from his compendium. Both al-Bukhari and
the editors of other collections of hadiths that appeared in the ninth century
were learned and painstaking scholars. Yet they have been widely criticized
during the last hundred years for assigning undue importance to the creden-
tials of the chain of authorities transmitting a particular hadith and paying too
little heed to the intrinsic merits or plausibility of the text itself. In any case, it
is often argued, the so-called science of verifying hadiths was useful chiefly for
making the study of genealogy and historical biography such a prominent feature in Islamic life; sifting the evidence more than two hundred years after the
event was bound to be so faulty that all hadiths might as well be considered
apocryphal. The judgment of an Indian Muslim, writing in the late nineteenth
century, is typical:

> The vast flood of traditions soon formed a chaotic sea. Truth and error,
> fact and fable mingled together in an undistinguishable confusion. Every
> religious, social, and political system was defended, when necessary, to
> please a Khalif or an Ameer to serve his purpose, by an appeal to some
> oral traditions. The name of Mohammad was abused to support all man-
> ner of lies and absurdities, or to satisfy the passion, caprice, or arbitrary
> will of the despots, leaving out of consideration the creation of any stan-
> dards of test. . . . I am seldom inclined to quote traditions having little or
> no belief in their genuineness, as generally they are unauthentic, unsup-
> ported, and one-sided.[7]

A generation later, a British scholar made a more generous evaluation: 20

> But however sceptical we are with regard to the ultimate historical value
> of the traditions, it is hard to overrate their importance in the formation
> of the life of the Islamic races throughout the centuries. If we cannot
> accept them at their face value, they are of inestimable value as a mirror
> of the events which preceded the consolidation of Islam into a system.
> Many of the political, dynastic, religious, and social differences which agi-
> tated Islam in the days of its imperial might are illustrated in traditions

---

[7]Moulavi Cheragh Ali, *The Proposed Political, Legal and Social Reforms in the Ottoman Empire and Other Mohammadan States* (Bombay, 1883), xix and 147, as quoted by Alfred Guillaume, *The Traditions of Islam* (Oxford: Clarendon Press, 1924) 29.

promulgated by the conflicting parties in the interest of their pretensions. In them we see how the rival forces of militarism and pacifism, asceticism and materialism, mysticism and literalism, free will and determination, strove fiercely for the mastery.[8]

21 Even a spurious hadith may reveal an issue that aroused feelings strong enough for men to put words in the mouth of the Prophet. And traditions such as the one quoted above, with its report of the Prophet's gentle treatment of the man who broke the ban on sexual activity during the daylight hours of Ramadan, endow the austere figure of Muhammad with warmth and humor.

The Last Judgment

22 There is little that is gentle or humorous, however, in the urgent warnings relayed by Muhammad in the early revelations of the Koran. Everyone must realize, he insists, especially the stubborn materialists and polytheists of Mecca, that the Last Judgment is no remote contingency but something that may have to be faced a few moments after death. The very titles of some suras are arresting: "The Terror" (56), "The Mustering" (59), "The Darkening" (81), "The Splitting" (82), "The Earthquake" (99), "The Clatterer" (101). The verses themselves convey the awfulness of the Last Day:

When heaven is split open,
when the stars are scattered,
when the seas swarm over,
when the tombs are overthrown,
then a soul shall know its works, the former and the latter. . . .
When the sun shall be darkened,
when the stars shall be thrown down,
when the mountains shall be set moving,
when the pregnant camels shall be neglected,
when the savage beasts shall be mustered,
when the seas shall be set boiling,
when the souls shall be coupled,
when the buried infant shall be asked for what sin she was slain,
when the scrolls shall be unrolled,
when heaven shall be stripped off,
when Hell shall be set blazing,
when Paradise shall be brought nigh,
then shall a soul know what it has produced[9]

23 Souls will be consigned to eternal punishment or reward:

Faces on that day humbled,
labouring, toilworn,
roasting at a scorching fire,
watered at a boiling fountain,

---

[8]Guillaume, *The Traditions of Islam*, 12–13.
[9]Arberry, *The Koran Interpreted*, II, suras 82 and 81, 328 and 326.

no food for them but cactus thorn
unfattening, unappeasing hunger.
Faces on that day jocund,
with their striving well-pleased,
in a sublime Garden,
hearing there no babble;
therein a running fountain,
therein uplifted couches
and goblets set forth
and cushions arrayed
and carpets outspread.[10]

Many Westerners have expressed shock not so much at the gruesome pun-   24
ishments of the Muslim hell as at the sensual delights of the Islamic paradise
with its "maidens good and comely, houris, cloistered in cool pavilions,
untouched before them by any man or jinn" and its promise of indulgence in
unique beverages ("no brows throbbing, no intoxication").[11] Yet, "the highest joys even there are spiritual," as Carlyle observed, and they may be
summed up in the word *salaam,* "peace." *Salaam alaykum* ("peace be upon
you, peace be with you") is the universal greeting among Muslims. Verse after
verse in the Koran insists that the peace of paradise is reserved for those who
have faith and who fear the Lord. The damned are the unbelievers, those who
deny the Last Judgment or commit the unforgivable sin of suggesting that God
could have partners.

Man and God

The Koran demanded that Muslims affirm the unity of God and warned Chris-   25
tians to abandon the doctrine of the Trinity because it violated the strict canon
of monotheism: "People of the Book, go not beyond the bounds in your religion, and say not as to God but the Truth. The Messiah, Jesus son of Mary,
was only the Messenger of God, and His Word that He committed to Mary,
and a Spirit from Him. So believe in God and His Messengers, and say not,
'Three.'"[12]

The Prophet, although entrusted with God's message, never claimed to   26
have the power that lies at the heart of the Christian view of Jesus—that of
interceding with God on behalf of man. Allah is, in effect, unapproachable and
incomprehensible. This concept of the deity goes far to account for the reputation of Muslims as fatalists, accepting with equal composure good fortune
or ill because both represent "the will of Allah."

But Islam is a religion of hope as well as of resignation. According to a   27
hadith, Muhammad stated that God had 99 "most beautiful" names in addition

---

[10]Arberry, *The Koran Interpreted,* II, sura 88, 336.

[11]Adapted from Arberry, *The Koran Interpreted,* II, suras 55 and 56, 253 and 254.

[12]Arberry, *The Koran Interpreted,* I, sura 4, 125.

to Allah and would admit to paradise any Muslims who had committed them all to memory. Aiding memorization is the "Islamic rosary," the "worry beads" that Muslims so often finger, which consist of a string of 99 beads, or one of 33 beads to be negotiated three times. The 99 names, drawn partly from the Koran and partly from the hadiths, stress both the stern and the gentle aspects of Allah. Here are the Koranic verses containing the 13 names heading the list:

He is the All-merciful, the All-compassionate,
He is the King, the All-holy, the All-peaceable,
the All-Faithful, the All-preserver,
the All-mighty, the All-compeller,
the All-sublime.
He is God,
the Creator, the Maker, the Shaper.
To Him belong the names Most Beautiful.[13]

Questions for Discussion and Your Reading Journal

The Prophet

1. In terms of modern-day conflicts between Arabs and Jews, what is significant and ironic about Muhammad the Prophet's ancestor Ishmael?

Teachings of Islam

1. How do the teachings of the Koran fit in with the revelations of the early Hebrew prophets and the teachings of Jesus?
2. What is the definition of "hadiths"? Do other religions tend to create their own forms of hadiths? Explain.
3. Who shall be inheritors of paradise and who shall be damned at the Last Judgment, according to the Islamic faith?
4. What does this text indicate is the proper relationship in Islam between humans and deity?

The Quran

To the Muslim believer, the Quran (sometimes spelled Koran) is more than a sacred book. Each of its verses and chapters (suras) is accepted as verbal revelation from the deity to Muhammad the Prophet. Because he could not write, Muhammad memorized them word for word, and only later were they written down. Thus, the Quran is sacred to Muslims in a

---

[13]Abridged from Sura 59. Arberry, *The Koran Interpreted*, II, 270. The complete list of the 99 may be found in *The Encyclopaedia of Islam*, new ed., s.v. al-Asma' al-Husna, and in Edwin Arnold's *Pearls of the Faith*.

different way than the Bible is to Christians. To believers, it is, word for word, the will and law of Allah. Great debate still surrounds the act of translating it to other languages for fear of changing the words and meaning of divine revelation. The selections here from sura 3 reflect Islam's acceptance of and borrowings from the Judeo-Christian heritage. The Arabic and Jewish peoples have a long, shared history since they have lived in the same lands at many points over time, Muhammad the Prophet would have been familiar with Jewish and Christian history like any other Arab of his time. However, the perspective he gives in these passages is different in significant ways from the perspective Christians hold, which, equally, is different from the perspective of the Jewish people themselves.

Reading Rhetorically

As with other religious examples of wisdom literature, the purpose of the Quran is to inspire and to uplift the thinking of its readers. However, an element of persuasion is also present throughout. Like other books in the Judeo-Christian tradition, the Quran takes as a given that its readers accept the existence of an all-powerful divine being who is keenly interested in the lives of its human creation. The following reading carries this common ground a step farther, showing through the language of the Quran how Muslims know about and teach of Jesus, son of Mary. Just as the Christian New Testament makes constant references to the Jewish Old Testament, so the Quran does to both collections of sacred writings. All three traditions claim the patriarch Abraham as a common ancestor. Hence it is not surprising that the message of each later tradition would grow out of the earlier ones. In the case of Islam, the common heritage is literal as well as spiritual. Muslims consider themselves the descendants of Abraham through his first son Ishmael, born from his second wife Hagar. The Jews trace their ancestry through Abraham's second son Isaac born from his first wife Sarah. The following Quranic reading draws liberally upon elements of Judeo-Christian heritage to present a new religious tradition.

Surely the true religion in the estimation of Allah is Islam, that is, complete submission to Him, and those who were given the Book disagreed only, out of mutual envy, after knowledge had come to them. Who so rejects the Signs of Allah should remember that Allah is swift at reckoning. (20)   1

Now if they should dispute with thee, say to them: I have submitted myself wholly to Allah, and also those who follow me. Say to those who have been given the Book and to those to whom no revelation has been vouchsafed: Do you submit yourselves to Allah also? If they submit they will surely be guided; but if they turn away, thy duty is only to convey the message. Allah is Watchful of His servants. (21)   2

To those who reject the Signs of Allah and seek to kill the Prophets and those from among the people who enjoin equity, without just cause, announce   3 thou a painful chastisement. These are they whose works shall come to naught in this world and the next, and they shall have no helpers. (22–23) . . .

4   Let not the believers take the disbelievers for intimate friends in preference to believers; whoever does that has no connection with Allah. Your only course is to keep away from them altogether. Allah warns you against His chastisement; and to Allah is your return. Warn them: Whether you keep hidden that which is in your minds, or disclose it, Allah knows it; and He knows whatever is in the heavens and whatever is in the earth. Allah has full power over all things. Beware of the day when everyone shall find confronting him all the good he has done and all the evil he has done. He will wish there were a great distance between him and the evil. Allah warns you against His chastisement; Allah is Most Compassionate towards His servants. (29–31) . . .

5   Call to mind when the angels said to Mary: Allah has exalted thee and purified thee and chosen thee from among all the women of thy time. Mary, be obedient to thy Lord and prostrate thyself before Him and worship Him alone with single-minded devotion along with those who worship. (43–44) . . .

6   Call to mind when the angels said to Mary: Allah, through His word, gives thee glad tidings of a son named the Messiah, Jesus son of Mary, honoured in this world and the next, and of those who are granted nearness to Allah. He shall admonish people in his early years and also in his ripe years, and he shall be of the righteous. Mary said: Lord, how shall I have a son, when no man has touched me? He answered: Such is the power of Allah, He creates what He pleases. When He decrees a thing, He says to it: Be; and it is. He will teach him the Book and the Wisdom and the Torah and the Gospel and will make him a Messenger to the children of Israel, bearing the message: I have come to you with a Sign from your Lord, that for your benefit, in the manner of a bird, I shall fashion, from among persons who are capable of receiving an impress, shapes and shall breathe into them a new spirit, then they will begin to soar like birds by the command of Allah; and I shall declare clean the blind and the leprous and shall bestow life on the spiritually dead, by the command of Allah; and shall announce to you what you will eat and what you will store up in your houses. In all this there is a Sign for you, if you will believe. I fulfil that which has been sent down before me, namely the Torah, and shall make lawful for you some of that which was forbidden you. I come to you with a Sign from your Lord; so be mindful of your duty to Allah and obey me. Verily, Allah is my Lord and your Lord; so worship Him. That is the straight path. (46–52)

7   When Jesus perceived their disbelief, he asked: Who will be my helpers in the cause of Allah? The disciples answered: We are helpers in the cause of Allah. We have believed in Allah, and bear thou witness we are obedient to Allah. They affirmed: Our Lord we have believed in that which Thou has sent down and we have become the followers of this Messenger, so write us down among the witnesses. (53–54)

8   The enemies of Jesus devised their plans and Allah devised His plan; Allah is the best of planners. Allah reassured Jesus: I shall cause thee to die a natural death, and shall exalt thee to Myself, and shall clear thee from the calumnies of those who disbelieve, and shall place those who follow thee above those who disbelieve, until the Day of Judgment; then to Me shall be your

return and I will judge between you concerning that wherein you differ. As for those who disbelieve, I will punish them with a severe punishment in this world and in the next, and they shall have no helpers; and as for those who believe and work righteousness, Allah will pay them their full desserts. Allah loves not the wrongdoers. That is what We recite unto thee of the Signs and the Wise Instructions. (55–59)

The case of Jesus in the sight of Allah is like unto the case of Adam. He 9 created him out of dust. He said concerning him: Be; and he began to be. This is the truth from thy Lord, so be thou not of those who doubt. Then whoso should dispute with thee concerning it, after that which has come to thee of divinely revealed knowledge, say to them: Come, let us call our sons and you call your sons, and let us call our women and you call your women, and let us call our people and you call your people, then let us pray fervently for the triumph of the truth and invoke the curse of Allah on those who lie. Most certainly this is the true account. There is none worthy of worship save Allah; and surely, it is Allah Who is the Mighty, the Wise. Then if they turn away, let them remember that Allah knows well those who create mischief. (60–64)

Say to the People of the Book: Let us agree upon one matter which is the 10 same for you and for us, namely, that we worship none but Allah, and that we associate no partner with Him, and that some of us take not others for lords beside Allah. Then, if they turn away, say to them: Bear ye witness that we have submitted to Allah. (65)

People of the Book, why do you dispute concerning Abraham, whereas the 11 Torah and Gospel were surely not sent down till after him? Will you not then understand? Hearken, you are those who have disputed about that whereof you had some knowledge; why do you now dispute about that whereof you have no knowledge at all? Allah knows and you know not. Abraham was neither a Jew nor a Christian; he was ever inclined to Allah and obedient to Him, and he was not of those who associate partners with Allah. Surely, the people closest to Abraham are those who followed him, and this Prophet and those who believe in him. Allah is the Friend of believers. (66–69)

Questions for Discussion and Your Reading Journal

1. According to the first verse of this text, what does "Islam" signify?
2. What does the Quran indicate was the mission of Jesus, the Messiah?
3. Does Allah seem to resemble the warrior God of the Old Testament or the God of love of the New Testament? Explain.
4. What other elements of the Judeo-Christian tradition do you find in this text?

KAHLIL GIBRAN

Kahlil Gibran (1883–1931) was born in Lebanon in a mountain village where the religious heritage was Maronite Christian (named after St. Maron, a fourth-century monk), but the cultural heritage and language were Arabic. Gibran's mother brought him to the United States when he was a boy, but his father remained behind in Lebanon. He grew up thus divided between Arab and Christian, Lebanese and American worlds. Influences from both worlds show up in his writings and paintings. His most famous work is The Prophet, *a somewhat biographical collection of 26 poetic essays that present his at once sensible and spiritual teachings on various day-to-day subjects (love, marriage, children, giving, eating and drinking, work, joy and sorrow, etc.). The selection that follows is upon the topic of religion.*

Reading Rhetorically

Gibran's reading is an excellent example of modern wisdom literature that makes no pretense of coming directly from a god or gods. Like wisdom literature in the Eastern tradition (Confucius' analects, the teachings of Lao-tzu, the enlightened insights of the Buddha), Gibran's writing is philosophical more than it is religious. And yet it is not the rational philosophy of Plato or Nietzsche (see earlier readings in this chapter). Rather, it takes a more mystical approach to ideas and human concerns, relying upon insight and inspiration to persuade readers of its inherent value. As with most pieces of wisdom literature, the author or authors assume that the worth of each idea will be self-evident in the very words conveying its meaning—for those who are ready to hear it. Note as you read any of the ideas that pertain to your own experience.

"Religion" from *The Prophet*

1   And an old priest said, Speak to us of Religion.

2   And he said:

3   Have I spoken this day of aught else?

4   Is not religion all deeds and all reflection,

5   And that which is neither deed nor reflection, but a wonder and a surprise ever springing in the soul, even while the hands hew the stone or tend the loom?

6   Who can separate his faith from his actions, or his belief from his occupations?

7   Who can spread his hours before him, saying, "This for God and this for myself; This for my soul, and this other for my body?"

8   All your hours are wings that beat through space from self to self.

8   He who wears his morality but as his best garment were better naked.

10   The wind and the sun will tear no holes in his skin.

11   And he who defines his conduct by ethics imprisons his song-bird in a cage.

12   The freest song comes not through bars and wires.

13   And he to whom worshipping is a window, to open but also to shut, has not yet visited the house of his soul whose windows are from dawn to dawn.

14   Your daily life is your temple and your religion.

15   Whenever you enter into it take with you your all.

Take the plough and the forge and the mallet and the lute, 16

The things you have fashioned in necessity or for delight. 17

For in revery you cannot rise above your achievements nor fall lower than 18
your failures.

And take with you all men: 19

For in adoration you cannot fly higher than their hopes nor humble your- 20
self lower than their despair.

And if you would know God be not therefore a solver of riddles. 21

Rather look about you and you shall see Him playing with your children. 22

And look into space; you shall see Him walking in the cloud, outstretch- 23
ing His arms in the lightning and descending in rain.

You shall see Him smiling in flowers, then rising and waving His hands in 24
trees.

Questions for Discussion and Your Reading Journal

1. Sum up as best you can what "religion" consists of for Gibran.
2. According to Gibran, how does one come to "know God"?
3. Which idea or insight do you find most appealing in this reading? Why?

RACE, GENDER, AND OPPRESSION

RIANE EISLER

Riane Eisler (1931–) is codirector for the Center for Partnership Studies and a lecturer on feminist issues. She is the author of Dissolutions: No-Fault Divorce, Marriage, and the Future of Women *(1977);* What the ERA Means to Your Life, Your Rights, and the Future *(1978); and* The Chalice and the Blade: Our History, Our Future *(1987). In the selection reprinted here, from an article published in 1985, Eisler challenges traditional interpretations of the origins of Western civilization. Using archaeological evidence of goddess worship in early European agricultural communities, she proposes that male-dominated hierarchical religions and societies have not always been the norm in the Western world, and she further theorizes about how the change from a female to a male deity might have taken place.*

Reading Rhetorically

Eisler's aim in this selection is to challenge long-held assumptions in the fields of religious history and of archaeology that God is male. With entire monotheistic religions traditions such as Judaism, Christianity, and Islam founded upon patriarchal and decidedly male interpretations of deity (that generally exclude women from holding priestly roles or decision-making power), it is no small task to argue persuasively that before God was Goddess. Eisler uses an argumentative style that incorporates logic, reasoning, and a great variety of evidence. In short, she adopts many of the same tools that males have used before her to argue in favor of a divine male god to attempt to turn their positions upside down. As you read, note how effective you think her argument is.

Our Lost Heritage: New Facts on How God Became a Man

1   In the nineteenth century, archeological excavations began to confirm what scholars of myth had long maintained—that goddess worship preceded the worship of God. After reluctantly accepting what no longer could be ignored, religious historians proposed a number of explanations for why there had been this strange switch in divine gender. A long-standing favorite has been the so-called Big Discovery theory. This is the idea that, when men finally became aware that women did not bring forth children by themselves—in other words, when they discovered that it involved their sperm, their paternity—this inflamed them with such a new-found sense of importance that they not only enslaved women but also toppled the goddess.

2   Today, new archeological findings—particularly post-World War II excavations—are providing far more believable answers to this long-debated puzzle. For largely due to more scientific archeological methods, including infinitely more accurate archeological dating methods such as radiocarbon and dendrochronology,[1] there has been a veritable archeological revolution.

3   As James Mellaart of the London University Institute of Archeology writes, we now know that there were in fact many cradles of civilization, all of them thousands of years older than Sumer, where civilization was long said to have begun about five thousand years ago.[2] But the most fascinating discovery about these original cultural sites is that they were structured along very different lines from what we have been taught is the divinely, or naturally, ordained human order.

4   One of these ancient cradles of civilization is Catal Huyuk, the largest Neolithic site yet found. Located in the Anatolian plain of what is now Turkey, Catal Huyuk goes back approximately eight thousand years to about 6500 B.C.E.—three thousand years before Sumer. As Mellaart reports, this ancient civilization "is remarkable for its wall-paintings and plaster reliefs, its sculpture in stone and clay . . ., its advanced technology in the crafts of weaving,

---

[1]Radiocarbon dating is a method of establishing the age of prehistoric artifacts by measuring the radioactivity of carbon; dendrochronology is a dating procedure based on counting the growth rings of trees.

[2]Mellaart, *The Neolithic of the Near East* (New York: Charles Scribner's Sons, 1975).

woodwork, metallurgy . . ., its advanced religion . . . , its advanced practices in agriculture and stockbreeding, and . . . a flourishing trade. . . ."[3]

But undoubtedly the most remarkable thing about Catal Huyuk and other   5
original sites for civilization is that they were *not* warlike, hierarchic, and
male-dominated societies like ours. As Mellaart writes, over the many centuries of its existence, there were in Catal Huyuk no signs of violence or deliberate destruction, "no evidence for any sack or massacre." Moreover, while
there was evidence of some social inequality, "this is never a glaring one." And
most significantly—in the sharpest possible contrast to our type of social organization—"the position of women was obviously an important one . . . with
a fertility cult in which a goddess was the principal deity."[4]

Now it is hardly possible to believe that in this kind of society, where,   6
besides all their other advances, people clearly understood the principles of
stockbreeding, they would not have also had to understand that procreation
involves the male. So the Big Discovery theory is not only founded on the fallacious assumption that men are naturally brutes, who were only deterred
from forcefully enslaving women by fear of the female's "magical" powers of
procreation; the Big Discovery theory is also founded on assumptions about
what happened in prehistory that are no longer tenable in light of the *really*
big discoveries we are now making about our lost human heritage—about
societies that, while not ideal, were clearly more harmonious than ours.

But if the replacement of a Divine Mother with a Divine Father was not   7
due to men's discovery of paternity, how did it come to pass that all our present world religions either have no female deity or generally present them as
"consorts" or subservient wives of male gods?

To try to answer that question, let us look more carefully at the new arche-   8
ological findings.

Logic would lead one to expect what ancient myths have long indicated   9
and archeology has since confirmed: that since life issues from woman, not
man, the first anthropomorphic deity was female rather than male. But logical
or not, this position was hardly that of the first excavators of Paleolithic caves,
some of whom were monks, such as the well-known Abbé Henri Breuil. They
consistently refused to see in the many finds of twenty-five-thousand-year-old
stylized female sculptures what they clearly were: representations of a female
divinity, a Great Mother. Instead, the large-breasted, wide-hipped, bountiful,
and often obviously pregnant women these men christened "Venus figurines"
were described either as sex objects (products of men's erotic fantasies) or
deformed, ugly women.[5] Moreover, in order to conform to their model of history as the story of "man the hunter" and "man the warrior," they refused to
see what was actually in the famous cave paintings. As Alexander Marshack
has now established, not only did they insist that stylized painting of tree

---

[3]Mellaart, *Catal Huyuk* (New York: McGraw-Hill, 1967). 11.

[4]Ibid., 69, 225, 553.

[5]See, for example, E. O. James, *The Cult of the Mother Goddess* (London: Thames and Hudson, 1959) and M. Gimbutas, "The Image of Woman in Prehistoric Art," *Quarterly Review of
Archeology,* December 1981.

branches and plants were weapons, they sometimes described these pictures as backward arrows or harpoons, chronically missing their mark![6] They also, as Andre Leroi-Gourhan noted in his major study of the Paleolithic, insisted on interpreting the already quite advanced art of the period as an expression of hunting magic, a view borrowed from extremely primitive contemporary societies like the Australian aborigines.[7]

10   Although Leroi-Gourhan's interpretation of the objects and paintings found in Paleolithic caves is in sexually stereotyped terms, he stresses that the art of the Paleolithic was first and foremost religious art, concerned with the mysterics of life, death, and regeneration.[8] And it is again this concern that is expressed in the rich art of the Neolithic, which, as Mellaart points out, not only shows a remarkable continuity with the Paleolithic,[9] but clearly foreshadows the great goddess of later Bronze Age civilizations in her various forms of Isis, Nut, and Maat in Egypt, Ishtar, Lillith, or Astarté in the Middle East, the sun-goddess Arinna of Anatolia, as well as such later goddesses as Demeter, Artemis, and Kore in Greece, Atargatis, Ceres, and Cybele in Rome, and even Sophia or Wisdom of the Christian Middle Ages, the Shekinah of Hebrew Kabalistic tradition, and, of course, the Virgin Mary or Holy Mother of the Catholic Church about whom we read in the Bible.[10]

11   This same prehistoric and historic continuity is stressed by UCLA archeologist Marija Gimbutas, whose monumental work, *The Goddesses and Gods of Old Europe,* brings to life yet another Neolithic civilization: the indigenous civilization that sprang up in the Balkans and Greece long, long before the rise of Indo-European Greece.[11] Once again, the archeological findings in what Gimbutas termed the civilizations of Old Europe not only demolish the old "truism" of the "warlike Neolithic" but also illuminate our true past, again showing that here, too, the original direction of human civilization was in some ways far more civilized than ours, with pre-Indo-Europeans living in far greater harmony with one another and the natural environment.

12   Moreover, excavations in Old Europe, like those unearthed in other parts of the ancient world, show that what brought about the onset of male dominance both in heaven and on earth was not some sudden male discovery. What ushered it in was the onslaught of barbarian hordes from the arid steppes and deserts on the fringe areas of our globe. It was wave after wave of these pastoral invaders who destroyed the civilizations of the first settled agrarian societies. And it was they who brought with them the gods—and men—of war

---

[6]Marshack, *The Roots of Civilization* (New York: McGraw-Hill, 1972).

[7]A. Leroi-Gourhan, *Prehistoire de l'Art Occidental* (Paris: Edition D'Art Lucien Mazenod, 1971).

[8]Ibid.

[9]Mellaart, *Catal Huyuk,* 11.

[10]See, for example, R. Eisler, *The Blade and the Chalice: Beyond War, Sexual Politics, and Fear,* work in progress; M. Stone, *When God Was a Woman* (New York: Harvest, 1976); E. Neumann, *The Great Mother* (Princeton: Princeton UP, 1955).

[11]M. Gimbutas, *The Goddesses and Gods of Old Europe* (Berkeley: U of California P, 1982).

that made so much of later or recorded history the bloodbath we are now taught was the *totality* of human history.

In Old Europe, as Gimbutas painstakingly documents, there were three major invasionary waves, as the Indo-European peoples she calls the Kurgans wiped out or "Kurganized" the European populations. "The Old European and Kurgan cultures were the antithesis of one another," writes Gimbutas. She continues:

> The Old Europeans were sedentary horticulturalists prone to live in large well-planned townships. The absence of fortifications and weapons attests the peaceful coexistence of this egalitarian civilization that was probably matrilinear and matrilocal.[12] . . . The Old European belief system focused on the agricultural cycle of birth, death, and regeneration, embodied in the feminine principle, a Mother Creatrix. The Kurgan ideology, as known from comparative Indo-European mythology, exalted virile, heroic warrior gods of the shining and thunderous sky. Weapons are nonexistent in Old European imagery; whereas the dagger and battleaxe are dominant symbols of the Kurgans, who, like all historically known Indo-Europeans, glorified the lethal power of the sharp blade.[13]

So while we are still commonly taught that it was to Indo-European invaders—such as the Aechaean warriors, celebrated by Homer, who eventually sacked Troy—that we owe our Western heritage, we now know that they in fact did not bring us civilization. Rather, they destroyed, degraded, and brutalized a civilization already highly advanced along wholly different lines. And, just as the factuality of how these truly savage peoples denoted both women and goddesses to the subservient status of consort or wife has now been established, the fact [that] they brought in warfare with them is also confirmed.

Once again, as when Heinrich Schliemann defied the archeological establishment and proved that the city of Troy was not Homeric fantasy but prehistoric fact, new archeological findings verify ancient legends and myths. For instance, the Greek poet Hesiod, who wrote about the same time as Homer, tells us of a "golden race," who lived in "peaceful ease" in a time when "the fruitful earth poured forth her fruits." And he laments how they were eventually replaced by "a race of bronze" who "ate not grain" (in other words, were not farmers) and instead specialized in warfare ("the all-lamented sinful works of Ares were their chief care").[14]

Perhaps one of the most fascinating legends of ancient times is, of course, that of the lost civilization of Atlantis. And here again, as with the once only legendary city of Troy, archeological findings illuminate our true past. For what new findings suggest is what the eminent Greek scholar Spyridon Martinatos

---

[12]In anthropology, *matrilinear* refers to descent through the female line; *matrilocal* pertains to residence with the wife's family.

[13]M. Gimbutas, "The First Wave of Eurasian Steppe Pastoralists in Copper Age Europe," *Journal of Indo-European Studies*, 1977, 281.

[14]Hesiod, quoted in J. M. Robinson, *An Introduction to Early Greek Philosophy* (Boston: Houghton Mifflin, 1968) 12–14.

already suspected in 1939: That the legend of a great civilization which sank into the Atlantic is actually the garbled folk memory of the Minoan civilization of Crete and surrounding Mediterranean islands, portions of which did indeed disappear into the sea after unprecedented volcanic eruptions sometime after 1500 B.C.E.[15]

18   First discovered at the turn of this century, the once unknown Bronze Age civilization of ancient Crete has now been far more extensively excavated. As Nicolas Platon, former superintendent of antiquities in Crete and director of the Acropolis Museum, who excavated the island for over thirty years, writes, Minoan civilization was "an astonishing achievement." It reflected "a highly sophisticated art and way of life," indeed producing some of the most beautiful art the world has ever seen. Also in this remarkable society—the only place where the worship of the goddess and the influence of women in the public sphere survived into historic times, where "the whole of life was pervaded by an ardent faith in the goddess Nature, the source of all creation and harmony"—there was still "a love of peace, a horror of tyranny, and a respect for the law."[16]

19   And once again, it was not men's discovery of their biological role in paternity that led to the toppling of the goddess. It was another, final Indo-European invasion: The onslaught of the Dorians, who, with their weapons of iron, as Hesiod writes, brought death and destruction in their wake.[17]

20   So the revolution in norms that literally stood reality on its head—that established this seemingly fundamental and sacrosanct idea that we are the creations of a Divine Father, who all by Himself brought forth all forms of life—was in fact a relatively late event in the history of human culture. Moreover, this drastic change in direction of cultural evolution, which set us on the social course that in our nuclear age threatens to destroy all life, was certainly not predetermined or, by any stretch of the imagination, inevitable. Rather than being some mystical mystery, it was the substitution of a force-based model of social organization for one in which both the female and male halves of humanity viewed the supreme power in the universe not as the "masculine" power to destroy but rather as the "feminine" power to give and nurture life.

21   Another popular old idea about this change was that it was the replacement of matriarchy with patriarchy. But my research of many years shows that matriarchy is simply the flip side of the coin to the *dominator* model of society, based upon the dominance of men over women that we call patriarchy. The real alternative to patriarchy, already foreshadowed by the original direction of human civilization, is what I have called the *partnership* model of social relations.[18] Based upon the full and equal partnership between the

---

[15]S. Martinatos, "The Volcanic Destruction of Minoan Crete," *Antiquity,* 1939, 13:425–439.

[16]N. Platon, *Crete* (Geneva: Nagel, 1966) 48, 148.

[17]Hesiod, see note 14.

[18]See, for example, R. Eisler, *The Blade and the Chalice;* R. Eisler, "Violence and Male-Dominance: The Ticking Time Bomb," *Humanities in Society,* Winter-Spring 1984, 7:1/2:3–18; R. Eisler and D. Loye, "The 'Failure' of Liberalism: A Reassessment of Ideology from a New Feminine-Masculine Perspective," *Political Psychology,* 1983, 4:2:375–391; R. Eisler, "Beyond Feminism: The Gylan Future," *Alternative Futures,* Spring-Summer 1981, 4:2/3:122–134.

female and male halves of our species, this model was already well-established a long time ago, before, as the Bible has it, a male god decreed that woman be subservient to man.

The new knowledge about our true human heritage is still meeting enormous resistance, with traditional "experts" from both the religious and academic establishments crying heresy. But it is a knowledge that, in the long run, cannot be suppressed. [22]

It is a knowledge that demolishes many old misconceptions about our past. It also raises many fascinating new questions. Is the real meaning of the legend of our fall from paradise that, rather than having transgressed in some horrible way, Eve should have obeyed the advice of the serpent (long associated with the oracular or prophetic powers of the goddess) and *continued* to eat from the tree of knowledge? Did the custom of sacrificing the first-born child develop after the destruction of this earlier world—as the Bible has it, after our expulsion from the Garden of Eden—when women had been turned into mere male-controlled technologies of reproduction, as insurance of a sort that conception had not occurred before the bride was handed over to her husband? [23]

We may never have complete answers to such questions, since archeology only provides some of the data and ancient writings, such as the Old Testament, were rewritten so many times, each time to more firmly establish, and sanctify, male control.[19] But what we do have is far more critical in this time when the old patriarchal system is leading us ever closer to global holocaust. This is the knowledge that it was not always this way: There are viable alternatives that may not only offer us survival but also a far, far better world. [24]

Questions for Discussion and Your Reading Journal

1. What is the "Big Discovery" (Paragraph 1) theory? What is one concrete reason that this theory is not convincing?
2. What was, according to Eisler, one of the most remarkable things about the Neolithic ruin Catal Huyuk?
3. Why did many early archaeologists fail to understand the significance of goddess-oriented artifacts?
4. Where does Eisler indicate our male-dominated, warlike heritage comes from, and what did it replace?
5. If ancient Indo-Europeans worshipped a divine goddess who was closely associated with nature and the giving of life, why is the Western world now almost entirely dominated by the worship of a male, fatherlike deity?
6. What does Eisler suggest is the danger of a male-dominated, warlike society in the 20th century?
7. What is matriarchy? How does the early society described by Eisler differ from a matriarchal society?
8. In your own words, explain what type of modern society we would be if our society were based on goddess worship.

---

[19]Ibid.

NINIAN SMART
AND RICHARD D. HECHT, EDS.

The following selection comes from Sacred Texts of the World, *an anthology edited by Ninian Smart and his colleague Richard D. Hecht. In this dialogue between the Buddha and his pupil Ānanda, the Buddha reveals his perceptions of the effect women would have upon his religion. At the time of this writing, nuns were permitted to join Buddhist monasteries but only under certain conditions that kept them in inferior positions of authority and separated from the male monks. Buddha predicted that women would bring about the downfall of Buddhism.*

Reading Rhetorically

It is more accurate to take the following reading as a general cultural statement of popular thinking in the early years of Buddhism rather than as a literal teaching of the Buddha. Either way, the challenges women face in patriarchal religions become evident in these lines. Even when women are permitted to participate in such religions, male bias against their spiritual abilities and natures often severely restricts the limited roles opened to them. The Buddhist writers of the following text seem to have some awareness of possible counter-arguments to the position they take against women. They supply example after example from day-to-day life to support their main claim, perhaps anticipating from the outset that half the human race would be inclined to disagree with them.

Women and the Order

1   Then the venerable[1] Ānanda drew near to where the Blessed One was; and having drawn near and greeted the Blessed One, he sat down respectfully at one side. And seated respectfully at one side, the venerable Ānanda spoke to the Blessed One as follows:

2   "Mahā-Pajāpatī of the Gautama clan, Reverend Sir, has accepted the eight weighty regulations; the sister of the mother of the Blessed One has become ordained."

3   "If, Ānanda, women had not retired from household life to the houseless one, under the Doctrine and Discipline announced by the Tathāgata, religion, Ānanda, would long endure: A thousand years would the Good Doctrine abide. But since, Ānanda, women have now retired from household life to the houseless one, under the Doctrine and Discipline announced by the Tathāgata, not long, Ānanda, will religion endure; but five hundred years, Ānanda, will

---

[1]**venerable** Worthy of honor and respect, usually due to age, achievements, or character. [Ed. note.]

the Good Doctrine abide. Just as, Ānanda, those families which consist of
many women and few men are easily overcome by burglars, in exactly the
same way, Ānanda, when women retire from household life to the houseless
one, under a doctrine and discipline, that religion does not long endure. Just
as, Ānanda, when the disease called mildew falls upon a flourishing field of
rice, that field of rice does not long endure, in exactly the same way, Ānanda,
when women retire from household life to the houseless one, under a doctrine
and discipline, that religion does not long endure. Even as, Ānanda, when the
disease called rust falls upon a flourishing field of sugarcane, that field of sugarcane does not long endure in exactly the same way, Ānanda, when women
retire from household life to the houseless one, under a doctrine and discipline,
that religion does not long endure. And just as, Ānanda, to a large pond a man
would prudently build a dyke, in order that the water might not transgress its
bounds, in exactly the same way, Ānanda, have I prudently laid down eight
weighty regulations, not to be transgressed as long as life shall last."

Questions for Discussion and Your Reading Journal

1. What main conclusion does the Buddha defend in this argument?
2. What premises does he offer to support this conclusion? Is the argument
   convincing?
3. Can you draw parallels between the Buddha's attitude toward women and
   attitudes toward women in other major world religions? Give examples
   from your own experience if possible.

NAILA MINAI

*Naila Minai's insights into the status of women in early Islamic culture
grow out of her own roots in the Islamic tradition and are broadened by
years of study and travel throughout the Western world. Where many
modern champions of women's rights tend to view Islam's treatment of
women in largely negative and stereotypic terms, Minai gives a more
positive perspective that emphasizes the improvements to women's lives
that Islam made possible among the tribal cultures of Arabia in the seventh and eighth centuries. This text provides a valuable look below the
surface of the Islamic teachings and beliefs overviewed in the two readings by John B. Christopher and in the selection from the Quran.*

Reading Rhetorically

It is commonly believed in parts of the West that Islam oppresses women.
Minai sets out to counter this stereotype. Through a historical look at the
roots of Islam and at the significant roles played by key women in the Prophet
Muhammad's family to establish and to preserve this religion, Minai offers a
compelling look at Islam as a champion of women's rights. The strength of her

position is buttressed by the scholarly nature of her work, which draws upon many historical sources. Perhaps the most effective rhetorical tool Minai draws upon is a "delayed thesis" approach to her argument. Note how she saves her most radical and forceful ideas to the very end of the reading. When she finally presents these ideas, she has had ample time to prepare better her readers through the thoroughness of her research both to respect and to accept her major points. As you read, note how effective you think this strategy is.

Women in Early Islam

"Woman is made hard and crooked like a rib."

—Arabian proverb popular
in the seventh century A.D.

"Women are the twin halves of men."

—The Prophet Muhammad

1   Khadija, an attractive forty-year-old Arabian widow, ran a flourishing caravan business in Mecca in the seventh century A.D., and was courted by the most eligible men of her society. But she had eyes only for an intelligent and hardworking twenty-five-year-old in her employ named Muhammad.[1] "What does she see in a penniless ex-shepherd?" her scandalized aristocratic family whispered among themselves. Accustomed to having her way, however, Khadija proposed to Muhammad and married him. Until her death some twenty-five years later, her marriage was much more than the conventional Cinderella story in reverse, for Khadija not only bore six children while co-managing her business with her husband, but also advised and financed him in his struggle to found Islam, which grew to be one of the major religions of the world.

2   It was a religion that concerned itself heavily with women's rights, in a surprisingly contemporary manner. A woman was to be educated and allowed to earn and manage her income. She was to be recognized as legal heir to her father's property along with her brother. Her rights in marriage were also clearly spelled out: She was entitled to sexual satisfaction as well as economic support. Nor was divorce to consist any longer of merely throwing the wife out of the house without paying her financial compensation.

3   This feminist bill of rights filled an urgent need. Meccans in the seventh century were in transition from a tribal to an urban way of life. As their town grew into a cosmopolitan center of trade, kinship solidarity had deteriorated, but municipal laws had not yet been fully established to protect the citizens. Women were particularly vulnerable, their rights closely linked with the tribal way of life their people had known before renouncing nomadism to settle in Mecca around A.D. 400. In nomadic communities of the desert a woman was not equal to a man. During famine a female could be killed at birth to increase her brother's food supply. However, if she managed to reach adulthood she had a better status in the desert than in the city, largely because her labors were

indispensable to her clan's survival in the harsh environment. While the men protected the encampment and engaged in trade, she looked after the herds and produced the items to be traded—meat, wool, yogurt, and cheese, all of which bought weapons and grains as well as other essentials. As a breadwinner the tribal woman enjoyed considerable political clout. Even if she did not always participate in council meetings, she made her views known. Only a fool refused to heed his womenfolk and risked antagonizing a good half of his tribe, with whom he had to live in the close confines of the camp and caravan.

If tribal discord was uncomfortable in the best of circumstances, it was   4 catastrophic during the battles that broke out frequently among the clans over pasture and watering rights or to avenge heroes slain by the enemy. With the battlefront so close to home, a woman was needed as a nurse, cheerleader, and even soldier. She was sometimes captured and ransomed or sold into slavery. If her tribesmen could not pay her captors the required number of camels in ransom, they valiantly stormed the enemy's camp to rescue her. These were men brought up on recitations of epic poems about brave warriors who rescued fair damsels in distress. Poets and poetesses of the tribe kept chivalry alive, constantly singing praises of heroism among their people and condemning cowardliness and disloyalty. No one who wanted a respectable place in his tribe could afford to ignore the ubiquitous "Greek chorus," for life without honor was worse than death to a nomad, who could not survive as an outcast in the desert.

Marriage customs varied from tribe to tribe,[2] but the most popular were   5 those that tended to maintain the woman's independence, if only incidentally, by having her remain within her family circle after marriage. If the husband was a close relative, the couple set up a conjugal tent near both of their parents. A husband who was not kin merely visited her at her home. In some clans women could be married to several visiting husbands at the same time. When the wife bore a child, she simply summoned her husbands and announced which of them she believed to be the child's father. Her decision was law. Actually, it did not matter greatly who the biological father was, since children of such unions belonged to the matrilineal family and were supported by communal property administered by her brothers or maternal uncles.

Life in the desert was so hard and precarious that some of the most impov-   6 erished tribes renounced nomadism to submit to a less independent existence in towns. Muhammad's ancestors, a segment of the Kinanah tribe, were among them. They settled down at the crossroads of important caravan routes in the place which is now Mecca, and prospered as middlemen under the new name of Quraysh. Their great wealth and power undoubtedly helped their deities extend their spiritual influence far beyond Mecca's boundaries and make Kaaba, their sanctuary, the most important shrine in central Arabia. As keepers of the shrine the leading Quraysh families grew immeasurably rich, but the wealth was not equitably distributed. As survival no longer depended on communal sharing and on women's contributing equally to the family budget, Meccans became more interested in lucrative business connections than in kinship ties. Glaring socioeconomic differences—unknown among nomads—emerged. Women lost their rights and their security.

7   If brothers went their separate ways, their sister who continued to live with them after marriage lost her home unless one of them took her and her children under his protection. A woman could not automatically count on her brothers to assume this duty, for with the rise of individualism the patrilineal form of marriage, which had coexisted with other marital arrangements in seventh-century Mecca, was gaining popularity. A self-made man tended to prefer leaving his property to his own sons, which sharpened his interest in ensuring that his wife bore only his children. The best way to guarantee this was to have her live under close supervision in his house. The woman thus lost her personal freedom, but the security she gained from the marital arrangement was precarious at best in the absence of protective state laws. Not only did she have to live at her in-laws' mercy, she could be thrown out of the house on her husband's whim. Khadija escaped such a fate because she was independently wealthy and belonged to one of the most powerful families of the Quraysh—a fact that must have helped her significantly to multiply her fortune.

8   It was against such a backdrop of urban problems that Islam was born.[3] Even though Muhammad lived happily and comfortably with his rich wife, he continued to identify with the poor and the dispossessed of Mecca, pondering the conditions that spawned them. He himself had been orphaned in early childhood and passed on from one relative to another. Since his guardians were from the poor and neglected branch of the Quraysh, Muhammad earned his keep as a shepherd from a very early age. But he was luckier than other orphans, for he at least had a place in loving homes and eventually got a good job with Kahadija's caravan, which allowed him to travel widely in the Middle East.

9   These journeys had a direct bearing on his spiritual growth and gave focus to his social concerns by exposing him to Christian monks and well-educated Jewish merchants. They intrigued him, for they seemed to have put into practice a monotheistic faith which a few Meccans of the educated circles were beginning to discuss. How did the Christian God inspire such diverse nationalities to worship Him alone? How did the Judaic God manage to unite widely dispersed Semitic groups under one set of laws which provided for the protection of women and children even in large cities? The astral deities that Muhammad's people inherited from their nomadic ancestors demanded offerings but gave nothing in return. After discussions with people of various faiths, Muhammad sought the ultimate solution to his community's problems in the solitude of a cave on Mount Hiraa overlooking Mecca, where he often retreated in his spare moments, with Khadija or by himself.

10   While meditating alone one day in the cave, Muhammad heard a voice which he believed to be the angel Gabriel's. "Proclaim in the name of thy Lord and Cherisher who created, created man out of a clot of congealed blood" (Quran, surah [chapter] xcvi, verses 1–2),[4] it said, pointing out that there was only one God and that man must serve Him alone. When Muhammad recovered from his ecstasy, he ran back, shaken, and described his experience to his wife. Having shared his spiritual struggles, Khadija understood that her husband had received a call to serve the one God whom the Christians and the Jews also worshipped. Bewildered and confused, Muhammad went on with

his daily work in the city and occasional meditations on Mount Hiraa. Again the voice commanded him to tell his people about the one omnipotent God, who would welcome believers into heaven and cast wicked people into hell. With Khadija's repeated encouragement, Muhammad finally accepted his prophetic call and devoted the rest of his life to preaching God's word as the new religion of Islam (which means *submission* [*to the will of God*]). Converts to it were called Muslims *(those who submit)*. They were not to be called Muhammadans, because they did not worship Muhammad, who was merely a human messenger for the one God. Though invisible and immortal, this God was named Allah after the Zeus of the old Meccan pantheon.

Numerous revelations that Muhammad received from Allah throughout   11 his life were compiled shortly after his death into the Muslim bible, named the Quran, which formed the basis for the Shariah, or Islamic law. A supplement to it was provided by the Hadith, or Muhammad's words, which were recorded over many years as his survivors and their descendants remembered them. Despite the exotic Arabic words in which it is couched, Islam's message is similar in its essentials to the one promulgated by Judaism and Christianity, and can be summed up by the Ten Commandments. *Allah,* after all, is but the Arabic name for the God worshipped by both Jews and Christians. But the rituals differed. Muhammad required his followers to obey the commandments through the practice of five specific rituals, called the pillars of Islam. A Muslim must (1) profess faith in one God; (2) pray to Him; (3) give alms to the poor; (4) fast during Ramadan, the month in the lunar calendar during which Muhammad received his first revelation; and (5) go on a pilgrimage to Mecca at least once in his lifetime (if he can afford to do so) to pay respects to the birthplace of Islam and reinforce the spirit of fellowship with Muslims from all over the world. Although these laws preached fairness and charity among all mankind, God—through Muhammad—preferred to establish specific guidelines to protect the interests of women.

Once he had united enough people under Allah to make a viable commu-   12 nity, Muhammad devoted an impressive number of his sermons to women's rights. In doing so, however, he did not attempt to fight the irreversible tide of urbanization. Nor did he condemn the trend toward patrimonial families, although they often abused women. Too shrewd a politician to antagonize Mecca's powerful patriarchs, he introduced a bill of rights for women which would not only ensure their protection under patriarchy but also reinforce the system itself so that it would stand as a mini-tribe against the rest of the world.

He did this mainly by providing for women's economic rights in marriage   13 in such a way that they had a financial stake in the system which constantly threatened to erode their independence. Upon marriage a man had to pay his bride a dowry, which was to be her nest egg against divorce or widowhood. While married to him, she could manage the dowry and all other personal income in any way that she pleased, exclusively for her own benefit, and will them to her children and husband upon her death. In her lifetime she did not have to spend her money on herself, or her children for that matter, since only the man was responsible for supporting his family. If the woman stayed married to her husband until his death, she also inherited part of his property.

While her share was less than her children's, she was assured of being supported by her sons in widowhood. By the same line of reasoning, her inheritance from her father was half that of her brother's: Her husband supported her, whereas her brother had to support his wife. The daughter's right to inherit tended to divide the patriarch's wealth, but the problem was customarily solved by having her marry a paternal first cousin. Falling that, the inheritance became a part of yet another Muslim family in the same tribe of Islam, united through faith rather than kinship. In either case, a Muslim woman with neither a paid occupation nor an inheritance enjoyed a modicum of financial independence, at the price of her submission to a patriarchal form of marriage.

14   But she was to be allowed to choose her own spouse, according to the Hadith: "None, not even the father or the sovereign, can lawfully contract in marriage an adult woman of sound mind without her permission, whether she be a virgin or not." This freedom was to be assured by a law that required the dowry to be paid to the bride herself. Since the parents were not to pocket it, as they often did before Islam, they were presumably above being "bought." But the brides' freedom remained largely theoretical, since most of them were barely ten years old when engaged to be married for the first time. Aysha, whom Muhammad married after Khadija's death, was only about six or seven years old when she was betrothed and about ten when she moved into her husband's house with her toys. Muhammad was not playing legal tricks on women, however. He did revoke the parents' choice of mate when their daughters complained to him about it.[5] Although parents were to be honored and obeyed, he made it clear that the grown-up daughter was to be respected as an individual—so much so that the marriage contract could be tailored to her specific needs: The bride could impose conditions on her contract. A cooperative wife, he pointed out, was the best foundation for a stable marriage.

15   Though Muhammad repeatedly preached compassion and love as the most important bonds of marriage, he also gave men financial enticements to keep the family together. The husband was allowed to pay only a part of the dowry upon marriage, with the balance payable upon divorce. If the dowry was large enough, the arrangement deterred the husband from throwing out his wife without substantial cause. In fact, under Islam he could no longer just throw her out. He had to pay her not only the balance of the dowry but also "maintainance on a reasonable scale" (Quran ii:241). He was also to support her through the ensuing *idda,* the three months of chastity which the Shariah asked her to observe in order to determine whether she was carrying his child. If pregnant, she was to be helped until she delivered and had nursed the infant to the point where he could be cared for by the husband's family. All of her children remained under the paternal roof. In a patriarchal society where men were not eager to support others' children or to provide employment for women, the child custody law assured children a decent home and enabled the divorcée to remarry more easily, but even an independently wealthy woman was forbidden to walk out of her husband's home with her children.

16   Any sexual behavior that would weaken the patriarchal system was strongly discouraged or made illegal. If the custom of taking a visiting husband was frowned upon, her taking more than one at a time was condemned

as adultery, which was punishable by whipping. Although men were also forbidden to sow wild oats, they could marry up to four wives and have as many concubines as they could afford. This law may have been partly a concession by Muhammad to the widely accepted custom among wealthy urban men, but he also saw it as a way to attach surplus women to the men's households for their own protection as well as to maintain social order. Due to frequent intertribal warfare and attacks on the merchants' caravans, women always outnumbered men. The conflict became increasingly serious as Muhammad's following grew large enough to threaten the purse and the prestige of the families who amassed fortunes from pilgrims to the Kaaba. So vicious were the attacks that in A.D. 622,[6] after Khadija died, Muhammad moved his budding Muslim community to Medina, an agricultural community without important shrines that would be threatened by Allah. Moreover, the perpetually quarrelling clans of Medina welcomed Muhammad because of his reputation as a just man and a skillful arbitrator.

Muhammad succeeded brilliantly in settling the clans' differences and won   17 a prominent place in Medina. This made Meccans even more determined to destroy him before he built up an alliance against them. Violent battles between the Muslims and the Meccans followed. Alliances and betrayals by various tribal factions during each battle engendered more battles, which decimated the Muslim community. The number of widows mounted to such catastrophic proportions after the battle fought at Uhud, near Medina, that God sent a message officially condoning polygamy: "Marry women of your choice, two, or three, or four." But He added, "If you fear that you cannot treat them equitably, marry only one" (iv,3). A polygamous husband was required to distribute not only material goods but also sexual attention equally among his wives, for sexual satisfaction, according to Muhammad, was every woman's conjugal right. Besides, a sexually unsatisfied wife was believed to be a threat to her family's stability, as she was likely to seek satisfaction elsewhere.

Unmarried men and women also posed a threat to Muhammad's scheme   18 of social order, which may be one reason why he frowned upon monasticism. Sexual instincts were natural, he reasoned, and therefore would eventually seek fulfillment in adultery* unless channeled into legitimate marriage. Wives and husbands were thus necessary for each other's spiritual salvation. "The curse of God be upon those women who remain unwed and say they will never marry," he said, "and a man who does not marry is none of mine."

Though the Quran abolished the ancient custom of stoning adulteresses to   19 death and called instead for public whipping—a hundred lashes administered to male and female offenders alike—Muhammad knew that the sexual double standard would single out women as targets of slander. After a bitter personal experience, he hastened to build safety features into his antiadultery and antifornication laws.

One day Aysha was left behind inadvertently by Muhammad's caravan   20 when she stepped away to look for a necklace that she had lost. She was brought back to the caravan the following morning by a man many years

---

*Here *adultery* refers to premarital as well as extramarital sex.

younger than her middle-aged husband, which set tongues wagging. Even Ali, Muhammad's trusted cousin and son-in-law, cast doubt on her reputation. The Prophet's faith in his wife was severely shaken. Aysha was finally saved when her husband fell into a trance, which indicated that he was receiving a message from God. Relief spread over his face. God had vouched for her innocence. The "affair of the slander," as it came to be known, was closed.[7] Four witnesses were henceforth required to condemn women of adultery, as against only two for business transactions and murder cases. Moreover, false witnesses were to be whipped publicly.

21   Other than false witnesses, violators of women's rights were not punished on this earth. The law would catch up with them in the next world, where they would be cast into the fire (an idea borrowed from the Christians). The good, on the other hand, would reside forever in a heavenly oasis with cool springs in shady palm groves where their every whim would be served by lovely dark-eyed houris. Like the Christian preachers who promised believers a heaven with pearly gates and haloed creatures floating about on white clouds, Muhammad merely presented images that would spell bliss to the common man. Though he did not specify who was going to serve the deserving women, probably for fear of offending their husbands, Muhammad guaranteed a place for them in paradise. Women had the same religious duties as men, and their souls were absolutely equal in God's eyes, with not even the responsibility for original sin weighing upon them. Islam rejects the idea of original sin altogether, claiming that every child is born pure. Nor does the Quran single out Eve as the cause of man's fall (though folklore in various parts of the Middle East does condemn her). According to the Quran, Allah tells both Adam and Eve not to eat the apple. "Then did Satan make them slip from the Garden" (ii,36). Allah scolds them both equally, but promises mercy and guidance when they repent.

22   Muhammad's decision to rely on each man's conscience to fulfill his Islamic obligation toward women reflected a realistic approach to legislation. He seems to have recognized how far he could carry his reforms without losing his constituents' support. In a city where women had neither economic nor political weight, men would take only so much earthly punishment for disregarding their rights. By the same token, they would not entirely give up their old prerogative of divorcing their wives for any cause without answering to a third party, or pay them more than comfortably affordable compensation. Muhammad therefore struck a compromise in his laws, but repeatedly emphasized the spirit of kindness and respect for women which was implied in them. When deprived of their true spirit, the laws were open to abuse, but were still better than no protection at all. For example, a man could legally divorce any number of wives without good cause if he met his financial obligations. But the amount of both the dowry and the alimony was determined purely by his conscience, and no court of law could enforce payment. Even if a man honestly did the best he could, the financial compensation that he paid supported the divorcée only for a short while unless he was extremely rich. This left at a disadvantage the older woman with diminished chances for remarriage. Muhammad therefore made a special virtue of marrying older women, and

stressed that God disliked divorce enormously. "A Muslim must not hate his wife," he said repeatedly, "and if he be displeased with one bad quality in her, let him be pleased with another which is good."[8] As a fellow husband, he tactfully sympathized with the local saying "Woman is made hard and crooked like a rib," but added, "If ye wish to straighten it, ye will break it."

Mothers, however, were above snide remarks. "Heaven lieth at the feet of mothers," said Muhammad, summing up God's repeated commands to love and respect mothers, and by extension all older women. Helping needy women was as great a virtue as fasting all day and praying all night.   23

"I have done a great crime. Is there any act by which I may repent?" a man asked Muhammad one day.   24

"Have you a mother?" the Prophet said.   25

"No," the man replied.   26

"Have you an aunt?"   27

"Yes."   28

"Do good to her, and your crime will be pardoned."   29

Daughters, often unwanted and killed at birth, were also treated with special tenderness by Muhammad, whose four surviving children were all girls. Female infanticide was outlawed. Education was to be open to girls as well as boys. The girl's interests were to be considered when marrying her off. "Marriage is a servitude," he pointed out, "therefore, let each one of you examine in what hands he places his daughter." In a society where women could not live unattached to a family, paternal duty did not end with the daughter's marriage. "Shall I point out to you the best of virtues?" Muhammad said. "It is your doing good to your daughter when she is returned to you having been divorced by her husband." Since daughters did not constitute old-age security for their parents, Muhammad could only promise their guardians special rewards in the next world. "Whoever hath a daughter and doth not bury her alive or scold her or prefer his male children to her, may God bring him into paradise," he said.   30

Women fared rather well under Muhammad's social reforms. Secure within the still-tribelike community of Islam, they not only took advantage of the rights granted them but fought to keep them. Although the Prophet had repeatedly stressed that learning was a "duty incumbent on every Muslim, male and female," women found themselves tied to housework and falling behind men in Muhammad's classes on religion. They petitioned Muhammad to set up a class for them at a mutually convenient time, and he obliged. At one of their meetings women objected that God's words were always addressed to men. Although in Arabic the masculine is used when referring to both men and women, Muhammad came back some time later with a revelation containing the "he or she" jargon that American feminists adopted thirteen centuries later: "The men who resign themselves to God and the women who resign themselves, and the believing men and the believing women, and the devout men and the devout women, and the men of truth and the women of truth, and the patient men and the patient women, and the humble men and the humble women . . . for them hath God prepared forgiveness and a rich recompense" (xxxiii,35).   31

32   A few of the learned women also acted as imams[9] (the equivalent of ministers in Islam, which does not have an ordained clergy). As he chose the most learned and respected man in a group to lead the prayers when he was absent, Muhammad appointed the most learned woman to lead when only women congregated for prayer. On the other hand, Umm Waraqah, one of the best students of the Quran, was asked to be imam for both the men and women of her large household. She did not set a precedent for later generations, however, since Muhammad never specified the conditions under which women could be imams. Today, women may lead only women. Those who are well versed in the Quran and the Hadith serve as imams and teachers mainly in sexually segregated societies.

33   Under Islam, poetesses rediscovered their role as historians, journalists, propagandists, social critics, and cheerleaders of their community. They celebrated the ideals which united their Islamic tribe, moved men to defend them against enemies, and sang of their victories. They eulogized those fallen in battle and elevated them to martyrdom, inspiring the living to avenge the dead and plaguing the conscience of those who transgressed the accepted code of ethics. The undisputed poet laureate in Muhammad's time was a woman named Al-Khansa.[10] She started her career as a typically promising young poetess, reciting at births, weddings, and funerals. She soon proved to be a prodigy who delighted in showing off her virtuosic skill in improvising verses, and regularly walked away with the highest prizes at the most prestigious poetry contest, held annually at the fair of Ukaz near Mecca. When she lost her brother in battle, everyone said that she became fully possessed by those spirits (jinn) who commune only with the best poets, for her grief unlocked verses that epitomized her people's suffering in their constant fight for survival. Al-Khansa eventually followed her sons to battle, reciting verses to arouse women and men to fight on for Islam.

34   Although most women fighters were poetesses and nurses who took up arms in self-defense or to avenge their loved ones' death, some volunteered as soldiers. The list of women warriors was in fact rather long, given the small size of the early Islamic community. Typical among them was Umm Umarah, one of Muhammad's earliest converts. She fought alongside her husband and sons in many battles, retiring only after she lost a hand. Like any old soldier, she was proud to show off her battle scars.

35   Perhaps the most endearing of the women veterans was Safiya, Muhammad's seventy-year-old aunt, who stood guard when the Muslim community in Medina was under siege. She noticed an enemy prowling around the weak point of the fortification. Unable to warn the men in time, she clubbed down the intruder herself.

36   The old chronicles and poems celebrating the daring exploits of these Amazons may not stand the scrutiny of today's historians in every detail, but they point out that the ideal woman in the mass media of early Islam was neither a housewife nor a sex object, but man's colleague. She would have been quite at home with Judith, Queen Esther, and Joan of Arc.

37   . . . The unspecified rights that women had enjoyed during Muhammad's time were chipped away gradually. But the meticulously detailed laws on mar-

ital and financial rights were too specific to be ignored entirely, and gave women a modicum of security and independence in the patriarchal family, which survived as a mini-tribe in the sprawling empire. Within the family circle women exerted considerable influence, not only on their men but also on the blossoming of Arab culture in the Middle Ages. An exceptional few followed Aysha's example and ruled the caliphs and their empire, which spread Islam to lands and peoples far beyond the Arabian peninsula.

Notes

1. For a detailed historical account in English of Muhammad's life and teachings, see W. Montgomery Watt, *Muhammad at Mecca* (Oxford, England: Oxford UP, Clarendon, 1953) and *Muhammad at Medina* (Oxford: Oxford UP, Clarendon, 1962). In his *Islam in Focus* (Indianapolis: American Trust, 1975), Dr. Hammudah Abdalati, who was a member of the Department of Islamic Culture at Al-Azhar University, one of the most prestigious universities for religious studies in the Islamic world, gives a thoughtful discussion of Islamic law.

2. Different types of marriage practiced among the Arabian tribes at the dawn of Islam are described in Watt, *Muhammad at Medina*, pp. 378–79, and in Gertrude H. Stern, *Marriage in Early Islam* (London: Royal Asiatic Society, 1939) 25. See also Diana Richmond, *Antar and Abla, a Bedouin Romance* (London: Quartet Books, 1978), for a romanticized portrayal of pre-Islam tribal life. The book deals with one of the most celebrated love stories of Arabia.

3. The problems of transition from a tribal to an urban way of life which Meccans experienced when Muhammad was growing up are detailed in Watt, *Muhammad at Medina*, chapter 3.

4. The English translations of the Quran are from A. Yusuf Ali, trans., *The Holy Quran* (Washington: American International, 1946). *The Koran*, J. M. Rodwell, trans. (London: Everyman Library, Kent, 1974), is also a worthwhile reference because it presents the surahs in the order in which they are believed to have been revealed to Muhammad, rather than arranged by length.

   Eventually different sects and schools formed around varying interpretations of the Quran and the Hadith. Muslim judges pronounced their own decisions on matters not covered by the Quran and the Hadith. Today the Shariah encompasses such decisions as well as the Quran and the Hadith, although the degree of importance accorded the decisions varies considerably from sect to sect. The Quran and the Hadith, however, remain the backbone of the Shariah in all sects. This book does not delve into sectarian nuances but focuses mainly on what the Quran says about women's rights. Some of Muhammad's pronouncements are quoted to supplement the Quran. Variations in the interpretation and application of the Shariah are discussed only where appropriate.

5. The independence that women enjoyed during Muhammad's time is documented by Nabia Abbott in *Aishah, the Beloved of Mohammed*

(Chicago: U of Chicago P, 1942). Pp. 110–11 describe Muhammad as a champion of women's right to choose their mates, even if this meant that he himself had to overrule the parent's choice.

6. The first year of Hegira, the Muslim era. Based on a lunar calendar, the hegira year is shorter than the solar year. A.H. 1401, for example, began on November 10, 1980, and will end on October 28, 1981. For a table converting A.H. to A.D. see Romeo Campani, *Calendario Arabo, Tabelle comparative delle Ere Araba e Christiano-Gregoriana mese per mese (Egira 1–1,318) e giorno per giorno (E.V. 1900–2000)* (Paris: Paul Geuthner, 1914).

7. The "affair of the slander" is described in greater detail in Abbott, p. 36.

8. Muhammad's sayings are excerpted from Muhammad ibn Muhammad al-Ghazali, "Le Livre des bons usages en matière de mariage," *Vivication des sciences de la foi*, Bibliothèque de la Faculté de Droit d'Alger, XVII, trans. I. Bercher and G. H. Bousquet (Paris: Maisonneuve, 1953), and Allama Sir Abdullah Al-Mamun al-Suhrawardy, *The Sayings of Muhammad* (New York: E. P. Dutton 1941).

9. Abbott, pp. 112–14.

10. For her life story and French translations of some of her poems, see Khansa bint Amr, *Le Diwan d'al Hansa, précédé d'une étude sur les femmes poètes de l'ancienne arabe per le P. de Coppier S. J.* (Beirut: Imprimerie catholique, 1889).

Questions for Discussion and Your Reading Journal

1. According to the second paragraph of Minai's text, what specific things did the "feminist bill of rights" in early Islam include?

2. For what reasons were women considered valuable in Arab tribal societies before the arrival of cities and urban-centered cultures?

3. What major problems did the movement toward urban cultures create for Arab women?

4. The prophet Muhammad, of course, was most directly responsible for developing the guiding themes of Islam. This text suggests, however, that an influential woman also helped shape Islam. Who was she and how did she contribute to the development of Islam?

5. This text argues that economic rights were an important advancement that Islam offered women. In your opinion, is it important for women to have economic rights equal to those of men? Why or why not?

6. When it came to marriage, in what way did Islam set up a double standard for men and women?

7. According to the biblical tradition, Eve bore responsibility for bringing about original sin by eating the forbidden apple. How does the Quran treat this same topic?

8. In important ways, this reading represents an extended argument by Minai. Sum up in one or two sentences what you interpret her argument to be. Are you convinced by this argument? Explain.

SULTANA YUSUFALI

Sultana Yusufali was a 17-year-old high-school student living in Toronto, Canada, when she wrote the following piece for the Toronto Star *newspaper. As a teenager and a Muslim woman, she and her family have kept her out of the public eye on this controversial issue, except for the preceding limited information that appeared in a byline with the publication of her essay.*

Reading Rhetorically

As a minority Arab woman in Western society, Yusufali comes to the issue of women's roles in Islam with an alternate perspective that she can anticipate is not shared by the majority of her readers. She knows from the start that her position on wearing the Islamic hijab will fly directly in the face of popular opinion in Canada. The success or failure of her argument rests as much upon how she presents herself as an Islamic woman as upon the logic, reasons, and evidence that she uses to support her position. Hers is a personal defense of her main point, that hijab "is actually one of the most fundamental aspects of female empowerment," a seemingly contradictory argument. As you read, note how she resolves the contradiction.

Why Do I Wear Hijab?

I probably do not fit into the preconceived notion of a "rebel." I have no visible tattoos and minimal piercings. I do not possess a leather jacket. 1

In fact, when most people look at me, their first thought usually is something along the lines of "oppressed female." 2

The brave individuals who have mustered the courage to ask me about the way I dress usually have questions like: "Do your parents make you wear that?" or "Don't you find that really unfair?" 3

A while back, a couple of girls in Montreal were kicked out of school for dressing like I do. It seems strange that a little piece of cloth would make for such controversy. Perhaps the fear is that I am harbouring an Uzi underneath it. 4

Of course, the issue at hand is more than a mere piece of cloth. I am a Muslim woman who, like millions of other Muslim women across the globe, chooses to wear the hijab. And the concept of the hijab, contrary to popular opinion, is actually one of the most fundamental aspects of female empowerment. 5

When I cover myself, I make it virtually impossible for people to judge me according to the way I look. I cannot be categorized because of my attractiveness or lack thereof. Compare this to life in today's society: We are constantly sizing one another up on the basis of our clothing, jewelry, hair and makeup. What kind of depth can there be in a world like this? Yes, I have a body, a 6 physical manifestation upon this Earth. But it is the vessel of an intelligent mind and a strong spirit.

7   It is not for the beholder to leer at or to use in advertisements to sell everything from beer to cars. Because of the superficiality of the world in which we live, external appearances are so stressed that the value of the individual counts for almost nothing.

8   It is a myth that women in today's society are liberated. What kind of freedom can there be when a woman cannot walk down the street without every aspect of her physical self being "checked out"? When I wear the hijab I feel safe from all of this. I can rest assured that no one is looking at me and making assumptions about my character from the length of my skirt. There is a barrier between me and those who would exploit me. I am first and foremost a human being, equal to any man, and not vulnerable because of my sexuality.

9   One of the saddest truths of our time is the question of the beauty myth and female self-image. Reading popular teenage magazines, you can instantly find out what kind of body image is "in" or "out." and if you have the "wrong" body type, well, then, you're just going to have to change it, aren't you? After all, there is no way that you can be overweight and still be beautiful. Look at any advertisement. Is a woman being used to sell the product? How old is she? How attractive is she? What is she wearing? More often than not, that woman will be no older than her early 20s, taller, slimmer and more attractive than average, dressed in skimpy clothing.

10   Why do we allow ourselves to be manipulated like this?

11   Whether the '90s woman wishes to believe it or not, she is being forced into a mold. She is being coerced into selling herself, into compromising herself. This is why we have 13-year-old girls sticking their fingers down their throats and overweight adolescents hanging themselves. When people ask me if I feel oppressed, I can honestly say no. I made this decision out of my own free will. I like the fact that I am taking control of the way other people perceive me. I enjoy the fact that I don't give anyone anything to look at and that I have released myself from the bondage of the swinging pendulum of the fashion industry and other institutions that exploit females.

12   My body is my own business. Nobody can tell me how I should look or whether or not I am beautiful. I know that there is more to me than that. I am also able to say "no" comfortably then people ask me if I feel as though my sexuality is being repressed.

13   I have taken control of my sexuality. I am thankful I will never have to suffer the fate of trying to lose/gain weight or trying to find the exact lipstick shade that will go with my skin colour. I have made choices about what my priorities are and these are not among them. So next time you see me, don't look at me sympathetically. I am not under duress or a male-worshipping female captive from those barbarous Arabic deserts. I've been liberated.

Questions for Discussion and Your Reading Journal

1. In her opening line, Yusufali indicates that she does not fit the "preconceived notion of a rebel." By the end of her essay do you begin to see her as a "rebel"? Why or why not?

2. In Paragraph 5, Yusufali argues that "the concept of hijab, contrary to popular opinion, is actually one of the most fundamental aspects of empowerment" for Muslim women. List all the evidence that she gives to support this position. Do you find her evidence convincing? Why or why not?

3. In Paragraph 8, Yusufali brands the counter-argument that "women in today's society are liberated," a "myth." After reading her reasons for making this claim, do you agree or disagree? Explain your position.

4. With her last sentence, Yusufali states, "I've been liberated." From what, exactly, has she been liberated?

5. Sum up in one or two paragraphs what you feel others can learn from Yusufali's essay about dealing with cultural stereotypes.

WAR AND PEACE

KAREN ARMSTRONG

Karen Armstrong (1946–) is a former Roman Catholic nun who left the order in 1969 to earn a degree at Oxford University in modern literature. She has written highly successful books that take readers into deeper understanding of the three great monotheistic faiths, Judaism, Christianity, and Islam; her works include Muhammad: A Biography of the Prophet *(1992);* A History of God *(1993); and* Jerusalem: One City, Three Faiths *(1996). She has also written a biography of Buddha (2001). She currently teaches part time at a rabbinical school in London.*

Reading Rhetorically

The following reading comes from a recorded conversation taped in 2002 in New York City where Armstrong joined an academic discussion of the rise of fundamentalist religions in recent years around the world. Although Armstrong uses an academic/expert approach to informing her readers of the nature of fundamentalism, there is also an element of persuasion that subtly works its way through the reading. By a careful choice of language and examples that show fundamentalism from the perspective of various fundamentalist groups themselves, she removes much of the negative bias that generally surrounds this topic. It is not that she attempts to persuade readers that they should embrace fundamentalism but, rather, that they should give this topic more serious consideration. Part of her rhetorical strategy for dealing with such a controversial topic is to hold her most important, and controversial, ideas until the end.

From "Fundamentalism and the Modern World"

1   Fundamentalism has erupted in every single major faith worldwide, not just in the Islamic world. The term "fundamentalism" was coined here in the United States, at the turn of the 20th century, when Protestant Christians said that they wanted to go back to the fundamentals of their faith. Sometimes Jews and Muslims, understandably, find it slightly offensive to have this Christian term foisted upon them, because they feel they have other objectives. It also suggests that fundamentalism is a kind of monolithic movement expressing the same kind of ideas and ideals.

2   Nevertheless, the term has come into popular parlance and tends to stand for a group of militant pieties that have erupted in every single major faith worldwide during the 20th century, first in Protestant fundamentalism. But also we have fundamentalist Judaism, Islam, Sikhism, Confucianism, Hinduism.

3   Fundamentalism is not simply extremism. Fundamentalism is not simply conservatism. Billy Graham, for example, would not be accepted as a fundamentalist by those who call themselves fundamentalists, nor would he call himself one. The Saudis, in Saudi Arabia, may be traditionalists but they're not, strictly speaking, fundamentalists.

4   We often see the words "fundamentalist terrorism" or "fundamentalist violence" put together. But only a tiny proportion of the people who might be called fundamentalists actually take part in acts of terror and violence. That's a very important distinction to make. Most people are simply struggling to live a religious life, as they see it, in a world that seems increasingly inimical to faith.

5   So what is fundamentalism? Fundamentalism represents a kind of revolt or rebellion against the secular hegemony of the modern world. Fundamentalists typically want to see God, or religion, reflected more centrally in public life. They want to drag religion from the sidelines, to which it's been relegated in a secular culture, and back to center stage.

6   Typically, fundamentalists have proceeded on a fairly common program. Very often they begin by retreating from mainstream society and creating, as it were, enclaves of pure faith where they try to keep the godless world at bay and where they try to live a pure religious life. Examples would include the ultra-orthodox Jewish communities in New York City or [Christians at] Bob Jones University or Osama bin Laden's camps.

7   In these enclaves, fundamentalist communities often plan, as it were, a counteroffensive, where they seek to convert the mainstream society back to a

more godly way of life. Some of them may resort to violence. Why? Because every fundamentalist movement that I've studied—in Judaism, Christianity, and Islam—is rooted in a profound fear. They are convinced, even here in the United States, that modern liberal secular society wants to wipe out religion in some way or is destructive to faith.

In some parts of the Muslim world, the modernization process has been   8
so accelerated and so rapid that secularism is very often experienced not as a liberating movement, as we have in the United States, but as a deadly assault upon faith. For example, when Ataturk was bringing modern Turkey into being, he closed down all the *madrasas,* the colleges of further education. He abolished all the Sufi orders and forced them underground, and forced all men and women to wear Western dress.

In Iran, the shahs used to make their soldiers go through the streets with bay-   9
onets, taking the women's veils off and tearing them to pieces in front of them. These modernizers wanted their countries to look modern. Never mind that the vast majority of the population, because of the rapid pace of the modernization process, had no understanding of modern institutions or modern ideals. Very often in these countries, only an elite had the benefit of a Western education.

In Eqypt, the chief mentor of Osama bin Laden, a man called Sayyid   10
Qutb, developed the form of fundamentalism that tends to be followed by most fundamentalists in the Sunni Muslim world. President Nasser had incarcerated thousands of members of the Muslim brotherhood, often without trial, and often for doing nothing more incriminating than handing out leaflets or attending a meeting. Sayyid Qutb went into the camp as a moderate. But after 15 years of hard labor, watching the brothers being executed, or being subjected to mental or physical torture, and hearing Nasser vow to relegate religion to the purely private sphere, he came to the conclusion that secularism was a great evil. Qutb was executed by President Nasser in 1966.

When people feel that their backs are to the wall and they're fighting for   11
survival, they can, very often, turn to violence. So fundamentalism often develops in a kind of symbiotic relationship with a modernity that is felt to be aggressive and intrusive.

Fundamentalism is not going back to the Dark Ages. We often treat fun-   12
damentalist movements as though they're harking back to some impossible, archaic, distant golden age. This is not true. These are essentially modern movements that could have taken root in no time other than our own.

The great changes of modernity mean that none of us can be religious in   13
the same way as our ancestors. We are, all of us, having to develop different forms of seeing our faiths. Every generation, ever since religion began, has had to reinterpret its traditions to meet the challenge of its particular modernity. But the challenges have been particularly great, especially during the 20th century. Fundamentalism is simply one of the attempts to rethink faith. The Ayatollah Khomeini was essentially a man of the 20th century. Instead of harking back to the Dark Ages, he was really introducing a revolutionary form of Shi'ism that was, in fact, as innovative as if the pope had abolished the Mass. But most of us didn't understand enough about Shi'ism to appreciate that.

14   Fundamentalist movements can also be modernizing. We're seeing in Iran the Islamic revolution—which seemed to us to throw off modernity—introduce into the country representational government, which Iranians were never allowed to have before. The institutions are highly flawed and imperfect but, under President Khatami, who sees himself working within the tradition of Khomeini, they are moving towards something democratic and modern.

15   It's no good ignoring fundamentalism with secularist or liberal disdain, as unworthy of serious consideration, hoping that it will somehow go away. Fundamentalism is an essential part of the modern scene and will be with us for some time. The fact that it is so ubiquitous, that it has erupted in almost every place where a modern, secular-style society has tried to establish itself—that again tells us something important about modernity. It suggests a great disenchantment that we must take seriously or ignore at our peril.

Questions for Discussion and Your Reading Journal

1. What is fundamentalism, exactly, and what religions does it affect, according to Armstrong?
2. What is the "counteroffensive" that fundamentalists launch and why do they do it?
3. What led Sayyid Qutb, the mentor of Osama bin Laden, to develop the Sunni Muslim form of fundamentalism?
4. Why do fundamentalists often turn to violence, according to Armstrong?
5. What does Armstrong mean when she says "Fundamentalism is simply one of the attempts to rethink faith"?
6. Does Armstrong seem to think that if we ignore fundamentalism it will eventually die out on its own? Explain.
7. Have you ever been around a fundamentalist movement or effort personally? What was it and what were its main concerns? Does Armstrong's overview help you understand it better? Explain.

MALISE RUTHVEN

Malise Ruthven was born in Dublin, Ireland, and is of Scotch-Irish descent. He studied English literature at Cambridge University in England, and Arabic language and culture in Jordan and the Middle East. He has worked as a BBC staff writer in London and as a freelance journalist and university lecturer in England and the United States. The reading included here comes from his book Islam in the World *(2000). He has published other noteworthy books on religion, including* The Divine Supermarket: Shopping for God in America *(1989), and* A Satanic Affair: Salman Rushdie and the Wrath of Islam *(1990).*

Reading Rhetorically

Ruthven aims to get his readers to look at the Islamic world-view in a new light. His personal experience in Jordan and the Middle East provide him with unusual tools for doing so. He starts with "the heavy, stressed rhythms of Western rock music" and compares them to "the complex rhythms and quarter tones of Eastern music" as an effective way to illustrate the cultural differences between the Arab world-view and the Western world-view. A focus on music quickly leads to language, and from there to analysis of the Quran. With each illustration and example, Ruthven leads his readers into deeper insight into Islam's most sacred book and into the religion itself. The difficult nature of this journey into Islam is perhaps best summed up by the frustrated and negatively charged response of Thomas Carlyle to the Quran, which Ruthven presents and discusses. By incorporating such counter-perspectives into Islamic culture with his own perspective, Ruthven anticipates the conceptual and language problems that his readers will face, and deals with them in advance. As you read, note the use of the counter-perspective and how effective you think it is.

The Quranic World-View

> "These are the signs of the Manifest Book
> We have sent it down as an Arabic
> Koran haply you will understand"
> —Quran 12:1–2 (tr. Arberry)

AN "ARABIC" QURAN

Few things are more indicative of the cultural differences between Europe and the Arab world than the sounds which emerge from the radio. In Europe the heavy, stressed rhythms of western rock music, punctuated by chat from fast-talking disc jockeys, create contrasting patterns which flash at the ear like so many multi-coloured neon signs. The aural world of Arab radio seems to operate within a much narrower range of frequencies. The complex rhythms and quarter-tones of eastern music are considerably more subtle than the strident impulses which hypnotize western listeners, while the language has a richness of tone and density of texture that seems to combine the warmth of a Bukhara carpet with the silken delicacy of Damascus brocade.

1

NOTE: All citations from the Quran in this chapter are from Muhammad Asad, *The Message of the Qur'ān* (Gibraltar, 1980), an English rendering of the so-called "Royal Egyptian" edition published in Cairo in 1337H/1918. *Suras* (chapters) and verses are rendered in accordance with standard academic practice—e.g. 3:28 signifies *sura* 3 (Äl 'Imrān), verse 28. Where I have changed Asad's wording I have signalled this with an asterisk*.

2   If Arabic is the key to this culture, the Quran is the key to Arabic. The language, if not invented, was specially developed for its transmission. The art of writing was rudimentary until the necessity for accurate versions of the Quran produced a dramatic evolution. According to Muslim tradition, the Prophet's utterances were first written down on whatever materials came to hand, such as shoulder-blades of camels, palm leaves, pieces of wood or parchment. These were later collected into *suras*, or chapters, under the supervision of the Prophet. No 'final' version of the text existed during his lifetime, for so long as he continued to receive revelations, the recension of God's Word was not complete.*

3   The final collection is supposed to have been made during the caliphate of 'Uthman, based on a text collated by the Prophet's principal secretary, Zaid ibn Thabit, and passed for safe-keeping to his widow, Hafsa, 'Uthman's daughter. Because of the manner in which rival versions of the same passages were being used as propaganda in the quarrels that had broken out inside the Muslim community, 'Uthman is supposed to have ordered an authorized version to be collected and copied, and all other variant texts destroyed. All present editions of the Quran (in which there are some slight variations, none of them important) are said to be based upon this so-called 'Uthmanic recension'. Some Western scholars have, however, radically questioned the Muslim account, using methods adapted from biblical textual analysis. They argue that the Quran as we know it was assembled at a much later date out of a fragmentary oral tradition deriving from the Arabian Prophet, but which also included a large quantity of exegetical or explanatory matter developed in the course of polemical disputes with Jews and Christians after the Arab conquest. This revisionist theory of the Quran has radical consequences for the early history of Islam, for it would suggest that the religious institutions emerged at least two centuries after Muhammad's time, to consolidate ideologically, as it were, the Arab conquest. It would mean that the Arabs, anxious to avoid becoming absorbed by the more advanced religions and cultures of the peoples they conquered, cast about for a religion that would help them to maintain their identity. In so doing they looked back to the figure of the Arabian Prophet, and attributed to him the reaffirmation of an ancient Mosaic code of law for the Arabs.

4   The revisionist theory has several attractions. It fits in with the available palaeographic evidence, which places the development of Arabic script much later than the Muslim sources. It provides an explanation of certain archaeological problems, such as the fact that the *qiblas* of certain early mosques in Iraq face Jerusalem rather than Makka. It would account for the absence of any references in Jewish sources to Madina as a place where the Torah was studied; and it would account for the repetitious and inconsequential character of the Quran which so exasperated Thomas Carlyle as well as countless others who have struggled through translations in various European languages: 'I must say, it is as toilsome reading as I ever undertook. A wearisome confused jumble, crude, incondite; endless iterations, long-windedness, entanglement . . . insupportable stupidity, in short! Nothing but a sense of duty could carry any European through the Koran!'

---

*We have retained the original punctuation. [Ed. note.]

Such words would smack of sacrilege, not just to the devout Muslim, but 5
to almost any Arab Christian, for whom the Quran, whatever religious truth
it contains, is the perfection of language. Basically, the historiographical controversy about the Quran's origins, regardless of its scientific merits, reflects
the same culture-gap which makes most Europeans dislike the sounds emitted
by Arab radio, because their ears, and minds, are ill-tuned to them. An assault
upon the Quran's authenticity is an assault upon an identity moulded by these
very repetitions and subtle inflexions.

In a special sense, the Arabs are a people moulded by their scripture. The 6
Hebrew and Christian texts were translated into Greek and Latin, and from
them diffused into other languages and cultures. European ideologies and
political movements no doubt owe much to biblical inspiration. The Mosaic
vision of a land promised by God may, consciously or otherwise, have influenced the utopian dreams of protestant settlers and communists, as well as
Zionists. But in all such cases many other cultural and political strands have
been present. In the West, after the Latin Church had lost its liturgical monopoly, such cultural and ultimately political pluralism was encouraged by the
translation of the Bible into different European tongues. Translation, which
contributed much to the formation of national identities in the West, was
made religiously possible by the pluralistic origins of the Bible itself, which
consists of most of the Hebrew scriptures plus an originally oral Aramaic tradition transcribed into Greek. For Christians the Word of God was manifested
in Christ's person, not in the language in which he revealed God's speech. Thus
in the earliest Christian centuries, national and regional squabbles took the
form of conflicts about the nature of this Person. The doctrine that the Quran
was the eternal and unalterable Word of God, revealed in Arabic (as the Quran
itself states on several occasions), prevented any such diffusion of the Muslim
scripture into the surrounding cultural landscape: the very intransigence with
which the Arabs defended the integrity of their text was decisive in maintaining a common Arab identity, which would otherwise have disintegrated, like
that of other nomadic conquerors both before and after Islam, into a multiplicity of new national groupings, such as occurred after Charlemagne in western Europe.

STRUCTURE OF THE QURAN

The most obvious difficulty for those brought up on the chronological sequences 7
of the Bible or Hindu epics is the absence of sustained narrative. The subject
matter, including stories of the earlier prophets, punishment stories about those
who failed to heed them, psalm-like lyric passages celebrating the manifestation,
of God's glory in nature, and the Leviticus-like legal prescriptions, appear to be
jumbled and diffused throughout the text. For instance, the Sura of Light contains one of the most celebrated passages in all mystical literature:

> God is the Light of the heavens and the earth. The parable of His light is, 8
> as it were, that of a niche containing a Lamp: the lamp is [enclosed] in
> glass, the glass [shining] like a radiant star: [A lamp lit from] a blessed

tree—an olive tree that is neither of the east nor of the west—the oil whereof [is so bright that it] would well-nigh give light [of itself] even though fire had not touched it: light upon light! (24:35)

9   The same *sura,* however, a few verses earlier, lays down details for the punishment of adulterers (100 lashes) and slanderers (80 lashes), and urges women not to 'swing their legs [in walking] so as to draw attention to their hidden charms'. This mixing of the sublime and the mundane, which Westerners might see as evidence of a 'consistent lack of logical structure', has in the didactic and liturgical context a powerful function. For, despite the proliferation of manuscripts of the Quran, and its extensive use in the highly developed art-form of calligraphic embellishment, it originated as a series of texts designed for oral transmission.

10   No one who has visited Cairo or any other great Arab Muslim city could fail to notice the position the Quran still occupies in the oral culture of the more traditionally minded sectors of society. Public recitations of the Quran are an important part of such social events as weddings, circumcisions, funerals, wakes and visits to the tombs of dead relatives on feast-days. At Cairo wakes, which are held on the evening of burial and successive Thursdays, male friends and relatives are to be found gathered in brightly lit marquees decorated with arabesques of red and white appliqué work. In the richer, more westernized, parts of the city, they will be seated on gilt salon chairs, of the kind used at concerts or fashion shows. The *muqri,* or professional Quran reciter, may be seated cross-legged on the ground, or loud-speakers may be linked to a microphone in a nearby mosque. Some of the *muqris* become extremely popular—and wealthy. Those who cannot afford to hire a live *muqri* are often to be seen playing their offerings on cassette radios.

11   Popular piety is still very much alive in Egypt and other Arab countries whose poverty has prevented them from succumbing to the blandishments of consumer capitalism. Taxi-drivers of the traditional kind, who would not dream of overcharging their Muslim passengers, will have the name of Allah on electric-coloured stickers on the facia board, or embroidered on pennants which festoon the interior like the tassles of a lampshade. The meandering nasal tones of the *muqri* will often be playing on the cassette machine, if the driver is especially pious. Cairo taxi-drivers include some of the most devout—as well as the most foul-mouthed—people in the world.

12   The esteem in which Arabs hold the Quran is not just the result of a religious dogma: it is due to the fact that many people find in its sonorous, rhyming prose an aesthetic pleasure of the kind Westerners usually discover in fine music or painting. Its dense elliptical style is a rich fund of aphorisms, its riddles and allegories the source of countless legends. Although there is a discernible variation in style between the short ecstatic passages from the earliest Makkan period and the much longer *suras* of the Madinese period, the seemingly chaotic organization of the material ensures that each of the parts in some way represents the whole. Good Muslims, especially those groomed for religious leadership, are required to memorize the whole of the Quran at a very early age. Since it consists of some 120,000 words divided into 114 *suras*

and 6,000 verses *(ayas)*, this is a considerable feat which, in the nature of things, many people fail to master. Nevertheless, almost any one of the *suras* will contain, in a more or less condensed form, the message of the whole. This is especially true of the chronologically later *suras* placed near the beginning, in which most of the legislation is to be found. An only partially memorized Quran will, therefore, contain as much as a conscientious but uneducated Muslim will find it necessary to know.

The illogical organization of the text in fact renders it more accessible, and   13
this is central to the Quran's didactic purpose. The more inaccessible the scripture, the greater the distinction between clergy and laity. While Sunni Islam certainly developed a rabbinical class of *ulama* with a superior knowledge of the text and its interpretation, the fact that a substantial part of it was known to everyone in society militated against the emergence of a spiritual elite comparable to the Catholic or Orthodox priesthoods.

Nevertheless, the need for such a class of interpreters was apparent from   14
an early stage. Many passages are obscure, and cannot be understood without reference to the substantial body of exegetical literature, derived from the oral *hadith*-traditions which came to be selected and written down around the third century of Islam. There are many allusions to events in the Prophet's career which can only be explained from these sources. Thus the punishment stories, composed from Arabian folklore and biblical materials, mostly date from the late Makkan and early Madinese periods, and are clearly intended as threats and warnings to the pagan Quraishis. The Madinese *suras* contain many references to such events as the division of the spoils after Badr, the cowardice of the 'hypocrites' at Uhud, the punishment of the Banu Nadir, Muhammad's marriages, and other events mentioned in the previous chapter.

The allusiveness of the Quran's style is, however, not confined to the cir-   15
cumstances of revelation. It is, in fact, integral to its didactic method, which could be described as a series of 'one-way dialogues' between God and the Prophet and between Muhammad and his auditors. The effect is not unlike listening to a person speaking on the telephone: one only hears half the conversation. The inaudible part of the discourse, Muhammad's unspoken questions, the arguments of his critics, and so forth, have to be reconstructed out of the exegetical literature, which draws on the vast body of *hadith*-tradition.

This exegetical literature became, in due course, a source of law: for only by   16
detailed study of the so-called 'occasions' of revelation could the general prescriptions and prohibitions contained in the Quran be given the force of law. This was especially necessary in the case of apparently contradictory statements, such as the prohibition on wine. Thus *sura* 16:67 clearly allows the drinking of wine:

> And [we grant you nourishment] from the fruit of date-palms and vines: from it you derive intoxicants as well as wholesome sustenance . . .

However, this is evidently contradicted by 2:219:   17

> They will ask thee about intoxicants and games of chance. Say: 'In both are great evil and some uses for men. But the sin in them is greater than their usefulness . . .'*

18 An even stronger prohibition occurs in 5:90–1:

> O you who have attained to faith! Wine, and games of chance, and idol-atrous practices, and the divining of the future are but a loathsome evil of Satan's doing: shun it then, so that you might attain a happy state! By means of wine and games of chance Satan seeks only to sow enmity and hatred among you, and to turn you away from the remembrance of God and from prayer. Will you not, then, desist?*

19 Without a chronology of revelation derived from the *hadith* literature, it would be impossible to determine whether wine was a possible benefit, an evil to be tolerated, or one to be prohibited absolutely. Although there was some disagreement about the order of some of the verses, the consensus was that 5:90, representing the strongest prohibition, was revealed after 2:219, and therefore overrules it; while 16:67 dates from the Makkan period, when Muhammad still allowed wine-drinking among his followers. One of the famous Quran commentators, Fakhr al-Din al-Razi, commenting on this passage, cites one of his predecessors:

> Al-Qaffal said that the wisdom of issuing the prohibition in these stages lies in the following: God knew that the people had been accustomed to drinking wine and drawing from it its many uses. Thus he also knew that it would be unbearable for them if he had prohibited them all at once [from the use of wine] and thus unquestionably [for this reason] he made use of these stages and kindness in the prohibition . . .

20 More abstruse legal points occur in commentaries on 2:172, where the flesh of swine is prohibited. Are the pig's bristles, used for sewing leather, included in the ban? This was a subject on which authorities disagreed. There was also disagreement concerning the meat of the hippopotamus, known to the Arabs as *khinzir al-ma,* 'water-swine.' Argument depended on whether the hippo's presumed 'swinishness' overruled its character as a water-creature, allowed under 5:96: 'Lawful to you is all water-game, and what the sea brings forth . . .'

21 In order to deal with a host of similar problems, the exegetes developed a doctrine of abrogation, based on 2:106: 'Any verse/message [*aya*] which We annul or consign to oblivion We replace with a better or similar one . . .' According to the great Persian grammarian and exegete, Abu al-Qasim al-Zamakhshari (d. 1144), the verse was revealed in response to a challenge from the unbelievers, who had said: 'Look at Muhammad, now he commands his companions to do something, and then forbids it to them and commands the opposite. He says one thing today and retracts it tomorrow!' Zamakhshari continues:

> To abrogate a verse means that God removes it by putting another in its place . . . Every verse is made to vanish whenever the well-being [of the community] requires that it be eliminated—either on the basis of the

---

*The translation of this Quranic quotation differs from that of Muhammad Asad.

wording or [by] virtue of what is right, or on the basis of both these reasons together, either with or without a substitute.

Zamakhshari belonged to the rationalistic school of theologians (Mu'-   22
tazilis) who believed that the Quran, having been 'created' in time, could be interpreted with considerable allowances made for time-bound changes due to historical and social conditions. The Mu'tazilis were eventually defeated after attempting unsuccessfully to impose their doctrines by force during the caliphate of al-Mamun (813–33), but the doctrine of abrogation survived in a more restricted form. Some modern authorities, including Muhammad Asad, have rejected it absolutely. The word 'aya', according to Asad, means in this context a 'message' rather than a Quranic verse, and therefore refers to the abrogation, by the whole Quran, of the earlier Hebrew and Christian scriptures.

The activities of the exegetes were very far from being confined to legal   23
problems. Only about 600 of the Quran's 6,000 verses deal with legislative matters. Stories of the earlier prophets and the punishments meted out to those who failed to heed them, ecstatic descriptions of God's power in nature and the eschatological passages about paradise, hell and the Day of Judgement occupy much of the rest. Sometimes the language is explicit and self-explanatory, at other times it is highly allusive and allegorical. The Quran itself is eloquent on this point:

> He it is who has bestowed upon thee from on high this divine writ, containing messages [*ayas*] that are clear in and by themselves, and those are the essence of the divine writ [*umm al-kitab*], as well as those that are allegorical. (3:7)

In his commentary on this passage Zamakhshari writes: 'If the [meaning of   24
the] entire Quran [were clearly] determined men would come to depend on it since it would be so easily accessible, and would turn away from what they lack—research and meditation through reflection and inference.'

The memorizing and study of the Quran, which occupied such a large part   25
of the traditional Muslim education, has always been regarded as the most meritorious of all religious activities. Assimilated and internalized through constant repetition, the sacred book became part of the Muslim's very being, the filter through which he received the world and its mental images. Just as Islamic philanthropy and the requirements of law gave rise to the splendid monuments of Islamic architecture—mosques, schools, hospitals, convents, public drinking fountains and other pious foundations—Quranic piety created out of the divine text literary artefacts comparable in many ways to the plastic images created out of medieval Christian piety. Thus Zamakhshari's embellishments to 19:16–22, where the annunciation and birth of Jesus are described, convey a typical medieval literalism. Here is the original text, slightly shortened, taken from Asad's translation:

> And . . . Lo! [Mary] withdrew from her family to an eastern place, and kept herself in seclusion from them, whereupon We sent to her Our angel of revelation, who appeared to her in the shape of a well-made human being. She exclaimed: 'Verily! I seek refuge from thee with the Most Gracious!

[Approach me not] if thou art conscious of Him. [The angel] answered: 'I am but a messenger of thy Sustainer [who says] "I shall bestow on thee the gift of a son endowed with purity."' Said she: 'How can I have a son when no man has ever touched me?—for never have I been a loose woman!' [The angel] answered: 'Thus it is: [but] thy Sustainer says: "This is easy for Me; and thou shalt have a son, so that We might make him a symbol unto mankind and an act of grace for Us."' And it was a thing decreed, and in time she conceived him and then she withdrew with him to a far-off place. (19:16–22)

26 Zamakhshari's embellishments to this passage are too long to give in full. But here is a condensed version:

27 Some say that Mary settled in an eastern place when she wanted to purify herself from menstruation, and that she concealed herself behind a wall, or perhaps something else that would keep her out of view. The place where she usually stayed was the mosque. As soon as she had her period, she went to the home of her maternal aunt; then, when she was again in the state of purity, she returned to the mosque. Now when she was at the place at which she customarily purified herself, the angel came to her as a young, smooth-faced man with pure countenance, curly hair, and a well-built body, without exhibiting a single blemish in his human appearance . . . He presented himself to her in the form of a man in order that she might have confidence in what he was to say and not flee from him. Had he appeared to her in the form of an angel, she would have fled from him and would not have been able to hear what he had to say. If Mary now sought refuge with God from this charming, towering, and handsome figure, then this shows that she was modest and pious. Through the appearance of the angel in this manner, Mary had undergone a test and her modesty was made certain . . .

28 According to Ibn 'Abbas [the Prophet's uncle and founder of the exegetical tradition] Mary found comfort in the words of the angel, and thus the latter approached near to her and breathed under her shift so that the breath reached into her womb and she became pregnant. Some say that the pregnancy lasted for six months . . . Others say that it lasted eight months and that beside Jesus no child capable of living ever came into the world after [only] eight months. Still others say that it lasted three hours. Some maintain that Mary was pregnant with Jesus for [only] one hour, that he was formed in one hour, and that she brought him into the world in one hour at sunset. According to Ibn 'Abbas the pregnancy lasted for [only] one hour. [Also] Mary is said to have brought Jesus into the world as soon as she became pregnant with him.

29 Some maintain that she became pregnant with him at the age of thirteen. It is also said that this occurred when she was ten years old, after she had had her period for two months previously. [Moreover] some say that every [newborn] infant cries and that Jesus is the only one who did not do this.

Like the Quran itself, which is constructed out of the same body of Ara- 30
bian, biblical and talmudic folklore, the *tafsirs* (commentaries) incorporated a
wide range of popular culture which made it accessible to the masses, and
hence intelligible across a broad spectrum of cultural assumptions. In this
respect the Quranic commentators fulfilled the function which Christianity
reserved for religious painting. The Sunni Muslim ban on representational art
drove the imaginative evocation of biblical texts (which forms the material of
western painting till after the Renaissance) into the realm of the footnote. As
with Christian art, such exegetical expression could acquire an inter-regional
character impossible for secular literature. Since the Quran was the 'speech of
God' and Arabic was the language through which he chose to communicate
his final messages to mankind, to translate it into other languages was tantamount to blasphemy. Non-Arab Muslims could only approach the Quran
through Arabic: in this manner the scripture continued to exercise its cultural
hegemony, ensuring that Arabic would remain the dominant language of intra-
Muslim communication long after Arabic speakers had ceased to be a numerical majority in the Islamic world.

Questions for Discussion and Your Reading Journal

1. What effect does it have for you that Ruthven opens a difficult essay on the
   Islamic world-view by comparing Islamic music to Western rock and roll?
2. Sum up the response of Thomas Carlyle to reading the Quran. How does
   Ruthven use his example of music to counter Carlyle's negative assessment
   of the Quran? Do you find this convincing? Explain.
3. How does Ruthven deal with the disappointment many Western readers
   feel when the Quran does not give them the "sustained narrative" that they
   have come to expect from the Bible?
4. Sum up the reasons Ruthven gives for why Muslims hold the Quran in such
   high esteem.
5. How do Muslim theologians deal with seeming contradictions in the
   Quran, according to Ruthven?
6. According to Ruthven, "the Quranic commentators fulfilled the function
   which Christianity reserved for religious painting." Why didn't Quranic
   painters fulfill this role with their own religious paintings?
7. Why is it still considered a sin in many places to translate the Quran?
8. What is the one most important insight that you gain about Islam from this
   reading? Explain your answer.

JOHN HALL

John Hall is a contemporary journalist who writes for the Baptist Standard *magazine, the "news journal for Texas Baptists" founded in 1888.
The Baptists are conservative Protestant Christians and considered by*

*many to be representative of fundamentalist tendencies in American reli-
gious culture. The purpose of the magazine is to present "stories of faith,
ministry and missions, analysis of religious controversy, Bible study,
inspiration and a guide to church and family life," with the mission to
"inspire, equip, and empower Christians to be disciples of Jesus Christ"
(http://www.baptiststandard.com). There are some 34 million Baptists in
the United States, making it the second-largest denomination in the
country. Both Jimmy Carter and George W. Bush are members of the
Baptist Church.*

Reading Rhetorically

The following reading represents an analysis by Hall, a Christian writer, of a
Muslim topic. The greatest challenge Hall faces as an advocate of his own religious group is to appear fair and evenhanded in his treatment of another religious group. He attempts this fairness through constant use of opposing points
and ideas. He also uses quotes and paraphrases from expert sources that qualify, or soften, the negativity of certain main claims made about Muslims. (Note
these as you read.) However, Hall's use of qualifiers is not intended to fully
negate the main point that his article makes overall, as his quotation from
Chancellor demonstrates: "Muslims are not more violent than Westerners, but
the use of violence comes more easily to Muslims." In the aftermath of 9/11
when Muslim terrorists killed some 3,000 Americans, Hall's topic is highly
charged emotionally for his fellow Christian readers. This allows him room to
appeal to emotion as much as to logic and to reasoning to persuade his audience to accept his main points.

Baptist Professors Don't See Islam as a "Peaceful" Religion

1   Islam is a "peaceful religion," President George W. Bush has assured the
American public on several occasions since the Sept. 11 terrorist attacks in
New York City and Washington, D.C.

2   Not so, say four Baptist experts on world religions, who characterize
Islam as drawing from both violent and non-violent streams.

3   Bush's assertion that Islam is "peaceful" is "ridiculous," said James Chancellor, professor of missions at Southern Baptist Theological Seminary in
Louisville, Ky., and an authority on numerous world religions.

4   "He's saying it for two reasons," Chancellor said. "He's saying it so the
United States will not be seen as attacking Muslims. He's also saying it to prevent attacks on Muslims."

5   While religions in the Western world have turned away from the normative use of violence to accomplish their goals, much of the Islamic world has
not made that transition, Chancellor explained. Muhammad, who Muslims

Religious students raise their hands to register their vote for a holy war against the U.S. at a madrassa (religious school) in Chaman, 81 miles northwest of Baluchistan's provincial capital of Quetta Sept. 24. © 2001 Reuters News Service.

believe was given the final word of Allah, was a warrior; therefore, Muslims can build a case for using violence to accomplish their objectives.

That does not mean all Muslims are violent people, Chancellor empha- 6 sized. "They are like everyone else. They want to raise a family. Muslims are not more violent than Westerners, but the use of violence comes more easily to Muslims."

Many devout Muslims are shocked that one of their own could commit 7 the atrocious acts attributed to Osama bin Laden and his followers in the al Qaeda terrorist network, Chancellor said.

That impression was echoed by Samuel Shahid, professor of missions at 8 Southwestern Baptist Theological Seminary in Fort Worth and director of the seminary's Muslim studies program.

"Most Muslims are people who want to live in peace," Shahid said. 9 "There are some fanatic leaders inside them who play on the religion and their religious emotions to promote violence."

Much like Christianity in the eyes of some outsiders, Islam presents a 10 conundrum for outsiders because its scriptures can be interpreted differently to support actions on both sides of a conflict, Shahid said.

"There are many verses in the Koran that talk about peace, and a lot of verses 11 talk about violence," he said. "It depends on the people. Some like to quote from the verses that emphasize peace and some from the verses on violence."

Chancellor believes whether or not a Muslim is violent depends on the 12 person. But Keith Parks, a veteran Baptist missions leader and former missionary to Indonesia, believes Muslim actions vary according to the amount of power they wield in a society. Where Muslims have political and social power, they are aggressive and controlling, Parks said. But when they are not in power, they present themselves as peaceful.

13   "They present themselves in the States as very peaceful, and the Koran has passages you can emphasize, but it also has passages that speak of converting infidels and ridding their country of infidels," Parks said. "They teach the jihad is a physical conflict, and if you die trying to destroy the infidels you are granted direct access to paradise. But there are many Muslims who would disagree."

14   Indeed, the entire subject of Islamic jihad is often misunderstood, added John Jonsson, a religion professor at Baylor University in Waco and an authority on world religions.

15   "We call it holy war. They call it pursuit of justice," he explained.

16   Although a majority of Muslims do not condone terrorist acts, a large percentage would support the ultimate goals terrorists seek to accomplish against the Western world, Chancellor said. They want at least neutrality from the West in dealings with Israel, and they want the United States to take its military out of Saudi Arabia. For Muslims, having U.S. troops in Saudi Arabia is equivalent to how Roman Catholics would perceive the placement of Muslim troops in the Vatican, Chancellor said.

17   In the current world situation, it is virtually impossible to separate Islam as a religion from Islam as a political system, added Parks.

18   "You cannot separate the religion from the government or society," he said. "It is a way of life. There is no idea of separation of church and state."

19   Chancellor agreed: "Muslims have not separated those worlds. It is consistent to achieve religious goals through politics."

20   This is confirmed by Terry Muck, author of a soon-to-be-published book called "The Pocket Guide to America's Religions."

21   "In a sense, the Islamic world is out of step with the current political trend of moving toward pluralistic democracies," Muck writes. "These democracies, fashioned largely after the United States model, have as one of their key characteristics the separation of church and state. This is not a congenial model for Muslim countries, where the ideal is not separation of church and state but the identification of the two under a single Muslim-dominated leadership structure."

22   In the Muslim world, Muck notes, "President Bush and Pope John Paul would be the same person."

23   For Muslims, this understanding has its roots in the role played by Muhammad himself, who was both a religious leader and political leader, Muck adds. "By incarnating both roles in his singular leadership style, Muhammad managed to unite—or set the stage for his immediate followers to unite—much of the most politically fractious geographies on earth, the Middle East."

24   Because of the intertwining of religious and political leadership in the Muslim world, Islam's religious teaching about jihad often takes on political ramifications, Muck explains.

25   Muslims have "a theological mandate to spread the influence of their religion worldwide," he notes. "This practice is included in a wider mandate to fully realize the injunctions of the Koran called jihad. Because Muslims do not have a strict separation between the theological and the political spheres, this missionary mandate is often indistinguishable from the political aims of Islamic governments."

Questions for Discussion and Your Reading Journal

1. What seems to be Hall's purpose for quoting President George Bush in his opening sentence?
2. As a Christian writer, does Hall attempt to be fair in his treatment of a Muslim topic? Give an example of this attempt at fairness.
3. Would you characterize the sentence "Muslims are not more violent than Westerners, but the use of violence comes more easily to Muslims" as a rhetorical appeal to logic and reason, or to emotion? Explain.
4. Hall starts off with the title "Baptist Professors Don't See Islam as 'Peaceful' Religion." Do all four Baptist professors clearly agree with this statement in the quotes that Hall presents?
5. After reading this magazine article, how would you respond to someone who said to you, "Islam is not a peaceful religion"?

ZAYN KASSAM

Dr. Zayn Kassam is a graduate of McGill University in Montreal, Canada, in Islamic studies. She currently holds the position of professor of religious studies at Pomona College in Claremont, California. She has received awards for distinguished teaching at Pomona College in areas that include Islamic philosophy, mysticism, gender, and literature. She currently has two book projects underway: one deals with Quranic interpretation in medieval Islamic philosophy; the other examines gender issues across the Muslim world. The following article was published in a book of readings by internationally respected experts entitled Terrorism and International Justice, *edited by James P. Sterba.*

Reading Rhetorically

As a college professor writing in a scholarly book on global terrorism and justice, Kassam can anticipate that her readers are highly educated people who are in positions with some authority to affect global events through their own writing, teaching, and consultant roles to government leaders. Many university students preparing themselves for leadership in government and politics may also be among her audience. It is for this educated audience that she writes. Instead of taking a firm position at the outset, she uses a question as her title: "Can a Muslim Be a Terrorist?" This allows her to take more of an investigative approach to a complex subject. Rather than telling her readers what they should think, she encourages them to join her in an exploration of ideas that can lead to their own insights. Throughout this journey into ideas, she organizes her points carefully so as to keep on a coherent path. Words like "first," "second," "third," and "fourth" show up regularly in subsequent paragraphs, leading from one major point to the next. As you read, think about how these signposts help guide you through the ideas, and whether or not they are helpful rhetorically.

Can a Muslim Be a Terrorist?[1]

1   Sure, why not, I wonder, for so can a Jew, a Hindu, a Sikh, a Catholic, or, indeed, a member of any faith. The difficult question is whether the religion with which terrorists are aligned actually teaches, promotes, or requires them to engage in terrorism as their religious duty. Painfully, for the majority of the world's Muslims, many contemporary headlines and opinion pieces in the news announce the verdict: Islam teaches jihad and honors suicide bombings with a safe passage-way to heaven replete with flowing rivers of milk and honey and the promise of doe-eyed virgins. Such a verdict contrasts with the view most Muslims themselves hold: They think of their religion as one of peace consequent upon the act of surrender *(islam)* to the divine being they consider synonymous with the God of the Hebrew Bible and the New Testament.

2   Despite the efforts of many academics who study Islam ("Islamologists" or "Islamicists") and journalists to show that the Quranic term "jihad" (literally, "struggle, effort") must be understood in its historical context, the term has come to signify a central tenet of the Islamic faith to the popular mind and conveys the notion that all Muslims are religiously predisposed to violence and hate. In a rhetorical gesture designed to replace Communism with Islam as the new other or enemy of Western civilization, the imaginary of the Muslim as unreasonable, rigid, and authoritarian continues to be projected in the popular media, whether through profiles of single Muslim men such as Saddam Hussein or Osama bin Laden or through characterizations of the entire faith of Islam, such as those articulated most recently by Franklin Graham, son of Reverend Billy Graham. In its seventh-century context, jihad was not directed against members of other monotheistic faiths but rather was to be conducted in response to the persecution visited upon the nascent Muslim community by the rulers of Mecca, the Quraysh, who perceived in Muhammad a direct threat to their political and economic hegemony. As such, then, jihad, or armed struggle, was not to be initiated except in response to an attack, or when no other course was feasible; only when these conditions were met was it permissible to take another human life during jihad. Nor was armed struggle, according to the narratives *(badith,* plural *abadith)* recorded in historical memory as depicting the words and actions of the Prophet to be considered the best aspect of religiosity, for the "greater jihad" was identified as the internal jihad or struggle against one's soul in the practice of righteousness. In its subsequent historical development, jihad against those outside the boundaries of Muslim domains was considered to be one of the responsibilities of the caliph or ruler, again only to be undertaken when the other side struck first or in defense, and never to be initiated by an individual, only by the ruler of the Islamic polity. Self-immolation is denounced in the Quran; a soldier who died defending the early Islamic community, on the other hand, was declared a martyr for defending his faith. There are parallels here with nascent Christian communities whose members were martyred by non-Christian state officials. Is every war in which a Muslim finds himself (or herself) a jihad? No. Muslims, in their variety of languages, have developed a vocabulary for wars that

are not undertaken in defense of their religion but rather in defense of their territory: the terms *jang* and *barb* are two such examples.

COLONIZATION AND ITS DISCONTENTS

Unfortunately, in the contemporary postcolonial world, such fine distinctions   3
have been lost on Muslims currently engaged in struggling for their causes, whatever they may be. There are several reasons for the coupling of religious language with the language of struggle. First and foremost, the otherizing by colonial powers of their Muslim populations, a process that has been documented by Edward Said and others, facilitated a delineation of the difference between the colonizers and the colonized in terms that were set up as religious, since the religion of Islam was blamed by the colonizers as responsible for the backwardness of the subject peoples, especially exemplified in the segregation of women from the public sphere. Such a discourse served to justify to home constituencies the continued presence of colonial powers in the colonies, as well as the need to civilize—and indeed Christianize—the backward infidel (notwithstanding the efforts made to squash suffragette movements in the home countries). Such an attitude built upon a long history of distrust and repugnance toward Muslims, going back as far as the Crusades with respect to the *religion* of the Muslims, and to the Graeco-Persian wars with respect to the *ethnicities* of such Muslims. Colonizing discourses also laid the parameters of any resistance to those colonizing powers within the language of a religious struggle for self-determination and self-rule. Since adherence to Islam was made responsible for the perceived backwardness of the subject peoples, the counterargument produced by those peoples was precisely that Islam would rescue them from subordination.

Second, despite the rhetoric of delivery of civilization tools to the subject   4
peoples, the intensely poor quality of educational, health, and civic services provided to the populations while simultaneously draining the subject territories of their natural and labor resources resulted in either slow development or maldevelopment of the human resources among subject peoples, in addition to eroding traditional cultures.

Thus, formerly colonized Muslim nations entered the era of independence   5
and self-rule beset with challenges that are likely to endure for some decades to come. The first of these challenges consists of the need to modernize given the fact that internal cultural processes of self-determination had lost much of their social and cultural, not to mention political, integrity in the intervention of the colonial powers. Such a historical intervention had introduced Western-style education and institutions, whether acquired at home or abroad, into the cultural frameworks of subject peoples, and newly emergent independent nations were well aware that their survival and ongoing viability as nations depended on their ability to be players in the Western hegemonic realm of economics and politics. The resulting agony over whether modernization entailed survival through a wholesale adoption of Western practices and ideologies or whether modernization was possible in a manner integrated into traditional cultural and religious praxis has been explored in the novels of Naguib Mahfouz, Yahya

al-Haqqi, Cheikh Hamidou Kane, Salman Rushdie, Attiya Hossein, Ismat Chhughtai, Aziz Necin, Orhan Pamuk, and Sadegh Hedayat, to mention just a few. Kane, for instance, in his novel *Ambiguous Adventure* articulates the struggle thus: "It suddenly occurs to us that, all along our road, we have not ceased to metamorphose ourselves, and we see ourselves as other than that we were. Sometimes the metamorphosis is not even finished. We have turned ourselves into hybrids, and there we are left. Then we hide ourselves, filled with shame."[2] A distinction must be made between modernization understood as technologization, and modernization understood as Westernization. For many Muslims, enjoying the fruits of scientific progress is seen as a form of divine bounty; Westernization, on the other hand, is fraught with issues of power and domination and exemplifies societies that have lost their moral moorings. Modernization as Westernization connotes secularization or the separation of religion from public life, especially politics, and herein lies the crux of the debate between Muslim modernists, who argue that religion should be separated from what is in the best interests of society (itself a laudable religious aim), and Muslim conservatives, who argue that indeed the best interests of society lie in the re-Islamization of public institutions, including the law.

6   Connected to the challenge of modernization lies a second challenge, the challenge of identity. Does modernization necessitate imbuing Western culture along with Western technology? Boroujerdi, writing on Iranian intellectual life,[3] makes an observation that could well be extended to the entire formerly colonized Muslim world, that is, that all things Western are necessarily mediated through the lens of the (unhappily) remembered colonized experience. The search for an authentically local form of modernization was on, and resistance to Western forms of modernization formed part and parcel of the quest for a national identity that was struggling to be modern in its use of technology and ability to parlay at the economic table of emergent globalization, and yet culturally resonant with its own history, social institutions, and peoples.

7   The relationship between largely Muslim-populated nations and Western nations was an uneasy one during much of the twentieth century. The end of colonization certainly did not spell the end of first European, and then American, influence in Muslim regions. While others in this book and elsewhere have more substantively explored such relationships, suffice it here to draw attention to several factors that militate against harmonious relationships unless addressed. One such factor relates to the consequences of carving up Palestine in order to create the country of Israel. The lack of reparation to displaced Palestinians, the continued Palestinian refugee camps, the building of settlements and military roads through internationally agreed-upon Palestinian territories, the uneven distribution of water in the Occupied Territories, the withholding of taxes from Palestinian enterprises, and the international upholding of the fiction that there are two equal and opposite "countries" struggling against each other are some of the reasons underlying the violence that is, unfortunately, now not only characteristic of but also a daily occurrence in the region. The massive American fiscal support of Israel and the largely unflagging European and American moral support of Israeli policies toward the Palestinians—who, until recently, comprised also a sizeable Chris-

tian population—have led to the perception that the "West" is still Crusader-like, antagonistic toward its formerly colonized Muslim peoples, and that the Western civilized world's rhetoric of democracy, human rights, international conventions, and fair play do not matter when it comes to Palestine.

Another factor relates to the Cold War, in which several Muslim nations became pawns in a larger power struggle between the forces of capitalism and the forces of communism, and in smaller power struggles between Muslim nations. The case of Afghanistan is particularly poignant, as its ability to chart its own course after the departure of the British remained continually at risk given its strategic positioning between Soviet Central Asian territories and the Middle East. The training of Afghani Mujahiddin through American- and Saudi-funded[4] (via Pakistan's Interservices Intelligence Directorate, ISI) installations and personnel accomplished several objectives: It gave the Afghans a sense of purpose in removing the Soviets from their soil, dovetailing with larger American interests in limiting Soviet spheres of influence. However, at the same time, in order to impel the Mujahiddin to fight, a connection had to be made between the notion of jihad and the liberation of Afghanistan; whether credible or not, a *Washington Post* article suggests that USAID-funded "textbooks filled with violent images and militant Islamic teachings, part of covert attempts to spur resistance to the Soviet occupation" were developed at the University of Nebraska (Omaha)'s Center for Afghanistan Studies.[5] John K. Cooley chillingly suggests that American, Pakistani, and Saudi funding and collaboration in support of Islamist groups was based on "(t)he tacit consensus . . . that the Muslim religion, fundamentally anti-Communist, if translated into politics, could be harnessed as a mighty force to oppose Moscow in the Cold War, in a world growingly polarized by that war."[6] Further, the recruitment of Muslims from outside of Afghanistan to assist in the effort led to the internationalization of ideologically driven militants now ready to take on the task of engaging in vigilante military activity should the rationale, however irrational, demand it. Once the Soviets had been forced out of Afghanistan, the land was left to its own devices, and in disarray, hence fertile ground for the Islamist recruitment, especially in the Afghan refugee *madrasahs* (literally, "a place in which to study," that is, school or classroom) along the Afghan-Pakistani border and the subsequent establishment of the Taliban who, in turn, provided ready fodder for the likes of Osama bin Laden. The rest is history. The smaller power struggle between the Pakistani need to have a pliable neighbor to the north in order to safeguard its borders to the south ensured their preference for Islamists rather than left-leaning Afghan leadership, thereby providing logistical and government support and encouragement to a politicized form of Islam rather than to Muslims who sought to modernize their country and address the challenges facing development without drawing religious norms into the equation. While this author is by no means advocating leftist as opposed to capitalist forms of economy, the point is that the support needed to address the problems of rebuilding Afghanistan was directed toward a small group that saw the answer in religiously fundamentalist terms rather than in drawing upon the rich intellectual-, creative-, and social justice-oriented heritage of prior Islamic societies.

9   A third factor relates to the politics of access to oil. The establishment of military bases in oil-bearing regions and the propping up of governments and leaders friendly to American and European interests have been detrimental to the growth of democracy and institutions devoted to social welfare in the region. One might wonder whether the discovery of oil has been a curse as it has assured American and other foreign intervention in the politics of the region.

10   Thus, challenges to Western culture, perceived as rapacious and self-serving—despite the attempt of courses on Western civilization that paint it as glorious, humanistic, and universalistic in its hopes of rights and dignity for all humans—were given voice more than fifty years ago, long before the Mujahiddin were trained in Afghanistan largely to serve Western purposes. Iranian thinkers such as Jalal Al-i Ahmed (d. 1969) in Iran coined the term gharbzadegi, literally "born of the West," but commonly translated as "westoxification." Other thinkers such as Abu al-Ala Mawdudi (d. 1979) in Pakistan and Sayyid Qutb (d. 1966) in Egypt, along with Ibn al-Wahhab's (d. 1792) interpretation of Islam (regnant in Saudi Arabia), contributed toward forming totalizing conceptualizations of what it means to be Muslim in a Muslim society governed by Muslim institutions. In all of these, the influence of the writings of the medieval Syrian jurist Ibn Taymiyya (d. 1328), who was left to languish in prison, are clearly apparent.

11   Thinkers such as these, whose Shiite parallel may be found in Iran's Ayatollah Khomeini and his successors, defined their visions of an Islamic "orthodoxy" that is exclusivist, anti-Western, and highly shariah oriented in the hopes of inculcating pride in the Islamic tradition in an attempt to create Islamic nations that would provide an alternate model to Western nations. Drawing upon the ideologies provided by such orthodoxy creationists, innumerable groups have sprung up all over the Islamic, and now Western, world, in the hopes of garnering political power that would ensure the running of Muslim states in a Muslim manner as defined by such ideologues, and thereby able to resist Western control over minds, resources, culture, and politics while simultaneously reinstating pride in Islam and self-governance—hence the definition of an Islamist as one who holds that every aspect of a Muslim's life must be governed by Islam through shariah law and whose ultimate aim is to take over the reins of both public and private life and to regulate these according to the particular legal regime of the orthodoxy creator to whom they subscribe. While all Islamists are Muslim, all Muslims are not Islamists. Further, while all Islamists subscribe to versions of the ideology stated here, the majority of these do not believe in utilizing physically violent means in achieving their aims, although some Islamist groups do have an organizational arm devoted to that purpose. A case in point is Hamas, whose main body concerns itself with the delivery of social services, while its militant arm, 'Izz al-Din al-Qasim, is often cited as responsible for what it considers "acts of justice" or retaliation.

12   Debate, discussion, and rhetorical as well as legal and military struggles ensued through much of the Islamic world in the twentieth century regarding the extent to which Islamic praxis, institutions, and ideologies should play a

role in civic life and societal organization. Efforts to "Islamize" already Muslim populations were thus carried out, for instance, in Pakistan, under the regime of General Zia ul-Haq (in command from 1976 to 1988), who placed a shariah bench in the law courts and moved to pass the Hudood Ordinances of 1979 (making rape and adultery practically synonymous), as well as the Shariat Bill in 1985 (passed in 1991), with their disastrous consequences for women. Similar efforts are also underway in Malaysia, the Sudan, and Nigeria, to name but a few. Perhaps the most obvious examples of an attempt to Islamicize all aspects of social, political and cultural interaction are in Iran and Afghanistan, the first under Khomeini and the second under the Taliban. While the two are by no means synonymous since Iran is Ithna Ashari or Twelver Shiite, whereas the Taliban espoused an extreme form of Sunni Islam, they are similar in their attempt to totalize their discrete understandings of "correct" Islam and Islamic praxis over all aspects of society and civic life.

THE REACH OF ISLAMISM

Why would Muslims seek to support such totalizing ideologies, such narrow understandings of a rich, diverse, and intellectually and culturally vibrant tradition expressed in the many historically discrete forms of Islam ("Islams," as dubbed by Aziz Al-Azmeh)[7] already present in the world? Part of the success experienced by Islamist groups is because of the widespread educational efforts funded in many instances by oil wealth, which do not hesitate to utilize modern technological advances for the purpose of da'wah, or missionizing. Part relates to the fact that religion is so deeply intertwined with cultural life as to be inseparable from it, and piety is a valued characteristic. Thus, many Muslims feel that they are advancing their piety through knowledge ('ilm) about their faith, and the notion that piety is best expressed through adherence to religious law (shariah) makes complete the hold of religion over every aspect of life. The lack of training in the humanities and in developing critical thinking skills in general education curricula means that religious instruction is virtually uncritically accepted as being divine in origin, and hence not to be questioned without earning the charge of being an infidel, perhaps among the worst offenses a Muslim could commit. Part of the success relies on the fact that many recruits to Islamist thinking are materially impoverished and feel that the slogan of the Islamists, that is, "Islam is the solution," will provide a panacea to their social discomfiture. Others, those who flock from the rural areas to the cities in pursuit of work opportunities or an education, deal with cultural dislocation by resorting to an ideology that will keep them safe from the cosmopolitan and uncertain nature of social relations in the city. Still others, the upwardly mobile young, faced with the often corrupt, inefficient and authoritarian governments that cannot provide adequate jobs, deliver social services, or political stability, let alone a presence on the world stage politically or with respect to globalization, find in the Islamist ideologies, varied as these are geographically, a platform on which to mount resistance both against their own regimes as well as at the hegemonic power of the West, especially the United States. And part of the success lies in the fact that many Islamist groups

13

provide much-needed education (albeit through the religious schools, the *madrasahs*), social services, a sense of community, a sense of direction and purpose, and a projection of a worldwide Muslim *ummah* (community) that must work toward establishing socially just societies on earth. While all of these provisions assist in motivating the ordinary pious Muslim recruited to the Islamist cause to turn into activists, and while such activism is usually directed at local causes, it is not difficult to see how such ideologies could easily be turned toward causes that go beyond the borders of any specific region. Access to military training and arms completes the capability for making a perceived just cause sufficient reason to engage in armed activity: ideology coupled with perceived causes coupled with arms and training. It would be untrue to say that all Islamists are trained to engage in armed combat, for perhaps many stop at introducing piety through the shariah into all aspects of their lives, just as it would be untrue to say that all militant Islamists are necessarily shariah observant, for if they were, then the Quranic principles of tolerance, compassion, pluralism, and sanctions against killing might be taken far more seriously.

14   Another factor that complicates the relationship of religion to armed struggle in Muslim societies is that often the perceived cause for activism is by itself sufficient justification for militant activism, and the participant happens to be a Muslim, but does not necessarily consider such activism to be religiously derived or rooted. Such might be the case for adherents of the People's Democratic Party in Afghanistan, or the leftist parties such as the Popular Front for the Liberation of Palestine in the Occupied Territories. Unfortunately, while some of our academic investigations are aware of the diversity of ideologies and motivations underpinning such activism, in the media all acts of terrorist or resistance activity are labeled Muslim, with the implication that the acts are religiously motivated. Compounding this widespread assumption that all Muslims are piously motivated is that the very language of resistance is indistinguishable from religious language, since the latter is so deeply imbedded in linguistic norms—a resonant example might be found in our "goodbye" ("God be with ye"). Nor, indeed, does the media acknowledge the sometimes variegated religious base of the population; for instance, the large numbers of Palestinian Christians who also might have participated or continue to participate in armed or militant struggle before their numbers dwindled to their present 10 percent have rarely been acknowledged by the media.

15   Several points must be made with respect to the reform and revivalist, and now Islamist, ideologies sweeping through the Muslim world and, given global migration patterns, through pockets of the Western world. First, it is not clear, despite the successes of such movements, what percentage these groups comprise in relation to the entire Muslim population (about 1.4 billion worldwide). Second, neither is it clear what percentage of these are militant or have access to arms. Our suspicion is that an overwhelming percentage simply remains within the boundaries of doing good works, on the one hand, and missionizing themselves and others to accept a narrowly defined, and shariah-bound form of Islam, on the other. Distressing as the latter is, it is not a militant threat but rather a social and civic threat, especially for women and for

minorities, and has the capacity to engender mistrust and intolerance of the West, and further, of its sister monotheisms, not to mention geographically proximate polytheisms and atheisms, both of which run contrary to much of the history and spirit of Islam. With respect to militarization, the question is, where does one find armed Islamists? It appears that before September 11, 2001, armed Islamists largely fought other Muslims, whether in Algeria (post-independence), Iran (post-Khomeini), Afghanistan (the Taliban), or Egypt (against Sadat), or participated in liberation struggles fighting largely non-Muslims in Israel, Kashmir, and possibly the Philippines. It is not clear whether the Muslims fighting in the Philippines, Chechnya, Bosnia, Albania, and Lebanon are Islamist in ideology, although clearly Islam serves as a group marker for a common cause (as might Catholicism in Ireland). In all cases, increasingly Islamist ideology is being paired with an armed struggle for liberation from perceived hostile forces. That is to say, while not all pious Muslims, Islamist or not, are militant, it is likely that in cases where militancy is advocated, the pool of willing participants appears to be drawn from Islamists. September 11 marked the first truly large-scale expression of anti-American sentiment, and one has to wonder whether such attacks were restricted to the particular virulent form of the ideology espoused by Osama bin Laden and are likely not to be undertaken by any others, or whether they sent out the message that they could be undertaken, albeit at a terrible cost. Many of the attacks on American embassies and personnel, according to media reports, appear to be traceable to Osama bin Laden, which would suggest that most other Islamists restrict themselves to their local causes as far as militancy goes.

Third, with respect to anti-Western rhetoric, it is true that current ideological articulations of Islam necessarily look at the West through the remembered lens of colonization and the current lens of globalization as well as political interference of the West in local affairs, especially in the oil-bearing and strategically located nations. However, from an educated and larger historical perspective, the Islamic world has long been intertwined with the Western world in a manner that has been enriching for the latter, just as the former has been enriched by the latter. For instance, much of the greatness of Islamic civilization during its golden age, from about the ninth century to the fifteenth, can be attributed to Muslim developments of classical learning found in Greek texts pertaining to the sciences, music, medicine, astronomy, philosophy, and so forth, that were translated into Arabic in the eighth and ninth centuries. Muslim reflections upon these texts, and the subsequent developments contributed by Muslims as they read, studied, and worked on texts originating in Hellenistic, Persian, Hebraic, and Indic (South Asian) sources contributed to efflorescence in all the disciplines known in that day. Such knowledge was then retransmitted back to Europe via Spain through translations made into Latin, and although barely credited in our history books, Muslim thinkers and texts written by Muslims played a significant role in facilitating the European Renaissance through a revitalization of European academies of learning after the Dark Ages. 16

One cannot imagine the development in astronomy without the astrolabes of Nasir al-Din Tusi or his contributions to algebra (the term itself derives 17 from the Arabic *al-jabr*), or architecture without the innovations of Rashid al-Din Sinan, or the ceramic techniques that went all along the Silk Road to China and beyond without the Persian tile makers and painters, or the intricate patterning and vegetable dye techniques of oriental fabrics and rugs without the tribal weavers spanning the Middle East and Central Asia, not to mention the many philosophical contributions to medieval philosophy, including the theology of St. Thomas Aquinas without an Ibn Rushd (Averroës). The medical canon of Ibn Sina (Avicenna) remained in European medical curricula up to the eighteenth century. All this is by way of noting that from a larger historical perspective, the Western world and the Islamic world have not always been Crusader-like antagonists in their interactions, as has been touted by some academics in fashion today, but rather that there have been periods of collaboration and, if not direct collaboration, certainly mutual enrichment. Thus for those on either side of the divide, whether Western or Islamist, to claim retrospectively a conflictual relationship between the two does disservice to the historical tradition and forgets that each is rooted in the other in almost every discipline, if not culturally.

18   Fourth, the Islamist (and there are many varieties belonging to this label) re-creation of all-encompassing shariah law as expressive of a Muslim's piety is a move both to counter the privatization of religion as well as to retroject a notion of a Golden Age of Islam that supposedly existed during the time of the Prophet and the first four caliphs when the Muslim community is thought to have lived in perfect obedience to Muhammad's religious and political authority (contrary to the historical Golden Age, which, as mentioned earlier, came later). At such a time, it is thought, the community was unified, all the Muslims lived in harmony with no dissenting opinions, and shariah law guided the actions of the community. As Nazih Ayubi has observed:

19   Today, when most salafis and some fundamentalists call for the implementation of shari'a, what they really have in mind is the implementation of the jurisprudence formulated by the early jurists. This jurisprudence has now been extracted from its historical and political context, and endowed with essentialist, everlasting qualities. The point is thus overlooked that this jurisprudence was in the first place a human improvisation meant to address certain political and social issues in a certain historical, geographical and social context. What is also often overlooked is that the main body of the official jurisprudence fulfilled a certain political function by imparting religious legitimacy to the government of the day, which had usually come to rule by force or intrigue and which, in its daily conduct, was not generally living up to the Islamic ideal.[8]

THE CONSEQUENCES OF ISLAMIZATION

20 Now, it is true that in some cases the application of Islamic law is an advance over tribal and feudally patriarchal forms of tribal council (*panchayat* or *jirga*) law observed in many parts of the Islamic world in which societies, especially rural societies, are still organized according to feudal structures that are inher-

ently patriarchal. A recent example of such tribal rulings is the notorious Pakistani case of a young rural woman who was ordered to be raped by four men as a consequence of her brother's being seen walking with a woman from a higher caste. But in the main, shariah law has exacted its own price in allowing loopholes for men in cases of honor killings (Pakistan, Jordan, among others); blurring the line between adultery and rape (Pakistan); leveling charges of apostasy and consequent forcible divorce against those who wish to initiate discussions of the role of religion in civic life (Egypt); invoking charges of heresy and hence death against the same in the infamous case of the author Taslima Nasreen (Bangladesh); and so forth.

Two consequences of shariah law application can be identified. The first is   21 that Muslim populations find themselves socially and sometimes physically terrorized by Islamists who seek to police not only the mode of dress worn by women and their comportment, but also attendance at the mosque for Muslim men, as well as the particular form of Islam espoused by the adherent. Thereby, Islamists attempt to remove all forms of Islam other than those promoted by their own ideology. In their attempts to enforce coercively their new orthodoxies, many historical variants of Islam find themselves under siege, whether they are the hybridized or syncretic Muslim mystically oriented traditions of South Asia, Indonesia/Malaysia, or Africa; discrete forms of Shiism (there are many forms of the latter in addition to the majority tradition found in Iran, commonly called Imami Shiism, Ithna Ashari Shiism, or Twelver Shiism); or Sufi (mystical) in their outlook and emphasis.

All of these run the risk of being supplanted either by a lately fashioned   22 puritanical form of Islam popularly known as Wahhabism or by ideologies such as those constructed by Mawdudi and Sayyid Qutb at times when Islamic countries were seeking to escape the lingering yoke of colonization. Wahhabism itself, no more than three centuries old (its earlier antecedents exercised little influence among the majority of Muslims), had its genesis in Saudi Arabia and was granted politically expedient support by the contenders for power at the turn of the twentieth century, displacing the hereditary claims to the leadership of Saudi Arabia. The role of Western nations, interested in pliable Saudi leadership given their interests in recently discovered oil, in facilitating the transition of Wahhabi-sympathetic Saudi leadership at that critical juncture, is not the subject of this essay. What is germane, however, is that oil funding makes it possible for Islamists, whether Wahhabi-, Mawdudi- or Sayyid Qutb-inspired, to establish or take over Quaranic schools or *madrasas* and disseminate their ideologies, all in the name of piety and in the interests of "education," a deeply cherished Islamic principle. It is a short step thence for militants to find an ever-ready pool of men (and women) to coerce and cajole surrounding populations, campaign against legal reforms, indeed, campaign for an Islamization of the law, not to mention an Islamization of all knowledge. Any opposition is effectively silenced by charges of heresy *(kufr)*, innovation *(bida'a)*, or "Westernization" (meaning "westoxification"), and governments find they have to barter certain civic rights and especially women's rights to the Islamists in order to gain legitimacy for their own often weak, embattled, and sometimes undemocratic rule.

23 The second is that shariah law, which is not a singular phenomenon, comprises several discrete systems of jurisprudence that took at least two centuries to develop in the Sunni cases and several centuries to develop in the Shiite cases. These are, as pointed out by Ayubi and others, specific to their historical, geographical, and political contexts. Given the principle that the intent of any legal system must be to safeguard the good of the societies to which it is applicable, surely it would make sense to construct legal systems, albeit in the spirit of cherished Islamic principles, that would attend to the very real issues and challenges facing Muslim populations today. A blind adherence, even with juristic intervention, to juridical systems developed a millenium ago in most cases does disservice to the very populations it seeks to protect simply because the historical, cultural, social, and political conditions under which Muslims live today are very different from those of the tenth-century Abbasid Empire under which several of the Sunni and to some extent Shiah legal systems developed. Furthermore, under the various dynastic rulers (Abbasid, Fatimid, Buyid, Ottoman, Mamluk, Mughal, to mention but a few), the administration of justice was continually modernized as changing circumstances required in contrast to the common misperception that "there is no separation of church and state in Islam." The various caliphs took under their control all aspects of law with the exception of law pertaining to prescribed religious duties such as the paying of *zakat* (a form of tithing), religious endowments, and family law. It is these latter that remained the preserve of religious jurists, whereas every other aspect of the law was overseen by the caliph's executives and given the stamp of religious legitimacy by dubbing the caliph both the religious leader of prayer *(imam)*, in whose name the Friday sermon was declared, and the chief political authority *(malik* or sultan). Juridical writings also, over time, created theories of Islamic states, in which the jurists speculated what an Islamic state should look like, bearing very little resemblance to what actually occurred historically. Unfortunately, for moderns reading such texts, the fine distinction between an envisioned Islamic state and its historical nonreality has been blurred. So, indeed, has the fact that the Quran has very little to say about the state. Rather, later legal texts are used as evidence, as is the shariah itself, that a utopian Islamic state existed at the time of the Prophet, complete with shariah laws, and should now be resuscitated through a program of re-education of Muslims worldwide.

24 Thus we have a conundrum: On the one hand, it is assumed that shariah law is divinely revealed and hence immutable as well as non-negotiable; on the other hand, the existence of several schools of shariah law, plus the fact that trained jurists declare in a *fatwa* (legal response) what is best suited to the particular case before the court, suggests that the jurist is, in fact, an interpreter of the vast resources he has before him (there are very few women jurists, hence the gendered pronoun), even though he claims to be upholding that which is divinely revealed. It is not difficult, then, to see that despite the fact that Islam claims to have no priestly class, a priestly caste has been created in the form of *fatwa*-issuing jurists who can block—or dictate—the administration of justice, using divinity as a shield to disengage from questions of whether their pronouncements are, in fact, in the best interests of society

(maslaba). This is particularly germane with respect to gender issues but becomes even more critical with respect to structuring civil societies in modern-day conditions. Since the creation of a just society was Muhammad's divinely inspired aim, in the interests of which the Quran accorded rights and responsibilities to Muslims, surely, it is now more critical than ever in postcolonial Muslim societies to encourage debate and discussion regarding how these challenges can be met within the spirit and intent of Islam rather than adhering to the cultural forms in which that spirit was articulated in seventh-century Arabian terms. But to suggest so is immediately silenced as an attempt to deny the eternal validity of the Quran—which is not what is intended by this author—and dismissed in the name of "tradition," as though tradition somehow has value and the changing circumstances of people do not, since many "traditions" continue to perpetuate inequities that run contrary to the principles and ethos of Islam. Thus, in sum, the second consequence of the application of shariah law is that the linkage of Muslim piety with an adherence to shariah law has made it extremely risky for Muslims to engage in open discussion and reflection of what it might mean to construct a civil society, or to construct legal systems that would be fair and just to all citizens in the modern state. Nor can there be any open or critically informed discussions of the role the religious institutions—given that Islam is not a monolithic faith—ought to play in public life. Witness, for instance, the persecution and then execution of the Sudanese Muslim thinker and theologian Muhammad Husayn Taha. The difficulties attached to examining such questions are especially unnerving when one considers that the ideologies of a well-funded few, armed with morally and sometimes physically coercive tools, silence a larger majority of Muslims for whom the necessities of life, peace, safety, hospitality, and the exercise of their divinely endowed faculties, including the capacity to think within the boundaries of moral accountability, are what matters most.

CONCLUDING REMARKS

I want now to bring these reflections to a close with a few observations. From the foregoing, a case can be made that revivalist and reform movements such as the many forms of Islamist ideology and praxis found in the world today stem in response to several variegated but interconnected factors. First, they embody the search for an authentic identity as part of a resistance strategy to colonization and postcolonial Western hegemony. Second, they mount a platform of resistance in protest of governments that perpetuate Western hegemony and/or Western-mediated control over natural resources (especially when such governments do not act in the people's interest but in exchange for Western support will allow the establishment of military bases to protect access to oil, as an example), political stances (especially over Israel and the Occupied Territories), and economic policies in the name of globalization and the politics of aid (considered to be favorable for the West but not for much of the rest of the world). Third, they construct a desire in their recruits to return to a retrospective Golden Age utopia supposedly articulated and implemented by the community of the Prophet in which a total Islamic polity

25

existed, pervading all areas of life. In so doing, they seek to overturn, infiltrate, or take over the government in order to provide such a society, and along the way, create civic conditions that are punitive toward Muslim minorities, members of other faiths, and women. Fourth, disappointed with the failure of their governments to provide the conditions necessary for healthy, vibrant societies, they provide social services unmet by the government in response to the poverty and material needs of the population.

26   If Islamist ideologies are to lose the moral and at times militant force they exercise over their recruits and over those they terrorize, then some of the very real concerns that feed and underlie such movements must be addressed by all those, Muslims and non-Muslims alike, who have a stake in civic societies, freedom of conscience, and democracy. Otherwise, as witnessed by the world on September 11, 2001, a Muslim, most likely an Islamist, can become a terrorist. Even though the Quran forbids it. There were Muslims killed in the Twin Towers, in direct violation of Quran 4:29, "and kill not one another." In a verse applicable to all Muslims as it remains unabrogated from a rule the Quran claims was laid down for the children of Israel, Quran 5:32 states, "whosoever kills a human being for other than manslaughter or corruption in the earth, it shall be as if he had killed all humankind, and who saves the life of one, it shall be as if he had saved the life of all humankind." Can the assertion of what constitutes "manslaughter" or "corruption" be left to the judgment of individuals not accountable to civic institutions? Surely not. This essay has sought to argue that violent, radically militant interpretations of Islam that consider jihad to be a religious duty, and that now seek to globalize jihad against those that do not, in their view, conform to their understanding of Islam, pose a significant threat to Muslims and non-Muslims alike. While such interpreters and interpretations of Islam run contrary to the largely peaceful and ethical stances taken by the majority of the world's diverse Muslims, nonetheless, their access to arms and networks makes their small number a sizeable source of risk. The colonial and postcolonial factors discussed here have fueled the albeit limited success such ideologies have had with most Muslims. To prevent such ideologies from gaining ground, a concerted effort must be made by liberal Muslims and non-Muslims alike to address the issues I have discussed, from which these ideologies draw support.

Notes

1. That is, one who resorts to violent means toward attaining a political end.
2. Cheikh Hamidou Kane, *Ambiguous Adventure* (Portsmouth, NH: Heinemann, 1963), pp. 112–113.
3. Mehrzad Boroujerdi, *Iranian Intellectuals and the West: The Tormented Triumph of Nativism* (Syracuse, NY: Syracuse University Press, 1996).
4. John K. Cooley, *Unholy Wars: Afghanistan, America and International Terrorism*, 2d ed. (London, Sterling, VA: Pluto Press, 2000), p. 5.
5. *Guardian Weekly*, March 28–April 3, 2002, p. 32, reprint of *The Washington Post* article titled, "From U.S., the ABCs of Jihad," by Joe Stephens and David B. Ottaway.

6. Cooley, *Unholy Wars*, p. 1.
7. Aziz Al-Azmeh, *Islams and Modernities* (London, New York: Verso, 1993).
8. Nazih M. Ayubi, *Political Islam: Religion and Politics in the Arab World* (London and New York: Routledge, 1991), p. 2.

Questions for Discussion and Your Reading Journal

1. In her first lines, what is Kassam's response to her title question?
2. According to Kassam, what has the word "jihad" come to mean in the popular thinking of non-Muslims, especially among Westerners?
3. In your judgment, why does Kassam bring up the issue of "Colonization and Its Discontents" early in her paper?
4. What are the four main points Kassam makes under the subhead "The Reach of Islam"?
5. What are the two consequences she identifies under the subhead "The Consequences of Islamization"?
6. How is Kassam's response to "Can a Muslim Be a Terrorist" different in the second paragraph of her "Concluding Remarks" from her original response in the first paragaph of the paper?

HERMANN HESSE

The works of Nobel Prize–winning Swiss author Hermann Hesse (1877–1962) embody his lifelong search for the "Way," the philosophy of life that would offer him spiritual fulfillment. His novels explore the mysteries of the human soul from many perspectives, Eastern and Western, and capture the anguish, the joy, and the serenity that characterize the struggle to discover truth. In "The Brahmin's Son," the first chapter of Siddhartha, *the young Siddhartha is unsatisfied with the teachings of Hinduism, for they leave many of his fundamental questions unanswered. As the chapter concludes, he sets out with his friend Govinda to join a group of wandering ascetics. The rest of the novel describes his disillusionment with the Samanas's way of life and his subsequent attempt to find satisfaction in a life of sensuality and earthly love. He realizes that he is only being distracted from his search for true self. Finally, with the help of a simple ferryman, he discovers that true wisdom can be found only within, and at last he achieves the peace and transcendence he has sought after for so many years.*

Reading Rhetorically

Hesse's "The Brahmin's Son" is historical fiction written in narrative mode. The story Hesse tells is a parallel to the story of the Buddha. His main character

Siddhartha carries the same first name as Siddhartha Gautama, the original Buddha ("Siddhartha" means "wish fulfilled" in Sanskrit). Siddhartha, like his namesake, attains enlightenment by the end of the book. Hesse seeks to convey the richness of ideas and human spiritual longing that characterizes the life story of the Buddha. By presenting these ideas and longings in story form, he is able to take readers deeper into them in a personal manner than a textbook description of the same events is likely to do.

The Brahmin's Son (From *Siddhartha*)

1   In the shade of the house, in the sunshine on the river bank by the boats, in the shade of the sallow wood and the fig tree, Siddhartha, the handsome Brahmin's son, grew up with his friend Govinda. The sun browned his slender shoulders on the river bank, while bathing at the holy ablutions, at the holy sacrifices. Shadows passed across his eyes in the mango grove during play, while his mother sang, during his father's teachings, when with the learned men. Siddhartha had already long taken part in the learned men's conversations, had engaged in debate with Govinda and had practiced the art of contemplation and meditation with him. Already he knew how to pronounce Om silently—this word of words, to say it inwardly with the intake of breath, when breathing out with all his soul, his brow radiating the glow of pure spirit. Already he knew how to recognize Atman within the depth of his being, indestructible, at one with the universe.

2   There was happiness in his father's heart because of his son who was intelligent and thirsty for knowledge; he saw him growing up to be a great learned man, a priest, a prince among Brahmins.

3   There was pride in his mother's breast when she saw him walking, sitting down and rising: Siddhartha—strong, handsome, supple-limbed, greeting her with complete grace.

4   Love stirred in the hearts of the young Brahmins' daughters when Siddhartha walked through the streets of the town, with his lofty brow, his kinglike eyes and his slim figure.

5   Govinda, his friend, the Brahmin's son, loved him more than anybody else. He loved Siddhartha's eyes and clear voice. He loved the way he walked, his complete grace of movement; he loved everything that Siddhartha did and said, and above all he loved his intellect, his fine ardent thoughts, his strong will, his high vocation. Govinda knew that he would not become an ordinary Brahmin, a lazy sacrificial official, an avaricious dealer in magic sayings, a conceited worthless orator, a wicked sly priest, or just a good stupid sheep amongst a large herd. No, and he, Govinda, did not want to become any of these, not a Brahmin like ten thousand others of their kind. He wanted to follow Siddhartha, the beloved, the magnificent. And if he ever became a god, if he ever entered the All-Radiant, then Govinda wanted to follow him as his friend, his companion, his servant, his lance bearer, his shadow.

That was how everybody loved Siddhartha. He delighted and made every- 6
body happy.

But Siddhartha himself was not happy. Wandering along the rosy paths of 7
the fig garden, sitting in contemplation in the bluish shade of the grove, washing his limbs in the daily bath of atonement, offering sacrifices in the depths of
the shady mango wood with complete grace of manner, beloved by all, a joy
to all, there was yet no joy in his own heart. Dreams and restless thoughts
came flowing to him from the river, from the twinkling stars at night, from the
sun's melting rays. Dreams and a restlessness of the soul came to him, arising
from the smoke of the sacrifices, emanating from the verses of the Rig-Veda,
trickling through from the teachings of the old Brahmins.

Siddhartha, had begun to feel the seeds of discontent within him. He had 8
begun to feel that the love of his father and mother, and also the love of his
friend Govinda, would not always make him happy, give him peace, satisfy
and suffice him. He had begun to suspect that his worthy father and his other
teachers, the wise Brahmins, had already passed on to him the bulk and best
of heir wisdom, that they had already poured the sum total of their knowledge
into his waiting vessel; and the vessel was not full, his intellect was not satisfied, his soul was not at peace, his heart was not still. The ablutions were good,
but they were water; they did not wash sins away, they did not relieve the distressed heart. The sacrifices and the supplication of the gods were excellent—
but were they everything? Did the sacrifices give happiness? And what about
the gods? Was it really Prajapati who had created the world? Was it not
Atman, He alone who had created it? Were not the gods forms created like me
and you, mortal, transient? Was it therefore good and right, was it a sensible
and worthy act to offer sacrifices to the gods? To whom else should one offer
sacrifices, to whom else should one pay honor, but to Him, Atman, the Only
One? And where was Atman to be found, where did He dwell, where did His
eternal heart beat, if not within the Self, in the innermost, in the eternal which
each person carried within him? But where was this Self, this innermost? It
was not flesh and bone, it was not thought or consciousness. That was what
the wise men taught. Where, then, was it? To press towards the Self, towards
Atman—was there another way that was worth seeking? Nobody showed the
way, nobody knew it—neither his father, nor the teachers and wise men, nor
the holy songs. The Brahmins and their holy books knew everything, everything; they had gone into everything—the creation of the world, the origin of
speech, food, inhalation, exhalation, the arrangement of the senses, the acts of
the gods. They knew a tremendous number of things—but was it worth while
knowing all theses things if they did not know the one important thing, the
only important things?

Many verses of the holy books, above all the Upanishads of Sama-Veda 9
spoke of this innermost thing. It is written: "Your soul is the whole world." It
says that when a man is asleep, he penetrates his innermost and dwells in
Atman. There was wonderful wisdom in these verses; all the knowledge of the
sages was told here in enchanting language, pure as honey collected by the
bees. No, this tremendous amount of knowledge, collected and preserved by

successive generations of wise Brahmins could not be easily overlooked. But where were the Brahmins, the priests, the wise men, who were successful not only in having this most profound knowledge, but in experiencing it? Where were the initiated who, attaining Atman in sleep, could retain it in consciousness, in life, everywhere, in speech and in action? Siddhartha knew many worthy Brahmins, above all his father—holy, learned, of highest esteem. His father was worthy of admiration; his manner was quiet and noble. He lived a good life, his words were wise; fine and noble thoughts dwelt in his head—but even he who knew so much, did he live in bliss, was he at peace? Was he not also a seeker, insatiable? Did he not go continually to the holy springs with an insatiable thirst, to the sacrifices, to books, to the Brahmins' discourses? Why must he, the blameless one, wash away his sins and endeavor to cleanse himself anew each day? Was Atman then not within him? Was not then the source within his own heart? One must find the source within one's own Self, one must possess it. Everything else was seeking—a detour, error.

10   These were Siddhartha's thoughts; this was his thirst, his sorrow.

11   He often repeated to himself the words from one of the Chandogya-Upanishads. "In truth, the name of Brahman is Satya. Indeed, he who knows it enters the heavenly world each day." It often seemed near—the heavenly world—but never had he quite reached it, never had he quenched the final thirst. And among the wise men that he knew and whose teachings he enjoyed, there was not one who had entirely reached it—the heavenly world—not one who had completely quenched the eternal thirst.

12   "Govinda," said Siddhartha to his friend, "Govinda, come with me to the banyan tree, We will practice meditation."

13   They went to the banyan tree and sat down, twenty paces apart. As he sat down ready to pronounce the Om, Siddhartha softly recited the verse:

> "Om is the bow, the arrow is the soul,
> Brahman is the arrow's goal
> At which one aims unflinchingly."

14   When the customary time for the practice of meditation had passed, Govinda rose. It was now evening. It was time to perform the evening ablutions. He called Siddhartha by his name; he did not reply. Siddhartha sat absorbed, his eyes staring as if directed at a distant goal, the tip of his tongue showing a little between his teeth. He did not seem to be breathing. He sat thus, lost in meditation, thinking Om, his soul as the arrow directed at Brahman.

15   Some Samanas once passed through Siddhartha's town. Wandering ascetics, they were three thin worn-out men, neither old nor young, with dusty and bleeding shoulders, practically naked, scorched by the sun, solitary, strange and hostile—lean jackals in the world of men. Around them hovered an atmosphere of still passion, of devastating service, of unpitying self-denial.

16   In the evening, after the hour of contemplation, Siddhartha said to Govinda: "Tomorrow morning, my friend, Siddhartha is going to join the Samanas. He is going to become a Samana."

17   Govinda blanched as he heard these words and read the decision in his friend's determined face, undeviating as the released arrow from the bow.

Govinda realized from the first glance at his friend's face that now it was beginning. Siddhartha was going his own way; his destiny was beginning to unfold itself, and with his destiny, his own. And he became as pale as a dried banana skin.

"Oh, Siddhartha," he cried, "will your father permit it?"   18

Siddhartha looked at him like one who had just awakened. As quick as lightning he read Govinda's soul, read the anxiety, the resignation.   19

"We will not waste words, Govinda," he said softly. "Tomorrow at daybreak I will begin the life of the Samanas. Let us not discuss it again."   20

Siddhartha went into the room where his father was sitting on a mat made of bast. He went up behind his father and remained standing there until his father felt his presence. "Is it you, Siddhartha?" the Brahmin asked. "Then speak what is in your mind."   21

Siddhartha said: "With your permission, Father, I have come to tell you that I wish to leave your house tomorrow and join the ascetics. I wish to become a Samana. I trust my father will not object."   22

The Brahmin was silent so long that the stars passed across the small window and changed their design before the silence in the room was finally broken. His son stood silent and motionless with his arms folded. The father, silent and motionless, sat on the mat, and the stars passed across the sky. Then his father said: "It is not seemingly for Brahmins to utter forceful and angry words, but there is displeasure in my heart. I should not like to hear you make this request a second time."   23

The Brahmin rose slowly. Siddhartha remained silent with folded arms.   24

"Why are you waiting?" asked his father.   25

"You know why," answered Siddhartha.   26

His father left the room displeased and lay down on his bed.   27

As an hour passed by and he could not sleep, the Brahmin rose, wandered up and down and then left the house. He looked through the small window of the room and saw Siddhartha standing there with his arms folded, unmoving. He could see his pale robe shimmering. His heart troubled, the father returned to his bed.   28

As another hour passed and the Brahmin could not sleep, he rose again, walked up and down, left the house and saw the moon had risen. He looked through the window. Siddhartha stood there unmoving, his arms folded; the moon shone on his bare shinbones. His heart troubled, the father went to bed.   29

He returned again after an hour and again after two hours, looked through the window and saw Siddhartha standing there in the moonlight, in the starlight, in the dark. And he came silently again, hour after hour, looked into the room, and saw him standing unmoving. His heart filled with anger, with anxiety, with fear, with sorrow.   30

And in the last hour of the night, before daybreak, he returned again, entered the room and saw the youth standing there. He seemed tall and a stranger to him.   31

"Siddhartha," he said, "why are you waiting?"   32

"You know why."   33

"Will you go on standing and waiting until it is day, noon, evening?"   34

35   "I will stand and wait."

36   "You will grow tired, Siddhartha."

37   "I will grow tired."

38   "You will fall asleep, Siddhartha."

39   "I will not fall asleep."

40   "You will die, Siddhartha."

41   "I will die."

42   "And would you rather die than obey your father?"

43   "Siddhartha has always obeyed his father."

44   "So you will give up your project?"

45   "Siddhartha will do what his father tells him."

46   The first light of day entered the room. The Brahmin saw that Siddhartha's knees trembled slightly, but there was no trembling in Siddhartha's face; his eyes looked far away. Then the father realized that Siddhartha could not longer remain with him at home—that he had already left him.

47   The father touched Siddhartha's shoulder.

48   "You will go into the forest," he said, "and become a Samana. If you find bliss in the forest, come back and teach it to me. If you find disillusionment, come back, and we shall again offer sacrifices to the gods together. Now go, kiss your mother and tell her where you are going. For me, however, it is time to go to the river and perform the first ablution."

49   He dropped his hand from his son's shoulder and went out. Siddhartha swayed as he tried to walk. He controlled himself, bowed to his father and went to his mother to do what had been told to him.

50   As, with benumbed legs, he slowly left the still sleeping town at daybreak, a crouching shadow emerged from the last hut and joined the pilgrim. It was Govinda.

51   "You have come," said Siddhartha and smiled.

52   "I have come," said Govinda.

Questions for Discussion and Your Reading Journal

1. Describe the concept of "Atman."
2. Who are the Brahmins?
3. Describe the role of sacrifice and ritual in Hindu life. How does Siddhartha feel about the rituals he performs?
4. Why is Siddhartha dissatisfied with Hinduism?
5. What does he hope to find with the Samanas?
6. Describe Siddhartha's relationship with his father and compare it to the relationship of mother and daughter in "No Name Woman" (p. 337). Discuss the sorts of conflicts young adults have with their parents today. How are these problems like the one Siddhartha experiences? How are they different?
7. Hesse used the name "Siddhartha" to suggest certain parallels between his character and Siddhartha Gautama, who became Buddha (see "Introduction to Buddhism," p. 662). What parallel do you see in this selection with the life of Buddha?

RABINDRANATH TAGORE

Rabindranath Tagore (1861–1941) was born in Calcutta and is the most famous member of a prestigious and artistically gifted family. At 17 he traveled to London to study English literature; after completing his education he returned to India. Tagore is renowned for his spirituality and advocation of religious tolerance, his powers of literary expression, and his dedication to the revival of India's cultural heritage. In the following poem Tagore expresses his feelings about religion. "False Religion" is his lament on the corruption of religion and on the atrocities committed "in the name of Faith." Like many of the poets represented in Chapter 3, Tagore is voicing concerns about his society: Spirituality, which should bring us peace and harmony, is too often used to justify hate, cruelty, and war.

Reading Rhetorically

"False religion" has been an explosive topic throughout human history. This accusation has resulted in conflicts between individuals, groups, peoples, and entire nations. It is nothing new to write about falsehood in religion. What is somewhat new, and certainly unique, about Tagore's approach to this sensitive topic is his use of the poetic form to give expression to ideas. Poetry generally aims to inspire and to enlighten its readers with unexpected insights, which are often expressed through the nontraditional use of language. Rhetorically, Tagore's use of poetry seeks to lift readers above the anger, hatred, and intolerance that far too often accompany the words "false religion."

False Religion

Those who in the name of Faith embrace illusion,
Kill and are killed.
Even the atheist gets God's blessing—
Does not boast of his religion;
With reverence he lights the lamp of Reason   5
And pays his homage not to scriptures,
But to the good in man.

The bigot insults his own religion
When he slays a man of another faith.
Conduct he judges not in the light of Reason;   10
In the temple he raises the blood-stained banner
And worships the devil in the name of God.

All that is shameful and barbarous through the Ages,
Has found a shelter in their temples—
Those they turn into prisons;   15

O, I hear the trumpet call of Destruction!
Time comes with her great broom
Sweeping all refuse away.

That which should make man free,
20 They turn into fetters;
That which should unite,
They turn into a sword;
That which should bring love
From the fountain of the Eternal,
25 They turn into prison
And with its waves they flood the world.
They try to cross the river
In a bark riddled with holes;
And yet, in their anguish, whom do they blame?

30 O Lord, breaking false religion,
Save the blind!
Break! O break
The altar that is drowned in blood.
Let your thunder strike
35 Into the prison of false religion,
And bring to this unhappy land
The light of Knowledge.

Questions for Discussion and Your Reading Journal

1. What is Tagore criticizing in this poem? (Cite specific passages.)
2. What is the danger of false religion? The value of true religion?
3. Summarize each stanza of the poem in your own words.
4. In what ways is this criticism of religion similar to Voltaire's criticism in the next reading, "Of Universal Tolerance"?
5. Why does Tagore capitalize words that are not usually capitalized?

VOLTAIRE

Voltaire, the pseudonym of François-Marie Arquet (1694–1777), was one of France's most famous and influential writers. He studied law for a time but made his mark as a dramatist and as a crusader against tyranny and bigotry. Candide, a satire on philosophical optimism, is his best-known work; it was adapted for the modern stage in a musical version by Leonard Bernstein. Voltaire's liberal religious opinions and his mockery of the political order often caused him difficulty; he was imprisoned in the Bastille for a year (1717) and fled from Paris to the countryside after the publication of his Lettres Philosophiques *(1734), in which he spoke out against established religious and political systems.*

His essay on Christian intolerance presented here reflects the attitudes of the 18th-century French Enlightenment, when reason, religious and intellectual tolerance, and freedom of expression came to be viewed as basic essentials of a civilized world. Benjamin Franklin, Tom Paine, and Thomas Jefferson were three prominent American figures who were much influenced by the Enlightenment ideas of men like Voltaire. This helps explain the deep note of tolerance in the U.S. Constitution as well as the fundamental separation of church and state in the American nation.

Reading Rhetorically

Voltaire penned the following essay during the 18th century in France. Although the power of the Catholic Church was decreasing, it was still a time when writers could be arrested and executed for challenging the ideas of religious leaders. Voltaire had already gotten himself into serious trouble with the Catholic fathers for questioning the Spanish Inquisition (in which some 60,000 people were put to death by the Church on charges of heresy). He had also proved the innocence posthumously of a French Protestant man put to death as a heretic by the Church in Southern France. In the following essay, Voltaire is writing not to an audience of Church fathers but, rather, to common people who lived in fear of the Church's power and who were hesitant to challenge it. Voltaire makes shrewd use of humor in this piece as a way of pulling in timid readers. His comic use of examples; exaggeration; and direct addresses to "Moslem" leaders, Buddhists, and Dominican Inquisitors are all intended to disarm the prejudices and fears of his audience. Note how he uses this humor to establish his *ethos* as he discusses a delicate—even dangerous—topic.

Of Universal Tolerance

It does not demand any great skill or highly developed eloquence to prove   1
that Christians ought to show tolerance for one another. I will go a step further: I will tell you that we ought to look upon all men as our brothers. What! Call a Turk my brother? A Chinaman my brother? A Jew? A Siamese? Yes, without hesitation; are we not all children of the same father and creatures of the same God?

But these people despise us; they treat us as idolaters! And what of it? I   2
will tell them they are quite wrong. It seems to me that I could shake up at least the arrogant assumptions of a high Moslem leader or the head of a Buddhist monastery if I were to say to them something like this:

"This little globe, which is no more than a dot, spins through space the   3
same as countless other globes, and we are lost in this immense vastness. Mankind, at about five feet of height, is unquestionably a rather small thing in all of creation. And yet one of these insignificant beings says to a few of his neighbors in Arabia or in South Africa: 'Listen to me, for the God of all these

worlds has enlightened me. There are nine hundred million little ants like us on the earth, but my anthill alone is dear to God; all the others are a source of disgust to him for all eternity; mine alone will know happiness, and all others will be forever miserable.'"

4   At that point they would stop me and ask who the madman was that spoke such foolishness. I would be obliged to answer them: "It is you yourselves." I would then attempt to calm them down, but that would be quite difficult.

5   Next I would speak to the Christians, and I would dare to tell, for example, a Dominican Inquisitor devoted to his faith: "Dear brother, you know that each province of Italy has its own way of talking and that people in Venice and Bergamo do not speak at all like those in Florence. The Academy of Crusca has set up the rules of the Italian language; its dictionary is a standard from which one must not stray, and Buonmattei's book of grammar is an infallible guide which must be followed; but do you believe that the consul of the Academy, or Buonmattei in his absence, would have been able, in good conscience, to cut the tongues out of all the Venetians and of all the Bergamese who would have persisted in speaking their own dialects?"

6   The Inquisitor would answer me: "There is a vast difference; here it is a question of the salvation of your soul: It is for your own good that the Grand Inquisitor orders your arrest upon the testimony of a single person, be he of the worst character and an outlaw to justice; that you have no lawyer to defend you; that the name of your accuser be not even known to you; that the Inquisitor first promise you mercy, and then condemn you; that he put you through five different tortures, and that afterwards you either be whipped, sent to the gallows, or burned at the stake. [Church leaders and influential Christian judges] are of exactly of this opinion, and this holy practice cannot suffer contradiction."

7   I would take the liberty of answering him: "My brother, perhaps you are right; I am convinced of the good you only wish to do me, but can I not be saved without all that?"

8   It is true that these absurd horrors do not stain the face of the earth every day, but they have been done frequently, and one could easily compile them into a book that would be much larger than the Gospels that condemn them. Not only is it quite cruel in this short life to persecute those who do not think like us, but I wonder if it isn't rather bold to pronounce their eternal damnation as well. It seems to me that it is not the business of momentary specks of insignificance, such as we are, to second guess the decrees of the Creator. I am far from fighting against the maxim "Outside of the Church there is no salvation"; I respect the Church and all that it teaches, but, in truth, do we know all of the ways of God and the extent of his mercy? Isn't it permitted to hope in him as much as to fear him? Isn't it enough to be faithful to the Church? Must each particular group take for themselves the rights of the Divine, and decide, in its place, the eternal fate of all men?

9   When we wear clothes in mourning for the king of Sweden, Denmark, England, or Prussia, do we say that we are in mourning for a damned soul that is eternally burning in hell? In Europe, there are forty million inhabitants who do not belong to the Church of Rome. Shall we say to each of them: "Sir, in

light of the fact that you are infallibly damned, I will neither eat, nor converse, nor have anything to do with you?"

What ambassador of France, when given audience with a Great Lord, will   10
say in the depths of his heart: His Highness will be infallibly burned during all of eternity because he has undergone circumcision? If he really believed that the Great Lord was a mortal enemy to God and the object of divine vengeance, would he be able to speak to him? Should he have been sent to see him? With what other man could one do business, what civil responsibilities could one carry out, if in effect one was convinced of this idea that he was dealing with the damned?

O schism-loving, worshippers of a merciful God! If you have cruel hearts,   11
if, while you adore him whose entire law consists of these words: "Love God and your neighbor," you have buried this sacred and pure law under meaningless arguments and incomprehensible disputes; if you have sown discord, here over a new word, there over a single letter of the alphabet; if you have attached eternal punishment to the omission of a few words, to the lack of a few ceremonies that other peoples could not know of, I would tell you with tears for all of mankind: "Come with me to the day where all will be judged and where God will reward each man according to his own works.

"I see all the dead from centuries past and from our own time appear   12
together in his presence. Are you certain that our Creator and Father will say to the wise and virtuous Confucius, to the lawmaker Solon, to Pythagoras, Zaleucus, Socrates, Plato, the divine Antonians, the benevolent Trajan, to Titus, to the best of mankind, to Epictetus, and to many others, the very models of men: 'Away with you, monsters, go suffer torments that are infinite in intensity and duration; let your suffering be as eternal as I am! And you, my beloved, Jean Châtel, Ravaillac, Damiens, Cartouche, etc. [Christian leaders with reputations for corruption, evil-doing, and villainous treatment of other humans], you who died with the prescribed ceremonies, sit on my right and share endlessly both my empire and my goodness.'"

You draw back with horror at these words; and, after they have escaped   13
me, I have nothing left to say to you.

Questions for Discussion and Your Reading Journal

1. What is satire? Discuss how this piece is satiric. (For example, what effect does the anthill comparison have?)
2. What might be Voltaire's reasons for using satire to treat a "sacred" subject?
3. Notice that Voltaire makes his argument for tolerance in part through narrative and direct address to religious and historical figures and to his readers. What effect does this approach have on you as a reader?
4. Explain the historical reference to the "Grand Inquisitor" (Paragraph 6). How does this reference give weight to Voltaire's argument?
5. Do you agree or disagree with Voltaire's idea of universal tolerance? Why or why not?

THE DALAI LAMA

The Dalai Lama (1935–) was born under the name Lhamo Dhondrub in a peasant village in northeastern Tibet. Little Lhamo was officially recognized at the age of 2 by Tibetan Buddhist spiritual leaders as a Bodhisattva, meaning he was considered by Tibetan Buddhists to be the reincarnation of the Buddha of Compassion and was meant to lead the people. The young boy was renamed Jetsun Jamphel Ngawang Lobsang Yeshe Tenzin Gyatso, which means Holy Lord, Gentle Glory, Compassionate, Defender of the Faith, Ocean of Wisdom. He became the spiritual leader of his people and is considered to be the 14th reincarnation of the original enlightened Dalai Lama, by which name he is known around the world. As a leader of his people, he has proven to be an exceptionally gifted and enlightened individual by any standards, religious or otherwise. In 1950 he took full political control of the Tibetan government at the age of 15 when China invaded and occupied the country. He was forced to flee Tibet in 1959 when relations with the Chinese worsened. He has since lived in exile in India and has led a decades-long struggle to free his homeland from Chinese occupation. Although hundreds of thousands of his people have died in the ongoing conflict with China, the Dalai Lama has not wavered from the pursuit of a peaceful resolution to the conflict. In 1989 his efforts as a peacemaker won him the prestigious Nobel Peace Prize and worldwide respect. The Nobel Prize Committee awarded him the prize with the following statement summing up much of his life's work:

> *The Committee wants to emphasize the fact that the Dalai Lama in his struggle for the liberation of Tibet consistently has opposed the use of violence. He has instead advocated peaceful solutions based upon tolerance and mutual respect in order to preserve the historical and cultural heritage of his people (http://www.tibet. com/DL/biography.html).*

The following reading presents a sample of the core ideas and the inner spirit that the Dalai Lama regularly shares with audiences around the world in his speeches, lectures, and writings.

Reading Rhetorically

The Dalai Lama's primary purpose in the following reading is to "enlighten" his readers. As a Buddhist leader in the world, he faces the rhetorical difficulty that his readers would naturally expect him to think of his own religion as the "best" path to enlightenment. He openly deals with this expectation by showing that he does not necessarily think this way in all cases, then, with a playful sense of humor, affirms that he does consider the Buddhist path a good one for himself to follow. Throughout his writing, it is his playful sense of self and his generous respect for others (a primary concept that Buddhists call *metta,* or "loving-kindness") that most characterizes his rhetorical appeal. As you read, note the words and phrases that he uses to establish this *ethos*.

Excerpts from *A Simple Path* and *An Open Heart*

A SIMPLE PATH

The Four Noble Truths are the very foundation of the Buddhist teaching. In fact, if you don't understand the Four Noble Truths, and if you have not experienced the truth of this teaching personally, it is impossible to practice Buddha Dharma. Therefore I am always very happy to have the opportunity to explain them. 1

Generally speaking, I believe that all the major world religions have the potential to serve humanity and develop good human beings. By "good" I mean that they have a good and more compassionate heart. This is why I always say it is better to follow one's own traditional religion, because by changing religion you may eventually find emotional or intellectual difficulties. 2

However, for those of you who really feel that your traditional religion is not effective for you then the Buddhist way of explaining things may hold some attraction. Maybe in this case it is all right to follow Buddhism. Generally, I think it is better to have some kind of religious training than none at all. If you really feel attracted to the Buddhist approach, and the Buddhist way of training the mind, it is important to reflect carefully, and only when you feel it is really suitable for you is it right to adopt Buddhism as your religion. 3

© Image Source/Superstock

There is another important point here. Human nature is such that sometimes, in order to justify our adoption of a new religion, we may criticize our previous religion and claim it is inadequate. This should not happen. Firstly, although your previous religion may not be effective for you, that does not mean it will fail to be of value to millions of other people. Since we should respect all human beings, we must also respect those following different religious paths. It is clear that for some people the Christian approach is more effective than the Buddhist one. It depends on the individual's mental disposition. We must therefore appreciate that potential in each religion, and respect all those who follow them. 4

5   The second reason is that we are now becoming aware of the many religious traditions of the world, and people are trying to promote genuine harmony between them. I think there are now many interfaith circles and the idea of religious pluralism is taking root. This is a very encouraging sign.

6   I wanted to begin with these points, because when I actually explain the Four Noble Truths, I have to argue the Buddhist way is the best! Also, if you were to ask me what the best religion is for me personally, my answer would be Buddhism, without any hesitation. But that does not mean that Buddhism is best for everyone—certainly not. Therefore, during the course of my explanation, when I say that I feel that the Buddhist way is best, you should not misunderstand me.

7   I would like to further emphasize that when I say that all religions have great potential, I am not just being polite or diplomatic. I have met genuine practitioners from other traditions. I have noticed a genuine and very forceful loving kindness in their minds. My conclusion therefore is that these various religions have the potential to develop a good heart.

8   Whether or not we like the philosophy of other religions isn't really the point. For a non-Buddhist, the idea of nirvana and a next life seems nonsensical. Similarly, to Buddhists the idea of a Creator God sometimes sounds like nonsense. But these things don't matter; we can drop them. The point is that through these different traditions, a very negative person can be transformed into a good person. That is the purpose of religion—and that is the actual result. This alone is a sufficient reason to respect other religions.

9   There is one last point. As you may know, Buddha taught in different ways, and Buddhism has a variety of philosophical systems. If the Buddha taught in these different ways, it would seem that he himself was not very sure about how things really are! But this is not actually the case; the Buddha knew the different mental dispositions of his followers. So even Buddha Shakyamuni very much respected the views and rights of individuals. A teaching may be very profound but if it does not suit a particular person, what is the use of explaining it?

AN OPEN HEART

Brothers and Sisters, Good Morning

10 I believe that every human being has an innate desire for happiness and does not want to suffer. I also believe that the very purpose of life is to experience this happiness. I believe that each of us has the same potential to develop inner peace and thereby achieve happiness and joy. Whether we are rich or poor, educated or uneducated, black or white, from the East or the West, our potential is equal. We are all the same, mentally and emotionally. Though some of us have larger noses and the color of our skin may differ slightly, physically we are basically the same. The differences are minor. Our mental and emotional similarity is what is important.

11   We share troublesome emotions as well as the positive ones that bring us inner strength and tranquillity. I think that it is important for us to be aware

of our potential and let this inspire our self-confidence. Sometimes we look at the negative side of things and then feel hopeless. This, I think, is a wrong view.

I have no miracle to offer you. If someone has miraculous powers, then I 12 shall seek this person's help. Frankly, I am skeptical of those who claim extraordinary powers. However, through training our minds, with constant effort, we can change our mental perceptions or mental attitudes. This can make a real difference in our lives.

If we have a positive mental attitude, then even when surrounded by hos- 13 tility, we shall not lack inner peace. On the other hand, if our mental attitude is more negative, influenced by fear, suspicion, helplessness, or self-loathing, then even when surrounded by our best friends, in a nice atmosphere and comfortable surroundings, we shall not be happy. So, mental attitude is very important: it makes a real difference to our state of happiness.

I think that it is wrong to expect that our problems can be solved by 14 money or material benefit. It is unrealistic to believe that something positive can come about merely from something external. Of course, our material situation is important and helpful to us. However, our inner, mental attitudes are equally important—if not more so. We must learn to steer away from pursuing a life of luxury, as it is an obstacle to our practice.

It sometimes seems to me that it is the fashion for people to put too much 15 emphasis on material development and neglect their inner values. We must therefore develop a better balance between material preoccupations and inner spiritual growth. I think it natural for us to act as social animals. Our good qualities are what I would call true human values. We should work at increasing and sustaining qualities like sharing with one another and caring for one another. We must also respect the rights of others. We thereby recognize that our own future happiness and welfare is dependent on the many other members of our society.

In my case, at the age of sixteen I lost my freedom, and at twenty-four I 16 lost my country. I have been a refugee for the past forty years, with heavy responsibilities. As I look back, my life has not been easy. However, throughout all these years, I learned about compassion, about caring for others. This mental attitude has brought me inner strength. One of my favorite prayers is

So long as space remains,
So long as sentient beings remain,
I will remain,
In order to help, in order to serve,
In order to make my own contribution.

That sort of thinking brings one inner strength and confidence. It has brought 17 purpose to my life. No matter how difficult or complicated things may be, if we have this type of mental attitude, we can have inner peace.

Again, I must emphasize that *we are the same!* Some of you may have the 18 impression that the Dalai Lama is somehow different. That is absolutely wrong. I am a human being like all of you. We have the same potential.

Spiritual growth need not be based on religious faith. Let us speak of sec- 19 ular ethics.

20   I believe that the methods by which we increase our altruism, our sense of caring for others and developing the attitude that our own individual concerns are less important than those of others, are common to all major religious traditions. Though we may find differences in philosophical views and rites, the essential message of all religions is very much the same. They all advocate love, compassion, and forgiveness. And even those who do not believe in religion can appreciate the virtues of basic human values.

21   Since our very existence and well-being are a result of the cooperation and contributions of countless others, we must develop a proper attitude about the way we relate to them. We often tend to forget this basic fact. Today, in our modern global economy, national boundaries are irrelevant. Not only do countries depend upon one another, but so do continents. We are heavily interdependent.

22   When we look closely at the many problems facing humanity today, we can see that they have been created by us. I am not talking of natural disasters. However, conflicts, bloodshed, problems arising out of nationalism and national boundaries, are all man-made.

23   If we looked down at the world from space, we would not see any demarcations of national boundaries. We would simply see one small planet, just one. Once we draw a line in the sand, we develop the feeling of "us" and "them." As this feeling grows, it becomes harder to see the reality of the situation. In many countries in Africa, and recently in some eastern European countries such as the former Yugoslavia, there is great narrow-minded nationalism.

24   In a sense the concept of "us" and "them" is almost no longer relevant, as our neighbors' interests are ours as well. Caring for our neighbors' interests is essentially caring for our own future. Today the reality is simple. In harming our enemy, we are harmed.

25   I find that because of modern technological evolution and our global economy, and as a result of the great increase in population, our world has greatly changed: it has become much smaller. However, our perceptions have not evolved at the same pace; we continue to cling to old national demarcations and the old feelings of "us" and "them."

26   War seems to be part of the history of humanity. As we look at the situation of our planet in the past, countries, regions, and even villages were economically independent of one another. Under those circumstances, the destruction of our enemy might have been a victory for us. There was a relevance to violence and war. However, today we are so interdependent that the concept of war has become outdated. When we face problems or disagreements today, we have to arrive at solutions through dialogue. Dialogue is the only appropriate method. One-sided victory is no longer relevant. We must work to resolve conflicts in a spirit of reconciliation and always keep in mind the interests of others. We cannot destroy our neighbors! We cannot ignore their interests! Doing so would ultimately cause us to suffer. I therefore think that the concept of violence is now unsuitable. Nonviolence is the appropriate method.

27   Nonviolence does not mean that we remain indifferent to a problem. On the contrary, it is important to be fully engaged. However, we must behave in a way that does not benefit us alone. We must not harm the interests of oth-

ers. Nonviolence therefore is not merely the absence of violence. It involves a sense of compassion and caring. It is almost a manifestation of compassion. I strongly believe that we must promote such a concept of nonviolence at the level of the family as well as at the national and international levels. Each individual has the ability to contribute to such compassionate nonviolence.

I have chosen a few lines that I feel would be acceptable to people of all 28 faiths and even to those with no spiritual belief. When reading these lines, if you are a religious practitioner, you can reflect upon the divine form that you worship. A Christian can think of Jesus or God, a Muslim can reflect upon Allah. Then, while reciting these verses, make the commitment to enhance your spiritual values. If you are not religious, you can reflect upon the fact that, fundamentally, all beings are equal to you in their wish for happiness and their desire to overcome suffering. Recognizing this, you make a pledge to develop a good heart. It is most important that we have a warm heart. As long as we are part of human society, it is very important to be a kind, warm-hearted person.

> May the poor find wealth,
> Those weak with sorrow find joy.
> May the forlorn find new hope,
> Constant happiness and prosperity.
>
> May the frightened cease to be afraid,
> And those bound be free.
> May the weak find power,
> And may their hearts join in friendship.

Questions for Discussion and Your Reading Journal

A Simple Path

1. A "golden rule" in Buddhism is "Never think or say that your own religion is best." How do the Dalai Lama's comments in the opening to "A Simple Path" reflect this attitude? In your opinion, what difference might it make if all religions adopted this golden rule?
2. Does he feel that when one adopts a new religion, it is acceptable to criticize one's old religion? Explain.
3. What, according to the Dalai Lama, is the "purpose of religion"?

An Open Heart

1. Does the Dalai Lama claim to have at least some miraculous power? Explain.
2. What does the Dalai Lama feel about solving problems with money and material benefits?
3. What are his feelings about how people so often divide themselves into "us" and "them" to deal with difficult situations?

4. The Dalai Lama argues that "the concept of war has become outdated." How does he support this claim? Do you find his argument convincing? Why or why not?

5. What one point in the Dalai Lama's teachings presented here do you find least insightful and/or valuable? Explain.

WRITING ASSIGNMENTS

A Creative Paper: Writing a Creation Story

TASK: Read at least three of the creation stories from around the world listed here and write answers to the questions that follow them in the textbook. Then write a two- or three-page creation story of your own that reflects your views on an ideal creation process. You may want to take into consideration the kind of deity involved, if there is one; how the act of creation took place; how living creatures fit into the creation process; and the roles women and men were given during or after the creation.

Paper Format

Use standard MLA style.

READINGS: (Select Any Three)

China: "Nu Kwa"
India: "Shakti"
Mesopotamia: Excerpt from *Enuma Elish*
Palestine: Genesis
Africa (Yoruba): "The Descent from the Sky"
North America: "The Iroquois Story of Creation"

Thinking Rhetorically about Your Audience and Purpose

In a creative writing activity such as this one, a sense of audience may or may not play a major role in shaping your ideas. You may simply be writing for yourself, imagining a creation story that fits your perceptions and your values concerning the nature of deity, the importance of nature, proper human relationships, and so on. However, if you plan to share your writing with someone else, such as the instructor and classmates, it can be useful to think first about your purpose. Do you want to reinforce your own religious heritage? Introduce a new and possibly more equitable creation story for men and women participants? Show a more nature-friendly creation? Explore an entirely new set of ideas? Having a basic sense of purpose in mind may help you write a narrative with more coherence and interest for others.

Writing Objectives

- You will gain deeper understanding of different religious views of human creation from around the world.
- You will practice using other people's ideas to inspire your own creative thinking and writing.
- You will practice organizing your own ideas into a coherent narrative.
- You will be expected to use Standard American English grammar and punctuation effectively to communicate your ideas.

Evaluative Criteria

- Does the essay show some awareness of the major themes that creation stories tend to treat?
- Does the essay show creativity of ideas?
- Is the paper organized into a coherent narrative that other readers can follow effectively?
- Does the paper use Standard American English grammar and punctuation effectively to communicate ideas?

A Comparison/Contrast Essay: Differing Views of Creation

TASK: Read two of the following creation stories that seem most interesting to you. Then write a two- or three-page comparison of the major ideas presented in the two readings. Use your own insights to point out areas where the two stories share similarities, as well as areas where their ideas are different. Organize your points and insights into a standard essay in MLA format.

READINGS: (Select Any Two)

China: "Nu Kwa"
India: "Shakti"
Mesopotamia: Excerpt from *Enuma Elish*
Palestine: Genesis
Africa (Yoruba): "The Descent from the Sky"
North America: "The Iroquois Story of Creation"

Thinking Rhetorically about Your Audience and Purpose

For this assignment, consider that your audience is rather evenly split between supporters of each of the creation stories that you treat. This means that you should try to be fair in your treatment of the authors as you point out the major similarities that they might have, as well as significant differences. As with all good essay writing, you will need to organize your writing into a coherent introduction, body, and conclusion. Your audience will also expect some sort of main idea statement (thesis statement) from you that tells them *why* they ought to read your essay. Do we learn something valuable, insightful, surprising, or useful from comparing the two authors? Be sure to spell this out to your audience early on in your essay.

Writing Objectives

- You will practice comparing and contrasting the ideas of two authors.
- You will incorporate your own insights into a reflective essay (containing an introduction with thesis statement/body/conclusion).
- You will be expected to use Standard American English grammar and punctuation effectively to communicate your ideas.

Evaluative Criteria

- Have you understood the main ideas from two readings?
- Are your own insights into the readings incorporated effectively into a comparison/contrast essay (containing an introduction with thesis statement/body/conclusion)?
- Does the essay demonstrate mastery of Standard American English grammar and punctuation throughout?

An Annotated Bibliography (Summary) Paper: Issues in Religion and Philosophy

Note to Student

An annotated bibliography is simply a bibliography with a succinct, one-paragraph summary of the main points and subpoints of each source. An annotated bibliography is an excellent way to demonstrate your understanding of texts that treat complex issues and themes. It is especially useful as the first step in writing a complete research paper; and your instructor may ask you to use this assignment as the beginning point of the research paper assignment that comes later in this chapter. More information and a sample Annotated Bibliography Paper are available in the Writing Assignments section of Chapter 2: Government and Politics.

TASK: Use the model provided in the Writing Assignments section of Chapter 2: Government and Politics to set up the proper MLA format of an annotated bibliography and to annotate (summarize) three readings on one of the following issues. Be sure to label each sentence in your annotation (main point, subpoint, example) as is done in the model. Labeling sentences will help you to organize your annotation in a clear and understandable manner. (The reading itself may have a rather different organizational pattern.) Once you have completed annotations of three sources from the following readings, conduct outside research (in the library or electronically) to find two more sources on your topic. *Your final annotated bibliography must have five total sources.*

Format

Use standard MLA format.

READINGS: Select any *three* readings under *one* of the following headings. Annotate those three texts.

Religion and Gender

Religion and Terrorism

Philosophy, Religion, and Tolerance

Science and Religion

Thinking Rhetorically about Your Audience and Purpose

It actually works out best to make yourself the audience for this assignment. Annotated bibliographies are most useful as a tool for mastering big ideas that you will dig into more deeply later as you write a research paper on the same topic, or as you continue on in a major field of study more generally. Having yourself as the audience means putting ideas down clearly and succinctly enough that when you review them later, they will still make sense to you. Note how the model annotated bibliography (in the Writing Assignments section of Chapter 2: Government and Politics) is structured so that you put the main point of a given article first, followed by supporting points and specific examples. Often articles themselves may not be organized so neatly. In some cases the main point may come somewhere in the middle or even at the end. This may work best for other authors as they develop big ideas in an extended article, but in your succinct annotation you should focus on simply grasping and writing down in an organized manner the one to four biggest ideas of the reading.

Writing Objectives

- You will practice reading critically for main ideas, supporting points, and examples.
- You will practice synthesizing full articles in succinct annotation format.
- You will practice using MLA source citation format.
- You will be expected to use Standard American English grammar and punctuation effectively to communicate your ideas.

Evaluative Criteria

- Do annotations show coherent understanding of main ideas, supporting points, and examples?
- Are annotations succinct and understandable?
- Is MLA source citation format used properly?
- Does the writing demonstrate mastery of Standard American English grammar and punctuation throughout?

A Summary and Response Essay: Critical Reading of Religious and Philosophical Texts

TASK: Write a two- to three-page paper that summarizes the ideas in *one* of the following readings. Include in your essay a personal response that assesses the most important idea(s) that you feel we can learn today from this religion or philosophy.

Paper Format

Use standard MLA style.

READINGS: Summarize and respond to the reading or readings that follow *one* of the following bullets.

Eastern Philosophies/Religions

- Hinduism "Muṇḍaka Upanishad" (India)
- Ninian Smart and Richard D. Hecht, Eds., "The Enlightenment of the Buddha: Buddhacarita" (India)
- Lao-tzu, "The Sayings of Lao-tzu" (China)
- Confucius, *The Analects* (China)

Western Philosophies

- Plato, "The Allegory of the Cave" (Greece)
- Chief Seattle, "Environmental Statement" (North America)
- Jean-Paul Sartre, "Existentialism" (France)
- Friedrich Nietzsche, Excerpt from *Beyond Good and Evil* (Germany)
- Paul Davies, Excerpt from *The Mind of God* (England)

Middle Eastern Religions

- Solomon, The Proverbs (Palestine)
- Matthew 10: 34–39, "Mission of Jesus"; Matthew 5–7, Sermon on the Mount (Palestine)
- John B. Christopher, "The Prophet," "The Teachings of Islam," (Arabia) The Quran
- Kahlil Gibran, "Religion" from *The Prophet*

Thinking Rhetorically about Your Audience and Purpose

This assignment asks not only that you summarize the main ideas of a one of the preceding readings but also that you offer a critical response to the ideas. This means that you must come up with your own insight about what is particularly interesting, important, or significant about the reading and ideas. Once you have this insight, you are faced with the rhetorical purpose of persuading your readers that it is a valid insight. Therefore, you will need to have some reasons from your own thinking as well as evidence from the reading to support your insight. If you work with these rhetorical concerns in mind from the start, you are likely to have a much more informative and insightful paper at the end.

Writing Objectives

- You will gain deeper understanding of important religious or philosophical ideas.
- You will practice integrating summary writing into a larger piece of writing.
- You will practice organizing ideas (of others and your own) into essay format with an introduction/thesis, body, and conclusion.
- You will be expected to use Standard American English grammar and punctuation effectively to communicate your ideas.

Evaluative Criteria

- Does the essay open with a clear introduction to the reading with enough background to help the audience follow the ideas being presented?
- Does the introduction contain a coherent thesis statement that presents your thoughtful response about what we have to learn from the reading?
- Does the body of the paper support and develop the main ideas in the introduction through an effective summary of the reading text and a presentation of your own insights?
- Does a concluding paragraph sum up effectively your response?
- Does the writing demonstrate mastery of Standard American English grammar and punctuation throughout?

Notes to the Student

Once you have read the text and have begun to formulate your summary and response, organize your writing into a coherent "essay." This means:

1. Start with a clear introductory paragraph or two that gives a little background to the ideas in your summary and that builds up to a thesis statement presenting your own ideas about what we have to learn from the reading. A thesis sentence with your insight(s) into what we have to learn today from this text should become the main focus of this paper. *Important tip:* Do not put more than one to three main ideas in your thesis statement. Focus on the most important ideas in the reading, or you risk overwhelming your audience members with unnecessary information. If they like what they hear from you, they can go and read more on the subject for themselves.

2. Next, use the body of the paper to summarize the reading in an organized manner that helps the audience understand the key points and ideas of the reading. There may be a number of less important points that you simply leave out. Also in the body, come back to your own main points from your thesis and develop them more fully with examples.

3. Finally, conclude with a final paragraph that pulls the summary of the author's ideas and your own insights together in a manner that closes the essay.

A Cultural Analysis Essay: Basic Cultural Values in Islam

TASK: Read the following articles on Islam and then write a three- to four-page analysis of the key values that seem to lie at the roots of this world religion. Organize your insights around a thesis statement that sums up the kind of worldview that these values come together to create and that gives some assessment of whether this is a religion that people of other religions should fear, as many seem to do in the current climate of global tensions. Use standard MLA essay format for the essay. Be sure to include a Works Cited page to document quotes, specific ideas, and facts that come directly from your reading sources.

READINGS

John B. Christopher, "The Prophet," "The Teachings of Islam" (Arabia) and The Quran
Malise Ruthven, "The Quranic World-view"
Kahlil Gibran, "Religion" from *The Prophet*
Naila Minai, "Women in Early Islam"

Thinking Rhetorically about Your Audience and Purpose

For this assignment, imagine that you are writing for people in the Western world who are not Muslims and who are eager to understand better the concern of many Muslims who feel that their religious culture is being misunderstood and threatened by the West. Use the insights that you gain about global basic Islamic values from the four readings to give your own best analysis of the core values that provide the foundation of Islamic culture. Also give your assessment of whether or not non-Muslims should fear this religion and the core values that sustain it.

Writing Objectives

- You will analyze the core values of Islam.
- You will also give an assessment of how valid the concerns of non-Muslims are who feel that Islamic values are a threat to global relations between peoples.
- You will present your ideas in a well-organized analytical essay.
- You will be expected to use Standard American English grammar and punctuation effectively to communicate your ideas.

Evaluative Criteria

- Does the essay demonstrate thoughtful analysis of Islam's core values?
- Are your insights organized into a coherent and insightful essay that presents, develops, and supports your main ideas?
- Does the essay demonstrate mastery of Standard American English grammar and punctuation throughout?

A Gender Analysis Essay: God and Gender

TASK: Read the following articles on religion and gender and then write a three- to four-page analysis of the roles women have held in certain major world religions over time. Organize your insights around a thesis statement that sums up not only the roles women have been given but also the degree to which they have been able to define these roles on their own terms. Use standard MLA essay format for the essay. Be sure to include a Works Cited page to document quotes, specific ideas, and facts that come directly from your reading sources.

READINGS

Creation Story: India: "Shakti"
Creation Story: Palestine: Genesis
Riane Eisler, "Our Lost Heritage: New Facts on How God Became a Man"
Ninian Smart and Richard D. Hecht, Eds., "Women and the Order"
Naila Minai, "Women in Early Islam"
Sultana Yusufali, Why Do I Wear Hijab?

Thinking Rhetorically about Your Audience and Purpose

For this assignment, imagine that you are writing for educated men and women who are aware that women have often had a less-than-equal position with males in the religious world. Use the insights that you gain about how and why this inequality has come about to inform your audience not only of the issue itself but of the future for women believers. Is there any indication in the readings that as time goes by women will gain more equal ground religiously, stay the same, or lose ground? Make a thesis statement out of your key ideas on this issue and then use the rest of the essay to develop and support your position.

Writing Objectives

- You will analyze a key issue involving major world religions.
- You will also give an assessment of the how valid the concern is that women are not always treated as equal to men by religious movements.
- You will present your ideas in a well-organized analytical essay (introduction with thesis statement/body/conclusion).
- You will be expected to use Standard American English grammar and punctuation effectively to communicate your ideas.

Evaluative Criteria

- Does the essay demonstrate thoughtful analysis of the issue?
- Are your insights organized into a coherent and insightful essay that presents, develops, and supports your main ideas (through an introduction with thesis statement/body/conclusion)?
- Does the essay demonstrate mastery of Standard American English grammar and punctuation throughout?

Synthesis of Sources Paper: Religion and Terrorism

TASK: Read the following articles and then write a three- to five-page synthesis of the differing ideas that the various authors offer for understanding the relationship between religion and terrorism in the modern world. Organize your paper into separate paragraphs that use quotes and examples from each of your sources to show the ideas of each author. Include an introductory paragraph and a concluding paragraph that present the overall issue to your readers and that give your own assessment of which authors offer the most compelling approaches to understanding the use of terrorism by various groups and nations in the world today. Use MLA paper format to cite and to document your sources. Note that your Works Cited page will contain only sources from this textbook. You are not expected to do outside library research for this paper

READINGS

Karen Armstrong, From "Fundamentalism and the Modern World"
Malise Ruthven, "The Quranic World-view"
Zayn Kassam, "Can a Muslim Be a Terrorist?"
John Hall, "Baptist Professors Don't See Islam as Peaceful Religion"
Arundhati Roy, Excerpts from *War Talk* (Chapter 2)

Thinking Rhetorically about Your Audience and Purpose

The readings for this assignment present different and often opposing positions on the connections between religions and terrorism. This is, of course, an issue that inflames and angers people. Write your paper for an audience of concerned people in your country and around the world who genuinely want to understand more about why religion does not seem to be an effective force for peace around the world. To the contrary, religious belief is often given as a justification for violence and terror in our town. Use your sources to give these readers valuable insights from a variety of perspectives from around the world on this important issue.

Writing Objectives

- You will synthesize the ideas and quotes from a variety of different viewpoints into a single essay.
- You will present your ideas in a well organized, coherent, and informative paper.
- You will use MLA format and style to cite and to document your papers properly.
- You will be expected to use Standard American English grammar and punctuation effectively to communicate your ideas.

Evaluative Criteria

- Do you effectively synthesize the ideas of a variety of writers into a single paper?
- Does the paper have an introduction that sets up the overall flow of the paper?
- Does the body of the paper develop the main point(s) of the introduction with quotes, examples, and ideas from individual authors?
- Does the conclusion sum up and close the key points of the paper effectively?
- Is MLA format and style used properly to cite and to documents sources?
- Does the essay demonstrate mastery of Standard American English grammar and punctuation throughout?

Critique of an Argument: Rhetorical Analysis in Religion and Philosophy

TASK: Analyze the strengths and weaknesses of one of the following argument essays, then write a two- to three-page critique of the argument. Organize your writing to systematically critique the key aspects of the article that make it persuasive or not persuasive. Do not try to analyze every single element of the essay. Rather, focus upon the two to four major points that make it a convincing or not a convincing argument. The main point of your essay should be to answer the questions *Is this argument convincing, and why, or why not?* Use standard MLA style to format your paper and to cite and document sources. You need only have one source for this paper.

READINGS

David Brooks, "Kicking the Secularist Habit"
Friedrich Nietzsche, Excerpt from *Beyond Good and Evil*
Paul Davies, Excerpt from *The Mind of God*
Riane Eisler, "Our Lost Heritage: New Facts on How God Became a Man"

Sultana Yusufali, "Why Do I Wear Hijab?"
John Hall, "Baptist Professors Don't See Islam as 'Peaceful' Religion"
Zayn Kassam, "Can a Muslim Be a Terrorist?"
Voltaire, "Of Universal Tolerance"
The Dalai Lama, Excerpts from *A Simple Path* and *An Open Heart*

Thinking Rhetorically about Your Audience and Purpose

As you begin this assignment, you may soon realize that you are, in effect, writing an "argument about an argument." Your task is to persuade your readers that the reading you critique is persuasive, not persuasive, or a mix of the two, and why. Do not get lost in the argument itself. For example, do not jump on board with the writer because you personally agree with the author's position. Rather, critique the way the author argues. Does he/she have sound reasons for his/her position? Does the author provide reliable and relevant evidence? Does he/she consider alternative views or is the argument one-sided? Whom, exactly, does the author seem to be writing for? Is she/he likely to be effective with that audience but not with other audiences? As you draft your critique, it might help to think of the author herself or himself as your best audience. Use your critique to point out the strengths and/or the weaknesses of the author's argument in a systematic manner that even she or he might find useful and informative.

Writing Objectives

- You will critique the argument of one author.
- You will present your ideas in a well-organized, coherent, and informative paper (i.e., contains an introduction with a main idea/thesis statement, a body, and a conclusion).
- You will use standard MLA style to format the paper and to document sources.
- You will be expected to use Standard American English grammar and punctuation effectively to communicate your ideas.

Evaluative Criteria

- Do you effectively critique one argument?
- Does the paper have an opening paragraph that introduces the topic and sets up the critique?
- Does the body of the paper develop the main point(s) of the critique with convincing reasons, appropriate quotes, and specific evidence from the readings?
- Does the conclusion sum up and close the key points of the paper effectively?
- Is MLA format and style used properly?
- Does the essay demonstrate mastery of Standard American English grammar and punctuation throughout?

Persuasive Writing Essay: Issues in Religion and Philosophy

TASK: Select one of the following readings and write a three- to four-page persuasive essay in which you respond with your own position on the issue. You may agree or disagree with the author. Whatever position you take, use evidence from your own experience and from the reading to support your points. Use standard MLA paper format and documentation style to cite and to document any of the sources that you use. You may have only one source for the paper.

READINGS: (Select One)

David Brooks, "Kicking the Secularist Habit"
Chief Seattle, "Environmental Statement"
Paul Davies, Excerpt from *The Mind of God*
Kahlil Gibran, "Religion" from *The Prophet*
St. Matthew 5–7, Sermon on the Mount
Riane Eisler, "Our Lost Heritage: New Facts on How God Became a Man"
Zayn Kassam, "Can a Muslim Be a Terrorist?"
Rabindranath Tagore, "False Religion"
Voltaire, "Of Universal Tolerance"

Thinking Rhetorically about Your Audience and Purpose

The attitudes that people have concerning religious and philosophical issues generally are deeply held and highly personal. To persuade others to think differently about a religion or a philosophical perspective that may have been handed down to them from generation to generation will not be an easy task. The ideal audience for this paper would be reasonable people who are open to new ideas and to learning about the perspectives of others. A manageable goal in this paper is to try to persuade reasonable people, such as many of your peers in the class you are taking, to reflect more deeply about a religious or philosophical topic. If you present a fair and balanced argument that expresses your ideas on any of the topics in the chosen reading, your audience is likely to be enlightened by your work even if it does not completely adopt your position.

Writing Objectives

- You will write a thought-provoking and persuasive essay.
- You will organize your ideas around a specific religious or philosophical issue and will develop and support a position upon the issue with concrete evidence from the reading and from personal experiences.
- You will use standard MLA style to format the paper and to document sources.
- You will be expected to use Standard American English grammar and punctuation effectively to communicate your ideas.

Evaluative Criteria

- Does the paper present a clear position upon an issue in religion or philosophy?
- Does the body of the paper develop the main point(s) of the argument with convincing reasons, appropriate quotes, and specific evidence from the reading and from personal experience?
- Is MLA format and style used properly?
- Does the essay demonstrate mastery of Standard American English grammar and punctuation throughout?

Persuasive Writing Research Paper: Issues in Religion and Philosophy

TASK: Review the topics and readings contained in the Religion and Philosophy chapter of this book. Select an issue from among these readings that interests you and conduct further research both by reading other articles in this book (other chapters often contain very relevant readings as well) and through library and/or electronic research. Early on in your research, formulate a research question on this topic that you would like to find a good answer to; then use your research paper both to answer your question and to convince your readers that your answer is a good one. Be careful that your research question is not simply a fact-based question (i.e., What are the basic principles of Christianity?) Rather, formulate an *issue-oriented* question (i.e., Why have women often been given secondary roles in the Christian faith?) (*Note:* This would be an ideal assignment in which to incorporate the Annotated Bibliography assignment given earlier in this chapter as a preliminary research step.)

Paper Length

Your paper should be 7 to 10 pages long.

Required Number of Sources

Use a minimum of 10 sources in this paper, including articles from this book, database sources, and Web sources (*Caution:* Many Web sources are neither reliable nor by reputable authors; be sure to base your research upon sources that are credible.)

Format and Style

Use MLA format and style to format the paper and to document your use of sources.

Thinking Rhetorically about Your Audience and Purpose

Often when students begin a research project, their primary concern is to learn more about a specific topic. This is a great place to begin . . . and a bad place to end. You need to do more than come up with a lot of facts about your topic. Encyclopedias and dictionaries give us the facts. The purpose of a good academic research paper is to offer your readers some clear and compelling idea of *what they should do with or about the facts you offer*. In short, it is not enough in a good research paper to tell your audience in great detail that one religious group or another is being oppressed or that a certain philosophy developed in a certain place. Rather, you should persuade your audience that it has something important to learn or something that it ought to do based upon looking at a specific religious issue or philosophical topic. For your audience, imagine a group of fellow students who are open and idealistic about having some sort of positive influence in the world. Use this research paper to persuade them that there is something valuable that they can learn or even that they can do to improve a situation that needs to be improved.

Writing Objectives

- You will write a persuasive research paper on a topic in religion or philosophy.
- You will use a minimum of 10 credible sources to support and develop your main points upon the research topic.
- You will use standard MLA style to format the paper and to document sources.
- You will be expected to use Standard American English grammar and punctuation effectively to communicate your ideas.

Evaluative Criteria

- Does the paper present a well-researched and persuasive argument upon a specific issue in religion or philosophy?
- Does the body of the paper develop the main point(s) of the argument with convincing reasons, appropriate quotes, and specific evidence from the readings and/or from personal experience?
- Are a minimum of 10 credible sources used and are they documented properly in MLA style?
- Does the essay demonstrate mastery of Standard American English grammar and punctuation throughout?

Persuasive Writing Research Paper:
Valuing the Contributions of a Religious Leader or Philosopher

TASK: Review the topics and readings contained in the Religion and Philosophy chapter of this book. Select a religious or a philosophical figure from among these readings who interests you and read that selection thoroughly. Then continue your study of this individual through library and/or electronic research. Early on in your research, formulate a research question on this topic that you would like to find a good answer to; then use your research paper both to answer your question and to convince your readers that your answer is a good one. Be careful that your research question is not simply a fact-based question (i.e., What were the basic teachings of Socrates?) Rather, formulate an *issue-oriented* question (i.e., Why do the basic teachings of

Socrates continue to have relevance to people today, some 2,400 years after his death?) (*Note:* This would be an ideal assignment in which to incorporate the Annotated Bibliography assignment given earlier in this chapter as a preliminary research step.)

Paper Length

Your paper should be 7 to 10 pages long.

Required Number of Sources

Use a minimum of 10 sources in this paper, including articles from this book, database sources, and Web sources. (*Caution:* Many Web sources are neither reliable nor by reputable authors; be sure to base your research upon sources that are credible.)

Format and Style

Use MLA format and style to format the paper and to document your use of sources.

Thinking Rhetorically about Your Audience and Purpose

Often when students begin a research project, their primary concern is to learn more about a specific topic. This is a great place to begin . . . and a bad place to end. You need to do more than come up with a lot of facts about your topic. Encyclopedias and dictionaries give us the facts. The purpose of a good academic research paper is to offer your readers some clear and compelling idea of *what they should do with or about the facts you offer.* In short, it is not enough in a good research paper to tell your audience in great detail the facts about the life and teachings of a certain religious leader or philosopher. Rather, you should persuade your audience that it has something important to learn or something that it ought to do, based upon the teachings and insights of a given person. For your audience, imagine a group of fellow students who are open and idealistic about having some sort of positive influence in the world. Use this research paper to persuade them that there is something valuable that they can learn or even that they can do to better understand and perhaps to improve the world.

Writing Objectives

- You will write a persuasive research paper on a religious or a philosophical figure.
- You will use a minimum of 10 credible sources to support and develop your main points upon the research topic.
- You will use standard MLA style to format the paper and to document sources.

- You will be expected to use Standard American English grammar and punctuation effectively to communicate your ideas.

Evaluative Criteria

- Does the paper present a well-researched and persuasive argument upon a specific figure in religion or philosophy?
- Does the body of the paper develop your main point(s) with convincing reasons, appropriate quotes, and specific facts from the readings?
- Are a minimum of 10 credible sources used and are they documented properly in MLA style?
- Does the essay demonstrate mastery of Standard American English grammar and punctuation throughout?

LITERARY CREDITS

Alperovitz, Gar, "The U.S. Was Wrong," from *The New York Times,* August 4, 1985, Op-Ed. Copyright © 1985 by The New York Times Company. Reprinted with permission. p. 536

Annan, Kofi, Nobel Peace Prize Lecture, December 10, 2001. Copyright © 2001 The Nobel Foundation. p. 117

Archibugi, Daniele and Iris Marion Young, "Envisioning A Global Rule of Law, pp. 158–170," from *Terrorism and International Justice,* edited by James P. Sherpa, copyright © 2003 by Oxford University Press, Inc. Used by permission of Oxford University Press, Inc. p. 169

Armstrong, Karen, "Fundamentalism and the Modern World," from sojo.net, http://www.sojo.net/index.dfm?action=magazine.article&issue=soj0203i&article-020310. Courtesy of Bill Hicks, Trinity Television and New Media. All rights reserved. p. 760

Berrall, Julia Smith, "The Garden: In the Time of the Pharaohs" from *The Garden: An Illustrated History.* Copyright © 1966 by Julia S. Berrall. Used by permission of Viking Penguin, a division of Penguin Books (USA), Inc. p. 376

Berry, Wendell, "A Citizens Response to the National Security Strategy of the United States of America," Online version. Copyright © The Orion Society. p. 162

Bollag, Burton, "A Confrontation with the Past: The Japanese Textbook Dispute," *American Educator,* pp. 22–27. Copyright © 2001 by Burton Bollag. Reprinted with permission from the Winter 2001 issue of the *American Educator,* the quarterly journal of the American Federation of Teachers. p. 557

Bring, Mitchell, and Josse Wayembergh, "Chinese Gardens" from *Japanese Gardens: Design and Meaning.* Copyright © 1981 McGraw-Hill, Inc. Reprinted by permission of McGraw-Hill, Inc. p. 383

Brookes, John, "The Concept of the Paradise Garden" from *Gardens of Paradise.* Copyright © 1987. Reprinted by permission of George Weidenfeld & Nicolson, Limited. p. 380

Brooks, David, "Kicking the Secularist Habit," *The Atlantic Online.* Copyright © 2003 The Atlantic Monthly. All rights reserved. p. 630

Capra, Fritjof, "The Tao of Physics" from *The Tao of Physics: An Exploration of the Parallels between Modern Physics and Eastern Mysticism* by Fritjof Capra, Third Edition, Updated. Copyright © 1975, 1983, 1991 by Fritjof Capra. Reprinted by arrangement with Shambhala Publications, Inc. 300 Massachusetts Avenue, Boston, Ma 02115. p. 474

Carson, Rachel, "The Obligation to Endure" from *Silent Spring* by Rachel Carson. Copyright © 1962 by Rachel L. Carson, renewed 1990 by Roger Christie. Reprinted by permission of Houghton Mifflin Co. All rights reserved. p. 478

Carter, Jimmy, Nobel Peace Prize Lecture, December 10, 2002. Copyright © 2002 The Nobel Foundation. p. 149

Christopher, John B., "Science in Islam" from *The Islamic Tradition* by John Christopher. Copyright © 1972 by John B. Christopher. Reprinted by permission of HarperCollins Publishers, Inc. p. 465

Christopher, John B., "The Prophet," "The Teachings of Islam," and "The Quran" *from The Islamic Tradition* by John B. Christopher. Copyright © 1972 by John B. Christopher. Reprinted by permission of HarperCollins Publishers, Inc. p. 723

Collins, Billy, "Introduction to Poetry," from *Sailing Alone Around the Room.* Copyright © 2001 Random House. Reprinted with permission. p. 305

Colson, Charles, "Just War, Preemption, and Iraq," from *Commentary on Break Point* with Charles Colson. From *Breakpoint,* September 10, 2002. Reprinted with permission of Prison Fellowship, P.O. Box 17500, Washington, DC 20041. www.breakpoint.org. p. 146

Confucius, "The Sacred Book of Confucius: Paternal Government," eds. Chu Chai and Chai Winber. Copyright © 1965 Carol Publishing Group, Reprinted with permission. p. 23

Conner, John, "The U.S. Was Right," from *The New York Times,* August 4, 1985, Op-Ed. Copyright © 1985 by The New York Times Company. Reprinted with permission. p. 535

Courlander, Harold, "The Descent from the Sky" from *Tales of Yoruba Gods and Heroes.* Copyright © 1973. Originally published by Crown Publishers. Reprinted by permission of the author. p. 648

Dalai Lama, excerpts from *A Simple Path: Basic Buddhist Teaching* by His Holiness the Dalai Lama, copyright © 1997, 2000. Reprinted by permission of HarperCollins Publishers, Ltd. p. 801

Dalai Lama, from *An Open Heart.* Copyright © 2001 by his Holiness The Dalai Lama. By permission of Little, Brown and Company, Inc. p. 802

Davies, Paul, "Mystical Knowledge" from *The Mind of God.* Reprinted with the permission of Simon & Schuster Adult Publishing Group. Copyright © 1992 by Orion Productions. p. 706

de Beauvoir, Simone, "Women as Other," and excerpts from *The Second Sex,* trans. by H.M. Parshley. Copyright © 1952 and renewed 1980 by Alfred A. Knopf, Inc. Reprinted by permission of the publisher. p. 196

Mellor, John W., "The Intertwining of Environmental Problems and Poverty" from *Environment*, Vol. 30:9, November, 1988. Copyright © 1988. Reprinted with permission of the Helen Dwight Reid Educational Foundation. Published by Heldref Publications, 1319 18th Street, NW, Washington, DC 20036-1802. p. 488

Memmi, Albert, "Racism and Oppression": by Albert Memmi. Reprinted with permission. p. 181

Moore, Marianne, "Poetry," from *Collected Poems 1935*. Copyright © 1063 by Macmillan Publishing. p. 312

Mundaka Upanishad (India) from Robert Ernest Humen, trans., (1931) *The Thirteen Principal Upanishads translated from the Sanskrit, with an Outline of the Philosophy of the Upanishads,* 2nd Edition revised, reprint 1993. Used by permission of Oxford University Press, Delhi. p. 655

Needham, Joseph, "Science and China's Influence on the World" from *The Legacy of China*, ed. Raymond Dawson. Copyright © 1064. Reprinted by permission of Oxford University Press. p. 462

Neruda, Pablo, "The United Fruit Co," trans. Ben Belitt, from *Selected Poems by Pablo Neruda*, Ben Belitt, trans. English translation copyright © 1961 by Ben Belitt. Used by permission of Grove/Atlantic Pres. p. 314

Nietzsche, Friedrich, *Beyond Good and Evil*, translated by Walter Kaufmann, copyright © 1966 by Random House, Inc. Used by permission of Random House, Inc. p. 697

Nyerere, Mwalimu Julius K., "The Basis of African Socialism" and "The Arusha Declaration and TANU's Policy on Socialism and Self-Reliance." Copyright © 1967, Reprinted by permission of Mwalimu Julius K. Nyerere. p. 83

Oppenheimer, Robert Julius, "The Scientist in Society," from *The Open Mind*. Copyright © 1955 by Robert J. Oppenheimer. Copyright renewed 1983 by Robert B. Meyer, Executor of the estate of Katherine Oppenheimer. Reprinted by permission of Simon & Schuster, Inc. p. 418

Orwell, George, "Shooting an Elephant" from *Shooting an Elephant and Other Essays* by George Orwell. Copyright © 1950 by Sonia Brownell Orwell and renewed 1978 by Sonia Pitt-Rivers, reprinted by permission of Harcourt Brace & Company. p. 189

Oskooii, Marzieh Ahmadi, "I'm A Woman" from *Echoes of Iranian Revolution* by Sharma. Vikas Publishing House PVT, Ltd. Used with permission. p. 321

Oxfam, Section 1 "An Overview of Globalization" taken from Oxfam report: *Globalization: Submission to the Government's White Paper on Globalization,* May, 2000. Reproduced with the permission of Oxfam GB, 274 Banbury Road, Oxford OX2 7DX, www.oxfam.org.uk. p. 108

Pie Chart: "Major Religions of the World Ranked by Number of Adherents." Copyright © Adherents.com. Courtesy of Preston Hunter. p. 625

Piercy, Marge, "The Common Living Dirt" from *Stone, Paper, Knife* by Marge Piercy. Copyright © 1982 by Marge Piercy. Reprinted by permission of Alfred A. Knopf, Inc. p. 371

Plato, "The Allegory of the Cave," from *The Republic* in *The Great Dialogues of Plato*, trans. by W.H.D. Rouse. Copyright © 1954, 1984. Used by permission of Viking Penguin, a division of Penguin Books USA, Inc. p. 684

Plato, excerpts from *The Republic* in *The Great Dialogues of Plato*, trans. by B. Jowett. Copyright © 1941 The Modern Library. Reprinted with permission. p. 29

Raven, Peter H., "Third World in a Global Future" from *Bulletin of the Atomic Scientists*, Vol. 40, No. 9, November, 1984, pp. 17–20. Copyright © 1984. Reprinted by permission of the author. p. 498

Rawks, John, "The Law of Peoples" with "The Idea of Public Reason Revisited." Reprinted by permission of the publisher from *The Law of Peoples* by John Rawls, pp. 27–30, 34–37, 41, Cambridge, Mass. Harvard University Press. Copyright © 1999 by the President and Fellows of Harvard College. p. 103

Reich, Robert, "Why the Rich are Getting Richer and the Poor, Poorer," from *The World of Nations*. Copyright © 1992 by Vintage Books. Reprinted with permission. p. 123

Rietveld, Merete, "Mutant Bacteria and the Failure of Antibiotics," *Genome News Network,* April 4, 2003. Copyright © 2000–2004 The Center for the Advancement of Genomics. p. 485

Roy, Arundhati, excerpts from *War Talk*. Copyright © 2003 by Arundhati Roy. Reprinted from Arundhati Roy, War Talk, (Cambridge: South End Press, 2003). p. 155

Royal Bank of Canada, "What Use Is Art?" from *Royal Bank of Canada Newsletter*. Reprinted with permission of the Royal Bank of Canada. p. 277

Rubin, Zeffrey A., Frank J. Provenzano, and Zella Luria, "The Eye of the Beholder: Parent's View on Sex of Newborns" from *American Journal of Orthopsychiatry,* 1974. Copyright © 1974 by the American Orthopsychiatric Association, Inc. Reproduced by permission. p. 569

Rukeyser, Muriel, "Letter to the Front" (excerpt) from *Collected Poems*. Copyright © 1978 by McGraw-Hill. Reprinted with permission of William Rukeyser. p. 351

Russell, Bertrand, "Grounds of Conflict" from *Religion and Science,* 1935. Reprinted by permission of Oxford University Press. p. 456

PHOTO CREDITS

INDEX